# The SAGE Handbook of
## Management Learning, Education and Development

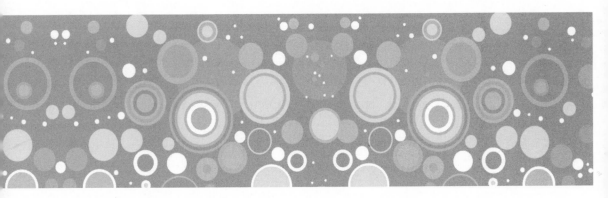

The SAGE
Handbook of

# Management Learning, Education and Development

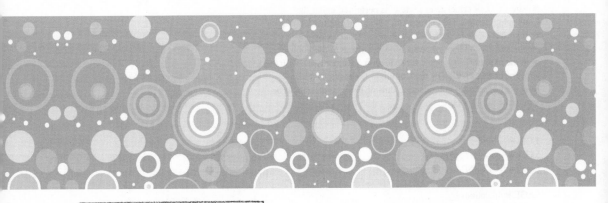

Edited by
# Steven J. Armstrong
## and Cynthia V. Fukami

Los Angeles • London • New Delhi • Singapore • Washington DC

© SAGE 2009

First published 2009

SAGE Publications Ltd
1 Oliver's Yard
55 City Road
London EC1Y 1SP

SAGE Publications Inc.
2455 Teller Road
Thousand Oaks, California 91320

SAGE Publications India Pvt Ltd
B 1/I 1 Mohan Cooperative Industrial Area
Mathura Road, Post Bag 7
New Delhi 110 044

SAGE Publications Asia-Pacific Pvt Ltd
33 Pekin Street #02-01
Far East Square
Singapore 048763

**Library of Congress Control Number: 2008929609**

**British Library Cataloguing in Publication data**

A catalogue record for this book is available from the British Library

ISBN 978-1-4129-3539-5

Typeset by CEPHA Imaging Pvt. Ltd., Bangalore, India
Printed in India at Replika Press Pvt. Ltd
Printed on paper from sustainable resources

# Dedication

To those in the world I am most indebted to – my wife Margaret, my daughter Sophie, and my mum Joan.

*Steven J. Armstrong*

To my family – Mark, Christine, Sarah, and Dad – my ongoing source of inspiration and humility.

*Cynthia V. Fukami*

# Contents

# Foreword

I have been 'professing' management within universities and through executive development programs for almost half a century. I offer two observations out of this experience in support of the importance of this Handbook. The first is this:

(1) Leaders within complex enterprises without contemporary management education and development are at a great disadvantage.

Let me cite but two suggestive examples.

I recall a number of years ago asking a group of business students to observe senior health care leaders conducting a problem solving effort dealing with a complex managerial decision challenge. These leaders were highly educated and exceptionally accomplished medical doctors just commencing a management program sponsored by the American College of Physician Executives. Yet, the business students were amazed at these leaders' untutored group behavior (forcing and smoothing) and limited decision-processing skills (acting on insufficient knowledge). The students were able to quickly identify the deficiencies, label the errors, and suggest alternative approaches that would have been more productive. The students were certainly neither brighter nor more gifted than the senior health care leaders they critiqued. Rather, they had the advantage of already being initiated into conventional management knowledge that the health care leaders were just beginning to learn.

The second example will resonate with academic readers of this handbook whose home discipline is management. Have you not observed in your own interaction with faculty, department chairs and academic administrators trained in disciplines outside the social sciences *experiencing* difficulties in organizing, processing decisions and engaging in collaborative behavior? However deficient my personal leadership when I was Dean of the Leavey School of Business, I felt privileged to have at my fingertips a repertoire of tools for analysis, protocols for processing group decision, and an understanding of helpful organizational arrangements that my academic colleagues not trained in management sciences lacked.

To use an analogy, whatever the weaknesses of western cultures, many immigrants from other countries struggle to enter the developed world because they perceive even greater deficiencies at home. In a similar fashion, those who have never been exposed to the concepts and developmental opportunities provided by management studies flock by the millions to community colleges, universities, corporate training programs, organizational development specialists and executive coaches for guidance. Their desire for management insight attests that our field is hardly a 'non-productive desert,' however apropos our own self-criticisms. Our lived experience testifies that education within a quality management program results in helpful knowledge when facing leadership challenges within organizations.

My second observation is this:

(2)    In addition to the rich knowledge content of management studies, we are in a moment of a radical paradigm
       transition in our understanding of how individuals learn and develop as leaders.

Again, let me cite but two examples.

Twice in my career I focused a sabbatical leave to retool my teaching. The first occasion
followed ten years of service as a dean. During that period of academic administration I did not
teach in my area of specialization – organizational innovation. So I devoted 1989 to visiting
gifted scholars, conversing regarding current research at knowledge centers, visiting doctoral
students, and sitting in on classes at other universities. During the decade I had been absent from
the classroom research had uncovered new findings and scholarly reflection had refined theory
and practice. But in truth, it was comfortable and relatively easy to fold these new developments
within the portfolio of knowledge I already held. What was startlingly different was the progress
in pedagogy.

Classroom learning was much less instructor-centered. Multimedia resources were not only
incorporated but expected. Experiential learning had been integrated. Group work within
teams was carefully constructed and modeled the new organizational realities wherein the
complexity of problems, the multidisciplinary nature of solution search, and the need for
boundary spanning across sub-specialties for implementation demanded new group skills. Thus,
students internalized from their experience in study teams the protocols that would be required
for organizational knowledge transfer. In short, approaches to teaching and learning that I had
only begun to think about had flowered during the decade of my absence from the classroom.
I discovered the most important challenges I faced in returning to the classroom were *teaching
and learning challenges*, not knowledge content challenges.

A decade later (1999) I once again undertook a Sabbatical, this time to prepare to address
the topic *Spirituality of Organizational Leadership*. Here I faced an entirely new arena
of knowledge. Spirituality intersects religious studies, the wisdom literatures, psychology,
East-West anthropology and human development. But again, there were additional teaching
and learning challenges. Religious studies and theology, but also medicine, psychology, social
work, and nursing were pioneering ahead of management how to address the intersections
of spirit, heart, body and mind. Fortunately, the organization *Contemplative Mind in Society*
and the *American Academy of Learned Societies* offered competitive fellowships providing
training in the integration of one important spiritual discipline, meditation/contemplative
practice, with classroom teaching. I was fortunate to receive a fellowship grant and during
the sabbatical year met with faculty in humanities, arts, architecture, law, psychology, religious
studies, etc. – a rainbow of disciplines from which gifted faculty exemplified models of how
they integrated spiritual disciplines within their teaching. Thus, once again, a challenging
aspect of preparation for a new teaching adventure was not simply the knowledge content.
Teaching in the interdisciplinary nexus of spirituality and management required a pedagogy
that integrated different dimensions of human experience than I had dealt with before in the
classroom.

To conclude, my personal experience testifies that preparation to profess in management
has moved beyond a restrictive focus on content. Examining new approaches to teaching and
learning must be part of preparation whether one is teaching in a college, university, corporate
or a consulting context. We can also expect that as technology continues to propel new modes
of communication the challenges will only accelerate.

The editors of this timely handbook eloquently make the scholarly case for the legitimacy of
*teaching and learning* as one central axis within the field of management. Here I have simply
testified that my own experience as a teaching scholar echoes their claim.

Our profession has always required of us an ascetic commitment to stay current with the ever-shifting knowledge content of management. It now requires we also incorporate this additional commitment to examine new approaches to teaching and learning. If we fail to do so, we will fail to generously serve those who come to us to drink from the well of management studies. As always this professional commitment requires both humility and selflessness.

Our calling (as teacher and scholar) is a profound personal challenge because it entails the continuous creation of a self.

Yet our mission can unfold properly only if we engage what has been put in front of us to do and to take on.

Thus, we can be grateful to the wise editors and exceptional authors who within this handbook share important insights. This seminal and summative anthology will help all of us dedicated to management education on behalf of a future generation be more aware of current knowledge regarding teaching and learning in the context of management studies.

Andre L. Delbecq
J. Thomas and Kathleen L. McCarthy
University Professor, Department of Management
Santa Clara University

# List of Contributors

**Khadija Al Arkoubi** is a doctoral candidate in Management at New Mexico State University in Las Cruces, New Mexico, USA. She holds a Master of Science degree in Human Resource Management (HRM) from the University of Manchester, UK. She was a lecturer in Human Resource Development at Al Akhawayn University in Ifrane, Morocco from 2002 to 2004. Before starting her academic career, Khadija was working as civil servant officer in the area of HRM in the Moroccan Ministry of Public Works. Her research interests include leadership, identity, storytelling, International Human Resource Management, and Development.

**J.B. (Ben) Arbaugh** is a Professor of Strategy and Project Management at the University of Wisconsin Oshkosh. He is the incoming Editor of *Academy of Management Learning & Education* and a past chair of the Academy of Management's Management Education and Development Division. Ben's research interests are in online management education, graduate-level management education, and the intersection between spirituality and strategic management research. Some of his recent publications include articles in *Academy of Management Learning & Education*, *Decision Sciences Journal of Innovative Education*, *Information & Management*, *Management Learning*, the *Journal of Management, Spirituality, and Religion*, and the *Journal of Management Education*.

**Steven J. Armstrong** is Director of Research and Professor of Organizational Behavior at Hull University Business School in the UK. After a successful career in the electronics industry he became a senior university lecturer in 1993 and received a PhD in organizational behavior from Leeds University Business School in 1999. His primary research interests focus on the relevance of cognitive style for improvements in workplace effectiveness but he is also interested in the scholarship of teaching and learning in a management context. Recent publications have appeared in the *Academy of Management Learning and Education*, *Journal of Management Studies*, *Journal of Occupational and Organizational Psychology*, *British Journal of Education Psychology*, *Journal of Business and Psychology*, *Small Group Research* and *Educational Psychology*. Steve is Past President of the Management Education and Development Division of the Academy of Management and a Council Member of the British Academy of Management where he serves as an Editor-in-Chief of the Academy's *International Journal of Management Reviews* (Wiley-Blackwell). He is also a Member of the Chartered Institute of Management and remains a Chartered Engineer, and a Member of the Institution of Engineering and Technology.

**Kaylene Ascough** is a Senior Research Officer and Project Manager in the UQ Business School at the University of Queensland. She has recently completed her Honours degree in Business Management. Her ongoing research interests are in ethical practice, emotions in the workplace, emotional intelligence and organizational culture and climate. Kaylene has an extensive history in organizational administration and support spanning over ten years and is the Managing Editor of the *Journal of Organizational Behavior*.

**Neal Ashkanasy** is Professor of Management in the UQ Business School at the University of Queensland. His Ph.D. is in Social and Organizational Psychology from UQ and he is a Fellow of the Society for Industrial and Organizational Psychology and the Australia and New Zealand Academy of Management. His research focuses on leadership, culture, ethics and, more recently, on the role of emotion in organizational life. He has published in journals such as the *Academy of Management Review*, the *Journal of Management*, and *Organizational Behavior and Human Decision Processes*. He is Editor-in-Chief of the *Journal of Organizational Behavior*, Associate Editor of *Academy of Management Learning and Education and Emotion Review*, and book series editor for *Research on Emotion in Organizations*. He administers two ListServs (Orgcult – The Organizational Culture Caucus; and Emonet – Emotions in Organizations), and is a past Chair of the Managerial and Organizational Cognition Division of the Academy of Management.

**Kathryn Aten** is a doctoral candidate in management in the Charles H. Lundquist College of Business at the University of Oregon. She received her Bachelor's degree from California Polytechnic State University-San Luis Obispo and a Master's degree from the Monterey Institute of International Studies. She also studied at the Universidad de Guadalajara and Instituto Tecnológico de Monterrey in Mexico. She currently teaches courses in management, negotiation, entrepreneurship, and international management. Her research explores the role of socio-cognitive institutions and national culture on the emergence and evolution of technology and innovation. She has presented papers at the Academy of Management National Meetings, the European Group for Organizational Studies, Association for Pacific Rim Universities Doctoral Student Conference, the West Coast Forum for Technology Entrepreneurship, and the United Nations-sponsored Business as an Agent of World Benefit Forum. She has also published in the *Journal of World Business*. Prior to her academic career, she worked in employee and management development for Apple Inc., Patagonia, Ralston Foods, and International Game Technology.

**James R. Bailey** is the Tucker Professor of Leadership and Director of Executive Development Programs at the George Washington University School of Business, and a Fellow in the Centre for Management Development, London Business School. He has been the recipient of many teaching distinctions, including the GWSB Outstanding Faculty Award in 2003, 2006 and 2007, and in 2006 was named one of the world's top ten executive educators by the International Council for Executive Leadership Development. He has published over 50 academic papers and case studies, and is the author or editor of several books, including the award-winning, best-selling *Handbook of Organizational and Managerial Wisdom* (with E. Kessler) and the forthcoming *Riding the Change Curve: Leading Through Transition*. He has designed and delivered hundreds of executive programmes for firms such as Nestlé, UBS, Morgan Stanley and Lucent Technologies. Dr Bailey is a frequent keynote speaker who has appeared on broadcast programmes for the BBC and Fox News Network, and whose work has been cited in such outlets as *Fortune, Forbes*, and *Business 2.0*. He currently serves as Editor-in-Chief of the *Academy of Management Learning and Education*.

**Myrtle P. Bell** is an Associate Professor of Management at the University of Texas at Arlington. She has degrees from the University of Notre Dame, Louisiana State University, and UT-Arlington. As a black American woman, Myrtle has been living and doing diversity work throughout her life. At present, her research focuses on diversity and social issues at work, including sexual harassment, disability, age, weight, appearance and religion as aspects of diversity, and effects of partner violence on women and work. Myrtle's research has appeared in leading academic journals and in numerous edited volumes. Her book, *Diversity in Organizations* (2007, Thomson), is the first comprehensive, research-based book of its kind for teaching diversity. Myrtle is the Professional Insights Editor of *Equal Opportunities International* and past chair of the Gender and Diversity in Organizations division of the Academy of Management.

**David M. Boje** is Bank of America Professor, and former Arthur Owens Anderson Professor in Business Administration in the Management Department at New Mexico State University. His main research is the interplay of story, strategy and complexity. He has published articles in *Administrative Science Quarterly, Management Science, Management Communication Quarterly, Organization Studies, Leadership Quarterly*, and other fine journals; see http://business.nmsu.edu/~dboje for more. He is President of Standing Conference for Management & Organization Inquiry (http://scmoi.org), editor of *Tamara Journal* (http://tamarajournal.com) and associated editor for *Qualitative Research in Organization & Management* (QROM). He serves on 13 other editorial boards when he is not riding his horse Nahdion in New Mexico.

**Richard E. Boyatzis** is Professor in the Departments of Organizational Behavior, Psychology, and Cognitive Science at Case Western Reserve University and in Human Resources at ESADE. Before becoming a professor, he was CEO of McBer and Company for 11 years and COO of Yankelovich, Skelly & White for two years. He is the author of more than 100 articles on sustained, desired change, intentional change theory, behaviour change, leadership, competencies, emotional intelligence, and thematic analysis. His books include: *The Competent Manager* (in two languages); *Transforming Qualitative Information* (in two languages); *Innovations in Professional Education* (with Scott Cowen and David Kolb; co-author of the international best-seller, *Primal Leadership*, with Daniel Goleman and Annie McKee (in 28 languages); co-author, *Resonant Leadership: Renewing Yourself and Connecting With Others Through Mindfulness, Hope, and Compassion*, with Annie McKee (in 18 languages); and co-author of *Becoming a Resonant Leader* (with Annie McKee and Fran Johnston). Professor Boyatzis has a B.S. in Aeronautics and Astronautics from MIT, and a M.S. and Ph.D. in Social Psychology from Harvard University.

**M. Ronald Buckley** is the J.C. Penney Company Chair of Business Leadership in the Michael F. Price College of Business, and Professor of Psychology at the University of Oklahoma. He received a Ph.D. in Industrial/Organizational Psychology from Auburn University. Buckley has research interests in, among other areas, organizational socialization processes and the performance evaluation process. He has published a number of articles in journals such as the *Academy of Management Review, Journal of Applied Psychology, Journal of Management, Personnel Psychology*, and *Organizational Behavior and Human Decision Processes*. During his 20 years in the field, Buckley has served on 25 doctoral dissertation committees and chaired eight.

**Robert Chia** holds a Sixth Century Chair in Management at the University of Aberdeen Business School where he teaches Business Strategy, International Management and Organizational Behaviour. He received his Ph.D. in Organization Studies from Lancaster University and publishes regularly in the leading international journals in organization and management studies. Robert initially trained as an aircraft engineer and has held senior positions in manufacturing management and human resource management for multinational corporations prior to embarking on an academic career. His research since then has been focused on the enhancement of life chances for all levels of society through the systematic analysis and understanding of the guiding principles underlying the general economy of effort involved in wealth creation.

**David Clutterbuck** is author of nearly 50 books on management and people development. He introduced the concept of structured mentoring to Europe in the early 1980s and has undertaken numerous studies into both fundamentals and practical application of mentoring. He co-founded the European Mentoring Centre, which evolved into the European Coaching and Mentoring Council, where he was until recently chair of the Research Committee. He is Visiting Professor at the coaching and mentoring faculties of both Sheffield Hallam and Oxford Brookes Universities. He led the development of the *International Standards for Mentoring Programmes in Employment* and leads an international consultancy, Clutterbuck Associates, specializing in helping organizations build sustainable capability in coaching and mentoring. He is currently working on his 12th and 13th books on coaching and mentoring – a second volume of *Techniques in Coaching and Mentoring* and a good practice guide to virtual coaching and mentoring.

**Ann L. Cunliffe** is currently Professor of Organization Theory at Hull University Business School and a Visiting Professor at Leeds and Strathclyde Universities. She was the Albert and Mary Jane Black Endowed Professor of Economic Development in the Anderson School of Management, University of New Mexico, and has held positions at California State University and the University of New Hampshire. Her recent publications include the book *Organization Theory*, collaborating with Mary Jo Hatch on the second edition of *Organization Theory: Modern, Symbolic, and Postmodern Perspectives*, and articles in the *Journal of Management Studies, Organization Studies, Human Relations*, and *Management Learning*. In 2002 she was awarded the 'Breaking the Frame Award' from the *Journal of Management Inquiry*, for the article 'that best exemplifies a challenge to existing thought'. Ann is currently Associate Editor for *Management Learning* and *Qualitative Research in Organizations and Management*, and is on the Editorial Boards of *Organization Studies, Human Relations*, the *Journal of Organizational Change Management*, the *Canadian Journal of Administrative Sciences*, and the *Scandinavian Journal of Management*. She received her Ph.D. and M.Phil. from Lancaster University, UK.

**Marie Dasborough** is an Assistant Professor of Organizational Behavior at School of Business, at the University of Miami, Florida, USA. She received her Ph.D. in Management from the University of Queensland, Australia in 2005. The quality of Marie's doctoral work has been recognized in the academic community. She was named the winner of the 2003 Kenneth E. Clark Student Research Award for the Best Graduate Student Paper on Leadership at the Center for Creative Leadership in Greensboro. She also received an honourable mention in the 2005 Jablin Dissertation Award competition for the Best Dissertation in Leadership (Jepson School of Leadership Studies at Richmond University, and the International Leadership Association). Her current research interests are in leadership, emotions at work, emotional intelligence, team emotional climate, workplace friendship, and the role of friendship ties on human resource selection decisions. This research has been published in journals such as *The Leadership Quarterly, International Journal of Human Resources Management, Journal of Education in Business*, and the *Asia Pacific Journal of Human Resources Management*. Marie currently serves on editorial boards for *Journal of Management, Journal of Organizational Behavior*, and *The Leadership Quarterly*.

**Kathy Lund Dean** is Associate Professor of Management at Idaho State University. She earned her Ph.D. in Organizational Behaviour, with a minor in ethics classics, from Saint Louis

University. Kathy has been active in both the *Organizational Behavior Teaching Society* and the *Academy of Management* for over a decade and is a founder of the *Academy*'s Management, Spirituality and Religion (MSR) interest group. Currently, she is researching non-traditional research methodologies (especially the use of art), business ethics and decision making, and the potential downsides of spirituality in the workplace. Her most common consulting work includes strategic planning and executive coaching. Her research has appeared in a wide variety of management journals and she has served as Associate Editor for the *Journal of Management Education* for six years. Prior to entering higher education, Kathy enjoyed a career in retail banking and was partner in a small commercial business. When not involved somehow with a manuscript, Kathy is a room parent for her kindergartner and pre-schooler boys. She also strategizes on how to spend more time skiing.

**Robert DeFillippi** is Professor and Director, Center for Innovation and Change Leadership, Suffolk University, Boston, USA. His scholarly writing focuses on project-based innovation and his empirical research spans many high technology, entertainment and business service industries. His pedagogic practice includes his design and co-ordination of the global MBA international internship projects at his university and his participation in the European consortium on Strategic Management of Projects, where he is an *Erasmus Mundus* visiting professor at Polytechicno di Milano and teaches Project-based Innovation and Knowledge Management within the consortium's Master's of Science programme. Professor DeFillippi is past chair of the Management Education and Development Division of the Academy of Management. He has also served as co-editor of the *Research in Management Education and Development* book series (Information Age Publishers) and has co-edited seven volumes in the series. He is also associate editor of the *International Journal of Management Reviews* and serves on the editorial board of *Management Learning*

**Gerald R. Ferris** is the Francis Eppes Professor of Management and Professor of Psychology at Florida State University. He received a Ph.D. in Business Administration from the University of Illinois at Urbana-Champaign. Ferris has research interests in the areas of social influence and effectiveness processes in organizations, and the role of reputation in organizations. He is the author of articles published in such journals as the *Journal of Applied Psychology, Organizational Behavior and Human Decision Processes, Organizational Dynamics, Personnel Psychology, Academy of Management Journal, Academy of Management Executive,* and *Academy of Management Review,* and from 1981 to 2003, he served as editor of the annual research series, *Research in Personnel and Human Resources Management.* In 2001, he was the recipient of the Herbert G. Heneman Jr Award for Career Achievement, Human Resource Division, Academy of Management, and in 2006 he received the Graduate Faculty Mentor Award from Florida State University. During over 25 years in the field, Ferris has served on 85 doctoral dissertation committees, and chaired 20.

**Charles J. Fornaciari** is a Professor of Management and the Uncommon Friends Chair in Ethics at Florida Gulf Coast University in Fort Myers, Florida. He has published over a dozen journal articles in areas such as the role of spirituality and religion in management, ethics in business education, corporate strategic change, affective learning techniques, and the use of technology in education. His work has appeared in journals such as *Journal of Organizational Change Management, Journal of Managerial Issues, Journal of Business Research, Journal of Management Education, Journal of Management, Spirituality and Religion,* the *Journal of Business Ethics Education,* and the *International Journal of Organizational Analysis.* Charles is also a recipient of the Organizational Behavior Teaching Society's prestigious New Educator Award. He currently serves as an associate editor for the *Journal of Management Education* and was an editorial review board member of the *Decision Sciences Journal of Innovative Education*.

**Cynthia V. Fukami** is Professor of Management at the Daniels College of Business, University of Denver in the US. In addition to her disciplinary contributions, Cindi has published some 12 articles, and made over 25 presentations at scholarly meetings, on the scholarship of teaching and learning. Cindi has served as Chair of the Academy of Management's Teaching Committee, and on the Board of Directors (two years as Board Chair) of the Organizational Behavior Teaching Society. She was Associate Editor of the *Journal of Management Education* from 1997–2000, and again from 2005–2007, and was an Associate Editor of *Academy of Management Learning and Education* from 2001–2005. She remains on both editorial boards. Cindi was appointed as a Fellow of the Carnegie Foundation for the Advancement of Teaching in 1999.

**Joan V. Gallos** is Professor of Leadership and University of Missouri Curators' Distinguished Teaching Professor at the Henry W. Bloch School of Business and Public Administration at the University of Missouri-Kansas City, where she has also served as Director of the Executive MBA, Professor and Dean of Education, Coordinator of University Accreditation, Special Assistant to the Chancellor for Strategic Planning, and Director of Higher Education Graduate Programs.Gallos holds a Bachelor's degree *cum laude* in English from Princeton and Master's and Doctoral degrees from the Harvard Graduate School of Education. She has published widely on leadership and management education; is co-author of two books, editor of two others, and creator of multiple sets of published teaching materials. She is recipient of both teaching and writing awards, and has served as president of the Organizational Behavior Teaching Society; as editor of the *Journal of Management Education*; and as Founding Director of the Truman Center for the Healing Arts, based at Kansas City's public hospital, which received the Business Committee for the Arts 2004 Partnership Award as the best partnership between a large organization and the arts.

**Silvia Gherardi** is full Professor of Sociology of Work at the Faculty of Sociology of the University of Trento, Italy. Her work has focused on issues associated with workplace learning and knowing, gender policies, labour conditions and social responsibility of enterprises. In recent years she has worked with theories of practice, aiming to develop a sociological approach to practice-based studies. Since 1993 she co-ordinates the Research Unit on Communication Organizational Learning and Aesthetics. Areas of interest include the exploration of different 'soft' aspects of knowing in organizations, with a peculiar emphasis for cognitive, emotional, symbolic, and linguistic aspects of organizational process. Currently the research unit that she co-ordinates is working on an Equal project on gender segregation, on a project focused on networks of interorganizational learning concerning the field of biotechnologies, and on a Master in gender politics. In 2005 she received the degree of 'Doctor Honoris Causa' from the Department of Social Sciences of the Danish Roskilde University.

**Grandon Gill** is an Associate Professor in the Information Systems and Decision Sciences department at the University of South Florida. He holds a doctorate in Management Information Systems from Harvard Business School, where he also received his MBA. His principal research focus is in the area of IS education, and he has published many articles describing how technologies and innovative pedagogies can be combined to increase the effectiveness of teaching across a broad range of IS topics. Currently, he teaches programming, database and managerial courses to both undergraduate and graduate students. He is also a Faculty Fellow at USF's *Center for 21st Century Teaching Excellence*.

**Vivien Hodgson** is a Professor of Networked Management Learning in the department of Management Learning and Leadership at Lancaster University Management School in the UK. She has written extensively on the use of computer-mediated communications and online learning in higher education as well as co-ordinated and participated in many 'e-learning' research projects and the evaluation of development projects. Between 1995 and 1998 she was seconded to the European Commission's 'Socrates' programme in Brussels where she was responsible for the Open and Distance Learning Action. She is the co-chair of international conference series 'Networked Learning'. She is interested in theoretical debates that exist around notions of critical management learning and constructionist approaches to learning together with researching how changes and advances in information and communications technology impact on the nature and experience of learning.

**George Allen Hrivnak Jr** is an instructor and Doctoral Fellow at The George Washington University School of Business. He holds a Master's degree in Adult Education from the University of South Florida and completed his undergraduate studies in business administration and Japanese at the Ohio State University. Prior to joining GW, he spent more than 12 years working in private industry, with extensive experience in leadership and business development roles which provide a practical grounding for his research and teaching. George leads undergraduate, graduate and executive courses in leadership, conflict management and negotiation, and other organizational topics. His research interests include leadership, leadership development, entrepreneurship development, identity, and social structures.

**Trav D. Johnson** is Associate Director of the Center for Teaching and Learning at Brigham Young University. He consults with faculty members, departments, and colleges to improve courses and programmes. He also helps direct the BYU online student rating system. Before joining the Center for Teaching and Learning, Trav was an assistant director in the BYU Faculty Center and also an adjunct instructor in the Instructional Psychology and Technology Department. He previously worked at the University of Illinois in the Office of Instructional Resources, American College Testing (ACT), Syracuse University in the Center for Instructional Development, and the University of Iowa – both in the Center for Teaching and the Center for Evaluation and Assessment. Trav's research and practice focus on improving teaching and learning, particularly through the use of faculty and course evaluation. His professional activities include numerous publications, conference presentations, and professional consultations on educational evaluation and improvement.

**Alice Kolb** is Adjunct Professor of Organizational Behavior at the Weatherhead School of Management, Case Western Reserve University. She is the President of Experience Based Learning Systems, Inc., a research and development organization devoted to research and application of experiential learning in organizations worldwide. She received her Ph.D. from Case Western Reserve University in Organizational Behavior. Her current work is focused on promoting learning in higher education through institution building. This work emphasizes approaching an educational institution's development by integrating development of curriculum, faculty, students and resources around a vision and mission that is focused on learning. Her research focus on learning spaces led to her 2005 paper 'Learning styles and learning spaces: Enhancing experiential learning in higher education' published in *Academy of Management Learning and Education*. Her upcoming publication, 'Learning to play, playing to learn: A case study of a ludic learning space', to be published in the *Journal of Organizational Change Management*, is part of her ongoing passion for creating spaces conducive to deep learning.

**David Kolb** is Professor of Organizational Behavior at the Weatherhead School of Management, Case Western Reserve University. He received his B.A. in Psychology, Philosophy and Religion at Knox College and his Ph.D. in Social Psychology from Harvard University. He is best known for his research on experiential learning and learning styles described in *Experiential Learning: Experience as the Source of Learning and Development*. Other books include, *Conversational Learning: An Experiential Approach to Knowledge Creation, Innovation in Professional Education: Steps on a Journey from Teaching to Learning*, and *Organizational Behavior: An Experiential Approach*. In addition he has authored many journal articles and book chapters on experiential learning. He currently serves on the editorial review boards of *Academy of Management Learning and Education, Human Relations, Simulation and Gaming*, and the *Journal of Management Development*. David's current research activities include studies of team learning, research on the cultural determinants of learning style and research on experiential learning in conversation. He is involved in a number of learning focused institutional development projects in education. David has received four honorary degrees recognizing his contributions to experiential learning in higher education.

**Gabriele Lakomski** is a Professor in the Graduate School of Education at the University of Melbourne, Australia. She is best known for her critical work on leadership and organizational learning in both public and private sector organizations. Trained in philosophy of science and epistemology, her research is based on the most recent scientific understanding of human knowledge acquisition and the processing of information, developed by connectionist cognitive science. In her work, Gabriele examines how such empirical knowledge affects current theories of organizational learning, leadership, organizational culture and change, as well as the training of managers and administrators. Her research programme includes the analysis of Knowledge Management (KM) as a new tool for managing organizational development and change with particular emphasis on what knowledge is, and on the human ability to codify and represent it. Gabriele is a member of the Academy of Management and is an executive member of the Academy's Management Education Division. She recently served as Senior Editor of *Organization Studies*, and is a member of the editorial board of *Management Learning*, among others.

**Roy J. Lewicki** is the Irving Abramowitz Memorial Professor of Business Ethics at the Max M. Fisher College of Business, the Ohio State University. Professor Lewicki maintains research and teaching interests in the fields of negotiation and dispute resolution, organizational leadership, and ethical decision making. Roy is an author or editor of 31 books in the areas of negotiation, conflict management, organizational justice and organizational change. His most recent books include *Negotiation* (5th edition, with B. Barry and D. Saunders), *Making Sense of Intractable Environmental Conflicts* (with B. Gray and M. Elliott), and *Mastering Business Negotiations* (with A. Hiam). He is also the author or co-author of over 80 book chapters and refereed journal articles. Roy is a past President of the International Association of Conflict Management. He is the recipient of the David Bradford Teaching Award from the Organizational Behavior Teaching Society, and the Distinguished Educator Award from the Academy of Management, as well as many teaching awards from the Ohio State University. He is the founding editor of *Academy of Management Learning and Education*. He is a graduate of Dartmouth College and received his Ph.D. from Columbia University.

**Kathryn Martell** (Ph.D. University of Maryland, B.A. University of Chicago) joined Montclair State University in 2002 as Associate Dean of the School of Business and Professor of Management. In addition to her teaching and Dean responsibilities, she has directed two BIE grants from the US Department of Education. Her projects using technology to link students in the US with students in other countries have received recognition from the AACSB (Midwest Regional Award for Curriculum Innovation), ACE (Special Recognition for Cost Effective Curriculum Programs), AAUA (International Award for Innovation in Higher Education), and the US Department of Education. Dr Martell is a nationally known expert on the topic of assessing student learning. She is a frequent speaker at AACSB (American Association of Collegiate Schools of Business) national and regional conferences. She developed the content for AACSB's online Assessment Resource Center (www.aacsb.edu/ARC). She recently edited a two-volume set *Assessment of Student Learning in Business Schools: Best Practices Each Step of the Way*, published by AACSB and the Association for Institutional Research. She has also published in *Human Resource Management*, *R&D Management*, *Industrial Management*, the *Labor Law Journal*, *Research in Higher Education*, *Journal of Teaching in International Business*, and the *Journal of Business Education*.

**Larry Michaelsen** (Ph.D. in Organizational Psychology from the University of Michigan) is David Ross Boyd Professor Emeritus at the University of Oklahoma, Professor of Management at Central Missouri State University, a Carnegie Scholar, a Fulbright Senior Scholar, and former editor of the *Journal of Management Education*. He is active in faculty development activities and has conducted workshops on teaching effectively with small groups in a wide variety of university and corporate settings. Dr Michaelsen has also received numerous college, university and national awards for his outstanding teaching and for his pioneering work in two areas. One is the development of Team-Based Learning (www.teambasedlearning.org). The other is an Integrative Business Experience (ibe.ucmo.edu) programme that links student learning in three core business courses to their experience in creating, funding and operating an actual start-up business whose profits are used to finance a hands-on community service project.

**Richard G. Milter** is Director of the MBA Fellows Program, Interim Chair of MBA Programs, and Professor of Management at the Carey Business School at Johns Hopkins University. Rick has consulted or served as a training facilitator or organization effectiveness specialist for dozens of corporations and government agencies around the globe. His research and publications are in the areas of executive judgment, group decision-making processes, management information systems, negotiation strategies, managerial ethics, leadership, and innovative learning platforms. He has served as editor-in-chief of the Springer Science and Business series *Educational Innovations in Economics and Business*, serves as associate editor of the Springer Publishing series *Advances in Business Education and Training*, and serves on the editorial boards of the Information Age Publishing series *Research in Management Education and Development* and the Springer Verlag Publishing series *Innovation and Change in Professional Education*.

**Luciara Nardon** is an Assistant Professor of Management at the Vlerick Leuven Gent Management School, Belgium. She has taught courses on international management in Denmark, Belgium, Brazil and the US. She received her Bachelor's degree in accounting from Universidade Federal do Rio Grande do Sul, Brazil, and a graduate degree in accounting from Fundação Getúlio Vargas, Brazil. In addition, she holds two Master's degrees in business from the Universidad de Ciencias Empresariales y Sociales, Argentina, and the Peter F. Drucker Graduate School of Management, Claremont Graduate University. She holds a Ph.D. in international management and strategy from the University of Oregon. Her recent research has been published in the *Journal of World Business*, *Organizational Dynamics* and *Advances in International Management*. She is also the co-author (with Richard M. Steers) of *Managing in the Global Economy* (2006, Sharpe) and 'The Culture Theory Jungle', a chapter in the *Handbook of Culture, Work, Organizations* (Cambridge University Press, forthcoming). Prior to her academic career, Professor Nardon worked as a director of control systems and strategic planning for companies in Brazil, Portugal, and the US.

**James O'Toole** is the Daniels Distinguished Professor of Business Ethics at the University of Denver's Daniels College of Business. Previously, at the University of Southern California's business school he held the University Associates' Chair of Management, served as Executive Director of the Leadership Institute, and was editor of *New Management* magazine. O'Toole's research and writings have been in the areas of leadership, philosophy, ethics, and corporate culture. He has addressed dozens of major corporations and professional groups, and has over 100 published articles. Among his 16 books, *Vanguard Management* was named 'One of the best business and economics books of 1985' by the editors of *BusinessWeek*. His latest books are *Creating the Good Life: Applying Aristotle's Wisdom to Find Meaning and Happiness* (2005), *The New American Workplace* (with Edward Lawler, 2006), and *Transparency* (with Warren Bennis and Daniel Goleman, 2008). O'Toole received his Doctorate in Social Anthropology from Oxford University, where he was a Rhodes Scholar. He served as a Special Assistant to Secretary of Health, Education and Welfare, Elliot Richardson, as Chairman of the Secretary's Task Force on Work in America, and as Director of Field Investigations for President Nixon's Commission on Campus Unrest. He won a Mitchell Prize for a paper on economic growth policy, has served on the Board of Editors of the *Encyclopaedia Britannica*, and was editor of *The American Oxonian* magazine. From 1994 to 1997 O'Toole was Executive Vice President of the Aspen Institute, and later, Mortimer J. Adler Senior Fellow at the Institute. He has also served as chair of the Booz/Allen/Hamilton Strategic Leadership Center. In 2007 he was named one of the '100 most influential people in business ethics' by the editors of *Ethisphere*, and one of 'the top 100 thought leaders on leadership' by *Leadership Excellence* magazine.

**Mustafa F. Özbilgin** is Professor of Human Resource Management at the Norwich Business School, University of East Anglia, UK, and director of the research centre, DECERe (Diversity and Equality in Careers and Employment Research). He researches on equality, diversity and inclusion at work from contextual and comparative perspectives. He has authored and edited a number of books, including *Global Diversity Management* (2008, Palgrave), *Career Choice in Management and Entrepreneurship* (2007, Edward Elgar), *Relational Perspectives in Organizational Studies* (2006, Edward Elgar), and *Banking and Gender* (2003, IB Tauris) and published numerous research papers and reports. He is editor of the journal *Equal Opportunities International* (Emerald Press). Having completed a Ph.D. in Organizational Sociology at the University of Bristol in 1998, he has previously worked at the University of Hertfordshire, UK, University of Surrey, UK, and at Queen Mary, University of London, as a lecturer in Employment Relations. He has held visiting researcher posts at CEPS-INSTEAD (Luxembourg), Cornell University, USA, and the Japan Institute of Labour and Policy.

**Mine Karataş Özkan** is a Lecturer in Entrepreneurship at the School of Management, University of Southampton, UK. Her research interests include nascent entrepreneurship from a learning perspective, social and science entrepreneurship, and diversity aspects of entrepreneurship and knowledge work. She has published a number of research papers and reports in these areas, and is currently authoring a book entitled *Nascent Entrepreneurship from a Learning Perspective* (2008, Edward Elgar). She completed a Ph.D. in Entrepreneurship at the University of Southampton in 2006, and has previously worked at the University of Derby, UK, as a researcher.

**Pamela L. Perrewé** is the Distinguished Research Professor and Jim Moran Professor of Management at the College of Business at Florida State University. She received a Ph.D. in

Management from the University of Nebraska – Lincoln. Dr Perrewé has focused her research in the areas of job stress, coping, organizational politics, emotion and personality. She has published several books, over 15 book chapters, and 80 journal articles in journals such as *Academy of Management Journal, Journal of Management, Journal of Applied Psychology*, and *Organizational Behavior and Human Decision Processes*. She is the co-editor of the annual series titled, *Research in Occupational Stress and Well Being*, published by Elsevier Science, Inc. Dr Perrewé has mentored many Ph.D. students over more than 23 years in the field, has served on 67 doctoral dissertation committees, and chaired 14.

**Tim O. Peterson** is Clinical Associate Professor of Business. He is also the Director of Mays Business Fellows, a premier undergraduate professional development programme focused on developing team-oriented leaders. He is the architect of the Transitions Program that develops the vital competencies needed by all employees. His research interests are leadership, work life competencies, the scholarship of teaching, and the application of information technology to organizational issues. He has published in the *Academy of Management Education and Learning, Academy of Management Executive, Performance Improvement Quarterly, Journal of Leadership Studies, Journal of Management Education*, and *Journal of Management Systems*. He earned his Ph.D. from Texas A&M University in 1988.

**Joe Raelin** holds the Asa. S. Knowles Chair of Practice-Oriented Education at Northeastern University and is a recognized scholar in the fields of work-based learning and leadership development. Formerly, he was Professor of Management at the Wallace E. Carroll School of Management. He received his Ph.D. from the State University of New York at Buffalo. His research has centred on executive and professional education and development. He is a prolific writer, having produced over 100 articles appearing in leading management journals. He is also a management consultant with over 30 years of experience working with a wide variety of organizational clients. His publications include *The Clash of Cultures: Managers Managing Professionals* (Harvard Business School Press, 1991), considered now to be a classic in the field of managing professionals; *Creating Leaderful Organizations:How to Bring Out Leadership in Everyone* (Berrett-Koehler, 2003); and the new edition of *Work-Based Learning: Bridging Knowledge and Action in the Workplace* (Jossey-Bass, 2008).

**Rebecca J. Reichard**, Ph.D., is Visiting Assistant Professor of Psychology at Claremont McKenna College and the Postdoctoral Research Fellow in Leadership at the Kravis Leadership Institute. Becky received her B.S. in Psychology from Missouri Western State University where she was also recently inducted into the Athletic Hall of Fame for her career playing women's basketball. She earned her doctorate in Business from the Gallup Leadership Institute, University of Nebraska-Lincoln. Dr Reichard has ongoing research on evaluating the impact of leadership and undergraduate leadership education, understanding the motivational aspects driving leader self-development, and building the development of global mindset.

**Michael Reynolds** is Emeritus Professor of Management Learning at Lancaster University Management School and has been director of full-time and part-time postgraduate programmes in the department of Management Learning and Leadership. His research interests are in illuminating differences between tutor intentions and students' experiences in experiential learning designs, and in the application of critical perspectives to management learning design. He was co-editor with John Burgoyne of *Management Learning: Integrating Perspectives In Theory And Practice* (1997) and with Russ Vince of *Organising Reflection* (2004) and the *Handbook of Experiential Learning and Management Education* (2007).

**Ronald E. Riggio**, Ph.D., is the Henry R. Kravis Professor of Leadership and Organizational Psychology and Director of the Kravis Leadership Institute at Claremont McKenna College. He received his B.S. in Psychology from Santa Clara University and M.A. and Ph.D. in Social/Personality Psychology from the University of California, Riverside. Professor Riggio is the author of over 100 books, book chapters, and research articles in the areas of leadership, assessment centres, organizational psychology and social psychology. His research work has included published studies on the role of social skills and emotions in leadership potential and leadership success, the use of assessment centre methodology for student outcome assessment, empathy, social intelligence and charisma. His most recent books are *The Practice of Leadership* and *The Art of Followership* (2007, 2008, Jossey-Bass), and *Transformational Leadership* (2nd edn), co-authored with Bernard M. Bass (2006, Erlbaum).

**Bob Rubin** is an Assistant Professor of Management at the Charles H. Kellstadt Graduate School of Business at DePaul University. Bob is an avid teacher specializing in the areas of organizational behaviour and human resource management. His current research interests include leadership, assessment, and management education. He has published in numerous books and leading academic journals including the *Academy of Management Journal, Personnel Psychology, The Leadership Quarterly, Journal of Organizational Behavior* and *Academy of Management Learning & Education*. Dr Rubin is currently an editorial board member for two journals, *Academy of Management Learning & Education* and *Journal of Leadership and Organizational Studies*. In addition, he recently co-authored a text titled *Developing Management Skills: What Great Managers Know and Do* focusing on building practical management capabilities in the classroom. Bob received his Ph.D. in Organizational Psychology from Saint Louis University.

**Eugene Sadler-Smith** is Professor of Management Development and Organizational Behaviour in the School of Management, University of Surrey. After a successful career in the gas industry, during which time he completed his Ph.D. under the supervision of Richard J. Riding, at the University of Birmingham, 1988–1992 (part-time) on the subject of cognitive styles, he became a university lecturer in 1994. His research interests at the moment are centred upon the role of intuitive judgement in management decision making and management development. His research has been published widely in peer-reviewed journals such as the *Academy of Management Executive, Academy of Management Learning and Education, British Journal of Psychology, Journal of Occupational & Organizational Psychology, Journal of Organizational Behavior, Management Learning* and *Organisation Studies*, and many others. He is author of *Learning and Development for Managers: Perspectives from Research and Practice* (2006, Blackwell), *Learning in Organisations: Complexities and Diversities* (with Peter J. Smith, 2006, Routledge) and *Inside Intuition* (2008, Routledge).

**Raymond Saner** is an expert in international management, economic and social development and organizational change management with more than 20 years of experience in the above fields as teacher, consultant and researcher. He is Professor at Basle University (Economics Department, 1988–present), and teaches at the World Trade Institute in Berne (2000–present) and in the Master in Public Affairs programme of Sciences in Paris (2005–present). Raymond Saner is co-founder of CSEND, a Geneva based NGRDO (non-governmental research and development organization, 1993–present), partner of Organizational Consultants Ltd, Hong Kong (consulting company, 1989–present), and has consulted international organizations such as WTO, the WB, UNDP, EBRD, ILO, UNICEF and BIS. He was the Swiss delegate to the ISO working group which drafted the ISO 10015 standard on training and has served as member of the peer review team which evaluated quality systems of Switzerland's professional schools and universities of applied sciences.

**D. Lynn Sorenson** is a professional teaching-and-learning consultant at Brigham Young University (BYU). For 15 years she served in the BYU Faculty Center where she was assistant director. She is currently assigned to the BYU Center for Teaching and Learning. Prior to joining BYU in 1992, she worked with L. Dee Fink in the University of Oklahoma Instructional Development Program. She has researched, presented and published numerous articles and book chapters on a variety of subjects – most recently, valuing the student voice in faculty and instructional development, classroom strategies to enhance student learning, (online) student ratings of instruction, and course design for the achievement of student learning outcomes. She has served on the board of directors, chaired conferences, and reviewed journal manuscripts for the Professional and Organizational Development (POD) Network in Higher Education. In addition, she has served as a council delegate to, and as conference chair for the International Consortium for Educational Development (ICED).

**Richard M. Steers** is Professor Emeritus of Organization and Management at the University of Oregon. He is a past President and Fellow of the Academy of Management and a Fellow of both the American Psychological Association and the American Psychological Society. He has published on various management topics, including work motivation, employee absenteeism and turnover, organizational effectiveness and international management. His most recent books include *Motivation and Work Behavior* (with Greg Bigley and Lyman W. Porter, 2003, McGraw-Hill), *Managing in the Global Economy* (with Luciara Nardon, 2006, M.E. Sharpe), and the *Handbook of Culture, Work, and Organizations* (with Rabi Bhagat; Cambridge University Press, forthcoming). In addition to his career at the University of Oregon, Professor Steers has taught at the Rotterdam School of Management and Nijenrode University (both in the Netherlands); Hanyang University (Korea); University of California, Irvine (USA); University of Cape Town (South Africa); and Oxford University (UK). Prior to his academic experience, he served in various management and employee development posts at the Dow Chemical Company.

**Michael Sweet** has worked in postsecondary faculty development since 1995, at universities and community colleges, and is currently an instructional consultant for the Division of Instructional Innovation and Assessment (DIIA) at the University of Texas at Austin. In over a decade of exposure to numerous classroom strategies, nothing has ignited Michael's interest like the motivational and instructional power of Team-Based Learning (TBL). As a result, Michael has an active research programme and publication history focusing mostly on the processes and outcomes of TBL in the college classroom. Michael recently co-edited a special issue of *Educational Psychology Review* on postsecondary collaborative learning research, and presents widely on practical ways to activate postsecondary learning.

**Russ Vince** is Professor of Leadership and Change in the School of Management and the School for Health, the University of Bath. His research interests are in management and organizational learning, leadership and change. His most recent books are: 'The Handbook of Experiential Learning and Management Education' (Oxford University Press, 2007), 'Rethinking Strategic Learning' (Routledge, 2004) and 'Organizing Reflection' (Ashgate, 2004). Russ is Editor-in-Chief of the international academic journal *Management Learning*. He is an International Advisor to the *Doctoral School of Organizational Learning*, Copenhagen, Denmark; Academic Director, the *Leading Consultation* programme, Paris, France; and a Member of the *Research Steering Committee* of the Association of Business Schools. Russ has worked as an Associate Consultant with the Ashridge Consulting Group and the International Institute for Organizational Change, Geneva. He is an internationally recognized expert in organizational learning and action learning.

**Suzanne Scaffidi Warell** has expertise in several disciplines including intercultural communication, foreign languages, graduate business education, and online learning. Recently, she has designed and delivered online MBA courses to impact intercultural sensitivity development for graduate students. These courses have utilized case study material gathered from her cross-cultural management research in Brazil, China, and India. Previously, she was a medical device consultant for over 13 years and coordinated and conducted educational programmes in the United States, South America, and Europe. Suzanne received a Bachelor of Arts from the University of Minnesota in Spanish and Speech Communications, a Master of Arts in Adult Education from Carroll College in Waukesha, Wisconsin, and a Ph.D. in Educational Policy and Leadership from Marquette University in Milwaukee, Wisconsin. She also attended the University of Seville, Spain, where she was an English tutor for medical students and acquired a working knowledge of Spanish, Portuguese and German languages.

**David A. Whetten** is the Jack Wheatley Professor of Organizational Studies and Director of the Faculty Development Center at Brigham Young University. Prior to joining BYU in 1994 he was on the faculty at the University of Illinois, Urbana-Champaign, for 20 years. He has published numerous articles and books on a variety of subjects – most recently on organizational identity and identification, theory development, and management education. His pioneering and award-winning management text, *Developing Management Skills*, co-authored with Kim Cameron, is in its seventh edition. He has also served as editor of the *Foundations for Organizational Science*, an academic book series, and the *Academy of Management Review*. In 1991 he was elected an Academy of Management Fellow, he received the Academy's Distinguished Service Award in 1994, and in 2004 he received the Academy of Management OMT Division Distinguished Scholar award. In addition, he served as President of the Academy of Management in 2000.

**Lichia Yiu** is co-founder and president of the Centre for Socio-Eco-Nomic Development, a Geneva-based research and development institute (CSEND, since 1993). She has designed and conducted management training and OD projects for European and North America-based multinational companies in North America, Europe and Asia, and has developed institutional development platforms to support public sector reforms in China, Slovenia, Vietnam, Russia and English-speaking African countries for the United Nations, WHO, ILO, EBRD and bilateral development aid agencies (SDC, GTZ, DANIDA, SIDA, NORAID, CIDA). She has published seven books and more than 40 articles in publications such as *American Academy of Management Executive*, *Advances in International Comparative Management*, *Human Resource Quarterly*, *Performance Improvement Quarterly*, *Public Sector Management*, and *International Journal of Human Resource Management*. She holds an M.A. and Ed.D. in counselling psychology from Indiana University, Bloomington, and a Post-doctoral Fellowship in organizational psychology from Teachers College, Columbia University, New York. Lichia Yiu was a member of the OECD team which assessed China higher education sector at national level and continues to provide research and consulting input for the OECD on quality aspects of higher education and on the link between education and employability.

# Past, Present and Future Perspectives of Management Learning, Education and Development

Steven J. Armstrong and Cynthia V. Fukami

## INTRODUCTION AND THEORETICAL OVERVIEW

The scholarship of management teaching and learning is increasingly being recognized as a field in its own right. Postgraduate courses in management learning are being offered in some of the most prestigious business schools around the world. The *Journal of Management Education*, founded in 1976 to serve as a forum for the improvement of management education in both classroom and corporate settings, continues to prosper, as does *Management Learning,* founded in 1978 to provide a forum for the understanding of learning in management and organizations. The US Academy of Management, regarded by many as the premier scholarly society in the discipline of management, has a division (Management Education and Development)

devoted to the field. Its membership, drawn from more than 40 nations, has increased by more than 75 per cent over the past ten years. The journal *Academy of Management Learning and Education* (AMLE) was launched in 2002 to sit alongside the Academy's other prestigious journals to address the scholarship of teaching and learning.

The time is now right to present an account of the 'state of the art' in management learning, education and development (MLED), to map out where the discipline is going, and to identify what are the key debates and issues that concern management educators. This *Handbook of Management Learning, Education and Development* (MLED) has therefore joined the series of Sage Handbooks that are recognised as benchmark volumes in their field in order to fulfil these important requirements. The book consists of original chapters by leading international scholars in the field from around the globe. A key dynamic of the handbook is a retrospective and prospective overview of the discipline, a critical assessment of past and present theory that also looks to the future. The handbook emphasizes the theoretical diversity within MLED by examining the integrity and intellectual coherence of the discipline, while also looking at resonances within and between its key components.

The focus of the handbook is on the education and development of managers, which will necessarily embrace theoretical aspects of individual and collective learning, the delivery of formal management education, and the facilitation of management development in educational and non-educational contexts. The interdisciplinary nature of the field is reflected in the contributions whose aims are to analyse, promote and critique the role of MLED to management understanding.

Each chapter offers a comprehensive, critical overview of aspects of the field, a discussion of key debates and research and a review of the emerging agendas in the topic area. Topics include the application of learning theories, theoretical advances about effective instructional and evaluation methods, innovations in the use of technology, both in the classroom and in virtual learning environments, and ways of developing practising managers in the context of lifelong learning.

Management is a practice that has to blend a good deal of experience with a certain amount of insight and some analysis (Mintzberg, 2004). It is not too difficult to imagine how analytical skills can be formally taught. It *is* difficult to imagine, however, how insight or the outcomes of management experience can be formally taught; and it is easier to imagine how they can derive from a developmental process. Herein lies the need for the use of two terms – 'management education' and 'management development' – and it is important to differentiate between these processes. Within this perspective, 'management education' is taken to imply formal learning which takes place under

the auspices of academic institutions within credit-bearing courses to enhance managers' analytic and critical skills. This type of learning is usually provided in organized, time-bounded and structured programmes. Such programmes sometimes emphasize the scientific aspects of management, but they are often criticized for spoon-feeding analysis and technique, and for being rather static in nature, emphasizing memory and repetition and being somewhat divorced from managerial reality. In contrast, informal learning, which is more closely associated with 'management development', is believed by some to offer a more effective approach by emphasizing on-the-job learning that occurs experientially in culturally embedded ways, situated in communities of practice within work-based organizations. Such learning is believed to result in the acquisition of tacit or procedural knowledge contributing to the art and craft of management, whereas formal education is believed to result in the acquisition of explicit or declarative knowledge. The former is believed to be more closely associated with successful managers.

Formal and informal learning approaches, however, should not be treated as being mutually exclusive. Instead, they should be regarded as being complementary and necessary components in the overall process of management learning. With this in mind, this handbook seeks to explore a variety of challenging approaches to the many diverse forms of management learning, linking new ideas and developments as a way of advancing both theory and practice. It seeks to identify and examine best practices in university-based management education programmes, and training and development processes in corporate, consultancy and independent college settings. The handbook, which is designed to appeal to academics, researchers, educators, programme directors, deans of business schools, advanced postgraduate students and practitioners in corporate education, is presented in three main parts. Part I covers theoretical aspects of knowledge acquisition in the context of management learning. It draws on other disciplinary fields such as philosophy, education, psychology and sociology, as well as organization theory, with a commitment to broadening and deepening our knowledge and understanding of the most relevant management theory. Part II is concerned with using theory to improve practice and promote ways of enhancing learning effectiveness in formal settings. The chapters in Part II explore a variety of learning and teaching phenomena, including potential use of the arts, cognitive styles and learning strategies, course design, technology in the classroom, distance learning, mentoring frameworks, culture and diversity issues, assessment and accreditation, problem and project based learning, team learning and importantly, the research-teaching nexus. Part III is concerned with exploring non-credit based management development through a variety of approaches and concepts, including reflexive practice, action learning, development of competencies, leadership development, coaching and mentoring, preparation of global business leaders and communities of practice. Part III finishes with a chapter that considers ways of assessing and accrediting these non-formal learning approaches. The handbook ends on a provocative note with the concluding chapter from James O'Toole that considers future perspectives of management learning, education and development in light of what has been presented in preceding chapters.

## HISTORICAL CONTEXT

Although there has been dramatic growth in the provision of management education and development programmes over the past century, there have also been increasing doubts over the relevance (Grey, 2004; Pfeffer and Fong, 2002) and effectiveness (Mintzberg, 2004) of their educational products. It has even been suggested that the field is on the verge of a paradigm shift (Whetten et al. Chapter 13 this volume) evidenced by the number of radical business school reforms being conducted around the world. To shed further light on this debate it is

helpful to consider the origins and history of business schools in general and management education in particular.

According to Engwall (2007) while there were early attempts to introduce economic disciplines into universities in Europe in the eighteenth century (e.g. Frankfurt-an-der-oder, Rinteln and Halle in Germany, 1727 and Uppsala, Sweden, 1741) the first notable institutions for academic business education began to appear in the middle of the nineteenth century as shown in Table 1.1.

Business colleges were also being founded in other parts of the world around this time, such as Tokyo (1887), Osaka (1901) and Kobe (1902) in Japan and also in India (1913). In the UK it was not until The British Institute of Management (founded in 1948) assembled a committee to address aspects of management education (Ivory et al., 2006) that interests began to accelerate (Tiratsoo, 1998). However, business education really began to gain momentum in the UK in the early 1960s following the Robbins Report in 1963 which called for two postgraduate business schools to be established. Shortly afterwards, a centre for business education was created at Warwick University and then two new business schools were founded within the universities of Manchester and London in 1965. By the 1970s, management education was being provided by 237 different institutions in the UK (Tiratsoo, 1998), and by the 1990s UK business schools brought in more than £400 million a year (Crainer and Dearlove, 1999) to the nation's economy. Engwall (2007) reports a similar proliferation of business schools across northern, central and eastern Europe and notes that the American model has played a dominant role in their development. For a more complete discussion of the history of management education, refer to Engwall (2007), Engwall and Zamagni (1998), and Warner (1997).

The roots of many of these business schools (despite others appearing in Europe at the same time, such as HEC in Paris and Handelshochschulen in Germany) can be traced back to the United States and

**Table 1.1    Institutions for Academic Business Education: Europe and United States**

| | |
|---|---|
| 1851 | University of Louisiana (US) |
| 1852 | University of Wisconsin (US); Institut Superieur de Commerce de l'Etat, Antwerp, Belgium; Institut Superieur de Commerce Saint Ignace, Antwerp, Belgium |
| 1854 | Ecole Superieure de Commerce, Paris, France |
| 1856 | Wiener Handelsakademie, Austria |
| 1866 | Ecole Superieure de Commerce, Mulhouse, France |
| 1867 | Scuola Superiore di Commercio, Venice, Italy |
| 1869 | Washington & Lee University, US |
| 1871 | Le Havre, France; Sciences Politiques, Paris, France |
| 1872 | Lyon, France; Marseille, France |
| 1874 | Bordeaux, France |
| 1881 | Ecole des Hautes Etudes Commerciales, Paris, France; Wharton School of Finance and Commerce, University of Pennsylvania |
| 1884 | Genoa, Italy |
| 1886 | Bari, Italy |
| 1892 | Lille, France |
| 1895 | London School of Economics, England; Rouen, France |
| 1896 | Nancy, France |
| 1897 | Montpellier, France |
| 1898 | Aachen, Germany; Leipzig, Germany; St Gallen, Switzerland; Vienna, Austria; University of California (US); University of Chicago (US) |
| 1900 | Budapest, Hungary; Dijon, France; Nantes, France; Amos Tuck School, Dartmouth (US); New York University (US) |
| 1901 | Cologne, Germany; Frankfurt, Germany |
| 1902 | Birmingham University, England; Bocconi, Milan, Italy |
| 1903 | Brussels, Belgium |
| 1904 | Manchester University, England |
| 1905 | Toulouse, France |
| 1906 | Berlin, Germany; Rome, Italy; Turin, Italy |
| 1908 | Mannheim, Germany; University College Dublin, Ireland; Columbia University (US); Harvard Business School (US) |
| 1909 | Stockholm School of Economics, Sweden |
| 1910 | Munich, Germany |
| 1911 | Finnish Business School, Helsinki, Finland |
| 1913 | Rotterdam, Neitherland |

*Source*: Adapted from: Engwall and Zamagni (1998) Reprinted with permission.

in particular to the Wharton School at the University of Pennsylvania when a Bachelor's degree in Business was initiated in 1881 by Joseph Wharton, an American businessman. Believed to be the first of the prominent business schools, it was founded, somewhat ironically, as we will demonstrate later, on

the basis of his criticisms of the 'learning by doing' approach common in colleges at that time. Wharton favoured a more structured and theoretical approach to management education (Sass, 1982). Wharton's criticisms were to be echoed nearly 80 years later in two landmark studies which were to change the face of management education. The first Master's degree in Business Administration (MBA) appeared at Dartmouth College's Tuck School of Business in the US in 1902. This school was established in 1900 by Edward Tuck, an international financier and philanthropist (Friga et al., 2003), at a time when there was explosive growth in commerce and industry. In 1908, the Harvard Business School launched its first MBA and Stanford followed suit in 1925. By 1915, there were approximately 40 business schools in the US and a year later the American Association of Collegiate Schools of Business, otherwise known as the AACSB, became the accrediting agency. The number of business schools then increased in the US five-fold to nearly 200 by 1925. Interestingly, most business professors at that time were either practising or retired corporate managers who focused on sharing lessons learned in the workplace (Friga et al., 2003).

This became known as the *trade school* approach to management education and drew major criticisms such as the one by sociologist Thorsten Veblen in 1918 cited in Engwall (2007: 11) as saying 'A college of commerce belongs in the corporation of learning no more than a department of athletics'. Nevertheless, this *trade school* approach continued through the first half of the twentieth century until massive reforms took place aimed at making business schools more academic and research oriented, like many other academic programmes at universities (Schmotter, 1998). Major driving forces behind these reforms were two landmark studies in the 1950s commissioned by the Ford Foundation (Gordon and Howell, 1959) and the Carnegie Corporation (Pierson, 1959) to review the state of management education. By today's standards, the Ford Foundation alone dedicated more than 250 million dollars to this effort (Friga et al., 2003). Essentially both of these studies argued that to give business schools more respectable academic underpinnings, they needed to shift their strategies to be more research focused and less vocational (Schlossman and Wechsler, 1998). Both reports called for the careful recruitment of staff whose credentials should include academic research. This gave rise to more rational, analytical decision-making approaches as the key to management education (Bach, 1959). The professionalization of management teaching that ensued brought about the domination of business functions such as finance, marketing, law, management science, and so on, but interestingly, not *management per se*. These reforms encouraged a scientific model of management education (Bennis and O'Toole, 2005). The strategies and structures of business schools today, both in the US (Mintzberg, 2004) and in Europe (Ivory et al., 2006), are almost identical to those established in the 1950s as a result of those two landmark studies.

Following these reforms, most leading universities now treat business schools as seriously as other long-standing schools. Their focus has switched from being vocational trade schools to being schools which conduct rigorous scientific research and adopt scientific principles to underpin the management education process. Some have argued, however, that the pendulum has swung too far from the trade school paradigm and that business schools have become too academic (Porter and McKibbin, 1988) and that it is now necessary to strike a balance between scientific rigour and practical relevance (Bennis and O'Toole, 2005: 98). In their *Harvard Business Review* article entitled 'How business schools lost their way', Bennis and O'Toole argue that this scientific model is predicated on the false assumption that business and management studies are an academic discipline like chemistry or physics when they should be viewed as a profession like medicine or law schools. In their pursuit to educate practitioners and to create knowledge through research, these schools deliberately engage with the outside world.

Faculty members are expected to be first rate scholars, but not to produce studies at arm's length from actual practice which is so often the case with business schools. They argue that business school professors know a lot about academic publishing, but few have ever worked in a real business. This contrasts sharply with medical schools, for example, where members of teaching faculty are often practising doctors. Bennis and O'Toole argue that no business school curricula reform will work until the scientific model is replaced by a more appropriate one rooted in the requirements of a profession – where the focus shifts towards integrating knowledge and practice. This controversy over academic rigour versus practical relevance of the learning attained in business schools has been widely discussed over the past two decades. We will now consider some of the major thrusts of those debates.

## Perceptions of the present state of management education and development

According to Chia (2005), the reforms which resulted in the domination of specialized business functions and the adoption of this scientific approach to problem solving have led to a functional 'silo type' disciplinary mentality (e.g. Marketing, Finance, HRM, Operations, etc.). Whereas some have argued that undergraduate programmes should continue to benefit from the depth and breadth of specialized learning (Campbell et al., 2006), others have argued persuasively for an integrated curriculum that breaks down the silos between functional subjects (Linder and Smith, 1992; Fukami et al., 1996; Michaelsen, 1999), especially for postgraduate programmes geared towards middle and upper level executives. Mintzberg (2004: 32) eloquently captures the consequence of the silo disciplinary mentality by asserting that, 'As businesses work valiantly to bust down the walls between their silos, business schools work valiantly to reinforce them'. He goes on to argue that these phenomena which characterize the curriculum lead to the passive ingestion of 'inert' ideas that pass for management education. In an address made at Cambridge University in 1912, Sir Alfred North Whitehead, mathematician and Professor of Philosophy of Science and Philosophy of Education said that, 'Above all things, we must be aware of "inert" ideas, that is to say ideas that are merely received into the mind without being utilised, or tested, or thrown into fresh combinations. Education with inert ideas is not only useless; it is above all things, harmful – Corruptio optimi, pessima'. Whitehead made similar assertions at a later address given to Harvard University Business School in 1928.

Despite consistent calls for change spanning more than a quarter of a century, some have argued that management education is still in a parlous state (Grey, 2004) and that the explosive growth it has witnessed has, paradoxically, been accompanied by a crisis of confidence (Armstrong and Sadler-Smith, 2008). This is manifested in debates about the direction of business and management education (Quinn Trank and Rynes, 2003), its effectiveness (Mintzberg, 2004) and serious doubts about the relevance of its educational product because 'neither possessing an MBA degree or grades earned in courses correlate with career success' (Pfeffer and Fong, 2002: 78). This is despite the undoubted huge commercial successes of business schools. Even more damning is evidence which suggests that engineering graduates are more likely to be managing others than management graduates, five years after graduation (CEML Report, 2002).

It has also been suggested that these major problems associated with management education arose following the reforms of the 1950s discussed above, when business schools were encouraged to place more emphasis on teaching students sets of analytical tools (Mintzberg, 2004). Some believe that these approaches led to students having the false perception that management problems can be defined as neat technical packages (Raelin, 1995). What to do with

the knowledge obtained from our educational experiences is often left out of the picture. Our graduates know a lot, but can't do anything (Fukami, 2007). One study reported that 73 per cent of the surveyed MBA programme graduates indicated that they made little use of what they had learned in the classroom on their first assignments as managers (McCall Jr et al., 1988). Some excellent companies, such as Southwest Airlines, do not recruit at leading business schools, and avoid hiring MBAs (Pfeffer and Sutton, 1999). Bennis and O'Toole (2005: 96) also criticize business schools for being too focused on 'scientific' research, hiring professors with limited real-world experience, and therefore graduating students who are ill-equipped to wrangle with complex, unquantifiable issues – 'in other words, the stuff of management'. Further problems arise from claims that business school research does not influence management practice either (Starkey and Madan, 2001; Pfeffer and Fong, 2002), calling into question the professional relevance of management scholarship. Problems deepen still further as other leading thinkers in the field, such as Donaldson (2002), identifies contradictions between theories and management education, and Goshal (2005), who called for better theorizing because bad management theories are destroying good management practice. Some have advocated the need for more radical challenges to prevailing mindsets through the contribution of critical management education (Grey, 2004) or through a marriage of critical management education and action-based learning as a way of innovating on the interplay of informal and formal learning (Reynolds and Vince, 2004). The proof of whether these ideas can be reasonably transformed into useful action, however, is questionable (Bailey, 2004). The problems reported here were eloquently captured by Starkey and Tempest (2005: 67) who suggested that 'the future of business schools is in doubt because its research and teaching missions are compromised – perhaps fatally'. As noted by Grey (2002), most would agree that a trained doctor or engineer has superior technical expertise and proficiency than someone without such training, and their professional credentials give them a more secure legal status. The impact of management education on equipping people to become better managers, however, is much more ambiguous and, lacking the same professional credentials as doctors, managers have diminished expert status in the eyes of the law.

However, laws, regulations, and policies have been shown to be relatively expensive and inefficient methods for promoting responsible conduct. One way to encourage responsible behaviour is to create a profession. But as O'Toole (Chapter 29 this volume) reminds us, 'whilst the founders of the early business schools such as Wharton, Tuck, and Dartmouth were public spirited men with the intent of turning management into a respected 'calling' that *hope* died shortly after World War II'. Today, for reasons highlighted by Khurana (2007) management isn't a profession. Sociologists have identified four common aspects across professions: a common body of knowledge; a system for certifying that individuals possess such knowledge before being licensed or allowed to practice; a commitment to use specialized knowledge for the public good; and a code of ethics with provisions for monitoring individual compliance with the code and a system of sanctions for enforcing it (Khurana et al., 2005). When we compare business management to more traditional professions, such as medicine or engineering, and apply these four aspects, we can see that management is found wanting. There is no solid common body of knowledge able to account for much of the social environment of business. There is neither a formal educational requirement nor a system of examination and licensing for aspiring members. An MBA is not a requirement for becoming a manager. Business managers are not universally committed to the public good, and finally, are not governed by a shared normative code (Khurana et al., 2005). Is it impossible to understand the unethical behaviour we have recently observed among our business leaders?

Thus, the investment of billions of dollars in business education around the world clearly has not fully paid off. The mere possession of a quantity of knowledge has not resulted in leaders who make good judgements. In higher education in general, and in business schools in particular, we have focused on disseminating information and knowledge and have neglected the ability of our graduates to translate theory into practice (Fukami, 2007). Is there hope for the future?

## SCHOLARSHIP IN MANAGEMENT EDUCATION AND DEVELOPMENT

There is hope for reversing the trend of the impotence of management education and it derives from the concept of the scholarship of teaching and learning (SOTL). Simply put, SOTL recognizes that teaching is an integral part of faculty scholarship. In other words, rather than thinking about teaching as the price to be paid to do research, SOTL considers teaching to be an important part of the job of the professor. SOTL was introduced largely through the work of Ernest Boyer, then President of the Carnegie Foundation for the Advancement of Teaching, in his book, *Scholarship Reconsidered* (1990). Boyer argued that the role of the university professor was broader than the traditional tripartite model of research, teaching and service. He proposed an alternative model that identified four separate but overlapping functions: the scholarship of discovery; the scholarship of integration; the scholarship of application; and the scholarship of teaching. The scholarship of discovery involves our traditional view of research, and refers to scholarly work that creates disciplinary knowledge through hypotheses testing and theory generation. The scholarship of integration relates to merging knowledge across disciplines, and the scholarship of application relates to applying disciplinary knowledge to solving real problems. The scholarship of teaching refers to the dissemination of disciplinary knowledge.

Although Boyer's work was directed towards higher education in general, it certainly addresses some of the dilemmas of management education outlined above. Graduates of business education programmes, either formal or informal, must be exposed to the most current body of knowledge in the various business disciplines, must be able to see the relationships across the various business disciplines and to understand how these various areas interact with an organization, and they must be able to solve important problems with this knowledge. Finally, our graduates will be more able to accomplish these critical goals if their faculty have concentrated on their learning as a similarly critical goal.

Business schools are particularly suited to SOTL because of the fundamental synergy between the substance of our disciplines and the substance of teaching. Using the disciplinary field of management as an example, we are a discipline in which *how* we teach, and the tools we use, most closely mirror important aspects of *what* we teach (Frost and Fukami, 1997). In short, the field of management is about understanding human behaviour in organizations as well as understanding the organizations themselves. Our classrooms can be thought of as organizations, and, as such, provide a real-time laboratory in which to illustrate, experiment with, but more importantly to model, most of our important disciplinary concepts. This observation is not lost on our students, who often recognize the parallels between the content we are delivering on effective management, and the process their professors use to manage their classroom and departments, interact with peers and conduct their personal lives (Billimoria and Fukami, 2002). Not to be sensitive to this connection would be a lost opportunity to develop, and to model, excellent practice. Thus, it will be critical for management educators to focus on both the content and process of our curricula.

Through his model of scholarship, Boyer elevated the status of teaching by recognizing that there is a set of problems inherent in teaching that are worth pursuing as an ongoing intellectual quest. And since this is an intellectual quest, we can use the same intellectual process we follow in our disciplinary work to improve our teaching and our students' learning. In other words, to use the term 'scholarship' towards our teaching implies that we apply the scientific process, and standards for evaluating our work in teaching, as we apply in our disciplinary research. Intellectual rigour is just as important to teaching as it is to our disciplinary research.

By a number of accounts, SOTL is on the rise (Schmidt-Wilk and Fukami, in press). There are required courses on teaching in doctoral programmes, there are sessions on teaching in doctoral consortia at professional conferences, there is the previously mentioned rise in membership of the Management Education and Development division of the Academy of Management, and there are abundant peer-reviewed outlets in which to publish SOTL. Given this platform, let us cast our eyes to the future.

## FUTURE PERSPECTIVES AND CHALLENGES

It is clear that business schools have been under a sustained attack, and for a variety of good reasons. More relevant management research has been called for because of the gap between rigorous academic research and its application in the world of the practising manager (Starkey and Madan, 2001). More relevant teaching approaches designed to attend to the needs of managers have also been called for – for more than 30 years (e.g. Argyris and Schön, 1974). Despite this, the long and vocal chorus of scepticism about the value of business schools shows no sign of abating (Grey, 2004). Nor do prospects for the future seem good (O'Toole, Chapter 29 this volume; Gioia and Corley, 2002). So, the six million dollar question is – what should we be doing differently? Let us first of all focus on the medium term.

Regarding teaching and learning, Mintzberg (2004) asserts that students learn the wrong things in the wrong ways. Some argue that this is due to the separation of learning from practice, leading to people being able to talk about practice rather than being competent practitioners (Armstrong, 2005). Chia (Chapter 2 this volume) suggests that controversies like these bring into focus the kind of knowledge that we teach, emphasizing that a crucial aspect that has not been sufficiently addressed is the nature of knowledge and knowing generally associated with MLED. He suggests that the form of knowledge taught in business schools is 'primarily that of *episteme* and *techné*; precise, linguistically explicit and verifiable forms of knowledge that emphasize logic, causality, meaning and representation'. Relying solely on this explicit representational form of knowledge in the education and development of managers is a mistake.

Management is more art than a science and effective managing happens where art (emphasizing insight), science (emphasizing analysis) and craft (emphasizing experience) meet (Mintzberg, 2004). It involves 'becoming aware, attending to, sorting out, and prioritizing an inherently messy, fluxing, chaotic world of competing demands that are placed on a manager's attention' (Chia, 2005: 1092). Managing is more an acquired coping capability than a science; more a set of skilled practices than a profession; more a phenomenon of method than a field of study. Dealing with a fuzzy chaotic world devoid of any sort of order, which Chia argues is so akin to managers' daily experiences, is where the components of tacit knowledge referred to as *phronesis* and *mētis*, become crucial in the MLED process. This is the sort of knowledge that people do not know they have (Forsythe et al., 1998), cannot be understood through direct articulation or introspection (Cooper and Sawaf, 1996; Morgan, 1986), is personal, profound, non-scientific and generated in the intimacy of lived experience (Baumard, 1999). Development of tacit knowledge in business schools is neglected at the expense of focusing too much on disseminating explicit knowledge and codified information (Fukami, 2007).

Knowing what to do is not enough, we need to help facilitate the conversion of knowledge into action (Pfeffer and Sutton, 1999).

Empirical studies have demonstrated significant correlations between tacit knowledge and managerial performance and success (Sternberg et al., 2000) and that tacit knowledge is what differentiates experts from novices (Armstrong and Mahmud, 2008; Nestor-Baker, 1999). The over-arching question, however, is if tacit knowledge is what distinguishes successful managers from others, how do we facilitate its acquisition? Some have argued for more innovative approaches to teaching, learning and assessment that require a radical andrological shift from tutor-driven teaching to near total participation and engagement of the learner – where students take significantly more responsibility for their own learning, and where there are higher levels of participation in social practice (Armstrong, 2007). Institutionalizing such approaches in the face of the existing teaching paradigm, however, remains a significant challenge. But the alternative is to continue to provide formal learning in organized, time-limited and structured ways, emphasizing the acquisition of content, and analysis and technique. The consequences are that we will continue to produce management graduates who display analytic detachment to the detriment of insight (Hayes and Albernathy, 1980) – and who engage in too much of a scientific approach to problem solving and managing (Mintzberg, 2004).

In the short-to-medium term then, we can consider doing different things to bring the management learner back to centrestage, and this handbook is designed to do just that. In an extensive review of the management education literature, Korpiaho et al. (2007) suggested that a fruitful conception of management education should not only resolve the tactical *how* issues, but should also address the political *what* and the moral *why* issues. They identified three categories of management education which they called *traditional*, *revised* and *alternative* forms. The first two of these are concerned with the mastering of scientific knowledge aimed at educating managers to succeed in their work. The *alternative* form suggests new, alternative goals for management education, 'namely the education of responsible citizens by means of service-learning, of critically reflective practitioners by means of action-based learning or politically conscious and active professionals by means of critical management education' (p. 12). This handbook captures some useful innovations and insights from a group of scholars dedicated to the improvement of management learning in order to redress some of the ailments of business schools discussed earlier and that also fit well with Korpiaho et al.'s *alternative* modes of learning. Some are based around 'action learning', 'experiential learning', 'collaborative learning', 'ethics and learning', 'critical management education' or 'problem-based' learning approaches. As one example of their potential utility, problem-based courses start with problems rather than with the exposition of disciplinary knowledge. Learning consists of real problems and groups work through projects with assistance from tutors or even work-based mentors. The learner poses the questions and discovers potential answers at the risk of making mistakes. Tacit knowledge is acquired through exposure and interaction within a work environment. Incorporating work-based problem scenarios into our curricula where tutors and work-based mentors are involved would not only enhance the learning process through the acquisition of managerial tacit knowledge but would also be helpful for developing relationships between business schools and businesses, and for bridging the relevance gap between research and practice.

If short-to-medium term strategies are to focus on doing different things, then longer-term strategies need to focus on doing things differently in order to bring about effective long-term reforms. More radical thinkers like Mintzberg (2004) have argued that it is time to break down the silos and put old paradigms out to pasture. Most business school curricula remain compartmentalized

by discipline such as marketing, finance, operations management and so on, following the reforms of the 1950s. This might just have been sensible when careers were characterized by vertical advancement in a single field, within a functionally divided bureaucracy. However, careers now cross boundaries of function, organization, industry, cultures and political borders. Some have therefore argued that management education should change accordingly by re-designing it in such a way that it is organized around the key constituencies that a manager needs to engage in order to be effective. Some schools are already beginning to take bold steps towards a more integrated curriculum (e.g. Yale Management School) by completely dismantling their previous offerings. Unless more schools begin to question the very purpose of their enterprises and the relevance of their educational product then we can continue to see the staggering statistics which led to Bennis and O'Toole's (2005) assertions that we currently fail to impart useful management skills, fail to install norms of ethical behaviour, fail to prepare leaders, and fail to lead our graduates into good management careers.

Institutional inertia theory, however, suggests that universities will be slow to change given internal politics and past successes. The overall consensus is that change will come slowly, particularly given the massive infrastructure and incentive programmes currently in place. However, according to Lyman Porter the comfortable period for business schools since the end of the Second World War is over. Almost none of the casual practices, procedures and assumptions about what we should be doing and how we should be providing education are likely to survive the next two decades (Porter, 2000). In the closing chapter of this handbook, however, O'Toole considers the most probable future scenario for business schools and suggests that the future still looks rather grim. He argues that the diversity of viewpoints and perspectives expressed in this handbook, for example, represents a perfect reflection of the fragmentation that exists in the field of management education; that deans of business schools need to change the assumption that good researchers equal good teachers and adopt a pluralistic model of professorial excellence; that decision makers need to address the question of what managers need to know, what skills they will need to possess to be successful in the future, and to mirror changes in the corporate world. He does not believe that there are any quick fixes for the problems with business schools but concludes that 'it avails no one to improve the delivery of a poor product'. Although he concedes that there is general agreement that the current dominant mode of management education is not working, there is also no agreement on what should replace it. Without agreement on the 'what', there can never be closure on the 'how', which leads to his forecast: '*Faute de mieux,* pluralism will be the wave of the future'.

Having considered some of the past, present, and future perspectives and challenges of management learning, education and development, we will now share with you the birth and subsequent development of the present handbook. We trust you will agree that it has undergone a rigorous process and will hopefully inspire future work in this crucially important field.

## CHARTING THE JOURNEY OF THE HANDBOOK'S DEVELOPMENT

### Phase 1

In May 2006 at the European Academy of Management meeting in Munich, Germany, Steve Armstrong was approached by an editor from Sage Publications (Kiren Shoman) and asked whether he would be interested in contributing to the series of Sage Handbooks that are recognized as benchmark volumes in their field. The subject would be management education and development. As someone who had spent several years in management positions in industry, then several more years in management education, and who was soon to become Division Chair and President of

the Management Education and Development Division of the Academy of Management, this conversation sparked immediate interest. Through his contacts in the Academy of Management it wasn't long before Steve identified an equally interested person in the US, Cindi Fukami. On 7 August 2005, the three of us (now four – including Maya) met at the Academy of Management Annual Meeting in Honolulu, Hawaii, to discuss the development of a formal proposal and to agree on timescales. The seeds were now sown.

### Phase 2

To help develop the proposal we reviewed the entire contents of the four major journals in Business/Management Education: *Academy of Management Learning and Education*; *Management Learning*; *Journal of Management Education*; *Journal of Management Development*. Additionally, we reviewed the previous ten years' titles of all papers, symposia and professional development workshop activities accepted by the Management Education and Development Division at the Academy of Management's annual meetings. We also referred to a previous review article from the field (Bilimoria and Fukami, 2002). This process enabled the editors to identify major themes, and names of leading authors associated with those themes. Outcomes of this process culminated in a detailed proposal in November 2005 and also led to the present structure of this handbook. The proposal was reviewed by six referees selected by the volume's editors which led to a further revision prior to formally submitting it to Sage Publications in January 2006 for their consideration. In March 2006 we received detailed reviews from 14 anonymous reviewers selected by Sage and the proposal was revised, resubmitted and then formally accepted by Sage in April 2006.

### Phase 3

An editorial board was assembled during May 2006 comprising members from Australia,

New Zealand, USA, Scandinavia, Mainland Europe and Japan. A formal contract was issued by Sage on 14 June 2006. Potential authors were approached to contribute to the handbook over the summer of 2006 and by October we had agreement from all of the present authors and the writing of chapters was initiated. We were now set to try to achieve a manuscript submission date of 30 November 2007. A significant number of draft chapters were received by July 2007 and the remainder arrived by September. All chapters were blind reviewed by at least two reviewers, and in some cases, three or four. Revised versions of the chapters began to arrive in October 2007 and the final ones were received by February/March 2008. Approximately 15 per cent of revised chapters went through a second review and revision cycle. The final manuscript was submitted to Sage on 31 March except for Chapters 1 and 29 which followed shortly afterwards. We will now turn to a brief description of the contents of the handbook.

## OVERVIEW OF PART I

Part I of the handbook covers theoretical aspects underpinning knowledge acquisition in the context of management learning. Areas covered include: the nature of knowledge and knowing; experiential learning theory; theory of distributed cognition in the context of collective learning; reflection, reflective practice and organizing reflection beyond the reflective practitioner; critical management education; development and use of collaborative learning approaches and designs; ethics pedagogy and its inclusion in business school curricula; and lastly a consideration of the implications of the pervasiveness of emotion in organizations from the point of view of learning and education, with an emphasis on the role of emotions and emotional intelligence training in leadership programmes.

Part I begins with a chapter (2) by Robert Chia that explores the nature of 'knowledge' and 'knowing' in the context of management learning, education and development.

Current controversies regarding the role of business schools revolve around the twin pillars of 'academic rigour' and the need for 'practical relevance' of the learning attained. Within this debate, this author brings into focus the kind of knowledge taught in business schools and argues that relying solely on explicit representational forms of knowledge emphasizing logic and causality (i.e. *episteme and techné*) in the education and development of management is a mistake. Instead, business schools should focus more on practical wisdom (*phronesis*) that leads to abilities in interpreting and adapting knowledge in a particular context, and other forms of practical knowing such as cunning intelligence (*métis*) that combines flair, wisdom, forethought, subtlety of mind, resourcefulness and various other skills acquired through experience. This leads us naturally into the next chapter which focuses on a theory of acquiring new knowledge from experience.

Experiential learning theory (ELT) has been widely used in management learning research and practice for almost four decades. Drawing on the work of prominent twentieth century scholars who gave experience a central role in their theories of human learning, ELT has led to the development of a dynamic, holistic model of the process of learning based on a learning cycle. The process is driven by the resolution of the dual dialectics of concrete experience-abstract conceptualization and active experimentation-reflective observation. Each is regarded as a dimension of cognitive growth. The experience-abstraction dimension represents how one prefers to grasp experiences and the action-reflection dimension represents how one prefers to transform experiences. New knowledge results from the combination of grasping and transforming these experiences. Chapter 3, by Alice and David Kolb, reviews current research and demonstrates how the key concepts from ELT can be used to examine management as a learning process operating at the level of the individual, the team and the organization and how they can also serve as useful tools for improving management learning, education and development.

Effective learning and knowledge creation in a management context often depends on rapid and effective learning at the organizational level. Some suggest that organizations learn only through individuals who learn, arguing that individual level cognitive constructs can be applied through the concept of collective mental models. Others favour a multi-level perspective, linking individual, group, and organization, or wider social perspectives to provide a more multi-faceted picture of organization learning. In Chapter 4, Gabriele Lakomski proposes a conception of learning for both the individual and the collective that is able to answer many of the difficulties traditionally raised about this distinction in the management/organizational learning and knowledge management literatures. This conception derives from contemporary explanations of human information processing, developed in contemporary cognitive neuroscience. Referred to as the theory of distributed cognition, this account acknowledges the social and contextual features of human cognition and opens up exciting research agendas that promise a healthy return on investment in our quest for a theory of collective learning that allows us to recast the traditional understanding of knowledge transfer – which is argued here to fall into place as a feature characteristic of all learning.

Reflection in learning, particularly when learning from experience, has become established as one of the key building blocks at the core of management and organizational learning theory. In Chapter 5 the theme of reflection in learning is introduced by Russ Vince and Michael Reynolds as a process which is bound up in a continuous relationship between reflection and action, where new knowledge is created through the transformation of experience (Kolb, 1984), and where the mind increases knowledge of itself and its workings. As the authors remind us, this relationship between reflection and action has inspired the two most well-known conceptual models in management learning known as Kolb's Learning Cycle (Chapter 3, this volume) and Schön's Reflective Practitioner.

However, the authors propose that we should be thinking beyond the reflective practitioners and highlight four perspectives that help us shift our understanding. These perspectives are referred to as *critical reflection, public reflection, productive reflection, and organizing reflection*. These are discussed in terms of their implications for theory and practice and each is exemplified with a concrete reference to a study as a way of situating discourse into practice.

In response to our earlier concerns about the crisis of confidence and chorus of scepticism surrounding management education, it has been suggested that some answers may come from Critical Management Education (CME). CME is a body of educational practice arising from the research tradition known as Critical Management Studies (CMS) and some say that it offers the kind of radical challenge to prevailing mindsets that is needed (Grey, 2004). While recognizing the many challenges facing it, in Chapter 6 David Boje and Khadija Al Arkoubi provide a historical overview of CME, drawing from its philosophical grounds reflected in critical theory, proposing a closer alliance of critical theory and critical pedagogy, and explicating tenets of CME before offering some ideas on how they can be translated into practice. The chapter identifies five major challenges of CME and offers suggestions on how these may be faced in order to open doors to a different practice of education.

Related to critical management education is the development of the theory of collaborative learning which is examined by Vivien Hodgson in Chapter 7. Its origins are linked to the advent and introduction of the concept of the learning community before exploring more current interests associated with collaborative learning in communities of practice. Underlying theoretical perspectives of collaborative approaches to learning are discussed in relation to claims that they are based on social processes of interaction which assume learning will be more effective as a result of dialogue and discussion with peers and others. The chapter also emphasizes the importance and relevance that collaborative learning approaches are believed to have for developing critical thinking and problem solving. In addition to providing a critical review of some of the key ideas and issues that are considered relevant when adopting such approaches, the chapter also identifies key areas for consideration when using collaborative approaches.

One of the more troubling aspects of recent business practice has been the lack of ethics and integrity observed in various high-profile companies such as Enron and Tyco. The apparent lack of ethical decision making in these and other companies has led, as we discussed earlier in this chapter, to criticism of business schools for not emphasizing the importance of integrity in preparing students for business careers. This is the focus of Chapter 8 where Charles Fornaciari and Kathy Lund-Dean review a broad base of literature from eight different streams and conclude that ethics can in fact be taught, and taught effectively. After making that case, they move on to providing explicit advice for adopting ethics pedagogy, which engages students in active learning. They conclude their chapter with ideas on how to address the continuing global debates on how to effectively include ethics in business school curricula.

Part I ends with Chapter 9 with Neal Ashkanasy, Marie Dasborough and Kaylene Ascough discussing the implications of the pervasiveness of emotions in organizations from the point of view of learning and education, with an emphasis on the role of emotions and emotional intelligence training in leadership programmes. The chapter contains a substantial review of the emotions and emotional intelligence literature, appropriately defining fundamental constructs and identifying some of the main issues in the field. The authors also include a useful review of how scholars have considered the role of emotions in the process of leadership. Issues surrounding emotional intelligence teaching are discussed together with how emotional skills may assist in the development of organizational leadership skills. The chapter concludes with a discussion of the implications of emotions and emotional intelligence

for management learning and education and directions for future development.

## OVERVIEW OF PART II

Part II covers opportunities for success in management education scholarship in a formal, credit-bearing classroom situation. The chapter topics in Part II reflect a very wide range of both traditional and innovative issues relating to the classroom (whether actual or virtual), including the use of visual, creative and performing arts, technology, distance learning, learning-centred course design, diversity, cognitive styles, teams and problem-based and project-based learning. In addition, Part II contains material on issues beyond the classroom, such as mentoring Ph.D. students, assessment and accreditation, and the nexus between research and teaching.

Part II begins with a chapter by Joan Gallos (10) on the potential uses of the arts in management teaching and learning, which invites readers to explore the many options for using the arts in the classroom. The chapter is divided into two parts. The first part is based on four assertions about the use of visual, creative and performing arts in teaching and learning: that they provide a rich, multi-cultural, and time-tested pedagogy, that they offer unique avenues for learning about complex behaviour in organizations, that they engender an openness and engagement in the learning process essential for deep understanding, and that they foster creativity and complex skills development. The second part of the chapter provides suggestions and caveats for effectively using the arts in management learning. In an interesting twist, the advice is tailored to career stages, from newcomers to seasoned veterans. Gallos concludes her chapter with the conclusion that arts-based pedagogy is well placed to develop the leaders of the future – leaders who will need hope and imagination.

Chapter 11, by T. Grandon Gill, focuses on one of the most intriguing trends of the last ten years, namely the use and preponderance of technology in teaching and learning.

In this chapter, Gill reflects on the impact of technology on teaching and learning goals. The range of technology discussed by Gill is extensive – ranging from presentation tools to simulations, to clickers, to cell phones, to table PCs. Predictions for the future suggest that more and more classroom technology tools will be developed, and that our future students will be from a virtual generation. Yet, in his conclusion, Gill notes that technology will not replace sound course design. In fact, the use of technology increases the need for sound course design. He concludes by offering a caveat that, to be effective, technology needs to be overtly linked to instructional objectives.

Closely related to the issue of technology in the classroom is the idea that students may no longer sit in a traditional classroom to learn. Many universities around the world are now delivering courses through online technologies. Chapter 12, by J. B. Arbaugh and S. S. Warell, provides a discussion of the state of the art of distance learning and web-based instruction. This review provides a summary of the research identifying the characteristics of online learning that will be most likely to result in positive learning outcomes. The authors find that, of all the factors studied, the behaviours of the participants are the strongest predictors of a successful online course. Arbaugh and Warell conclude their chapter with suggestions for future research on online management education and learning.

The next chapter (13) by David Whetten, Trav Johnson and Lynn Sorenson, is directed towards the shift of attention from 'teaching' to 'learning'. In order to adjust to this shift, they propose an approach to learning-centred course design. Based on principles of adult learning, this process includes significant learning objectives, developmental learning assignments, and engaging learning activities. Students learn best when they are working towards significant learning goals, not comprehension, when course requirements are aligned with learning goals rather than rote memory and recall, and when they are engaged in the process of learning. The authors offer a number of suggestions for accomplishing each of these three ends, and finish with a discussion of the importance of both the teacher and the student in the learning process.

Chapter 14, by Gerald Ferris, Pamela Perrewé, and Ronald Buckley, is focused on an overlooked but equally important aspect of teaching and learning, namely, the role of mentoring Ph.D. students. Ironically, most of the emphasis on teaching and learning is directed towards undergraduate and Master's level education. Ideas and suggestions on developing doctoral students are largely ignored by the literature. This chapter aims to fill that gap by exploring literatures on apprenticeship and mentoring, looking at both sides of the relationship: student and professor. The authors build a stage model of doctoral student development, and offer recommendations for effective activities in each stage. They conclude that the future of management teaching and learning is dependent on the effective mentoring of doctoral students.

Another important topic in Part II is incorporating diversity into management education. This is the topic of Chapter 15, by Myrtle Bell, Mustafa Özbilgin and Mine Karataş-Özkan. The authors recognize that pressures created by demographic trends and our global economy, as well as by individual and collective efforts to end discrimination, have combined to produce an interest in effectively managing diversity. Despite attempts to regulate diversity through legislation, discrimination still exists, and thus diversity is an important aspect for lifelong learning in management. The authors do a masterful job of outlining the complexities of how we learn about diversity, both in our lives and in our educational institutions, and offer concrete suggestions for effective diversity learning.

The next chapter (16), by Eugene Sadler-Smith, focuses on cognitive styles and learning strategies. Cognitive styles may be used effectively in the management classroom because they can affect appropriate learning strategies for the student, instructional design for the instructor, and the overall effectiveness of the learning process. Moreover, awareness of cognitive styles suggests that *how* students learn may be as important as *what* they learn. Lifelong learning is thus likely to be enhanced if students practise the necessary skills to learn continuously. Following his review and critique of the current state of research on cognitive styles, Sadler-Smith offers a duplex model of cognitive style, acknowledging both the analytical and intuitive modes of processing information. He concludes his chapter with the implications of the duplex model for management learning and education.

One of the most important recent trends in management education has been the use of teams in the classroom. Whether used to enrich students' understanding, or to build the skill of working within teams to prepare students' for future careers, it is easy to conclude that business students will not graduate from school without significant experience in teamwork. However, it is probably fair to say that just being put in a team does not build team skills, and so it is important for instructors to manage teams effectively in the classroom. This is the topic of Chapter 17, where Larry Michaelsen, Tim Peterson and Michael Sweet present a model of Team-Based Learning, an 'intensive and extensive' approach to using teams in the classroom. Their chapter gives an overview of team-based learning, the four defining principles of team-based learning, and a map for implementing team-based learning.

One of the promising ways to increase relevance in the classroom is to use problem-based and project-based learning approaches. This is the topic of Chapter 18, by Robert DeFillippi and Richard Milter. Based on several streams of learning theory, problem- and project-based learning allows students the opportunity to put theoretical knowledge into action, which increases the effectiveness of learning. DeFillippi and Milter present best practices of both approaches, including advice on how to implement these strategies into the classroom. Despite their promise, the use of problem- and project-based learning does present challenges, and the authors

discuss a number of these. They conclude by encouraging the increased use of these techniques for effective management learning.

As discussed earlier in this chapter, accrediting bodies have had a significant influence on the content and process of management learning in formal contexts. Currently, accrediting bodies have started to increase pressure for assurance of learning of our students. For a number of reasons, colleges and universities have been somewhat reluctant to participate in assessment activities. Chapter 19, by Robert Rubin and Kathryn Martell, addresses this critical topic. In particular, Rubin and Martell offer both clear interpretation and guidance on current AACSB requirements and helpful advice about best practices in assessment of assurance of learning. Included in their chapter is a table that classifies common assessment learning outcomes.

Part II ends with a particularly provocative chapter (20) by Roy Lewicki and James Bailey on the relationship between research and teaching. Over the years, there has been much speculation, and prognostication, but little research on the relationship between two of the more important activities of faculty in higher education. Lewicki and Bailey provide a systematic examination of this question and explore the assumptions that underlie this relationship. They identify tensions and compatibilities between research and teaching, and suggest that institutional pressures from our definitions of scholarship and from our traditional reward systems, serve to perpetuate a tension between these two activities. They conclude by calling for cultural change in management education so that research and teaching can effectively co-exist.

## OVERVIEW OF PART III

Part III explores important aspects of management development in a non-credit based learning context. Areas covered include: the importance of reflexivity in management learning; action learning and related modalities that conceive of practice as having its own epistemology; competency development related to effective managers and leaders; best practices and theoretical and empirical advances in leadership development; applications, benefits and efficacy of coaching and mentoring as forms of development intervention in organizations; interaction learning models that allow managers to learn cultures 'on the fly' when engaging in multicultural assignments and interactions; a proposition to reverse the concept of a community of practice to practices of a community leading to a wider understanding of practice-based studies; and lastly a consideration of assessment, accreditation and quality certification schemes associated with non-formal management development in the context of recurrent and lifelong learning.

Part III begins with a chapter (21) by Ann Cunliffe that explores the meaning of reflexivity, why it is important to managers and management learning, and how reflexive practice can be encouraged and supported. Being self-reflexive is about questioning our ways of thinking, being, relating and acting. Personal reflexivity involves reflecting on ways in which one's beliefs, values, interests, experiences and social identities shape the world around us. It is also about seeking to understand how we relate and act with others as a way of shaping our social realities. It is about questioning how we make sense of our surroundings and stimuli, and examining how we can act responsibly and ethically. Reflexivity is argued to be a cornerstone for ethical and responsive management. Social constructionist and deconstructionist approaches to reflexivity are explored in this chapter, but irrespective of one's orientation, the author makes very clear why reflexive practice is fundamentally and crucially important to both management practice and the process of management learning.

The next chapter (22) by Joe Raelin focuses on a cluster of strategies that are located within an emerging tradition in management development that sees practice as having its own epistemology. Where learning is generated from human interaction arising from engagement in real-world work problems, and concurrent reflection on experience can expand and create knowledge as well as improving practice. The author traces the roots of action learning to the work of Dewey (1897) and Lewin (1946) before providing a detailed account of its principles and advantages arising from engagement in solution of real-world work problems. As well as leading to performance improvements, advantages include an estimated return on investment of between 5 and 25 times its cost, a likelihood of adding to an organization's institutional memory, knowledge transfer across generations of employees, or even a shift in organizational culture. Following a detailed exposition of action learning, including a discussion of outcomes, design of action learning projects, and the use of learning teams as a primary vehicle for providing collective reflection, the author then turns to other principal action modalities. These include action research, action science, developmental action inquiry, co-operative inquiry, critical action learning, and global action learning where it is demonstrated that the experience of working with a global cross-cultural team can present participants with critical lessons in intercultural competence.

Competencies are defined as 'the underlying characteristics of a person that lead to or cause effective and outstanding performance' (Boyatzis, 1982). Important competencies fall into the three clusters of: cognitive intelligence competencies; emotional intelligence competencies; and social intelligence competencies. Although various combinations of these competencies have been shown to predict effectiveness in leadership and management throughout the world, there has been a dearth of longitudinal research into the effectiveness of trying to develop them.

In Chapter 23, Richard Boyatzis argues that the competencies related to outstanding leaders, managers and professionals can be developed in adults, but it is not easy. He then draws on more than 20 years of data to show that whereas an MBA education or management training can help people develop these competencies, we cannot use the typical lecture and discussion methods with their focus on knowledge acquisition only. Nor can we use the 'data dump and run' approach typical of assessment and feedback processes in training. Instead, a more holistic approach is needed, and the change process that seems to work most effectively draws on 'Intentional Change Theory' from a complexity perspective (Boyatzis, 2006).

In Chapter 24 George Hrivnak, Rebecca Reichard and Ron Riggio review some of the major theoretical and empirical advances in leadership development. These are compared with the dominant trends and best practices of leadership development in organizations in an attempt to identify points of congruence and disconnect. Building on this foundation of current understanding the authors then offer an alternative approach to leadership development by providing a model which does not offer a specific set of method-ologies or instructional tools *per se*, but rather a framework to incorporate the various modalities in a thoughtful, goal-driven, and comprehensive approach designed to achieve specific, measurable, individual and organiza-tional objectives. The chapter concludes with recommendations for future efforts to advance relevant research, to focus the teaching of leadership in the university classroom, and to improve the efficacy of current and future leadership development programmes in practice.

Coaching and mentoring are increas-ingly being recognized as crucially impor-tant instruments for promoting learning and development and for raising management competencies in many large and medium sized organizations. In Chapter 25, David Clutterbuck explores the origins, applications, benefits and efficacy of coaching and mentor-ing as forms of development intervention in organizations. Differences between coaching and mentoring and formal versus informal systems are defined. Benefits are consid-ered for the four categories of beneficiary: organization, learner, mentor/coach, and line manager. The evolution of coaching and men-toring relationships is also discussed around

the five stages of initiation, goal setting, progress making, winding up, and moving on. Other areas of importance that are covered include core competencies of coaching and mentoring; team coaching; virtual coaching and mentoring; effective coaching and men-toring programmes; creating a coaching and mentoring culture; measuring the impact of coaching and mentoring; and the role of standards and professional bodies.

As today's business environment becomes increasingly global, experts have advocated that managers cultivate a global mindset. However, in today's rapidly changing, multi-cultural business environment managers are often required to interact with multiple cultures with little time to immerse themselves in the foreign context. In Chapter 26, Kathryn Aten, Luciara Nardon, and Richard Steers consider the role of management development in preparing global business leaders for dealing with these challenges. It is argued that traditional immersion methods of developing cross-cultural knowledge are insufficient and that managers operating in a multi-cultural environment require a more efficient path that allows them to learn cultures 'on the fly' in the course of (rather than prior to) engaging in multi-cultural assignments and interactions. As a potential solution to the dilemma, the authors present an intercultural interaction learning model. Implications of the model for management development are then discussed before identifying the skills required for learning cultures 'on the fly', and offering examples of experiential exercises to develop those skills. Some perspectives of learning are viewed as social processes embedded in everyday routines and interactions within the surrounding contexts. One example includes the theory of situated learning (Brown et al., 1989; Lave and Wenger, 1991), which emphasizes the interaction between individual learning, practice and everyday work tasks. A second example is the theory of communities of practice (Brown and Duguid, 1992; Wenger, 1999) which stresses the term community and social relationships around the learner.

In Chapter 27 Silvia Gherardi provides a historical trajectory of the concept of communities of practice, originally born within a predominantly anthropological literature, but now firmly rooted in management studies. The chapter then discusses a literature that proposes a reversal of the concept, from community of practice to practices of a community, leading to a wider understanding of practice-based studies. The reversal is more than a play on words and shifts attention to how practical knowledge is enabled in situated contexts of action.

Chapter 28, by Lichia Yiu and Raymond Saner, focuses on assessment and accreditation of non-formal management education and development programmes. Although there have been major criticisms of business schools for failing to educate and develop true managers, the growing field of non-formal management education has eluded the critical eye of scholars and researchers. This is despite the fact that the field has grown in size without adequate quality assessments and almost without any form of accreditation systems. This chapter provides a resource for those interested in this under-researched and under-published field by closely examining these issues, identifying various assessment tools, questioning whether management training institutions should be subject to quality certification schemes, and raising various sets of questions that beg further inquiry and answers.

The handbook's concluding chapter by James O'Toole offers us a future perspective of management education. Its author looks through the distorted lens of the present and trains his telescope on the most probable scenario for business schools of the future. To help with this, a focus is established on the traditional American MBA which has the longest history, the most available information, and is the model for most formal business school programmes around the world. Drawing on a range of criticisms, including those from business school deans, O'Toole observes that their concerns appear mutually consistent, indicating that the chances of them all being right is rather high.

At the core of all their arguments is a call for the reconceptualization and redefinition of the very purpose of management education.

In search of what needs to be done, O'Toole then combs through the articles in this handbook concluding that while thoughtful readers will find something that is personally useful to fit every interest and bias, they will also find something that is idiosyncratically upsetting. He refers to the diversity of viewpoints and perspectives in the handbook which he believes represents a perfect reflection of the fragmentation that exists in the field of management education. He then moves on to argue that the central problem of management education is the corrosive impact of 1950s managerialism, 1970s management science, and 1990s investment capitalism driving out the original purpose of business schools which was to create a true profession of management with the higher purpose of public service similar to the law, medicine, or even theology professions. We are reminded that the agent of change was the Ford Foundation which used its significant financial leverage to bring about radical curricular reforms which led to a decline in the importance of teaching and a greater emphasis being placed on publishing discipline-based research in 'A' grade journals. O'Toole argues this has had a devastating impact on the quality of teaching and he calls for a pluralistic model of professorial excellence as one way of improving the quality of business school offerings. Boyer's (1990) vision of scholarship is recommended as one model for advancement.

The role of assessment and accreditation of business schools is also presented as a corrosive element which is preventing much needed advancement. With no equivalent to professional associations such as those representing legal and medical professions, its nearest equivalent is the American Assembly of Collegiate Schools of Business (AACSB). This is reckoned by O'Toole to be a misguided and poor substitute with an over-emphasis on rigour of assessment where the trivial is quantified and the more important hard-to-measure aspects are ignored. He floats the idea that the AACSB could accredit schools that use the best assessment methods, while decertifying those that concentrate their resources on doing the right things for their stakeholder – this is especially ironic when one considers the full definition of the AACSB acronym. He goes on to argue that it would make more sense to measure what graduates have retained from their educational experience, what aspects they use in their careers, or how business school education affects later executive behaviours. A clear disjuncture is articulated between what AACSB assesses and the true metrics of learning.

Having teased out some important problems, O'Toole then turns his attention to the apparent lack of purpose of business schools and regards this as *the* major problem. Accepting that the content of this handbook offers great ideas that may enhance learning, he makes the important point that many of its authors are concerned about *how* to teach when there is little agreement about *what* to teach. For example, what does it mean to be an educated manager?; what is the purpose of the MBA degree?; what is the essential core content of an MBA curriculum? He does acknowledge, however, that the handbook is about management learning and not about curricular reform and concedes that its authors are quite right to have focused on alternative modes of learning within the existing dominant paradigm. In the longer term a radical paradigm shift is needed where business school decision makers rethink their assumptions about the marriage of 'the why', 'the what' and 'the how' of management education. If they know 'the why' O'Toole argues that they will have the essential guidance to choose 'the how' – method following vision, not vice versa. But so far, there is little evidence that deans are willing to break with established norms and take control of their own destiny by creating bold and innovative programmes. Instead, they do little other than to tinker at the margins with what everyone else is doing, which merely attempts to improve the delivery of a poor product.

O'Toole concludes that whereas there is general agreement that the dominant mode of management education isn't working, there is no agreement on *what* should replace it. There can therefore be no closure on the *how*, which leads him to feel that there is no single future of management education but, instead, a plurality of futures.

With that said, we offer this handbook as a state of the current affairs of this discipline, as we initially set out to do. It is our firm hope that others will find these collected chapters compelling, and will set out to address the many needs that are outlined for the future. For two things appear to us to be certain: students will continue to enter our formal and informal management education programmes, and the world will continue to need their wisdom. For them, we continue our quest.

# REFERENCES

Argyris, C. and Schön, D. (1974) *Theory in Practice*. San Francisco: Jossey-Bass.

Armstrong, S.J. and Sadler-Smith, E. (2008) 'Learning on demand, at your own pace, in rapid bite-sized-chunks: The future shape of management development?' *Academy of Management Learning and Education*, 7(4).

Armstrong, S.J. (2005) 'Postgraduate management education in the UK: Lessons from or lessons for the US model?', *Academy of Management Learning and Education*, 4 (2): 229–35.

Armstrong, S.J. (2007) 'Re-thinking management education: From cognition, to action, to learning', *Research Memorandum* (75), The Business School, University of Hull, Hull, UK.

Armstrong, S.J. and Mahmud, A. (2008) 'Experiential learning and the acquisition of managerial tacit knowledge', *Academy of Management Learning and Education*, 7 (3): 189–208.

Bach, G.L. (1959) 'Managerial decision making as an organizing concept', in F.C. Pierson (ed.) *The Education of American Businessmen: A Study of University-College Programmes in Business Administration*. New York: McGraw-Hill.

Bailey, J. (2004) 'Arranging marriages between theoretical positions', *Academy of Management Learning and Education*, 3 (4): 440–1.

Baumard, P. (1999) *Tacit Knowledge in Organizations*. London: Sage Publications.

Bennis W.G. and O'Toole, J. (2005) 'How business schools lost their way', *Harvard Business Review*, May: 96–104.

Bilimoria, D. and Fukami, C. (2002) 'The scholarship of teaching and learning in the management sciences', in Mary Taylor Huber and Sherwyn P. Morreale (eds), *Disciplinary Styles in the Scholarship of Teaching and Learning: Exploring Common Ground*. Washington, DC: American Association for Higher Education, pp. 125–42.

Boyatzis, R.E. (1982) *The Competent Manager: A Model for Effective Performance*. New York: John Wiley & Sons.

Boyatzis, R.E. (2006) 'Intentional change theory from a complexity perspective', *Journal of Management Development*, 25 (7): 607–23.

Boyer, E. L. (1990) *Scholarship Reconsidered: Priorities of the Professoriate*. Princeton, NJ: The Carnegie Foundation for the Advancement of Teaching.

Campbell, N.D., Heriot, K.C. and Finney, R.Z. (2006) 'In defence of silos: An argument against the integrative undergraduate business curriculum', *Journal of Management Education*, 30 (2): 316–32.

CEML (2002) *Management and Leadership Abilities: An analysis of texts, testimony and practice*. London: Council for Excellence in Management and Leadership.

Chia, R. (2005) 'The aim of management education: Reflections on Mintzberg's managers not MBAs', *Organization Studies*, 26 (7): 1090–2.

Cooper, R. and Sawaf, A. (1996) *Executive EQ: Emotional Intelligence in Leadership and Organizations*. New York: Grossett/Putnam.

Crainer, S. and Dearlove, D. (1999). *Gravy Training: Inside the Business of Business Schools*. San Francisco: Jossey-Bass.

Donaldson, L. (2002) 'Damned by our own theories: Contradictions between theories and management education', *Academy of Management Learning & Education*, 1 (1): 96–106.

Engwall, L. (2007) 'The anatomy of management education', *Scandinavian Journal of Management*, 23 (1): 4–35.

Engwall, L. and Zamagni, V. (1998) *Management Education in Historical Perspective*. Manchester: Manchester University Press.

Forsythe, G., Hedlund, J., Snook, S., Horvath, J., Williams, W., Bullis, R., Dennis, M. and Sternberg, R. (1998) 'Construct validation of tacit knowledge for military leadership', Paper presented at the *Annual Meeting of the American Educational Research Association*, San Diego, California, April 13–17, 1998. Available: http://www.aera.net/divisions/i/home/ForsythePaper.pdf

Friga, P.N., Bettis, R.A. and Sullivan, R.S. (2003) 'Changes in graduate management education and new business school strategies in the 21st century', *Academy of Management Learning and Education*, 2 (3): 233–49.

Frost, P. J. and Fukami, C. V. (1997) 'Teaching effectiveness in the organizational sciences: Recognizing and enhancing the scholarship of teaching', *Academy of Management Journal*, 40: 1271–81.

Fukami, C.V. (2007) 'Can wisdom be taught?' in E.H. Kessler and J.R. Bailey (eds), *Handbook of Organizational Wisdom*, Thousand Oaks, CA: Sage Publications, forthcoming.

Fukami, C.V., Clouse, M.L., Howard, C.T., McGowan, R.P., Mullins, J.W., Silver, W.S., Sorensen, J.E., Watkins, T.L. and Wittmer, D.P. (1996) 'The road less travelled: The joys and sorrows of transdisciplinary team teaching', *Journal of Management Education*, 20: 409–10.

Gioia, D. and Corley, K.G. (2002) 'Being good versus looking good: business school rankings and the circean transformation from substance to image', *Academy of Management Learning and Education*, 1 (1): 107–20.

Gordon, R.A. and Howell, J.E. (1959) *Higher Education for Business*. New York: Columbia University Press.

Grey, C. (2002) 'What are business schools for? On silence and voice in management education', *Journal of Management Education*, 26 (5): 496–511.

Grey, C. (2004) 'Reinventing business schools: The contribution of critical management education', *Academy of Management Learning & Education*, 3 (2): 178–86.

Goshal, S. (2005) 'Bad management theories are destroying good management practice', *Academy of Management Learning and Education*, 4: 75–91.

Hayes, R.H. and Albernathy, W.J. (1980) 'Managing our way to economic decline', *Harvard Business Review*, July–August: 67–77.

Ivory, C., Miskell, P., Shipton, H., White, A., Moeslein, K. and Neely, A. (2006) 'UK business schools: Historical contexts and future scenarios', Summary Report from an EBK/AIM Management Research Forum, Advanced Institute of Management Research: London.

Khurana, R., Nohria, N. and Penrice, D. (2005) 'Management as a profession', in Jay W. Lorsch, Leslie Berlowitz and Andy Zelleke (eds), *Restoring Trust in American Business*, produced by the American Academy of Arts & Sciences and published by The MIT Press.

Khurana, R. (2007) *From Higher Aims to Hired Hands. The Social Transformation of American Business*

*Schools and the Unfulfilled Promise of Management as a Profession*. Princeton University Press.

Kolb, D. (1984) *Experimental Learning: Experience as the Source of Learning and Development*. Englewood Cliffs, NJ: Prentice Hall.

Korpiaho, K., Paivio, H. and Rasanen, K. (2007) 'Anglo-American forms of management education: A practice-theoretical perspective', *Scandinavian Management Journal*, 23 (1): 36–65.

Linder, J. and Smith, H. (1992) 'The complex case of management education', *Harvard Business Review*, September/October: 16–33.

McCall, Jr, Morgan, W., Lombardo, M.M. and Morrison, A.M. (1988) *The Lessons of Experience: How Successful Executives Develop on the Job*. Lexington, MA: Lexington Book.

Michaelsen, L. (1999) 'Integrating the core business curriculum: An experienced based solution', *Selections*, 15 (2): 9–17.

Mintzberg, H. (2004) *Managers Not MBAs. A Hard Look at the Soft Practice of Managing and Management Development*. San Francisco: Barrett-Koehler Publishers, Inc.

Morgan, G. (1986) *Images of Organization*. Beverly Hills: Sage.

Nestor-Baker, N. (1999) 'Tacit knowledge in the superintendency: An exploratory analysis', (Doctoral dissertation, The Ohio State University). University Microfilms International Dissertation Services, AAT 9941397.

Pfeffer, J. and Fong, C. (2002) 'The end of business schools? Less success than meets the eye', *Academy of Management Learning & Education*, 1 (1): 78–95.

Pfeffer, J. and Sutton, R.I. (1999) 'Knowing what to do is not enough: Turning knowledge into action', *California Management Review*, 42: 83–108.

Pierson, F.P. (1959) *The Education of American Businessmen: A Study of University-College Programmes in Business Administration*. New York: McGraw-Hill.

Porter, L. (2000) 'Observations on business education', *Selections*, 16 (2): 29–30.

Porter, L. and McKibbin, L.E. (1988) *Management Education and Development: Drift or Thrust in the 21st Century?* New York: McGraw-Hill.

Quinn Trank, C. and Rynes, S.L. (2003) 'Who moved our cheese? Reclaiming professionalism in business education', *Academy of Management Learning & Education*, 2 (2): 189–205.

Raelin, J. (1995) 'Reformulating management education: Professional education, action learning, and beyond', *Selections*, Graduate Management Admissions Council, Autumn, 20–31.

Reynolds, M. and Vince, R. (2004) 'Critical management education and action-based learning: Synergies and contradictions', *Academy of Management Learning & Education*, 3 (4): 442–56.

Sass, S.A. (1982) *The Pragmatic Imagination: A History of the Wharton School, 1881–1981*. Philadelphia: University of Pennsylvania Press.

Schmidt-Wilk, J. and Fukami, C. (in press) 'In search of balance between relevance and rigor', in Charles Wankel and Robert DeFillippi (eds), *Being and Becoming a Management Education Scholar*, Volume 7, *Research in Management Education and Development Series*.

Schlossman, S.M. and Wechsler, H. (1998) 'The new look: The Ford foundation and the revolution in business education', *Selections*: The magazine of the graduate management admission council, 14 (3): 8–28.

Schmotter, J.W. (1998) 'An interview with Dean B. Joseph White', *Selections*, 14 (2): 22–6.

Starkey, K. and Madan, P. (2001) 'Bridging the relevance gap: Aligning stakeholders in the future of management research', *British Journal of Management*, 12: 3–26.

Starkey, K. and Tempest, S. (2005) 'The future of the business school: Knowledge, challenges, and opportunities', *Human Relations*, 58 (1): 61–82.

Sternberg, R.J., Forsythe, G.B., Hedland, J., Horvath, J.A., Wagner, R.K., Williams, W.M., Snook, S. and Grigorenko, E.L. (2000) *Practical Intelligence in Everyday Life*. New York: Cambridge University Press.

Tiratsoo, N. (1998) 'What you need is a Harvard: The American influence on British management education', in T. Gourvish and N. Tiratsoo (eds), *Missionaries and Managers: American Influences on European Management Education, 1945–1960*. Manchester, UK: Manchester University Press.

Warner, M. (1997) 'Industrialisation, management education and training systems: A comparative analysis', in M. Warner (ed.), *Comparative Management: Critical Perspectives on Business and Management*, Vol. 1. London: Routledge, North American Management: 106–27.

Whitehead, A.N. (1929) *The Aims of Education and Other Essays*. Macmillan: New York.

PART I

# Management Learning: Theoretical Aspects of Learning and Knowledge Aquisition

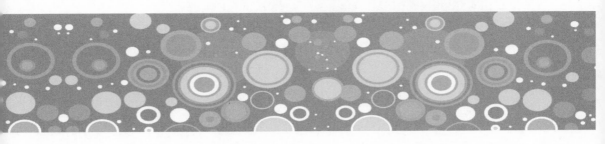

# 2

# The Nature of Knowledge and *Knowing* in the Context of Management Learning, Education and Development

Robert Chia

The ordinary practitioners ... live "down below" ... their knowledge ... is as blind as that of lovers in each other's arms.

(Michel de Certeau, *The Practice of Everyday Life*, 1984: 93)

## Abstract

This chapter explores the nature of knowledge and elaborates on how and why formal knowledge that is traditionally taught in business schools differs qualitatively from the kind of *knowing* possessed by management practitioners. We argue that this epistemological rupture between knowledge and *knowing* is intimately linked to a widely held explanatory stance in management academia that we term here the *building* world-view in which knowledge is construed as a product of conscious cognition and mental representation. Such a view is circumscribed by Aristotle's discussion of *episteme* and *techné* and presupposes that an actor has first to *construct* mental representations and models of the world prior to any practical engagement with it. We contrast this world-view with an alternative *dwelling* world-view whereby representational knowledge is not assumed to precede social engagement, but is deemed to emerge as a locus of understanding in the course of material social practices. Such a *dwelling* world-view suggests that knowledge is not some transferable, representational commodity. Rather, it is grown, re-grown and incorporated into the *modus operandi* of an individual through material social practices. Such a form of *tacit* practical knowing is encapsulated by *phronesis* and *mētis*, two epistemological terms which remain relatively unexplored in management studies. A *dwelling* world-view enables us to better appreciate the unarticulated *knowing* world of management practitioners in contrast to the knowledge-based world of management academia. This then leads us to explore the broader implications of such forms of knowing for the practice of Management Learning, Education and Development.

In this chapter we explore the nature of knowledge and knowing and elaborate on how and why formal knowledge that is traditionally taught in business schools differs qualitatively from the kind of practical *knowing* possessed by management practitioners. Understanding this basic incompatibility between formal knowledge and *tacit* knowing enables us to explore its wider implications for Management Learning, Education and Development. We maintain that this epistemological rupture between knowledge and *knowing* results from the translation of practitioner experiences into the logic, vocabulary and interpretive frameworks of academia in order to meet the demands of rigour and scholarship in management research. It is thus the overall epistemological stance adopted in academic research that is at issue here and not merely a question of the research perspective adopted. Thus, *whether an objectivist/positivist or subjective/interpretive methodological stance is adopted in research*, both these approaches are united by a common core presupposition: *that conscious cognition, meaning and mental representation necessarily precede purposive productive action.* Both positivism and interpretivism remain very much within the epistemological mould circumscribed by Aristotle's discussion of *episteme* and *techné* in *Nichomachean Ethics* 6. There, a 'reasoned state' of cognitive awareness on the part of actors is presupposed (Aristotle, in Dunne, 1993: 249–53) to be the proper basis of knowledge. Knowledge is thus only considered so if it is expressed linguistically in terms of principles, causes or actor meanings and intentions. Thus, for both *episteme* and *techné*, explanatory coherence is a vital dimension of any knowledge claim.

In addition to *episteme* and *techné*, however, Aristotle also posited (though less emphatically) the existence of *phronesis* (practical wisdom) as a form of personal knowing which differs qualitatively from

*episteme* and *techné* but which nevertheless shapes and disposes an individual and 'expresses the kind of person that one is' (Dunne, 1993: 244). Whereas *episteme* and *techné* imply the explicitness and transmissability of knowledge, *phronesis* alludes to a form of personal knowing that is more supple, less formulable and which emerges through a person's striving. It is hence something that is inseparable from an individual's entire cultural attitude and predisposition. Although both *episteme* and *techné* can be consciously learnt and hence can be *forgotten*, '*phronesis* cannot' (Aristotle, *Nichomachean Ethics, 6.5.1140b28–30*, in Dunne, 1993: 265) since it is already part of an individual's make-up. It is a kind of knowledge whose whole finality is intrinsically directed towards individual expression-in-action. Unlike *episteme* or *techné* where it is possible to make a distinction between intention and behaviour and hence between what one *is* and what one *does*, in *phronesis* it is precisely this distinction that is denied: in phronetic knowing, what one *does* is inextricable from what one *is*. This intimate relationship between *being* and *doing* makes *phronesis* extremely difficult to apprehend and hence it remains very much an unexplored feature in management academic research.

Moreover, recent studies of pre-Socratics Greek culture and society, including especially the insights expressed in Homer's *Iliad* and Hesiod's *Theogony* (Detienne and Vernant, 1978) suggest the existence of yet another form of practical *knowing* of which even Plato and Aristotle remained surprisingly silent on. In their scholarly treatise, Detienne and Vernant called this form of 'cunning intelligence' *mētis*. *Mētis* is 'a type of intelligence and of thought, a way of knowing; it ... combines flair, wisdom, forethought, subtlety of mind, deception, resourcefulness, vigilance, opportunism, various skills and experience acquired over years. It is applied to situations which are transient, shifting, disconcerting and ambiguous' (Detienne and Vernant, 1978: 4). *Mētis* corresponds to what we mean when we say that someone is 'street-smart' or who seems able to 'get away with things' or 'get out of difficult situations' with cunning and ease. Both *phronesis* and *mētis* remain unexplored and hence unacknowledged in the Management Learning, Education and Development debate. Yet they are vital qualities of an effective management practitioner.

Our task in this chapter is to resuscitate these relatively forgotten insights on knowledge and *knowing* and to show that they are vital to our appreciation of the richness of tacit knowing possessed by management practitioners. Drawing from the seminal works of the German philosopher Martin Heidegger and the Heideggerian commentator Hubert Dreyfus, as well as eminent sociologist/social anthropologists such as Pierre Bourdieu, Michel de Certeau and Tim Ingold, we identify two distinct epistemological stances which we, following Heidegger (1962, 1971), term the *building* and *dwelling* world-views. In the former *building* mode it is presumed that the actor-manager has first a need to '*construct* mental representations and models of the world prior to any practical engagement with it' (Ingold, 2000: 178). Conscious, deliberate, *purposeful* action (Chia and Holt, 2006: 648) is presupposed in all managerial circumstances so that recourse to actor meanings and interpretations provide the basis for management research accounts. We maintain that both *episteme* and *techné* are predicated upon this *building* world-view. From this world-view, knowledge is generated through acts of interpretation on the part of the researcher of the practitioner's own narrated (i.e. interpretive) accounts. This double-interpretive act generates a theoretical 'distancing' of the researcher from the actual scene of practice. The meanings and intentions of actors and their ostensibly *purposeful* actions replace the practice itself as the primary foci of analysis and explanation while the latter remains unexamined.

In the *dwelling* mode, on the other hand, practitioner awareness is frequently (though not always) characterized by a *being-in-the-world* (Heidegger, 1962; Dreyfus, 1991); a state of 'non-thematic circumspective absorption' which precludes deliberate conceptualization, reflection and mental representation. Under such circumstances, a being is assumed to be totally absorbed and unthinkingly immersed, *like lovers in each other's arms*, in his/her surrounding and hence acts accordingly relying more on cultivated tendencies and habituated disposition than on conscious forethought. On this account, people are assumed to be intimately and inextricably intertwined with their surroundings in all its complexities so that their everyday activities are better understood as practical 'wayfinding' (Hutchins, 1995) than as cognitively 'mapping' and representing their practical situations. Here, actor intentions and meanings are not deemed to drive *purposive* actions. Instead, in the course of everyday practical coping actors habitually and unthinkingly generate action pathways that radiate outwards from their concrete existential circumstance. This *dwelling* world-view construes knowing in terms of *phronesis* and, *mētis* and enables us to view practical knowing as something that is unconsciously 'absorbed', 'grown' and re-grown, incorporated into the *modus operandi* of the individual, through repeated material social practice rather than something consciously taught or learnt. Such a *dwelling* world-view allows us to capture more authentically and faithfully the practical *knowing* and oftentimes *unarticulated* world of management practitioners as opposed to the knowledge-based world of management academia.

The creation of this distinction between a *building* and a *dwelling* world-view and hence the epistemological stances associated with each enables us to distinguish academic *knowledge* from practical *knowing*. *Episteme/techné* expresses a detached and contemplative form of knowledge which is precise and formulable and can be articulated, communicated and transmitted in the educational process whereas *phronetic/mētistic* forms of knowing are inarticulate and hence only transmissible through exemplification via a *modus operandi*. This understanding then leads us to explore the implications of an alternative *dwelling* epistemological stance for Management Learning, Education and Development. We show that adopting a *dwelling* stance towards knowing opens up new avenues for exploring pedagogical priorities; one that emphasizes the practice of managing, not so much as concerning spectacular, well-designed and decisive action, but rather one exemplified by ongoing, mundane and unheroic forms of everyday practical coping that surprisingly oftentimes prove to be efficacious and ultimately transformational in their overall conduct.

## THE QUEST FOR KNOWLEDGE: THE EPISTEMOLOGICAL LEGACY OF WESTERN THOUGHT

> ... knowledge and expertise belong rather to skill than to experience ... the skilled know the cause, whereas the experienced do not. For the experienced know the 'that' but not the 'because'. (Aristotle, *The Metaphysics*, trans, Lawson-Tancred, 1998: 5)

Beginning with the Greek philosophers, Plato was perhaps the first to attempt a systematic inquiry into the nature of knowledge, defining the latter as an awareness of abstract, universal ideas and forms existing independently of a knowing subject. Unlike Socrates before him, who was sceptical about the possibility of attaining certain knowledge and hence revelled in revealing the latent ignorance in himself and in others, Plato assumed that systematic cumulative knowledge was possible and set about elaborating on the conditions that would make such knowledge certain. Where Socrates advocated the acceptance of ignorance as a necessary human condition, Plato sought the ultimate foundations of knowledge in the essential and unchanging furniture of the universe. In the *Republic* he makes a distinction between an ephemeral world of mere *appearance* and an underlying invisible realm of perfect *unchanging forms* (pure justice, goodness, truth, beauty, equality). All reality derives from this ultimate realm of unchanging

forms, resembling it in some way or other, and ultimately returning to it. The task of epistemology, therefore, is to take us from mere *opinions* to a proper foundational *knowledge* of relations in the world through the accurate mental representation of these perfect unchanging forms existing beyond our everyday comprehension.

Plato's successor, Aristotle, although more sanguine in accepting that there are different forms of knowledge that can be identified, including especially *phronesis* as we have seen, nevertheless insisted on the superiority of *episteme* and *techné* as the founding basis of proper knowledge. For Aristotle, proper knowledge concerns true logical statements about what exists. Thus, for Aristotle, it is not being practically competent or 'hands-on' that makes one knowledgeable but possession of a detached universal understanding of the underlying causes of phenomena. Ultimately, despite the differences in their emphasis, both Plato and Aristotle assumed that knowledge can only be called so if it is logically and rigorously arrived at and presupposed the possession of mental representations mirroring an external reality.

Since Plato and Aristotle, two broad philosophical outlooks and dispositions have dominated the problem of knowledge in the West. First, is a tendency to take *episteme* (linguistically articulated generalizations using propositional forms) and *techné* (precise, measurable, codifiable instruction) as the primary forms of knowledge, reducing all knowledge, intelligence and abilities to possession of such *explicit* modes of comprehension. Second, there is an instinctive tendency to 'moralize' these forms of knowledge. This tendency to link knowledge with *virtue* began with Socrates who insisted that no one who knows the Good wittingly does ill and this intimate association of knowledge with virtue was subsequently taken up in the Christian neoplatonism of the Middle Ages through the influence of St Augustine. For neoplatonists like St Augustine, the pursuit of knowledge was as much a moral as an intellectual enterprise. Its aim was not just to learn facts about the world or to develop cognitive skills but also to shape one's life (Raphals, 1992). The goal of self-cultivation – spiritual, mental and physical – was integral to the search for certain knowledge.

Although the sceptics of the seventeenth and eighteenth centuries questioned the medieval claims to knowledge and the methods of discussing it, they crucially did not *challenge its definition*. Locke, Descartes and Kant continued to privilege theoretical knowledge over practical *knowing* and to associate true knowledge with essences that could be described and defined in words. This legacy of knowledge as linguistically coded mental representation was reinforced by Descartes in what is now recognized as the Cartesian split between mind and matter. Descartes believed that we can gain knowledge independently of our sense experience because reason is superior to experience as a source of knowledge. Although other Enlightenment philosophers, such as John Locke and David Hume, have insisted that we have no source of knowledge other than through our sense experience, and although a number of recent alternative approaches such as hermeneutics, phenomenology and critical realism have more latterly made their appearance on the epistemological scene, the idea of the mind as a mirror and knowledge as mental representation (Rorty, 1980) remains deeply entrenched in much of academic research and theorizing. It is this dominant view of knowledge as linguistically articulated claims arising solely from contemplation, cognition and mental representation that underpins much of the literature on Management Learning, Education and Development and this tends to exclude other forms of knowing, including especially the *tacit* practical wisdom (*phronesis*) and 'cunning intelligence' (*mētis*) of ordinary management practitioners who, in the course of their everyday practical coping, are required continuously to learn to adapt, adjust and 'make do' *in situ* often relying on their instincts, habits, ingenuity and guile to bring about favourable outcomes.

Moreover, the moral dimension associated with proper knowledge has persisted and this is well exemplified by the suspicious reaction to Machiavelli's English translation of *The Prince* when it first appeared in 1640 (Raphals, 1992). Because the book delved into the less savoury use of practical intelligence and cunning rather than more 'virtuous' practices to effect desired political outcomes, it was seen as incompatible with the high moral spirit associated with proper knowledge. Moreover, as Detienne and Vernant (1978) argue forcefully, although other forms of knowing such as *mētis* played a major role in Greek culture and mythology and held an important influence on Greek values and beliefs, it has curiously never been studied theoretically by ancient Greek scholars. *Mētis* is conspicuous by its absence. Western epistemological pursuits have therefore tended to concentrate on explicit theoretical knowledge not simply because it is viewed as being more rigorous, robust and reliable, but also because the seemingly clandestine nature and apparent 'deviousness' of practical knowing and intelligence make them morally repugnant and hence unworthy of serious study and scholarship.

In summary, what we have are two distinct epistemological predispositions which have profound implications for our understanding of Management Learning, Education and Development. On the one hand, the idea of knowledge as explicit, linguistically codifiable mental representations locatable in the minds of conscious individual agents has prevailed. On the other hand, a moralizing tendency meant that only knowledge properly arrived at through rigorous reflection and conjecturing and clearly aimed at the Good of humanity, whatever that may mean, was considered legitimate. What this implies is that other forms of knowing, including especially the embodied skills, proficiency, resourcefulness and ingenuity of practitioners that enabled them to pragmatically 'get by' on a day-to-day basis remain for the most part excluded from serious epistemological considerations. It is this excluded dimension that constitutes what we mean by practical *knowing* in the context of Management Learning, Education and Development.

## TWO MODES OF EXPLANATION: THE BUILDING AND DWELLING WORLD-VIEWS

The world of our experience is, indeed, continually and endlessly coming into being around us as we weave … it has no 'inside' or 'outside' … Only if we are capable of weaving, only then can we make. (Ingold, 2000: 348)

In an evocative essay entitled 'Building, Dwelling, Thinking' in his book collection *Poetry, Language, Thought*, the German philosopher Martin Heidegger (1971) poses the question of what it means to build and to dwell. Conventionally, we might consider building to precede dwelling so that houses, for instance, are first built before we may then dwell in them. Heidegger, however, tackles the issue through an exhaustive exercise in etymology and comes to the surprising conclusion that 'We do not dwell because we have built, but we build and have built because we dwell … *Only if we are capable of dwelling, only then can we build*' (Heidegger, 1971: 148, emphasis original). In other words, for Heidegger, it is only through the physical experience of actual living in and coping with the exigencies of a multitude of situations – of *being-in-the-world* – that we subsequently develop the capacity for distancing, reflection, linguistic articulation, cognitive representation and conscious thought. The capacity to build involves intellectual distancing and forethought but this is only possible because we have always already experienced dwelling in the variety of circumstances we found ourselves in the past. The latter mode of engagement with the world precedes the former. Thus, it is only by taking the individual-in-its-environment continually generating forms that eventually become crystallizations of human *purposive* activities as our starting point of analysis that we can then begin to fully appreciate

what knowing-in-practice is really about. Before, we are able to conceptualize, design and theorize, we are firstly practically coping dwellers totally immersed unthinkingly in our day-to-day-activities. We dwell before we design and build. We act *purposively* before we develop conscious, *purposeful* plans of action (Chia and Holt, 2006: 648).

To begin to appreciate fully how a *building* world-view differs from a *dwelling* world-view it is helpful to recall an illuminating illustration provided by the socio-biologists Humberto Maturana and Francisco Varela in their seminal book entitled *Autopoiesis and Cognition* (1980). Maturana and Varela describe the example of two contrasting but equally successful approaches to building a house to demonstrate two distinct epistemological stances; one arising from an observer domain, the other from an *autopoietic* (i.e. the organism reaching out to the environment) world-view.

Let us suppose that we want to build two houses. For such a purpose we have two groups of thirteen workers each. We name one of the workers of the first group as the group leader and give him a book which contains all the plans of the house showing, in the standard way the layout of walls, water-pipes, electric connections, windows, etc, … the workers study the plans and under guidance of the leader, construct the house approximating continuously the final stage prescribed by the description. In the second group, we do not name a leader, we only arrange the workers in a starting line in the field and give each of them … only neighbourhood instructions. These instructions do not contain words such as house, pipes or windows, nor do they contain drawings or plans of the house to be constructed; they only contain instructions of what a worker should do in different positions and in the different relationships in which he finds himself as the position changes … the end result in both cases is the same, namely, a house. (Maturana and Varela, 1980: 54)

In the first case, the workers knew in advance through the design plans, linguistically coded instructions and representations what they were expected to construct and followed accordingly producing successfully the desired outcome. In the second group, however, there was no end-view representation of what was to be accom- plished, nor was it necessary to have such a priori knowledge. Rather, what was coded and internalized was an effective process:

> that constitutes a path of changing relationships which if carried out through … (invariably) results in a system with a domain of interaction which has no intrinsic relationship with the beholding observer. That the (external) observer should call this system a house is a feature of his cognitive domain, not that of the system itself. (Maturana and Varela, 1980: 54, our emphasis)

The point Maturana and Varela is making is that from an *autopoietic* perspective (what we here call the *dwelling* world-view) the practi- cal ability to successfully construct a house or run a business does not necessarily presuppose detached planning, distancing, linguistic jus- tification, or cognitive representation. Unlike a researcher/observer the practitioner is not disposed to standing outside his/her situation and to survey it with a detached eye the way an academic does. Rather what preoccupies him/her is how to respond *in situ* to the changing relationships he/she encounters in a manner that ensures the smooth and productive functioning of his/her everyday world. This is what characterizes a *dwelling* mode of engagement, a mode that generates an internal logic of practice (Bourdieu, 1990) that is effectively incompatible with a world of academia intent on seeking coherent explanations. Much of academic research obscures 'the logic of practice in the very moment in which it tries to offer it' (Bourdieu, 2002: 19). It cannot grasp 'the principles of practical logic without forcibly changing their nature' (Bourdieu, 1990: 90). *This is because within the dwelling mode, the logic of practice exists only to facilitate action, not explanation.* And, even when business practitioners are *retrospectively* asked to make sense of their own practices by researchers, they often unwittingly 'conceal even from their own eyes, the true nature of their own practical mastery' (Bourdieu, 2002: 19). The pressure, on the part of practitioners, to offer justification retrospectively for actions taken in the heat of the moment, 'in conditions

which exclude distance, perspective, detach- ment and reflexion' (Bourdieu, 1990: 82), often leads to a betrayal of the real reasons for actually doing so.

For the most part of their practical lives, the managers' overall disposition is that of practical coping and problem-solving, not abstract representation or justification. The material and social world around them do not appear as free-standing objects to be scrutinized, mentally represented in the mind and only then purposefully utilized. Rather, they '*interiorize* these things and … *dwell in them*' (Polanyi, 1969: 148, emphasis original). They become so much a part of managerial life that a 'primordial relationship … with the object (i.e. the material and social world)' (Heidegger, 1962: 98) exists.

However, unlike the smooth and unobtru- sive practical coping that characterizes the *dwelling* mode a certain distancing of the individual from the phenomena apprehended takes place during what Heidegger (1962) calls a 'breakdown' or disturbance of that process. By 'breakdown', Heidegger means a jolt to consciousness. This may happen when the results of our actions surprise us – whether positively or negatively. Only then do we take a step back to reflect and assess its significance. Only then do we move from the *dwelling* to a *building* mode of engagement assigning terms, concepts and linguistic categories as well as identities, meanings and functions to help explain to ourselves *retrospectively* what has actually happened. In other words, it is a disruption to our smooth, mundane and unspectacular everyday functioning '*that alerts our consciousness and attention and causes us to stand back and survey our circumstance*' (Chia and Holt, 2006: 642, emphasis original). Only then does meaning, deliberate intention and a *purposeful*, means-ends logic of action take over. In other words, it is the experience of dissonance (whether positive or negative) which prompts distancing, reflection and conscious action and brings us from a *dwelling* to a *building* epistemological stance.

The essence of this distinction between the *building* and *dwelling* modes of existence is captured in de Certeau's book *The Practice of Everyday Life*. Here, de Certeau (1984: 91–3) finds himself at the top of the ill-fated World Trade Centre in New York musing on the distinction between the view looking down on the city and enjoying the voyeuristic pleasures of seeing it all neatly laid out below as one would view a map of a city, and the perspective of the city as most ordinary people would experience it at the street level. Unlike the detached, transcendent observer looking from atop the building, the pedestrians on the streets down below do not have a map-like view of the city but instead experience a series of migrational outlooks generating horizons of comprehension that are continuously evolving and changing as they actually walk the streets at 'ground zero': unthinkingly and deftly avoiding traffic, sidestepping and negotiating their way around obstacles, ignoring the honking, but noticing the displays on the sidewalk, passing by, reaching towards, and generally 'muddling through' (Lindblom, 1959) on their way to work. This is the creative experience of weaving spaces, events and situations together in a subjective self-referential manner. The richness of experiences involved in such pedestrian journeys cannot be captured by static maps, tracing routes or locating positions since maps, routes and positions are typically forms of fixing and pinning down the flux and flow of everyday life. The pedestrians 'down below' having no privileged 'birds-eye' view must act by 'reaching out' from wherever they find themselves feeling their way towards a satisfactory resolution of their immediate circumstances.

De Certeau here is making a vital distinction between the knowledge of a 'tourist' researcher/observer and that form of intimate knowing which results from being totally immersed in negotiating, overcoming and resolving material circumstances as they arise. On the one hand, it presupposes the ability to survey, abstract, fix and define. On the other, there is the kind of *knowing* that is locally adaptive and inventive and that emerges from the immediate need to continuously revise, adjust and make do according to the situation.

In other words, it presumes that individuals in the intimacy of their *dwelling* situations, like a fish in water, can only operate 'blow by blow ... (they must) accept the chance offerings of the moment, and seize on the wing the possibilities that offer themselves at any given moment' (de Certeau, 1984: 37). Rather than relying on a pre-established 'map' of action or some grand 'strategy', this kind of local practical knowing manifests itself in small, unheroic and seemingly inconsequential moves: 'tactics' requiring ingenuity, wit, trickery, surprise and opportunistic poachings. *Timeliness* in intervention is a crucial weapon of such 'tacticians'.

In articulating this important distinction between 'strategic' knowledge and 'tactical' *knowing* de Certeau expresses the same insight on the difference between the *building* and *dwelling* world-views that we are proposing here. Like the walkers de Certeau describes many successful managerial practitioners (especially those who have never been to business schools, and we must remember that there are still millions of successful business people all over the world who have never heard of nor bothered about an MBA qualification) do not generally rely on the kind of formalized planning, organizing and decision making taught in the business school curriculum to guide their actions and decisions. Rather, they 'feel their way *through* a world that is itself ... continually coming into being' (Ingold, 2000: 155). Self and world (e)merge in the concrete activities of managerial coping so much so that like social skills, managerial skills are 'passed ... through individuals without necessarily passing through consciousness' (Dreyfus, 1991: 27). 'Decisions' and 'actions' emanate from being *in situ* and occur *sponte sua*. Here, the efficacy of action in achieving successful outcomes does not depend upon some pre-designed plan of action but results from continuous timely and ongoing adjustment and adaptation to local circumstances. This is the kind of *knowing* exemplified by *phronesis* and *mētis*.

Both the *building* and the *dwelling* modes co-exist in the actual practice of managing.

Yet, to date, it has been the former that has dominated the attention of management academic researchers and this is because of the overwhelming commitment to the idea of knowledge as detached mental representation. The *involved* management practitioner, like the pedestrian, however, is more like a blind person attempting to negotiate his/her way around an unfamiliar room. He/she *does not* and *need not* have a 'bird's-eye' view of the room to successfully deal with his predicament. Instead, with the aid of a walking stick (a prosthetic device which extends and reaches out to feel the world around him/her) he/she is able to successfully find his/her way around. Similarly, the management practitioner develops a local insider's 'feel' for the problem situation he/she finds him/herself in and responds accordingly using all the means immediately available to effect a satisfactory resolution. This is the management practitioner's *dwelling* view of the world: one in which detached seeing and contemplation gives way to an immersed guileful and opportunistic form of doing involving *phronesis* and *mētis*.

## PRACTICAL *KNOWING*: PHRONESIS AND MĒTIS

*phronesis* is the result of experience and social practice. *Phronesis* is singular, idiosyncratic ... It is personal, and has profound meaning only for the individual who has lived the experience. (Baumard, 1999: 53)

*mētis* ... refers to a particular type of intelligence, an informed prudence. (Detienne and Vernant, 1978: 11)

In his useful and stimulating discussion of *Tacit Knowledge in Organizations*, Philippe Baumard (1999) develops Nonaka and Takeuchi's (1995) discussion of the value of explicit knowledge and tacit knowing in the knowledge-creation process. Baumard distinguishes between *episteme*, *techné*, *phronesis*, and *mētis* as we have done here. For Baumard, both *episteme* and *techné* are forms of knowledge that can be 'written, recorded, validated and protected by a firm'

(Baumard, 1999: 22). Indeed both terms appear to be used interchangeably among the Greeks as Nussbaum (1986: 94) notes. We have seen that both *episteme* and *techné* are codifiable forms of knowledge that presuppose linguistic articulation and that both arise from adopting a *building* world-view.

*Phronesis,* on the other hand, is a know-how capability 'born from the experience of social practice' (Baumard, 1999: 22). Unlike *episteme*, or *techné*, *phronesis* is acquired through immersion, acquisition and internalizing of such practices and this does not necessarily pre-suppose acquiring formal explicit knowledge (universal or particular) about a practice. Such a non-explicit form of *knowing* is generated in the immediate intimacy of lived experience, acquired through trial and error and hence does not lend itself to scientific validation or precise codification. *Phronesis*, therefore, is the *tacit* form of prudent practical intelligence and wisdom that underlies the ability to perform appropriately in defined social circumstances.

Similarly, *mētis*, as we have seen, is also a form of *tacit* knowing. And, like the *episteme/techné* couplet, both *phronesis* and *mētis* share many common aspects even though a distinction between the two is frequently made. Recent attention on the existence of *mētis* as a yet unexamined form of practical knowing was first drawn by Marcel Detienne and Jean-Pierre Vernant (1978) whose discussion of 'cunning intelligence' in Greek culture and society has now become a classic reference for serious scholars of Western thought and social practice. The kind of knowing associated with *mētis* is 'furtive, discretionary and simultaneous, it spurns idealizations and established representations' (Baumard, 1999: 54). It is the kind of knowing required to 'escape puzzling and ambiguous situations' (Detienne and Vernant, in Baumard, 1999: 64). It is applied to situations that are 'transient, shifting, disconcerting and ambiguous, situations that do not lend themselves to precise measurement, exact calculation or rigorous logic' (Detienne and Vernant, in Baumard, 1999: 65). In management and organizational research, Baumard (1999) is to be credited for first drawing our attention to this obscured form of knowing which is crucial to our understanding of management practice and hence for our re-evaluation of the relevance of contemporary Management Education. To appreciate the importance of this, however, we need to explore both *phronesis* and *mētis* in greater depth.

In their original study of Greek culture and society, Detienne and Vernant (1978) identified a form of primordial 'knowing' that encapsulates the internalized resourcefulness, imaginative integration and guile of living creatures as part of their survival instinct. Take the 'fishing frog' as an example.

> The fishing frog is a sluggish creature with a soft body and a hideous aspect. Its mouth opens exceedingly wide. Nevertheless it is a possessor of *mētis*, for all that and it is *mētis* that procures its food. What it does is crouch, motionless, deep in the wet mud. Then it stretches out a little fleshy appendage which grows below its lower jaw; the appendage is thin, white and has an unpleasant smell. The frog waves it about continuously, using it as a bait to attract small fish. As soon as these catch sight of it they fall on it in order to seize it. Then, imperceptibly, the frog draws this sort of tongue back towards it and continues to wave it gently about a couple of finger-lengths away from its mouth. Without the slightest suspicion that it is a trap the little fish follow the bait. Soon they are swallowed up one after another within the wide jaws of this huge mouth ... The domain of *mētis* is one ruled by cunning and traps. It is an ambiguous world composed of duplicity and deceit. (Detienne and Vernant, 1978: 28–9)

*Mētis* operates through 'duplicity' and 'disguise' concealing its true lethal nature beneath a reassuring exterior. It is characterized by three crucial aspects: (1) the quality of agility, suppleness, swiftness, mobility; (2) dissimulation, the art of seeing without being seen or acting without being seen to act; and (3) vigilance and alertness. In fishing, for example, it is the *mētistic* guile of the fish that obliges the fisherman to 'deploy an intelligence full of finesse' (Detienne and Vernant, 1978: 33).

Although Detienne and Vernant, and by implication Baumard, tend to equate *mētis* with deliberate 'duplicity' and 'deceit', and

hence to imply conscious intentional action on the part of the fishing frog, it is hard to imagine such a creature operating in this deliberate *purposeful* manner without resorting to an insidious anthropomorphism. It is more appropriate to think of *mētis* as an inherited 'mindless' coping capability that has been gradually refined and 'unconsciously' passed on from one generation of fishing frogs to another. And, this kind of primordial 'knowing' is made more understandable from the *dwelling* worldview that we are advocating here. Both *mētis* and *phronesis* are predicated upon the direct bodily acquisition of skills in a manner which does not involve conscious learning or explicit articulation. But whereas *phronesis* is 'practical but not inherently oblique, devious or indirect', *metic* intelligence operates with a 'peculiar twist'; it reflects the ability to attain a surprising reversal of situations (Raphals, 1992: 5). Yet, like the *episteme/techné* couplet, this distinction between *phronesis* and *mētis* is not always observed. *Phronesis* and *mētis* are often used interchangeably in a manner similar to *episteme* and *techné*.

The Yale political scientist and social anthropologist James Scott in his seminal book *Seeing Like a State* appears to embrace this latter view when he insists that 'all human activities require a considerable degree of *mētis*' (Scott, 1998: 313). For Scott, 'Knowing how and when to apply the rules of thumb *in a concrete situation* is the essence of *mētis*' (Scott, 1998: 317, emphasis original). Scott describes the experience of European settlers in North America thus:

> When the first European settlers in North America were wondering when and how to plant New World cultivars, such as maize, they turned to the local knowledge of their Native American neighbours for help. They were told ... to plant corn *when the oak leaves were the size of a squirrel's ear.* Embedded in this advice, however folkloric its ring is today, is a finely observed knowledge of the succession of natural events in the New England spring. For Native Americans, it was this *orderly* succession of, say, the *skunk cabbage appearing, the willows beginning to leaf, the red-winged blackbird returning,* and the first hatch of the

*mayfly* that provided a readily observable calendar of spring. (Scott, 1998: 311–12, our emphasis)

It appears from Scott's description that the term *mētis* is generally employed for what others like Raphals (1992) and Baumard (1999) would consider to be more characteristic of *phronesis*: a form of local 'know-how' that does not rely on devious and indirect means. Whichever the case, it is clear that this kind of practical *knowing* derives from living within and becoming intimately acquainted with local conditions 'on the ground' and not from some detached observer's point of view. In other words, they can only arise from a *dwelling* mode of existence. What is common to both *mētis* and *phronesis*, therefore is a particularly heightened sensitivity to the importance of *timing* and the *timeliness* of action and intervention. Not only 'know-how' but 'know-when' is crucial for successful intervention. *Mētis*, in particular, suggests an acute sensitivity and absorbed awareness of how immersed in a given set of circumstance one finds oneself, one can still achieve strategic advantage through alertness, ingenuity, guile and opportunism and hence to transform unfavourable circumstances into favourable outcomes. Both *mētis* and *phronesis* operates on the unexpressed premise that reality and language cannot be understood (or manipulated) in straightforward 'rational' terms but must be approached by 'subtlety, indirection, and even cunning' (Raphals, 1992: 5). Both *mētic* intelligence and *phronesis*, to use the words of Bourdieu (1990: 53), are a consequence of *habitus*; a style, demeanour, and culturally mediated set of predispositions inscribed onto material bodies that result in a propensity to act in a manner congruent with the demands of shifting social situations. Such a *habitus* generates competent practices 'without presupposing a conscious aiming at ends or an express mastery of the operations' (Bourdieu, 1990: 53). It is a capability inscribed and inherited by social agents via the process of socialization; grown and re-grown in each individual rather than through deliberate purposeful training, much in the same manner that the 'fishing frog'

has 'learnt' how to fish successfully. It is clear that the frog's actions are in no way 'deliberate' and 'intentional' in the sense generally associated with human actions. Rather it is an inherited predisposition.

What all this discussion regarding the two forms of knowledge (i.e. *episteme/techné* and *phronesis/mētis*) does imply is that beneath the aura of instrumental rationality, conscious intentionality and purposefulness, as biological organisms, humans have unconsciously acquired, in the evolutionary process, a survivalist instinct in the form of a 'mindless' practical coping capacity which has remained theoretically unexamined since the time of the ancient Greeks. That such qualities are more universal than generally acknowledged has led de Certeau to observe that these *phronetic* and *mētistic* abilities:

> correspond to an ageless art which has not only persisted through the institutions of successive political orders but … present in fact a curious analogy, and a sort of immemorial link, to the simulations, tricks, and disguises that certain fishes or plants execute with extraordinary virtuosity … They maintain formal continuities and the permanence of *a memory without language, from the depths of the oceans to the streets of our great cities*. (de Certeau, 1984: 40, our emphasis)

Both *phronesis* and *mētis* are forms of practical *knowing* involving a 'memory without language' or representation. This would explain how and why animals in the wild instinctively *know* how to survive the constant dangers surrounding them. Socio-biological studies show, for example, that reindeer in the Finnish Lapland have developed a ploy whereby on pursuit by predatory wolves, there comes a moment when the reindeer stops dead momentarily in its track and turns to face its adversary who, altogether surprised by the manoeuvre, also stops. Both pursuer and pursued gather themselves for the final decisive phase of the episode when the deer turns to flight and the wolf rushes to overtake it. Since it is the deer that takes the initiative in moving first, it has a slight head start giving it an advantage in fleeing from the wolf's grasp. This momentary hesitation on the part of the wolf is just sufficient to facilitate the reindeer's successful escape from almost certain death. In this rudimentary sense the animal can be said to *know* how to deal with predatory threats to its survival (Ingold, 2000). Both *phronesis* and *mētis* are primordial intelligences, forms of knowing that are peculiarly sensitive to time, duration and simultaneity and hence particularly well suited for dealing with transient, shifting, disconcerting and ambiguous situations that are common to management practitioners but that are an anathema to all academic researchers.

## KNOWLEDGE AND KNOWING: IMPLICATIONS FOR MANAGEMENT LEARNING, EDUCATION AND DEVELOPMENT

We enunciate two educational commandments, 'Do not teach too many subjects', and again, 'What you teach, teach thoroughly ... Whatever interests attaches to your subject-matter must be evoked here and now ... What education has to impart is an intimate sense for the power of ideas, for the beauty of ideas ... I mean the sense for style. (Whitehead, 1932: 2–19)

Sumantra Ghoshal (2005) has tirelessly argued against the prevailing conception of knowledge held within business schools which is governed by what we call here *episteme* and *techné*. The presumption is that use of such representational structures produces proper reliable knowledge that is then transmitted to students who are subsequently encouraged to 'apply' them in practice. Truth-seeking knowledge-creation necessarily precedes and hence guides practical action. Knowing 'what' and 'why' precedes 'knowing how to'. But this representational truth-seeking orientation is not just restricted to *objectivist/positivist* accounts only. It is also what motivates the more recent *interpretive* approaches that seek to capture the true meanings of actions and decisions in the intentions of actors. Researching singular cases with the promise of offering a rich and 'thick description' of managerial goings

on has become a popular alternative to the traditional positivist forms of knowledge-creation in management research.

Yet, even here, the epistemological stance of such descriptions and interpretations remain problematic because it retains an unwavering faith in the reliability of language to adequately capture the subtle nuances of managerial actions. But asking managers for their reasons for acting is not such a straight-forward affair as we have previously argued. Such interpretive acts still tend to exclude or overlook the tacit, unspoken, inarticulate and often unmeasurable understandings possessed by individuals that are historically and culturally shaped and that are idiosyncratic and invisible in their influence on behaviour. The unspoken and performative nature of practice involving complexity, chance and contradictory elements will typically resist the formulation of a neat comprehensive account of meaning and intention. We have attempted to show that this process of filtration and distortion of practitioner *knowing* takes place in the course of translating lived experiences from the 'shop-floor' to the MBA classrooms via the causal logic and system of representation employed in academic explanations. When pressed by researchers, even highly experienced management practitioners are generally unable to give a consistent and coherent account of their judgements and decisions and are thus forced to 'regress to the level of a beginner' stating the more obvious and well-known aspects of their practice that are familiar and understandable to both the researcher and researched. In so accounting for his/her actions, the manager is 'forced to remember rules he or she no longer uses' (Dreyfus and Dreyfus, 2005: 788).

This epistemological 'slippage' from pure practical action to 'justification' is aided by an indiscriminate 'drift' from a *dwelling* mode of comprehension-in-action on the part of the practitioner to a *building* mode of explanation where *episteme* and *techné* govern the basis of understanding. The practical expertise demonstrated in *phronesis* and *mētis* cannot be logically and linguistically captured but can be *demonstrated*: materially *exemplified* through the manner of approach, demeanour and disposition of the individual practitioner. This crucial insight allows us now to move on to address the question of what implications this would have for Management Learning, Education and Development.

In his illuminating reflections on the *Aims of Education*, the philosopher Alfred North Whitehead reminds us of the true function of education, including especially Management Education: 'Education is the acquisition of the art of the utilisation of knowledge' (Whitehead, 1932: 6). Note the emphasis. It is *not* about the acquisition of knowledge. Rather it is about the cultivation of the *art* of using knowledge effectively. The task of education as the etymology of the term 'educe' suggests, is to *draw out* the mental powers, imagination and 'zest for life' (Whitehead, 1932) of the individual. Education is a formative process involving the cultivation of the whole person; his/her overall attitude, manner of behaviour, dispositional tendency, and social sensitivity. And this is done not so much by emphasizing the content taught, which serves as useful vehicles of learning, but by 'evoking' imaginative participation and comprehension on the part of the learner. This is the crucial difference between 'training' and 'education': the former deals with content expertise and the latter with the cultivation of an individual's overall attitude, 'style', and disposition.

For Whitehead, 'style' is not some superficial and arbitrary embellishment but is something distinctive about an individual which is cultivated and honed in the educational process. It is central to our being and identity for it governs our *habitus* and *modus operandi*: the way we set about instinctively dealing with things around us in a manner congruent with a deep sense of who we are. Style in this finest sense: 'is the last acquirement of the educated mind; it is also the most useful. It pervades the whole being. The administrator with a sense for style hates waste; the engineer with a sense for style economizes his materials. The artisan with a sense for style prefers good work. Style is the ultimate morality of the mind' (Whitehead, 1932: 19).

Style, like *phronesis* is not something one 'has' but something one *is*. Something as elusive as style, cannot be 'taught', using linguistic symbols and representations, but it can be learnt and internalized through exemplification. It corresponds to a certain form of *tacit* knowing that we associate with *phronesis* and *mētis*. It is cultivated largely *unconsciously* through exemplification in the educational process. But what do we mean by exemplification and how can it be communicated in the Management Education process?

Exemplification implies exemplary behaviour, demeanour, observed tendencies and predispositions on the part of the expert, master or teacher that is oftentimes unconsciously communicated to the student/ apprentice/disciple in the pedagogical process. For example, learning how to write scholarly journal articles entails not merely a mastery of the subject matter, but also the assiduous cultivation of the more subtle skills of articulation and persuasion which is often unconsciously learnt from one's intellectual mentor and/or Ph.D. supervisor – vaguely passed on as 'scholarship' within the academic system. All established scholars *tacitly* know that attention to the seemingly mundane and less important details like spelling, punctuation, sentence structure, use of examples, thoroughness of referencing, logical flow of the argument, etc. go a long way towards making a piece of work more persuasive and compelling irrespective of its actual content. For this reason, we may disagree completely with a piece of work but nevertheless (often grudgingly) acknowledge the seriousness of its scholarship. This same 'subsidiary awareness' (Polanyi, 1969) of the persuasive power of a 'hidden order' in a piece of work or a performance is something well understood by artists and art theorists. It is what makes for the acute vision of great artists who are able to tap into this tacit understanding. 'There are other forms in a painting unseen ... but which nevertheless exerts great influence. I refer to the almost microscopic, scribbles which make up the technique of a great draftsman or the brushwork of a great painter' (Ehrenzweig, 1965: 29). What makes great artists great is often not that which the layperson imagines. Rather, 'A truly nervous seemingly uncontrolled "handwriting" that resists all deliberate mannerisms and tricks is highly valued by artists and art lovers. In some mysterious way it expresses the artist's personality better than his more considered composition' (Ehrenzweig, 1965: 28–9). What Ehrenzweig is pointing to is that there is a large element of hidden persuasive power in any field of endeavour that occurs unconsciously and which therefore implicitly shapes the mood, personality, *modus operandi* and disposition of an individual affected by it. In the process of immersion in this aesthetic experience, learning takes place but almost indirectly and serendipitously rather than by deliberate design. Similarly, in any stimulating encounter such as a good lecture, the student internalizes what the expert/ master/teacher *does* and how it is done more than what he/she says. Individual style is cultivated through observation and imaginative integration on the part of the student learning and imitating the teacher/expert.

Thus, successful learning of this *habitus* or predisposition can only occur through *indirect* communication by 'a faculty whose members themselves wear their learning with imagination' (Whitehead, 1932: 145). Hence, 'The whole art in the organisation of a university is the provision of a faculty whose learning is lighted up with imagination' (Whitehead, 1932: 145–6). 'It is the function of the scholar to evoke into life wisdom and beauty which, apart from his magic, would remain lost' (Whitehead, 1932: 147). This is what marks out learning a practice such as management: learning through the emulation of predispositions, orientations and attitudes of already skilful others, rather than through direct explicit instruction. These highly-skilled others stand in relation to their knowledge as stewards; people whose learning has been gradually and painfully accumulated, honed and refined through their ongoing struggle to solve

(or dissolve) problems immediately at hand, rather than through preoccupying themselves with causal explanations regarding what is true or false.

Achieving proficiency and mastery in any specific practice, including business management and entrepreneurship, does not presuppose the need for formal training or knowledge. The Bill Gates, Steve Jobs, Alan Sugars and Lee Ka Shings of this world never needed any formal business school training to be successful. But they certainly did learn good management practice capabilities, unconsciously through observation and imitating the good practices of others whom they looked up to or admired. Such forms of *tacit* knowing are 'passed on silently from body to body … it is only by being an apprentice to one's parents and teachers that one gains … practical wisdom (*phronesis*)' (Dreyfus, 2001: 48). *Phronesis* and *mētis*, knowing 'how to' and 'when to' entails developing sensitivity and awareness to local situations through observing significant others. A child, for instance, learns how to behave appropriately: how to express joy, gratitude, disappointment and frustration; how to behave with others in social situations; how to defer gratification and win approval; and even how to get away with things, not so much from formal instruction as from acute observation and imitation:

> The child imitates not 'models' but other people's actions. Body *hexis* speaks directly to the motor function, in the form of pattern of postures … in all societies, children are particularly attentive to the gestures and postures which, in their eyes, express everything that goes into making an accomplished adult – a way of walking, a tilt of the head, facial expressions, ways of sitting and of using implements … (Bourdieu, 2002: 87)

Much of human action performed on a day-to-day basis relies on the acquisition of this *habitus* and this is essentially non-deliberate and does not presume conscious mental activity, images or representations (Dreyfus, 1991: 82). Instead, through the *exemplification* of parents, masters and teachers, children, apprentices, interns as well as MBA students are able to learn a style or predisposition for dealing with situations they encounter. Their learning involves a 're-education of attention' (Chia, 2004) and hence the cultivation of a heightened sensitivity and awareness to goings-on. Whereas, in the traditional forms of knowledge it is presumed that what unifies and gives meaning and continuity to each action is the existence of an explicit purpose or end-goal; in a *dwelling* mode, what unifies and gives consistency to a pattern of behaviour is the social internalizing of a certain *style of engagement*; a way of disposing oneself towards and dealing with the world. This is accomplished not through spectacular heroic examples, but through a slow unheroic process of 'silent' unspectacular learning that relies primarily on the observance and imitation of exemplary behaviour.

Given this, the business school's emphasis on detached analysis and understanding in acquiring formal causal knowledge overlooks the need to encourage direct immersion, emotional involvement and risk-taking in encouraging individual personal growth and in mastering the *art* of management. Such displays of vulnerability, risk-taking and emotional involvement are not usually exemplified by faculty members in business school teaching environments. But it is exactly this detachment and risk-aversion which is often unconsciously and unintentionally transmitted as exemplary behaviours to management students in business schools. Little surprise, therefore, that business schools appear to be producing MBA graduates that are overly conservative in their thinking and predictably alike in their mentalities and hence ill-equipped for the challenges of the real world (Mintzberg, 2004). This is especially the case for MBAs in areas such as finance where the legendary Warren Buffett is reported to have joked that 'he would like to fund university chairs in the Efficient Market Hypothesis, so that the professors would train even more misguided financiers whose money he could win' (Mandlebrot and Hudson, 2004: 12). Buffett and George Soros are two successful financial speculators who have an acute sense

of *phronesis* and *mētis* that is sadly lacking in business schools. These constitute the missing elements in the pedagogical priorities of Management Learning, Education and Development. It is, then, by supplementing *episteme* and *techné* with *phronesis* and *mētis* that business schools will better develop a practice-based ethos and so warranting their claim to be practically relevant and engaged with, everyday business life.

This must be done by faculty members, not through what they teach in their curriculum, but through the manner by which they serve as exemplars for students to emulate. Instead of just being detached 'scholars' primarily concerned with the representative contents of what they research and/or teach, they must also be proficient practitioners of *phronesis* and *mētistic* intelligence displaying the virtuosity of their performance and practical coping through exemplification in the classroom: the flair, enthusiasm, inventiveness and subtlety of thought they show in drawing together disparate elements of management into a kaleidoscopic understanding of the phenomenon of management; the risk-taking intellectual boldness and entrepreneurialism they exemplify in their imaginative engagement with the world of ideas; and the resourcefulness, vigilance and opportunism they demonstrate in enjoining students in the act of discovery and learning.

In effect, what we are advocating is that business school professors actually develop and display their imaginative capacity and enthusiasm in capitalizing on the transient, shifting, and ambiguous pedagogical situations they find themselves in the course of transmitting knowledge. This is the true value of any formal university education. Enthusiasm, inventiveness and imagination are 'contagious diseases' which cannot be 'taught' but can only be *exemplified*. It is through such inclinations, enthusiasm and predispositions displayed by faculty members and the manner in which they exemplify their skill, care, concern and approach in engaging with, dealing and assessing an idea, concept or theory and how that works in practice that students learn the practical skills of *phronesis* and *mētis*. Therein lie the seeds of the answer to the question of relevance of business schools to the business community.

## CONCLUSION

There has been much discussion and debate surrounding the practical relevance of business school education in recent times. Current controversies regarding the role of business schools have tended to revolve around the twin pillars of 'academic rigour' and the need for practical 'relevance' of the learning attained in business schools. The debate brings into focus the kind of knowledge taught in business schools and the apparent lack of practical value of such knowledge (Bennis and O'Toole, 2005; Ghoshal, 2005; Grey, 2005; Pfeffer and Fong, 2004; Starkey et al., 2004). In our previous discussion above we have emphasized that a crucial aspect that has not been sufficiently addressed is the nature of knowledge and knowing generally associated with Management Learning, Education and Development. We have tried to show that the form of knowledge generated in traditional management research and which is taught in business schools is primarily that of *episteme* and *techné*; precise, linguistically explicit and verifiable forms of knowledge that emphasizes logic, causality, meaning and representation. We have argued that this form of knowledge presumes a *building* worldview in which knowledge is viewed from an external observer's vantage point and this remains the case even with interpretive forms of research.

Relying solely on this explicit representational form of knowledge (i.e. *episteme* and *techné*) in the education and development of managers, we suggest, is a mistake. Management is fundamentally a set of skilled and internalized *social practice*, more an art than a science. It involves reaching out from where one finds oneself: becoming aware, attending to, sorting out, and prioritizing an inherently messy, fluxing, chaotic world of competing demands that are placed on a manager's attention. 'Active perceptual

organization and the astute allocation of attention is a central feature of the managerial task' (Chia, 2005: 1092). Managerial action and sense-making takes place from *within* a given set of circumstance that the manager finds him/herself in. As such, managing is more an acquired coping capability than a science; more a set of skilled practices than a profession; more a phenomenon of method than a field of study. This is where *phronesis* and *mētis* become crucial in the Management Learning, Education and Development process.

## REFERENCES

Aristotle (1998) *Metaphysics* (trans. H. Lawson-Tancred). London: Penguin.

Baumard, P. (1999) *Tacit Knowledge in Organizations*. London: Sage.

Bennis, W. and O'Toole (2005) 'How business schools lost their way', *Harvard Business Review*, May.

Bourdieu, P. (1990) *The Logic of Practice*. Cambridge: Polity Press.

Bourdieu, P. (2002) *Outline of a Theory of Practice*. Cambridge: Cambridge University Press.

Chia, R. (2004) 'Re-educating attention: What is foresight and how is it cultivated?', in H. Tsoukas and J. Shepherd (eds), *Managing the Future: Foresight in the Knowledge Economy*. Oxford: Blackwell Publishing.

Chia, R. (2005) 'The aim of management education: Reflections on Mintzberg's "Managers not MBAs" ', *Organization Studies*, 26 (7): 1090–2.

Chia, R. and Holt, R. (2006) 'Strategy as practical coping: A Heideggerian perspective', *Organization Studies*, 27 (5): 635–55.

De Certeau, M. (1984) *The Practice of Everyday Life*. Berkeley: University of California Press.

Detienne, M. and Vernant, J.P. (1978) *Cunning Intelligence in Greek Culture and Society*. Sussex: The Harvester Press.

Dreyfus, H. (1991) *Being-in-the-World*. Cambridge, MA: MIT Press.

Dreyfus, H. (2001) *On the Internet*. London: Routledge.

Dreyfus, H.L. and Dreyfus, S.E. (2005) 'Expertise in real world contexts', *Organization Studies*, 26: 779–92.

Dunne, J. (1993) *Back to the Rough Ground: Phronesis and Techné in Modern Philosophy and in Aristotle*. London: University of Notre Dame Press.

Ehrenzweig, A. (1965) *The Hidden Order of Art*. Berkeley: University of California Press.

Ghoshal, S. (2005) 'Bad management theories are destroying good management practices', *Academy of Management Learning and Education*, 4 (1): 75–91.

Grey, C. (2005) *A Very Short, Fairly Interesting, and Reasonably Cheap Book about Studying Organizations*. London: Sage.

Heidegger, M. (1962) *Being and Time*. Oxford: Basil Blackwell.

Heidegger, M. (1971) *Poetry, Language, Thought*. Trans. A. Hofstader. New York: Harper & Row.

Hutchins, E. (1995) *Cognition in the Wild*. Cambridge, MA: MIT Press.

Ingold, T. (2000) *The Perception of the Environment*. London: Routledge.

Lindblom, C.E. (1959) 'The science of muddling through', *Public Administration Review*, 19: 79–88.

Machiavelli, N. (1640/1981) *The Prince*. Trans. G. Bull. New York: Penguin.

Mandlebrot, B. and Hudson, R.L. (2004) *The Misbehaviour of Markets*. London: Profile Book Ltd.

Maturana, H. and Varela, F. (1980) *Autopoiesis and Cognition: The Realization of the Living*. Dordrecht: Reidel.

Mintzberg, H. (2004) *Managers not MBAs*. London, New York: Prentice-Hall.

Nonaka, I. and Takeuchi, H. (1995) *The Knowledge Creating Company*. New York: Oxford University Press.

Nussbaum, M. (1986) *The Fragility of Goodness: Luck and Ethics in Greek Tragedy and Philosophy*. Cambridge: Cambridge University Press.

Pfeffer, J. and Fong, C. (2004) 'The business school "business": Some lessons from the US experience', *Journal of Management Studies*, 41 (8): 1501–20.

Polanyi, M. (1969) 'Sense-giving and sense-reading', in M. Green (ed.) *Knowing and Being*. London: Routledge, Keegan, Paul.

Raphals, L. (1992) *Knowing Words: Wisdom and Cunning in the Classical Traditions of China and Greece*. Ithaca and London: Cornell University Press.

Rorty, R. (1980) *Philosophy and the Mirror of Nature*. Oxford: Blackwell.

Scott, J.C. (1998) *Seeing Like a State: How Certain Schemes to Improve the Human Condition Have Failed*. New Haven and London: Yale University Press.

Starkey, K., Hatchuel, A. and Tempest, S. (2004) 'Rethinking the business school', *Journal of Management Studies*, 41 (8): 1521–31.

Whitehead, A.N. (1932) *The Aims of Education*. London: Williams & Norgate.

# 3

# Experiential Learning Theory: A Dynamic, Holistic Approach to Management Learning, Education and Development

Alice Y. Kolb and David A. Kolb

## Abstract

Experiential learning theory (ELT) has been widely used in management learning research and practice for over 35 years. Building on the foundational works of Kurt Lewin, John Dewey and others, experiential learning theory offers a dynamic theory based on a learning cycle driven by the resolution of the dual dialectics of action/reflection and experience/abstraction. These two dimensions define a holistic learning space wherein learning transactions take place between individuals and the environment. The learning space is multi-level and can describe learning and development in commensurate ways at the level of the individual, the group, and the organization. This approach is illustrated by reviewing current research on individual learning styles and managerial problem solving/decision making, the process of team learning and organizational learning. We describe how ELT can serve as a useful framework to design and implement management education programs in higher education and management training and development.

## INTRODUCTION

The organizational behavior and management fields for many years have focused on performance as the primary validation touchstone for their theories and concepts. In the twenty-first century, however, we have begun to see a shift in focus away from measures of organizational and managerial performance that are often limited and subject to short-term manipulation at the expense of long-term sustainability. In the new perspective organizations are seen as learning systems and the management process is viewed as a process of learning. Learning lies at the core of the management process when learning is defined holistically as the basic process of human adaptation. This broad definition subsumes more specialized managerial processes such as entrepreneurial learning (Corbett, 2005, 2007; Poltis, 2005); strategy formulation (Ramnarayan and Reddy, 1989; Van Der Heijden, 1996; Kolb et al., 1986); creativity (Brennan and Dooley, 2005; Boyle et al., 1991; Ogot and Okudan, 2006; Potgieter, 1999); problem solving and decision making (Donoghue, 1994; Jervis, 1983; Kolb, 1984; Selby et al., 2004); and leadership (Robinson, 2005; Kayes et al., 2005a).

For over 35 years research based on experiential learning theory (ELT–Kolb 1984; Kolb and Kolb, 2007a,b) has been an advocate for and contributor to this shift in perspective. Experiential learning theory draws on the work of prominent twentieth century scholars who gave experience a central role in their theories of human learning and development – notably John Dewey, Kurt Lewin, Jean Piaget, William James, Carl Jung, Paulo Freire, Carl Rogers and others – to develop a dynamic, holistic model of the process of learning from experience and a multi-linear model of adult development. ELT is a dynamic view of learning based on a learning cycle driven by the resolution of the dual dialectics of action/reflection and experience/abstraction. It is a holistic theory that defines learning as the major process of human adaptation involving the whole person. As such, ELT is applicable not only in the formal education classroom but in all arenas of life. The process of learning from experience is ubiquitous, present in human activity everywhere all the time. The holistic nature of the learning process means that it operates at all levels of human society, from the individual, to the group, to organizations and to society as a whole. Research based on ELT has been conducted all around the world supporting the cross-cultural applicability of the model.

Research on experiential learning in management has used ELT to describe the management process as a process of learning by managers, teams and organizations for problem solving and decision making, entrepreneurial opportunity seeking and strategy formulation. It has also had a major influence on the design and conduct of educational programs in management training and development and formal management education. After a review of the basic concepts of experiential learning theory – the cycle of experiential learning, learning style, learning space and the developmental model of learning – we describe how the process of management can be viewed as a learning process. Research on the use of ELT to study managerial behavior, teams, and organizations is reviewed. Next, applications to training and development and formal management education are described. The final section includes a summary, evaluation of the theory and future directions for research and application of ELT.

## EXPERIENTIAL LEARNING THEORY

ELT integrates the works of the foundational experiential learning scholars around six propositions which they all share:

(1) *Learning is best conceived as a process, not in terms of outcomes.* To improve learning in higher education, the primary focus should be on engaging students in a process that best enhances their learning – a process that includes feedback on the effectiveness of their learning efforts: '… education must be conceived as a continuing reconstruction of experience … the process and goal of education are one and the same thing.' (Dewey 1897: 79)

(2) *All learning is re-learning.* Learning is best facilitated by a process that draws out the students' beliefs and ideas about a topic so that they can be examined, tested and integrated with new, more refined ideas.

(3) *Learning requires the resolution of conflicts between dialectically opposed modes of adaptation to the world.* Conflict, differences, and disagreement are what drive the learning process. In the process of learning one is called upon to move back and forth between opposing modes of reflection and action and feeling and thinking.

(4) *Learning is a holistic process of adaptation.* It is not just the result of cognition but involves the integrated functioning of the total person – thinking, feeling, perceiving and behaving. It encompasses other specialized models of adaptation from the scientific method

to problems solving, decision making and creativity.

(5) *Learning results from synergetic transactions between the person and the environment.* Stable and enduring patterns of human learning arise from consistent patterns of transaction between the individual and his or her environment. The way we process the possibilities of each new experience determines the range of choices and decisions we see. The choices and decisions we make to some extent determine the events we live through, and these events influence our future choices. Thus, people create themselves through the choice of actual occasions they live through.

(6) *Learning is the process of creating knowledge.* ELT proposes a constructivist theory of learning whereby social knowledge is created and recreated in the personal knowledge of the learner. This stands in contrast to the 'transmission' model on which much current educational practice is based where pre-existing fixed ideas are transmitted to the learner.

## THE CYCLE OF EXPERIENTIAL LEARNING

ELT defines learning as 'the process whereby knowledge is created through the transformation of experience. Knowledge results from the combination of grasping and transforming experience' (Kolb, 1984: 41). The ELT model portrays two dialectically related modes of grasping experience – Concrete Experience (CE) and Abstract Conceptualization (AC) – and two dialectically related modes of transforming experience – Reflective Observation (RO) and Active Experimentation (AE). Experiential learning is a process of constructing knowledge that involves a creative tension among the four learning modes that is responsive to contextual demands. This process is portrayed as an idealized learning cycle or spiral where the learner 'touches all the bases' – experiencing, reflecting, thinking and acting – in a recursive process that is responsive to the learning situation and what is being learned. Immediate or *concrete experiences* are the basis for observations and *reflections*. These reflections are assimilated and distilled into *abstract concepts* from which new implications for action can be drawn. These implications can be *actively tested* and serve as guides in creating new experiences (see Figure 3.1).

Jung discovered the universal mandala symbol in many cultures and religions

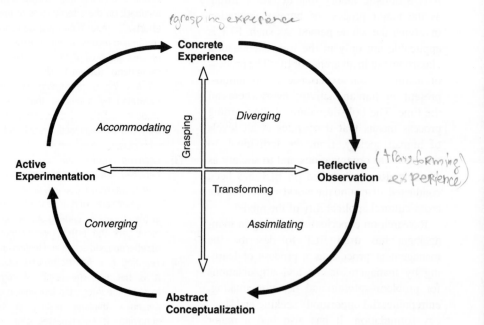

**Figure 3.1    Experiential learning cycle**

throughout time representing this holistic, dynamic cycle of learning. Mandala means circle, an eternal process where endings become beginnings again and again. 'The mandala form is that of a flower, cross, or wheel with a distinct tendency towards quadripartite structures', (Jung, 1931: 100). It often represents dual polarities, the integration of which fuels the endless circular process of knowing. 'Psychologically this circulation would be a "turning in a circle around oneself": whereby all sides of the personality become involved. They cause the poles of light and darkness to rotate ...' (p. 104). In their theories of experiential learning William James and Paulo Freire describe their views about the integration of these of the concrete/abstract and action/reflection dialectics.

William James proposed radical empiricism as a new philosophy reality and mind which resolved the conflicts between nineteenth century rationalism and empiricism, the philosophies of idealism and materialism. For James, everything begins and ends in the continuous flux and flow of experience. His philosophy of radical empiricism was based on two coequal and dialectically related ways of knowing the world – 'knowledge of acquaintance' based on direct perception and 'knowledge about' based on mediating conception. In radical empiricism, direct perception has primacy since all concepts derive their validity from connection to sense experience. Concepts, however, have priority in controlling human action because they often enable us to predict the future and achieve our desires. James (1977: 243) draws attention to the importance of this co-equal relationship when he says:

We thus see clearly what is gained and what is lost when percepts are translated into concepts. Perception is solely of the here and now; conception is of the like and unlike, of the future, and of the past, and of the far away. But this map of what surrounds the present, like all maps, is only a surface; its features are but abstract signs and symbols of things that in themselves are concrete bits of sensible experience. We have but to weigh extent against content, thickness against spread,

and we see that for some purposes the one, for other purposes the other, has the higher value. Who can decide off-hand which is absolutely better to live and to understand life? We must do both alternately, and a man can no more limit himself to either than a pair of scissors can cut with a single one of its blades.

While the conceptualizing/experiencing dialectic described by James is recognized by the Brazilian educator Paulo Freire, by stressing the importance of naming one's own experience in dialogue with others, he and other critical theorists give primary emphasis to praxis, the transformative dialectic between reflection and action – reflection informed by action and action informed by reflection. He writes powerfully about the dynamics of this dialectic:

As we attempt to analyze dialogue as a human phenomenon. ... Within the word we find two dimensions, reflection and action, in such radical interaction that if one is sacrificed – even in part – the other immediately suffers. ... When a word is deprived of its dimension of action, reflection automatically suffers as well; and the word is changed into idle chatter, into verbalism, into an alienated and alienating 'blah'. ... On the other hand, if action is emphasized exclusively, to the detriment of reflection, the word is converted into activism. The latter action for action's sake negates the true praxis and makes dialogue impossible. (Freire, 1992: 75–8)

In *The Art of Changing the Brain: Enriching Teaching by Exploring the Biology of Learning,* James Zull, a biologist and founding director of CWRU's University Center for Innovation in Teaching and Education (UCITE), sees a link between ELT and neuroscience research, suggesting that this process of experiential learning is related to the process of brain functioning, '... concrete experiences come through the sensory cortex, reflective observation involves the integrative cortex at the back, creating new abstract concepts occurs in the frontal integrative cortex, and active testing involves the motor brain. In other words, the learning cycle arises from the structure of the brain.' (Zull, 2002: 18).

## LEARNING STYLE

The concept of learning style describes individual differences in learning based on the learner's preference for employing different phases of the learning cycle. Because of our hereditary equipment, our particular life experiences, and the demands of our present environment, we develop a preferred way of choosing among the four learning modes. We resolve the conflict between being concrete or abstract and between being active or reflective in patterned, characteristic ways. ELT posits that learning is the major determinant of human development and how individuals learn shapes the course of their personal development. Previous research (Kolb, 1984) has shown that learning styles are influenced by personality type, educational specialization, career choice, and current job role and tasks.

A recent study (Joy and Kolb, 2007) has shown relationships between learning style and culture of birth and residence. Analysis of country ratings on individual cultural dimensions suggests that individuals tend to have reflective learning styles in countries that are high in uncertainty avoidance and active learning styles in countries that are high in in-group collectivism. Individuals tend to have abstract learning styles in countries that are high in uncertainty avoidance, future orientation, performance orientation and institutional collectivism. Yamazaki (2004, 2005) has identified learning style cultural influences as well.

Much of the research on ELT has focused on the concept of learning style using the Learning Style Inventory (KLSI) to assess individual learning styles (Kolb, 1971, 1985, 1999). While individuals tested on the KLSI show many different patterns of scores, previous research with the instrument has identified four learning styles that are associated with different approaches to learning: Diverging, Assimilating, Converging, and Accommodating. The following summary of the four basic learning styles is based on both research and clinical observation of these patterns of KLSI scores (Kolb, 1984, 1999).

An individual with diverging style has CE and RO as dominant learning abilities. People with this learning style are best at viewing concrete situations from many different points of view. It is labeled 'Diverging' because a person with it performs better in situations that call for generation of ideas, such as a 'brainstorming' session. People with a Diverging learning style have broad cultural interests and like to gather information. They are interested in people, tend to be imaginative and emotional, have broad cultural interests, and tend to specialize in the arts. In formal learning situations, people with the Diverging style prefer to work in groups, listening with an open mind and receiving personalized feedback.

An individual with an assimilating style has AC and RO as dominant learning abilities. People with this learning style are best at understanding a wide range of information and putting it into concise, logical form. Individuals with an Assimilating style are less focused on people and more interested in ideas and abstract concepts. Generally, people with this style find it more important that a theory has logical soundness than practical value. The Assimilating learning style is important for effectiveness in information and science careers. In formal learning situations, people with this style prefer readings, lectures, exploring analytical models and having time to think things through.

An individual with a converging style has AC and AE as dominant learning abilities. People with this learning style are best at finding practical uses for ideas and theories. They have the ability to solve problems and make decisions based on finding solutions to questions or problems. Individuals with a Converging learning style prefer to deal with technical tasks and problems rather than with social issues and interpersonal issues. These learning skills are important for effectiveness in specialist and technology careers. In formal learning situations, people with this style prefer to experiment with new ideas, simulations, laboratory assignments and practical applications.

An individual with an accommodating style has CE and AE as dominant learning abilities. People with this learning style have the ability to learn from primarily 'hands-on' experience. They enjoy carrying out plans and involving themselves in new and challenging experiences. Their tendency may be to act on 'gut' feelings rather than on logical analysis. In solving problems, individuals with an Accommodating learning style rely more heavily on people for information than on their own technical analysis. This learning style is important for effectiveness in action-oriented careers such as marketing or sales. In formal learning situations, people with the Accommodating learning style prefer to work with others to get assignments done, to set goals, to do field work and to test out different approaches to completing a project.

Recent theoretical and empirical work shows that the original four learning style types can be refined to show nine distinct style types (Eickmann et al., 2004; Kolb and Kolb, 2005a; Boyatzis and Mainemelis, 2000). David Hunt and his associates (Abbey et al., 1985; Hunt, 1987) identified four additional learning styles which they identified as Northerner, Easterner, Southerner, and Westerner. In addition, a Balancing learning style has been identified by Mainemelis et al. (2002) that integrates AC and CE and AE and RO.

## LEARNING SPACES

The concept of learning space elaborates further the holistic, dynamic nature of learning style and its formation through transactions between the person and environment. The idea of learning space builds on Kurt Lewin's field theory and his concept of life space. For Lewin, person and environment are interdependent variables, a concept Lewin translated into a mathematical formula, B=f(p,e) where behavior is a function of person and environment and the life space is the total psychological environment which the person experiences subjectively. Lewin introduced a number of concepts for analysis

of the life space and a person's relationship to it that are applicable to the study of learning spaces, including position, region, locomotion, equilibrium of forces, positive and negative valence, barriers in the person and the world, conflict and goal.

Three other theoretical frameworks inform the ELT concept of learning space. Urie Bronfrenbrenner's (1977, 1979) work on the ecology of human development has made significant sociological contributions to Lewin's life space concept. He defines the ecology of learning/development spaces as a topologically nested arrangement of structures each contained within the next. The learner's immediate setting, such as a course or classroom, is called the *microsystem*, while other concurrent settings in the person's life, such as other courses, the dorm or family, are referred to as the *mesosystem*. The *exosystem* encompasses the formal and informal social structures that influence the person's immediate environment, such as institutional policies and procedures and campus culture. Finally, the *macrosystem* refers to the overarching institutional patterns and values of the wider culture, such as cultural values favoring abstract knowledge over practical knowledge, that influence actors in the person's immediate microsystem and mesosystem. This theory provides a framework for analysis of the social system factors that influence learners' experience of their learning spaces.

Another important contribution to the learning space concept is situated learning theory (Lave and Wenger, 1991). Like ELT, situated learning theory draws on Vygotsky's (1978) activity theory of social cognition for a conception of social knowledge that conceives of learning as a transaction between the person and the social environment. Situations in situated learning theory like life space and learning space are not necessarily physical places but are constructs of the person's experience in the social environment. These situations are embedded in communities of practice that have a history, norms, tools and traditions of practice. Knowledge resides, not in the individual's head, but in communities of practice. Learning is thus a process of becoming a member of a community of practice through legitimate peripheral participation (e.g. apprenticeship). Situated learning theory enriches the learning space concept by reminding us that learning spaces extend beyond the teacher and the classroom. They include socialization into a wider community of practice that involves membership, identity formation, transitioning from novice to expert through mentorship and experience in the activities of the practice, as well as the reproduction and development of the community of practice itself as newcomers replace old-timers.

Finally, in their theory of knowledge creation, Nonaka and Konno (1998) introduce the Japanese concept of 'ba', a 'context that harbors meaning', which is a shared space that is the foundation for knowledge creation. 'Knowledge is embedded in *ba,* where it is then acquired through one's own experience or reflections on the experiences of others' (Nonaka and Konno, 1998: 40). Knowledge embedded in *ba* is tacit and can only be made explicit through sharing of feelings, thoughts and experiences of persons in the space. For this to happen, the *ba* space requires that individuals remove barriers between one another in a climate that emphasizes 'care, love, trust and commitment'. Learning spaces similarly require norms of psychological safety, serious purpose, and respect to promote learning.

In ELT the experiential learning space is defined by the attracting and repelling forces (positive and negative valences) of the two poles of the dual dialectics of action/reflection and experiencing/conceptualizing, creating a two dimensional map of the regions of the learning space. An individual's learning style positions them in one of these regions depending on the equilibrium of forces among action, reflection, experiencing and conceptualizing. As with the concept of life space, this position is determined by a combination of individual disposition and characteristics of the learning environment. The LSI measures an individual's preference for a particular region of the learning space, their home region so to speak. The regions of the ELT learning space offer a typology of the different types of learning based on the extent to which they require action vs. reflection, experiencing vs. thinking thereby emphasizing some stages of the learning cycle over others.

The ELT learning space concept emphasizes that learning is not one universal process but a map of learning territories, a frame of reference within which many different ways of learning can flourish and interrelate. It is a holistic framework that orients the many different ways of learning to one another. The process of experiential learning can be viewed as a process of locomotion through the learning regions that is influenced by a person's position in the learning space. One's position in the learning space defines their experience and thus defines their 'reality'.

## DEVELOPMENT AND DEEP LEARNING

The ELT developmental model (Kolb, 1984) defines three stages: (1) *acquisition*, from birth to adolescence where basic abilities and cognitive structures develop; (2) *specialization*, from formal schooling through the early work and personal experiences of adulthood where social, educational, and organizational socialization forces shape the development of a particular, specialized learning style; and (3) *integration* in mid-career and later life where non-dominant modes of learning are expressed in work and personal life. Development through these stages is characterized by increasing complexity and relativism in adapting to the world and by increased integration of the dialectic conflicts between AC and CE and AE and RO. Development is conceived as multi-linear based on an individual's particular learning style and life path – development of CE increases affective complexity, of RO increases perceptual complexity, of AC increases symbolic complexity, and of AE increases behavioral complexity (see Figure 3.2).

A study by Clarke (1977) of the accounting and marketing professions illustrates the ELT developmental model. The study compared the learning styles of cross-sectional samples

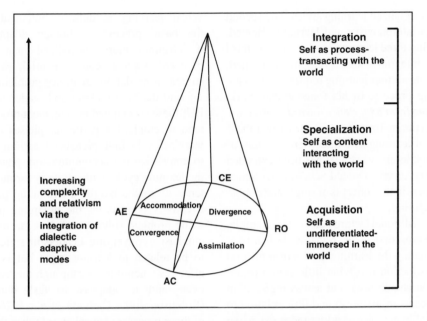

**Figure 3.2   The experiential learning theory of growth and developement**

of accounting and marketing students and professionals in school and at lower, middle and senior level career stages. The learning styles of marketing and accounting students were similar, being fairly balanced on the four learning modes. Lower level accountants had convergent, abstract and active learning styles, and this convergent emphasis was even more pronounced in middle-level accountants, reflecting a highly technical specialization. The senior level accountants, however, became more accommodative in learning style, integrating their non-dominant concrete learning orientation. Clark found a similar pattern of development in the marketing profession. Gypen found the same move from specialization to integration in his study of the learning styles of a cross-sectional sample of social work and engineering alumni from early to late career:

As engineers move up from the bench to management positions, they complement their initial strengths in abstraction and action with the previously non-dominant orientations of experience and reflection. As social workers move from direct service into administrative positions they move in the opposite direction of the engineers. (Gypen, 1981: ii)

In ELT the concept of deep learning is introduced to describe the developmental process learning that fully integrates the four modes of the experiential learning cycle – experiencing, reflecting, thinking and acting (Jensen and Kolb, 1994; Border, 2007). Deep learning refers to the kind of learning that leads to development in the ELT developmental model. ELT suggests that the basic learning styles represent specialized and limited ways of learning. Following Jung's theory that adult development moves from a specialized way of adapting towards a holistic integrated way, deep learning is seen as moving from specialization to integration. Integrated deep learning is a process involving a creative tension among the four learning modes that is responsive to contextual demands. This is portrayed as an idealized learning cycle or spiral where the learner 'touches all the bases' – experiencing, reflecting, thinking and acting – in a recursive process that is responsive to the learning situation and what is being learned.

Development towards deep learning is divided into three levels. In the first level learning is registrative and performance oriented, emphasizing the two learning modes of the specialized learning styles. The second level is interpretative and learning oriented, involving three learning modes, and the third level is integrative and development oriented, involving all four learning modes in a holistic learning process. In his foundational work, *Learning from Experience toward Consciousness*, William Torbert (1972) described these levels of learning as a three-tiered system of feedback loops; work that has been extended by Chris Argyris, Donald Schön, Peter Senge and others in the concepts of single and double loop learning.

The traditional lecture course, for example, emphasizes first level, registrative learning, accentuating the learning modes of reflection and abstraction involving little action (often multiple choice tests that assess registration of concepts in memory) and little relation to personal experience. Adding more extensive learning assessments that involve practical application of concepts covered can create second level learning involving the three learning modes where reflection supplemented by action serve to further deepen conceptual understanding. Further addition of learning experiences that involve personal experience such as internships or field projects create the potential for third level integrative learning (cf. Kolb, 1984, Chapter 6). As a counter example, an internship emphasizes registrative learning via the modes action and experience. Deeper interpretative learning can be enhanced by the addition of activities to stimulate reflection such as team conversation about the internship experience and/or student journals. Linking these to the conceptual material related to the experience adds the fourth learning mode, abstraction and integration though completion of the learning spiral.

## MANAGEMENT AS A LEARNING PROCESS

ELT offers a way to study management as a learning process that is dynamic and holistic, operating at the level of the individual, the team and the organization.

When learning is defined holistically as the basic process of human adaptation, it subsumes more specialized managerial processes such as entrepreneurial learning, strategy formulation, creativity, problem solving and decision making and leadership. In ELT these specialized management processes tend to emphasize particular phases of the learning cycle. Entrepreneurial learning tends to emphasize the accommodating phases of the learning cycle while strategy formulation tends to emphasize the assimilating phases. Creativity emphasizes the diverging phases while problem solving and decision making emphasize converging. Leadership style tends to be related to learning style but is most effective when it moves through the learning cycle and is adaptive to task demands (Robinson 2005; Carlsson et al., 1976). All of these processes are enhanced when the full cycle of learning is followed. For example Corbett (2007) found that in the opportunity identification phase of the entrepreneurial process an abstract orientation is helpful in addition to an active orientation. We begin with research describing individual managerial learning as a process of problem management. Next research on experiential learning in teams is reviewed followed by the ELT approach to organizational learning.

## MANAGERIAL PROBLEM SOLVING AND DECISION MAKING

Kilmann has argued that problem solving is central to the managerial role:

> One might even define the essence of management as problem-defining and problem-solving, whether the problems are well-structured, ill-structured, technical, human, or even environmental. Managers of organizations would then be viewed as problem managers, regardless of the types of products and services they help their organizations provide. (Kilmann, 1979: 214)

As we have noted, the experiential learning cycle is a holistic model of adaptation that encompasses more specialized models of the adaptive process. Numerous studies have examined the relationship between learning styles and problem solving behavior (Armstrong and McDaniel, 1986; Donoghue, 1994; Grochow, 1974; Hendrick, 1979; Jervis, 1983; Katz, 1990; McCormick, 1987; Sanley, 1987; Selby et al., 2004; Wessel et al., 1999; Yonutas, 2001). One example is Stabell's (1972) study of portfolio managers in the trust department of a large Midwestern bank. One aim of his study was to discover how the learning styles of investment portfolio managers affected their problem solving and decision making in the management of the assets in their portfolios. He found a strong correspondence between the type of decisions these managers faced and their learning styles. More specifically, he found that nearly all of the managers in the investment advisory section of the department, a high-risk, high-pressure job (as indicated by a large percentage of discretionary accounts, and a high performance and risk orientation on the part of clients) had accommodative learning styles (scoring very high on the AE and CE LSI scales). On the other hand, the managers in the personal trust section, where risk and performance orientations were low and there were few discretionary accounts and fewer holdings in common stock, scored highest on reflective observation. He was also able to identify differences, on the basis of their KLSI scores, in the way managers went about making investment decisions. He focused his research on differences between managers

with concrete (CE) learning styles and abstract (AC) learning styles. He asked these managers to evaluate the importance of the information sources they used in making decisions and found several interesting differences. First, concrete managers cited more people as important sources (colleagues, brokers and traders), while the abstract managers listed more analytically oriented printed material as sources (economic analysis, industry and company reviews). In addition, concrete managers sought services that would give them a specific recommendation that they could accept or reject, while the abstract managers sought information they could analyze themselves in order to choose an investment. This analytic orientation of the abstract managers is further illustrated by the fact that they tended to use more information sources in their decisions than the concrete managers.

These studies of learning style and problem solving, along with other problem solving research, have been integrated into an idealized problem-solving process model that describes the fully functioning person in optimal circumstances (Kolb, 1983, see Figure 3.3). Ineffective problem solving deviates from the ideal because of personal habits and style as well as situational constraints such as time pressure. The model has four stages that correspond to the four stages of the learning cycle – Situation Analysis (CE), Problem Analysis (RO), Solution Analysis (AC), and Implementation Analysis (AE). Each stage of the model has an opening

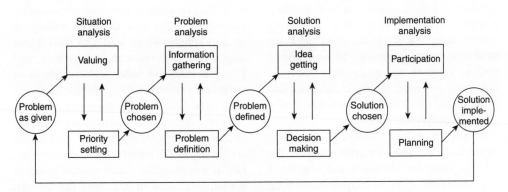

**Figure 3.3   The ELT problem management model**

'green mode' and closing 'red mode' phase. This two-phase process of divergent opening and convergent closing has been shown to operate in studies of the learning and problem solving process (McCarthy, 1987; Lingham, 2004; Jules, 2007).

In Situation Analysis, where the immediate situational context is examined to determine the right problem to work on, the green mode is Valuing and the red mode is Priority Setting. People who are strong in this stage emphasize feeling over thinking and are good at relating to others; they are often good intuitive decision makers and function well in unstructured situations; they have an open-minded approach to life.

In Problem Analysis, the stage where the problem is defined in terms of the essential variables or factors that influence it, the green mode is Information Gathering and the red mode is Problem Definition. Managers who are effective in this stage emphasize understanding as opposed to practical application, a concern with what is true or how things happen as opposed to what is practical, an emphasis on reflection as opposed to action. They like to rely on their own thoughts and feelings to form opinions. People with this orientation value patience, impartiality, and thoughtful judgment.

In Solution Analysis, the stage where possible solutions are generated and their feasibility for solving the problem is examined against the criteria defined in the previous stage, the green mode is Idea Getting and the red mode is Decision Making. People who are strong in this stage emphasize thinking as opposed to feeling, a concern with building general theories as opposed to intuitively understanding facts. They enjoy and are good at systematic planning, manipulation of abstract symbols and quantitative analysis; they value precision, the rigor and discipline of analyzing ideas, and the aesthetic quality of a neat, conceptual system.

In Implementation Analysis, the stage where tasks essential for implementing the solution must be identified and organized into a coherent plan with appropriate time deadlines and follow-up evaluations, the

green mode is Participation and the red mode is Planning. Managers who are strong in this stage actively influence others and change situations. They are more interested in practical applications than they are in understanding; that is they are more interested in doing things than in observing. People with an active experimentation orientation enjoy and are good at getting things accomplished. They are willing to take some risk to achieve their objectives; they also value having an impact and influence on the environment around them and like to see results.

## TEAM LEARNING

The experiential approach to learning in teams has a long and rich history dating back to the 1940s and Kurt Lewin's research on group dynamics. Lewin's discovery of the T-group is worth examining. From this work emerged three key insights that have framed research on the experiential approach to team learning as it has evolved over the years: (1) the pivotal role of reflective conversation; (2) the theory of functional role leadership; and (3) the experiential learning process as the key to team development.

*To learn from their experience, teams must create a conversational space where members can reflect on and talk about their experience together.* In the summer of 1946, Lewin and his colleagues designed a new approach to leadership and group dynamics training for the Connecticut State Interracial Commission. The two-week training program began with an experiential emphasis encouraging group discussion and decision making in an atmosphere where staff and participants were peers. The research and training staff gathered extensive notes and recordings of the group's activities. They met each evening to analyze the data collected during the day's meetings. Although it was the scientific norm to analyze research objectively without the subjective involvement of the participants, Lewin was receptive when a small group of participants asked to join these discussions. One of the staff members in attendance was Ronald Lippitt, who described what happened in a discussion attended by three trainees:

> Sometime during the evening, an observer made some remarks about the behavior of one of the three persons who were sitting in – a woman trainee. She broke in to disagree with the observation and described it from her point of view. For a while there was quite an active dialogue between the research observer, the trainer, and the trainee about the interpretation of the event, with Kurt an active questioner, obviously enjoying this different source of data that had to be coped with and integrated. ... The evening session from then on became the significant learning experience of the day, with the focus on actual behavioral events and with active dialogue about differences of interpretation and observation of the events by those who had participated in them. (Lippitt, in Kolb, 1984: 9)

By creating a conversational space where staff in analytic, objective roles could integrate their ideas with the experiences and observations of active group participants, Lewin and his colleagues discovered the self-analytic group and with it a powerful force for team learning and development.

A team can develop a composite image of itself by developing the capacity to reflect on its experience through conversations that examine and integrate differences in members' experiences on the team. This shared image, which Mills (1967) calls executive consciousness, becomes a guiding light that enables the team to learn and shape itself to respond effectively to the challenges of its mission and environment. A team that cannot see itself accurately is ultimately flying blind. To develop executive consciousness a team needs to create a hospitable conversational space. Members need to respect and be receptive to differing points of view; to take time to reflect on consequences of action and the big picture; and to desire growth and development (Baker et al., 2002).

*As a team develops from a group of individuals into an effective learning system, members share the functional roles necessary for team effectiveness.* In 1948, Kenneth Benne and Paul Sheats described a new concept of team roles and team leadership based on the first National Training Laboratory in Group Development. In contrast to the then-prevailing idea that leadership was a characteristic of the person and that teams should be led by a single leader, Benne and Sheats discovered that mature groups shared leadership. While initially group members were oriented to individual roles focused on satisfying their personal needs, they later came to share responsibility for team leadership by organizing themselves into team roles. Some roles focused on task accomplishment, such as initiator-contributor, information seeker, coordinator, and evaluator-critic; other roles focused on group building and maintenance, such as encourager, compromiser, standard setter, and group-observer. While members tended to choose roles based on their personality dispositions, they also were able to adopt more unfamiliar roles for the good of the group (Benne and Sheats, 1948).

*Teams develop by following the experiential learning cycle.* The laboratories in group development, or T-groups as they came to be known, were based on a model of learning from experience known as the laboratory method. This model was typically introduced by the group trainer as follows:

> Our goal here is to learn from our experience as a group and thereby create the group we want to be. We will do this by sharing experiences together and reflecting on the meaning of these experiences for each of us. We will use these observations and reflections to create a collective understanding of our group, which will serve to guide us in acting to create the kind of group experience that we desire. In ELT, the process of learning from experience ... shapes and actualizes developmental potentialities. (Kolb, 1984: 133)

Theodore Mills (1967) describes team development as successive stages in the sophistication of a team's ability to learn. At the higher stages of his model, a team develops a system of executive consciousness. 'Consciousness is gained through adding to the function of acting the functions of observing and comprehending the system that is acting' (p. 19). At this level, team members take on an executive role following the experiential learning cycle: 'He [sic] experiences, observes, and assesses the realities of the momentary situation. He acts and assesses the consequences of his action upon the group's capability of coping with immediate demands and future exigencies' (p. 90). All team members can take the executive role, forming what Mills calls the executive system, 'the group's center for assessment of itself and its situations, for arrangement and rearrangement of its internal and external relations, for decision making and for learning, and for 'learning how to learn' through acting and assessing the consequences of action' (p. 93). Thus, experiential learning and engagement in the learning cycle provide the mechanisms by which teams can transition from lower to higher developmental stages.

Current research, involving different methodologies and different educational and workplace populations, has shown that ELT is useful in understanding team learning and performance. Studies support the proposition that a team is more effective if it follows the learning cycle in its work process and emphasizes all four learning modes.

Summarized below are studies of team member learning style, team roles, and team norms.

*Team member learning style.* There have been numerous studies that have investigated the impact of team member learning style diversity on team effectiveness. Most find that teams whose members have different learning styles are more effective than homogeneous learning style teams (Hall, 1996; Halstead and Martin, 2002; Kayes, 2001; Jackson, 2002; Sandmire and Boyce, 2004; Sharpe, 2001; Wolfe, 1977). For example, Jackson studied the learning styles of ongoing workgroup team members who participated in a paired team competition. The exercise was designed to require teamwork skills. Results showed that teams with balanced learning styles performed better. In 17 of the 18 team pairs, the winning team average score was higher than that of the losing team. Jackson concluded, 'Designing teams that reflect the dynamic nature of team activities has great appeal in that it gives all team members a more equal opportunity to contribute and a more equal opportunity to be valued. ... The process model advocates that different team members lead in different team activities or learning situations (2002: 11).

A study by Jules (2007) examined the influence of both learning style diversity and experiential learning team norms on team performance in a survey of 33 work teams from six different industries. Overall, both team member learning style diversity and experiential learning work norms were positively related to a team's ability to make decisions, to achieve its goals and to overall team performance. However, learning style diversity was not related to team experiential learning norms, suggesting that other factors than member composition such as team leadership, team task or organization culture influence team norms. This was supported by the fact that learning style diversity was positively related to performance in teams with routine tasks, and unrelated to performance in teams with non-routine tasks and experiential team norms were more strongly related to performance in teams with non-routine tasks.

*Team roles.* A number of studies have examined the theory of functional role leadership using the ELT framework (Fernandez, 1986, 1988; McMurray, 1998; Gardner and Korth, 1999). Park and Bang (2002) studied the performance of 52 Korean industrial work teams using the Belbin team role model, which is conceptually linked to ELT (Jackson, 2002). They found that the best-performing teams were those whose members adopted at a high level all nine of Belbin's roles covering all stages of the learning cycle. They also found that teams with roles that matched the particular stage of a team's work/learning process performed best. Lingham (2004) in a study of the conversational space norms of 49 educational and work teams found that teams performed more poorly with members who were less satisfied and who felt more psychologically unsafe when the team had a single leader as opposed to sharing leadership.

*Team norms.* Carlsson, Keane, and Martin used the ELT learning cycle framework to analyze the bi-weekly reports of research and development project teams in a large consumer products corporation. Successful project teams had work process norms that supported a recursive cycling through the experiential learning cycle. Projects that deviated from this work process by skipping stages or being stuck in a stage 'indicated problems deserving of management attention' (1976: 38).

Two studies have explicitly examined team conversational learning spaces with norms that support the experiential learning cycle. Wyss-Flamm (2002) selected from a management assessment and development course three multicultural student teams who rated themselves as high in psychological safety, defined as the ability of the team to bring up and talk about difficult or potentially psychologically uncomfortable issues. Three of the teams rated themselves as low in psychological safety. Through intensive individual and team interviews, Wyss-Flamm analyzed the teams' semester-long experience. In teams with high psychological safety, the conversations followed a recursive experiential learning cycle: differences were experienced among team members, examined through reflective juxtaposition that articulated learning and culminated in either an integration of the differences or an affirmation of the contrast. Teams with low psychological safety tended to have early disturbing incidents that limited conversation and made the conversational flow more turbulent and conflict filled. Lingham (2004) found that the more the teams supported the experiential learning cycle through norms that focused their conversation on interpersonal diverging (concrete experience and reflective observation) and task-oriented converging (abstract conceptualization and active experimentation), the better they performed, the more satisfied they were with their membership on the team, and the more they felt psychologically safe to take risks on the team.

Other studies of educational teams (Gardner and Korth, 1997; Pauleen et al.,

2004) have found that interventions aimed at the introduction of experiential learning norms facilitated learning and transfer of learning.

*Education for team learning.* Kayes et al. (2005a) have integrated the above research and other group theories into a theory of experiential learning in teams that focus on six aspects of team functioning – purpose, membership, roles, context, process and action. Based on this theory, the Kolb Team Learning Experience (KTLE – Kayes et al., 2004) was created as a structured written simulation through which team members learn about team functions while engaging in the processes of knowledge creation, reflection, critical thinking, and action taking. Thus, team members learn how to learn as the team progresses through activities and problems in the team-learning workbook. The team is encouraged to experience all stages of the learning cycle multiple times and reflect on its ability to continually experience these stages. As the team learns, it increases its ability to operate at higher developmental stages within its functional aspects of purpose, membership, roles, context, process, and action taking (Kayes et al., 2005b).

## ORGANIZATIONAL LEARNING

Since its first formulation (Kolb, 1976) the ELT approach to organizational learning has been elaborated by a number of scholars (Dixon, 1999; Hayes and Allinson, 1998; Huczynski and Boddy, 1979); Kay and Bawden, 1996; Kim, 1993; Ramnarayan and Reddy, 1989; Lahteenmaki, Toivonen and Mattila, 2001; Leroy and Ramanantsoa, 1997; Mumford, 1991; Popper and Lipshitz, 2000; Simonin, 1997; Thomas, 2002; Zhang et al., 2006). Easterby-Smith (1997) in his typology of contemporary organizational learning theories classifies the ELT approach as a human development, psychological and organization development approach along with the theories of Nonaka (1994); Argyris (1992); Dixon (1999); Kim (1993); Mumford (1991) and Revans (1971, 1980).

True to its Lewinian social psychology origins, organization learning in ELT is seen as a transactional process between individuals and their environment and between the organization and its environment.

A central issue for most organizational learning scholars is the relationship between individual learning and organizational learning. In *The Organizational Learning Cycle* Nancy Dixon translates the individual learning cycle of experiential learning to the organizational level by introducing the concept of dialogue (Dixon, 1999) or conversational learning (Baker et al., 2002) in the reflection and conceptualization phases of the individual learning cycle describing organizational learning as a cycle where employee direct experiences and mental maps (CE, Nonaka's tacit knowledge) are shared in dialogue (RO), interpreted collectively to create collectively shared meaning (AC, explicit knowledge) as the basis for responsible action (AE). Thus the team learning from experience process described in the previous section becomes a pivotal linking pin between individual and organizational learning.

At the individual level, learning from experience leads to a 'match' between the individual and their immediate organizational environment, i.e. their work and functional work setting. Through learning from previous experiences that lead to choice of and/or placement into jobs and on-the-job learning to meet job demands, managers achieve a fit between their skills and their job demands that produces effective performance (Sims, 1981, 1983). The Learning Skills Profile (Boyatzis and Kolb, 1991, 1995, 1997) was developed as a holistic typology of learning skills associated with the phases of the experiential learning cycle to assess skills and job demands in commensurate terms. These job demand/learning skill profiles have been used to assess skill development needs for management training and development programs (Kolb et al., 1986; Smith, 1990; Rainey et al., 1993).

At the organizational level, learning is a process of differentiation and integration focused on mastery of the organizational environment. The organization differentiates itself into specialized units charged with dealing with one aspect of the organizational environment; marketing deals with the market and customers, R&D with the academic and technological community, etc. This creates a corresponding internal need to integrate and coordinate the specialized units.

Because specialized units need to relate to different aspects of the environment they develop characteristic ways of working together, different styles of learning, problem solving and decision making. In fact, Lawrence and Lorsch (1967: 11) define organizational differentiation as 'the difference in cognitive and emotional orientation among managers in different functional departments. From a learning perspective these represent differences in learning style. Previous research has shown that educational specialization is a primary determinant of learning style (Kolb, 1984; Kolb and Kolb, 2005b; Joy and Kolb, 2007). Interestingly, in these studies business majors tend on average to end up in the middle of the learning style grid with no particular specialized style. However, research on the relationship between learning style and business functional specialty has shown consistent patterns of differentiation (Loo, 2002a,b; Biberman and Buchanan, 1986; Jervis, 1983; Novin et al., 2003; Rowe and Waters, 1992). Results from these and other studies suggest that the accommodating learning style is characteristic of people in sales and of general managers while the assimilating style is characteristic of those in the planning, research and development and finance specialties. Accountants, production managers and engineers tend to be converging in their learning style while people in marketing, human resources and organization development tend to have diverging styles. These associations are of course not perfect; every function tends to have managers with different styles in it. This is important both for learning within the functional team and for integration and communication with other functions. For example, Kolb (1976) found that those managers in marketing who deviated from the dominant accommodating style by having an assimilating style communicated better with the assimilative R&D department. The reverse was also true of accommodating managers in R&D.

Organizations have numerous ways of achieving integration, such as strategic management, vision, leadership, organization culture and cross-functional teams. All of these mechanisms are designed to resolve conflicts between specialized units and achieve a coherent direction for the organization. Too often this integration is achieved through domination of one functional mentality in the organization culture. An example is the case of an electronics firm started by a group of entrepreneurial engineers who invented a unique product (Osland et al., 2007). For a number of years they had no competition and when some competition appeared in the market they continued to dominate because of their superior engineering quality. It became a different story when stiff competition appeared and their very success created new problems when the management approaches of a small intimate company didn't work in a large organization with operations all over the world. The engineering mentality of the organization made specialists in marketing, finance and human resources, who were brought in to help the organization, feel like second-class citizens. The organization's strength, its engineering expertise, had become its greatest weakness. Jervis (1983) provides other similar case examples from his studies of U.K. management teams. For example, in a senior manufacturing management team with managers who had accommodating learning styles, the group was seen as pursuing a 'butterfly' strategy' which concentrated on idea generation and action and lacked systematic convergent evaluation of projects.

From the ELT perspective organizational learning requires that the opposing perspectives of action/reflection and concrete involvement/analytical detachment are valued and integrated into a process that follows the whole learning cycle and is adaptive to changing environmental challenges (Ramnarayan and Reddy, 1989).

## EXPERIENTIAL LEARNING IN MANAGEMENT EDUCATION

There is a long history of experiential learning methods in management training and education dating back to the popularity of Lewin's laboratory training methods for teaching group dynamics in the 1960s. Although the traditional 'T-Group' is now seldom used, training programs and courses based on the experiential learning cycle are widespread and commonplace. The first management textbook based on experiential learning was published in 1971 (Kolb, Rubin and McIntyre, 1971b) and is now in its 8th edition (Osland et al., 2007). The workbook resulted from testing the feasibility of Lewin's experiential learning methods for teaching organizational behavior. This workbook provides simulations, role plays, and exercises (concrete experiences) that focus on central concepts in organizational behavior, providing a common experiential starting point for participants and faculty to explore the relevance of behavioral concepts for their work. Each chapter is organized around the learning cycle providing the experience, structured reflection and conversation exercises, conceptual material and personal application assignments.

Research on learning styles has shown that managers on the whole are distinguished by strong active experimentation skills and weaker reflective observation skills. Business faculty members (and professors in general) usually have the reverse profile. In traditional management education methods, the conflict between scholar and practitioner learning styles is exaggerated because the material to be taught is filtered through the learning style of faculty in their lectures or presentation and analysis of cases. Students are 'one down' in their own analysis because the data are secondhand and already biased. In the experiential learning approach, this filtering process is reduced because teacher and students alike are observers of immediate experiences that they both interpret according to their own learning style. In this approach to learning, the teachers' role is that of facilitators of a learning process that is basically self-directed. They help students to experience in a personal and immediate way the phenomena in their field of specialization. They stand ready with alternative theories and concepts as students attempt to assimilate their observations into their own conception of reality. They assist in deducing the implications of the students' concepts and in designing new 'experiments' to test these implications through practical, real-world experience.

To bridge the gap in learning styles, the management educator must respond to pragmatic demands for relevance and the application of knowledge, while encouraging the reflective examination of experience that is necessary to refine old theories and to build new ones. In encouraging reflective observation, the teacher is often seen as an interrupter of action – as a passive 'ivory tower' thinker. This is, however, a critical role in the learning process. If the reflective observer role is not internalized by the learners themselves, the learning process can degenerate into a value conflict between teacher and the student, each maintaining that theirs is the right perspective for learning. The diverse learning style composition of students in any given learning environment suggests a need for an equally diverse learning processes and strategies. Understanding individual learning style can be considered as the entry point through which learners enter a particular learning space and continue to actively move around the space to acquire complex knowledge and skills.

There are two goals in the experiential learning process. One is to learn the specifics of a particular subject, and the other is to learn about one's own learning process. These goals present challenges associated with adoption and implementation of experiential methods in classrooms. Most frequently encountered challenges are associated with the integration of experiential learning methods into the instructors' current teaching preferences and practices (Hickcox, 2002). Experiential learning methods place equal emphasis on content and process involved in the acquisition of knowledge and skills. As a consequence,

in comparison to a more traditional course format, experiential learning methods require a considerable amount of time and commitment in preparation of courses. They may also require smaller class sizes in order to accommodate various experiential activities, and they call for holistic assessment methods that adequately evaluate all facets of student learning (Mellor, 1991; Sprau and Keig, 2001).

In 1987, Svinick and Dixon published an influential paper describing a comprehensive instructional model to deal with the constraints and challenges instructors and students encounter in the face of adopting experiential learning as the instructional design framework. The model offers an instructional design approach that incorporates a broad range of classroom activities that lead students through the full cycle of learning, thus giving instructors a rich array of instructional choices as well as the benefit of offering students a more complete learning experience gained from multiple perspectives. Additionally, it offers a useful model that responds to one of the key challenges of the experiential methods – adapting teaching strategies to student readiness to engage in experiential learning. As the model in Figure 3.4 suggests, instructors are able to design their classroom activities based upon how much student involvement would be appropriate. Activities at the outer rim of the learning cycle allow for greater student involvement, while those close to the center involve limited student participation.

The following studies conducted in the fields of accounting, business and management, and marketing describe examples of the current state of the art in the use of ELT in course design.

Siegel et al. (1997) conducted a controlled field experiment to test the effectiveness of video simulation as a way to integrate experiential learning theory in the teaching of auditing in their accounting course. The videotape used in the experiment followed the principles of experiential learning in teaching the fundamental steps in auditing. The results of the experiment indicated

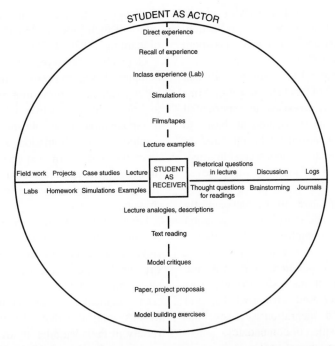

**Figure 3.4   Degree of direct student involvement in various teaching methods**
*Source*: Adapted from: Svinick, M.D. and Dixon, N.M. (1987). The Kolb model modified for classroom activities. *College Teaching*, 35 (4): 141–6. Reprinted with permission of the Helen Dwight Reid Educational Foundation. Published by Heldref Publications, 1319 Eighteenth St., NW, Washington, Dc 20036-1802. Copyright © (1987).

significantly higher examination scores for the experimental groups supporting the value of experiential learning for improving effectiveness in teaching auditing.

Specht (1991) examined the effect of an experiential learning method in student learning in an undergraduate accounting course compared to another class conducted using a traditional lecture method. The results revealed no significant differences in short-term learning between the two course formats; however, the experiential class demonstrated retention of knowledge over a six-week period whereas a significant decrease in the scores of the lecture class was observed. The authors concluded that students in the experiential learning classroom may have formed a better understanding of the concepts, thus successfully retaining knowledge better than students in the lecture class.

In applying experiential learning in his accounting course Umapathy (1985) underscores the importance of the role of

the experiential instructor for a successful adoption and implementation of experiential learning curricula. Experiential exercises have proven to be effective in generating considerable student involvement and participation in the learning process, with increased student capacity to retain knowledge for a longer period of time.

Certo designed a series of experiential training activities for an undergraduate management course based on the four dimensions of the learning cycle. In conducting those activities, the instructor assumed the role of an experiential facilitator by 'encouraging high levels of student participation; creating a learning environment conducive to learn new behaviors; providing theoretical clarification; and emphasizing both content and process' (1976: 22). In a later study he further articulates the value of experiential learning as a methodology of education that focuses on the whole person and emphasizes the critical role of the facilitator as an active experiential instructor who blends with a proper balance experience, reflection, conceptualization, and action in the classroom activities (Certo, 1977).

In order to respond to mounting criticism of the inadequacy of business education Sims and Sauser (1985) proposed an experiential learning model as a theoretical basis to design management curricula intended to develop managerial competencies in business students. The authors offer seven core principles that need to be in place if such curricula are to be successfully implemented: (1) ability to face new situation and problems; (2) emphasis on both theory and practice; (3) opportunity to have a direct managerial experience; (4) relevant and reliable assessment methods; (5) effective feedback; (6) increased self-knowledge; and (7) reflection and integration as a key final step in the acquisition of competency.

In his organizational behavior course McMullan and Cahoon (1979) applied Kolb's experience-based learning evaluation instrument. The Personal Application Memo (PAM) was designed to raise student awareness of the distinct learning process involved at each step of the learning cycle. For example, students often have difficulty in differentiating objective experiences from personal reactions to those experiences. Similarly, an individual's tendency to focus only on personally useful concepts make it difficult for them to discriminate between abstract conceptualization and active experimentation in a given situation. By discriminating between the abstract conceptualizing and the active experimentation students will be forced to clarify the implicit assumptions and values that guide their actions. The PAM requires students to rigorously evaluate their own learning process and encourage behavioral patterns that lead to meaningful and purposeful actions. Such rigorous examination of one's learning process was foreign to most of the students and consequently frustrating to many. PAM activities made the familiar and obvious way of learning uncertain and problematic for most of them. As the authors suggest, 'such a situation is ripe for learning,

challenging students to move beyond the safety of their predictable and familiar ways of learning' (1979: 457).

Gopinah and Sawyer (1999) developed a computer-based enterprise simulation based on experiential learning in a business course to bridge the gap between knowledge and its application in the business world. The results of the simulation show that the recursive nature of experiential learning promotes strategic decision making and group behavior consistent with long-term strategy.

Lengnick-Hall and Sanders (1997) designed a learning system in the graduate and undergraduate level management courses structured around the learning cycle to give students a variety of ways to master each segment of the course material. Results indicate that despite the wide variety in their learning styles, experiences, academic levels, and interests, students demonstrated consistently high levels of personal effectiveness, organizational effectiveness, ability to apply course materials, and satisfaction with both course results and learning process. The study also showed learning style differences in student ratings of various outcome measures; divergent learners rated their personal effectiveness higher than the non-divergent learners, while assimilating learners rated the lowest on the same outcome measure. Converging learners, on the other hand, rated their ability to apply course material significantly higher than did the non-converging learners, an indication of their tendency to seek out opportunities to apply what they have learned. Looking at the positive learning outcomes generated by the courses, the authors contend that high-quality learning systems are the ones in which extensive individual differences are matched with a variety of options in learning methods, thus creating opportunities for student behavioral, emotional, and intellectual transformation of lasting impact.

Dissatisfied with the application of experiential methods in the business classrooms, Dyer and Schumann developed an experiential learning laboratory classroom applied to their marketing course:

> We believe that, to date, the application of experiential methods in the business classroom has frequently been incomplete and has therefore diluted the promise of experiential process. Educators have spent their time 'parroting' the instructional approaches of other teachers rather than 'partnering' experience and knowledge as intended by experiential learning models and the traditional laboratory method. (1993: 32)

In order to create a true laboratory experience in marketing classrooms, the authors developed the Knowledge/Experience Integration Learning Model in the senior-level marketing advertising/promotion class. In this class, the text assignments and lectures were integrated with experiences generated from two types of learning tasks, multiple group projects and multiple individual case studies. The traditional performance evaluations (multiple choice and essay exams) were eliminated altogether to give central focus on the recursive cycle of lecture, discussion, feedback, and hands-on experiences. At the completion of the course students reported increased level of critical thinking abilities and capacity to apply and connect theoretical knowledge with real-life business application.

From the above research and the ELT concept of learning space we have created the following principles for the promotion of experiential learning in education (Kolb and Kolb, 2005, 2006):

*Respect for Learners and their Experience* – We refer to this as the Cheers/Jeers continuum. At one end learners feel that they are members of a learning community who are known and respected by faculty and colleagues and whose experience is taken seriously, a space 'where everybody knows your name'. At the other extreme are learning environments where learners feel alienated, alone, unrecognized and devalued.

*Begin Learning with the Learner's Experience of the Subject Matter* – The cognitive constructivist theories of Piaget and Vygotsky emphasize that people construct new knowledge and understanding from what they already know and believe based on their previous experience.

*Creating and Holding a Hospitable Space for Learning* – To learn requires facing and embracing differences; be they differences between skilled expert performance and one's novice status, differences between deeply held ideas and beliefs and new ideas or differences in the life experience and values of others. These differences can be challenging and threatening, requiring a learning space that encourages the expression of differences and the psychological safety to support the learner in facing them.

*Making Space for Conversational Learning* – Human beings naturally make meaning from their experiences through conversation. Yet genuine conversation in the traditional lecture classroom can be extremely restricted or non-existent. Making space for good conversation as part of the educational process provides the opportunity for reflection on and meaning making about experiences that improves the effectiveness of experiential learning.

*Making Spaces for Acting and Reflecting* – Learning is like breathing; it involves a taking in and processing of experience and a putting out or expression of what is learned. Yet many programs in higher education are much more focused on impressing information on the mind of the learner than on opportunities for the learners to express and test in action what they have learned.

*Making Spaces for Feeling and Thinking* – Current brain research offers convincing research evidence that reason and emotion are inextricably related in their influence on learning and memory. Indeed it appears that feelings and emotions have primacy in determining whether and what we learn. Negative emotions such as fear and anxiety can block learning, while positive feelings of attraction and interest may be essential for learning. To learn something that one is not interested in is extremely difficult.

*Making Space for Inside-out Learning* – Linking educational experiences to the learner's interests kindles intrinsic motivation and increases learning effectiveness. Learning spaces that emphasize extrinsic reward can drive out intrinsically motivated learning.

*Making Space for Development of Expertise* – Research on expert learners shows that effective learning requires not only factual knowledge, but the organization of these facts and ideas in a conceptual framework and the ability to retrieve knowledge for application and transfer to different contexts. Such deep learning is facilitated by deliberate, recursive practice on areas that are related to the learner's goals.

*Making Space for Learners to Take Charge of their own Learning* – Many students enter higher education conditioned by their previous educational experiences to be passive recipients of what they are taught. Making space for students to take control of and responsibility for their learning can greatly enhance their ability to learn from experience.

## EVALUATION OF ELT RESEARCH

ELT was developed following Lewin's plan for the creation of scientific knowledge by conceptualizing phenomena through formal, explicit, testable theory. In his approach 'before a system can be fully useful the concepts in it have to be defined in a way that (1) permits the treatment of both the qualitative and quantitative aspects of phenomena in a single system, (2) adequately represents the conditional-genetic (or causal) attributes of phenomena, (3) facilitates the measurement (or operational definition) of these attributes, and (4) allows both generalization to universal laws and concrete treatment of the individual case' (Cartwright, 1951: ix). A theory developed by this process can be a powerful instrument for stimulating and focusing scholarly research conversation.

Since its first statement in 1971 (Kolb, 1971; Kolb et al., 1971), there have been many studies using ELT to advance the theory and practice of experiential learning. Since ELT is a holistic theory of learning that identifies learning style differences among different academic specialties, it is not surprising to see that ELT research is highly interdisciplinary, addressing learning and educational issues in

many fields. An analysis of the 1,004 entries in the 1999 bibliography (Kolb et al., 2001) shows 207 studies in management, 430 in education, 104 in information science, 101 in psychology, 72 in medicine, 63 in nursing, 22 in accounting and 5 in law. About 55 percent of this research has appeared in refereed journal articles, 20 percent in doctoral dissertations, 10 percent in books and book chapters, and 15 percent in conference proceedings, research reports, and others. Since 2000 ELT research in these fields around the world has more than doubled. The current experiential learning theory bibliographies (Kolb and Kolb, 2007a,b) include over 2,500 entries.

Included are research studies from every region of the world with many contributions coming from the U.S., Canada, Brazil, the U.K., China, India, Australia, Japan, Norway, Finland, Sweden, the Netherlands, and Thailand. These studies support the cross-cultural validity of ELT and the KLSI and also support practical applicability across cultures. The KLSI has been translated into many languages, including English, Spanish, French, Portuguese, Arabic, Russian, Dutch, German, Swedish, Chinese, Romanian, Persian, Thai, and Japanese. The value of the holistic ELT framework for understanding cultural differences has been shown in a number of studies on cross-cultural management (Kayes et al., 2005; Kayes et al., 2006; Yamazaki and Kayes, 2004; Yamazaki and Kayes, 2007).

There have been two comprehensive reviews of the ELT literature, one qualitative and one quantitative. In 1991 Hickox extensively reviewed the theoretical origins of ELT and qualitatively analyzed 81 studies that focused on the application of the ELT model as well as on the application of the concept of learning style in accounting and business education, helping professions, medical professions, post-secondary education and teacher education. She concluded that overall 61.7 percent of the studies supported ELT, 16.1 percent showed mixed support, and 22.2 percent did not support ELT. In 1994 Iliff conducted a meta-analysis of 101 quantitative LSI studies culled from 275 dissertations and 624 articles that were qualitative, theoretical, and quantitative studies of ELT and the

Kolb Learning Style Inventory (LSI, Kolb 1971, 1985, 1999a, 2005). Using Hickox's evaluation format he found that 49 studies showed strong support for the LSI, 40 showed mixed support and 12 studies showed no support. About half of the 101 studies reported sufficient data on the LSI scales to compute effect sizes via meta-analysis. Most studies reported correlations that fell in the .2 to .5 range for the LSI scales. In conclusion Iliff suggested that the magnitude of these statistics is not sufficient to meet standards of predictive validity, while noting that the LSI was not intended to be a predictive psychological test like IQ, GRE or GMAT. The LSI was originally developed as a self-assessment exercise and a means for constructing validation of ELT. Judged by the standards of construct validity ELT has been widely accepted as a useful framework for learning centered educational innovation, including instructional design, curriculum development, and life-long learning. Academic field and job classification studies viewed as a whole also show a pattern of results consistent with the ELT structure of knowledge theory.

Most of the debate and critique in the ELT/LSI literature has centered on the psychometric properties of the LSI. Results from this research have been of great value in revising the LSI in 1985, in 1999 and again in 2005 (Kolb and Kolb 2005b). Recent critique has been more focused on the theory than the instrument examining the intellectual origins and underlying assumptions of ELT from what might be called a critical theory perspective where the theory is seen as individualistic, cognitivist, and technological (e.g. Vince, 1998; Holman et al., 1997; Hopkins, 1993). Kayes (2002) has reviewed these and other critics of ELT and offered his own critique of the critics. He suggests that critics have overlooked the role of Vygotsky's social constructivist learning theory in the ELT theory of development and the role of personal knowledge and social knowledge in experiential learning. He proposes an extension of ELT based on Lacan's post-structuralist analysis that elaborates the fracture between personal and social knowledge and the role that language plays in shaping experience.

## SUMMARY

The key concepts from ELT – the learning cycle, learning style, learning space, deep learning and development – can be used to examine management as a learning process at the level of the individual, the team and the organization. They can also serve as useful tools to design and implement management education programs in higher education and management training and development. Research on ELT has today reached a level of maturity around the world such that the key challenges ahead lie in the application and institutionalization of these practices in order to improve management education, learning and development.

## ACKNOWLEDGEMENT

Figure 3.4 from *College Teaching* 35 (4): 141–6, 1987. Reprinted with permission of the Helen Dwight Reid Educational Foundation. Published by Heldref Publications, 1319 Eighteenth St., NW, Washington, DC 20036–1802. Copyright © 1987.

## REFERENCES

Abbey, D.S., Hunt, D.E. and Weiser, J.C. (1985) 'Variations on a theme by Kolb: A new perspective for understanding counseling and supervision', *The Counseling Psychologist*, 13 (3): 477–501.

Argyris, C. (1992) *On Organizational Learning.* Oxford: Blackwell.

Armstrong, P. and McDaniel, E. (1986) 'Relationships between learning styles and performance on problem-solving tasks', *Psychological Reports*, 59: 1135–8.

Baker, A., Jensen, P. and Kolb, D.A. (2002) *Conversational Learning: An Experiential Approach to knowledge Creation.* Westport, CT: Quorum Books.

Benne, K.D. and Sheats, P. (1948) 'Functional roles of group members', *Journal of Social Issues*, 4 (2): 41–9.

Biberman, N.J. and Buchanan, J. (1986) 'Learning style and study skills differences across business and other academic majors', *Journal of Education Business*, 61 (7): 303–7.

Border, L.L.B. (2007) 'Understanding learning styles: The key to unlocking deep learning and in-depth teaching', *NEA Higher Education Advocate*, 24 (5): 5–8.

Boyatzis, R.E. and Kolb, D.A. (1991) *Learning Skills Profile*. TRG Hay/McBer, Training Resources Group. 116 Huntington Avenue, Boston, MA 02116, trg_mcber@haygroup.com.

Boyatzis, R.E. and Kolb, D.A. (1997) 'Assessing individuality in learning: The Learning skills profile', *Educational Psychology*, 11 (3–4): 279–95.

Boyatzis, R.E., Cowen, S.S. and Kolb, D.A. (eds) (1995) *Innovation in Professional Education: Steps in a Journey From Teaching to Learning*. San Francisco: Jossey-Bass.

Boyatzis, R.E. and Mainemelis, C. (2000) 'An empirical study of pluralism of learning and adaptive styles in a MBA Program', (Working paper). Department of Organizational Behavior, Case Western Reserve University, Cleveland, OH.

Boyle, E.J., Geiger, M.A. and Pinto, J.K. (1991) 'Empirical note on creativity as a covariate of learning style preference', *Perceptual and Motor Skills*, 73: 265–6.

Brennan, A. and Dooley, L. (2005) 'Networked creativity: A structured management framework for stimulating management innovation', *Technovation*, 25: 1388–99.

Bronfrenbrenner, U. (1977) 'Toward an experimental ecology of human development', *American Psychologist*, July: 513–30.

Bronfrenbrenner, U. (1979) *The Ecology of Human Development*. Cambridge, MA: Harvard University Press.

Carlsson, B., Keane, P. and Martin, J.B. (1976) 'R & D organizations as learing systems', *Sloan Management Review*, 17: 1–15.

Cartwright, D. (ed.) (1951) *Field Theory in Social Science: Selected Theoretical Papers by Kurt Lewin*. New York: Harper Torchbooks.

Certo, S.C. (1976) 'The experiential exercise situation: A comment on instructional role and pedagogy evaluation', *The Academy of Management Review*, 1 (3): 113–16.

Certo, S.C. (1977) 'Stages of the Kolb-Rubin-McIntire experiential learning model and perceived trainee learning: A preliminary investigation'. Paper presented at the Academy of Management Proceedings.

Clarke, D. (1977) *A Study of the Adequacy of the Learning Environment for Business Students in Hawaii in the Fields of Accounting and Marketing*. (Unpublished manuscript). University of Hawaii-Manoa.

Corbett, A.C. (2005) 'Experiential learning within the process of opportunity identification and exploitation', *Entrepreneurship Theory and Practice*, 29 (4): 473–91.

Corbett, A.C. (2007) 'Learning asymmetries and the discovery of entrepreneurial opportunities', *Journal of Business Venturing*, 22: 97–118.

Dewey, J. (1897) 'My pedagogic creed', *The School Journal*, LIV(3): 77–80.

Dixon, N.M. (1996) *Perspectives on Dialogue: Making Talk Developmental for Individuals and Organizations*. Center for Creative Leadership.

Dixon, N.M. (1999) *The Organizational Learning Cycle. How We Can Learn Collectively*. (3rd edn). London: McGraw-Hill.

Donoghue, M.L. (1994) 'Problem solving effectiveness: The relationship of divergent and convergent thinking', Unpublished doctoral dissertation, University of Massachusetts.

Dyer, B. and Schumann, D.W. (1993) 'Partnering knowledge and exercise: The business classroom a laboratory', *Marketing Education Review*, 3 (Summer): 32–3.

Easterby-Smith, M. (1997) 'Disciplines of organizational learning: Contributions and critiques', *Human Relations*, 50 (9): 1085–113.

Eickmann, P., Kolb, A. and Kolb, D.A. (2004) 'Designing learning', in R. Boland and F. Calopy (eds), *Managing as Designing: Creating a New Vocabulary for Management Education and Research*. Stanford CA: Stanford University Press.

Fernandez, C.L. (1986) *Role elaboration: The influence of personal and situational factors*. [unpuplished qualifying paper]. Cleveland, OH: Department of Organizational Behavior, Case Western Reserve University.

Fernandez, C.L. (1988) *Role Shaping in a High-Tech Organization Using Experiential Learning Theory*. Unpublished Doctoral Dissertation, Department of Organizational Behavior, Case Western Reserve University, Cleveland, OH.

Freire, P. (1992) *Pedagogy of the Oppressed*. New York: Continuum.

Gardner, B.S. and Korth, S.J. (1997) 'Classroom strategies that facilitate transfer of learing to the workplace', *Innovative Higher Education*, 22 (1): 45–60.

Gardner, B.S. and Korth, S.J. (1999) 'A framework for learning to work in teams', *Journal of Education for Business*, 74 (1): 28–33.

Gopinah, C. and Sawyer, J.E. (1999) 'Exploring the learning from an enterprise simulation', *Journal of Management Development*, 18 (5): 477–89.

Grochow, J. (1974) 'Cognitive style as a factor in the use of interactive computer systems for decision support'. Unpublished doctoral dissertation, Massachusetts Institute of Technology, Cambridge, MA.

Gypen, J.L.M. (1981) 'Learning style adaptation in professional careers: The case of engineers and social workers'. Unpublished doctoral dissertation, Case Western Reserve University, Cleveland, OH.

Hall, J. (1996) 'Training in teamwork for students of library and information studies', *Education for Information*, 14 (1): 19–30.

Halstead, A. and Martin, L. (2002) 'Learning styles: A tool for selecting students for group work', *International Journal of Electrical Engineering Education*, 39 (3): 245–52.

Hayes, J. and Allinson, C.W. (1998) 'Cognitive style and the theory and practice of individual and collective learning in organizations', *Human Relations*, 51 (7): 847–71.

Hendrick, H.W. (1979) 'Differences in group problem solving behavior and effectiveness as a function of abstractness', *Journal of Applied Psychology*, 65: 518–25.

Hickcox, L.K. (2002) 'Personalizing teaching through experiential learning', *College Teaching*, 50 (4): 123–8.

Holman, D., Pavlica, K. and Thorpe, R. (1997) 'Rethinking Kolb's theory of experiential learning in management education: The contribution of social constructionism and activity theory', *Management Learning*, 28 (2): 135–48.

Hopkins, R. (1993) 'David Kolb's experiential learning-machine', *Journal of Phenomenological Psychology*, 24 (1): 46–62.

Huczynski, A. and Boddy, D. (1979) 'The learning organization: An approach to management education and development', *Studies in Higher Education*, 4 (2): 211–22.

Hunt, D.E. (1987) 'Beginning with ourselves in interpersonal relations', in D.E. Hunt (ed.), *Beginning with Ourselves*. Cambridge, MA: Brookline Press.

Jackson, C.J. (2002) 'Predicting team performance from a learning process model', *Journal of Managerial Psychology*, 17 (1): 6–13.

James, W. (1977) 'Percept and concept: The import of concepts', in J. McDermott (ed.), *The Writings of William James*. Chicago: University of Chicago Press.

Jensen, P. and Kolb, D. (1994) 'Learning and development', in M. Keeton (ed.), *Perspective in Experiential Learning*. Chicago: Council for Adult and Experiential Learning (CAEL).

Jervis, P. (1983) 'Analyzing decision behavior: Learning models and learning styles as diagnostic aids', *Personnel Review*, 12: 26–38.

Joy, S. and Kolb, D.A. (2007) 'Are there cultural differences in learning style?' (Working paper), Department of Organizational Behavior, Case Western Reserve University.

Jules, Claudy (2007) 'Diversity of member composition and team learning in organizations'. Unpublished Ph.D. dissertation, Case Western Reserve University.

Jung, C.G. (1931) 'Forward and commentary', in R. Wilhelm (Trans.), *The Secret of the Golden Flower*. New York: Harcourt Brace and World.

Katz, N. (1990) 'Problem-solving and time: Functions of learning styles and teaching methods', *Occupational Therapy Journal Research*, 10 (4): 221–36.

Kay, R. and Bawden, R. (1996) 'Learning to be systematic: Some reflections from a learning organization', *The Learning Organization*, 3 (5): 18–25.

Kayes, D.C. (2001) 'Experiential learning in teams: A study in learning style, group process and integrative complexity in ad hoc groups'. Unpublished doctoral dissertation, Case Western Reserve University, Cleveland, OH.

Kayes, D.C. (2002) 'Experiential learning and its critics: Preserving the role of experience in management education', *Academy of Management Learning and Education*, 1 (2): 137–49.

Kayes, A.B., Kayes, D.C. and Yamazaki, Y. (2006) 'Transferring knowledge across cultures: A learning competencies approach', *Performance Improvement Quarterly*, 18 (4): 87–100.

Kayes, D.C., Kayes, A.B. and Yamazaki, Y. (2005) 'Essential competencies for cross-cultural knowledge absorption', *Journal of Managerial Psychology*, 20 (7): 578–89.

Kayes, A.A., Kayes, D.C., Kolb, A.Y. and Kolb, D.A. (2004) *The Kolb Team Learning Experience: Improving Team Effectiveness Through Structured Learning Experiences*. Boston: Hay Resources Direct.

Kayes, A.B., Kayes D.C. and Kolb, D.A. (2005a) 'Experiential learning in teams', *Simulation and Gaming*, 36 (3): 330–54.

Kayes, A.B., Kayes D.C. and Kolb, D.A. (2005b) 'Developing teams using the Kolb team learning experience', *Simulation and Gaming*, 36 (3): 355–63.

Kilmann, R. (1979) 'Problem management: A behavioral science approach', in G. Zaltman (ed.), *Management Principles for Non-Profit Agencies and Organizations*. American Management Association

Kim, D.H. (1993) 'The link between individual and organizational learning', *Sloan Management Review*, Fall: 37–50.

Kolb, A.Y. and Kolb, D.A. (2007a) *Experiential Learning Theory Bibliography: 1971–2005*. www.learningfromexperience.com

Kolb, A.Y. and Kolb, D.A. (2007b) *Experiential Learning Theory Bibliography: Recent Research 2005–2007*. www.learningfromexperience.com

Kolb, A.Y. and Kolb, D.A. (2006) 'A review of multidisciplinary application of experiential learning theory in higher education', in R. Sims and S. Sims, (eds), *Learning Styles and Learning: A Key to Meeting the Accountability Demands in Education*. Hauppauge, NY: Nova Publishers.

Kolb, A.Y. and Kolb, D.A. (2005) 'Learning styles and learning spaces: Enhancing experiential learning in higher education', *Academy of Management Learning and Education*, 4 (2): 193–212.

Kolb, D.A. (1971) 'Individual learning styles and the learning process'. Working Paper #535–71, Sloan School of Management, Massachusetts Institute of Technology.

Kolb, D.A. (1976) 'On management and the learning process', *California Management Review*, 18 (3): 21–31.

Kolb, D.A. (1983) 'Problem management: Learning from experience', in S. Srivastva (ed.), *The Executive Mind*. San Francisco: Jossey-Bass.

Kolb, D.A. (1984) *Experiential Learning: Experience as the Source of Learning and Development*. Englewood Cliffs, NJ: Prentice-Hall.

Kolb, D.A. (1985) *Learning Style Inventory, Revised Edition*. Boston, MA: McBer and Company.

Kolb, D.A. (1999) *Learning Style Inventory, Version 3*. Boston, MA: Hay Resources Direct. 116 Huntington Avenue, Boston, MA 02116, trg_mcber@haygroup.com.

Kolb, D.A. (2005) *The Kolb Learning Style Inventory – Version 3.1: Self Scoring and Interpretation Booklet*. Boston, MA: Hay Resources Direct.

Kolb, D.A., Boyatzis, R.E. and Mainemelis, C. (2001) 'Experiential learning theory: Previous research and new directions', in R. Sternberg and L. Zhang (eds), *Perspectives on Cognitive Learning, and Thinking Styles*. Mahwah, NJ: Lawrence Erlbaum Associates.

Kolb, D.A., Lublin, S., Spoth, J. and Baker, R. (1986) 'Strategic management development: Using experiential learning theory to assess and develop managerial competence', *The Journal of Management Development*, 5 (3): 13–24.

Kolb, D.A., Rubin, I.M. and McIntyre, J. (1971) *Organizational Psychology: An Experiential Approach*. Englewood Cliffs, NJ: Prentice-Hall.

Lahteenmaki, S., Toivonen, J. and Mattila, M. (2001) 'Critical aspects of organizational learning research and proposals for its measurement', *British Journal of Management*, 12 (2): 113–29.

Lave, J. and Wenger, E. (1991) *Situated Learning: Legitimate Peripheral Participation*. Cambridge, UK: Cambridge University Press.

Lawrence, P. and Lorsch, J. (1967) *Organization and Environment*. Boston, MA: Division of Research, Harvard Business School.

Lengnick-Hall, C.A. and Sanders, M.M. (1997) 'Designing effective learning systems for management education: Student roles, requisite variety, and practicing what we teach', *Academy of Management Journal*, 40 (6): 1334–68.

Leroy, F. and Ramanantsoa, B. (1997) 'The cognitive and behavioral dimensions of organizational learning in a merger: An empirical study', *Journal of Management Studies*, 34 (6): 871–94.

Lingham, T. (2004) 'Developing a measure of conversational learning spaces in teams', Unpublished doctoral dissertation, Department of Organizational Behavior, Case Western Reserve University, Cleveland, OH.

Loo, R. (2002a) 'A meta-analytic examination of Kolb's learning style preferences among business majors', *Journal of Education for Business*, 77 (5): 25–50.

Loo, R. (2002b) 'The distribution of learning styles and types for hard and soft business majors', *Educational Psychology*, 22 (3): 349–60.

Mainemelis, C., Boyatzis, R. and Kolb, D.A. (2002) 'Learning styles and adaptive flexibility: Testing experiential learning theory', *Management Learning*, 33 (1): 5–33.

McCarthy, B. (1987) *The 4-Mat System: Teaching to Learning Styles with Right/Left Mode Techniques*. Barrington, IL: Excel, Inc.

McCormick, S.Y. (1987) 'Nurse education and nursing student learning style match and its effect on the problem solving ability of the nursing student'. Unpublished doctoral dissertation, North State Texas University.

McMullan, W.E. and Cahoon, A. (1979) 'Integrating abstract conceptualizing with experiential learning', *The Academy of Management Review*, 4 (3): 453–8.

McMurray, D. (1998) 'Learning styles and organizational behavior in Japanese EFL classrooms', *Journal of Fukiri Prefectural University*, 13: 29–45.

Mellor, A. (1991) 'Experiential learning through integrated project work: An example from soil science', *Geography in Higher Education*, 15 (2): 135–49.

Mills, T. (1967) *The Sociology of Small Groups*. Englewood Cliffs, NJ: Prentice-Hall.

Mumford, A. (1991) 'Individual and organizational learning: Balance in the pursuit of change', *Studies in Continuing Education*, 13 (2): 115–25.

Nonaka, I. (1994) 'A dynamic theory of organizational knowledge creation', *Organizational Science*, 5 (1): 14–37.

Nonaka, I. and Konno, N. (1998) 'The concept of "ba": Building a foundation for knowledge creation', *California Management Review*, 40 (3): 40–54.

Novin, A.M., Arjomand, L.H. and Jourdan, L. (2003) 'An investigation into the preferred learning styles of accounting, management, marketing and general business majors', *Teaching and Learning*, 18 (1): 24–31.

Ogot, M. and Okudan, G.E. (2006) 'Systematic creativity methods in engineering education: A learning styles perspective', *International Journal of Engineering Education*, 22 (3): 566–76.

Osland, J.S., Turner, M.E., Kolb, D.A. and Rubin, I.M. (2007) *Organizational Behavior: An Experiential Approach* (8th edition). Upper Saddle River, NJ: Pearson, Prentice-Hall.

Park, W. and Bang, H. (2002, March 26–7) 'Team role balance and team performance'. Paper presented at the Belbin Biennial Conference, 'Changing Role of Management in the 21st Century', Clare College, Cambridge.

Pauleen, D.J., Marshall, S. and Egort, I. (2004) 'ICT-supported team-based experiential learning: Classroom perspectives', *Education + Training*, 46 (2): 90–9.

Poltis, D. (2005) 'The process of entrepreneurial learning: A conceptual framework', *Entrepreneurship Theory and Practice*, 29 (4): 399–424.

Popper, M. and Lipshitz, R. (2000) 'Organizational learning – Mechanisms, culture, and feasibility', *Management Learning*, 31 (2): 181–96.

Potgieter, E. (1999) 'Relationship between the whole-brain creativity model and Kolb's experiential learning model', *Curationis*, 22 (4): 9–14.

Rainey, M.A., Hekelman, F., Galazka, S.F. and Kolb, D.A. (1993, February) 'Job demands and personal skills in family medicine: Implications for faculty development', *Family Medicine*, 25: 100–3.

Ramnarayan, S. and Reddy, N.M. (1989) 'Institutional learning: The essence of strategic management', *Vikalpa*, 14 (1): 21–33.

Revans, R.W. (1971) *Developing Effective Managers: A New Approach to Management Education*. London: Blond & Briggs.

Revans, R.W. (1980) *Action Learning: A New Approach for Managers*. London: Blond & Briggs.

Robinson, J. (2005) 'Individual learning styles and their relationship to leadership styles'. Unpublished Ph.D. dissertation Claremont Graduate School.

Rowe, F.A. and Waters, M.L. (1992) 'Can personality-type instruments profile majors in management programs?' *Journal of Education for Business*, 68 (1): 10–15.

Sandmire, D.A. and Boyce, P.F. (2004) 'Pairing of opposite learning styles among allied health students: Effects on collaborative performance', *Journal of Allied Health*, 33 (2): 156–63.

Sandmire, D.A., Vroman, K.G. and Sanders, R. (2000) 'The influence of learning styles on collaborative performances of allied health students in a clinical exercise', *Journal of Allied Health*, 29 (3): 143–49.

Sanley, J.D. (1987) 'An examination of student learning styles and learning modalities on problem solving success'. Paper presented at the Annual Meeting of the National Science Teachers' Association, Washington, D.C.

Selby, E.C., Treffinger, D.J. Isakson, S.G. et. al. (2004) 'Defining and assessing problem solving style: Design and development of a new tool', *Journal of Creative Behavior*, 38 (4): 221–43.

Sharp, J.E. (2001, October 10–13) 'Teaching teamwork communication with Kolb learning style theory' [session F2C1]. Presented at the 31st ASEE/IEEE Frontiers in Education Conference, Reno, NV.

Siegel, P.H., Khursheed, O. and Agraval, S.P. (1997) 'Video simulation of an audit: An experiment in experiential learning theory', *Accounting Education*, 6 (3): 217–30.

Simonin, B.L. (1997) 'The importance of collaborative know-how: An empirical test of the learning organization', *Academy of Management Journal*, 40 (5): 1150–74.

Sims, R.R. (1981) 'Assessing competencies in experiential learning: A person-job congruence model of effectiveness in professional careers'. Unpublished doctoral dissertation, Case Western Reserve University, Cleveland, OH.

Sims, R.R. (1983) 'Kolb's experiential learning theory: A framework for assessing person-job interaction', *Academy of Management Review*, 8 (2): 501–8.

Sims, R.R. and Sauser Jr., W.I. (1985) 'Guiding principles for the development of competency-based curricula', *The Journal of Management Development*, 4 (5): 51–65.

Smith, D. (1990) 'Physician managerial skills: Assessing the critical competencies of the physician executive. Unpublished doctoral dissertation, Department of Organizational Behavior, Weatherhead School of Management, Case Western Reserve University, Cleveland, OH.

Specht, L.B. (1991) 'The differential effects of experiential learning activities and traditional lecture class in accounting', *Simulation and Gaming*, 22 (2): 196–210.

Sprau, R. and Keig, L. (2001) 'I saw it in the movies: Suggestions for incorporating film and experiential learning in the college survey history course', *College Student Journal*, 35 (1): 101–12.

Stabell, C.B. (1972) 'Project on the impact of conversational computer systems. Cognitive style in portfolio management'. Unpublished paper, Sloan School of Management.

Svinick, M.D. and Dixon, N.M. (1987) 'The Kolb model modified for classroom activities'. *College Teaching*, 35 (4): 141–6.

Thomas, G.F. (2002) 'Individual and organizational learning: A developmental perspective on Gilsdorf, Rymer and ABC', *The Journal of Business Communication*, 39 (3): 379–87.

Torbert, W.R. (1972) *Learning from Experience: Toward Consciousness.* New York: Columbia University Press.

Umapathy, S. (1985) 'Teaching behavioral aspects of performance evaluation: An experiential approach', *The Accounting Review*, 60 (1): 97–108.

Van Der Heijden, K. (1996) *Scenarios. The Art of Strategic Conversation.* John Wiley and Sons.

Vince, R. (1998) 'Behind and beyond Kolb's learning cycle', *Journal of Management Education*, 22 (3): 304–19.

Vygotsky, L.S. (1978) *Mind in Society: The Development of Higher Psychological Processes*, in M. Cole, V. John-Steiner, S. Scribner and E. Souberman (eds), Cambridge, MA: Harvard University Press.

Wessel, J., Loomis, J., Pennie, S., Brook, P., Hoddinott, J. and Aherne, M. (1999) 'Learning styles and perceived problem-solving ability of students in a baccalaureate physiotherapy programme', *Physiotherapy Theory and Practice*, 15 (1): 17–23.

Wolfe, J. (1977) 'Learning styles rewarded in a complex simulation with implications for business policy and organizational behavior research'. Paper Presented at the Academy of Management, University of Illinois.

Wyss-Flamm, E.D. (2002) 'Conversational learning and psychological safety in multicultural teams'. Unpublished doctoral dissertation, Department of Organizational Behavior, Case Western Reserve University, Cleveland, OH.

Yamazaki, Y. (2005) 'Learning styles and typologies of cultural differences: A theoretical and empirical comparison', *International Journal of Intercultural Relations*, 29 (5): 521–48.

Yamazaki, Y. (2004) 'An experiential approach to cross-cultural adaptation: A study of Japanese expatriates' learning styles, learning skills, and job satisfaction in the United States'. Unpublished doctoral dissertation. Department of Organizational Behavior, Case Western Reserve University, Cleveland, OH.

Yamazaki, Y. and Kayes, D.C. (2004) 'An experiential approach to cross-cultural learning: A review and integration of success factors in expatriate adaptation', *Academy of Management Learning Education*, 3 (4): 354–79.

Yamazaki, Y. and Kayes, D.C. (2007) 'Expatriate learning: Exploring how Japanese managers adapt in the United States', *The International Journal of Human Resource Management*, 18 (8): 1373–95.

Yonutas, D.N. (2001) 'Impact of analogical versus logical representations of theoretical concepts on recall and problem-solving performances of concrete and abstract thinkers'. Doctoral dissertation, University of Florida.

Zhang, M., Macpherson, A. and Jones, O. (2006) 'Conceptualizing the learning process in SME's: Improving innovation through external orientation', *International Small Business Journal*, 24 (3): 299–323.

Zull, J.E. (2002) *The Art of Changing the Brain: Enriching Teaching by Exploring the Biology of Learning.* Sterling, VA: Stylus.

# 4

# Collective Learning and Knowledge Transfer

Gabriele Lakomski

## Abstract

In this chapter a conception of learning is proposed for both the individual and the collective that is able to answer many of the difficulties traditionally raised about this distinction in the organizational learning and knowledge management literatures. This conception derives from contemporary explanations of human information processing, developed in contemporary cognitive neuroscience. Also known as the theory of distributed cognition, this account acknowledges the social and contextual features of human cognition, and therefore presents the beginnings of a new theory of collective learning. Such a theory also allows us to recast the traditional understanding of knowledge transfer, premised on the classical view of cognition and information processing, which turns out as too narrow to explain human cognition. What has been named the 'problem of transfer' can more productively be understood as a form of situated learning, as partially recognized in von Hippel's term 'sticky' knowledge. It is argued that an explanation based on our most advanced knowledge of human learning will enable us to provide better founded advice regarding the physical as well as social conditions of the creation
of organizational knowledge. Subsequently, we will also be able to offer better advice on how to structure, and therefore manage, organizational knowledge more profitably.

## INTRODUCTION

The idea of collective learning, most commonly expressed in the concept of organizational learning, presented an important conceptual and practical advance in organizational studies in the 1970s and is traditionally associated with the work of Argyris and Schön (1996). Subsequently, much discussion about individual and organizational learning, as well as learning in communities, has taken place that sought to clarify the distinctions and relations between these various conceptions (see Dierkes et al. (2001) *Handbook of Organizational Learning and Knowledge*).

About 20 years after Argyris and Schön's (1978) classic text the concept of Knowledge Management arrived on the organizational theory scene (see Wiig, 1993, 2000; Cortada and Woods, 1999, 2000; Prusak, 1997).

A further theoretical development has now emerged in that connections have been made between organizational learning and Knowledge Management in another important *Handbook* that carries both terms in its title (Easterby-Smith and Lyles, 2003a,b; Vera and Crossan, 2003).

The belief that organizational or collective learning and knowledge provide competitive weapons to generate productivity and secure organizational survival is now widely accepted in management thinking (e.g. Nonaka and Takeuchi, 1995). In this chapter, no sharp distinction is drawn between 'collective' and 'organizational' learning. While collective learning can mean learning in networks, teams or communities in the present context it refers to *learning at the interpersonal level,* and in so far as such learning is directed towards common learning or working outcomes it shades over into organizational learning (de Laat and Simons, 2002). Knowledge generated as a result of such learning needs to be managed effectively since its 'creation and use would accelerate a company's natural rate of learning, allow it to outpace competitors and create value for both customers and shareholders' (Lucier and Torsilieri, 2001: 232). It follows that the so-called transfer of knowledge, too, needs to be managed well to contribute to the better use of knowledge created.

Despite general agreement on the importance of collective learning or knowledge in modern economies, our understanding of how collectives learn, and how knowledge transfers remain contentious issues. There is disagreement in the organizational learning literature on what it means to talk about an organization as a learning entity, aptly described in Argyris and Schön's (1996) memorable phrase: What is an organization that it may learn? For some the point is moot because organizations do not have brains and therefore are incapable of learning. Others continue to struggle with understanding how the learning of an individual can 'transmute' into that of a collectivity, as is evidenced in the writing of many organizational learning theorists. Coupled with these difficulties

is the very idea and *modus operandi* of knowledge transfer. To date the transfer of knowledge seems to be characterized by a traditional transmission model that assumes that knowledge sent from point A is received at point B and understood unambiguously, as intended.

In this chapter I argue that we can make progress on both fronts if we draw on the best interdisciplinary knowledge about learning and transfer that is available, especially in the field of cognitive neuroscience and the theory of distributed cognition. Cognitive neuroscience explains how human organisms are able to acquire information from their natural and created environments, and how it is processed (e.g. Rumelhart, 1993), while the theory of distributed cognition expands the notion of individual cognition to include features of our environments such as artefacts, objects, space, and other human beings as part of the human cognitive system (e.g. Hutchins, 1996). Cognition thus extended allows us to understand better how collectivities learn and work in context. Such understanding in turn has direct consequences for the traditional notion of transfer. Transfer can now be understood as a form of situated learning, as partially recognized by Brown and Duguid (1999, 2000).

An explanation based on our most advanced, *causal* knowledge of human individual and collective learning, it is argued, will enable us as researchers and practitioners of management and management learning to provide better founded advice regarding the physical and social conditions of the creation of individual and organizational knowledge, and how it is shared and appropriated. Subsequently, we will also be able to structure, and therefore manage, organizational knowledge more profitably. Finally, concern with 'transfer' will give way to creating better organizational environments that facilitate new learning on site.

This chapter departs from traditional accounts of (organizational) learning as represented in the cognitive perspective of organizational theorists such as March and Simon (1958), for example. The differences between the older (psychological–behavioural) tradition and the new approach to cognition are complex, but the major difference lies in contemporary neuroscience's broader understanding of what cognition consists of and how it is 'produced' by real biological brains. Such was not the concern of the older tradition that relied heavily on the symbol processing computer model of the mind/brain to explain human cognition and considered it the private property of the individual.

Concerns with the architecture and processing functions of real biological brains seem a long way away from management or social science investigations generally (but see Strauss and Quinn, 1997). What may at first sight be an unusual way to approach the issues under consideration is an initial exploration of the engine-room of the mind/brain to begin to understand the nature of the cognitive machinery that makes possible what humans routinely do: learn, create knowledge, share it, manage organizations. The primary justification for the neuroscientific approach adopted here is that it enables us to base accounts of collective, i.e. interpersonal and organizational learning and knowledge transfer on actual, real human capabilities which include the ability to process symbols such as language but are not identical with that ability. In other words, it allows us to get at the cause of learning as best as science tells us.

The central focus of this chapter is therefore on human cognition, how it is created by the individual mind/brain and how cognition is shared between human agents, whether tacitly or explicitly, to use the terminology of Knowledge Management. Importantly, cognition is also *socially distributed*. The descriptor 'distributed' here refers to the distribution of cognitive activity both within the skull in the sense in which information is processed in parallel and at several locations in the brain, as well as beyond the skull; the environments in which we find ourselves – whether human-made or natural – strongly determine what we can know, and how we can act. Powerful as brains are, they are nevertheless limited in their computational capacities. No one person can keep 'in mind' what it takes to run a modern company. As a result we 'outsource' knowledge by creating external structures, be they expert systems, or the kinds of organization that fall into the domain of the social sciences. Viewed from this perspective, 'mind' and 'world' are inextricably linked with boundaries that are rather more fluid than firm (see Clark, 2001).

The recognition of the importance of the cultural and contextual features as integral parts of cognition is not peculiar to the theory of distributed cognition. It has been acknowledged in *situated learning or action*, an umbrella description for a number of approaches that derive mainly from cultural anthropology, ethnomethodology, discourse analysis, and interpretive social science. Where this perspective differs from distributed cognition is that it remains agnostic about the fine-grained causal mechanisms of cognition that make culture possible in the first place (Lakomski, 1999; Strauss and Quinn, 1997).

The theory of distributed cognition combines both the causal account of its genesis with the external, cultural, and thus provides a more comprehensive framework for the present discussion. More detail on these issues will be raised later, but much is also left out. Many of the traditional legitimate concerns of sociologists, political scientists and organizational theorists cannot be dealt with in this context. Issues of power and organizational hierarchies and their influence on learning and knowledge transfer, for example, have to await treatment at a later stage pending further explorations of 'cognition in the wild', to borrow Hutchins's (1996) now classical term.

## ORGANIZATIONAL LEARNING REVISITED

In their introduction to the Special Issue on Organizational Learning in 1991, Cohen and Sproull (1991: i) laid out the two major issues that were confronting theorists interested in organizational learning:

First, better theories of learning will provide a positive alternative to rational choice assumptions. Much empirical work on both individual behavior and organizational processes rests on a negative theme of counterevidence to rational actor assumptions. ... This produces a peculiar intellectual schizophrenia. ... [that does not lead to] proposing a positive theoretical alternative.

Second, better theories of learning will more gracefully accommodate the effects of history and timing on organizational events and on the beliefs of organizational actors.

Despite the fact that these observations were made more than a decade ago, it would be fair to say that their salience has not diminished. In this section the central claims and arguments on behalf of organizational learning will be revisited in the positive spirit indicated above. Unlike Weick and Westley's (1997: 440) provocative argument that defines organizational learning as an oxymoron, because 'organizing and learning are essentially antithetical', the end result of the argument presented here will be that organizing and learning are different sides of the same coin: producing effective practice and ongoing organizational change.

Organizational learning, within the context of organizational theory, may well be the most ambitious attempt to explain how a complex collectivity functions. It is therefore hardly surprising that the field is so vast in scope, and that it suffers from an absence of conceptual clarity and theoretical coherence. For some, it (and the idea of a learning organization) has become 'a management Rorschach test' (Ulrich, Jick and Von Glinow, 1993), while others argue that it will only get to centre stage in organization theory when it successfully answers three questions, posed by Miner and Mezias (1996: 91–2): '(1) Who or what is doing the learning? (2) What are the key learning processes? [And] (3) When is learning valuable?' Only when these are answered satisfactorily will organizational learning be

'ugly duckling no more' (Miner and Mezias, 1996).

These questions are central for the whole enterprise, but they can only be addressed properly if one question is answered first: what is the nature of human cognition, and how do we learn? In the organizational learning literature human learning is simply presumed to happen without explanation. To be more precise, a specific version of learning is implicitly accepted, that which presumes that humans predominantly learn through the use of symbols such as language, and that learning and cognition consists in the successful processing of such symbols. This will be discussed in more detail later. Suffice it to note in the present context that even such prominent theorists as Argyris and Schön (1996: 4–6) have little to say about learning, human cognition and its origin and nature.

There are many good overviews that discuss the challenges of organizational learning,[1] and this is not the place to give chapter and verse. What is of most interest here are the main analytical difficulties in the concept of organizational learning itself. Is organizational learning *learning as new knowledge or insight* (e.g. Argyris and Schön, 1996; Hedberg, 1981); does it comprise *new structures, new systems, mere actions,* or a combination of all of the above? It is striking that such concepts as learning, adaptation, change, innovation, and unlearning are all used to account for *organizational* learning, with the end effect that nothing has been clarified in regard to the main issue.

A further important point is lack of clarity regarding the value, direction of, as well as threats to, organizational learning, and problems of implementation. A broad range of definitions of organizational learning accompanies lack of clarity regarding important analytical distinctions. Consider the following three that represent both the theoretical assumptions of their designers but also highlight shared elements.

Dodgson (1993: 377), for instance, provides a good example since his definition contains most features on which theorists tend to agree:

> Learning ... relates to firms, and encompasses both processes and outcomes. It can be described as the ways firms build, supplement and organize knowledge and routines around their activities and within their cultures, and adapt and develop organizational efficiency by improving the use of the broad skills of their workforces.

Compare this with Argyris and Schön's (1996: 180) definition which is also broad but offers pragmatist elements such as inquiry and its ongoing application to the means-ends continuum:

> [Organizational learning] includes notions of organizational adaptability, flexibility, avoidance of stability traps, propensity to experiment, readiness to rethink means and ends, inquiry-orientation, realization of human potential for learning in the service of organizational purposes, and creation of organizational settings as contexts for human development.

And speaking from within the behavioral science tradition, Levitt and March (1988: 319) note:

> Organizational learning is ... routine-based, history-dependent, and target-oriented. Organizations are seen as learning by encoding inferences from history into routines that guide behavior.

While Dodgson dodges the issue of learning and cognition altogether, assuming *organizational* learning from the start, Argyris and Schön incorporate pragmatic elements into their approach to organizational learning that are helpful in so far as pragmatist philosophy is naturalistic in its orientation; human learning is characterized by biological-evolutionary features, and is ongoing and open-ended. In Levit and March's definition, organizational learning is, simply put, learning by experience. I revisit these different approaches at a later stage.

It is generally but not unanimously agreed that (1) learning has positive consequences, and includes learning from error; (2) the organization learns as a whole while the learning of individuals is not identical with organizational learning, a distinction sometimes blurred; and (3) learning occurs throughout the organization, happens at different speeds and comprises both lower-level and higher-level learning. This kind of distinction, although shared by many writers, has become most prominent in Argyris and Schön's (1996) distinction of single-loop and double-loop learning. According to Argyris and Schön, learning starts when the organization notices a mismatch between expectation and outcome, such as the occurrence of a shortfall of production target. The organization can respond in at least two ways: either by 'instrumental learning that changes strategies of action or assumptions underlying strategies in ways that leave the values of a theory of action unchanged' (Argyris and Schön, 1996: 20); or by engaging in double-loop learning which is more far-reaching in its consequences because it requires the change of the organization's values and norms, as well as ways of doing things. Double-loop learning 'results in a change in the values of theory-in-use, as well as in its strategies and assumptions' (Argyris and Schön, 1996: 21). The third kind of learning is a variation of double-loop learning, called deutero-learning. This basically means 'learning how to learn' and allows organization members to '*discover and modify the learning system that conditions prevailing patterns of organizational inquiry*' (Argyris and Schön, 1996: 29. Italics in original), a kind of learning, the authors note, that is extremely rare, if known at all.

Implicit in the above characterizations of the different types of learning is another distinction that has become a stock-in-trade concept in organizational theory, the distinction between an organization's theory of action and its two modes of representation: espoused theory as opposed to the theory-in-use. A theory of action is the kind of organizational road map including its organizational chart, policy statements and job descriptions. It is the organization's window to the world as found on its website and also incorporates its strategies for action, the norms it accepts and its underlying assumptions. The official (re)presentation of itself is counteracted by its theory-in-use, whose main feature is that it is tacit and represents the way organization members actually go about doing their work. It is here that the organization 'lives', as opposed to what the organization explicitly states about itself. Methodologically speaking, studying organization members' theories-in-use means studying their tacit knowledge, or their practice that cannot be rendered explicit, i.e. translated into explicit description since the core feature of a theory-in-use is that it is not conscious, or consciously known. As Argyris and Schön put it,

> A theory-in-use is not a 'given' ... In the case of organizations, a theory-in-use must be constructed from observation of the patterns of interactive behavior produced by individual members of the organization, insofar as their behavior is governed by formal or informal rules for collective decision, delegation, and membership. (Argyris and Schön 1996: 14)

In addition to the numerous difficulties in terms of analytic distinctions, definitions and assumptions in organizational learning, there are also agreements regarding general problematic issues. Organizations are relatively good at single-loop learning but double-loop or deutero-learning has not been detected, at least as far as Argyris and Schön are concerned. Among the many inhibitors to learning Levitt and March's (1988) competency traps are well known, as is superstitious learning, which only appears to be an instance of successful learning, but in fact is not, because it fails to draw the correct connection between actions and outcomes.

The preceding brief outline of the main features characteristic of organizational learning showed up enough complexity to cast doubt on the validity of the whole enterprise. And yet, researchers do agree that organizations learn: there is some awareness of the complexities though. Argyris and Schön (1996: 42–3) make reference to the fact that practitioners' causal inquiry consists in 'their situation-specific inferences of design, efficient, or pattern causality', that is, in their constructing causal stories which, as prototypes, are carried over from old to new

situations (reflective transfer). They do not explain, however, how it is that organizational actors can construct such patterns at all. In the next section, I want to take a closer look at the issue of learning and cognition directly.

## LEARNING AND COGNITION AS SYMBOL PROCESSING

It is of course recognized in the OL literature that it is important to know how the individual acquires knowledge and learns, and indeed the prevailing tradition in organizational learning theory is that of the *cognitive perspective*, most prominently represented by March and Simon (1958); Argyris and Schön (1996); Simon (1991) and Newell and Simon (1972). Indeed, when Miner and Mezias (1996: 91) note that 'Much popular work on organizational learning seems to assume that learning goes on in the heads of individuals', they might have had Simon's definition of learning in mind:

> All learning takes place inside individual human heads; an organization learns in only two ways: (a) by the learning of its members, or (b) by ingesting new members who have knowledge the organization didn't previously have. (Simon, 1991: 125).

Concentrating on the core problem of learning and cognition, Simon's view is particularly important because it is so prominent in organizational and administration theory, and in classical Artificial Intelligence. Above all, it is of considerable but not often acknowledged relevance that the modern division of labour also harbours a *division of cognitive labour* (see Hutchins, 1996; Evers and Lakomski, 2000; Lakomski, 2005). One of the few researchers in the field of organizational theory who did recognize this explicitly are March and Simon (1958). Their definition of cognition as symbol processing is the view to be discussed in the following because it has been, and continues to be, highly influential in organizational (learning).

Returning to the above quote, Simon emphasizes that we must not reify the organization in terms of attributing 'knowing' or 'learning' to it, but that we treat organizational learning as an *aggregate*, made up of the learning stored either in individual heads, or in files or databases. What makes learning 'organizational' is represented by phenomena that 'go beyond anything we could infer simply by observing learning processes in isolated individuals'. The task is to understand those kinds of consequences and phenomena, under conditions of *bounded rationality*, that is, we are never in possession of all the facts and always labour under conditions of uncertainty. In Simon's view then, organizational learning is an aggregate of individual learning whose representations go beyond what could have been garnered from individual learning. Individual learning is conceived of as social in the sense that information is transferred from one organization member to another, or to a group.

Working backwards from the aggregate that is organizational learning – learning or knowledge people have in their heads, or is stored in files or databases, and is 'transmitted' between them – what facilitates individual learning in the first place, what is meant by 'transmission', and how is it accomplished? The cognitive perspective provides specific answers to these questions that are enshrined in the so-called Physical Symbol System Hypothesis (PSSH). Proposed by Anderson (1983), Newell and Simon (1972, 1976) and Simon (1979), the hypothesis is put forward to postulate that human knowledge and rationality consist in the ability to manipulate linguistic and quasi-linguistic symbols in the head. The emphasis is on the internal processing structures of the brain and the symbolic representations of mind. It is worthwhile to quote Simon (1990: 3) in full to get an appreciation of the boldness of the hypothesis:

[It] *states that a system will be capable of intelligent behavior if and only if it is a physical symbol system....* [it] is a system capable of inputting, outputting, storing, and modifying symbol structures, and of carrying out some of these actions in response to the symbols themselves. 'Symbols' are any kinds of patterns on which these operations can be performed, where some of the patterns denote actions (that is, serve as commands or instructions).... Information processing psychology claims that intelligence is achievable by physical symbol systems and only such systems. From that claim follow two empirically testable hypotheses: 1. That computers can be programmed to think, and 2. That the human brain is (at least) a physical symbol system.

Translated into less formal language, computers are appropriate models for the human mind and its operations. Indeed, and astonishingly, 'A physical symbol system has the necessary and sufficient means for general intelligent action' (Newell and Simon, 1976: 87). 'Mindware' (our mental 'stuff' such as feelings, thoughts, and intuitions) is equated with 'software' (Clark, 2001), nothing more goes on in the brain than can be modelled by a computer, and physical symbol systems are all there is to human thought and intelligence. But what do these systems amount to?

To begin with, 'symbols' are not merely verbal or linguistic in form, but may 'designate words, mental pictures, or diagrams, as well as other representations of information' (Vera and Simon, 1993, 10). Although the story is rather long and complicated, the short version suffices for our purposes (e.g. Clark, 2001, Ch. 2; for those wanting more detail, see especially Rosenbloom et al., 1992). The story can best be told via describing SOAR, possibly the most famous project that endeavours to implement such intelligent (= physical symbol) systems computationally. SOAR is an architecture designed to process symbol systems, or, put simplistically, to 'mimic' intelligent thought via a computer program.

Based on a production memory that consists of a range of 'if-then' condition-action scenarios, SOAR when confronted by a specific problem (encoded in 'scripts' of commonly occurring events, such as ordering food in a restaurant) is able to 'call up' all relevant stored knowledge/facts from its production memory, and then by applying a decision procedure, is able to arrive at a specific action to be performed. It is part of SOAR's functions to determine the problem space consisting of situations and actions that can be performed and that lead to further states, until a solution may be found. Here it is important to note that all condition-action scenarios are derived from knowledge stored in the long-term production memory. Also, and this is relevant for our purposes, 'learning' in SOAR (and like systems) is achieved by means of a 'uniform learning mechanism, known as "chunking", in which a successful sequence of subgoal generations can be stored away as a single unit' (Clark, 2001: 33). On encountering a problem later that seems similar, these chunked sequences of action can be called up as a whole without wasting time searching.

Summing up, intelligence, according to SOAR, is to be found at the level of deliberative thought, and 'consists in the retrieval of symbolically stored information and its use in processes of search. Such processes involve the generation, composition, and transformation of symbolic structures until the specified conditions for a solution are met' (Clark, 2001: 33). 'Learning', on this account consists of calling up previously encoded information for action when encountering a situation that resembles an earlier one encoded in a script. As an aside, let us note here that the symbol processing rationale has been the centre piece of first generation Knowledge Management and expert systems, and continues to be influential in terms of assuming that explicit, i.e. propositional knowledge, is easy to 'move' because it can be encoded, as discussed above, and is thus readily communicable to others.

In so far as this is one important way to represent human knowledge, there is justification in emphasizing the work that can be done by expert systems, or generally by the transmission of encoded knowledge or information in Knowledge Management systems. But this is not the whole story, and the reasons why it is not will be discussed in the following.

## THINKING BEYOND THE SKULL

The cognitive perspective as described and exemplified in the kind of information processing model represented by SOAR has worked reasonably well with regard to limited kinds of problems, such as retrieving information for crossword puzzles and playing chess, and despite its purported success and extensive testing over previous decades, its creators concede that there are some irksome problems left unresolved. The most interesting is that as Simon (1995: 5) put it, while we know a lot about the 'software of thinking', information processing says little about its 'hardware', or 'wetware'. More generally, Newell et al. (1996: 127) single out the following issues: (1) 'acquiring capabilities through development, of living autonomously in a social community, and of exhibiting self-awareness and a sense of self … '; (2) how to square the cognitive architecture they defend with biological evolution which puts a premium on perceptual and motor systems; and (3) how to integrate emotion, feeling and effect into cognitive architecture. In a nutshell, what is at issue is the demarcation between cognition and learning and the world in which humans do their thinking and acting. It is the kind of situation so vividly described by Minsky (1994: 101):

> Imagine yourself sipping a drink at a party while moving about and talking with friends. How many streams of processing are involved in shaping your hand to keep the cup level, while choosing where to place your feet? How many processes help choose the words that say what you mean while arranging those words into suitable strings … what about those other thoughts that clearly go in parallel as one part of your mind keeps humming a tune while another sub-mind plans a path that escapes from this person and approaches that one.

Mind as 'an assortment of subagencies' (Minsky), or as Clark (2001) is fond of saying, 'a bag of tricks', are references to a different way of representing, and explaining, what goes on 'under the bonnet'. What is immediately obvious in the cognitive perspective is that the mind's contents are reckoned to be symbolic and semantically transparent, with no reference to the biological brain, and secondly, that the world has a very limited role to play in cognition, if any. Put another way, the relation between the individual and the organization/world in the traditional view, is as Elkjaer (2003: 42) notes, comparable to the relation between soup and bowl, '... the soup does not shape the bowl, and the bowl does not alter the substance of the soup'. Both remain analytically separate. As we now know, however, neither assumption stands on firm ground.

First, the difficulties related by Newell et al. above show every indication of being so serious that they cannot be solved within the framework of the physical symbol system hypothesis, or, to put the matter differently, the biological brain has everything to do with how we think. In fact, following Hutchins' (1996: 363 onwards) line of argument, it is a mistake to believe that the physical symbol system architecture models individual cognition. What is modelled is the operation of a socio-cultural system, composed of formal manipulations of abstract systems, from which the human actor has been removed.

A simple example will make clear what is meant. Relating the story of Alan Turing, Hutchins points out that Turing's self-reflections on how he performed his computations and solved mathematical problems, initially meant that the model cognitive system was a real human being, Turing, engaged in manipulating symbols either manually or by using his eyes. The interaction of person, Turing, with the symbols – mathematical or logical – meant something computational has happened. Here it is important to note that 'the cognitive properties of the human are not the same as the properties of the system that is made up of the human in interaction with these symbols. It is true to say that the properties of the human in interaction with the symbols produce some kind of computation, but one should not infer from this that that computation is happening inside the person's head' (Hutchins, 1996: 361). Cognition never simply happens 'in the head'. Turing's great discovery, as it were,

was to eliminate the embodied actions of the mathematician who concretely manipulated symbols external to himself, as well as the environment in which such actions took place, and to leave behind an abstract system of symbols manipulable without reference to any biological agent. It is in this way that symbols 'got into the head', and became identified with human problem-solving and cognition generally. Just to make it quite clear what the essence of the symbol system hypothesis is: it represents a model of the operation of a socio-cultural system from which is absent a flesh-and-blood-human being who did the manipulation in the first place. What we encounter here, is, as Dreyfus (1994: x–xi) observes:

> An old rationalist dream ... GOFAI [good old fashioned artificial intelligence] is based on the Cartesian idea that all understanding consists in forming and using appropriate symbolic representations. For Descartes, these representations were complex descriptions built up of primitive ideas or elements. Kant added the important idea that all concepts are rules for relating such elements, and Frege showed that rules could be formalized so that they could be manipulated without intuition or interpretation.

A biologically realistic account of cognition that includes symbol processing but is not identical with it is proposed by contemporary cognitive science or connectionism, in particular artificial neural net research. (An excellent overview on connectionism is the entry in the open access *Stanford Encyclopaedia of Philosophy*). We now know that human brains do not think like computers.[2] In light of the extensive interconnectivity of the human brain in terms of whole systems of neural nets, we are able to process information and carry out computation tasks in parallel and at speed (parallel distributed processing, or PDP). The brain's ability to activate prototypes in response to whatever external (as well as internal) input it receives makes us good at pattern recognition and completion. It allows us to make plans, identify faces, recall and recognize relevant information, and to understand speech (Tienson, 1990: 382).

The details of neural net architecture are highly complex, but generally speaking, the pattern of activation (prototype), which, say, is Coco, the cat, would consist in the strength of the connection between neuronlike processors, or their weight. Coco the cat is thus internally (i.e. in my brain) represented in the connection strengths obtaining in a particular neuronal configuration. In neural nets many units or processors are involved in enacting representation, hence representations are *distributed*. Information in connectionist systems is actively represented as a pattern of activation and is not stored as data structures. It is 'stored' in its weights, and this means that it is created and re-created as the situation requires. Repeated appearances of Coco would mean that my brain re-creates the relevant pattern of activation that allows me to 'recognize' my cat.

Learning on the connectionist account, then, consists in the changing of the weights, a very different account from that offered by the symbol system perspective. Representations in connectionist systems do not have a syntactic structure. According to what we now know about how our brain functions, it can be said that human cognition and reason includes linguistic-symbolic representation (as conceived in the physical symbol system hypothesis), but that such representation is only a minor part of cognition which is much more associative in nature.

To reiterate the two most important points that emerged from the previous comments: (1) we know from contemporary connectionism that humans are able to manipulate symbols but that such activity does not account for all human cognition, and (2) human cognition is not confined by the individual skull. The latter development needs further explication in that it is central to a reworked notion of what it means for a collection of humans to learn.

## COGNITION AS SOCIALLY DISTRIBUTED

Recent work in the theory of distributed cognition has begun to outline the manner in which cognition is embodied and embedded.[3] By this is meant that cognition is shaped by the affordances and constraints of the situation in which human agents find themselves, and it is in this sense that it is *socially distributed*. It is important to be clear about the meaning of 'distributed' in distributed cognition because it is commonly taken to be mere spatial, geographical, or functional distribution. In the full-blown sense employed by the theory of cognition, as evidenced in the work of Hollan et al., brains, despite their remarkable capacities, can suffer overload; for that reason, external distribution, or 'offloading' is a biological necessity. We lighten computational load by 'outsourcing' features of complex problem solving and learning (Kirsh, 2000, 2001). The other point to make is that the environment is not merely a passive recipient but has a far more active and cognitive role to play.

Some examples are in order to relate these abstract considerations to ordinary practice. The first describes a simple, everyday occurrence. Most of us, when asked to multiply two three-digit numbers in our heads, grab a pencil and paper, and carry out certain procedures in writing on the paper. If we use our calculator, other manual operations apply. In either case, we externalize what we had in our minds by manipulating written symbols on the page or the calculator (e.g. de Léon, 2002). To carry out the required operations, hand and eye motor co-ordination is necessary, and the whole process can be described something like this: '(1) setting up the problem in a physical form; (2) doing the correct manipulations in the right order; and (3) supplying the products for any two integers, which can be done easily from memory' (Giere and Moffatt, 2003: 3). What is operative here is a distributed cognitive *system* that performs the multiplication, in which you, the actor forms one part, in addition to the produced external representation, and the means to produce it, i.e. pencil, paper, or calculator.

The second example derives from Hutchins' famous cognitive ethnography *Cognition in the Wild* (1996) in which he describes what is involved in navigation near land, or 'pilotage'. What happens is as follows:

> Sailors on either side of the ship telescopically record angular locations of landmarks relative to the ship's gyrocompass. These readings are then passed on, for example by the ship's telephone, to the pilothouse where they are combined by the navigator on a specially designed chart to plot the location of the ship. In this system, no one person could possibly perform even just these three tasks in the required time interval. And only the navigator, and perhaps his assistant, knows the outcome of the task until it is communicated to others in the pilothouse.

> (Giere and Moffatt, 2003: 3)

This example makes clear how closely human actors are integrated into a whole complex cognitive system of which they are a part. In particular, the social structure, which comprises the culture of the navy, is highly significant as it enables the smooth co-ordination of the various functions. Another feature of the navy culture is that of rank in that it facilitates fast and accurate action as the result of issuing orders. It can be seen in this example that the way in which cognition is distributed is determined largely by its social components.

The third example is one provided by Tyre and von Hippel (1997) in their empirical study of the process of problem solving involving new production equipment during early factory use (see Lakomski, 2005: 110–13, in the context of discussing transfer).

Unlike the two earlier examples, this study locates itself theoretically in what has been labelled the *situated learning* perspective that, despite variations in the assumptions of its advocates and different theoretical contexts, nevertheless emphasizes the importance of *learning in context*.[4] It is not possible in the current discussion to examine this particular rich perspective, which consists of a range of complex views and terminologies (but see Lakomski, 1999). Suffice it to note here that *situated learning* has contributed enormously to expanding the notion of human cognition

beyond what goes on 'in the head' to the social world of the actor. Although writers such as Lave note that cognition is indeed distributed over mind, body and activity as well as culturally organized settings, there is no account of the human cognitive machinery that makes this possible in the first place. This point is important because while situations do indeed facilitate some actions and not others given specific affordances, these have to be recognized, that is, interpreted as such by an actor. Put differently, situations have no interpretive facility, but humans do on the basis of their information acquisition and processing capacities. It is in this strongly interdependent and relational way that individual cognition merges, or 'bleeds' into the environment (or other human actors) which in turn determines what is or is not possible to do or to think. Tyre and von Hippel's study is in this context an excellent example because it describes the reality of workplace learning and the complexities of the many situational features – between multiple locations and agents, agents and agents, and objects and agents – that make up, as we might now say, the *distributed cognitive system* that enables possible successful implementation of new technology. In other words, what Tyre and von Hippel describe coheres well with the explanatory framework of distributed cognition in that both perspectives are explicitly interested in what agents *actually do* in the solving of their problems, what use they make of the resources in their environments, and what new understandings are generated in doing so, as became evident in Hutchins' pilotage example.

The specific focus of their study is the introduction of new production machines into factory contexts, the problems that were encountered in the two sites of the study, and the adaptations that were undertaken to solve users' problems which included machine malfunction, unsatisfactory processing of parts, and other problems with convenience or efficiency. Adaptations made comprised 'modifications to hardware or software elements of the machine or to users' procedures, as well as adjustments in engineers' and users' beliefs about cause-and-effect relationships' (Tyre and von Hippel, 1997: 74).

The authors note at the outset that a study of adaptive learning makes it obvious that agents 'incorporate codified abstract theory into local, informal routines, freely adapting it as they work on actual problems in their particular social and physical circumstances' (Tyre and von Hippel, 1997: 72). In other words, there is no sharp divide between explicit, codified knowledge and tacit practice. (The complex interplay between explicit and procedural or tacit knowledge is extended by Sahdra and Thagard, 2003, in their connectionist account of how molecular biologists acquire specific commonly used laboratory techniques.)

A further, central assumption in Tyre and von Hippel's study is that the physical environment in which problem solving takes place is a constitutive element of it. This coheres with the earlier point about the significance of the external features of a distributed cognitive system. Hence, the authors argue, not only are locations important individually, but since there are often shifts between different locations, such movements are important phenomena to study because we need to know why they happen. Indeed, that their study would take the form of an investigation into problem solving *locations* only emerged after they observed the frequent visits production engineers undertook between the development lab and the factory and back, round trips that were costly in time and resources. The same problem, in other words, required investigation in the two different sites before it could be solved. In addition, *how* the actors used their physical settings to learn about and resolve problems became an important focal point of study.

It was observed that different settings afforded different clues about the problem, indeed about the kind of problem it was in the first place, and where it was located. This depended in turn on the different technologies and other physical features available to the engineers who did the investigating. What emerged as very important was that no location in itself – laboratory or factory

site – contained sufficient insights or clues that led to solving the problem. Furthermore, surprisingly, problem solution did not especially depend on the participants' discussing the issue, but apparently was tied more closely to watching, trying things out, noticing things and generally 'doing'. It was more in the nature of the actual location that determined what kind of array of problem solving features were available, such as who was available to talk to, what the nature of that interaction was, or was turning into, and what could be known and learnt in the situation. Given that different situations have different affordances in the sense just described, Tyre and von Hippel state that there is a cumulative effect in learning. Just why and how the physical setting is so important in problem solving activities is summarised well below:

1. Technical experts and users tend to be attuned to see different things in a given setting necessitating moving backwards and forwards between locations to 'discover' clues that the others had not noticed/seen; clues are embedded in the contexts.
2. Skills that could be used by experts depended partly on where they stood and on the resources available there; e.g. engineers are not familiar with local factory idiosyncrasies that might affect machine performance.
3. The physical setting not only determined what problem solvers could see, it also determined what tools are available for use, which is itself important in that successful tool use is part of the engineer's expertise; in addition, the setting also influenced behavior in terms of the tacit rules and assumptions that prevail there which include interactions with the other problem solvers on site.
4. The physical setting is important in that it affords learning in, as well as between, settings.

(Tyre and von Hippel, 1997: 76 onwards)

The learning process described is thus dynamic and iterative and involves the knowledge made available by particular settings *and* the knowledge the production engineers have in their heads. Unlike the rather narrow description of problem solving as representation in terms of mental frameworks or computational models 'in the head', the adaptive learning model offered by Tyre and von Hippel expands the 'net of cognition' considerably. They recognize the physical settings with their embedded clues as constitutive of learning and problem solving, and the way in which experts are able to make use of them and of the specialized tools available.

The previous examples served to indicate both the richness and complexity of distributed cognitive systems that make it possible to see more clearly why cognition is not confined within the skull of the individual, and indeed how far we might have to go to draw the boundary between mind and world. In addition, what is commonly called 'transfer' appears to be closely related to the kind of learning in context, or adaptive learning, that was discussed in previous sections. In the section to follow the phenomenon of transfer itself will be considered, and how it might now be appraised in light of the discussion on human cognition and learning.

## UNPACKING THE BLACK BOX OF KNOWLEDGE TRANSFER

The parlous state of our knowledge of transfer is well signalled by the fact that the National Science Foundation (NSF) of the United States thought it appropriate and necessary in 2002 to make the study of transfer of learning a priority area for research. It considered it so important that it laid out a research agenda for the future, based on the fact that 'we now know much more about human cognition (of which transfer is a subset)...' (NSF, 2002: 3–4).

Research on transfer has a considerable history (e.g. Thorndike, 1923), and despite numerous investigations, especially in (social) psychology and education, the jury is still out on (1) what exactly it means and (2) whether it occurs or not, and if it does, why it does. As Barnett and Ceci (2002: 612) point out in their comprehensive review, 'there is little agreement ... about the nature of transfer, the extent to which it occurs, and the nature

of its underlying mechanisms'. Much of the confused situation in this field of study relates to a matter of definition: how in fact can we define this phenomenon clearly and thus unify our understanding of the occurrence of transfer?

This is not the place to provide an extensive discussion.[5] This section focuses instead on the conception of *far* transfer that 'refers both to the ability to use what was learned in one setting to a different one as well as the ability to solve novel problems that share a common structure with the knowledge initially acquired' (NSF, 2002: 3). Implicit in this general definition are two concepts that are important: similarity and representation. Briefly, the former is a central notion shared in otherwise diverse accounts and suggests that 'People solve problems better if they have previously solved similar problems ... People learn more easily if they have previously learned similar or related information ...' (Robins, 1996: 186).

Despite terminological differences and unclear assumptions, there nevertheless appears to be a consensus in so far as successful transfer is said to depend on 'certain aspects of the situation, including the content to be transferred and the context to which it is transferred ... aspects of the physical, social, and semantic contexts exert significant sources of variation on cognitive performance, including but not limited to transfer (Barnett and Ceci, 2002: 632). Given the explanatory framework of distributed cognition discussed above, as well as the arguments advanced by the situated learning or cognition perspective (e.g. Greeno et al., 1993), the conclusion Barnett and Ceci arrive at from within the dominant psychological view coheres well with these insights, at least in general outline.

Concern with knowledge transfer has, of course, also been discussed in the management literature since transfer proved as elusive in organizational-industrial contexts as it did in other work or education contexts. Ever since the management of organizational knowledge has come into focus there have been concerns regarding the difficulties of knowledge transfer (e.g. Lakomski, 2005; Wenger et al., 2002; Dixon, 2000; Attewell, 1992). The issue became prominent in relation to revising the traditional understanding of how new technology is diffused by making use of von Hippel's (1994) concept of *stickiness* that served as something of a watershed. Broadly understood, and as exemplified in the case studies by Tyre and von Hippel (1997) above, the notion directed attention to the real difficulties of transfer – the complexities of (multiple) locations, agents and their understandings, and the time and costs involved – factors that had either been considered as unimportant or were significantly underrated in traditional implementation models, following the Shannon-Weaver model of communication. The idea of stickiness seems to have become widely accepted as a better account of why transfer does not happen smoothly, or why it does not happen at all. In addition, rather than understanding 'sticky' transfer as applying only to difficult transfers of knowledge, stickiness, so Szulanski and Capetta (2003) argue, is a feature of all transfer. Their insight is important in that it expands the idea of stickiness in a way that gives appropriate acknowledgement to the constraints and affordances of each situation in which transfer is expected to take place.

Departing from traditional accounts of transfer of organizational knowledge that considered difficult transfer an anomaly, Szulanski and Capetta (2003) broaden the conception of stickiness by developing a typology based on the notion of 'stickiness as eventfulness'. In essence, this notion indicates the degree of difficulty experienced in a transfer, where *eventfulness* denotes the kinds of critical, observable incidents that accompany transfer in all its phases. Szulanski and Cappetta (2003) identify four phases of transfer, beginning with initiation, moving to implementation and 'ramp up', where unexpected problems can still be rectified, and finally, to integration. In their view, it is possible to anticipate the degree of stickiness to some extent through prior planning or experimenting in set conditions before the

new knowledge is introduced ('learning before doing'). This phase is followed by 'learning by doing' in which unexpected problems are solved that appear when the new knowledge has been put to use. However, the extent to which implementation activities can be planned 'depends on the depth of understanding of the practice, that is, on causal ambiguity' (Szulanski and Cappetta, 2003: 520). This is a critically important point, and refers to the observation that replication or successful integration of a new technology may fail because of the specific idiosyncratic features of the new transfer situation. We tend to know only after transfer has taken place what knowledge was needed, in part due to the fact that tacit knowledge is always involved. It is not possible in principle to have the knowledge relevant for transfer beforehand, because we cannot anticipate what knowledge might be useful in advance. This state of affairs leads Szulanski and Cappetta (2003: 522–3) to conclude the following:

> If results cannot be precisely reproduced elsewhere because of differences in environmental conditions and if there exist[s] causal ambiguity about the inner workings of productive knowledge then problems that arise in the new environment have to be solved *in situ* through costly trial and error.

Szulanski and Cappetta's conclusion that stickiness is the order of the day, in the sense that there are always more or less complicated problems arising out of the process that need to be solved, especially where complex technology is at issue (see Eveland and Tornatzky, 1990), offers a more differentiated perspective on what happens in organizational contexts. Their realization that 'Transfers of knowledge involve unending problem solving' (Szulanski and Carpetta, 2003: 527) *in situ* provides a more naturalistic account than was offered by mainstream transfer research, whether supported from psychology, or the signalling metaphor of the traditional diffusion model.

The question that emerges quite naturally, given the various examples of 'transfer' and the conditions that appear to determine its success or lack thereof, is whether it is still appropriate to speak of transfer at all since the diffusion of (technological) knowledge turns out to be a matter of learning on site by both individuals and by collectives (see Sole and Edmondson, 2002; Attewell, 1992).

## CONCLUSION

It is now time to draw together the strands of what are the beginnings of a new account of collective learning and transfer developed in the previous pages. It is an understatement to note that the discussion has been broad-based and has drawn on disciplines not usually encountered in management discussions. It has also raised theoretical and empirical issues of immense proportions that await more fine-grained and substantive research across a range of disciplinary fields of studies. In the present context no more could be accomplished than to point out some of the complexities and note what knowledge is available to throw light on problems of perennial concern in knowledge management and organizational theory alike. In this sense, the present chapter is also a 'generic' contribution about *how* to study knowledge management.

To begin with, the most important insight is that delivered by the theory of distributed cognition, that helps us understand that cognition is neither 'owned' by an individual nor is it located in the skull. In accordance with our biological capacities, cognition is 'spread' or distributed across humans, artefacts, 'the world', and the relationships holding between them. There is no sharp inside/outside demarcation where cognition is concerned. Human agents are, in other words, embedded in cognitive systems that they determine, but that also determine them in return. *An organization on the connectionist account is a system of socially distributed cognition.* The traditional problem in organizational learning between individual and group level, interpersonal, learning can now be rephrased as follows. Individual cognition can be modelled by whole (assemblies of) networks, while group cognition, as a system of socially distributed

cognition, can be modelled by *communities of networks*, as has been demonstrated by Hutchins (1991). If we understand group or collective cognition in this manner, then the issue for organizational learning is: how do these networks interact with one another, and can we detect differences in their interactions, given differences in the social organization of communal networks? Simply put: do groups know more than the individuals who comprise them, and if so, what might be the optimal way to maximize group cognition for organizational problem-solving? Solving this issue is of central importance for organizational learning, because:

> ... if groups can have cognitive properties that are significantly different from those of the individuals in the group, then differences in the cognitive accomplishments of any two groups might depend entirely on differences in the social organization of distributed cognition and not at all on differences in the cognitive properties of individuals in the two groups
>
> (Hutchins, 1991: 285; see also Hutchins, 1996, Chapter 5).

Here issues such as power and organizational hierarchy, which are specific features of the social organization, pose challenges for the theory of distributed cognition that await future exploration.

It is hardly overemphasizing the point to say that research into this area matters because of its practical organizational consequences, such as, for example, planning for the successful diffusion of new technology. While our understanding of group cognition and how best to structure it to maximize problem-solving are big issues for future theoretical and empirical research in management and cognitive science, the causal, naturalistic account of cognition denotes the scientifically best defensible starting-point because it coheres with natural human capacities.

Secondly, the extension of cognition 'into the environment', that is the recognition that we think through and with human-created as well as natural objects, as we saw, expands our understanding of how situationally placed agents manage to accomplish what they do in the physical and social settings in which they find themselves. To put this point differently, the environment is an active participant in knowing. Here, a further rich area of study is the exploration of the *context of work*, as foreshadowed by Kirsh (2001). We do not yet understand how cognition is distributed in the workplace, such as an office, for example. Uncovering what Kirsh calls 'the deep structure' of context, that is the underlying structure or context for specific work done in well-used work spaces, would be an important step towards understanding, and designing, appropriate processes for introducing, say, new technologies in new sites that may improve adoption, and thereby reduce costs. There are already some examples of what such studies might look like, especially in relation to shift handovers which are important organizational events requiring continuity in the handling of complex situations. For example, shift handovers have been studied in medical care (e.g. Xiao, 2005; Galliers et al., 2006), emergency medical dispatch (Furniss and Blandford, 2006), space mission control (e.g. Patterson and Woods, 2001), and in manufacturing (Grusenmeyer, 1995).

Thirdly, how can management scholars and students study such complex theoretical and empirical matters? First and foremost, the case for truly interdisciplinary study has become evident in this chapter, if anything has. If we take it seriously, consequences for the structuring of programmes of study follow, as well as for the academic preparation of professors of management, and especially for those who profess Knowledge Management. Methodologically, the best way to get at the richness and complexities of interactions between humans and the objects of their own making are *cognitive ethnographies* as developed by Rogers and Ellis (1994). The broad goal of such ethnographies is to account for how distributed systems are co-ordinated by analysing the various contributions of the environment in which work activity takes place. These include the representational media, such as instruments, displays, manuals, and navigation charts,

the interactions of individuals with each other and their interactional use of artefacts. Cognitive ethnographies provide a theoretical and methodological framework for analysing complex, socially distributed work activities of which a diversity of technological artefacts and other tools are an indispensable part. Particularly important is that the central unit of analysis is the collection of individuals and artefacts and their relations to each other in a particular work practice.

Finally, what of transfer? As already recognized in the psychological literature, transfer is seen as a subset of cognition. And as we saw, cognition is highly decentralized and distributed across many agents – both human and material. Even though there may be overt similarities between situations, every situation is always subtly different. As the saying goes, 'you cannot step into the same river twice'. Among other issues, it is this phenomenon that we encountered in the transfer situations described by Tyre and von Hippel, as well as by Szulanski and Capetta. On the present account, and while there is much left over for future discussion, 'transfer' falls into place as a feature characteristic of all learning. Once it is recognized that it is not the individual, or the group, who carry 'their' knowledge from one situation into the next, and once we bring into focus the properties of situations with all their affordances as well as constraints, as argued by the theory of distributed cognition, the traditional concept and the 'problem of transfer' loses its salience. Since every situation encountered by an agent is always subtly different and therefore 'new' despite surface similarities, and since not even hindsight can tell us exactly what kind of knowledge was in fact required to carry out a task such as implementing new technology successfully, we face ongoing '*adaptive reorganization in a complex system*', as Hutchins (1996: 289) puts it. In other words, we face the requirement of ongoing learning, in the much expanded sense in which we explored learning and cognition in this chapter.

Although it is early days yet in terms of spelling out the intricacies of 'cognition in the wild', the theory of distributed cognition opens up exciting research agendas that promise a much better return on investment since they start from the premise of our natural talents, and maximizing natural talent must surely rank highly among the goals of any organization.

## NOTES

1 For comprehensive discussions see Argyris and Schön, 1996; Hedberg, 1981; Fiol and Lyles, 1985; Huber, 1996; Dodgson, 1993; Weick and Westley, 1997; Miner and Mezias, 1996; Crossan et al., 1999; Levitt and March, 1988; Friedman et al., 2005; Shipton, 2006; Weick, 2002; also Evers and Lakomski, 2000, Ch. 5; Cook and Yanow, 1996.

2 Good introductions are Churchland (1988, Ch. 7); Churchland (1989, Ch. 10); Rumelhart and McClelland (1986); Dreyfus (1994); Hutchins (1996); Evers and Lakomski (1996, Chs. 7 and 8); Lakomski (2005).

3 See Rogers and Ellis (1994); Salomon (1997); Cole and Engeström (1997); Clark (1997, 2001, 2003); Hollan et al. (2000); Giere (2002); Special Issue of Cognitive Systems Research (2002); Giere and Moffatt (2003); Bereiter (1997); St Julien (1997).

4 For example, Wenger et al. (2002); Salomon (1997); Chaiklin and Lave (1993); Lave (1991); Lave and Wenger (1991); Resnick (1991); Resnick et al. (1991); Rogoff and Lave, (1984).

5 For relevant work on critical aspects from a social, psychological and education perspective see, for instance, Resnick et al. (1991); Detterman and Sternberg (1993); Sternberg and Frensch (1993); Lave (1997); Dienes and Altmann (1997); Bransford et al. (1999); Gott et al. (1993); Mosel (1957).

## REFERENCES

Anderson, J.R. (1983) *The Architecture of Complexity.* Cambridge, MA: Harvard University Press.

Argyris, C. and Schön, D.A. (1978) *Organizational Learning II.* Reading, MA: Addison-Wesley. Republished in 1996.

Attewell, P. (1992) 'Technology diffusion and organizational learning: The case of business computing', *Organization Science,* 3 (1): 1–19.

Bereiter, C. (1997) 'Situated cognition and how to overcome it', in D. Kirshner and J.A. Whitson (eds), *Situated Cognition.* Hillsdale, NJ: Lawrence Erlbaum Associates.

Barnett, S.M. and Ceci, S.J. (2002) 'When and where do we apply what we learn?: A taxonomy for far transfer', *Psychological Bulletin,* 128 (4): 612–37.

Bransford, S.M., Brown, A.L. and Cocking, R.R. (1999) *How People Learn: Brain, Mind, Experience, and School.* Washington, DC: National Academy Press.

Brown, J.S. and Duguid, J. (2000) 'Organizing knowledge', in D.E. Smith (ed.), *Knowledge, Groupware and the Internet.* Boston: Butterworth-Heinemann.

Brown, J.S. and Duguid, J. (1999) 'Organizational learning and communities-of-practice', in M.D. Cohen and L.S. Sproull (eds), *Organizational Learning.* Thousand Oaks, CA: Sage.

Chaiklin, S. and Lave, J. (eds) (1993) *Understanding Practice – Perspectives on Activity and Context.* Cambridge: Cambridge University Press.

Churchland, P.M. (1988) *Matter and Consciousness.* Cambridge, MA: MIT Press.

Churchland, P.S. (1989) *Neurophilosophy.* Cambridge, MA: MIT Press.

Clark, A. (2001) *Mindware.* New York: Oxford University Press.

Clark, A. (2003) *Natural-Born-Cyborss.* Oxford: Oxford University Press.

Clark, A. (1997) *Being There: Putting Brain, Body, and World Together Again.* Cambridge, MA: The MIT Press.

Cohen, M.D. and Sproull, L.S. (1991) 'Editors' introduction', *Organization Science,* 2 (1): i–iii.

Cole, M. and Engeström, Y. (1997) 'A cultural–historical approach to distributed cognition', in G. Salomon (ed.), *Distributed Cognitions, Psychological and Educational Considerations.* Cambridge: Cambridge University Press.

Cook, S.D.N. and Yanow, D. (1996) 'Culture and organizational learning', in M.D. Cohen and L.S. Sproull (eds), *Organizational Learning.* Thousand Oaks, CA: Sage.

Cortada, J.W. and Woods, J.A. (eds) (2000) *The Knowledge Management Yearbook 2000–2001.* Boston: Butterworth-Heinemann.

Cortada, J.W. and Woods, J.A. (eds) (1999) *The Knowledge Management Yearbook 1999–2000.* Boston: Butterworth-Heinemann.

Crossan, M.M., Lane, H.W. and White, R.E. (1999) 'An organizational learning framework: From intuition to institution', *The Academy of Management Review,* 24 (3): 522–37.

De Laat, M. and Simons, R.-J. (2002) 'Collective learning: Theoretical perspectives and ways to support networked learning', *European Journal of Vocational Training,* 27: 13–24.

De Léon, D. (2002) 'Cognitive task transformations', *Cognitive Systems Research,* 3: 349–59.

Detterman, D. and Sternberg, R. (1993) *Transfer on Trial.* Norwood, NJ: Ablex Publishing Co.

Dierkes, M., Ariane Berthoin, A., Child, J. and Nonaka, I. (eds) (2001) *Handbook of Organizational Learning and Knowledge.* Oxford: Oxford University Press.

Dienes, Z. and Altmann, G. (1997) 'Transfer of implicit knowledge across domains: How implicit and how abstract?' in D. Berry (ed.), *How Implicit is Implicit Learning?* Oxford: Oxford University Press.

Dixon, N. (2000) *Common Knowledge.* Cambridge, MA: Harvard Business School Press.

Dodgson, M. (1993) 'Organizational learning: A review of some literatures', *Organization Studies,* 14 (3): 375–94.

Dreyfus, H.L. (1994) *What Computers Still Can't Do.* Cambridge, MA: MIT Press.

Easterby-Smith, M. and Lyles, M.A. (eds) (2003a) *Handbook of Organizational Learning and Knowledge Management.* Oxford: Blackwell.

Easterby-Smith, M. and Lyles, M.A. (2003b) 'Watersheds of organizational learning and knowledge management', in M. Easterby-Smith and M.A. Lyles (eds), *Handbook of Organizational Learning and Knowledge Management.* Malden, MA: Blackwells.

Elkjaer, B. (2003) 'Social learning theory: learning as participation in social processes', in M. Easterby-Smith and M.A. Lyles (eds), *Handbook of Organizational Learning and Knowledge Management.* Malden, MA: Blackwells.

Eveland, J.D. and Tornatzky, L. (1990) 'The deployment of technology', in L. Tornatzky and M. Fleischer (eds), *The Processes of Technological Innovation.* Lexington, MA: Lexington Books.

Evers, C.W. and Lakomski, G. (2000) *Doing Educational Administration.* Oxford: Elsevier.

Evers, C.W. and Lakomski, G. (1996) *Exploring Educational Administration.* Oxford: Elsevier.

Evers, C.W. and Lakomski, G. (1991) *Knowing Educational Administration.* Oxford: Elsevier.

Fiol, C.M. and Lyles, M.A. (1985) 'Organizational learning', *Academy of Management Review,* 10 (4): 803–13.

Friedman, V.J., Lipshitz, R. and Popper, M. (2005) 'The mystification of organizational learning', *Journal of Management Inquiry,* 14 (1): 19–30.

Furniss, D. and Blandford, A. (2006) 'Understanding emergency medical dispatch in terms of distributed cognition: a case study', *Ergonomics,* 49 (12–13): 1174–1203.

Galliers, J., Wilson, S. and Fone, J. (2006) 'A method for determining information flow breakdown in clinical systems', *International Journal of Medical Informatics,* 13: 1–9.

Giere, R.N. (2002) 'Discussion note: Distributed cognition in epistemic cultures, *Philosophy of Science,* 69 (December): 1–8.

Giere, R.N. and Moffatt, B. (2003) 'Distributed cognition: Where the cognitive and social merge', *Social Studies of Science,* 33 (2): 1–10.

Gott, S.P., Parker Hall, E., Pokorny, R.A., Dibble, E. and Glaser, R. (1993) 'A naturalistic study of transfer: Adaptive expertise in technical domains', in D. Detterman and R. Sternberg (eds), *Transfer on Trial.* Norwood, NJ: Ablex Publishing Co.

Greeno, J.G., Moore, J.L. and Smith, D.R. (1993) 'Transfer of situated learning', in D.K. Detterman and R.J. Sternberg (eds), *Transfer on Trial: Intelligence, Cognition, and Instruction.* Norwood, NJ: Ablex Publishing Co.

Grusenmeyer, C. (1995) 'Shared functional representation in cooperative tasks – the example of shift changeover', *International Journals of Human Factors in Manufacturing,* 5 (2): 163–76.

Hedberg, B. (1981) 'How organizations learn and unlearn', in P.C. Nystrom and W.H. Starbuck (eds), *Handbook of Organizational Design.* Oxford: Oxford University Press.

Hollan, J., Hutchins, E. and Kirsh, D. (2000) 'Distributed cognition: Toward a new foundation for human–computer interaction research', *ACM Transactions on Computer–Human Interaction,* 7 (2): 174–96.

Huber, G.P. (1996) 'Organizational learning', in M.D. Cohen and L.S. Sproull (eds), *Organizational Learning.* Thousand Oaks, CA: Sage.

Hutchins, E. (1996) *Cognition in the Wild.* Cambridge, MA: The MIT Press.

Hutchins, E. (1991) 'The social organization of distributed cognition', in L.B. Resnick, J.M. Levine, and S.D. Teasley (eds), *Perspectives on Socially Shared Cognition.* Washington, DC: American Psychological Association.

Kirsh, D. (2001) 'The context of work', *Human–Computer Interaction,* 16: 305–22.

Kirsh, D. (2000) 'A few thoughts on cognitive overload', *Intellectica,* 1 (30): 19–51.

Lakomski, G. (2005) *Managing without Leadership. Towards a Theory of Organizational Functioning.* Elsevier: Oxford.

Lakomski, G. (1999) 'Symbol processing, situated action, and social cognition: Implications for research and methodology', in J.P. Keeves and G. Lakomski (eds), *Issues in Educational Research.* Oxford: Elsevier.

Lave, J. (1997) 'The culture of acquisition and the practice of understanding', in D. Kirshner and J.A. Whitson (eds), *Situated Cognition.* Hillsdale, NJ: Lawrence Erlbaum Associates.

Lave, J. (1991) 'Situating learning in communities of practice', in L.B. Resnick, J.L. Levine and S.D. Teasley (eds), *Perspectives on Socially Shared*

*Cognition.* Washington, DC: American Psychological Association.

Lave, J. and Wenger, E. (1991) *Situated Learning.* Cambridge: Cambridge University Press.

Levitt, B. and March, J.G. (1988) 'Organizational learning', *Annual Review of Sociology,* 14: 319–40.

Lucier, C.E. and Torsilieri, J.D. (2001) 'Can knowledge management deliver bottom-line results?' in I. Nonaka and D. Teece (eds), *Managing Industrial Knowledge.* London: Sage.

March, J. and Simon, H.A. (1958) *Organizations.* New York: Wiley.

Miner, A.S. and Mezias, S.J. (1996) 'Ugly duckling no more: Pasts and futures of organizational learning research', *Organization Science,* 7 (1): 88–99.

Minsky, M. (1994) 'Society of mind: A response to four reviews', in W. Clancey. S, Smoliar and M. Stefik (eds), *Contemplating Minds.* Cambridge, MA: MIT Press.

Mosel, J. (1957) 'Why training programs fail to carry over', *Personnel,* 56–64.

National Science Foundation (2002) *Transfer of Learning: Issues an Research Agenda.* Report of Workshop by J. Mestre, University of Massachusetts-Amherst.

Newell, A. and Simon, H.A. (1976) 'Computer science as empirical enquiry: symbols and search', in M.A. Boden (ed.), (1990) *The Philosophy of Artificial Intelligence.* Oxford: Oxford University Press.

Newell, A. and Simon, H.A. (1972) *Human Problem Solving.* New York: Prentice-Hall.

Newell, A., Rosenbloom, P.S. and Laird, J.E. (1996) 'Symbolic architectures for cognition', in M.I. Posner (ed.), *Foundations of Cognitive Science.* Cambridge, MA: MIT Press.

Nonaka, I. and Takeuchi, H. (1995) *The Knowledge-creating Company.* New York: Oxford University Press.

Patterson, E. and Woods, D. (2001) 'Shift changes, updates, and the on-call architecture in space shuttle mission control', *Computer Supported Cooperative Work,* 10: 317–46.

Prusak, L. (ed.) (1997) *Knowledge in Organizations.* Boston: Butterworth-Heinemann.

Resnick, L.B. (1991) 'Shared cognition: Thinking as social practice', in L.B. Resnick, J.M. Levine, and S.D. Teasley (eds), *Perspectives on Socially Shared Cognition.* Washington, DC: American Psychological Association.

Resnick, L.B., Levine, J.M. and Teasley, S.D. (eds) (1991) *Perspectives on Socially Shared Cognition.* Washington, DC: American Psychological Association.

Robins, A. (1996) 'Transfer in cognition', *Connection Science,* 8 (2): 185–203.

Rogers, Y. and Ellis, J. (1994) 'Distributed cognition: An alternative framework for analysing and explaining collaborative working', *Journal of Information Technology,* 9 (2): 119–28.

Rogoff, B. and Lave, J. (eds) (1984) *Everyday Cognition: Its Development in Social Context.* Cambridge, MA: Harvard University Press.

Rosenbloom, P., Laird, J., Newell, A. and McCarl, R. (1992) 'A preliminary analysis of the SOAR architecture as a basis for general intelligence', in D. Kirsh (ed.), *Foundations of Artificial Intelligence.* Cambridge, MA: MIT Press.

Rumelhart, D.E. (1993) 'The architecture of mind: A connectionist approach', in M.I. Posner (ed.), *Foundations of Cognitive Science.* Cambridge, MA: MIT Press.

Rumelhart, D.E. and McClelland, J.L. (eds) (1986) *Parallel Distributed Processing.* Volumes I & II. Cambridge, MA: The MIT Press.

Sahdra, B. and Thagard, P. (2003) 'Procedural knowledge in molecular biology', *Philosophical Psychology,* 16 (4): 477–98.

Salomon, G. (ed.) (1997) *Distributed Cognitions, Psychological and Educational Considerations.* Cambridge: Cambridge University Press.

Shipton, H. (2006) 'Cohesion or confusion? Towards a typology for organizational learning research', *International Journal of Management Reviews,* 8 (4): 233–52.

Simon, H.A. (1995) 'New decomposability and complexity: How a mind resides in a brain', in H. Morowitz and J.L. Singer (eds), *The Mind, the Brain, and Complex Adaptive Systems.* New York: Addison-Wesley.

Simon, H.A. (1991) 'Bounded rationality and organizational learning', *Organization Science,* 2 (1): 125–34.

Simon, H.A. (1990) 'Invariants of human behavior', *Annual Review of Psychology,* 41: 1–19.

Simon, H.A. (1979) *The Sciences of the Artificial.* Cambridge, MA: The MIT Press.

Sole, D. and Edmondson, A. (2002) 'Situated knowledge and learning in dispersed teams', *British Journal of Management,* 13: 17–34.

*Stanford Encyclopaedia of Philosophy,* http://plato. stanford.edu/entries/cognitive-science

Sternberg, R.J. and Frensch, P.A. (1993) 'Mechanisms of transfer', in D. Detterman and R. Sternberg (eds), *Transfer on Trial.* Norwood, NJ: Ablex Publishing Co.

St. Julien, J. (1997) 'Explaining learning: The research trajectory of situated cognition and the implications of connectionism', in D. Kirshner and J.A. Whitson (eds), *Situated Cognition.* Hillsdale, NJ: Lawrence Erlbaum Associates.

Strauss, C. and Quinn, N. (1997) *A Cognitive Theory of Cultural Meaning*. Cambridge, MA: Cambridge University Press.

Szulanski, G. and Cappetta, R. (2003) 'Stickiness: Conceptualising, measuring, and predicting difficulties in the transfer of knowledge within organizations', in M. Easterby-Smith and M.A. Lyles (eds), *Handbook of Organizational Learning and Knowledge Management*. Oxford: Blackwell.

Thorndike, E.L. (1923) 'The influence of first year Latin upon the ability to read English', *School Sociology*, 17: 165–68.

Tienson, J.L. (1990) 'An introduction to connectionism', in J.L. Garfield (ed.), *Foundations of Cognitive Science: The Essential Readings*. New York: Paragon House.

Tyre, M. and von Hippel, E. (1997) 'The situated nature of adaptive learning in organizations', *Organization Science*, 8 (1): 71–83.

Ulrich, D., Jick, T. and Von Glinow, M.A. (1993) 'High-impact learning: Building and diffusing learning capability', *Organizational Dynamics*, (Autumn): 52–67.

Vera, D. and Crossan, M. (2003) 'Organizational learning and knowledge management: Toward an integrative framework', in M. Easterby-Smith and M.A. Lyles (eds), *Handbook of Organizational Learning and Knowledge Management*. Malden, MA: Blackwells.

Vera, A.H. and Simon, H.A. (1993) 'Situated action: A symbolic interpretation', *Cognitive Science*, 17: 7–48.

von Hippel, E. (1994) ' "Sticky information" and the locus of problem solving: Implications for innovation', *Management Science*, 40 (4): 429–39.

Weick, K. (2002) 'Puzzles in organizational learning: An exercise in disciplined imagination', *British Journal of Management*, 13: 7–15.

Weick, K.E. and Westley, F. (1997) 'Organizational learning: Affirming an oxymoron', in S.R. Clegg, C. Hardy, and W.R. Nord (eds), *Handbook of Organization Studies*. London: Sage.

Wenger, E., McDermott, R. and Snyder, W.M. (2002) *Cultivating Communities of Practice*. Cambridge, MA: Harvard Business School Press (HBSP).

Wiig, K.M. (1993) *Knowledge Management Foundations*. Arlington, TX: Schema Press.

Wiig, K.M. (2000) 'Knowledge Management: An emerging discipline rooted in a long history', in C. Despres and D. Chauvel (eds), *Knowledge Horizons: The Present and Promise of Knowledge Management*. Boston, MA: Butterworth-Heinemann.

Xiao, Y. (2005) 'Artifacts and collaborative work in health care: Methodological, theoretical, and technological implications of the tangible', *Journal of Biomedical Informatics*, 38: 26–33.

# 5

# Reflection, Reflective Practice and Organizing Reflection

Russ Vince and Michael Reynolds

Reflection is the practice of periodically stepping back to ponder the meaning to self and others in one's immediate environment about what has recently transpired. It illuminates what has been experienced by both self and others, providing a basis for future action. It thus constitutes the ability to uncover and make explicit to oneself and to one's colleagues what one has planned, observed, or achieved in practice. In particular, it privileges the process of inquiry leading to an understanding of experiences that may have been overlooked. Experiences can be composed of actions, beliefs, and feelings.

(Raelin, 2001: 11)

The word reflection is a representation of human consciousness, both individual and collective. From a philosophical point of view, reflection refers to 'the process or faculty by which the mind has knowledge of itself and its workings' (OED, 1993: 2521). This process or faculty is bound up in an inevitable and continuous relationship between reflection and action. Therefore, reflection is also defined as 'the action of turning (back) or fixing the thoughts on some subject...' in order to learn (OED, 1993: 2521).

Reflection is one of the key building blocks of human learning; it has become established at the core of management and organizational learning; and the relationship between reflection and action has inspired the two most well-known conceptual models in management learning and management education (Kolb's 'Learning Cycle' and Schön's 'Reflective Practitioner'). In this chapter, we discuss reflection and management learning, paying particular attention to ideas and approaches that have attempted to move beyond the notion of the reflective practitioner.

## REFLECTION, LEARNING AND EXPERIENCE: SOME KEY THEORIES AND PERSPECTIVES

The philosopher John Dewey is arguably the founding father of our modern conceptualization of reflection in management learning and his ideas continue to influence recent interpretations. For Dewey, thought and action were, or ideally should be, inextricably connected:

> Thinking includes all of these steps – the sense of a problem, the observation of conditions, the formation and rational elaboration of a suggested conclusion, and the active experimental testing. (1916: 151)

Anticipating something of the spirit of the developments we describe in this chapter, Dewey conceived of this perspective on learning as of greater significance than a process of problem solving. His vision was of an educational process that had reflection and action linked at its core, and was the means by which individuals gained 'a personal interest in social relationships and control' – a platform for social change to a more democratic social order and preparation for membership of it (p. 99).

Drawing on Dewey's ideas, Lindeman (1947) later developed a concept of learning which recast education as a process of 'utilising knowledge, feelings and experience in problem solving' (p. 53). For Lindeman, learning through experience complemented other educational methods because it involved the application of ideas and theories at the point where they become necessary in making sense of particular situations, problems or events. As such it provided the basis for subsequent action.

> True learning, that is learning which is associated with the problems of life, is a twofold process which consists of knowledge on the one hand, and the use of knowledge on the other. (Lindeman, 1935: 44)

Through these authors the meaning of reflection has been refined to signify a process in which we distance ourselves from an event in order to make sense of it, providing a conscious and thoughtful connection between ideas and experience, past experience and future action. Applied but not limited to problem solving, reflection has been established at the core of learning as a process both of drawing on and developing new ideas. To reflect is to make thoughtful and productive use of otherwise un-coded

experience (Usher, 1985), a process 'whereby knowledge is created through the transformation of experience' (Kolb, 1984: 38). Other authors have elaborated different modes of reflection on the experience of events and of individuals' responses to them: such as recognizing what seems to work and what doesn't; being aware of associated feelings; of judgements made and on what basis; and of the ideas, values and assumptions which influence the interpretations made of the experience (Vince, 1998).

The appeal of these ideas in a professional context is in linking learning with action and experience – in contrast with the academic tradition where they can seem disconnected or at least delayed until the benefits of the educational process might be realized in later work experience. This sense of immediacy, of the connection with the practicalities, problems and challenges of work and of the possibilities of learning in and from the experience of work has resulted in the current prominence of reflection-based experiential learning, especially in management development and more recently in organizational learning. The influence of these ideas has become widespread and can be seen in 'structured' activities, where reflection on contrived experience is used to underpin attempts to improve managers' practice, including, for example, simulations, 'outdoor' management development, group conferences and action learning.[1]

Reflective approaches have proved appealing to professional practitioners because they raise the likelihood of the learning being 'relevant', particularly if they are situated in day-to-day work experience. Exactly how relevant is open to question. Dehler (1998) argues that the demand for relevance, however understandable, is one way in which the practice of management is rationalized through the insistence on practical solutions to felt problems (p. 85). Dehler's point is that such a response is only of short-term value compared with one which embraces the tensions inherent in the complexity of organizations. He argues that ready 'solutions' tend to deny such tensions and in turn, deny access to the emotions and politics that both promote and limit learning in organizations.

The challenge for the academy is the assumption that learning based on experience might be regarded with an authority traditionally granted to institutionally legitimized theory and research. This represents a fundamental change in emphasis in thinking about how people learn, one which would appear to respond directly to the perceived shortcomings of the academic tradition. Personal and professional experience assume validity as a source of learning and of ideas. Such a perspective has provided the basis for the concept of 'self-directed learning' (Knowles, 1984) and for an even more radical possibility, of ideas as co-authored between managers and academics, as well as or even instead of, the more usually assumed hierarchical arrangement between them (Cunliffe, 2001; Elliott and Reynolds, 2002).

## The reflective practitioner

Schön's work on reflective practice (1983, 1987) epitomizes the characteristics of a theory and practice of learning which is based on re-connecting ideas and experience through reflection. His elaboration of the concept of the 'reflective practitioner' brings to the fore the tacit element involved in learning and in particular the idea that reflection is not only retrospective, but becomes an element of the experience *per se*. Schön described this as:

> on-the-spot surfacing, criticizing, restructuring, and testing of intuitive understanding of experienced phenomena; often it takes the form of a reflective conversation with the situation. (1983: 241–2)

Schön's early research (his doctoral thesis) was influenced by the writing of John Dewey. His subsequent ideas were the result of his study of professionals – which goes some way to explaining why they have greatly influenced the practice of professional education and development. Experience is connected to evaluation during a 'conversation' with the situation in which the person draws on previous understandings, some of

which are tacit, which is to say mysterious to both themselves and to others. Schön's concept of the reflective practitioner underpins the development of theory and practice of reflection in ways which emphasize the importance of the organizational context as well as of personal psychology. Schön was critical of the technical rationality which he saw as characterizing organizational problem solving, and which paid insufficient attention to ends as well as means. He wrote of the significance of interrogating the assumptions on which professional practice was based through reflecting on the 'norms' and 'appreciations' which underpin judgements and actions. Thus the practitioner should reflect

> ... on the feeling for a situation which has led him to adopt a particular course of action, on the way he has framed the problem he is trying to solve, or on the role he has constructed for himself within a larger institutional 'context'. (op. cit. p. 62)

In practical terms this involved both 'reflection-in-action' and 'reflection-on-action'. The former has been described as 'thinking on our feet'. It involves reviewing experiences, feelings and assumptions in order to create new ways of understanding and acting within a situation as it unfolds. The reflective practitioner uses rather than excludes things that often seem irrelevant to rational processes of problem solving, for example the surprise, puzzlement, or confusion inherent within a situation.

Reflection on experience therefore implies a critique of situations, which provides the opportunity to experiment in ways that might produce new understanding or action (Schön, 1983). 'Reflection-on-action' is a process of inquiry that comes later and involves, for example, the writing up of recordings, reviews of group sense-making and the formation of themes and/or questions. The expectation placed on the reflective practitioner is to make sense of a situation in different ways. Human actors often take refuge in practised and habitual ways of thinking and working in established procedures and familiar approaches. Efforts to see the unfamiliar within the everyday allows the individual to confront habits and attachments and to change those aspects of working thought and practice that are taken-for-granted. The ability, for example, to draw upon a range of metaphors, images and emotions; to engage aesthetically as well as rationally; and to see relational dynamics within situations, allows for the generation of different ways of thinking and acting within practice.

There is little doubt that the idea of the reflective practitioner has made a profound contribution to the ways the theory and practice of reflection have developed. It often speaks very clearly to individuals' experience, and particularly in terms of the generative possibilities of making change at work. However, the notion of the reflective practitioner has also been used in unreflective ways by trainers and facilitators in management education and development. The concept has been very widely applied, often uncritically, drawing on individualized perspectives which cannot adequately address complex organizational and political processes. It is perhaps the critical intent at the heart of the original challenge to technical rationality made by Schön that is most easily lost. This is not only about the continued dominance of rational approaches to management, but also about the focus of reflection in organizations on individuals' responsibility for their own improvement through reflecting 'back' on situations (Vince, 2002).

In the past decade, through research and increasingly through application, the concept of reflection has been elaborated in recognizably different ways. These developments demonstrate a shift in perspective which re-emphasizes the critical and collective dimensions of thought and action in both educational and organizational contexts. In the following section of the chapter, we highlight four perspectives that have helped to shift our understanding of reflection beyond that of the reflective practitioner. These are: critical reflection; public reflection; productive reflection; and organizing reflection. We discuss these both in terms of their implications for theory and for practice.

# BEYOND THE REFLECTIVE PRACTITIONER

## *Critical reflection*

Although there have always been dissident, if peripheral voices questioning the accepted curriculum within management education, it was not until the 1990s that these gained recognition as a clearly defined movement. Exemplified in the collection of papers published by Alvesson and Willmott (1992) there was a significant shift in emphasis as the dominant theme exercising business school academics of 'what is the best way to do this?' was countered with the question 'but is this what we should be doing?'. The reasons for the growth of this movement, conveniently described as 'Critical Management Studies' (CMS), and the reason why it came to prominence at this time are complex, and as Fournier and Grey (2000) point out, the movement is far from homogeneous, both in its theoretical positions and its propositions for practice.

A key element of CMS is the consciousness of the crucial role which managers exercise within society and that, simply refining solutions to technical problems – a 'narrow, instrumental form of rationality' (Alvesson and Willmott, 1992: 1) – is not a sufficient objective for management educators. Their role should also be to raise questions about purpose and intent and about the assumptions which underpin organizational structures and practices. Consequently, the practice of reflection is involved with examining organizational aims and processes through ideas and analytical perspectives which are capable of such inquiry. CMS, while still not the dominant discourse in management education, has become an established alternative through writing, research and increasingly through practice, and its specific focus on pedagogy is also represented in a growing body of theory and practice as 'Critical Management Education' (CME). Early projects in CME can be seen in the collection of papers by French and Grey (1996) and since then in numerous contributions to *Management Learning* and the *Journal of Management Education*. Perriton (2007) has summarized and critiqued this movement, its origins and influences.

Central to these developments is the concept of 'critical reflection', a perspective through which events, actions and intentions are evaluated and influenced. Critical reflection owes much to previous explanations of the reflective process, but is an approach to questioning which is informed by conceptual frameworks which are social and political. What critical reflection adds is an *outward* questioning of discourses inherent in the structures and practices in which professional practice is embedded. For 'critical' management educators, instrumental approaches are seen as providing inadequate support for managers wishing to understand and engage with – materially, morally and socially – an increasingly complex environment.

Critical perspectives which have been applied within management education show a range of influences which include poststructuralist, feminist, Marxist and postcolonial frameworks. Our account in this chapter summarizes an interpretation which has been shaped more by Critical Theory (Habermas, 1973) as reflected in the fields of management education (Alvesson and Willmott, 1992) and of continuing education (Hindmarsh, 1993). The goal of Critical Theory can be summarized as:

The emancipatory potential of reason to reflect critically on how the reality of the social world, including the construction of the self, is socially produced and, therefore, open to transformation. (Alvesson and Willmott, 1992: 435)

A key element of this perspective, critical reflection entails an examination of social and political 'taken-for-granteds', and of historical and contextual factors. It is emancipatory in that it advocates the examination of purposes, motives and vested interests so as to construct the basis of a more just society in which people have more control over decisions and practices which affect them.

From this position, all generalized observations and prescriptions on social structures and practices are regarded as 'interested' rather than neutral, and attempts 'to pass off sectional viewpoints as universal, natural, classless, timeless' are to be questioned (Gibson, 1986: 172). The theory and practice of reflection is thereby developed in order to examine processes of power and control which may be implicit in taken-for-granted aspects of policy and practice – whether in an organizational or an educational context. In management education, this has implications for both the ideas presented in the curriculum and for other aspects of pedagogy such as educational methods and teacher–student relations (Reynolds, 1998).

Reflection has been traditionally thought of as a disciplined approach to making sense of and learning from experience, or as the basis of making considered and informed choices between alternative courses of action. Such processes have tended to be concerned with technical, individualized perspectives, leaving unquestioned the social and political 'givens' such as purpose or the organizational arrangements in which they are embedded. The characteristics of critical reflection which distinguish it from other versions of reflection can be summarized as follows:

- The fundamental task of critical reflection is to identify and question taken-for-granted beliefs and values, particularly those which have become unquestioned or 'majority' positions. It is a process of making evaluations, often moral ones, and not simply exercising judgements of a practical, technical nature.
- Critical reflection pays particular attention to the analysis of power relations and relations between power and knowledge. Regardless of the particular perspective a critical approach is based on, it will emphasize the value of questioning and challenging existing structures and practices – including whether the function of management education is to reinforce existing power relations in organizations or to transform them.
- From a reflexive position, questioning our own practice is important too, entertaining the possibility that research data or established theory are not the only or necessarily the most significant bases for learning. Managers' collective experience has equal validity – particularly if understood critically

in ways that highlight its political, emotional and ethical components as well as its conceptual or technical aspects.

- It has been a long-standing criticism of management education that it has been overly influenced by individualistic – chiefly psychological – perspectives. Working, managing and learning involve social and cultural processes as well as their personal and psychological counterparts.[2] A critical approach implies a focus on a collective, situated (contextually specific) process that assists inquiry into actual and current organizational projects and projections. This enables managers to question critically organizational practices within their specific situation.[3]

It has seemed for some time as though these principles were limited to the development of theory. Nor is the approach without some acknowledgment of its limitations and pitfalls (Reynolds, 1999; Perriton, 2004). But there is currently a significant body of examples where critical perspectives are applied to existing practices within management learning such as action-based approaches to learning (Willmott, 1997; Reynolds and Vince, 2004a) and to the development and application of critical pedagogies within postgraduate management programmes (see for example Trehan and Rigg, 2007; Gold et al., 2002).

We can provide an example of an encounter with critical reflection. A professional consultant who had worked in management development for a number of years based her work largely on experiential learning methods. Course participants were involved in practical activities, most of which involved working in groups. The activities, indoor and outdoor, provided the experiences from which, in subsequent reflective sessions, participants learnt about their behaviour and characteristics as group members and leaders. Taking time out in order to deepen her own understanding of her professional practice and ideas, the consultant undertook a period of postgraduate study in management learning. During this programme, which included experience-based learning methods supported by critical perspectives, she developed an interest in ideas which placed more emphasis

on the classroom as a political arena and on the social discourses which were implicit in her practices as tutor, course designer and facilitator of group activities. She reflected on her own role in unilaterally deciding on the designs in which she involved participants and the parallels in management style she was exemplifying. She became increasingly aware of the related constructs of course 'groups' and management 'teams' and the way in which apparently participative structures looked less liberal in the light of ideas which highlighted the potential dynamics of coercion and surveillance.

Most significant to the consultant was her reflexive critique of the theoretical basis for her design and facilitation, as well as the restricted range of ideas she was drawing on in her development work with managers. Her initial response was to feel incapacitated by these insights. What had seemed – in the tradition of experiential learning – to be the natural approach in putting participants into group exercises which would mirror their work experience, now seemed fraught with the possibility that she was reinforcing the processes of hierarchy and coercion she had intended her educational practice to contest. After an initial period of professional paralysis, her practice was to change as a result of these 'critically informed' insights. Her design and facilitation came to reflect a broader platform of informing ideas, ideas more likely to help herself and her participants to understand the social and political complexity of groups, both on her development programmes and in the workplace.

## Public reflection

The second approach to reflection we highlight in our model of reflection as 'beyond the reflective practitioner', emphasizes the transformational potential of collective reflection. In an exemplary paper, Joe Raelin (2001) carefully and clearly outlines the argument for collective reflection. He refers to this as 'public reflection' since it is necessarily undertaken in the company of others, and as a result, creates different interpersonal dynamics of accountability, authority and learning. In his paper he explains why we need reflection in organizations that goes beyond the individual to engage with experience generated collectively – for example, in project teams, internal groups and organizational subsystems. He gives four explanations of the need to address the relationship between reflection and learning with and through the involvement of others.

First, we are often unaware of the consequences of our behaviour. Public reflection can bring these consequences to our attention in ways that might transform behaviour. Second, there is a gap between what we say we will do and what we actually do in organizations. Public reflection is a necessary part of making this gap both visible and discussable, and in order to make change possible. Third, we are often selective or biased in the information we obtain and/or communicate. Public reflection allows us to become aware of judgement errors that arise as a consequence of bias and to attempt to correct them. Finally, collectively reinventing the wheel is useful sometimes because prior solutions may not fit with new problems and issues. Public reflection provides an environment within which we can distinguish 'what is measured and critical from that which might be self-fulfilling and self-justificatory' (Raelin, 2001: 15).

Public reflection captures the personal and political complexities of organizational life and asks that they be considered as crucial components in the improvement or even the transformation of policy and practice. For example, while public reflection can bring the consequences of behaviour to our attention in ways that might transform it, there is also the possibility of reinforcing behaviour, of retrenched positions and highly defended individuals. This paradox, that attempting to learn and change can paralyze as well as produce learning and change, is at the heart of an understanding of authority and leadership in context. Public reflection encourages engagement with those others who are similarly caught up in the distinctive political processes that organizations and organizing create, and that continuously shape 'the way we do things here' (Vince, 2004).

The two key components of public reflection are: the willingness of people to confront themselves and to create alternative interpretations of their own constructed reality (see also Cunliffe, Chapter 21, this volume). Such willingness is the basis of an understanding and practice of authority that is free from individual defensiveness and the regressive political consequences of this defensiveness in action. This revised notion of authority then provides an emotional base for people to distinguish themselves when necessary from their social context. It provides the necessary political environment for individuals to risk putting forward ideas and suggestions that might not be accepted by their community; to risk isolating themselves in the service of transformation. Public reflection invites the consideration of data 'beyond our personal, interpersonal, and organizational taken-for-granted assumptions'. Reflection 'in public' makes the questioning of assumptions more likely because it acknowledges the role of difference and dissent in improvement.

Public reflection is important because it creates both individual and collective momentum. 'It influences both the environment and also the speaker him or herself' (Kets de Vries and Balazs, 1998: 614), by creating external accountability at the same time as giving public voice to personal intent. It is an approach that explicitly links the impact of organizational politics on the individual – for example, the tendency towards caution and blame (Vince and Saleem, 2004) with the impact individuals can make (collectively) on organizational politics. Thus, public reflection as a learning process 'can help us review and alter any misconstrued meanings arising out of uncritical half-truths found in unconventional wisdom or in power relationships' (Raelin, 2001: 12–13).

An example of reflection 'in public' can be found in Reynolds and Vince (2004a), where we discuss the case of an international utilities company that wanted to revise the way they reflected on organizational bids for contracts because they realized that the knowledge and expertise generated in Bid Teams was poorly linked to improvements in practice. Where bids had failed, reflection was ignored because organizational members did not want to dwell on their failure. Where bids had been a success, organizational members wanted to enjoy their success rather than reflect on it. This was not seen as a failure of the groups themselves to reflect, rather as a failure in the ability of the organization to support reflection as an integral part of the process of bidding for contracts. This raised the question of how the knowledge (about the procedures and dynamics of the bidding process) that was being lost could be recaptured. The company used an action-based approach that was integrated into each Bid Team. All Bid Teams started to include an 'action researcher' (a role taken up by one of the existing members, who received training and support) whose job it was to record the process from beginning to end, to initiate discussions at each meeting on the group's processes and behaviour, and to pay attention to the politics that were having an impact on the team both from outside and from within. It was clear that this approach was not always easy or welcome within teams. Some team leaders thought that the action researchers were being critical of them; it took time for team members to understand that there was more happening in the team than the task at hand; and the action researchers often found it difficult to say what their inquiry had raised, as well as being believed when they did. However, despite these difficulties, the knowledge from both successful and unsuccessful bids was given public voice in the organization. The public expression of this knowledge could assist in the practical task of evaluating the bidding process. It was also a method to surface and examine the assumptions, emotions and politics that shaped both the bidding process and the review of bids.

## Productive reflection

The third approach to reflection emphasizes the dual goals of productivity and quality of working life. 'Reflection is far from being an isolating act of solely personal benefit, it is a key to learning to improve production and to making life at work more satisfying' (Boud et al., 2006: 2). The aim of productive reflection is to balance the needs and ambitions of customers, investors and personnel through learning, competence development, creativity and innovation. In this sense, the focus for reflection is the learning potential of work itself, and the development and implementation of collective learning activities that change work practices to enhance productivity and to underpin improvements in personal engagement and meaning in work. Such changes include reflective practices that underpin the decentralization of management, the flattening of hierarchies, broadening employee capacity, and critical engagement in quality enhancement.

Productive reflection has similar goals to public reflection. Both public reflection and productive reflection signify a shift from the individual to the collective level of reflection and they are concerned with building on and embedding critical reflection in organizations. However, while public reflection is concerned with situating reflection in the political complexities of organizations and transforming authority relations, productive reflection focuses on how competence is distributed inside companies and the processes of monitoring and intervention that are constructed to link competence to productivity and work satisfaction (Boud et al., 2006). Productive reflection asks for the creation of collective links into the production process in any given workplace. It seeks to be generative, both in relation to work outcomes and personnel, recognizing that people within organizations can be active in both work and learning.

The key elements in productive reflection are an organizational rather than individual intent and a collective rather than individual orientation. Reflection is necessarily contextualized in work and therefore reflective practices should not be considered separately from the situation and organizational purposes for which they are used. This means that actual practices will vary greatly from organization to organization and that companies will create distinctive reflective practices that emerge from and further inform their own knowledge about what they do and how to improve both knowledge and production. Productive reflection is an organizing process, and reflection is not confined to any one group in an organization (e.g., the HR Department), but rather makes use of the distributed expertise within the organization, a form of expertise that is too often ignored or undervalued. Reflection is not seen as something that can be operationalized in the service of management approaches or techniques, nor is it seen as a process that can be controlled in order to lead towards pre-directed outcomes. Rather, productive reflection has a developmental character with an intention to build agency among participants; to promote confidence that they can act together in meaningful ways; and that they can develop their own repertoire of approaches to meet future challenges. Productive reflection sees reflection as an open, unpredictable process, it is dynamic (it is likely to change over time) and it is unlikely that it can be turned into 'formal interventions to improve learning at work' (Boud et al., 2006: 167).

However, an example of productive reflection that is based on intervention can be found in Gherardi and Poggio (2006). The authors worked with a large local authority organization in Northern Italy. The organization had invited them to design their in-house training for women managers to improve female leadership. The training was delivered as four, five-day workshops, addressing themes that represented the core of leadership (rationality, control, decision making, strategic thinking) 'and their opposite'. These 'opposite' themes included: 'leadership's relationship with power, recognition of its conflictual dimensions, the importance of learning to recognize and understand emotions connected with the exercise of authority' (p. 186). The authors used narratives to stimulate memory of experiences; they asked participants to develop their own narratives of their experience as women leaders; and then to engage with these narratives collectively.

They used this narrative process as critical reflection on the politics of knowledge. Therefore,

> reflection and group analysis of situations in which the participants wielded authority in organizations furnish occasions for self-knowledge which involves not only the cognitive, cultural and affective dimensions of the individuals concerned but also the strategic and structural ones of the organization. The main assumption within productive reflection is that the group is a crucial learning resource because it enables different experiences to be shared and compared. (p. 186)

In this process, narrative encouraged the development of 'retrospective glance' at what might have been created in previous experience, but not yet noticed. They found that this process of reflection was productive for the individuals involved because it provided the reflective space for remembering within the context of the collective experience of women leaders within organizational power relations. They also identified an organizational process relating to knowledge productivity; that it is necessary for organizations to support a style of intervention that is by its nature critical of the status quo.

## Organizing reflection

The final approach to reflection we highlight is 'organizing reflection' (Vince, 2002; Reynolds and Vince, 2004b). The notion of organizing reflection emerged from a critique of the current theory and practice of reflection. It is similar to the other approaches we have mentioned, based on critical and collective reflection rather than individual reflective practice. Organizing reflection supports a shift from a view of reflection as a key element of individual learning and the application of learning, and towards a view of reflection as an organizing process, one that takes account of social and political processes at work in the organization of reflection in the workplace. In particular, this approach argues for the transformation of implicit approaches to reflection in organizations, where the responsibility for reflection is often located with the individual, either to do it for her/himself (when there's time), or to be responsible for the review of other individuals' performance, mostly in relation to people within subordinate roles. Less emphasis would be placed on reflection as the task of individuals, and more emphasis on creating collective and organizationally focused processes for reflection. The question that organizations face therefore is not only how the collective knowledge generated through organizing can be captured and utilized through reflection, but also, what are the emotional and political processes in the organization that prevent or severely limit processes of reflection?

An example of an attempt at 'organizing reflection' can be found in Nicolini et al. (2004). The authors' intervention linked action learning sets and whole-system change conferences. It was designed in order to explore how reflection might be understood as a stable and self-sustaining feature of organizing, and they focused particularly on the problem of addressing 'the power conditions that would allow the result of reflection to be implemented to produce organizational effects' (p. 87). Their project, with middle managers in a UK Health Authority, emphasized two levels on which reflection can be organized and addressed. First, in addition to creating several Reflection Action Learning Sets (RALS) for individual managers, they also built in the ability to mobilize dialogue between sets. They call this interaction between sets 'the structure that reflects'. Second, this organizing structure of reflection provided the agenda from which to engage with key decision makers within three 'whole-system change conferences'. They refer to this as 'the structure that connects', a space where the outputs of reflective practices could be communicated and aired (publicly) in the presence of senior managers, and thereby linked to power conditions that might support the implementation of the results of reflection.

In this example, the authors tried to situate reflective practice overtly in the context of work-based power relations. They did

this initially by recognizing that there is an impact on organizational dynamics when action learning sets are brought together into 'a structure that reflects'. They then sought to air these collective reflections in the organization as a whole. The importance of this structure in terms of the relationship between reflection and power was emphasized when most of the key decision makers in the organization did not turn up to the large change conference. The authors realized that their intervention was itself a mirror of the organizational dynamics that they were attempting to challenge. It was built on an assumption that all organizational members (not directly involved in RALS) were part of a reflective process. They conclude:

> herein, lies a powerful practical lesson. Designing organizational reflection activities and promoting them in such a way that exempts the sponsors from being part of the reflective practices, deprives them of the experience of learning, and exposes a paradox of reflection being promoted at one level and denied at another. Inevitably, this will have practical repercussions and will be played out by the participants as they pick up and enact this inner contradiction. (p. 99)

Therefore, the authors integrate action learning and critical reflection and provide an example of how action learning, as an organizing process, can reveal, engage with *and* reproduce the various power relations that surround attempts to learn.

Organizational groups and sub-systems can be seen as a part of the process of making reflection 'public' and 'productive'. However, they are also environments where unexpressed and unconscious organizational dynamics are enacted to protect organizational members from the consequences of reflection. Reflection and the production of new knowledge and actions necessarily confront established ways of working, as well as habitual authority relations and leadership approaches. Complex emotional, social and political relations are mobilized when organizational members meet. Making at least some of these relations overt is one way to reflect on and to change the organizational dynamics that undermine rather than support reflection. One phrase which has been used of this approach to reflection is that it attempts to 'unsettle conventional practices' (Cunliffe and Easterby-Smith, 2004) through a reflexive perspective on the interplay between learning and organizing. Organizing reflection is linked explicitly to notions of reflexivity. We will not discuss the notion of reflexivity further here, since Ann Cunliffe covers this subject fully in Chapter 21 of this volume. There is an important overlap between the chapters on reflection and reflexivity, and we would encourage the reader to engage with both chapters in order to understand the future study of reflection.

## SUMMARY: THE CRITIQUE AND DEVELOPMENT OF REFLECTION

In this final section of the chapter we summarize and present the four approaches we have outlined as a combined response to the future development of the theory and practice of reflection. In the previous section we addressed what is distinctive about these approaches to reflection. However, we also think of them as a complementary set of ideas, which together comprise a new perspective on reflection, one that we expect to make

an impact both in theory and in practice (Figure 5.1).

Theories and approaches to critical reflection provide a conceptual base from which to develop reflection beyond the reflective practitioner. Critical reflection involves the (outward) questioning of discourses implicit in the procedures, practices and structures which make up professional and organizational work. The key shift implied in critical reflection is from a concern with individuals' ability or responsibility to reflect within an organizational context, towards collective responsibility for reflective practice on organizing assumptions and practices. In addition to their physical and rational structures, organizations are built and maintained (emotionally, politically and relationally) from, for example, habits and attachments, established ways of working, rules and routines, political imperatives, techniques for compliance and demands for consensus. A critical perspective emphasizes the importance of collective reflection on emotional, moral, social and political as well as material considerations. The function of such reflection is to improve reflexive capabilities within organizations, to ensure that organization can create 'structures that reflect' (Nicolini et al., 2004) and to create the possibility of 'unsettling' established ways

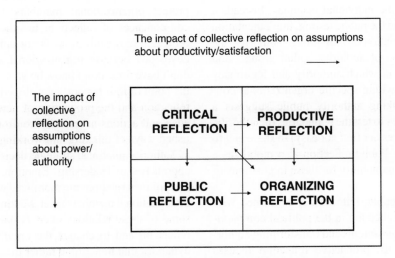

**Figure 5.1   The Organization of reflection: beyond the reflective practitioner**

of working in support of change (Cunliffe: Chapter 21, this volume).

Critical reflection implies a collective orientation towards the questioning of assumptions. However, the idea of continuously questioning the assumptions that underpin organizing/organization is an impractical notion unless it is targeted at key aspects of organizing. Two of these have been identified in the literature as 'public reflection' (questioning assumptions about power/authority relations) and 'productive reflection' (questioning assumptions about the relationship between productivity and work satisfaction). Public reflection encourages engagement with those others who are similarly caught up in the distinctive political processes that organizing creates, thereby seeking to make such processes both visible and subject to change. Reflection 'in public' makes the questioning of assumptions more likely because the act of giving voice to underlying assumptions can make them contestable. However, the extent to which organizational power relations allow assumptions to be contested varies considerably within different organizational contexts. Public reflection explicitly acknowledges the role of difference and dissent in improvement, and thereby seeks to offer an expanded view of authority relations. Authority is not a feature of individual behaviour or character, nor is it contained within the role that the individual occupies. Instead, it arises from the public testing, implementation and negotiation of individuals' authority; the negotiation of authority within groups; and the ways in which authority and legitimacy combine within specific organizational contexts. Making authority public suggests a willingness to test the boundaries of authority, making it easier (but not easy) to share and to distribute. Public reflection also mobilizes a wider accountability for those in positions of authority.

While public reflection is concerned with situating reflection in the political complexities of organizations and transforming authority relations, productive reflection focuses on how knowledge/competence is distributed inside companies and the processes of monitoring and intervention that are constructed to link competence to productivity and work satisfaction. Productive reflection is generated from some key questions. For example: how does an organization make use of the existing knowledge produced through established ways of working when 'we don't have time to reflect'? How can expertise be distributed throughout an organization when organizational members have to compete for resources? What collective practices for reflection can be developed to promote collaboration between organizational members and confidence in the legitimacy of individual and collective voice? Productive reflection has a general aim, which is to maximize the learning potential of work by asking such questions. Learning might be available to individuals as part of collective activity, but also may be organizational in nature, having an impact on established learning mechanisms as well as creating new ones. In addition, the aim of productive reflection is to tie together collective processes of reflection on what and how productivity is achieved, with the search for ways of improving people's work satisfaction.

Organizing reflection adds another dimension, which is that organizations are often environments where reflection is ignored or unwanted; where unexpressed and unconscious organizational dynamics are enacted to remove opportunities to reflect or to protect organizational members from the consequences of reflection. In other words, reflection in organizations is not only poorly developed because organizational members don't have time, don't know how, or don't see the point of it. It is poorly developed because reflection and the production of new knowledge and actions necessarily confront established ways of thinking and working, as well as authority relations, strategic decisions and approaches to leadership. Emotional, social and political relations are mobilized whenever organizational members meet. Making at least some of these relations overt is one way to reflect on and to change the organizational dynamics that undermine rather than support reflection. Organizing reflection is an attempt to link collective reflection with thinking about the impact of reflexivity in organizations. In Figure 5.1, 'organizing reflection' is shown as feeding back into critical reflection because it has helped both to critique and elaborate the concept in the organizational context.

## CONCLUSION

The evolution of the theory and practice of reflection can be seen to represent a crucial shift in the importance attached to reflection as looking 'back' into something past. Based on the work of John Dewey, earliest interpretations emphasized the importance of reflection in learning, and in particular in learning from experience, as a means of preparation for living and working in a society characterized by democratic values. Later developments placed more emphasis on the role of history and context in influencing an individual's growing sense of identity – including the assumptions and perspectives which they used to make sense of experience and to plan future action. Theoretically and practically therefore, these developments reflect the transition from a purely psychological perspective on reflection and learning, to one in which context and history are seen as factors which shape and influence learning, to the perspective represented in this chapter, which is of the individual inseparable from history and context, shaping and being shaped by the discursive practices which comprise life and work within communities and the workplace.

We observed at the start of the previous section that the four developments of reflection we have summarized share common ground and together constitute a distinctive contemporary approach to both the theory of reflection and reflective practice. Our final thoughts are about how our understanding of reflection links explicitly to Management Learning, Education and Development.

Firstly, in management and business schools there are implications for which knowledge is counted as authoritative because it has been authorised. Critical perspectives are a central element in the academic tradition, but as proponents of CMS point out, not always shared by management schools. In the same way that public reflection in an organizational context would focus on authority relationships, we as educators should be prepared to examine authority relations in the classroom, as well as the ways we teach leadership and help managers and management students understand power relations at work. This, reflexively, means that through public reflection leaders' accountability is given more emphasis, whether in the workplace or in the management school programme. Secondly, productive reflection means examining and being accountable for, the relationship between the outcome of an enterprise, whether at work or in education, and its relationship to satisfaction and work–life balance. These also are issues that as teachers we are perhaps more inclined to research and theorize than to apply to our own 'workplace'.

In the context of organizations, reflection in its different but related aspects should be an essential part of the day-to-day life of managers, not a disconnected, separate activity but an integral part of learning, supported by structures and the culture of the workplace, affecting decisions and choices, policies and activities and the politics and emotion associated with them. In this way to be reflective is not a technique, learned and sometimes applied, but part of what it means to be a manager. We believe that in this way organizing reflection represents both a critique and a development of 'critical' reflection in elaborating the practical ways it can be applied – both at work and in management education programmes. Our responsibility is to research and develop the practice of organizing reflection, to find examples of it at work, and to be able to see these processes reflected in our pedagogy.

## NOTES

1 For recent developments in experiential learning in management education see Reynolds and Vince, (2007).

2  See Kayes (2002) for an extended discussion and critique of these positions.

3  For a development and application of these principles see Reynolds and Vince (2004a).

# REFERENCES

Alvesson, M. and Willmott, H. (eds) (1992) *Critical Management Studies*. London: Sage.

Boud, D., Cressey, P. and Docherty, P. (eds) (2006) *Productive Reflection at Work*. London: Routledge.

Cunliffe, A.L. (2001) 'Managers as practical authors: Reconstructing our understanding of management practice', *Journal of Management Studies*, 38 (3): 351–71.

Cunliffe, A.L. and Easterby-Smith, M. (2004) 'From reflection to practical reflexivity: Experiential learning as lived experience', in M. Reynolds and R. Vince (eds), *Organizing Reflection*. Aldershot: Ashgate.

Dehler, G. (1998) '"Relevance" in management research: A critical reappraisal', *Management Learning*, 29: 69–89.

Dewey, J. (1916) *Democracy and Education*. New York: Macmillan.

Elliott, C. and Reynolds, M. (2002) 'Manager-educator relations from a critical perspective', *Journal of Management Education*, 26: 512–26.

Fournier, V. and Grey, C. (2000) 'At the critical moment: Conditions and prospects for critical management studies', *Human Relations*, 53 (1): 7–32.

French, R. and Grey, C. (eds) (1996) *Rethinking Management Education*. London: Sage.

Gherardi, S. and Poggio, B. (2006) 'Feminist challenges to mainstream leadership through collective reflection and narrative', in D. Boud, P. Cressey and P. Docherty, (eds), *Productive Reflection at Work*. London: Routledge.

Gibson, R. (1986) *Critical Theory and Education*. London: Hodder & Stoughton.

Gold, J., Holman, D. and Thorpe, R. (2002) 'The role of argument analysis and story telling in facilitating critical thinking', *Management Learning*, 33 (3): 371–88.

Habermas, J. (1973) *Theory and Practice*. Boston: Beacon Press.

Hindmarsh, J.H. (1993) 'Tensions and dichotomies between theory and practice: A study of alternative formulations', *International Journal of Lifelong Education*, 12 (2): 101–15.

Kayes, D.C. (2002) 'Experiential learning and its critics: Preserving the role of experience in management learning and education', *Academy of Management Learning and Education*, 1 (2): 137–49.

Kets de Vries, M.F.R. and Balazs, K. (1998) 'Beyond the quick fix: The pychodynamics of organizational transformation and change', *European Management Journal*, 16 (5): 611–22.

Knowles, M. (1984) *The Adult Learner: A Neglected Species*. Houston: Gulf.

Kolb, D.A. (1984) *Experiential Learning: Experience as the Source of Learning and Development*. Englewood Cliffs, NJ: Prentice-Hall.

Lindeman, E. (1935) 'The place of discussion in the learning process', in S. Brookfield (ed.) (1987), *Learning Democracy: Eduard Lindeman on Adult Education and Social Change*. London: Croom Helm.

Lindeman, E. (1947) 'Methods of democratic adult education', in S. Brookfield (ed.), (1987), *Learning Democracy: Eduard Lindeman on Adult Education and Social Change*. London: Croom Helm.

Nicolini, D., Sher, M. Childerstone, S. and Gorli, M. (2004) 'In search of the "Structure that Reflects": Promoting organizational reflection practices in a UK health authority', in M. Reynolds and R. Vince (eds), *Organizing Reflection*. Aldershot: Ashgate.

Perriton, L.J. (2004) 'A reflection of what exactly? Questioning the use of "critical" reflection in management education contexts', in M. Reynolds and R. Vince (eds), *Organizing Reflection*. Aldershot: Ashgate.

Perriton, L.J. (2007) 'Really useful knowledge? Critical management education in the UK and the US', *Scandinavian Journal of Management*, 23: 66–83.

Raelin, J.A. (2001) 'Public reflection as the basis of learning', *Management Learning*, 32 (1): 11–30.

Reynolds, M. (1998) 'Reflection and critical reflection in management learning', *Management Learning*, 29 (2): 183–200.

Reynolds, M. (1999) 'Grasping the nettle: Possibilities and pitfalls of a critical management pedagogy', *British Journal of Management*, 10 (2): 171–84.

Reynolds, M. and Vince, R. (2004a) 'Critical management education and action-based learning: Synergies and contradictions', *Academy of Management Learning and Education*, 3 (4): 442–56.

Reynolds, M. and Vince, R. (eds) (2004b) *Organizing Reflection*. Aldershot: Ashgate.

Reynolds, M. and Vince, R. (eds) (2007) *Handbook of Experiential Learning and Management Education*. Oxford: Oxford University Press.

Schön, D.A. (1983) *The Reflective Practitioner: How Professionals Think in Action*. London: Maurice Temple Smith.

Schön, D.A. (1987) *Educating the Reflective Practitioner*. San Francisco: Jossey-Bass.

Trehan, K. and Rigg, C. (2007) 'Working with experiential learning: A critical perspective in practice', in M. Reynolds and R. Vince (eds), *Handbook of Experiential Learning and Management Education*. Oxford: Oxford University Press.

Usher, R.S. (1985) 'Beyond the anecdotal: Adult learning and the use of experience', *Studies in the Education of Adults*, 7 (1): 59–74.

Vince, R. (1998) 'Behind and beyond Kolb's learning cycle', *Journal of Management Education*, 22 (3): 304–19.

Vince, R. (2002) 'Organizing reflection', *Management Learning*, 33 (1): 63–78.

Vince, R. (2004) *Rethinking Strategic Learning*. London: Routledge.

Vince, R. and Saleem, T. (2004) 'The impact of caution and blame on organizational learning', *Management Learning*, 35 (2): 131–52.

Willmott, H. (1997) 'Making learning critical: Identity, emotion, and power in processes of management development', *Systems Practice*, 10 (6): 749–71.

# 6

# Critical Management Education Beyond the Siege

David M. Boje and Khadija Al Arkoubi

## Abstract

Management education has been dominated by managerialism and its underlying assumptions (rationality, efficiency, performativity, control, objectivity, etc.). Although some management scholars have denounced management orthodoxies and have provided illuminating critiques of business curricula and their ingrained pedagogies, their efforts have yet to achieve the promised emancipatory journey for educators, students, and citizens. *Critical Management Education* (CME) is at impasse, unable to liberate management teaching from the siege of managerialist capitalism, and the corporatization and deskilling of the university. While we recognize the many challenges facing CME, we outline and explain its tenets and offer some ideas on how they can be translated into practice.

## INTRODUCTION

*Critical Management Education (CME)* arose in the 1990s (Perriton and Reynolds, 2004) to counter the managerialist orientation in business schools. Managerialism is an ideology of performativity (work until you drop), efficiency (people defined as expendable resources), and commitment to short-term, bottom-line decision criteria. CME questions these ethical assumptions, and seeks to liberate management education to be more inclusive of a variety of stakeholder voices and a myriad of issues, including the environment, labor, community, multiculturalism, racial/ethnic diversity, and social concerns.

CME rebels against the positivist, dogmatic management education models and is well grounded in the social and moral roles of education. Although it has been influenced by a number of academic disciplines including Critical Theory (CT), critical theory (ct lowercase),[1] Critical Pedagogy (CP) and Critical Management Studies (CMS), it is still searching for its soul.

CT can be defined as the theories and methods of the Frankfurt School between 1923 and end of World War II. 'ct' (lowercase) typically refers to subsequent critical theories, theorists, and methods originated since the 1970s. CP stands for the branch of education known as Critical Pedagogy, initiated by Paulo Freire in the 1960s. CMS (Critical Management Studies) is a branch of scholarship that is informed by CT, ct, and most recently by CP. CMS has led to writers and teachers developing texts and materials for Critical Management Education (CME).

In this chapter, we first offer an historical overview on CME drawing from its philosophical grounds reflected in the Frankfurt School Critical Theory (known as CT) (*Zeitschrift für Sozialforschung, 1932–1939*), and later work, in contemporary 'critical theory' 'ct'. Second, we propose closer alliance of CT, ct, and critical pedagogy, 'CP'. Third, we explore the meaning of *critical,* in CT, ct and CP, and *critical thinking* approaches that are prominent in managerialism. Fourth, we explicate tenets of CME such as, ethics of answerability, commitment to emancipation/transformation, diffusion of power in the classroom, promotion of multiculturalism, and the belief in multidisciplinary approaches. Finally, we identify some challenges of CME and offer suggestions on how these may be faced.

## FOUNDATIONS OF CRITICAL MANAGEMENT EDUCATION (CME)

### Critical Theory (CT): the Frankfurt School

CT designates the philosophy, theory, and practice of the directors and associates of the Frankfurt School Institute for Social Research. Boje (2007a) asserts that there were three phases: the inception, the aestheticization of critical theory, and the search for enlightenment.

### Phase 1 of CT: the inception

In the First Phase of CT, Theodor Wiesengraund Adorno and Max Horkheimer were directors of the Frankfurt School Institute for Social Research. Besides Adorno and Horkheimer, Walter Benjamin, Erich Fromm, Henry Gossmann, Arkadij Gurland, Otto Kirchheimer, Leo Lowenthal, Herbert Marcuse, Franz Newmann, Freidrich Pollock, and successor Jürgen Habermas are recognized as the main figures of CT. The Frankfurt School was founded in Frankfurt in 1923, but it was Horkheimer's directorship after 1931 that gave it prominence. Horkheimer and Adorno focused on an empirical and historically ground interdisciplinary research program to overcome the inadequacies of Hegelian, Marxist, and Kantian theories. Horkheimer's (1974) *Critique of Instrumental Reason* (a collection of his writings from mid-40s to 1967) asserted that business goals once achieved become instrumental means to new goals, and that this progression is without ethical moorings. Reason without spiritual (transcendentally reflexive) substance becomes the curse of science made into technology instrumentally deployed by business and public administration. Horkheimer (1974) for a time thought that CT would, after Nazism's defeat, begin a new day of 'authentically human history' brought about by 'reforms or revolution.' Yet new forms of dictatorship emerged.

Adorno and Horkheimer are particularly critical of Immanuel Kant's (1781) '*Kritik der reinen Vernunft*' (*Critique of Pure Reason*). There was hope that the Enlightenment could be salvaged in critical interdisciplinary projects. Horkheimer's (1933) essay '*Materialismus und Moral*' (*Materialism and Morality*) is the first CT materialist critique of Kantian ethics. Horkheimer (1933/1993: 25) points out how the Kantian doctrine of the categorical imperative anticipates the end of morality, and helps it along by making a 'distinction between interest and duty.' Adorno (1963/2000) talks about it as the distinction between Kant's ethics of conviction, and an ethics of responsibility. Boje (2007a) argues that industrial revolution gave way to the post-industrial revolution of late modern capitalism, Kant's writings on Moral Philosophy have been transformed to achieve currency in a field known as 'Business Ethics' in the Academy of Management, and Public Administration Ethics, in the Academy of Public Administration. Horkheimer's (1933/1993: 25) critique is the basis for an ethics of responsibility. Horkheimer's challenge is how can any 'society of isolated individuals' acting with ethics of conviction bring about meaningful change in the social order (Horkheimer, 1933/1993: 25)? At the close of the first phase of CT, it was business as usual for the capitalist and Marxist-inspired states: exploitation reined. Horkheimer's and Adorno's (June 1947) introduction could well be describing our contemporary situation. Public opinion has become a commodity, which is manipulated to keep attention away from depravation and oppression by language manipulations.

## Phase 2 of CT: the aestheticization of critical theory

The Second Phase of CT (1947–1970) began with Adorno and Horkheimer's (1944) *Dialectic of Enlightenment*. It is regarded as a turning point in CT implying the aesthetic critique of the Culture Industry. The Nazi fascism of World War II left them disillusioned about the prospects for any positive program of empirical interdisciplinary study. Clearly, their goal of ultimate emancipation from fascism lies elsewhere than scientific Enlightenment. They turned to more Weberian and Nietzchean skepticism to contend with the dark reality of post World War II. In particular, Phase 2 work indicates a distrust of state and corporate control over the culture industry. Adorno (1963/2000: 170) ends his series of 1963 lectures by declaring, 'There is no ethics [...] in the administered world.' Adorno says he owes Nietzsche 'the greatest debt' for his skepticism (p. 172).

The second phase was characterized by the critique of the mass culture that is in reality embedded in an elitist hierarchical society where privileged people prevail culturally and socially. Both Adorno and Horkheimer were working with an 'inner circle' composed of Marcuse, Lowenthal, Fromm and Benjamin. This circle initiated some of the most critical analyses of ideology ever produced (Kellner, 1990). Having the intention to promote transition towards socialism, scholars under this circle denigrated capitalist ideologies in research and theory. They attacked mass culture, such as literature, music, magazines, films, TV, radio, etc. and other artifacts of the culture industry. They also fostered the necessity of developing the sociology of mass culture and were persuaded that cultural phenomena are the translation and reflection of the whole socio-economic structure. In fact, according to Adorno and Horkheimer, a theory of culture should involve the processes of production, reproduction, distribution, exchange and consumption (Held, 1980).

## Phase 3 of CT: the search for enlightenment

The third Phase of CT (1970–1980s) is characterized by the leadership of Jürgen Habermas. We would argue that Habermas has turned the clock back to redeem the First Phase of CT. Habermas seeks the Enlightenment ideal, an emancipatory potential attainable by neo-Kantian moral philosophy applied to social science. This can be seen in Habermas' communicative ethics. More recently Habermas picks up on Luhmann, as well as Parsons in a turn that can only be described as structural functionalist system theory. The result is that whereas Horkheimer and Adorno (as well as Fromm and Marcuse) were moving away from formal, absolutist, universalistic ethics to one that Bakhtin (1990, 1993) calls an ethics of answerability, Habermas is headed to the other direction. He fearlessly criticized positivism and its contribution to the 'technocratization' of the social consciousness. He turned his back to the methodology of the exact sciences and based his work on hermeneutics (interpretive methodology of human sciences). He believed that critical theory of society is capable of ensuring order, reason, truth and justice. Following Kant's position, Habermas pointed out that moral obligation requires that we always give up our selfish interests when they clash with universal ones (Ingram, 1987). However, his discourse on ethics has shifted away from Kant's categorical imperative into moral argumentation. The latter suggests that the *sine qua non* condition for a norm to be valid is its satisfaction of everyone's interests. Therefore, unlike Kant, who promoted a monological and solitary consciousness, Habermas concentrated on a collective moral consciousness characterized by perspective-taking and inclusion of the community interests (Habermas, 1991).

In sum, CT stands for the three phases of theory and research of the Frankfurt School founders and associates. Each phase has its characteristics and pioneers. While there are disagreements, all converge in the pursuit of social justice and a critique of managerialist approaches to capitalism.

## CONTEMPORARY CRITICAL THEORY (CT)

It is important to develop the current directions in 'ct' that were ignored by the Frankfurt School CT. Critical theory (ct) has given credentials to the feminist movement and is characterized by women's contributions. In fact, one of the major problems with CT is its lack of female scholarship. For example, Adorno, Horkheimer, and key male associates, including Walter Benjamin, Henry Gossmann, Arkadij Gurland, Eric Fromm (often excluded by CT historians), Otto Kirchheimer, Leo Lowenthal, Herbert Marcuse, Franz Newmann, and Freidrich Pollock, and successor Habermas dominated CT. With little ct there has been more female authorship. However, several feminists have contributed not usually cited in 'ct' reviews: Susan Bordo, Judith Butler, Hélène Cixous, Donna Haraway, Lucé Irigaray, and Julia Kristeva (see Boje, 2007b for a review).

Over the decades there has been an increase in feminist ct scholarship, beginning with Calás and Smircich (1996) and Townley (1993, 1994). The critical theory (ct) has resulted in the movement of 'Critical Management Studies' (CMS) that focuses more superficially on gender as well as ethnic and racial diversity, postcolonialism, and multiculturalism. A complete review is beyond the scope of this chapter, as the literature is so prolific that we can barely scratch the surface.

The 'ct' writing began its inroad into management studies in the 1970s with focus on new-Marxism, hegemony, and labor process (Benson, 1977; Braverman, 1974; Gramsci, 1971; Wood and Kelley, 1978), expanded in the 1980s, broke loose in the 1990s with the growing application of Foucault's work, and the 2000s taking more focus on narrative, discourse, and rediscovering CT ethics (see the list below for more information on the scholars who contributed to ct in the 1980s, 1990s and 2000s). This emphasis shows the proliferation and the growing impact of 'ct' on all disciplines, including management education.

In sum, what is occurring now is some resurgence of interest in difference in early phases of CT, and implications of ct scholarship in gender, diversity, and multiculturalism. In addition, there is now interdisciplinary work to develop a more Critical Pedagogy (CP). We explore these conditions next.

## CRITICAL MANAGEMENT EDUCATION (CME) AND ALLIANCE OF CT, *ct* AND CRITICAL PEDEGOGY (CP)

We would like to acknowledge and encourage the growing intertwinement of CMS with CP. From the 1970s through the early 1990s, CMS and CP have remained separate disciplines, with a paucity of cross-citation. All roads of CP lead to Paulo Freire (1972).

CP is grounded in the struggle for social justice, democracy, and the most humane precepts of life. Paulo Freire, the father of CP,

**Table 6.1   Development of 'ct' in recent decades[1]**

| Decades | Key areas | Pioneers |
|---|---|---|
| 1980s | Critique of capitalism; managerial bias in accounting; doing critical management research methods | Clegg (1981, 1989); Clegg and Dunkerley (1980); Ferguson (1984); Jermier (1985); Knights and Willmott (1986a,b, 1988, 1989); Knights et al. (1985); Littler (1982, 1984); McCarthy (1981); Steffy and Grimes (1986); Shor (1980). Thompson (1989); Tinker (1985); Willmott and Knights (1989). |
| 1990s | Managerialism in TQM; critical storytelling; critical human relations | Adler (1990); Adler et al. (2006); Alvesson (1990); Boje (1995); Boje and Dennehy (1993); Boje and Winsor (1993); Calás (1993, 1994); Calás and Smircich (1991, 1993, 1999); Collins (1995); Deetz (1992); Forester (1993); Fulop and Linstead (1999); Hardy and Clegg (1996); Hassard et al. (1998, 1999); Jermier (1998); Jermier et al. (1994); Parker (1999); Thompson (1990); Townley (1993, 1994); Willmott (1993, 1998) |
| 2000s | Racial and ethnic diversity; spectacles of capitalism | Boje (2000; 2001a–c; 2002, 2004, 2006, 2007a–e, 2008); Boje and Al Arkoubi, (2005); Boje and Cai, (2004, 2005); Boje et al. (2005); Boje et al. (1999); Boje and Rosile, (2003); Delbridge (2006); Edwards and Collinson (2002); Hassard et al. (2001); Hassard et al. (2000); Knights and Willmott (2000, 2007) ; Knights et al. (2003); Mills et al. (2006); Mills et al. (2005); Parker (2002); Prasad (2003); Thompson and McHugh (2002); Thompson and Newsome (2004); Thompson and Smith (2001); Tinker (2002); Vurdubakis, and Willmott (2001); Willmott (2003, 2005). |

[1] The references in this table can be found at http://business.nmsu.edu/~dboje/655/CMS_guide.htm. We apologize for leaving anyone's work out. See also Academy of Management CMS interest group http://group.aomonline.org/cms/Resources/Bibliography/cmsbib.htm.

regarded education as a way to transform and liberate the human kind. He fought against oppression and sought to develop students who are capable of taking actions and changing their own realities. At the heart of the Freirean philosophy is the courage to alter one's own identities in a sharp contradiction with the dominating, oppressing and widely held assumptions. Therefore, students are always exhorted to develop subject positions and act as critical analysts and change agents.

In terms of Critical Management Pedagogy (CMP) we will limit our review to commentaries on critical theory reforms in management education and the university. CMS has just begun to develop its own teaching texts, and pedagogy materials. In fact, since the 1990s, critical theorists (i.e. Alvesson and Deetz, 2000; Alvesson and Willmott, 1992, 1996; Boje, 1994, 1996; Ehrensal, 2001; Fenwick, 2001, 2005; Humphries and Dyer, 2005; Grey, 2004; French and Grey, 1996; Grey and Mitev, 1995; Humphries and Dyer, 2005; Monaghan, 2001; Parker and Jary, 1995; Reed, 2002; Reynolds, 1999;

Summers et al., 1997; Thompson, 2005; Willmott, 1997) started to demystify the role of educational institutions, especially business schools, as agents of regulation and control of organizations and people. They denounced the utilitarian and technical trend in knowledge transfer and the focus on a purely positivistic worldview. They also deplored the prevailing wave of celebrating capitalism, shareholders' profit maximization, and enforcement of managers' hegemony in the educational act. For them, schools should be deemed the sites of critical learning, and social, political, and cultural emancipation. Schools are supposed to prepare critical citizens, who can voice their opinions with courage, and otherwise challenge the embedded assumptions of instrumental society.

The CMS movement is heavily influenced by Freire's (1972) CP, which according to Perriton and Reynolds (2004: 108) still deserves further attention:

> Critical pedagogy [...] is a minority and marginalized activity within management education that

deserves to be more widely recognized and adopted. Although there has been a proliferation of literature on management learning, especially in terms of techniques of teaching, the efforts of critical pedagogues in ME have rarely been articulated and consequently we suspect their practice probably occurs in a fragmented and ad hoc manner.

As with CMS, CP took off in the 1970s with work by Stanley Aronowitz (1973, 1977; Aronowiz and Giroux, 1985), developed in the 1980s, and the 1990s, Henry Giroux (1991); bell hooks (1994), Peter McLaren (1995), and Maxine Greene (1996). Unlike CT, there is more early reference by CP to critical feminist work by Hannah Arendt (1959). In the main, ct will cite some of the same CT scholars, such as Habermas (1972) and Marcuse (1966), and in ct work by Braverman (1974). There seems less CP focus on work by Horkheimer, Adorno, or Fromm.

The focus in CP is on taking back the classroom from predatory capitalism. Accordingly, Aronowitz and Giroux (1991: 76) have regarded schools as 'places where a sense of identity, worth, and possibility is organized through the interaction among teachers, students, and texts'. At the heart of this process lies the andragogy (the theory of adult learning as developed by Malcolm Knowles) to be embraced. The latter should reinforce the perception of schools as 'democratic public spheres' where administrators, students and teachers play the role of 'public intellectuals' who continuously challenge the existing assumptions in an attempt to expand 'civic courage', and permanently transform public life (Aronowitz and Giroux, 1991).

While unfolding our story of CT, ct, and CP, one cannot ignore Ghoshal's outcry against teaching bad management theories and their moral implications on management practice: 'our theories and ideas have done much to strengthen the management practices that we are all now so loudly condemning' (Ghoshal, 2005: 75). More than that, Ghoshal suggests that 'by propagating ideologically inspired amoral theories, business schools have actively freed their students from any sense of moral responsibility' (p. 76).

One hears echoes of Horkheimer and Adorno. Therefore, there are problematic issues in management education that one cannot deny. These include for instance, encountering students who are deprived from sense of ethics and do not recognize their roles in their communities or societies, the commodification of management education and the engagement of management academics in the game of sustaining educational models that promote management orthodoxies. Certainly one can point to corporatization of the university, with presidents and deans, demanding salaries like those of corporate CEOs, and turning the university into McUniversity, as common ground of CP and ct.

Does 'educational theory and practice stand at an impasse' as Giroux (1997: 71) claims? How can we liberate education from the siege (Aronowitz and Giroux, 1985) that many want purposefully or aimlessly to sustain?

Our story is still unraveling and we think it's time to raise questions for both ct and CP. First, we share with you our understanding of critical management education (CME) focusing mainly on its tenets and underlying assumptions. Second, we explore its content and andragogy, and finally we identify some of the challenges of CMS and CP, and offer some suggestions on how these may be faced.

## WHAT IS CRITICALITY?

When exploring the concept 'critical thinking' versus CT, ct, or CP, one must first be clear about the sense of the word 'critical'.

In conventional managerialism, critical may be viewed as arming students with problem-solving skills and training them to look for unconventional, even creative remedies to crises and difficulties they face in the business environment. In CMS or CP, on the other hand, being critical means students (and faculty) recognizing their agency as citizens, their complicity in systems of production and commodification in a world where 95 percent of the population of the world is

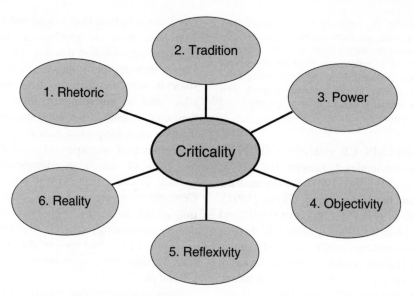

**Figure 6.1   Six dimensions of being critical**

below common poverty line designations for advanced corporate nations.

In this next section we adapt and extend Mingers (2000) specification of four dimensions of the meaning of critical, that is a skepticism towards rhetoric, tradition, power and objectivity. Besides these aspects we like to add two more elements: being critical towards oneself (reflexivity) and towards the reality where education takes place (see Figure 6.1). While some students may attain all these dimensions, their level of general criticality may vary according to the educational system they went through, their worldview, degree of maturation, dominant intellectual/epistemological paradigm and accumulated ontological experiences in life.

Rhetoric:   The critique of rhetoric or critical thinking is the simplest level that reflects the ability to assess others' arguments, opinions, and use of the language in a logical, abstract as well as reflective ways. This aspect is what business schools and management departments run after and try to promote in their educational systems. Although we recognize critical thinking as defined by Mingers (2000) as fundamental, we feel

compelled to add the term discourse with small 'd' and big 'D' (Alvesson and Karreman, 2000). Small 'd' discourse is talk and text in social contexts and practice. Big 'D' discourse is focused on broader cultural and historically situated language systems.

The term discourse has been vastly controvertible (Grant et al., 1998; Fairhurst, 2007). Whether it is a talk or a text, for us, discourse involves several ways of expression (speech, myth, story, essay, conversation, dialogue, account, metaphors, tropes, etc.) that require careful attention to be understood, analyzed, reflected upon, deconstructed and reconstructed. We don't include at this level of criticality Discourse with big 'D' which is a general system of thought developed in a particular historical time (Foucault, 1980) or 'critical Discourse' as in the work of Fairclough. We are somewhat suspicious of big 'D' and little 'd' as a duality, one we think that managerialism can continue to exploit, keeping 'critical thinking' confined to problem solving, while the source of problems are in the material conditions, and the logics of the political economy. It is the interaction between micro-discourse and macro-Discourse and the necessity for students to be able to engage in a critical (de)construction of knowledge and reality that we consider as essential for criticality.

**Tradition:**  Skepticism towards tradition or conventional wisdom infers challenging our deep assumptions and taken-for-granted attitudes and views about traditions and customs, whether they are embedded in organizations or are well rooted in societies concerning gender, race, ethnicity, and how the Other (e.g. individuals belonging to a minority) is treated. Often, it is easier in critical thinking to adhere to these common and majority held managerial or market forces values rather than critiquing or even opposing them because they are very much promoted by powerful groups and supported by the weight of the tradition. Does CMS dare to deconstruct them as a way of initiating change and overcoming the inertia of the status quo, right in the classroom, as is done routinely in CP?

**Power:**  In critical thinking, one is supposed to be skeptical of the one dominant view and seek a more Bakhtinian polyphony (multiple voices), and difference in meanings and perspectives (polysemy). In CP and CMS, de-power consists of teaching students that there is no one 'correct' answer, otherwise 'they will never dare to question the 'validity of their teachers' (Mingers, 2000: 226). And if they don't feel the courage to challenge teachers' authority and opinions in the academic setting, they will be deprived in the future from the power to think differently in their organizations or societies. More than that, they will easily accept oppression of their free will, ideas, individuality, and personal voice, etc. The result of critical thinking is submission to authority, to people in leadership, to teachers, etc. Conversely, learning to deal in a dialogic way with other perspectives is extremely critical and necessary for any growth process: 'We must share each other's excess in order to overcome our mutual lack' (Bakhtin, 1990: xxvi). Boje (2001a) called for a restitution that overcomes the cast of dualities, hierarchical thinking, and hegemonic reasoning. He emphasized the

need to hear from marginal voices (rebellious people, employees in the lowest ranks of the hierarchy, minorities, etc.).

**Objectivity:**  The final aspect of critical thinking according to Mingers (2000) is being skeptical of knowledge and objectivity. By contrast in CMS and CP, it is about recognizing that there is no value free knowledge and that the construction of knowledge and the processing of information are always subjective and subject to power structures and interest groups in particular context (Foucault, 1980; Freire, 1970). Which knowledge gets to be promoted and propagated and which one gets to be marginalized or even silenced depends heavily on political agendas. In the process of learning, Weick (2007: 6) suggests that we should focus on dropping our tools to gain wisdom. In critical thinking metaphor, story and trope are just tools for efficiency and performativity. He states: 'Learning to drop one's tools to gain lightness, agility, and wisdom tend to be forgotten in an era where leaders and followers alike are preoccupied with knowledge management reengineering (Boje, 2006), acquisitions and acquisitiveness. Nevertheless, human potential is realized as much by what we drop, as what we acquire.'

**Reflexivity:**  Being critical towards oneself entails first a capacity to develop an awareness of oneself at individual, relational and collective levels. Second, it requires an understanding of our present/actual self and the possible one (the one to which we aspire). One's level of reflexivity can heavily contribute to our transition towards the possible self and will always play a key role in our growth and transformation. Critical theory work by Ricoeur (1992) looks at how narrative identity is one of sameness being dialectic with selfhood. Identity stories (or narratives) solicit our obligation to take action, to recognize our connection of selfhood on a moral plane to others. In sameness identity there is a distancing, a standing back from the other, and the kinds of apathetic world we live in is the result. Without reflexivity, learning about selfhood in the world of others will be hindered. If one refuses or does not know how to be critical towards oneself, one will be unable to develop awareness about others. Critical thinking without reflexivity on one's selfhood, one's complicity, and solicitude to act when one encounters a story of other beings negatively affected our shared life on the plant. For Ricoeur (1992: 218–19), as with Adorno and Horkheimer, Kant's 'follow your maxim', falls short, in the individualist world.

Reality:    Critical thinking is not about context, especially not about one's citizenship in the world. CP is focused upon being skeptical towards the reality where education takes place. This means being fully aware of one's citizenship and one's role as a critical citizen. In CMS, questioning the structural factors influencing the general educational context becomes very relevant. These factors may include among others, historical, cultural, economic, social, and political facts that seem to be excluded in critical thinking. Critical thinking is too focused in small reality, what we call small 'r'. Small 'r' refers to students' own personal context as producers, consumers, and individuals complicit in global capitalism. The micro-little 'r' needs to be tightly related to the other Reality (with the big R) and reflect the different ways in which people are oppressed globally.

It is worth noting that all these six aspects of criticality are interwoven and they interact with each other in a strong way. From a CP or CMS perspective, we believe students need to develop a sufficient courage and skills to be active members in the act of constructing Reality (with a big 'R') by recognizing the complicity of small 'r'. No one of them can be seen in isolation of the others. Criticality is a whole that is beyond any dichotomies or dual thinking of CT and ct, big D and little d, and big R and little r. It is in the-in-between that the actions of solicitude and answerability take place, recognizing complicity of the selfhood in more dialectic relationship to the narratives of sameness. Nonetheless, one may develop different levels of competency related to each aspect of criticality. It is up to critical management and CP educators to develop teaching methods and content that help students acquire and improve their competency level pertaining to criticality dimensions.

Now that we have clarified our underlying assumptions regarding criticality, we shall elucidate what we consider as tenets of CME.

## TENETS OF CRITICAL MANAGEMENT EDUCATION

We offer five tenets of critical management education based upon the first three sections of our chapter (see Figure 6.2). These

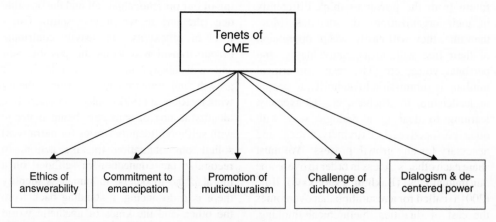

**Figure 6.2    Tenets of critical management education**

are: ethics of answerability, commitment to emancipation, promotion of multiculturalism, challenge of dichotomies and boundaries, and de-centered power. Each one of them is explained below. All of them are in line with the meaning of criticality exposed above and they have a common philosophical ground with CP and CMS.

## Ethics of answerability

Answerability is Bakhtin's term that implies responsibility and accountability of the individual towards self and the other. It is a whole philosophy of life and of the act that 'can only be a moral philosophy' (Bakhtin, 1993: 56). It is about authoring our answers through acts that reinforce ethics, question injustice, oppression, commodification of the society, and design new projects that create the potential for legitimizing and gratifying the deepest needs and desires of human beings. Answerability requires critical moral beings who have skillfully learned how to position themselves *vis-à-vis* immorality, how to courageously craft their ideas and actions to serve others in their societies. It is the greatest gift an educator may have because it is based on bravery, self-sacrifice and a permanent willingness to improve our social environment. It is very sad to notice though that the prevailing model of education does not encourage educators to be answerable or to promote a culture of answerability in their institutions. Boje (2006) states that: 'The problem with this line of ethical theory and practice is that it ignores the teachings of "ethic of answerability" to get involved and change the status quo, that it's impossible to lead the good moral life within a society or global capitalism that leads the bad moral life. For practical business purposes, contemporary Business Ethics and Public Administration Ethics endorse a *Supposed Right to Lie* and *a Right to Exploit.*'

Educators who transfer not only knowledge but also values seem to be complicit in disseminating amoral ideological beliefs (Ghoshal, 2005). They are fulfilling their roles as employees of business or management schools and act 'in a spirit of managerialism' (Watson, 1999: 3). Managerialism is founded on a technical view of organizations and regards management as a politically neutral/technical activity. Therefore, management education within this paradigm is 'the acquisition of techniques regardless of the context of their application' (Grey and Mitev, 1995: 74). Managers get the privilege to impose their worldview, enforce their control and come up with technical solutions to problems that are deeply grounded in issues related to power, race, class, gender, unfairness, human dignity, etc.

Cheit (1985: 50) reviewed more than 200 articles on MBA programs and codified all the critiques. His findings fall into four categories: programs emphasize the wrong model, ignore important work, fail to meet society's needs, and foster undesirable attitudes. A program's content is oftentimes more concentrated on control, efficiency and greater effectiveness that meet the demands of the accreditation requirements and fall under the wrong model of management education (Porter and McKibbin, 1988). The latter is heavily reliant on economics and quantitative methodologies that are far, most of the time, from handling complexity, uncertainty, uniqueness and value/power clashes (Schon, 1983). Conversely, managers need to be exposed as students and learners to ethical issues. They need to gain awareness about how their potential position, power, values, understandings of the world affect others' lives. In a similar vein, management academics have to be wholly conscientious of their impact on their students' ethical growth and answerability development.

Pfeffer (1997, 2005) called business academics to be solicitous towards the values they teach and warned them against turning universities into knowledge factories that are producing limited technical competencies without consideration of ethics that serve the society as whole. In CME, the responsibility of academics and scholars to educate should be regarded primarily as a moral imperative that is well embedded in the praxis of ethics.

## Commitment to emancipation and transformation

There is a strong belief in CME that learning and teaching should challenge the existing reality rather than sustain it (Grey and Mitev, 1995) and that historically the focal principle of CME has been the praxis (Fenwick, 2005; Freire, 1973). Commitment to this combination of reflexivity and social collective actions lies at the heart of individual and societal transformation: 'Indeed in the tradition of critical pedagogy, learning is a process through which personal and group consciousness are transfigured to unveil a world of oppression, through praxis, a dialectic of critical reflection and practical action, learners commit to its reform' (Grey and Mitev, 1995: 32). Unfortunately, in the dominant model of management education, functional analyses that address practical organizational problems are the ones that are more accepted while analyses that challenge the structural order (political, ethical, social, cultural, etc.) and question the philosophical underpinnings of organizations and management are deemed to be dangerous and are therefore avoided (Kellie, 2004; Pfeffer, 1997).

Nevertheless, historically, the original vision of Joseph Wharton when he endowed the business school at University of Pennsylvania was to ingrain management in the social fabric of people's life and seek their general well-being (Grey, 2004). This noble aim cannot be achieved without emancipating ourselves and our students from the rigidity of fixation, without challenging our believed truths, and without 'dropping our tools'. Weick (2007: 15) eloquently stated that 'your students are likely to remain among the sane if they learn to drop their tools, and you maintain your own lightness as you teach excellence'. Teaching excellence is teaching against rigidity, conformism and taken-for-granted assumptions. This may occur through creating a relaxed free atmosphere where students can feel liberated from all kinds of fear (academic/ideological, political, social, psychological, etc). Without this freedom (that we should initiate) in our academic institutions, it is less likely that our students become effective social agents in their communities. In the words of Palmer (1998: 19–20): 'Institutions reform slowly, and as long as we wait, depending on "them" to do the job for us – forgetting that institutions are also "us" – we merely postpone reform and continue the slow slide into cynicism that characterizes too many teaching careers.' Learning is the domain of discovery, risk, surprise, puzzle, creation, unlimited territories, change and transformation. If we fail to liberate our students' potential and open the doors large in front of their growth, then they will remain imprisoned in their own fears and will be probably incapable of becoming critical citizens.

## Promotion of multiculturalism

Palmer (1998) pointed out that teaching requires a deep understanding of the inner sources of both the intent and the act. It is also about being cognizant of our identity as a teacher and deepest self as a human being. Thus, one of the ethics of CME is to recognize differences and celebrate them to bring about depth and richness. This tenet is about creating a sense of relatedness, relationality and connectedness with the others that are different than us in a way or another. It is about believing that our being in this world depends on them and our actions are never completed and successful without them, their help and their appreciation. Embracing CME entails a full belief in your authentic identity without faking or looking down to others' identities. Yet, management teaching and learning reality is pretty shocking. In the US, the politics of identity are ongoing. Complaints of discrimination related to race, gender, ethnicity, religious background, color, political membership, ideological convictions, cultural origin, etc. are quite numerous, while there is a majority that intentionally or unconsciously enjoys privileges. Attending to multicultural issues in the US is still marginal and a far-reached objective.

Far from the US and in the rest of the world, business schools following the

American model and adopting English as the language of teaching have mushroomed, celebrating the American educational model and the American cultural hegemony. On the other hand, the local identities, the social, cultural, economic and political concerns in these societies have been overlooked and/or marginalized at the expense of promoting a corporate identity that is aligned with the giant American corporations' identities. It is very sad to notice that management students in several corners of the world are being molded according to the American model and that the number one priority in American education is to make the US number one in the market place. An alternative proposed by Giroux (1993: 20) is:

> to educate students to live in a multicultural world, face the challenge of reconciling difference and community, and addressing what it means to have a voice in shaping one's future is part of a broader task of deepening and extending the imperatives of democracy and human rights on both a national and global level.

Promoting multiculturalism is all about initiating and consolidating multicultural literacy based on a dialogic classroom where students discursively and reflexively negotiate their identities (Hesford, 1999).

## Challenge of dichotomies and boundaries

A central assumption to CME, as we regard it, is the perception of the student and the teacher as whole human beings who cannot be deprived from their wholeness. Fostering the belief in fragmentation, scattering, and dichotomy within the individual during the teaching and learning process is confining the relationship of both teachers and students to the world, and negating the strong interaction between the basic and the most fundamental components of the human fabric: the heart, the mind and the spirit. Palmer (1998: 4) has eloquently expressed this point:

> Reduce teaching to intellect and it becomes a cold abstraction; reduce it to emotions and it becomes

narcissistic; reduce it to the spiritual and it loses its anchor to the world. Intellect, emotion, and spirit depend on each other for wholeness. They are interwoven in the human self and in education at its best, and we need to interweave them in our pedagogical discourse as well.

The dominant education model emphasizes the cerebral activity, rationality and logical thinking. Many teachers are cautious to let emotions interfere in the learning act because they are perceived as weakness while any discussion involving spirituality and/or religion is deemed to be unacceptable. Moreover, the 'either or' axiom is fully embraced and enacted by both teachers and students. Getting over this dualistic thinking is what CME needs to achieve.

Another key assumption that we want to instigate in CME is the engagement in multidisciplinary learning/teaching and the defeat of educational boundaries and all kinds of narrow/discipline-centric thinking. This should be based on the encouragement of interdisciplinary inquiry and the perception of management education as well grounded in the other disciplines and the integration of business schools within the other institutions in the Academy. There are three boundaries that we need to cross according to Costigan (2003: 14): (1) boundaries of common sense and constructivist educational orientation, (2) boundaries of artificially construed subject disciplines and (3) boundaries between schools of education and schools of arts and sciences (we can add here business schools). The main advantage of crossing the boundaries is allowing ourselves and our students to see the world from different lenses, and uncover/explore the hidden perspectives that are never present or clear within one discipline, school, or paradigm.

## Dialogism and de-centered power

One of the focal tenets of CME is the belief in an egalitarian liberatory learning agenda and process where values of equality, participation, and collaboration are shared and celebrated. Dialogism is a Bakhtinian concept that involves sharing power in the classroom and allowing all the voices to be heard. It is a way to transform social interactions in the classroom and sensitize students about relations in their larger environment (Ira and Freire, 1987). Thus, students in CME are not passive submissive learners who fear the autocratic teacher, but they are at the heart of the learning process. They co-create knowledge along with the teacher. The dynamics created to help them share their perspectives, express their opinions and interpretations of the world are central to the CME community because these dynamics promote difference and respect and support their way of acting on reality.

In a dialogic community, both the teacher and the student preserve their uniqueness and sense of self, but they both have the courage to listen and accept opinions that may be opposite to their cherished beliefs. Central to these principles of self-awareness, motivation to learn and having a stand in the world is the distinction of Knowles (1990) between pedagogy and andragogy. The former implies the education of children while the latter refers to adult education.

The dialogic classroom is the terrain where shared inquiry based on mutual respect is fostered. Mutual respect means seeking connectedness, and relatedness, without merging. It is listening to people in their wholeness without violating their space or having any intention of control or domination. Our perception of mutual respect is well reflected by Josselson's (1996: 93) in the following way:

> This 'moving with' (as opposed to 'getting ahead of' or 'gaining control of') others has not been encouraged. It is clear that we have come to the edge of our capacity as a species to wield power over one another or to solve problems with force and domination. Either we live interdependently or we all vanish. Our survival necessitates seeing what connects us, looking at what occupies the space between us.

This way both parties can transcend their own boundaries and self-limitations.

## THE CHALLENGES FOR CME

How can critical management academics legitimize CME in their institutions and overcome some of the ethical dilemmas they might themselves be subject to? We organize an answer around five challenges for CME: teaching and working in the Margins, the 'I' and the 'Other' in the classroom, the content of management education, and curricula development, and bridging the gap between theory and practice. We chose these themes, because we believe they are central to repositioning CME in today's world.

### Teaching and working in the margins

Perriton and Reynolds (2004: 73) have pointed out that critical management educators (CMEs) find themselves a minority in their academic institutions where the managerialist functionalist worldview is strongly embraced and perceived as aligned with the global trend of management in the world: 'We might already have acknowledged the painful truth that, just outside the margins of the articles we write that so proudly outline our "critical" approaches, we are embedded in an educational system that both profits from and promotes the managerialist agenda we like to believe we are combating.' Thus CMEs find themselves isolated, sometimes harshly criticized by their colleagues who belong to the overriding paradigm. Besides, their courses are not a part of a whole curriculum based on the same perspective. Therefore, in the middle of their struggle against the dominant system, their voices do not get fully listened to and their influence on their academic and business environment turns to be partial.

While CMEs believe in their moral responsibility and their role in acting on reality, they live unfortunately in the margins and feel continuously compelled to engage in power negotiations. Their professional identities are torn between ensuring an academic comfort in the institutions where they work and being change agents in their classrooms, communities and societies.

A major consequence of this situation is the position CMEs adopt *vis-à-vis* their students and the learning/teaching process.

## The 'I' and the 'Other' in the classroom

CMEs believe in their role in engaging their students in critical learning where the dialectics between critical reflection and action should unfold opening doors to the praxis to shake the structural order and engage in reform. This strong stance may be based on the assumption of an ideological supremacy that can be very hard to be accepted by some students. In the words of Fenwick (2005: 33): 'How can an educator ethically justify such radical intervention in others' beliefs, identities, and values? Furthermore, what views can be tolerated? How can a posture of critique be adopted that is not also somewhat despotic, intolerant of intolerance, and therefore controlling?'

Indeed, we cannot ignore the clashes that may occur between the critical teacher and students whose identities have been manipulated throughout their educational experiences and different socialization processes. Students might find themselves in an existentialist state characterized by loss and confusion. They might sympathize with the liberatory discourse at the same time that they accumulate feelings of fear of failure of their future emancipatory endeavours (Alvesson and Willmott, 1996). The dynamics of the interactions between the 'I' (teacher) and the 'Other' (students) in the classroom becomes the story of different subjectivities and torn identities trying to create meanings and define potential prospective actions with some chances of success.

Several authors (Fenwick, 2005; Grey, 1996; Reynolds, 1999), for instance, have warned against the 'blind' adoption of critical pedagogy (CP) where CMEs continue to 'impose' their discourse and rationalize it regardless of students' resistance. In this case, it is the dark side of CP that will emerge and threaten both teachers and students. The former will suffer from the negative corollaries of adopting a doctrinarian standpoint and imposing it instead of working with students and appreciating the benefits of a progressive dialogic relationship. Students, on the other hand, may develop a discomfort with both the content and the pedagogy (Currie and Knights, 2003), they may doubt their right and worthiness to challenge their teachers (Reynolds, 1999) and may wonder how they would fit in the global market when they graduate.

Having recognized these risks, it is useful now to reiterate the necessity of being permanently aware of avoiding them through developing:

> the willingness to see one's own world from other perspectives, the willingness to engage with them, the willingness to work things through in a positive spirit, the willingness to risk critique not just from within, but also beyond one's own intellectual and professional world, the willingness to go on giving relentlessly of oneself, and the willingness to go on undercutting one's own social and professional identity as one takes on the conflicting perspectives of one's own frameworks. (Barnett, 1997: 169)

This basic challenge of identity is also related to the perceived roles of students and teachers. To keep away from any sort of domination, imposition or coercion in the learning process we should avoid talking about teaching and replace it with the concept of 'dialogic inquiry' where both CMEs and students learn collaboratively and take turns to voice their concerns, opinions, positions, emotions, and stories. In the words of Michel Novak: 'We are always living out a story. There is no way to live a storyless [...] life.' (Aronowitz and Giroux, 1991: 128) Yet, it is fundamental to be able to unveil it, reflect on it, learn from it and develop a stance *vis-à-vis* the world.

## The content of management education and curricula development

It is very sad to notice that the management curricula around the world are all standardized and follow the Anglo-American model and seem to be Western ethnocentric. It is also bizarre as Currie and Knights (2003) noted that cultural otherness is not given some intellectual space in most typical MBA programs. One of the key challenges for CMEs is how to act on the content of management education to make it as diverse as possible and reflective of the concerns, specificities, cultural values, heritage and contextual characteristics of the learners.

Although, CMEs are not always involved in the development of management education curricula, another challenge for them is to go beyond the disciplinary boundaries and expose students to a myriad of knowledge domains. This will provide, according to Giroux (1997), a space for critical discourse and will set up the foundation for students to learn how to discuss issues in a problematic way. Moreover, the different paradigmatic perspectives explored will serve as a source for insights and an opportunity to recognize difference and appreciate how conflicting positions and understandings play a crucial role in creating shared meanings (Bartunek et al., 1983).

### Bridging the gap between theory and practice

One of the key issues that many critical theorists have raised, including Alvesson and Wilmott (1996), and Fenwick (2005), is the tension that CMEs may create among students between theory and practice. While the theoretical discourse tries heavily to challenge the technicist/managerialist trend, the reality of organizations promotes profitability, competitivity, performativity, etc. Also, other educators in the same institution foster managerial theories and activities that are celebrating the capitalistic system, and students feel this fragmentation just by going from one course to the other. Another problem phrased by Watson (1999: 8) is that critical academics may 'talk about these ideas in language which few people understand' with the result that the ideas have 'no chance of being implemented'.

Several suggestions have been offered to close this gap between theory and practice. Some of them include the creation of strong links between the academy and the workplace (Boud and Solomon, 2002); emphasizing students', experiences (Fenwick, 2005); adopting critical action learning where students conduct field projects in volunteering organizations and engage in reflexive conversations about them in their classes (Alvesson and Willmott, 1996; Cunliffe, 2002; Fenwick, 2003; 2005; Foley, 2001); undertaking organizational ethnographies to research organizational members in their everyday practice and getting closer to their lived experiences (Samra-Fredericks, 2003); interpreting and negotiating in class the narratives collected and deciding about what may work and can be integrated in organizations and what may not. Indeed, conducting ethnographies and appreciating the use of stories have been suggested by multiple academics (i.e. Boje, 2006; Fineman and Gabriel, 1994; Willmott, 1994) who insisted on the need to care about emotions and feelings, and derive insightful meanings from experiences that would inform future actions.

The challenges of CME are tightly related to the main components of education in general. These are: the teacher, the student, the content and the process. These should never be seen as compartmentalized. It is the deep understanding of how these components interact in a complex academic setting in a complex world that will provide every critical academic with the agency to contribute to transformation.

## CONCLUSION

CME is the story of a group of approaches that are beginning to pay dialogic attention to one another. There is agreement that managerialism must be challenged with a variety of ethical voices. There is disagreement over the particular approach to ethics. For example, Habermas (phase 3 CT, which is a reincarnation of phase 1 Kantian ethics) turns back to the unfinished projects of Enlightenment, in such areas as a communicative rationality. The varieties of contemporary 'ct' perspectives have put a stronger focus on feminism, diversity, multiculturalism, and postmodern approaches which question the underlying universal ethics of Enlightenment projects.

We have suggested that CME can benefit from a closer relationship to CP. The issue facing CME is how to translate 'critical' into management education. What CME can learn from CP is to develop the student's understanding on how their lives (and roles) are complicit in the fabric of socioeconomic life.

Each of the CT and ct disciplines has its storylines, characters, concerns, context, and a history of ideological struggles. The multistory is still unfolding and sincerely searching for new and better avenues that would help academics, students, professionals, managers, institutions, communities, political actors, etc. to transcend their interests, constricted calculations, fixed ideologies, narrow terrains, and so forth to embrace the essence of human life in its wholeness and hold up front the human dignity in the world.

The field of CME has inherited strong philosophical principles and ethea from both critical theory movements 'CT' and 'ct', critical pedagogy and critical management studies. It can still benefit from an interactive and closer relationship between all of them while being open to a multidisciplinary inquiry that considers the major historical, political, social, economic, and cultural developments in the world.

While there is a frenetic search for a sustainable economic development in many corners of the world, there should be a parallel search for alternatives to efficiency, competition, performativity, consumption, and exploitation. Privileging a new political, economic, social and cultural system based on justice, human well-being and respect of human dignity entails a new educational order that challenges the well-embedded assumptions and goes beyond the quick fixes. CME is a good alternative when it is fully embraced and supported. It is true that it won't radically change the practice of management overnight, but it will at least contribute to the critical education of new generation of managers and citizens.

In a complex, McDonaldized world, several challenges of CME that relate to the subject (teacher and student), content and the process of teaching and learning remain undefeated. Nevertheless, it is quite clear that a strong belief in the tenets of CME as outlined above will open doors to a different practice of education. This practice will radically refute the mere commodification of educational products in a serious attempt to get out of the box of managerialism and overcome the blind followership of the current world socioeconomic order. A powerful commitment to the ethics of answerability, emancipation, multidisciplinary exploration of issues, diffusion of power, social justice and challenge of dualistic dichotomic thinking will certainly take CME beyond the siege of managerialism and will encourage every critical management educator to start the first step of the thousand mile journey.

We have major concerns about the encroachment of managerialism into university education. In the United States, the corporatization of the university is a movement, which is gaining ground. University presidents are acting as if they are CEOs; academic freedom of students and faculty has lost ground to hierarchical administered curriculum and governance. In Australia (and elsewhere) government is defining and administering the research agenda of universities. University ranking systems in the UK follow a managerialist ideology. In these times there is greater need than ever before for critical management education.

## NOTE

1 CT ct is a well-known distinction in Critical Management studies to designate important transitions in the Frankfurt School (CT) from more recent work in ct.

## REFERENCES

Adler, P.S. (1990) 'Marx, machines and skill', *Technology and Culture*, 31 (4): 780–812.

Adler, P.S., Forbes, L.C, and Willmott, H. (2006) 'Critical management studies: Premises, practices, problems and prospects'. Unpublished draft for annals of the *Academy of Management*, Nov. 2.

Adorno, Theodor W. (1963/2000) *Problems of Moral Philosophy*. Stanford, CA: Stanford University Press. First published in German, 1996; English version 2000. Based upon 17 lectures (7 May 1963 through 25 July 1963).

Adorno, T.W. and Horkheimer, M. (1944) *Dialectic of Enlightenment*. Trans. John Cumming. London & New York: Verso, 1979.

Alvesson, M. (1990) 'Organization: From substance to image?', *Organization Studies*, 11 (3): 373–94.

Alvesson, M. (1994) 'Critical theory and consumer marketing', *Scandinavian Journal of Management*, 10 (3): 291–313.

Alvesson, M. and Deetz, S. (2000) *Doing Critical Management Research*. London: Sage.

Alvesson, M. and Karreman, D. (2000) 'Varieties of discourse: On the study of organizations through discourse analysis', *Human Relations*, 53 (9): 1125–49.

Alvesson, M. and Willmott, H. (1992) 'Critical theory and management studies: An introduction', in M. Alvesson and H. Willmott (eds), *Critical Management Studies*. London: Sage Publications, pp. 1–20.

Alvesson, M. and Willmott, H. (1996) *Making Sense of Management: A Critical Introduction*. London: Sage.

Arendt, H. (1959) *The Human Condition*. Garden City, NY: Doubleday.

Aronowitz, S. (1973) *False Promises*. New York: McGraw-Hill.

Aronowitz, S. (1977) 'Mass culture and the eclipse of reason. The implications for pedagogy', *College English*, April: 768–74.

Aronowitz, S. and Giroux, H. (1985) *Education Under Siege*. Westport, CN: Greenwood, Bergin-Garvey.

Aronowitz, S. and Giroux, H. (1991) *Postmodern Education: Politics, Culture and Social Criticism*. Minneapolis: University of Minnesota Press.

Bakhtin, M.M. (1990) *Art and Answerability: Early Philosophical Essays*. Michael Holquist and Vadim Liapunov (eds), trans. Vadim Liapunov. Austin: Texas University Press.

Bakhtin, M.M. (1993) *Toward a Philosophy of the Act*. Trans. and notes by Vadim Liapunov, Michael Holquist and Vadim Liapunov (eds). Austin: Texas University Press.

Barnett, R. (1997) *Higher Education: A Critical Business*. Bristol, PA: The Society for Research into Higher Education and Open University Press.

Bartunek, J.M., Gordon, J.R. and Weathersby, R.P. (1983) 'Developing "complicated" understanding in administrators', *Academy of Management Review*, 8: 273–84.

Benson, J.K. (1977) 'Organizations: A dialectical view', *Administrative Science Quarterly*, 22: 1–21.

Boje, D.M. and Dennehy, R. (1993) *Managing in the Postmodern World: America's Revolution Against Exploitation*. Dubuque, IA: Kendall Hunt Publishing.

Boje, D.M. (1994) 'Organizational storytelling. The struggles of pre-modern, modern and postmodern organisational learning discourses', *Management Learning*, 25 (3): 433–61.

Boje, D.M. (1995) 'Stories of the storytelling organization: A postmodern analysis of Disney as "Tamara-land"', *Academy of Management Journal*, 38 (4): 997–1035.

Boje, D.M. (1996) 'Management education as a panoptic cage', in R. French and C. Grey (eds), *Rethinking Management Education*. London: Sage. pp. 76–93.

Boje, D.M. (2000) 'Nike corporate writing of academic, business, and cultural practices', *Management Communication Quarterly*, 4 (3): 507–16.

Boje, D.M. (2001a) *Narrative Methods for Organizational and Communication Research*. London: Sage.

Boje, D.M. (2001b) 'Carnivalesque resistance to global spectacle: A critical postmodern theory of public administration', *Administrative Theory and Praxis*, 23 (3): 431–58.

Boje, D.M. (2001c) 'Las Vegas spectacles: Organization power over the body', *Management*, 4 (3): 201–7. Special issue on Deconstructing Las Vegas at http://www.dmsp.dauphine.fr/management/PapersMgmt/43Boje2.html

Boje, D.M. (2002) *Critical Dramaturgical Analysis of Enron Antenarratives and Metatheatre*. Plenary keynote presentation to 5th International Conference on Organizational Discourse: From Micro-Utterances to Macro-Inferences, 24th–26th July (London).

Boje, D.M. (2004) *Grotesque Method*. Published in Proceedings (edited by Henri Savall, Marc Bonnet and Michel Peron) of First International Conference (Lyon, France); Co-sponsored Conference, Research methods Division, Academy of Management: Crossing Frontiers in Quantitative and Qualitative Research Methods. Vol. II pp. 1085–114.

Boje, D.M. (2006) 'The dark side of knowledge reengineering meets narrative/story', *Organization Journal*, Book Review, *Knowledge Management and Narratives: Organizational Effectiveness through Storytelling*, edited by Georg Schreyögg and Jochen Koch. Berlin: Erich Schmidt Verlag GmbH and Co.

Boje, D.M. (2008) *Storytelling Organizations*. London: Sage.

Boje, D.M. (ed). (2007a) 'Contributions of CT ethics for business and public administration', in *Critical Theory Ethics for Business and Public Administration*. NC: Information Age Press (in press).

Boje, D.M. (2007b) 'Story ethics', in D.M. Boje (ed). *Critical Theory Ethics for Business and Public Administration*. NC: Information Age Press (in press).

Boje, D.M. (2007c) 'Dialogism in management research', in Richard Thorpe, Luiz Mountinho and Graeme Hutchinson (eds), *Sage Dictionary of Management Research*, forthcoming.

Boje, D.M. (2007d) 'Exploitation'. Entry to appear in S. Clegg and J. Bailey (eds), *International Encyclopedia of Organization Studies*. London: Sage.

Boje, D.M. (2007e) Chapter 17: 'Globalization Antenarratives', in Albert Mills, Jeannie C. Helms-Mills and Carolyn Forshaw (eds), *Organizational Behavior in a Global Context*. Toronto: Garamond Press.

Boje, D.M. and Al Arkoubi, K. (2005) 'Third cybernetic revolution: Beyond open to dialogic system theories', *Tamara Journal*, 4 (4): 139–51.

Boje, D.M. and Cai, Y. (2004) 'McDonald's: Grotesque method and the metamorphosis of the three spheres: McDonald's, McDonaldland, and McDonaldization', *Metamorphosis Journal*, 3 (1): 15–33.

Boje, D.M. and Cai, Y. (2005) 'A Laclau and Mouffe discursive critique of McJob', in Nico Carpentier (ed.), *Discourse Theory and Cultural Analysis*. London: Sage.

Boje, D.M., Enríquez, E., González, M.T. and Macías, E. (2005) 'Architectonics of McDonald's cohabitation with Wal-Mart: An Exploratory study of ethnocentricity', *Critical Perspectives on International Business Journal*, 1 (4): 241–62.

Boje, D.M., Luhman, J. and Baack, D. (1999) 'Hegemonic tales of the field: A telling research encounter between storytelling organizations', *Journal of Management Inquiry*, 8 (4): 340–60.

Boje, D.M. and Rosile, G.A. (2003) 'Life imitates art: Enron's epic and tragic narration', *Management Communication Quarterly*, 17 (1): 85–125.

Boje, D.M., Rosile, G.A., Durant, R.A. and Luhman, J.T. (2004) 'Enron spectacles: A critical dramaturgical analysis'. Special Issue on Theatre and Organizations edited by Georg Schreyögg and Heather Höpfl, *Organization Studies*, 25 (5): 751–74.

Boje, D.M. and Winsor, R. (1993) 'The resurrection of Taylorism: Total quality management's hidden agenda', *Journal of Organizational Change Management*, 6 (4): 57–70.

Boud, D. and Solomon, N. (eds) (2002) *Work-based Learning: A New Higher Education?*

Buckingham: Society for Research into Higher education and Open University Press.

Braverman, H. (1974) *Labor and Monopoly Capital*. New York: Monthly Review Press.

Calás, M.B. (1993) 'Deconstructing charismatic leadership: Re-reading Weber from the darker side', *Leadership Quarterly*, 4: 305–28.

Calás, M.B. (1994). 'Minerva's Owl?: Introduction to a thematic section on globalization', *Organization*, 1: 243–48.

Calás, M.B. and Smircich, L. (1991) 'Voicing seduction to silence leadership', *Organization Studies*, 12: 567–602.

Calás, M.B. and Smircich, L. (1993) 'Dangerous liaisons: The "feminine-in-management" meets "globalization" ', *Business Horizons*, 36 (2): 71–81.

Calás, M.B. and Smircich, L. (1996) 'From the Woman's point of view: Feminiist approaches to organizational studies', in S.R. Clegg, C. Hardy and W.R. Nord (eds), *Handbook of Organization Studies*. London: Sage. pp. 218–57.

Calás, M.B. and Smircich, L. (1999) 'Past postmodernism? Reflections and tentative directions', *Academy of Management Review*, 24 (4): 649–71.

Calás, M.B. and Smircich, L. (2006) 'From the woman's point of view ten years later: Towards a feminist organization studies', in S.R. Clegg, C. Hardy, T.B. Lawrence and W.R. Nord (eds), *The Sage Handbook of Organization Studies* (2nd edn). London: Sage, pp. 284–346.

Cheit, E.F. (1985) 'Business schools and their critics', *California Management Review*, 27 (3): 43–62.

Clegg, S. (1981) 'Organization and control', *Administrative Science Quarterly*, 26 (4): 545–62.

Clegg, S.R. (1989) *Frameworks of Power*. London: Sage.

Clegg, S. and Dunkerley, D. (1980) *Organization, Class and Control*. London: Routledge & Kegan Paul.

Collins, D. (1995) 'A socio-political theory of workplace democracy: Class conflict, constituent reactions and organizational outcomes at a gain sharing facility', *Organization Science*, 6 (6): 628–44.

Costigan, A. (2003) 'Educational foundations: Building the case for communication', in D. Kaufman, D.M. Mauss and T.A. Osborn, *Beyond the Boundaries: A Transdisciplinary Approach to Learning and Teaching*. London: Praeger/Greenwood. pp. 13–33.

Cunliffe, A.L. (2002) 'Reflexive dialogical practice in management learning', *Management Learning*, 33 (1): 35–61.

Currie, G. and Knights, D. (2003) 'Reflecting on a critical Pedagogy in MBA education', *Management Learning*, 34 (1): 27–49.

Deetz, S. (1992) *Democracy in the Age of Corporate Colonization: Developments in Communication and* the *Politics of Everyday Life*. Albany, NY: State University of New York Press.

Dehler, G.E., Welsh, M.A. and Lewis, M.W. (2001) 'Critical pedagogy in the "New Paradigm" ', *Management Learning*, 32 (4): 493–511.

Delbridge, R. (2006) 'Extended review: The vitality of labour process analysis', *Organization Studies*, 27 (8): 1209–19.

Edwards, P. and Collinson, M. (2002) 'Empowerment and managerial labor strategies', *Work and Occupations*, 29: 271–90.

Ehrensal, K.N. (2001) 'Training capitalism's foot soldiers: The hidden curriculum of undergraduate business education', in E. Margolis (ed.), *The Hidden Curriculum in Higher Education*. New York/London: Routledge. pp. 97–113.

Fairhurst, G.T. (2007) *Discursive Leadership in Conversation with Leadership Psychology*. London: Sage Publications.

Fenwick, T. (2001) 'Ethical dilemmas of transformative pedagogy in critical management education. Stream 20 activism and teaching', Critical Management Studies Conference. Unpublished document.

Fenwick, T. (2003) 'Emancipatory potential of action learning: A critical analysis', *Journal of Organizational Change Management*, 16 (6): 619–32.

Fenwick, T. (2005) 'Ethical dilemmas of critical management education within classrooms and beyond', *Management Learning*, 36 (1): 31–48.

Ferguson, K.E. (1984) *The Feminist Case Against Bureaucracy*. Philadelphia: Temple University Press.

Fineman, S. and Gabriet, Y. (1994) 'Changing rhetorics: Traditional and "alternative" organizational behaviour textbooks', *Organization*, 1 (2): 375–99.

Foley, G. (2001) *Strategic Learning: Understanding and Facilitating Organizational Change*. Sydney: Centre for Popular Education.

Forester, J. (1993) *Critical Theory: Public Policy and Planning Practice*. Albany, NY: State University of New York Press.

Foucault, M. (1980) *Power/Knowledge: Selected Interviews and Other Writings 1972–1977*. Brighton: Harvester Press.

Fournier, V. (2006) 'Breaking from the weight of the eternal present: Teaching organizational difference', *Management Learning*, 37 (3): 295–311.

Freire, P. (1970) *Pedagogy of the Oppressed*. New York: Continuum International Publishing.

Freire, P. (1972) *Pedagogy of the Oppressed*. New York: The Seabury Press.

Freire, P. (1973) *Education for Critical Consciousnesss*. (Trans. Myra Bergman Ramos). New York: Continuum.

French, R. and Grey, C. (1996) *Rethinking Management Education*. London: Sage Publications.

Fulop, L. and Linstead, S. (eds) (1999) *Management: A Critical Text*. London: Macmillan.

Ghoshal, S. (2005) 'Bad management theories are destroying good management practices', *Academy of Management Learing and Education*, 4 (1): 75–91.

Giroux, H.A. (1991) 'Border pedagogy and the politics of modernism/postmodernism', *Journal of Architectural Education*, February: 69–79.

Giroux, H.A. (1993) *Living Dangerously: Multiculturalism and the Politics of Difference*. New York: Peter Lang.

Giroux, H.A. (1997) *Pedagogy and Politics of Hope: Theory, Culture, and Schooling*. Boulder, CO: Westview Press.

Gramsci, A. (1971) *Selections from the Prison Notebooks*. Trans. Q. Hoare and G. Nowell-Smith. New York: International Publishers.

Greene, M. (1996) 'In search of a critical pedagogy', in P. Leistyna, A. Woodrum and S.A. Sherblom (eds), *Breaking Free: The Transformative Power of Critical Pedagogy*. Cambridge, MA: Harvard Educational Review. pp. 13–30.

Grey, C. (1996) 'Towards a critique o managerialism: The contribution of Simone Weil', *Journal of Management Studies*, 33 (5): 592–611.

Grey, C. (2004) 'Reinventing business schools: The contribution of critical management Education', *Academy of Management Learning and Education*, 3 (2): 178–86.

Grey, C. and Mitev, N. (1995) 'Management education: A Polemic', *Management Learning*, 26: 73–90.

Grant, D., Keenoy, T. and Oswick, C. (1998) 'Organizational discourse: Of diversity, dichotomy and multi-disciplinary', in D. Grant, T. Keenoy, and C. Oswick (eds), *Discourse and organization*. London: Sage. pp. 1–13.

Habermas, J. (1972) *Knowledge and Human Interests*. Trans. J.J. Shapiro. London: Heinemann.

Habermas, J. (1991) *Moral Consciousness and Communicative Action*. Cambridge: MIT Press.

Hardy, C. and Clegg, S.R. (1996) *Some Dare Call it Power: Handbook of Organization Studies*. London: Sage.

Hassard, J., Hogan, J. and Rowlinson, M. (2001) 'From labor process theory to critical management studies', *Administrative Theory and Practice*, 23 (3): 339–62.

Hassard, J., Holliday, R. and Willmott, H. (1998) *Body and Organization: Toward the Organization Without Organs*. London: Sage.

Hassard, J., Kelemen, M. and Forrester, P. (2000) 'BPR and TQM: Convergence or divergence', in H. Willmott and D. Knights (eds.), *The Re-engineering Revolution*. London: Routledge.

Held, D. (1980) *Introduction to Critical Theory: Horkheimer to Habermas*. Berkeley, CA: University of California Press.

Hesford, W.S. (1999) *Framing identities: Autobiography and the Politics of Pedagogy*. Minneapolis, US: The University of Minnesota Press.

hooks, b. (1994) *Teaching to Transgress Education as the Practice of Freedom*. New York/London: Routledge.

Horkheimer, M. (1933/1993) *Materialism and Morality*. Translated by G. Frederick Hunter, Matthew S. Kramer, and John Torpey, with introduction by G.F. Hunter. London/Cambridge, MA: The MIT Press.

Horkheimer, M. (1974) *Critique of Instrumental Reason*. Translated by Mathew J. O'Connell et al. New York: The Seabury Press (A Continuum Book). First published in German in 1967.

Horkheimer, M. (1947) *Eclipse of Reason*. New York: The Seabury Press.

Humphries, M. T. and Dyer, S. (2005) 'Introducing critical theory to the management classroom: An exercise building on Jermier's "Life of Mike"', *Journal of Management Education*, 29 (1): 169–95.

Ingram, D. (1987) *Habermas and the Dialectic of Reason*. Yale: Yale University Press.

Jermier, J. (1985) 'When the sleeper awakens: A short story extending themes in radical organization theory', *Journal of Management*, 11 (2): 67–80.

Jermier, J. (1998) 'Introduction: Critical perspectives on organizational control', *Administrative Science Quarterly*, 43 (2): 235–56.

Jermier, J., Nord, W. and Knights, D. (eds) (1994) *Resistance and Power in the Workplace*. London: Routledge.

Josselson, R. (1996) *The Space Between us: Exploring the Dimensions of Human Relationships*. Thousand Oaks, CA: Sage.

Kant, I. (1781/1900) *Critique of Pure Reason*. Introduction by translator, J.M.D. Meiklejohn and special introduction by Brandt V.B. Dixon. New York: The Colonial Press.

Kant, I. (1785/1993) *Grounding for the Metaphysics of Morals: On A Supposed Right to Lie Because of Philanthropic Concerns*. Translated by James W. Ellington. Indianapolis, IN: Hackett Publishing Company. 1785 in German, 1993, 3rd edn, English.

Kellner, D. (1990) 'Critical theory and ideology critique', in R. Roblin (ed.), *The Aesthetics of the Critical Theorists: Studies on Benjamin, Adorno, Markuse and Habermas*. Lewiston: Edwin Mellen Press.

Kellie, J. (2004) 'Management education and management development: Widening participation or narrowing agenda?', *Journal of European Industrial Training*, 28 (8/9): 676–88.

Knights, D. and Willmott, H. (eds) (1986a) *Managing the Labour Process*. Aldershot: Gower.

Knights, D. and Willmott, H. (eds) (1986b) *Gender and the Labour Process*. Aldershot: Gower.

Knights, D. and Willmott, H. (eds) (1988) *New Technology and the Labour Process*. New York: Macmillan.

Knights, D. and Willmott, H. (eds) (1989) *Labour Process Theory*. New York: Macmillan.

Knights, D. and Willmott, H. (1999) *Management Lives: Power and Identity in Contemporary Organizations*. London: Sage.

Knights, D. and Willmott, H. (eds) (2000) *The Re-Engineering Revolution? Critical Studies of Corporate Change*. London: Sage.

Knights, D. and Willmott, H. (2007) *Introducing Organizational Behavior and Management*. London: Thomson Learning.

Knights, D., Noble, F. and Vurdubakis, T. <http://www.lums.lancs.ac.uk/profiles/theo-vurdubakis/> and Willmott, H. (2001) 'Chasing shadows: Control, virtuality and the production of trust', *Organization Studies*, 22 (2): 311–36.

Knights, D., Willmott, H. and Collinson, D. (eds) (1985) *Job Redesign: Critical Perspectives on the Labour Process*. Aldershot: Gower.

Knowles, M. (1990) *Adult learning* (4th edn). Houston, TX: Gulf.

Levy, D.L. and Egan, D. (2003) 'A neo-Gramscian approach to corporate political strategy: Conflict and accommodation in the climate change negotiations', *Journal of Management Studies*, 40 (4): 803–30.

Littler, C. (1982) *The Development of the Labour Processes in Capitalist Societies*. London: Heinemann.

Littler, C. (1984) 'Soviet-type societies and the labour process', in K. Thompson (eds), *Work, Employment and Unemployment*. Milton Keynes: Open University. pp. 87–96.

Marcuse, H. (1966) *Ethics and Revolution. Ethics and Society: Original Essays on Contemporary Moral Problems*, R.T. de George (ed.). Garden City, NY: Anchor.

Marcuse, H. (1972) *Counterrevolution and Revolt*. London: Allen Lane.

Marx, K. (1867) *Capital: A Critique of Political Economy*. Vol. 1. The Process of Capitalist Production. Trans. S. Moore and E. Averling. F. Engles (ed.). New York, NY: International Publishers. First published 1867, English 1967.

McCarthy, T. (1981) *The Critical Theory of Jürgen Habermas*. Cambridge, MA: MIT Press.

McLaren, P. (1995) *Critical Pedagogy and Predatory Culture: Oppsitional Politics in a Postmodern Era.* London, New York: Routledge.

Mills, A.J., Simmons T., Jean C. and Mills, H. (2005) *Reading Organization Theory: A Critical Approach to the Study of Organizational Behaviour and structure* (3rd edn). Orchard Park, NY: Broadview Press.

Mills, A.J., Jean, C., Mills, H., Forshaw, C. and Bratton, J. (2006) *Organizational Behavior in a Global Context.* Orchard Park, NY: Broadview Press.

Mingers, J. (2000) 'What is it to be critical? Teaching a critical approach to management undergraduates', *Management Learning,* 31 (2): 219–37.

Monaghan, C.H. (2001) 'Silence, voice, and resistance in management education'. Stream 20: Activism and Teaching. Paper presentation at Critical Management Studies Conference # 3, unpublished.

Palmer, P. (1998) *The Courage to Teach: Exploring the Inner Landscape of a Teacher's Life.* San Francisco: Jossey-Bass.

Parker, M. (1999) 'Capitalism, subjectivity and ethics: Debating labour process analysis', *Organization Studies,* 20 (1): 25–45.

Parker, M. (2002) *Against Management.* Oxford: Polity.

Parker, M. and Jary, D. (1995) 'The McUniversity: Organization, management and academic subjectivity', *Organization,* 2 (2): 319–38.

Perriton, L. and Reynolds, M. (2004) 'Critical management education: From pedagogy of possibility to pedagogy of refusal', *Management Learning,* 35 (1): 61–77.

Pfeffer, J. (1997) *New Directions for Organization Theory: Problems and Prospects.* New York: Oxford University Press.

Pfeffer, J. (2005) 'Why do bad management theories persist? A comment on Ghoshal', *Academy of Management Learning and Education,* 4 (1): 96–100.

Plato (406 BC) *The Phaedrus* (Jowett, B. Trans 1999). Mineola, NY: Dover Publications.

Porter, L.W. and McKibbin, L.E. (1988) *Management Education and Development: Drift or Thrust into the 21st Century?* New York: McGraw-Hill.

Prasad, A. (ed.) (2003) *Postcolonial Theory and Organisational Analysis.* Basingstoke: Palgrave Macmillan.

Reed, D. (2002) 'Management education in an age of globalization: The need for critical perspectives', in C. Wankel and R. DeFillippi (eds), *Rethinking Management Education for the 21st Century.* Greenwich, CT: Information Age Publishing.

Reynolds, M. (1999) 'Grasping the nettle: Possibilities and pitfalls of critical management pedagogy', *British Journal of Management,* 9: 171–84.

Ricoeur, P. (1992) *Oneself as Another.* Trans. by Kathleen Blamey. Chicago/London: The University of Chicago Press.

Samra-Fredericks, D. (2003) 'A proposal for developing a critical pedagogy in management from researching organizational members' everyday practice', *Management Learning,* 34 (3): 291–312.

Schon, D.A. (1983) *The Reflective Practitioner: How professionals think in action.* New York: Basic Books.

Shor, I. (1980) *Critical Teaching and Everyday life.* Boston, MA: South End Press.

Shor, I. (1992) *Empowering Education; Critical Teaching for Social Change.* Chicago/London: The University of Chicago Press.

Shor, I. and Freire, P. (1987) 'What is "the dialogic method" of teaching?', *Journal of Education,* 169 (3): 11–31.

Steffy, B.D. and Grimes, A.J. (1986) 'A critical theory of organization science', *Academy of Management Review,* 11 (2): 322–36.

Summers, D., Boje, D., Dennehy, R. and Rosile, G. (1997) 'Deconstructing the organizational behavior text', *Journal of Management Education,* 21 (3): 343–60.

Thompson, P. (1989) *The Nature of Work* (2nd edn). London: Macmillan.

Thompson, P. (1990) 'Crawling from the wreckage: The labour process and the politics of production', in D. Knights and H. Willmott (eds), *Labour Process Theory.* London: Macmillan.

Thompson, P. (2005) 'Brands, boundaries and band-wagons: A critical reflection on critical management studies', in C. Grey and H.C. Willmott (eds), *Critical Management Studies: A reader.* Oxford: Oxford University Press.

Thompson, P. and McHugh, D. (2002) *Work Organizations* (3rd edn). London: Palgrave.

Thompson, P. and Newsome, K. (2004) 'Labour process theory, work and the employment relation', in B. Kaufman (ed), *Theory and the Employment Relationship.* Champagne, IL: Industrial Relations Research Association. pp. 133–62.

Thompson, P. and Smith, C. (2001) 'Follow the redbrick road: A reflection on pathways in and out of the labour process debate', *International Studies of Management and Organization,* 30 (4): 40–67.

Tinker, T. (1985) *Paper Prophets: A Social Critique of Accounting.* New York: Praeger.

Tinker, T. (2002) 'Specters of Marx and Braverman in the twilight of postmodernist labour. Process research work', *Employment and Society,* 16 (2): 251–81.

Townley, B. (1993) 'Foucault, power/knowledge, and its relevance for human resource management', *Academy of Management Review,* 18 (3): 518–45.

Townley, B. (1994) *Reframing Human Resource Management*. London: Sage.

Watson, T.J. (1999) 'Beyond Managism: negotiated narratives and critical management education in practice', Paper presented in the First International Conference on Critical Management Studies, University of Manchester, July 14–16, 1999.

Weick, K. (2007) 'Drop your tools: On reconfiguring management education', *Journal of Management Education*, 31 (1): 5–16.

Willmott, H. (1993) 'Strength is ignorance; slavery is freedom: Managing culture in modern organizations', *Journal of Management Studies*, 30 (4): 515–53.

Willmott, H. (1997) 'Critical management learning', in J. Burgoyne and M. Reynolds (ed), *Management Learning: Integrating Perspectives in Theory and Practice*. London: Sage. pp. 161–76.

Willmott, H. (1998) 'Re-cognising the other: Reflections on a new sensibility in social and organizational studies' in R. Chia (ed), *In the Realm of Organization: Essays for Robert Cooper*. London: Routledge.

Willmott, H. (2003) 'Organization theory as a critical science? Forms of analysis and "new organizational forms" ', In H. Tsoukas and C. Knudsen (ed), *The Oxford Handbook of Organization Theory*. Oxford: Oxford University Press. pp. 88–112.

Willmott, H. (2005) 'Theorizing contemporary control: Some poststructuralist responses to some critical realist questions', *Organization*, 12 (5): 747–80.

Willmott, H. and Knights, D. (1989) 'Power and subjectivity at work: From degradation to subjugation in social relations', *Sociology Review*, 23 (4): 535–58.

Wood, S. and Kelly, J. (1978) 'Toward a critical management science', *Journal of Management Studies*, 15: 1–24.

# 7

# Collaborative Learning

Vivien E. Hodgson

## Abstract

This chapter examines the development and use of collaborative learning within management learning, education and development. Collaborative approaches to learning have a relatively long history in management learning and education. Early examples of collaborative learning approaches and designs are linked to the advent and introduction of the idea of the learning community in the 1980s. Also discussed is the more current and prevalent interest that are associated with collaborative learning in communities of practice and online learning communities. As described in the chapter the advent of technology supported learning communities has seen an increased resurgence and development of interest in collaborative learning and has become a key site and context for pedagogical thinking and research about collaborative learning. The chapter looks at underlying theoretical perspectives of collaborative approaches to learning which it claims are based on social processes of interaction which assume learning will be more effective as a result of dialogue and discussion with peers and others. As explained, collaborative learning is frequently often associated with social constructionist views of learning. In addition, the social orientation intrinsic to collaborative learning is for some, although by no means all, linked to emancipatory and critical pedagogy thinking and ideas. Some of the educational thinking and theories upon which collaborative approaches are based are described. A critical review is provided of some of the key ideas and issues considered significant when adopting collaborative approaches to learning and key areas are identified for consideration when using collaborative approaches.

## INTRODUCTION

The term 'collaborative learning' is used to describe educational approaches where students work together in small groups towards, it is often assumed, a common goal. There is a lot of evidence to suggest that collaborative learning contributes to the development of critical thinking and problem solving, which is why it is considered relevant and important for management learning, education and development (MLED).

Recent interest in collaborative learning has become increasingly associated with the rapid development and interest in web-based and technology enhanced education programmes. The adoption and use of collaborative learning in online learning communities is frequently claimed to be one of the potential real benefits from such courses and programmes.

Collaborative learning has, however, been an established part of management learning, education and development approaches since the 1970s where it was most associated with the ideas of Learning Communities (Heron, 1974; Pedler, 1981). However, until the 1990s much of the research and interest in collaborative learning tended to be at the school level and not so much within higher education or MLED.

Interest in collaborative learning is generally associated with emancipatory and humanistic approaches to education where students are encouraged to be responsible for one another's learning as well as their own. Thus, it is assumed, the success of one student helps other students to be successful. An early interesting discussion of collaborative learning is that of Douglas Barnes (1976) in his book *From Communication to Curriculum* in which he describes how in open collaborative social relationships school pupils make frequent use of one another's contributions by extending or modifying them. Importantly, as identified by Barnes, social relations and communication have always been seen as significant aspects of collaborative learning approaches.

To this extent collaborative learning is conceptually and theoretically associated with social constructionist and relational views of learning. In addition, the social orientation intrinsic to collaborative learning links it to emancipatory and critical pedagogical thinking and ideas.

In this chapter I describe some of the educational thinking and theories upon which collaborative approaches are based, provide a critical review of some of the ideas and issues considered significant when adopting collaborative approaches to learning, and identify key areas for consideration when using collaborative approaches. I will discuss both the perceived benefits as well as resistance and potential issues to be aware of when engaging in collaborative learning. In particular I will discuss in more detail that collaborative learning is not a simple matter of creating discussions in small groups in order to increase interest: it involves and assumes a range of complex and important pedagogical, learning and relational concepts and ideas.

## THEORETICAL BACKGROUND AND CONTEXT OF COLLABORATIVE LEARNING

Communication and dialogue underpin the intentions and idea of collaborative learning as a pedagogical design for critical thinking and learning. The importance of communication and dialogue for radical and emancipatory approaches to learning has a long history and is frequently seen to be influenced by the work and ideas of educationists such as John Dewey (1916), Eduard Lindeman (1926) through to the work of Paulo Freire (1972) and Henry Giroux (1983) as well as more recent radical educationist, such as Elizabeth Ellsworth (1989), Robin Usher (1992), Jennifer Gore (1993) and Stephen Brookfield (1995). The political significance and nature of education for democracy and critical emancipation underpins much of the writings of Dewey, Lindeman, Freire and Giroux although it is not always prominent in the writing and thinking about management learning, education and development or even about collaborative learning. However, in an approach based on social interaction which claims one of its main benefits to be the development of critical thinking, it is hard to separate it from at least an implicit critical and emancipatory agenda. At this time when many would claim such an agenda and approach to management education has never been more important, collaborative learning potentially offers an important pedagogical approach for MLED. As Freire points out in *Pedagogy of the Oppressed*,

> Only dialogue which requires critical thinking is capable of generating critical thinking. Without dialogue there is no communication, and without communication there can be no true education. (1972: 65)

To date the more radical aspects of the thinking of educationists such as Freire,

Lindeman and Dewey has not been easy to recognize in many of the dominant methods and approaches to management education. It is clear that the work of John Dewey, in particular, has in other respects had a significant impact. Dewey (1916: 9) advocated that relevance and significance should be placed on the learners' experience and that it was undesirable to create a 'split between the experience gained in more direct associations and what is acquired in school, that is, formal education'.

It was Kolb's interpretation of Dewey's ideas on the importance of the relationship between experience, action and reflection that led to the development of the Kolb learning cycle (Kolb and Fry, 1975; Kolb, 1984). Schön's idea of the reflective practitioner (Schön, 1983) equally came from his interpretation of Dewey's work. These ideas have clearly been very influential within management education. However, arguably less influential has been the significance Dewey also placed on the importance of communication as a social process that changes understanding and experience and impacts on the nature of society. As he states:

> To be recipient of a communication is to have an enlarged and changed experience. One shares in what another has thought and felt and in so far, meagrely or amply, has his own attitude modified. Nor is the one who communicates left unaffected. (Dewey, 1916: 5)

As he goes on to say,

> All communication is like art. It may well be said, therefore that any social arrangement that remains vitally social, or vitally shared, is educative to those who participate in it. (Dewey, 1916: 6)

Equally, Lindeman's (1926) concern for a critical understanding of experiences and situations placed emphasis on the potential of collaborative and informal educational processes for people to question taken-for-granted ideas, beliefs, values and behaviors.

From Eduard Lindeman's (1926) work through to Malcolm Knowles (1975) a move can be seen within adult education towards collaborative approaches that emphasize self-directed learning and taking responsibility for one's own learning. Building on from Lindeman's ideas, Brookfield (1994), however, points to the political and socio-cultural aspects that arise if an uncritical approach to self-directed learning is adopted. The unequal distribution of power and control between learners and educators within intended liberal and humanistic educational process has come to be seen as a significant element for learning approaches where learners are invited to take greater responsibility for their learning. (See also Gore, 1993; Ellsworth, 1989) This is a significant and often unaddressed issue when using collaborative learning and learning community approaches.

More recently the emerging interest and development of critical management studies (CMS) and, more specifically, critical management education (CME) has seen a clearer acknowledgement of the more radical agendas of the likes of Dewey, Lindeman and Freire. This has included recognition of the importance and impact of power and control in pedagogy and learning, though Reynolds (1997), after Giroux (1983), suggests engagement with this work is often at the level of radical pedagogical content and not radical pedagogical process as associated with critical pedagogical methods and educational approaches.

Collaborative learning can be examined through a range of other theories and ideas about education and learning other than those associated with emancipatory and critical pedagogy. In the following sections I will examine the various ways that collaborative learning and learning communities have come to be discussed and written about, particularly in the context of MLED.

## DEVELOPMENT OF COLLABORATIVE LEARNING APPROACHES WITHIN MELD

It is possible to identify a number of key influences on the way ideas and thinking about the role and significance of collaborative learning have evolved within management learning, education and development. One of the earliest was thinking about learning communities, for example, in the work of John Heron (1974) and Mike Pedler (1981). Two other slightly later developments are the interrelated and associated interests in situated, social learning theory (SLT) and communities of practice (CoPs) that developed based on the work of Lave and Wenger (1991), Brown and Duguid (1991), Lave and Chaiklin (1993) and others in the late 1980s and early 1990s. Another important influence is the development of critical pedagogy ideas based on the work of Freire (1972), Giroux (1983) and Habermas (1981), among others, into critical management studies and critical management education (for example, French and Grey (1996), Reynolds (1997, 1999a,b) and Wilmot (1997)). Although this work is discussed elsewhere in this handbook in its own right, it is important to recognize the relationship of both SLT and critical pedagogy to the theory and practice of collaborative learning approaches within management learning, education and development. Finally, and most recently, the work associated with online learning and networked management learning (NML) (Arbaugh, 2000; Borthick and Jones, 2000; Brower, 2003; Hodgson and Watland, 2004) has come to see collaborative learning within learning communities as one of the key and significant benefits to be gained from online discussions within distance or virtual management education programmes. Networked management learning is an area of work where an increasing amount of research focuses on the process and benefits of collaborative learning and learning communities. This research adopts a social constructionist emphasis and interest on language and the construction of meaning through dialogue drawing on the work and thinking of, for example, Bahktin (1986); Gergen (1973); Shotter (1994) and Fairclough (2003). This is in addition to recognizing the importance and relevance of social presence (Garrison, 1997; Stacey, 1999) and relationships and trust (Underwood, 2003; McConnell, 2005).

I will look in turn at each of these development and their influences upon the theory and thinking about collaborative learning within management education.

## THE LEARNING COMMUNITY

The idea of Learning Community has long been established as an approach within management education and precedes the now equally prevalent concept of communities of practice (CoP) associated with the work of Lave and Wenger (1991) onwards. Pedler (1981) explains that the Learning Community is a management development design that involves bringing together a group of people as peers to meet personal learning needs primarily through a sharing of resources and skills offered by those present. According to Pedler, the learning community approach rests on two major principles:

- That each individual takes primary responsibility for identifying and meeting his own learning needs.
- That each person is responsible for helping others identify and meet their needs and for offering themselves as a flexible resource to the community.

From Pedler's discussion of the origins and development of Learning Community it is clear that the learning community idea is based on a set of ideas and thinking different from those of communities of practice (CoP) associated with situated learning theory. According to Pedler the idea of Learning Community stems from two post-war movements, one concerned with learning and the other with therapy. As he explains, experiential learning groups, such as T-groups or encounter training, began to proliferate in the late 1940s and had the explicit purpose of being for personal growth and development in terms of self-image, interpersonal relationships and self-direction.

The second movement and influence stems from therapy and the idea of therapeutic communities which is generally accredited originally to Maxwell Jones and his work on therapeutic communities at Henderson Hospital in the UK. In therapeutic communities, Pedler explains, the boundaries between the therapist and patients are blurred in order to share decision making and encourage people to act as therapists for one another. According to Pedler, both experiential learning groups and therapeutic community groups place an emphasis on the values of community, close relationships and comradeship; confronting rather than ignoring problems; encouraging individual self-development and direction, together with community self-government.

As Pedler points out, in both instances there is a tension between the individual and support of others – the personal and the communal – which is equally present in learning communities. Learning communities and their associated tensions are believed by their advocates to give learners in them the potential to access a richer more varied field of resources and interpretations of meaning. The emphasis in learning communities on self-development and direction is similar to that already discussed by Lindeman (1926) as well as Knowles (1975). This emphasis, together with that of community self-government challenges more conventional approaches to learning where the teacher is seen/expected to decide on matters of pedagogy and curriculum. The tensions and challenges within learning communities means, however, that they remain a potentially uncomfortable and time-consuming way to operate as Pedler suggested in 1981. Potential for discomfort and the additional time required is a common feature and characteristic of collaborative learning and can lead to resistance to its use by both learners and educators, as will be discussed more below.

The Learning Community approach offers, however, a set of principles and a framework for supporting collaborative learning. As Pedler explains, the intention/idea of the Learning Community is to provide (after Torbert, 1978) a 'liberating structure' that allows greater responsibility and participation in the learning process. Pedler suggests

that many of the critical questions about the Learning Community as an educational design cohere around the role of the trainer, convenor or instigator – who becomes the focus for issues of leadership and direction in a situation where the aim is to help participants to achieve greater measure of self-direction and control over their development. Torbert, he says, refers to this as the deliberate irony of liberating structures.

John Heron (1982) identified other potential anomalies and power differentials that are endemic in any learning community design with respect, in particular, to assessment processes. As Heron explained, assessment is the most political of all educational processes and is the area where issues of power are most at stake. He felt that if there was no collaboration on assessment processes then staff exerted a stranglehold that would inhibit the development of collaboration with respect to other processes. Heron (1982) pointed out that generally speaking tutors exercise unilateral, intellectual authority in assessment even in otherwise learner centred courses.

Hodgson and Reynolds' study of the learner's experience of the dynamics of the learning community largely confirmed this view, commenting that:

So, for example, although the intention was to transform the tutor–student relationship within the programme, the tutors' ultimate control over assessment mitigated against this. Tutors were seen both as traditional authority figures and, on occasions, as failing to exercise their authority. (1987: 155)

Referring to the programme that they studied, Hodgson and Reynolds explain changes to the assessment system were consequently introduced:

The assessment procedure has also become more collaborative in an attempt to bridge the constraints and expectations of the academic community and more democratic philosophy of the course design. (1987: 157)

Attention to the power differentials and control associated with embedded socio-cultural structures and processes, such as assessment, within collaborative and partic-ipative learning approaches like the Learning Community are not always acknowledged or their importance recognized. The issue of power and control within learner centred approaches based on emancipatory values and ideas have come to be discussed much more, however, in the growing critical manage-ment education literature (French and Grey, 1996; Reynolds, 1999a,b; Fournier and Grey, 2000; Reynolds and Trehan, 2003; Fenwick, 2005).

## SITUATED LEARNING THEORY AND COMMUNITIES OF PRACTICE

Ideas about the Learning Community are located in an essentially psychodynamic and individual view of the learner who, it is assumed, benefits from the challenges and support gained through collaboration with others in a learning community. More recently, thinking about learning commu-nities has become associated with a more socio-cultural view of learning and an interest in concepts arising out of situated learning theory (SLT) where the ideas of 'situated learning' (SL) and 'communities of practice' (CoP) (Lave and Wenger, 1991) have developed along a less individual-ized, more socially orientated perspective on learning.

In SLT learning is seen as participation in a community and becoming a recognized member of a community. Translated into the experience of management education, this can be interpreted as learning through participation in the pedagogy and curriculum of a given educational programme. Through this participation 'students' learn how to be a participant or member of a given knowledge community and acquire the language and an identity that is recognized by that community. Increasingly, the terms 'learning community' and 'communities of practice' get used interchangeably as metaphors for describing the ideas and intentions of collaborative learning approaches. The theories and con-cepts associated with SLT and CoPs are undoubtedly helpful for analyzing, examining and understanding the process of collabora-tive learning. It is not, however, simply a case of being able to superimpose the idea of CoP upon educational practice(s) such as collaborative learning.

SLT has, potentially, a greater explanatory power than an intention to identify how to develop particular learning outcomes, such as critical thinking. Edwards (2005), similar to some other writers on the use of SLT and CoPs ideas within educational contexts, points out:

> It is not clear how the community of practice metaphor deals with learning something new. It provides a compelling account of learning as socialization into existing beliefs, values and practices but does not offer an account of how new knowledge is produced. (Edwards, 2005: 57)

Edwards' comments emerges within the context of a UK national funded teaching and learning project (cf. James and Brown, 2005) that was concerned with the analy-sis of research approaches to examine the relationship between teaching approaches and learning outcomes. Edwards' interest is in looking at learning outcomes at the level of the individual and where learning 'is a change of state, which alters how we act on the world and in turn changes it by our actions'. Edwards clearly acknowledges the socio-cultural dimension and significance of CoPs for how and what we learn but feels that on its own CoP as a metaphor for learning does not do justice to the intricacies of the relationship between mind and the world and knowing what is learnt by the individual, a point which brings us back to the purpose of educational approaches that have emancipa-tory and democratic intentions, as suggested is the case for collaborative learning. There are no such intentions suggested or assumed as prerequisite in the literature on communities of practice.

Contu and Wilmott (2003) also suggest that within many adoptions of the idea of CoPs the issue of power relations is not given sufficient attention: within the socio-cultural view of SLT, learning is about identity construction and, as they point out, also power. Lave and Wenger (1991) themselves refer to and recognize the importance of unequal power relationships within CoPs and the impact this has on situated learning and the construction of identity. Contu and Wilmott explain actions that comprise learning are within SLT 'conceived to be embedded in their historical conditions of possibility, and language is understood to be the principal medium of communication for the (re)production of social practices' (Contu and Wilmot 2003: 287). Their paper alerts us to the importance of power, communication and language in the ideas of Lave and Wenger (1991). It again reminds us that CoP as a metaphor and explanation for learning does not suppose or assume an emancipatory or liberal educational agenda. Without attention to the social practices that are (re)produced it can not be assumed that educational approaches claiming a CoP approach support or encourage critical thinking.

In her own work Edwards (2005) draws on Vygotsky (1997) and Leont'ev (1978) who she explains eroded the distinction between mind and the world, arguing that mind is revealed in action on the world. They were not simply concerned with learning to become a member of a community, they were interested in how we might transform our worlds through our increasingly informed actions on them. A key aspect of Vygotsky's and Leont'ev's work is the recognition of the importance of language. As Edwards comments:

> He (Vygotsky) argued that language carries the concepts we use when acting on, and trying to make sense of, the world. (Edwards, 2005: 53)

Gherardi et al. (1998) adopt a similar Vygotskian language-related perspective to SLT and CoP and claim that newcomers are both a product and a producer of the social reality they are part of and live in and that 'language is both the medium for becoming "competent" in the carrying out of a practice' and at the same time 'a way to modify that practice by talking about it, questioning, arguing, proposing, mediating and supporting

an alternative way of doing' (p. 283). Gherardi et al. are primarily concerned with understanding the social processes of how people learn in organisations and the 'notion of situated curriculum'.

Edwards and Gherardi et al. direct us once again to the significance and importance of communication and language in the learning process. Only Contu and Wilmott, however, explicitly draw attention to the significance given to unequal power relations in language and communication within SLT and within participation in communities of practice.

As SLT and CoPs ideas are increasingly adopted and used within educational practice, it is important to remind ourselves that they do not by definition embrace emancipatory or liberal educational intentions. They do, however, offer us important insights into the way learning occurs and how meaning and knowledge are situational and socially constructed.

## ONLINE COLLABORATIVE LEARNING

The idea of learning communities and communities of practice is increasingly being used in the context of technology supported learning models and approaches. In many online or e-learning initiatives they have become strongly associated with collaborative learning approaches, for example, Cousin and Deepwell, 2005; Ebersole, 2003; Garrison and Anderson, 2003; Nichani, 2000.

Even earlier there was a belief that computer-mediated communication and online discussions offered new potential for democratic and collaborative approaches to learning that encouraged critical thinking and problem solving (Hiltz, 1986; Boyd, 1987; Boshier, 1990; Harasim, 1990). Gokhale (1995) concluded that where the educational purpose was to enhance critical thinking and problem solving collaborative learning was demonstrated as beneficial.

This assumed potential of technology supported collaborative learning was seen as significant and relevant for MLED

(Johansen, 1988; Hodgson and McConnell, 1992). As Leidner and Jarvenpaa (1995) commented:

> In the domain of business education, decision-making skills including analytical and problem solving skills and communication skills are seen as critical. We might therefore speculate that methods requiring interaction and student involvement would be preferred over traditional methods. Thus, the informating up or transforming technologies with the corresponding collaborative or constructivist models might be ways to improve the quality of business education. (Leidner and Jarvenpaa, 1995: 280)

As technology becomes an undistinguishable part of work and life, this is a view increasingly adopted. Borthick and Jones (2000) suggested that collaborative discovery learning online prepares students for work in environments in which new problems are the norm and professionals work collaboratively to solve them in virtual spaces. Alvai and Gallupe (2003) also found greater levels of critical thinking skills for online students involved in collaborative interaction and discussions.

Brower (2003) claims that discussions in online communities met the benefits of collaborative learning, which she lists as,

1  Giving students the opportunity to raise questions for clarification of principles and issues raised in the reading material.
2  Enhancing the applicability of the course material through students' sharing of personal work experience in which concepts were demonstrated.
3  Adding to the applicability of the theoretical concepts as students pose problems they currently face in their workplace and peers and faculty provide advice on how to analyze and deal with difficult situations.
4  Providing an appropriate forum for students to ask questions and raise counter arguments.
5  Keeping students and faculty connected in the learning process for accountability purposes.

Alvai and Gallupe (2003), Borthick and Jones (2000), and Brower (2003) all offer support for MLED online collaborative and learning community based learning approaches.

However, they and other researchers agree that there is still much that we need to understand about online collaborative learning, including more about some of the potential negative processes of collaboration that, for example, lead to a kind of censorship where certain students' postings/comments do not get read or responded to (Brower, 2003). Other researchers claim that there can be resistance from students for many reasons, among them grade pressure and a lack of trust in both the instructor and classmates (Underwood, 2003). There is also a reticence from educators who resist after unsuccessful attempts at implementing collaborative approaches owing to student resistance, time constraints and other problems encountered (Keeley and Shemberg, 1995; Underwood, 2003). These are all problems regularly associated with learning community approaches generally.

Another area seen to be important is that of social presence online and the development of trust (Stacey, 1999; Swan, 2002; Garrison and Anderson, 2003). McConnell (2005) explains that without attention to developing trustful relationships, which in turn support and foster collaborative work, members of the groups are less likely to feel engaged with each other or feel that they have been involved in a truly collaborative learning experience. As he states:

> Collaborative e-learning groups exhibit complex dynamics and diverse learning processes and outcomes. Pedagogical designers who ask learners to work in such groups need to be aware of this. It is all too easy for teachers to include group work in a collaborative learning design in the assumption that the technology itself will support the work of the group. (McConnell, 2005: 39)

Often not acknowledged in discussions on resistance and problems encountered is their relationship to unequal power relations in learning communities, as identified by Heron (1981) and more recently by Contu and Wilmott (2003). And, as we discuss in more detail in Hodgson and Reynolds (2005), how being a member of a community (including a learning community and/or a community of practice) usually entails subjugation to its core values and norms of behaviour, and to deviate from these in resisting assimilation is to run the risk of becoming marginalized in order that the integrity of the community is preserved. As we comment in that paper:

> 'Normocentricity' is thus enforced and dissent outlawed (Noddings, 1996: 254). This is just as much the case in participative pedagogies, especially if they entail students and tutors sharing in decision-making and planning. This process is more interactive than might be expected in more conventional, more tutor-directed programme designs. As a consequence of being in the social and political processes of a participative pedagogy, difference – whether structural (gender, role, age, etc.) or of preferred ways of working – can result in some students becoming isolated or marginalized. (Hodgson and Reynolds, 2005: 16)

We describe, after Reynolds (2000), if collaborative learning pedagogy, virtual or otherwise, is to reflect less hierarchical, more participative principles, it needs to avoid the more coercive characteristics of 'community'.

It needs, we claim, to demonstrate the following features:

- The structure and design of the course will support recognition of differences that emerge rather than contribute to their avoidance or suppression.
- Differences of values, circumstance, belief, role or interest will be central to the life and learning of the participants.
- These differences will be the basis of, and provide support for, multiple (and changing) sub-communities.
- Such differences will be the focus for understanding, debate and dispute – rather than become targets for assimilation, reconciliation or the grounds of marginalizing minority interests. (Hodgson and Reynolds, 2005)

It is important not to lose sight that collaborative learning in online communities depends ultimately on processes of relational dialogue. It is through online dialogue that we construct meaning about who we are and what is acceptable knowledge within a given social and cultural context. As Contu and Wilmott (2003) imply, hierarchies and inequalities are structured and re-structured through interaction/dialogue and social norms are (re)produced. In the online communities literature there has been a tendency to foreground communication (and collaboration) at the expense of recognizing the continuing importance that social categories, such as nationality, race and gender have in dialogical exchanges.

Ferreday et al. (2006) claim online collaboration that adopts a critical relational dialogue perspective can provide learners with opportunities to articulate their social and cultural experiences and to develop critical thinking. This takes place through questioning and challenging existing work practices and organizational conditions, especially taken-for-granted assumptions embedded in both theory and professional practice (Reynolds and Vince, 2004). Dialogue also offers learners an opportunity to learn to listen to others' goals and interests. This critical relational dialogue view of online learning is explicitly acknowledged in the idea and concept of Networked Management Learning (Hodgson and Watland, 2004). In Networked Management Learning (NML) the emphasis is on learning that emerges from relational dialogue with others in either learning networks or communities. I shall discuss this further in the next section.

## NETWORKED MANAGEMENT LEARNING

Discussions of SLT emphasize the relationship between learning and participation in CoPs. And although, as already discussed, the importance of communication and language is acknowledged, it is not necessarily foregrounded or unequal power relations given sufficient attention. Within the developing field of networked management learning the emphasis is more explicitly on learning that emerges from relational dialogue with others in either learning networks or communities.

NML aligns itself with a social constructionist view of the world and the social constructionist emphasis on language and the construction of meaning (Berger and Luckman, 1966; Gergen, 1973). Social constructionists (Shotter, 1994; Gergen, 1999) stress the importance of understanding 'different interests' without searching for the 'most relevant' perspective. Cunliffe (2001) uses such a perspective to make sense of management practice to examine how managers apparently construct a sense of who they are and move others to talk or act in different ways through dialogical practices. Similarly, in NML the focus is on such dialogical practices but specifically within the context of online collaborative learning conversations.

Within NML power, age, gender, identity, socio-cultural norms and language and discourse are all recognized as important dimensions and influences on collaborative learning community processes and the experience of taking and sharing of responsibility. Language and discourse are seen to be key and the medium through which relations of power and control are practised (Fairclough, 2003). Language is seen as the means by which learners construct reality, establish social relations, act in relation to each other, and develop their professional identity.

Bakhtin's ideas on dialogical speech (Bakhtin, 1986) are pertinent and helpful in considering the importance of dialogue in online collaborative learning. A number of authors have drawn on Bakhtin's work for understanding and analyzing online communication and learning (e.g. McKenna, 2005; Dysthe, 2002; Mitra and Watts, 2002; Koschmann, 1999). Similarly, Shotter and Cunliffe (2001) and Cunliffe (2001) draw on Bakhtin in their work on 'managers as practical authors'.

In Ferreday et al. (2006) we describe Bakhtin's view that, 'because of its simplicity and clarity, dialogue is a classic form of speech communication' (Bakhtin, 1986: 72). What is significant in Bakhtin's position is that he sees every utterance as dialogical and a real unit of speech communication. As he comments, 'real-life' dialogue is orientated towards the response of the other/s, and every utterance has an absolute beginning and end marked by the speaker beginning to speak or write, and finishing. Consequently, for Bakhtin the important feature of an utterance, compared to other equivalent language unit (e.g. a sentence) is that the listener or reader takes an active responsive attitude towards it.

Bakhtin states, 'Sooner or later what is heard and actively understood will find its response in the subsequent speech or behaviour of the listener' (Bakhtin, 1986: 69). It is the assumed responsive position of the listener/reader to an utterance (either implicit or explicit) that makes all speech/text dialogical. Even a monological utterance, according to Bakhtin, is filled with dialogic overtones.

Bakhtin claims that every utterance has two aspects: the relation between the message and the messages that precede and follow it; and the addressivity of the message, that is, to whom it is directed. As he explains, the composition and the style of an utterance will depend on the imagined addressee. How the speaker/writer views the addressee will in turn influence the choice of speech genre used, and this will vary depending, for example, on the personal proximity of the addressee to the speaker/writer. Where there is deep confidence or trust in the addressee the speaker/writer is more likely to adopt a familiar or intimate tone.

Bakhtin's ideas on the dialogical nature of all communication and more specifically the choice of speech genre used are relevant and helpful for examining closer and understanding better the discourse of collaborative learning exchanges and discussions. His point that where there is trust in the addressee the speaker/writer is more likely to adopt a familiar or intimate tone, allows us to identify the difference and consequences of different speech genre used in online interactions. His ideas relate equally to earlier points on the importance of time and effort required to ensure that confidence and trust are allowed to develop and also whether the voice of the other is heard. That is, if collaborative learning in a learning community is to function in such a way that other voices are present and are open to the other and is to avoid what Mann (2005) refers to as a 'dynamic of compliance'.

Interestingly, in view of the earlier discussion on Vygotsky and the importance he places on language, Cheyne and Tarulli say that Vygotsky's and Bakhtin's views of dialogue are different and suggest different possibilities (Cheyne and Tarulli, 1999: 28). They claim that Vygotsky sees the purpose of dialogue in terms of consensus to the position of authority/expert: 'the ideal speech situation is one in which the shared "given" is maximal and misunderstanding is minimized. This is a view of dialogue in which the task is a faithful replication by a listener of the information contained in the speech of the speaker'. Dialogue in this view is seen as 'a cooperative enterprise aimed at an ever greater agreement' (1999: 11).

For Bakhtin the concept of expert is more problematic, thus offering greater possibilities for an understanding of dialogue in the context of critically reflective collaborative learning. From such a critically reflective perspective NML is more critical of both the assumption that knowledge is transmitted from expert to novice, and that the purpose of dialogue can or should be to produce consensus.

Bakhtin's ideas are further developed in Fairclough's (2003) work on critical discourse analysis; indeed a key idea in the work of both Bakhtin and Fairclough is that of different voices in a text or discourse and the position of oneself (Self) to 'the Other'.

Bakhtin and Fairclough both imply that in order to build on our understanding of how identity and knowledge is constructed within collaborative learning communities it is necessary to pay attention to the idea that through dialogue we construct meaning about who we are as well as create norms and values that determine what is seen as acceptable knowledge within a given social and cultural context. In addition, as already mentioned, Ferreday et al. (2006) argue we need to be aware of the extent to which hierarchies and inequalities are structured and re-structured through interaction/dialogue; also the way social norms are reproduced, and to recognize the importance that social categories such as nationality, race and gender have on voice, be it that of Self or of 'the Other'.

In other words, dialogue and dialogical speech (like CoPs discussed earlier) cannot be assumed to be a taken-for-granted emancipatory, ideal or good thing. Equally this is the case for collaborative learning. Without attention to and critical reflection on the performative and structuring dimensions of language/discourse used and positions taken, collaborative learning has the potential to be as oppressive as any other hierarchical or authoritarian educational approach.

## SUMMARY

In this chapter I have emphasized the importance and relevance that collaborative learning approaches are believed to have for developing critical thinking and problem solving. I have shown that it is an approach that is related and associated to participatory and emancipatory pedagogies within MLED. It is an approach that can be found within a number of different contexts and pedagogical designs, most notably that of the Learning Community and more recently online and networked management learning.

Collaborative learning is embedded in socio-cultural processes where dialogue and language are the means through which learners construct reality, establish social relations, act in relation to each other and develop their professional identity. This involves complex and diverse dynamics that can be uncomfortable and time consuming. There are issues in all social situations and processes, including within education, of unequal distribution of power and control. In collaborative learning approaches, if ignored, this inequality can lead to a dynamic of compliance as identified by Mann (2005).

In her exploration of learning communities Mann claims there is frequently the pull of naturalized norms and assumptions about how to be communicating in learning situations. These norms and assumptions, she points out, can inhibit questioning and challenge. The resultant outcome, she writes is:

> potentially ideological nature of particular communicative events within the educational context; the power of the other in shaping the identity of the individual in the group; and a dynamic of compliance which may pull teachers and learners towards a surface form of harmony in order to get through the business of the class without too much damage to oneself. (Mann 2005: 50)

The danger of focusing on getting through the business of the class without too much damage to oneself is potentially a real one for learners and teachers alike within the context of collaborative learning communities. This is, however, a dysfunctional and unsatisfactory situation from a learning perspective and negates the potential benefits assumed of collaborative learning. It is thus important for a learning community to consider ways to find the space and time to come to know and trust the other and for each person to find their voice.

Following Reynolds (2000) and Hodgson and Reynolds (2005) programme designers who seek to adopt collaborative learning approaches based on less hierarchical and more participative forms of pedagogy should consider the following points:

- Does the structure and design of the course support recognition of differences that emerge rather than contribute to their avoidance or suppression?
- Is there time given and opportunities to form relationships, to listen and to come to know 'the Other'?
- Do differences become grounds for exploration and dialogue and, if need be, changing the social and academic aspects of the programmes? Or do they become targets for assimilation or the basis for marginalization and exclusion?
- Do tutors acknowledge the power they hold due to their role in assessment, and effects on relations within the community?
- Do tutors or facilitators through their interventions support sense-making? Are they as aware of their role in this as they should be?

Attention to the above will not dissolve or remove the tensions and difficulties that will inevitably arise when engaged in critical collaborative learning approaches. They will, at least, assist in avoiding a dynamic of compliance. At best they will contribute to collaborative learning being used to produce and construct new understanding and ways of being in the world.

## ACKNOWLEDGEMENTS

I would like to thank Steve Armstrong and Cynthia Fukami for their invitation to write this chapter as well as the unnamed reviewers and Linda Perriton and Michael Reynolds for their valuable and useful comments on an earlier draft. Also thanks to Morgan Tanton for her invaluable feedback and comments.

## REFERENCES

Alvai, M. and Gallupe, R.B. (2003) 'Using information techology in learning: Case studies in business and management education', *Academy of Management Learning and Education*, 2 (2): 139–53.

Arbaugh, B. (2000) 'Virtual classroom versus physical classroom: An exploratory study of class discussion patterns and student learning in an asynchronous Internet-based MBA course', *Journal of Management Education*, 20 (19): 213–34.

Bakhtin, M. (1986) *Speech Genres and Other Late Essays*. C. Emerson and M. Holquist (V.W. McGee, Trans.). Austin, TX: University of Texas Press.

Barnes, D. (1976) *From Communication to Curriculum*. London: Penguin.

Berger, P. and Luckman, T. (1966) *The Social Construction of Reality*. London: Penguin.

Borthick, A.F. and Jones, D.R. (2000) 'The motivation for collaborative discovery learning online and its application in an information systems assurance course', *Issues in Accounting Education*, 15 (2): 181–210.

Boshier, R. (1990) 'Socio-psychological factors in electronic networking', *International Journal of Lifelong Education*, 9 (1): 49–64.

Boyd, G.M. (1987) 'Emancipative Educational Technology', *Canadian Journal of Educational Communication*, 16 (2): 167–72.

Brookfield, S. (1994) 'Tales from the dark side: A phenomenography of adult critical reflection', *International Journal of Lifelong Education*, 13 (3): 203–16.

Brookfield, S. (1995) *Becoming a Critically Reflective Teacher.* San Francisco: Jossey-Bass.

Brower, H.H. (2003) 'On emulating classroom discussion in a distance-delivered OBHR course: Creating an on-line community', *Academy of Management Learning and Education,* 2 (1): 22–36.

Brown, J.S. and Duguid, P. (1991) 'Organisational learning and communities of practice: Toward a unified view of working, learning and innovation', *Organization Science,* 2 (1): 40–56.

Cheyne, J.A. and Tarulli, D. (1999) 'Dialogue, difference and voice in the zone of proximal development', *Theory and Psychology,* 9: 5–28.

Contu, A. and Willmott, H. (2003) 'Re-embedding situatedness: The importance of power relations in learning theory', *Organization Science,* 14: 283–96.

Cousin, G. and Deepwell, F. (2005) 'Designs for networked learning; A communities of practice perspective', *Studies in Higher Education,* 30 (1): 57–66.

Cunliffe, A.L. (2001) 'Managers as practical authors: Reconstructing our understanding of management practice', *Journal of Management Studies,* 38 (3): 351–71.

Dewey, J. (1916) *Democracy and Education.* New York: Macmillan.

Dysthe, O. (2002) 'The learning potential of a web-mediated discussion in a University Course', *Studies in Higher Education,* 27 (3): 339–52.

Edwards, A. (2005) 'Let's get beyond community and practice: The many meanings of learning by participating', *The Curriculum Journal,* 16 (1): 49–65.

Ebersole, S.E. (2003) 'Online learning communities: Connecting with success', *The Journal of Education, Community and Values*: Interface on the Internet, http://bcis.pacificu.edu/journal/2003/09/ebersole.php, accessed 21/08/2007.

Ellsworth, E. (1989) 'Why doesn't this feel empowering: Working through the repressive myths of critical pedagogy', *Harvard Educational Review,* 59 (3): 297–324.

Fairclough, N. (2003) *Analysing Discourse: Textual Analysis for Social Research.* London/New York: Routledge.

Ferreday, D., Hodgson, V. and Jones, C. (2006) 'Dialogue, language and identity: Critical issues for networked management learning', *Studies in Continuing Education,* 28 (3): 223–39.

Fenwick, T. (2005) 'Ethical dilemmas of critical management education: Within classrooms and beyond', *Management Learning,* 36 (1): 31–48.

Fournier, V. and Grey, C. (2000) 'At the critical moment: Conditions and prospects for critical management studies', *Human Relations,* 53 (1): 7–32.

Freire, P. (1972) *Pedagogy of the Oppressed.* Harmondsworth: Penguin.

French, R. and Grey, C. (1996) *Rethinking Management Education.* Thousand Oaks, CA: Sage.

Garrison, D.R. (1997) 'Computer conferencing: The post-industrial age of distance education', *Open Learning,* 3–11.

Garrison, D.R. and Anderson, T. (2003) *E-Learning in the 21st Century: A Framework for Research and Practice.* London & New York: RoutledgeFalmer.

Gergen, K.J. (1973) 'Social psychology as history', *Journal of Personality and Social Psychology,* 26 (2): 309–20.

Gergen, K.J. (1999) *An Invitation to Social Construction.* London: Sage.

Gherardi, S., Nicolini, D. and Odella, F. (1998) 'Towards a social understanding of how people learn in organizations', *Management Learning,* 29 (3): 273–97.

Giroux, H. (1983) *Theory and Resistance in Education.* London: Heinemann Education Books.

Gokhale, A.A. (1995) 'Collaborative learning enhances critical thinking', *Journal of Technology Education,* Available: http://scholar.lib.vt.edu/ejournals/ JTE/jte-v7n1/gokhale.jte-v7n1.html. accessed 25/02/2008.

Gore, J.M. (1993) *The Struggles for Pedagogies.* New York: Routledge.

Habermas, J. (1981) *The Theory of Communicative Action, Vol 11.* Boston: Beacon Press.

Harasim, L. (1990) 'Online education: An environment for collaboration and intellectual amplification', in L. Harasim (ed.) *Online Education: Perspectives on a New Environment.* New York: Praeger Publishers. pp. 39–66.

Heron, J. (1974) 'The concept of a peer learning community', *Human Potential Research Project.* University of Surrey.

Heron, J. (1981) 'Self and peer assessment for managers', in T. Boydell, and M. Pedlar (eds), *Management Self Development, Concepts and Practices.* Farnborough: Gower.

Hodgson, V. and McConnell, D. (1992) 'IT-based open learning: A case-study in management learning', *Journal of Computer Assisted Learning,* 8 (3): 136–58.

Hodgson, V.E. and Reynolds, P.M. (2005) 'Consensus, difference and "multiple communities" in networked learning', *Studies in Higher Education*, 30 (1): 11–24.

Hodgson, V.E. and Reynolds, M. (1987) 'The dynamics of the learning community: Staff intention and student', in D. Boud and V. Griffen (eds), *Understanding Adult Learning from the Learner's Perspective*. London: Kogan Page.

Hodgson, V.E. and Watland, P. (2004) 'Researching networked management learning', *Management Learning*, 35 (2): 99–116.

Hiltz, S.R. (1986) 'The "Virtual Classroom": Using computer-mediated communication for university teaching', *Journal of Communication*, 36 (2): 95–104.

James, M. and Brown, S. (2005) 'Grasping the TLRP nettle: Preliminary analysis and some enduring issues surrounding the improvement of learning outcomes', *The Curriculum Journal*, 16 (1): 7–30.

Johansen, R. (1988) *Groupware: Computer Support for Business Teams*. New York: Free Press.

Keeley, S.M. and Shemberg, K. (1995) 'Coping with student resistance to critical thinking', *College Teaching*, 43: 140–6.

Knowles, M. (1975) *Self-Directed Learning: A Guide for Learners and Teachers*. New York: Association Press.

Kolb, D.A. (1984) *Experiential Learning: Experience as the Source of Learning and Development*. Englewood Cliffs, NJ: Prentice-Hall.

Kolb, D.A. and Fry, R. (1975) 'Toward an applied theory of experiential learning', in C. Cooper (ed.), *Theories of Group Process*. London: John Wiley.

Koschmann, T. (1999) 'Toward a dialogic theory of learning: Bakhtin's contribution to understanding learning in settings of collaboration', *Proceedings of Computer Support for Collaborative Learning*, USA. pp. 308–13.

Knowles, M. (1975) *Self-Directed Learning: A Guide for Learners and Teachers*. Englewood Cliffs: Prentice-Hall/Cambridge.

Lave, J. and Chaiklin, S. (1993) *Understanding Practice: Perspectives on Activity and Context*. Cambridge: Cambridge University Press.

Lave, J. and Wenger, E. (1991) *Situated Learning: Legitimate Peripheral Participation*. Cambridge: Cambridge University Press.

Leidner, D.E. and Jarvenpaa, S.L. (1995) 'The use of information technology to enhance management school education: A theoretical view', *MIS Quarterly*, 19 (3): 265–91.

Leont'ev, N. (1978) *Activity, Consciousness, and Personality*. Trans. Marie J. Hall. Prentice-Hall, available at http://www.marxists.org/archive/leontev/works/1978/ accessed 25/02/2008.

Lindeman, E.C. (1926) *The Meaning of Adult Education*. New York: New Republic.

Mann, S.J. (2005) 'Alienation in the learning environment: A failure of community?' *Studies in Higher Education*, 30 (1): 43–55.

McConnell, D. (2005) 'Examining the dynamics of networked e-learning groups and communities', *Studies in Higher Education*, 30 (1): 23–40.

McKenna, C. (2005) 'Words, bridges and dialogue; issues of audience and addressivity in online communication', in R. Land, and Siân Bayne (eds), *Education in Cyberspace*. London: RoutledgeFalmer.

Mitra, A. and Watts, E. (2002) 'Theorizing cyberspace: The idea of voice applied to the internet discourse', *New Media & Society*, 4 (4): 379–498.

Nichani, M.R. (2000) 'Learning through social interactions' (Online communities), Elearningpost.com, http://www.elearningpost.com/images/uploads/comm.pdf, accessed 21/08/2007.

Noddings, N. (1996) 'On community', *Educational Theory*, 46: 245–67.

Pedler, M. (1981) 'Developing the learning community', in T. Boydell and M. Pedler (eds), *Management Self-Development: Concepts and Practices*. Aldershot: Gower.

Reynolds, M. (1997) 'Towards a critical management pedagogy', in J.G. Burgoyne and P.M. Reynolds (eds) *Management Learning: Integrating Perspectives in Theory and Practice*, London: Sage. pp. 312–28.

Reynolds, M. (1999a) 'Grasping the nettle: Possibilities and pitfalls of a critical management pedagogy', *British Journal of Management*, 10 (2): 171–84.

Reynolds, M. (1999b) 'Critical reflection and management education: Rehabilitating less hierarchical approaches', *Journal of Management Education*, 23 (5): 537–53.

Reynolds, M. (2000) 'Bright lights and the pastoral idyll', *Management Learning*, 31: 67–81.

Reynolds, M. and Trehan, K. (2003) 'Learning from difference?' *Management Learning*, 34 (2): 163–80.

Reynolds, M. and Vince, R. (2004) 'Critical management education and action-based learning: Synergies and contradictions', *Academy of Management Learning & Education*, 3 (4): 442–56.

Schön, D.A. (1983) *The Reflective Practitioner: How Professionals Think in Action*. London: Maurice Temple Smith.

Shotter, J. (1994) *Conversational Realities: Constructing Life Through Language*. London: Sage.

Shotter, J. and Cunliffe, A.L. (2001) 'Managers as practical authors: Everyday conversations for action', in D. Holman and R. Thorpe (eds), *Management and Language*. London: Sage Publications.

Stacey, E. (1999) 'Collaborative learning in an online environment', *Journal of Distance Education/ Revue de l'enseignement à distance*, available at http://cade.icaap.org/vol14.2/stacey.html accessed 25/02/08.

Swan, K. (2002) 'Building learning communities in online courses: The importance of interaction', *Education, Communication & Information*, 2 (1): 23–49.

Torbert, W.R. (1978) 'Educating towards shared purpose, self direction and quality work', *Journal of Higher Education*, 49 (2): 109–35.

Usher, R. (1992) 'Experience in adult education: A post modern critique', *Journal of Philosophy of Education*, 26 (2): 201–15.

Underwood, J.D.M. (2003) 'Student attitudes towards socially acceptable and unacceptable group working practices', *British Journal of Psychology*, 94: 319–37.

Willmott, H. (1997) 'Making learning critical: Identity, emotion, and power in processes of management development', *Systems Practice*, 10 (6): 749–71.

Vygotsky, L.S. (1997) 'Consciousness as a problem for the psychology of behaviour', in *The Collected Works of L.S. Vygotsky*. Vol. 3. New York: Plenum. pp. 63–79.

# 8

# State of the Art:
# Ethics and Learning

Charles J. Fornaciari and Kathy Lund Dean

## Abstract

This chapter explores wide-reaching research streams that both support unequivocally the positive outcomes of ethics education and challenge current pedagogical norms. We assert that the debate about whether we can teach ethics has been irrationally persistent and offer evidence that teaching ethics parallels teaching other topical areas in which we have taken for granted that there are lasting learning and behavioral outcomes for students. Research in ethics and its impact on organizational life, personal life, and myriad forms of decision-making has been undertaken in disparate arenas such as workplace spirituality, economics, leadership, neuroscience, and clinical psychology. We discuss the major outcomes from eight distinct and lively research streams, examining implications for ethics pedagogy. Overwhelmingly, we find evidence supporting the position that the future of teaching ethics lies in engaging students creatively, experientially, and even physiologically. 'Traditional' forms of passive pedagogy must give way to immersion-based, holistic educational models in which the professor plays a significant role in norming and modeling expected prosocial behaviors for students. We conclude the chapter by exploring the calls for change that are gaining attention and urgency, put forth by various stakeholders in the conversation about ethics education.

The debate over whether business ethics may be taught has been irrationally perpetuated. It is irrational because we predicate much of our teaching profession on the idea that what students take away from the classroom will in fact be applied in their working lives. We believe we may teach students to be more effective leaders, better accountants, more creative programmers. Why not more ethical in their business dealings? We believe the persistence of skepticism is at least partly due to the tension between *possibility* and *limitation*.

Business school topics are fundamentally about possibility, about creativity, about the best and brightest gaining the most. The market mindset we embrace is built on vast horizons, limitless potential and blue skies. For example, Marketing studies potential sales niches and future product-based revenue streams; Management focuses on high-functioning teams and innovative competitive advantage; Finance studies market gains and wealth accumulation techniques.

Ethics, though, labors under the reputation as a delimiter, an unfortunate constraint on the possibilities – a limitation to be avoided. Making ethically-defensible decisions in the workplace adds yet another layer of complexity in an already dizzyingly complex organizational context. The persistently short-term orientation of corporate outcomes, like quarterly earnings and dramatically shortened average CEO tenures, make ethics – a long-term construct – seem like a quaint nicety that is out of touch with real-world pressures. And, because academic and popular press attention to business ethics seems to come in fits and starts, depending on how high-profile the corporate ethics violations are (such as in the mid-1980s with downsizing and Michael Milkin, and in the post-Enron era of the early 21st century), it is no wonder that behaving ethically in the workplace is considered an aberration to business as usual.

The state of the art in ethics education research is a rich and increasingly varied body of work that understands ethics education matters, but with little agreement on how much or how we should measure success. The literature also insists that change is needed in ethics education, particularly at a post-secondary level, but the calls fall along a continuum of how holistic and systemic change must be. And, as expected, there is an enormous divergence of variables to be manipulated to fix ethics education.

Ethics education matters when we consider Adam Smith's original conceptualization of markets and capitalistic activity in three distinct ways. His biggest worry was the proliferation of unethical actors in a market system and insisted on 'no force, no fraud' as a main capitalistic norm. Even Milton Friedman, who has been misunderstood as the poster-child for what some have considered pure capitalism, wrote of the need for fair market play without the taint of fraudulent activity (Friedman, 1970). Secondly, although markets have self-correcting mechanisms that

punish unethical behavior, there is a lag factor that makes the self-corrections *ex post facto* events. By the time the market corrects, the hurt has already been inflicted and *ex ante* learning opportunities for preventing future abuses quickly grow cold.

Lastly, after the multi-pronged collusion among Enron executives, its Board of Directors, Andersen's audit team, and layers of employees that secured the firm's failure, confidence in the check-and-balance mechanisms we took for granted in the market economy has been shattered. Interest in ethical behavior has taken a decidedly personal turn after the investor community realized institutions would no longer protect its interests. We are left with the understanding that post-secondary education is part of the solution to an increasingly broken market apparatus.

Throughout the chapter, we are defining 'effectiveness' in ethics education as being able to positively affect students' ethical decision-making ability *and* subsequent behaviors in organizational settings. The (illogical) gap between behavioral expectations in other disciplines and those in ethics discussed in the first paragraph of the chapter notwithstanding, we observe that the crux of the outcry about ethics educational efforts coalesces around what former business students are *doing* in organizations. The ethics breaches only matter when others are harmed, thus, we write from the vantage point of where the ethics educational rubber hits the organizational behavior road – the decisions our former students are making and the actions they are taking.

The crucial connector in this paradigm is predicated on the idea that students accept the learning and change opportunities we make available to them. Indeed, isn't all promise of behavioral change, whether with employees, clients, patients, family or students, predicated on such an acceptance? Although some may view this as controversial, we believe that learning and sensemaking (Schwandt, 2005) rest within the 'target' of our educational efforts.

Thus, if we may make one overall, composite statement with respect to the state of the art in ethics education, it is this: education does matter. The debate about whether educational efforts have any effects on subsequent student behaviors has been steadily waning in favor of evidence that the level at which students get ethics instruction may leave fundamentally lasting imprints on their thoughts, deeds, and futures (see for example, Balotsky and Steingard, 2006; Driscoll and Finn, 2005; and O'Fallon and Butterfield, 2005 for a snapshot of this literature).

## EVIDENCE OF EDUCATIONAL EFFECTIVENESS

Immediately after the ethics scandals perpetrated by companies over the last several years, ethics education, and specifically post-secondary ethics educational efforts, received a deluge of academic and popular attention. While popular consensus indicated that business education has persistently failed to enact in students norms of ethical corporate behavior, the literature paints a different picture. For the remainder of the chapter we examine some of the major sources of evidence in very different arenas that buttress the notion that educational efforts can positively inform students' ethical behaviors. We end the chapter examining varied exhortations for change and critically assess their potential to achieve the change each promises, pointing to future research opportunities.

## LESSONS FROM EXPERIENTIAL LEARNING THEORY FOR ETHICS EDUCATION

Experiential learning theory (ELT) has long advocated the benefits of moving students from passive receptors to active participants in their own learning and for the lasting impressions that such pedagogy engenders. Although radical when Dewey promoted it a century ago (Dewey, 1897/1959; 1928/1959, 1938) and still tangential when Kolb put out his seminal version of it (Kolb, 1984), ELT's

immense improvements on passive learning models have steadily gained devotees. ELT research has shown a battery of learning improvements including increased retention of learning objectives, better understanding of complex organizational systems, better verbal communication skills and increased emotional intelligence.[1]

ELT's promise for ethics education is increased empathy, better understanding of how decisions trigger systemic impacts, better understanding of power relationships and their possible abuses, increased ability to defend one's views to a group, and increased congruence of personal and work values systems. All of these learning opportunities parallel ethics constructs and the behaviors we believe are 'ethical' (Balotsky and Steingard, 2006; Trevino and Brown, 2004; Weaver and Agle, 2002).

Perhaps the greatest promise lies in immersion pedagogies, one dimension of ELT, and one that has been formulated into a variety of models. While ELT pedagogies are at root process-oriented, immersion pedagogies take process even further. For example, service-learning and its concordant reflection work have been established as almost unparalleled in helping students experience the organizational and emotional nuances that fundamentally affect decision making. Kenworthy-U'ren and Peterson (2005) chronicle service-learning's holistic impacts, following Zlotkowski's (2001) tireless efforts to institutionalize service-learning programs. Others (e.g., Godfrey et al., 2005; McCarthy et al., 2002) offer evidence of student-reported learning outcomes that reach far beyond sterile recall of leadership theories or motivational models due to the service-learning opportunities provided. Ethical impact may be observed in students' increased identification with the other; experience with organizational holism; experiential contact with social power norms; and awareness of communication patterns and their impacts.

Reflection is being integrated into all disciplines in business education, not just management. Accounting, for example, utilizes student reflection as a source of learning how to accept and learn from failure (e.g., Gracia and Jenkins, 2002). Reflection offers insights into how affect impacts decisions – an irreplaceable addition to the rational-analytic model so often proffered as how decisions are made in organizations (Mintzberg, 2004; Mintzberg and Westley, 2001). When students encounter their organizational 'job' as service providers they see firsthand and in real time what immediate impact managerial decisions have on workers. Ethical maturity requires such internalization of understanding, and the literature tells us how much more successful service-learning is at gaining that internalization than passive teaching techniques.

Dehler (2006) chronicles how action science connects and personalizes learning to workplace activities. He notes that action science as a pedagogical tool[2] adds robustness to process, rather than content (p. 642) and thus provides significant transferability for potential student takeaways. In this context, action science fosters an iterative, problem-based learning opportunity that ultimately results in practical outcomes that students may apply in many different organizational situations. Similar to service-learning, action science requires reflection to add completion to the learning process and as such provides a framework for evaluating, among other activities, the rightness or wrongness of potential workplace behaviors.

> In other words, where the traditional teaching-centered approach privileges textbook learning for use later, that is, toward practice, action research begins with practice and works the other way, that is, toward knowledge. (2006: 642)

Using action science as an experiential learning tool in the classroom allows students to develop, clarify, critically examine and 'test' their own knowledge-relevant basis for evaluating action, a crucial component for operationalizing a moral compass in organizational settings not designed to honor individual limits.

ELT has been continuously honed for increased creativity and application breadth. Kolb's newer work focuses on creating learning spaces defined by conversation among students (Baker et al., 2002; Kolb et al., 2005). Dialoguing as a learning experience is grounded in affect: How will others respond to my comments? Will I sound stupid? Can I justify my position? What do I do when others disagree with me? Content almost completely aside, facilitating conversations among peers creates process-based competencies that develop students' understanding of their own beliefs, values and perhaps most importantly for ethics, their own limits.

Other process-oriented incarnations of ELT that offer significant ethics learning opportunities include peer evaluations, in-class simulations such as the Power Game (Bolman and Deal, 1979)[3], and role-plays. For each, there is a responsible process for both students as well as for facilitators, and like conversational learning, the content of each is perhaps subsumed to how the journey towards outcomes goes. For example, Marcic et al. (2001) offer observer feedback questions for framing discussion about role-plays – a vulnerable student experience wherein careless comments may devastate a classmate. Those authors also offer a six construct framework for evaluating peers that focuses on the process of engaged group behavior, helping students understand their responsibilities to each other in defined, measurable and actioned ways.

Repeated exposure to and accountability for sound and kind process follow students long after the content itself has faded, shaping their decisions towards the 'other.' This is the continued promise of ELT.

## LESSONS FROM SERVANT-LEADERSHIP FOR ETHICS EDUCATION

Greenleaf's (1977) conceptualization of servant-leadership described, 'a natural feeling' to serve others in organizational life (p. 13) and has since almost defined leadership idealism. Largely owing to the serious American corporate ethics breaches, servant-leadership as a viable alternative to prevailing leadership paradigms is experiencing a renewal of interest (ASHE, 2006). The servant model is inherently ethical owing to its other-orientation (Collier, 2006; Hamilton and Bean, 2005); leaders who are concerned about negative impacts on others, who lead only to serve others, and whose leadership focus is to harness the creative and responsible energies of others will not fall prey to the self-indulgent forces for ethical compromise in organizational settings.

The servant model is also inherently active and requires energy directed towards developing others, which is often inconsistent with our national cultural orientation constructs as defined by Hofstede, as well as with pervasive workplace reward systems that recognize individual achievements. Teaching under a servant-leadership paradigm is thus akin to swimming upstream in the rapid cultural river that is organizational norming. However, Greenleaf and others who have written on the model (e.g., Audi and Murphy, 2006; Sauser, Jr., 2005) acknowledge its fundamental grounding in the concept of power and how power is used to both enhance and stall organizational and personal goals. Grounding servant-leadership in power offers realism by engaging in a commonly understood organizational 'language.' A power basis also offers a way to pedagogically tackle the practical idealism of serving others in a leadership context.

Hamilton and Bean (2005) detail how servant-leadership is embedded into Synovus Financial Corporation (www.synovus.com), representing significant commitment to developing managers who practice the servant model. Three levels of leadership education build upon each other and are holistically faithful to practicing servant-leadership at every organizational level. Interestingly, every program requires an action-learning project, further immersing participants into the servant ideals and helping Synovus managers understand causal

attributes as well as detractors from real-world servant-leadership practice. Everything about Synovus is predicated on executives who use servant-leadership to manage others, showing students the importance of fit and consistency when advocating for ethical leadership. Rewarding managers based upon how responsibly they wield organizational influence is a remarkably salient 'alternative data point' for students immersed in traditional thinking about power and influence.

Collins' (2001) *Good to Great* is a recent incarnation of the servant-leader model. Collins utilizes accessible business language, stories and analogies to help us understand what he calls, 'Level 5 Leadership' or leaders who 'channel their ego needs away from themselves and into the larger goal of building a great company... A Level 5 leader blends extreme personal humility with intense personal will' (Collins, n.d.). Power and ego are closely aligned and when power/ego needs are out of whack, the entire organization suffers.

*Good to Great* reads like a workbook rather than an academic framework and Collins' website (www.jimcollins.com) contains actionable information including assessments, notes to prompt discussion, video clips, analytic tools, and even homework exercises to help Level 5 Leadership seekers see how the model works in real life and in real time. The transferability difficulty, however, is that unless an organization undertakes Collins' model on an *organizational* level, the chances for individual success – an apple in a sea of oranges – are slim. Level 5 Leadership and servant-leadership are very similar in approach, ideals, and implementation difficulties. Level 5 Leadership, however, builds on the servant model in that it focuses more holistically on the organizational context as supportive of the leader's efforts, while in the classic servant model, the leader is more of a maverick change agent on an individual level.

Locander and Luechauer's (2006) brief piece discusses such potential mismatches and frames power as the buttress of organizational action. They note the about-face that ascribing to a servant-leadership model requires, in that, although we have based our last 25 years of teaching about organizational power on techniques for gaining as many organizational resources as possible, we now need to '… embrace the paradox that the best way to get power is to give it away' (p. 45). Thus, they address head-on one of the culturally problematic elements of servant-leadership – that it is invisible and unremarkable in a self-aggrandizing and achievement-oriented milieu.

Students must be shown the upsides of the servant model's potential while we also acknowledge the cultural giveaways. Thus, servant-leadership ethics pedagogy might entail a directed internship experience wherein students practice orienting their energy towards making those around them better. Coupled with reflection work and structured debriefs, first-hand understanding of the servant model is most consistent with what Greenleaf might expect.

Servant-leadership 'works' when consistently applied and embedded, and when applying servant-leadership pedagogy, ethics instructors must reflect the model's holism to do it and students' learning justice. Teaching servant-leadership is active, expressive and demanding because we have to model it unswervingly.

## LESSONS FROM SPIRITUALITY, RELIGION AND THE WORKPLACE FOR ETHICS EDUCATION

This literature investigates relationships between spirituality, religion and right action in two ways: how religiosity and how morality influence ethical action. Specific religious traditions are usually used as the constructs because researchers believe spirituality is too individualized to reliably measure (e.g., Baker and Wang, 2004). Researchers are interested in how one's religious or spiritual beliefs influence decision making and behaviors in the workplace. The general orientation is that stronger religiosity or spiritual engagement will positively correlate

with ethical decision making and, more importantly, behavior.

O'Fallon and Butterfield's (2005) empirical ethics decision-making literature review revealed 14 findings that used religion as an independent variable among studies published between 1996 and 2003. Nine found positive empirical relationships between some religion construct (i.e., reported religious affiliation, level of church attendance, etc.) and ethical decision making. In their review, Weaver and Agle (2002) indicate that while the evidence is generally in favor of religiosity positively influencing ethics, there are major variations in how religiosity was operationalized as well as how ethics was empirically measured. Drawing on identity theory and concepts of role expectations, Weaver and Agle indicate that two moderators influence whether 'religious' people will indeed behave in ethical ways: salience of religious self-identity and individual motivation for being religious (p. 90). They call for more creative research methodologies to more deeply explain how religiosity influences ethical decision making and behaviors; the literature generally notes the limitations of observable, self-reported constructs like church attendance to proxy 'religiousness' of respondents.

Although the research work spans many populations, from students to business executives to health care workers, older and newer work alike contends with the same significant methodological problem confronting this type of research: the relationship between 'intent' and subsequent 'action.' Kohlberg struggled with it as did Rest and his colleagues; Ajzen's (1985) seminal work tried to bridge the gap. Weber and Gillespie (1998) found that empirical links that Ajzen and others found between intent and action represented 'weak to moderate correlation' (p. 462). Singhapakdi et al. (2000) found that religiousness influences personal moral philosophy and intention to act correctly but also found the behavioral link to be elusive.

It is fruitful to note the fundamental challenges ethics pedagogy faces in trying to link the outcomes of traditional instructional approaches such as exposure to models and case analyses (see Lund-Dean and Beggs, 2006, for a more complete discussion) with teaching right action; adding a religious or spiritual construct muddies the waters considerably. The literature acknowledges the gap between what one espouses (especially in a religious context) and intends to do, and what one ultimately does. de Graaf (2006) asserts that, 'No one's actions are based on only conscious decisions solely based on explicit moral values' (p. 247), and points to the importance of organizational context when actors weigh ethical matters. Thus, de Graaf uses discourse as his data gathering technique, creating a continuum of meaning between 'representation[s] of reality' and their 'consequences for action' (p. 250). Most importantly, de Graaf found that 'worldview narratives' including spiritual perspectives, help us understand how identity, normative positions, and context inform ethical decision-making (p. 254).

King (2006) reports on eight in-depth interviews that show overtly spiritual and religious influences on managerial decision-making and management styles. King sought to exemplify how these orientations positively impacted the manager's job; the lack of well-rounded reporting is salient, but methodologically he illustrated the gains in understanding that can be made using text analysis in the context of our research questions.

Newer research is trending towards more creative methodological directions, helping educators see a richly expanded source of potential ethics conversations and activities for learning. For instance, King's work acknowledges the role of context in ethical decision making and Delbecq's seminal works advocate using one's religious community as support for tough decisions, overtly recognizing organizational pressures that serve to sway one from making decisions in concert with religious or spiritual ideals (e.g., Delbecq, 1999, 2005).

Pedagogically, the implications are clear – ethics instructors must move away from values-free rhetoric towards not only acknowledging spiritual and religious life in organizations but integrating millennia-old

traditions of decision-making holism. In Delbecq's leadership courses, managers learn to meditate quietly and reflect on decisions made. Fry (2006) requires students to engage with spiritually-nourishing practices such as spending time in nature or practicing yoga while Trott (2006) requires multiple reflection writing assignments and interviews with spiritually mature executives. Thus, training future organizational leaders and actors moves outside the rational-analytic pedagogical box and taxes our abilities as instructors to get more engaged with our own paradigmatic teaching limitations. We discuss more about these limitations in the next section.

## LIMITATIONS OF THE RATIONAL ACTOR MODEL AS IT IMPACTS ETHICS EDUCATION

Our discussion so far has focused on management ethics education firmly grounded in the behavioral and social sciences. The front-edge work in ethics education that we have highlighted requires a holistic shift in considering the nature of learners *per se*. Although there is no shortage of evidence that active social science pedagogy is superior to passive, in general pedagogical practices have been more traditional than innovative. For example, the popularity of cases as a pedagogical tool for exploring ethics issues in the management classroom can be directly connected to the underlying behavioral science paradigm typically found in business schools of the 'rational actor' decision-maker gathering facts, assessing alternatives, and making an informed decision (Greenhalgh, 2007; Mintzberg, 2004; Mintzberg and Westley, 2001; Reynolds, 2006). Indeed, it is almost *de rigueur* that ethics texts include a selection of cases for students to apply to some decision-making model.[4]

As noted, the rational actor paradigm starts with the premise that decision making and behaviors are based on careful analysis of the information at hand. Here, humans, and thus their brains, are simply 'computers' that take in information, processes it and output optimal decisions (Pressman, 2006). If the brain is indeed a computer-like machine for the purpose of rational decision making, then ethics becomes a matter of which 'program' gets fed into the computer to resolve the problem – utilitarianism, rights and duties, justice and so on. Of course this approach directly produces two of the greatest obstacles regarding ethics education today.

The first obstacle emerges as a debate over moral relativism and absolutism. If ethics is relative, then education simply becomes a matter of exposing students to various models [programs] and teaching them the relevant decision-making tools and then 'hoping for the best', whatever that may be. If ethics is absolute, then education becomes the search for universal principles followed by the subsequent teaching and application of those principles and the judging of whether we have managed to uphold them in our decisions.

The second obstacle deriving from the rational actor model is whether ethics can be taught in a manner to produce behavioral change. If the brain is a fully fixed machine by the time students reach college, then is it really possible to reprogram all this 'wiring' within the classroom to produce change? Many management educators have traditionally answered 'no', and as a result, the measure of success in ethics teaching becomes something different. Instead of the hoped for, but rarely measured behavioral change (Balotsky and Steingard, 2006), 'success' gets denigrated into concepts such as 'exposure', 'understanding' and 'ability to apply a decision-making model to a case'.

Combined, these issues often lead educators down a dark path that essentially buttresses the notion that ethics education does not matter. In effect, the limitations of the underlying paradigm are translated directly as limitations into how we traditionally teach ethics, and consequently, the process becomes a reinforcing self-defeating circle. If we acknowledge the limitations of the rational actor model, it offers us the opportunity to look far beyond our social scientific fields for

some of the greatest possibilities for potential advances in business ethics education. This is perhaps most evident in the groundbreaking work emerging from the neurosciences, cognitive and clinical psychology and economics, all of which provide strong empirical challenges to the efficacy of viewing humans as rational decision makers. The next three sections explore the implications for future management ethics education based on the work emerging from these fields.

## LESSONS FROM NEUROSCIENCE FOR ETHICS EDUCATION

Neuroscientific research has moved away from the notion of the brain as a 'fixed computer-like machine' to a richer understanding of its functioning, and consequently, its impact on human behavior. Recent neuroscience advances show that the brain can and does undergo physical changes in its structure and operation during a person's adult lifetime, and not simply as the result of extreme events such as accident-induced traumas (G. Carr, 2006; Siegel, 2007). Further, these effects operate in both directions – brain changes can produce behavioral changes and behavioral changes can produce brain changes. These insights have the potential to profoundly impact ethics education if its focus is behaviorally-directed.

For example, ample evidence exists that empathy, a precursor to ethical behavior, has at least a partial basis in evolutionary biology both in primates such as chimpanzees (de Waal, 1996, 2006; Mendez, 2006) and in humans (L. Carr et al., 2003; Hauser, 2006; Mendez, 2006; Siegel, 2007) in addition to its psychological constructs that are so heavily explored in the behavioral sciences. While empathy has traditionally been viewed as a social construction among 'advanced' humans, some argue that evolutionary biology is the basis for ensuring the proper functioning of social communities that in turn aids in the long-term survival of the community and species – what Hauser (2006) calls our 'moral grammar'. According to

Hauser, moral grammar is universal despite its apparent surface variations: 'When we judge an action as morally right or wrong, we do so instinctively, tapping a system of unconsciously operative and inaccessible moral knowledge' (2006: 419–20).

For Hauser, experience plays a key role in the process of learning this grammar: 'The role of experience is to instruct the innate system, pruning the range of possible moral systems down to one distinctive moral signature. This type of instructive learning is characteristic of countless biological processes' (p. 422). Hauser does not provide much detail concerning what constitutes experience. He does argue that, 'many of the principles underlying our moral judgment are inaccessible conscious reflection' (p. 423) and, 'the systems that generate intuitive moral judgments for our actions are often in conflict with the systems that generate principled reasons for our actions' (p. 418). However, the above, combined with Hauser's arguments that the biological imperatives of cooperation and reciprocity serve as the basis of our moral makeup, and that moral behavior requires us to tap into the right biological impulses, does provide some insight to what constitutes these experiences. We will address them shortly.

While neuroscience has demonstrated that brain physiology can have a direct impact on the formation of values and subsequent behaviors, it has also produced evidence that certain experiences induce changes in how the brain functions. Just as an ongoing program of physical training enables a person to run faster and longer, some activities can produce striking brain changes. Much of this relatively recent research has given rise to the concept of 'neuroplasticity' – changes in the brain's physical structures and operations as a response to experiences. Neuroscientist Ulyings notes:

Progress in brain development allows development of cognitive capabilities and, in its turn, the exercising of cognitive capabilities shapes further brain development. Some capabilities (such as binocular vision) can only be developed within rather limited sensitive or critical developmental periods. For other capabilities, such as 'experience' learning in a so-called enriched environment, such restricted developmental time windows do not exist (e.g., Ulyings, 2001) because of the plasticity potential of the underlying brain circuitry elements necessary for these abilities. (2006: 60)

Ulyings (2006: 73) further asserts:

'Experience' learning requires local dendritic and synaptic alterations. This kind of plasticity does not stop in adulthood. This does not imply that the capacity for plasticity remains unchanged during life. In practice, a decline with age has been observed in the paradigm of the so-called environmental enrichment. On the other hand, specially designed strategies might be necessary to obtain (better) plastic changes in adult learning. (e.g., Bergan et al., 2005)

While much of the direct research on neuroplasticity occurs at too basic of a level (e.g., the brain's restructuring to adapt to vision loss) to be directly applicable for management education, applied findings supporting Hauser's and Ulyings's insights concerning experience are being illustrated by research into mental activities, known by names ranging from meditation to mindfulness, that can serve as an aid to making ethics instruction more effective. These 'experience' techniques all fundamentally involve their practitioners fully engaging themselves in the current moment by consciously observing their own thought processes, and thus disengaging their minds from operating through rationalized and automatic judgment routines, and ultimately achieving higher states of self-awareness [see for example Begley's (2007: 14) definition of Buddhist 'meditation' and Siegel's (2007: 10) definition of 'mindfulness'].

Proponents have often argued for the positive physiological and psychological benefits of the practices. Transcendental Meditation advocates, for example, have long argued for its ability to produce increases in 'health, world peace, more energy, happiness, creativity, and inner peace' (http://www.tm.org/). The results historically have not garnered widespread attention within the business education community, perhaps due to inconsistent applications of research methods (Begley, 2007: 215), or the tendency for the research to be reported in conjunction with specific spiritual traditions (e.g., Balotsky and Steingard, 2006; Delbecq, 2000; Falque and Duruau, 2004). It appears, however, that many of the obstacles regarding beliefs about the brain–mind connection are being overcome or disregarded as the neuroscience community has begun to use its techniques and tools (including the use of advanced brain imaging equipment such as fMRI and EEG machines) to explore the relationship. For example, Hauser (2006) details how many different neurobiological studies have shown physical evidence of targeted brain activity when people evaluate ethical dilemmas (pp. 219–25).

Neurobiologist Siegel (2007: 337–62) argues mindfulness activities promote the growth of brain fibers responsible for functions ranging from emotional balance to empathy to self-insight, and to morality. Increases in these fibers in turn increase neural integration, empathetic relationships and coherence of mind, thus increasing overall well-being. Likewise, Begley (2007) reports on studies examining the meditative practices of experienced Buddhist monks, often in direct comparison to novices. Much of this research is helping to break down the formally dominant paradigm of 'neurogenetic determinism' (Begley, 2007: 252–3) and is beginning to convincingly establish empirical relationships between meditation and factors such as happiness and compassion (Begley, 2007: 242).

It is becoming clear from neuroscientific research that brain physiology, which directly affects behavior, can also demonstrably be altered through a number of experience practices to have impacts on the factors related to ethical behavior. So, what can it tell us about ethics education? First, as Siegel (2007) asserts, these mindfulness techniques need not be tied to any specific faith traditions, thus enabling them to be used in a variety of contexts, such as secular classrooms. Second, these techniques can help cultivate increased

attention and emotional regulation, reduce stress and foster a sense of well-being and compassion. In short, their appropriate use can allow us to tap into our biological imperatives for moral behavior.

The challenge for ethics education from neuroscience research is to translate the 'appropriate' experience practices such as meditation and mindfulness (but also techniques such as Yoga, Tai Chi and Chi Gong) into classroom activities to simultaneously stimulate our universal moral grammar *and* to alter the brain to reduce our developed rationalizations that impede moral behavior. The essences of many of these techniques, such as silence, introspection, mind quieting, and ego separation are often foreign to management education practices which often tend to emphasize exactly the opposite approaches: *active* student involvement in the classroom; individual *competition* [ego building]; temporary cooperation to *achieve a short-term self-interested goal*; and a preference for *hands-on action*. Likewise, many of these techniques also often require some type of formal training, both for students and teachers, before they can be effectively practiced. Finally, results often do not arise instantaneously, and thus the classroom component becomes a long-term starting point.

Even for those unwilling, or unable, to take the step of engaging themselves and their students in these specific experience practices in the classroom, Siegel (2007) argues that many of the same benefits can still accrue if we were to adopt a 'fourth r' – reflection – to education in addition to its three common r's (reading, 'riting, and 'rithmetic). Siegel likens this to Langer's (cf. 1989, 2000) well-documented mindfulness theory of education (which in turn is closely related to our reflection discussion earlier), but also includes activities not typically associated with the management classroom that can aid in the development of awareness and subsequent improved ethical decision making such as 'art, music, dance, writing, psychotherapy, touch (e.g., massage, acupuncture) and sports' (Siegel, 2007: 267–8).

## LESSONS FROM PSYCHOLOGY FOR ETHICS EDUCATION

Related to, but still separate from, neuroscientific research is the work from cognitive and clincial psychology, which essentially attempts to understand brain structures [at a more macro/systems level than the neuroscientists] and how they are involved in complex interactions with emotions, decisions, and behaviors, with the ultimate goal of designing treatments to produce long-term sustainable change (Prochaska and DiClemente, 1992). In direct contrast to many management teachers, who still argue today about the effectiveness of ethics education to produce behavioral change, clinical psychologists have *long* based their work on the foundational assumption that the therapist can help the patient engage in real behavioral change:

> The goal of interpersonal therapy is for the therapist and client to identify, clarify, and establish alternatives to the rigid and self-defeating evoking style of the client. Their task is to replace constricted, extreme transactions with more flexible and clear communications adaptive to the changing realities of specific encounters. (Kiesler, 1982: 15)

Of particular interest to management educators is Frank's assertion that:

> All psychotherapeutic methods are elaborations and variations of age-old procedures of psychological healing. These include confession, atonement, absolution, encouragement, positive and negative reinforcements, modeling, and promulgation of a particular set of values. These methods become embedded in theories as to the causes and cures of various conditions which often become highly elaborated. (1985: 49–50)

The goal of this section is not to produce a comprehensive review of the voluminous work in the psychological sciences, but rather to ask ourselves what lessons we can garner for ethics education from a discipline that shares so many similarities with management, yet reaches such a fundamentally different conclusion about its ultimate effectiveness. The starting point is the recognition that, like so many of the critiques described in

this manuscript, psychology does not place a great deal of emphasis on humans as 'rational actors' (Stanovich and West, 2000). Rather, it acknowledges that many of our behaviors are automatic, irrational, impulsive, and often based on an historical pattern of maladaptive behaviors and beliefs. Thus, behavioral change results from an ongoing process of actions and reflections that are ultimately designed to help the patient form new habits and patterns. Consequently, two important lessons emerge from psychology for ethics educators.

First is the notion that change results first from identifying maladaptive habits and behaviors and then engaging in an ongoing process of developing more well-adjusted approaches to the world. This is in marked contrast to the 'rational actor' view of the business education world which so heavily focuses on the provision of 'new skills' rather than the attunement of old skills or behaviors – we prefer to focus on teaching students how to learn to conduct a Five Forces analysis in Strategy rather than working on diagnosing and improving their current individual abilities as environmental scanners (a fundamental prerequisite for conducting a Five Forces analysis).

This approach also contrasts greatly with many management classroom techniques that revolve around tests for student comprehension, ability to apply and so on. Thus, psychology informs us that to be effective, management educators must move to a much more diagnostic approach to teaching rather than a 'transmit and check' approach. Thus, it may not be effective for most students to lecture on the importance of ethical behavior, nor may it be particularly beneficial to expose them to decision-making models and hope they are more ethical as a result. Instead, psychology suggests that instructors will have to spend time trying to understand the unique circumstances behind each student's ethical bearing and then helping the student develop strategies to maximize his/her own ethical behavior.

Second, psychology suggests a crucial time component is necessary to produce any real behavioral change. This causes us to reconceptualize the 'debate' so in vogue over the past decade of whether business ethics is best taught as a module in content-specific classes or as a standalone course (see Lund Dean, Beggs, and Fornaciari, 2007, for a summary of this debate). If true behavioral change is going to occur, ethics must be delivered and reinforced over time, as with what we witness with the ongoing instruction and *immersion* in the honor codes at military service academies like West Point (http://www.usma.edu/committees/honor/) and Annapolis (http://www.usna.edu/OfficerDevelopment/honor/honorconcept.html) in the United States. In this context, psychology informs immersion techniques in three crucial ways: the message(s) are consistent, applied over a long period of time (in our example, over the course of the cadet's four-year academy career), and reinforced by all members of the organization.

These two lessons can be derived from the work of Vallacher and Wegner and their colleagues (cf. Kozak et al., 2006; Vallacher and Wegner, 1985, 1987; Vallacher et al., 1992; Wegner and Vallacher, 1986) in Action-Identification Theory (AIT). AIT suggests a complex interaction exists between a person's self-image and their actions. In short:

> People do what they think they are doing. Ordinarily, they would prefer to think about their acts in the most encompassing way possible. But when they cannot perform an act so broadly conceptualized, they concern themselves with thinking of the detail of the act. (Wegner and Vallacher, 1986: 550)

From an applied ethics education perspective, this suggests that in order for a person to perceive himself as being 'good' and consequently acting 'good', then a series of activities designed to build and reinforce that perception, engaged in over time, will ultimately lead to a broadening and deepening of that perception as well as leading to the person ultimately undertaking actions to reinforce that self-concept, thus producing a virtuous cycle (Mathews and Fornaciari, 1999, 2001).

Furthermore, as another example, Epstein's Cognitive Experiential Self Theory (CEST) (cf. Epstein, 1994, 2000; Epstein and Pacini, 2000/2001; Pacini and Epstein, 1999) suggests that individuals learn best and lastingly when presented with information in a manner that bypasses the 'short-term rational actor' portion of the brain, and instead connects to the affective elements of the brain/memory system, where long-term behavioral change starts. From an ethics education perspective, it is easy to combine the insights of AIT with CEST to begin to conceptualize effective pedagogy as a series of experiential activities designed to be learned, reinforced, and lived over time, with the ultimate goal of supporting the development of core moral virtues.

Likewise, psychology's conception of the role of the therapist has important insights for ethics education practitioners. Greenberg et al. argue that the therapist's role is to:

> hear, see and understand clients as they are at that moment and to stimulate experiential processing rather than attempting to formulate hypotheses about clients' internal dynamics or to change or modify clients' cognitions and behaviors ... the therapist continuously attempts to provide an optimal environment for the type of flexible cognitive/affective processing required in therapy. (1993: 3–4)

This view, combined with Frank's (1985) description of therapy, suggests a more active role is required of the teacher in the ethics education process than is typically inferred in management education. Although, we have all heard about the exhortation that educators should not be 'sages on the stage but rather guides on the side', much of our focus on the process still revolves around techniques for increasing student involvement in their own education. Even within this chapter we have called upon students to perform service learning, to engage in structured reflection, to meditate, to practice Tai Chi, to name just a few advanced techniques. However, the argument is clear that if many of these techniques are to be effective, then like therapists, the teacher needs to deeply build the foundation. For example, educators will have to model the outcomes they wish their students to achieve: we must do service learning if we require it of our students; we must meditate along with our students; and we must create practice trust, empathy, and integrity if we want our students to internalize these behaviors and values. In short, psychology tells us that if we desire our students to engage in active learning to improve their ethical dispositions, then we must also actively teach.

## LESSONS FROM BEHAVIORAL ECONOMICS FOR ETHICS EDUCATION

A capitalism maxim is that individuals pursue enlightened self-interest. This tenet asserts that rational individuals, when faced with competing choices in a world of scarce resources, will deliberately choose those actions or goods which maximize their own long-term utility, or 'happiness' (Kahneman and Thaler, 2006).

Even though economists have long demonstrated the problematic assumptions behind 'completely rational' decision-making (cf. a sampling of works from these Nobel Prize winning economists: Kahneman, 2003a; Kahneman, 2003b; Kahneman and Thaler, 2006; Simon, 1955; Smith, 2003; Tversky and Kahneman, 1986), the underlying belief that individuals attempt to consciously choose those actions that maximize their own proscription of happiness has remained essentially unchallenged within the discipline. *De gustibus non est disputandum* ('one does not quarrel over taste') is one of economics' most basic principles, and the question of how those tastes are derived has historically been treated as a question uninteresting enough to economists to be left to other disciplines to solve (Stigler and Becker, 1977).

Given that economists traditionally view tastes as 'fixed' (Kahneman and Thaler, 2006), and concurrently that individuals maximize happiness, traditional economic thinking dictates that most individuals will not make choices that inevitably wind up hurting themselves in the long run (Pressman, 2006;

Robins, 1932). This logic forms the basis of the argument that many capitalists proffer against engaging in unethical behavior. While some 'unethical' choices may result in a short-term gains, in the long run they wind up costing more than benefiting – a firm will not make misrepresentations to maximize short-term sales because of the potential reputation and sales costs that could ensue if the misrepresentations were to become public. The literature, both in economics and ethics, is replete with assertions that essentially follow the structure of this argument. Arce (2004: 264) notes 'no less than five Nobel laureates and the father of modern economics recognize the importance of ethical behavior for the functioning of the marketplace, and the ethical behavior within firms for productive efficiency' (before he ironically demonstrates that most managerial economics textbooks are bereft of significant coverage of the topic).

However, what happens to the economic theory of ethical behavior if the notion of individuals as 'utility maximizers', turns out to be inaccurate? Advances in 'behavioral', or 'happiness', economics are beginning to grasp the implications of this idea. In short, the field is demonstrating that people experience many difficulties in attempting to determine their own happiness, and their gauges are often susceptible to being shifted due to a variety of circumstances, some of which are as inconsequential as time of day, state of hunger or recent hours of sleep achieved (Kahneman and Krueger, 2006; Kahneman and Thaler, 2006). This suggests that people often make decisions that work against their own long-term happiness, even when they believe that they are working in their own best interests (Kahneman and Thaler, 2006; Pressman, 2006).

For example, Kahneman and Krueger (2006) reveal the following well-documented conditions regarding happiness that are significantly different from what is usually proscribed in the business classroom:

- 'rank in the income distribution or in one's peer group is more important than the level of income' (p. 8)

- 'measurements of temperament and personality typically account for much more of the variance of reported life satisfaction than do life circumstances' (p. 8)
- there is a 'relatively small and short-lived effect of changes in most life circumstances on reported life satisfaction' (p. 14)
- 'large increases in the standard of living have almost no detectable effects on life satisfaction or happiness' (p. 15)
- 'long-run well-being is not closely related to one's circumstances and opportunities' (p. 16)

These conditions serve to substantially invalidate the commonly held business maxim of 'he who dies with the most toys wins', and strongly demonstrates that humans are essentially poor decision makers with respect to understanding what truly makes us happy. Furthermore, these findings provide strong empirical insights into the causes of a number of well-documented problems of individual behavior within firms. These issues form the basis of Social Comparison Theory's (Festinger, 1954) investigation into the perpetual cycle of disenchantment and a suspicion that the 'other guy' has more than we do (cf. Goodman, 2007). They are also the root of many of the problems documented in Equity Theory (Adams, 1963, 1965) where we make flawed and necessarily imperfect equity calculi when we contextualize our economic accomplishments with our referent group (cf. Wheeler, 2002).

It is easy to imagine situations where individuals experience anxieties of underachievement in outcomes received and consequently engaging in unethical and self-gaining behaviors at the expense of everyone else given the problems documented by SCT and EQ. Given the behavioral economists' insights into the roots of these problems, what are the implications for ethics education? In short, an extension of the happiness research would be the argument that the key to improving ethical behavior is not necessarily training students to be 'more aware' of ethical dilemmas in individual and firm contexts than they were previously and then teaching them how to apply macro level rational

decision models (such as utility) to maximize ethical outcomes (the 'head on' approach prevalent in much business ethics education today).

Rather, they would suggest the use of a more 'indirect' micro level approach, such as training students how to better determine and truly measure their own individual happiness. As discussed, a primary postulate of behavioral economics is not that people choose to be unethical, but rather that they are too fallible in their decision-making processes along the bumpy path of enlightened self-interest. Consequently, 'ethics training' would involve activities designed to either help people uncover their true preferences or to help them avoid the biases and errors in judgment inherent in decision making. Fortunately, economists have produced a huge number of applied texts, so the aspiring ethics professor need not look far for practical guidance on the topic. For example Hogarth's (1987) and Bazerman's (2005) texts continue to stand as classic primers, along with the texts of Kahneman and his colleagues (Gilovich et al., 2002; Kahneman, Slovic et al., 1982; Kahneman and Tversky, 2000).

## SYSTEMS, STRUCTURES AND ETHICS – CALLS FOR CHANGE

Throughout this chapter we have attempted to show that, while there is little convergence among what observers consider to be the shortcomings of ethics education, there is consensus that ethics education must change. Those who advocate for ethics education from their particular vantage point such as psychology or neuroscience are, after all, advocating for approaches that they believe will positively affect ethical behaviors once students leave the classroom. If we re-visit the equivocation of whether ethics education matters, even supporters of ethics education concede that organizational actors are not being given 'correct' tools with which to make defensible decisions once in organizations. It is the 'how' of ethics education that is currently being debated with relish.

At the risk of too rough a generalization, we notice a bi-modal response to how ethics education should look going forward. Internationally, scholars advocate for completely reconfiguring ethics instruction. This means rejecting the current curriculum and pedagogical system completely and starting from scratch. Lund Dean, Beggs, and Fornaciari (2007) describe how critical management studies (CMS) has altered the lens through which ethics educational efficacy is being viewed. Dehler and his colleagues (Dehler, 2006; Dehler et al., 2001) and Hendry are among those international scholars who want to use ethics education to deconstruct the *status quo*, asserting that the values structure within the current economic system is too embedded to fix:

> At the core of the [current business] model is a conception of the business enterprise as a mechanism for coordinating economic inputs and activities and of the manager as a morally neutral technician engaged in a world of purely rational problem solving in the pursuit of efficiency... In a central and critically important sense, however, morality is now what management is all about. (Hendry, 2006: 269, 273)

For Hendry, the fix is business curricula based in the liberal arts, not in courses that perpetuate the above, flawed view of managers. For Dehler et al. deconstruction begins with 'de-centering' the classroom to engage both student and professor on equal epistemological grounding (p. 502) – a model with profound implications for ethics learning.

More broadly, other international scholars embed ethics education not within a classroom or curricular context but within nothing short of a global context. Zsolnai (2007) reports on the 2006 Europe–Asia Dialogue on Business, Ethics and Spirituality conference in which panelists' unit of analysis, if you will, was the global business community. In an age of interdependence and global transparency, worldwide speakers stressed the long-term obligations of business actors and each businessperson's duty in supporting the growing global business infrastructure.

We may contrast the international calls for change with American calls for change. Among American scholars, deconstructing the current system is not a point of discussion. Recent American scholarship (e.g., Hartman, 2006; Heath et al., 2005; Kolb et al., 2005) accepts the current system as too embedded to fundamentally alter and so makes recommendations for ethics education within the current system. For example, Hartman (2006) believes that ethics education cannot reach every student (p. 69) and that case-based dialectic may 'hopefully' (p. 79) help students to recognize potentially hazardous organizational situations.

The pedagogical implication of the international vs. American viewpoint is that the international advocacy is sweeping, but offers very few if any details for actually effecting pedagogical change. The American suggestions are ultimately incremental, but offer clear nuts-and-bolts how-tos (e.g., Greenwood, 2000; Kolb et al., 2005; Williams and Dewett, 2005).

In examining the differences in the academic communities' responses, we may note some of Hofstede's work being operationalized. The American bias towards individualism and short-term orientation would in effect preclude any large-scale, societal-level advocacy for change. One manifestation of this may be seen in the almost complete absence of longitudinal work examining how and if educational efforts, cultural shifts or demographics have affected ethical behavioral changes.

## CONCLUSIONS AND FUTURE DIRECTIONS

As we asserted earlier, our operationalized ethics education paradigm defines effective as the ability to positively affect our students' ethical behavior in organizations. We believe we have shown that changed behaviors, more accountability in behaviors, better ability to assess right and wrong within organizational frameworks and cultures that do not generally stop to evaluate personal moral codes is possible by fundamentally altering our pedagogy towards active and experiential immersion methods. No matter what vantage point we take to examine the state of the art in ethics learning research, the message is unequivocal that we must honor the internalized learning that only active and experiential models have shown to fulfill. Ethics learning is not only cognitive, but it is emotive, complex, physiological, and contextual. Delivery methods matter. We believe this position falls somewhere in the middle of current international (sweeping) and American (incremental) change advocacy with the crucial advantage of being doable.

Part of this is expanding our definitions of what 'ethics' means. For example, professor modeling is a little discussed and researched aspect of teaching right behavior (Kolb et al., 2005). Do we insist on students being on time for class and for appointments, only to ourselves routinely skip office hours? Do we promptly act on academically dishonest behavior when it occurs with our students, or do we let it slide due to the hassles of documentation and potentials for conflict? How we respond every day to seemingly pedestrian occurrences sends messages much more powerful than anything we can say. See McCabe et al.'s (2006) compelling empirical evidence for the power of peer and superior modeling when MBAs – current and future managers – make decisions about what is acceptable and what is not.

The deeper issue is that effective and lasting ethics education requires that we dispense with the folly that our teaching does not matter for student behaviors once they leave our classrooms. Consistent with creating behavioral change in other disciplines, we believe that we can, in fact, make lasting imprints on our students in terms of right behavior, in terms of expectations of morally-aligned management decisions, and in terms of reflecting on and operationalizing organizational actions that best impact others. Adam Smith has been telling us since the beginning that we must embrace ethics to make this system work. If we embrace Smith's system, which we do, why do we ignore his admonitions that ethics is embedded within, part and parcel to, the capitalistic system?

Research-wise, then, we need longitudinal understanding of what managers consider when attempting to resolve ethical dilemmas. We need a firmer understanding of the contextual stimuli that encourage right actions or let wrong actions slip by. We need less silos over integrative research and invite our colleagues in the disciplines examined in this essay to work with us for a holistic understanding of how ethical learning and correlative behaviors happen.

Finally, we need to stop being defensive about ethics and view it paradigmatically as an enabler rather than a delimiter. In the long run, right behaviors enhance business outcomes. The trick is to convince a culturally short-term-oriented business cycle that continuing as-such is foundationally destructive and perpetuates incentives to behave in self-interested and impact-blind ways.

## NOTES

1 A review of ELT research is beyond the scope of this essay. Please see, for examples of models and outcomes, Mintzberg, (2004); Baker et al. (2002); Belcheir (2003); Dworkin (1959); Mathews and Fornaciari (1999); Munro and Rice-Munro (2004); Theroux and Kilbane (2004); Zlotkowski (2001).

2 For an in-depth discussion of the action research project Dehler uses, please see the *Journal of Management Education* article. Describing it here is beyond the scope of this chapter.

3 The *Journal of Management Education* is the premier outlet for detailed learning simulations in a section of the journal specifically devoted to publishing them. Please examine *JME* for myriad examples of in-class simulation opportunities.

4 The advantages, and disadvantages, of using cases as a pedagogical tool to teach rational actor decision-making are well-documented elsewhere (cf. Greenhalgh, 2007; Lundberg et al., 2001), so we will not dwell on them here.

## REFERENCES

Adams, J.S. (1963) 'Toward an understanding of inequity', *Journal of Abnormal and Social Psychology*, 65: 422–36.

Adams, J.S. (1965) 'Inequity in social exchange', in L. Berkowitz (ed.), *Advances in Experimental Social Psychology* (Vol. 2). New York: Academic Press. pp. 267–99.

Ajzen, I. (1985) 'From intentions to actions: A theory of planned behavior', in J. Kuhl and J. Beckmann (eds), *Action Control: From Cognition to Behavior*. New York: Springer-Verlag. pp. 11–39.

Arce, M.D.G. (2004) 'Conspicuous by its absence: Ethics and managerial economics', *Journal of Business Ethics*, 54 (3): 261–77.

ASHE (2006) 'Revolutionary concepts of leadership', *ASHE Higher Education Report*, 31 (6): 71–99.

Audi, R. and Murphy, P.E. (2006) 'The many faces of integrity', *Business Ethics Quarterly*, 16 (1): 3–21.

Baker, A.C., Jensen, P.A. and Kolb, D.A. (eds) (2002) *Conversational Learning: An Experiential Approach to Knowledge Creation*. Westport, CT: Quorum.

Baker, M. and Wang, M. (2004) 'Examining connections between values and practice in religiously committed U.K. clinical psychologists', *Journal of Psychology and Theology*, 32 (2): 126–36.

Balotsky, E.R. and Steingard, D.S. (2006) 'How teaching business ethics makes a difference: Findings from an ethical learning model', *Journal of Business Ethics Education*, 3 (1): 1–30.

Bazerman, M. (2005) *Judgment in Managerial decision-making* (6th edn). New York: John Wiley and Sons.

Begley, S. (2007) *Train Your Mind, Change Your Brain*. New York: Ballantine Books.

Belcheir, M.J. (2003) *Active Learning in and out of the Classroom: Results from the National Survey of Student Engagement* (ERIC Educational Resource Clearinghouse). Boise, ID: Boise State University.

Bergan, J.F., Ro, P., Ro, D. and Knudsen, E.I. (2005) 'Hunting increases adaptive auditory map plasticity in adult barn owls', *Journal of Neuroscience*, 25 (42): 9816–20.

Bolman, L. and Deal, T.E. (1979) 'A simple – but powerful – power simulation', *Exchange*, 4 (3): 38–42.

Carr, G. (2006) 'A survey of the brain: Who do you think you are?' *The Economist*, 381: 3–4.

Carr, L., Iacoboni, M., Dubeau, M.-C., Maziotta, J.C. and Lenzi, G.L. (2003) 'Neural mechanisms of empathy in human beings', *Proceedings of the National Academy of Sciences*, 100 (9): 5497–502.

Collins, J. (2001) *Good to Great: Why Some Companies make the Leap ... and Others Don't*. New York: HarperCollins.

Collier, J. (2006) 'The art of moral imagination: Ethics in the practice of architecture', *Journal of Business Ethics*, 66 (2/3): 307–17.

Collins, J. (n.d.). 'Level 5 Leadership', Retrieved 4/27/07, from http://www.jimcollins.com/lab/level5/index.html

de Graaf, G. (2006) 'Discourse and descriptive business ethics', *Business Ethics: A European Review*, 15 (3): 246–58.

de Waal, F. (1996) *Good Natured: The Origins of Right and Wrong in Humans and Other Animals*. Cambridge, MA: Harvard University Press.

de Waal, F. (2006) 'Morally evolved: Primate social instincts, human morality, and the rise and fall of "veneer theory"', in F. de Waal (ed.), *Primates and Philosophers: How Morality Evolved*. Princeton, NJ: Princeton University Press. pp. 1–80.

Dehler, G.E. (2006) 'Using action research to connect practice to learning: A course project for working management students', *Journal of Management Education*, 30 (5): 636–69.

Dehler, G.E., Welsh, M.A. and Lewis, M.W. (2001) 'Critical pedagogy in the "new paradigm"', *Management Learning*, 32 (4): 493–511.

Delbecq, A.L. (1999) 'Christian spirituality and contemporary business leadership', *Journal of Organizational Change Management*, 12 (4): 345–49.

Delbecq, A.L. (2000) 'Spirituality for business leadership: Reporting on a pilot course for MBAs and CEOs', *Journal of Management Inquiry*, 9 (2): 117–28.

Delbecq, A.L. (2005) 'Spiritually-informed management theory: Overlaying the experience of teaching managers', *Journal of Management Inquiry*, 14 (3): 242–46.

Dewey, J. (1897; 1959) 'My pedagogic creed', in M.S. Dworkin (ed.), *Dewey on Education: Selections*, Vol. 3. New York: Teachers College at Columbia University. pp. 19–32.

Dewey, J. (1928; 1959) 'Progressive education and the science of education', in M.S. Dworkin (ed.), *Dewey on Education: Selections*, Vol. 3. New York: Teachers College at Columbia University. pp. 113–26.

Dewey, J. (1938) *Experience and Education*. New York: Macmillan.

Driscoll, C. and Finn, J. (2005) 'Integrating ethics into business education: Exploring discrepancies and variability among professors and students', *Journal of Business Ethics Education*, 2 (1): 51–69.

Dworkin, M.S. (ed.) (1959) *Dewey on Education*, Vol. 3. New York: Teachers College, Columbia University.

Epstein, S. (1994) 'Integration of the cognitive and psychodynamic unconscious', *American Psychologist*, 49: 709–24.

Epstein, S. (2000) 'The rationality debate from the perspective of cognitive-experiential self-theory, *Behavioral and Brain Sciences*, 23 (5): 671–71.

Epstein, S. and Pacini, R. (2000/2001) 'The influence of visualization on intuitive and analytical information processing', *Imagination, Cognition, and Personality*, 20 (3): 195–216.

Falque, L. and Duruau, V.J. (2004) 'Managerial discernment: An examination in the case of employee appraisal', *Journal of Management, Spirituality, and Religion*, 1 (1): 51–76.

Festinger, L. (1954) 'A theory of social comparison processes', *Human Relations*, 7 (2): 117–40.

Frank, J.D. (1985) 'Therapeutic components shared by all psychotherapies', in M.J. Mahoney and A. Freeman (eds), *Cognition and Psychotherapy*. New York: Plenum Press. pp. 49–80.

Friedman, M. (1970, September 13) 'The social responsibility of business is to increase its profits', *New York Times Magazine*, 32–3.

Fry, L.J. (2006) 'Leadership course syllabus' (pp. post to MSR-L list).

Gilovich, T., Griffin, D. and Kahneman, D. (eds) (2002) *Heuristics and Biases: The Psychology of Intuitive Judgment*. New York: Cambridge University Press.

Godfrey, P.C., Illes, L.M. and Berry, G.R. (2005) 'Creating breadth in management education through service-learning', *Academy of Management Learning and Education*, 4 (3): 309–23.

Goodman, P.S. (2007) 'Special issue on social comparison processes', *Organizational Behavior and Human Decision Processes*, 102 (1): 1–2.

Gracia, L. and Jenkins, E. (2002) 'An exploration of student failure on an undergraduate accounting programme of study', *Accounting Education*, 11 (1): 93–107.

Greenberg, L.S., Rice, L.N. and Elliott, R. (1993) *Facilitating Emotional Change: The Moment-by-Moment Process*. New York: Guilford Press.

Greenhalgh, A.M. (2007) 'Case method teaching as science and art: A metaphoric approach and curricular application', *Journal of Management Education*, 31 (2): 181–94.

Greenleaf, R.K. (1977) *Servant-Leadership: A Journey into the Nature of Legitimate Power and Greatness*. New York: Paulist.

Greenwood, M.R. (2000) 'The study of business ethics: The case for Dr. Seuss', *Business Ethics: A European Review*, 9 (3): 155–62.

Hamilton, F. and Bean, C.J. (2005) 'The importance of context, beliefs and values in leadership development', *Business Ethics: A European Review*, 14 (4): 336–47.

Hartman, E.M. (2006) 'Can we teach character? An Aristotelian answer', *Academy of Management Learning and Education*, 5 (1): 68–81.

Hauser, M.D. (2006) *Moral Minds: How Nature Designed Our Universal Sense of Right and Wrong*. New York: HarperCollins.

Heath, E., Hutton, B., Thorne McAlister, D., Petrick, J. and True, S. (2005) 'Panel: Philosophies of ethics education in business schools', *Journal of Business Ethics Education*, 2 (1): 13–20.

Hendry, J. (2006) 'Educating managers for post-bureaucracy: The role of the humanities', *Management Learning*, 37 (3): 267–81.

Hogarth, R. (1987) *Judgement and Choice* (2nd edn). New York: John Wiley and Sons.

Kahneman, D. (2003a) 'Maps of bounded rationality: Psychology for behavioral economics', *The American Economic Review*, 93 (5): 1449–75.

Kahneman, D. (2003b) 'A psychological perspective on economics', *The American Economic Review: Papers and Proceedings of the One Hundred Fifteenth Annual Meeting of the American Economic Association*, 93 (2): 162–8.

Kahneman, D. and Krueger, A.B. (2006) 'Developments in the measurement of subjective well-being', *The Journal of Economic Perspectives*, 20 (1): 3–24.

Kahneman, D., Slovic, P. and Tversky, A. (eds) (1982) *Judgment under Uncertainty: Heuristics and Biases*. New York: Cambridge University Press.

Kahneman, D. and Thaler, R.H. (2006) 'Anomalies: Utility maximization and experienced utility', *Journal of Economic Perspectives*, 20 (1): 221–34.

Kahneman, D. and Tversky, A. (eds) (2000) *Choices, Values, and Frames*. New York: Cambridge University Press.

Kenworthy-U'ren, A.L. and Peterson, T.O. (2005) 'Service-learning and management education: Introducing the "WE CARE" approach', *Academy of Management Learning and Education*, 4 (3): 272–77.

Kiesler, D.J. (1982) 'Interpersonal theory for personality and psychotherapy', in J.C. Anchin and D.J. Kiesler (eds), *Handbook of Interpersonal Psychotherapy*. New York: Pergamon Press. pp. 3–24.

King, S.M. (2006) 'The moral manager: Vignettes of virtue from Virginia', *Public Integrity*, 8 (2): 113–33.

Kolb, D.A. (1984) *Experiential Learning: Experience as the Source of Learning and Development*. Englewood Cliffs, NJ: Prentice-Hall.

Kolb, R., LeClair, D., Pelton, L., Swanson, D.L. and Windsor, D. (2005) 'Panel: The role of ethics in business curricula', *Journal of Business Ethics Education*, 2 (1): 5–12.

Kozak, M.N., Marsh, A.A. and Wegner, D.M. (2006) 'What do I think you're doing? Action identification and mind attribution', *Journal of Personality and Social Psychology*, 90: 543–55.

Langer, E.J. (1989) *Mindfulness*. Cambridge, MA: Da Capo Press.

Langer, E.J. (2000) 'Mindful learning', *Current Directions in Psychological Science*, 9 (6): 220–3.

Locander, W.B. and Luechauer, D.L. (2006) 'Trading places: How do you practice servant-leadership in an exchange-driven world?' *Marketing Management*, 15 (3): 43–5.

Lund Dean, K. and Beggs, J.M. (2006) 'University professors and teaching ethics: Conceptualizations and expectation', *Journal of Management Education*, 30 (1): 15–44.

Lund Dean, K., Beggs, J.M. and Fornaciari, C.J. (2007) 'Teaching ethics and accreditation: Faculty competence, methods and assessment', *Journal of Business Ethics Education*, 4: 5–26.

Lundberg, C.C., Rainsford, P., Shay, J.P. and Young, C.A. (2001) 'Case writing reconsidered', *Journal of Management Education*, 25 (4): 450–63.

Marcic, D., Seltzer, J. and Vaill, P. (eds) (2001) *Organizational Behavior: Experiences and Cases* (6th edn). Cincinnati: South-Western.

Mathews, C.S. and Fornaciari, C.J. (1999) *Understanding the Use of Feature Films in Classroom Learning*. Paper presented at the Academy of Management Meetings.

Mathews, C.S. and Fornaciari, C.J. (2001) *Using Action Identification Theory in the Classroom to Develop Student Moral Behavior*. Paper presented at the Organizational Behavior Teaching Conference.

McCabe, D.L., Butterfield, K.D. and Trevino, L.K. (2006) 'Academic dishonesty in graduate business programs: Prevalence, causes, and proposed action', *Academy of Management Learning and Education*, 5 (3): 294–305.

McCarthy, A.M., Tucker, M.L. and Lund-Dean, K. (2002) 'Service-learning: Creating community', in C. Wankel and R. DeFillippi (eds), *Rethinking Management Education for the 21st Century*, Vol. I. Greenwich, CT: Information Age. pp. 63–86.

Mendez, M.F. (2006) 'What frontotemporal dementia reveals about the neurobiological basis of morality', *Medical Hypotheses*, 67: 411–18.

Mintzberg, H. (2004) *Managers, Not MBAs: A Hard Look at the Soft Practice of Managing and Management Development*. San Francisco: Berrett-Koehler.

Mintzberg, H. and Westley, F. (2001) 'Decision-making: It's not what you think', *MIT Sloan Management Review*, 42 (3): 89–93.

Munro, R.A. and Rice-Munro, E.J. (2004) 'Learning styles, teaching approaches, and technology', *Journal for Quality and Participation*, 27 (1): 26–32.

O'Fallon, M.J. and Butterfield, K.D. (2005) 'A review of the empirical ethical decision-making literature: 1996–2003', *Journal of Business Ethics*, 59 (4): 375–413.

Pacini, R. and Epstein, S. (1999) 'The relation of rational and experiential information processing styles to personality, basic beliefs, and the ratio-bias phenomenon', *Journal of Personality and Social Psychology*, 76 (6): 972–87.

Pressman, S. (2006) 'Kahneman, Tversky, and institutional economics', *Journal of Economic Issues*, 40 (2): 501–6.

Prochaska, J. and DiClemente, C. (1992) 'The transtheoretical approach', in J. Norcross and M. Goldfried (eds), *Handbook of Psychotherapy Integration*. New York: Basic Books. pp. 300–34.

Reynolds, S.J. (2006) 'A neurocognitive model of the ethical decision-making process: Implications for study and practice', *Journal of Applied Psychology*, 94 (4): 737–48.

Robins, L. (1932) *An Essay on the Nature and Significance of Economic Science*. London: Macmillan.

Sauser, Jr., W.I. (2005) 'Ethics in business: Answering the call', *Journal of Business Ethics*, 58 (4): 345–57.

Schwandt, D.R. (2005) 'When managers become philosophers: Integrating learning with sensemaking', *Academy of Management Learning and Education*, 4 (2): 176–92.

Siegel, D.J. (2007) *The Mindful Brain: Reflection and Attunement in the Cultivation of Well-Being*. New York: W.W. Norton and Company.

Simon, H. (1955) 'A behavioral model of rational choice', *Quarterly Journal of Economics*, 69 (1): 99–118.

Singhapakdi, A., Marta, J.K., Rallapalli, K.C. and Rao, C.P. (2000) 'Toward an understanding of religiousness and marketing ethics: An empirical study', *Journal of Business Ethics*, 27 (4): 305–19.

Smith, V.L. (2003) 'Constructivist and ecological rationality in economics', *The American Economic Review*, 93 (3): 465–508.

Stanovich, K.E. and West, R.F. (2000) 'Individual differences in reasoning: Implications for the rationality debate?' *Behavioral and Brain Sciences*, 23 (5): 645–55.

Stigler, G.J. and Becker, G.S. (1977) 'De Gustibus Non Est Disputandum', *The American Economic Review*, 67 (2): 76–90.

Theroux, J. and Kilbane, C. (2004) 'The real-time case method: A new approach to an old tradition', *Journal of Education for Business*, 79 (3): 163–7.

Trevino, L.K. and Brown, M.E. (2004) 'Managing to be ethical: Debunking five business ethics myths', *Academy of Management Executive*, 18 (2): 69–81.

Trott, D.A. (2006) 'Leadership course syllabus' (pp. post to MSR-L list).

Tversky, A. and Kahneman, D. (1986) 'Rationality in psychology: The contrast with economics rational choice and the framing of decisions', *The Journal of Business*, 59 (4, Part 2: The Behavioral Foundations of Economic Theory), S251–S278.

Ulyings, H.B.M. (2001) 'The human cerebral cortex in development', in A.F. Kaverboer and A. Gramsbergen (eds), *Handbook of Brain and Behavior in Human Development*. Amsterdam: Kluwer Academic. pp. 63–80.

Ulyings, H.B.M. (2006) 'Development of the human cortex and the concept of 'critical' or 'sensitive' periods', *Language and Learning*, 56 (supplement): 59–90.

Vallacher, R.R. and Wegner, D.M. (1985) *A Theory of Action Identification*. Hillsdale, NJ: Lawrence Erlbaum Associates.

Vallacher, R.R. and Wegner, D.M. (1987) 'What do people think they're doing? Action identification and human behavior', *Psychological Review*, 94 (1): 3–15.

Vallacher, R.R., Wegner, D.M., McMahan, S.C., Cotter, J. and Larsen, K.A. (1992) 'On winning friends and influencing people: Action identification and self-presentation success', *Social Cognition*, 10: 335–55.

Weaver, G.R. and Agle, B.R. (2002) 'Religiosity and ethical behavior in organizations: A symbolic interactionist perspective', *Academy of Management Review*, 27 (1): 77–97.

Weber, J. and Gillespie, J. (1998) 'Differences in ethical beliefs, intentions, and behaviors: The role of beliefs and intentions in ethics research revisited', *Business and Society*, 37 (4): 447–67.

Wegner, D.M. and Vallacher, R.R. (1986) 'Action identification', in R.M. Sorrentino and E.T. Higgins (eds), *Handbook of Motivation and Cognition: Foundations of Social Behavior*. New York: Guilford. pp. 550–82.

Wheeler, K.G. (2002) 'Cultural values in relation to equity sensitivity within and across cultures', *Journal of Managerial Psychology*, 17 (7): 612–27.

Williams, S.D. and Dewett, T. (2005) 'Yes, you can teach business ethics: A review and research agenda', *Journal of Leadership and Organizational Studies*, 12 (2): 109–20.

Zlotkowski, E. (2001) 'Mapping new terrain: Service-learning across the disciplines', *Change* (January/February): 25–33.

Zsolmai, L. (2007) 'Business, ethics and spirituality Europe–Asia views', *Business Ethics: A European Review*, 16 (1): 87–92.

# 9

# Developing Leaders: Teaching about Emotional Intelligence and Training in Emotional Skills

Neal M. Ashkanasy, Marie T. Dasborough
and Kaylene W. Ascough

Despite years of denial, management scholars are now recognizing that emotions and affect comprise an inescapable component of organizational life (Barsade and Gibson, 2007). The *Free Dictionary* defines emotion as 'A mental state that arises spontaneously rather than through conscious effort and is often accompanied by physiological changes.'[1] If it is indeed the case that emotions 'arise spontaneously', then this clearly will have major ramifications for the way people behave in general, and in their working life in particular. In this chapter we discuss the implications of the pervasiveness of emotion in organizations from the point of view of learning and education, with an emphasis on the role of emotions and emotional intelligence training in leadership programs. To accomplish this, we first define emotions, and then we review the recent literature on emotions as it pertains to organizational settings. In particular, the controversial notion of emotional intelligence has attained wide prominence, especially in the practitioner literature (e.g., Goleman, 1998), so we deal with this topic in some depth in this chapter, including a definition of emotional intelligence, discussion of the ongoing controversy, and elucidation of the role of emotion intelligence in the context of leadership. We then discuss issues surrounding emotional intelligence teaching, and specifically discuss how emotional skills may assist in the development of organizational leadership skills. We conclude with a discussion of the implications of emotions and emotional intelligence for management learning and education, and discuss some directions for the future development of this field.

## THE RISE AND RISE OF EMOTION IN ORGANIZATIONS AS A FIELD OF STUDY

Over the past two decades, there has been an almost exponential increase in research interest and productivity in the field of emotion in organizations. This upsurge began in the 1980s with sociological studies of emotional labor (Hochschild, 1983), and renewed research into mood and affect by social psychologists (e.g., see Alice Isen and colleagues' work on positive effect, e.g., Isen and Means, 1983). Other seminal studies from the 1980s (with an organizational focus) included Van Maanen and Kunda's (1989) ethnographic studies of culture and emotion, and Rafaeli and Sutton's (1987, 1989) studies of emotional labor. Sutton and Rafaeli (1988) was particularly noteworthy. This study of emotional labor in service encounters was the recipient of the *Academy of Management Journal*'s 1989 Best Paper Award.

The pace stepped up in the early 1990s, with notable articles covering a range of different topics by Albrow (1992); Baron (1993); George (1990); Hosking and Fineman (1990); Isen and Baron (1991); Pekrun and Friese (1992); and Wharton and Erickson (1995), as well as an influential edited book by Fineman (1993). Seminal articles in the organizational field published in the mid-1990s by Ashforth and Humphrey (1995), who called for more recognition of the role played by emotion, especially in leadership; and Weiss and Cropanzano's (1996) introduction of Affective Events Theory further accelerated the trend. These were complemented by best-selling books by neurobiologist Damasio (1994) on the mind-body nexus, Goleman (1995) on emotional intelligence, Le Doux's (1996) seminal work on the central role of the amygdale in emotional responding, and the establishment of the Emonet (Emotion in Organizations Network) listserv in 1997 (http://www.uq.edu.au/emonet/).

By the close of the twentieth century, the volume of literature addressing emotion in organizational settings stepped up even further, including special issues of journals (e.g., Ashkanasy, 2004; Fisher and Ashkanasy, 2000; Fox, 2002; Humphrey, 2002a; Weiss, 2001, 2002); edited books (e.g., Ashkanasy et al., 2000a; Ashkanasy et al., 2002; Fineman, 2000; Härtel et al., 2005; Lord et al., 2002; Payne and Cooper, 2001), and Brief and Weiss's chapter in the 2002 *Annual Review of Psychology*. The annual book series, *Research on Emotion in Organizations*, first published in 2005, is now up to its third volume.[2] Indeed, by 2003, Barsade et al. (2003) had declared that the study of organizational behavior was in the midst of an 'affective revolution'. Finally, from an educational point of view, recognition of the study of emotions in organizations as a legitimate field in itself came with the inclusion of a standalone chapter on 'Emotions and Moods' in the best-selling[3] OB textbook (Robbins and Judge, 2007).

And even as we write this chapter, the prevalence of research into emotion in organizations continues to develop. This is reflected in established conferences such as the Emonet-sponsored biannual 'International Conference on Emotions and Worklife', conference tracks on the topic (e.g., annual conference of the European Academy of Management or EURAM), and a plethora of papers on emotion in organizations presented at major international conferences including the annual meetings of the Academy of Management (http://www.aomonline.org) and the Society for Industrial and Organizational Psychology (http://siop.org). For organizational behavior scholars, the message is clearly that emotions, affect and moods now constitute central concepts in our understanding of behavior at work.

## DEFINING AFFECT, EMOTIONS AND MOODS

Surprisingly, scholars seem to have great difficulty in deciding how to define emotion. We prefer to take the view that emotions are derived from human neurobiology. For example, and consistent with the online definition we gave in the introductory paragraph to this chapter, Fischer et al. (1990) define emotion as a 'discrete, innate, functional, biosocial action and expression system' (p. 84). Ashkanasy et al. (2000b) separate emotion into internal and external manifestations. In this model, internal manifestations of emotion constitute the subjective feelings of emotions that individuals experience as a result of an emotion-eliciting stimulus. This feeling is, in turn, processed cognitively, resulting in the conscious expression of emotion. At the same time, however, emotions are also experienced as a sub-conscious level (see Damasio, 1994; Le Doux, 1996) resulting in external manifestations of emotion such as respiration rate, facial expression, and posture. In this latter respect, humans constantly struggle to regulate their emotions (see Gross et al., 2006).

It is also important to differentiate moods from emotion. While both are classified under the rubric of *affect*, emotions are discrete responses to particular objects or occurrences and are generally of a relatively short duration

(Frijda, 1986). Moods, on the other hand, tend to be relatively long-lasting, and are not generally object-focused. Still, moods are important, insofar as they infuse cognitive thinking processes (Forgas, 1995) and thus deeply influence an individual's judgment processes.

## UNDERSTANDING EMOTIONS IN THE WORKPLACE: A 5-LEVEL MODEL

In order to present a fuller understanding of the pervasiveness of emotion and its effects in organizations, Ashkanasy (2003a) devised a five-level model. The five levels are (see also Figure 9.1):

*Level 1.* Neuropsychological and cognitive correlates of emotion at the within-person level of analysis.
*Level 2.* Individual differences in emotion at the between-persons level of analysis.
*Level 3.* Perception and communication of emotion at the dyadic (relationships) level of analysis.

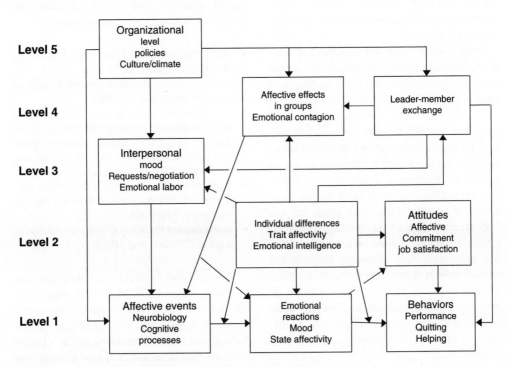

**Figure 9.1 The five-level model of emotion in organizations**
*Source*: (Ashkanasy and Ashton-James, 2007)

Level 4.   Management and promulgation of emotion at the group level of analysis.

Level 5.   Emotional climate at the organizational level of analysis.

*Level 1* of the model is based essentially on the neurobiology of emotion (see Ashkanasy, 2003b), which is still in the process of being understood (e.g., see Frijda et al., 2006). Neurobiologists, such as Antonio Damasio (1994) and Joseph Le Doux (1996), continue to unravel the essential relationships between emotion and every aspect of human behavior and intellect. From the organizational perspective, this is reflected in Weiss and Cropanzano's (1996) Affective Events Theory, which holds that organizational environments generate 'affective events' also known as 'hassles' and 'uplifts', which engender positive or negative emotional reactions in organizational members.[4] These emotional reactions in turn engender both direct ('impulsive') and indirect behavioral reactions (positive or negative). These indirect behaviors (e.g., intention to turnover, intentional poor productivity) are the result of attitudes (e.g., job satisfaction, commitment) that derive from the members' emotional reactions.

*Level 2* deals with between-person variables, or individual differences. From an emotions perspective, the most pertinent of these are state or trait positive and negative affect (Watson and Tellegan, 1985) and emotional intelligence (Mayer and Salovey, 1997). Positive and negative state/trait affect describe an individual's penchant to be in a positive or negative affective state, either as a personality-type trait (trait affect) or as a short-lived contingent state (state affect). The affect construct is usually described using a circumplex based on axes of positive and negative affect, although Russell and Carroll (1999) argue that a more accurate representation is based on dimensions of positive–negative valence and strong–weak activation.[5] (We discuss emotional intelligence in more detail in the next section of this chapter.)

*Level 3* deals with the interpersonal or social exchange level of analysis, focusing in particular on emotional recognition in the human face. Citing Ekman's work in general (e.g., Ekman, 1999), and a study by Frank et al. (1993) in particular, Ashkanasy (2003a) argues that people make a key distinction between feigned and real smiles that, in workplace settings, can be important. For instance, in a study involving conflicting facial and verbal communication in performance appraisal feedback, Newcombe and Ashkanasy (2002) found that perception of facial expression counted more than verbal feedback, with the strongest (negative) response elicited when positive verbal feedback was combined with a negative facial expression. More recently, Althoff and Ashkanasy (2004) found that female observers more accurately decoded facial expressions in a boardroom scenario and that this effect was mediated by emotional intelligence.

*Level 4* captures emotional processes at the group-level of analysis, including leadership (especially leader-member exchange or LMX, see Graen and Uhl-Bien, 1995) and emotional contagion (Hatfield et al., 1992). Moreover, recent research into emotional contagion processes in work teams has shown that:

- team emotion is promulgated through emotional contagion (Barsade, 2002);
- team leaders communicate emotional states to their followers (Sy et al., 2005);
- leader-member exchange relationships impact on team-member exchange relationships (TMX, Seers, 1989), in a process involving group and team member affect (Tse, Dasborough and Ashkanasy, 2008; Tse and Dasborough, 2008);
- team members' emotional states affect their leaders' affective states and effectiveness (Tee and Ashkanasy, 2007); and
- teams develop the ability to recognize emotion as a group (Elfenbein et al., 2007).

Finally, *Level 5* refers to the role of emotion at the organizational level, reflecting what De Rivera (1992) has termed 'emotional climate'. Ashkanasy and Nicholson (2003) have also studied the phenomenon of 'climate of fear', and demonstrated that climate was distinguishable from organizational culture in the organizations they studied, in that climate varied by site within organizations, while culture varied across organizations, but not within each organization. In addition, climate in this study was a measure of affective reactions, while the measures of culture related more to organizational artifacts and values. More recently, Kimberley and Härtel (2007) described the role played by organizational-level emotions in facilitating a climate of trust.

In summary of Ashkanasy's (2003a) 5-level model, it is clear that emotions play a key role as a determinant of human attitudes and behaviors at every level of organizational functioning. Ashkanasy (2003b) points out further that this level of embeddedness is explained in terms of the fact that emotion is a fundamental neurobiological property of human beings. Every thought humans have and every behavior they execute is affected in some way by emotional substrates. Muraven and Baumeister (2000) argue further that emotional regulation is in itself effortful, resulting in physical depletion similar to physical exertion. If this is so, then teaching students about emotion and its role in organizations would seem to be imperative in management education.

Of the variables discussed within the 5-level model, the one that has attracted most attention in both the popular and academic literature is emotional intelligence. In this respect, emotional intelligence has been characterized by Ashkanasy and Daus (2002: 81) as follows:

1 Emotional intelligence is distinct from, but positively related to, other intelligences.
2 Emotional intelligence is an individual difference, where some people are more endowed, and others are less so.
3 Emotional intelligence develops over a person's life span and can be enhanced through training.
4 Emotional intelligence involves, at least in part, a person's abilities to effectively identify and to perceive emotion (in self and others), as well as possession of the skills to understand and to manage those emotions successfully.

We discuss this variable in more detail in the next section.

## EMOTIONAL INTELLIGENCE

Since its introduction in 1990 by Salovey and Mayer (1990)[6] and subsequent popularization by Goleman (1995), interest in emotional intelligence, especially in organizational settings, has increased exponentially. At the time of writing, for example, a *Google* search for 'emotional intelligence' resulted in more than two million hits. Despite this level of popularity among the lay population, however, emotional intelligence has been the subject of criticism in the academic literature for ten years. This criticism began with an article by intelligence researchers Davies et al. (1998) published in the *Journal of Personality and Social Psychology*. Although this piece has been highly cited,[7] it was arguably premature, as it predated many of the more important developments in the field. Despite the continued developments in the field, criticism of emotional intelligence applications in organizational settings continues to be scathing. Locke (2005), for example, uncompromisingly declared the whole concept to be 'invalid' (p. 425), while Landy (2005) regards emotional intelligence as simply a continuation of public fascination with the discredited idea of 'social intelligence' (Thorndike, 1920). In responding to these critics, Ashkanasy and Daus (2005) pointed out that the protagonists appear to be directing their ire towards popular models of emotional intelligence that do not in fact conform to the Mayer and Salovey (1997) definition of the construct.[8] In this respect, Ashkanasy and Daus defined three 'steams' of emotional intelligence conceptualization and research as follows.

*Stream 1.* Emotional intelligence in this stream conforms to the definition given by Mayer and Salovey (1997) and is measured using the 'abilities' test developed by the authors in conjunction with consultant David Caruso (Mayer et al., 2002), known as the *MSCEIT* (Mayer, Salovey, Caruso Emotional Intelligence Test). Mayer and Salovey defined emotional intelligence as comprising four 'branches': (1) ability to perceive emotion, both in self and in others;

(2) ability to assimilate emotion into the cognitive processes underlying thought; (3) ability to understand emotion and its consequences; and (4) ability to manage and thereby to regulate emotion, again in self and others. The MSCEIT comprises a series of eight test scales (two for each branch) that purport to be measures of emotional intelligence ability, in much the same way that an IQ test measures intellectual mental abilities. The 'right' answers to the test items are either based on a set of consensus norms (N = 5000), or scores obtained from a panel of 80 'experts' who were in fact members of the selective *Society for Research on Emotions* (see http://www.isre.org). Of course, whether these answers are 'right' in reality remains a bone of contention (e.g., see Davies et al., 1998), but emerging evidence (e.g., see Daus and Ashkanasy, 2005) seems to support the validity and reliability of the MSCEIT in organizational applications.

*Stream 2.* Emotional intelligence in Stream 2 purports to conform to the Mayer and Salovey (1997) four-branch definition, but is measured using self-report questionnaires (e.g., Brackett et al., 2006; Jordan et al., 2002; Schutte et al., 1998; Wong and Law, 2002) or, more rarely, using peer-reports (e.g., Jordan and Ashkanasy, 2006). Of course, the major point of contention with this approach is that self-reports of emotional intelligence are inherently suspect (see Mayer, 2004 for discussion of this issue). Nonetheless, results using self-report (Stream 2) measures in organizational settings have been impressive (e.g., see Jordan and Troth, 2004; Law et al., 2004; Offermann et al., 2006).

*Stream 3.* Models of emotional intelligence in this stream are differentiated from the model used in Streams 1 and 2, based on the Mayer and Salovey (1997) definition. The Stream 3 models are often referred to as 'mixed models' of emotional intelligence, insofar as they tend to introduce aspects of personality into the construct. Some well-known examples include the EQi (Bar-On, 1997), the Emotional Competency Index (ECI; Sala, 2002), the Emotional Intelligence Questionnaire (EIQ: Dulewicz et al., 2003)

and the Swinburne University Emotional Intelligence Test (SUEIT: Palmer and Stough, 2001). *Consistent with Ashkanasy and Daus (2005), we do not regard any of the Stream 3 models as valid representations of emotional intelligence.* All include elements of personality and other individual difference constructs, and most depart radically from Mayer and Salovey's (1997) conceptualization. While these measures may be handy consulting tools, we fail to see how a particular defined construct can be represented by other (at best) remotely related constructs.

In summary, and consistent with Jordan et al. (2006), we regard only the Stream 1 and 2 approaches (which are based on the Mayer and Salovey, 1997, four-branch representation of emotional intelligence) as valid representations of emotional intelligence. Thus, as we note in the following sections of this chapter, claims for any results based on Stream 3 measures are going to be of doubtful authenticity. Moreover, we do not recommend that the Stream 3 models be taught, except in a comparative context with the more valid Mayer and Salovey (1997) model of emotional intelligence represented in Streams 1 and 2.

Next, we discuss the role of emotions and emotional intelligence in leadership. We outline the empirical research exploring the emotional aspects of leadership in organizations, and explain how emotional intelligence has been examined as a predictor of leadership effectiveness.

## EMOTIONS IN LEADERSHIP

### Historical perspectives on emotions in leadership

Early empirical work on the field of leadership implicitly touched on emotional aspects of leadership behaviors, yet there was no explicit mention of follower emotions evoked by leaders. The Ohio State Leadership studies and the Michigan Leadership studies of the 1950s highlighted task-oriented behaviors versus relations-oriented behaviors (Yukl, 2005).

These relations-oriented behaviors are socio-emotional in nature; however, there was no reference to the emotions of followers in these studies. With regards to follower outcomes, satisfaction and productivity were the key outcome variables of interest during this early stage.

Similar to management research in general, most leadership research traditionally empha-sized cognitive processes, with emotions as a basis for influence only coming to the spotlight since emotions came to prominence in research in the late 1980s (as we noted earlier in this chapter; see also Yukl, 2005). The recent advances in our understanding and appreciation of emotion in workplace settings that we noted earlier have shifted the focus from purely behavioral and cognitive processes to emotions, a perspective that has been neglected to date by most scholars of leadership (e.g., see Ashforth and Humphrey, 1995; Ashkanasy and Tse, 2000; George, 2000). This shift has been long overdue because, as Humphrey (2002b) has empha-sized, leadership is intrinsically an emotional process, whereby leaders recognize and evoke employees' emotional states, seeking to man-age employees' emotional states.

In an early general discussion of emotion in the workplace, Ashforth and Humphrey (1995) explained that leaders need to be able to evoke follower emotion, in order to achieve their task of creating and maintaining a system of shared meanings. Ashforth and Humphrey also discuss the idea of 'symbolic management', noting that this 'is largely dependent upon the evocation of emotion' (p. 111). They also suggest that, when employees are emotionally charged by a call from their leaders, they are less likely to view the call as being an attempt by the leader to be manipulative.

Early work identifying emotional consequences of leadership was related only to charisma (see George, 2000 for a discussion); however, since employee behavior and productivity are directly affected by their emotional states (Ashkanasy, Härtel and Daus, 2002), it is now considered imperative to consider follower emotional responses to organizational leaders. At a basic level, since leadership involves interpersonal relationships in the workplace, the relationship between a leader and his or her follower is inherently emotional in nature (Dasborough, 2006). As George (2000) argues, leadership is a particularly emotion-laden process, with emotions entwined with the social influence process.

## Emotions in leadership development

Day (2000) has reviewed the concept of leadership development as a distinct field, distinguishing between intrapersonal char-acteristics of individual leaders and the interpersonal processes of leadership as a relational process. Day identified McCauley, Moxley, and van Velsorto (1998) as the origi-nators of this concept, and defined leadership development as 'expanding the collective capacity of organizational members to engage effectively in leadership roles and processes' (p. 582). Importantly, he specifically listed emotional self-awareness and self-regulation as critical skills for leadership development. This idea was subsequently fleshed out by Caruso and Wolfe (2004), who based a leadership development model on the four-branch Mayer and Salovey (1997) model of emotional intelligence abilities, and suggested how training can be used to enhance these abilities to improve leadership effectiveness.

## Empirical contributions: leadership as a source of affective events

With a focus now on emotional aspects of leadership, empirical studies are being conducted to explore the types of emotional responses followers have to their leaders. As we noted earlier in this chapter, many of these studies are based on affective events theory (AET: Weiss and Cropanzano, 1996). According to this theory, leaders are sources of affective events in the workplace (Brief and Weiss, 2002), bringing about both positive and negative emotional responses in followers during their interactions with them in the workplace. In the context of leadership, for example, when leaders recognize employee efforts, they can induce employee self-pride, as well as enthusiasm for the job (see Basch and Fisher, 2000; Dasborough, 2006; Grandey et al., 2002). Leaders can also evoke strong negative emotions, for example when mishandling employee discipline (Ball et al., 1992). In this section, we outline findings from a range of empirical studies demonstrating the emotional side of leadership.

In more recent applications of AET in leadership research, Gaddis et al. (2004) and Newcombe and Ashkanasy (2002) examined leaders' negative feedback as an affective event. The authors of both studies reported that subordinates' attitudes and performance were influenced by the nature of the failure feedback and the emotional response of the subordinate to the feedback. Thus, in terms of AET, leader behavior can be seen as an affective event in the workplace producing positive and negative emotions in employees.

Dasborough (2006) has since empirically demonstrated a whole range of emotional responses of employees to specific organizational leader behaviors. In her qualitative study, she viewed leaders as sources of both positive and negative affective events for followers. Dasborough found that, when it came to recalling emotional incidents, employees remembered more negative incidents than positive incidents, and they recalled them more intensely and in more detail than positive incidents.

When leaders express their own emotions, this too can be a source of affective events for followers (e.g., see Newcombe and Ashkanasy, 2002). Leaders need to be able to manage their own emotions. Prati et al. (2003) discuss how a lack of emotional control by a leader can be perceived by followers as a weakness, and this may be related to leader ineffectiveness. Leaders should aim to be in control over their emotions, especially negative emotions, which might transfer from themselves to their followers via emotional contagion. In this respect, several studies have empirically demonstrated emotional

contagion from leaders to followers (Bono et al., 2007; Cherulnik et al., 2001; Lewis, 2000; Sy et al., 2005).

Leaders also need awareness of the emotional content in the messages they are delivering, and to manage their emotional expressions when delivering the message. Newcombe and Ashkanasy (2002) found that positive messages and message-congruent leader affect results in more positive member ratings of the leader. They found that, if message content and leader affect are incongruent, then the leader's expression may appear manipulative, resulting in perceptions of lower quality LMX.

When leaders express negative emotions, the result is a reduction in follower liking for the leader, and more negative evaluations of the leader (Gaddis et al., 2004; Glomb and Hulin, 1997; Lewis, 2000). These effects depend on the specific type of emotion being expressed and the gender of the leader expressing them. For example, female leaders will receive higher ratings than male leaders in the case of expressing sadness; while male leaders will receive higher ratings than female leaders in the case of expressing anger (Lewis, 2000). Lewis explains this in terms of the gender norms that exist, and follower expectations around these norms.

These empirical studies have examined follower emotional responses to leadership. Next, we focus in on the most *emotional* leadership theory, the theory of transformational leadership.

## Empirical contributions: transformational leadership and emotion

There are numerous theories of leadership in organizations (see Bass, 1990). Transformational leadership theory has been one of the most widely studied theories, and has been consistently argued as being the most effective type of leadership (see Bass and Riggio, 2005, for an up-to-date review). In comparison to transactional leaders, transformational leadership involves heightened emotions in followers, and the nature of influence is more emotion-based. Antonakis (2004) argues that transformational leaders generate affective links with their followers, and that this is a result of the leaders' vision and moral convictions, combined with their courage and confidence.

Transformational and charismatic leaders have a positive emotional impact on their followers and their success as leaders is determined by managing their follower's emotions (Ashkanasy and Tse, 2000). Leaders rated high on charisma and transformational leadership behaviors by their followers are often associated with followers reporting higher levels of positive emotions (Bass and Riggio, 2005). The energetic positive emotions experienced by followers, such as excitement and enthusiasm, may be the reason why they rate the leaders as being effective (Bono and Ilies, 2006; Damen et al., 2008).

Empirical demonstrations of transformational leadership also provide support for these arguments. McColl-Kennedy and Anderson (2002) found that sales representatives (who worked under a transformational leader) had higher sales and this was explained by the representatives' felt optimism and frustration. Further support for the association between transformational leadership and positive emotions was provided by Dasborough (2006). In her field sample of employees, Dasborough found that, to evoke positive emotional responses, leaders displayed behaviors associated with transformational leadership (individualized consideration, inspirational motivation, intellectual stimulation, and charisma or idealized influence: Bass and Riggio, 2005). Specifically, Dasborough (2006) found that the following leader behaviors had positive emotional consequences: 'awareness and respect' (individualized consideration), 'empowerment' (intellectual stimulation), 'motivation and inspiration' (inspirational motivation), 'reward and recognition' (individual consideration).

De Cremer (2006) examined the effect of procedural justice and transformational leadership style on followers' emotions. He found that procedural justice and transformational leadership style interacted to influence followers' self-esteem and emotions, such that the positive relationships between procedural justice and emotions were more pronounced when the leadership style was high in transformational behavior. Given these and earlier findings, we conclude that the evidence supports the idea that transformational leaders have an emotional impact on their followers.

## Emotional intelligence and leadership

Given the affective nature of leadership, attention has turned to emotional abilities of leaders as a means of improving leadership effectiveness. Early leadership studies have shown that the emotional maturity of leaders is associated with their effectiveness (Bass, 1990). In more recent times, a range of emotional abilities have been explored. Of these, and despite the concerns we noted earlier in this chapter, emotional intelligence has received considerable attention by leadership researchers. This is in contrast to other emotion-related variables such as emotion recognition (Newcombe and Ashkanasy, 2002; Rubin et al., 2005) and empathy (Kellett et al., 2006), which have not been as popular as the broader construct of emotional intelligence.

The underlying assumption of those who view emotional intelligence as important in leadership is that the skills required for leaders to be effective depend in part on the ability of leaders to understand and manage emotions (Cooper and Sawaf, 1997). Goleman et al. (2002) explain that effectively dealing with emotions may contribute to how a leader can effectively motivate employees, and to deal with their needs in the workplace. As Kellet et al. (2006) state, the ability of leaders to display emotions can influence how followers perceive them. In turn, this can influence their relationships with followers over the long term (see Dasborough and Ashkanasy, 2002).

George (2000) was the first to provide a detailed discussion of the central role of emotions and emotional intelligence in the leadership process. She based her arguments on the ability model of emotional intelligence (Mayer and Salovey, 1997). George made a substantial contribution to the literature, by being the first to propose how emotional intelligence specifically contributes to effective leadership. In particular, George explained how emotional skills contribute to the development of collective goals and objectives; instilling in others an appreciation of the importance of work activities; generating and maintaining enthusiasm, confidence, optimism, cooperation, and trust; encouraging flexibility in decision making and change; and establishing and maintaining a meaningful identity for an organization.

Although there are many supporters of the link between emotional intelligence and leadership, there remain some harsh critics. Antonakis (2004), for example, claims that people have been 'hoodwinked' in regard to the claims made about the necessity of emotional intelligence for leadership and organizational performance. To clarify our position on this matter, we argue that, while emotional intelligence abilities may not be an absolute necessity, these abilities do assist with the social aspects of leadership which involve emotions. As reported earlier, leadership is an emotional process involving social interaction and influence. Hence, emotional intelligence abilities may be of use to individuals wishing to manage these emotional aspects of the workplace. We acknowledge nonetheless that there may be some circumstances in which these skills may not be as useful, as for example, in the case of an external leader with little social interaction with followers.

## Empirical support for emotionally intelligent leaders

Specifically, George (2000) explained that when it comes to the development of collective goals and objectives, the affective state of the leader may influence the content of their vision. Positive emotions have been shown in a range of empirical studies to enhance creativity (see Isen and Baron, 1991). Hence, leaders may use their emotional intelligence to boost positive emotions and moods in order to

assist with developing their innovative vision for the organization. Further, George argues that emotionally intelligent leaders who can manage the emotions of their employees can garner positive employee emotions such as enthusiasm and confidence. These positive emotions may then be used to establish commitment to the vision, and help to develop a collective identity (see also Ashkanasy and Ashton-James, 2007).

The majority of the early empirical work on emotional intelligence and leadership, however, has been based on the Stream 3 (mixed) models of emotional intelligence, and was conducted by management consultants. Some of these studies have made unsubstantiated claims about the connection between emotional intelligence and effective leadership. For example, Goleman et al. (2002) concluded astonishingly that emotional intelligence may contribute 80 to 90 percent of the competencies that distinguish outstanding from average leaders. Despite this and other claims by some consulting groups, there still remains a dearth of scholarly empirical evidence to support this statement (see Antonakis, 2004).

Sosik and Megerian (1999) explain that emotional intelligence has recently gained popularity as a potential underlying attribute of effective leadership. Along with this popularity, scholarly research has begun to emerge examining the connection between emotional intelligence and leadership. There are strong arguments for the connection between the abilities based model of emotional intelligence (Stream 1) and leadership ability, especially in the case of the more 'emotional' transformational leadership style. Daus and Ashkanasy (2005) outline these arguments, and state that this is an exciting area of research in organizational behavior. They report scholarly empirical studies that demonstrate the association between transformational leadership and the abilities based model of emotional intelligence; however, these are mostly conference papers and unpublished manuscripts. Initial empirical evidence does provide some support for the role of emotional intelligence abilities in promoting transformational leadership behaviors, and hopefully with time, more empirical studies will make their way into peer-reviewed journals. Next, we outline some of the published work in this field.

In a Stream 3 study by Palmer et al. (2000), preliminary evidence was found for the relationship between EI and effective leadership. Based on their work, they suggest that the ability to monitor and manage emotions within oneself and others may be an underlying competency of transformational leadership. Despite their promising findings, they call for caution, as do Moss et al. (2006) who also conducted field studies on emotional intelligence and leadership behaviors. They found mixed support for the role of emotional intelligence, and conclude that emotional intelligence may enhance the ability of managers to adapt their leadership style appropriately, but only in some contexts.

Wong and Law (2002) argue that supervisors with high emotional intelligence and maturity are more likely to be psychologically supportive of their followers, because such supervisors are more sensitive to feelings and emotions, both of themselves and their followers. Their (Stream 2) field study provides some preliminary support for researchers who have proposed the importance of leader emotional intelligence. Specifically, they found that the emotional intelligence of leaders is positively related to the job satisfaction and extra-role behavior of followers. While this is a promising finding, they did not find support for the hypothesized connection between leader emotional intelligence and follower performance, arguably the most important outcome indicative of leadership effectiveness. Hence, similar to Palmer et al. (2000), and Moss et al. (2006), caution is again called for.

Within team contexts, the results of empirical studies on emotional intelligence and leadership have been more positive, specifically in regard to leader emergence. Leadership emergence is considered to have a logical tie with emotional intelligence, and this has even been stated by critics of the emotional intelligence construct, such as Frank Landy (see Daus and Ashkanasy, 2005). Emotional intelligence has been examined

as a predicator of emergent team leadership by Pescosolido (2002); Wolff et al. (2002); Pirola-Merlo et al. (2002); and Dasborough et al. (2007). All of these scholars provide justification for the relevance of emotional skills for the emergence of team leaders. Here, the focus is on leader emergence, and not leader effectiveness (as indicated by follower performance or satisfaction for example), and it is within a team context.

Kellett et al. (2006) also examined emotional abilities and effective leadership within a team context, using a Stream 2 approach to emotional intelligence and peer ratings of leadership behaviors. In their study, they found support for the importance of emotional skills, especially empathy, in the development of follower perceptions of task and relations oriented leadership. Given their findings, and earlier supportive findings for the role of emotional intelligence in team leadership, it seems that the prevalence of face-to-face interactions with leaders and followers in teams may result in a stronger need for emotional skills within teams.

Outside of the team context, there have also been some promising developments. Rosete and Ciarrochi (2005) examined leadership and emotional intelligence in a small field study. Their research was based on the ability based model of EI (Stream 1) using the MSCEIT measure of EI. They found that higher emotional intelligence was associated with higher leadership effectiveness. Building on from this work, and also using the ability based model (Stream 1), Kerr and colleagues (2006) examined the association of emotional intelligence and leadership effectiveness (as measured by subordinates). Their results are also promising, with support for emotional intelligence being a predictor of leadership effectiveness. Further, they found that the branches of emotional intelligence had different levels of predictive power. The ability to perceive emotions and to use emotions were the strongest predictors of leadership effectiveness. This study and the one by Rosete and Ciarrochi before it paved the way forward in learning more about emotional intelligence and leadership.

Utilizing an ability-based measure of emotional intelligence (Stream 1) and subordinate ratings of leadership effectiveness overcome many of the problems associated with other types of measures. The measures used in previous studies do raise questions over the validity of the results.

To improve the empirical research on emotional intelligence and leadership, we support the call by Antonakis (2004) for researchers to request target leaders to complete measures of cognitive ability, personality, and emotional intelligence, and followers/peers/bosses to assess the leadership of the target leader. This would enable the testing of emotional intelligence discriminant validity, incremental validity, and construct validity, and would avoid social desirability bias. It would ensure that the association between leadership and emotional intelligence is not merely an artifact of a single respondent assessing independent and dependent items on a single survey. While Antonakis (2004) predicts that the 'EI boat' will 'suffer a calamity of titanic proportions', we argue that when measured according to Stream 1 (the ability based test of EI), emotional intelligence is indeed a useful and valid predictor of leadership and is a tool that can be utilized to aid in the education of future organizational leaders.

In the final section of this chapter, we turn to the issue of educating about emotions and emotional intelligence. We outline the concerns and the suggestions by scholars in the field. We also explain the current methods being utilized to assist in developing individual's emotional abilities, such as emotional literacy. We then report findings from a study of teaching about emotional intelligence within the context of leadership education.

## TEACHING ABOUT EMOTIONS AND EMOTIONAL INTELLIGENCE

### Teaching emotions

Although emotional capacities may be partly influenced by genetic factors and early development, many scholars argue that there is room for further development (e.g., see Lopes et al., 2006; Moriarty and Buckley, 2003). Lopes and his colleagues (2006) maintain further that learning to manage emotions and relationships with others is a lifelong process. In this case, Dunlop (1984) suggests that such education provides individuals with a selection of tools to assist with dealing with their own and others' emotions. As we have earlier argued (e.g., see Forgas, 1995), emotions and moods have a pervasive influence on all mental activity, so the availability of tools for better managing emotions has implications also for cognitive functioning and behavior. Consequently, understanding of our own and others' emotions and their effects, or what Denzin (1984) refers to as 'emotional ways of knowing', deserve our attention.

In the specific instance of the workplace, Thomson (1998) has made the case that learning about emotion contributes to what he calls 'emotional capital', and that this in turn, creates the basis for business success. Thomson (1998) suggests further that, by encouraging learning about emotion, the organization becomes more human 'in the most amazing and positive way' (p. 22). Thus, training in emotional skills may enhance work performance. Lopes et al. (2006) have shown that emotion training for leaders is likely to be most effective if it induces leaders to pay more attention to the feelings and concerns of others, and thereby enhances their understanding of others' motives and behavior. Steiner and Perry (1999) believe that everyone has something to learn about their emotions, and consequently managers can enhance their effectiveness in the workplace through acknowledging and managing feelings. Therefore, managers should strive to acquire a degree of emotional literacy in order to be effective in their roles as organizational leaders (Fineman, 1997).

As an example of a typical teaching syllabus, leading emotions researcher Anat Rafaeli includes an 'Emotions in Organizations' syllabus available on her website.[9] The syllabus provides a broad coverage of the field, including an introduction to the fundamentals of positive and negative emotions, and models of emotion. Other topics include monitoring and control of emotions in organizations, emotional labor, the effects (outcomes) of emotions, emotion and culture and emotional intelligence. Rafaeli asks her students to read published studies of emotion in organizational contexts, covering both employee and customer emotional responses and emotional abilities. The studies cover a wide range of research approaches in the field of emotions, including surveys, experiments, observations, event analysis and qualitative analysis.

Another leading emotions researcher, Quy Hui, has developed a program for teaching emotions to senior managers as a component of INSEAD Management School's 'Challenge of Leadership' Executive Education Program.[10] Hui uses detailed case examples to demonstrate how top managers' understanding and empathetic management of emotion can be the key to organizational success and failure. In particular, by using realistic case studies, students are encouraged to think about how the concepts are going to apply to their own organizational problems and issues.

Thus, and as Ashkanasy and Daus (2002) argue, teaching about emotions in an organizational context may be seen as integral to leadership development. Still, while some pioneers in emotions scholarship are making progress, and there is a growing volume of research demonstrating the effects of emotions within the organization (Ashkanasy, 2003b), there is still little to show exactly how emotional abilities can be developed and what impact that development then has on the organization (e.g., see Wong et al., 2007).

## Teaching emotional intelligence

Ashkanasy and Daus (2002) assert that training programs involving emotional intelligence are the key to the development of emotional capacities in organizations. Indeed, there is a virtual plethora of consultants and training organizations offering emotional intelligence training programs (see http://www.emotionaliq.org/EI-Workshops.htm, for example). Clarke (2006) has pointed out, however, that the evidence demonstrating the actual impact of training in emotional intelligence on performance related outcomes

is rare. Still, it is hard to ignore the volume of literature claiming that emotional intelligence is beneficial to leaders, and as such, training programs focused on enhancing leaders' emotional intelligence should be pursued (for example see Bagshaw, 2000; Dulewicz and Higgs, 1999; Langley, 2000; Rozell et al., 2002; Sy and Côté, 2004; Welch, 2003).

Kunnanatt (2004) claims that the goal of emotional intelligence training is to facilitate individuals in developing self-knowledge about who they are and where they stand in the world of emotions, in order to guide them smoothly towards interpersonal success. He believes that a carefully drafted emotional intelligence training program changes both the inside aspects and the outside relationships of participants, and cultivates a host of virtues and attributes, including better attitudes, clearer perceptions, and productive affiliations.

MSCEIT co-developer David Caruso has put together a suite of emotional intelligence training courses (see Caruso and Salovey, 2004). Topics include: MSCEIT overview, emotional blueprint, emotionally intelligent feedback, the emotionally intelligent manager, emotional intelligence and change, and emotional intelligence and teams.[11] As one would expect, Caruso's training courses are built around the Mayer and Salovey (1997) four-branch model of emotional intelligence, and involve administration of the MSCEIT (Stream 1). Caruso teaches course participants about each of the four branches of emotional intelligence, and then uses exercises as a means to develop skills in each of the four areas. Finally, Caruso has participants apply their learning to case study scenarios as well as cases from their own experience.

Murray et al. (2006) have also developed training programs based on the Mayer-Salovey four-branch model. Their program consists of a two-day interactive workshop format that includes specific activities that address each of the four branches, including training in perception of emotional 'micro-expressions' (Ekman, 1999); introduction to emotional contagion and 'organizational stories' (Van Buskirk and McGrath, 1992); teaching understanding of emotions through knowledge of emotional transitions (Mayer et al., 2001); and skills training related to emotion management (Caruso and Salovey, 2004). In a series of experimental studies in a large organization, Murray and her colleagues (2006) demonstrated that the training had positive results on team performance.

Cherniss and Adler (2000) outline a number of similar programs', which they called 'model programs'. These programs consisted of two prevailing techniques for teaching emotional intelligence. The first is a workshop format, similar to the Murray et al. (2006) format described above, and conducted over varying timeframes of one- or two-day block seminars, to a series of sessions over a more extended period of time (e.g., once a week for six weeks). In these group training models, trainers employ a variety of methods such as lectures, group discussions, and role play exercises to facilitate emotional intelligence training.

The other popular format is one-on-one coaching sessions where the emotional intelligence trainer meets with a manager for personal development training. The executive coaching model described by Cherniss and Adler (2000) is an example of this technique. In this program, participants go through an initial one- or two-day diagnostic assessment and feedback session, followed by a coaching phase that involves usually one day of training per month for approximately six months.

Despite all the encouraging progress outlined above, we note that many of the studies reporting positive findings that training can have an impact in developing emotional intelligence are in fact based on the Stream 3 (mixed) models of emotional intelligence (Ashkanasy and Daus, 2005) and not on the Stream 1/2 (ability) approach. Many of these studies seem to provide impressive results (e.g., see also Hein, 2004) perhaps because, as we noted earlier, these authors are often consultants with access to large samples. However, these Stream 3 studies lack the scientific validity and credibility to be published in high quality journals. Clarke (2006) argues further that training based on the Stream 3 models of emotional intelligence

run the risk of undermining the potential benefits that might be gained from training or development programs based on the more valid ability model.

In light of this argument, Wong et al. (2007) tested the abilities based concept of emotional intelligence in order to shed some light on if an individual can develop abilities in emotional management and regulation. These authors claim that the key to discovering whether emotional intelligence can be effectively trained is found in the definition of the emotional intelligence construct. They argued that, if emotional intelligence is accepted as a set of abilities as presented by Mayer and Salovey (1997), then there is a possibility that emotional intelligence may be developed or enhanced by training programs. Based on a Stream 2 approach (i.e., using the Wong and Law, 2002, self-report instrument) these authors asked whether nurture or nature constructs are more important in development of emotional intelligence capabilities. By investigating the impact a full-time parent has on the development of their child, Wong et al. (2007) provided evidence that parental nurturing did indeed enhance emotional intelligence. They concluded that, because emotional intelligence is determined in essence from numerous exogenous sources, including family and social environment, there remains considerable scope for development of alternative whole-of-life models of emotional intelligence training. In other words, rather than viewing emotional intelligence as something that can be developed in a specific training program, it may be more useful to regard it as a set of skills/competencies that develop over an individual's lifetime (see also Mayer et al., 2001).

## Teaching emotional literacy rather than 'intelligence' per se

A further issue that needs to be addressed is whether it makes sense at all to speak of teaching 'intelligence' *per se*. Mayer and Dobb (2000), for example, argue that, with a few exceptions, it probably does not. These authors point out that *intelligence* refers to a *capacity* to learn. It means that there are differences among people in emotional processing. Emotional intelligence relies on knowledge of emotional processes and information-processing skills (e.g., see Lopes et al., 2006). The problem here, as Clarke (2006) has observed, is that emotional intelligence is more than likely derived from genetic inheritance and home nurturance (see also Wong et al., 2007), and therefore may not be a skill or competency that can necessarily be developed through education.

Emotional literacy, on the other hand, is the constellation of understandings, skills, and strategies that a person can develop and nurture from infancy throughout an entire lifetime (Bocchino, 1999). Thus, emotional intelligence becomes the capacity to which an individual can develop emotional literacy. Therefore, the higher an individual's emotional intelligence, the more able s/he is to process emotional information accurately and efficiently and to increase emotional literacy. Therefore, although training in emotional skills is beneficial to leaders in general, such training would be more effective and enhanced in those high in emotional intelligence. This line of argument is also consistent with authors such as Perkins (1995) who argue that intelligence can be developed though expansion of inherent intelligence capacities.

## Teaching emotional awareness and emotional intelligence to develop leaders

While there is a myriad of emotional intelligence training programs for organizational leaders advertised by consultants, there is little published scholarly research on the impact of teaching about emotional intelligence on leadership. Ashkanasy and Dasborough (2003) conducted an empirical study to asses the impact of such training in a classroom setting focused on leadership. Ashkanasy and Dasborough measured emotional intelligence of student participants using both an ability-based test

(Stream 1) and self-report (Stream 2) measures of emotional intelligence. They found that teaching about emotions and emotional intelligence in the leadership class had an impact on subsequent team performance. Similar to the field studies on emotional intelligence and leadership emergence in teams discussed earlier in this chapter, Ashkanasy and Dasborough's findings in regards to teaching about the role of emotional intelligence and leadership, again suggests that this is more important in social settings such as workplace teams.

## IMPLICATIONS, FUTURE RESEARCH DIRECTIONS AND CONCLUSION

It is clear from the foregoing discussion that, despite all the hyperbole we read in popular literature, we still have a long way to go before we can conclude that emotional intelligence training is truly effective. As we have argued, intelligence is a capacity for performance, and is derived from a person's genetic background and home nurturance. On the other hand, there is no reason that an individual cannot be trained to use his or her intelligence, even defined as a capacity, more effectively. The studies that we have reviewed in this chapter give hope that emotional skills can be developed, and there are encouraging signs that these skills lead to better performance outcomes for individuals and teams. Moreover, based on Ashkanasy's (2003a) five-level model, this also has the potential to lead to improved organizational performance.

Nonetheless, and as we noted earlier, we are witnessing an 'affective revolution' in organizational behavior and management (Barsade et al., 2003), including the inclusion of chapters on the topic in leading textbooks. A consequence of this is that there will be increasing attention paid to emotions and affect, both in the workplace and in the classroom. We predict therefore that management classes and organizational training programs will see an introduction of the topics of emotions, and emotional intelligence as an individual difference variable, that are worthy of study. Further, such lessons will become invaluable to the study of leadership, especially within the context of teams.

It is still early days in the study of emotion and emotional intelligence, and our knowledge of how to incorporate these constructs in learning and education programs is still developing. As we outlined at the beginning of this chapter, the study of emotion in organizational settings in general and emotional intelligence in particular, does not have a long history, and we are still on a steep learning curve. Recent findings based on fMRI technology, for example, are redefining important aspects of our understanding of the emotional brain (Gazzaniga, 2004). Clearly, there are limitless possibilities in this field.

We believe that the new developments in the field are going to continue to develop our ideas about the nature and effects of emotions, and especially emotional intelligence. As Barsade (2002) outlines, there is still a deeply embedded prejudice against including non-intellectual constructs in our understanding of organizational behavior. Until Simon's (1976) seminal work on bounded rationality, organizations were assumed to be inherently 100 percent rational, with no place for emotion whatsoever. More recently, scholars have begun to recognize that emotion most likely plays a role in decision processes and behavior at every level of organizational functioning, including CEO's strategic decision-making at the very top (Ashkanasy and Ashton-James, 2002; Daniels, 1998).

One impediment to the development of the field, however, continues to be the ongoing animosity towards emotional intelligence, especially in some academic quarters (e.g., see Antonakis, 2004; Landy, 2005; Locke, 2005). As we have pointed out in this chapter (see also Ashkanasy and Daus, 2005), these negative attitudes have arisen largely because of the exaggerated claims made for emotional intelligence, many of which have not stood up in scientific testing (Jordan et al., 2006), and the proliferation of Stream 3 models. Hopefully, however, the message about the scientifically valid abilities model of emotional intelligence, based on the Mayer and Salovey (1997) four-branch model of emotional intelligence, and embodied in the Stream 1 and 2 approaches is getting though, both in scholarship (i.e., through our efforts) and in educational programs such, as those by Caruso and Huy described earlier in this chapter.

At the same time, we do not want to be seen to be dogmatic about this. As our knowledge of emotion increases in the wake of yet-undiscovered advances, reasons to modify or maybe even abandon altogether the Mayer and Salovey model may emerge. As Jordan et al. (2003) have pointed out, the whole concept of emotional intelligence is still in a developmental phase, and is still therefore open to new ideas and change. The important thing here is that such advances need to be based on scientific and empirically tested models, rather than on exaggerated popular claims.

In conclusion, and as we have shown in this chapter, consistent with Ashkanasy's (2003a) 5-level model, emotions have been shown to play a significant role at every level of organizational functioning. In particular, there is a great deal of interest in the connection between emotional intelligence and leadership, and some promising findings are emerging. Moreover, there are some early indications that emotional intelligence training, or more correctly worded, emotional literacy training, can have beneficial effects in leadership programs.

Nonetheless, we still advise caution. At this point in time there is too little empirical evidence for us to be certain about the efficacy of teaching about emotional intelligence in leadership training. Part of the problem lies in the definition and measurement of emotional intelligence, and part of the problem lies in the definition of what exactly is 'effective leadership'. Still, although we cannot say how or to what extent emotional intelligence contributes to effective leadership, we do know from empirical research that leadership involves emotions, and emotional skills may be beneficial for leaders in the workplace, especially those within team contexts. Hence, leadership training and development programs to enhance leadership effectiveness should still incorporate these emotion based skills, but caution is still necessary before making any concrete claims of regarding emotional intelligence and leadership.

## ACKNOWLEDGEMENT

Figure 9.1 was published in 'Positive emotion in organizations: A multi-level framework' by N.M. Ashkanasy and C.E. Ashton-James in *Positive Organizational Behaviour: Accenting the Positive at Work* by C.L. Cooper and D. Nelson (eds), pp.57–73. Copyright Elsevier (2007).

## NOTES

1 http://www.thefreedictionary.com/emotion (accessed June 14, 2007).

2 See http://www.elsevier.com/wps/find/bookdescription.cws_home/BS_REO/description#description.

3 Based on Amazon.com search, June 14, 2007.

4 Although 'hassles' and 'uplifts' are often mentioned in reference to AET, Weiss and Cropanzano did not in fact use either term in their 1996 article.

5 Despite all the controversy between Watson and Tellegen and Russell and Carroll (e.g., see Russell and Carroll, 1999; Watson and Tellegen, 1999), the two perspectives can be shown to be functionally identical using simple 45-degree axis rotation.

6 The term 'emotional intelligence' was, in fact, introduced by Payne (1985) in his doctoral dissertation, but this work was not developed further. Salovey and Mayer (1990) developed their concept of emotional intelligence independently, and this is generally regarded as the seminal article in the field.

7 We found 173 citations recorded in SSCI; and 269 recorded in Google Scholar™ (as at Dec. 1, 2007).

8 The articles by Locke and Landy and responses by Ashkanasy and Daus were published in a 'Point-Counterpoint' issue of the *Journal of Organizational Behavior* (introduced by Spector, 2005), which followed a debate on this topic at the 2003 annual meeting of the Society for Industrial and Organizational Psychology (see Daus and Ashkanasy, 2003).

9 http://iew3.technion.ac.il/Home/Users/anatr/emotion_syllabus.pdf, (visited June 14, 2007).

10 http://executive.education.insead.edu/challenge%5Fleadership/ (visited June 14, 2007).

11 http://www.emotionaliq.com/ (visited June 14, 2007).

## REFERENCES

Albrow, M. (1992) *'Sine ira et studio* – or do organizations have feelings?', *Organization Studies*, 13: 313–29.

Althoff, J. and Ashkanasy, N.M. (2004, April) 'Determinants of accurate perception of facial expressions in the boardroom', Paper presented at the Annual Meeting of the Society for Industrial and Organizational Psychology (SIOP), Chicago, Illinois, USA.

Antonakis, J. (2004) 'On why "emotional intelligence" will not predict leadership effectiveness beyond IQ or the "big five": An extension and rejoinder', *Organizational Analysis*, 12: 171–82.

Ashforth, B.E. and Humphrey, R.H. (1995) 'Emotion in the workplace: A reappraisal', *Human Relations*, 48: 97–125.

Ashkanasy, N.M. (2003a) 'Emotions in organizations: A multilevel perspective', in F. Dansereau and F.J. Yammarino (eds), *Research in Multi-level Issues: Multi-level Issues in Organizational Behavior and Strategy* (Vol. 2). Oxford, UK: Elsevier/ JAI Press, pp. 9–54.

Ashkanasy, N.M. (2003b) 'Emotions at multiple levels: An integration', in F. Dansereau and F.J. Yammarino (eds), *Research in Multi-level Issues: Multi-level Issues in Organizational Behavior and Strategy* (Vol. 2). Oxford, UK: Elsevier/JAI Press, pp. 71–81.

Ashkanasy, N.M. (ed.) (2004) 'Special issue on emotions and performance', *Human Performance*, 17(2).

Ashkanasy, N.M. and Ashton-James, C.E. (2005) 'Emotion in organizations: A neglected topic in I/O Psychology, but with a bright future', in G.P. Hodgkinson and J.K. Ford (eds), *International Review of Industrial and Organizational Psychology*, Vol. 20. Chichester, UK: John Wiley and Sons, pp. 221–68.

Ashkanasy, N.M. and Ashton-James, C.E. (2007) 'Positive emotion in organizations: A multi-level framework', in C.L. Cooper and D. Nelson (eds), *Positive Organizational Behavior: Accenting the Positive at Work*. Chichester, UK: John Wiley and Sons. pp. 57–73.

Ashkanasy, N.M. and Dasborough, M.T. (2003) 'Emotional awareness and emotional intelligence in leadership teaching', *Journal of Education in Business*, 79: 18–22.

Ashkanasy, N.M. and Daus, C.S. (2002) 'Emotion in the workplace: The new challenge for managers', *Academy of Management Executive*, 16: 76–86.

Ashkanasy, N.M. and Daus, C.S. (2005) 'Rumors of the death of emotional intelligence in organizational behavior are vastly exaggerated', *Journal of Organizational Behavior*, 26: 441–52.

Ashkanasy, N.M. and Nicholson, G.J. (2003) 'Climate of fear in organizational settings: Construct definition, measurement, and a test of theory', *Australian Journal of Psychology*, 55: 24–9.

1

Ashkanasy, N.M., Härtel, C.E.J. and Daus, C.S. (2002) 'Diversity and emotion: The new frontiers in organizational behavior research', *Journal of Management*, 28: 307–38.

Ashkanasy, N.M. and Tse, B. (2000) 'Transformational leadership as management of emotion: A conceptual review', in N. Ashkanasy, C.E.J. Härtel and W.J. Zerbe (eds), *Emotions in the Workplace: Research, Theory, and Practice*. Westport, CT, Quorum Books. pp. 221–35.

Ashkanasy, N.M., Härtel, C.E.J. and Zerbe, W. (eds) (2000a) *Emotions in the Workplace: Research, theory, and Practice*. Westport, CT: Quorum.

Ashkanasy, N.M., Härtel, C.E.J. and Zerbe, W.J. (2000b) 'Emotions in the workplace: Research, theory, and practice. Introduction', in N.M. Ashkanasy, C.E.J. Härtel and W. Zerbe (eds), *Emotions in the Workplace: Research, Theory, and Practice*. Westport, CT: Quorum Books. pp. 3–18.

Ashkanasy, N.M., Zerbe, W. and Härtel, C.E.J. (eds) (2002) *Managing Emotions in the Workplace*. Armonk, NY: ME Sharpe.

Bagshaw, M. (2000) 'Emotional intelligence: Training people to be affective so they can be effective', *Industrial and Commercial Training*, 32: 61–5.

Ball, G.A., Trevino, L.K. and Sims, H.P. Jr. (1992) 'Understanding subordinate reactions to punishment incidents: Perspectives from justice and social affect', *The Leadership Quarterly*, 3: 307–33.

Baron, R.A. (1993) 'Affect and organizational behavior: When and why feeling good (or bad) matters', in J.K. Murnighan (ed.), *Social Psychology in Organizations: Advances in Theory and Research*. Englewood Cliffs, NJ: Prentice Hall. pp. 63–88.

Barsade, S.G. (2002) 'The ripple effect: Emotional contagion and its influence on group behavior', *Administrative Science Quarterly*, 47: 644–75.

Barsade, S.G. and Gibson, D.E. (2007) 'Why does affect matter in organizations?' *Academy of Management Perspectives*, 21: 36–59.

Barsade, S.G., Brief, A.P. and Spataro, S.E. (2003) 'The affective revolution in organizational behavior: The emergence of a paradigm', in J. Greenberg (ed.), *Organizational Behavior: The State of the Science*. Mahwah, NJ: Lawrence Erlbaum Associates. pp. 3–52.

Basch, J. and Fisher, C.D. (2000) 'Affective events-emotions matrix: A classification of work events and associated emotions', in N.M. Ashkanasy and C.E.J. Härtel, W.J. Zerbe (eds), *Emotions in the Workplace: Research, Theory, and Practice*. Westport, CT: Quorum. pp. 36–48.

Bass, B.M. (1990) *Bass and Stogdill's Handbook of Leadership: A Survey of Theory and Research*. New York: Free Press.

Bass, B.M. and Riggio, R.E. (2005) *Transformational Leadership*. Mahwah, NJ: Lawrence Erlbaum Associates.

Bocchino, R. (1999) *Emotional Literacy: To Be a Different Kind of Smart*. Thousand Oaks, CA: Sage Publications.

Bono, J.E. and Ilies, R. (2006) 'Charisma, positive emotions, and mood contagion', *The Leadership Quarterly*, 17: 317–34.

Bono, J., Foldes, H.J., Vinson, G. and Muros, J.P. (2007) 'Workplace emotions: The role of supervision and leadership', *Journal of Applied Psychology*, 92: 1357–67.

Brackett, M.A., Rivers, S.E., Shiffman, S., Lerner N. and Salovey P. (2006) 'Relating emotional abilities to social functioning: A comparison of self-report and performance measures of emotional intelligence', *Journal of Personality and Social Psychology*, 91: 780–95.

Brief, A.P. and Weiss, H.M. (2002) 'Organizational behavior: Affect in the workplace', *Annual Review of Psychology*, 53: 279–307.

Caruso, D.R. and Salovey, P. (2004) *The Emotionally Intelligent Manager: How to Develop and use the Four Key Emotional Skills of Leadership*. San Francisco: Jossey-Bass.

Caruso, D.R. and Wolfe, C.J. (2004) 'Emotional intelligence and leadership development', in D.V. Day, S.J. Zaccaro and S.M. Halpin (eds), *Leader Development for Transforming Organizations: Growing Leaders for Tomorrow*. Mahwah, NJ: Lawrence Erlbaum Associates. pp. 237–63.

Cherniss, C. and Adler, M. (2000) *Promoting Emotional Intelligence in Organizations*. Alexandria: American Society for Training and Development.

Cherulnik, P.D., Donley, K.A., Wiewel, T.S.R. and Miller, S.R. (2001) 'Charisma is contagious: The effect of leaders' charisma on observers' affect', *Journal of Applied Social Psychology*, 31: 2149–59.

Clarke, N. (2006) 'Emotional intelligence training: A case of caveat emptor', *Human Resource Development Review*, 5: 422–41.

Cooper, R.K. and Sawaf, A. (1997) *Executive EQ: Emotional Intelligence in Leadership and Organizations*. New York: Grosset/Putman.

Damasio, A.R. (1994) *Descartes' Error: Emotion, Reason, and the Human Brain*. New York: Avon Books.

Damen, F., van Knippenberg, B. and van Knippenberg, D. (2008). 'Affective match: Leader emotional displays, follower positive affect, and follower performance', *Journal of Applied Social Psychology*. 38: 868–902.

Daniels, K. (1998) 'Towards integrating emotions into strategic management research: Trait affect and perceptions of the strategic environment', *British Journal of Management*, 9: 163–8.

Dasborough, M.T. (2006) 'Cognitive asymmetry in employee emotional reactions to leadership behaviors', *The Leadership Quarterly*, 17: 163–78.

Dasborough, M.T. and Ashkanasy, N.M. (2002) 'Emotion and attribution of intentionality in leader-follower relationships', *The Leadership Quarterly*, 13: 615–34.

Dasborough, M.T., Thomas, J. and Bowler, W.M. (2007, August) 'Utilizing your social network and emotional skills to emerge as the team leader', Paper presented at the Academy of Management Annual Meetings, Philadelphia, PA.

Daus, C.S. and Ashkanasy, N.M. (2003) 'Will the real emotional intelligence please stand up? On deconstructing the emotional intelligence "debate" ', *The Industrial and Organizational Psychologist*, 41: 69–72.

Daus, C.S. and Ashkanasy, N.M. (2005) 'The case for an ability-based model of emotional intelligence in organizational behavior', *Journal of Organizational Behavior*, 26: 453–66.

Davies, M., Stankov, L. and Roberts, R.D. (1998) 'Emotional intelligence: In search of an elusive construct', *Journal of Personality and Social Psychology*, 75: 989–1015.

Day, D.V. (2000) 'Leadership development: A review in context', *The Leadership Quarterly*, 11: 581–613.

De Cremer, D. (2006) 'When authorities influence followers' affect: The interactive effect of procedural justice and transformational leadership', *European Journal of Work and Organizational Psychology*, 15: 322–51.

De Rivera, J. (1992) 'Emotional climate: Social structure and emotional dynamics', *International Review of Studies of Emotion*, 2: 197–218.

Denzin, N. (1984) *Understanding Emotions*. San Francisco: Jossey-Bass.

Dulewicz, S.V. and Higgs, M.J. (1999) 'Can emotional intelligence be measured and developed?' *Leadership and Organization Development Journal*, 20: 242–52.

Dulewicz, S.V., Higgs, M.J. and Slaski, M. (2003) 'Emotional intelligence: Content, construct and concurrent validity', *Journal of Managerial Psychology*, 18: 405–20.

Dunlop, F. (1984) *The Education of Feeling and Emotion*. London: Allen and Unwin.

Ekman, P. (1999) 'Facial expressions', in T. Dalgleish, M.J. Power and J. Mick (eds), *Handbook of Cognition and Emotion*. New York: Wiley. pp. 301–20.

Elfenbein, H.A., Polzer, J.T. and Ambady, N. (2007) 'Team emotion recognition accuracy and team performance', in C.E.J. Härtel, N.M. Ashkanasy and W.J. Zerbe (eds), *Research on Emotion in Organizations*, Vol. 3. *The Functional Role of Emotion in Organizations*. Oxford, UK: Elsevier/ JAI Press. pp. 89–119.

Fineman S. (ed.) (1993) *Emotion in Organizations*. London: Sage.

Fineman, S. (1997) 'Emotion and management learning', *Management Learning*, 28: 13–25.

Fineman, S. (ed.) (2000) *Emotion in Organizations* (2nd edn). London: Sage.

Fischer, K.W., Shaver, P.R. and Carnochan, P. (1990) 'How emotions develop and how they organize development', *Cognition and Emotion*, 4: 81–127.

Fisher, C.D. and Ashkanasy, N.M. (eds) (2000) 'Special issue on emotions in work life', *Journal of Organizational Behavior*, 21(3).

Forgas, J.P. (1995) 'Mood and judgment: The Affect Infusion Model (AIM)', *Psychological Bulletin*, 117: 39–66.

Fox, S. (ed.) (2002) 'Special issue on emotions in the workplace', *Human Resource Management Review*, 12(2).

Frank, M.G., Ekman, P. and Friesen, W.V. (1993) 'Behavioral markers and recognizability of the smile of enjoyment', *Journal of Personality and Social Psychology*, 64: 83–93.

Frijda, N. (1986) *The Emotions*. Cambridge, UK: Cambridge University Press.

Frijda, N.H., Manstead, A.S.R. and Bem, S. (eds) (2006). *Emotions and Beliefs: How Feelings Influence Thoughts (Studies in emotion and social interaction)*. New York: Cambridge University Press.

Gaddis, B., Connelly, S. and Mumford, M.D. (2004) 'Failure feedback as an affective event: Influences of leader affect on subordinate attitudes and performance', *The Leadership Quarterly*, 15: 663–86.

Gazzaniga, M.S. (2004) *The Cognitive Neurosciences III*. Cambridge, MA: MIT Press.

George, J.M. (1990) 'Personality, affect, and behavior in groups', *Journal of Applied Psychology*, 76: 299–307.

George, J.M. (2000) 'Emotions and leadership: The role of emotional intelligence', *Human Relations*, 53: 1027–55.

Glomb, T.M. and Hulin, C.L. (1997) 'Anger and gender effects in observed supervisor-subordinate dyadic interactions', *Organizational Behavior and Human Decision Processes*, 75: 281–307.

Goleman, D. (1995) *Emotional Intelligence: Why it can Matter More than IQ*. New York: Bantam.

Goleman, D. (1998) *Working with Emotional Intelligence*. New York: Bantam.

Goleman, D., Boyatzis. R. and McKee, A. (2002) *Primal Leadership: Realizing the Power of*

*Emotional Intelligence*. Cambridge, MA: Harvard Business School Press.

Graen, G.B. and Uhl-Bien, M. (1995) 'Development of leader-member exchange (LMX) theory of leadership over 25 years: Applying a multi-level multi-domain perspective', *The Leadership Quarterly*, 6:219–47.

Grandey, A.A., Tam, A.P. and Brauburger, A.L. (2002) 'Affective states and traits in the workplace: Diary and survey data from young workers', *Motivation and Emotion*, 26: 31–55.

Gross, J.J., Richards, J.M. and John, O.P. (2006) 'Emotion regulation in everyday life', in D.K. Snyder, J.A. Simpson and J.N. Hughes (eds), *Emotion Regulation in Families: Pathways to Dysfunction and Health*. Washington DC: American Psychological Association. pp. 13–35.

Härtel, C.E.J., Zerbe, W.J. and Ashkanasy, N.M. (eds) (2005) *Emotions in Organizational Behavior*. Mahwah, NJ: Lawrence Erlbaum Associates.

Hatfield, E., Cacioppo, J. and Rapson, R.L. (1992) 'Primitive emotional contagion', *Review of Personality and Social Psychology*, 14: 151–77.

Hein, S.J. (2004, April) 'Emotional intelligence and performance of CEOs of high-growth companies', in P. Papadogiannia and S.J. Hein (co-chairs), *Emotional Intelligence and its Impact on Job Performance*. Symposium presented at the annual meeting of the Society for Industrial and Organizational Psychology, Los Angeles, CA.

Hochschild, A.R. (1983) *The Managed Heart: Commercialization of Human Feeling*. Berkeley, CA: University of California Press.

Hosking, D. and Fineman, S. (1990) 'Organizing processes', *Journal of Management Studies*, 27: 583–604.

Humphrey, R.H. (2002a) 'Special issue on emotions and leadership', *The Leadership Quarterly*, 13(5).

Humphrey, R.H. (2002b) 'The many faces of emotional leadership', *The Leadership Quarterly*, 13: 493–504.

Isen, A.M. and Baron, R.A. (1991) 'Positive affect as a factor in organizational-behavior', *Research in Organizational Behavior*, 13: 1–53.

Isen, A.M. and Means, B. (1983) 'The influence of positive affect on decision-making strategy', *Social Cognition*, 2: 18–31.

Jordan, P.J. and Ashkanasy, N.M. (2006) 'Emotional intelligence, emotional self-awareness, and team effectiveness', in V.U. Druskat, F. Sala and G.J. Mount (eds), *The Impact of Emotional Intelligence on Individual and Group Performance*. Mahwah, NJ: Lawrence Erlbaum Associates. pp. 145–63.

Jordan, P.J. and Troth, A.C. (2004) 'Managing emotions during team problem solving: Emotional intelligence

and conflict resolution', *Human Performance*, 17: 195–218.

Jordan, P.J., Ashkanasy N.M. and Härtel, C.E.J. (2003) 'The case for emotional intelligence in organizational research', *Academy of Management Review*, 28: 195–97.

Jordan, P.J., Ashton-James, C.E. and Ashkanasy, N.M. (2006) 'Evaluating the claims', in K.R. Murphy (ed.), *A Critique of Emotional Intelligence: What are the problems and how can they be fixed?* Mahwah, NJ: Lawrence Erlbaum Associates. pp. 198–210.

Jordan, P.J., Ashkanasy, N.M., Härtel, C.E.J. and Hooper, G.S. (2002) 'Workgroup emotional intelligence: Scale development and relationship to team process effectiveness and goal focus', *Human Resource Management Review*, 12: 195–214.

Kellett, J.B., Humphrey, R.H. and Sleeth, R.G. (2006) 'Empathy and the emergence of task and relations leaders', *The Leadership Quarterly*, 17: 146–62.

Kerr, R., Garvin, J., Heaton, N. and Boyle, E. (2006) 'Emotional intelligence and leadership effectiveness', *Leadership and Organization Development Journal*, 27: 265–79.

Kimberley, N. and Härtel, C.E.J. (2007) 'Building a climate of trust during organizational change: The mediating role of justice perceptions and emotion', in C.E.J. Härtel, N.M. Ashkanasy and W.J. Zerbe (eds), *Research on Emotion in Organizations: The Functional Role of Emotion in Organizations* (Vol. 3). Oxford, UK: Elsevier/JAI Press. pp. 237–64.

Kunnanatt, J.T. (2004) 'Emotional intelligence: The new science of interpersonal effectiveness', *Human Resource Development Quarterly*, 15: 489–95.

Landy, F.J. (2005) 'Some historical and scientific issues related to research on emotional intelligence', *Journal of Organizational Behavior*, 26: 411–24.

Langley, A. (2000) 'Emotional intelligence: A new evaluation for management development?', *Career Development International*, 5: 177–83.

Law, K.S., Wong, C.S. and Song, L.J. (2004) 'The construct and criterion validity of emotional intelligence and its potential utility for management studies', *Journal of Applied Psychology*, 89: 483–96.

Le Doux, J. (1996) *The Emotional Brain*. New York: Simon and Schuster.

Lewis, K.M. (2000) 'When leaders display emotion: How followers respond to negative emotional expression of male and female leader', *Journal of Organizational Behavior*, 21: 221–34.

Locke, E.A. (2005) 'Why emotional intelligence is an invalid concept', *Journal of Organizational Behavior*, 26: 425–31.

Lopes, P.N., Côté, S. and Salovey, P. (2006) 'An ability model of emotional intelligence: Implications for assessment and training', in F. Sala, V.U. Druskat and G. Mount (eds), *Linking Emotional Intelligence and Performance at Work: Current Research Evidence with Individuals and Groups*. Mahwah, NJ: Lawrence Erlbaum Associates. pp. 53–80.

Lord, R.G., Klimoski, R.J. and Kanfer, R. (eds) (2002) *Emotions in the Workplace: Understanding the Structure and Role of Emotions in Organizational Behavior*. San Francisco: Jossey-Bass.

Mayer, J.D. (2004) 'A classification system for the data of personality psychology and adjoining fields', *Review of General Psychology*, 8: 208–19.

Mayer, J.D. and Dobb, C.D. (2000) 'Educational policy on emotional intelligence: Does it make sense?' *Educational Psychology Review*, 12: 163–83.

Mayer, J.D. and Salovey, P. (1997) 'What is emotional intelligence?' in P. Salovey and D.J. Sluyter (eds) *Emotional Development and Emotional Intelligence: Educational Implications*. New York: Basic Books. pp. 3–31.

Mayer, J.D., Salovey, P. and Caruso, D.R. (2002) *Mayer-Salovey-Caruso Emotional Intelligence Test (MSCEIT) Users Manual*. Toronto, Canada: MHS Test Publishers.

Mayer, J.D., Salovey, P., Caruso, D.R. and Sitarenios, G. (2001) 'Emotional intelligence as a standard intelligence', *Emotion*, 1: 232–42.

McCauley, C.D., Moxley, R.S. and van Velsor, E. (eds) (1998) *The Center for Creative Leadership Handbook of Leadership Development*. San Francisco: Jossey-Bass.

McColl-Kennedy, J.R. and Anderson, R.D. (2002) 'Impact of leadership style and emotions on subordinate performance', *The Leadership Quarterly*, 13: 545–59.

Moriarty, P. and Buckley, F. (2003) 'Increasing team emotional intelligence through process', *Journal of European Industrial Training*, 27: 98–100.

Moss, S., Ritossa, D. and Ngu, S. (2006) 'The effect of follower regulatory focus and extraversion on leadership behavior', *Journal of Individual Differences*, 27: 93–107.

Muraven, M. and Baumeister, R.F. (2000) 'Self-regulation and depletion of limited resources: Does self-control resemble a muscle?' *Psychological Bulletin*, 126: 247–59.

Murray, J.P., Jordan, P.J. and Ashkanasy, N.M. (2006, May) 'Emotional intelligence training: Theoretical and practical issues', in J.P. Murray and N.M. Ashkanasy (co-chairs), *Emotional Intelligence and Workplace Training Interventions*. Symposium presented at the Annual Meeting of the Society for Industrial and Organizational Psychology (SIOP), Dallas, TX.

Newcombe, M.J. and Ashkanasy, N.M. (2002) 'The role of affect and affective congruence in perceptions of leaders: An experimental study', *The Leadership Quarterly*, 13: 601–14.

Offermann, L.R., Bailey, J.R., Vasilopoulos, N.L., Seal, C. and Sass, M. (2004) 'The relative contribution of emotional competence and cognitive ability to individual and team performance', *Human Performance*, 17: 219–43.

Palmer, B. and Stough, C. (2001) *Workplace SUEIT: Swinburne University Emotional Intelligence Test – Descriptive Report*. Melbourne, Australia: Organisational Psychology Research Unit, Swinburne University.

Palmer, B., Walls, M., Burgess, Z. and Stough, C. (2000) 'Emotional intelligence and effective leadership', *Leadership and Organization Development Journal*, 22: 5–10.

Payne, R.L. and Cooper, C.L. (eds) (2001) *Emotions at Work: Theory, Research, and Applications for Management*. Chichester, UK: Wiley.

Payne, W.L. (1985) 'A study of emotion: Developing emotional intelligence; self-integration; relating to fear, pain and desire (theory, structure of reality, problem-solving, contraction/expansion, tuning in/coming out/letting go)', Unpublished doctoral dissertation. Cincinnati, OH: The Union for Experimenting Colleges and Universities (now The Union Institute).

Pekrun, R. and Friese, M. (1992) 'Emotions in work and achievement', *International Review of Industrial and Organizational Psychology*, 7: 153–200.

Perkins, D. (1995) *Outsmarting IQ: The Emerging Science of Learnable Intelligences*. New York: The Free Press.

Pescosolido, A.T. (2002) 'Emergent leaders as managers of group emotion', *The Leadership Quarterly*, 13: 583–99.

Pirola-Merlo, A., Härtel, C., Mann, L. and Hirst, G. (2002) 'How leaders influence the impact of affective events on team climate and performance in RandD teams', *The Leadership Quarterly*, 13: 561–81.

Prati, L.M., Douglas, C., Ferris, G.R., Ammeter, A.P. and Buckley, M.R. (2003) 'Emotional intelligence, leadership effectiveness, and team outcomes', *International Journal of Organizational Analysis*, 11: 21–40.

Rafaeli, A. and Sutton, R.I. (1987) 'Expression of emotion as part of the work role', *Academy of Management Review*, 12: 23–37.

Rafaeli, A. and Sutton, R.I. (1989) 'The expression of emotion in organizational life', in L.L. Cummings and B.M. Staw (eds), *Research in Organizational Behavior* (Vol. 11). Greenwich, CT: JAI Press. pp. 1–42.

Robbins, S.P. and Judge, T.A. (2007) *Organizational Behavior* (12th edn, Chapter 8). Englewood Cliffs, NJ: Prentice-Hall.

Rosete, D. and Ciarrochi, J. (2005) 'Emotional intelligence and its relationship to workplace performance outcomes of leadership effectiveness', *Leadership and Organization Development Journal*, 26: 388–99.

Rozell, E.J., Pettijohn, C.E. and Parker, R.S. (2002) 'An empirical evaluation of emotional intelligence: The impact on management development', *The Journal of Management Development*, 21: 272–89.

Rubin, R.S., Munz, D.C. and Bommer, W.H. (2005) 'Leading from within: The effects of emotion recognition and personality on transformational leadership behavior', *Academy of Management Journal*, 48: 845–58.

Russell, J.A. and Carroll, J.M. (1999) 'On the bipolarity of positive and negative affect', *Psychological Bulletin*, 125: 3–30.

Sala, F. (2002) *'Emotional Competence Inventory (ECI) Technical Manual'*, Boston, MA: McClelland Center for Research and Innovation. http://www.eiconsortium.org/research/ECI_Tech_Manual.pdf. (Accessed June 15, 2007).

Salovey, P. and Mayer, J.D. (1990) 'Emotional intelligence', *Imagination, Cognition, and Personality*, 9: 185–211.

Schutte, N.S., Malouff, J.M., Hall, L.E., Haggerty, D.J. Cooper, J.T., Golden, C.J. and Dornheim, L. (1998) 'Development and validation of a measure of emotional intelligence', *Personality and Individual Differences*, 25: 167–77.

Seers, A. (1989) 'Team-member exchange quality: A new construct for role-making research', *Organizational Behavior and Human Decision Processes*, 43: 118–35.

Simon, H.A. (1976) *Administrative Behavior: A Study of Decision-Making Processes in Administrative Organization*, (3rd edn). New York: Free Press.

Sosik, J.J. and Megerian, L.E. (1999) 'Understanding leader emotional intelligence and performance', *Group and Organization Management*, 24: 367–91.

Spector, P.E. (2005) 'Introduction: Emotional intelligence', *Journal of Organizational Behavior*, 26: 409–10.

Steiner, C. and Perry, P. (1999) *Achieving Emotional Literacy*. London, Bloomsbury Publishing.

Sutton, R.I. and Rafaeli, A. (1988) 'Untangling the relationship between displayed emotions and organizational sales: The case of convenience stores', *Academy of Management Journal*, 31: 461–87.

Sy, T. and Côté, S. (2004) 'Emotional intelligence: A key ability to succeed in the matrix organization', *The Journal of Management Development*, 23: 437–55.

Sy, T., Côté, S. and Saavedra, R. (2005) 'The contagious leader: Impact of the leader's mood on the mood of group members, group affective tone, and group processes', *Journal of Applied Psychology*, 90: 295–305.

Sy, T., Tram, S. and O'Hara, L.A. (2006) 'Relation of employee and manager emotional intelligence to job satisfaction and performance', *Journal of Vocational Behavior*, 68: 461–73.

Tee, E.Y.J. and Ashkanasy, N.M. (2007, April) 'The interactive effects of leader neuroticism and team mood on leader performance and decision speed', Paper presented at the Annual Meeting of the Society for Industrial and Organizational Psychology (SIOP), New York, USA.

Thomson, K.M. (1998) *Emotional Capital: Capturing Hearts and Minds to Create Lasting Business Success*. Oxford, UK: Capstone Press.

Thorndike, E.L. (1920) 'Intelligence and its uses', *Harper's Magazine*, 140: 227–35.

Tse, H.M. and Dasborough, M.T. (2008) 'A study of exchange and emotions in team member relationships', *Group and Organization Management: An International Journal*, 33: 194–215.

Tse, H.M., Dasborough, M.T. and Ashkanasy, N.M. (2008) 'A multilevel analysis of team climate and interpersonal exchange relationships at work', *The Leadership Quarterly*, 19: 195–211.

Van Buskirk, W. and McGrath, D. (1992) 'Organizational stories as a window on affect in organizations', *Journal of Organizational Change Management*, 5: 9–24.

Van Maanen, J. and Kunda, G. (1989) ' "Real feelings": Emotional expression and organizational culture', in L.L. Cummings and B.M. Staw (eds), *Research in Organizational Behavior* (Vol. 11). Greenwich, CT: JAI Press. pp. 43–103.

Watson, D. and Tellegen, A. (1985) 'Towards a consensual structure of mood', *Psychological Bulletin*, 98: 219–35.

Watson, D. and Tellegen, A. (1999) 'Issues in the dimensional structure of affect. Effects of descriptors, measurement error, and response formats: Comment on Russell and Carroll (1999)', *Psychological Bulletin*, 125: 601–10.

Weiss, H.M. (ed.) (2001) 'Special issue – Affect at work: Collaborations of basic and organizational research', *Organizational Behavior and Human Decision Process*, 86(1).

Weiss, H.M. (ed.) (2002) 'Special issue on emotional experiences at work', *Motivation and Emotion*, 26(1).

Weiss, H.M. and Cropanzano, R. (1996) 'Affective events theory: A theoretical discussion of the structure, causes and consequences of affective experiences at work', in B.M. Staw and L.L. Cummings (eds), *Research in Organizational Behavior* (Vol. 19). Greenwich, CT: JAI Press. pp. 1–74.

Welch, J. (2003) 'The best teams are emotionally literate', *Industrial and Commercial Training*, 35: 168–70.

Wharton, A.S. and Erickson, R.J. (1995) 'The consequences of caring: Exploring the links between women's job and family emotion work', *Sociology Quarterly*, 36: 273–96.

Wolff, S.B., Pescosolido, A.T. and Druskat, V.U. (2002) 'Emotional intelligence as the basis of leadership emergence in self-managing teams', *The Leadership Quarterly*, 13: 505–22.

Wong, C.S. and Law, K.S. (2002) 'The effect of leader and follower emotional intelligence on performance and attitude: An exploratory study', *The Leadership Quarterly*, 13: 243–74.

Wong, C.S., Foo, M.D., Wang, C.W. and Wong, P.M. (2007) 'The feasibility of training and development of EI: An exploratory study in Singapore, Hong Kong and Taiwan', *Intelligence*, 35: 141–50.

Yukl, G.A. (2005) *Leadership in Organizations* (6th edn). Englewood Cliffs, NJ: Prentice-Hall.

# PART II

# Management Education: In a Formal Learning Context

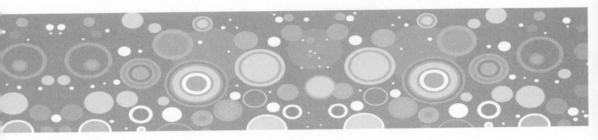

# 10

# Artful Teaching: Using the Visual, Creative and Performing Arts in Contemporary Management Education[1]

Joan V. Gallos

## Abstract

This chapter examines the diverse and powerful uses of the arts in teaching and learning, their contribution to the scholarship and practice of management education and development, and the growing fit between arts-infused pedagogies and the learning needed for organizational and leadership effectiveness in a competitive global world. The chapter explores the arts as a time-tested pedagogy for: (1) exploring human nature and modern organizational life; (2) facilitating deep cognitive, socio-emotional, and behavioral growth; and (3) fostering creativity and the development of complex skills. It ends with caveats and suggestions for the effective use of arts-based pedagogies in management education and development.

This chapter explores the use of the visual, creative and performing arts in management education, and development. Its purpose is two-fold: to examine both theory and practice – the *why* and the *how* – needed to appreciate the power and possibilities of management teaching strategies that employ or are fundamentally informed by artistic methods, approaches, or ways of knowing and understanding the larger world. No single chapter can illustrate all the ways that different artistic media have or can be used to foster significant learning and skills development across the organizational and management sciences, nor the reasons for choosing among them. Rather, this chapter is intended as a creative invitation to reflect on possibilities – the array of options for using the arts in management teaching and learning, their contributions to scholarship and practice, and the growing fit between arts-based pedagogies and all that is needed for success in today's – and tomorrow's – competitive global world.

The chapter is organized around four basic assertions that have been informed by learning theory, organizational best practices, and 30 years of classroom and executive teaching with the arts across sectors and nations. Teaching activities that employ products or processes from the visual, creative, and performing arts:

- provide a rich, multi-cultural, and time-tested instructional pedagogy that has evolved over time to reflect a growing understanding of people and organizations;
- offer unique avenues for learning about the fundamental complexities of human nature and of modern organizational life;
- engender an openness and engagement in the learning process that facilitate deep cognitive, socio-emotional, and behavioral growth; and
- foster creativity and the complex skills development that are increasingly important for innovation and contemporary organizational leadership.

The first part of this chapter examines the four assertions and provides a larger context for understanding the issues. It explores the increasingly diverse and multi-dimensional ways in which the arts, artistic sensibilities, and aesthetic ways of knowing have informed and been incorporated into management education and development; and draws on specific examples from teaching through literature and through films to illustrate key pedagogical concerns. Appreciating the power and possibilities in using the arts requires recognizing the rich – and often unacknowledged – history of influence that artistic practices, elements, and understandings have had on management pedagogy. They have challenged the traditional logical-rational paradigm (Nissley, 2002) that has historically framed the field from its early turn-of-the-century roots in scientific management. And they have served as tacit catalysts to broaden the ontological, teleological, and epistemological foundations of the field and to expand the meaning, values, and purposes of management teaching and training. Use of the arts has evolved beyond borrowing artistic practices and metaphors – an emphasis on

integrating selected arts products, approaches, and language into teaching methods to illustrate theory or encourage reflection on it – to encouraging students to immerse themselves deeply in 'making art' or partnering with artists in order to foster the creativity, artistic mindsets, and aesthetic sensibilities historically associated with artists and are now essential for 21st century business success (Adler, 2006; Canton, 2007; Edwards, 2008; Pink, 2005; Seifter, 2004).

The second part of the chapter supports educators in their ongoing work. It contains caveats and suggestions for effectively using the arts in management learning. The chapter's intent is to serve readers at different career stages. For newcomers, it offers an introduction to the opportunities in using different media and ways to get started. For seasoned veterans, it suggests resources to expand teaching options and learning outcomes. The chapter ends with a reminder of the important role of arts-based teaching for the creation of a management pedagogy of hope and imagination.

## EXPLORING THEORY AND PRACTICE: UNDERSTANDING THE ISSUES AND OPTIONS

When power leads men towards arrogance, poetry reminds him of his limitations.

When power narrows the areas of man's concern, poetry reminds him of the richness and diversity of his existence. When power corrupts, poetry cleanses. For art establishes the basic human truth which must serve as the touchstone of our judgment. (John F. Kennedy)[3]

Management education and development practices that employ artistic methods and approaches are neither experimental nor a recent innovation. Learning through the arts has a long and proud global track record. It encourages creativity and the developmental capacities needed to translate abstract information into innovative and actionable knowledge (e.g., Gardner, 1984, 1993, 1994a,

1994b; Jensen, 2001). It also facilitates multi-level cognitive and socio-emotional growth that is wider and deeper than can be measured by grades or test scores (Fiske, 1999). A brief look at selected highlights frames the use of the arts in management learning as rich, multi-cultural, and time-tested. It identifies the role of artistic thinking and practices in expanding ways of knowing, of discovering, and of defining managerial effectiveness and the training necessary for it. It also illustrates an ongoing evolution in pedagogical strategies, methods, and options for the field.

## Providing a rich, multi-cultural, and time-tested pedagogy

The human need to express the abstract through the concrete is deeply rooted, and theater and storytelling have long been central media for learning, communication, and social development. Storytelling is fundamental to the search for human meaning, as well as a socially economic vehicle for conveying beliefs and values, for learning from experience, and for inspiring social action (Bateson, 1995; Bennis and Levinson, 1996; Denning, 2005, 2007). Theater – storytelling's close cousin – is at its core a social art. It integrates text with visual imagery and interpretive performance to frame common struggles in the collective human experience and to probe universal political, religious, social, and moral issues. At their best, theater and storytelling instruct and entertain: they offer humanity opportunities to step back and see itself across time, space, and cultures. This role for theater has been so broad and universally understood that *theater* has often been used as a metaphor for life itself (Wickham, 1992), and theater arts and approaches have long served as powerful hermeneutic devices for understanding another's point of view and its origin and as sources of individual and social development.

Ancient Greeks and Romans, for example, used drama and the literary arts to educate their citizenry, explore moral teachings, examine the human condition, and foster socialization. The early Greeks studied leadership and organizing as none before them (Clemens and Mayer, 1999). And classical Greek theater, poetry, and histories are creative and enduring testimonials to the strength of their contributions in understanding human nature, the delicate balance between individual freedom and social order, and strategies for eliciting individual effort in service to community goals. The Greeks intuitively knew what contemporary research on social movements has proven: collective action requires a vehicle for communicating a 'script' on how a populace should frame and make sense of its world (Benford and Snow, 2000; Benford and Hunt, 1992). The religious links in ancient Greek theater – drama and theater were an outgrowth of rites celebrating the annual festival of Dionysus (Wickham 1992) – made the choice and power of the medium as significant as the message.

Plato even launched his own school to foster a drama-infused alternative to the lecture method of instruction – the dominant teaching strategy of the day. His famous dialogues were its foundation. Plato's new teaching method combined structured inquiry, discussion, and case analysis with the theatrical elements of character, plot, and setting. It built on a form of two-performer mime cultivated by the Sicilian poets Sophron and Epicharmus, whose work Plato was known to admire (Ausland, 1997). Plato saw no reason to separate entertainment from instruction (Smith, 2001). His methods were an early form of integrative learning as reflected in the contemporary *teaching for understanding* movement (e.g., Brandt, 1993; Wiske, 1997) – and a precursor to modern-day case teaching. Plato was not alone in recognizing the power of dramatic tension, theater arts, inquiry, and forensics for student motivation, learning, and developmental growth. While Plato was perfecting his teaching strategies in Greece, for example, dialogue-centered education in pre-colonial Africa was in full force, combining the use of tribal legends, proverbs, character-driven myths, and riddles to test judgment, develop reasoning skills, and probe the origin of the tribe and humanity (Mazonde, 2007; Miller, 2007). And for centuries, nations and cultures around the world have transferred values and the wisdom of elders across the generations through their music, dance, traditional crafts, and epic tales.

Across medieval Europe, for example, minstrels, court jesters, and theater troupes spoke truth to power and used stories, plays, and analogies to teach leadership lessons – a tradition that has continued across time and culture and is reflected in the theater's long history as 'a constant source of anxiety the world over to leaders of Church and State alike' (Wickham, 1992: 11). Armed with a conviction that the arts can change the world, for example, the Market Theater was established in Johannesburg in 1978 to challenge apartheid. The theater company staged controversial productions that kept the politically charged issues of the day before South African audiences – like exiled South African playwright Athol Fugard's *The Island* set in the Robben Island prison where Nelson Mandela was being held. The company's policies of open seating also challenged government bans on different races attending performances together without a permit. The government's refusal to take punitive action against the artists became a visible symbol for the role of the arts in community education and for the power of non-violent resistance through artistic expression (*Kansas City Repertory Theater*, 2007).

Turning to examples closer to the academic home front and the history of contemporary management education, instructional methods that draw on arts practices and mindsets have evolved in scope, purpose, and medium over much of the last century. The cumulative changes have paralleled theoretical advances in our understandings of people, complexity, and organizing. They also reflect – and help us chart – important shifts in beliefs about the essential nature and purpose of management education, core curricular content, the focus of student learning, and appropriate paths to success. The arts – and not just the

sciences – have been an essential partner for management pedagogy throughout its history and an important vehicle for staying true to the field's core mission: preparing people for effective professional practice.

In the 1920s, for example, faculty at the Harvard Business School (HBS) pioneered the instructional use of stories – they called them *cases* – to anchor theory in practice. Cases were revolutionary in their early days, offering students opportunity to immerse themselves in real world problems for a 'what if' experience: assume the role of key actors in a situation and play out alternative versions of the original drama. Although the case teaching method was not invented at Harvard – Barnes et al. (1995) remind us of Talmudic traditions – the pedagogy is closely identified with the university. In 1870, Christopher Columbus Langdell experimented at Harvard Law School with teaching through discussion of court cases and legal documents. He later made case teaching and the Socratic method the school's standard pedagogy when he became its dean (Eliot, 1920). Langdell's successor, James Ames, completed his work and is widely regarded as the scholar who perfected the case method of instruction (Griswold, 2007). HBS faculty drew on the experiences of their law faculty colleagues in adapting the case method for business education.

HBS cases were initially developed to emphasize decision making and the integrated nature of learning. Instructors do students a disservice, the HBS logic went, when they separate knowledge acquisition from application and make learning a two-step process – acquire information and then return to it later to explore how (and if) it can be applied. Over time, however, additional benefits became obvious – enhanced communication skills, creativity, self-confidence, risk taking, and comfort with action in the face of ambiguity. 'The case method of teaching and the HBS legacy of success in entrepreneurship are inseparable,' notes Jeffrey Cruikshank (2007). 'The curriculum is constantly refreshed with stories about problems that demand an action from the students – they learn to think like entrepreneurs. Here's the problem, you define the problem, but that's not enough: What are you going to do about it and how?'

Early cases were simple workplace stories. Today's cases are more like good dramas with clear plot lines, integrated narratives, and detailed background information. Many are written with an omniscient narration style that enables readers to see into the reasoning and internal reactions of key players, and are infused with dramatic tension – often ending with a 'cliff hanger' to bring students emotionally into the scenario. Many are part of a sequence that explores different facets and stages of resolution in a complex situation. In the 1980s, the Hartwick Institute (2007) launched efforts to facilitate the use of great works of literature, history, philosophy and poetry from various cultural traditions in management teaching: a wide variety of excerpts were organized by management topic, made available in single case formats like those available through other business case clearing houses, and supported by teaching notes for instructors. Multimedia and video cases (e.g., Higgins, 2007) followed with advances in technology that took the pedagogy into the visual age and well beyond its early roots.

The 1930s saw the focus of business education shift to an emphasis on the development of a managerial *persona* and public speaking skills with the impact of Dale Carnegie (1936) and others. Voice training, attention to image and managerial presence, and opportunities to rehearse the manager's role – learning to praise, to use tact, to encourage others to believe your idea is their own, and to become what William Whyte (1956) would later critique as the quintessential 'organizational man' – became important. The Carnegie period sowed seeds for a new view of managerial success and of the preparation needed for it. Professional effectiveness now included skilled performance in the theater of work life – how well managers understood and played their roles – and management itself was now on the road to becoming 'a performing art' (Vaill, 1989). The Carnegie period anchored theater

arts training techniques into management and leadership development and led to decades of interest in how to encourage and assess skilled performance, role effectiveness, and the presentation of self at work. Carnegie's classic *How to Win Friends and Influence People* (1936) is still the all-time, best-selling management book: it has been in print for 70 years and sold more than ten million copies.

The 1940s was a fertile period for instructional innovation, and management education benefited from advances by the military in the area of simulated learning environments and context-specific role playing. The 'Assessment Centers,' developed for the selection and training of intelligence agents during World War II, took the Carnegie era's interests in role preparation to a higher level. The Centers focused on eliciting appropriate, improvised behavioral responses in complex, albeit simulated situations – not statements of intention or answers to 'what if' questions about a case or work situation. The Centers underscored the complexity in behaving consistently with intentions and in the face of context-specific pressures. They also emphasized the linkages among evaluation of personal competencies, skills practice, feedback on performance, and learning. Assessment Center training activities included participation in leaderless groups in vigorous outdoor settings; role-plays involving enemies, confederates, or escaped prisoners; stress interviews; and more (Bray, 2007). Center methods and their philosophical underpinnings migrated into management education after the war. They helped to anchor experiential education, context-based learning, and a focus on differentiating the skill components of managerial effectiveness.

The human relations movement of the 1950s and 1960s took role playing, improvisation, and experiential training exercises beyond their military forms and uses and rooted them as instructional mainstays in management learning. The methods created 'safe,' staged opportunities for managers to see themselves in action across a variety of situations; understand the power and implications of their choices; and thereby enhance self-awareness, decision-making, and relationship skills. The developments paralleled the birth of organization development (OD), the introduction of dramaturgical metaphors into management science lexicons by sociologist Irving Goffman (1959) and others to describe work organizations, and a wealth of new organizational theories emphasizing the human side of enterprise – the importance of fit between individual and organization; the distinction between intention and action; the human capacity for blindness in the face of incompetence; and a revised definition of professional effectiveness that rested on the principles of free and informed choice. In this kind of professional world, expectations for managerial success shifted dramatically – as did teaching and training requirements for mastering them. Emphasis on behavioral options and personal choice empowered managers and morphed them into proactive and collaborative professionals – partners with their organizations in co-creating workplaces that foster openness to learning and consistency among beliefs, values and actions (Argyris, 1964). Effective management teaching and learning now required attention to the development of 'actionable' knowledge and authenticity. The era also anchored the need for new and creative pedagogies to minimize human defensiveness (Argyris, 1985), maximize reflection-in-action (Schon, 1983), and engage learners in generative discovery of long-term personal value (Freire, 1970).

In response to that call, a wealth of arts-related teaching-learning innovations were introduced in the 1970s and 1980s. The new methods reflected developments in organizational theory, in change management practices, and in laboratory education. They also reflected important shifts in beliefs about time, space, and organizing. The period, for example, saw growing appreciation for the socio-cultural roots of organizing in the evolution of a 'symbolic perspective' on organizations. The symbolic perspective was a theoretical construct introduced by Bolman and Deal (1978, 1984, 1995, 2003) to unify the research contributions of individuals who questioned many of the assumptions upon which previous theories of organization were based – most notably that organizational behavior is explicitly purposive and that organizations function and are structured in linear and intendedly rational ways. While those whose work fell under the symbolic banner would not describe themselves as 'symbolists,' their contributions shared important similarities (Gallos, 1982). They implicitly built on core ideas about organizational ethos introduced decades earlier in the classic work of William Whyte (1956), expanded the interdisciplinary nature of the OB theory base by incorporating ideas from fields like symbolic interactionism (Blumer, 1969) and cultural anthropology, and shared consistent philosophical underpinnings in phenomenology and the social construction of reality (Berger and Luckmann, 1972).

The core of the symbolic theory base can be traced to two primary sources. One was a body of theory emanating from Stanford University. This included work by individuals (e.g., Leavitt, 1975; March, 1978; Pascale, 1978) as well as coherent sets of ideas from two major research studies: (1) a five-year study of California public schools at the Stanford Center for Research and Development in Teaching (e.g., Davis et al., 1977; Deal and Derr, 1979; Meyer and Rowen, 1977); and (2) explorations of the college presidency and decision making in higher education (e.g., Cohen and March, 1974; March and Olsen, 1976). A second source centered on contributions from social, political, and behavioral scientists writing at the time about 'ideas in good currency' (Rein and Schon, 1976). This included seminal works on organizational culture (e.g., Schein, 1985; Deal and Kennedy, 1982), as well as theories advancing organizational ambiguity, stories, symbols, and meaning systems (e.g., Clark, 1972; Edelman, 1977; Feldman and March, 1981; Kamens, 1977; Lindblom, 1974; Mintzberg, 1975; Morgan, 1980; Pfeffer, 1976; Rowe, 1974; Westerlund and Sjostrand, 1979; Weick,

1976, 1978, 1980). Work from both sources coincided with noted shifts on the larger scholarly landscape:

- the incorporation of Eastern philosophies and thinking into Western conceptions of general science (e.g., Holbrook, 1981); physics (e.g., Capra, 1975); organizations (e.g., Ouchi, 1981); and health (e.g., Ohasi, 1976);
- greater appreciation of qualitative research methodologies within the academy (e.g., Argyris, 1980; the special issue on qualitative methods in the *Administration Science Quarterly*, 24,4: 1979);
- grassroots movements for individual and organizational transformation through balance, integration, and expanded global consciousness (e.g., Ferguson, 1980).

The symbolic perspective encouraged the development and use of a host of arts-based educational methods and practices to probe individual, cultural, and organizational meaning systems. These included activities like story telling; use of myths, fables, and ethnic lore; the writing of autobiographies, personal cases, organizational histories, and ethnographies; exercises related to language use and choice, especially metaphor; creative, visual, and performing arts activities to tap into tacit knowledge of self and the world; use of literature and plays – reading, seeing, performing, or writing them – to stimulate creative problem solving and reflections on diversity and cross-cultural issues; and study of organizational artifacts to illuminate context, cultural assumptions, and the power of rituals and ceremonies. Playing-based activities using art or building materials, script writing, and scenario building to plan and 'try out' the future were introduced and encouraged new perspectives toward time and learning. These methods not only asked managers to learn about and from the *here-and-now*, but they also offered opportunities to 'rehearse the future' in hopes of avoiding costly errors in judgment (Schwartz, 1991).

The practitioner world of organizational change added to the mix with its own evolving set of arts-based change strategies and with OD's redefinition of itself as a transformational 'art.' Mirvis (2006) argues that the creative, performing, and visual arts have played an increasingly important role in advancing OD thinking and global practice and have kept the field vibrant and alive in today's multi-cultural world. In addition, literary criticism and arts scholarship provided insights and models for assessing the non-linear nature of complex organizational change. Artistic media, like video documentaries, performance art, or storytelling became non-traditional assessment tools themselves (Mirvis, 1980).

OD practitioners developed a wide variety of arts methods and practices to stimulate the organizational diagnosis, reflection, and visioning needed for complex systems change. Those included use of music and song-writing, drawing, mask-making, dance, storytelling, clowning, reflections on classical art works, sculpture, and more. The arts were also employed as metaphors to describe and explore complex system and change dynamics: transformation as a three-act drama (Tichy and Devanna, 1986), management as a performing art (Vaill, 1989), the dance of blind reflex (Oshry, 1996), the dance of power (Oshry, 1999), the dance of change (Senge et al., 1999), leader as conductor (Zander and Zander, 2000), leader as architect (Bolman and Deal, 2003), and organizational change as design (Cameron, 2003) to name a few. Theater arts and storytelling methods were at the foundation of large-scale organizational interventions like Search Conferences (Weisbord and Janoff, 1995), whole system participatory experiences (Bunker and Alban, 2006), staged events to dramatize and visually illustrate the *what if* of organizational choices (e.g., Mirvis et al., 2003), and multi-cultural learning journeys for global consciousness and leadership development within multinational corporations (Mirvis and Gunning, 2006; Mirvis and Ayas, 2008). Permeable boundaries have always existed between OD and management education – sometimes the same professionals are involved in both kinds of work. It is no surprise then that many OD arts-based interventions have been adapted for individual learning and growth, and vice versa.

The 1970s and 1980s also brought recognition of the limitations of T-groups methods – the 'training groups' at the core of the human relations movement – and the development of a new generation of laboratory education. The new methods relied heavily on 'living theater' experiences to access truths about human systems. Barry Oshry's *power labs* (Oshry, 1996, 1999; Sales, 2006), for example, immersed people in a multi-day simulated society where participants lived out their assigned role at the top, middle or bottom of a social hierarchy under conditions and with available resources and constraints similar to those experienced by individuals living daily in similar circumstances. Oshry's simulated societies served dual purposes: they provided participants with opportunities to act out social inequality and to create and test alternatives. Bolman and Deal, inspired by Oshry, designed power simulations for classroom use requiring less staging and time (Bolman and Deal, 1979; Bolman, 2007). William Torbert created *The Theater of Inquiry* (1989) and mounted large-scale interactive performances described as simultaneous 'performance art, conceptual art, and hermeneutic art' (Torbert, 2007). *The Theater* invited participants to become both actor and audience in a participatory drama to 'live out' inquiry into their own social roles, internal paradoxes, and life possibilities. Torbert's *Alchemist Workshops* continued the same pedagogical traditions.

Common to these kinds of activities is learning from immersion in some variation of playfulness and theater – the *as if* nature of the activities providing the psychological safety needed to investigate theories-in-use (Argyris and Schon, 1972) and the social freedom to experiment with new ones. Equally important for the purpose of this chapter, the activities are underpinned by a philosophy of multi-level learning while making art – and signal a turning point in the history of management education from seeing the arts as metaphors and vehicles for conveying theory content to acknowledging that professionally-relevant

learning can come from intense participation in them.

## Fostering creativity and skills for a complex global world

> Innovation in the *post-Google generation* is often catalyzed by those who cross a conventional line so firmly drawn between the arts and the sciences. (David Edwards)[5]

The two decades surrounding the change to the new millennium have been characterized by a shift in the fundamental relationship between the arts and management and by a radical transformation from a focus on art as teaching method to artistry as a learning outcome. Forces outside the academy have largely propelled the changes, with four of particular note:

1  The increasing role of creativity and aesthetics in the economy and in contemporary lifestyles that has elevated the status of and interests in the arts across sector, ethnic, cultural, and social lines (Florida, 2005; Ray and Anderson, 2000).

2  The emergent body of brain research showing that engagement in the arts encourages the simultaneous development of multiple neurobiological systems and enhances complex cognitive, socio-emotional, and creative capacities (e.g., Jensen, 2001; Levitin, 2006) – exactly the capabilities identified as needed across sectors in today's complex, global world.

3  Arts-based learning and planning projects initiated by businesses that have modeled a new partnership with the arts – and offered the academy greater license in designing more intensive arts-based approaches to management education and development.

4  Growing appreciation for the spiritual side of enterprise that has continued to blur traditional boundaries between the rational and the expressive in the workplace.

These shifts parallel theorizing by management scholars on complexity, the emergent nature of organizations, and the positive organizational sciences – all of which adds weight to the calls for new leaders who know how to foster creativity, respect artistry, and 'attract' existing system energy and interests to new visions and possibilities (Hatch, 1997; Hatch et al., 2005).

Scholars have long described leading and managing as an art (e.g., De Pree, 2004; Morgan et al., 2004; Senge, 2006; Townsend and Gebhardt, 1999; Vaill, 1989). The term *art,* however, has been used largely as a default descriptor reflecting the complex social nature of leading and managing that makes both hard to define and enact as a normal science (Kuhn, 1996) – if leading and managing aren't science, then they must be art. The demands of global commerce, however, have asked contemporary scholars and educators to take the *art* in the art of managing more seriously.

Constant turnover in the production and consumption of goods in the worldwide market economy has increased the scope and pace of change, the need for capable leaders to manage it, and the pressures to innovate (Canton, 2007; Pink, 2005). In such an environment, continuous improvement – the 20th century business strategy of incrementally advancing existing products and processes – is insufficient. Inventing the next 'new new thing' (Lewis, 1999) now drives success – or failure if the advance comes from a current competitor or a newcomer to the field. Innovation is an artistic design task, not an administrative or analytical function; and it draws on a willingness to look beyond the conventional, inventiveness, and creative imagination historically seen as the primary domain and competencies of practicing artists (Adler, 2006). A session on global competitiveness at the 2004 Davos World Economic Forum framed well the challenge to contemporary educators: if creativity is highly valued in business and there are no easy ways to teach it, then 'how can the use of artistic competencies and communication forms contribute to organizational change and new product development?' and 'what can business leaders learn from artists?'[6]

The questions propose a new kind of pedagogical partnership between the arts and the management sciences and reflect the emerging reality that today's complex problems beg for increasingly creative solutions. The scientist and the artist may seem like strange bedfellows in complex problem-solving; however, their complementary approaches to truth and understanding – scientists embrace the proven and peer-reviewed, artists seek the original and untried – offer opportunities for deep 'crossover learning' that can spark innovation, curiosity, and the courage to tackle and resolve tough social, cultural, political, and technological challenges (Edwards, 2008). For management educators, this translates into pedagogical practices that enable students to: (1) engage in art making and deep art experiences in order to learn the creative thinking, aesthetic sensibilities, and mindsets of an artist; (2) partner on projects with artists who can challenge the assumptions and problem-solving approaches implicit in traditional management theory and practice; or (3) do both. Wider societal forces even predispose students to embrace these opportunities.

Technology and the knowledge economy have propelled the rise of a *creative class* – people in diverse fields who 'create' for a living. In the United States, Richard Florida (2002) estimates that 38 million people across sectors and industries live and work in many of the same ways that have historically defined the artist's life – and that this percentage of the workforce has doubled since 1980. Studies of Generation Y (e.g., Chester, 2002; Martin, 2007) and of the growing number of individuals embracing a 'cultural creatives' lifestyle (Ray and Anderson, 2000) confirm the trend will continue.

Time, space, professional development, collegiality, motivation, and the meaning of work have changed for the creative class and for their more aesthetically-inclined cousins – as have leisure and lifestyle choices that impact the economy and larger cultural ethos. To appreciate the magnitude of the shifts, for example, contrast the corporate culture, jobs, work life, and workers at IBM in the 1960s to the same at Google today. 'The Top Ten Reasons to Work At Google' and the company's on-line worklife video (Google, 2007) speak volumes about wedding artistry and productivity. So does the rebirth of Apple under the creative leadership of Steve Jobs and through its 'sexy' designs for products like the iPod and iPhone that create 'passionate' users (Young, 2005).

Competitive advantage for 21st century organizations rests in their ability to finish strong in the new global race for talent (Florida, 2005): to attract, develop, and retain 'creative human capital' who in turn can innovate and differentiate a company's products and services from those of its competitors. In such a world, boundaries have shifted in defining experiences relevant for business success (Seifter and Buswick, 2005; Seifter, 2004). Artistic processes and mindsets, partnerships with artists, arts-based pedagogies and planning activities, and arts-infused corporate cultures now easily fall within the new boundaries. Bob Lutz, the hard-hitting, tough negotiating, cigar smoking, ex-marine fighter pilot signaled a new day when as Chairman of General Motors North America he publicly defined the GM mission as art – 'I see us being in the art business. Art, entertainment, and mobile sculpture which, coincidentally, also happens to provide transportation' (Hakim, 2001).

In addition, increasing global prosperity and the proliferation of affordable goods and services have altered social, cultural, and economic life around the world in ways never seen before (Prahalad, 2006; Pink, 2005). The result is a shift from lifestyles largely focused on survival to ones involving expanded consumer choices – choices that are increasingly driven by intangibles like novelty, artistic appeal, and emotional 'added value.'

Aesthetics is also becoming more prominent relative to other goods. When we decide how next to spend our time or money, considering what we already have and the costs and benefits of various alternatives, 'look and feel' is likely to top our list. We don't want more food, or even more restaurant meals – we're already maxed out. Instead, we want tastier, more interesting food in an appealing environment. It's a move from physical quantity to intangible, emotional quality. (Postrel, 2007)

A parallel rise in respect for the spiritual side of enterprise adds support for expanding traditional boundaries in the business world. The workplace spirituality movement itself emerged within the world of practice – outside the university and largely outside the central thrust of mainstream churches, temples, and synagogues (Delbecq, 2008) – to respond to yearnings for significance and contribution. The arts have always served as an embodiment of meaning-making and a vehicle for self-discovery and expression. Bolman and Deal (1995), for example, proposed a 'revolution' to cultivate spirit and soul at work – infuse poetry, literature, music, art, theater, dance, history, and philosophy into corporate culture, education, and training. The artist's passion, creativity, commitment, and courage to look beyond illusion offer a model for a powerful and satisfying 21st century leadership of hope, possibility, and aspiration (Adler, 2006).

Finally, recognizing that 21st century success will require more than business as usual, an increasing number of businesses and corporations have chosen to bring artists and artistic processes into their companies. Examples are plentiful and diverse. They include activities and ongoing partnerships with poets, designers and architects, dancers, musicians, theater professionals, and visual artists (see examples in the special edition on business and the arts in the *Journal of Business Strategy*, 2005; as well as in Adler, 2006; Darso, 2001, 2004, 2005; Pink, 2005). Technology, globalization, and economic incentives to off-shore mundane, repetitive, or analytic tasks mean that work and work role will continue to evolve for blue collar and for white collar workers. The future belongs to individuals who are inventive and flexible – and to the organizations that can attract, train, retain, and nurture them. We are moving beyond the information age where people have been rewarded largely for their analytic skills, warns Daniel Pink (2005), and into a conceptual age where leadership means finding new possibilities and opportunities from within the competitive crunch. Skills for the conceptual age include capacities for:

1 **Design** – how to wed function with strong aesthetics.
2 **Storytelling** – how to influence through compelling narrative, not simple data.
3 **Creating symphony** – how to combine distinctive elements into an innovative whole.
4 **Empathy** – how to inform logic with an understanding of human nature and needs.
5 **Play** – how to embrace humor, lightheartedness, and the creative potential in joyful experimentation.
6 **Making meaning** – how to look beyond accumulation and the acquisition of things and fact for significance, contribution, and spiritual fulfillment.

According to the editors of the *Harvard Business Review*, top corporations are now recruiting at arts and design schools, and the Master in Fine Arts degree is on the road to fast becoming the new MBA (*HBR Editors*, 2004). Bottom-line, contemporary management education serves its students well when it teaches them how to act and work like artists (Austin and Devin, 2003).

A number of leading business schools are responding: Harvard, Wharton, MIT, INSEAD, University of Chicago, Stanford, Oxford, Cranfield, and Copenhagen, to name a few. As in industry, university approaches vary. INSEAD, for example, partners with the Art Center College of Design in Pasadena, California, to foster the development of a 'design mentality' and service skills for its graduates (Nussbaum and Tiplady, 2007). MIT focuses on acting and performance (Flaherty, 2002). University of Chicago business students write, produce, and showcase a film, while Cranfield students immerse themselves in Shakespeare (Adler, 2006). Wharton partners with the world-renowned Pilobolus Dance Company. A required part of its MBA curriculum has leaders-in-training learning through avant-garde dance and choreography (Pilobolus, 2007). Harvard and Stanford business schools seek to build leadership character through literature. Both have done

so for more than 20 years (Badaracco, 2006; March and Weil, 2005; Sucher, 2007a,b).

## Exploring the complexities of human nature and organizational life: using literature

Literature is an extension of life not only horizontally, bringing the reader into contact with events or locations or persons or problems he or she has not otherwise met, but also, so to speak, vertically, giving the reader experience that is deeper, sharper, and more precise than much of what takes place in life. (Martha Nussbaum)[7]

Art ... is, before all, to make you see. (Joseph Conrad)[8]

The brief historical review reminds educators that a variety of artistic forms have been employed in educating professionals across centuries and cultures. The use of literature remains a mainstay – and for good reason. Good fiction, Annie Dillard (1988) concludes, reveals more about the world, human nature, and modern thinking than the academic sciences and the other art forms combined. Fiction is 'a subtle pedagogy' that deals deeply and solely with the human experience (Dillard, 1982: 155). Writers paint with words that reflect the world as we know it – culture, nature, feelings, behaviors, and ideas. They describe that world with focus and precision. And as we read their descriptions word by word, we slow life down: study it and our reactions to it. Literature also lets us view events from multiple perspectives – our own, the writer's, and the various characters in the story or play – increasing our understandings of human diversity; the impact of time, culture, and experience; and the frames of reference we use to make sense of all that.

Fiction, asserts Dillard, 'traffics in understanding' (1982: 163) – and understanding one's internal and external worlds is at the heart of effective management. The major challenges of work life – understanding others in context, motivating and influencing, managing enduring differences, recognizing the roots of competing interests and conflicts, generating productive alternatives to complex problems, and the list goes on – 'are echoes of critical issues of life more generally,' asserts James G. March, the distinguished organizational theorist who taught a popular, literature-based leadership course at the Stanford Graduate School of Business from 1980 until his retirement in 1995 (March and Weil, 2005: 1). Professional effectiveness in a fast-paced, global world requires deep thinking about self and others in context, about enduring differences, and about the dynamics of an ever-shifting organizational landscape. Good management education provides opportunities to develop those multi-level diagnostic skills. Literature is a perfect vehicle, asserts March (March and Weil, 2005), to lay out the 'grand dilemmas' of human existence in an accessible form and to invite students to compare their solutions to those of others.

The health sciences, for example, have a long and broad history of encouraging the use of literature – the reading and writing of it – for professional development and renewal: the medical humanities are a well-established curricular tradition in medical education. Robert Coles (1989) asserts that fiction and storytelling powerfully deepen the inner life of those who work on life's interpersonal boundaries. They offer insights into the role of learning and growth in disappointment and suffering, historical perspectives on the meaning of care and service, and more. Coles and Testa (2002), for example, created an anthology of literary works for health care professionals to explore the ethical and procedural dilemmas that flow from major scientific advances and changes in medicine. Literature nurtures skills in observation, analysis, diagnosis, empathy, and self-reflection – capacities essential for professional effectiveness in any field. It also provides outlets to channel work-related stress and emotions – as necessary for managers and leaders as for clinical caregivers (Frost, 2003). Literary giants like William Carlos Williams, Anton Checkhov, W. Somerset Maugham, and John Keats were all physicians. Prestigious medical journals like the *Journal of the American Medical Association, Lancet,* and *Annals of Internal Medicine* regularly publish literary works by practicing physicians, and many health care clinicians are also published poets (e.g., Breedlove, 1998; Campo, 1994, 1996).

Finally, literature offers a powerful, behind-the-scenes look into organizational life in all its complexities. The increasing demands of modern life challenge adult developmental capacities, concludes psychologist Robert Kegan (1998), and we are all literally 'in over our heads' as we sort through life's demands with cognitive and socio-emotional capacities and strategies learned for a simpler time. In today's complex world, we do students a disservice as management educators when we convey the illusion of simplicity or control with models and theories that portray the workplace as linear, rational, neat, and tidy. Human nature is complicated, and social processes like leadership and management are steeped in ambiguity and choice. Good literature acknowledges that and plays out human struggles in their fullness.

Use of literature also embraces the interdisciplinary imperative at the heart of effective leadership. It 'emancipates' a pluralistic field, concludes William Howe (1996), from the stranglehold of narrow, discipline-centered models and acknowledges that solutions to complex problems are always interdisciplinary in nature. Literary devices like character and plot invite students into the middle of a complicated fray and make them privy to information, thoughts, and reasoning processes – perspectives hard to find in business books and texts. Leadership and management always seem simpler when viewed from the outside. Internal struggles, confusion, ambiguity, and doubts of the soul, however, are par for the course (Delbecq, 2008). Leadership looks more like the gritty and human process that it is – and less glamorous and heroic – when seen through the difficult choices of compelling characters in action.

As an example, *The Secret Sharer*[9] by Joseph Conrad offers a powerful portrait of leadership development from the inside out. Readers are privy to the inner struggles of a young sea captain seeking to understand what he must do to rise to the leadership challenge. When used with graduate students at a large public university, the students easily find parallels between the captain's leadership struggles and their own – and the captain's framing of his fears and challenges gives students language and a comfortable entry point to talk about their own. Like many of the students, the captain has technical know-how – training from a top seafaring academy and solid experience as first mate on comparable vessels – but is untested in translating all that into action. At the helm for the first time, he is surprised by what he finds – and finds out about himself. Leading is a lot harder than expected: followers must be earned, the pace of the work is fast and steady, decisions are often made in the face of ambiguity, and mistakes can be costly to the leader and the entire enterprise. Leadership is lonely work – and Conrad's straight-forward prose enables students to 'feel' this and to see its impact on the captain's decisions. By the end of the story and class activities connected to it, students understand cognitively and emotionally that leadership engages mind, heart, body, and soul – and that even the most prepared are never fully certain they will succeed until tested.

Conrad's story, however, is hopeful and infused with undertones of compassion for the captain which enables the students to recognize that effective leaders need patience, persistence, and support to serve others and their organizations well. The captain faces his vulnerabilities head on. He embraces self-reflection, accepts his limitations, and digs deep to find inner strength. He finds a confidant, albeit a controversial partner, to build his courage. He builds skills as a reflective practitioner (Schon, 1983) – a hard concept for many students to grasp without seeing it in practice – and learns by examining his impact on those around him. By the story's end, the captain feels ready to take the helm – self-aware, confident, and humble. By talking about the captain – and themselves in the process – students move a step forward themselves. They are empowered by the contemporary parallels in a story set almost a century ago, are excited by new insights into leadership and themselves, and learn a model for using literature in their ongoing learning and development. This happens even for students who have limited background in the humanities and for those who are not regular readers of fiction. Comments from course evaluations include statements like:

'Loved the literature! Awesome.'

'When we started the course, I couldn't figure out why we were reading stories and plays but when we started discussing them, I saw things that I never would have from a textbook.'

'Every week I'd do the reading and the written assignment, sure that I had nailed the story. Then we'd discuss it in class and I'd see things totally different. Every week I went home smarter than when I came.'

'I want to go back and read all the things I read in high school and college that never meant much to me then. I just never got it before.'

Conrad's story is short in length but rich enough for exploring a host of issues beyond those already mentioned: the meaning of leadership character and resolve, leader as facilitator of adaptive change (Heifetz, 1994), leadership passages (e.g., Dotlich et al., 2008; Bennis and Thomas, 2002), decision making under stress, healthy followership, power and influence, integrity, organizational justice, inner spiritual growth, balancing personal needs and a larger common good, and more. And it is, of course, only one literature choice for exploring any of the above issues – or many others.

There are resources available to build both instructor confidence in using literature and a list of relevant readings. Howe (1996) examines the liberating nature of literature for leadership education with examples from plays, poems, and fiction. Coles (1989) and Clemens and Mayer (1999) discuss the larger issues in using literature and suggest specific works. Coles and Testa's (2002) anthology contains pieces useful for discussing professional development, managerial, and leadership concerns. In fact, it was Robert Coles who introduced literature-based teaching to the Harvard Business School in the 1980s through his work across Harvard professional schools – law, architecture, education, divinity, design, and government – to promote professional development through stories and storytelling (Sucher, 2007b).

Other options include volumes in which experienced faculty discuss their literature-based courses. These are triple wins: a course design, reading suggestions, and teaching strategies. James March outlines his Stanford course in *On Leadership* (March and Weil, 2005) and discusses use of Shakespeare's *Othello*, Shaw's *Saint Joan*, Tolstoy's *War and Peace*, and Cervantes's *Don Quixote*. Joseph Badaracco (2006) and Sandra Sucher (2007a) explore their versions of the Harvard Business School leadership course. Sucher (2007b) has also created a student text that contains background information, prework, and assignments – a good learning resource for instructors too. The Hartwick Humanities in Management Institute (Hartwick, 2007) makes excerpts from larger works easy to identify and use. Teaching notes include management themes, teaching strategies, discussion questions, social and historical background, relevant management and leadership theories, and a short bibliography.

## Fostering openness, engagement in learning, and skills development: using films and video

The chapter's fourth proposition asserts that teaching with and through the arts engenders openness and engagement that facilitate deep learning and growth. No practice illustrates this better than teaching with films and video, and the general principles and caveats for doing that effectively apply to the other arts media as well. For more than a quarter century, films and video have been a mainstay in management learning, and the progression in use and impact parallels advances in technology (Champoux, 1999).

The 1970s, for example, saw the constraints of film reels, cumbersome projectors, and movie options largely limited to training and educational media (Smith, 1973). The 1980s brought the video cassette recorder (VCR), the proliferation of easily available feature films, simple advances like *rewind* and *fast forward* for selecting film segments, and the capacity to 'tape' commercial television as a way to garner timely and diverse material. Digital video disks (DVDs) improved quality and fidelity, saved tedious tape queuing and rewinding, and replaced bulky and breakable cassettes. By the 1990s, films and movie segments were a staple in university and corporate instruction (Lacho et al., 1991; Lee, 1987). Today, Pod casting, You-Tube, and other online technologies add to the ease with which films and video can be identified, shared, and viewed. In addition, advances in digital cameras and editing software have increased options for student filmmaking – from short segments that illustrate concepts to larger film projects, like those at the University of Chicago Graduate School of Business (Adler, 2006), that add the learning benefits from art making to the mix.

With the evolution of technology came growing recognition that film and video work well with different student learning styles. The visual nature of the media adds a feel of reality to instruction through concrete and visual portraits of abstract concepts; it also enables people to see the application of ideas or strategies across situations (Champoux, 1999). Research tells us that people learn abstract, unusual, or new concepts more easily when they are presented to them in both verbal and visual forms (Solomon, 1979a, 1979b, 1983) – and by extension when they present them through a film project to others. And like engagement with other visual arts, viewing films – or making them – enhance perception, cognition, emotional and cultural awareness, and an appreciation of aesthetics – all of which are relevant for the classroom and beyond (Jensen, 2001).

There are a host of reasons why movies and films engage students – excitement in connecting to a popular film or already known commodity, anticipated pleasure in seeing a clip or its actors, curiosity about the film choice or its intended use, opportunity to see another's visual interpretation of a book or lesson, or maybe simple contrast in the media use to regular teaching modes. The elevated levels of engagement lead to increased attention and interest in learning, knowledge acquisition and integration, and skills development (Marx and Frost, 1998). This is especially true for media-savvy students who have grown up in technologically rich and media intensive environments (Gioia and Brass, 1985–1986).

Teaching well with film segments requires attention to distinctive features in the learning process. Movies, for example, offer simultaneous visual imagery and sound that move along at a predetermined pace. In contrast, printed matter allows readers to return to material that is confusing, reread content with which they have low familiarity, and skim familiar information. Readers, therefore, tacitly control their own pace and approach to learning, both avoiding boredom and choosing the right balance for themselves to master confusing, new, or dense material (Shebilske and Reid, 1979). Since films are continuous – unless stopped by the instructor or by the student if he or she is watching alone – learning can only occur if there is a 'window of cognitive engagement' (Kozma, 1991). That is most apt to happen when lesson content is at an intermediate level of difficulty for the learner – both overly simple and highly complex content will lead to lower rates of attention and, as a result, reduced comprehension (Huston and Wright, 1983). All this suggests special attention in preparing students to view a film and in choosing video clips. Hooper and Hannafin (1991) call this attending to 'orienting functions' and identify two specific types: (1) a *cognitive orienting function* where learners are prepared to view a film by being asked to focus on key points or ideas; and (2) an *affective orienting function* where instructors select film segments to create strong emotional responses and thereby motivate interest in and recall of the larger teaching points.

Educators have long been concerned with achieving appropriate levels of mental effort and concentration for learning, and this becomes especially important when using video. People used to watching television for relaxation and entertainment invest less mental effort in viewing a learning video than in learning from print medium (Cennamo, 1993; Solomon, 1983). However, simple instructions to watch for a certain idea or concept – Hooper and Hannafin's cognitive orienting – lead to greater mental effort and higher achievement scores when compared to students instructed to view the same segment for enjoyment (Solomon and Leigh, 1984). Familiar scenes from popular films or television just 'go down easy' with students of all ages (Marx and Frost, 1998). They launch difficult discussions; enhance analytical, diagnostic, and critical thinking skills; and create 'sticky' learning – visual metaphors of organizational dynamics that are etched in student minds. Bottom-line, strong cognitive orienting activities combined with the affective arousal of a carefully chosen film increase student comprehension *and* motivation to learn. A closer look at the use of one feature film, *A Beautiful Mind*, illustrates how and why.

The movie features Russell Crowe as MIT math professor John Nash and Jennifer Connelly as his student. Crow's character is mathematically gifted but interpersonally challenged and plagued with bouts of psychosis. Connelly's character is smart in mathematics and in life. A possible teaching scene begins with Nash being reminded by his office mates that he will teach his first college class shortly. Without preparation, Nash rushes into the classroom. He is greeted by a noisy jackhammer outside the open classroom window. Despite hot weather and student pleas, he shuts the window. Nash then throws the assigned text in the wastebasket and turns to write complex math equations on the blackboard. While writing he mutters, 'Personally, I think this class will be a waste of your and, what is infinitely worse, my time.'

Suddenly, the Connelly character stands up. She makes eye contact with the professor and opens the window. She hails the foreman with a friendly 'Excuse me' and explains that it is hot with the windows closed but noisy with them open. She gingerly suggests that the workers might take a short break until class is over. The foreman smiles and adjourns the group for lunch. Connelly returns to her seat. Crowe acknowledges her intervention in math terms: 'As you will find in multivariate calculus, there is often a number of solutions to any given problem.'

The scene lasts two minutes, but contains an abundance of verbal and non-verbal behaviors useful for exploring a concept like emotional intelligence [EI]. Since research shows that learning from films requires multiple activities that reinforce the central learning goals (Marx and Meisel, 2006), a possible design for using the clip – and a model for others of an instructor's choice – might include the following:

1   *State the central learning goal.* Begin with a brief introduction to the linkages between EI and skilled management (Goleman et al., 2002).
2   *Provide a simple conceptual introduction to the theory.* Lay out the four domains of EI (self-awareness, social awareness, self-management, relationship management) and competencies for each domain (see Goleman et al., 2002: 39).
3   *Orient students with pre-viewing questions. Show the film. Lead a general discussion.* Ask students to watch the clip and assess the overall emotional intelligence of the two main characters. Because differences between characters are so stark, almost everyone can identify that the Connelly character exudes EI and Crowe's shows little if any.
4   *Divide the class into four sub-groups and have each group view the film again with a different set of focal questions.* Ask one group to view the second showing only from the domain and skill set of *self-awareness,* a second group for *social awareness,* a third for *self-management,* and the fourth group *relationship management.*
5   *Provide opportunity for small group discussion.* Class members can count-off by threes within their assigned domain groups. Ask the new trios to discuss the attributes of both characters from the perspective of their assigned domain.
6   *Build on the experience with other activities to extend and reinforce learning.* Collect observations from a few of the trios. Ask all the trios to write out their observations on a printed worksheet and submit it for class credit. Administer an emotional intelligence self-assessment questionnaire to individual students, and collect those as well.

Variations on this design have been used in a number of teaching situations, including at the beginning of a 500 student, introductory management course at a large public university. In the latter case, the learning activities evolved from several earlier iterations that were less than effective. Herein is the beauty and power of the arts in management education for instructor and student. Experimentation leads to increased instructor comfort, versatility, and confidence. Increased comfort and options bring instructor playfulness and greater willingness to fine-tune in response to different student audiences, needs, and learning styles. Students in turn respond with 'heightened learner arousal' (Hooper and Hannafin, 1991) and a different level of engagement and openness generated by the combination of surprise and pleasure in learning through enjoyment. As Plato reminded us centuries ago, learning and enjoyment need not be separated. When used effectively, films and video enhance learning in ways unavailable through traditional pedagogies and instructional methods.

Champoux (1999, 2001, 2003) and Clemens and Wolfe (2000) provide support and guidance for using films in management learning. Their works contain movie recommendations, as well as good beginning and end points for selected scenes, possible teaching topics, and discussion questions. *Management Live! The Video Workbook* (Marx et al., 1991) is another resource – and one of the first texts designed to empower instructors to identify video segments consistent with their teaching goals, styles, and values. Additional resources include scholarly articles on teaching with video such as those that explore teaching with animated films like *The Lion King* and *Toy Story* (e.g.,

Champoux, 2001; Comer, 2001) or that examine how to teach about complex social processes like managing diversity (Bumpus, 2005) or increasing individual capacities to reframe experience (Gallos, 1993a). The searchable *Journal of Management Education* (OBTS, 2007) database offers a host of articles that provide film possibilities and teaching designs. Students themselves are also a good source: they will have suggestions or can be asked to integrate relevant film clips in class presentations or projects. And a growing body of research and practice supports educators in organizing student filmmaking projects within courses or training programs (e.g., Kearney and Schuck, 2005, 2003; Hakkarainen and Saarelainen, 2005).

## SUPPORTING THE EFFORTS: TEACHING EFFECTIVELY WITH THE ARTS

Sufficient evidence and grounded experience attest to the power and contribution of arts-based pedagogies in management teaching, learning, and development. Research shows improvement in learning-related factors like motivation, enjoyment, attendance, grades, communication skills, and openness to new ideas (Fiske, 1999). In addition, learning through deep experiences – opportunities to make art, study the art-making process with practicing artists, or work on diverse projects in collaboration with artists – encourages the development of complex skills that are highly relevant for today's – and tomorrow's – workforce.

Students ... will likely develop a willingness to imagine and explore ideas that have not existed before. Art-making students will be willing to explore uncertainty, delaying closure or early solutions in favor of sustaining judgment and enhanced process. Students will learn alternative thinking. They'll be more willing to explore opposing ideas, multiple perspectives, and unexpected points of view. They'll become more compassionate about others' feelings. They'll appreciate better other cultures and alternative ways of thinking. (Jensen, 2001: 116)

What can help management educators and trainers maximize such high quality learning and development? This chapter concludes with suggestions and warnings to assist instructors in improving the odds of success. It closes with a reminder as to the importance of why.

Effective teaching with the arts shares a number of characteristics with all good teaching. Learning is strongest with tight coordination among learning **goals** (what instructors expect students to *know* at the end of a lesson), **objectives** (what they expect students to be able to *do* with the knowledge), **activities** (the teaching designs that best enable students to meet those goals and objectives), and **assessment** (how to evaluate whether the intended learning has taken place). When teaching with the arts, close attention to learning objectives and assessment is even more vital. High student energy, enjoyment, or espoused epiphanies do not necessarily mean deep understanding or clarity about how to integrate and use the new knowledge. Multiple activities that tackle different aspects of a topic in different ways and test for understanding along the way – individual and group, written and oral, large and small group, self-reflection and abstract conceptualization, general discussions and more specialized analyses, as illustrated in the *A Beautiful Mind* example earlier in the chapter – help and also respond to learning style differences. So does instructor clarity about the level of understanding and use of knowledge expected from students.

Instructors have a range of options in determining student learning objectives – from simple recall or comprehension of facts through higher order learning like the sophisticated integration of the new knowledge or creation of an innovative product as a result of it. Bloom's classic taxonomy of learning, the six-tiered model for classifying levels of complexity in thinking and knowing, is a helpful reminder that increasingly complex learning – like that expected from many arts-based teaching activities – requires a strong foundation in the basics first. Making a short film to demonstrate application of a complex management topic, for example, may be fun and engaging but cognitively overwhelming for students without structured activities to assist them in acquiring and integrating relevant knowledge first. Anderson and Krathwohl (2001: 67–8) lay out a framework based on Bloom's work that can guide the design of sequential learning and assessment activities to move students' work through the steps to integrated learning and toward the development of higher level thinking skills.

- **Level 1: Remembering**: recalling relevant knowledge.
- **Level 2: Understanding**: grasping the meaning from oral, written, and visual information.
- **Level 3: Applying**: using information in new or concrete situations to solve problems or complete tasks.
- **Level 4: Analyzing**: breaking down material into parts, determining how the parts relate to one another and to an overall whole.
- **Level 5: Evaluating**: making judgments, comparisons, and critiques using criteria and standards.
- **Level 6: Creating**: putting parts and elements together to form a coherent whole; reorganizing elements into a new pattern or structure through planning or producing.

The hierarchical nature of the framework means that higher levels of thinking and knowing – like those required, for example, in comparing, contrasting and evaluating the usefulness of multiple theories in a case situation – imply complete mastery of lower level steps and skills.

There are numerous applications of Bloom's taxonomy and its use: Krumme (2007) provides a list of resources and links. A guide for developing test and assessment questions for each of Bloom's six levels is also helpful (University of Victoria Counseling Services, 2007). Resources on student-centered learning (e.g., Fink, 2003) provide additional suggestions for better aligning learning goals, objectives, activities, and assessment.

Complex learning takes time as learners sort through the full intricacies and meaning of their experiences. This is especially true in arts-based teaching that offers opportunity for learning on multiple levels:

conceptual, procedural, psychomotor, and socio-emotional. Beware the temptation to undermine the rich possibilities in the teaching medium by rushing things or by telling students what they *should* have learned. When using films, for example, show a short segment and leave plenty of time for activities centering on it rather than use limited class time to show the whole film. Effective arts-based teaching is always learner-centered. Its power comes from student engagement, discovery, and developmental growth – and those take time. The pace of discovery and the meaning of development also differ among learners.

The media content or the process of engaging it, for example, can evoke strong affective responses for some learners. Management learning through the arts may be new or different enough to raise confusion or defenses: developmental capabilities influence student capacities for dealing with ambiguity and with experience-based learning (Gallos, 1993b). Affective reactions – be they positive or negative – are all grist for the learning mill, and instructor patience and good facilitation skills are essential to make that so. Important learning may be taking place for students below the surface – and despite student protests. Learning works best when instructors have patience and 'walk in their students' shoes' – respect and link to student experiences, frame the purpose of activities in language that students understand and see as relevant, and inquire into learner reactions. Most arts methodologies will work with most audiences; but engineers or accountants, for example, may need different orientating and processing activities for a session on collaboration with the Pilobolus dance troupe than arts administrators.

There is messiness in complex learning: learners explore at different rates and with different interests and experiences, instructional designs that work with one group flop with another, and anyone can be closed to the learning he or she most needs (Argyris, 1991). Experimentation, flexibility, and a lighthearted spirit are foundations for successful arts-based learning – and instructors help students stay playful and open to learning and discovery when they are. As discussed, instructor planning and preparation are essential; but so are trial-and- error, risk taking, willingness to model learning, and a good sense of humor. Experimentation and experience build teacher and learner confidence. But instructors beware! Students steeped in traditional pedagogies can perceive a dichotomy between fun and learning, and that may make it hard for them to initially bring the cognitive discipline needed – another reason to include strong 'cognitive orienting' with every activity (Hooper and Hannafin, 1991).

Finally, effective teaching with the arts benefits from a variety of creative resources. The internet and technology have expanded options and ease of access. The Gutenberg Project (2007), for example, has thousands of e-books and e-short stories available for students to download, and the Gutenberg DVD and CD Projects are growing. Independent films, short subjects, documentaries, streaming videos, and other public domain media are available through sites like Google Video and elsewhere. And virtual tours of the world's great art museums make activities like selecting a piece of art as a vehicle for self-reflection or presentation of self (e.g., Heracleous and Jacobs, 2008) a simple desktop assignment.[10]

## Closing thoughts: toward a pedagogy of hope and imagination

For more than half a century, Maxine Greene, William F. Russell Professor in the Foundations of Education *emerita* at Columbia University, founder and former director of the Center for Social Imagination at Teachers College, and longtime philosopher-in-residence at the Lincoln Center Institute for the Arts in Education, has advocated broadly and widely for the central role of the arts in learning across social classes, sectors, and age groups (e.g., Greene 1995a, 1995b, 1997, 2007). Her rationale has been consistent. Encounters with the arts are transformational: they engage learners and bring people in closer touch with themselves, with the world, and with new possibilities. Imagination is

an expression of the human passion for possibility – and a powerful source of hope, promise, and creative action.

Greene (2007) reminds us what the great educational philosopher John Dewey recognized long ago. Facts, figures, and theories are 'dead and repellent things' until human imagination engages them in its search for an alternative future. The arts and the humanities open the mind and the heart to facilitate that process.

> Engaged in this search, many of us turn to the several arts, not because Goya or Virginia Woolf or Toni Morrison or Mozart or Michelangelo holds solutions the sciences and the social sciences do not, but because an encounter with an art form demands a particular kind of interchange or transaction between a live human consciousness and a painting, say, or a novel, or a sonata that becomes a work of art or may be realized as art depending on the reader's or perceiver's willingness and readiness to grasp what is being offered. And to grasp it may mean a transformation of a sort – a changed perspective, a new mode of understanding. (2007: 2)

The arts and humanities must, therefore, be central to any curriculum, asserts Greene. But they are especially important in contemporary society and in a world where yesterday's pride and certainties have given way to 'endless ambiguities and negations' (2007: 2). The world is rapidly changing and not always in the ways that many would wish. Technology facilitates 24/7 media images and graphic reminders that many of the changes bring loss, suffering, confusion, and feelings of powerlessness. Education through the arts encourages agency. It counters passivity and models the capacity to see, to imagine, and to hope – arouses people to look at themselves and the world through new eyes and with 'consciousness of beginnings rather than closures' (Greene, 2007: 2). A pedagogy of hope and imagination seems only right for management education and important in training today's – and tomorrow's – leaders. In fact, they expect nothing less.

Students tell us that they need and want experiences that engender deep and personal learning. They share a common dream at the start of each new course, Richard Light (2001,

2004) found in his multi-year research study of students at 25 colleges in the Harvard Assessment Project. 'Details vary, but the most common hope students express is that each class, by its end, will help them to become a slightly different person in some way' (2001: 47). Arts-based teaching provides a route to that. No pedagogy is more powerful in firing developmental growth, imagination, and hope.

## NOTES

1  I thank Professor Bob Marx at the University of Massachusetts-Amherst for his contribution to this chapter's spirit and substance. His experiences teaching with films and videos inform the emotional intelligence case example.

2  October 26, 1963, Amherst College. John F. Kennedy's speech in honor of the late poet Robert Frost can be read or heard at http://arts.endow.gov/about/Kennedy.html The author regrets the historical use of 'man' to represent the experiences of both men and women.

3  Edwards, D. (2008) *Artscience: Creativity in the Post-Goggle Generation.* Boston: Harvard University Press.

4  From the Forum session program description for 'If An Artist Ran Your Business,' January 22, 2004 led by Lotte Darso, Research Manager for the Creative Alliance Learning Lab in Denmark. Panelists: photographer Yann Arthus-Bertrand; film director Shekhar Kapur; Hermitage Museum director Mikhail Piotrovsky; and actor Chris Tucker.

5  Nussbaum, M. (1990) *Love's Knowledge: Essays on Philosophy and Literature.* New York: Oxford University Press: 48.

6  Conrad, J. (1976) 'The Condition of Art' in Morton Dauwen Zabel (ed.). *The Portable Conrad* (revised edition). New York: Penguin: 651.

7  This short story is available as a free download at the Project Gutenberg at http://www.gutenberg.org/etext/220

8  I thank Professor Nancy Adler of McGill University for her contributions to this list: the British Museum in London http://www.britishmuseum.org/default.aspx; the Egyptian Museum in Cairo www.egyptianmuseum.gov.eg; the Guggenheim Museums in New York City http://www.guggenheimcollection.org/index.html or Bilbao, Spain http://www.guggenheim-bilbao.es/secciones/la_coleccion/fondos_propios.php?idioma=es; The Hermitage in Moscow www.hermitagemuseum.org; the Louvre in Paris, France www.louvre.fr; The Metropolitan Museum of Art in New York City www.metmuseum.org; the Museu Nacional del Prado in Madrid, Spain http://

museoprado.mcu.es; the Shanghai Art Museum in Shanghai, China www.echinaart.com; the Tokyo National Museum in Japan www.tnm.jp

## ACKNOWLEDGEMENT

David Edwards quote (page 194) from Harvard University Press catalog copy for *Artscience: Creativity in the Post-Google Generation* by David Edwards, Cambridge, MA: Harvard University Press.

Martha Nussbaum quote (page 197) reprinted by permission of Oxford University Press, Inc.

## REFERENCES

Adler, N.J. (2006) 'The arts & leadership: Now that we can do anything, what will we do?' *Academy of Management Learning & Education,* 5 (4): 486–99.

Anderson, L.W. and Krathwohl, D.R. (2000) *A Taxonomy for Learning, Teaching and Assessing.* Boston: Allyn & Bacon.

Argyris, C. (1964) *Integrating the Individual and the Organization.* New York: Wiley.

Argyris, C. (1980) *Inner Contradictions of Rigorous Research.* New York: Academic Press.

Argyris, C. (1985) *Strategy, Change and Defensive Routines.* Boston: Pitman.

Argyris, C. (1991) 'Teaching smart people how to learn', *Harvard Business Review.* Reprint 91301.

Argyris, C. and Schon, D. (1972) *Theory in Practice: Increasing Professional Effectiveness.* San Francisco: Jossey-Bass.

Ausland, H.W. (1997) 'On reading Plato mimetically', *American Journal of Philology,* 118 (3): 371–416.

Austin, R. and Devin, L. (2003) *Artful Making.* Upper Saddler River, NJ: Prentice-Hall.

Badaracco, J. (2006) *Questions of Character: Illuminating the Heart of Leadership through Literature.* Boston: Harvard Business School Press.

Barnes, L.B., Christensen, C.R. and Hansen, A. (1995) *Teaching and the Case Method* (3rd edn). Boston: Harvard Business School Press.

Bateson, M.C. (1995) *Peripheral Visions: Learning along the Way.* New York: Harper.

Benford, R.D. and Hunt, S.A. (1992) 'Dramaturgy and social movements: The social construction and communication of power', *Sociological Inquiry,* 62 (1): 36–55.

Benford, R.D. and Snow, D.A. (2000) 'Framing processes and social movements: An overview and assessment', *Annual Review of Sociology*, 26: 611–39.

Bennis, W.G. and Levinson, H. (January 1996) 'The leader as storyteller', *Harvard Business Review*. Reprint # 96102.

Bennis, W.G. and O'Toole, J. (May 2005) 'How business schools lost their way', *Harvard Business Review*. Reprint # R0505F.

Bennis, W.G. and Thomas, R.J. (2002) 'The crucible of leadership', *Harvard Business Review*, 80 (9): 39–45.

Berger, P. and Luckmann, T. (1972) *The Social Construction of Reality*. Garden City: Doubleday.

Blumer, H. (1969) *Symbolic Interactionism: Perspective and Method*. Berkeley: University of California Press.

Bolman, L.G. (2007) 'Teaching Resources', Accessed July 2, 2007 at www.leebolman.com

Bolman, L.G. and Deal, T.E. (1978) 'The symbolic perspective on organizations', Unpublished manuscript, Harvard University.

Bolman, L.G. and Deal, T.E. (1979) 'A simple but powerful power simulation', *Exchange: The Organizational Behavior Teaching Journal*, 4: 38–42.

Bolman, L.G. and Deal, T.E. (1984) *Modern Approaches to Understanding and Managing Organizations*. San Francisco: Jossey-Bass.

Bolman, L.G. and Deal, T.E. (1995) *Reframing Organizations*. San Francisco: Jossey-Bass.

Bolman, L.G. and Deal, T.E. (2003) *Reframing Organizations: Leadership, Artistry, and Choice*. San Francisco: Jossey-Bass.

Brandt, R. (1993) 'Teaching for understanding: A conversation with Howard Gardner', *Educational Leadership*, 50 (7): 4–7.

Bray, D.W. (2007) *Centered on Assessment*. Retrieved August 14, 2007, from http://www.assessmentcenters.org/articles/centeredonassess.asp.

Breedlove, C. (1998) *Uncharted Lines: Poems from the Journal of the American Medical Association*. New York: Ten Speed Press.

Bumpus, M.A. (2005) 'Using motion pictures to teach management: Refocusing the camera lens through the infusion approach to diversity', *Journal of Management Education*, 29 (6): 792–815.

Bunker, B. and Alban, B. (2006) 'Large group interventions and dynamics', in J.V. Gallos (ed.), *Organization Development*. San Francisco: Jossey-Bass.

Cameron, K. (2003) 'Organizational transformation through architecture and design', *Journal of Management Inquiry*, 12: 88–92.

Cameron, K., Dutton, J. and Quinn, R. (eds) (2003) *Positive Organizational Scholarship*. San Francisco: Jossey-Bass.

Campo, R. (1994) *The Other Man Was Me: A Voyage to the New World*. New York: Arte Publico Press.

Campo, R. (1996) *What the Body Told*. Durham, NC: Duke University Press.

Canton, J. (2007) *The Top Trends That Will Reshape the World in the Next 20 Years*. New York: Plume/Penguin.

Capra, F. (1975) *The Tao of Physics*. New York: Bantam Books.

Carnegie, D. (1936) *How to Win Friends and Influence People*. New York: Simon & Schuster.

Cennamo, K.S. (1993) 'Learning from video: Factors influencing learners' preconceptions and invested mental effort', *Educational Technology Research and Development*, 41 (3): 33–45.

Champoux, J.E. (1999) 'Film as a teaching resource', *Journal of Management Inquiry*, 8 (2): 206–16. Retrieved March 7, 2003, from http://proquest.umi.com/pdqweb.

Champoux, J.E. (2001) 'Animated films as a teaching resource', *Journal of Management Education*, 25 (1): 79–100.

Champoux, J.E. (2003) *At the Movies: Organizational Behavior*. Mason, OH: South-Western.

Chester, E. (2002) *Employing Generation Why?* Lakewood, CO: Tucker House.

Clark, B. (1972) 'The organizational saga in higher education', *Administrative Science Quarterly*, 17: 178–784.

Clemens, J. and Mayer, D. (1999) *The Classic Touch: Lessons in Leadership from Homer to Hemingway*. Chicago: Contemporary Books.

Clemens, J. and Wolfe, M. (2000) *Movies to Manage By*. Boston: McGraw-Hill Trade.

Cohen, M. and March J.G. (1974). *Leadership and Ambiguity*. New York: McGraw-Hill.

Coles, R. (1989) *The Call of Stories: Teaching and the Moral Imagination*. Boston: Houghton Mifflin.

Coles, R. and Testa, R. (2002) *A Life in Medicine: A Literary Anthology*. New York: The New Press.

Comer, D.R. (2001) 'Not just a Mickey Mouse exercise: Using Disney's *The Lion King* to teach leadership', *Journal of Management Education*, 25 (4): 430–36.

Conrad, J. (2007) *The Secret Sharer*. Retrieved March 28, 2007, from Project Gutenberg http://www.gutenberg.org/etext/220.

Cruikshank, J. (1987) *A Delicate Experiment: The Harvard Business School 1908–1945*. Boston: Harvard Business School Press.

Cruikshank, J. (2005) *Shaping The Waves: A History of Entrepreneurship at Harvard Business School*. Boston: Harvard Business School Press.

Cruikshank, J. (2007) 'Shaping a legacy: Cruikshank chronicles the history of entrepreneurship at HBS'.

Retrieved August 10, 2007 from http://www.hbs.edu/ entrepreneurship/newbusiness/2005spring_1.html.

Darso, L. (2001) *Innovation in the Making*. Copenhagen, Denmark: Copenhagen Business School Press.

Darso, L. (2004) *Artful Creation: Learning-Tales of Arts-in-Business*. Frederiksberg, Denmark: Forlaget Samfundslitteratur.

Darso, L. (2005) 'International opportunities for artful learning', *Journal of Business Strategy*, 26 (5): 58–61.

Davis, M. et al. (1977) *The Structure of Educational Systems*. Palo Alto: Stanford Center for Research and Development in Teaching.

Deal, T. and Derr, B. (1979) 'Toward a contingency theory of change in education: Organizational structure, process and symbolism', in E. King (ed.), *Education for Uncertainty*. London: Sage.

Deal, T. and Kennedy, A. (1982) *Corporate Culture*. Reading, MA: Addison Wesley.

Delbecq, A. (2008) 'Spirituality and leadership effectiveness: Inner growth matters', in J.V. Gallos (ed.), *Business Leadership* (2nd edn). San Francisco: Jossey-Bass.

Denning, S. (2005) *The Leader's Guide to Storytelling: Mastering the Art and Discipline of Business Narrative*. San Francisco: Jossey-Bass.

Denning, S. (2007) *The Secret Language of Leadership: How Leaders Inspire Action through Narrative*. San Francisco: Jossey-Bass.

De Pree, M. (2004) *Leadership is an Art*. New York: Currency.

Dillard, A. (1988) *Living by Fiction*. New York: Harper.

Donaldson, J.W. (2004) *The Theater of the Greeks: A Treatise on the History and Exhibition of the Greek Drama*. Whitefish, MT: Kessinger Publishers.

Dotlich, D.L., Noel, J.L. and Walker, N. (2008) 'Learning for leadership: Failure as a second chance', in J.V. Gallos. *Business Leadership* (2nd edn), San Francisco: Jossey-Bass.

Edelman, M. (1977) *The Symbolic Uses of Politics*. Madison: University of Wisconsin Press.

Edwards, D. (2008) *Artscience: Creativity in the Post-Goggle Generation*. Boston: Harvard University Press.

Eliot, C.W. (1920) 'Langdell and the law school', *Harvard Law Review*, 33 (4): 518–25.

Feldman, M. and March, J. (1981) 'Information in organizations as signal and symbol', *Administrative Science Quarterly*, 26 (2): 186–206.

Ferguson, M. (1980) *The Aquarian Conspiracy: Personal and Social Transformation in the 1980s*. Los Angeles: J.P. Tarcher.

Fink, D.L. (2003) *Creating Significant Learning Experiences*. San Francisco: Jossey-Bass.

Fiske, E. (ed.). (1999) *Champions of Change: The Impact of the Arts on Learning*. Washington, DC: The Arts

Education Partnership and the President's Committee on the Arts and Humanities.

Flaherty, J. 2002. 'If they can't get jobs, there's summer stock', *New York Times*, Business Diary, section 3, page 4, December 15, 2002.

Florida, R. (2002) *The Rise of the Creative Class*. New York: Basic Books.

Florida, R. (2005) *The Flight of the Creative Class: The New Global Competition for Talent*. New York: Harper Business.

Freire, P. (1970) *Pedagogy of the Oppressed*. New York: Continuum Publishing.

Frost, P.J. (2003) *Toxic Emotions at Work*. Boston: Harvard Business School Press.

Gallos, J.V. (1982) *Exploration of an Uncharted Terrain: Gender Stereotypes and Symbolic Views of Organization*. Cambridge, MA: Harvard Graduate School of Education.

Gallos, J.V. (1993a) 'Teaching about reframing with films and videos', *Journal of Management Education*, 17 (1): 127–32.

Gallos, J.V. (1993b) 'Understanding the organizational behavior classroom: An application of developmental theory', *Journal of Management Education*, 17 (4): 423–39.

Gardner, H.E. (1984) *Art, Mind and Brain: A Cognitive Approach to Creativity*. New York: Basic Books.

Gardner, H.E. (1993) *Creating Minds: An Anatomy of Creativity Seen Through the Lives of Freud, Einstein, Picasso, Stravinsky, Eliot, Graham, and Gandhi*. New York: Basic Books.

Gardner, H.E. (1994a). *The Arts and Human Development*. New York: Basic Books.

Gardner, H.E. (1994b) *Creating Minds: An Anatomy of Creativity Seen Through the Lives of Freud, Einstein, Picasso, Stravinsky, Eliot, Graham, and Gandhi*. New York: Basic Books.

Gioia, D. and Brass, D. (1985–1986) 'Teaching the TV generation: The case for observational learning', *Organizational Behavior Teaching Review*, 10 (2): 11–18.

Goffman, E. (1959) *The Presentation of Self in Everyday Life*. New York: Doubleday.

Goleman, D., Boyatzis, R. and McKee, A. (2002) *Primal Leadership: Realizing the Power of Emotional Intelligence*. Boston: Harvard Business School Press.

Google (2007) 'The top ten reasons to work at Google and video', Retrieved May 14, 2007, from http://www.google.com/jobs/working.html.

Greene, M. (1995a) *Releasing the Imagination: Essay on Education, the Arts, and Social Change*. San Francisco: Jossey-Bass.

Greene, M. (1995b) 'Art and imagination: Reclaiming the sense of possibility', *Phi Delta Kappan*,

**209**

76:5, 378–82. Accessed December 10, 2007 at http://www.maxinegreene.org/articles.php

Greene, M. (1997) 'Teaching as possibility: A light in dark times', *Journal of Pedagogy, Pluralism and Practice* 1:1. Accessed December 10, 2007 at http://gayleturner.net/Maxine%20Greene.pdf

Greene, M. (2007) 'Toward a pedagogy of thought and a pedagogy of imagination', Accessed December 15, 2007 at http://www.maxinegreene.org/articles.php

Griswold, E.N. (2007) 'The Harvard Law Review: Glimpses of its history as seen by an afficionado', Retrieved June 29, 2007, from http://www.harvardlawreview.org/Centennial.shtml

Gutenberg Project (2007) Accessed December 16, 2007 at http://www.gutenberg.org/wiki/Main_Page

Hakkarainen, P. and Saarelainen, T. (2005) 'Towards meaningful learning through designing, producing and solving digital video-supported cases with students', in G. Richards (ed.), *Proceedings of World Conference on E-Learning in Corporate, Government, Healthcare, and Higher Education*. Chesapeake, VA: AACE. pp. 2081–2104.

Hakim, D. (2001) 'An artist invades stodgy G.M.: Detroit wonders if the "Ultimate Car Guy" can fit in', *New York Times*, October 19, 2001. Retrieved August 23, 2007, from http://select.nytimes.com/search/restricted/article?res=F40F14F8395A0C7A8DDDA9094D9404482.

Hatch, M.J. (1997) 'Jazzing up the theory of organizational improvisation', *Advances in Strategic Management*, 14: 181–91.

Hatch, M.J., Kostera, M. and Kozminski, A.K. (2005) *The Three Faces of Leadership: Manager, Artist, Priest*. London: Blackwell.

Hartwick Humanities in Management Institute (2007) Retrieved July 10, 2007, from http://www.hartwickinstitute.org/hhmi_faq.htm.

Harvard Law School History Project (2005) 'The report of the Harvard Law School History Project 2004–2005', Retrieved August 12, 2007, from http://www.law.harvard.edu/programs/pdfs/2005_HLS_History_Project.pdf

HBR Editors (Feb 2004) 'Breakthrough ideas for 2004: The HBR list', *Harvard Business Review*, Reprint # R0402A.

Heifetz, R.A. (1994) *Leadership Without Easy Answers*. Cambridge, MA: Harvard University Press.

Heracleous, L. and Jacobs, C.D. (2008) 'Playing with serious intent: Creative strategy and strategic leadership development', in J.V. Gallos (ed.), *Business Leadership: A Jossey-Bass Reader*. San Francisco: Jossey-Bass.

Higgins, M. (2007) 'Building careers foundation project', Harvard Business School. Retrieved August 1, 2007, from http://www.people.hbs.edu/mhiggins/index.html.

Holbrook, B. (1981) *The Stone Monkey: An Alternative Chinese Scientific Reality*. New York: William Morrow and Company.

Hooper, S. and Hannafin, M.J. (1991) 'Psychological perspectives on emerging instructional technologies: A critical analysis', *Educational Psychologist*, 26 (1): 69–95.

Howe, W. (1996) 'Leadership vistas: From the constraints of the behavioral sciences to emancipation through the humanities', *Journal of Leadership Studies*, 3 (2): 32–69.

Huston, A.C. and Wright, J.C. (1983) 'Children's processing of television: The informative functions of formal features', *American Psychologist*, 38: 835–43.

Jensen, E. (2001) *Arts with the Brain in Mind*. Alexandria, VA: ASCD.

JME (2007) 'Access to search the *Journal of Management Education* archives is available through the Organizational Behavior Teaching Society website', Retrieved August 24, 2007, from http://www.obts.org/journal-8.html.

Kamens, D.H. (1977) 'Legitimizing myths and education organizations: Relationship between organizational ideology and formal structures', *American Sociological Review*, 42 (2): 208–19.

Kansas City Repertory Theater (2007) 'Understanding South Africa. Dramaturgy notes for "The Syringa Tree", production', April 27, 2007–May 27, 2007.

Kearney, M. and Schuck, S. (2003) 'Teachers as producers, students as directors: Why teachers use student generated videos in their classes', Proceedings from the Apple University Consortium Conference. Accessed December 10, 2007 at http://www.ed-dev.uts.edu.au/personal/mkearney/homepage/acrobats/auc05.pdf

Kearney, M. and Schuck, S. (2005) 'Students in the director's seat: Teaching and learning with student generated video', Proceedings from Educational Media Conference. Accessed December 10, 2007 at http://www.ed-dev.uts.edu.au/personal/mkearney/homepage/acrobats/edmedia05.pdf

Kegan, R. (1998) *In Over Our Heads: The Mental Demands of Modern Life*. Cambridge, MA: Harvard University Press.

Kozma, R.B. (1991) 'Learning with media', *Review of Educational Research*, 61: 79–211.

Krumme, G. (2007) *Major Categories in the Taxonomy of Educational Objectives: Bloom 1956*. Accessed December 14, 2007 at http://faculty.washington.edu/krumme/guides/bloom1.html

Kuhn, T. (1996) *The Structure of Scientific Revolutions*. Chicago, IL: University of Chicago Press.

Lacho, K.J., Herring, R.A. and Hartman, S.J. (1991) 'The video age: An analysis of classroom use of video technology by management professors', Paper submitted to the Southern Management Association, Management Education Track.

Leavitt, H. (Summer 1975) 'Beyond the analytic manager', *California Management Review.*

Lee, C. (1987) 'Where the training dollars go', *Training*, 24 (10): 51–65.

Lewis, M. (1999) *New New Thing: A Silicon Valley Story.* New York: Norton.

Levitin, D. (2006) *This is Your Brain on Music: The Science of Human Obsession.* New York: Plume.

Light, R. (2001) *College Students Speak Their Minds.* Cambridge, MA: Harvard University Press.

Light, R. (2004) *Making the Most of the College Years.* Cambridge, MA: Harvard University Press.

Lindblom, C.E. (1974) 'The science of muddling through', *Public Administration Review*, 52: 79–80.

Maier, M. (1992) *A Major Malfunction: The Story Behind the Space Shuttle Challenger Disaster.* Albany, NY: The Research Foundation of the State University of New York.

March, J.G. (1978) 'Bounded rationality, ambiguity and the engineering of choice', *Bell Journal of Economics.*

March, J.G. and Olsen, J. (1976) *Ambiguity and Choice in Organizations.* Norway: Universitetsforlaget.

March, J.G. and Weil, T. (2005) *On Leadership: A Short Course.* London: Blackwell Publishing Limited.

Martin, P. (2007) *Renaissance Generation.* Avon, MA: Adams Media.

Marx, R.D. and Frost, P.J. (1998) 'Toward optimal use of video in management education: Examining the evidence', *Journal of Management Development.* 17 (4): 243–50.

Marx, R.D., Frost, P.J. and Jick, T. (1991) *Management Live! The Video Workbook.* Englewood Cliffs, NJ: Prentice-Hall.

Marx, R.D. and Meisel, S.I. (Mar 2006) 'Ei, Ei, Oh: Teaching emotional intelligence in the classroom', Paper presented at the Mid-Atlantic Organizational Behavior Teaching Conference, March 25, 2006, La Salle University, Philadelphia, PA.

Mazonde, I.H. (2007) 'Culture and education in the development of Africa', Accessed May 23, 2007 at http://unpan1.un.org/intradoc/groups/public/documents/IDEP/UNPAN003347.pdf

Meyer, J. and Rowan, B. (1977) 'Institutionalized organizations: Formal structure as myth and ceremony', *American Journal of Sociology*, 83: 340–63.

Miller, J. (2007) *Cross-X: The Amazing True Story of How the Most Unlikely Team from the Most Unlikely of Places Overcame Staggering Obstacles at Home and at School to Challenge … Community on Race, Power, and Education.* New York: Picador.

Mintzberg, H. (1975) 'The manager's job: Folklore and fact', *Harvard Business Review* (July–Aug).

Mirvis, P.H. (1980) 'The art of assessing the quality of work life', in E. Lawler, D. Nadler and C. Cammann (eds), *Organizational Assessment.* New York: Wiley.

Mirvis, P.H. (2006) 'Revolution in OD: The new and the new new things', in J.V. Gallos (ed.). *Organization Development: A Jossey-Bass Reader.* San Francisco: Jossey-Bass.

Mirvis, P.H. and Ayas, K. (2008) 'Enhancing the psycho-spiritual development of leaders: Lessons from leadership journeys in Asia', in J.V. Gallos (ed), *Business Leadership* (2nd edn). San Francisco: Jossey-Bass.

Mirvis, P.H. and Gunning, L. (2006) 'Creating a community of leaders', in J.V. Gallos (ed.), *Organization Development.* San Francisco: Jossey-Bass.

Mirvis, P.H., Ayas, K. and Roth, G. (2003) *To the Desert and Back: The Story of one of the Most Dramatic Business Transformations on Record.* San Francisco: Jossey-Bass.

Morgan, G. (1980) 'Paradigms, metaphors and puzzle-solving in organizational theory', *Administrative Science Quarterly*, 25 (4): 605–22.

Morgan, H., Harkins, P. and Goldsmith, M. (2004) *The Art and Practice of Leadership Coaching.* New York: Wiley.

Nissley, N. (2002) 'Arts-based learning in management education', in C. Wankel and R. DeFillippi (eds), *Rethinking Management Education for the 21st Century.* Charlotte, NC: Information Age Publishing.

Nussbaum, B. and Tiplady, R. (2005) 'Where MBAs learn the art of blue skying', *Business Week*, April 18, 2005. Retrieved May 28, 2007, from http://www.businessweek.com/magazine/content/05_16/b3929040_mz011.htm

Ohasi, W. (1976) *Do-it-Yourself Shiatsu.* New York: E.P. Dutton.

Oshry, B. (1996) *Seeing Systems: Unlocking the Mysteries of Organizational Life.* San Francisco: Berrett Koehler.

Oshry, B. (1999) *Leading Systems: Lessons from the Power Lab.* San Francisco: Berrett Koehler.

Ouchi, W. (1981) *Theory Z.* New York: Avon Books.

Pascale, R. (1978) 'Zen and the art of management', *Harvard Business Review* (Mar–Apr).

Peters, T. and Waterman, R.H. (1985) *In Search of Excellence.* Boston: Nathan Tyler Productions.

Pfeffer, J. (1976) 'The effects of uncertainty on the use of social influence in organizational decision making', *Administrative Science Quarterly*, 21: 227–45.

Pilobolus (2007) 'The leadership workshop', Retrieved May 23, 2007 from http://www.pilobolus.com/Institute%20Activities.

Pink, D.H. (2005) *A Whole New Mind: Why Right-Brainers Will Rule the Future*. New York: Riverhead Books.

Postrel, V. (2007) 'Interview with the author', Retrieved August 21, 2007, from http://www.dynamist.com/tsos/q&a.html.

Prahalad, C.K. (2006) *The Fortune at the Bottom of the Pyramid: Eradicating Poverty Through Profits*. Philadelphia, PA: Wharton Business Press.

Ray, P. and Anderson, S. (2000) *The Cultural Creatives: How 50 Million People are Changing the World*. New York: Three Rivers Press.

Rein, M. and Schon, D. (1976) 'Problem setting in policy research', Unpublished paper, MIT.

Rowe, A.J. (Aug 1974) 'The myth of the rational decision maker', *International Management*.

Sales, M.J. (2006) 'Understanding the power of position: A diagnostic model', in J.V. Gallos (ed.), *Organization Development*. San Francisco: Jossey-Bass.

Schechner, R. (2003) *Performance Theory*. London: Routledge.

Schein, E. (1985) *Organization Culture and Leadership* (1st edn). San Francisco: Jossey-Bass.

Schon, D. (1983) *The Reflective Practitioner: How Professionals Think in Action*. New York: Basic.

Schwartz, P. (1991) *The Art of the Long View*. New York: Doubleday.

Seifter, H. (2004) 'Artists help empower corporate america', *Arts and Business Quarterly Online*, Spring 2004. Retrieved May 15, 2007, from http://www.americansforthearts.org/private_sector_affairs/arts_and_business_council/abut_us/newsletters/2004/spring.asp

Seifter, H. and Buswick, T. (2005) 'Editor's note: Arts-based learning in business', *Journal of Business Strategy*, 26 (5): 4–5.

Senge, P. (2006) *The Fifth Discipline: The Art & Practice of The Learning Organization*. New York: Currency.

Senge, P., Kleiner, A., Roberts, C., Ross, G. and Smith, B. (1999) *The Dance of Change*. New York: Doubleday.

Shebilske, W.L. and Reid, L.S. (1979) 'Reading eye movements, macrostructure and comprehension', in P.A. Kolers, M.E. Wrostad, and H. Bouma (eds), *Processing of Visible Language*. New York: Plenum.

Smith, D.D. (1973) 'Teaching introductory sociology by film', *Teaching Sociology*, 1: 48–61.

Smith, M.K. (2001) 'Dialogue and conversation: The encyclopaedia of informal education', Retrieved from www.infed.org/bibio/b-dialog.htm.

Solomon, G. (1979a) *Interaction of Media, Cognition, and Learning: An Exploration of How Symbolic Forms Cultivate Mental Skills and Affect Knowledge Acquisition*. San Francisco: Jossey-Bass.

Solomon, G. (1979b) 'What does it do to Johnny? A cognitive-functionalistic view of research on media', in G. Solomon and R.E. Snow (eds), *Commentaries on Research in Instructional Media*, 33–62. Bloomington: School of Education, Indiana University.

Solomon, G. (1983) 'The differential investment of mental effort in learning from different sources', *Educational Psychologist*, 18 (1): 42–50.

Solomon, G. and Leigh, T. (1984) 'Predispositions about learning from print and television', *Journal of Communication*, 34: 119–35.

Sucher, S. (2007a) *Teaching the Moral Leaders: A Guide for Instructors*. London: Routledge.

Sucher, S. (2007b) *The Moral Leader: Challenges, Tools, and Insights*. London: Routledge.

Tichy, N. and Devanna, M.A. (1986) *The Transformational Leader*. New York: Wiley.

Townsend, P.L. and Gebhardt, J.E. (1999) *Five-Star Leadership: The Art and Strategy of Creating Leaders at Every Level*. New York: Wiley.

Torbert, W.R. (1989) 'Leading organizational transformation', in R. Woodman and W. Passmore (eds), *Research in Organizational Change and Development (Vol. 3)*. Greenwich, CT: JAI Press.

Torbert, W.R. (2007) 'Major influence on my work', Accessed June 10, 2007 at http://www2.bc.edu/~torbert/4_maj_infl.html

University of Victoria Counseling Services (2007) *Bloom's Taxonomy*. Accesses December 15, 2007 at http://www.coun.uvic.ca/learning/exams/blooms-taxonomy.html

Vaill, P.B. (1989) *Managing as a Performing Art: New Ideas for a World of Chaotic Change*. San Francisco: Jossey-Bass.

Volckmann, R. (2005) 'Alchemist at work: Two sessions with Bill Torbert', *Integral Leadership Review*, 5, December. Retrieved August 10, 2007, from http://www.integralleadershipreview.com/archives/2005_12/2005_12_announce_torbertalchemist.html.

Weick, K. (1976) 'Educational organizations as loosely coupled systems', *Administrative Science Quarterly*, 12: 1–19.

Weick, K. (1978) 'The spines of leadership', in L. Pondy (ed.), *New Perspectives on Leadership*. Durham, NC: Duke University Press.

Weick, K. (1980) 'Loosely coupled systems: Relaxed meanings and thick interpretations', Unpublished paper, Cornell University.

Weisbord, M. and Janoff, F. (1995) *Future Search: Finding Common Ground for Action in Organizations and Communities.* San Francisco: Berrett-Koehler.

Westerlund, G. and Sjostrand, S. (1979) *Organizational Myths.* New York: Harper & Row.

Wickham, G. (1992) *A History of the Theater.* New York: Phaidon Press.

Wiske, M.S. (1997) *Teaching for Understanding: Linking Research with Practice.* San Francisco: Jossey-Bass.

Whyte, W.H. (1956) *The Organization Man.* New York: Doubleday.

Young, J.F. (2005) *iCon Steve Jobs: The Greatest Second Act in the History of Business.* New York: Wiley.

Zander, R.S. and Zander, B. (2000) *The Art of Possibility.* Boston: Harvard Business School Press.

# Technology in the Classroom

T. Grandon Gill

There is a quiet revolution taking place in today's management education classrooms. Although web-enabled online learning has captured more media attention, the incremental changes in how we teach that are being enabled by today's emerging classroom technologies will – for many faculty members – require far greater adjustments than the transition from face-to-face to online delivery. Indeed, to use today's classroom technologies effectively, fundamental changes in teaching philosophy and processes are often required.

In this chapter, we explore classroom technologies and how they can impact instructional goals. We begin by identifying a number of different technologies, including presentation tools, simulations, audience response systems (a.k.a. clickers), communications tools and ink-based computer tools, such as Tablet PCs. We then examine the role such technologies can play in achieving a variety of instructional goals. These observations lead to one of the key conclusions of the chapter: that the importance of sound course design (as well as its potential complexity) grows dramatically as classroom technologies are introduced. Finally, we consider how the expanding portfolio of

classroom technologies is likely to impact the future of business education.

## EXAMPLES OF CLASSROOM TECHNOLOGIES

The range of classroom technologies – proven and potential – is so great and changes so rapid that it would be a pointless exercise to attempt to catalog them here. Instead, we will consider a broad portfolio of widely used and promising technologies, presented in Table 11.1, with the expectation that the analysis presented can be generalized to other technologies. The items are sorted according to the 'category' column, which provides insights into how the technology would be deployed. Institution, for example, signifies institutional involvement, either through facilities infrastructure (e.g., academic computing-installed equipment) or through policy (e.g., requiring students in certain programs to have a laptop). The remaining categories identify technologies that are typically acquired by an individual instructor or an individual student. The maturity column of the table refers to the degree to which the technology has demonstrated its potential in higher education,

**Table 11.1  Selected technologies relevant to classroom activities**

| Technology | Description | Category | Maturity |
|---|---|---|---|
| Projection System | Technology used for projecting documents and computer screen. | Institution | Established |
| Student Workstations | Individual workstations for students, either supplied by the university or required by a program. | Institution | Established |
| Course Management System | Tool for controlling, distributing and creating online content, such as blackboard. | Institution | Established |
| Telecast and Interactive TV | TV studio facilities built into a classroom for recording or remote transmission. | Institution | Established |
| Intelligent Whiteboards | Whiteboards capable of controlling a computer and archiving content written or drawn by the instructor. | Institution | Emerging |
| Audience Response System | 'Clicker' system allowing students to submit multiple choice responses and results to be displayed and/or graded. | Institution | Emerging |
| Tablet PC Network | Laptop displays capable of recording on screen drawings and transferring them back and forth between students and the instructor. | Institution | Experimental |
| Presentation Tools | Software tools, such as MS PowerPoint, used to create and display presentations. | Instructor | Established |
| Computer Simulations | Programs modeling real-world phenomena for demonstration or participative exercises. | Instructor | Established |
| Animated Screen Capture | Software that captures activities on the screen, along with narration, then renders the results in multimedia format. | Instructor | Emerging |
| Digital content available commercially, online and in repositories | Instructional assets that are prepared by other developers and shared. These may either be commercially available (e.g., as part of a textbook), available online (e.g., web sites, podcasts) or included in repositories (e.g., Merlot). | Instructor | Emerging |
| Synchronous Voice/Video Links | Tools allowing audio and video streams to be shared between the classroom and external locations. | Instructor | Emerging |
| Instant Messenger | A tool for sending computer-to-computer text messages. | Instructor | Emerging |
| Instructor Tablet PC | A laptop supporting digital ink that can be used for presentation, media creation and grading purposes. | Instructor | Experimental |
| Recording | Digital recording device capable of capturing classroom audio. | Student | Established |
| Cell Phone | Cellular handset also capable of still and live motion photography, text messaging and limited web access. | Student | Established |
| Electronic Notes | Note taking software that includes ink and text input, synchronization of recorded speech and notes, note sharing, and full text search of notes. | Student | Experimental |
| Virtual Worlds | Online environments where individuals can interact using simulated figures known as avatars. | (All) | Experimental |

particularly business education. In line with the portfolio objective, established technologies, emerging technologies and experimental technologies are all represented.

## INSTRUCTIONAL OBJECTIVES

There is little point to employing classroom technologies if they are not intended to achieve some instructional goal. For the purposes of this chapter, we will break these goals into six categories, developed by the author after years of serving as a mentor to nearly a hundred faculty members implementing technologies in their own classrooms. These goals are identified in Table 11.2, under the headings how, when, what, where, if and who. We now consider how the technologies presented in Table 11.1 impact these goals.

**Table 11.2   Common instructional goals for classroom technologies**

| Heading | Related question | Technology goal |
| --- | --- | --- |
| How | How does the instructor communicate with students in the classroom? | Enabling communication patterns |
| When | When is classroom content available to students? | Archiving content for later study |
| What | What forms of presentation are used to communicate content? | Increasing effective information transfer rates |
| Where | Where does classroom content come from and go to? | Leveraging instructional assets |
| If | If students are comprehending and retaining the content being presented in the classroom. | Assessing instructional effectiveness in real time |
| Who | Who is primarily responsible for the instruction and learning taking place in the classroom? | Stimulating alternative learning modalities |

## 1 How: enabling communications patterns

One of the biggest impacts of classroom technologies involves changes in how we communicate. Although the stereotypical college class consists of a lecturer standing in front of a group of students, there are actually many different patterns of communication that can take place in a classroom setting. Using network terminology, we can identify four broad categories:

- Standalone: Independent work by a student.
- Broadcast: One-way communication from instructor to students, as in the case of a mass lecture. Certain uses of case studies, most notably lecturing a case, theorizing a case and illustrating a case (Rangan, 1996), also principally employ the broadcast pattern.
- Star: Supports bi-directional interactions between the instructor (the hub) and individual students, as would occur in a Q&A session. In some processes, such as a review session, the questions may come from the students. In others, such as a Socratic dialog, the instructor may be posing the questions

as a teaching technique. The pattern also typifies the case method as employed at institutions such as Harvard Law School, where 'This entire process puts the instructor front and center. It is very much hub-and-spoke: the professor exercises a firm, controlling hand and virtually all dialogue includes her. There are few student-to-student interchanges' (Garvin, 2003: 59).

- Peer-to-peer: Supports direct communications between students. Classroom group participation activities, such as 'the Beer game', generally fit this model, as do classic business school case discussions, where 'a primary goal is to encourage student-to-student dialogue' (Garvin, 2003: 61).

One important role that classroom technology can play is to encourage communications patterns beyond the traditional lecture. Table 11.3 summarizes how different patterns can be enabled by different technologies.

For standalone classroom activities, the student workstation is clearly one of the most relevant technologies. This area will be discussed further when we consider enabling alternative learning modalities. Course management system technology, such as Blackboard or Moodle, is a useful adjunct to the workstation in the classroom context, since it allows the instructor to distribute content and administer quizzes.

Not surprisingly, many of the most ubiquitous and enduring classroom technologies (e.g., projection systems, telecasts and presentation tools, such as PowerPoint) are particularly well suited to broadcast communications, such as the traditional lecture.

Some technologies that have been introduced only recently are particularly suitable for facilitating back and forth interactions between instructions and students – the star pattern. The Tablet PC (Gill, 2007a), for example, allows an instructor to ink on the screen, which can significantly increase his or her ability to respond to complex questions, particularly in disciplines where diagrams or equations are routinely used. Another recent entry into this space is the intelligent whiteboard, such as the Smart Board™, which allows annotations to be made over video steams and remote control

**Table 11.3   Patterns facilitated by different technologies**

| Pattern | Commonly employed technologies | Comments |
|---|---|---|
| Standalone | Student Workstations<br>Course Management System | Technologies that facilitate independent activities and content distribution. |
| Broadcast | Projection System<br>Telecast<br>Presentation Tools | Technologies that facilitate one-way communications between instructor and students. |
| Star | Instructor Tablet PC<br>Intelligent Whiteboard<br>Synchronous Voice/Video Links<br>Instant Messenger | Technologies that facilitate Q&A.<br>Technologies for assessing instructional effectiveness (Goal 5) also frequently support this pathway. |
| Peer-to-peer | Cell Phone<br>Virtual Worlds | Technologies that enable student-to-student communications or collaboration in the classroom. Technologies enabling alternative learning modalities (Goal 6) also frequently support this pathway. |

of computer applications using the board as a giant digitizing tablet.

Another technology that the author has observed facilitating star interactions in large classrooms is Instant Messenger (IM). Although most commonly used in online settings, IM can also be used to allow students to send text-based questions to instructors or each other. The technology is freely available from a variety of vendors, including AOL, Yahoo and Microsoft. This tool can be particularly effective in large lecture hall settings, where students can submit text questions that appear on the main screen using a laptop or personal digital assistant (PDA).

One potential advantage offered by IM Q&A communications is that some students, intimidated by the thought of speaking out in front of a large auditorium full of people (the course using IM observed by the author had about 350 students attending each session), may feel comfortable using the technology to pose a question. The technology also offers a number of disadvantages. It is easy for the instructor to forget to disable IM and, in consequence, questions may pop up at inopportune time, as well as personal communications unrelated to the class being taught.

Another example of technologies facilitating classroom star interactions – as well as having obvious applications to online settings – are synchronous audio and video chat (as provided by applications such as Elluminate and Skype). These can allow

visitors to interact with a class from another location. In one example observed by the author, a case study protagonist who was unable to attend the actual first discussion of the case, participated in the classroom discussion using an Elluminate connection. In another example, iMac computers were used to connect a classroom music course with musicians at remote sites. The potential application of this type of instructor-initiated technology to business courses is great; whereas it is often difficult to get case study participants or business experts to take the time necessary for physical travel to a classroom, arranging a 15–30 minute guest appearance is likely to be far simpler.

Technologies that facilitate peer-to-peer interactions in the classroom fall into two categories: those that establish a communications channel and those that support inherently collaborative activities (to be discussed under the alternative learning modalities goal). In the former category, good examples are the cell phone and the previously mentioned IM. The cell phone is an extraordinarily versatile technology that typically provides text messaging, color displays, embedded cameras, video capture and limited web access in addition to its original voice calling functionality.

In the classroom, cell phones present both opportunities and challenges. On the opportunities side, text messaging can provide a valuable tool for distributing announcements and may also be utilized by audience response systems. Where the instructor permits it, they can also serve as a convenient tool for archiving classroom content. For example, they can be used to make recordings, and photographs of conventional white boards can be taken by students, reducing the need for electronic boards or digital ink.

Cell phones also introduce a great many classroom challenges. The most obvious of these is the potential for distraction offered by incoming calls or text-messaging activities. The technology also provides tools that can be applied to cheating. For example, students may photograph exams, email them to other students outside the classroom, and, finally, receive answers in the form of text messages. Photographs stored in the phone can also contain notes or other information not permitted in closed-book tests. The cell phone's ability to surreptitiously photograph or film classroom activities may also present privacy concerns, as well as the intellectual property concerns raised by recordings. Although some faculty have chosen to require students to turn off cell phones during class, such policies are hard to enforce and – for some students – being without constant communication is, itself, a distraction.

Although we have yet to see concrete examples of this in a business education setting, it is quite plausible that virtual worlds such as Second Life™ – already producing considerable excitement in the distance learning community (Cross et al., 2007) – may eventually become equally useful as a technology for peer-to-peer activities in classroom settings where students have workstations. Within these virtual worlds, participants are depicted as digital forms referred to as avatars (which may resemble the participant or be entirely dissimilar) that can interact with other avatars in their immediate vicinity, principally through voice chat – although audio capabilities are being introduced. In Second Life, these interactions take place in settings known as islands, which include representations of physical buildings, common areas, streets, transportation facilities and so forth. Participants in the community can create their own buildings,

possessions and decorations, all of which can also be purchased from other participants. These worlds also support thriving economies based upon their own currencies. These virtual currencies can, in turn, be purchased and exchanged for real currencies through legal and extra-legal means.

There are a number of ways that communities such as Second Life might be employed in a classroom setting. The communication proximity mechanisms (i.e., you can only interact with individuals within a certain radius) may actually facilitate the creation of breakout sessions and other peer-to-peer activities that can be hard to accommodate in a typical classroom – and nearly impossible when collaboration across classrooms is desired. They could also provide a venue for guests providing a richer potential interaction than voice connections alone. Detailed recreations of real-world settings, such as the Louvre Museum, are also becoming increasingly common in these worlds. Some day, perhaps, operations management faculty members will take students on a plant tour of a virtual facility developed so as to depict a real factory setting with perfect accuracy.

## 2 When: archiving content for later study

In a higher education setting, it is more or less assumed that a substantial fraction of student learning will take place outside of the classroom. As a result, many technologies have been developed that can serve to archive content for later study, either as a primary or secondary function. Table 11.4 contains a number of examples of such technologies. Such technologies may be supplied by the institution, the instructor or the student.

Institution-supplied technologies include facilities for distributing content (e.g., a course management system, as previously mentioned) and for recording content. In the recording context, the TV studio has been used by universities since the 1950s, allowing lectures to be produced and then rebroadcast.

From a pedagogical standpoint, the value of such classroom recordings is likely to

**Table 11.4   Classroom technologies serving archival purposes**

| Technology | Remarks |
| --- | --- |
| Course Management System | Provides convenient tool for distributing archived content. |
| Telecast and Interactive TV | Televised content and interactive sessions can be recorded and replayed at later times. |
| Intelligent Whiteboards | Activities performed on intelligent whiteboards can be recorded and redistributed for later use. |
| Presentation Tools | Software tools, such as MS PowerPoint, make it easy to distribute outlines as handouts or archived content. |
| Animated Screen Capture | Lectures can either be prepared strictly for archival purposes or can be recorded for later replay in a classroom setting. |
| Recording | Digital recording device capable of capturing classroom audio, typically used by students. The capability is frequently bundled with other devices (e.g., cell phones, laptops). |
| Electronic Notes | Note taking software that includes ink and text input, synchronization of recorded speech and notes, note sharing, and full text search of notes. Typically used by students. |

mirror the use of film and television for teaching purposes, a subject that has been a matter of extensive study. Reviews of the research suggest two general findings: (1) The effectiveness of television in teaching is not heavily dependent on production quality; the instructor in front of a chalkboard seems to be as effective as heavily produced and scripted segments, if not more so (McKeachie, 1990); and (2) There is little evidence of significant difference between the effectiveness of televised lectures when compared with conventional lectures (Seels et al., 2004), although critics are quick to point out that most studies in this area controlled far too few variables to be considered conclusive.

Instructor supplied archiving technologies include both presentation tools – such as MS PowerPoint – and a variety of other tools (e.g., portable document format, scanning,

even word processing documents), that allow lecture notes to be distributed to students for later study. It is also possible for instructors to capture both audio and video streams from lectures using inexpensive animated screen capture technologies (Gill, 2007b), which make recordings of both screen activities and narration that can later be deployed on the web. Because the intelligent whiteboard also allows recordings of classroom sessions to be produced, that technology can also be used in this manner.

Student-supplied technologies for archiving content include digital recorders, which may be standalone devices or may be incorporated into other devices such as cell phones or laptops. In addition, sophisticated note taking software, such as Microsoft's OneNote (Gill, 2007a), allows students to mix digital ink, typing and other content types (e.g., web links) into a single, searchable document. Such tools also allow audio recordings of classroom activities to be synchronized with note taking.

## 3  What: increasing effective information transfer rates

Many classroom technologies expand the realm of what types of content may be presented to students. When used in this manner, the objective is often to increase the rate of information transfer, both by adding a visual channel to the instructor's spoken lecture and eliminating the time formerly required to write the information on a chalkboard or whiteboard (the most basic of the classroom technologies). There is a substantial body of education theory suggesting that such multichannel communication can be beneficial to learning. This is particularly true where one channel provides cues for interpreting the other channel (Moore et al., 2004), as would be the case where bullet points on a slide help cue what is important in an instructor's lecture or where a narrative channel explains what is going on in a video clip. Examples of technologies supporting the increased effective information transfer rate objective, both of which have been previously discussed, are presented in Table 11.5.

**Table 11.5   Classroom technologies supporting knowledge transfer rates**

| Technology | Remarks |
| --- | --- |
| Projection System | Allows visual cues to be supplied along with lecture. Also allows prepared multimedia content to be played. |
| Telecast and Interactive TV | Televised content and other professionally prepared material may increase transfer efficiency. |
| Presentation Tools | Allows visual cues to be provided along with lectures and reduces class time required to create content on whiteboards. |

**Table 11.6   Technologies for leveraging instructional resources**

| Technology | Remarks |
| --- | --- |
| Course Management System | Provides venue for distributing previously created instructional resources. Many tools, including blackboard, provide the capability of copying a course for later reuse, reducing design and setup time. |
| Telecast and Interactive TV | TV studio facilities built into a classroom can be used to simulcast to multiple sites and recorded sessions can be replayed. |
| Animated Screen Capture | Recorded lectures and walkthroughs can be replayed outside the classroom. Recorded software demonstrations can be used to reduce the need for lab time. |
| Synchronous Voice/VideoLinks | Audio and video streams to be shared between the classroom and external locations, reducing the need for classroom space. |
| Digital content available commercially, online and in repositories | Instructional assets that are prepared by other developers. These come in many forms, and may include text-based assets, lecture slides, media clips, exercises, special purpose software. |

## 4  Where: leveraging instructional assets

There is a long tradition of employing classroom technologies to permit scarce instructional assets to be spread across a larger number of students. Such scarcity often manifests itself as a shortage of facilities (e.g., classroom space, lab space), instructors or financial resources. Central to addressing such scarcity are the twin questions of 'where': where does instructional content come from and where is it available? For example, archiving technologies – allowing instructional content to be reused or revisited at a different location – can address both classroom and instructor scarcity. Technologies supporting broadcast communication patterns – allowing a larger number of students to be reached in a single session – can also serve the same purpose. Where facilities are scarce, technologies facilitating blended learning can also be used to reduce classroom time required per student, changing where much of the student's learning occurs. Examples of technologies that are commonly employed in this manner are presented in Table 11.6.

It is also possible to leverage resources by changing where classroom content originates. Digital resources prepared by other instructors are rapidly becoming established as an important source of classroom technology content. Textbooks must increasingly include lecture slides and test banks if they are to be marketable. The web has become a major source of instructional assets – web pages, podcasts, video clips – that can be displayed in the classroom. Commercial repositories, such as Merlot (http://www.merlot.org/merlot/index.htm), now provide peer-reviewed access to lesson plans, exercises, media clips, software tools, and activities appropriate for the classroom in all disciplines, including business.

As technology opens up new sources of instructional assets, intellectual property (IP) issues become increasingly important. There are two general concerns here: preserving the IP rights of others and preserving the instructor's own IP rights. With respect to the rights of others, the 'fair use' doctrine has generally been applied in the classroom context. By the U.S. Copyright Office's own admission, the 'distinction between "fair use" and infringement may be unclear and not easily defined' (U.S. Copyright Office, 2006).

Moreover, at many institutions, such as the author's, what constitutes fair use may be defined at the college, or even department level. The risk the instructor runs is that content to which fair use obviously applies when incorporated into a slide that is projected on a classroom screen may constitute infringement if the same slide is given to students. Another concern, particularly when university computers are used in a classroom setting, is that unintended student activities during class time – such as file sharing or downloading – may infringe on copyrights. The recording industry, in particular, has recently become highly aggressive in pursuing such cases at universities. At this time, it is unclear what obligation, if any, the instructor might have to ensure classroom technologies are not utilized for such purposes during class time.

Of greater concern to many instructors may be the preservation of their own IP rights. At issue here are the many classroom technologies that can be used to record, archive and distribute class-related materials and activities. Interestingly, in the U.S. – unlike many European countries – the presumption is that the copyright for content created on a work-for-hire basis generally belongs to the employer. In academia, however, standard practice always has been to cede these rights to faculty members, so as to motivate them to continue developing and publishing their research, textbooks and other creative efforts. Where the situation becomes grey, however, is where content that is directly classroom related is involved – such as lecture notes and recorded lectures. In the context of distance learning, where similar issues have surfaced, the university typically claims ownership: one survey reported that only 11 percent of faculty members owned the content they created, while 24 percent reported joint university-faculty ownership (Berg, 2000). In the context of classroom technologies, there is no evidence from the literature that such a consensus exists. The typical faculty member is unlikely to lose sleep over the highly improbable situation where university stakes a claim to royalty streams produced by his or her PowerPoint lecture slides. Where a

valid concern would exist, however, is in situations were the university were to demand the right to reuse prepared course content (slides, multimedia, exercises) for subsequent offerings of a course. Such a scenario is quite plausible in the U.S., where it routinely occurred in the context of distance learning, though perhaps less likely in many other countries.

## 5 If: assessing instructional effectiveness in real time

A particularly important group of emerging classroom technologies is intended to provide real-time feedback to instructors regarding the state of student learning. These prove particularly suited for addressing the question of *if the student is learning*, a natural complement to the question of *what is being presented*. Some examples of technologies particularly relevant to this goal are presented in Table 11.7.

A technology that is rapidly becoming widespread goes under the heading of audience response systems (although many other names, such as electronic voting systems, are also used). The technology involves two components: a hardware component and a software component. The hardware component consists of a keypad that allows students to enter multiple-choice replies in response to questions posed by the instructor. The hardware may be hard-wired in the classroom or may be wireless, using either infrared frequencies (like a TV remote), radio frequencies,

**Table 11.7   Technologies for assessing instructional effectiveness in real time**

| Technology | Remarks |
|---|---|
| Audience Response System | Instructor can request student responses in multiple choice or short answer (available in some system configurations) format. |
| Tablet PC Network | Laptop systems capable of recording onscreen drawings and transferring them back and forth between students and the instructor. |

or – in the case of some vendors – may be a virtual application run on a student's PC. The software component allows the instructor to pose questions, collect responses, and then display, grade (if appropriate) and save results. Many systems, such as eInstruction's CPS™ and Turning Technologies' TurningPoint™, offer relatively seamless integration with presentation software, such as Microsoft's PowerPoint®. In addition, we are increasingly seeing integration with CMS system grade books.

Audience response technologies can be used in support of a broad range of communications patterns. Although their most natural use is in a star configuration, they can also be used to encourage classroom and pre-class independent activities (through quizzes and examinations administered with the technology), broadcast patterns (where survey results from previous groups are incorporated into lectures), and even peer-to-peer patterns in which students work in groups as part of the process of coming up with responses.

At the author's institution, a significant effort has been made to disseminate audience response technology across all disciplines. Part of the motivation for this effort was the versatility demonstrated by the technology in early pilot tests. Promising uses included:

- Attendance tool: The technology allows attendance to be taken in large classes with minimal effort – even permitting spot checks to be made at various points in a class session.
- Inducement for pre-class independent activities: Using the technology in quiz mode, students can be required to answer multiple choice questions on assigned readings or activities. Such quizzes appeared to have an impact even where no explicit weight was assigned to the results. For example, in a case-method class taught by the author, the majority of students agreed that knowing a quiz on required case preparation would be given impacted the degree to which they prepared – despite the fact that it was understood that the quiz results were not generally considered as part of class participation.
- Formative assessment: In a number of courses, audience response quiz results are used by the instructor as a tool for formative learning assessment, useful in pacing classes and determining when material needed review. In end-of-semester surveys, the vast majority of students viewed this type of assessment as positively impacting their learning. This type of activity can be generated individually or in small groups. The benefits of this type of activity are also among the most well documented in the literature (particularly in medicine), with use of the technology in this manner often leading to gains in later summative measures (Gill et al., 2006).
- Eliciting attitudes on sensitive subjects: In a number of courses where the technology has been observed by the author, such as those relating to human sexual behavior and criminology, the technology has allowed surveys of sensitive issues (e.g., homosexuality, the death penalty) to be conducted anonymously. This type of survey tends to increase student engagement in large lecture classes. Results can also be compared with previous classes or with national polls on the same subject.
- Eliciting attitude changes: In one of the author's classes, students are assigned to debate topics in management information systems (Gill, 2006). Although given a choice of their assigned topics, students had no choice in whether they were assigned to the pro or con team. As part of the debate protocol, students were surveyed before and after each debate to determine if the random assignments to pro or con teams impacted the attitudes of team members – with results showing that they did not – and to measure the degree to which a particular debate changed the opinion of the class as a whole.

Despite their versatility and proven success, there are presently some limitations associated with audience response technologies. First, there are still quite a number of competing vendors and, in the absence of a single institutional standard, pockets of incompatible systems can easily develop. Second, except where hardwired installations are present, students are normally responsible for the costs of the transmitter technologies. While the per-class costs drop considerably when adoption is widespread, these costs can be substantial (~\$30/class) in cases where a single instructor adopts the technology. It is reasonable to expect that such costs are likely to drop significantly as time progresses. In addition to the economies of scale that are likely to occur as the technology becomes more widely adopted, some vendors are already making the technology available on PCs, as previously noted. Configurations that respond to cell phone text messages are also becoming available. These developments will, in the long run, reduce the need to acquire specialized hardware in order to participate in audience response system classes.

A final drawback of audience response systems – and likely the most significant one – is that the technology is largely limited to multiple choice responses. For some disciplines – particularly the sciences and quantitative business disciplines, such as statistics and introductory finance – the burden placed on the instructor by such a limitation may not be terribly great, since coming up with a correct answer may require substantial application and analysis-level reasoning. For many disciplines, however, the need to specify a set of answers could lead to a tendency to pose recall-based questions. The author found, for example, that it is much easier to ask questions that identify the student's mastery of case facts prior to a discussion than it is to ask multiple choice questions that determine how effectively the student has synthesized the case to produce a sensible judgment of how the protagonist should proceed.

When using audience response systems – as well as other technologies that provide direct feedback to the instructor regarding what is being learned in a classroom context – a common instructor reaction is dismay. Eric Mazur, the renowned physicist at Harvard who is also well known for his pioneering work with audience response technology in an introductory physics course, described the phenomenon as follows:

I suddenly realized that many students didn't understand what I had just told them. I knew immediately that I would have to spend more time explaining that material. Before [using the technology], I would have gone on to the next topic and increased the number of students that I left behind. (Cromie, 2006)

A typical result of this realization is a reduction in total course content, with greater focus on mastery.

Another technology that extends facilities real-time assessment is the Tablet PC network, where each student or small group of students is given a Tablet PC and software allowing communication between students and the instructor. The resulting configuration dramatically expands the capabilities of the audience response system by allowing the instructor to pose questions that require essay responses (including program code and mathematical computations). Classroom Presenter (CP), developed at the University of Washington (Simon et al., 2004), is an example of such an application. In a CP setup, software resident on student machines connects to software resident on the instructor's machine. In addition, there is a public display that allows the instructor to display selected individual student responses.

Although clearly an experimental technology – particularly in management education – major technology players, including Microsoft and Hewlett Packard, are currently investing millions into researching educational uses of Tablet PC technology. As a participant in some of the earliest of these studies aimed at business education, the author had the opportunity to observe the use of these technologies in several different classroom settings. The results showed important benefits to using ink-based approaches. For example:

- In an MS in MIS graduate capstone class, Tablet PC networks were contrasted audience response systems. Statistical analysis of the results, which contrasted a clicker-only class, a tablet-only class and a class where use of clickers and tablets were split 50-50 found significant differences in the degree to which: (a) use of the technology motivated case preparation (with tablets scoring higher), (b) use of the technology during case discussions added value (61 percent for clickers agreeing, versus 88 percent for Tablet PCs), and (c) significant differences in the overall perceived value of the course as a whole, with the Tablet PC section having the highest score.
- In a database course, Tablet PCs and CP were used in exercises involving code writing and

drawing diagrams (both very hard to implement without ink-based technologies). When students were surveyed near the end of the course about how they would like to see the course changed, the strongest response was to include more similar exercises.

- In an MBA MIS course, students were asked to annotate their pre-discussion case analyses with new insights they gained during the discussion. These were then submitted electronically at the end of class, for instructor review. Not only did the instructor find these extremely useful in making formative assessments of how the course was proceeding, students also reacted extremely positively to the course design and awarded the instructor exceptionally high evaluation scores.
- In an undergraduate business programming class, CP-enabled activities replaced traditional lectures (with all lecture and reading content being moved online, to be accessed outside of class time). This was accompanied by substantial improvements in retention rate (with the percent of the class receiving A-B-C grades rising from historical averages of around 60 percent to over 90 percent), increases in the amount of material completed by a typical student, and a dramatic jump in instructor evaluations. While it is not clear the degree to which the tablet network contributed to these improvements, since other changes in course format, content and delivery were made concurrently, the use of CP was definitely an important part of the overall change in course design.

These examples clearly demonstrate how the Tablet PC's ability to solicit less structured student responses can be used to encourage higher level activities. Moreover, by saving student responses to CP questions or inked comments made during discussions, the instructor is given a powerful tool for assessing student engagement in peer-to-peer activities.

Weighed against the highly positive educational outcomes observed, early experiments with Tablet PC networks also had a number of drawbacks. Most important of these, since relatively few students (or institutions) have Tablet PC technology, establishing the necessary setup demands substantial investment on the part of institutions or students. Another drawback relates to the fragility of

the technology: Tablet PCs are more easily damaged than conventional laptops. Finally, because Tablet PC users remain a small market, relatively few software packages have been developed that specifically take advantage of the technology's unique capabilities. Although important strides have been made in this direction, particularly by Microsoft (who have incorporated Tablet functionality into new versions of its operating systems and Office suite), the fact remains that educational software that supports classroom use of Tablet PCs is scarce, and that which is available tends to be prone to a fair number of software bugs.

In the long term, many of these issues are likely to be resolved. It is reasonable to expect that the reliability of the technologies will improve with time and broader usage. We are also seeing attempts to achieve results similar to a Tablet PC network without requiring students to acquire unusual hardware. For example, it is possible to achieve a networking effect similar to that of CP using a web-based technology, Ubiquitous Presenter (UP; Wilkerson et al., 2005), that requires an instructor Tablet PC, but allows students to interact with the screen using conventional workstations or laptops. Versions of CP that allow non-Tablet interactions are also being introduced.

## 6 Who: stimulating alternative learning modalities

The last category of instructional goal that can be enabled through the use of classroom technology we will discuss is that of stimulating different learning modalities. Of particular interest here is who is at the center of classroom activities. Within the distance learning literature (see Chapter 12), it has long been accepted that many techniques work best when the instructor takes a less directive role and more of the student's learning is either derived from peers or from self-directed inquiry. Technology can, however, enable similar changes in instructional approach within the classroom environment.

An important element of the underlying theory that justifies the use of differing modalities is that a typical group of students is likely to have a wide range of learning styles (Hawk and Shah, 2007), and that no single approach to instruction is likely to meet individual needs. In addition, many modes of instruction – most notably, lectures – are generally seen to have diminishing effectiveness when employed over extended blocks of time, although probably more than the 10–15 minutes of effectiveness commonly cited in the literature (Wilson and Korn, 2007). Thus, establishing a portfolio of learning modalities is likely to be the most effective classroom approach if all students are to benefit. Some examples of classroom technologies particularly suited for alternative learning modalities are presented in Table 11.8.

Computer simulations and games are a particularly ubiquitous example of technologies used to stimulate alternative forms of learning in business education. Simulations are programs that use the computer to model some real-world phenomenon. In a classroom setting, they most often are used in the form of a game in which teams of students compete in a simulated environment.

The use of computer-based simulations has a long history in business programs. At Harvard Business School, for example, a computer simulation game, developed in the late-1960s was played through the 1980s. In that game, teams were formed and, for an entire week, competed in a simulated industry setting. One of the interesting aspects of the game was the degree to which lessons outside

### Table 11.8   Classroom technologies supporting alternative learning modalities

| Technology | Remarks |
| --- | --- |
| Computer Simulations | Simulations include models of real-world phenomena that allow students to participate in virtual environments, often presented in the form of a game. |
| Student Workstations | Individual workstations for students, either supplied by the university or required by a program, that allow instructor designated activities to be conducted during class time. |

of the traditional curriculum – such as security and ethical standards of behavior – found their way into the game, and the national press (e.g., Moore, 1982).

The nature of tools for developing and running simulations varies considerably. Some are, essentially, toolkits that allow the instructor or the student to model agent behaviors and then determine the impact on industry dynamics (e.g., Robertson, 2005). These typically require a reasonably steep learning curve in order to create meaningful experiences. Others incorporate built-in assumptions and may include a substantial amount of explanatory content, such as video, and may be viewed as being more along the lines of a walkthrough (e.g., Wolfe, 2004). The most advanced simulation games offer substantial opportunities for peer-to-peer interaction – indeed, they usually mandate it. Because multi-player simulations uniformly require that students deal with complex interrelated choices in an environment characterized by considerable uncertainty, they tend to require the development of higher-level skills. For this reason, we often see them utilized near the end of graduate programs, perhaps in a capstone setting (e.g., Zantow, 2005).

There is often a choice as to whether or not to limit simulation technology to the classroom, or to assign it as an outside-of-class activity. Although the nature of licensing agreements may mandate a lab-only venue, the choice is often in the hands of the instructor. A particular factor that argues strongly for classroom use, at least part of the time, involves the exceptional difficulty in assessing the student learning that occurs as a result of participating in a multi-player simulation. Included among the confounding factors are: (1) Simulation teams often are formed in groups, reducing individual visibility. (2) In a multi-player environment, just as is the case for a business environment, a perfectly viable strategy may fail in some circumstances owing to competitor behavior. This makes performance in the game suspect as the sole criterion for assessing the quality of play. (3) Many environments have a steep technological learning curve, a type of learning that is not necessarily an intended outcome of the game. This means that early moves that have a deleterious impact on team performance may not be reflective of management learning. (4) Unless games are played repeatedly, it is hard to assess if learning is actually occurring. This is a general problem with higher level/tacit knowledge, not limited to simulation settings. Although some of these may be addressed through post-game debriefing and peer assessments, the author has observed that these types of assessment are frequently subject to student gaming of a different sort.

When played in a classroom setting, the instructor can informally observe the actions of the players, and listen in on group discussions and planning activities. These types of observations can both be enlightening and, in many ways, are more authentic – in a real world sense – than a process wherein team members are asked to assess each other. This type of informal observation would be very hard to make in the context of an online activity, since requiring groups to set up an online meeting (e.g., text chat or synchronous conference) at a specified time pretty much contradicts the meaning of informal.

Another example of a technology that fosters alternative learning modalities is student workstations. Most typically, such workstations occur in the context of a computer lab classroom or in institutional settings where students are required to own a laptop and bring it to class. Because of the general purpose-nature of the technology, it can be applied under many different communications patterns (e.g., Murray, 1999) and to enable many different types of learning activities. Using spreadsheet technology as an example, students could work spreadsheet problems individually (standalone), following the directions of the instructor to develop a spreadsheet (broadcast), use the spreadsheets to answer instructor-posed questions (star) or work out problems in small groups (peer-to-peer).

Despite their versatility, there are many potential drawbacks to students accessing computers during business classes (Murray, 1999). In communications terms, the problem seems to be that the computers encourage independent activities – but not necessarily the independent activities intended by the instructor. To combat such non-class activities, the instructor may benefit from wandering around the classroom to cast a casual glance at the on-screen activities of the members of the class. Unfortunately, many types of classroom activities (particularly those involving broadcast patterns) require frequent interactions with a central workstation that tend to inhibit such instructor mobility in the classroom. Another philosophy that is commonly applied in these situations is to require students to close up their laptops or turn off their systems except during specifically designated exercises. The drawbacks of this approach are that it prevents any useful interactions with the computers that might have otherwise occurred during non-exercise periods and that considerable class time may be eaten up by the process of starting up computers when exercises are to be conducted. Infrequent use of individual computers may also encourage students to risk leaving their computers behind instead of bringing them to class. Thus, when the technology is actually needed, a substantial fraction of the class may be without.

## COMPLEXITY OF COURSE DESIGN

Course design has always been a mixture of art and science. The continuing evolution of classroom technologies has not changed this situation, nor is it likely to. For as long as there has been education, instructors have always had to figure out ways to balance the six goals explored in the previous section. Thus, it is reasonable to claim that technology has not given us any fundamentally new designs for classroom teaching. What it has done, however, is to vastly increase the number of options available for achieving desired outcomes.

There is no mechanical procedure that can be used to design the optimal use of technology in a particular classroom setting. (Indeed, it is not even clear that the term 'optimal' is meaningful in such a context, since it is likely that any approach that works perfectly for one student will fall short of meeting the needs of another.) As a starting point, however, it is possible to assess the consistency of the particular learning outcomes desired for the course mesh with the instructional goals and associated technologies employed in the course design. The most widely used framework for classifying learning outcomes is the taxonomy proposed by Bloom (1956). Originally devised as a tool to help educators better communicate what they meant by vague terms such as 'thinking' and 'problem solving', Bloom's Taxonomy divides skills into six levels. The lower-level skills, such as *knowledge* and *comprehension*, principally involve the effective acquisition and storage of explicit knowledge. The mid-level skills, *application* and *analysis*, describe the ability to apply such knowledge in meaningful ways. The highest levels, *synthesis* and *evaluation*, involve the ability to generate and choose between alternatives as problems become increasingly ill-defined. It should be pointed out that the use of levels in this context is not meant to imply that one type of cognitive skill is in some way 'superior' to another. It can be assumed, however, that successful synthesis and evaluation are likely to benefit from the accumulation of skills at the lower-levels. In the management education literature, this is sometimes presented in terms of earlier stages of a program focusing on conveying explicit knowledge – the readily conveyed and testable skills of the lower four levels – while later stages emphasize acquisition of tacit knowledge (Greiner et al., 2003) – which would include decision making in an ambiguous environment where perfect information is unavailable.

Table 11.9 summarizes an approximate mapping between the Bloom levels and the six instructional goals presented earlier. The effectiveness of broadcast patterns, particularly lecture, has been studied extensively in

**Table 11.9 Bloom levels and instructional goals**

| Pattern | Communication patterns | Instructional goals |
|---|---|---|
| Knowledge | Broadcast | Archiving Content Increased Information Transfer Rate Leveraging Instructional Assets |
| Comprehension Application Analysis | Star | Assessing Instructional Effectiveness in Real Time |
| Synthesis Evaluation | Peer-to-Peer | Alternative Learning Modalities |

the education literature. The general conclusion reached has been:

Lecture tends to be at least equal to, and often more effective than, discussion for immediate recall of factual information. (McKeachie, 1990: 190)

With respect to the remaining instructional goals, those involving archiving content, increasing knowledge transfer rates and leveraging scarce instructional assets all seem to be particularly knowledge-directed.

The star and peer-to-peer patterns both exist on the continuum of student-centered teaching methods, which appear to be most effective in achieving 'the more subtle, "higher level" outcomes rather than factual knowledge' (McKeachie, 1990: 191). The star pattern would be exemplified by instructor-directed discussions or recitation sections, also associated with the instructional goal of acquiring real-time feedback from students, which can lead to better scores on examinations (McKeachie, 1990). Such examinations, in turn, are generally most effective at objectively assessing comprehension, analysis and application.

Student-directed discussions, in contrast, represent a peer-to-peer pattern and force the participants to confront considerable ambiguity and contradiction as a consequence of the multiple perspectives involved. As a result, they are frequently central to educational approaches whose objective is to refine the highest order skills, such as evaluation and judgment (e.g., Christensen et al., 1992). Such pedagogical approaches, being very different from the traditional lecture, typically involve the final goal: enabling alternative learning modalities.

Effective course design involves understanding the complex interaction between the nature of the content to be conveyed, the students and the instructor. What the availability of classroom technologies has done is to vastly increase the number of interactions that need to be considered in design: technology-content, technology-student and technology-instructor interactions are all relevant. While rules of thumb such as those presented in Table 11.9 are oversimplifications, they can be useful in helping course designers avoid two risks: (1) that the potential of the technologies will be ignored because they are both unfamiliar and represent a departure from the status quo; and (2) that the decision to employ a particular set of technologies will precede the choice of instructional goals to be accomplished – leading to a situation where the technology drives the pedagogy. Just because a tool like PowerPoint makes it easier to lecture doesn't mean that we should do more lecturing.

## FUTURE DIRECTIONS: CLASSROOM TECHNOLOGY IN MANAGEMENT EDUCATION

In considering how the use of classroom technologies is likely to evolve over the coming decade, two trends need to be considered: technological and social. On the technological side, we can reasonably expect to see Moore's Law – that the cost per unit of computing power will drop by 50 percent every 18 to 24 months – continuing for another decade or two. What this means, in a practical sense, is that our ability to render video and sound, compress it, and disseminate it, could easily increase by a factor of 100 by the year 2020. That means that we'll be capable of generating content that would, today, be considered cinema quality. The same applies

to our ability to run complex simulations, create virtual environments in which to interact, and build intelligent learning systems that offer students a rich interactive learning experience. Moreover, we can expect that the level of connectivity that is available to our students will grow correspondingly (e.g., what is considered lower-end broadband service today is roughly ten times faster than it was just five years ago). From a practical standpoint, the changes mean that the incremental value of the classroom experience compared to the live Internet broadcast will diminish to the extent that the large lecture hall could easily become obsolete. Experienced instructors may argue that the signals they get from students in the live setting are invaluable, making the face-to-face lecture infinitely superior. If they are like most of us, however, they will get a rude awakening when they test what the student nods of understanding actually mean using questions posed through audience response technology or networked Tablet PCs. The experience is humbling.

On the social side, the generation that is coming of age for business education, sometimes referred to as the 'virtual generation' (Proserpio and Gioia, 2007), has been weaned on the computer. They have grown up with the notion that online interactions, such as massive multi-player games and social networks, are recreation. They communicate effortlessly using the special language of text messaging and IM, while viewing the lengthy discourse associated with e-mail as being old-fashioned. For them, the classroom is associated with work. It is naive of us to believe that the observed student preference for enrolling in distance learning sections at many institutions (including the author's) is purely a consequence of the desire to do less work. To keep these students in the classroom, we need to offer them something very special.

In parallel with generational trends, the nature of business education is dramatically changing, particularly on the graduate side. There is a strong trend away from full-time MBA programs and towards executive education, part-time programs, corporate degrees and modular offerings (Friga et al., 2003). All of these transitions imply students who are likely to be working full time while pursuing their degree. For these students, convenience and flexibility will be of paramount concern. For them, the minute benefits that a classroom lecture experience would offer when contrasted with its higher quality online counterpart will not justify the logistical effort entailed. We already see such trends taking place; witness the growth in institutions such as the University of Phoenix, where employers pay about 40 percent of student tuition despite its lack of AACSB accreditation (Kimball-Stanley, 2006).

Do these trends spell the end of business classroom education? Not necessarily. If the classroom management education is to survive, however, it is going to have to reposition itself so as to do things that online education cannot do particularly well. Specifically, the lecture – which, itself, replaced more intimate tutorials a century ago as a result of the need to transfer knowledge simultaneously to more students – is likely to be replaced by peer-to-peer group activities that will be much harder to accomplish online. Indeed, the author has already seen strong evidence that working professionals welcome such a change. Group work can easily become an anathema to such individuals because of the demands it places on their scarce discretionary time. Setting aside regularly scheduled face-to-face time when everyone in a group is required to be available provides a welcome relief; at least, it has to the author's students.

If these trends materialize as the author predicts, the technologies employed in the classroom can be expected to evolve in parallel. We can expect to see greater use of technologies that encourage peer-to-peer interaction, such as Tablet PC networks and simulation activities. We are likely to see managerial technologies, such as group decision support systems, return to the classroom (where they initially originated). Low tech activities, such as case discussions and student presentations, should also continue to play an important role. To these activities, however, technology may be able to grant us greater access to remote students and actual case participants.

One interesting side effect of the changing role of the classroom in management education may be a rethinking of the programmatic timing of classroom activities. Where classroom teaching is used to facilitate all communications patterns, there is really no need to change the amount of classroom time scheduled as students move from the introductory to advanced levels of a program. Where the classroom is used principally to facilitate peer-to-peer activities, on the other hand, there may be reason to expect that such activities would be more beneficial in the later stages of a program (where synthesis and evaluation skills are being emphasized) as opposed to the earlier stages.

Another important implication of such transformations in management education will be a significant change in the role played by the instructor. In distance learning, the phrase 'sage on the stage versus guide on the side' is sometimes used. Rather than being at the center of the star, the instructor needs to become more of a facilitator in the classroom context. For some, such as those whose pedagogy of preference revolves around peer-to-peer patterns such as case discussions, such a role will become completely natural. For those who are used to a more instructor-directed style of teaching, the transition will require a considerable amount of attitudinal change, if it is to be achieved.

## CONCLUSIONS

Technology does not, by itself, teach anything. It can, however, be employed in ways that facilitate nearly every type of learning. To accomplish its objectives, however, technology must be employed as part of an overall course design. In the classroom, the principal challenge that an instructor faces is not how to operate the technology – that is a lower level skill that can be mastered in a fairly predictable amount of time.

Rather, the instructor must strive to employ technology in a manner that fits the goals that he or she has established for student learning. In doing so, however, there is a danger. Some classroom technologies, such as the ubiquitous PowerPoint, are seductive in their tendency to promote certain patterns of instruction. The instructor must guard against allowing such technologies to drive their goals and the manner in which they teach.

## REFERENCES

Berg, G.A. (2000) 'Early patterns of faculty compensation for developing and teaching distance learning courses', *Journal of Asynchronous Learning Networks*, 4 (1): 62–74.

Bloom, B.S. (ed.) (1956) *Taxonomy of Educational Objective, Handbook I: Cognitive Domain*. New York: Longman.

Christensen, C.R., Garvin, D.A. and Sweet, A. (eds) (1992) *Education for Judgment: The Artistry of Discussion Leadership*. Boston: HBS Press.

Cromie, W.J. (2006) 'Harvard launches wireless classroom: Lessons in the palm of your hand', *Harvard University Gazette*, 2/23/06. Retrieved on 6/4/2007 from http://www.news.harvard.edu/gazette/2006/02.23/05-eclassroom.html

Cross, J., O'Driscoll, T. and Trondsen, E. (2007) 'Another life: Virtual worlds as tools for learning', *eLearn Magazine*. Retrieved on 6/6/07 from http://elearnmag.org/subpage.cfm?section=articles&article=44-1

Friga, P.N., Bettis, R.A. and Sullivan, R.S. (2003) 'Changes in graduate management education and new business school strategies for the 21st century', *Academy of Management Learning and Education*, 2 (3): 233–249.

Garvin, D.A. (2003) 'Making the case: Professional education for the world of practice', *Harvard Magazine*, September-October, 106 (1): 56–65, 107.

Gill, T.G. (2006) 'A learner-centered capstone course for a MIS Master's degree program', *Decision Line*, 37 (2): 4–6.

Gill, T.G. (2007a) 'Using the tablet PC for instruction', *Decision Sciences Journal of Innovative Education*, 5 (1): 183–90.

Gill, T.G. (2007b) 'Quick and dirty multimedia', *Decision Sciences Journal of Innovative Education*, 5 (1): 197–206.

Gill, T.G., El-Rady, J. and Myerson, M. (2006) 'Classroom response units in human sexual behavior', *Informing Faculty*, 1 (4): 1–26.

Greiner, L.E., Bhambri, A. and Cummings, T.G. (2003) 'Searching for a strategy to teach strategy', *Academy of Management Learning and Education*, 2 (4): 402–20.

Hawk, T.F. and Shah, A.J. (2007) 'Using learning style instruments to enhance student learning', *Decision Sciences Journal of Innovative Education*, 5 (1): 1–19.

Kimball-Stanley, A. (2006) 'Students like online degrees, but some employers wary', *Knight Ridder Tribune Business News*. Washington: Vol. Nov 5: 1.

Moore, D.M., Burton, J.K., Myers, R.J.K., Berry, L. and Horn, L.J. (2004) 'Multiple-channel communications: The theoretical and research foundations of multimedia', in D.H. Johanssen, *Handbook of Research on Educational Communications and Technology* (2nd edn). Mahwah, NJ: Earlbaum. pp. 979–1005.

Moore, T. (1982) 'Industrial espionage at the Harvard B-School', *Fortune*. Sept. 6, 106 (5): 70–3.

Murray, M.P. (1999) 'Advancing the integration of new technologies into the undergraduate teaching of economics', *The Journal of Economic Education*, 30 (3): 308–21.

McKeachie, W.J. (1990) 'Research on college teaching: The historical background', *Journal of Educational Psychology*, 82 (2): 189–200.

Proserpio, L. and Gioia, D.A. (2007) 'Teaching the virtual generation', *Academy of Management Learning & Education*, 6 (1): 69–80.

Rangan, K. (1996) 'Choreographing a case class', *Case 9-595-074*. HBS Publishing.

Robertson, D.A. (2005) 'Agent-based modeling toolkits: NetLogo, RePast, and Swarm', *Academy of Management Learning & Education*, 4 (4): 525–7.

Seels, B., Fullerton, K., Berry, L. and Horn, L.J. (2004) 'Research on learning from television', in D.H. Johanssen (ed.), *Handbook of Research on Educational Communications and Technology*. (2nd edn). Mahwah, NJ: Earlbaum. pp. 249–334.

Simon, B., Anderson, R., Hoyer, C. and Su, J. (2004) 'Preliminary experiences with a tablet PC-based system to support active learning in computer science courses', *9th ITICSE, June 2004*, Leeds, UK. pp. 213–17.

U.S. Copyright Office. (2006) 'Fair use', *FL-102 Revised July 2006*. Retrieved on 6/4/2007 from http://www.copyright.gov/fls/fl102.html

Wilkerson, M., Griswold, W.G. and Simon, B. (2005) 'Ubiquitous presenter: Increasing student access and control in a digital lecturing environment', *SIGCSE'05*,

*February 23–27, 2005,* St. Louis, Missouri, USA. pp. 116–20.

Wilson, K. and Korn, J.H. (2007) 'Attention during lectures – beyond ten minutes', *Teaching of Psychology,* 34 (2): 85–9.

Wolfe, J. (2004) 'Two computer-based entrepreneurship experiences: An essay review', *Academy of Management Learning & Education,* 3 (3): 333–9.

Zantow, K., Knowlton, D.S. and Sharp, D.C. (2005) 'More than fun and games: Reconsidering the virtues of strategic management simulations', *Academy of Management Learning & Education,* 4 (4): 451–8.

# 12

# Distance Learning and Web-Based Instruction in Management Education

J.B. Arbaugh and S.S. Warell

## Abstract

This chapter examines the variables found to be most influential in predicting success in online management education and assesses the current state of this body of research. The first part of the chapter reviews research findings on technological characteristics, course participants and their behaviors, and course design and structure to identify the characteristics most influential for positive course outcomes in the context of management education. Perhaps due to the focus of the management education literature on instructional practice over course design issues, most of the literature has found that participant behaviors generally are the strongest predictors of course outcomes. The chapter's concluding section identifies areas where future research emphasis is particularly warranted. These areas of emphasis include: 1 A need for testing emerging theoretical frameworks of online management education and grounding subsequent research in such frameworks; 2 More rigorous research methods and designs; 3 Increased attention to blended learning environments; 4 More cross-disciplinary studies to help identify and better understand the unique challenges of conducting management education in technology-mediated environments.

## INTRODUCTION

After a relatively slow start, the pace of research in online management education has increased rapidly during the first decade of the 21st century. Journals such as *Academy of Management Journal*, *MIS Quarterly*, and *Decision Sciences* at least partially addressed online learning in special issues on management education during the mid-to-late 1990s (Alavi et al., 1995; Alavi et al., 1997; Leidner and Jarvenpaa, 1995; Warkentin et al., 1997; Webster and Hackley, 1997). A review of management education publications such as the *Journal of Management Education*, *Management Learning*, *Journal of Education for Business*, and *Business Communication Quarterly* shows that online learning received limited attention until 1999. As a result, earlier literature reviews on online learning in management education were forced to be highly dependent upon literatures from other disciplines (Arbaugh and Stelzer, 2003; Salas et al., 2002). However, due in significant part to the introduction of the journals *Academy of Management Learning and Education* and *Decision Sciences Journal of Innovative Education*, the pace of this research stream has quickened. Since 2000, *AMLE, DSJIE, JME,* and *ML* collectively have published over 40 research articles on technology-mediated learning, and scores of articles on the subject in the context of management education have appeared in other journals. During the past 10–15 years, this research has progressed from narratives of single-course experiences (e.g., Bailey and Cotlar, 1994; Berger, 1999; Dumont, 1996; Ellram and Easton, 1999; Taylor, 1996) and reports of emerging uses of online technologies for management education (e.g., Bigelow, 1999; Budd, 2002; Rahm and Reed, 1997; Shrivastava, 1999) to studies of increasing conceptual (Proserpio and Gioia, 2007; Rungtusanatham et al., 2004), methodological (Arbaugh, 2005b; Klein et al., 2006; Webb et al., 2005), qualitative (Alavi and Gallupe, 2003; Brower, 2003), and/or quantitative rigor (Arbaugh and Benbunan-Fich, 2006; Arbaugh and Rau, 2007; Martins and Kellermanns, 2004; Sitzmann et al., 2006). Clearly this topic is developing rapidly into a delineated body of work for management education research.

Online management education programs incorporate information technology that combines satellite broadcasting with videoconferencing, the Internet, and PC networking for a hands-on management experience (Wankel and DeFillippi, 2003). The successful integration of these technologies (Martins and Kellermanns, 2004) and the factors that lead to effective online instruction have been studied by numerous scholars in management education (Arbaugh, 2000c, 2001, 2004, 2005b; Bocchi et al., 2004; Clouse and Evans, 2003; Conaway et al., 2005; Eom et al., 2006). Factors found to influence student acceptance of coursework using Web-based

information and communication technologies into the instructional processes include perceived incentives to use it, perceived faculty encouragement to use it, and peer encouragement to use it. It has also been argued that awareness of the technology's capabilities, availability of technical support, and prior computer and Web-based experience were positively related to perceived ease of use of technology (Lowe and Holton, 2005; Martins and Kellermanns, 2004). The theoretical and conceptual frameworks proposed by several authors suggest that online delivery formats are highly supportive of the use of asynchronous methods and collaborative learning activities (Alavi and Gallupe, 2003; Alavi et al., 1997; Leidner and Jarvenpaa, 1995; Rungtusanatham et al., 2004).

Online management programs are being implemented into business curricula regularly, and many business schools have invested heavily in these initiatives (Dos Santos and Wright, 2001; Ives and Jarvenpaa, 1996; Leidner and Jarvenpaa, 1995; Shrivastava, 1999). However, although substantial progress has been made in the last decade, there are numerous issues yet to be addressed sufficiently in this rapidly emerging stream of management education research. Topics requiring additional attention include increased methodological rigor (Arbaugh and Benbunan-Fich, 2006; Bernard et al., 2004), further testing of existing theoretical frameworks (Alavi and Leidner, 2001), focused consideration of blended learning environments (Graham, 2006; Bonk et al., 2006), and analysis of the unique contributions of program-level, discipline-level, and content effects (Warell and Arbaugh, 2007). The rest of this chapter presents a review of the research on technological characteristics of online courses, the characteristics and roles of students and instructors, and the learning processes essential to quality online management education courses. A structural framework of the chapter is provided in Table 12.1. The chapter concludes with a discussion of the issues for further research and suggests a research agenda for business educators.

**Table 12.1   Chapter framework**

| Technological characteristics | Participant characteristics | Course structure and conduct characteristics |
|---|---|---|
| 1. Technology Acceptance and Online Management Education | 1. Students | 1. Online vs. Face-to-face Learning |
| 2. Use and Variety of Media | A. Age | 2. Blended Learning |
| | B. Gender | 3. Discipline/Course Level Effects |
| | C. Prior Online Learning Experience | 4. Participant Interaction |
| | D. Skill Level with Technology | A. Interaction with Content |
| | E. Learning Style | B. Interaction with Instructors |
| | 2. Instructors | C. Interaction with Peers |
| | | D. Interaction with Interface |
| | | 5. Collaborative Learning |

Significant issues for future research
1  Greater use and testing of theoretical framework
2  'Upgraded' measures of technology
3  More robust research methods
4  Program-level effects
5  Uniqueness of online management education relative to other disciplines
6  Instructor effects in online management education
7  Global perspectives on online management education

## TECHNOLOGICAL CHARACTERISTICS OF ONLINE MANAGEMENT EDUCATION

Although much of the literature in online management education has lacked a common framework, this is not the case in the area of user perceptions of the electronic communication systems. Several studies in management education research have used the Technology Acceptance Model (TAM) as a grounding framework, either in its original form (Davis, 1989) or in the extended model (Venkatesh and Davis, 2000). The TAM contends that actual system usage is predicated on users perceiving a technology to be both useful and easy to use. These perceptions influence the users' intentions to use the technology, which in turn influences whether they actually will use it. This research suggests that although it may have limited predictive power for novice online learners or early course management systems (Arbaugh, 2000c; Arbaugh and Duray, 2002), the TAM has emerged as a useful framework for explaining course management system usage and satisfaction with the Internet as an educational delivery medium (Landry et al.,

2006). Martins and Kellermanns (2004) found that although perceived usefulness and perceived ease of use of WebCT did influence students' attitudes toward the software and its usage, peer encouragement to use the system was an even stronger influence. Davis and Wong (2007) found that perceived usefulness and ease of use had moderate effects on student intentions to use the CECIL system at the University of Auckland, but that student perceptions of flow and playfulness of the system (which, in turn, was highly influenced by the speed of the software) was a stronger predictor of intentions to use. In studies of relatively experienced online learners, Arbaugh (2004, 2005b) found that perceived usefulness and ease of use of blackboard increased dramatically between the first and subsequent online course experiences, and that these variables significantly predicted student satisfaction with the Internet as an educational delivery medium. However, because studies examining a possible TAM-learning relationship have yet to find significant results, the TAM has been less useful for predicting learning outcomes (Arbaugh, 2000c, 2005b).

## USE AND VARIETY OF MEDIA

Although the impacts of various types of media in online learning environments have been studied extensively in the instructional design and technology literatures (Hall et al., 2003; Wisher and Curnow, 2003), they have been relatively ignored in the online management education literature. Historically, web-based management education courses have relied extensively on text-based transmission of course content and discussion. This is true for a number of reasons, such as historically limited bandwidth, concerns over minimum hardware/software requirements for students, and the learning curve required for both students and instructors. Such factors may, in part, explain why initial studies of course management software found that e-mail-driven systems produced higher learning outcomes than did multimedia systems (Alavi et al., 2002). However, with increasing bandwith availability and the introduction of wireless and virtual reality technologies (Kirkley and Kirkley, 2006), alternatives to the purely text-based online learning environment are increasing rapidly. As a result, management education researchers are beginning to examine the effects of differing types of media on online course outcomes. In one of these initial studies, Arbaugh (2002) found that the use of varying numbers of audio and/or video clips in a study of 13 web-based courses was not a significant predictor of either student learning or course satisfaction. However, subsequent studies have shown that media variety positively predicts delivery medium satisfaction (Arbaugh and Rau, 2007), and both positively (Arbaugh, 2005b) and negatively (Arbaugh and Rau, 2007) predicts student learning.

## PARTICIPANT CHARACTERISTICS AND BEHAVIORS IN ONLINE MANAGEMENT EDUCATION STUDENTS

Although some researchers have designed instruments and approaches to test for whether students are adequately prepared to take online courses (Parnell and Carraher, 2003; Schniederjans and Kim, 2005), most studies in online management education to date have focused on programs that do not conduct pre-screening assessments. One benefit of such an approach is that the results of the findings have higher generalizability. The more commonly examined student characteristics include age, gender, prior online learning experience, technological skill level, and learning styles.

*Age.* Although some research suggests that online learners on average tend to be older than traditional students (Hiltz and Shea, 2005), student age either tends not to be examined or is found to have little relationship to course outcomes in online management education. Perhaps this relative lack of research attention to age effects in management education is due to the course level constraints imposed by the research designs. Presently, there are few studies that examine undergraduate and graduate courses simultaneously (see Benbunan-Fich and Hiltz, 2002, for an exception); therefore age effects tend to be either right- or left-censored. However, there is increasing evidence that student age may not matter in online management education. Although a few limited scale recent studies have found positive age effects (i.e., Silberg and Lennon, 2006), the vast majority of recent studies have found no relationship between student age and online course outcomes in management education (Anstine and Skidmore, 2005; Arbaugh, 2002, 2005b; Hwang and Arbaugh, 2006; Lu et al., 2003; Webb et al., 2005; Williams et al., 2006). Although some might interpret this non-finding as a victory for the age neutrality of online management education, we believe that the state of this research is more indicative of a lack of methodological rigor that we will discuss in detail later in this chapter.

*Gender.* Men's and women's language use in online communication can lead to mis-understandings, as computer-mediated communication does not provide physical cues to signal biological gender. Men generally choose language that is more direct and confrontational, while women choose to be less hostile and more personal (Wolfe, 1999). For example, women's language use in online courses tends to develop social interdependence (Tannen, 1990) and enhance conversation (Jaffe et al., 1995), which men may view as evidence of women's lesser credibility and intelligence (Stewart et al., 1999). Often online communicators unconsciously present information about their gender in their interactions (Herring, 2001). Although media often can filter language, gender-related characteristics found in face-to-face environments also are found in computer-mediated communication (Ferris, 1996; Herring, 2000, 2001).

Gender effects have received more research attention than have age effects in studies of online management education. Previous reviews of the online management education literature suggest that women were slower to adopt the computer as an information tool, but certainly had caught up to men in electronic communication usage by the beginning of the 21st century (Arbaugh and Stelzer, 2003). However, although initial studies of gender effects in online management education suggested that the medium was a female-friendly environment (Arbaugh, 2000b, 2000d), more recent research suggests that findings on gender effects may be inconclusive. Some studies have found that women tend to perform better than men in technology-assisted courses and/or have more positive attitudes toward online learning (Cybinski and Selvanathan, 2005; Friday et al., 2006; Silberg and Lennon, 2006). Hwang and Arbaugh (2006) found that in blended management education courses, men were much more likely to seek feedback by asking questions in class, while women were more likely to seek feedback through regular and intense participation in online forums. Conversely, in a study of over 50 online MBA courses, Arbaugh (2005b) found that men reported higher perceived learning. Other studies have found no relationship between gender and learning outcomes (Anstine and Skidmore, 2005; Arbaugh and Rau, 2007; Larson, 2002; Williams et al., 2006). Other research

suggests that gender effects may be subject to the instructional methods employed in a course. Although they found no gender-based differences in final grades, Benbunan-Fich and Arbaugh (2006a) found that men reported higher perceived learning in courses delivered in an objectivist instructional mode. Collectively, these studies provide more support for online management education being gender neutral than being age neutral, but this conclusion is based upon a somewhat limited number of studies.

*Prior Online Learning Experience.* Initial studies of online management education reported positive reactions as well as isolation, anxiety, and frustration with the experience from both students and instructors (Arbaugh, 2000b; Berger, 1999; Chizmar and Walbert, 1999; Hara and Kling, 2000; McGorry, 2002; Salmon, 2000). However, as the use of technology has become more prevalent in management education (Fornaciari et al., 1999; Proserpio and Gioia, 2007) and subsequent studies have been able to include learners with more varied amounts of online learning experience, more positive results have begun to emerge (Arbaugh, 2005a; Arbaugh and Duray, 2002; Drago et al., 2005). However, these improvements in student attitudes toward online management education may not require extensive online experience. In an analysis of students that participated in online learning surveys for up to seven online MBA courses, Arbaugh (2004) found that the most significant changes in student perceptions of the flexibility, interaction, course software, and general satisfaction with the Internet as an educational delivery medium occurred between the first and second course. Kock et al. (2007) recently found that although performance differences in online and classroom-based offerings of the same course were present in their initial stages, these performance differences were gone by the time the classes were completed. Allan's (2007) study found that novice adult online learners do encounter an initial learning curve of being overwhelmed with keeping up with the course, but that they were able to take more control of their time as they became more familiar with the delivery medium. This type of learning curve may explain why prior student online experience was not a predictor of course outcomes in subsequent research (Arbaugh and Benbunan-Fich, 2007; Arbaugh and Rau, 2007; Davis and Wong, 2007; Williams et al., 2006). The increased availability and accessibility of technology also may be reducing student anxiety toward technology-mediated learning. Recent studies have found that students less experienced with virtual learning environments were favorably disposed toward the prospect of future online learning activities (Cappel and Hayden, 2004; Clark and Gibb, 2006; Dineen, 2005; Walker and Jeurissen, 2003). Such seemingly divergent findings suggest that it is important for researchers to control for prior online learning experience when designing their studies.

*Skill with Technology.* Perhaps it is because much of online management education now is conducted using a course management system (Martins and Kellermanns, 2004), but technological skill level generally has not been a predictor of online learning outcomes (Arbaugh and Benbunan-Fich, 2007; Berry, 2002; Clark and Gibb, 2006; Lemak et al., 2005; Yoo et al., 2002). However, skill with technology may have indirect effects on course outcomes. Davis and Wong (2007) found that technological skill level influenced students' sense of playfulness or flow with an online course management system, which in turn influenced their perceptions of the usefulness of the system and their intentions to use it. Such findings suggest that skill level with technology may be a significant predictor only in virtual learning environments that do not employ course management systems. However, with forecasts of online learning becoming increasingly mobile due to the use of wireless technologies and handheld devices (Bonk et al., 2006), technological skill level could become an important factor for future research to examine.

*Learning Styles.* May and Short (2003) suggested that faculty should address the issue of learning style differences in online undergraduate management courses by providing content in a variety of formats and using multiple types of assignments to assess learning. Although the concept of tailoring instructional approaches to student learning styles is not new to management education or online learning (Armstrong, 2000; Armstrong et al., 2004; Hiltz and Shea, 2005; Riding and Sadler-Smith, 1992), research directly examining the effects of learning styles in online management education is surprisingly limited. Those studies that have examined learning style in management education have tended to find that it is not a strong predictor of course outcomes (Drago et al., 2005; Lu et al., 2003; Marks and Sibley, 2006). Eom and colleagues (2006) recently found that students with visual and read/write learning styles were more satisfied with the Internet as a delivery medium and were more likely to feel that learning outcomes in online courses were at least comparable to those in classrooms than were students with other learning styles. Even in this study, the conclusions for business students are somewhat limited because they comprised less than 25 percent of the respondents. One possible explanation for the lack of a relationship between learning style and learning outcome may be degree program-related. The studies finding no relationship at all were conducted using samples of MBA students in program formats other than a full-time classroom-based setting. It is quite likely that such students already have been socialized regarding the appearance and uses of electronic communication through their work experiences (Atkinson and Kydd, 1997; Gefen and Straub, 1997); therefore they may be able to adapt more readily than undergraduate students to online learning environments.

## INSTRUCTORS

Faculty have long been considered to be the 'neglected resource' in distance education (Dillon and Walsh, 1992). Unfortunately, to date this also appears to be the case in online management education research (Alavi and

Gallupe, 2003). Studies that examine effects such as faculty age, gender, ethnicity, and/or skill level are essentially non-existent. This is because, in part, many published studies used the same instructor or a small number of instructors, thereby limiting opportunities for variance in instructor characteristics (Anstine and Skidmore, 2005; Webb et al., 2005). However, as more robust research designs have been developed, opportunities for examining faculty characteristics have increased. One faculty characteristic that has begun to receive research attention is prior online teaching experience. To date, research suggests that at worst, prior online teaching experience is not a bad thing. Instructor online experience may be a strong predictor of student satisfaction with the Internet as an educational medium and a strong predictor of learning relative to subject matter effects (Arbaugh, 2005a; Arbaugh and Rau, 2007; Drago et al., 2002), but its effects appear to be less significant for learning than are behavioral characteristics such as participant interaction (Arbaugh, 2005b).

Collectively these studies suggest that individual characteristics, be they of learners or of instructors, may not be consistent predictors of course outcomes in online management education. This suggests that characteristics such as course design, structure, and conduct may be more significant factors, to which we turn our attention.

## ONLINE COURSE STRUCTURE, DESIGN, AND CONDUCT

### Online vs. face-to-face courses

Although 'online vs. face-to-face' learning experiences generated numerous studies in management education around the beginning of the 21st century (e.g., Alavi et al., 1997; Arbaugh, 2000b; Berry, 2002; Bigelow, 1999; Clouse and Evans, 2003; Dellana et al., 2000; Friday et al., 2006; McLaren, 2004; Piccoli et al., 2001; Warkentin et al., 1997), there is increasing evidence in management education that online learning is as effective, and may be even more effective, than classroom-based learning. Even initial differences in learning outcomes of the two delivery media appear to diminish as students acquire familiarity with online learning (Kock et al., 2007). Much of this evidence is the result of two recent meta-analyses. Zhao and colleagues' (2005) analysis of 51 journal articles comparing distance and classroom courses found that studies published after 1998 showed significantly higher learning outcomes for distance courses, and that there was no significant difference between distance and classroom graduate courses. Furthermore, they found that business courses were more likely than other disciplines to find positive outcomes for distance education. More specific to online and classroom business training and/or education courses, Sitzmann and colleagues' (2006) recent meta-analysis found that web-based instruction was 6 percent more effective than classroom instruction for teaching declarative knowledge. They found that the two methods essentially were equal for teaching procedural knowledge, and learners generally were satisfied equally with both methods as education delivery mediums. Although some studies with conflicting results suggest concerns regarding the performance of students online in more quantitatively-oriented courses (Anstine and Skidmore, 2005; Cybinski and Selvanathan, 2005; Grandzol, 2004), these findings collectively suggest somewhat conclusively that online learning is a viable means of instruction in management education. Such findings also suggest that introducing online activities into face-to-face courses could even be beneficial, resulting in what are increasingly being referred to as blended learning environments (Bonk and Graham, 2006).

## BLENDED LEARNING ENVIRONMENTS

Although recent publications suggest that research in blended learning is a recent phenomenon (Bonk and Graham, 2006; Picciano and Dziuban, 2007), a closer examination of the management education literature suggests that studies of blended learning actually have been taking place for some time. Initial research in management education suggests encouraging results for the use of blended learning environments. Introducing online elements or exercises has been positively associated with course outcomes in numerous studies (Balotsky and Christensen, 2004; Clouse and Evans, 2003; Ford et al., 2007; Hwang and Arbaugh, 2006; Webb et al., 2005), and blended courses have fared well in studies comparing them with classroom and online courses (Klein et al., 2006; Terry, 2007; Webb et al., 2005). Other benefits of blending in management education include increased confidence in working in virtual project teams (Dineen, 2005), increased learner control of the educational experience (Klein et al., 2006), and enhanced dialogue skill development (Eveleth and Baker-Eveleth, 2003). Initial research also has identified characteristics that influence successful blending, including faculty-driven rather than administration-driven blending initiatives (Alavi and Gallupe, 2003), student peer encouragement (Martins and Kellermanns, 2004), the perceived usefulness of course management systems for accessing content (Landry et al., 2006; Martins and Kellermanns, 2004), the use of experiential learning exercises (Pauleen et al., 2004; Proserpio and Gioia, 2007), and adequate technical and administrative support (Alavi and Gallupe, 2003; Yoo et al., 2002).

To date, much of the research in blended management education environments suggests similar issues and results as those in online environments. Although the flexibility of blending often is mentioned as an advantage (Cappel and Hayden, 2004; Graham, 2006), concerns about isolation and transferability of particular concepts to the online environment also persist (Patel and Patel, 2006). This suggests that continued study of online management education environments will provide insights not only for effective delivery of online courses, but also for faculty and administrators seeking to blend online and classroom-based content.

## DISCIPLINE/COURSE- LEVEL EFFECTS

To date, although some authors have made compelling arguments for why management education-related topics such as organizational behavior are quite amenable to online delivery (Bigelow, 1999; Meisel and Marx, 1999), comparative studies of discipline- and course-level effects have been somewhat limited. Initial studies suggest disciplinary effects may not have as large an effect on learning outcomes as do instructor experience and behaviors (Arbaugh, 2005a; Drago et al., 2002), but that disciplinary effects may have a strong effect on student satisfaction with online learning. Arbaugh and Rau (2007) recently found that disciplinary effects explained 67 percent of the variance in student satisfaction with the educational delivery medium in a sample of 40 online MBA courses. Initial evidence also suggests that non-quantitative courses may be better received than quantitative courses online, but whether this is due to the delivery medium, the subject matter, or both is still unclear (Anstine and Skidmore, 2005; Arbaugh and Rau, 2007).

Very few studies of online management education have examined both undergraduate and MBA students simultaneously (see Lemak et al., 2005 as an example of such a study that examined distance education via compressed video). However, comparing results of studies using undergraduate vs. graduate business samples suggest some preliminary results. These studies suggest that the behaviors of undergraduate management students in online environments may be more peer driven (Baugher et al., 2003; Hwang and Arbaugh, 2006; Martins and Kellermanns, 2004), in part because undergraduates may be less self-disciplined (Clark and Gibb, 2006). Initial evidence also suggests that online environments may be friendlier to introverted undergraduates than to extroverts (Fornaciari and Matthews, 2000; Schniederjans and Kim, 2005). Conversely, MBA students appear to be rather self-motivated in the online environment (Patel and Patel, 2006). Therefore, the flexibility of asynchronous communication has proven to be particularly attractive for this student population (Arbaugh, 2000a; Arbaugh and Duray, 2002; Dunbar, 2004; Marks et al., 2005). Also, participant interaction appears to be particularly important in MBA courses (Arbaugh, 2005b; Arbaugh and Rau, 2007; Benbunan-Fich and Arbaugh, 2006b; Bocchi et al., 2004; Brower, 2003; Dineen, 2005; Hartman et al., 2002; Peltier et al., 2003; Lemak et al., 2005; Williams et al., 2006; Yukselturk and Top, 2005–2006), a topic that is discussed in the following section.

## PARTICIPANT INTERACTION IN ONLINE MANAGEMENT EDUCATION

Collaborative group activity, or the 'interactivity' among and between online participants, is an essential characteristic that distinguishes online courses from other traditional classroom-based face-to-face learning activities (Garrison and Anderson, 2003), and is the most frequently discussed topic among online educators. It may consist of a learner accessing a page of text via an Internet interface and reading the content, or it may require the learner and learning system to respond dynamically to each other (Hirumi, 2004). The design and sequence of e-learning activities must be meaningful to students to promote online interaction. Since learning is largely a social activity and humans are social animals, many students need group activity to make their learning meaningful (Leonard and DeLacey, 2002).

Unlike traditional face-to-face formats, which tend to feature the instructor as a 'talking head' with little input from the group, interactions of various kinds are at the center of the online learning experience, particularly in management education (Mundell and Pennarola, 1999). Interactions and group activity facilitate building online communities through the creation of social and cognitive presence, thus promoting the acquisition of knowledge and the realization of higher-order learning outcomes (Swan, 2002). Online interaction research falls into

four areas: interaction with content (Moore, 1989), interaction with instructors (Moore, 1989), interaction with peers (Moore, 1989), and interaction with the interface or CMS (Hillman et al., 1994). Next, we review the extent to which each area has been examined in online management education.

*Interaction with Content.* Studies of design principles, design factors, and differing kinds of content suggest certain criteria that promote effective online learning. For example, learning concepts vs. techniques is likely to elicit multiple perspectives and disciplined inquiry based on reflection and interaction (Benbunan-Fich and Hiltz, 1999; Garrison and Anderson, 2003; Parker and Gemino, 2001; Picciano, 2002). Although learner-content interaction has been relatively underexamined in online management education, emerging theoretical frameworks are considering it more explicitly (Hardaway and Scamell, 2005; Peltier et al., 2003). Rungtusanatham and colleagues' (2004) typology specifically addresses issues such as learner control of content and opportunities for double loop learning. Such conceptual treatments suggest that learner-content interaction in management education may receive greater research attention in the near future.

*Interaction with Instructors.* Survey data on interactions with instructors point to strong correlations between learners' perceived interactions, perceived learning, and overall course satisfaction in other disciplines (Jiang and Ting, 2000; Picciano, 1998; Richardson and Swan, 2003; Swan et al., 2000). Instructors' roles such as managerial, social, pedagogical, and technical (Berge, 1995), organizational, social, and intellectual (Paulsen, 1995), and instructors' abilities to facilitate discussions (Rossman, 1999), are cited as factors that contribute to successful online learning experiences. The changing roles and teaching presence of instructors also dictate successful course outcomes (Anderson et al., 2001; Shea et al., 2003; Shea et al., 2004). Teaching presence and the importance of 'restrained presence' have been found to influence the direction of cognitive and social processes in collaborative learning activities (Vandergrift, 2002; Wu, 2003). An instructor's ability to realize personally meaningful and educationally worthwhile student outcomes depends on student perceptions of supportive, timely, and appropriate feedback (Kashy et al., 2003; Riccomini, 2002).

In contrast with learner-content interaction, learner-instructor interaction has received substantial attention in online management education research. The findings of this research emphatically suggest that learner-instructor interaction is one of the strongest predictors of student learning (Arbaugh, 2000c, 2005b; Arbaugh and Benbunan-Fich, 2007; Drago et al., 2002; Bocchi et al., 2004; Eom et al., 2006) and delivery medium satisfaction (Arbaugh, 2000a, 2002, 2005b; Eom et al., 2006; Hartman et al., 2002). In fact, results from some studies suggest that learner-instructor interaction may be the primary variable for predicting online course learning outcomes (Arbaugh and Rau, 2007; Marks et al., 2005).

*Interaction with Peers.* Compared with more traditional forms of instruction, students perceive online discussion to be more equitable and more democratic (Harasim, 1990; Levin et al., 1990; Mundell and Pennarola, 1999), and more reflective and mindful (Hiltz, 1994; Poole, 2000). They also link perceived learning with the percent of the course grade based on discussion (Hawisher and Pemberton, 1997; Jiang and Ting, 2000; Picciano, 1998; Swan et al., 2000).

Studies have found that participants in asynchronous communication project their identities into their communications and create social presence (Garrison et al., 2001; Gunawardena and Zittle, 1997; Poole, 2000; Richardson and Swan, 2003; Anderson et al., 2001; Walther, 1994). In terms of interaction and performance, perceived social presence, perceived interactions, and perceived learning all are correlated (Picciano, 2002), but perceived social presence is not correlated with either actual interactions or actual performance. The researchers suggest that students who perceive high social presence from peer participants and instructors perform

significantly better in online courses (Shea et al., 2003, 2004).

Studies that have examined learner-learner interaction in online management education generally have found that it positively predicts course learning outcomes (Arbaugh, 2002; Arbaugh and Rau, 2007; Borthick and Jones, 2000; Larson, 2002; Peltier et al., 2003; Williams et al., 2006; Yukselturk and Top, 2005–2006) and that it tends to increase as a course progresses (Driver, 2002; Eveleth and Baker-Eveleth, 2003; Yoo et al., 2002). However, whether it is a stronger predictor than learner-instructor interaction is unclear because studies that have examined both have produced mixed results. Some studies have found that learner-learner interaction is the stronger predictor (Arbaugh, 2002; Peltier et al., 2003), and others have found that learner-instructor interaction is the stronger predictor (Arbaugh and Rau, 2007; Marks et al., 2005). Regardless of which is the direct predictor, it is clear that even in settings where learner-learner interaction is the stronger predictor, instructors still play at least a structural role through the manner in which they design and organize the course, and their role as content expert should not be underestimated (Arbaugh and Hwang, 2006; Brower, 2003; Sarker and Nicholson, 2005). Therefore, findings in the area of participant interaction strongly suggest the importance of instructors in online management education.

*Interaction with the Interface.* Although some researchers question whether learner-interface interaction is a distinctive construct or a component of other types of interaction (Anderson, 2003), advances in mobile technologies and increased use of blended learning environments suggest that the dimension will be increasingly important and more likely to be a distinct dimension of online management education in the future (Bonk et al., 2006; Proserpio and Gioia, 2007). Interface studies of multimedia learning provide scientific explanations on the effectiveness of differing media combinations for supporting student learning (Mayer, 2001). The conclusions from multiple studies from other disciplines replicated over 20 years suggest that people learn better from animation and narration and that better transfer occurs when the pace of the presentation is learner controlled. Numerous experimental studies examine virtual media systems and find that various interfaces may support student problem-solving better than traditional print-based sources (Chang et al., 2002; Gutl and Pivec, 2003; Lin, 2002).

To date, learner-interface interaction has yet to receive the attention that interaction between participants has in online management education research. Initial studies have shown mixed support for learner-interface interaction and course outcomes in online management education research. A study of senior managers by Alavi and colleagues (2002) suggests that interfaces that incorporate features commonly used in work settings may yield higher learning outcomes than do more robust, proprietary interfaces. Arbaugh and Benbunan-Fich (2007) found that learner-interface interaction predicted both perceived learning and delivery medium satisfaction, but Arbaugh and Rau (2007) found support only for its relationship to perceived learning.

*Collaborative Learning.* A report called *Collaborative Learning in Web-based Instruction* (Comeaux et al., 1998) suggests that Internet-based technology tools can enhance collaborative learning activities. The authors discuss the importance of integrating student communication interactions to facilitate learning (as cited in Spires and Jaeger, 2002):

> Students think and act in ways that promote their own learning and that of others. Collaborative learning is enhanced when students are fully engaged in the activities of the class, are engaged with each other and the subject matter and take risks (p. 3).

An online collaborative learning environment can challenge students to use discussion and debate to offer explanations, interpretations, and resolutions to problems (Alavi, 1994). It can promote an active construction of knowledge with members of the learning community and an internalization of meaning and understanding (Whipp et al., 2002). The discussion and interaction can reveal multiple perspectives and enable the student community to arrive at a more comprehensive conception and understanding of knowledge (Alavi, 1994; Mezirow, 1991).

Although several early studies and frameworks supported the use of collaborative learning in online management education (Alavi, 1994; Alavi et al., 1995; Alavi et al., 1997; Benbunan-Fich, 2002; Chidambaram, 1996; Hodgson and McConnell, 1995; Leidner and Jarvenpaa, 1995; Shrivastava, 1999), research comparing its effectiveness to other teaching and learning approaches has been surprisingly lacking until relatively recently. A multi-disciplinary three-year study that included business courses (Hiltz et al., 2000) found support for collaborative learning approaches. More recent research directly examines the assumption that collaborative approaches are the desired method for online management education and suggests a need for distinctions between delivering course content and student learning activities. A recent critique of the role of community in online management learning (Hodgson and Reynolds, 2005) argues that instead of enhancing learning, the push to build 'community' may in fact limit learning because of pressures for consensus and conformity. They advocate creating subgroups that allow learners to encourage and support the ability to cultivate and learn from differences. Studies by Arbaugh and Benbunan-Fich (2006, 2007) and Benbunan-Fich and Arbaugh (2006a/b) suggest that online management education courses designed with the combination of objectivist-oriented content delivery mechanisms and collaborative learning activities instead of purely collaborative approaches produce the most positive course outcomes.

## SIGNIFICANT ISSUES FOR FUTURE RESEARCH

Including an entire chapter devoted to the state of research in online management education is noteworthy; such was not possible less than a decade ago. Clearly this literature has come a very long way in a relatively short time. A summary, by section, of the most noteworthy findings of our review is presented in Table 12.2. However, although this review suggests that there has been significant progress made in online management education research during the first decade of the 21st century, it is clear that this is still an emerging body of research in need of substantially enhanced conceptual linkages and methodological refinement (Arbaugh and Benbunan-Fich, 2004;

Hodgson and Watland, 2004a, 2004b). The following paragraphs provide suggestions for future researchers interested in studying online management education.

## GREATER USE AND TESTING OF THEORETICAL FRAMEWORKS

One of the more surprising conclusions from this review is the extent to which the research has been conducted without the grounding of conceptual frameworks of online learning to

**Table 12.2   Significant findings of the review**

Technological characteristics:
1  Technology Acceptance and Online Management Education - TAM is the most commonly used theoretical framework in online management education research, but the TAM-course outcome relationship varies substantially across studies.
2  Use and Variety of Media – As online learning evolves beyond text-based only formats, media variety is beginning to receive research attention.

Participant characteristics:
1  Students
    (a) Age – Student age generally has been neither examined nor found to be a significant predictor of management education course outcomes.
    (b) Gender – Several initial studies found online learning in management education to be female friendly, but recent research on gender effects has been inconclusive
    (c) Prior Online Learning Experience – As more learners become experienced in online learning, we are beginning to see that experience effects predict learning outcomes.
    (d) Skill Level with Technology – Skill with technology hasn't had direct effects on online learning outcomes, but it may have indirect effects.
    (e) Learning Style – Learning styles have not received much research attention in online management education, and those studies that have examined it tend not to find a relationship between learning style and course outcomes.
2  Instructors – There has been very little research on instructor effects in online management education. The research that does exist suggests a relationship between prior instructor online experience and course outcomes.

Course structure and conduct characteristics:
1  Online vs. Face-to-face Learning – At worst, online management education yields outcomes equivalent to classroom education, and recent meta-analyses suggest that online learning may yield superior outcomes in business education courses.
2  Blended Learning – Blended learning environments tend to fare well in studies comparing them with purely online and purely classroom-based learning environments.
3  Discipline/Course Level Effects – Disciplinary effects have received limited attention in online management education, as have course/program-level effects.
4  Participant Interaction
    (a) Interaction with Content – Relatively unexamined in online management education, although it is considered in emerging theoretical frameworks.
    (b) Interaction with Instructors – Probably the strongest predictor of learning outcomes in online management education research to date.
    (c) Interaction with Peers – Another strong predictor of learning outcomes in online management education, but findings regarding its importance relative to interaction with instructors are inconclusive.
    (d) Interaction with Interface – Has yet to receive extensive research attention in online management education, but trends toward mobile learning suggest it will become increasingly important.
5  Collaborative Learning – Initial research found support for the use of collaborative learning approaches in online management education, but recent studies suggest that distinctions need to be made between content delivery mode and learning/assessment activities.

(Hodgson and Watland, 2004a). In earlier times, this could have been excused by factors such as the lack of general theories of management education (Lemak et al., 2005) or a still emerging cadre of researchers or online management education (Arbaugh and Benbunan-Fich, 2004). However, as this review suggests, the validity of such rationale is now long past, especially if one operates in 'internet time.' There are several frameworks that can be used to drive future research, from both within and outside management education. Leidner and Jarvenpaa's (1995) virtual learning spaces framework has been oft-cited, but yet to be substantially operationalized. Initial studies that have been grounded in the framework suggest that it is useful for explaining online learning outcomes (Arbaugh and Benbunan-Fich, 2006; Benbunan-Fich and Arbaugh, 2006b). Other conceptual frameworks derived in management education settings that could influence future research include Alavi and Leidner's (2001) cognitive information processing model, Benbunan-Fich's (2002) pedagogy-location-mode model, Rungtusanatham and colleagues' (2004) content-delivery-learning model, Sharda and colleagues' (2004) Computer Supported Collaborative Learning in Immersive Presence (CSCLIP) framework, and DeLone and McLean's (2003) information systems success model, adapted for e-learning by Holsapple and Lee-Post (2006). A framework that is gaining acceptance amongst education scholars is the Community of Inquiry framework (Garrison et al., 2000). This framework posits that effective online learning is a function of the interaction of three elements: teaching presence, social presence, and cognitive presence. Initial studies using this framework in online management education research have yielded promising results (Arbaugh, 2007; Arbaugh and Hwang, 2006; Heckman and Annabi, 2005) and encourage use of the framework for grounding of future studies.

Although further theory-grounded research certainly will be welcome, we think that future online management education researchers face a significant challenge in developing, applying, and operationalizing theoretical frameworks that comprehensively capture all the factors that influence online learning. Frameworks grounded in the information systems often focus on the technological aspects of online learning to the neglect of interaction of participants or the nature of course content. Frameworks grounded in educational theory often focus on the behaviors of course participants to the neglect of technological or disciplinary effects. Frameworks driven by the instructional design literature tend to focus on the development and positioning of course content to the neglect of how participants use the content or the technological platforms upon which the content is placed. Trying to capture each of these dimensions as comprehensively as those from the particular disciplines would likely result in data collection tools that are so long and require so much time to complete that they would either result in disastrous response rates or severely limit the sampling frame of studies to single course samples. Therefore, we particularly applaud the recent efforts of scholars that have developed frameworks that consider each of these dimensions generally and relatively efficiently, such as those by Rungtusanatham and colleagues (2004), Benbunan-Fich and colleagues (2005), and Wan and colleagues (2007). Although such orientations may not capture individual elements as precisely as their disciplinary adherents might like, they do allow us to examine the entirety of the online learning experience relatively efficiently and facilitate interaction between disparate perspectives.

## 'UPGRADED' MEASURES OF TECHNOLOGY

As mentioned previously, the operationalization of the TAM presently is the predominant measure for technological effects in online management education research. However, future use of the TAM in online management education research is subject to two significant concerns. First, the management information systems literature is moving toward more comprehensive and integrative models of technology adoption, specifically the Unified Theory of Acceptance and Use of Technology (UTAUT) model (Venkatesh et al., 2003). UTAUT integrates perspectives from eight theoretical frameworks of technology adoption into one parsimonious framework which suggests that behavioral intention of technology adoption is predicted by performance expectancy, effort expectancy, social influence and facilitating conditions, and moderated by age, gender, prior experience with the technology, and the extent to which adoption of the technology is voluntary. In addition to measuring constructs related to technology adoption, we are encouraged that this framework incorporates moderator variables that we feel should be used as control variables in studies of online management education regardless of whether a researcher is examining technology-related issues. Modified versions of the UTAUT survey items already have been used to examine attitudes toward and intention to use WebCT by marketing students (Robinson, 2006), and we encourage its adoption for examining attitudes toward technology in studies of online management education.

Second, although we support the usage of such frameworks, we feel that they likely will need to be modified for studying online learning environments. Consistent with the development of the theory driving models of technology adoption, such approaches tend to focus on whether a person will use the course management system. Given that participation in online discussions commonly is used as a grading criterion for these courses (Palloff and Pratt, 2001), questions regarding voluntary usage may not be completely appropriate or the primary factor for examining the role of technology in the online learning environment. This suggests that if variables predicting technology adoption are to be useful for predicting online learning effectiveness, future scholars will need to develop stronger conceptual linkages among the factors driving the decision to use a technology, usage of the technology, and

direct linkages to those drivers and course outcomes.

We also see a need for future online management education researchers to broaden their study of technological effects to include conceptualizations from other disciplinary perspectives. As the variety of media used in online courses becomes more diverse (Arbaugh, 2005b; Proserpio and Gioia, 2007), measures of technology will need to address more than participant attitudes toward the course management system. Therefore, measures of technological effects in online management education might be better studied by using measures with other conceptual grounding. Perhaps borrowing approaches from the educational literature, such as Mayer's (2006) Multimedia Learning Theory, would provide additional relevant measures.

Finally, as mobile technologies become increasingly common and broadband capacities continue to improve, it is likely that questions related to learner-interface interaction will become increasingly important to online management education (Bonk et al., 2006). Ironically, this situation could provide opportunities for online learning researchers to draw upon research on historical methods of distance education. As video capabilities via the Internet improve, will findings initially developed from research on distance courses in management education using compressed/interactive video technologies (i.e., Alavi et al., 1997; Brindle and Levesque, 2000; Lemak et al., 2005; Webster and Hackley, 1997; Yoo et al., 2002) find renewed relevance as we attempt to address questions of media variety?

## MORE ROBUST RESEARCH METHODS

The first decade of the 21st century has seen substantial progress in methodological approach in online management education research. From consisting primarily of anecdotal single course experiences at the end of the 20th century, studies that include advanced methodological and analytical rigor such as multi-course, multi-disciplinary samples

(Arbaugh, 2005a; Friday et al., 2006), multilevel modeling approaches (Arbaugh and Benbunan-Fich, 2006), structural equation modeling (Davis and Wong, 2007; Martins and Kellermanns, 2004; Hwang and Arbaugh, 2006), rigorous control variables (Anstine and Skidmore, 2005; Arbaugh, 2005b), and multiple case studies (Alavi and Gallupe, 2003) are becoming increasingly common. However, although there has been progress, methodological rigor in this research stream often leaves much to be desired. Many published empirical studies fail to include even basic control variables such as age and gender, neglect to test for non-response bias, and/or rely on relatively small samples. Sample sizes of less than 100 still are not uncommon. Although these issues will likely be resolved as the field continues to mature, it merits mention that the methodological bar for this research stream is rising rapidly, whether the methods are quantitative or qualitative in nature. In fact, multiple method approaches may be necessary to advance the field appropriately (Hodgson and Watland, 2004b; Warell and Arbaugh, 2007), and researchers entering the field would be well advised to prepare accordingly. Recently, Allan (2007) provided an example of such approaches, combining the use of a survey, content analysis of participant discussion postings, and participant interviews to examine visualizations of time in networked learning communities. Considering methodological concerns regarding distance education in general (Bernard et al., 2004; Tallent-Runnels et al., 2006), this is an area where management education research has an opportunity to play a leadership role in advancing online learning research across disciplines.

## PROGRAM-LEVEL, DISCIPLINARY EFFECTS, AND ONLINE MANAGEMENT EDUCATION

Related to the point of enhanced methodological rigor is the need for more comprehensive research samples. For the most part, online learning research generally appears to operate under the assumption that course content or program level does not impact effective online learning practice. However, studies that have examined both undergraduate and graduate students have found differences in the learning outcomes of those groups (Benbunan-Fich and Hiltz, 2002). Because samples for studies of online management education tend to be exclusively graduate or undergraduate students, researchers and practitioners are left to speculate regarding differences in teaching these student populations. Therefore, studies that examine undergraduate and graduate student populations simultaneously would be particularly helpful, especially if the research incorporates findings from multiple institutions.

Future online management education researchers also could assist instructors immensely by identifying characteristics that distinguish management education from other disciplines for teaching in online settings. Although management education is hardly alone among disciplines in its failure to adequately consider the impact of 'subject matter' effects in online learning (Arbaugh, 2005a; Sarker and Nicholson, 2005; Wallace, 2002), a potential consequence of this inattention could be an over-reliance upon using the same instructional approaches for teaching topics within the management discipline. Although few would disagree that subjects such as Human Resources and Strategic Management require different instructional skills and approaches, the lack of research on examining such differences could lead some to conclude that these subjects could be taught in a similar manner online. Early attempts were made in articulating structural and delivery challenges for subjects such as organizational behavior (Bigelow, 1999), and recent research on the role of intuition in management education (Burke and Sadler-Smith, 2006) raises questions regarding educational characteristics that are unique to management education. Perhaps the organizational e-learning and training literature could be a source for useful insights regarding this question (DeRouin et al., 2005).

Such research will also likely require substantial qualitatively oriented efforts to identify these characteristics (Hodgson and Watland, 2004a; Warell and Arbaugh, 2007). The Community of Inquiry framework has benefited from such efforts to qualitatively ground its dimensions (Garrison et al., 2000; Garrison and Cleveland-Innes, 2005; Garrison et al., 2006), and those seeking to identify nuances of online management education are encouraged to follow this approach.

## INSTRUCTOR CHARACTERISTICS AND ONLINE MANAGEMENT EDUCATION

Although researchers have given substantial attention to student attitudes and perceptions in online learning, it appears that at least in management learning and education, instructors remain a relatively neglected resource (Dillon and Walsh, 1992). Beyond the interview approaches employed by Coppola and colleagues (2002) and Liu and colleagues (2005, 2007), instructor characteristics typically are not considered in online management education research. Additional studies of instructors in online management education environments could provide several benefits. First, such studies could help identify what demographic, dispositional, and behavioral characteristics are particularly desirable for online instructors. Although some researchers have designed instruments and approaches to test whether students are prepared adequately to take online courses (Parnell and Carraher, 2003; Schniederjans and Kim, 2005), similar approaches for screening potential online faculty have not been advocated. Second, such research could help faculty determine whether their pedagogical practices are having the desired effects, and whether their own perceptions of their teaching are consistent with their students' perceptions. Third, such studies would provide instructors with evidence as they lobby administrators to make changes in incentives and resource allocations to support online teaching and learning appropriately.

Advances in the study of faculty in online management education would not be difficult to include in future research. A first step could include variables such as age, gender, and prior teaching experience similar to studies that include these measurements for students. Subsequent research on faculty could include studies of faculty attitudes, perceptions, and behaviors.

## GLOBAL PERSPECTIVES ON ONLINE MANAGEMENT EDUCATION

Finally, we believe more research needs to study international and global perspectives of online management education. Paralleling the historical development of graduate management education, most studies of online management education to date have used either North American or United Kingdom research settings (for examples of other settings, see Clark and Gibb, 2006; Painter-Morland et al., 2003; Walker and Jeurissen, 2003; Yoo et al., 2002; and Yukselturk and Top, 2005–2006). However, as management education becomes a more global phenomenon, the generalizability of findings in this area of research to other regions of the world should receive increasing scrutiny. As more schools seek to deliver education via the Internet to a global audience, seek to develop indigenous online courses and degree programs, and create collaborative ventures with schools in other countries, opportunities for studies of online learning in cross-cultural or multi-national contexts certainly will increase.

## CONCLUSION: IN SEARCH OF BOUNDARY SPANNERS

In this chapter, we have identified emerging themes from a field of research that is advancing quite rapidly. Even with the rapid pace of advance, it is unfortunate that researchers in one area are not finding research in other areas that would inform their efforts. Based upon our review, we believe that future online management education researchers will need to be conversant not only with this emerging literature stream, but also with the literatures of education theory, information systems, instructional design, training and development, and discipline-based research of at least one management topic. Rather than leaving future research in this field up to a yet-to-be-conceived group of superhumans, we propose the more modest approach of encouraging researchers with interests in those streams to work together. For instance, those with interests and background in educational theory might work with more discipline-based management researchers; those from information systems perspectives could work with instructional designers; and so on. In addition to creating interesting work, these boundary spanners (Adams, 1976) likely would accelerate the rate at which the community of researchers coalesce around common measures of variables, particularly learning outcomes (Wan et al., 2007). Granted, such efforts will require a great deal of work, but this type of effort is required if research in management education is to gain the legitimacy and respect afforded discipline-based management research.

# REFERENCES

Adams, J.S. (1976) 'The structure and dynamics of behavior in boundary spanning roles', in M.D. Dunnette and L.M. Hough (eds), *The Handbook of Industrial and Organizational Psychology*. Palo Alto, CA: Consulting Psychologists Press. pp. 1175–99.

Alavi, M. (1994) 'Computer-mediated collaborative learning: An empirical evaluation', *MIS Quarterly*, 18: 159–74.

Alavi, M. and Gallupe, R.B. (2003) 'Using information technology in learning: Case studies in business and management education programs', *Academy of Management Learning and Education*, 2: 139–53.

Alavi, M. and Leidner, D.E. (2001) 'Research commentary: Technology-mediated learning – A call for greater depth and breadth of research', *Information Systems Research*, 12 (1): 1–10.

Alavi, M., Marakas, G.M. and Yoo, Y. (2002) 'A comparative study of distributed learning environments on learning outcomes', *Information Systems Research*, 13: 404–15.

Alavi, M., Wheeler, B.C. and Valacich, J.S. (1995) 'Using IT to re-engineer business education: An exploratory investigation of collaborative telelearning', *MIS Quarterly*, 19: 293–312.

Alavi, M., Yoo, Y. and Vogel, D.R. (1997) 'Using information technology to add value to management education', *Academy of Management Journal*, 40: 1310–33.

Allan, B. (2007) 'Time to learn? E-learners' experiences of time in virtual learning communities', *Management Learning*, 38: 557–72.

Anderson, T. (2003) 'Modes of interaction in distance education: Recent developments and research questions', in M.G. Moore and W.G. Anderson (eds), *Handbook of Distance Education*. Mahwah, NJ: Lawrence Erlbaum Publishers. pp. 129–44.

Anderson, T., Rourke, L., Garrison, D.R. and Archer, W. (2001) 'Assessing teaching presence in a computer conferencing context', *Journal of Asynchronous Learning Networks*, 5 (2). Retrieved December 10, 2004 from http://www.aln.org/publications/jaln/v5n2/v5n2_anderson.asp

Anstine, J. and Skidmore, M. (2005) 'A small sample study of traditional and online courses with sample selection adjustment', *Journal of Economic Education*, 36: 107–27.

Arbaugh, J.B. (2000a) 'Virtual classroom characteristics and student satisfaction in internet-based MBA courses', *Journal of Management Education*, 24: 32–54.

Arbaugh, J.B. (2000b) 'Virtual classroom versus physical classroom: An exploratory comparison of class discussion patterns and student learning in an asynchronous internet-based MBA course', *Journal of Management Education*, 24: 207–27.

Arbaugh, J.B. (2000c) 'How classroom environment and student engagement affect learning in internet-based MBA courses', *Business Communication Quarterly*, 63 (4): 9–26.

Arbaugh, J.B. (2000d) 'An exploratory study of the effects of gender on student learning and class participation in an internet-based MBA course', *Management Learning*, 31: 533–49.

Arbaugh, J.B. (2001) 'How instructor immediacy behaviors affect student satisfaction and learning in web-based courses', *Business Communication Quarterly*, 64 (4): 42–54.

Arbaugh, J.B. (2002) 'Managing the on-line classroom: A study of technological and behavioral characteristics of web-based MBA courses', *Journal of High Technology Management Research*, 13: 203–23.

Arbaugh, J.B. (2004) 'Learning to learn online: A study of perceptual changes between multiple online course experiences', *The Internet and Higher Education*, 7: 169–82.

Arbaugh, J.B. (2005a) 'How much does "subject matter" matter? A study of disciplinary effects in on-line MBA courses', *Academy of Management Learning and Education*, 4: 57–73.

Arbaugh, J.B. (2005b) 'Is there an optimal design for on-line MBA courses?' *Academy of Management Learning and Education*, 4: 135–49.

Arbaugh, J.B. (2007) 'An empirical verification of the Community of Inquiry framework', *Journal of Asynchronous Learning Networks*, 11 (1): 73–85.

Arbaugh, J.B. and Benbunan-Fich, R. (2004) 'In defense of quantitative methods to research networked management learning: A reply to Hodgson and Watland', *Management Learning*, 35: 117–24.

Arbaugh, J.B. and Benbunan-Fich, R. (2006) 'An investigation of epistemological and social dimensions of teaching in online learning environments', *Academy of Management Learning and Education*, 5: 435–47.

Arbaugh, J.B. and Benbunan-Fich, R. (2007) 'Examining the influence of participant interaction modes in web-based learning environments', *Decision Support Systems*, 43: 853–65.

Arbaugh, J.B. and Duray, R. (2002) 'Technological and structural characteristics, student learning and satisfaction with web-based courses: An exploratory study of two MBA programs', *Management Learning*, 33: 231–47.

Arbaugh, J.B. and Hwang, A. (2006) 'Does "teaching presence" exist in online MBA courses?' *The Internet and Higher Education*, 9: 9–21.

Arbaugh, J.B. and Rau, B.L. (2007) 'A study of disciplinary, structural, and behavioral effects on course outcomes in online MBA courses', *Decision Sciences Journal of Innovative Education*, 5: 63–93.

Arbaugh, J.B. and Stelzer, L. (2003) 'Learning and teaching via the web: What do we know?', in R. DeFillipi and C. Wankel (eds), *Educating Managers with Tomorrow's Technologies*. Greenwich, CT: Information Age Publishing. pp. 17–51.

Armstrong, S.J. (2000) 'The influence of individual cognitive style on performance in management education', *Educational Psychology*, 20 (3): 323–39.

Armstrong, S.J., Allinson, C.W. and Hayes, J. (2004) 'The effects of cognitive style on research supervision: A study of student-supervisor dyads in management education', *Academy of Management Learning and Education*, 3: 41–63.

Atkinson, M. and Kydd, C. (1997) 'Individual characteristics associated with World Wide Web use: An empirical study of playfulness and motivation',

*The DATA BASE for Advances in Information Systems*, 28 (2): 53–62.

Bailey, E.K. and Cotlar, M. (1994) 'Teaching via the internet', *Communication Education*, 43: 184–93.

Balotsky, E.R. and Christensen, E.W. (2004) 'Educating a modern business workforce: An integrated educational information technology process', *Group and Organization Management*, 29 (2): 148–70.

Baugher, D., Varanelli, A. and Weisbord, E. (2003) 'Student hits in an internet-supported course: How can instructors use them and what do they mean?' *Decision Sciences Journal of Innovative Education*, 1: 159–79.

Benbunan-Fich, R. (2002) 'Improving education and training with Information Technology', *Communications of the ACM*, 45 (6): 94–9.

Benbunan-Fich, R. and Arbaugh, J.B. (2006a) 'Gender differences in online courses', in E.M. Trauth (ed.). *Encyclopedia of Gender and Information Technology* Hershey, PA: IDEA Group Publishing. pp. 570–76.

Benbunan-Fich, R. and Arbaugh, J.B. (2006b) 'Separating the effects of knowledge construction and group collaboration in web-based courses', *Information and Management*, 43: 778–93.

Benbunan-Fich, R. and Hiltz, S.R. (1999) 'Effects of asynchronous learning networks: A field experiment', *Group Decision and Negotiation*, 8: 409–26.

Benbunan-Fich, R. and Hiltz, S.R. (2002) 'Correlates of effectiveness of learning networks: The effects of course level, course type and gender on outcomes', *Proceedings of the 35th Hawaii International Conference on System Sciences*, 1–8.

Benbunan-Fich, R., Hiltz, S.R. and Harasim, L. (2005) 'The online interaction learning model: An integrated theoretical framework for learning networks', in S.R. Hiltz and R. Goldman (eds), *Learning Together Online: Research on Asynchronous Learning Networks*. Mahwah, NJ: Erlbaum. pp. 19–37.

Berge, Z. (1995) 'Facilitating computer conferencing: Recommendations from the field', *Educational Technology*, 35 (1): 22–30.

Berger, N.S. (1999) 'Pioneering experiences in distance learning: Lessons learned', *Journal of Management Education*, 23: 684–90.

Bernard, R., Abrami, P.C., Lou, Y. and Brokhovski, E. (2004) 'A methodological morass: How can we improve the quality of quantitative research in distance education?' *Distance Education*, 25: 175–98.

Berry, R.W. (2002) 'The efficacy of electronic communication in the business school: Marketing students' perceptions of virtual teams', *Marketing Education Review*, 12 (2): 73–78.

Bigelow, J.D. (1999) 'The web as an organizational behavior learning medium', *Journal of Management Education*, 23: 635–50.

Bocchi, J., Eastman, J.K. and Swift, C.O. (2004) 'Retaining the online learner: Profile of students in an online MBA program and implications for teaching them', *Journal of Education for Business*, 79: 245–53.

Bonk, C.J. and Graham, C.R. (2006) *The Handbook of Blended Learning: Global Perspectives, Local Designs.* San Francisco, CA: Pfeiffer.

Bonk, C.J., Kim, K-J and Zeng, T. (2006) 'Future directions of blended learning in higher education and workplace learning settings', in C.J. Bonk and C.R. Graham (eds), *The Handbook of Blended Learning: Global Perspectives, Local Designs.* San Francisco: Pfeiffer. pp. 550–67.

Borthick, A.F. and Jones, D.R. (2000) 'The motivation for collaborative discovery learning online and its application in an information systems assurance course', *Issues in Accounting Education*, 15: 181–210.

Brindle, M. and Levesque, L. (2000) 'Bridging the gap: Challenges and prescriptions for interactive distance education', *Journal of Management Education*, 24: 445–57.

Brower, H.H. (2003) 'On emulating classroom discussion in a distance-delivered OBHR course: Creating an on-line community', *Academy of Management Learning and Education*, 2 (1): 22–36.

Budd, J.W. (2002) 'Teaching labor relations: Opportunities and challenges of using technology', *Journal of Labor Research*, 23: 355–74.

Burke, L.A. and Sadler-Smith, E. (2006) 'Instructor intuition in the educational setting', *Academy of Management Learning and Education*, 5: 169–81.

Cappel, J.J. and Hayden, R.L. (2004) 'Evaluating e-learning: A case study', *Journal of Computer Information Systems*, 44 (4): 49–56.

Chang, K.E., Sung, Y.T. and Chiou, S.K. (2002) 'Use of hierarchical hyper-concept maps in web-based courses', *Journal of Educational Computing Research*, 27 (4): 335–53.

Chidambaram, L. (1996) 'Relational development in computer-supported groups', *MIS Quarterly*, 20: 143–63.

Chizmar, J.F. and Walbert, M.S. (1999) 'Web-based learning environments guided by principles of good teaching practice', *Journal of Economic Education*, 30 (3): 248–64.

Clark, D.N. and Gibb, J.L. (2006) 'Virtual team learning: An introductory study team exercise', *Journal of Management Education*, 30: 765–87.

Clouse, S.F. and Evans, G.E. (2003) 'Graduate business students' performance with synchronous and asynchronous interaction e-learning methods',

*Decision Sciences Journal of Innovative Education*, 1: 181–202.

Comeaux, P., Huber, R., Kasprzak, J. and Nixon, M. (1998, November) *Collaborative Learning in Web-based Instruction (ED427693).* Paper presented at the Webnet 98 World Conference of the WWW, Internet, and Intranet Proceedings, Orlando, FL.

Conaway, R.N., Easton, S.S. and Schmidt, W.V. (2005) 'Strategies for enhancing student interaction and immediacy in online courses', *Business Communication Quarterly*, 68 (1): 23–35.

Coppola, N.W., Hiltz, S.R. and Rotter, N.G. (2002) 'Becoming a virtual professor: Pedagogical roles and asynchronous learning networks', *Journal of Management Information Systems*, 18 (4): 169–89.

Cybinski, P. and Selvanathan, S. (2005) 'Learning experience and learning effectiveness in undergraduate statistics: Modeling performance in traditional and flexible learning environments', *Decision Sciences Journal of Innovative Education*, 3: 251–71.

DeLacey, B.J. and Leonard, D.A. (2002) 'Case study on technology and distance in education at the Harvard Business School', *Educational Technology and Society*, 5 (2): 13–28.

Davis, F. (1989) 'Perceived usefulness, perceived ease of use and user acceptance of information technology', *MIS Quarterly*, 13: 319–40.

Davis, R. and Wong, D. (2007) 'Conceptualizing and measuring the optimal experience of the elearning environment', *Decision Sciences Journal of Innovative Education*, 5: 97–126.

Dellana, S.A., Collins, W.H. and West, D. (2000) 'Online education in a Management Science course: Effectiveness and performance factors', *Journal of Education for Business*, 76 (1): 43–7.

DeLone, W.H. and McLean, E.R. (2003) 'The DeLone and McLean model of information systems success: A ten-year update', *Journal of Management Information Systems*, 19 (4): 9–30.

DeRouin, R.E., Fritzsche, B.A. and Salas, E. (2005) 'E-learning in organizations', *Journal of Management*, 31: 920–40.

Dillon, C.L. and Walsh, S.M. (1992) 'Faculty: The neglected resource in distance education', *American Journal of Distance Education*, 6 (3): 5–21.

Dineen, B.R. (2005) 'TeamXchange: A team project experience involving virtual teams and fluid team membership', *Journal of Management Education*, 29: 593–616.

Dos Santos, B.L. and Wright, A.L. (2001) 'Internet-supported management education', *Information Services and Use*, 21 (2): 53–64.

Drago, W., Peltier, J. and Sorensen, D. (2002) 'Course content or the instructor: Which is more important in online teaching?' *Management Research News*, 25 (6/7): 69–83.

Drago, W., Peltier, J., Hay, A. and Hodgkinson, M. (2005) 'Dispelling the myths of online education: Learning via the information superhighway', *Management Research News*, 28 (6/7): 1–17.

Driver, M. (2002) 'Investigating the benefits of web-centric instruction for student learning – An exploratory study of an MBA course', *Journal of Education for Business*, 77: 236–45.

Dumont, R. (1996) 'Teaching and learning in cyberspace', *IEEE Transactions on Professional Communication*, 39 (4): 192–204.

Dunbar, A.E. (2004) 'Genesis of an online course', *Issues in Accounting Education*, 19: 321–43.

Ellram, L.M. and Easton, L. (1999) 'Purchasing education on the Internet', *Journal of Supply Chain Management*, 35 (1): 11–19.

Eom, S.B., Wen, H.J. and Ashill, N. (2006) 'The determinants of students' perceived learning outcomes and satisfaction in university online education: An empirical investigation', *Decision Sciences Journal of Innovative Education*, 4 (2): 215–35.

Eveleth, D.M. and Baker-Eveleth, L.J. (2003) 'Developing dialogue skill – A qualitative investigation of an online collaboration in a team management course', *Journal of Education for Business*, 78: 228–33.

Ferris, S.P. (1996) 'Women online: Cultural and relational aspects of women's communication in on-line discussion groups', *Interpersonal Computing and Technology*, 4 (3/4): 29–40.

Ford, M.W., Kent, D.W. and Devoto, S. (2007) 'Learning from the pros: Influence of web-based expert commentary on vicarious learning about financial markets', *Decision Sciences Journal of Innovative Education*, 5: 43–63.

Fornaciari, C.J. and Matthews, C.S. (2000) 'Student personality types and predispositions toward distance education', in S.J. Havlovic (ed.), *Academy of Management Best Papers Proceedings*, MED A1–A6.

Fornaciari, C.J., Forte, M. and Matthews, C.S. (1999) 'Distance education as strategy: How can your school compete?' *Journal of Management Education*, 23: 703–18.

Friday, E., Friday-Stroud, S.S., Green, A.L. and Hill, A.Y. (2006) 'A multi-semester comparison of student performance between multiple traditional and online sections of two management courses', *Journal of Behavioral and Applied Management*, 8 (1): 66–81.

Garrison, D.R. and Anderson, T. (2003) *E-Learning in the 21st Century: A Framework for Research and Practice*. London: RoutledgeFalmer.

Garrison, D.R., Anderson, T. and Archer, W. (2000) 'Critical inquiry in a text-based environment: Computer conferencing in higher education', *The Internet and Higher Education*, 2: 87–105.

Garrison, D.R., Anderson, T. and Archer, W. (2001) 'Critical thinking, cognitive presence, and computer conferencing in distance education', *American Journal of Distance Education*, 15 (1): 7–23.

Garrison, D.R. and Cleveland-Innes, M. (2005) 'Facilitating cognitive presence in online learning: Interaction is not enough', *American Journal of Distance Education*, 19: 133–48.

Garrison, D.R., Cleveland-Innes, M., Koole, M. and Kappelman, J. (2006) 'Revisiting methodological issues in the analysis of transcripts: Negotiated coding and reliability', *The Internet and Higher Education*, 9 (1): 1–8.

Gefen, D. and Straub, D.W. (1997) 'Gender differences in the perception and use of E-mail: An extension to the technology acceptance model', *MIS Quarterly*, 21 (4): 389–400.

Graham, C.R. (2006) 'Blended learning systems: Definition, current trends, and future directions', in C.J. Bonk and C.R. Graham (eds), *The Handbook of Blended Learning: Global Perspectives, Local Designs*. San Francisco: Pfeiffer. pp. 3–21.

Grandzol, J.R. (2004) 'Teaching MBA statistics online: A pedagogically sound process approach', *Journal of Education for Business*, 79: 237–44.

Gunawardena, C. and Zittle, F. (1997) 'Social presence as a predictor of satisfaction within a computer mediated conferencing environment', *American Journal of Distance Education*, 11 (3): 8–26.

Gutl, C. and Pivec, M. (2003) 'A multimedia knowledge module virtual tutor fosters interactive learning', *Journal of Interactive Learning Research*, 14 (2): 231–58.

Hall, R.H., Watkins, S.E. and Eller, V.M. (2003) 'A model of web-based design for learning', in M.G. Moore and W.G. Anderson (eds), *Handbook of Distance Education*. Mahwah, NJ: Erlbaum. pp. 367–76.

Hara, N. and Kling, R. (2000) 'Student distress in a web-based distance education course', *Information Communication and Society*, 3 (4): 557–79.

Harasim, L. (1990) 'Online education: An environment for collaboration and intellectual amplification', in L. Harasim (ed.), *On-line Education: Perspectives on a New Environment*. New York: Praeger. pp. 133–69.

Hardaway, D.E. and Scamell, R.W. (2005) 'Use of a technology-mediated learning instructional approach for teaching an introduction to information technology course', *Journal of Information Systems Education*, 16 (2): 137–45.

Hartman, J., Lewis, J.S. and Powell, K.S. (2002) 'Inbox shock: A study of electronic message volume in a distance managerial communication course', *Business Communication Quarterly*, 65 (3): 9–28.

Hawisher, G.E. and Pemberton, M.A. (1997) 'Writing across the curriculum encounters asynchronous learning networks or WAC meets up with ALN', *Journal of Asynchronous Learning Networks*, 1 (1).

Heckman, R. and Annabi, H. (2005) 'A content analytic comparison of learning processes in online and face-to-face case study discussions', *Journal of Computer-Mediated Communication*, 10 (2), article 7. Retrieved January 4, 2007, from http://jcmc.indiana.edu/vol10/issue2/heckman.html

Herring, S.C. (2000) 'Gender differences in CMC: Findings and implications', CPSR Newsletter, 18(1). Retrieved May 16, 2003, from http://www.cpsr.org/publications/newsletters/issues/2000/Winter2000/herring.html

Herring, S.C. (2001) 'Gender and power in online communication', Retrieved May 16, 2003, from http://slis.indiana.edu/CSI/WP/WP01-05B.html

Hillman, D.C.A., Willis, D.J. and Gunawardena, C.N. (1994) 'Learner-interface interaction in distance education: An extension of contemporary models and strategies for practitioners', *American Journal of Distance Education*, 8 (2): 30–42.

Hiltz, S.R. (1994) *The Virtual Classroom: Learning Without Limits via Computer Networks.* Norwood, NJ: Ablex Publishing Corporation.

Hiltz, S.R. and Shea, P. (2005) 'The student in the online classroom', in S.R. Hiltz and R. Goldman (eds), *Learning Together Online: Research on Asynchronous Learning Networks.* Mahwah, NJ: Erlbaum. pp. 145–68.

Hiltz, S.R., Coppola, N., Rotter, N., Turoff, M. and Benbunan-Fich, R. (2000) 'Measuring the importance of collaborative learning for the effectiveness of ALN: A multi-measure, multi-method approach', *Journal of Asynchronous Learning Networks*, 4 (2).

Hirumi, A. (2004) *Multimedia Instructional Systems Design I.* (Web-based Distance Education Course (http://webct.ucf.edu). Orlando, FL: University of Central Florida, Department of Instructional Technology.

Hodgson, V. and McConnell, D. (1995) 'Co-operative learning and development networks', *Journal of Computer Assisted Learning*, 11 (4): 210–24.

Hodgson, V. and Reynolds, M. (2005) 'Consensus, differences, and "multiple communities" in networked learning', *Studies in Higher Education*, 30 (1): 11–24.

Hodgson, V. and Watland, P. (2004a) 'Researching networked management learning', *Management Learning*, 35 (2): 99–116.

Hodgson, V. and Watland, P. (2004b) 'The social constructionist case for researching networked management learning: A postscript and reply to Arbaugh and Benbunan-Fich', *Management Learning*, 35 (2): 125–32.

Holsapple, C.W. and Lee-Post, A. (2006) 'Defining, assessing, and promoting e-learning success: An information systems perspective', *Decision Sciences Journal of Innovative Education*, 4: 67–85.

Hwang, A. and Arbaugh, J.B. (2006) 'Virtual and traditional feedback-seeking behaviors: Underlying competitive attitudes and consequent grade performance', *Decision Sciences Journal of Innovative Education*, 4: 1–28.

Ives, B. and Jarvenpaa, S.L. (1996) 'Will the Internet revolutionize business education and research?' *Sloan Management Review*, 37 (3): 33–41.

Jaffe, J.M., Lee, Y.E., Huang, L. and Oshagan, H. (1995) 'Gender, pseudonyms, and CMC: Masking identities and baring souls', Paper submitted for presentation to the 45th Annual Conference of the International Communication Association, 1995, Albuquerque, New Mexico. Retrieved July 30, 2003, from http://members.iworld.net/yesunny/genderps.html

Jiang, M. and Ting, E. (2000) 'A study of factors influencing students' perceived learning in a Web-based course environment', *International Journal of Educational Telecommunications*, 6 (4): 317–38.

Kashy, D.A., Albertelli, G., Bauer, W., Kashy, E. and Thoennessen, M. (2003) 'Influence of non-moderated and moderated discussion sites on student success', *Journal of Asynchronous Learning Networks*, 7 (1). Retrieved December 20, 2007, from http://www.sloan-c.org/publications/JALN/v7n1/v7n1_kashy.asp

Kirkley, J.R. and Kirkley, S.E. (2006) 'Expanding the boundaries of blended learning: Transforming learning with mixed and virtual reality technologies', in C.J. Bonk and C.R. Graham (eds), *The Handbook of Blended Learning: Global Perspectives, Local Designs.* San Francisco: Pfeiffer. pp. 533–49.

Klein, H.J., Noe, R.A. and Wang, C. (2006) 'Motivation to learn and course outcomes: The impact of delivery mode, learning goal orientation, and perceived barriers and enablers', *Personnel Psychology*, 59: 665–702.

Kock, N., Verville, J. and Garza, V. (2007) 'Media naturalness and online learning: Findings supporting both the significant- and no-significant-difference perspectives', *Decision Sciences Journal of Innovative Education*, 5: 333–55.

Landry, B.J.L., Griffeth, R. and Hartman, S. (2006) 'Measuring student perceptions of blackboard using the technology acceptance model', *Decision Sciences Journal of Innovative Education*, 4: 87–99.

Larson, P.D. (2002) 'Interactivity in an electronically delivered marketing course', *Journal of Education for Business*, 77: 265–69.

Leonard, D. A. and Brian J. DeLacey (2002) 'Designing hybrid online/in-class learning programs for adults', Harvard Business School Working Paper Series, No. 03-036.

Leidner, D.E. and Jarvenpaa, S.L. (1995) 'The use of information technology to enhance management school education: A theoretical view', *MIS Quarterly*, 19: 265–91.

Lemak, D.J., Shin, S.J., Reed, R. and Montgomery, J.C. (2005) 'Technology, transactional distance, and instructor effectiveness: An empirical investigation', *Academy of Management Learning and Education*, 4: 150–9.

Levin, J., Kim, H. and Riel, H. (1990) 'Analyzing instructional interactions on electronic message networks', in L. Harasim (ed.), *Online Education: Perspectives on a New Environment*. New York: Praeger. pp. 185–213

Lin, C.H. (2002) 'Effects of computer graphics types and epistemological beliefs on students' learning of mathematical concepts', *Journal of Educational Computing Research*, 27 (3): 265–74.

Liu, X., Bonk, C.J., Magjuka, R.J., Lee, S. and Su, B. (2005) 'Exploring four dimensions of online instructor roles: A program level case study', *Journal of Asynchronous Learning Networks*, 9 (4): 29–48.

Liu, X., Magjuka, R.J., Bonk, C.J. and Lee, S. (2007) 'Does sense of community matter? An examination of participants' perceptions of building learning communities in online courses', *Quarterly Review of Distance Education*, 8 (1): 9–24.

Lowe, J.S. and Holton, E.F. III. (2005) 'A theory of effective computer-based instruction for adults', *Human Resource Development Review*, 4 (2): 159–88.

Lu, J., Yu, C-S. and Liu, C. (2003) 'Learning style, learning patterns, and learning performance in a WebCT-based MIS course', *Information and Management*, 40: 497–507.

Marks, R.B., and Sibley. S.D. (2006). 'Distance education and learning styles: Some interesting results.' *Journal of College Teaching & Learning*, 3(3): 71–80.

Marks, R.B., Sibley, S. and Arbaugh, J.B. (2005) 'A structural equation model of predictors for effective online learning', *Journal of Management Education*, 29: 531–63.

Martins, L.L. and Kellermanns, F.W. (2004) 'A model of business school students' acceptance of a web-based course management system', *Academy of Management Learning and Education*, 3: 7–26.

May, G.L. and Short, D. (2003) 'Gardening in cyberspace: A metaphor to enhance online teaching and learning', *Journal of Management Education*, 27: 673–93.

Mayer, R.E. (2001) *Multimedia Learning*. New York: Cambridge University Press.

Mayer, R.E. (2006) 'Ten research-based principles of multimedia learning', in H.F. O'Neil and R.S. Perez (eds), *Web-based Learning: Theory, Research, and Practice*. Mahwah, NJ: Erlbaum. pp. 371–90.

McGorry, S.Y. (2002) 'Online, but on target? Internet-based MBA courses – A case study', *The Internet and Higher Education*, 5: 167–75.

McLaren, C.H. (2004) 'A comparison of student persistence and performance in online and classroom business statistics experiences', *Decision Sciences Journal of Innovative Education*, 2: 1–10.

Meisel, S. and Marx, B. (1999) 'Screen-to-screen versus face-to-face: Experiencing the differences in management education', *Journal of Management Education*, 23: 719–31.

Mezirow, J. (1991) *Transformative Dimensions of Adult Learning*. San Francisco: Jossey-Bass.

Moore, M.G. (1989) 'Three types of interaction', *American Journal of Distance Education*, 3 (2): 1–6.

Mundell, B. and Pennarola, F. (1999) 'Shifting paradigms in management education: What happens when we take groups seriously?' *Journal of Management Education*, 23: 663–83.

Painter-Morland, M., Fontrodona, J., Hoffman, W.M. and Rowe, M. (2003) 'Conversations across continents: Teaching business ethics online', *Journal of Business Ethics*, 48: 75–88.

Palloff, R. and Pratt, K. (2001) *Lessons from the Cyberspace Classroom*. San Francisco: Jossey-Bass.

Parker, D. and Gemino, A. (2001) 'Inside online learning: Comparing conceptual and technique learning performance in place-based and ALN formats', *Journal of Asynchronous Learning Networks*, 5 (2): 64–74.

Parnell, J.A. and Carraher, S. (2003) 'The Management Education by Internet Readiness (MEBIR): Developing a scale to assess personal readiness for internet-mediated management education', *Journal of Management Education*, 27: 431–46.

Patel, C. and Patel, T. (2006) 'Exploring a joint model of conventional and online learning systems', *E-services Journal*, 4 (2): 27–46.

Pauleen, D.J., Marshall, S. and Egort, I. (2004) 'ICT-supported team-based experiential learning: Classroom perspectives', *Education + Training*, 46 (2): 90–9.

Paulsen, M.P. (1995) 'Moderating educational computer conferences', in Z.L. Berge and M.P. Collins (eds), *Computer-Mediated Communication and the Online*

*Classroom in Distance Education*. Creskill, NJ: Hampton Press.

Peltier, J.W., Drago, W. and Schibrowsky, J.A. (2003) 'Virtual communities and the assessment of online marketing education', *Journal of Marketing Education*, 25: 260–76.

Picciano, A.G. (1998) 'Developing an asynchronous course model at a large, urban university', *Journal of Asynchronous Learning Networks*, 2 (1).

Picciano, A.G. (2002) 'Beyond student perceptions: Issues of interaction, presence, and performance in an online course', *Journal of Asynchronous Learning Networks*, 6 (1), Retrieved January, 6, 2006, from http://www.sloan-c.org/publications/jaln/v6n1/pdf/v6n1_picciano.pdf

Picciano, A.G. and Dziuban, C.D. (eds) (2007) *Blended Learning: Research Perspectives*. Needham, MA: Sloan-C.

Piccoli, G., Ahmad, R. and Ives, B. (2001) 'Web-based virtual learning environments: A research framework and a preliminary assessment of effectiveness in basic IT skills training', *MIS Quarterly*, 25: 401–26.

Poole, D.M. (2000) 'Student participation in a discussion-oriented online course: A case study', *Journal of Research on Computing in Education*, 33: 162–77.

Proserpio, L. and Gioia, D.A. (2007) 'Teaching the virtual generation', *Academy of Management Learning and Education*, 6: 69–80.

Rahm, D. and Reed, B.J. (1997) 'Going remote: The use of distance learning, the World Wide Web, and the Internet in graduate programs of public affairs and administration', *Public Productivity and Management Review*, 20 (4): 459–71.

Riccomini, P. (2002) 'The comparative effectiveness of two forms of feedback: Web-based model comparison and instructor delivered feedback', *Journal of Educational Computing Research*, 27 (3): 228–31.

Richardson, J.C. and Swan, K. (2003) 'Examining social presence in online courses in relation to students' perceived learning and satisfaction', *Journal of Asynchronous Learning Networks*, 7 (1), Retrieved June 1, 2004, from http://www.aln.org/publications/jaln/v7n1/index.asp

Riding, R.J. and Sadler-Smith, E. (1992) 'Type of instructional material, cognitive style and learning performance', *Educational Studies*, 18: 323–40.

Robinson, L. Jr. (2006) 'Moving beyond adoption: Exploring the determinants of student intention to use technology', *Marketing Education Review*, 16 (2): 79–88.

Rossman, M. (1999) 'Successful online teaching using asynchronous learner discussion forum', *Journal of Asynchronous Learning Networks*, 3 (2).

Rungtusanatham, M., Ellram, L.M., Siferd, S.P. and Salik, S. (2004) 'Toward a typology of business education in the internet age', *Decision Sciences Journal of Innovative Education*, 2: 101–20.

Salas, E., Kosarzycki, M.P., Burke, C.S., Fiore, S.M. and Stone, D.L. (2002) 'Emerging themes in distance learning research and practice: Some food for thought', *International Journal of Management Reviews*, 4 (2): 135–53.

Salmon, G. (2000) 'Computer-mediated conferencing for management learning at the Open University', *Management Learning*, 31: 491–502.

Sarker, S. and Nicholson, J. (2005) 'Exploring the myths about online education in information systems', *Informing Science Journal*, 8: 55–73.

Schniederjans, M.J. and Kim, E.B. (2005) 'Relationship of student undergraduate achievement and personality characteristics in a total web-based environment: An empirical study', *Decision Sciences Journal of Innovative Education*, 3: 205–21.

Sharda, R., Romano, N.C. Jr., Lucca, J.A., Weiser, M., Scheets, G., Chung, J.-M. and Sleezer, C.M. (2004) 'Foundation for the study of computer-supported collaborative learning requiring immersive presence', *Journal of Management Information Systems*, 20 (4): 31–63.

Shea, P.J., Fredericksen, E.E., Pickett, A.M. and Pelz, W.E. (2003) 'A preliminary investigation of "teaching presence" in the SUNY learning network', in J. Bourne and Janet C. Moore (eds), *Elements of Quality Online Education: Into the Mainstream*. Needham, MA: Sloan-C. pp. 279–312

Shea, P.J., Fredericksen, E.E., Pickett, A.M. and Pelz, W.E. (2004) 'Faculty development, student satisfaction, and reported learning in the SUNY learning network', in T.M. Duffy and J.R. Kirkley (eds), *Learner-Centered Theory and Practice in Distance Education: Cases from Higher Education*. Mahwah, NJ: Lawrence Erlbaum Associates. pp. 343–77.

Shrivastava, P. (1999) 'Management classes as online learning communities', *Journal of Management Education*, 23: 691–702.

Silberg, D. and Lennon, K. (2006) 'Developing leadership skills: Online versus face-to-face', *Journal of European Industrial Training*, 30 (7): 498–511.

Sitzmann, T., Kraiger, K., Stewart, D. and Wisher, R. (2006) 'The comparative effectiveness of web-based and classroom instruction: A meta-analysis', *Personnel Psychology*, 59: 623–64.

Spires, M.S. and Jaeger, J. (2002) 'A survey of the literature on ways to use web-based and Internet instruction most effectively: Curriculum and program planning (ED477459)'. Paper presented to Programs for Higher Education, Nova Southeastern University.

Stewart, C.M., Shields, S.F., Monolescu, D. and Taylor, J.C. (1999) 'Interpersonal computing and technology: An electronic journal for the 21st century, 7, 1-2', Retrieved May 1, 2003, from http://www.emoderators.com/ipct-j/1999/n1-2/stewart.html

Swan, K. (2002) 'Building learning communities in online courses: The importance of interaction', *Education, Communication and Information*, 2 (1): 23–49.

Swan, K., Shea, P., Fredericksen, E., Pickett, A., Pelz, W. and Maher, G. (2000) 'Building knowledge building communities: Consistency, contact, and communication in the virtual classroom', *Journal of Educational Computing Research*, 23: 389–413.

Tallent-Runnels, M.K., Thomas, J.A., Lan, W.Y. Cooper, S., Ahern, T.C., Shaw, S.M. and Liu, X. (2006) 'Teaching courses online: A review of the research', *Review of Educational Research*, 76: 93–135.

Tannen, D. (1990) *You Just Don't Understand: Men and Women Conversation*. New York: Morrow.

Taylor, J. (1996) 'The continental classroom: Teaching labour studies online', *Labor Studies Journal*, 21: 19–38.

Terry, N. (2007) 'Assessing instruction modes for Master of Business Administration (MBA) courses', *Journal of Education for Business*, 82 (4): 220–5.

Vandergrift, K.E. (2002) 'The anatomy of a distance education course: A case study analysis', *Journal of Asynchronous Learning Networks*, 6 (1): 76–90.

Venkatesh, V. and Davis, F.D. (2000) 'Theoretical extension of the technology acceptance model: Four longitudinal field studies', *Management Science*, 46: 186–204.

Venkatesh, V., Morris, M.G., Davis, G.B. and Davis, F.D. (2003) 'User acceptance of information technology: Toward a unified view', *MIS Quarterly*, 27: 425–78.

Walker, R. and Jeurissen, R. (2003) 'E-based solutions to support intercultural business ethics instruction: An exploratory approach in course design and delivery', *Journal of Business Ethics*, 48 (1): 113–26.

Wallace, R.M. (2002) 'Online learning in higher education: A review of research on interactions among teachers and students', *Education, Communication, and Information*, 3 (2): 241–80.

Walther, J. (1994) 'Interpersonal effects in computer mediated interaction', *Communication Research*, 21 (4): 460–87.

Wan, Z., Fang, Y. and Neufeld, D.J. (2007) 'The role of information technology in technology-mediated learning: A review of the past for the future', *Journal of Information Systems Education*, 18 (2): 183–92.

Wankel, C. and DeFillippi, R. (eds) (2003) *Educating Managers With Tomorrow's Technologies*. Greenwich, CT: Information Age Publishing.

Warell, S.S. and Arbaugh, J.B. (2007, April) 'Developing intercultural sensitivity through an online MBA course', Paper presented at the American Educational Research Association Conference, Chicago, IL.

Warkentin, M.E., Sayeed, L. and Hightower, R. (1997) 'Virtual teams versus face-to-face teams: An exploratory study of a web-based conference system', *Decision Sciences*, 28: 975–96.

Webb, H.W., Gill, G. and Poe, G. (2005) 'Teaching with the case method online: Pure versus hybrid approaches', *Decision Sciences Journal of Innovative Education*, 3: 223–50.

Webster, J. and Hackley, P. (1997) 'Teaching effectiveness in technology-mediated distance learning', *Academy of Management Journal*, 40: 1282–309.

Whipp. J., Schweizer, H. and Hayslett, C.H. (2002) 'Quality control in online courses: Using a constructivist framework', *Computers in the Schools*, 18 (3/4): 143–58.

Williams, E.A., Duray, R. and Reddy, V. (2006) 'Teamwork orientation, group cohesiveness, and student learning: A study of the use of teams in online distance education', *Journal of Management Education*, 30: 592–616.

Wisher, R.A. and Curnow, C.K. (2003) 'Video-based instruction in distance learning: From motion pictures to the internet', in M.G. Moore and W.G. Anderson (eds), *Handbook of Distance Education*. Mahwah, NJ: Erlbaum. pp. 315–30.

Wolfe, J. (1999) 'Why do women feel ignored? Gender differences in computer-mediated classroom interactions', *Computers and Composition*, 16: 153–66.

Wu, A. (2003) 'Supporting electronic discourse: Principles of design from a social constructivist perspective', *Journal of Interactive Learning Research*, 14 (2): 167–84.

Yoo, Y., Kanawattanachai, P. and Citurs, A. (2002) 'Forging into the wired wilderness: A case study of a technology-mediated distributed discussion-based class', *Journal of Management Education*, 26: 139–63.

Yukselturk, E. and Top, E. (2005–2006) 'Reconsidering online course discussions: A case study', *Journal of Educational Technology Systems*, 34 (3): 341–67.

Zhao, Y., Lei, J., Yan, B., Lai, C. and Tan, H.S. (2005) 'What makes the difference? A practical analysis of research on the effectiveness of distance education', *Teachers College Record*, 107 (8): 1836–84.

# 13

# Learning-Centered Course Design

David A. Whetten, Trav D. Johnson, and D. Lynn
Sorenson

## Abstract

According to authoritative sources, higher education is undergoing a paradigm shift, from a focus on teaching to a focus on student learning. Indications of this shift in focus include a heightened interest in the predictors of student learning and what is referred to as learning-centered course design. This integrated approach to planning a course is guided by three design questions: 1 What do I believe is most important for students in this course to learn? 2 How can I reliably assess students' mastery of these intended learning outcomes? 3 Which experiences during the course will contribute the most to their learning? In line with these questions, the course-design process outlined in this chapter consists of the following core elements, or steps: formulate *significant* learning objectives, construct *developmental* learning assessments, and select *engaging* learning activities. It also requires proper *alignment* of learning objectives, activities and assessments, as well as acute sensitivity to the *learning context*. It is expected that this introduction to learning-centered course design will be useful for novice and seasoned management teachers,
alike, irrespective of what, how, who, or where they teach.

According to higher education scholars, colleges and universities, generally, are undergoing a significant shift in educational priorities, from focusing on teaching to focusing on learning (Barr and Tagg, 1995; Campbell and Smith, 1997; Davis, 1993; Diamond, 1998; Halpern, 1994; Halpern and Hakel, 2002, 2003; Svinicki, 1999). While good teaching fosters good learning, teaching does not automatically translate into learning. 'Learning can and often does take place without the benefit of teaching – and sometimes even in spite of it – but there is no such thing as effective teaching in the absence of learning – that is, 'Teaching without learning is just talking' (Angelo and Cross, 1993: 3). Furthermore, research shows that the time professors invest in improving their teaching does not necessarily translate into greater student learning (Boice, 1991). In fact, as suggested by the comparison

**Table 13.1   Recent paradigm shift in higher education**

|  | Teaching focus | ⟶ | Learning focus |
|---|---|---|---|
| Orienting questions | • What do I want to teach?<br>• How can I cover the designated course material? | | • What do students need to learn?<br>• How can we accomplish specific learning objectives? |
| Teacher's role | • Provide/deliver instruction<br>• Transfer knowledge to students<br>• Classify and sort students | | • Produce learning<br>• Elicit student discovery and construction of knowledge<br>• Develop each student's competencies and talents |
| Success criteria | • Teacher's performance<br>• Inputs, resources | | • Students' performance<br>• Learning, student-success outcomes |
| Assumption about teachers | • Any expert can teach | | • Teaching is complex and requires considerable training |

*Source*: Adapted from Barr and Tagg, *Change*, Nov/Dec 1995, pp. 16–17. Reprinted with permission of the Helen Dwight Reid Educational Foundation. Published by Heldref Publications, 1319 Eighteenth St., NW, Washington, DC 20036-1802. Copyright © (1995).

between the teaching and learning paradigms in Table 13.1, efforts focused on what *teachers* do in the classroom can, as likely as not, reduce the opportunity for student learning.

As with most paradigm shifts, the changes illustrated in Table 13.1 have required many college professors to rethink their assumptions about the relationship between the roles of teacher and student and the associated activities of teaching and learning. It is noteworthy that the growing emphasis on learning-centered teaching has been the subject of several articles in the management education literature, including Hall (1994), Mundhenk (2004), and Ramsey and Fitzgibbons (2005). As suggested by Table 13.1, the teaching-learning paradigm shift includes two components: from a focus on what the *teacher does* to what *students do* during a course, and from a focus on the performance of the teacher (faculty evaluation) to the performance of the students (student learning). In her book, *Learner-Centered Teaching*, Mary Ellen Weimer (2002) admonishes professors to focus 'attention squarely on learning: what the student is learning, how the student is learning, the conditions under which the student is learning, whether the student is retaining and applying the learning, and how the current learning positions the student for future learning' (p. xvi).

It is noteworthy that this paradigm shift was in part inspired by significant advances in our understanding of adult learning. For example, the study of learning within the fields of psychology and education now includes brain imaging research as well as controlled studies of learner style X content to be learned X learning modality interactions (Bransford et al., 2000; Halpern and Hakel, 2002, 2003). Of particular note, a task force of learning authorities on student learning was assembled in the mid-1980s to synthesize the burgeoning body of knowledge regarding what helps college student learn. At the conclusion of their deliberations, they produced a report entitled, 'Seven principles for good practice in undergraduate education' (Chickering and Gamson, 1987, 1991; Sorcinelli, 1991; Gamson, 1995). While these principles originally envisioned a traditional classroom setting, they have since been applied to courses involving extensive use of technology (Brown, 2000; Chickering and Ehrmann, 1996; http://www.tltgroup.org/programs/seven.html). One indication of the Seven Principles report's effect on higher education is its influence on the design of the National Survey of Student Engagement (NSSE), a survey that has been utilized by over 1,200 colleges to assess the quality of student learning and engagement (Kuh and Vesper, 1997). The Seven Principles are summarized in Table 13.2. We will refer to it and other research on student learning throughout the chapter.

One of the striking features of this table is what is not included – namely, items

**Table 13.2    Seven principles for good practice in undergraduate education**

Effective teaching…
1. Encourages teacher-student contact
2. Encourages cooperation among students
3. Encourages active learning
4. Gives prompt feedback
5. Emphasizes time on task
6. Communicates high expectations
7. Respects diverse talents and ways of learning

Summary of Chickering and Gamson (1987).

explaining effective teaching in terms of individual differences among teachers. None of these predictors of student learning is dependent on a certain personality profile or teaching style. For example, one does not have to be gregarious, spontaneous, or witty to provide prompt feedback or to allow students opportunities to learn from their mistakes. By contrast, these principles of effective teaching and learning generally reflect choices teachers make while planning a particular course. Said differently, most of the significant predictors of student learning shown in Table 13.2 are things that can and should be incorporated into a carefully-crafted course plan. For example, all of the following are tied to the design of course activities and assignments: active learning, student cooperation, diverse learning approaches, time on task, and high expectations. Even the amount of faculty–student contact and the promptness of feedback on assignments often reflect specific pre-course plans for 'out-of-class teaching,' including office hours, correcting exams and assignments, and meeting with project groups.

One of the strongest endorsements of the course design view of effective teaching comes from an extensive study of students' college experiences, known as the Harvard Assessment Seminars. This study encompassed 1,600 student and 65 faculty interviews at 25 colleges and universities. Richard Light (2001), the study director, offered the following summary comment: 'The best part of these examples [of exceptional teaching] is that they rarely depend on inborn or immutable personality traits of any given faculty member. Rather, students identify certain *planned*

*efforts* these special professors made' (p. 105, italics added).

Regarding these 'planned efforts,' L. Dee Fink (2005), past-president of the US-based association for faculty development professionals, said:

> When we teach, we engage in two closely related, but distinct, activities. First, we design the course by gathering information and making a number of decisions about the way the course will be taught. Second, we engage in teacher–student interactions as we implement the course we have designed…. In order to teach well, one must be competent in both course design and teacher–student interactions.
>
> However, of these two activities, our ability to design courses well is usually the most limiting factor. Most of us have had little or no training in how to design courses. In addition, during the last two decades, research on college teaching and learning have led to some new ideas about course design that have, in essence, 'raised the bar' in terms of what is possible.

## LEARNING-CENTERED COURSE DESIGN

We now turn to the central focus of the chapter: outlining a systematic process for incorporating the predictors of student learning, including those in Table 13.2, into the design of management courses (Whetten, 2007; Richlin, 2006; deVry and Brown, 2000; Diamond, 1998; Hall, 1994). Learning-centered course design is distinguished by three key design questions: (1) What do I believe is most important for students in this course to learn? (2) How can I reliably assess students' mastery of these learning outcomes? (3) Which experiences during the course will contribute the most to student learning?

Building on these questions, a systematic, integrated process for designing what Fink (2003) calls significant learning experiences is shown in Figure 13.1 (adapted from Fink, 2003).[1] This model contains three design elements: *significant* learning objectives, *developmental* learning assessments, and *engaging* learning activities. The connecting arrows highlight the importance of aligning learning objectives, assessments,

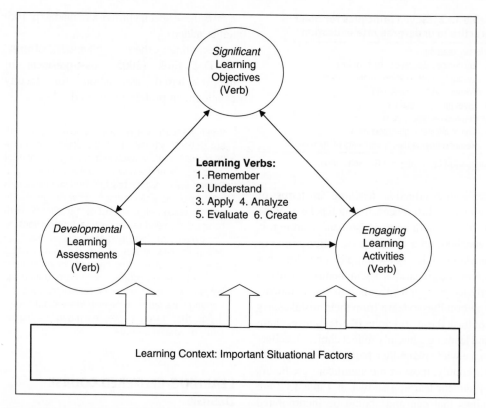

**Figure 13.1   Components of effective course design. Adapted from Fink (2003): 62.**

and activities to produce a coherent learning experience. As we'll discuss later, the list of learning verbs at the center of the figure can guide the *alignment* process. Figure 13.1 also underscores the need to design a course with a particular *learning context* in mind. Given that, logically, this is the first step in the design process we'll use it as our starting point.

## BEGIN WITH A SYSTEMATIC ASSESSMENT OF THE LEARNING CONTEXT

Anyone who has taught the same course to undergraduates and graduate students, or to full-time and part-time students, or in a domestic and an international educational program, or who has attempted to adapt an in-class course to an online learning environment recognizes the importance of this

initial step in the course planning process. Fink (2003: 69) suggests that a comprehensive approach to course design should include a thorough understanding of key situational factors, including the following:

- Specific context of the teaching and learning situation: size of the class, location of the course in the curriculum, number and length of class periods, how the course material will be delivered – classroom instruction, online, combination of instruction and discussion-group sections.
- Expectations of external groups: expectations of society at large for this type of education, applicable state or professional society standards, curriculum-wide learning goals specified by encompassing degree program.
- Nature of the subject, e.g., convergent (working towards a single right answer) vs. divergent (working towards equally valid interpretations), primarily cognitive vs. a significant skill-development component, field is relatively stable vs. changing rapidly.

- Characteristics of the learners: age, familiarity with the subject matter, full-time or part-time students, work-related experience, reasons for enrolling in this course, learning styles, cultural background.
- Characteristics of the teacher: relevant content-related experience, skills and knowledge, previous teaching experience, number of times the teacher will likely teach the course, understanding of the teaching and learning process.
- Special pedagogical challenges: any factors that might get in the way of the teacher and students making this a significant learning experience.

## FORMULATE SIGNIFICANT, EXPLICIT LEARNING OBJECTIVES

With an understanding of the learning context in mind teachers are prepared to formulate a learning plan. The careful choice of learning objectives is the most important step in this process because it informs all other aspects of the planning process. As summarized in Table 13.3, by specifying what skills, understanding, or abilities students are expected to gain from their learning experience explicit learning objectives provide a wide range of benefits for both teachers and students. Importantly, from a course design perspective, they guide the careful selection of topics, assignments, readings, activities, and assessments, and they make it possible for teachers and students to know if the desired learning has been achieved.

The course-design literature speaks of 'learning goals,' 'learning objectives,' or 'learning outcomes.' Sometimes these terms are used interchangeably; at other times specific distinctions are made among them.[2] In any case, teachers should specify what they expect their students to learn, or more specifically, how they expect their students will be changed by this learning experience and what they should be able to *do* upon completion of the course.

It is noteworthy that in an intensive study of 63 exceptional college teachers across a variety of disciplines, Ken Bain (2004) found that these teachers shaped the learning environments for their students by first asking questions like: 'What should my students be able to do intellectually, physically, or emotionally as a result of their learning?' (p. 49). One professor explained: 'Some students do well in school but still do not develop a good understanding or the capacity to think or to think about their own thinking. I'm trying to figure out how to move those students from mere performance to levels of deeper and more meaningful learning' (p. 53). A Sociology professor realized that the learning students needed was not merely memorizing rules but rather to inductively pull together patterns from multiple examples. In addition, he wanted his students 'to develop an empathetic understanding of the diverse cultural heritage in which they lived, and to emerge from his class with increased abilities – and confidence

### Table 13.3    Benefits of clearly stated learning objectives

1. Fairness in both testing and grading is facilitated.
2. The goals of the course, its content, and the evaluation procedures are both consistent and interrelated.
3. Objectives allow evaluators to determine which practices and materials are effective and which are not.
4. The emphasis is changed from what faculty members must cover to what a student should be able to do as a consequence of instruction.
5. A logical instructional structure is communicated by identifying a sequence of objectives and thus content – that is, the student must be able to do *a* before he or she can do *b*.
6. Communication among faculty and between faculty and support staff is improved.
7. Self-evaluation by the students is encouraged because they know what is expected of them.
8. Efficient student learning is facilitated and anxiety is reduced because the students are provided with direction and they know what the instructional priorities are.
9. Students understand how the course relates to other courses and to institutional goals.

Adapted from Diamond (1998): 128–9.

in those abilities – to think sociologically and communicate their thoughts to others' (p. 61).

Further support for emphasizing relevant learning objectives comes from a stream of research examining the relationship between students' motivation to learn and their beliefs about the personal relevance of the course to their personal lives and educational objectives (Bransford et al., 2000; Bulte et al., 2006). This instrumental connection was also a key finding of the Harvard Assessment Seminars study (Light, 2001): 'Faculty members who had an especially big impact [on students] are those who helped students make connections between a serious curriculum, on the one hand, and the students' personal lives, values, and experiences on the other' (p. 110).

One of the implications of these findings is that the explicit use of course learning objectives provides a natural opportunity for teachers to explain the benefits of mastering the course learning objectives. Indeed, college professors should treat this as one of their most significant teaching opportunities and responsibilities. One of the best ways for management professors to demonstrate course relevance is to invite accomplished practitioners to make the case for them (Sorenson, 2001, 2006). Another strategy is to highlight the links between course learning outcomes and data reporting the predictors of manager or organizational performance (see Introduction in Whetten and Cameron, 2007).

Learning objectives typically follow the convention of specifying a **subject** (students), a *learning verb* (what students will do), and an *object* (content matter). For example: '**Students** will be able to *recognize* the *three different types of interpersonal conflict* and *apply type-appropriate conflict resolution practices.*' The contemporary scholarship on learning outcomes focuses primarily on the learning verb (e.g., Fink, 2003) and emphasizes the value of 'higher-order' learning – often equated with 'significant' learning. In Table 13.4, examples of higher-order learning verbs are listed under the 'Application' heading (see, Anderson and Krathwohl, 2001).

To identify suitable learning objectives for a particular course, teachers may ask themselves questions such as: What are the three or four most important things I hope students will master during this course? What do students in this course need to learn in order to be prepared for subsequent courses? What would I like my students to do consistently five years from now? How can students develop a love of this subject matter that will foster a commitment to life-long learning? Assuming that students will master the content of this course, how might they use it to accomplish something important in organizational settings? In addition, Diamond suggests that teachers ask a colleague to pose the following question: 'If I'm your student, what do I have to do to convince you that I'm where you want me to be at the end of this lesson, unit, or course?' (1998: 134).

In line with these questions, we now turn to the practical matter of crafting learning objectives that are both meaningful and measurable, and, hence, are capable of guiding course-design decisions. A common belief held by college teachers, especially among those teaching particularly difficult or complex subjects, is that students can't apply something they don't understand. While this is true by definition, it is also true that students achieve a deeper level of understanding when they are required to apply what they are learning. Thus, comprehension should be viewed as a means to achieve deeper student learning, rather than as an end in itself. Viewed in this way, in highly technical courses, comprehension is something to be achieved quickly and efficiently, preparing students for higher learning opportunities. Therefore, as noted in Table 13.4, learning objectives should focus on what students will be able to apply, analyze, evaluate, or create, with the acknowledgement that remembering and understanding the relevant course content is a critical prerequisite.

In less-technical courses, the relationship between comprehension and application is often somewhat different. For example, if the objectives of a management course target personal insight, interpersonal relationships, moral development, or other so-called 'soft skills,' application is often a prerequisite

**Table 13.4   A taxonomy of learning objectives (verbs)**

| Comprehension | | Application | | | |
|---|---|---|---|---|---|
| Remember | Understand | Apply | Analyze | Evaluate | Create |
| Recognize, Recall | Interpret, Classify, Summarize, Compare, Explain | Execute, Implement | Differentiate, Organize, Attribute | Check, Critique | Generate, Plan, Produce |
| Retrieve relevant knowledge from long-term memory | Construct meaning from instructional messages, including oral, written, and graphic | Carry out or use a procedure in a given situation | Break material into parts and relate to one another and to larger structure/ purpose | Make judgments based on criteria and standards | Put elements together to form a coherent, functional whole; reorganize into new patterns |

*Source*: From Anderson, Lorin W. et al. *Taxonomy For Learning, Teaching and Assessing: A Revision of Bloom's Taxonomy of Educational Objectives*, Complete Edition, 1/e. Published by Allyn And Bacon, Boston, MA. Copyright © 2001 by Pearson Education. Adapted by permission of the publisher.

for comprehension; understanding comes from doing (Kolb, 1984). In these cases, student comprehension is enhanced by making explicit the expected application learning outcome for a given learning activity and providing students with opportunities to reflect on what they've learned from their participation.

In summary, students learn best when they are working to accomplish personally significant, explicit learning goals and when comprehension is not the primary objective of a course (Duit and Treagust, 1998; Kolb, 1984; Roth, 1998). Focusing course design on competencies that are personally relevant for students is one of the most direct ways to ensure that a course is both learning- and learner-centered. Indeed, management professors might experiment with inviting students to specify some, or even all, of their learning goals. This approach is particularly appropriate for advanced or part-time students, and for highly diverse groups of students. For example, at the beginning of a course students might be given an extensive pre-test, assessing their level of understanding and/or proficiency and then they may be invited to design a series of learning activities tailored to their individual learning needs (see Whetten and Campbell-Clark, 1996, and Akin, 1991 for more systematic discussions of this process). The point here is that whether a teacher is designing the same set of learning experiences for all students in a course, or students are

designing personalized learning experiences, proven learning principles should be used to guide the learning design process.

## USE VALID DEVELOPMENTAL ASSESSMENTS OF STUDENT LEARNING

The second step of the learning-centered course design process involves determining how best to assess student mastery of each learning outcome and to design learning assessments that foster further learning. Admittedly, focusing on how students will be evaluated may seem counterproductive to some professors; after all, a major obstacle to student learning seems to be students' singular focus on grades and their associated preoccupation with 'Is this going to be on the test?' While teachers may yearn for students whose motivation for learning extends beyond their course grades – even in introductory courses – it is important to understand that intrinsic motivation is not a necessary requirement for achieving stated learning outcomes. In fact, students' preoccupation with grades can actually be an asset to learning rather than a liability. As a wise colleague astutely observed, 'There is nothing wrong with "teaching to the test" if the test accurately reflects the course's learning objectives.' In brief, learning-centered course design encourages students and teachers alike to view graded tests and assignments as opportunities to ascertain how well a course's learning objectives are being achieved.

Implied in this view of assessment is a critical principle of effective learning: if students are going to be assessed on their attainment of specified outcomes, they should have ample opportunity to practice and receive feedback on the skills and understanding needed to achieve these expectations. This approach to learning is exemplified by the best college teachers. These teachers 'see examinations as extensions of the kind of work that is already taking place in the course. Teachers prepare students to do certain kinds of intellectual work, not to be good test takers. The examinations ask students to do that work. The goal is to establish congruity between the intellectual objectives of the course and those that the examination assesses' (Bain, 2004: 162).

To help in the selection of effective, outcome-appropriate learning assessments, consider questions like the following:

- Given the stated learning outcomes for this course, how can I best assess student learning?
- How can I effectively assess higher-order learning outcomes?
- How can I assess learning in ways that enhance and extend, rather than culminate, students' involvement with the subject matter?
- During our next re-accreditation process, if I were asked to provide evidence of learning for this course, what would be the best evidence I could provide?

In reporting the results of the Harvard Assessment Seminars, Light (2001) reported several findings that he considered surprising. One of these had to do with assessment:

> ... I expected students to prefer courses in which they work at their own pace, courses with relatively few quizzes, exams, and papers until the end of the term. Wrong again. A large majority of students say they learn significantly more in courses that are highly structured, with relatively many quizzes and short assignments. Crucial to this preference is getting quick feedback from professors – ideally with an opportunity to revise and make changes before receiving a final grade. In contrast, students are frustrated and disappointed with classes that require only a final paper. How can we ever improve our work, they ask, when the only feedback comes after a course is over, and when no revision is invited? (Light, 2001: 8)

While the notion that learning assessments should stimulate further learning seems self-evident, research and experience show that this element of learning-centered course design is the hardest to implement effectively and consistently (Wiggins, 1998; Walvoord and Anderson, 1998). Truth be told, many teachers are as preoccupied with grading as their students are with grades. Specifically, too often our overriding concern in selecting course assignments and tests is to produce a certain grade distribution at the end of the course, to limit the amount of time spent grading assignments and tests, and to minimize students' complaints about their grades.[3]

Inspired by another view of learning assessment from scholars such as Weimer (2002) and Angelo and Cross (1993), management professors can approach assessments with a focus on increasing student learning. This might involve having students take quizzes alone and then in groups (Michaelsen et al., 2004; Michaelsen et al., 1994), allowing them to resubmit graded papers or repeat tests (Jacobs and Chase, 1992), and implementing cumulative and problem-solving tests (Huba and Freed, 2000). Or, it might involve inviting a panel of practicing managers to critique student presentations of semester-long group projects, or, for part-time students, emphasizing on-the-job application assignments.

Compared with multiple-choice exams, we can't ignore the fact that application-oriented papers and essay questions seem to place the grader in double jeopardy: they take longer to grade and students are more likely to challenge their grades. Fortunately, authorities on this subject have identified ways to reduce both grading time and student complaints (Davis, 1993; McBeath, 1992; Stevens and Levi, 2005; Walvoord and Anderson, 1998). Here's a sampler of useful ideas.

- Use a grading rubric. A rubric is a scoring tool that divides an assignment or exam answer into its component parts and describes acceptable and unacceptable levels of performance for each of those parts (Stevens and Levi, 2005). If there are 15 points available for a particular short essay question, they might be broken down into three sets of 5 points, each associated with a specific evaluation standard related to a learning objective (e.g., effectively apply course material in problem analysis and recommendations). If it is distributed and discussed before the test, the value of the rubric is enhanced as a learning tool. Even better, it can be used to guide formative learning activities leading up to the exam, such as homework assignments and small-group discussions or mini-projects.
- Give selective, detailed, developmental feedback. Not every student will benefit from the same comment, and no one benefits from general comments like 'good job,' or 'dig deeper.' Experienced graders are able to identify the most common mistakes that students make on a particular assignment and formulate one or two helpful suggestions for each. Working with a repertoire of these comments accumulated over time, they are able to efficiently give students instructive feedback.

For the assessment 'workhorse' in management courses – multiple choice tests – teachers can significantly increase the quality of their test questions by following a few basic rules (see, Davis, 1993; Haladyna, 1999; McBeath, 1992). In addition, it is possible to write multiple-choice test items that assess higher-order learning outcomes. For example, test items can include scenarios with alternative intervention strategies or problem statements paired with alternative solutions (Walvoord and Anderson, 1998; McBeath, 1992).

It is important to point out that not all assessments of learning need to be graded. It is both appropriate and instructive for students to gauge their learning progress through formative self-assessments, feedback from peers, performance on practice tests, and so forth. Teachers may also ask students to rate themselves on course objectives that are difficult to grade, such as objectives related to character development, moral judgment, and integrity.

To summarize, possibly the greatest impact teachers can have on learning involves the thoughtful selection of course requirements. These expectations signal *what* teachers believe is most important to learn, as well as *how* students should approach the learning experience. A decision to focus assessments only on student recall and comprehension, for whatever reason, constitutes a significant opportunity cost. Think of it this way: we undermine the credibility of our claims that mastering the content of management courses has important, long-term implications for on-the-job performance if during the course all we assess is students' ability to recall key terms and theories.

## SELECT LEARNING ACTIVITIES THAT FOSTER ACTIVE, ENGAGED LEARNING

The planning sequence followed in this chapter reflects what Wiggins (1998) calls 'backwards design,' in that decisions about learning assessment should precede decisions about learning activities. Course readings, activities, and projects thus function as opportunities for students to prepare for graded assignments and tests. Stated differently, using the metaphor of a journey the recommended course planning process is guided by three questions asked in a particular sequence: 'What is our intended destination?' 'How will we know when we've arrived?' 'How are we going to get there?'

Learning theory experts have advised teachers for decades that learning is promoted by active involvement – reflected in the quip: 'passive learning is an oxymoron' (Marchese, 1998). Students who are invited to actively explore course content are more likely to achieve specified learning goals and to internalize what they have learned (Auster and Wylie, 2006; Sherwood, 2004). Thus, rather than listening to teachers *cover* important concepts in a course, students should be encouraged to *uncover* the concepts themselves.

In an effort to increase student involvement it is standard practice for management professors to shorten their lectures in favor of extended class and small group discussion, as well as in-class group exercises. While this is a step in the right direction, it is important to not equate activity with learning – to not decouple 'active' from 'active learning.' Said differently, although learning is enhanced by involvement, not all involvement produces learning. Too often, teachers act as if 'active learning' means 'any activity occurring in a learning context.' This misconception tends to promote activity-centered rather than learning-centered courses. The hallmark of learning-centered courses is that teachers can articulate how each and every planned learning activity enhances their students' ability to demonstrate mastery of particular course learning outcomes.

As management professors dispassionately evaluate their favorite learning activities, they may find that these activities are not as effective in promoting student learning as they had assumed. It is important to keep in mind that when students report 'We learned a lot' from a classroom exercise their unstated frame of reference is generally, 'Compared with listening to you talk for 45 minutes,' rather than, 'Relative to mastering learning objective #2.'

As a way of reinforcing the intended, instrumental link between expected learning outcomes and designed learning activities, teachers can introduce learning activities, in the syllabus or in class, as designed 'learning links,' connecting previously specified learning objectives and upcoming learning assessments. When introduced in this fashion, post-activity discussion is more likely to focus on how prepared students feel they are to apply what they are learning to specific post-course situations, and to perform well on upcoming course assessments, which are designed to simulate those situations. Thus, in a module on motivation a management teacher might ask, 'What did you learn from this activity about how to effectively diagnose the cause(s) of poor performance, as introduced in the reading?' 'How might your diagnosis have been different if the person/situation/relationship

had been \_\_\_\_\_, instead of \_\_\_\_\_?' 'How would you rate your ability to diagnose complex work-related performance problems at this point?' 'What would help you improve?'

Although most discussions of active learning focus on classroom activities, it is important that a learning-centered course design addresses out-of-class activities as well (e.g., readings, papers, group projects). In fact, based on extensive interviews with students Light (2001) found that out-of-class learning activities were highly valued and generally contributed more to student learning than in-class activities. Here are two particularly illuminating examples:

> We asked some graduating seniors this question: 'Which courses had the biggest impact on your learning, why was this impact so big, and exactly how were these courses structured?' The results were eye-opening. We learned that *how* students study and do their homework assignments outside of class is a far stronger predictor of engagement and learning than particular details of their instructor's teaching style. 'The design of homework really matters. Specifically, those students who study outside of class in small groups of four to six, even just once a week, benefit enormously' (pp. 51–2).
>
> 'Students identify the courses that had the most profound impact on them as courses in which they were required to write papers, not just for the professor, as usual, but for their fellow students as well' (p. 64). 'The relationship between the amount of writing for a course and students' level of engagement – whether engagement is measured by time spent on the course, or the intellectual challenge it presents, or students' interest in it – is stronger than any other course characteristic' (p. 55).

It follows that these assignments need to be carefully designed, focusing on what will best help students achieve specific learning objectives. Out-of-class assignments may include online or computer-based components. Technology, if used effectively, can significantly enhance active learning in out-of-class settings (DeLacey and Leonard, 2002; Garrison, 2003; Huang and Zhou, 2006).

There are several excellent resources available for teachers seeking a broader repertoire of learning activities, including McKeachie and Svinicki (2005); Davis (1993); Bonwell and Eison (1991); Wilkerson and Gijselaers (1996); and Sutherland and Bonwell (1996). Here are some examples that are particularly relevant for management courses (see, Finan, 2004; Peterson, 2004; Sherwood, 2004; Michaelson et al., 2004; Auster and Wylie, 2006; Raelin and Coghlan, 2006):

- Facilitate student interaction with the teacher and with classmates through provocative class discussions, team projects, small group work, presentations, and peer feedback.
- Give bonus 'class participation' points for comments that are explicitly linked to the assigned readings ( pro, con, exception to the rule, etc.)
- Encourage direct application of the course material in on-the-job settings and discuss the results with the class.
- Provide class time for students to practice what they've learned, via job-like simulations, exercises and role-plays.
- Assign study groups a course-related management decision (e.g., human resources, operations, strategy) and have a representative of each group announce and defend their decision in class – explaining how their action reflects the related course material.
- Require students to teach a subject to others, preferably individuals who could directly apply what they learn to solve on-the-job problems.
- Assign time for reflection, including students completing 'minute papers' at the end of a class period (see Angelo and Cross, 1993) and/or the ongoing use of learning portfolios or journals.
- Use problem-based learning to entrain the meta-skills of effective diagnosis, principled analysis, and systematic comparison.
- Organize part-time students (e.g., distance-learning or evening courses) into consulting groups and have them identify and remedy a specific problem within one of their organizational work groups.

The selection of effective learning activities for courses that are taught online or as a blend of online and in-class learning requires special attention. Indeed, it is generally believed among course design authorities that the less central the teacher is to the day-to-day learning experience the more care needs to be given to designing that experience. In line with this observation, readers designing online or blended courses are invited to explore the emerging sub-field within the management education literature devoted to this subject (e.g., Hodgson, 1997; Arbaugh & Duray, 2002; Brower, 2003; Hodgson and Watland, 2004; and Marks et al., 2005).

As illustrated by the earlier comments from students about the value of out-of-class assignments, student feedback is the best source of information about the effectiveness of learning activities in a course. Consistent with the learning predictor of 'time on task' introduced in Table 13.2, teachers might ask their students at the end of a learning module or semester to report how much time they spent on specific assignments, on preparing for each test, and so forth. It is particularly important to ask them how much they feel various activities and assignments contributed to their mastery of particular course learning objectives.

In summary, learning-centered courses are feedback-rich courses. Students are given ample opportunity to practice before being assessed, and teachers are continuously seeking feedback about the what, why, and how of their students' learning experience. Feedback from students is invaluable for enhancing the learning-focus of a course over time. It also helps teachers using unconventional teaching strategies or unusual or difficult course requirements justify these choices to a group of new students.[4]

## ALIGN COURSE DESIGN ELEMENTS SYSTEMATICALLY AND CONTINUOUSLY

Having discussed each of the three elements of learning-centered course design (objectives, assessments, and learning activities), we now direct our attention to the critical matter of alignment among the course design elements. The results of a recent survey at Brigham Young University (BYU) highlight the importance of aligning course objectives, assessments, and activities. When graduating seniors were asked to evaluate their educational experience, one of their top complaints was that, in too many cases, what was required on tests did not reflect the course description, the stated learning objectives, nor what the teacher had led them to believe was important to learn. Apparently this misalignment problem is not limited to BYU courses. In summarizing research on educational effectiveness, Alan Cohen (1987) explains:

> Lack of excellence in American schools is not caused by ineffective teaching, but mostly by misaligning what teachers teach, what they intend to teach, and what they assess as having been taught. ...Presently, we find no other construct that consistently generates such large effects [on student learning], which is probably why the idea of instructional alignment is so well-entrenched in the conventional wisdom of instructional designers, even if not in the programs currently found in most classrooms. (p 19)

The wagon wheel is an apt visual analogy for the course alignment process – using suitable learning-activity spokes to connect the learning-objectives hub with the learning-assessments rim. Viewed in this manner, learning activities help students understand what a particular learning objective entails. In addition, when course activities prepare students for graded assessments, students appreciate not being surprised by the content or format of a test, and they are motivated to take seriously the preparatory learning experiences.

One of the most effective and practical tools for aligning course components is the consistent use of 'learning verbs,' as introduced earlier in conjunction with Figure 13.1 and Table 13.4. Suppose one course learning objective is to help students *apply* certain principles of effective interpersonal relations. To achieve alignment between this stated objective and the course activities and assessments, the teacher may use the word 'apply' in test questions and assignments, as well as in grading rubrics for written or oral reports. Likewise, if

students' ability to *evaluate* the reasons for various managerial decisions will be assessed using case analysis, learning activities should include practice in analyzing cases and making informed 'evaluative' judgments. When designing learning objectives, activities and assessments, a teacher should consistently use verbs from the same category (Table 13.4) such as Analyze, Differentiate, Organize, Attribute. The consistent use of learning verbs as 'learning markers' throughout a course syllabus helps students understand what they are expected to learn, how they will learn it, and how learning achievement will be assessed.

Table 13.5 illustrates the use of another effective and simple alignment tool. In this illustration, the alignment between learning objectives and learning activities is examined, as well as alignment between learning objectives and individual test items. Obviously, a more complete form of this assessment would include both verbs and objects (e.g., *integrate* motivation theories, *critique* leadership theories). The intent here is to illustrate how a stated commitment to a particular learning objective should be reflected in subsequent course-design choices. With regard to the cells in the matrix of Table 13.5, the number of course elements that should support a given learning objective depends on how much emphasis the teacher places on each. The purpose of this alignment check is to ensure that what the students are experiencing during a course reflects the teacher's carefully considered intentions and objectives.

In the case of blended courses (i.e., courses that have both online and face-to-face components), there are some additional alignment considerations. While some learning activities and assessments are best accomplished in face-to-face settings, others may be more suitable for individuals or groups of students working in an online environment. Therefore, in blended courses, each activity or assessment needs to be aligned with the optimal learning modality (e.g., online, face-to-face) as well as with other elements of the course (Shea, 2007).

**Table 13.5 Course alignment diagnostic test**

| Course Assignments | Learning objectives | | |
|---|---|---|---|
| | Understand | Apply | Create |
| Attendance | X | | |
| Group project | | X | X |
| Term paper | X | X | X |
| Exams | X | X | |
| Journal | | X | X |

| Test Questions | Learning objectives | | |
|---|---|---|---|
| | Understand | Apply | Create |
| Question#1 | X | | |
| Question#2 | X | X | |
| Question#3 | X | | |
| Question#4 | X | X | |
| Question#5 | X | | X |

## CONCLUSION

A central theme in the higher education teaching and learning literature for the past decade has been the so-called paradigm shift from a teaching focus to student-learning focus. Hallmarks of this shift in focus have been a heightened interest in the predictors of student learning and an accompanying increase in attention to effective, comprehensive course-design.

The learning-centered course planning process outlined in this chapter can be summarized as a set of design principles. To enhance student learning:

- Focus course planning primarily on what *students will do* in and out of class.
- Plan to explain what students are *expected to learn,* how their *learning will be assessed,* and how course activities are designed to *facilitate student learning.*
- Be prepared to justify each and every course design decision, in terms of its *relevance for student learning.*
- Center the planning process in a carefully selected, course-defining set of *explicit learning objectives.*
- Give preference to the use of *significant* (application-oriented) learning objectives, *developmental* learning assessments, and *engaging* learning activities.
- Ensure that course components are *properly aligned.* Using the wagon-wheel configuration

analogy, connect the *learning objectives hub* with the *learning assessment rim,* using *learning activity spokes.*
- Exercise *sensitivity to key situational conditions,* including the *needs of the students* taking the course, the broader *program learning goals,* and the *learning modality* selected for the course.

Finally, this chapter's focus on course design is intended to underscore, not diminish the contribution that teachers make to the learning process. It is built on the presumption that teachers care deeply about what their students need to learn, and it provides teachers with a set of 'best practices' for how they can realize their highest aspirations for student learning. We concur with Fink that while course design and teacher–student interaction are both important contributors to student learning, new or experienced university teachers looking to significantly increase student learning would do well to plan each and every component of their courses with that outcome in mind.

## NOTES

1 There are several distinctive and salutary features of Dee Fink's course design methodology: 1 It explicitly adopts a higher-education perspective. 2 It is informed by contemporary research on the antecedents of student learning. 3 It was written with professors, rather than education students, in mind. Planning guides adapted from Fink (2003) can be found at ctl.byu.edu.

2 For example, it is generally acknowledged that learning goals are broader in scope and more abstract than learning objectives and that learning outcomes is a generic term applying to both goals and objectives. Thus, the term learning goals is more often used in conjunction with program-level design and learning objectives with course-level design. It is important to note that while our focus is on course-level design, these design principles and practices can be applied at the program-level and at the level course modules.

3 Experienced management professors will no doubt detect an inherent tension between a learning-centered view of student assessment and the conventional approach to grading in higher education. While a discussion of the merits of criterion-referenced grading (competence-based) versus norm-referenced grading (curve-based) are beyond the scope of this chapter, interested readers are referred to: Suski (2004) and Walvoord and Anderson (1998).

4 In passing, research on student ratings of teachers suggests that students give teachers requiring an above-average workload high marks *if* they perceive that the extra work translated into increased learning (Marsh, 2001).

## ACKNOWLEDGEMENT

Table 13.1 from *Change* 13–25 (November–December), 1995. Reprinted with permission of the Helen Dwight Reid Educational Foundation. Published by Heldref Publications, 1319 Eighteenth St., NW, Washington, DC 20036–1802. Copyright © 1995.

Table 13.4 from Anderson, Lorin W. et al. *Taxonomy For Learning, Teaching and Assessing: A Revision of Bloom's Taxonomy of Educational Objectives*, Complete Edition, 1/e. Published by Allyn and Bacon, Boston, MA. Copyright © 2001 by Pearson Education. Adapted by permission of the publisher.

## REFERENCES

Akin, G. (1991). Self-directed learning in introductory management, *Journal of Management Education*, 15(3), 295–312.

Anderson, L.W. & Krathwohl, D.R. (eds) (2001). *A Taxonomy for Learning, Teaching, and Assessing: A revision of Bloom's taxonomy of educational objectives.* San Francisco: Longman.

Angelo, T.A. & Cross, K.P. (1993). *Classroom Assessment Techniques: A handbook for college teachers* (2nd ed.). San Francisco: Jossey-Bass.

Arbaugh, J.B. & Duray, R. (2002). Technological and structural characteristics, student learning and satisfaction with web-based courses: An exploratory study of two MBA programs, *Management Learning*, 33, 231–47.

Auster, E.R. & Wylie, K.K. (2006). Creating active learning in the classroom: A systematic approach, *Journal of Management Education*, 30(2), 333–53.

Bain, K. (2004). *What the Best College Teachers Do.* Cambridge, MA: Harvard University Press.

Barr, R.B. & Tagg, J. (1995, November–December). From teaching to learning: A new paradigm for undergraduate education. *Change*, 13–25.

Boice, R. (1991). Quick starters: New faculty who succeed. in M. Theall & J. Franklin (eds), *Effective Practices for Improving Teaching: New directions for teaching and learning*, 48, San Francisco: Jossey-Bass, pp. 111–21.

Bonwell, C.C. & Eison, J.A. (1991). *Active Learning: Creating excellence in the classroom.* Washington, DC: George Washington University Press.

Brower, H.H. (2003). On emulating classroom discussion in a distance delivered OBHR course: creating an on-line community, *Academy of Management Learning and Education*, 2(1), 22–36.

Brown, D.G. (ed.) (2000). *Teaching with Technology: Seventy-five professors from eight universities tell their stories.* Bolton, MA: Anker.

Bransford, J.D., Brown, A.L. & Cocking, R.R. (eds) (2000). *How People Learn: Brain, mind, experience, and school.* Washington, DC: National Academy Press.

Bulte, A.M.W., Westbroek, H.B., de Jong, O. & Pilot, A. (2006). A research approach to designing chemistry education using authentic practices as contexts, *International Journal of Science Education*, 28(9), 1063–86.

Campbell, W.E. & Smith, K.A. (eds) (1997). *New Paradigms for College Teaching.* Eina, MN: Interaction Book Company.

Chickering, A. & Ehrmann, S.C. (1996). Implementing the Seven Principles: Technology as Lever. *AAHE Bulletin*, 3–6.

Chickering, A.W. & Gamson, Z.F. (1987). Seven principles for good practice in undergraduate education, *AAHE Bulletin*, 39, 3–7.

Chickering, A.W. & Gamson, Z.F. (eds) (1991). Applying the Seven Principles for Good Practice in Undergraduate Education. *New Directions for Teaching and Learning*, 47.

Cohen, S.A. (1987, November). Instructional alignment: Searching for a magic bullet. *Educational Researcher*, 16–20.

Davis, B. (1993). *Tools for Teaching.* San Francisco: Jossey-Bass.

DeLacey, B.J. & Leonard, D.A. (2002). Case study on technology and distance in education at the Harvard Business School, *Educational Technology and Society* 5(2), 13–28.

deVry, J.R. & Brown D.G. (2000). A framework for redesigning a course, in D.G. Brown (ed.) *Teaching with Technology.* Bolton, MA: Anker.

Diamond, R.M. (1998). *Designing and assessing Courses and Curricula: A practical guide* (Rev. ed.). San Francisco: Jossey-Bass.

Duit, R. & Treagust, D.F. (1998). Learning in science – from behaviourism toward social constructivism and beyond, in B.J. Fraser & K.G. Tobin (eds), *International handbook of science education: Part 1.* Dordrecht, The Netherlands: Kluwer.

Finan, M.C. (2004). Experience as teacher: Two techniques for incorporating student experiences into a course. *Journal of Management Education, 28*(4), 478–91.

Fink, L.D. (2003). *Creating Significant Learning Experiences.* San Francisco: Jossey-Bass.

Fink, L.D. (2005). *A self-directed guide to designing courses for significant learning.* Retrieved December 20, 2007 from http://cfaes.osu.edu/about-us/pdf/ self-directedguidetocoursedesign-deefink.pdf.

Gamson, Z.F. (1995). The seven principles for good practice in undergraduate education: A historical perspective in S.R. Hatfield (ed.), *The Seven Principles in Action: Improving undergraduate education* Boston, MA: Anker, pp. 1–8.

Garrison, D.R. (2003). Cognitive presence for effective asynchronous online learnng: The role of reflective inquiry, self-direction, and metacognition, in J. Bourne & J.C. Moore (eds), *Elements of Quality Online Education: Practice and direction.* New York: Sloan-C.

Haladyna, T.M. (1999). *Developing and Validating Multiple-choice Test Items* (2nd ed.). Mahwah, NJ: Lawrence Erlbaum Associates.

Hall, F.S. (1994). Management education by design. *Journal of Management Education, 18*(2), 182–97.

Halpern, D. (ed.) (1994). *Changing College Classrooms: New teaching and learning strategies in an increasingly complex world.* San Francisco: Jossey-Bass.

Halpern, D.F. & Hakel, M.D. (2002). *Applying the Science of Learning to the University and Beyond: New Directions for Change, No. 89.* Jossey-Bass.

Halpern, D.F. & Hakel, M.D. (2003). Applying the science of learning to the university and beyond. *Change,* July–August, 37–41.

Hodgson, V. (1997). New technology and learning: Accepting the challenge, in J. Burgoyne & M. Reynolds (eds), *Management learning: Integrating Perspectives in theory and practice.* London: Sage. pp. 215–25.

Hodgson, V. & Watland, P. (2004). Researching networked management learning. *Management Learning, 35*(2), 99–116.

Huang, R. & Zhou, Y. (2006). Designing blended learning focused on knowledge category and learning activities: Case studies from Beijing Normal University, in C.J. Bonk & C.R. Graham (eds), *The Handbook of Blended Learning: Global perspectives, local designs.* San Francisco: Pfeiffer.

Huba, M.E. & Freed, J.E. (2000). *Learning-centered Assessment on College campuses: Shifting the focus from teaching to learning.* Boston, MA: Allyn & Bacon.

Jacobs, L.C. & Chase, C.I. (1992). *Developing and Using Tests Effectively: A guide for faculty.* San Francisco: Jossey-Bass.

Kolb, D.A. (1984). *Experiential Learning: Experience as the source of learning and development.* Englewood Cliffs, NJ: Prentice Hall.

Kuh, G.D. & Vesper, N. (1997). A comparison of student experiences with good practices in undergraduate education between 1990 and 1994. *The Review of Higher Education, 21,* 43–61.

Light, R.J. (2001). *Making the Most of College: Students speak their minds.* Cambridge, MA: Harvard University Press.

Marchese, T.J. (1998). The new conversations about learning insights from neuroscience and anthropology, cognitive science and workplace studies. *New Horizons for Learning, 3*(4). [Online] New Horizons for Learning. Available: http://www.newhorizons.org

Marks, R.B., Sibley, S. & Arbaugh, J.B. (2005). A structural equation model of predictors for effective online learning. *Journal of Management Education, 29,* 531–63.

Marsh, H.W. (2001). Distinguishing between good (useful) and bad workloads on students' evaluations of teaching. *American Educational Research Journal, 38*(1), 183–212.

McBeath, R.J. (ed.) (1992). *Instructing and Evaluating in Higher Education: A guidebook for planning learning outcomes.* Englewood Cliffs, NJ: Educational Technology Publications.

McKeachie, W.J. & Svinicki, M. (2005). *Teaching Tips: Strategies, research, and theory for college and university teachers* (12th ed.). Boston: Houghton-Mifflin.

Michaelson, L.K., Fink, L.D. & Watson, W.E. (1994). Pre-instructional minitests. *Journal of Management Education, 18,* 32–44.

Michaelson, L.K., Knight, A.B. & Fink, L.D. (2004). *Team-based learning: A transformative use of small groups in college teaching.* Sterling, VA: Stylus.

Mundhenk, L.G. (2004). Toward an understanding of what it means to be student centered: A new teacher's journey. *Journal of Management Education, 28*(4), 447–62.

Peterson, T.O. (2004). So you're thinking of trying problem based learning?: Three critical success factors for implementation. *Journal of Management Education, 28*(5), 630–47.

Raelin, J.A. & Coghlan, D. (2006). Developing managers as learners and researchers: Using action learning and action research. *Journal of Management Education, 30*(5), 670–89.

Ramsey, V.J. & Fitzgibbons, D.E. (2005). Being in the classroom. *Journal of Management Education, 29*(2), 330–56.

Richlin, L. (2006). *Blueprint for learning: Constructing college courses to facilitate, assess, and document learning.* Sterling, VA: Stylus Publishing.

Roth, W. (1998). Teaching and learning as everyday activity, in B.J. Fraser & K.G. Tobin (eds) *International Handbook of Science Education: Part 1.* Dordrecht, The Netherlands: Kluwer.

Shea, P. (2007). Towards a conceptual framework for learning in blended environments, in A.G. Picciano & C. Dziuban (eds), *Blended Learning: Research perspectives.* New York: Sloan-C.

Sherwood, A.L. (2004). Problem-based learning in management education: A framework for designing context. *Journal of Management Education, 28*(5), 536–57.

Sorcinelli, M.D. (1991). Research findings on the seven principles. *New Directions for Teaching and Learning, 47,* 13–26.

Sorenson, D.L. (2001). Guest speakers: agony or ecstasy. *Focus on Faculty, 9*(2), 4.

Sorenson, D.L. (2006). When you are the guest lecturer. *Focus on Faculty, 14*(1), 4.

Stevens, D.D. & Levi, A.J. (2005). *Introduction to Rubrics: An assessment tool to save grading time, convey effective feedback, and promote student learning.* Sterling, VA: Stylus.

Suski, L. (2004). *Assessing for Student Learning.* San Francisco: Anker Publishing.

Sutherland, T.E. & Bonwell, C.C. (eds) (1996). Using active learning in college classes: A range of options for faculty. *New Directions for Teaching and Learning, 67.* San Francisco: Jossey-Bass.

Svinicki, M. (ed.) (1999). Teaching and learning on the edge of the millennium: Building on what we have learned. *New Directions for Teaching and Learning, 80.* San Francisco: Jossey-Bass.

Walvoord, B.E. & Anderson, V.J. (1998). *Effective Grading: A tool for learning and assessment.* San Francisco: Jossey-Bass.

Weimer, M. (2002). *Learner-Centered Teaching: Five key changes to practice.* San Francisco: Jossey-Bass.

Whetten, D.A. (2007). Principles of effective course design: What I wish I had known about learning-centered teaching 30 years ago. *Journal of Management Education, 31,* 339–57.

Whetten, D.A. & Campbell-Clark, S. (1996). An integrated model for teaching management skills. *Journal of Management Education, 20,* 152–81.

Whetten, D.A. & Cameron, K.S. (2007). *Developing Management Skills* (7th ed.). Upper Saddle River, NJ: Prentice Hall.

Wiggins, G. (1998). *Educative Assessment: Designing assessments to inform and improve student performance.* San Francisco: Jossey-Bass.

Wilkerson, L. & Gijselaers, W.H. (eds) (1996). Bringing problem-based learning to higher education: Theory and practice. *New Directions for Teaching and Learning, 68.* San Francisco: Jossey-Bass.

# 14

# Mentoring Ph.D. Students within an Apprenticeship Framework

Gerald R. Ferris, Pamela L. Perrewé, and
M. Ronald Buckley

## Summary

Despite its importance in the education industry, little has been written about how to train, educate, and mentor graduate students in pursuit of a Ph.D. Consequently, inconsistency has tended to characterize professor–Ph.D. student mentoring processes and outcomes, perhaps affecting the time-to-completion of degree and also the student attrition rate. The purpose of this chapter is to address this need by providing some guidance on the process of training, educating, and mentoring Ph.D. students using a modeling, coaching, scaffolding, and fading framework. We characterize this as a collaborative dyadic mentoring process within an apprenticeship framework, and draw upon theory and research in mentoring, behavior modeling, social learning theory, and organizational politics to explicate the process dynamics in the professor/mentor-Ph.D. student/protégé relationship. Through this analysis, we attempt to provide a better understanding of the perspectives of both the professor/mentor and Ph.D. student/protégé, and how the apprenticeship/mentoring process can be best designed to maximize protégé development, degree completion, and subsequent career effectiveness.

Every year, thousands of new Ph.D. students in numerous fields of study are hooded in commencement ceremonies at universities across the world. As a highly labor-intensive process, the training and education of Ph.D. students is a costly venture, owing to the relatively few students that any one professor can educate and mentor at one time. In light of the aforementioned facts, and the sizable financial investment in this process, the logical conclusion would be that there is volume upon volume of training techniques, educational tips, and other published material on 'best practices' for developing Ph.D. students. There is not!

As Gordon (2003) has commented, and Mitchell (2007) has seconded, there is an overabundance of advice for those who pursue a Ph.D., accompanied by minimal advice for the effective advising and mentoring of Ph.D. students. The sober fact is that very little material exists concerning how to train, educate, or mentor Ph.D. students, perhaps at least partially due to the misguided belief that this is just something that we as Ph.Ds should know how to do.

Mitchell (2007: 237) presented a plethora of data collected by others indicating that our doctoral students 'believe that our training has failed to prepare them for their professional careers.' Importantly, in the context of Ph.D. supervision, the relationship between the student and advisor has a direct effect upon important performance outcomes for the nascent Ph.D. (Armstrong et al., 2004; Cummings, 1996).

The purpose of this chapter is to address the aforementioned gap by providing some guidance on the process of training, educating, and mentoring Ph.D. students. Van Dyne (1996) cogently developed the differentiation between mentoring processes as they occur in business and in academia, with the major difference occurring with respect to businesses valuing 'fit' and academia valuing socialization. Recently, a number of models for this process have been suggested. We agree with Ferris (2003) that the appropriate model for doctoral supervision can best be described as a collaborative partnership model, as opposed to the corporate manager model suggested by Vilkinas (2002).

We characterize the Ph.D. student mentoring process within an apprenticeship framework, and draw upon our experience, as well as theory and research in mentoring, to examine the dynamic processes within the relationship. Through this analysis, we attempt to provide a better understanding of the perspectives of both the mentor and protégé, and how the apprenticeship/mentoring process can be best designed to maximize protégé development,

degree completion, and subsequent career effectiveness, as well as developing and preserving a high-quality mentor–protégé relationship.

We would be remiss if we did not mention a caveat regarding the perspective and focus taken in the development of this chapter. In this chapter, our approach is decidedly American centric, because we (i.e., the authors of this chapter) all are affiliated with American universities. Importantly, mentoring practices demonstrate greater differences across programs and countries than within (Wang, 2001). Wright et al. (2007) have elucidated the myriad supervisory styles used with respect to doctoral supervision. The American model of Ph.D. development involves a substantial coursework component followed by a dissertation. The United Kingdom (UK) model, which also is used in countries such as Australia and New Zealand, involves appreciably less coursework. The American model is organized around teams or committees of mentors. The UK model typically involves one primary supervisor/advisor and one associate supervisor/advisor, whose role is to ensure that what is essentially a 3–4 year full-time research project, that generates new insight, is completed.

Despite the desire to unify education systems across the world, according to the Bologna Process, each country in Europe seems to have its own distinct way of training/mentoring/supervising Ph.D. students. This led Kehm (2004: 297) to conclude that 'even in those countries that have a more structured doctoral education, insufficient supervision has been a continuous concern.' Further, she stated that many in Europe are now looking at 'abolishing the traditional apprenticeship model' in favor of the more structured training that we have been using in the United States. We might suggest that our international colleagues implement some of the training methodologies discussed in this chapter if their intention is to move away from the strict apprenticeship model, and toward more of a collaborative partnership model that we implement in our doctoral training. This perspective combines the most effective aspects of mentoring and development within a broader apprenticeship framework.

In our examination of Ph.D. education and mentoring, we agree with the assumptions made by Bowen and Rudenstine (1992), regarding the design of Ph.D. programs, when they stated: 'The design, oversight, evaluation, and careful monitoring of graduate programs make an enormous difference to the quality of the educational experience, the morale and progress of students, and the extent to which human and financial resources are used effectively' (p. 267). So, although our concerns in this chapter focus more on the dyadic professor–Ph.D. student education and mentoring process, we assume that this takes place within a context of collective faculty accountability.

## AMBIGUITY AND INCONSISTENCY IN THE PROFESSOR–PH.D. STUDENT INTERACTION CONTEXT

By its very nature, the professor–Ph.D. student interaction context is ambiguous, with only distal goals guiding the interactions, but seriously lacking in proximal processes to achieve the long-term goals. Combined with the lack of formal guidelines or generally agreed upon procedures for developing Ph.D. students in a mentoring context, we see considerable inconsistency in the approaches taken by faculty in training and developing their Ph.D. students. Indeed, as noted by Kennedy (1997): 'To this well-furnished suite of challenges, most mentors come entirely unprepared at the beginnings of their careers. Beyond observation, doctoral and post-doctoral programs typically include nothing at all by way of training in this vital aspect of academic life. In the vacuum, the new Ph.D.s have little choice but to observe those around them and accept whatever model is provided to them by their mentors' (p. 98).

With such ambiguity about how to approach Ph.D. development, different styles emerge,

ranging from awful and dysfunctional, involving abusive behavior, to benign neglect by professors who simply do nothing at all, to very effective working relationships, whereby students benefit greatly from the active involvement and guidance of knowledgeable and skilled mentors. Kennedy (1997) argued that: 'The interaction between advanced student and faculty mentor is complex, and presents its own set of hazards and challenges. There are tensions between a growing independence on the part of the student and various needs that may be felt by the professor' (pp. 97–8).

The very characteristics of this relationship, which involve close and frequent interaction among people of high intelligence and great interests, but unequal status, suggest that there is the opportunity for inspirational guidance at the one extreme, and conflicts and difficulties at the other. It appears that there are some who possess a natural tendency to understand how to be an effective mentor of Ph.D. students, and others who do not. Again, making reference to Kennedy (1997: 108): 'There is no formula for discharging the academic duties involved in being a good mentor. Knowing when to be demanding and when to be flexible and forgiving is a skill possessed by the best.'

## THE APPRENTICESHIP MODEL OF INDIVIDUAL DEVELOPMENT

### The apprenticeship concept in historical perspective

Dating back to ancient times, the concept of apprenticeship has been a persistent pedagogical approach, separate from formal education provided in the school systems, learning a trade or craft working under the guidance and direction of a skilled craftsman or master (Randi, 2000). Through observation of experts and guided practice, apprentices would gradually move from performing simple tasks all the way to taking on responsibility for completing such tasks independently. As noted by

Randi (2000), 'this type of apprenticeship persisted throughout the middle ages to Colonial America and continues today in vocational education apprenticeships' (p. 220).

In recent years, the concept of apprenticeship has been expanded beyond the acquisition of physical skills, to also include cognition and the efforts to identify and communicate the underlying thought processes that are involved in specific tasks (Randi, 2000). This concept has been referred to as 'cognitive apprenticeship,' and Collins et al. (1989) developed a model to characterize its features, which is based upon the four aspects of traditional apprenticeship. These components of the model, which are particularly pertinent to educational environments, are: '*modeling*, in which apprentices observe masters demonstrating how to perform tasks; *scaffolding*, in which masters support apprentices in carrying out tasks; *coaching*, in which masters coach apprentices through a wide range of activities; and *fading*, in which masters gradually remove support, increasing apprentice's responsibility' (Randi, 2000: 220). We believe that this is an effective framework around which to organize many of our thoughts in this chapter.

The apprenticeship framework, as noted above, implies a strong role played by the master craftsman, skilled tradesperson, or experienced mentor. Therefore, the study of the mentoring process serves as an underlying theme within the apprenticeship model, and critical to developing a more informed understanding of the professor–Ph.D. student interaction and development process.

**Table 14.1   The apprenticeship framework**

| 1 | MODELING | Developing expectations about our field |
|---|---|---|
| 2 | SCAFFOLDING | Learning opportunities/effective feedback |
| 3 | COACHING | Skill building/individual development |
| 4 | FADING | Redefining mentor/protégé roles |

## Mentoring process and content

The concept of mentoring has been around for a long time, in various ways, shapes, and forms, and in many different fields. In Greek mythology, Mentor was the wise and experienced friend of Odysseus, who served to educate and care for his son (Randi, 2000). Thus, most generally agree that mentoring involves some aspects of overseeing another's learning and development, offering advice, establishing trust, guiding, challenging, motivating, encouraging, supporting, all within some progression of time and activity whereby 'mentors initiate apprentices into a field, providing support until the apprentices become competent and independent' (Randi: 221).

Employees in organizations experience understanding, learning, and sense making, which are critical to effectiveness, and organizational scientists have actively researched the formal and informal mechanisms through which such learning and understanding are transmitted. Furthermore, mentoring has emerged as a principal mechanism for disseminating information and building savvy and understanding regarding how and why things work the way they do in organizations (e.g., Noe et al., 2002; Wanberg et al., 2003).

Both formal and informal learning goes on in mentoring relationships, and whereas much research has examined the learning of declarative knowledge, mentoring only more recently has been viewed as the most likely way that employees are educated about procedural knowledge issues, including politics in the organization. Perrewé et al. (2002) suggested that political skill development is a critical function of mentoring relationships, and Noe et al. (2002) argued that the role of mentoring in building protégé political skill was an important area of investigation.

Additionally, these researchers argued that an important outcome of mentoring is the visibility and exposure of protégés, which can occur through access to important social and work networks provided by mentors. Lankau and Scandura (2002) suggested that the individual learning that goes on in mentoring relationships tends to focus on work content as well as social and political competencies. Simply doing a good job is not going to lead to long-term effectiveness if individuals do not develop an understanding and savvy about career positioning, networking, and opportunity creation (Perrewé and Nelson, 2004).

Some learning that goes on in mentoring relationships can be transmitted through observation of role models through social learning processes (Ferris et al., 1994). Socializing protégés into the informal norms, rules, and nuances of behavior in organizations can be told, but frequently modeled behaviors by mentors are akin to social learning in action (Bandura, 1977). Research has demonstrated not only the social learning of work values but also supervisory style (Weiss, 1977, 1978). Protégés observe particularly salient incumbent employees (e.g., mentors), and they imitate or model their behavior.

This latter point suggests that it is important to select someone who not only has a keen interest and set of effective mentoring skills, but also one who has an established reputation. Such a mentor can provide high-quality instruction and skill building, as well as role modeling of effective professional behavior. In addition, such mentors can be quite helpful in effectively placing their Ph.D. students in faculty positions at institutions congruent with competencies and aspirations.

## Mentoring in doctoral programs

Developing an understanding of mentoring in professor–Ph.D. student relationships in graduate school certainly can borrow extensively from the theory and research on mentoring discussed in the previous section, and we liberally make use of such information in this section of the chapter, and those to follow (for other sources, see e.g., Huwe and Johnson, 2002). Beyond doctoral seminars, there is much learning that goes on in the professor–Ph.D. student mentoring interactions that focuses on a variety of topics, issues, and skill-building experiences. These settings are where students learn the craft of research, and all that it entails, including one of the most important skills of learning to write for a scientific audience (i.e., the journals).

Additionally, scholars recently have addressed the nature and degree of politics in graduate school and academic careers, suggesting that just being smart is not enough, but that political skill also is needed to effectively navigate such turbulent and complex contexts, with the implication that this skill building needs to come from professor/mentors (e.g., Ferris, 1998; Hawley, 2003; Kirchmeyer, 2005). As we discuss issues related to politics in graduate school and academic careers, we wish to emphasize that, indeed, a keen understanding of the political dynamics in academic environments is very important, as are the skills necessary to navigate such politics. However, research skills, experience, and productivity also are very important, and go a long way toward distinguishing the most effective academics throughout their careers. The point we wish to emphasize is that research skill building and political skill together reflect the best portfolio, and superior in nature than either skill set by itself.

Kirchmeyer (2005) conducted an interesting investigation that tested a performance versus a political perspective on protégé career success. The performance perspective is the more traditional view that mentors influence protégé career success indirectly through skill building and performance. Alternatively, the political perspective suggests that protégé career success can be impacted by mentoring directly, and need not be mediated by performance. This perspective is drawn from Pfeffer's (1981) view that political skill can contribute directly to advancement at least as much (or more) as can performance, and from Ferris and Judge's (1991) arguments that mentors build protégé social and political skill, embed them in their extensive social networks, and thus send powerful signals to the marketplace of the protégés' reputation, ability, and fit. Kirchmeyer found support for the political perspective whereby mentoring demonstrated direct effects on protégé career success, not mediated by performance.

Cable and Murray (1999) studied the tournament or contest perspective (e.g., publication success, authorship priority, etc.) versus the sponsored mobility perspective (i.e., prestige of Ph.D. department and eminence of one's dissertation chairperson) in prediction of university faculty hiring of new professors. Contrary to previous research in this area, they reported that the tournament or contest mobility model best predicted hiring decisions. However, even though the research record and other contest variables predicted most effectively, the eminence of the dissertation chairperson (i.e., a sponsored mobility variable) significantly predicted the prestige of job offers received by the newly minted Ph.D.s. This suggests, as we saw in the previous section on mentoring in organizations, that the reputation and prestige of the mentor can be a significant factor not only in the quality of mentoring received and skills developed, but also in the subsequent job search and career effectiveness decisions.

One issue that emerges at the outset in this area is that not all dissertation chairs necessarily are mentors, but instead serve merely as advisors to the students, and guide them through the dissertation research process. Indeed, Hawley (2003) argued that only exceptional dissertation chairs deserve to be called mentors. Most chairs are merely advisors and do a reasonable job of overseeing course work progression and research projects. She argued that mentors do much more than simply provide direction, but instead they make a greater commitment and become much more involved with the students and their unique circumstances. Mentors accompany their protégés throughout the entire process, and make professional and emotional investments in their students.

More directly addressing the nature of politics in graduate school and in dealing specifically with faculty, Hawley (2003) provided the following hints, observations, and advice for individuals who have made the decision to enroll in a Ph.D. program. She advises the new Ph.D. student that the journey is more than intellectual; it is intensely emotional and ego-threatening within a highly political environment. The unfortunate reality is that the ranks of ABDs (i.e., Ph.D. students who have completed All But Dissertation) are filled with intelligent, but politically naive, people who never learned how to navigate their way through the dissertation process (Hawley, 2003).

Hawley (2003) goes on to characterize the Ph.D. program environment, and the ambiguity and politics that can emerge. 'A major problem with the doctoral environment is that it is fraught with double messages. One day you are treated as a colleague and the next day a 'go-fer,' sometimes by the very same person! You follow a promising hunch and are praised by a committee member only to be chastised by your chair for venturing too far out on your own … you need great tolerance for ambiguity to cope with the situation. This requires a tough and resilient ego that is not easily bruised and can bounce back quickly after setbacks. Some cope by saying to themselves, 'If I can learn to play the game, I'll get through this' (Hawley, 2003: 26). 'While it may sound cynical, I must admit there are game-playing aspects to earning a Ph.D. The first rule is that you accept the role of a neophyte … a talented, creative, and motivated neophyte, but a neophyte nevertheless. Such a role is probably most distasteful to the student who has held a position of authority in the outside world and must quickly adjust to the relatively powerless status of a student' (p. 26).

Hawley (2003) argued that successful students must have more than 'book smarts,' they must also have 'street smarts.' This means they must be intellectually and emotionally resilient, conscientious, and able to accurately read the political environment in which they have to function. Unfortunately, this creates problems for the new generation of students, who, according to Levine (2005), are quite politically naive (see discussion of generational issues in a later section of this chapter). One mechanism for helping doctoral student protégés to develop, both academically as well as politically, is through the management of mentor–protégé expectations.

## Modeling effective behavior through the development of mentor–protégé expectations

Perhaps one of the most important aspects of successful mentor–protégé relationships is managing and communicating expectations (Perrewé and Zellars, 2006, 2007). Early in a program of study, realistic expectations must be developed. For example, our expectations for our Ph.D. students include excellence in coursework, teaching, and research. Furthermore, our expectations also include pursuing faculty positions at the best research universities possible, upon completion of the Ph.D. It is the responsibility of mentors to clearly communicate these types of expectations. For example, if a doctoral student would like to pursue organizational consulting after obtaining the Ph.D., it is our responsibility to counsel this student out (i.e., best done prior to admitting this student) and into another program that supports this goal, and is better equipped for developing this type of career. Thus, good mentors need to know not only their personal expectations for students, but also the general expectations of the Ph.D. program.

Furthermore, if a Ph.D. student expresses interest in attaining a position at a more teaching-oriented versus research-oriented university, this should be made clear to potential academic mentors. Some mentors may be supportive of this as a vocation, whereas others may be less supportive. This expectation must be communicated to avoid unrealistic expectations. A good mentor understands how time-consuming it is to train, educate, and mentor Ph.D. students. When mentors invest time developing Ph.D. students to conduct high-quality research, only to find they are not interested in going to the best

research university possible, such mentors most likely will both be disappointed and irritated.

However, it is the mentor's responsibility to determine the goals of their Ph.D. students. If students have preferences (or constraints) regarding where they will take their first academic position, it is imperative to be honest with the mentor. For example, if a Ph.D. student prefers a certain part of the country or has a spouse who also has a career that must be considered, this must be communicated to the mentor. Just as doctoral students should not be expected to 'read their professors' minds,' and automatically understand the academic culture and norms, professors should not be expected to intuitively know the constraints and/or preferences of their Ph.D. students.

Communicating expectations is a critical aspect of a doctoral program. There may not be one consistent model even within a specific doctoral program, because professors may have different philosophies about training Ph.D. students. However, it is important for both mentors and protégés to communicate their expectations for each other. Interestingly, research has found that academic mentors and doctoral protégés often have different types of expectations regarding the type of support the mentor should provide (Young and Perrewé, 2000). Academic mentors believed they should provide primarily instrumental support for their Ph.D. student protégés. This means mentors believed they should train Ph.D. students, for example, in understanding the empirical and conceptual research in their area of expertise, help develop their thinking in theory, research design, and data analysis, and, perhaps, assist them with their teaching and interpersonal presentation style. Ph.D. student protégés believed their mentors should provide primarily emotional social support, such that mentors would listen to their concerns, help them to alleviate their stress, and teach them how to cope with academic pressures.

Clearly, these differences in the types of mentoring support expected from the mentor and protégé perspectives could represent a recipe for disaster if there is minimal communication about such expectations. Although the best mentor may be one who can provide both types of support for Ph.D. students, not all mentors possess these skills. Doctoral students should consider the type of support most needed prior to committing to a mentor. Professors should consider what they can and/or are willing to offer their doctoral students before committing to serve as a mentor. We need to mention here that the discretion in the 'joining up process' (i.e., pairing of mentor and protégé) described is mostly an American phenomenon. In many such systems (e.g., Europe, Asia, and Australia) in the world, there is little choice with respect to a mentor, and the mentoring relationship holds fast throughout the entire academic program.

Toward the end of their Ph.D. program, protégés need to understand that their career choices reflect their mentor, which may well be one of the most misunderstood aspects of the mentor–protégé relationship. Doctoral students who are completing their programs of study want to obtain the faculty position they most prefer. On the surface, this makes perfect sense. However, if a student has worked with a mentor, and each has a different expectation about what is best for the protégé's career, their discussions about what type of academic position is best for the student might prove to be a very frustrating experience for both. Furthermore, it is important to be honest with one another. It does no good for a mentor to work with a Ph.D. student 'hoping' that the student's expectations eventually will match up with their own. Nor is it productive for Ph.D. students to tell their mentors just 'what they want to hear.' Clearly communicating expectations, and doing so early in the relationship, is paramount for a healthy mentor–protégé relationship.

Finally, mentors differ on the amount of social capital they are willing to expend on their Ph.D. students. As a general rule, the more protégés mirror the expectations of their mentors, the more likely mentors will be willing to utilize their social capital to help students. For example, mentors utilize their social capital by calling colleagues to ask them to consider their students for potential jobs, encouraging colleagues to involve their doctoral students in professional conference programs, introducing their students to prestigious colleagues at conferences, and including their Ph.D. students in research and publication opportunities.

These are just a few of the ways in which mentors can demonstrate a positive impact on protégés' careers. Although it is important for good mentors to invest the time and energy to engage in these types of activities in order to maximize Ph.D. student development and network building, it is just as important for protégés to understand that such investments are not made devoid of obligation. Assuming protégés have multiple opportunities, mentors most likely will expect that protégés will pursue those job opportunities for which they have been preparing.

When mentors leverage their social capital with colleagues, they are essentially putting their own reputations on the line in order to do so. Mentors, who invest a lot of time, energy, and social capital in their Ph.D. students, do so with an expectation of a return on their investment. Whether right or wrong, Ph.D. student protégés are a reflection of their faculty mentors, and this is a reality that needs to be taken seriously by both parties. Indeed, as a job candidate and/or a new professor in the field, you are frequently identified by who you studied under (i.e., your Ph.D. advisor/mentor) and where you received your Ph.D. (e.g., He's a Smith student from UCLA).

We have discussed the importance of mentors and protégés meeting each other's expectations, and we argue that this is the cornerstone of a successful mentor–protégé relationship. In the next section, we examine the faculty mentor–Ph.D. student protégé relationship within an apprenticeship framework. The notion of met expectations is a theme that is integrated throughout this discussion.

## Apprenticeship model in professor–Ph.D. student mentoring interactions

What we address directly in this section of the chapter is the nature of professor–Ph.D. student mentoring within an apprenticeship framework. Although such dyadic academic relationships may appear to be quite informal, Kennedy (1997) noted that 'they require at least as much planned effort and special skill as the lecture and the seminar, but they also embody the greatest risk of failure' (p. 116). This section has a personal tone because it is based primarily on our 25 years of experience mentoring Ph.D. students at six major universities.

*Providing coaching and learning opportunities.* The philosophy of Ph.D. student development we propose involves a multi-dimensional approach, which includes content-based learning, mastery of statistics and methodology, active involvement in the research process, development of oral and written communication skills, and socialization experiences, all woven together in an apprenticeship framework. Indeed, this is an individual development model, which suggests that strategically orchestrated investments in Ph.D. student development should yield the desired return on investment of a highly valued resource in the academic labor marketplace.

We might mention that whereas professors' overarching philosophy of Ph.D. student development should be consistent across students, within that framework, there is the need to make situational adjustments and adapt one's approach to the knowledge, prior experience, and style of individual students. Therefore, the overall philosophy, at a broad level, tends to be a 'one-size-fits-all,' but the experiences and approach developed for each student are tailored to each specific student.

Ph.D. students typically spend four years (sometimes five years) in our doctoral program, and during that time, the apprenticeship model employs a combination of coursework/seminars, intensive independent studies, and research assistantship experiences, whereby the new student gradually is exposed to, and held accountable for, actually conducting and executing more of the research project as they acquire and hone their scholarly skills. The process is highly labor-intensive, where we spend considerable time with our Ph.D. students in one-on-one sessions that range from discussions of specific theoretical and methodological approaches, to the development of writing and presentation skills for preparing their work for presentation at conferences and journal publication.

The expectations set for new students are high and rigorous. They are told to expect to work harder than they ever have, to take advantage of opportunities presented to them, to take a 'knowledge/skill-development-mentality,' not a 'coursework-achievement-mentality,' and to plan on being in a position to submit their research papers (i.e., working under our supervision) for presentation at conferences, and to journals for publication. Finally, they are told to expect to do all of this within the 4–5 year period typically allotted, and to finish their dissertations in time to go through the hooding ceremony at commencement so they leave with degree in hand. It is important for students to realize that leaving before degree completion is not an option.

Because effective mentoring relies upon the nature of the mentor–protégé relationship, we suggest that effective relationships between professor/mentors and Ph.D. students/protégés are characterized by some common characteristics that include trust, commitment, loyalty, accountability, flexibility, and support. Positive regard seems important to such relationships, as does mutual respect. In fact, former American Psychological Association (APA) President, and founder of positive psychology, Martin Seligman, recently spoke at the annual APA convention on the topic of mentoring in academic settings. 'He espoused a mentoring philosophy in line with his area of expertise: "Emphasize the positive and offer room to grow." His views stem from what psychologists know about how children's creativity spikes when they are in a secure, positive environment' (Chamberlain, 2006: 60).

In 2006, the American Psychological Association created a presidential task force 'Centering on Mentoring,' which was challenged to expand our understanding of mentoring in scientific and professional training and development endeavors. An early outcome of that task force's work is the document, *Introduction to Mentoring: A Guide for Mentors and Mentees,* which provides a very useful discussion of basic issues in mentoring. Some of the ideas discussed in that document, particularly with regard to stages of mentoring, have been integrated with our own ideas in formulation of the basic stages in the evolution of the professor–student mentoring relationship.

*Coaching experiences: The initiation and planning phase.* We set up a gradual progression of experiences over time designed to build research understanding and skills, as well as a working knowledge of the key issues involved in career progress and success after leaving the program. We schedule regular (e.g., weekly) standing meetings to discuss progress on their research projects, dissertation, and so forth. This builds in a formal accountability mechanism that should stimulate a regular progression of activity, goals to be met, and projects to be completed on time. Furthermore, inclusive here are time-to-degree goals for dissertation completion, which historically has been a problem, along with doctoral program attrition, where folks just drop out, or remain ABD forever (Bowen and Rudenstine, 1992).

We also balance out the delicate tensions or dilemmas in accountability of 'creativity vs. conformity' (Ferris et al., 1995). We want to create a structured and temporally-sensitive context that regulates activity on a consistent schedule of progression, yet is flexible and open enough to encourage creativity and innovation – sort of an environment of 'structured flexibility.'

We create simulations to use as a training and development tool whereby students are taught to work through a simulated activity of, say, mimicking professional activities they will have to perform after they get their degrees and are professors (e.g., presenting papers at conferences, practice job talks to build presentation skills, practice critically reviewing papers for journals under supervision, etc.). Such experiences reinforce the notion of 'behavioral consistency,' which says that the best predictor of future behavior is past and present behavior in similar situations (Wernimont and Campbell, 1968).

We ensure that students obtain some teaching experience, but not too much (Bowen and Rudenstine, 1992), as more time should be spent in research assistantships building scholarly skills and records. However, this issue of getting Ph.D. students out of the classroom and doing research more will continue to be an ongoing point of contention in many programs where Ph.D. students as teachers become such an attractive source of 'cheap labor' that college and university administrators cannot resist due to its efficiency.

*Progression, evaluation, and tracking: The development phase.* As we saw in the previous section, years 1 and 2 of the Ph.D. program in the organizational sciences involve content mastery and evaluation through doctoral seminars, and then preliminary examinations. Also included in that initial phase is teaching for the first time, and getting involved in research at a modest, but progressively measured, level. Certainly, progress is expected and assessed during the initiation phase. However, because everything is new and unfamiliar, and considerable student time is devoted to listening, observing, and attending research meetings with others, expectations for progression are lower, and there is greater flexibility, patience, and tolerance.

During years 3 and 4 (and possibly 5, in some cases), there is more focus on research experience by requiring the student to take on responsibility for larger parts of the total process of research and writing. During this period, there is also more involvement in presenting work at professional conferences and submitting research papers for publication review to journals. Ideally, near the end of year 3, the student should defend a dissertation proposal, and then proceed, during year 4, with the execution, write-up, and defense of the doctoral dissertation.

Very important in the development phase of the professor/mentor–Ph.D. student/protégé relationship is the provision of focused, specific feedback from mentor to protégé, certainly handled always in a humane and constructive manner. Areas in need of improvement and development need to be identified in order to expect the student to change. However, handling the feedback in a non-threatening way will help the student see this process as a natural opportunity for development, and less likely to become paralyzed in non-activity for fear of scathing criticism.

Indeed, the careful provision of constructive feedback is a very important consideration, as noted by Kennedy (1997): 'Apprentice scholarship is a time of trying out new ideas and testing creative limits. Sometimes the new ideas are bad or even silly. Veterans become used to the harsh public fate of bad ideas, but neophytes can be scared into a kind of unproductive trance if one of their first real creations is treated roughly. Criticizing with respect and turning a poorly structured question into a good one are among the skills that good mentors are able to utilize regularly' (p. 108).

An additional point about regular feedback and evaluation is important here, and it pertains to the monitoring of students' performance and progress in the program. Specifically, faculty need to be able to make evaluative determinations as soon as possible regarding students who are struggling so seriously in the program that they will not be able to make it through (Bowen and Rudenstine, 1992). Unfortunately, sometimes such students are allowed to drift or become totally lost because faculty members do not monitor students' behavior, performance, and tracking diligently enough. Furthermore, early identification of student problems and deficiencies are critical in proposing remediation steps and courses of action which can get the student back on track.

*Building scaffolding for future success.* The content of mentoring during the latter part of the students' doctoral studies continues to focus on research skill building and experience, scholarly writing style, and building one's own research portfolio. Additionally, the focus shifts a bit to the job market, and what to expect when interviewing for faculty positions upon degree completion. If orchestrated effectively, and good planning, progression, evaluation, and tracking are realized, the beginning of the final year in the Ph.D. program should see the student developing into a promising young scholar, with the beginnings of a good professional portfolio of research and teaching.

Discussions and activities then focus on skill building in research presentations, staging simulated 'job talks' for the student, with departmental faculty serving as the audience, who pose challenging questions and issues with which the student must grapple, much like when interviewing for a job during a campus visit. Mentors provide information on what to expect during the 1–2 day campus visits, knowing what kind of questions to expect, and learning what to ask. The practicalities and politics of faculty hiring also are topics of discussion at this time.

Often characterized as a two-stage fit process, stage one focuses on person–job fit, and involves reflecting all of the knowledge, skills, and abilities to effectively perform the job of professor; that is, possess a Ph.D. from a good university, demonstrate evidence of research and teaching effectiveness, and show strong letters of recommendation. Stage one fit gets your name placed on the short list of job candidates who are invited for campus visits, where stage two fit occurs. Stage two fit focuses on person–group fit, and although during the campus visits there are continued assessments of research and teaching skills, a major focus is on collegiality and how the candidate fits in with the group/department faculty.

The old saying in faculty hiring seems to be: 'Hire the best person you can, but never hire a jerk!' As the term 'jerk' is inherently multidimensional in nature, frank discussions are initiated between mentor and student regarding how to avoid being perceived as arrogant, condescending, dismissive, defensive, or self-interested (for a more specific discussion of the two-stage fit process in hiring decisions, see Judge and Ferris, 1992).

*Fading away and moving to the background.* Throughout the student's Ph.D. program, but particularly during this last phase of development, the mentor involves the student in his/her own network of colleagues at other universities, including former Ph.D. students who are now professors and may have their own Ph.D. students. The latter connections take on an 'extended family' feel, where the former Ph.D. students lend assistance and support to the student, and expands his/her own social and professional network (Chamberlain, 2006).

The final several months of a student's Ph.D. program should involve a transition phase where the mentor works with the student at ensuring the completion of the dissertation, and also begins to wrap up existing projects, thus gaining a gradual sense of closure on the graduate school phase of development. This also points toward preparation for the next phase of becoming a professor, where students may soon be directing the development of Ph.D. students themselves. This is where the mentor role can begin to fade, and a different type of relationship can be developed.

There are numerous issues with which Ph.D. students must be familiar and aware, that bear on professional activity in the field, and which can meaningfully impact career effectiveness. Unfortunately, much of this information is never taught in seminars, and there are few books one can read to self-educate. Issues such as dealing and working with journal editors and reviewers on submitted work, learning how to provide constructively critical feedback when reviewing journal submissions as a reviewer, and so forth get communicated in effective professor– student mentoring interactions, but may

get forgotten or neglected in other mentor relationships.

It is important to understand that, to some extent, the transmission of such information and skill development can be formalized somewhat through the regular meeting of 'pro-seminars' or 'professional development workshops' offered for Ph.D. students and orchestrated by faculty. These can be ongoing weekly sessions throughout the academic year, with topics ranging widely and issues emerging both systematically and opportunistically.

*Mentoring beyond Ph.D. completion: The redefinition phase.* When the rationale, goals, and objectives of a professor mentor–Ph.D. student protégé relationship are achieved, thus rendering the conditions of that relationship null and void, then the relationship can be either formally terminated, or redefined into a different type of relationship. This redefinition phase may take on different forms. One form is when the mutual respect and affection have continued to develop, and the traditional mentor–protégé teaching and coaching relationship is replaced by a friendship or affable colleagueship, whereby the two parties continue to work together on research in the future. For some, the relationship lasts the remainder of their careers.

Another form of relationship redefinition occurs when some degree of interpersonal conflict emerges because the mentor continues to be directive, and the protégé is striving for greater independence. Acknowledgment of the problem and its causes by both parties may result in a period of distance, yet mutual respect, in the working relationship, which may be either temporary or permanent. Some protégés have a strong need to put both physical and psychological distance between themselves and their mentors, and to develop their own unique identity and reputation independent of the mentors.

Most certainly, it is desirable for new Ph.D.s to develop their own scholarly identity and reputation so that they are not marginalized by being perceived too extensively as simply a 'student of so-and-so.' The key issue here is the degree of distance and fading that works best for them. Good mentors hold frank, open discussions with their protégés regarding how the protégé's research record is likely to be perceived and evaluated at promotion and tenure time if there has been too much co-authored work. Thus, identification with one's mentor can reflect a nonlinear relationship with job performance and career effectiveness, helping new Ph.D.s up to a point, but then becoming dysfunctional as perceived by others. The key is to be able to predict the inflection in the curve, when it breaks downward and begins to harm the protégé.

The nature of an effective post-Ph.D. mentoring relationship can concern itself with many things, but typically it is less focused on protégé learning and more on career management, building an effective program of research, networking and positioning, and goal setting and planning for 3, 5, and more years out. The mentor serves as both a career advisor and a research colleague, simultaneously working on collaborative projects with the protégé, and also providing advice regarding the selection and sequencing of projects in order for the protégé to build a *program* of research in an area of inquiry, and the establishment of an independent research identity and reputation.

Consensus clearly seems to suggest that mentor–protégé relationships progress through a reasonably well-defined set of stages (modeling, coaching, scaffolding, and fading), and that the final stage marks some kind of dissolution of the old relationship and/or redefinition and development of a new type of relationship. It is difficult to put a timetable on this process, but good mentors seem to know when the time is right to redefine the relationship.

As Hawley (2003) noted: 'Good mentors, like good houseguests, know when it is time to go. When the journey is over and the traveler has reached her destination, the original relationship has served its purpose. It must be replaced with a different one reflecting the new Ph.D.'s altered status. Wise mentors more or less consciously make

this transition with each graduate, gladly relinquishing a student in favor of gaining a colleague. Others seem to lack the ego strength to surrender a relationship in which the balance of power is so unquestionably on their side' (p. 57).

## RECOMMENDATIONS AND FINAL THOUGHTS

Hopefully, we have impressed upon the readers of this chapter at least three central points. First, we make the point that (i.e., certainly supported by some data and facts) that training and developing Ph.D. students is a critically important (and costly) part of the higher education industry. Second, despite its importance, there has been little published regarding how to conduct such training and development systematically and effectively. Third, we provided our collective ideas for how the professor–Ph.D. student mentoring relationship can unfold and progress within the context of a collaborative apprenticeship framework.

### Additional challenges

*Friendships between the mentor and protégé.* Simply put, professor mentors and Ph.D. student protégés should not be friends; that is, at least not in the beginning of their working relationship. Nothing can disrupt a working relationship more than for the mentor and protégé to become too close. First, there needs to be an understanding that the mentor is the person who advises and guides the protégé. If protégés believe their mentor is their close friend, this puts them equal in status and can erode the mentor's ability to advise and guide the student. If protégés believe they are of equal status as their mentor, they are much less likely to accept the advice of the mentor (i.e., especially if it goes against their wishes, and sometimes it does).

Second, if mentors begin to have protégé friendships, this can negatively affect their ability to objectively evaluate and develop their students. Clearly, this is not to say that mentors and protégés should not like each other and enjoy each other's company. However, there is a very important distinction between developing a good working relationship, characterized by a healthy degree of professional distance, and being too close, which impairs judgment and objectivity, and results in unhealthy mentor–protégé relationships. Of course, toward the end of the protégé's program or after the protégé has taken a job, this relationship may very well become a relationship characterized by closeness and friendship.

*Multi-student mentoring.* We need to use the forgoing discussion as a way to move from just an examination of the dyadic mentoring situation, to a more realistic doctoral training setting where a single professor may be working with and mentoring as many as three, four, or five Ph.D. students at a time, who most likely are at different stages of development and points in their Ph.D. programs. This raises questions of individual student time allocation from the professor, and the progression of working in a group or team setting with other, perhaps more advanced, Ph.D. students.

Also, this might raise the issue of 'layering' or setting up layers or levels of mentoring, whereby a new student might work on a research project with a professor and a senior Ph.D. student, and sometimes all meet together to discuss and teach, but other times the senior student takes on responsibility for providing new students basic information; that is, sort of the same way coaches use veteran players to teach the rookies new things. This also may have advantages of reducing the possibility for intimidation, where new students might be a bit intimidated having to always deal with the senior professor, and might deal more comfortably with another Ph.D. student, albeit a more advanced and skilled student.

Successful mentors have a basic philosophy of training Ph.D. students that doesn't change, yet they also need to make individual adjustments based on the nuances, personal characteristics, and so forth of each student. Some take a firmer hand right away, and others need a gentler manner

to ease them into the process. Some need more support, and others are naturally more independent. Good mentors are able to read these signs early and make adjustments, adapt, and calibrate the specific approach tailored to the students' needs (within the general philosophy), much like Graen suggested in his Leader-Member Exchange (LMX) theory of leadership (e.g., Graen and Uhl-Bien, 1995).

*Generational issues.* Levine (2005) has argued that our new generation job applicant (i.e., our twixters) is not demonstrating a readiness for, and fit with, the demands of contemporary work organizations. Levine says that the new generation potential employees about to enter the work world are simply not prepared for the rigors of pursuing goals, a career direction, and the regularity of full-time employment. These new generation twixters seem to lack the social and psychological preparedness to engage fully in career endeavors, and commit to long-term career goals. Furthermore, such youngsters seem to lack the capacity to delay gratification, think long term, and make important decisions.

Levine (2005) said that 'It takes more than ability and drive to succeed as a startup adult. You have to be sensitive to the needs and desires of the people you work with and for' (p. 56). He said that such individuals often have no idea about the political realities of their job or organization. Levine goes on to state: 'To succeed, it is not enough to know a lot, work hard, and turn out quality products or services. You need to make yourself liked, and you have to show you like the people you want to have like you. That's politics' (p. 192).

So, extending Levine's (2005) observations to the current generation of Ph.D. students, we might conclude that because they are not very aware of the political realities of organizational environments, nor have much skill or competence in dealing with such issues, discussions of the politics of doctoral education and academic careers becomes important subject matter for discussion in professor–Ph.D. student mentoring relationships.

Compounding the generational issues raised by Levine (2005) are the tendencies of today's young adults to be much more self-centered and narcissistic (Twenge, 2006). Such issues seemingly can cause serious problems for Ph.D. students in mentoring relationships when they need to be given critical feedback sometimes, and may not be used to ever being told they are anything but perfect! This is a time for mentors to realize that protégés need both instrumental as well as social support to move them forward. Mentors need to recognize these generational differences and work with students so that they do not take constructive criticism as an assault on them, but instead as a learning experience intended to benefit.

*Success in the organization sciences.* Currently, there is disagreement in the published literature concerning those skills necessary for scholarly success in the organization sciences. Some agree with the contentions of Glick et al. (2007), that there are significant barriers to the launching and development of a successful academic career. We find ourselves agreeing that it is difficult but considerably more optimistic with respect to the career prospects of our students in this field (e.g., Ferris et al., in press). We believe that there are many different career paths that can be carved out by our students that will yield a successful and rewarding career in terms of teaching and research. We believe that our training should be done in the context of developing students who will make different contributions in terms of teaching and research at universities that are in line with their capabilities. Furthermore, our students need to believe that they are trained for success so that they have a chance to be successful.

*Faculty training and evaluation.* So, what recommendations can we make for the future? Well, we believe it is long past time that we regard mentoring Ph.D. students as a naturally intuitive set of competencies that faculty will simply 'pick up on their own.' These are acquirable skills and learnable content which should be taught to new professors, perhaps as part of junior faculty development programs. Such development

programs will need to be placed within the context of an expanded faculty performance evaluation system that formally rewards Ph.D. student mentoring along multiple dimensions (e.g., reduced drop-out rate, reduced time to degree, placement quality, publication records of Ph.D. students, etc.). Indeed, Bowen and Rudenstine (1992) argued 15 years ago that faculty should be formally evaluated regarding their performance as mentors or advisors, with particular reference to directing or advising dissertation research.

Without such a systemic framework acknowledging its importance, training Ph.D. students will be perceived as 'not really counting,' as noted in this excerpt from Hawley (2003): 'Time spent with students doesn't show up on the books anywhere, so it doesn't count, not even as teaching. The implicit statement is that it isn't important and this is bound to be reflected in student–faculty relationships. Because the system really discourages it, it takes the most dedicated faculty member to commit high-quality time to students. Many give them short shrift and concentrate instead on their own research which *is* rewarded by the administration' (p. 62).

## CONCLUSION

We might characterize Ph.D. students as miniature private enterprises (e.g., Bob, Inc.), who arrive in the program with certain human capital knowledge, skill, ability, and experience assets (i.e., raw materials). The intention of the structured and informal mentoring experiences that take place over the next four or five years is to make strategic investments in the development of those assets designed to lead to a successful teacher/researcher. Indeed, if done well, this process is designed to maximize the return on investments realized through placement in high-quality university faculty positions, and the students' development of premier research records and teaching success. Although these more tangible returns represent quite positive outcomes, good mentors will tell you that their greatest reward is the pride and satisfaction they experience when a student does well and enjoys a good career.

Therefore, as we have seen, the professor–Ph.D. student mentoring relationship is quite special, and can reflect very positive outcomes for both, particularly when the mentor takes a special interest in, and develops a degree of identity with, a particular student. Kennedy (1997) perhaps said it best when stating that: 'These interactive relationships are where the most meaningful and memorable influences arise. These are also the relationships that many faculty members find the most rewarding. There is a special joy in watching a student succeed brilliantly with a difficult problem; and sometimes an equal joy in helping a limited or troubled student overcome a handicap' (p. 116). When this occurs, there can be very rewarding and beneficial consequences for both professor and student, which benefits us and our field.

# REFERENCES

American Psychological Association Presidential Task Force Centering on Mentoring (2006) *Introduction to Mentoring: A Guide for Mentors and Mentees.* Washington, DC: American Psychological Association.

Armstrong, S.J., Allinson, C.W. and Hayes, J. (2004) 'The effects of cognitive style on research supervision: A study of student-supervisor dyads in management education', *Academy of Management Learning and Education,* 3: 41–63.

Bandura, A. (1977) *Social Learning Theory.* Englewood Cliffs, NJ: Prentice-Hall.

Bowen, W.G. and Rudenstine, N.L. (1992) *In Pursuit of the Ph.D.* Princeton, NJ: Princeton University Press.

Cable, D.M. and Murray, B. (1999) 'Tournaments versus sponsored mobility as determinants of job search success', *Academy of Management Journal,* 42: 439–49.

Chamberlain, J. (2006) 'Shared wisdom: Three generations of mentors and protégés discussed their insights on good mentoring', *Monitor on Psychology,* 37: 60–1.

Collins, A., Brown, J.S. and Newman, S.E. (1989) 'Cognitive apprenticeship: Teaching the crafts of reading, writing, and mathematics', in L. Resnick (ed.), *Knowing, Learning, and Instruction: Essays*

*in Honor of Robert Glaser.* Hillsdale, NJ: Lawrence Erlbaum. pp. 453–94.

Cummings, L.L. (1996) 'The development of doctoral students: Substantive and emotional perspectives', in P.J. Frost and M.S. Taylor (eds), *Rhythms of Academic Life: Personal Accounts of Careers in Academia.* London: Sage. pp. 147–52.

Ferris, G.R. (1998) *Politics in Graduate School and Academic Careers.* Invited presentation in the New Doctoral Student Consortium, Academy of Management, 58th Annual National Meeting, San Diego.

Ferris, G.R. and Judge, T.A. (1991) 'Personnel/Human Resources Management: A political influence perspective', *Journal of Management,* 17: 447–88.

Ferris, G.R., Fedor, D.B. and King, T.R. (1994) 'A political conceptualization of managerial behavior', *Human Resource Management Review,* 4: 1–34.

Ferris, G.R., Ketchen, D.J. and Buckley, M.R. (in press) 'Making a life in the organization sciences: No one said it was going to be easy', *Journal of Organizational Behavior.*

Ferris, G.R., Mitchell, T.R., Canavan, P.J., Frink, D.D. and Hopper, H. (1995) 'Accountability in human resource systems', in G.R. Ferris, S.D. Rosen and D.T Barnum (eds), *Handbook of Human Resource Management.* Oxford, UK: Blackwell Publishers. pp. 175–96.

Ferris, W.P. (2003) 'Why the partnership model's usefulness far exceeds that of the client model: Reply to Armstrong', *Academy of Management Learning and Education,* 2: 375–7.

Glick, W.H., Miller, C.C. and Cardinal, L.B. (2007) 'Making a life in the field of organization science', *Journal of Organizational Behavior.* Available at http://www3.interscience.wiley.com/cgi-bin/jissue/80002833

Gordon, P.J. (2003) 'Advising to avoid or cope with dissertation hang-ups', *Academy of Management Learning and Education,* 2: 375–7.

Graen, G.B. and Uhl-Bien, M. (1995) 'Development of leader-member exchange (LMX) theory of leadership over 25 years: Applying a multi-level, multi-domain perspective', *The Leadership Quarterly,* 6: 219–47.

Hawley, P. (2003) *Being Bright is Not Enough: The Unwritten Rules of Doctoral Study.* Springfield, IL: Charles C Thomas, Publishers.

Huwe, J.M. and Johnson, W.B. (2002) *Getting Mentored in Graduate School.* Washington, DC: American Psychological Association.

Judge, T.A. and Ferris, G.R. (1992) 'The elusive criterion of fit in human resources staffing decisions', *Human Resource Planning,* 15: 47–67.

Kehm, B.M. (2004) 'Developing doctoral degrees and qualifications in Europe: Good practice and issues of concern', in J. Sandlak (ed.),

A Comparative Analysis Doctoral Studies and Qualifications in Europe and the United States: Status and Prospect. UNESCO-CEPES Studies on Higher Education, pp. 279–98. Available at http://www.cepes.ro/publications/pdf/Doctorate.pdf

Kennedy, D. (1997) Academic Duty. Cambridge, MA: Harvard University Press.

Kirchmeyer, C. (2005) The effects of mentoring on academic careers over time: Testing performance and political perspectives', Human Relations, 58: 637–60.

Lankau, M.J. and Scandura, T.A. (2002) 'An investigation of personal learning in mentoring relationships: Content, antecedents, and consequences', Academy of Management Journal, 45: 779–90.

Levine, M. (2005) Ready or Not, Here Life Comes. New York: Simon and Schuster.

Mitchell, T.R. (2007) 'The academic life: Realistic changes needed for business school students and faculty', Academy of Management Learning and Education, 6: 236–51.

Noe, R.A., Greenberger, D.B. and Wang, S. (2002) 'Mentoring: What we know and where we might go', in G.R. Ferris and J.J. Martocchio (eds), Research in Personnel and Human Resources Management (Vol. 21). Oxford, UK: JAI Press/Elsevier Science. pp. 129–73.

Perrewé, P.L. and Nelson, D.L. (2004) 'Gender and career success: The facilitative role of political skill', Organizational Dynamics, 33: 366–78.

Perrewé, P.L., Young, A.M. and Blass, F.R. (2002) 'Mentoring within the political arena', in G.R. Ferris, M.R. Buckley and D.B. Fedor (eds), Human Resources Management: Perspectives, Context, Functions, and Outcomes (4th ed). Englewood Cliffs, NJ: Prentice-Hall. pp. 343–55.

Perrewé, P.L. and Zellars, K.L. (2006) Mentoring in Professor–Ph.D. Student Interactions. Professional Development Workshop, Annual Meeting of the Southern Management Association, Clearwater, FL.

Perrewé, P.L. and Zellars, K.L. (2007) Faculty Mentorship. Professional Development Workshop, New Doctoral Consortium, Annual Meeting of the Academy of Management, Philadelphia, PA.

Pfeffer, J. (1981) Power in Organizations. Boston: Pitman.

Randi, J. (2000) 'Apprenticeship', in A.E. Kazdin (ed.), Encyclopedia of Psychology (Vol. 1). New York: Oxford University Press and American Psychological Association. pp. 220–22.

Twenge, J.M. (2006) Generation Me: Why Today's Young Americans are More Confident, Assertive, Entitled – and More Miserable than Ever Before. New York: Free Press.

Van Dyne, L. (1996) 'Mentoring relationships: A comparison of experiences in business and academia', in P.J. Frost and M.S. Taylor (eds), Rhythms of Academic Life: Personal Accounts of Careers in Academia. London: Sage. pp. 159–73.

Vilkinas, T. (2002) 'The Ph.D. process: The supervisor as manager', Education and Training, 44: 129–37.

Wang, J. (2001) 'Contexts of mentoring and opportunities for learning to teach: A comparative study of mentoring practice', Teaching and Teacher Education, 17: 51–73.

Wanberg, C.R., Welsh, E.T. and Hezlett, S.A. (2003) 'Mentoring research: A review and dynamic process model', in J.J. Martocchio and G.R. Ferris (eds), Research in Personnel and Human Resources Management (Vol. 22). Oxford, UK: JAI Press/Elsevier Science. pp. 39–124.

Weiss, H.M. (1978) 'Social learning of work values in organizations', Journal of Applied Psychology, 63: 711–18.

Weiss, H.M. (1977) 'Subordinate imitation of supervisor behavior: The role of modeling in organizational socialization', Organizational Behavior and Human Performance, 19: 89–105.

Wernimont, P.F. and Campbell, J.P. (1968) 'Signs, samples, and criteria', Journal of Applied Psychology, 52: 372–6.

Wright, A., Murray, J.P. and Geale, P. (2007) 'A phenomenographic study of what it means to supervise doctoral students', Academy of Management Learning and Education, 6: 429–38.

Young, A.M. and Perrewé, P.L. (2000) 'What did you expect? The mediating role of met expectations in the mentor–protégé relationship', Journal of Management, 26: 611–32.

# 15

# Diversity in the Context of Lifelong Learning

Myrtle P. Bell, Mustafa F. Özbilgin and
Mine Karataş-Özkan

## Summary

In this chapter, we explore diversity in the context of lifelong learning, with a focus on learning as an ongoing process throughout one's life in formal and informal environments, and an investigation of how diversity learning can be effectively integrated into formal education and training. We begin by defining diversity from an interdisciplinary perspective in order to explain its multifaceted nature. Next, we briefly discuss attempts to reduce discriminatory practices through formal legislation. We then consider how the early and variety of diversity learning can work to reduce effectiveness of legislation and of management learning, in particular, learning about management and human resources processes in which non-dominant group members may be disadvantaged by erroneous, stereotypical beliefs. We also discuss how diversity learning is and should be infused into formal learning processes, with an emphasis on including learning from extant diversity scholarship and empirical evidence to counteract stereotypical beliefs.

The changing demographic makeup of global workforce and the enactment and expansion of anti-discriminatory legislation in many countries have brought about significant research attention on the increasing diversity of the workers. Increases in life expectancy, improved human capital of women and minority groups, and efforts to combat discriminatory practices have contributed to noticeable changes in the composition of labor markets. As a result, much diversity learning occurs in work settings, as people interact with others who are different; however, such settings are only one of many settings in which diversity learning takes place.

## DEFINING AND DOCUMENTING DIVERSITY

Contributions to the field of diversity learning are many, and come from distinct disciplines such as education, law, sociology, psychology, anthropology, history, and political science. Our aim in this chapter is to bring insights from across these disciplinary lines to reveal the trans-disciplinary and multi-faceted nature of diversity learning. For the purposes of this chapter, diversity is defined as real or perceived differences among people that affect their interactions and relationships (Dobbs, 1996). We specifically focus on real or perceived differences among people that are based on power or dominance relations between identity groups (e.g. 'the collectivities people use to categorize themselves and others' – Konrad, 2003: 7), which exist in some form worldwide. Although the term 'diversity' is sometimes perceived as appropriate only from a Western viewpoint, when defined in this way, the rationale for viewing it as a universal concept is more apparent. Internationally, the existence of widespread discrimination, dominance, marginalization, and colonization of people based on race, ethnicity, gender, religion, sexual orientation, age, and numerous other factors deem the concept of diversity relevant internationally (Bell, 2007).

With recognition of the demographic variety across the world's populations, the normalization of white able-bodied males as ideal workers has been ethically, legally, and socially challenged. However, the legacy of systemic discrimination has by no means been eradicated (Bell, 2007; Goldman et al., 2006). Nevertheless, the intensifying mobility of capital and the search for ever cheaper labor has generated a range of instrumental interests to exploit the demographic make-up of populations and their serviceability for employment purposes. Where labor shortages are high, an increased interest in female, elder, non-white, disabled and other 'non-traditional' workers is more evident. The collective and individual struggles of the workers with marginal backgrounds to seek equality and access to positions of power and influence at work have also played a role. It appears that there are dual mechanisms of capitalist desires seeking to exploit new forms of labor and individual/collective forms of resistance to

discrimination working in tandem to generate the management practices which we come to call 'Diversity Management' today.

## DEMOGRAPHIC CHANGES ACROSS POPULATIONS

Demographic changes across the world's population, resulting from changes in birth and mortality rates, immigration, and changes in healthcare, are challenging homogeneity at work. In the United States, for example, the workforce now comprises increasing numbers of women, minorities, older workers, gay, lesbian, bisexual, transgender, and transsexual workers, people with disabilities, and those with caring responsibilities. As predicted some two decades ago, the majority of net new entrants to the U.S. workforce are now women and minorities (e.g. Johnston and Packer, 1987). More recently, McCuiston et al. (2004: 73) predicted that this trend will continue and that 'women, people of color and ethnic minorities will represent over 50 percent of all new entrants to the U.S. workforce by 2008,' owing to a complex set of conditions that govern labor market dynamics. As the 'baby-boomers' age and remain in the workforce, and fewer younger workers are added, the mean age of the U.S. workforce is increasing. Similarly, the British workforce is increasingly diverse. Estimates suggest that 80 percent of the workforce growth between 2004 and 2010 will be women (Armitage and Scott, 1998). Along with more women, the British workforce is aging, proportions of ethnic minorities are increasing, and work and family issues (e.g. parenting, elder care) are gaining importance (Gallagher and O'Leary, 2007; Williams and Jones, 2005). As in the U.S. and Britain, in Canada and Mexico workforce growth is small when compared with growth in previous periods, and in Spain, Italy, Germany, France, Japan, and South Africa, declines in the population of working adults are projected for 2010 through 2050 (Bell, 2007). These population changes herald significant changes, e.g., reorganization of work and life due to skills shortages, which in turn will render the need to appreciate workers from all backgrounds imperative, rather than a luxury of choice.

## ATTEMPTS TO REDUCE DISCRIMINATORY PRACTICES

Clearly, workplaces are, and will continue to be, more diverse in the future than in the past, particularly as women, minority ethnic workers, and other underrepresented groups are making inroads in sectors, organizations, and positions of hierarchy and influence from which they were traditionally excluded. However, this diversity may come at a cost if effective measures are not taken to eradicate prejudice, discrimination, and biases that reduce individual and organizational effectiveness and to help different groups learn to work well together. Despite increasing diversity in some areas, women, minorities, and other non-dominant group members continue to experience the glass ceiling, confinement to low-wage and low-status jobs, to be held to higher performance standards, and are often sexually and racially harassed (e.g. Goldman et al., 2006; Lyness and Heilman, 2006; Moss and Tilly, 2001; Shaffer et al., 2000; Stauffer and Buckley, 2005; see also Bell, 2007 for descriptions of numerous U.S. lawsuits and settlements involving race, sex, age, religious, disability, and appearance discrimination). Such practices necessitate active measures to counteract them and to reduce their negative effects (e.g. lowered morale, turnover, absence, etc.).

## ANTI-DISCRIMINATION LEGISLATION

There have been numerous efforts worldwide to counteract discriminatory practices. The Convention on Elimination of all forms of Discrimination against Women (CEDAW, 1995) was signed by high-ranking representatives and ministers of over 150 countries. The International Labour Organization (2003) has issued a Declaration on Fundamental Principles and Rights at Work focusing on

the elimination of workplace discrimination. Further, numerous countries have implemented progressive national legislations that seek to address many aspects of inequality and discrimination. The key point about these legal changes is that the national policy makers are cognizant of the significant demographic changes and challenges that are marking labor markets of the 21st century and of people's fundamental rights to equity and work.

In the U.S., legislation exists to provide some legal protections based on race, ethnicity, sex, age, religion, and disability. In Britain, similar legislation provides protection against six strands of discrimination. In South Africa, legislation prohibits unfair discrimination against people of color, people with disabilities, and women. As these three examples indicate, legislation from distinct areas attempts to provide some protection from discrimination and to reduce inequality. Similar legislation exists in countless countries around the world. People's organizational experiences cannot always be regulated through legislation, however, and are influenced by various factors outside of legislative control, including strongly held attitudes and beliefs about diversity issues that are learned early, and through the life course.

## DIVERSITY LEARNING THROUGH THE LIFE COURSE: INFORMAL LEARNING

### Social difference codes and socialization

Diversity learning begins very early, before one reaches school age, and continues throughout the life course. Ridgeway (2006: 180) argues that *social difference codes* present bottom-up processes which account for the way inequalities become self-organizing:

> Social difference codes are widely shared cultural beliefs that delineate the socially significant distinctions among people on the basis of which a society is structured and inequality is organized. Examples are occupation, race or gender. Social difference

codes provide cultural schemas for enacting social relations on the basis of a given difference by indicating the attributes by which people may be categorized according to the distinction and the traits and behaviors that can be expected as a result.

Similar to social difference codes, *socialization* is the process by which social institutions, including families, friends, organizations, and the media form and shape expectations of acceptable behaviors, occupations, jobs, and attire by gender (Bell, 2007) and ethnicity (Wallace, 2007). The most studied form of socialization is *gender role socialization*. Research indicates that the gender role socialization of children begins very early; expectant mothers speak more softly to females in the womb than they do to males (Smith, 2000). Parents describe newborn girl babies as delicate and soft, but describe similarly sized newborn boys in masculine, stronger terms (Smith, 2000). After birth, males and females continue to receive gender differentiated messages about appropriate behavior, play, appearance, and occupations. Once children are in school, gender-based differential treatment, experiences, and learning continue. In pleasure reading materials, for example, characters are sometimes twice as likely to be male as female and when present, female characters often play subordinate roles to male characters (see Davis and McDaniel, 1999; Witt, 1996). This socialization teaches lessons that girls are less valuable than boys and that their jobs (e.g. secretary, nurse) are less important than jobs of boys (e.g. manager, physician).

Through socialization from their parents, teachers, and society, and through observation of the world around them, both male and female children learn that there are appropriate behaviors, fields of study, and jobs for men and for women (e.g. Dunn, 1999; Evans and Davies, 2000). While women receive more undergraduate degrees than men, women's degrees are more likely to be in education and health; men are more likely to earn degrees in science and engineering (Freeman, 2004). These 'choices'

contribute to sex segregation of jobs and to the persistent wage gap between men and women that exists in countries around the world (Anker, 1998). Half of all workers around the world seek jobs that are at least 80 percent sex segregated (Anker, 1998). In the U.S., children learn from an early age that while men are dentists, women are dental hygienists. Men are university professors, but women are elementary school teachers. Women are secretaries and receptionists, while men are managers and executives. These life socialization lessons advantage men and disadvantage women in earnings, job security, status and prestige. For example, the average earnings of elementary school teachers, 85 percent of whom are women, are $44,300. The average earnings of public university full professors, 88 percent of whom are men, are $84,100. Dentists, who are primarily men, earn an average of $133,350 per year, while dental hygienists, primarily women, earn $57,790 per year (Dunn, 1999; U.S. Census Bureau, 2003). Similar wage penalties exist across other strands of social distinction (e.g. Gallagher and O'Leary, 2007). Furthermore, these patterns are long-standing and have been the focus of public policy for over 50 years in Europe (Treaty of Rome) and the U.S.

Unfortunately, socialization experiences often lead values and beliefs to be internalized and habitualized in ways which may prevent them being questioned even in the face of contradictory empirical evidence or real-life experience. Therefore, the internalization of biases, prejudices, and cultural myths often operates to deem inequalities across strands of difference largely invisible (Özbilgin and Woodward, 2003). If perceptible, these inequalities may be viewed as rational and acceptable, particularly since they are learned from such a young age and through so many media, and work to influence one's self-perception. Gendered and racialized forms of self-perception and status beliefs may have an impact on the outcome of assessment results. Research in simulated settings suggests that supposedly gender-neutral processes of assessment may generate gendered outcomes due to the impact of gendered status beliefs (Correll, 2001) which are enacted in social and educational encounters. Steele and Aronson's (1995) research on stereotype threat clearly documents the negative effects of stereotype activation on the test performance of different groups.

## FORMAL LEARNING

Diversity learning also occurs in formal settings, across all disciplines of social sciences. Each discipline has its own view on diversity issues, however. While sociology examines social diversity, psychological approaches often focus on individual differences. From the perspective of economics, demographic diversity is studied in the context of dynamics of diversity in markets (e.g. human capital, supply and demand for certain workers). Political scientists are interested in issues of social cohesion and integration as aspects of diversity that require regulation. Similarly, and more relevant to our interest in this chapter, the field of business management has also developed a keen interest in diversity as it relates to regulation and management of diversity in work settings and in the curriculum of business and management schools.

Constructs and concepts of demographic diversity and diversity learning are highly emotive in nature, engendering a range of emotional reactions as they call for attitudinal and behavioral changes among learners. Even the presentation of most established, sound findings in the field may invoke emotional responses such as denial, confrontation, reconciliation, and advocacy. In addition, even in formal settings, many outside factors impede the diversity learning process and the effect of outside influences on diversity learning is substantially greater than the effects of such influences on other areas. While students of human resources, for example, may feel they 'know' how best to select employees to be hired, they are less likely to be strongly and emotionally resistant to learning about the utility of structured interviews than they

are about learning some aspects of diversity and certainly to the possibility that they themselves may be the carriers of racist, sexist, ageist, or other prejudices. In addition, again using structured interviews as an example, beliefs about certain groups may work against learning (and transferring learning) about structured interviews. If one believes, for example, that women are less committed workers because of family responsibilities, one may be less willing to relinquish the attachment to a 'gut feel' about a male employee being suited to a particular job requiring significant travel. If one believes that older workers are unable to learn new skills (Smith, 2001), one is less likely to invest in training them. These beliefs are key components of diversity-related attitudes and behaviors that affect individuals and shape jobs and organizational structures.

Beliefs about certain groups also extend to one's views of 'merit,' which is commonly used in management decision making. The discourse of 'merit' is saturated with archetypes of gender, ethnicity, disability, and sexual orientation. In their national study of recruitment agencies in the UK, Özbilgin and Tatli (2007a: 67) reveal that the meritocratic discourse of 'the best person for the job' falsely assumes that identification of merit in recruitment decisions would be free from biases. To the contrary, this discourse serves as a mechanism which conceals these inherent biases and silences critical voices from the margins:

Our research revealed that the level of equality and diversity awareness of private sector agencies can be summarised as gender blindness as well as blindness to other strands of diversity. The outcome of this is an unintentional gender bias and indirect and covert discrimination. Coupled with the discourse of 'best person for the job', which accepts that jobs are unquestioningly gender blind, more subtle forms of gender bias which relate directly to the structuring of jobs, workplaces and temporal and spatial arrangements of work remain unchallenged by the private recruitment agencies.

Cockrell et al. (1999) argue that multiculturalism in classrooms requires teachers to develop certain skills which recognize the significance of cross-cultural experience, gender, and belief in shaping diversity experiences of students. In recent years, there has been an explosion of curriculum development activities in the field of diversity in work settings. There are now dedicated courses offered at undergraduate, postgraduate, and doctoral study levels. There are a large number of books and journals published in the field and countless organizational training programs, consultancy projects, and management initiatives which focus on diversity learning. Many professional bodies in the field of human resources, marketing, accounting, and sales provide advice to their members on diversity issues and public, private, and third sector agencies seek to impact on diversity issues in organizational settings. Employers, trade unionists, as well as organizational actors such as diversity managers, specialists, advocates, and champions work to provide diversity learning and management activities across the industrialized countries. Looking at the scope of the range of diversity learning activities and actors involved in the process, it is possible to speak of a 'diversity industry' (Özbilgin and Tatli, 2007b) which is geared to provide diversity learning in order to facilitate changes in work organizations. In the following sections, we consider specific diversity learning programs.

## University programs

Drawing on a study conducted in the United States, Engberg (2007) argues that structured diversity learning across all disciplines of study engenders positive outcomes including improved intergroup learning among students across races. The study also suggests that students acquire pluralistic skills, especially in the engineering and life sciences disciplines through diversity learning. The work of Patricia Gurin and her colleagues at the University of Michigan also clearly documents the benefits of formalized diversity learning efforts. In longitudinal research she and her colleagues found that diverse students who interacted with and learned from each other in meaningful ways viewed diversity as not

necessarily being divisive, saw commonality in values, and were able to take the perspective of others (Gurin et al., 2004).

Blackmore (2006: 193) explains that schools have a role to play in promoting a model of diversity:

> If the concept of diversity is to be mobilized in ways that will produce greater equity, it needs to be located within broader notions of the role of schools in democratic pluralistic societies in terms of citizen formation, an analysis of how structural and cultural inequality occurs and how privilege works, and a theory of social justice that provides principles that will inform policy and practice locally as well as centrally.

The predominant accrediting body for schools of business in the United States, the Association to Advance Collegiate Schools of Business International (AACSB), has explicitly included requirements that member institutions have diversity embedded in their course content. Specifically, AACSB requires that 'commitment to the concept that diversity in people and ideas enhances the educational experience in every management education program' (AACSB, 2007). The AACSB pointedly includes diversity in a broad context, for its affiliated schools around the world, providing stimuli for such schools to ensure to include diversity components in their educational programs. In business schools internationally, it is possible to find complete undergraduate and postgraduate courses in managing diversity, equal opportunities, and discrimination law.

There are also ways in which people learn about diversity issues in university settings without these being the sole focus of an entire class. Indeed, diversity learning is more common when we consider the range of classes that incorporate aspects of diversity. University classes that include diversity content, such as human resources, organization behavior, principles of management, and ethics may have a diversity chapter, an overall perspective, or may include a section on 'equal opportunity laws.' Such courses serve many purposes, among these, the most common would be the raising of awareness regarding diversity issues including recognition of demographic changes and social, economic, and legal structures that regulate diversity in organizational and national settings.

## Industry training

In addition to formal learning in university settings, many firms have diversity training either in-house or outsourced by diversity training companies. A national survey of 285 diversity managers in the UK identified that 67 percent of the organizations have taken positive steps by providing awareness training and carrying out employee attitude surveys (Tatli et al., 2007). Learning and awareness activities are the most common activities of diversity management in the UK (see Figure 15.1).

Tatli et al. also asked where diversity managers had acquired their expertise and knowledge on diversity. The majority of the diversity officers in the study reported acquiring their expertise through work experience and external training. This is an indication of the absence of formal routes to professional education in the field. Diversity networks, in-house training, and formal education also appear as other sources of learning and expertise for diversity officers (see Table 15.1).

**Table 15.1  How did you gain the expertise required for your current role in diversity management?**

| Source of expertise | Count |
| --- | --- |
| Work experience | 185 |
| External training | 145 |
| Diversity networks | 106 |
| In-house training | 99 |
| Formal education | 91 |

Tatli et al. (2007): 19.

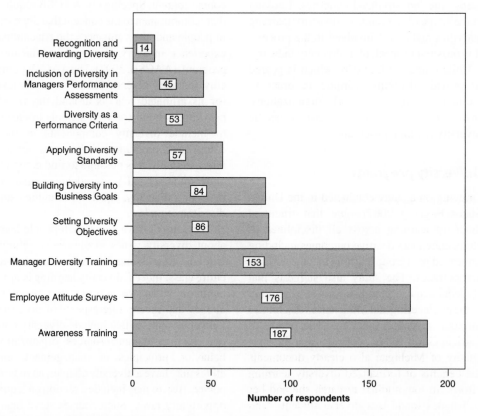

**Figure 15.1  Which of the following diversity activities does your organization have?**
*Source*: Tatli et al. (2007): 14.

Diversity training and education are considered to be effective strategies for managing diversity in organizations of all kind, particularly international organizations. Several studies show that diversity training is a growing area of concern for many multinational corporations (Littlefield, 1995; Wentling and Palma-Rivas, 1999) because many of them face specific diversity-related challenges, including group member differences in beliefs, perceptions, and experiences (Thomas and Proudford, 2000) and inter and intragroup biases and stereotypes (Dass and Parker, 1996; Combs and Luthans, 2007). This calls for transformation of diversity training programs from a primary focus on legal and regulatory compliance to recognition of the performance impact and the multiple effects on the bottom line (Richard, 2000).

## DIVERSITY TRAINING, EDUCATION, OR BOTH?

Definitions of diversity training are contingent upon the way in which organizations define diversity and how the concept of diversity is understood in organizations. Wheeler (1994) notes that diversity training can be conceptualized as training and education to raise awareness about individual differences and changes in the workforce and as a way to create behavioral changes that are required to work and manage effectively within a diverse workforce. This conceptualization does not differentiate between education and training. We suggest that diversity education is an approach with a long-term focus, and that it should be embedded in the organizational culture and human resources management strategies, policies, and practices. It can be achieved at various levels, including raising awareness of differences and creating synergies based on individual differences and competencies. On the other hand, diversity training, as does other training, sometimes has a short-term focus (Bohlander and Snell, 2004) with immediate action points for departments and individuals. Diversity training initiatives can be used as an efficient method to influence interactions of

employees with diverse coworkers and clients (Wentling and Palma-Rivas, 2000; Combs and Luthans, 2007). A well-designed diversity training program should tie together and complete an employment training repertoire and address diversity issues, for instance, stereotype reduction and change in attitudes toward differences by taking an inclusive approach and concurrent behavioral change. The content and methods of diversity training programs should aim to impact on the cognitive disposition of trainees and transferability of what has been learned in training to work setting.

Prejudices and biases toward others are often emotionally and socially charged perceptions that are irrational and abstract (Cox and Beale, 1997; Bell, 2007). Hence, it is difficult to identify and fully change them in a training environment. The attitudes, thinking, and intentions of individuals can be influenced through such training so that individuals reach an acknowledgement of differences between people and in their organizational experiences. They should also view the differences between people as sources of synergy in effective undertaking of the tasks that will generate positive diversity outcomes. In organizations, the role of the HR function and the training of HRM professionals are crucial in ascertaining design and implementation of diversity training on a broad organizational scale.

Academics and practitioners alike point out the liabilities of poor diversity training, which can be harmful rather than helpful in advancing the cause of diversity (Hemphill and Haines, 1997; Hite and McDonald, 2006). The objectives of diversity training initiatives should be carefully thought-out and its content and methods should be in constructive alignment with these objectives. Such objectives may include raising awareness of individual feelings about diversity, disseminating information about diversity-related legal issues and policies, developing skills for a diverse workforce, and applying these skills in undertaking organizational tasks effectively and implementing organizational change (Holvino et al., 2004; Hite and

McDonald, 2006). The implementation and outcomes can vary widely in depth and quality. As noted by Hite and McDonald (2006), diversity training has an additional complexity of addressing, and challenging most of the time, not only the roots of organizational culture (inclusiveness of policies and practices), but also the beliefs, values, and dispositions of individual members (their prejudices, biases, and stereotypes). Implementing training can yield potential rewards but poor content and ineffective methods can cause problems that are extremely difficult to overcome.

Cox's (2001) model provides a summative framework for effective design and implementation of diversity education and training. The model integrates the following components: leadership support, research and measurement, education, management systems alignment, and follow-up. The significance of leadership commitment to the longevity and success of diversity education and training endeavors can be combined with another factor, management systems alignment, that requires policies and procedures that reinforce diversity by changing organizational practice, being part of a larger systemic intervention (e.g. 'diversity management').

Embedding diversity education in organizations and schools will help to eradicate erroneous perceptions about diversity that are often widely held. It is only then possible to design specific training programs that address various ways of acknowledging diversity, overcoming racist, sexist, ageist, homo-philic and homosocial tendencies at work, and creating synergistic and effective group interactions in diverse employee and student populations. Therefore, we suggest that there is a need to shift from training, with its short-term orientation, to diversity education in organizations and classrooms. Diversity education can provide comprehensive frameworks with a long-term focus, to instill knowledge and educate employees or students in order to promote positive work climates. *Training and education* are part of a diversity management program that will seek to achieve 'full integration of

members of minority social categories into the social, structural, and power relationships of an organization or institution' (Brewer et al., 1999: 337). Alone, diversity training does not imply any background change in system-level structure, decision making, or organizational ethos (Pendry et al., 2007), as would diversity management in a broader systemic manner.

## CONTENT OF TRAINING AND EDUCATION PROGRAMS

Specific content of training programs varies by the needs of the specific organization. Ideally, education should encompass details on the historical and long-standing issues that affect different groups' societal status. For example, in the United States, slavery and the legacy of legal segregation, discrimination, and exclusion against Blacks continue to affect their current status. Near annihilation and colonization of indigenous people in the U.S., Canada, New Zealand, and Australia have had long-term negative effects on Native people but many are unaware of the history and current influences of such treatment. In addition, research evidence about different key groups can be helpful in eradicating stereotypes and misperceptions. For example, data on the propensity of women to work, regardless of the existence of young children (e.g. Bell, 2007), the negative individual and organizational effects of sexual harassment (Fitzgerald et al., 1997; Miner-Rubino and Cortina, 2007), and the performance of people with disabilities and older workers (Czajka and DeNisi, 1988; Kite et al., 2005) can help increase data-based knowledge and understanding of diversity issues. Thus, stereotype reduction is an expected consequence of training and education. Formal diversity learning, as a result of diversity education and training programs, may affect strong, entrenched beliefs and values in cognitive processes. Personal biases and learned stereotypes toward certain groups can be challenged as a part of such learning process.

Diversity self-efficacy can also be a consequence of diversity training and education. Combs and Luthans (2007: 92) refer to 'diversity self-efficacy' as 'the perception and belief that one can marshal the necessary motivation, cognitive resources, and courses of action to change behaviors and successfully attain diversity goals and initiatives in communities and work environments.' This concept shows resonances with Bandura's (1997) self-efficacy principles, which focus on developing competence blocks in several task domains. Diversity self-efficacy can be viewed as similar to other forms of efficacy which all reference confidence in individual skills to perform a task domain.

Lastly, diversity learning may provide insights into organizational structures which are conducive to create diversity cultures (Bassett-Jones et al., 2007). Diversity learning therefore may help students as incipient managers and employers to see the potential of diversity management in achieving organizational goals and in improving business performance.

## INFLUENCES OF THE DEMOGRAPHICS OF THE RESEARCHER, TEACHER, OR TRAINER

Social research should transcend the false dichotomy between the objective structures of the world and the subjective experience of individuals (Bourdieu, 1977; see also Özbilgin and Tatli, 2005), as any research project is shaped by the assessments of measurable properties of the external world as well as by the interests and experiences of researchers. In the case of diversity concerns, particular interests driven by one's own experiences uniquely qualify the teacher while also affecting her or his credibility. Some students may view a woman of color, for example, as having a personal agenda or 'chip on her shoulder' and as not being objective. On the other hand, others may view her as knowing more about the topic and thus as being more believable. Some students may view a white male as having

no true knowledge about or experience with diversity issues, while others may see his (apparent) lack of self-interest as making him more credible. The complex relationship between the researcher and the object and subject of research presents unique challenges to diversity learning. A researcher, teacher, or trainer must be aware of the identities that she or he brings to the table, and aware of the role played by those identities in her or his work.

## CONCLUSION

The changing demographic makeup of workers is one of the significant challenges facing many organizations in the contemporary world. Organizations that recognize the need to fully develop their employees in order to remain competitive are responding to such changes by implementing a variety of different initiatives to help this increasing diversity be a positive, rather than negative factor (Baytos, 1995; Wentling and Palma-Rivas, 1999). Diversity should be effectively managed in order to eradicate prejudice, discrimination, biases and help different individuals work better by creating synergies based on differences for better organizational performance. As a result of rising importance of diversity management, there have been numerous efforts internationally to counteract discriminatory practices in organizations. Progressive legislations, policies, and strategies have been put in place in order to address inequality and discrimination.

Given the significance of diversity management, we have focused on diversity learning in this chapter. Diversity learning is described as a continual process that takes place over a life span through informal and formal learning. Informal learning occurs usually through socialization experiences that lead values and beliefs to be internalized and habitualized in ways which may prevent them being questioned. Such internalization of biases and prejudices results in inequalities across strands of difference to operate invisibly (Özbilgin and Woodward, 2003). Diversity learning also takes place in formal settings, such as schools, universities, and institutions. This can be facilitated by effective diversity education and training programmes with a long term and embedded strategic focus in organizations. We argue that diversity education and training should be a subset of overarching diversity management strategy in organizations, recognizing that our diversity learning begins early in life and is often fraught with strongly held misperceptions, errors, and biases. It is only through conscious, concerted, purposeful, and continual intervention that this lifelong learning can be leveraged to generate individual and organizational benefits.

# REFERENCES

AACSB (Association to Advance Collegiate Schools of Business) (2007) 'Eligibility procedures and accreditation standards for business accreditation', Accessed 6/15/07 from http://www.aacsb.edu/accreditation/standards.asp.

Anker, R. (1998) *Gender and Jobs: Sex Segregation of Occupations in the World*. Geneva: International Labour Organization.

Armitage, B. and Scott, M. (1998) 'British Labour Force Projections: 1998–2011', *Labour Market Trends*, 106 (6): 281–97.

Bandura, A. (1997) *Self-efficacy: The Exercise of Control*. New York: Freeman.

Bassett-Jones, N., Brown, R. and Cornelius, N. (2007) 'Delivering effective diversity management through effective structures', *Systems Research and Behavioral Science*, 24: 59–67.

Baytos, L.M. (1995) *Designing and Implementing Successful Diversity Programs*. Englewood Cliffs, NJ: Prentice-Hall.

Bell, M. (2007) *Diversity in Organizations*. Mason, OH: Thomson South-Western.

Blackmore, J. (2006) 'Deconstructing diversity discourses in the field of educational management and leadership', *Educational Management Administration & Leadership*, 34 (2): 181–99.

Bohlander, G.W. and Snell, S. (2004) *Managing Human Resources* (13th edn). Mason, OH: South-Western Publishers.

Bourdieu, P. (1977) *Outline of Theory of Practice*. Cambridge: Cambridge University Press.

Brewer, M.B., Hippel, W.V. and Gooden, M.P. (1999) 'Diversity and organizational identity: The problem

of entrée after entry', in D.A. Prentice and D.T. Miller (eds), *Cultural Divides: Understanding and Overcoming Group Conflict*. New York: Sage Publications.

Czajka, J.M. and DeNisi, A.S. (1988) 'Effects of emotional disability and clear performance standards on performance ratings', *Academy of Management Journal*, 31: 394–404.

Cockrell, K., Placier, P., Cockrell, D. and Middleton, J. (1999) 'Coming to terms with "diversity" and "multiculturalism" in teacher education: Learning about our students, changing our practice', *Teaching and Teacher Education*, 15 (4): 351–66.

Combs, G.M. and Luthans, F. (2007) 'Diversity training: Analysis of the impact of self-efficacy', *Human Resource Development Quarterly*, 18: 91–120.

Correll, S.J. (2001) 'Gender and the career choice process: The role of biased self-assessments', *American Journal of Sociology*, 106: 1691–1730.

Cox, T.H. (2001) *Creating the Multicultural Organization: A Strategy for Capturing the Power of Diversity*. San Francisco, CA: Jossey-Bass.

Cox, T.H. and Beale, R. (1997) *Developing Multicultural Competence: Readings, Cases and Activities*. San Francisco: Jossey-Bass.

Dass, P. and Parker, B. (1996) 'Diversity as a strategic issue', in E.E. Kossek and S.A. Lobel (eds), *Managing Diversity: Human Resource Strategies for Transforming the Workplace*. Malden, MA: Blackwell.

Davis, A. and McDaniel, T. (1999) 'You've come a long way, baby – or have you? Research evaluating gender portrayal in recent Caldecott-winning books', *Reading Teacher*, 52: 532–6.

Dobbs, M.F. (1996) 'Managing diversity: Lessons from the private sector', *Public Personnel Management*, 25: 351–68.

Dunn, D. (1999) 'Women: The fifty-one percent minority', in A.G. Dworkin & R.J. Dworkin (eds), *The Minority Report*. Orlando, FL: Harcourt Brace.

Evans, L. and Davies, K. (2000) 'No sissy boys here: A content analysis of the representation of masculinity in elementary school reading textbooks', *Sex Roles*, 42: 255–70.

Engberg, M. (2007) 'Educating the workforce for the 21st century: A cross disciplinary analysis of the impact of the undergraduate experience on students' development of a pluralistic orientation', *Research in Higher Education*, 48 (3): 283–317.

Fitzgerald, L.F., Drasgow, R., Hulin, C.L., Gelfand, M.J. and Magley, V.J. (1997) 'Antecedents and consequences of sexual harassment in organizations: A test of an integrated model', *Journal of Applied Psychology*, 82: 578–89.

Freeman, C.E. (2004) *Trends in Educational Equity of Girls and Women*. (NCES 2005-016) US Department of Education. National Center for Education Statistics. Washington, DC: US Government Printing Office.

Gallagher N. and O'Leary, D. (2007) *Recruitment 2020: How Recruitment is Changing and Why it Matters*. London: DEMOS.

Goldman, B.M., Gutek, B.A., Stein, J.H. and Lewis, K. (2006) 'Employment discrimination in organizations: Antecedents and consequences', *Journal of Management*, 32: 786–830.

Gurin, P., Nagda, B.A. and Lopez, G.E. (2004) 'The benefits of diversity in education for democratic citizenship', *Journal of Social Issues*, 1: 17–34.

Hemphill, H. and Haines, R. (1997) *Discrimination, Harassment, and the Failure of Diversity Training: What to Do Now*. Westport, CT: Quorum Books.

Hite, L.M. and McDonald, K.S. (2006) 'Diversity training pitfalls and possibilities: An exploration of small and mid-size US organizations', *Human Resource Development Journal*, 9 (3): 365–77.

Holvino, E., Ferdman, B.M. and Merrill-Sands, D. (2004) 'Creating and sustaining diversity and inclusion in organizations: Strategies and approaches', in M.S. Stockdale and F.J. Crosby (eds), *The Psychology and Management of Workplace Diversity*. Oxford: Blackwell. pp. 245–76.

International Labour Organization (2003) 'Declaration on fundamental principles and rights at work,' http://www.ilo.org/dyn/declaris/DECLARATIONWEB. INDEXPAGE, accessed 12/02/07.

Johnston, W.B. and Packer, A.H. (1987) *Workforce 2000*. Indianapolis, IN: Hudson Institute.

Kite, M.E., Stockdale, G.D., Whitley, B.E. Jr. and Johnson, B.T. (2005) 'Attitudes toward older and younger adults: An updated meta-analytic review', *Journal of Social Issues*, 61: 241–66.

Konrad, A.M. (2003) 'Defining the domain of workplace diversity scholarship', *Group and Organization Management*, 28 (1): 4–17.

Littlefield, D. (1995) 'Managing diversity seen as core domestic value', *People Management*, 1: 6, 15.

Lyness, K.S. and Heilman, M.E. (2006) 'When fit is fundamental: Performance evaluations of upper-level female and male managers', *Journal of Applied Psychology*, 91: 777–85.

McCuiston, V.E., Wooldridge, B.R. and Price, C.K. (2004) 'Leading the diverse workforce: Profit, prospects and progress', *Leadership and Organization Development Journal*, 25: 73–92.

Miner-Rubino, K. and Cortina, L.M. (2007) 'Beyond targets: Consequences of vicarious exposure to misogyny', *Journal of Applied Psychology*, 92: 1254–69.

Moss, P. and Tilly, C. (2001) *Stories Employers Tell: Race, Skill, and Hiring in America*. New York: Russell Sage Foundation.

Özbilgin, M. and Tatli, A. (2005) 'Book review essay: Understanding Bourdieu's contribution to organization and management studies', *Academy of Management Review*, 30 (4): 855–69.

Özbilgin, M. and Tatli, A. (2007a) *Opening up Opportunities through Private Sector Recruitment and Guidance Agencies*. Manchester: Equal Opportunities Commission, Paper No. 50.

Özbilgin, M. and Tatli, A. (2007b) 'Diversity management as calling: Sorry, it's the wrong number', in Iris Koall, Verena Bruchhagen and Friederiike Höher (eds), *Diversity Outlooks – Managing Diversity zwischen Ethik, Business Case und Antidiskriminierung*, LIT-Verlag, Münster, Hamburg.

Özbilgin, M. and Woodward, D. (2003) *Banking and Gender*. London and New York: IB Tauris Publishers.

Pendry, L.F., Driscoll, D.M. and Field, S. (2007) 'Diversity training: Putting theory into practice', *Journal of Occupational and Organizational Psychology*, 80: 27–50.

Richard, O.C. (2000) 'Racial diversity: Business strategy, and firm performance: A resource based view', *Academy of Management Journal*, 43: 164–77.

Ridgeway, C.L. (2006) 'Social relational contexts and self-organizing inequality', in O. Kyriakidou and M.F. Ozbilgin (eds), *Relational Perspectives in Organization Studies*. Cheltenham: Edward Elgar. pp. 180–96.

Tatli, A., Özbilgin, M. and Worman, D. (2007) *State of the Nation: Survey of Diversity Management Practices and Policies in the UK*. London: Chartered Institute of Personnel and Development (CIPD).

Shaffer, M.A., Joplin, J.R.W., Bell, M.P., Oguz, C. and Lau, T. (2000) 'Gender discrimination and job-related outcomes: A cross-cultural comparison of working women in the United States and China', *Journal of Vocational Behavior*, 57: 395–427.

Smith, D. (2000) *Women at Work: Leadership for the Next Century*. Upper Saddle River, NJ: Prentice-Hall.

Smith, D.J. (2001) 'Old enough to know better: Age stereotypes in New Zealand', in I. Glover and M. Branine (eds), *Ageism in Work and Employment*. Aldershot: Ashgate Publishing. pp. 219–35.

Stauffer, J.M. and Buckley, M.R. (2005) 'The existence and nature of racial bias in supervisory ratings', *Journal of Applied Psychology*, 90: 586–91.

Steele, C. and Aronson, J. (1995) 'Stereotype threat and the intellectual test performance of

African Americans', *Journal of Personality and Social Psychology*, 69: 797–811.

Thomas, D.A. and Proudford, K.L. (2000) 'Making sense of race relations in organizations: Theories for practice', in R.T. Carter (ed.), *Addressing Cultural Issues in Organizations: Beyond the Corporate Context*. Thousand Oaks, CA: Sage Publications.

Wallace, D.M. (2007) 'It's a M-A-N Thang: Black male gender role socialization and the performance of masculinity in love relationships', *The Journal of Pan African Studies*, 1 (7): 11–22.

Wentling, R.M. and Palma-Rivas, N. (1999) 'Components of effective diversity training programmes', *International Journal of Training and Development*, 3: 215–26.

Wentling, R.M. and Palma-Rivas, N. (2000) 'Current status and trends of diversity initiatives in the workplace', *Human Resources Development Quarterly*, 11: 35–60.

Wheeler, M.L. (1994) 'Diversity training', research report number 1083–94RR. New York: The Conference Board.

Williams, L. and Jones, A. (2005) *Changing Demographics*. The Work Foundation.

Witt, S. (1996) 'Traditional or androgynous: An analysis to determine gender role orientation of basal readers', *Child Study Journal*, 26: 303–18.

# 16

# Cognitive Styles and Learning Strategies in Management Education

Eugene Sadler-Smith

## Abstract

In this chapter I define cognitive styles and learning strategies, and review and critique three dimensions of cognitive style, namely representation (verbalizer-imager), organization (wholist-analytical) and processing (analysis-intuition) of information. Extant frameworks appear to be wanting in terms of a combination of reliability and validity of style measurement, commonality of conceptual framework and theoretical bases, and the extent to which they acknowledge the integrated and interdependent nature of human thinking. I offer a duplex framework for cognitive style which draws heavily upon dual-process theory and consists of two complementary information processing modes: (1) analytical: affect-free, slow in operation, fast in formation, serial and detail-focused, cognitively demanding, abstract/symbolic, and open to conscious awareness; (2) intuitive: affect-laden, fast in operation, slow in formation, parallel and holistic, cognitively undemanding, imagistic/narrative based, unavailable to conscious awareness. I outline some of the implications of the duplex model for management

learning, education and training with regard to issues of development of self-awareness, meta-cognitive skills, whether to match or mismatch instruction to the learner, and the promotion of dialogue between instructors and learners.

A cognitive style is an individual's habitual approach to representing, organizing and processing information (Hayes and Allinson, 1994, 1996; Messick, 1984; Riding and Rayner, 1998; Sternberg, 1997; Tennant, 1988). A learning strategy is defined as 'operations and procedures that the learner may use to acquire, retain and retrieve different kinds of knowledge and performance', and may involve representational capabilities, selectional capabilities and self-directional capabilities (Rigney, 1978: 165). If executed effectively such strategies may help to place the acquisition, development and application of knowledge and skills more in the control of the learner and hence facilitate the transition from lower-order, primary (habitual) cognitive functioning to a higher-order executive level of functioning (Riding and Rayner, 1998: 98).

Cognitive styles are important for three reasons: (1) a personal knowledge of cognitive styles is an important first step in the development of learning strategies which may be called upon to overcome the limitations of one's habitual style of thinking; (2) from the educators' perspective, awareness of the impact that individual differences in learning and thinking can have may allow the incorporation of style-related factors into the instructional design of management education and training programs; and (3) incorporating the findings of cognitive styles research into the pedagogy of management education has the potential to enhance the quality of the management learning experience.

At a more general level these issues are important within a management learning paradigm predicated on the assumption that the processes of *how* managers learn are as important as the content of *what* they learn. One objective of management learning ought to be to equip managers with cognitively based learning strategies that enable them to understand their own thinking and learning processes and thereby develop and practice the necessary skills to learn continuously in professional and personal contexts over their lifespan. By addressing the pedagogical issues raised by cognitive styles research management educators may help develop what Argyris (1962) termed learn*ing* managers as well as learn*ed* managers.

## CONCEPTUAL BACKGROUND

Cognitive style is a structural property of the cognitive system itself and as such forms an enduring basis for behavior (Messick, 1984). Cognitive style differs from personality in that style operates at the level of a 'cognitive control' in between personality (one of a number of 'primary sources', the others being knowledge and cognitive history, reasoning ability and gender) and cognitive inputs and outputs (Riding, 2001: 68). Cognitive style

differs from ability in that it focuses on how 'intelligence' is directed or how one performs specific cognitive tasks rather than how much intelligence an individual has or whether one is generally capable of performing specific cognitive tasks (Renzulli and Dai, 2001). Both ability and style may affect performance on a given task; the effect of style may be positive or negative depending upon the nature of the task, whereas the effect ability in general is likely to be positive across tasks (Riding, 1997).

The emergence of cognitive styles as a particular area of interest in management (Allinson et al., 2001; Allinson and Hayes, 1996; Hayes and Allinson, 1994, 1996; Hodgkinson and Sadler-Smith, 2003) has several likely causes but may be attributed in part to the perceived need for managers to assimilate, process and respond to increasing volumes of information in complex and uncertain environments – a key cognitive competence for managers in the 21st century (Hodgkinson and Clarke, 2007). Cognitive styles have been studied in a range of organizational phenomena including decision making behavior (Scott and Bruce, 1995), strategic cognition (Hodgkinson and Sparrow, 2002), entrepreneurship (Allinson et al., 2000; Sadler-Smith, 2004), interpersonal and group processes (Allinson et al., 2001) and learning and development (Riding, 2001; Sadler-Smith, Allinson et al., 2000; Sternberg, 1997).

Cognitive styles are generalized habits (Messick, 1984) that are applied spontaneously across situations. For the purposes of this chapter they are taken to be synonymous with 'thinking styles' ('a preferred way of thinking' Sternberg, 1997: 18) but are distinct from learning styles.[1] Strategies differ from styles in that the former are selected from amongst alternative approaches in response to situational demands (Renzulli and Dai, 2001: 34) whilst the latter are applied habitually. For example, a habitual reliance upon lengthy and time-consuming rational analysis in a way that is invariant across tasks would reflect an analytical cognitive style, whilst the calculated and deliberate use of visual imagery as a representational mode contingent upon the nature of the task would reflect a visualizer strategy. Sternberg and Grigorenko (2001) drew a further distinction between style and strategy in terms of the degree of consciousness involved: styles often operate without the individual's awareness (they may be said to operate non-volitionally and non-consciously), whereas strategies are volitional and involve a conscious choice between alternatives (for example, to 'zoom in' and focus on detail, or 'zoom out' to obtain a whole view).

Since the inception of systematic research into cognitive style over half a century ago which focused primarily upon perceptual style, summarized by Witkin et al. (1977), the concept of cognitive style has broadened to encompass a number of other aspects of cognition and latterly the role of affect (feeling) also (Allinson and Hayes, 1996; Epstein, 1994). Critical reviewers of the styles literature (Coffield et al., 2004; Hayes and Allinson, 1994; Riding and Rayner, 1998) have remarked upon the negative impact that the proliferation of cognitive style constructs and labels has had upon the field. There is a surfeit of constructs and measures, some of which duplicate existing theories or labels, or fail to take the extant literature, or each other, into account sufficiently well. Riding and Rayner (1998) have argued that there is a need to integrate more fully the various models of styles and strategies of learning and thinking.

## THREE DIMENSIONS OF COGNITIVE STYLE

As a first step in exploring cognitive style as a meaningful and relevant component of management learning's theory and method it is necessary to identify those style constructs that have a convincing conceptual framework, robust empirical basis, and that are pertinent to management learning research and practice. Using these criteria and drawing upon the principles suggested by Curry (1983, 2000),

Riding and Cheema (1991) and Sternberg and Grigorenko (1997) three dimensions of style will be the main focus of the first part of the chapter, namely: (1) *representation* of information, for example as words or as images (the verbal-imagery dimension of style, referred to by researchers as VI[2]); (2) *organizing* of information, for example into wholes or parts, corresponding to 'whole/global versus part/local' organization (the wholist-analytical (WA) dimension of style); and (3) *processing* of information, for example on the basis of 'hard data' or 'gut feel', corresponding to rational analytical and intuitive processing (which will be referred to here as an intuition-analysis (IA) dimension of style).

Two well-known models are excluded from this analysis on the grounds that their remit is broader than purely cognitive style: (1) Kirton's (1989) Adaption-Innovation (AI) theory is a comprehensive model of problem solving and creativity in which stylistic differences are but one element; (2) the *Myers-Briggs Type Indicator (MBTI)* (Myers, 1962), which some find hard to distinguish from a 'conventional, paper-and-pencil personality inventory' (Sternberg, 1997: 145), is designed around a set of Jungian personality-based constructs, some of which overlap with cognitive style. The overall assessment of the *MBTI* by Coffield et al. (2004) was that the construct validity of the opposing pairs of styles (for example, sensing-versus-intuiting) is controversial, and the direct relevance of the 16 *MBTI* types for learning is unclear. Readers are referred to Kirton (1989) and Gardner and Martinko (1996) for detailed reviews of the extensive body of management-related research concerning both to AI theory and the *MBTI*.

## MODE OF REPRESENTATION OF INFORMATION: THE VERBAL-IMAGERY (VI) DIMENSION OF COGNITIVE STYLE

The notion of individual differences in the ability to visualize has a lengthy history in psychology. Gardner described anecdotal reports of individual variations in visualization ranging from the inventor Nikola Tesla's accounts of being able to build and test his inventions in his 'mind's eye' (thus obviating in his case the need for blueprints), to Aldous Huxley's admission that words did not evoke a picture in his mind and that 'only by an effort of will could he evoke even a faint image' (Gardner, 1983: 187–8). Riding and his co-researchers have posited a verbal-imagery dimension of cognitive style that draws a simple distinction between 'thinking in pictures or [thinking in] words' (Rayner and Riding, 1997: 7) but with the acknowledgement that in spite of having such a preference 'most individuals are capable of using either a visual or a verbal mode of representation' (Riding and Rayner, 1998: 41).

In terms of its antecedents Rayner and Riding (1997) cited a stream of research from Francis Galton and William James in the late 19th century (Galton, 1883; James, 1890) through Bartlett (1932), to Paivio's dual-coding theory (Paivio, 1969, 1971) and Richardson's verbaliser-visualizer model (1977) and Riding's notion of verbal-imagery (VI) processing style (assessed directly, rather than via self-report, in one of the three subtests of the *Cognitive Styles Analysis (CSA)*, see Riding, 1991[3]). The concept of a verbal-visual (VI) dimension of cognitive style, and the underpinning notion of mode of representation of information, relates directly to the role played by mode of présentation of information in a learning situation (the stimulus), and to storage in the various components of the memory system (working memory and declarative and episodic long-term storage).

The VI sub-test of the *CSA* assesses an individual's habitual mode of representation based upon how quickly he or she is able to make judgments relating to semantic conceptual category membership (for example, 'spring is a season') compared to speed of response in judgments relating to visual appearance (for example, 'snow is white') (see Riding, 2001: 49–50). The precursors of the *CSA*, such as Paivio's

(1971) *Individual Differences Questionnaire (IDQ)* and Richardson's (1977) *Verbalizer Visualizer Questionnaire (VVQ)*, were self-report. Other researchers have also chosen to use introspective, self-report measures of verbal and visual styles; for example, Smith and Woody (2000) used the *Styles of Processing* scale (*SOP*) when comparing multimedia and traditional teaching approaches.

As far as the effects upon learning go, a number of researchers have explored the interaction of the VI style and mode of presentation of information and its effect on learning preferences and performance. For example, the computer presentation of information in a text-plus-picture format was better for imagers (in terms of learning performance) than the same information in a text-plus-text format (Riding and Douglas, 1993). In the same study in the text-plus-picture condition 50 percent of imagers used illustrations as part of their answers to problems compared with 12 percent of verbalizers. Moreover, imagers appear to be able to recall highly visually descriptive text better than acoustically complex and unfamiliar text (Riding and Rayner, 1998). The VI dimension of style is also related to learners' preferences for particular instructional media or modes of presentation. Riding and Watts (1997) presented participants with a choice of three alternative instructional formats ('unstructured verbal', 'structured verbal' and 'structured pictorial') and observed that most verbalizers selected the verbal version whilst most imagers selected the pictorial version. On the basis of these and a number of other studies, conducted for the most part in high school or college settings, Riding (2001: 61) concluded that 'imagers generally learn best from pictorial presentations whereas verbalizers learn best from verbal presentations'. Smith and Woody (2000: 223) found that students who prefer visual presentation of information (as implemented in multimedia programs) over verbal presentation of information will benefit more from multimedia instruction than those who are less visually-oriented.

This leads to a discussion of an important but perhaps contentious concept in the styles literature – the matching hypothesis. It states that when the mode of representation or the organization of information matches the learner's cognitive style learning performance will be superior to that in the un-matched condition (Riding and Douglas, 1993). Instructional matching strategies that may be used to accommodate the verbal and imagery styles respectively include the verbal presentation of information to accommodate the verbalizer style and the visual presentation of information to accommodate the imager style. It is argued that through this adaptive approach the processing loads that are imposed upon individuals' working memory will be lower than in the mis-matched condition (since the mode will match the learner's primary style) and thereby require lower 'processing power' (the emphasis on working memory overlooks the non-conscious processing of information – see below). Adaptation to style is feasible in a number of ways, for example through the use of computer-assisted learning programs in which the style of the learner may be assessed and instruction offered in a mode that is commensurate with the individual's style. Riding and Sadler-Smith (1992) made an early attempt devising such a system, and in a series of experimental studies observed interactions between styles, mode and structure of presentation, and learning outcome.

The matching hypothesis has proven problematic in styles research for a number of reasons. Firstly, the interactions of cognitive style and instructional treatment tend to be more complex than predicted by a simple interpretation of the matching hypothesis (for example, it is not uncommon for three-way interactions to be presented, for example Riding and Sadler-Smith, 1992). Secondly, overall evidence in favor of the matching hypothesis is not unequivocal and there is no published research in management learning *per se* which offers strong supporting evidence for 'the match'. For example, Massa and Mayer (2006) in an experimental study involving college students and non-college adults which employed a battery of 14 cognitive measures relating to the verbalizer-visualizer dimension including tests of cognitive style did not find any strong support for the matching hypothesis. Thirdly, the concept of 'matching' is itself problematic not only in cognitive styles research, but in the related domain of learning styles given that one of the espoused aims of learning styles pedagogy is to 'stimulate style growth' through 'controlled style mismatching' (Riding and Rayner, 1998: 58). Styles research is unclear about whether, and under what circumstances, it is better to match or to mis-match the style of the learner and the mode of presentation.

## MODE OF ORGANIZATION OF INFORMATION: THE WHOLIST-ANALYTICAL (WA) DIMENSION OF COGNITIVE STYLE

A problem that often faces managers is one of 'information overload' that is, when faced with an overwhelming amount of information only part of it can be processed and acted upon at any one time. This creates a dilemma: on the one hand managers need to be able to attend to detailed aspects of the situation, on the other hand there is a need to be able to stand back and retain an overall perspective in a holistic fashion and not become swamped in detail and minutiae (Hodgkinson and Sparrow, 2002: 196). A fundamental premise of a number of models of cognitive style is that individuals exhibit preferred approaches for organizing information that may vary in terms of 'seeing the parts' or 'seeing the whole' (this may be termed generically a wholist-analytical (WA) cognitive style dimension). This idea may be traced to the middle decades of the 20th century when Witkin and his co-workers identified a construct that they labeled 'psychological differentiation' and developed an associated theory, that of 'field dependence-independence' (FDI) considered by many to be the antecedent of modern cognitive styles research (Sternberg and Grigorenko, 2001). FDI was based on the observation that disembedding a simple shape from a more complex background (a perceptual competence termed 'field independence') was easier for some individuals than for others and was also related to competence in other (non-perceptual) problem solving tasks. A bipolar dimension was postulated, the extremes of which were termed field dependence (FD) indicating a greater reliance on external frames of reference, and field independence (FI) indicating a greater reliance on internal frames of reference. Witkin and his co-workers developed a series of tests including the body adjustment test, the rod and frame test, and a suite of paper-and-pencil embedded figures tests (EFTs). A summary of the origins and development of the FDI program of research may be found in Witkin, Moore, Goodenough and Cox (1977) and Sternberg and Grigorenko (2001: 4–7).

Despite being the bedrock of several decades of cognitive styles research the FDI construct has been criticized on two grounds. Firstly, that measures of field dependence-independence (for example the Embedded Figures Test, EFT) correlate with intelligence (Goldstein and Blackman, 1978; MacLeod, Jackson and Palmer, 1986; McKenna, 1984). These observations led Sternberg to argue, 'a significant portion of the genetic variance in field dependence-independence [up to 60 percent] is explainable by genetic variation in intelligence' (1997: 7). The second criticism leveled by Riding and Rayner (1998) is that the Embedded Figures Test and its variants such as the Group Embedded Figures Test (GEFT) fail to assess both poles of the field dependence-field independence continuum; that is field dependence (FD) is merely inferred from a low field independence (FI) score (since the EFT-type measures do not include a direct assessment of FD).

In the wake of these difficulties, attempts to revitalize the 'whole/part' notion in cognition and rationalize the number of style constructs in which it is important have led researchers to postulate a super-ordinate WA dimension of cognitive style. The WA dimension consists of two contrasting modes of organizing information – whether individuals 'take the whole view or see things in parts' (Rayner and Riding, 1997: 7). The WA cognitive style dimension is bi-polar and subsumes perceptual functioning (Witkin, 1962), holist and serialist thinking (Pask and Scott, 1972) and overlaps with 'local' and 'global' processing (Sternberg, 1997 – see below). It represents the habitual mode in which an individual organizes information: some individuals will organize information into its component parts (described as 'analytics'), whilst others will retain a global or overall view (described as 'wholists') (Riding, 1997: 30).

A number of tests of this dimension are available, some of which overcome the limitations of self-report (Caldwell, 2006) by directly assessing wholist-analytical perceptual functioning (Witkin, 1962; Riding, 1991) whilst others continue to rely upon Likert-scaled items (Sternberg and Wagner, 1991). As implemented in the *CSA*, and like its complement the VI dimension, the WA dimension of cognitive style does not appear to correlate with intelligence (Riding and Pearson, 1994), Kolb learning style[4] (Sadler-Smith, 2001) or academic performance (Sadler-Smith, 1997). Moreover, differences are qualitative rather than absolute in that each pole of the dimension has its own strengths and weaknesses. From a pedagogical and problem-solving perspective, for wholists there is the danger that the distinction between the parts of a topic may become blurred, whereas for analytics, the separation of the whole into its parts may mean that one aspect of a situation may be focused on at the expense of others and hence its overall importance exaggerated (Riding, 2001).

As with the VI dimension of cognitive style, Riding has postulated that WA operates at the level of a cognitive control and interacts with the structure of teaching material to affect learning performance. In the experimental study referred to previously Riding and Sadler-Smith (1992) observed an interaction between the two dimensions of thinking style (verbal-imagery × wholist-analytical) and structure of material (three instructional designs which varied in terms of the use of structural devices such as overviews and also presentation mode) in their effect upon recall performance in a computer-based learning package. Riding and Al-Sanabani (1998) observed an interaction between wholist-analytical style and gender in their effect upon performance for learning from materials that varied in terms of the use of headings and sub-divisions of textual content. Sadler-Smith and Riding (1999) explored the learning preferences of business and management undergraduates and observed that analytics preferred to have control over learning for themselves whereas the wholists had no preference.

In parallel with these developments which emanated mainly from the UK, in North America Sternberg (1997) and his co-researchers developed a comprehensive and elaborate theory of individual differences in thinking (cognitive) styles termed 'Mental Self Government' (MSG) since it reflected the ways in which people 'somehow govern or manage their everyday activities' (Sternberg and Zhang, 2001: 199) – an assumption that Coffield et al. (2004) describe as 'metaphorical' and for which 'no evidence is offered' (2004: 110). The theory is conceptualized as comprising 13 styles that fall along five dimensions: functions (legislative, executive and judicial); forms (monarchic, hierarchic, oligarchic and anarchic); levels (local and global); scope (internal and external); leanings (liberal and conservative). A detailed consideration is beyond the scope of this chapter and readers are referred to Sternberg (1997: 27–75) for a full description and to Zhang and Sternberg (2001: 199–201) for an overview. A number of the cognitive functions associated with Sternberg's MSG styles appear to overlap with the wholist-analytical styles considered thus far. For example, a monarchic style is characterized by focusing on one thing at a time ('I like to deal with major issues or themes, rather than details or facts', Sternberg, 1997: 45), a local style is concerned with working at the level of fine detail ('I pay more attention to the parts of a task than to its overall effect or significance', Sternberg, 1997: 62), whilst a global style is more concerned with attention to the overall

picture ('I tend to pay little attention to details', Sternberg, 1997: 60). The local and global scales of the MSG inventory (Sternberg and Wagner, 1991) have been shown to be valid for US samples in that they are correlated with other theoretically related measures such as the *Gregorc Style Delineator* and the *Myers Briggs Type Indicator*, but uncorrelated with SAT (and hence distinct from ability) (Zhang and Sternberg, 2001).

Sternberg (1997: 64–5) argues that although most people tend to be either more local or more global in their style of thinking, a key to successful problem solving in many situations lies in the ability to be able to traverse levels often by pairing-up with someone more adept at the other level. Failure to do so may result in, for example, idea formation being favored at the expense of idea implementation, or issues getting very efficiently (and quickly) 'pinned-down' at the expense of setting-out the global issues when there is the absence of the whole view.

## MODE OF PROCESSING INFORMATION: THE INTUITION-ANALYSIS (IA) DIMENSION

Like several other researchers, Allinson and Hayes (1996) recognized the need for rationalization in styles research, and with this in mind they argued that there is a single and fundamental dimension of cognitive style which over-arches and is super-ordinate to a number of other constructs, for example: analytic, deductive, rigorous, constrained, convergent, formal and critical versus synthetic, inductive, expansive, unconstrained, divergent, informal, diffuse and creative (Nickerson et al., 1985). Allinson and Hayes labeled this over-arching construct the intuition-analysis (IA) dimension of cognitive style, and described the two poles of this dimension thus:

Intuition, characteristic of the right brain orientation, refers to immediate judgement based on feeling and the adoption of a global perspective. Analysis, characteristic of the left brain orientation, refers to judgement based on mental reasoning and a focus on detail. (Allinson and Hayes, 1996: 122)

The model as originally described is based on the theoretical premise of brain hemisphericity – that is 'right-left patterns [that] are not merely transient' (ibid.) and which manifest themselves as follows:

Intuitivists (right brain dominant) tend to be relatively nonconformist, prefer an open-ended approach to problem solving, rely on random methods of exploration, remember spatial images most easily, and work best with ideas requiring overall assessment. Analysts (left-brain dominant) tend to be more compliant, favour a structured approach to problem solving, depend on systematic methods of investigation, recall verbal material most readily and are especially comfortable with ideas requiring step by step analysis. (Allinson and Hayes, 1996: 122)

Readers are referred to Coffield et al. (2004) for a summary and positive evaluation of the instrument developed by Allinson and Hayes (1996) – the *Cognitive Style Index (CSI)* – in terms of: (1) reliability: internal consistency and test-retest reliability are both high; (2) validity: the *CSI* correlates with relevant scales from other instruments (including the *Myers-Briggs Type Indicator, MBTI*), an effect of job level on *CSI* scores has been observed across a number of studies (greater seniority is associated with higher levels of intuition) and success in entrepreneurship and business venturing; and (3) implications for pedagogy: matched styles are often effective in mentoring relationships. They concluded their assessment of the Allinson and Hayes model and *CSI* thus:

The constructs of analysis and intuition [as measured by the *CSI*] are relevant to decision making and work performance in many contexts, although the pedagogical implications of the model have not been fully explored. The *CSI* is a suitable tool for researching and reflecting on teaching and learning, especially if treated as a measure of *two factors* rather than one. (Coffield et al., 2004: 89, italics added)

Coffield et al. (2004) are alluding to the fact that despite Allinson and Hayes' *CSI* being the instrument of choice of those which they reviewed, the fundamental precept adhered to by its authors of a bipolar intuition-analysis dimension of cognitive style (Hayes et al., 2003) has not gone unchallenged to the extent that there are two opposing views with regard to the nature of this important dimension of cognitive style.

## SUMMARY AND CRITIQUE

The various cognitive styles researchers whose work has been discussed thus far have each provided their own distinctive conceptual framework, presented empirical evidence in support of the underlying conceptual bases of their work, and offered conclusions which have implications for the pedagogy of management learning. Notwithstanding these achievements, made on the basis of several decades of research, a number of important questions remain unanswered, and new questions are raised. Amongst the principal questions to which styles researchers must provide convincing answers if their work is to impact in meaningful ways on management learning theory and practice are those which pertain specifically to: (1) reliability and validity of style measurement: several of the models reviewed exhibit a number of weaknesses in this regard (Peterson et al., 2003; Hodgkinson and Sadler-Smith, 2003); (2) commonality of conceptual framework and shared theoretical basis: the study of cognitive style would benefit considerably from a unifying model or conceptual framework (Sternberg, 1997: 149), and an underpinning by a coherent and current body of psychological theory; and (3) the integrated and interdependent nature of human thinking: a number of authors have argued that a vital learning and managerial competence is the ability to take decisions and solve problems in cognitively versatile ways which integrate different modes of thinking (Coffield et al., 2004;

Hodgkinson and Sparrow, 2002; Louis and Sutton, 1991).

## RELIABILITY AND VALIDITY OF STYLE MEASUREMENT

The computer-presented *Cognitive Styles Analysis (CSA)* (Riding, 1991), one of the few direct measures of cognitive style, was designed to overcome assessment problems associated with the various embedded figures tests (with respect to the WA dimension) and drawbacks of self-report rating scales (Riding and Rayner, 1998; Riding, 2001). The *CSA* is based upon an integration of the wholist-analytical (WA) and the verbal-imagery (VI) dimensions of cognitive style, and consists of separate sub-tests for each dimension. Peterson et al. (2003) examined the *CSA*'s internal consistency and its stability using parallel forms, test-retest and split half analyses. Kline (1991: 45) suggests that the correlation ($r$) between scores on the same test taken on different occasions should be at least 0.70. Regrettably, in Peterson et al.'s study of the *CSA* observed correlations were low ($0.07 \leq r \leq 0.36$). This and their other findings led them to conclude that in its current form the *CSA* 'is not reliable or internally consistent', and only by doubling the length of the WA sub-test does this element alone become more reliable and more stable (Peterson et al., 2003: 890). Riding (2003) criticized Peterson et al.'s study on the grounds of sampling, test conditions, test-retest interval and in particular the fact that the *CSA* version they used was not a test of the published form of the *CSA per se* (Peterson et al. constructed their own version of the test). Nonetheless the research by Peterson and her colleagues does raise questions with regard to the *CSA*'s reliability, and in particular of the VI sub-test.

The internal consistency and test-retest reliability of the *Cognitive Style Index (CSI)* (Allinson and Hayes, 1996) in its original form is well-established (Allinson and Hayes, 2000; Allinson et al., 2000;

Allinson et al., 2001; Murphy et al., 1998; Sadler-Smith, Spicer et al., 2000). However, at a more fundamental level the validity of the intuition-analysis dimension of cognitive style as a bipolar construct has been called into question. In essence there are two competing views: Allinson and Hayes (1996) assert that analysis and intuition are opposite ends of a unidimensional, bipolar continuum – referred to by Hodgkinson and Sadler-Smith (2003) as the 'unitary' conception of intuition-analysis cognitive style (an analysis style *versus* an intuition style). An alternative position, labeled 'complex', asserts that intuition-analysis cognitive style is better conceived as two separate, albeit inter-correlated, unipolar constructs (an analysis dimension *and* an intuition dimension). Using data from over 900 participants in a series of exploratory and confirmatory factor analyses Hodgkinson and Sadler-Smith (2003) found that a two factor ('complex') model provides a better approximation of responses to the *CSI* than does a single factor ('unitary') model. They argued that this provided compelling evidence in favor of the disaggregation of a unitary intuition-analysis dimension into separate, albeit correlated, intuition and analysis components, a view with which Coffield et al. (2004: 88) concurred:

> Despite the claims of its authors [Allinson and Hayes], the *CSI* has been shown to measure two related, albeit multifaceted, constructs. We believe that the basically sound psychometric properties of the *CSI* would be further improved if the revised two-factor scoring system proposed by Hodgkinson and Sadler-Smith (2003) were generally adopted.

This conclusion is vital in the light of the fact that Coffield et al. (2004) reviewed 13 of the most influential style models and concluded that the *CSI* had the best evidence for reliability and validity of all the models they studied (including Herrmann's 'whole brain' model and *Herrmann Brain Dominance Instrument (HBDI)*, the *MBTI*, Riding's model of cognitive style and *CSA*, and Sternberg's theory of Mental Self-Government and *Thinking Styles Inventory*). Overall these findings suggest that a multi-faceted ('complex') formulation based upon independent but complementary styles, such as intuition and analysis, which can be measured using reliable and valid self-report scales, but ideally using non-self-report methods, would represent a significant advance in the assessment of cognitive style and in cognitive styles research more generally.

## COMMONALITY OF CONCEPTUAL FRAMEWORK AND SHARED THEORETICAL BASIS

One of the problems that Sternberg (1997: 149) identifies with the 'theory' of styles is that there is 'usually no unifying model or metaphor that integrates the various styles, not only between theories, but even within theories'. Riding's conceptual frame is clear and unequivocal, consisting of two orthogonal dimensions, VI and WA, between which the observed correlations are consistently low and non-significant ($r = \pm0.10$, see: Riding and Rayner, 1998: 100). As noted earlier, Riding's theoretical basis is a systems model (the 'cognitive control model') consisting of a number of elements: primary sources (knowledge and cognitive history, reasoning ability, personality sources and gender); cognitive control (cognitive style); cognitive input (working memory); cognitive output (learning and coping strategies); external; world (experiences and observed behaviors). Within this model cognitive style provides a 'representational interface' between the internal sources and the external environment. Notwithstanding the logic of the model in itself, precisely how the hypothesized function of 'cognitive control' via style (Riding, 2001: 68) relates explicitly to models of working memory (Baddeley, 1997), long-term working memory (Ericsson and Kintsch, 1995), non-conscious processing of information (Reber, 1993) or personality (given that relationships with neuroticism are suggested – see Riding, 2001: 66) are unclear.

The extent to which Riding's more recent work (Riding, 2002) which incorporates a measure of working memory capacity (the *Information Processing Index, IPI*) addresses these issues remains to be seen.

When taken in isolation the various models of style often possess the virtues of elegance (for example, the orthogonality of VI and WA dimensions), conceptual simplicity (for example, the unitary nature of IA), and face validity (for example, the metaphor of 'government'). However, this conceptual clarity becomes somewhat obfuscated when the models are scrutinized collectively. As has already been noted, the concepts of 'local' and 'global' as used by Sternberg (1997) in the MSG theory share many of the features of the whole/part distinction embodied in Riding's WA dimension. When one adds to this the definition and operationalization of the notion of 'analysis' in the *CSI* model (Allinson and Hayes, 1996) the difficulties are, to say the least, compounded. If 'analysis' (Allinson and Hayes, 1996) and 'analytical' (Riding, 2001) refer to similar psychological constructs we might expect there to be a statistically significant positive correlation between Allinson and Hayes' *CSI* scores and Riding's *CSA* WA scores (high scores indicate an analytic style on the *CSA* and the *CSI*). Empirical data suggest otherwise: Sadler-Smith, Spicer et al. (2000) observed a near zero correlation ($r = +0.05$) between *CSI* scores and *CSA* WA scores. As Coffield et al. (2004: 42) noted the reliability questions raised by Peterson et al. (2003) in relation to the *CSA* may be one of the reasons why correlations of WA with other measures have often been close to zero. In an unpublished manuscript Sadler-Smith scored the Allinson and Hayes *CSI* as two separate intuition and analysis scales according the revised procedure suggested by Hodgkinson and Sadler-Smith (2003) and computed Pearson correlations with Sternberg's *MSG* local and global scales.[5] Whilst the correlations were low, it is perhaps encouraging that there appeared to be some degree of convergence in the 'local/analytical' and 'global/intuitive' constructs as independently defined and operationalized by Allinson and Hayes (1996) and Sternberg (1997).

## THE INTEGRATED AND INTERDEPENDENT NATURE OF HUMAN THINKING

Polarization of cognitive functioning is inherent in the Riding model (verbal-versus-visual style, and wholist-versus-analytical style) and the Allinson and Hayes' model (and intuition-versus-analysis) of cognitive style. An analogy which can be used is that of a child's see-saw – it is impossible to be 'up' or 'down' at both ends simultaneously, hence for example more of analysis means less of intuition and one can therefore, only exercise a high level of intuition at the expense of a reduction in analytical reasoning – the processes contest and oppose rather than integrate and harmonize. Following this line of reasoning, Coffield et al (2004: 42) argue with regard to the *CSA* that there are conceptual problems with VI in that most tasks make demands on verbal and non-verbal processing, and that in reality these are interdependent or integrated aspects of thinking. Coffield et al. (2004) also drew a comparison between the WA dimension and Bloom's (1956) elements of analysis and synthesis in the taxonomy of educational objectives for the cognitive domain (knowledge, comprehension, application, analysis, synthesis and evaluation). They argue that the wholist style shares some of the features of synthesis which in Bloom's terms is a less simple (i.e. higher level) process than analysis but nonetheless interdependent with it. Moreover 'we simply do not know enough about the interaction and interdependence of analytic and holistic thinking in different contexts to claim that they are opposites' (Coffield et al., 2004: 42). At a more general level some psychologists have called into question the simplistic dichotomization and polarization of human information processing. Reber (1993) argued that it is important to have an appreciation of the differences between implicit and explicit learning, but it is quite

another thing to 'allow ourselves to be seduced by what we can call, for want of a better name, "the polarity fallacy"' and thereby treat different modes of cognition as completely separate and independent rather than interactive components in a 'cooperative process' (Reber, 1993: 23).

## CONCLUSION

In the light of these observations, limitations and criticisms it may be concluded that if the concept of cognitive style is to achieve its potential to make a more meaningful contribution to management learning research it must have valid and reliable methods of assessment, be based on a unifying conceptual model and be attuned to the integrated and versatile nature of the cognitive competencies required of managers in the 21st century. The current position is that a number of the available methods of cognitive style assessment are beset by problems of reliability, validity and convergence, and no common conceptual framework appears to be drawn upon which acknowledges recent advances in cognitive and social psychology and cognitive neuroscience. Styles researchers have yet to take advantage of the new generation of imaging techniques such as PET and fMRI which may help shed light upon the biological nature of stylistic differences. Moreover, the notion of bipolarity is often employed in a way which fails to acknowledge and accommodate the integrated nature of human cognition and problem solving, all-too-often dominates both the conceptualization and the operationalization of cognitive style.

## A DUPLEX MODEL OF COGNITIVE STYLE

The question of whether human beings represent, organize and process information in ways served by different cognitive systems manifested as two different modes of thought has been debated in psychology from James, Freud and Jung up to the present time.

The ramifications have been felt in related fields including management; for example AT&T executive and author of *The Functions of the Executive* (1938), Chester I. Barnard subdivided mental processes into two groups, logical and non-logical. According to Barnard the latter are incapable of being expressed in words or in reasoning, and are so unconscious, complex and rapid that they cannot be analyzed by the person within whose brain they take place; they represent the handling of a mass of experience or a complex of abstractions 'in a flash' (Barnard, 1938). In a similar vein Herbert Simon, Nobel prize-winning cognitive scientist and author of *Administrative Behavior* (1947/1997), was concerned both with the limits of rational reasoning processes (that rationality is 'bounded') and with the role of intuition and affect in management decision making (the 'reasons that underlie unreason'). He described intuitions as analyses which have become frozen into habit and as a capacity for rapid response through pattern recognition. The detailed issues as they pertain to intuitive judgment in management are discussed more fully elsewhere (Dane and Pratt, 2007; Hodgkinson et al., 2008; Sadler-Smith and Sparrow, 2007; Sinclair and Ashkanasy, 2005), but in essence Allinson and Hayes' model of cognitive style and the attendant debate is a recent manifestation of the longer-standing question concerning the operation of 'two minds': one computational, logical and rational and the other heuristic, non-logical (as opposed to illogical) and intuitive.

Sloman (2002) argues that an obvious solution to the conundrum (of 'either/or') is to conceive of the mind in both ways; that it has dual aspects conforming to the processes of an associative system (characterized by intuition, fantasy, creativity, imagination, visual recognition, experientiality and associative memory) and a rule-based system (characterized by deliberation, explanation, abstract symbolic representation, and formal analysis with verification and ascription of purpose), a distinction supported by various sources of evidence (Sloman, 2002: 383–4).

At a more inclusive level the properties of Sloman's associative and rule-based distinction may be conjoined and subsumed within two-process (dual) theories of reasoning, generically labeled 'System 1 processes' and 'System 2 processes' respectively (Stanovich and West, 2000). Stanovich and West (2000) identify a number of such dual process theories predicated upon the System 1 and System 2 distinction. For example, Epstein (1994) in the Cognitive Experiential Self Theory (CEST) distinguishes between two information-processing systems, an experiential system and a rational system: (1) The experiential system is a learning system which operates automatically, pre-consciously, non-verbally, rapidly, effortlessly, and concretely. It is holistic[6] and is associated with affect and operates on the basis of schemas acquired from lived experiences. Intuition is the operation of the experiential system. (2) The rational system is an inferential logical system which operates consciously, primarily verbally, slowly, and effortfully. The rational system is abstract, analytic, and affect-free and evolutionarily the more recent of the two systems (Epstein, 1994, 2004). The generic properties of System 1 and System 2 as outlined by Stanovich and West (2000) and the specific properties of the rational and experiential systems (Epstein, 1994) are summarized in the upper portions of Table 16.1.

In the Cognitive Experiential Self Theory (CEST) the degree to which either system dominates thought and behavior is a function of: (1) the extent to which the situation is associated with a customary way of responding; (2) the degree of emotional involvement; (3) experiential dominance based on repeated amounts of relevant experience; and (4) 'individual differences in *preference* for relying on one system more than the other' (Epstein et al., 1996: 391, italics added). Epstein et al. (1996) constructed two separate self-report scales to assess preferences for experiential and rational processing with the aim of empirically resolving whether such preferences are unimodal ('I believe in trusting my hunches' and 'I would prefer a task that is intellectual,

**Table 16.1  A dual process framework for cognitive style**

*GENERIC DESCRIPTIONS AND EXAMPLES*

| System 1 | System 2 | Source |
|---|---|---|
| Associative; holistic; automatic; undemanding of cognitive capacity; relatively fast operation; acquisition by biology, exposure and personal experience | Rule-based; analytic; controlled; demanding of cognitive capacity; relatively slow operation; acquisition by cultural and formal tuition | Stanovich and West (2000) |
| Experiential | Rational | Epstein (1994) |
| Recognition-primed decisions | Rational choice strategy | Klein (1998) |
| X-system | C-system | Lieberman et al. (2004) |
| Imagistic-nonverbal | Verbal | Paivio (1969, 1971) |
| Implicit cognition | Explicit learning | Reber (1993) |
| Associative system | Rule-based system | Sloman (2002) |
| Slow learning memory system / Associative processing mode | Fast-binding memory system/Rule-based processing mode | Smith and DeCoster (1999) |

*EPSTEIN COGNITIVE EXPERIENTIAL SELF-THEORY*

| Experiential system | Rational system | Source |
|---|---|---|
| Holistic; automatic; effortless; affective; associationistic; mediated by 'vibes' from past events; concrete images, metaphors, narratives; more rapid, immediate action; slower, more resistant to change; changes with repetitive/intense experience | Analytic; intentional, effortful; logical; mediated by conscious appraisal of events; abstract symbols, words, numbers; slower, delayed action; changes more rapidly; changes with strength of argument, new evidence. | Epstein et al. (1996) |

*LIEBERMAN SELF-KNOWLEDGE SYSTEMS*

| Reflexive (X) system | Reflective (C) system | Source |
|---|---|---|
| Parallel processing; fast operating; slow learning; non-reflective consciousness; sensitive to subliminal presentations; spontaneous processes; typically sensory; phylogenetically older | Serial processing; slow operating; fast learning; reflective consciousness; insensitive to subliminal presentations; intentional processes; typically linguistic; phylogenetically older | Lieberman (2007) |

*DUPLEX MODEL OF COGNITIVE STYLE*

| Intuitive system | Analytical system | Sources |
|---|---|---|
| Affect-laden; comparatively fast in operation, slow in formation; parallel and holistic; involuntary; cognitively undemanding; imagistic/narrative-based; unavailable to conscious awareness | Affect-free; comparatively slow in operation, fast in formation; serial and detail-focused; intentional; cognitively demanding; abstract/symbolic-based; open to conscious awareness | Epstein (1994); Lieberman (2007); Sloman (2002); Smith and DeCoster (1999); Stanovich and West (2000) |

difficult and important to one that is somewhat important but does not require much thought') rather than an *a priori* assumption, as in the *CSI* and the *MBTI*, of bimodality ('I am more of a thinking-type person than a feeling-type person'). Epstein and his colleagues developed and tested the *Rational Experiential Inventory* (*REI*) by combining a reliable and valid measure of rational processing (Cacioppo and Petty's (1982) 'Need for cognition' (*NFC*) scale) with a new scale which they called 'Faith in Intuition' (*FII*). The verbal-visual distinction which is to be found in dual coding theory ('images and verbal processes are viewed as alternative coding systems or modes of representation', Paivio, 1971: 8) which Riding drew upon as a theoretical basis for the VI dimension is also recognized as antecedent to dual processing theory (Epstein et al., 1996: 390). The representational mode of visualization is encapsulated in the *REI* by a number of items, for example: 'I often have clear visual images of things' and 'I am good at visualizing things'.

As well as being potentially helpful in the understanding, diagnosis and treatment of various psychopathologies, Epstein et al. (1996) speculate that CEST and the *REI* may also be helpful in understanding a person's receptivity to different kinds of communication, for example:

> Appeals to emotions, personal experience and the use of concrete examples could be more effective for people who process information primarily in the intuitive mode, whereas presenting facts and logical arguments could be more effective for individuals who process information primarily in the analytic mode. (Epstein et al., 1996: 390)

This in effect restates the matching hypothesis from the perspective of CEST, but it is by no means clear whether matching mode of presentation to the requirements of the different information processing systems turns out be more effective than mis-matching. As we have seen in relation to other models of cognitive style, the evidence in favor of the match is far from unequivocal and significant effects are often

a result of complex two-way and three-way interactions. This question is one which requires further theoretical elaboration ('why should matching be more effective than mis-matching?') and empirical investigation ('is matching more effective than mis-matching?'). Moreover, in the same way that rational processing can be disaggregated into various sub-components (such as mathematical and verbal) Epstein et al. (1996: 403) speculated that there may also be a number of experiential (intuitive) sub-components (for example, visualization, imagination and aesthetic sensibility).

Dual process theories and the System 1/System 2 distinction provide a simple and compelling conceptual framework for a duplex model of cognitive style based upon the parallel workings of an intuitive system and an analytical system which contribute jointly to a cooperative process. The two modes of thought are qualitatively different in terms of the kinds of data upon which they draw, their operating principles and their outcomes (Smith and DeCoster, 1999). Moreover, there is accumulating evidence that different brain structures appear to be activated when these different modes of thought are engaged (see Kruglanski and Orehek, 2007). The term 'intuitive' is preferred over 'experiential' for three reasons: firstly, the term intuition has greater currency in management research; secondly, intuition subsumes experientiality; and thirdly, intuition is the operation of the experiential system (see: Epstein, 2004). The term 'analytical' is preferred over 'rational' because there are strong elements of rationality in both systems (Slovic et al., 2004). This view is predicated on the evolutionary argument that it was a phylogenetically more ancient intuitive system which had a rationality of purpose (Sadler-Smith, 2008) that equipped *Homo sapiens* with some of the skills necessary to survive and evolve during the last 200 millennia or so:

> Long before there was probability theory, risk assessment, and decision analysis, there were intuition, instinct, and gut feeling to tell us

whether an animal was safe to approach or the water was safe to drink. As life became more complex and humans gained more control over their environment, analytic tools were invented to 'boost' the rationality of our experiential thinking. Subsequently, analytic thinking was placed on a pedestal and portrayed as the epitome of rationality. (Slovic et al., 2004: 313).

To summarize: the analytical system is affect-free, comparatively slow in operation, comparatively fast in formation, serial and detail-focused, intentional, cognitively demanding, abstract/symbolic-based, and accessible to conscious awareness. The intuitive system, on the other hand, is affect-laden, comparatively fast in operation, comparatively slow in formation, parallel and holistic, involuntary, cognitively undemanding, imagistic/narrative-based, and unavailable to conscious awareness (see lower portion of Table 16.1). Moreover, the two systems are connected in that intuition (sometimes manifested as 'analyses frozen into habit') draws upon implicit and explicit learning experiences compressed into expertise which reveals itself as the involuntary, affectively-charged, holistic informed intuitive judgments which experts are able to exercise in complex, time-pressured and judgmental situations (Dane and Pratt, 2007; Sadler-Smith, 2008).

With regard to the self-reported assessment of individual differences in preferences for the analytical mode or the intuitive mode there are several instruments which have exhibited acceptable levels of reliability. The *CSI* consists of 38 trichotomous (true/uncertain/false) items which are scored to derive a single index (0 through 76; lower scores are more intuitive, higher scores more analytic). As discussed earlier, there are a number of problems that have been identified with this instrument: firstly, factor analyses suggest that a unifactoral model is not tenable (Backhaus and Liff, 2007; Hodgkinson and Sadler-Smith, 2003); secondly, when scored as recommended by Coffield et al. (2004) as two separate scales, in spite of the acceptable levels of reliability, the intuition and analysis components are not independent (reported correlations are

moderate and statistically significant). Other candidate instruments for the assessment of cognitive style within a duplex framework include the *Rational Experiential Inventory (REI)* (Epstein et al., 1996) and the *Linear-Nonlinear Thinking Style Profile (LNTSP)* (Vance et al., 2007).

The *REI* exists in both long (31 item) and short (ten-item) forms. The *REI* has a compelling conceptual and theoretical basis (in dual process theory) and there are emerging connections to neuro-scientific explanations of the neural substrates of two systems (see Kruglanski and Orehek, 2007; Lieberman, 2007). Psychometrically the *REI* appears to be a reliable and valid instrument for the assessment of two independent constructs ('Need for Cognition' and 'Faith in Intuition') reflecting the operation of the intuitive and analytical systems. In spite of the *REI*'s undoubted strengths there are a number of problems as observed by Hodgkinson et al. (2006). Firstly, whilst the two main scales (NFC and FII) seem to reflect accurately the overall construct definition (two independent dimensions of intuition/experientiality and analysis/rationality) it appears unclear whether or not a third factor to that emerged in Hodgkinson et al.'s (2006) research represented a true substantive factor as opposed to a method factor. Secondly, the *REI* measures predominantly the affective aspects of intuition (for example: 'I trust my initial feelings about people') and there may be a case for expanding (as was also noted by Epstein et al., 1996) for coverage of other aspects of the intuitive system's domain, for example, the aesthetic and imagistic elements (including visualization – see Paivio, 1971).

Vance et al. (2007) reported the development and validation of a self-report diagnostic instrument for measuring individuals' linear and non-linear thinking styles (the *Linear-Nonlinear Thinking Style Profile* or *LNTSP*) which they claim is of 'potential beneficial use for management education and business practices' (Vance et al., 2007: 167). The four *LNTSP* scales exhibit satisfactory reliability ($0.70 \leq \alpha \leq 0.87$) and convergent validity with respect to the *MBTI* and the *CSI* (when scored conventionally, i.e. unifactorially). The authors assert that the *LNTSP* may provide managers and other professionals with valuable insights into their cognitive flexibility and degree of balance in their use of linear (rationality, logic, analysis) and non-linear (intuition, insight, creativity) thinking styles. Further research is required with respect to the construct validity of the *LNTSP* and its predictive validity.

One assumption of the duplex model is that individual managers will exhibit a preference (a set level) for relying on the intuitive or the analytical system (see Epstein et al., 1996). An implication of this is that managers may be classified as one of the four types identified by Hodgkinson and Clarke (2007): (1) high analytic/low intuitive managers may be characterized as 'detail conscious' and are driven by a compulsion to pore over minutiae and analyze, sometimes to the point of 'analysis paralysis'. Whilst to focus on detail has undoubted strengths in many situations, in taking it to extremes one may overlook the bigger picture and ignore intuition; (2) low analytic/high intuitive managers are 'big picture conscious' and may be pre-occupied with 'seeing the wood rather than the trees'; (3) low analytic/low intuitive managers are 'non-discerning' to the extent that they deploy 'minimal cognitive resources' and rely upon received wisdom or the opinions of others (Hodgkinson and Clarke, 2007: 247); and (4) high analytic/high intuitive managers are cognitively versatile, able to 'see the wood' and 'see the trees' and deploy rational and analytical processing with equal facility. If analysis and intuition are well-developed preferences then it is likely that the majority of managers fall into the 'detail conscious' or 'big picture conscious' categories; therefore one of the aims of management education and training should be to endow managers with a cognitive versatility whereby they are able to deploy strategies in ways that go beyond their set level of intuition or analysis and are commensurate with the task.

## GENERAL IMPLICATIONS OF COGNITIVE STYLES FOR TEACHING AND LEARNING STRATEGIES

As has been argued, several of the most popular models of cognitive style are beset by limitations of varying degrees of severity. The duplex model attempts to overcome these by presenting a conceptual framework for cognitive style which has its theoretical basis in dual process theories of cognition and which subsumes, albeit to varying degrees, the functions of representation, organization and processing of information. The model recognizes the integrated and interdependent nature of human thinking; moreover valid and reliable instruments are available for the assessment of intuitive and analytical processing. These are easy to administer and interpret in organizational settings (for example, the *CSI*, *LNTSP* and *REI*). The implications for teaching and learning strategies of cognitive styles in general and of the duplex model in particular will now be considered.

In general terms research-based knowledge of cognitive style has several potential implications for teaching and learning, summarized by Coffield et al. (2004: 119–26):

*Increased self-awareness*: a knowledge of cognitive styles may enable individuals to 'see and to question their long-held habitual behaviors' (Sadler-Smith, 2001: 300) which may impact upon not only the efficacy of their learning but also their decision-making and problem-solving behavior in general. Self-awareness of cognitive style may also form the basis of personal and career guidance and counseling (Hayes and Allinson, 1994). Self-awareness on the part of instructors may help them to reflect upon and adapt their practices on the basis of a theory of cognition and individual difference.

*Meta-cognition*: individuals can be trained to monitor and evaluate their selection and use of various learning-related behaviors building on an increased self-awareness resulting from the identification of their preferred ways of representing, organizing and processing information. Riding and Sadler-Smith (1997) presented a model of meta-cognition in which learners may be trained to sense their level of comfort with a learning situation, and selecting an informational mode or structural form which best suits them or reconfiguring the mode and structure in such a way as to reduce the information processing load.

*A lexicon of learning*: knowledge of cognitive styles can provide learners and teachers with a terminology with which to engage in a dialogue relating to their preferences, causes of success and failure and the teacher-student relationship (Coffield et al., 2004). It must be borne in mind, however, that without a coherent and scientifically robust conceptual framework at its foundation any such lexicon may be of little pedagogical value.

*To match or not to match*: the question of whether to match teaching and learning strategy to cognitive style or not-to-match is a more contentious one than the issues of self-awareness, meta-cognition and dialogue, and any firm recommendation is difficult to justify on the basis of the available scientific evidence. Perhaps the best that can be achieved given the current state of knowledge relating to the matching hypothesis is to adopt a 'cognitive belt-and-braces' approach (Riding and Sadler-Smith, 1997): that is to configure teaching and learning strategies in such a way that learners are for some of the time able to operate safely inside their 'cognitive comfort zone', but are at other times guided to move away from their habitual mode of thinking into cognitively unfamiliar territory in much the same way as various learning style theorists recommend in relation to the learning cycle (Honey and Mumford, 1986; Kolb, 1984).

## SPECIFIC IMPLICATIONS OF THE DUPLEX MODEL

The duplex model has a number of implications both for the teaching strategies used by management educators, and the strategies employed by learners themselves.

*Rectifies analytical bias in management education*: traditional management education, as practiced in most business schools, emphasizes the development of logical, 'rational' and analytical skills, and it could even be argued that these curricula are biased in favor of the analytical system and the analytic cognitive style. However, an important and indeed long-standing challenge for management education (Taggart and Robey, 1981; Taggart and Valenzi, 1990) is to recognize and accept the importance of the intuitive system, and to devise ways of integrating knowledge of it into the curriculum in order to develop managers' intuitive awareness and enhance their intuitive capabilities (Sadler-Smith and Shefy, 2004). Various researchers have made suggestions for how this might be achieved (Hogarth, 2001; Klein, 1998, 2003; Robinson, 2006). Sadler-Smith and Burke (2008) and Sadler-Smith and Shefy (2007) suggest a number of activities which could be successfully incorporated into the management education curriculum, including: dispelling myths about intuition as a sixth sense, journaling intuitions and developing cognitive maps, scrutinizing intuitions and giving good feedback, being aware of biases in heuristics and intuitive judgment, and 'giving the rational mind a reprieve' through the techniques of mind by-pass.

*The context of management and learning*: managers in the 21st century face frequent and unexpected changes in their internal and external environments, they therefore need to be able to adapt, flex and change. Meta-cognition provides a basis for personal adaptation to new and changing environments, a corollary of this is that too great an emphasis upon the development of a single mode of thinking (and traditionally the accent has been put upon analysis) may instill cognitive rigidity and inertia and constrain the personal adaptability that the business environment demands of managers. Managers call upon intuitive judgments in those situations which require people-oriented decisions, quick decisions, unexpected decisions, uncertain or novel situations, and situations where there is a lack of explicit clues (Burke and Miller, 1999). Where there is an absence of an informed or educated intuition, such judgments may be practiced covertly and without the constructive feedback which is essential for the development of informed intuition (Hogarth, 2001). Without a honing of the expertise through focused and deliberate practice which is the bedrock of good intuitive judgment (Ericcson and Charness, 1994) intuitions may be misinformed and potentially perilous, and of no more value than guesses.

*Further opportunity for the integration of affect and emotion into management education*: affect is a principal feature of the experiential system. The acknowledgement of the role that affect plays in learning may be addressed by reference to intuition *per se* (see above) but also via the incorporation of emotional intelligence (EI) into management education and training. The subject of EI is hotly debated, however; Ashkanasy and Daus (2002) argue that it is safe to work on the assumptions that EI involves the ability to identify and perceive emotions in the self and others, and the skills to understand and manage them is an individual difference which is distinct from, but positively related to, other 'intelligences' and develops over the life span and is 'trainable' via specific affective domain practices (Ashkanasy and Dasborough, 2003; Boyatzis et al., 2002). Further work is required to explore the relationships between affect as it manifests itself in intuitive judgment and emotions and the relationship between being 'emotionally intelligent' and 'intuitively intelligent'.

*Integrated nature of management decisions and problems*: analytic and intuitive cognitive styles are qualitatively different; each has its own strengths and weaknesses, and the problems and decisions which confront managers are likely to require a synthesis of the processes of the intuitive and the analytical systems (Hodgkinson and Clarke, 2007). There are few tasks which require analytical solutions or intuitive judgments exclusively. More often than not intuition can alert an experienced practitioner to anomalies in a computation, whilst an analytical check may be used to moderate levels of confidence in intuitively-derived

judgments. The polarization favored by some cognitive styles researchers of a 'unitary' persuasion logically precludes the union of opposites. A more complex, flexible and theoretically parsimonious view allows for the union of intuition and analysis and the development of learning strategies to augment individuals' habitual and preferred ways of representing, organizing and processing information.

## CONCLUSION

Over a quarter of a century ago Mintzberg (1976) argued that one of the keys to organizational effectiveness lies in a synthesis of clear-headed logic and powerful intuition. Mintzberg and Gosling (2002: 64) criticized contemporary management education for the undue emphasis that it gives to 'drill' in the various business functions and the inculcation of analytical decision-making skills, when in reality most critical management decision-making tasks center upon problems that are not neatly packaged, well-structured, quantifiable and amenable to computational solutions (Schön, 1983; Shapiro and Spence, 1997). Khatri and Ng (2000: 58) asserted that rational analysis is a useful and indispensable tool in strategy making but that 'strategic decision-making has to take into account both rational and intuitive processes'. In a similar vein Senge (1990) argued that whilst rationality is not opposed to intuition, logical analysis often implies that cause-and-effect are close in time and space whereas in reality temporal and spatial relationships are much more complex and better understood by intuitive as opposed to analytical judgment.

If we accept the view that business schools have a long and distinguished tradition of educating managers in analytical thinking, the question is raised how might the balance be redressed so that the curriculum of the business school develops managers' abilities to understand intuitive thinking and use it in more effective ways? Cognitive styles research and the duplex model in particular offer one possible way in which the business school curriculum might engage other cognitive and affective faculties which go beyond the verbal, sequential and analytical and into imagistic, holistic and intuitive realms.

Management education's theory and method has very successfully embraced experiential learning theory (Kolb, 1984) and the related notion of learning style (Honey and Mumford, 1986; Kolb, 1984). It may however be underplaying the significance of dual process theories and the related notion of cognitive style at a time when: (1) neurological research and a new generation of brain-imaging techniques are rapidly expanding scientists' understanding of the neural circuitry which underpins decision making, problem solving and learning (Bechara, 2004; Bechara et al., 2000; Damasio, 1994; Jung-Beeman et al., 2004; Lieberman, 2007; Springer and Deutsch, 1998); (2) perspectives from evolutionary psychology, whilst controversial in some quarters (Rose and Rose, 2000), are adding new insights to the understanding of cognition, emotion and learning (Dunbar, 2004; Nicholson, 1998; Reber, 1993; Slovic et al., 2004); and (3) dual process theories provide a coherent conceptual framework in which to place a pedagogy based upon managerial cognition (Epstein, 1994; Sloman, 2002; Smith and DeCoster, 1999; Stanovich and West, 2000). By failing to acknowledge these issues management educators run the risk of overlooking some of the most important developments in the current body of scientific knowledge relating to human cognition.

Louis and Sutton (1991) argued that the development of the capability to 'switch cognitive gears' is a highly desirable outcome for management education. The recognition, acknowledgement and accommodation of cognitive style-related differences is but one means of enabling individuals to develop strategies that complement their habitual style, allow them to go beyond their 'set level'

and therefore enable them to change mental gear commensurate with the circumstances they face. One potential outcome of such an endeavor is that, as well as developing as *learned* managers with the necessary depth of functional knowledge, managers may also acquire a self-knowledge and the associated meta-cognitive skills that will enable them to grow holistically throughout their lives as *learning* managers.

## ACKNOWLEDGEMENTS

The author is grateful for the comments of the editors, two anonymous reviewers and, in particular, the detailed and constructive feedback provided by Eva Cools on an earlier draft of this chapter.

## NOTES

1 A number of models of learning style focus upon the learning process itself and, according to Riding and Rayner (1998: 50–1), fall into four main groups: experiential learning-based models; orientation to study-based models; instructional preference; and cognitive skills and learning strategy development. In this chapter I will not be concerned with the former three models, choosing instead to treat strategy as a category in itself and distinct from learning style (which have a learning process orientation, including the experiential model of Kolb) or cognitive (thinking) styles *per se*.

2 A full list of acronyms is to be found at the end of the chapter.

3 Imagery in this context can involve mental representation in any of the sensory modalities but most often refers to visual imagery (Sternberg, 1999: 217).

4 As measured using the *Learning Styles Inventory* (*LSI*) (see Kolb, 1984). All correlations (r) between VI and WA and the four Kolb scales were ≤ ±0.11 and non-significant (Sadler-Smith, 2001).

5 Readers should contact the author for further details of the study.

6 It should be stressed that the experiential/intuitive system does not have a monopoly on holistic, non-analytical thinking; it is entirely feasible to engage in non-linear thinking in ways that are under conscious control (for example, creative and divergent thinking, the deliberate use of imagery, etc.).

## LIST OF ACRONYMS

| | |
|---|---|
| AI | Adaptor Innovator |
| C | Reflective |
| CEST | Cognitive Experiential Self Theory |
| *CSA* | Cognitive Styles Analysis |
| *CSI* | Cognitive Style Index |
| EFT | Embedded Figures Test |
| FD | Field Dependence |
| FDI | Field Dependence Independence |
| FI | Field Independence |
| FII | Faith in Intuition |
| fMRI | functional Magnetic Resonance Imaging |
| *MBTI* | Myers Briggs Type Indicator |
| MSG | Mental Self Government |
| NFC | Need for Cognition |
| *REI* | Rational Experiential Inventory |
| VI | Verbal Imagery |
| VMPC | Ventro Medial Prefrontal Cortex |
| WA | Wholist Analytic |
| X | Reflexive |

## REFERENCES

Allinson, C.W. and Hayes, J. (1996) 'The cognitive style index: A measure of intuition-analysis for organizational research', *Journal of Management Studies*, 33: 119–35.

Allinson, C.W. and Hayes, J. (2000) 'Cross-national differences in cognitive style: Implications for management', *International Journal of Human Resource Management*, 11 (1): 161–70.

Allinson, C.W., Armstrong, S.J. and Hayes, J. (2001) 'The effects of cognitive style on leader-member exchange: A study of manager-subordinate dyads', *Journal of Occupational and Organizational Psychology*, 74: 201–20.

Allinson, C.W., Chell, E. and Hayes, J. (2000) 'Intuition and entrepreneurial performance', *European Journal of Work and Organizational Psychology*, 9 (1): 31–43.

Argyris, C. (1962) *Interpersonal Competence and Organizational Effectiveness*. Homewood, I: Dorsey.

Ashkanasy, N.M. and Dasborough, M.T. (2003) 'Emotional awareness and emotional intelligence in leadership training', *Journal of Education for Business*, September/October: 18–22.

Ashkanasy, N.M. and Daus, S.D. (2002) 'Emotion in the workplace: The new challenge for managers', *Academy of Management Executive*, 16 (1): 76–86.

Backhaus, K. and Liff, J.P. (2007) 'Cognitive style index: Further investigation of the factor structure with an American student sample', *Educational Psychology*, 27 (1): 21–31.

Baddeley, A.D. (1997) *Human Memory: Theory and Practice*. Hove: Psychology Press.

Barnard, C.I. (1938) *The Functions of the Executive*. Cambridge, MA: Harvard University Press.

Bartlett, F.C. (1932) *Remembering: A Study in Experimental and Social Psychology*. Cambridge: Cambridge University Press.

Bechara, A. (2004) 'The role of emotion in decision-making: Evidence from neurological patients with orbito-frontal damage', *Brain and Cognition*, 55: 30–40.

Bechara, A. Tranel D. and Damasio, H. (2000) 'Characterization of the decision-making deficit of patients with ventro-medial prefrontal cortex lesions', *Brain*, 123: 2189–202.

Bloom, B.S. (1956) *Taxonomy of Educational Objectives. Handbook 1: The Cognitive Domain*. New York: Longman.

Boyatzis, R.E., Stubbs, E.C. and Taylor, S.N. (2002) 'Learning cognitive and emotional intelligence competencies through graduate management education', *Academy of Management Learning and Education*, 1 (2): 150–62.

Burke, L. and Miller, M. (1999) 'Making intuitive decisions: Demystifying the process', *Academy of Management Executive*, 13 (4): 91–9.

Cacioppo, J.T. and Petty, R.E. (1982) 'The need for cognition', *Journal of Personality and Social Psychology*, 42: 116–31.

Caldwell, A.B. (2006) 'Maximal measurement or meaningful measurement: The interpretive challenges of the MMPI-2 restructured clinical (RC) scales', *Journal of Personality Assessment*, 87 (2): 193–201.

Coffield, F., Moseley, D., Hall, E. and Ecclestone, K. (2004) *Learning Styles in Post 16 Learning: A Systematic and Critical Review*. London: Learning and Skills Council.

Curry, L. (1983) 'An organization of learning styles theory and constructs', *ERIC Document Retrieval Service*, TM 830 554.

Curry, L. (2000) 'Review of learning style, study approach and instructional preference research in medical education', in R.J. Riding and S.G. Rayner (eds), *International Perspectives on Individual Differences (1): Cognitive Styles*. Stamford, CT: Ablex Publishing.

Damasio, A.R. (1994) *Descartes' Error: Emotion, Reason and the Human Brain*. New York: HarperCollins.

Dane, E. and Pratt, M.G. (2007) 'Exploring intuition and its role in managerial decision making', *Academy of Management Review*, 32 (1): 33–54.

Dunbar, R. (2004) *The Human Story*. London: Faber.

Epstein, S. (1994) 'Integration of the cognitive and the psychodynamic unconscious', *American Psychologist*, 49: 709–24.

Epstein, S. (2004) 'Intuition from the perspective of cognitive-experiential self-theory', *5th Heidelberg Meeting on Judgment and Decision Processes 'Intuition in Judgment and Decision Making'*, University of Heidelberg, February 19–22, 2004.

Epstein, S., Pacini, R., Denes-Raj, V. and Heier, H. (1996) 'Individual differences in intuitive-experiential and analytical-reasoning thinking styles', *Journal of Personality and Social Psychology*, 71: 390–405.

Ericsson, K.A. and Charness, N. (1994) 'Expert performance: Its structure and acquisition', *American Psychologist*, 49: 725–47.

Ericsson, K.A. and Kintsch, W. (1995) 'Long-term working memory', *Psychological Review*, 102: 211–45.

Galton, F. (1883) *Inquiries into Human Faculties and its Development*. London: Macmillan.

Gardner, H. (1983) *Frames of Mind: The Theory of Multiple Intelligences*. New York: Basic Books.

Gardner, W.L. and Martinko, M.J. (1996) 'Using the Myers-Briggs Type Indicator to study managers: A literature review and research agenda', *Journal of Management*, 22: 45–83.

Goldstein, K.M. and Blackman, S. (1978) *Cognitive Style*. New York: Wiley.

Hayes, J. and Allinson, C.W. (1994) 'Cognitive style and its relevance for management practice', *British Journal of Management*, 5: 53–71.

Hayes, J. and Allinson, C.W. (1996) 'The implications of learning styles for training and development: A discussion of the matching hypothesis', *British Journal of Management*, 6: 63–73.

Hayes, J., Allinson, C.W., Hudson, R.S. and Keasey, K. (2003) 'Further reflections on the nature of intuition-analysis and the construct validity of the Cognitive Style Index', *Journal of Occupational and Organizational Psychology*, 76: 269–78.

Hodgkinson, G.P. and Clarke, I. (2007) 'Exploring the cognitive significance of organizational strategizing: A dual-process framework and research agenda', *Human Relations*, 60: 243–55.

Hodgkinson, G.P. and Sparrow, P.R. (2002) *The Competent Organization: A Psychological Analysis of the Strategic Management Process*. Buckingham: Open University Press.

Hodgkinson, G.P., and Sadler-Smith, E. (2003) 'Complex or unitary? A critique and empirical re-assessment of the Allinson-Hayes Cognitive Style Index', *Journal of Occupational and Organizational Psychology*, 76: 243–68.

Hodgkinson, G.P., Langan-Fox, J. and Sadler-Smith, E. (2008) 'Intuition: A fundamental bridging construct in the behavioural sciences', *British Journal of Psychology*, 99: 1–27.

Hodgkinson, G.P., Sadler-Smith, E. and Sinclair, M. (2006) 'More than meets the eye? Intuition and analysis revisited', Paper presented at the *Annual Academy of Management Meeting*, Atlanta, Georgia, August, 2006.

Hogarth, R.M. (2001) *Educating Intuition*. Chicago: The University of Chicago Press.

Honey, P. and Mumford, A. (1986) *The Manual of Learning Styles*. Maidenhead: Peter Honey.

James, W. (1890) *The Principles of Psychology*. London: Macmillan.

Jung-Beeman, M., Bowden, E.M., Haberman, J., Frymiare, J.I., Arambei-Liu, S. and Greenblatt, R. (2004) 'Neural activity when people solve problems with insight', *Public Library of Science (Biology)*, 2 (4): 0500–0510.

Khatri, N. and Ng, H.A. (2000) 'The role of intuition in strategic decision-making', *Human Relations*, 53: 57–86.

Kirton, M.J. (1989) 'A theory of cognitive style', in M. Kirton (ed.), *Adaptors and Innovators: Styles of Creativity and Problem Solving*. London: Routledge. pp. 1–36.

Klein, G. (1998) *Sources of Power*. Cambridge, MA: MIT Press.

Klein, G. (2003) *Intuition at Work*. New York: Doubleday.

Kline, P. (1991) *Intelligence: The Psychometric View*. London: Routledge.

Kolb, D.A. (1984) *Experiential Learning*. Englewood Cliffs, NJ: Prentice-Hall.

Kruglanski, A.W. and Orehek, E. (2007) 'Partitioning the domain of social inference: Dual mode and systems models and their alternatives', *Annual Review of Psychology*, 58: 291–316.

Lieberman, M.D. (2007) 'Social cognitive neuroscience: A review of core processes', *Annual Review of Psychology*, 58: 259–89.

Lieberman, M.D., Jarcho, J.M. and Satpute, A.B. (2004) 'Evidence-based and intuition-based self-knowledge: An fMRI study', *Journal of Personality and Social Psychology*, 87: 421–35.

Louis, M.R. and Sutton, R.I. (1991) 'Switching cognitive gears: From habits of mind to active thinking', *Human Relations*, 44: 55–76.

MacLeod, C.M., Jackson, R.A. and Palmer, J. (1986) 'On the relation between spatial ability and field dependence', *Intelligence*, 10: 141–51.

Massa, L.J. and Mayer, R.E. (2006) 'Testing the ATI hypothesis: Should multimedia instruction accommodate verbalizer-visualizer cognitive style?'

*Learning and Individual Differences*, 16 (4): 321–35.

McKenna, F.P. (1984) 'Measures of field dependence: Cognitive style or cognitive ability?' *Journal of Personality and Social Psychology*, 47: 593–603.

Messick, S. (1984) 'The nature of cognitive styles: Problems and promise in educational practice', *Educational Psychologist*, 19: 59–74.

Mintzberg, H. (1976) 'Planning on the left side, managing on the right', *Harvard Business Review*, July–August: 49–58.

Mintzberg, H. (2004) *Managers not MBAs*. San Francisco: Berrett-Koehler.

Mintzberg, H. and Gosling, J. (2002) 'Educating managers beyond borders', *Academy of Management Learning and Education*, 1: 64–76.

Murphy, H.J., Kelleher, W.E., Doucette, P.A. and Young, J.D. (1998) 'Test-retest reliability and construct validity of the Cognitive Style Index for business undergraduates', *Psychological Reports*, 82: 595–600.

Myers, I.B. (1962) *The Myers-Briggs Type Indicator Manual*. Princeton, NJ.: Educational Testing Service.

Nicholson, N. (1998) 'How hardwired is human behavior?' *Harvard Business Review*, July–August: 135–47.

Nickerson, R., Perkins, D. and Smith, E. (1985) *The Teaching of Thinking*. Hillsdale, NJ: Erlbaum.

Paivio, A. (1969) 'Mental imagery in associative learning and memory', *Psychological Review*, 76: 241–63.

Paivio, A. (1971) *Imagery and Verbal Processes*. New York: Holt, Rinehart & Winston.

Pask, G. and Scott, B.C.E. (1972) 'Learning strategies and individual competence', *International Journal of Man-Machine Studies*, 4: 217–53.

Peterson, E.R., Deary, I.J. and Austin, E.J. (2003) 'The reliability of Riding's Cognitive Style Analysis test', *Personality and Individual Differences*, 34: 881–91.

Rayner, S. and Riding, R.J. (1997) 'Towards a categorization of cognitive styles and learning styles', *Educational Psychology*, 17: 5–28.

Reber, A.S. (1993) *Implicit Learning and Tacit Knowledge: An Essay on the Cognitive Unconscious*. New York: Oxford University Press.

Renzulli, J.S. and Dai, D.Y. (2001) 'Abilities, interests and styles as aptitudes for learning: A person-situation interaction perspective', in R.J. Sternberg and L.F. Zhang (eds), *Perspectives on Thinking, Learning and Cognitive Styles*. Mahwah, NJ: LEA.

Richardson, A. (1977) 'Verbalizer-visualizer: A cognitive style dimension', *Journal of Mental Imagery*, 1: 109–25.

Riding, R.J. (1991) *Cognitive Styles Analysis*. Birmingham: Learning and Training Technology.

Riding, R.J. (1997) 'On the nature of cognitive style', *Educational Psychology*, 17: 29–50.

Riding, R.J. (2001) 'The nature and effects of cognitive style', in R.J. Sternberg and L.F. Zhang, (eds), *Perspectives on Thinking, Learning and Cognitive Styles*. Mahwah, NJ: LEA.

Riding, R.J. (2002) *School Learning and Cognitive Style*. London: David Fulton Publishers.

Riding, R.J. (2003) 'On the assessment of cognitive style: A commentary on Peterson, Deary, and Austin', *Personality and Individual Differences*, 34: 893–7.

Riding, R.J. and Al-Sanabani, S. (1998) 'The effect of cognitive style, age, gender and structure on recall of prose passages', *International Journal of Educational Research*, 29: 173–85.

Riding, R.J. and Cheema, I. (1991) 'Cognitive styles – An overview and integration', *Educational Psychology*, 11: 193–215.

Riding, R.J. and Douglas, G. (1993) 'The effect of cognitive style and mode of presentation on learning performance', *British Journal of Educational Psychology*, 63: 297–307.

Riding, R.J. and Pearson, F. (1994) 'The relationship between cognitive style and intelligence', *Educational Psychology*, 14: 413–25.

Riding, R.J. and Rayner, S.G. (1998) *Cognitive Styles and Learning Strategies*. London: David Fulton.

Riding, R.J. and Sadler-Smith, E. (1992) 'Type of instructional material, cognitive style and learning performance', *Educational Studies*, 18: 323–40.

Riding, R.J. and Sadler-Smith, E. (1997) 'Cognitive style and learning strategies: Some implications for training design', *International Journal of Training and Development*, 1: 199–208.

Riding, R.J. and Watts, M. (1997) 'The effect of cognitive style on the preferred format of instructional material', *Educational Psychology*, 17: 179–83.

Rigney, J.W. (1978) 'Learning strategies: A theoretical perspective', in H.F. O'Neil (ed.), *Learning Strategies*. New York: Academic Press.

Robinson, L.A. (2006) *Trust your Gut: How the Power of Intuition Can Grow your Business*. Chicago: Kaplan Publishing.

Rose, H. and Rose, S. (eds) (2000) *Alas Poor Darwin: Arguments Against Evolutionary Psychology*. London: Jonathan Cape.

Sadler-Smith, E. (1997) 'Learning style: Frameworks and instruments', *Educational Psychology*, 17: 51–64.

Sadler-Smith, E. (2001) 'The relationship between learning style and cognitive style', *Personality and Individual Differences*, 30: 609–16.

Sadler-Smith, E. (2008) *Inside Intuition*. Abingdon: Routledge.

Sadler-Smith, E. and Burke, L.A. (2008) 'Fostering intuition in management education: Activities and resources', *Journal of Management Education* (in press).

Sadler-Smith, E. and Riding, R.J. (1999) 'Cognitive style and instructional preferences', *Instructional Science*, 27: 355–71.

Sadler-Smith, E. (2004) 'Cognitive style and the performance of small and medium sized enterprise', *Organization studies*, 25: 155–82.

Sadler-Smith, E. and Shefy, E. (2004) 'The intuitive executive: Understanding and applying "gut feel" in decision-making', *The Academy of Management Executive*, 18 (4): 76–92.

Sadler-Smith, E. and Shefy, E. (2007) 'Developing intuitive awareness in management education', *Academy of Management Learning and Education*, 6 (2): 1–20.

Sadler-Smith, E. and Sparrow, P.R. (2007) 'Intuition in organizational decision-making', in G.P. Hodgkinson and W.H. Starbuck (2006) (eds), *The Oxford Handbook of Organizational Decision-Making*. Oxford: Oxford University Press. pp. 304–23.

Sadler-Smith, E., Allinson, C.W. and Hayes, J. (2000) 'Cognitive style and learning preferences: Some implications for CPD', *Management Learning*, 31: 239–56.

Sadler-Smith, E, Spicer, D.P. and Tsang, F. (2000) 'The Cognitive Style Index: A replication and extension', *British Journal of Management*, 11: 175–81.

Schön, D.A. (1983) *The Reflective Practitioner: How Professionals Think in Action*. New York: Basic Books.

Scott, S.G. and Bruce, R.A. (1995) 'Decision making style: The development and assessment of a new measure', *Educational and Psychological Measurement*, 55: 818–31.

Senge, P.M. (1990) *The Fifth Discipline: The Art and Practice of the Learning Organization*. London: Century Business.

Shapiro, S. and Spence, M.T. (1997) 'Managerial intuition: A conceptual and operational framework', *Business Horizons*, January–February: 63–8.

Simon, H.A. (1947/1997) *Administrative Behavior*. New York: Macmillan.

Sinclair, M. and Ashkanasy, N.M. (2005) 'Intuition: Myth or a decision-making tool?' *Management Learning*, 36 (3): 353–70.

Sinclair, M., Sadler-Smith, E. and Hodgkinson, G.P. (2007) 'The role of intuition in strategic decision making', in A. Costanzo and R.B. McKay (eds), *The Handbook of Research on Strategy and Foresight*. Cheltenham, UK: Edward Elgar (in press).

Sloman, S.A. (2002) 'Two systems of reasoning', in T. Gilovich, D. Griffin and D. Kahneman (eds), *Heuristics and Biases: The Psychology of Intuitive Judgment*. New York: Cambridge University Press. pp. 379–96.

Slovic, P., Finucane, M.L., Peters, E. and MacGregor, D.G. (2004) 'Risk as analysis and risk as feelings: Some thoughts about affect, reason, risk and rationality', *Risk Analysis*, 24: 311–22.

Smith, E.R. and DeCoster, J. (1999) 'Associative and rule based processing', in S. Chaiken and Y. Trope (eds), *Dual-Process Theories in Social Psychology*. New York: Guilford Press. pp. 323–36.

Smith, S.M. and Woody, P.C. (2000) 'Interactive effect of multimedia instruction and learning styles', *Teaching of Psychology*, 27: 220–23.

Springer, S.P. and Deutsch, G. (1998) *Left Brain, Right Brain: Perspectives from Cognitive Neuroscience*. New York: W.H. Freeman & Co.

Stanovich, K.E. and West, R.F. (2000) 'Individual differences in reasoning: Implications for the rationality debate?' *Behavioral and Brain Sciences*, 23: 645–726.

Sternberg, R.J. (ed.) (1988) *The Nature of Creativity*. Cambridge: Cambridge University Press.

Sternberg, R.J. (1997) *Thinking Styles*. Cambridge: Cambridge University Press.

Sternberg, R.J. (1999) *Cognitive Psychology*. Fort Worth, TX: Harcourt Brace College Publishers.

Sternberg, R.J. and Grigorenko, E.L. (1997) 'Are cognitive styles still in style?' *American Psychologist*, 52: 700–12.

Sternberg, R.J. and Grigorenko, E.L. (2001) 'A capsule history of theory research on styles', in R.J. Sternberg and L.F. Zhang (eds), *Perspectives on Thinking, Learning and Cognitive styles*. Mahwah, NJ: LEA. pp. 1–22.

Sternberg, R.J. and Wagner, R.K. (1991) *Mental Self-Government Thinking Styles Inventory*. Unpublished Manual.

Sternberg, R.J. and Zhang, L. (eds) (2001) *Perspectives on Thinking, Learning and Cognitive Styles*. Mahwah, NJ: LEA.

Taggart, W. and Robey, D. (1981) 'Minds and managers: On the dual nature of human information processing and management', *Academy of Management Review*, 6: 187–95.

Taggart, W. and Valenzi, E. (1990) 'Assessing rational and intuitive styles: A human information processing metaphor', *Journal of Management Studies*, 27: 149–72.

Tennant, M. (1988) *Psychology and Adult Learning*. London: Routledge.

Vance, C.M., Groves, K.S., Paik, Y. and Kindler, H. (2007) 'Understanding and measuring linear-nonlinear thinking style for enhanced management education and professional practice', *Academy of Management Learning and Education*, 6 (2): 167–85.

Witkin, H.A. (1962) *Psychological Differentiation: Studies of Development*. New York: Wiley.

Witkin, H.A., Moore, C.A., Goodenough, D.R. and Cox, P.W. (1977) 'Field dependent and field independent cognitive styles and their educational implications', *Review of Educational Research*, 47: 1–64.

Zhang, L.F. and Sternberg, R.J. (2001) 'Thinking styles across cultures: Their relationship with student learning', in R.J. Sternberg and L.F. Zhang (eds), *Perspectives on Thinking, Learning and Cognitive Styles*. Mahwah, NJ: LEA.

# 17

# Building Learning Teams: The Key to Harnessing the Power of Small Groups in Management Education

Larry Michaelsen, Tim O. Peterson and Michael Sweet

## INTRODUCTION

Post-secondary educators have been using small groups to facilitate learning some time and in a wide variety of ways (e.g. for comparative discussion of different approaches, see Fink 2004; Johnson et al., 2007; Millis and Cottell, 1998). In management education, small groups are most often used to enrich students' understanding of course concepts and in one of two ways. Probably the most common is as a supplement to lecture/discussion or case-based courses and involves assigning a group project and/or presentation (with much or all of the work to be done outside of the class). The other is using the experiential group activities (typically during class time) to provide illustrations of and as a basis for discussing applications

of course concepts. Team-Based Learning (TBL), by contrast, represents both a more intensive and a more extensive strategy for using small groups for three reasons. First, group work is central to both exposing students to and enhancing their ability to apply the course content. Second, the vast majority of the group work takes place during class time. Third, management courses taught with TBL typically involve both multiple group assignments and a variety of in-class experiential activities. In some ways TBL is similar to Problem-Based Learning (PBL). One of the significant differences is that where TBL begins with the content and then moves to the problem, PBL begins with the problem and then moves to the content (Peterson, 2004). However, both approaches focus on students being able to apply knowledge to solve problems: something organizations lament that new organizational members lack (Holt and Willard-Holt, 2000.) This chapter begins with a very brief overview of TBL, in order to ground the reader in the basics so they can most benefit from the detailed discussions that follow. We next discuss the four defining principles of TBL as an instructional strategy, and then walk the reader through the practical steps required to implement TBL. Finally, we review some of the benefits that students, administrators and faculty can expect from a successful implementation of TBL.

## A BROAD OVERVIEW OF TBL

The primary learning objective in TBL is to go beyond simply 'covering' content and focus on ensuring that students have the opportunity to *practice using course concepts to solve problems*. As any experienced manager will tell you – a theoretical understanding of the forces at play in a situation is a very different kind of knowledge than being able to actually put that understanding to use and make a good decision in the midst of the situation. The education literature refers to this distinction as the difference between conceptual and pro-cedural knowledge (e.g., Krathwohl, 2002) and the goal of TBL is to provide students with both kinds of knowledge. Therefore, although some time in the TBL classroom is spent on ensuring that students master the course content, the vast majority of class time is used for team assignments that focus on using course content to solve the kinds of problems that students are likely to face as they take on management roles in the workplace. Figure 17.1 outlines generally how time in one unit of a TBL course is organized.

In a TBL course, students are strategically organized into permanent groups (for the entire term) and the course content is organized into 5–7 major units (typically 5–7). Before *any* in-class content work, students must read assigned materials because each unit begins with the Readiness Assurance Process (RAP). The RAP consists of a short

test (over the key ideas from the readings) which students first complete as individuals, then they take the exact same test again as a team, coming to consensus on team answers. Students receive immediate feedback on the team test and they then have the opportunity write evidence-based appeals if they feel they can make valid arguments for their answer to questions which they got wrong. The final step in the RAP is a 'lecture' (usually very short and always very specific) through which the instructor clarifies any misperceptions of the material which may still remain as indicated by team test performance and the appeals. The rest of the learning unit is spent with students putting course content to use.

Readers familiar with post-secondary small group learning will see similarities between TBL and other small group instructional practices, especially problem-based learning (PBL). The two instructional strategies have a similar goal: students in both PBL and TBL classrooms learn to use course material to make context-driven decisions. In practice, however, the approaches differ in two impor-tant ways. First, the two formats sequence their instructional activities in reverse. While PBL immerses students in problems through which they must work together in order to identify and then discuss relevant course concepts, TBL requires students to first review, discuss and clarify course concepts, and only then become immersed in difficult problems through which they must work together. Importantly, it is the process by which students perform the work preceding their immersion in a problem – the RAP – that sets TBL apart from any other instructional practice. The second, and more practice-based difference between the PBL and TBL is that PBL tends to require a smaller teacher–student ratio to ensure that the discussion in student groups follows a productive track, is scalable to classes of several hundred students (Fink, 2004).

In addition to the authors who in combi-nation have had over 2,000 teams in our own classes, teachers in a wide variety of situations are finding that a well-crafted implementation of four defining principles of TBL can bring

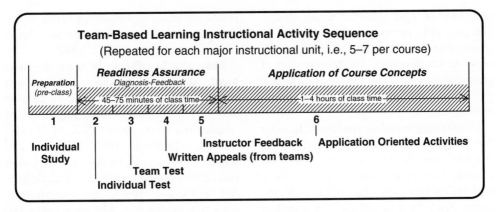

**Figure 17.1**

about student engagement and performance they had so far been unable to achieve using other instructional strategies. These include well over 100 disciplines (e.g., Aarestad and Moewes, 2004; McInerney, 2003; Meeuwsen, 2002; Michaelsen et al., 2007; Trytten, 1999; Weeks, 2003), in classes of up to 400 students, in a diverse array of cultural settings (e.g., Cragin, 2004; Popovsky, 2004) and even in classes composed of students whose physical handicaps require them to converse using the American Sign Language (Nakaji, 2004). Understanding these four principles is essential to a successful implementation of TBL, so a discussion of these principles follows next.

## THE FOUR DEFINING PRINCIPLES OF TEAM-BASED LEARNING

Shifting from simply familiarizing students with course concepts to requiring that students actually use those concepts to solve problems is no small task. Making this shift requires changes in the roles of both instructors and students. The instructor's primary role shifts from dispensing information to designing and managing the overall instructional process, and the students' role shifts from being passive recipients of information to one of accepting responsibility for the initial exposure to the course content so that they will be prepared for the in-class

team work. Changes of this magnitude do not happen automatically and, based on past experience, may even seem to be dreams rather than achievable realities. There are, however, surprisingly reliable outcomes when the four defining principles of TBL are successfully implemented. These defining principles are:

- **Groups** – groups must be properly formed *and* managed.
- **Accountability** – students must be accountable for the quality of their individual *and* group work.
- **Feedback** – students must receive frequent *and* timely feedback.
- **Assignment Design** – group assignments must promote both learning *and* team development.

When these four principles are implemented in a course, the stage is set for student groups to evolve into cohesive learning teams. This section briefly explores each of these principles.

## DEFINING CHARACTERISTIC 1 – GROUPS MUST BE PROPERLY FORMED *AND* MANAGED

Forming effective groups requires that the instructor oversee the formation of the groups so that he or she can manage three important variables. One is ensuring that the groups have adequate resources to draw from in completing their assignments and approximately the same level of those resources across groups. The second is preventing the formation of groups whose membership characteristics are likely to interfere with the development of group cohesiveness. The third is ensuring that groups have the opportunity to *develop* into learning teams.

**Distributing member resources**. In order for groups to function as effectively as possible, they should also be as diverse as possible. Each group should contain a mix of student characteristics which might make the course easier or more difficult for a student to do well in the course (e.g. previous course work and/or course-related practical experience) as well as demographic characteristics like gender, ethnicity, and so on. The goal here is to equip groups to succeed, as well as populate them with members who will bring different perspectives to the task. Findings in both group dynamics research (e.g., Brobeck et al., 2002) and educational research (e.g., Chan et al., 1997) illuminate the positive impact of diverse input in problem-solving *discussions* on both learning and performance. When group members bring many different perspectives to a task, their process of collaborative knowledge-building in pursuit of consensus is powerful to watch. In addition, although member diversity initially inhibits both group processes and performance, it is likely to become asset when members have worked together over time and under conditions that promote group cohesiveness (Watson et al., 1993).

**Minimizing barriers to group cohesiveness – avoiding coalitions**. Coalitions within a group are likely to threaten its overall development. In newly-formed groups, either a previously established relationship between a subset of members in the group (e.g. boyfriend/girlfriend, fraternity brothers, etc.) or the potential for a cohesive subgroup based on background factors such as nationality, culture or native language can form a 'voting block' within the group and burden it with insider/outsider tension which plagues the group all term. Because it is human nature to seek out similar others, allowing students free reign in forming their own groups practically ensures the existence of potentially disruptive subgroups (Fiechtner and Davis, 1985; Michaelsen and Black, 1994).

**Time – a key factor in team development**. Any group dynamics textbook will tell you that groups need time to develop into high-performing teams, regardless of whether you favor sequential/life-cycle models (e.g., Tuckman, 1965; Tuckman and Jensen, 1977), cyclic models (e.g., Worchel et al., 1994), equilibrium models (e.g., Gersick and Hackman, 1990), or adaptive/non-sequential models (e.g., McGrath, 1991). For this reason, students should stay in the same group for the entire course. Although even a single well-designed group assignment usually produces a variety of positive outcomes, only when students work together over time can their groups become cohesive enough to evolve into self-managed and truly effective learning teams.

## DEFINING CHARACTERISTIC 2 – STUDENTS MUST BE ACCOUNTABLE FOR THE QUALITY OF THEIR INDIVIDUAL *AND* GROUP WORK

In lecture classes, there is no real need for students to be accountable to anyone other than the instructor. By contrast, TBL students are accountable to both the instructor and their teammates for the quality and quantity of their individual work. Further, teams are also accountable for the quality and quantity of their work as a unit. (For a review of the effects of accountability on an array of social judgments and choices, see Lerner and Tetlock, 1999).

**Accountability for individual pre-class preparation**. Lack of preparation places clear limits on both individual learning and team development. If several members of a team come unprepared to contribute to a complex group task, then the team as a whole is far less likely to succeed at that task, cheating its members of the learning the task was designed to stimulate. *No amount of discussion can overcome absolute ignorance.*

Furthermore, lack of preparation also hinders the cohesiveness development because those who do make the effort to be prepared will resent having to 'carry' their peers. As a result, the effective use of learning groups clearly requires individual students be made accountable for class preparation.

**Accountability for contributing to their team**. The next step is ensuring that members contribute time and effort to group work. In order to accurately assess members' contributions to the success of their teams, it is imperative that instructors involve the students themselves in a peer assessment process. That is, members should be given the opportunity to evaluate one another's contributions to the activities of the team. Contributions to the team include activities such as: individual preparation for team work, reliable class attendance, attendance at team meetings that may have occurred outside of class, positive contributions to team discussions, valuing and encouraging input from fellow team members, and so on. Peer assessment is essential because team members are typically the only ones who have enough information to evaluate accurately one another's contributions.

**Accountability for high quality team performance**. The third significant factor in ensuring accountability is developing an effective means to assess team performance. There are two keys to effectively assessing teams. One is using assignments that require teams to create a 'product' that can be readily compared across teams and with 'expert' opinions, and the other is using procedures to ensure that such comparisons occur frequently and in a timely manner. We provide practical suggestions for how to achieve both of these outcomes below.

## DEFINING CHARACTERISTIC 3 – STUDENTS MUST RECEIVE FREQUENT *AND* IMMEDIATE FEEDBACK

Immediate feedback is the primary instructional lever in TBL for two very different reasons. First, feedback is *essential* to content learning and retention – a notion that not only makes intuitive sense but is also well documented in educational research literature (e.g., Bruning et al., 1994; Kulik and Kulik, 1998; Hattie and Timperlie, 2007). Second, immediate feedback has tremendous impact on group development (for a review, see Birmingham and McCord, 2004).

## DEFINING CHARACTERISTIC 4 – TEAM ASSIGNMENTS MUST PROMOTE BOTH LEARNING *AND* TEAM DEVELOPMENT

The most fundamental aspect of designing team assignments that promote both learning and team development is ensuring that they truly require group interaction. In most cases, team assignments will generate a high level of interaction if they: 1 Require teams to use course concepts to *make decisions* that involve a complex set of issues and, 2 Enable teams to *report their decisions* in a simple form. When assignments emphasize making decisions, most students chose to complete the task by engaging each other in a give-and-take content-related discussion. By contrast, assignments that involve producing complex output such as a lengthy document often limit both learning and team development because of the typically impact intra-team discussions in two different ways. First, discussions are likely to be much shorter because students are likely to feel an urgency to get going on the 'real' work – creating the product that is to be graded. Second, instead of focusing on content-related issues, they are likely to center on how to divide up the work. Thus, complex products outputs such as a lengthy document seldom contribute to team development because they are likely to have been created by individual members working alone on their part of the overall project.

**Conclusion – Part I**. By adhering to the four defining principles of TBL – careful design of one's groups, accountability, feedback, and assignments – teachers create a context that promotes the quantity and quality of interaction required to transform groups into highly effective learning teams. Appropriately forming the teams puts them on equal footing and greatly reduces the possibility of mistrust from pre-existing relationships between a subset of team members. Holding students accountable for preparation and attendance motivates team members to behave in pro-social ways that build cohesiveness and foster trust. Using RAPs and other assignments to provide ongoing and timely feedback on both individual and team performance enables teams to develop confidence in their ability to capture the intellectual resources of all their members. Assignments that promote both learning and team development motivate members to challenge each others' ideas for the good of the team. Also, over time students' confidence in their teams grows to the point that they are willing and able to tackle difficult assignments with little or no external help.

### Implementing Team-Based Learning

Effectively using TBL typically requires redesigning a course from beginning to end, and the redesign process should begin well before the start of the school term. The redesign process involves making decisions about and/or designing activities at four different points in time. These are: (1) Before class begins; (2) The first day of class; (3) Each major unit of instruction; and (4) Near the end of the course. In this section, we discuss the practical steps a TBL instructor takes at each of these points in time, but for a treatment that is even more detailed and practical, the interested reader is directed to Michaelsen et al. (2002, 2004).

### Before class begins

Traditionally management education, particularly in undergraduate programs, has tended to separate knowledge acquisition from knowledge application both between and within courses. In the early phases of most programs,

for example, students take a series of lecture-based foundational courses in which they are expected to absorb a great deal of knowledge that the will then later (sometimes much later) be asked to put to use. In fact, even within higher-level courses, students often spend much of the term absorbing knowledge that they don't put to use until a final project that is due just prior to final exams.

TBL, however, uses a fundamentally different knowledge-acquisition/knowledge-application model. With TBL, students repeat the knowledge-acquisition/knowledge-application cycle several times *within each individual course*. With TBL, students individually study the course content, discuss it with their peers and the instructor (see the Readiness Assurance Process below) and immediately apply it in solving problems much like those they will face in professional practice. Thus, students in TBL courses develop a much better sense of the relevance of the material because they seldom have to make unreasonably large inferences about when and how the content might become useful in 'the real world.' Rather than being filled with libraries of 'inert knowledge' (Whitehead, 1929) from which they then later must extract needed information with great effort, students walk away from TBL courses having already begun the practical, problem-solving process of learning to use their knowledge in context.

This benefit, however, does not occur by accident. Designing a successful TBL course involves making decisions related to first identifying and clustering instructional objectives, and then designing a grading system around those objectives.

**Identifying instructional objectives: The process of 'backward design.'** Designing a TBL course requires instructors to 'think backward.' What do we mean by 'think backward?' In most forms of higher education, teachers design their courses by asking themselves what they feel students need to *know*, then telling the students that information, and finally testing the students on how well they absorbed what they were told. In contrast, TBL courses are planned around what you want students to be able to *do* when they have finished your course, and only then what they need to know in order to do that. Wiggins and McTighe (1998) coined the term 'backward design' to describe this method of course design, and it is the method which enables the instructor to build a course which provides students with both declarative and procedural knowledge (in other words, conceptual knowledge *and* the ability to use that knowledge in decision making). This is a useful distinction, but for those of us who have taught with conceptual familiarization as our goal, it can be surprisingly difficult to identify what exactly you want your students to be able to *do* upon completion of a given course. However, the following question is a good place to start.

*What are the students who really 'get it' doing which shows you they get it?* Imagine you are working shoulder-to-shoulder with a former student who is now a junior colleague. In a wonderful moment you see them do something that makes you think 'Hey! They *really* got from my class what I *wanted* them to get – *there's the evidence right there!*' When designing a course 'backward,' the question you ask yourself is: *What, specifically, is that evidence?* What could a former-student be doing in a moment like that to make it obvious they really internalized what you were trying to teach them and are putting it to use in the world?

For every course there are several answers to this question and these different answers will correspond to the 'macro' units of the re-designed version of the course. A given real-world moment will likely demand knowledge from one part of a course but not another, so for any given course, you should brainstorm about a half-dozen of these proud moments in which a former student is making it obvious that they really learned what you wanted them to learn. For now, don't think about the classroom; just imagine they are doing something in a real organizational context. Also, don't be afraid to get too detailed as you visualize these moments – in fact come up with as many details as you can about *how* this former student is doing what they

are doing, what *decisions* they are making, in what *sequence*, under what *conditions*, and so on.

These detailed scenarios become useful in three ways. First, the actions taking place in the scenarios will help you organize your course into units. Second, the scenarios will enable you to use your class time to build students' applied knowledge instead of inert knowledge. Third, the details of the scenario will help you design the criteria for the assessments upon which you can base your students' grades.

Once you have brainstormed your 'Aha! They get it!' scenarios and the details that accompany them, now let's step into the classroom. Those half-dozen or so scenarios are what you want your students to be able to *do* when they are done with your class. These are your instructional objectives and they often involve making decisions that are based on insightful applications of the concepts from your course. Now you are ready to ask three more questions:

1  **What will students need to *know* in order to be able to *do* those things?** Answers to this question will guide your selection of a text book, the contents of your course-packet, experiential exercises, and are likely to prompt you to provide supplementary materials of your own creation or simply reading guides to help students focus on what you consider most important in the readings or lab findings. In addition, it will be key in developing questions for the Readiness Assurance Process.

2  **While solving problems, what knowledge will students need to make decisions?** Answers to this question will help you import the use of course knowledge from your brainstormed 'real world' scenarios into the classroom. You may not be able to bring the actual organizational settings in which your scenarios occurred into the classroom (although computer simulations, video – including full-length feature films, and especially requiring students to learn business by *doing* business (see Miller, 1991 and Michaelsen and McCord, 2006) are coming much closer to approaching 'real'), but you can provide enough relevant information about those settings to design activities which require your students to face the same kinds of problems and make

the same kinds of decisions they will make in the clinical and laboratory settings.

3 **What *criteria* separate a well-made decision from a poorly-made decision using this knowledge?** Answers to this question will help you begin building the measures you will use to determine how well the students have learned the material *and* how well they can put it to use under specific conditions.

In summary, TBL leverages the power of action-based instructional objectives to not only expose students to course content, but also give them practice using it. When determining an instructional objective, it is crucial to know how you are going to assess the extent to which students have mastered that objective. Some teachers feel that designing assessments first removes something from the value of instruction – that it simply becomes 'teaching to the test.' Our view is that yes, you absolutely *should* teach to the test, as long as the test represents (as closely as possible) the real use to which students will ultimately apply the course material: what they are going to *do with* it, not just what they should *know about* it.

**Designing a grading system**. The other step in re-designing the course is to ensure that the grading system is designed to reward the right things. An effective grading system for TBL must: (1) provide incentives for individual contributions and effective work by the teams, as well as (2) address the equity concerns that naturally arise when group work is part of an individual's grade. The primary concern here is typically borne from past group work situations in which students were saddled with 'free riding' team members and have resented it ever since. Students worry that they will be forced to choose between getting a low grade or carrying their less able or less motivated peers. Instructors worry that they will have to choose between grading rigorously and grading fairly.

Fortunately, many of the above concerns are alleviated by a grading system in which a significant proportion of the grade is based on: (1) Individual performance, (2) Team performance, and (3) Each member's contributions

to the success of their teams. As long as that standard is met, the primary remaining concern is that the relative weight of the factors is acceptable to both the instructor and the students. (Assigning relative weight is addressed in the next section.)

## The first hours of class: getting started on the right foot

Activities that occur during the first few hours of class are critical to the success of TBL. During that time, the teacher must see that four objectives are accomplished. The first objective is ensuring that students understand *why* you (the instructor) have decided to use TBL and what that means about the way the class will be conducted. The second objective is to actually form the groups. The third and fourth objectives include alleviating students' concerns about the grading system and setting up mechanisms to encourage the development of positive group norms.

**Introducing students to TBL**. Because the roles of both the instructor and the students are so fundamentally different from traditional instructional practice, it is absolutely critical that students understand both the rationale for using TBL and what that means about the way the class will be conducted. Educating the students about TBL requires (at a minimum) providing students with an overview of the basic features of TBL, how TBL affects the role of the instructor and their role as students and why they are likely to benefit from their experience in the course. This information should be printed in the course syllabus, presented orally by the instructor and *demonstrated* by one or more activities.

In order to foster students' understanding of TBL, we typically use two activities. The first involves explaining the basic features of TBL using overhead transparencies (or a PowerPoint presentation) including a discussion of the way in which learning objectives for this course will be accomplished through the use of TBL, as compared to a course that is taught with a more traditional approach. The second activity which, with class periods of less than an hour, might occur on day 2, involves using part of the first class as a demonstration of a Readiness Assessment Test (see below) using either the course syllabus or a short reading on TBL and/or about some potentially useful ideas such as what helps and hinders team development or strategies for giving helpful feedback (see Michaelsen and Schultheiss, 1988) as the 'content' material to be covered.

**Forming the groups**. As discussed above, when forming groups, one must consider the course-relevant characteristics of the students and the potential for the emergence of sub-groups. As a result, the starting point in the group formation process is to gather information about specific student characteristics that will make it easier or more difficult for a student to succeed in *this* class. For a particular course, characteristics that could make it easier for a student to succeed might include such things as previous relevant course work or practical experience, access to perspectives from other cultures, etc. Most commonly, student characteristics making it more difficult for them to succeed are the absence of those that would make it easier, but might include such things as a lack of language fluency.

We recommend actually forming the groups in class in the presence of the students as a means of avoiding student concerns about ulterior motives the instructor may have had in forming groups. We begin the group formation process by simply asking questions about the factors that are important to group success. For a class in organizational behavior, typical questions could include, 'How many years have you worked as a manager?' 'What is your major?' 'How many of you attended high school outside of the United States?', etc. Students respond to each of the questions either orally or with a show of hands. Then, we create a 'stratified' sampling frame by having students possessing a series of specific assets to form a single line around the perimeter of the classroom with the rarest and/or most important category at the front of the line. After students are lined up, we have them count-off down the line by the total number of groups (5–7 members) in the class. All 'ones' become Group 1,

all 'twos' become Group 2, etc. Following this procedure rapidly creates heterogeneous (and approximately equivalent-ability) teams. (For a graphic depiction of this process, see Sweet, 2007, and for a more detailed explanation and video demonstration see www.teambasedlearning.org.)

**Alleviating student concerns about grades**. The next step in getting started on the 'right foot' with TBL is to address student concerns about the grading system. Fortunately, student anxiety based on previous experience with divided-up group assignments largely evaporates as students come to understand two of the essential features of TBL. One is that two elements of the grading system create a high level of individual accountability for pre-class preparation, class attendance and devoting time and energy to group assignments – counting individual scores on the Readiness Assurance Tests and basing part of the grade on a peer evaluation. The other reassuring feature is that team assignments will be done *in class* and will be based on thinking, discussing, and deciding, so it is highly unlikely that one or two less-motivated teammates members can put the group at risk.

Many choose to alleviate student concerns about grades by directly involving students in 'customizing' the grading system to *this* class. Students become involved by participating in an exercise called 'Setting Grade Weights' (Michaelsen et al., 1981 – see Appendix B of Michaelsen et al., 2002, 2004). Within limits set by the instructor, representatives of the newly-formed teams negotiate with one another to reach consensus (i.e., all of the representatives must agree) on a mutually acceptable set of weights for each of the grade components: individual performance, team performance, and members' contributions to the success of their teams. After an agreement has been reached regarding the grade weight for each component, the standard applies for all groups for the remainder of the course.

**Ensuring content coverage: The Readiness Assurance Process**. As described in the introduction of this chapter, each unit of a TBL

**Table 17.1    Readiness Assurance Process**

1  **Assigned Readings**. In most instances, students are initially exposed to concepts through assigned readings.
2  **Individual Test**. Additional exposure during the individual test helps reinforce students' memory of what they learned during their individual study (for a discussion of the positive effects of testing on retention see Nungester and Duchastel, 1982).
3  **Team Test**. During team tests students orally elaborate the reasons for their individual answer choices. As a result, they are exposed to peer input that aids in strengthening and/or modifying their schemata related to the key course concepts. In addition, they gain from acting in a teaching role (for a discussion of the cognitive benefits of teaching see Bargh and Schul, 1980; Slavin and Karweit, 1981).
4  **Appeals**. During this step, teams are given the opportunity to restore credit on both the team and individual tests (for the members of their team). As a result, they are highly motivated to engage in a focused re-study of troublesome concepts from the readings.
5  **Oral Instructor Feedback**. Steps 1–4 enable the instructor to learn of any specific misunderstandings in relation to the key concepts covered in the test. In step 5, he or she provides corrective feedback and instruction aimed at resolving any misunderstandings that remain after the students have done the focused review in preparing their appeals.

course begins with a Readiness Assurance Process (RAP), occurring at least 5–7 times per term. The RAP provides the foundation for individual and team accountability and has five major components: 1 Assigned readings; 2 Individual tests; 3 Group tests; 4 An appeals process; and 5 Instructor feedback (Table 17.1). In a very complex and ambiguous problem based class such as Managing and Leading during Crisis, one of the authors has used RAPs to ensure the students have a good grasp of the team development process, so the focus could remain on the problem of solving potential organizational crises. Though we described this process briefly above, the following paragraphs provide a more detailed treatment of each of these components.

*Assigned readings*. Prior to the beginning of each major instructional unit, students are given reading and other assignments that should contain information on the concepts and ideas that must be understood to be able to solve the problem you identified for this unit in the backward design activity (see above). Students are to complete the assignments and come to the next class period prepared to take a test on the assigned materials.

*Individual test*. The first in-class activity in each instructional unit is an individual Readiness Assurance Test (iRAT) over the material contained in the pre-class assignments. The iRATs typically consist of multiple-choice questions that, in combination, enable the

instructor to assess whether or not students have a sound understanding of the *key* concepts from the readings. As a result, the iRAT questions should focus on foundational concepts (and avoid picky details), but be difficult enough to create discussion within the teams.

*Team test*. When students have finished the iRAT, they turn in their answers (which we recommend scoring during the team test) and immediately proceed to the third phase of the Readiness Assurance Process, the gRAT. During the third phase, students re-take the *same test*, but this time the teams must reach agreement on the answers to each test question and immediately check the correctness of their decision using an IF-AT® self-scoring answer sheet (see Figure 17.2) that provides real-time feedback on each team decision. With the IF-AT® answer sheets, students scratch off the covering of one of four (or five) boxes in search of a mark indicating they have found the correct answer. If they find the mark on the first try, they receive full credit. If not, they continue scratching until they do find the mark, but their score is reduced with each unsuccessful scratch. This allows teams to receive partial credit for proximate knowledge.

The IF-AT® answer sheets are an effective way to provide timely feedback on the **team** RATs (not the iRATs – otherwise, members would know the answers before the team test and discussion would be pointless).

**Essential Principles for Designing and
Implementing Effective Group Assignments**

$$\boxed{\text{Individual Work}} \times \boxed{\text{Small Group Discussion}} \times \boxed{\text{Total Class Discussion}} = \text{Impact on Learning}$$

**To obtain the maximum impact on learning, assignments at each stage should be characterized by "3 S's":**

- **Same problem** – Individuals/groups should work on the same problem, case, or question.
- **Specific choice** – Individuals/groups should be required to use course concepts to make a specific choice.
- **Simultaneously report** – If possible, individuals/groups should report their choices simultaneously.

**Figure 17.2**

Further, using the IF-AT® answer sheets makes it possible to provide real-time content feedback to multiple (in fact many) without requiring them to maintain the same work pace.

Getting real-time feedback from the IF-AT® provides two key benefits to the teams.

- Real-time feedback enables members to correct their misconceptions of the subject matter. Finding a star immediately confirms the validity of their choice, but finding a blank box lets them know they have more work to do.
- Real-time feedback promotes both the ability and the motivation for teams, with no input from the instructor, to learn how to work together effectively. In fact, those who have used the IF-ATs for their tRATs have learned that doing so virtually eliminates any possibility that one or two members might dominate team discussions. 'Pushy' members are only one scratch away from embarrassing themselves and quiet members are one scratch away from being validated as a valuable source of information and two scratches away from being told that they need to speak up.

The impact of the IF-AT® on team development is immediate, powerful, and extremely positive. In our judgment, using the IF-ATs with the gRATs is the single most effective tool one can use to promote both concept understanding and cohesiveness in learning teams and anyone who doesn't use them will

miss a sure-fire way to increase their ability to successfully implement TBL.

*Appeals.* At this point in the Readiness Assurance Process, students proceed to the fourth phase. This phase gives students the opportunity to refer to their assigned reading material and appeal any questions that were missed on the group test. That is, students are allowed to do a focused re-study of the assigned readings (this phase is 'open-book') to 'challenge' the teacher about their responses on specific items on the group test or about confusion created by either the quality of the questions or inadequacies of the pre-class readings. Discussion among group members is usually very animated while the students work together to 'build a case' to support their appeals. The students must produce compelling evidence to convince the teacher to award credit for the answers they missed on the group test. Teachers listening to students argue the fine details of course material while writing team appeals report being convinced their students learn more from appealing answers they got wrong than from confirming the answers they got right. As an integral part of the Readiness Assurance Process, this appeals exercise provides yet another review of the readings.

*Instructor Feedback.* The fifth and final part of the Readiness Assurance Process involves oral feedback from the instructor. This feedback comes immediately *after* the appeals process and allows the instructor to clear up any confusion students may have about any of the concepts presented in the readings. As a result, input from the instructor is typically limited to a brief, focused review of only the most challenging aspects of the pre-class reading assignment.

*The Readiness Assurance Process in Summary.* The Readiness Assurance Process allows instructors to minimize class time often used to cover material that students can learn on their own. Time is saved because the instructor's input occurs *after* students have: 1 Individually studied the material; 2 Taken an individual test focused on key concepts from the reading assignment; 3 Re-taken the same test as a member of a learning team; and 4 Completed a focused re-study of the most difficult concepts. A cursory review of team-test results illuminates for instructors which concepts need additional attention so that he or she can correct students' misunderstandings. In contrast to the concerns many instructors express about 'losing time to group work' and not being able to cover as much content, many teachers report being able to cover *more* with the Readiness Assurance Process than they can through lectures (e.g. Knight, 2004). Leveraging the motivational power and instructional efficiency of the Readiness Assurance Process leaves the class a great deal of class time to develop students' higher level learning skills as they tackle multiple and challenging application-oriented assignments.

Beyond its instructional power, the Readiness Assurance Process is the backbone of TBL because of its effect on team development. The Readiness Assurance Process is the single most powerful team development tool we have ever seen because it *promotes team development* in four specific areas. First, starting early in the course (usually the first few class hours) the students are exposed to immediate and unambiguous feedback on both individual and team performance. As a result, each member is explicitly accountable for his or her pre-class preparation. Second, because team members work face-to-face, the impact of the interaction is immediate and personal. Third, students have a strong

vested interest in the outcome of the group and are motivated to engage in a high level of interaction. Finally, cohesiveness even continues to build during the final stage of the process, that is, when the instructor is presenting information. This is because, unlike lectures, the content of the instructor's comments is determined by students' choices/actions during the Readiness Tests. Thus, the instructor's comments provide either positive reinforcement (thus, they celebrate together) or corrective instruction (thus, particularly in the presence of other groups, is an external threat).

Even though the impact of the Readiness Assurance Process on student learning is limited primarily to ensuring that they have a solid exposure to the content, it also increases students' ability to solve difficult problems for two reasons. First, by encouraging pre-class preparation and a lively discussion, the RAP builds the intellectual competence of team members. Second, because they have immediate performance feedback, the experience of working together during gRAT and in preparing appeals enhances their ability and willingness to provide high quality content feedback to one another. As a result, the Readiness Assurance Process provides a practical way of ensuring that, even in large classes, students are exposed to a high volume of immediate feedback that, in some ways, can actually be better than having a one-on-one relationship between student and instructor.

**Promoting higher-level learning: Group Application Assignments**. The final stage in the TBL instructional activity sequence for each unit of instruction is using one or more assignments that provide students with the opportunity to deepen their understanding by having groups use the concepts to solve some sort of a problem. These application assignments must both foster accountability and foster give-and-take discussion first within and then between groups, and designing these assignments is probably the most challenging aspect of implementing TBL.

We have identified four practical assignment characteristics – fondly referred to as

**Four Keys for Creating and Managing
Group Assignments**

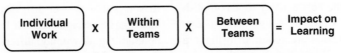

To obtain the maximum impact on learning, assignments
at each stage should be characterized by "4's":

○ **Significant Problem.** Individuals/groups should work on a
  problem that is significant to students.

○ **Same Problem.** Individuals/groups should work on the same
  problem, case or question.

○ **Specific Choice.** Individuals/groups should be required to use
  course concepts to make a specific choice.

○ **Simultaneous Report.** Whenever possible individuals and groups
  should report their choices simultaneously.

**Figure 17.3**

the '4 S's' – that, in combination, constitute guidelines for creating and implementing effective group assignments. These are: 1 Assignments should always be designed around a problem that is *significant to students*; 2 All of the students in the class should be working on the *same* problem; 3 Students should be required to make a *specific* choice; and 4 Groups should *simultaneously* report their choices (Figure 17.3). Further, these procedures apply to all three stages in which students interface with course concepts – individual work prior to group discussions, discussions within groups, and whole-class discussion between groups. The '4 S's' are explained in the following paragraphs.

*Key #1 – Significant [to students] problem.* Effective assignments must capture students' interest. Unless assignments are built around what students see as an interesting and/or relevant problem, most students will view what they are being asked to do as 'busy work' and will put forth the minimum effort required to get a satisfactory grade. Fortunately, unlike many disciplines in which one of the greatest challenges is convincing students that the subject is of value (e.g. history, literature, etc.), by placing the problems in a context that students have encountered and/or believe they will encounter in the future, management instructors can

create assignments that students will see as significant.

*Key #2 – Same problem.* One of the essential characteristics of an effective group assignment is the necessity for discussion both *within* and *between* groups. It is through such discussions that students receive immediate feedback regarding the quality of their own thinking both as individuals and teams.

In order to facilitate such an exchange, groups must have a common frame of reference. That commonality is derived from working on the same problem, that is, the same assignment/learning activity. Unless everyone is working on the same problem there is no basis for comparison, first between group members, and then between groups. Further, having everyone work on the same problem is necessary for students to be able to give and receive peer feedback on their own thinking and their performance as a learning team.

*Key #3 – Specific choice.* As previously discussed, cognitive research shows that learning is greatly enhanced when students are required to engage in higher-level thinking (e.g., Mayer, 2002; Pintrich, 2002; Scandura, 1983). In order to challenge students to process information at higher levels of cognitive complexity, we must provide them with assignments that create those challenges. We must, as the saying goes, 'lead them into situations which they can only escape by thinking.'

In general, the best activity to accomplish this goal is to word the assignment in such a way that students are required to make a specific choice. While the terminology may sound vague, we find it useful to think of the situation faced by a jury as a metaphor for a good group assignment. Juries are presented with a 'problem' of having to sort through a complex set of issues and evidence and come up with a verdict – guilty or not guilty. Similarly, effective assignments in management courses might require students to make specific decisions such as, 'Which power base (French and Raven, 1959) did X use to influence Y to ____?' (in an organizational behavior course), 'Which PERT chart link offers the greatest potential for accelerating the completion date for [a specific project]? (for a course in Operations and/or Project Management), etc. (For a much more thorough discussion of 'make-a-specific-choice' assignments and a rationale as to why they work so well in promoting both student learning and team development, see Chapter 3 of Michaelsen et al., 2002, 2004, Michaelsen and Sweet, 2007).

*Key #4 – Simultaneous reports.* Once groups have made their choices, they can share the result of their thinking with the rest of the class in one of two ways: sequentially or simultaneously. One significant disadvantage of sequential reporting is that the initial response often has a powerful impact on the subsequent discussion because later-reporting teams change their answer in response to what seems to be an emerging majority view – even if that majority is wrong.

This phenomenon, which we call 'answer drift,' (Sweet, Michaelsen and Wright, in press) limits both learning and team development for a variety of reasons. One is that it is most likely to occur when the problems being discussed have the greatest potential for producing a meaningful discussion. That is because the more difficult and/or ambiguous the problem, the greater the likelihood that: 1 The initial response would be incomplete or even incorrect;

and 2 Subsequent groups would be unsure about the correctness of their answer. Another reason is that answer drift discourages give-and-take discussions because later-responders deliberately downplay differences between their initial answer and the one that is being discussed. Finally, sequential reporting limits accountability because the only group that is truly accountable is the one that is forced to open the discussion.

On the other hand, requiring groups to simultaneously reveal their answers virtually eliminates the main problems that result from sequential reporting. For example, in a human resource management course, a typical assignment would involve requiring teams to choose (from a list of 6 or 7 employees – see Key #3) who they think should be laid off first from a set of complex and conflicting performance data provided on each employee. Then, one simultaneous report option (others are discussed in Sweet, Michaelsen and Wright, in press) would be for instructor to signal the teams to simultaneously hold up a card with the name of the employee on it corresponding to their choice. This simultaneous public commitment to a specific choice increases both learning and team development because each team is: 1 Accountable for their choice; 2 Motivated to defend their position and; 3 The more difficult the problem, the greater the potential for disagreements that are likely to prompt give-and-take discussion.

Several examples of potential application-focused assignments meeting these criteria are shown in Table 17.2. In each case, the assignment requires teams to use course concepts to make a complex decision that can be represented in a simple form. As a result, because each of these assignments could be implemented so that teams could receive prompt and detailed *peer* feedback on the quality of their work they would also enhance both learning and team development. Learning is enhanced because students would be forced to re-examine and possibly modify their assumptions and/or interpretations of the facts and the teams become more cohesive as they pull together in an attempt to defend their position.

**Table 17.2   Examples of decision-based assignments**

From a list of 2–5 plausible, but differentially defensible, outcomes that are related to concepts from the course, have teams choose the one that would be *most* (or least) affected by (plug in an example from the list below):

☐ A specific failure to complete a deliverable on time [in a course in project management or decision making].

☐ A cut in training budget requiring a reorganization of the department [in a course in human resource management or training].

☐ A specific increase in market share due to a competitor dropping out of the market [in a course in strategy].

## Near the end of the term

Although TBL provides students with multiple opportunities for learning along the way, instructors can solidify and extend student understanding of both course content and group process issues by using specific kinds of activities near the end of the term. These are activities that cause students to reflect on their experience during the semester. Their reflecting is focused on several different areas. In most cases, these end-of-the-semester activities are aimed at reminding students of what they have learned about: 1 Course concepts; 2 The value of teams in tackling intellectual challenges; 3 The kinds of interaction that promotes effective team work; and 4 Themselves.

**Reinforcing content learning**. One of the greatest benefits of using TBL is also a potential danger. Since so little class time is aimed at providing students with their initial exposure to course concepts, many fail to realize how much they have learned. In part, this seems to result from the fact that, with TBL, the volume of their lecture notes is far less than in normal courses. As a result, many management students are somewhat uneasy and some may actually feel that they have been cheated even in situations in which they are aware of the fact that the scores from TBL sections on 'common' midterm exams were significantly higher than scores from non-IBE sections. As a result, on

an ongoing basis – and especially near the end of the course – instructors should make explicit connections between end-of-course exams and the RAT questions and application assignments. In addition, an effective way to reassure students is devoting a class period to a concept review. In its simplest form this involves: 1 Giving students an extensive list of the concepts from the course; 2 Asking them to individually identify any concepts that they don't recognize; 3 Compare their conclusions in the teams; and 4 Review any concepts that teams identify as needing additional attention.

**Learning about the value of teams**. Concerns about better students being burdened by less motivated or less able peers are commonplace with other group-based instructional approaches. TBL, however, enables instructors to provide students with compelling empirical evidence of the value of teams for tackling difficult intellectual challenges. For example, in taking both individual and team RATs, students generally have the feeling that the teams are outperforming their own best member, but they are seldom aware of either the magnitude or the pervasiveness of the effect. Near the end of each term, we create a transparency that shows five *cumulative* scores from the RATs for each team – the low, average and high member score, the team score and the difference between the highest member score and the team score (e.g. see Michaelsen et al., 2004: 163). Most students are literally stunned when they see the pattern of scores for the entire class. In the past 20 years, over 99.95 percent of the nearly 2,000 teams in our classes have outperformed their own best member by an average of nearly 11 percent. In fact, in the majority of classes, the lowest team score in the class is higher than the single best individual score in the entire class (e.g., see Michaelsen et al., 1989).

**Recognizing effective team interaction**. Over time, teams get increasingly better at ferreting out and using members' intellectual resources in making decisions (Watson et al., 1991). However, unless instructors use an activity that prompts members to explicitly think about group process issues, they are likely to miss an important teaching opportunity. This is because most students, although pleased about the results, generally fail to recognize the changes in members' behavior that have made the improvements possible.

We have used two different approaches for increasing students' awareness of the relationship between group processes and group effectiveness. The aim of both approaches is to have students reflect on how and why members' interaction patterns have changed as their team became more cohesive. One approach is an assignment that requires students to individually: 1 Reflect on how the interactions among team members have changed over time and formulate a list of 'members' actions that made a difference'; 2 Share their lists with team members; and 3 Create a written analysis that summarizes the barriers to their team's effectiveness and what was done to overcoming them. The other, and more effective approach, involves the same assignment but, having students prepare along the way by keeping an ongoing 'log' of observations about how their team has functioned (see Hernandez, 2002).

**Learning about themselves: The critical role of peer evaluations**. One of the most important contributions of TBL is that it creates conditions that can enable students to learn a great deal about the way they interact with others. In large measure, this occurs because of the extensive and intensive interaction within the teams. Over time, two important things happen. One is that members really get to know each others' strengths and weaknesses. This makes them better at teaching each other because they can make increasingly accurate assumptions about what a given teammate finds difficult and how best to explain it to them. The other is that, in the vast majority of teams, members develop such strong interpersonal relationships that they feel morally obligated to provide honest feedback to each other.

Although students learn a great deal about themselves along the way, the instructor can have a significant positive impact on many students' understanding of themselves by using a well-designed peer evaluation process. This involves collecting data from team members on how much and in how they feel others have contributed to their learning and making the information (but not who provided it) available to individual students.

Some TBL practitioners feel strongly that collecting and feeding back peer evaluation data should occur two or more times during the term (usually in conjunction with major team assignments). Others favor involving teams in developing peer evaluation criteria part way through the term but only collecting the peer evaluation data at the very end of the term. The biggest advantage of collecting and feeding back peer evaluation data along the way is that it gives students the opportunity to make changes. One potential disadvantage is that – depending upon how one handles mid-term peer evaluations – having students formally evaluate each other can measurably disrupt the team development process.

**Encouraging the development of positive team norms**. Learning teams will only be successful to the extent that individual members prepare for and actually attend class. We have learned, however, that when we provide students with ongoing feedback on attendance and individual RAT scores, the link between pre-class preparation and class attendance team performance is so obvious that we can count on norms promoting pre-class preparation and attendance pretty much developing on their own. One very simple, yet effective, way to provide such feedback to the students is through the use of team folders. The folders should contain an ongoing record of each member's attendance, along with the individual and team scores on the RATs and other assignments (see Appendix D-B1.1 in Michaelsen et al., 2002, 2004). The act of recording the scores and attendance data in the team folders is particularly helpful because it ensures that every team member knows how every other team member is doing. Further, promoting a public awareness of the team scores further fosters norms favoring individual preparation and regular attendance because doing so invariably focuses attention on the fact that there is always a positive relationship between individual preparation and attendance and team performance.

## Benefits of team-based learning

In part, because of its versatility in dealing with the problems associated with the multiple teaching venues in management education, TBL produces a wide variety of benefits for students, for management education administrators, and for individual faculty members who are engaged in the instruction process.

## Benefits for students

In addition to ensuring that students master the basic course content, TBL enables a number of outcomes that are virtually impossible in a lecture-based course format and rarely achieved with any other small-group based instructional approach. With Team-Based Learning:

1 Most students progress well beyond simply acquiring factual knowledge and achieve a depth of understanding that can only come through solving a *series* of problems that are too complex for even the best students to complete through their individual effort. Virtually every student develops a deep and abiding appreciation of the value of teams for solving difficult and complex and real-world problems.
2 Many students gain profound insights into their strengths and weaknesses as learners and as team members.
3 Compared to a traditional curriculum, faculty members in a wide variety of contexts have observed that introducing TBL enables the 'at risk' students (probably because of the increased social support and/or peer tutoring) to successfully complete and stay on track in their course work.

## Benefits from an administrative perspective

Many of the benefits for administrators are related to the social impact of the fact that the

vast majority of groups develop into effective learning teams. With team-based learning:

(1) Almost without exception, the groups develop into effective *self-managed* learning teams. As a result, the faculty and/or professional staff time used for training facilitators and involved in team facilitation is minimal.
(2) TBL is highly cost-effective since it can be successfully employed in large classes and across the entire spectrum of management courses.
(3) Using the kinds of assignments that are characteristic of TBL virtually eliminates administrators' frustrations in dealing with the aftermath (and even legal implications) that often occur when interpersonal hostilities develop to the point that groups are incapable of doing effective work.

## Benefits for faculty

There is tremendous benefit to the faculty who use TBL. Because of the student apathy that seems to be an increasingly common response to the traditional lecture-based instruction, even the most dedicated faculty tend to burn out. By contrast, TBL prompts most students to engage in the learning process with a level of energy and enthusiasm that transforms classrooms into a place of excitement that is rewarding for both them and the instructor. With team-based learning:

1 Instructors seldom have to worry about students not being in class or failing to prepare for the work that he or she has planned.
2 When students are truly prepared for class, interacting with them is much more like working with colleagues than with the 'empty vessels' that tend to show up in lecture-based courses.
3 Because instructors spend much more time listening and observing than making formal presentations, they develop many more personally rewarding relationships with their students.

When the instructor adopts the, 'it's about learning, *not* about teaching' view of the education process that is a normal outcome of the 'backward-design' aspect of TBL, instructors and students tend to become true partners in the education process.

## REFERENCES

Aarestad, B.J. and Moewes, D.S. (2004) 'Incorporating learning styles into team-based learning'. Paper presented at the SUN Conference on Teaching and Learning, University of Texas, El Paso, March.

Birmingham, C. and McCord, M. (2004) 'Group process research: Implications for using learning groups', in L.K. Michaelsen, A.B. Knight and L.D. Fink (eds), *Team-Based Learning: A Transformative Use of Small Groups in College Teaching*. Sterling, VA: Stylus. pp. 73–93.

Birmingham, C. and Michaelsen, L.K. (1999) 'Conflict resolution in decision making teams: A longitudinal study'. Paper presented at the Midwest Academy of Management, Chicago, IL.

Brobeck, F.C., Kerschreiter, R., Mojsich, A., Frey, D. and Schulz-Hardt, S. (2002) 'The dissemination of critical, unshared information in decision-making groups: The effects of pre-discussion dissent', *European Journal of Social Pscyhology*, 32: 35–56.

Bargh, J.A. and Schul, Y. (1980) 'On the cognitive benefits of teaching', *Journal of Educational Psychology*, 74 (5): 593–604.

Bruning, R.H., Schraw, G.J., and Ronning, R.R. (1994) *Cognitive Psychology and Instruction* (2nd edn). Englewood Cliffs, NJ: Prentice-Hall.

Chan, C., Burtis, J. and Bereiter, C. (1997) 'Knowledge building as a mediator of conflict in conceptual change', *Cognition and Instruction*, 15 (1): 1–40.

Cragin, J.P. (2004) 'Team-based learning in international situations', in L.K. Michaelsen, A.B. Knight and L.D. Fink (eds), *Team-Based Learning: A Transformative Use of Small Groups in College Teaching*. Sterling, VA: Stylus. pp. 173–82.

Feichtner, S.B. and Davis, E.A. (1985) 'Why some groups fail: A survey of students' experiences with learning groups', *The Organizational Behavior Teaching Review*, 9 (4): 58–71.

Fink, L.D. (2004) 'Beyond small roups: Harnessing the extraordinary power of learning teams', in L.K. Michaelsen, A.B. Knight and L.D. Fink (eds), *Team-Based Learing: A Transformative Use of Small Groups in College Teaching*. Sterling, VA: Stylus. pp. 169–72.

French, J.R.P. and Raven, B.M. (1959) 'The basis of social power', in D. Cartwright (ed.), *Studies in Social Power*. Ann Arbor, MI: Institute for Social Research. pp. 150–87.

Gersick, C. and Hackman, J.R. (1990) 'Habitual routines in task-performing groups', *Organizational Behaviour and Human Decision Processes*, 47: 65–97.

Hattie, J. and Timperley, H. (2007) 'The power of feedback', *Review of Educational Research*, 77 (1): 81–112.

Hernandez, S.A. (2002) 'Team-based learning in a marketing principles course: Cooperative structures that facilitate active learning and higher level thinking', *Journal of Marketing Education*, 24 (1): 45–75.

Holt, D.G. and Willard-Holt, C. (2000) 'Let's get real: Students solving authentic corporate problems', *Phi Delta Kappan*, 82: 243–46.

Johnson, D.W., Johnson, R.T., and Smith, K. (2007) 'The state of cooperative learning in postsecondary and professional settings', *Educational Psychology Review*, 19 (1): 15–29.

Knight, A.B. (2004) 'Team-based learning: A strategy for transforming the quality of teaching and learning', in L.K. Michaelsen, A.B. Knight and L.D. Fink (eds), *Team-Based Learning: A Transformative Use of Small Groups in College Teaching*. Sterling, VA: Stylus. PP. 197–208.

Krathwohl, D.R. (2002) 'A revision of bloom's taxonomy: An overview', *Theory into Practice*, 41 (4): 212–18.

Kulik, J.A. and Kulik, C.C. (1988) 'Timing of feedback and verbal learning', *Review of Educational Research*, 58 (1): 79–97.

Lerner, J.S. and Tetlock, P.E. (1999) 'Accounting for the effects of accountability', *Psychological Bulletin*, 125 (2): 255–75.

McGrath, J.E. (1991) 'Time, interaction, and performance (TIP): A theory of groups'. *Small Group Research*, 22 (2): 147–74.

McInerney, M.J. (2003) 'Team-based learning enhances long-term retention and critical thinking in an undergraduate microbial physiology course', *Microbiology Education Journal*, 4 (1): 3–12.

Mayer, R.E. (2002) 'Rote versus meaningful learning', *Theory into Practice*, 41 (4): 226–32.

Meeuwsen, H.J. (2002) 'The effective use of learning teams in the classroom', *Journal of Sport and Exercise Psychology*, 24 *(Suppl.)* (S4): 15.

Michaelsen, L.K. and Black, R.H. (1994) 'Building learning teams: The key to harnessing the power of small groups in higher education', in S. Kadel and J. Keehner (eds), *Collaborative Learning: A Sourcebook for Higher Education, Vol. 2*. State College, PA: National Center for Teaching, Learning and Assessment.

Michaelsen, L.K. and Schultheiss, E.E. (1988) 'Making feedback helpful', *The Organizational Behavior Teaching Review*, 13 (1): 109–13.

Michaelsen, L.K. and Sweet, M. (2007) 'Fundamental principles and practices of team-based learning', in L.K. Michaelsen, D.X. Parmelee, K.K. McMahon and R.E. Levine (eds), *Team-Based Learning for Health Professions Education: A Guide to Using Small Groups for Improving Learning*. Sterling, VA: Stylus. pp. 9–34.

Michaelsen, L.K., Cragin, J.P. and Watson, W.E. (1981) 'Grading and anxiety: A strategy for coping', *Exchange: The Organizational Behavior Teaching Journal*, 6 (1): 8–14.

Michaelsen, L.K., Knight, A.B. and Fink, L.D. (2002) *Team-Based Learning: A Transformative Use of Small Groups*. Westport, CT: Praeger.

Michaelsen, L.K., Knight, A.B. and Fink, L.D. (2004) *Team-Based Learning: A Transformative Use of Small Groups in College Teaching*. Sterling, VA: Stylus.

Michaelsen, L.K and McCord, M. (2006) 'Teaching business by doing business: An interdisciplinary faculty-friendly approach', D. Robertson and L. Nilson (eds). in *To Improve the Academy: Resources for Faculty, Instructional and Organizational Development*. Stillwater, OK: New Forums Press. pp. 238–53.

Michaelsen, L.K., Watson, W.E. and Black, R.H. (1989) 'A realistic test of individual versus group consensus decision making', *Journal of Applied Psychology*, 74 (5): 834–9.

Michaelsen, L.K., Parmelee, D.X., McMahon, K.K. and Levine, R.E. (eds) (2007) *Team-Based Learning for Health Professions Education: A Guide to Using Small Groups for Improving Learning*. Sterling, VA: Stylus Publishing.

Miller, J.A. (1991) 'Experiencing management: A comprehensive, "hands-on" model for the introductory management course', *Journal of Management Education*, 15 (2): 151–73.

Millis, B.J. and Cottell, P.G. (1998) '*Cooperative Learning for Higher Education Faculty*. Phoenix, Arizona: Oryx Press.

Nakaji, M.C. (2004) 'A dramatic turnaround in a classroom of deaf students', in L.K. Michaelsen, A.B. Knight and L.D. Fink (eds), *Team-Based Learning: A Transformative Use of Small Groups in College Teaching*. Sterling, VA: Stylus. pp. 125–32.

Nungester, R.J. and Duchastel, P.C. (1982) 'Testing versus review: Effects on retention', *Journal of Applied Psychology*, 74 (1): 18–22.

Peterson, T.O. (2004) 'So you're thinking of trying problem based learning? Three critical success factors for implementation', *Journal of Management Education*, 28 (5): 630–47.

Pintrich, P.R. (2002) 'The role of metacognitive knowledge in learning, teaching, and assessing', *Theory into Practice*, 41 (4): 219–25.

Popovsky, J. (2004) 'Using team-based learning in a very traditional, cultural, and institutional context',

in L.K. Michaelsen, A.B Knight and L.D. Fink (eds), *Team-Based Learning: A Transformative Use of Small Groups in College Teaching*. Sterling, VA: Stylus. pp. 169–72.

Scandura, J.M. (1983) 'Instructional strategies based on the structural learning theory', in C.M. Reigeluth (ed.), *Instructional Design Theories and Models*. pp. 213–46.

Slavin, R.E. and Karweit, N.L. (1981) 'Cognitive and affective outcomes of an intensive student team-based learning experience', *Journal of Experimental Education*, 50 (1): 29–35.

Sweet, M. (2007) 'Forming fair groups', in L.K. Michaelsen, D.X. Parmelee, K.K. McMahon, and R.E. Levine, (eds), *Team-Based Learning for Health Professions Education: A Guide to Using Small Groups for Improving Learning*. Sterling, VA: Stylus. pp. 32–4.

Sweet, M.S., Michaelsen, L.K. and Wright, C. (2008) 'Simultaneous report: A reliable method to stimulate class discussion', *Decision Sciences Journal of Innovative Education*, 6 (2): 469–73.

Tryteen, D.A. (1999, November 10–13). 'Progressing from small group work to coorperactive learning: A case study from computer science', Paper presented at the ASEE/IEEE Frontiers in Education Conference, San Juan, Puerto Rico.

Tuckman, B.W. (1965) 'Developmental sequences in small groups', *Psychological Bulletin*, 63: 384–99.

Tuckman, B.W. and Jensen, M.A.C. (1977) 'Stages in small group development revisited', *Group and Organizational Studies*, 2: 419–27.

Watson, W.E., Kumar, K. and Michaelsen, L.K. (1993) 'Cultural diversity's impact on group process and performance: Comparing culturally homogeneous and culturally diverse task groups', *The Academy of Management Journal*, 36 (3): 590–602.

Watson, W.E., Michaelsen, L.K. and Sharp, W. (1991) 'Member competence, group interaction and group decision-making: A longitudinal study', *Journal of Applied Psychology*, 76: 801–9.

Weeks, W. (2003, September) 'Incorporation of active learning strategies in the engineering classroom', Paper presented at the ASEE Midwest Section Meeting, University of Missourri-Rolla.

Whitehead, A. (1929) *The Aims of Education*. Cambridge, UK: Cambridge University Press.

Wiggins, G. and McTighe, J.H. (1998) *Understanding by Design*. Columbus, OH: Merrill Prentice-Hall.

Worchel, S., Wood, W. and Simpson, J.A. (eds) (1992) *Group Process and Productivity*. Newbury Park, CA: Sage Publications.

Worchel, S., Wood, W. and Simpson, J.A. (eds) (1992) *Group Process and Productivity*. Newbury Park, CA: Sage Publications.

# 18

# Problem-Based and Project-Based Learning Approaches: Applying Knowledge to Authentic Situations

Robert DeFillippi and Richard G. Milter

## Abstract

This chapter focuses upon applications of problem-based and project-based learning approaches to management education (course credit, undergraduate and post graduate degree credit programs, and intervention activities). The chapter opens by first presenting the intellectual origins of these two approaches. Learning theory influences include experiential learning (e.g., Barrows and Tamblyn, 1976; Schmidt, 1983; Kolb, 1984), adult learning (Mezirow, 1991), action learning (Revans, 1982), pragmatic learning (Dewey, 1933), action research (Lewin, 1946), action science (Argyris and Schon, 1974; 1978), and constructivist learning perspectives (Savery and Duffy, 1995; Perotti et al., 1998). The chapter provides examples of how management education has been impacted by the use of problem-based and project-based learning. It also discusses the applications of the approaches in student field work projects, service learning projects, consulting projects, internships, and virtual project e-learning applications. Current best practices of both approaches are highlighted including the specific methodologies used in the implementation for management education. The chapter provides an outlook for how these approaches will continue to impact the future of management education and the challenges that will be addressed.

## INTRODUCTION

Problem-based, project-based (or project-driven) learning are closely related learner-centered approaches whose commonalities outweigh their differences. These approaches stand in stark contrast to the more commonly practiced university methods with heavy emphasis on lecturing and classroom discussion on assigned readings. Case work interaction approximates some elements of project-driven learning (namely engaging the student in a decision-making or problem-solving situation) but the static nature of written cases stands in contrast to the less stable and more dynamic character of real-world project tasks and collaboration on specific problem challenges. In essence both project and problem-based learning are grounded in practice and in student engagement with real-world problem and project challenges that require students to learn by doing. As both approaches incorporate inquiry as a key element of their learning frameworks, they share the perspective of the 'wheel of learning' as introduced by Charles Handy (1995). This perspective includes reflection as a required element in the learning process. Both approaches use an inquiry-based learning methodology, which is the initial event in the Handy learning wheel. Handy posits that all learning begins with an inquisitive mind. With project and problem-based learning approaches the learners develop questions as a direct result of their contextual involvement in authentic situations.

In this respect, both approaches have much in common with action learning methodologies (Revans, 1982) that are separately addressed elsewhere in the handbook (see Raelin, Chapter 22 this volume) and with constructivist approaches to learning (Savery and Duffy, 1995; Perotti et al., 1998).

The constructivist perspective posits that cognitive conflict or puzzlement is the stimulus for learning and determines the organization and nature of what is learned; knowledge is socially negotiated. Constructivism is a particularly appropriate learning orientation when learning is ill-defined (Duffy and Jonassen, 1991) or when 'there is no single right or wrong answer' (Rungtusanatham et al., 2004: 100). Further, constructivism as a learning approach contributes to the development of behavioral competencies such as problem-solving or decision-making skills,

both of which necessitate a high level of flexibility in responding to changing demands to learn new content and methods appropriate to the evolving requirements of the project task. Hence, constructivist teaching designs are most appropriate where 'the learner is exploring complex scenarios and applying problem-solving skills to ambiguous situations' (Rungtusanatham et al., 2004: 112).

In the constructivist problem/project-learning environment the student takes control of setting his/her own learning goals (Clark, 2001; Leidner and Jarvenpaa, 1995; Papastergiou, 2006; Waddill, 2006). Since constructivism embraces the viewpoint that reality for the learner is based on the learners' experiences and perceptions, the facilitator becomes just that. She should not force a point of view (Leidner and Jarvenpaa, 1995; Poole, 2000). Constructivism impacts the design of instruction when it includes the following: (1) anchor all learning activities to a larger task or problem; (2) support the learner in developing ownership for the overall problem or task; (3) design an authentic task; (4) design the task and the learning environment to reflect the complexity of the environment they will function in at the end of the learning; (5) give the learner ownership of the process used to develop a solution; (6) design the learning environment to support and challenge the learner's thinking; (7) encourage testing ideas against alternative views and alternative contexts; and (8) provide opportunity for and support reflection on both the content learned and the learning process (Perotti et al., 1998).

In summary, project- and problem-based learning methods draw upon a constructivist perspective on learning, in which students are responsible for constructing meaning from their own experience. In each mode, education is thus learner-centered rather than teacher-directed. Indeed, the role of the instructor is more focused on providing facilitation and social and technical support than explicit direction or knowledge transfer. Instead, the demands of the problem or project challenge become the driver for student self-organizing, action, and reflection.

These drivers include the learning deadlines and deliverables that are specified in the learning assignment.

## PROBLEM-BASED LEARNING

Problem-based learning (PBL) is an approach to education in which students learn collaboratively by confronting authentic and current problems. Initially developed in the mid-1960s at McMaster University, courses are organized thematically rather than by discipline, often by a small team of instructors having different disciplinary backgrounds (Barrows, 1983, 1985). It has been proposed that 'the principal idea behind problem-based learning is … that the starting point for learning should be a problem, a query, or puzzle that the learner wishes to solve' (Boud, 1985: 13). The direction of the learning enterprise in PBL is based upon inquiry. American writer John Steinbeck once stated that 'we frequently search for answers, when we should be developing better questions.' This inquiry mode of learning coupled with a full appreciation for the prior knowledge of the learner provides the foundation for a PBL approach.

The key characteristics of a PBL approach outlined by Gijselaers (1996) include:

- Problems serve as a stimulus for learning.
- Learning is constructive and not a receptive process – learning occurs as new learning is associated with existing knowledge networks.
- Knowing about knowing (meta-cognition) affects learning – What am I going to do? How am I going to do it? Did it work?
- Social and contextual factors influence learning – understanding how and when to use knowledge is as important as the knowledge itself.
- Problems reflect world situations or professional practice.
- Small group work encourages student collaboration and independence.
- Students learn to share their ideas and share responsibility.
- Students learn to question their own assumptions about their reality.

- Conflicting views as part of discussion facilitate understanding.
- PBL may not be suitable for all types of learning and topic areas.
- Educators must have confidence in the students that they will use their time wisely and can be trusted to carry out the required tasks on time.
- Problems are encountered before all relevant knowledge has been acquired, not after it.

The final bulleted statement (above) points to the basic nature of the PBL approach, that encountering problems leads learners to ask questions that drive their search for meaning and learning. This is fundamental to the approach as it provides a very different role for the faculty member involved in the process. The role of the educator becomes more of a 'guide by the side' involved in facilitating knowledge and skill acquisition than the more traditional role of 'sage on the stage' which is exhibited by information dissemination, the prominent activity of most lecture-based educational formats.

Citing a 1980 book by Springer Publishing, Gijselaers supports the premise recognized by many researchers that acknowledges Howard Barrows, MD, as the most prominent figure to move PBL into the arena of medical education. Barrows and his colleagues at the McMaster University Faculty of Health Sciences in Canada introduced the PBL approach in the 1960s. It has become an instructional method of choice for a growing number of medical schools around the globe. The growth of PBL activities in medical education has been charted most rigorously by the work of Schmidt (1983) and his colleagues at Maastricht University in the Netherlands over the past 35 years. The use of PBL approaches in medical education has been employed by a growing number of universities, each putting their signature on the application. A network developed by Schmidt and his colleagues at Maastricht University, has helped to secure a home for medical educators around the globe who are seeking innovative methods to train health professionals. The early use of PBL in medical education is chronicled by Albanese and

Mitchell (1993) as they provide insights into issues of implementation and the results of early comparisons between the PBL approach and traditional classroom activities.

Barrows (1983, 1985) developed a PBL approach to medical education at Southern Illinois University (SIU) where he also developed a Center for PBL that reached out to other educational institutions including primary schools. The influence of the PBL programs in medical education at McMaster, SIU, and Maastricht University were foundational to the continued development of PBL in other institutions and across other disciplines. Schmidt and his colleagues, for example, strongly influenced Gijselaers as he led the development of PBL programs in the Business School of Maastricht University. The efforts of the researchers and faculty at Maastricht University have had considerable influence on the implementation of PBL within the field of management education. In a chapter titled 'Perspectives on Problem-Based Learning' Gijselaers (1995) outlines the goals, basic features, instructional tools, and institutional structures that are exhibited in early PBL approaches in schools of business and management.

Adopted by many business schools around the world over the past 15 years, PBL has been an important tool, linking student learning and actual business practice. One of the earliest applications of this alternative learning methodology in a US business school setting is reported by Stinson (1990) where he describes the approach as 'integrated contextual learning' that is situated in practice and reiterative by design. In a later example the business school at Curtin University of Technology (Australia) launched a program to better equip students with the range of skills that they need in their professional life. This program, titled 'The professional skill project,' aimed to identify and define specific professional skills that were needed by graduates and develop a professional skill portfolio template, to enable students to demonstrate what skills they learned during their degree courses (Dickie, 1999). More recently, a large Dutch information technology company has integrated into their new hire development program a PBL platform where all employees spend three weeks at a major university in the US addressing problem challenges designed to enhance their business consulting skills (Van Doorn and Milter, 2005).

One of the primary investigators of PBL and similar approaches in education has been Tom Duffy, currently director of instructional systems technology at the School of Education at Indiana University. His 1995 *Educational Technology* article with John Savery is perhaps the most referenced work on PBL applications. Savery and Duffy (1995) provide a framework for understanding PBL as an instructional approach and highlight several implementation strategies in various educational settings. The use of PBL models for instruction has also been adopted in schools of architecture, law, social work (Boud and Feletti, 1991), and engineering (De Graff and Kolmos, 2006; Boud and Feletti, 1991). More closely related to management education, examples of the use of PBL have been documented in a US university accounting course (Barsky et al., 2003), an economics course in Ireland (Forsythe, 2002), a cross-curricular experience at a university in the UK (Brassington and Smith, 2000), a corporate MBA program in Malaysia (Yost and Keifer, 1998), and an undergraduate business program in Sweden (Soderlund, 1998).

Influenced by his early educational research in medical education and the success of the network for medical educators developed by Schmidt, Gijselaers founded a network where his colleagues at the Faculty of Economics and Business Administration might share, learn, and collaborate on new innovations in instructional models. When the value of such collaboration took hold and expanded, the EDiNEB (Educational Innovations in Economics and Business) Network was formed in 1993, supported by a Foundation at Maastricht University (then University of Limburg) with members from around the globe. In the early years, many of the activities of the EDiNEB Network centered on PBL theory, practices, and learning methodologies.

The inaugural international conference, in December of 1993, was titled 'The Case of Problem-Based Learning.' It was held at the University of Limburg, an institution that was founded on the premise that all instruction would use PBL methods.

## Applying PBL methods in a university setting

The specific PBL method used at Maastricht University is called the Seven Jump Step. Using the Seven Jump Step students are divided into groups of between 5 and 12 with one person appointed as a Chair and another as a Minutes Secretary. The Chair and Minutes Secretary can be rotated at each session. The role of the Chair is to guide the discussions of the group, but all students should be involved in the discussions. The instructor hands out the problem to the Chair who distributes it to the rest of the group. The following 7 steps (also provided by Gijselaers, 1996) are then tackled:

1    The Chair and the group read the problem; the Chair will ask if any of the group do not understand any of the vocabulary in the problem – not concepts or theories but literally the vocabulary. Any queries can be resolved through the use of a dictionary.
2    The Chair asks the group to identify what they think the problem statement is about. At this stage, students may be clueless about the depth of the knowledge inherent in the statement but this will become clearer as the process continues. Some of the answers therefore may be naive or ignorant but this does not matter. The educator must resist the temptation at this point of stepping in and offering any form of knowledge transmission.
3    A brainstorm session is held to ascertain what, if anything, is known (or is believed to be known) about the subject matter by any of the students at this point in time.
4    The Minutes Secretary identifies the key issues that have been discussed. The Chair ensures that a clear list of what is known, what is unclear and what needs to be investigated in more detail is established. This is designed to help the group understand the issues surrounding the problem.
5    The group members agree on their learning objectives and the tasks that they will have to carry out before the next meeting.
6    Individual Study – members of the group collect the information identified in step 5. There is a choice of two routes here – either each student should tackle his or her own learning objectives, or each student covers all the learning objectives. The latter is more time consuming and may be off-putting for students and avoid inculcating the collaborative team-based learning experience. However, the former option may result in gaps in an individual's knowledge and understanding. The educator can provide a list of references to help guide students in their line of investigation.
7    The group members meet for the second time. The Chair asks the Minutes Secretary to read out the learning objectives and each student has the opportunity to present their research to the rest of the group. It is suggested that this can be done either formally, i.e. in turn, or through group discussion.

At the end of the seven steps, it is the responsibility of the Minutes Secretary to write up the summary of the investigation and the conclusions drawn. A copy of the document is made available for each member of the group. It is important therefore that the process ensures that every person in the group is Secretary/Joint Secretary at least once. The process will therefore provide each student with a piece of written work for assessment. The educator can, at their discretion, identify a series of criteria for less formal assessment – contribution to the discussion, role of the Chair, quality of the individual research carried out and so on. To avoid the problem of non-attendance, marks can be awarded for regular attendance, which contributes toward the final assessment total.

Once the process has been completed, the groups can do a presentation of their findings and a discussion can be facilitated on why there were different solutions to the same problem and what we can learn from these different solutions about the problem. The cycle then continues with the presentation of another stimulus problem. A particular problem provides the context for learning new information and serves as a stepping-stone for students to acquire knowledge about the general problem-domain. In this final stage of Problem-Based Learning, the tutor may also demonstrate how conceptual knowledge about issues addressed in this problem can be used in the analysis. This enables students to observe how knowledge from one problem may be transferred to new problem situations (Gijselaers, 1996).

In North America a major initiative in problem-based learning was developed in the late 1980s at the College of Business at Ohio University (Milter and Stinson, 1995; Stinson and Milter, 1996). This program was built on an evolving platform that started with integrating major core elements in an approach referred to as 'integrated contextual learning' and moving to problem-based learning, and finally as it became a program-wide initiative it was called project-based action learning (Day and Stinson, 1990; Milter, 2002). Although the early work in these approaches at Ohio University targeted the MBA programs, the practice cascaded into the ranks of the undergraduate curriculum (the main mission of the OU College of Business) into a program called 'The Business Cluster' that uses PBL to integrate marketing, management, information systems, communication, and business law (Perotti et al., 1998). For recent comprehensive reviews of PBL approaches for management education, see Smith (2005); Hallinger and Bridges (2007).

## PROJECT-BASED LEARNING

Project-based learning in this chapter refers to the theory and practice of student or learner engagement in time-limited, goal-directed activities negotiated with a project client or sponsor that generate both externally validated performance outcomes and individual and collective learning (DeFillippi, 2001). Student projects offer an ideal situation to provide problem-solving opportunities that present real-world problems that are scaled back so that they are doable in the confines of the classroom. Project-based learning can also be thought of as learning through a series of activities based in authentic, real-world problems in which the learner has some degree of control over the learning environment and the design of the learning activities (Morgan, 1987; MacGregor, 2005). Typically, these project work activities are enacted outside the classroom and their performance in work settings qualifies project-based learning as a variant of work-based learning (Raelin, 2000). Raelin (2000) identifies the roots of work-based learning and by extension, project-based learning, in experiential learning (e.g., Kolb, 1984) and adult learning (Mezirow, 1991). Additionally, the project-based learning perspective owes much to pragmatic learning perspectives associated with Dewey (1933), who argued for experimenting in the real world.

The most extensive North American applications of project-based learning have arisen in Kindergarten through grade 12 educational settings (Blumenfeld et al., 1991). The practice of project-based learning in middle school and secondary school settings has been encouraged in North America by non-profit advocacy organizations such as the Buck Institute for Education, which has created a handbook for project-based learning that it makes available to middle school and high school teachers (Thomas et al., 1999). Project-based learning theory and practice applications to university based management education have strong roots in the UK, where some of the earliest and most extensive project-based learning initiatives have occurred.

One of the earliest studies on project-based learning (Adderley et al., 1975: 1) describes project-based learning as emphasizing:

- the solution of a problem;
- initiative by the student or group of students;
- that commonly results in an end product (e.g., thesis, report, design plans, computer programme and model);
- work often goes on for a considerable length of time;
- teaching staff are involved in an advisory role.

The first and third items concerning the focus on a problem around which to organize activities resulting in a final project are considered to be the most essential features of project-based learning, and these same two characteristics are emphasized by Blumenfeld et al. (1991) in their review of project-based learning. These early discussions of project-based learning do not distinguish between project-based learning and problem-based learning. However, recent reviewers of project-based learning argue that a key distinction is that project-based learning involves the construction of a concrete artifact or project deliverable (e.g. the draft of a design or an end product) as an outcome of project work (Helle, Tynjala and Oklinuora, 2006). Problem-based learning approaches, on the other hand, may use a problem that is more limited in scope or duration.

Project-based learning draws from several different action-based learning perspectives. One influence includes the action learning writings of Reg Revans (1982). The basic assumption of action learning is that 'managers learn best by taking action and reflecting on the action' (Revans, 1998). Another action-based influence is Lewin's (1946) action research and its underlying assumption that knowledge will be used in the service of action. These action research perspectives have been subsequently employed in the design and implementation of learning projects (Coghlan, 2001). Also influential are some core assumptions and practices of action science, associated with Chris Argyris and Donald Schon (1974, 1978). Action science intervention requires that project participants engage in significant self-reflection on their learning assumptions or theories-in-use. Such reflection generally occurs under the guidance of a skilled facilitator.

Project-based learning theory and practice tends to draw upon many of the same cognitive learning perspectives that underlie action learning. Smith (2001) identifies the following relevant schools of cognitive theory for action learning and its application to project-based interventions: distributed cognition theory (Dede, 1996), cognitive flexibility theory

(Spiro et al., 1988), situated cognition theory (Perret-Clermont, 1993), and meta-cognition theory (Flavell, 1976). A detailed comparison of project-based learning assumptions to other psychological learning perspectives can be found in DeFillippi and Ornstein (2003).

When applied to management education, project-based learning has specific implications for instructional design. Typically, students work on a semi-structured or open-ended assignment that requires some engagement outside the classroom setting with real-time primary information sources, project client, or project sponsor. The teacher acts as a facilitator, perhaps providing access to project opportunities, perhaps providing resources (content, context, or process) and advice (often a mix of coaching, mentoring, and consulting) to students. The students (most frequently working in small teams) assume responsibility for designing and implementing activities focused on creating a set of project deliverables for their client. Knowledge is created through student project involvement, which provides the experiential basis for student reflection and dialogue on the inter-relationships between theoretical knowledge and its action implications when knowledge is put into practice. Project-based learning thus provides a learning context in which teachers can help students increase their skills and knowledge through cooperative learning and collaborative problem solving and reflection (DeFillippi and Wankel, 2005).

Some project-based learning theorists further emphasize the shared learning that arises within the community of reflective practitioners (Schön, 1983) when collaborating in project-based learning activities (Ayas and Zeniuk, 2001). The community of practice tradition is associated with Etienne Wegner (1998) and this perspective explicates how learning occurs naturally through people's social participation in the practices of social communities and through their construction of identities in relation to these communities. Within this community of practice tradition, project-based learning develops as participants change their membership from more peripheral project roles to more central positions within a project community. However, the opportunity for such project-based community learning requires that an educational institution provide its students the opportunity to participate in a multiplicity of projects over an extended period of time so that a community of student project practitioners may arise. As we will see shortly, only some institutions make such a substantial commitment to project-based learning in their curriculum design.

Morgan (1983) describes three general models of project work for educational purposes: *Project exercises*, which require students to apply knowledge already acquired to an academic issue in a subject area already familiar to them, such as might occur as an end of semester assignment; *project component*, which is typically inter-disciplinary in nature and often related to 'real-world' issues, such as a required 'capstone project' for integrating learning in a degree program, concentration or major; and *project orientation*, which denotes an entire curriculum philosophy or program based on the use of projects. A recent example of project orientation is the Johns Hopkins MBA Fellows program, whereby students complete their program of studies through a blended format of intensive residencies and project-based collaboration. For some universities, project-based student learning is the exception to a classroom-based learning culture. However, project-based learning is more than a technique. In recent years, an increasing number of business schools have heeded the call for greater relevance by instituting programs of instruction that are centrally focused on project-learning (Rickards et al., 2005; Coombs and Yost, 2004). Although the conceptual language of Morgan has lost some currency, the range of project-based learning practices summarized by this tripartite classification retains some useful distinctions regarding the range of project-learning engagement within a business school educational curriculum.

The centerpiece of project-based learning is the project, which is a complex task to address a set of client or sponsor relevant questions or problems. Projects typically involve students in design, problem solving, decision making, and/or investigative activities. These activities are typically undertaken by students operating with varying degrees of autonomy over extended periods of time. The project generally culminates in deliverables to some project client or sponsor, in the form of a written report, physical artifacts (e.g. prototype), and/or oral presentation (Smith and Dodds, 1997).

Project-based learning has many applications in management education and management development, including leadership development (Thompson and Bleak, 2007), action learning (Yorks, 2005), action research (Coghlan, 2001), consulting, (Clifford et al., 2005), internships (Brace-Govan and Powell, 2005), service learning (Ayas and Mirvis, 2005), and university based online learning programs (Milter, 2002). Several of these applications (consulting, internships, and service learning) have become staples of the management education curricula and these merit more detailed consideration within the limits imposed upon this review chapter.

Service-learning has become one of the major arenas for project-based learning, with many universities instituting service-learning programs and providing students course credit for participation in projects that typically serve local and often resource-poor communities and not-for-profit organizations and their constituencies. The National Society for Experiential Education defines service learning as 'any carefully monitored service experience in which a student has intentional learning goals and reflects actively on what he or she is learning throughout the experience' (Kendall and Associates, 1990: 3). A service-learning project is usually embedded in a course as an assignment and is not paid for by the service organization, and service-learning projects typically require students to reflect on their experience in terms of what they have learned about theories and concepts presented in class, and how it has impacted their lives (McCarthy et al., 2002).

Management education journals and other academic outlets are devoting increasing attention to service learning projects with four special issues on service-learning led by management educators in (1) the *Journal of Business Ethics* special issue in 1996, (2) the *Academy of Management Learning and Education* special issue in 2005, (3) the special issue of the *International Journal of Case Method Research and Application* in 2006, and (4) the 2008 special issue of the *Journal of Management Education* (Fornaciari and Kenworthy-U'Ren, 2007). Also, the American Association of Higher Education (AAHE) has sponsored a discipline-specific book series on service-learning, with one of the books, *Working for the Common Good: Concepts and Models for Service-Learning in Management*, focused solely on service-learning in management education (Godfrey and Grasso, 2000).

Closely related to service learning projects are consulting projects, which may serve a wide array of client organizations, both not-for-profit and for-profit and the constituencies served may range from disadvantaged clientele to fast track executive managers in training (Ayas and Mirvis, 2005). Adams and Zanzi (2004) found that the use of field projects in management consulting courses in top tier schools increased from 18.3 percent to 30.9 percent during the 2001–2003 time period. When evaluating all AACSB accredited MBA programs, Adams and Zanzi (2004) also reported the use of field consulting projects in management consulting courses was 15.3 percent in 2003 (a significant increase over 2002), indicating that the use of consulting field projects is beginning to attract a wider audience than just the elite business schools in North America.

One of the first management education institutions to commit to project-based learning was Manchester Business School, which has fostered the connection between management education and project-based experiential learning since 1965. The *Manchester Method* incorporates subject-based lectures with group projects in live settings; students take increasing responsibility throughout the MBA program for project acquisition, management, and delivery; student assessment necessarily incorporates project ambiguity in order to reflect group success over student-to-student competition. Furthermore, experiential features of the program are introduced from the beginning of the program (Rickards et al., 2005).

## ASSESSING LEARNING IN PBL AND PROJECT-BASED APPROACHES

Much has been published about the values and differences of PBL and project-based learning approaches compared to more traditional methods of instruction. Some research suggests little difference between the PBL approach and more conventional instruction when one examines content acquisition – that is, standard measures for checking that students incorporate the stated knowledge elements – show a fairly level playing field between the two approaches (Albanese and Mitchell, 1993; Vernon and Blake, 1993). The real difference between the problem/project-based approach and more conventional approaches is that the former targets the application of the knowledge. In a meta-analysis on research efforts that have targeted an evaluation of PBL methods, it is suggested that PBL approaches trump conventional methods when the goal is to expand the expertise of higher level learning (Gijbels and others, 2005).

Assessing learning in PBL and project-based activities follows the logic of other constructivist interventions, as students' self-reflective journals are an important vehicle for the assessment of individual learning (Honebein, 1996). Moreover, the nature of student learning on projects is likely to involve 'double loop' learning, as students not only learn specific elements of virtual project work but also learn about how their own behavioral tendencies are aids and hindrances to team effectiveness, and thus each project participant is encouraged to become a more reflective practitioner

(Argyris and Schon, 1974). These forms of student learning exist alongside but outside of any external appraisals of the quality of the project deliverables by internship project sponsors, faculty advisors, and other stakeholders in the project assignment. It is an axiom of project-based learning that individual or group learning may arise independently of any external appraisal of project technical or commercial success (DeFillippi et al., 2006). However, students report significantly greater development of meta-adaptive skills (e.g. learning to learn) than in conventional teaching designs (Lizzio and Wilson, 2004).

Helle et al. (2006) have examined the impact of project-based learning in post-secondary education based on a review of 22 articles published between 1966 and 2000. Of these articles, only two assessed learning outcomes from project-based learning. Barab et al. (2000) examined the learning of ten students in a project-based astronomy course to the previous year's astronomy course taught by the same teacher using a lecture method. The article reported that students in the project-based course performed better on questions requiring conceptual understanding. The second study was Fell (1999) and it involved a 360-degree evaluation of the learning by adult students in agricultural extension training. Results indicated that all respondents felt that work-based projects were one of the keys to successful completion of the course. The most frequently mentioned outcome was a gain in self-confidence.

Stewart (2007) investigated the link between self-directed learning readiness and project-based learning outcomes with a culturally diverse class of international Masters students in engineering management. Stewart posited that because project-based learning activities typically feature fewer structured learning activities and require more self-directed learning tasks, then those international students who are more predisposed to engage in self-directed learning (SDL) would be more able to benefit from project-based learning methods. In his questionnaire survey of 26 students (65 percent of class) completing an engineering management course, a linear regression analysis provided evidence that SDL readiness was a key enabler for achieving learning outcomes from project-based learning. In particular, having high self-management skills was shown to be the most significant and reliable predictor for achieving learning outcomes from project-based experiences.

Clearly these findings barely rise above the level of self-reports on practice, and further research is required to assess the learning benefits from project-based teaching methods. Van Noort and Romme (2005) suggest that conventional assessment methods, such as multiple-choice testing of pre-and post-course information, do not adequately assess the learning benefits from student engagement with the types of complex learning outcomes from solving the ill-structured problems typical in project-based learning. Therefore, they recommend alternative methods of assessment that make greater use of self and co-assessment (Dochy et al., 1999) and are grounded in a student-approved system for assessment from multiple assessor perspectives, including the academic supervisor, students, subject matter instructors, and the client-owner of the project problem (Muir, 1996).

Each stakeholder offers distinctive perspectives on project learning benefits according to assessment criteria appropriate to their stakeholder position. For example, the project client assesses the usefulness and relevance of the project findings and recommendations, the course instructor evaluates the project team's utilization of concepts and tools from the targeted subject matter, and the students assess the degree to which the project experience impacted their individual development. Also, team members evaluate each other's degree of cooperation and contribution in performing project work and serving as effective team members.

Assessing learning is most appropriately separated out from success on a specific product developed for the client. You could, for example, fail miserably on the development of the client product and yet learn a great deal. Although the novice learning facilitator might not see this distinction, it is important for educators to zero in on the actual learning achieved and not be overly influenced by the power of the final products delivered to the client.

In both PBL and project-based learning approaches it is important that faculty members assist learners to reflect on and draw learning from their experiences in the context of the problem/project. This activity, often referred to as 'decontextualizing' is vital as the learners need to test their ability to transfer the knowledge and skills gained via the problem/project work. The reason for placing some of this responsibility on the faculty is that, given a good problem/project design, the learners tend to get so thoroughly engaged in the process of working within the frame of the specific problem/project context, that they frequently lose sight of the greater learning significance. This reflective activity typically follows some form of individual assessment where learners are tasked with demonstrating an ability to transfer knowledge and skills gained via the problem/project into a new and unrelated context. The same learning outcomes targeted in the design of the problem/project remain as targets for the assessment activity. Successful completion of the problem/project assignment does not necessarily document individual learning across the targeted learning outcomes. Assessment devices for management education should mirror situations found in the practice of managing.

Four comprehensive reviews have assessed the effectiveness of problem-based learning in medical education (Albanese and Mitchell, 1993; Colliver, 2000; Dochy et al., 2003; Vernon and Blake, 1993). The results from these reviews suggest that there is a small but significantly positive effect of PBL on measures of medical student diagnostic ability. PBL interventions also appear to generate higher measures of student satisfaction (Norman and Schmidt, 2000). Most importantly, there is evidence that although students may acquire slightly less medical knowledge

that can be recalled in a standardized testing format, they remember more of the knowledge acquired for purposes of applying it in clinical practice through problem-based learning methods (Dochy et al., 2003).

This experience is matched by management education environments that use problem-based or project-based approaches where students who have learned knowledge and skills in practice tend to 'hit the ground running' when they are placed in real management situations. Because (as was mentioned above) the design of problems and projects follows a constructivist tradition and meets the requirements for being authentic, current, and engaging as stimulants for learning, the assessment of learning should also follow this rationale. Finally, the assessment provides an opportunity for the learners to demonstrate their newly gained knowledge and skills in the same way they learned them and in the same way they will be called to use them in genuine situations. Rarely does a business executive step into their office and find that a 'case for the day' has been placed on their desk. More typically, business leaders deal continuously with messy and often ambiguous problems and projects that demand a full integration of their business knowledge and skills.

Evaluation of problem-based and project-based learning methods can also be illuminated by inspecting best practices. Although there are many educators carrying the banner of problem-based and project-based approaches to management education, there are fewer business schools using these approaches on a broader programmatic level. At the program level, it is possible to identify some best practices in problem- and project-based learning. A best practice example in the use of PBL approaches on a total program level in management education is the Faculty of Economics and Business Administration at Maastricht University, which has been a leader for over 20 years. A best practice example in the use of project-based learning is the Carey Business School at Johns Hopkins University, which has developed a client-based approach to learning in several of the MBA programs including the innovative MBA Fellows program. These two examples do not reflect the full scope and variety of problem/project-based methods but do represent two institutions that have placed a premium on learner-centered approaches to management education and have a solid core of faculty who subscribe to and act on the principles demonstrated in this chapter.

## CRITICISMS OF PBL AND PROJECT-BASED LEARNING APPROACHES

In the above section we reviewed the important element of assessing learning that results from the activities involved in PBL and project-based learning approaches. In this section we turn our attention to some criticisms that have been directed toward PBL and project-based learning approaches. Because of its wide application in a variety of management education settings, project-based learning has become subject to post-modernist criticism. Garrick and Clegg (2001) worry that project-based learning focuses too much on the instrumental and performative elements of project work and in the process undermines the more emancipatory elements of authentic learning. Rhodes and Garrick (2003) build on this earlier critique and extend their concern to the instrumental focus of project-based learning interventions on measurable outcomes based upon cognitive psychology and positivist methodology. They raise important questions that suggest a more critical perspective on project-based learning:

1 Why are we doing this project?
2 Do we understand the project's unintended consequences?
3 Does our project view people merely as resources to achieve corporately defined ends?
4 To what extent do educators account for the way that the (project) attempt(s) to exert control over people's subjectivity?
5 How does this project affect what I do and who I am? How much freedom do I and others have to be active in constructing our own subjectivities?

6 What are the ethical dimensions and consequences of our actions?

In response to the first critical question of why are we doing this project, Heitman (1996) identifies four primary project learning motives: professional, humanitarian, critical thinking, and subject matter understanding. Different stakeholders in the educational marketplace may produce different subsets of these motives, and some recent criticisms of project-based learning are concerned that professional socialization motivations may be taking a dominant position in universities relative to the goals of fostering critical thinking, humanitarian service goals, or deeper understanding of a discipline or practice (Garrick and Clegg, 2001; Rhodes and Garrick, 2003). Our experience with different business school programs utilizing project learning suggests that there is a lively interplay between the achievements of multiple purposes from project-based learning in higher education. Thus, the relative priority placed upon each of the professional, critical, humanitarian, or subject matter mastery learning purposes is a contested terrain where different institutions and even different educators within the same institution are likely to enact different priorities and trade-offs in implementing project-based learning purposes.

Rhodes and Garrick raise important critical issues facing the application of project-based learning methods to management education. Without downplaying the importance of these concerns, it may be reassuring to revisit several of the intellectual foundations of project-based learning, whose practice can help mitigate the performative risks suggested by critical theorists its critics. First, project-based learning is not solely based on individualistic cognitive perspective. Indeed, it is fair to characterize project-based learning as having a deep foundation in constructivist theories that emphasize self-defined learning as a critical goal of project-based teaching methodologies (Rungtusanatham et al., 2004). Moreover the strong self-reflective component of most project-based learning methods provides a safeguard against student participants losing control over their subjectivity.

The ethical dimension of project-based learning has always been a component of enlightened learning design. Service learning projects that benefit decidedly non-corporatist interests are a leading form of project-based learning opportunities in universities and such projects are now being applied to a wide range of management education audiences (Dumas, 2002). McCarthy, Tucker, and Dean (2002) assert that service learning projects often have a strong civic engagement component that can empower student project participants and their community clientele. These socially responsible service-based learning projects, while originating in US educational practice, are now beginning to spread into European management educational settings (Voort, 2003).

## SIMILARITIES AND DIFFERENCES

As suggested previously, problem and project-based learning approaches have much in common. In both cases, education is learner-centered rather than teacher-directed. The role of the problem-based or project-based instructor is more focused on providing facilitation and social and technical support than explicit direction or knowledge transfer. In both problem-based and project-based approaches the nature of the context should be: (1) authentic; (2) current; and (3) engaging. Authentic means that the problem/project represents in a genuine fashion the type of issue that would be faced by a manager or business leader. Current means that the problem/project is appropriate to the present day business environment, not a case study with archival history. Engaging means that there is relevance to the learner and that the learner can derive some intrinsic motivation for their work in that environment. Although it may be more pronounced in project-based approaches, · problems in both problem and project-based environments often entail a multidisciplinary design. Management issues rarely present

themselves in neatly defined packages sorted by discipline. The demands and challenges of the problem or project are the ultimate driver for student self-organizing and self-direction. However, there are a few systematic differences worth noting between problem-based and project-based learning approaches.

Problem-based learning applications tend to employ instructor-designed or instructor-selected problems whose content is selected by the instructor to provide a specific type of learning opportunity for the student population. Hence, problem-based learning interventions have a quality of standardization that allows them to be employed with relatively larger numbers of learners, and these problems can be re-used over time. Additionally, because these learning assignments are selected and controlled by the instructor, these assignments may be customized to fit many types of learners, ranging from first year undergraduates to full time master's level to experienced practitioners and executives. It is the instructor control over task assignment that allows for a matching of the complexity and content of the assigned problem to the backgrounds and course content objectives of the targeted classroom audience. Lastly, the utilization of instructor designed and selected problems allows for the development of a rich tool kit of problem assignments, supporting materials, and teaching protocols that can be elaborated and refined with each re-use of the same set of problem-based teaching tools.

By way of contrast, the project-based learning intervention more typically requires a negotiation of the learning assignment (project goals and deliverables) between the individual student or team of students and their project sponsor or client. The role of the instructor in these project-based interventions is typically to mediate between the student project participants and the project client or sponsor. The client/sponsor is typically a real-world organization that is making available at least limited access to its data, people, and support resources in return for a set of deliverables (typically a written report and oral presentation of findings) that they negotiate with the project team. Within project-based learning interventions, the actual negotiation of project deliverables is considered a valuable learning opportunity for the project participants, and the skills of self-presentation and negotiation are sometimes explicitly reviewed and taught in a classroom setting prior to the student's engagement with a project client or sponsor (Fleenor et al., 2005).

Because project-based learning applications typically include client negotiations over project deliverables and project presentations to external clients or project sponsors, such project-based practices are typically limited to upper level undergraduate or postgraduate (master's level) students, who have sufficient interpersonal maturity and communications skills to interact productively with their project clients or sponsors. Where less experienced undergraduates engage in such project assignments, the role of the instructor may include more direct mediation with the project client and the active coaching and supervision of the written report preparations and rehearsing of student oral presentations prior to their delivery to a client or sponsor audience.

## NEW ROLES FOR NEW CHALLENGES

Problem- and project-based learning perspectives are confronting both students and faculty instructors with new roles and new challenges. Students face the challenge of having to play multiple roles in problem- or project-based learning contexts. Johnston (2005) suggests that students engaged in project learning must learn to play the roles of ready learner, coach, contributor, team member, and academic scholar, and each of these roles pose complementary challenges for their faculty instructor.

As a ready learner, students must learn to develop realistic expectations of how their current skills and experiences match up with the requirements of the problem or project assignment, which may have much less of the structure and much more ambiguity in performance requirements than they have experienced in traditional classroom settings. The project instructor thus plays a complementary role of helping students' transition into a less structured learning environment.

As coach, students must learn to engage in dialogue as a co-inquirer and co-learner with their teacher, who plays the role of coach rather than the more traditional role of disseminator of information. See Clutterbuck's Chapter 25 in this volume for further details on coaching in management development.

As contributor, students must learn to make contributions not only to task accomplishment but also to each other's learning. The processes of reflection that are part of most project- or problem-based learning activities are intended to reinforce this role, and faculty may also encourage such reflection through their own demonstration of reflective practices and values.

As team member, students must learn how to work effectively in teams. A major challenge with today's teamwork is the increasing diversity of students now attending institutions of higher learning. This diversity provides a much greater opportunity for students to learn how different cultural and national experiences may impact one's approach to teamwork and project task assignments. However, these same opportunities also pose a new set of challenges to the project team facing near term time pressures for accomplishment of required tasks. Consequently, teachers can help students by serving as process facilitators as they work through some of the conflicts and frustrations that arise during team-based problem/project work.

Finally, in their roles as academic scholars, students must learn how their project work can be a means to apply concepts and tools learned in their academic course work. It is this application of knowledge to action that makes both problem- and project-based learning so important to professional development.

## CONCLUSION: PBL AND PROJECT-BASED LEARNING FOR THE 21ST CENTURY

Problem and project-based learning is also being transformed by the advent of new online and distance learning tools and practices. Discussion, collaboration, and learning communities via online interaction are the new elements of problem- and project-based e-learning interventions (Lou and MacGregor, 2006). The online discussion board is becoming the cyber-place where problem- and project-based learning is recorded and reflected upon (Milter, 2003). Some benefits of asynchronous threaded discussion include: accommodating geographically distant learners (Ahern and El-Hindi, 2000), providing added time for reflection (Arbaugh and Duray, 2002), developing through online interactions a learner's social negotiation skills (Harman and Koohang, 2005), and creating transparent group deliberations for all participants to see (Schwartzman, 2006). Additional insights on the role of learning and web-based instruction are available in Chapter 12 by Arbaugh and Warell this volume.

The higher education marketplace has become much more competitive with students having an abundance of performance information and rapid changes in educational patterns: more part-time students, mature students and students with varied backgrounds, the new developments in e-learning and increasingly sophisticated learning technologies, and new trends influence the university education systems. Technology is the key factor: triggering the changes in education. In both education and training there is a shift, which offers flexibility in relation to time, pace of entry and exit. E-learning and Internet are seen as ideal media to create a global village (Miller, 1996).

Ohio University has been a leader in utilizing as an educational tool Second Life, which is an Internet-based virtual world launched in 2003, developed by Linden Research, Inc (commonly referred to as Linden Lab), that came to international attention via mainstream

news media in late 2006 and early 2007. Ohio University was one of only a few other universities – Harvard among them – to offer experiences beyond the classroom. Recently more than 300 universities, including Harvard and Duke, are using Second Life as an educational tool. Some educators conduct entire distance-learning courses there; others supplement classes. With the online Second Life software the users are able to explore, build, collaborate, learn, trade, and participate in activities as part of a virtual society. Users act in Second Life as they would in the real world. Ohio University Without Boundaries (OUWB) is researching the effectiveness of virtual technology in education. According to Christopher Keesey, OUWB project manager, Ohio University is unique in its approach: 'We're not just moving the classroom into Second Life. We're innovating learning beyond what's already going on in the classroom with educational games, learning kiosks, student organizations, and arts experiences,' he said. At Ohio University, users create avatars—images of characters they can use to move around and interact with other users.

PBL and Project-Based Learning oriented courses can be enhanced with e-learning and Second Life Education learning tools (Land and Greene, 2000). Colleges are adopting new technologies and their application to learning to help them improve productivity, manage planned growth, and help reconstruct the curriculum. Universities need to change to accommodate the impact of technology on learning and the emerging sensibilities of the millennium generation, which is more mobile, technology savvy and electronic social network oriented than many of their predecessor learning cohorts (Falvo and Pastore, 2005).

The near future promises to be as unpredictable as the near past. This requires educators to continuously tap into the trend lines to gauge the requisite knowledge and skill sets to meet the future challenges of business organizations. True, some static knowledge and age-old remedies may remain useful into that uncertain future. But the dynamic nature of most industries today demands that business leaders constantly seek to upgrade their professional tool kits. Like business leaders, management educators should continuously seek appropriate environments and methods for learning. Many techniques and methods are suggested or referenced in this book, and their use can be integrated with the practices and tools described in this chapter.

# REFERENCES

Adderley, K., Askurin, C., Bradbury, P., Freeman J., Goodlad, S., Greene, J., Jenkins, D., Rae, J. and Uren, O. (1975) *Project Methods in Higher Education.* SRHE working party in teaching methods. Techniques group. Guildford, Surrey, Society for Research into Higher Education.

Adams, S.M. and Zanzi, A. (2004) 'Academic development for careers in management consulting', *Career Developmental International*, 9 (6): 559–77.

Ahern, T.C. and El-Hindi, A.E. (2000) 'Improving the instructional congruency of a computer-mediated small-group discussion: A case study in design and delivery', *Journal of Research on Computing in Education*, 32: 385–400.

Albanese, M.A. and Mitchell, S. (1993) 'Problem-based learning: A review of literature on its outcomes and implementation issues', *Academic Medicine*, 68: 52–81.

Arbaugh, J.B. and Duray, R. (2002) 'Technological and structural characteristics, student learning and satisfaction with web-based courses: An exploratory study of two on-line MBA programs', *Management Learning*, 33 (3): 331–48.

Argyris, C. and Schon, D.A. (1974) *Theory to Practice: Increasing Professional Effectiveness.* San Francisco, CA: Jossey-Bass.

Argyris, C. and Schon, D.A. (1978) *Organizational Learning: A Theory of Action Perspective.* Reading: MA: Addison-Wesley.

Ayas, K. and Zeniuk, N. (2001) 'Project-based learning: Building communities of reflective practitioners', *Management Learning*, 32 (1): 61–76.

Ayas, K. and Mirvis, P. (2005) 'Educating managers through service learning projects', in C. Wankel and R. DeFillippi (eds), *Educating Managers Through Real World Projects*. Greenwich CT: Information Age Publishing. pp. 93–114.

Barab, S.A., Hay, K.E., Squire, K., Barnett, M., Schmidt, R., Karrigan, K. Yamagata-Lynch, L.,

and Johanson, C. (2000) 'Virtual solar system project: Learning through a technology-rich, inquiry-based, participatory learning environment', *Journal of Science Education and Technology*, 9 (1): 7–25.

Barrows, H.S. (1983) 'Problem-based, self-directed learnings', *Journal of the American Medical Association*, Vol. 250: 3077–80.

Barrows, H.S. (1985) *How to Design a Problem-based Curriculum for the Preclinical Years.* New York: Springer Publishers.

Barrows, H.S. and Tamblyn, R.M. (1976) 'An evaluation of problem-based learning in small groups utilizing simulated patient', *Journal of Medical Education*, 51: 52–6.

Barsky, N.P., Catanach, A.H. and Stout, D. (2003) 'A PBL framework for introductory management accounting', in A. Bentzen-Bilkvist, W. Gijselaers, and R. Milter (eds), *Educating Knowledge Workers for Corporate Leadership: Learning into the Future*, Dordrecht: Kluwer Academic Publishers. Vol. 7: pp. 3–19.

Blumenfeld, P.C., Soloway, E., Marx, R.W., Krajcik, J.S., Guzdial, M. and Palincsar, A. (1991) 'Motivating project-based learning: Sustaining the doing, supporting the learning', *Educational Psychologist*, 26: 369–98.

Boud, D. (1985) 'Problem-based learning in perspective', in D. Boud (ed.), *Problem-based Learning in Education for the Professions*. Sydney: HIgher Education and Development Society of Australia.

Boud, D. and Feletti, G. (eds) (1991) *The Challenge of Problem-Based Learning.* New York: St. Martin's Press.

Brace-Govan, J. and Powell, I. (2005) 'Real world transfer of professional knowledge: A modification to internship learning', in C. Wankel and R. DeFillippi (eds), *Educating Managers through Real World Projects*. Greenwich CT: Information Age Publishing. pp. 144–7.

Brassington, F. and Smith, A. (2000) 'Competitions and problem-based learning: The effect of an externally set competition on a cross-curricular project in marketing and design', in L. Borghans, W. Gijselaers, R. Milter and J. Stinson (eds), *Business Education for the Changing Workplace*, Vol. 5. Dordrecht: Kluwer Academic Publishers. pp. 187–208.

Clark, L.J. (2001) 'Web-based teaching: A new educational paradigm', *Intercom*, 48, 20–3.

Clifford, P.G., Farran, J.H and Lodish, L (2005) 'Wharton's global consulting practicum: Interdependence, ambiguity and reflection', in C. Wankel and R. DeFillippi (eds), *Educating Managers through Real World Projects*. Greenwich CT: Information Age Publishing. pp. 3–24.

Colliver, J. (2000) 'Effectives of problem based learning curricula', *Academic Medicine*, *75*: 259–66.

Coghlan, D. (2001) 'Insider action research projects: Implications for Practising Managers', *Management Learning*, 32 (1): 49–60.

Coombs, G. and Yost, E. (2004) 'Teaching international business through international student consulting project', in C. Wankel and R. DeFillippi (eds), *The Cutting Edge of International Management Education*. Greenwich CT: Information Age Publishing. pp. 285–305.

Day, W.A. and Stinson, J.E. (1990) 'Educating tomorrow's managers through integrated contextual learning', *Professions Education Researcher Notes*, 1990.

Dede, C. (1996) 'Emerging technologies and distributed learning', *American Journal of Distance Education*, 10 (2): 4–36.

DeFillippi, R.J. (2001) 'Introduction: Project-based learning, reflective practices and learning outcomes', *Management Learning*, 32 (1): 5–10.

DeFillippi, R., and Ornstein, S. (2003) 'Psychological perspectives underlying theories of organizational learning', in M. Easterby-Smith and M. Lyles, *Handbook of Organizational Learning and Knowledge*. Oxford, UK: Blackwell Press. pp. 19–37.

DeFillippi, R. and Wankel, C. (2005) 'Real world projects and project-based learning pedagogies', in C. Wankel and R. DeFillippi (eds), *Educating Managers through Real World Projects*. Greenwich CT: Information Age Publishing. pp. xi–xxiv.

DeFillippi, R., Arthur, M.B. and Lindsay, V. (2006) *Knowledge At Work: Creative Collaboration in the Global Economy*. Oxford, UK: Blackwell Publishers.

De Graff, E. and Kolmos, A. (2006) *Implementing Change in PBL*. The Netherlands: Sense Publishers.

Dewey, J. (1933) *How We Think*. Chicago: Regenery.

Dickie, L. (1999) 'The problem-based learning: The Rubik's cube of experimental inquiry. *10th PBL Conference*, Curtin University of Technology, Australia.

Dochy F., Segers M. and Buehl M. (1999) 'The relation between assessment practices and outcomes of studies: The case of research on prior knowledge', *Review of Educational Research*, 69 (2): 147–88

Dochy, F., Segers, M., Van den Bossche, P. and Gijbels, D. (2003) 'Effect of problem based learning: a meta-analysis', *Learning and Instruction*, 13 (5): 533–68.

Duffy, T.M. and Jonassen, D.H. (1991) 'Constuctivism: New implications for instructional technology', *Educational Technology*, 21 (5): 7–12.

Dumas, C. (2002) 'Community-based service-learning: Does it have a role in management education', *International Journal of Value-Based Management*, 15 (3): 249–64.

Falvo, D. and Pastore, R. (2005) 'Exploring the relationship between learning styles and technological collaborations', in C. Crawford et al. (eds), *Proceedings of Society for Information Technology and Teacher Education International Conference 2005*. Chesapeake, VA: AACE. pp. 3167–72

Fell, R.F. (1999) 'Adult learning and action learning – A real workplace learning approach', *Journal of Agricultural Education and Extension*, 6 (2): 73–82.

Flavell, J.H. (1976) 'Metacognitive aspects of problem solving', in L.B. Resnick (ed.), *The Nature of Intelligence*. Hillsdale, NJ: Erlbaum. pp. 231–5.

Fleenor, C.P., Raven, P.V. and Ralston, J. (2005) 'Project-based International Business Consulting', in C. Wankel and R. DeFillippi (eds), *Educating Managers through Real World Projects*. Greenwich CT: Information Age Publishing. pp. 25–46.

Fornaciari, C.K. and Kenworthy-U'Ren, A.L. (2007) Special issue: 'A "How-To" issue on service-learning in management education', *Journal of Management Education*, *31*: 859.

Forsythe, F.P. (2002) 'The role of problem based learning and technology support in a spoon-fed undergraduate environment', in T. Johannessen, A. Pedersen, and K. Petersen (eds), *Teaching Today the Knowledge of Tomorrow*, Vol. 6. pp. 147–61.

Garrick, J. and Clegg, S. (2001) 'Stressed-out knowledge workers in performative times: A postmodern take on project-based learning', *Management Learning*, 32 (1): 119–34.

Gijbels, D., Dochy, F., Van den Bossche, P. and Segers, M. (2005) 'Effects of problem-based learning: A meta-analysis from the angle of assessment', *Review of Educational Research*, 75 (1): 27–61.

Gijselaers, W.H (1996) 'Connecting problem-based practices with educational theory', in L. Wilkerson and W.H Gijselaers (eds), *Bringing Problem-Based Learning to Higher Education: Theory and Practice*. San Francisco: Jossey-Bass.

Gijselaers, W. (1995) 'Perspectives on problem-based learning', in W. Gijselaers, D. Tempelaar, P. Keizer, J. Blommaert, E. Bernard, and H. Kasper (eds), *Educational Innovations in Economics and Business Administration: The Case of Problem-Based Learning*. Dordecht: Kluwer Academic Publishers. pp. 39–52.

Godfrey, P.C. and Grasso, E.T. (2000) *Working for the Common Good: Concepts and Models for Service-Learning in Management*. Herndon, VA: Stylus Publishing.

Hallinger, P. and Bridges, E. (2007) *A Problem-based Approach for Management Education: Preparing Managers for Action*. New York: Springer Publishing.

Handy, C. (1995) 'Managing the dream', in S. Chawla and J. Renesch (eds), *Learning Organizations: Developing Cultures for Tomorrow's Workplace*. Portland, OR: Productivity Press. pp. 44–55.

Harman, K. and Koohang, A. (2005) 'Discussion board: A learning objective', *Interdisciplinary Journal of Knowledge and Learning Objects*, 1: 67–77.

Heitman, G. (1996) 'Project-oriented study and project-organized curricula: A brief review of intentions and solutions', *European Journal of Engineering Education*, 21: 121–32.

Helle, L., Tynjala, P. and Olkinuora, E. (2006) 'Project-based learning in post-secondary education-theory, practice and rubber sling shots', *Higher Education*, 51: 287–314.

Honebein, P.C. (1996) 'Seven goals for the design of constructivist learning environments', in B.G. Wilson (ed.), *Constructivist Learning Environments: Case Studies in Instructional Design*. Englewood Cliffs, NJ: Educational Technology Publications. pp. 11–24.

Johnston, T.C. (2005) 'The role of the student in project learning', in C. Wankel and R. DeFillippi (eds), *Educating Managers through Real World Projects*. Greenwich CT: Information Age Publishing. pp. 333–58.

Kendall, J.C. and Associates (eds) (1990) *Combining Service and Learning: A Resource Book for Community and Public Service*. Raleigh, NC: National Society for Internships and Experiential Education. pp. 1–33.

Kolb, D.A. (1984) *Experiential Learning as the Source of Learning and Development*. Englewood Cliffs, NJ: Prentice-Hall.

Land, S.M. and Greene, B.A. (2000) 'Project-based learning with the world wide web: A qualitative study of resource integration', *Educational Technology Research and Development*, 48 (1): 45–68.

Leidner, D.E. and Jarvenpaa, S.L. (1995) 'The use of information technology to enhance management school education: A theoretical view', *MIS Quarterly*, 19 (3): 265–91.

Lewin, K. (1946) 'Action research and minority problems', *Journal of Social Issues*, 2 (4): 34–46.

Lizzio, A. and Wilson, K. (2004) 'Action learning in higher education: An investigation of its potential to develop professional capability', *Studies in Higher Education*, 29 (4): 469–88.

Lou, Y. and MacGregor, S.K. (2006) 'Enhancing project-based learning through online between-group collaboration', *Educational Research and Evaluation*, 10 (4–6): 419–44.

McCarthy, A., Tucker, M.L. and Dean, K.L. (2002) 'Service-learning: Creating community', in C. Wankel, and R. DeFillippi (eds), *Rethinking Management Education for the 21st Century*. Greenwich, CT: Information Age Publishing. pp. 63–88.

MacGregor, S.K. (2005) 'Online project-based learning: How collaborative strategies and problem solving processes impact performance', *Journal of Interactive Learning Research*, 16 (1): 83–107.

Mezirow, J. (1991) *Transformative Dimensions of Adult Learning*. San Francisco: Jossey-Bass.

Miller, S. (1996) *Civilizing Cyberspace: Policy, Power and the Information Superhighway*. ACM Press.

Milter, R.G. (2002) 'Developing an MBA online degree program: Expanding knowledge and skills via technology-mediated learning communities', in P. Comeaux (ed.) *Communication and Collaboration in the Online Classroom: Examples and Applications*, Bolton, MA: Jossey-Bass, Anker Publishing. pp. 3–22.

Milter, R.G. (2003) 'Developing learning communities via asynchronous collaborative platforms', *Proceedings of the E-Learn 2003 World Conference on E-Learning in Corporate, Government, Healthcare, and Higher Education*, Phoenix, AZ, November 7–11. pp. 649–51.

Milter, R.G. and Stinson, J.E. (1995) 'Educating leaders for the new competitive environment', in W. Gijselaers, D. Tempelaar, P. Keizer, J. Blommaert, E. Bernard, and H. Kasper (eds), *Educational Innovation in Economics and Business Administration: The Case of Problem-Based Learning*. Norwell, MA: Kluwer Academic Publishers. pp. 30–8.

Morgan, A. (1983) 'Theoretical aspects of project-based learning in higher education', *British Journal of Educational Technology*, 14 (1): 66–78.

Morgan, A. (1987) 'Project work in open learning', in M. Thorpe and D. Grugeon (eds), *Open Learning for Adults*. Harlow, London: Longman. pp. 245–51.

Muir, C. (1996) 'Using consulting projects to teach critical-thinking skills in the business communication', *Business Communication Quarterly*, 59 (4): 77–88.

Norman, G.R. and Schmidt, H.G. (2000) 'Effectivness of problem-based learning curricula: Theory, practice and paper darts', *Medical Education*, 34: 721–28.

Papastergiou, M. (2006) 'Course management systems as tools for the creation of online learning environments: Evaluation from a social constructivist perspective and implications for their design', *International Journal of E-Learning*, 5 (4): 593–623.

Perotti, V.S., Gunn, P.C., Day, J.C. and Coombs, G. (1998) 'Business 20/20: Ohio University's Integrated Business Core', in R.G. Milter, J.E. Stinson and W.H. Gijselaers (eds), *Educational Innovation in*

*Economics and Business III: Innovative Practices in Business Education.* Dordrecht: Kluwer Academic Publishers. pp. 169–88.

Perret-Clermont, A.N. (1993) 'What is it that develops?' *Cognition and Instruction, 11:* 197–205.

Poole, D.M. (2000) 'Student participation in a discussion-oriented online course: A case study', *Journal of Research on Computing in Education, 33:* 162–77.

Raelin, J.A. (2000) *'Work-Based Learning: The New Frontier of Management Development.* New Jersey: Prentice-Hall.

Revans, R.W. (1982) *The Origin and Growth of Action Learning.* Brickley, UK: Chartwell-Bratt.

Revans, R.W. (1998) 'Sketches of action learning', *Performance Improvement Quarterly,* 11 (1): 23–7.

Rhodes, C. and Garrick, J. (2003) 'Project-based learning and the limits of corporate knowledge', *Journal of Management Education,* 27 (4): 447–71.

Rickards, T., Hyde, P.J. and Papamichail, K.N (2005) 'The Manchester method: A critical review of a learning experiment', in C. Wankel and R. DeFillippi (eds), *Educating Managers through Real World Projects.* Greenwich CT: Information Age Publishing. pp. 241–54.

Rungtusanatham, M., Ellram, L., Siferd, S. and Salik, S. (2004) 'Toward a typology of business education in the Internet age', Decision Sciences. *Journal of Innovative Education,* 2 (2): 101–20.

Savery, J.R. and Duffy, T.M. (1995) 'Problem-based learning: An instructional model and its constructivist framework', *Educational Technology, 35:* 31–8.

Schön, D.A. (1983) *The Reflective Practitioner: How Professionals Think in Action.* New York: Basic Books, HarperCollins Publishers.

Schmidt, H.G. (1983) 'Problem-based learning: Rationale and description', *Medical Education, 17:* 11–16.

Smith, P.A.C. (2001) 'Action learning and reflective practice in project environments that are related to leadership development', *Management Learning,* 32 (1): 31–48.

Smith, G.F. (2005) 'Problem-based learning: Can it improve managerial thinking?' *Journal of Management Education,* 29 (2): 357–78.

Smith, B. and Dodds, R. (1997) *Developing Managers through Project-Based Learning.* Aldershot/Vermont: Gower.

Soderlund, M. (1998) 'Problem-based learning, interpersonal orientations and learning approaches: An empirical examination of a business education program', in D. Tempelaar, F. Wiedersheim-Paul and E. Gunnarsson (eds), *In Search of Quality.* Educational Innovation in Economics and Business II, Dordrecht: Kluwer Academic Publishers. Vol. 2. pp. 155–70.

Spiro, R.J., Coulson, R.L., Feltovich, P.J. and Anderson, D.K. (1988) 'Cognitive flexibility: Advanced knowledge acquisition in ill-structured domains', *Proceedings of the Tenth Annual Conference of the Cognitive Science Society.* Hillsdale, NJ: Erlbaum.

Stewart, R.A. (2007) 'Investigating the link between self-directed learning readiness and project-based learning outcomes: The case of international Masters students in an engineering management course', *European Journal of Engineering Education,* 32 (4): 453–65.

Stinson, John E. (1990) 'Integrated contextual learning: Situated learning in the business profession', *American Education Research Association,* April 16, ED 319 330.

Stinson, J.E. and Milter, R.G. (1996) 'Problem-based learning in business education: Curriculum design and implementation issues', in W. Gijselaers and L. Wilkerson (eds), *New Directions in Teaching and Learning in Higher Education.* San Francisco, CA: Jossey-Bass, *68:* 33–42.

Schwartzman, R. (2006) 'Virtual group problem solving in the basic communication course: Lessons for online learning', *Journal of Instructional Psychology,* 33 (1): 3+.

Thomas, J.W., Mergendoller, J.R. and Michaelson, A. (1999) *Project-based Learning: A Handbook for Middle and High School Teachers.* Novato, CA: The Buck Institute for Education.

Thompson, K.J. and Bleak, J. (2007) 'The leadership book: Enhancing the theory-practice connection through project-based learning', *Journal of Management Education,* 31 (2): 278–91.

Van Doorn, M. and Milter, R.G. (2005) 'Adapting a face-to-face training program to a distance delivery model: A case study of a professional training program', in R.G. Milter, V.S. Perotti and M.R. Segers (eds). *Educational Innovation in Economics and Business IX: Breaking Boundaries for Global Learning.* Berlin: Springer: Science + Business Media. pp. 221–36.

Van Noort, M. and Romme, G. (2005) 'Assessing performance in projects from different angles', in C. Wankel and R. DeFillippi (eds), *Educating Managers through Real World Projects.* Greenwich CT: Information Age Publishing. pp. 359–63.

Vernon, D.T.A. and Blake, R.L. (1993) 'Does problem-based learning work? A meta-analysis of evaluative research', *Academic Medicine,* 550–63.

Voort, J.M. van der (2003) *Integrating Service Learning into the Business Curriculum.* Rotterdam: Rotterdam School of Management.

Waddill, D.D. (2006) 'Action E-Learning: An exploratory case study of action learning applied online', *Human Resource Development International,* 9 (2): 1–15.

Wegner, E. (1998) *Communities of Practice: Learning, Meaning, and Identity.* Cambridge, UK: Cambridge University Press.

Yorks, L. (2005) 'Action learning as a vehicle for management development and organizational learning: Empirical patterns from practice and theoretical implications', in C. Wankel and R. DeFillippi (eds), *Educating Managers Through Real World*

*Projects.* Greenwich, CT: Information Age Publishing. pp. 183–12.

Yost, E.B. and Keifer, J.L. (1998) 'Application of problem-based learning pedagogy to management education', in R. Milter, J. Stinson, and W. Gijselaers (eds), *Innovative Practices in Business Education,* Dordrecht: Kluwer Academic Publishers. Vol. 3. pp. 283–99.

# 19

# Assessment and Accreditation in Business Schools

Robert S. Rubin and Kathryn Martell

## Abstract

Business school mission statements routinely purport to promote some form of learning. Indeed, for most business schools, few issues are more mission-critical than the inculcation of competencies most important for the practice of management. Despite this significance, systematic efforts to demonstrate student acquisition of such knowledge and skill are not universally practiced. With increasing pressure for accountability from a multitude of stakeholders, business schools are being challenged to provide direct and systematic evidence of student learning. This chapter is intended to synthesize and augment knowledge of formal assessment practices within business schools and its role in the accreditation process. Specifically, current requirements and evidence to demonstrate student learning towards accreditation by the AACSB (Association to Advance Collegiate Schools of Business) are presented. In addition, the chapter details prevailing best-practices in assessment and discusses many of the perils often encountered along the way.

In the past few decades, higher education has been increasingly scrutinized by multiple stakeholders calling for improved accountability regarding the quality of education provided. Indeed, governments, students, accrediting bodies and the media to name a few are taking institutions to task for their inability to derive critical evidence indicative of educational achievement (Cabrera, Colbeck & Terenzini, 2001). Institutions have responded by attempting to develop measurements to capture the now well-known academic tripartite of research, service and teaching. Not surprisingly, of these major educational domains, institutions receive perhaps the most inquiries regarding their teaching and learning practices (Cabrera et al., 2001). Logically, external stakeholders peering into the ivory tower are concerned about what is in their view, the key role of the university: produce students who are more capable going out than they were coming in. Undeniably, stakeholders desire some assurance that their educational investment will provide the espoused returns institutions claim and are increasingly less willing to rely on vague promises of achievement and quality.

To date, however, many institutions have been rather reluctant to allow such external examinations of the sort being requested, choosing rather to rely on proxies (e.g., reputation, acceptance ratios, proportion of faculty with Ph.D.s etc.) as indicators of educational value. Such alterative measures are now being called into question. For example, in a controversial 2006 report commissioned by the United States Secretary of Education Margaret Spellings, the commission notes, 'There is inadequate transparency and accountability for measuring institutional performance, which is more and more necessary to maintaining public trust in higher education' (U.S. Department of Education, 2006: 13). Accordingly, the commission's recommendations call for an overhaul of an institutional system that is primarily reputation-based to one that is performance-based. This would include, for instance, a 'consumer-friendly information database ... to enable students, parents, policymakers and others to weigh and rank comparative institutions' (p. 20). Comprising such a system would be data obtained from national standardized college learning tests to allow for comparability across universities. True to the commission's goals, major efforts are underway in the United States to create a national standardized college learning assessment (Kingsbury, 2007). Such trends and actions are creating considerable tension among institutional administrators and faculty who argue passionately for a continued system of independence from government oversight but also recognize the social and economic realities at play. In all, these trends are likely to continue and will have considerable impact on institutions' ability to survive and thrive (Cabrera et al., 2001).

In response to the escalation for accountability, accrediting bodies are contemporaneously increasing pressure for universities to provide greater assurance of learning. Collegiate schools of business and their respective accrediting bodies have by no means been immune to these broader accountability trends. Perhaps no other institution has had a greater influence on the practice of learning assessment in business schools than the premier accrediting body, the Association for the Advancement of Collegiate Schools of Business (AACSB). The AACSB publishes a set of standards according to a minimum threshold concept. That is, they set out standards of which schools must demonstrate their minimal achievement. It does not establish a system of ranking or 'aspirational' standards, leaving schools to define their own standards of quality. Though these standards used to be quite broad, consistent with the broader trends, the most recent standards require institutions to complete assurance of learning measures that determine *direct* educational achievement (Thompson, 2004). Thus, institutions who state that they train certain managerial capabilities must present primary evidence that those skills have indeed been learned. As such, schools of business are being asked more and more to provide *prima facie* evidence of success.

With the above background in mind, the purpose of the present chapter is three-fold. First, we sought to briefly discuss the trends in management education leading to increased calls for learning assessment. Second, we provide an explication of the nature of accreditation standards and their associated requirements regarding assessment. Third, we sought to clarify methods for accomplishing assessment on programmatic level in schools of business, highlighting common traps along the way. In all, the chapter is an attempt to provide the reader with information that can be useful in understanding and applying learning assessment techniques in a dynamic institutional environment.

## ACCOUNTABILITY IN SCHOOLS OF BUSINESS

Opportunities to systematically acquire managerial competencies are usually quite limited.

In most organizations, 70–90 percent of management learning occurs through informal work experiences, training and mentoring (Pfeffer & Sutton, 2000; Tannenbaum, 1997). Although it should be noted that trial and error and informal experiences are effective, they tend to be somewhat inefficient means that require substantial investments, multiple years and ability to synthesize unsystematic learning (Rubin, Baldwin & Bommer, 2002). With such limited access to systematic development, individuals hoping to acquire capabilities more efficiently are increasingly relying on university-based management education. The steady rise in graduate management education degrees awarded annually is quite reflective of this trend (Pfeffer & Fong, 2002).

The extraordinary growth in management education in the last few decades has had the added benefit for business schools of increased economic prosperity (Pfeffer & Fong, 2002). Indeed, as of the year 2000, 341 accredited schools of business offered graduate degrees in management representing well over 100,000 degrees awarded each year (Pfeffer & Fong, 2002). Needless to say, graduate management education is big business. Despite the rapid growth of business schools and the large numbers of newly minted MBAs produced yearly, the perceived value in the workplace of the MBA as a differentiating factor in managerial success remains high. In a recent survey (GMAC, 2006), corporate recruiters ($n = 1{,}270$) indicated that 40 percent of all new hires in 2005 held MBA degrees. In addition, these recruiters indicated that they would provide additional compensation and benefits to their MBA hires in the future and that starting salaries would continue to rise at a faster pace than non-MBA recruits. In all, individuals and organizations alike are increasingly turning to, and relying on, the business school market-place for management skills and education. Such reliance on universities for broad managerial training is in part a mark of success in the long progression toward the professionalization of the management discipline (Porter & McKibbin, 1988).

Though business schools are enjoying unprecedented growth and economic prosperity, such 'success' has brought with it a whole new set of challenges. Fueled by evidence suggesting holding a graduate degree in management provides little extrinsic value (e.g., Pfeffer & Fong, 2002), a broad set of stakeholders, including governments, students, funding agencies, accrediting bodies and organizations, are escalating their demand for increased accountability. Following simple logic, stakeholders purport that like any organization, investors ought to be able to determine some relative return on their investments. That is, management education ought to be viewed as a consumer-driven product (Zell, 2005). Regardless of the reason, however, the movement toward increased accountability in management education for what is being taught and learned is ubiquitous. Below, we briefly summarize the key accountability issues as emanating from three key business school stakeholders: students, organizations and the media.

With this consumer-model in mind (Gross & Hogler, 2005), it comes as no surprise that student criticism toward business schools tends to focus on the methods used to develop future managers for the 'real world.' For example, Trank and Rynes (2003) noted that students are increasingly emphasizing employability as salient curriculum factors resulting in negative attitudes toward organizational behavior, human resources, management and anything that is not perceived as 'useful' in gaining employment. As such, students report decreasing tolerance for management theory (Trank & Rynes, 2003) and models. Following such logic, students routinely rank management courses at the bottom of the list of important courses in the business curriculum (Rynes & Trank, 1999). In addition, students' demand for curriculum that will land them jobs has impacted the evaluation system whereby faculty provide 'easy' courses in exchange for high course ratings. As a result, failures are rare and high rates of grade inflation exist (Pfeffer & Fong, 2002; Zell, 2001). Moreover, recent research has shown that students exert considerable pressure on administrators to eliminate required management courses resulting in a curricula that is actually less relevant to managerial job requirements (Rubin & Dierdorff, in press). As such, students place significant pressures on faculty and administrators by asserting the criteria they believe to be most relevant in the assessment of success.

Magnifying the above concerns, organizations are exerting strong pressures on business schools to revamp their approach to training their future managers. Of particular salience is the move toward commodification of knowledge resulting in the training of tools and techniques that benefit organizations in the short-term (Trank & Rynes, 2003). That is, in order to meet organizations' immediate needs in technology and specific job-focused arenas, organizations exert pressure on business schools to provide job candidates who can hit the ground running. As a result, business schools have increasingly turned to specialized programs and courses to provide job candidates who know how to use a particular tool, but may be less certain about the underlying complexities of the tool (Trank & Rynes, 2003). Perhaps the most visible pressure from organizations, however, emanates from corporate recruiters. Recruiters routinely assert that MBA programs need to do a better job at inculcating knowledge and skills as they relate to 'soft-skills' such as leadership, communication and interpersonal skills (Eberhardt, McGee & Moser, 1997; GMAC, 2006). Yet, research consistently demonstrates that recruiters select primarily on technical or 'hard-skill' competencies, to the exclusion of soft-skills.

Perhaps the most recent, influential and controversial stakeholder seeking to establish accountability is that of the media (Elsbach & Kramer, 1996; Gioia & Corley, 2002). In the form of business school rankings (e.g., *Business Week*, *Financial Times* etc.), the media has imposed its own set of standards that have to some extent virtually taken the place of any other indicators of success. Further, media rankings have become

some of the most important variables that influence driving both student and recruiter choices (Safón, 2007). So critical are media rankings that they have been shown to factor heavily in administrative decisions such as curriculum design (Elsbach & Kramer, 1996) and retaining Deans (Fee, Hadlock & Pierce, 2005). From the perspective of the media, rankings are standardized, consumer-friendly and useful in helping prospective students, organizations and recruiters compare business school quality. As such, the media believe that such rankings make schools more accountable and establish a level playing field. In the process, however, Trank and Rynes note, 'other than recruiter and student impressions, most other media measures of quality reflect either incoming student quality ... or factors that vary by geographic locations ... rather than measures of curriculum or teaching quality' (p. 197).

Taken collectively, organizations, recruiters, students, faculty, the media, the government and others all seem to be laying claim to the criteria from which business school quality will be judged and ultimately will be held accountable. As noted above, pressures from these stakeholders for accountability are not simply a business school problem but follow the more general trends toward accountability. However, many disciplines such as medicine and law are a bit more shielded from such accountability pressures since their respective accreditation oversight (i.e., American Bar Association and American Medical Association) is highly standardized and drives program curriculum. Despite its role as the largest business school accreditation body, and unlike these other accrediting bodies, the AACSB is increasingly less inclined to enforce a unilateral approach to management education (Porter & McKibbin, 1988). Instead, the AACSB has been recently favoring flexible 'mission-based' standards that squarely places the onus of accountability at the institution level (Trank & Rynes, 2003). While the merits of such an approach can be debated, this approach does significantly impact the process by which institutions may attempt on the one hand to deal with their multiple stakeholder pressures for accountability, and on the other hand to maintain their accreditation status. At the center of this tension are assessment standards and process. In the next section, we describe this process in depth.

## ACCREDITATION AND ASSURANCE OF LEARNING

In the field of management education, the AACSB International and the European Quality Improvement System (EQUIS) are considered the premier accrediting bodies. Together, they have been responsible for the accreditation of over 600 schools of business worldwide. Although somewhat different labels for standards are often used, their approach to accreditation generally follows a comparable process (Urgel, 2007). For example, both bodies engage in a thorough review process in which institutions engage in self-study and teams of assessors perform an on-site visit evaluation of the school's compliance with the standards. Further, most salient to the present chapter, both bodies require evidence that student learning has taken place. Because of these relative similarities, in the present chapter we chose to focus primarily on the larger of the two bodies, the AACSB.

Currently, 549 business schools hold AACSB accreditation, including 93 schools located in 30 countries outside of the US. AACSB schools comprise roughly one-third of business schools in the US, and 15 percent of business schools worldwide (AACSB, 2007). Once accredited, schools maintain their accreditation status every five years with required reports and peer review. The AACSB is routinely involved in public relations activities promoting the value of management education in general, and of AACSB accreditation in particular, to students, businesses, and the general public. The visibility and advocacy of the organization is an attempt to ensure accreditation adds value to the school's reputation.

In order to achieve accreditation, business schools must satisfy a set of standards

(the current version has 21 standards) related to the school's strategic planning and resource allocation, faculty resources (including an evaluation of their research), and the quality and management of the curriculum. The most recent accreditation standards were passed by a membership vote in April 2003. The set of standards focusing on the quality of the curriculum are called 'Assurance of Learning' (standards 15–21). This choice of name reflects the emphasis on the assessment of student learning in attaining or maintaining accreditation. Prior to 2003, schools satisfied concerns over the quality of their curriculum by documenting their teaching and their curriculum review processes. Typically, schools would develop a matrix that would demonstrate how their business curriculum aligned with the topics and skill development that the AACSB considered mandatory. Many schools relied heavily on proxy data from students, alumni, and employers to further document the quality of their programs. Thus, 'curriculum quality was evaluated primarily by inputs (e.g., Do we teach it?) and indirect outcome measures (e.g., student and alumni self-assessments: Do you think you learned it?)' (Martell, 2007: 189).

This approach is no longer sufficient for AACSB accredited schools – schools must provide 'hard evidence' that their students are achieving the learning goals that form the basis for the curriculum. According to Milton Blood, former Director for Accreditation at AACSB, this is a significant change from the prior standards. In fact, he deemed it the most significant change between the 1990 standards and the 2003 standards remarking, '… the establishment of learning goals is going to be one of the greatest changes in how schools behave… . It is [an] evolutionary [change], but it is a very distinct change' (Thompson, 2004: 429). While the reaction of those tasked with implementation was predictably negative, compliance with the AACSB AoL standards provides an opportunity to respond to critics of higher education discussed above. The new standards require business schools to respond directly by proving their students are learning. A recent survey (Pringle & Michel, 2007) reveals that many business schools would not be expending considerable effort to document their students' learning directly if not required by outside entities. Clearly, most business schools needed a push other than public criticism to provide direct evidence of the educational value of their degree programs. The AACSB clearly had this intention in mind, as evidenced by their language:

> Few characteristics of the school will be as important to stakeholders as knowing the accomplishment levels of the school's students when compared against the school's learning goals... . Assurance of learning to demonstrate accountability (such as in accreditation) is an important reason to assess learning accomplishments. Measures of learning can assure external constituents such as potential students, trustees, public officials, supporters, and accreditors, that the organization meets its goals. (AACSB, 2007: 60)

While the AoL standards did not figure prominently in the debate during the two-year review process, they have emerged as a key challenge for many schools seeking to maintain their accreditation. Very few schools had systems in place in 2003 that would meet the new requirements; furthermore, the assessment process set forth in the standards was so foreign that many schools were at a loss for where to begin:

> As schools began to digest the new standards, a realization dawned that the AoL requirements were a major departure from what had been required in the past. The switch from indirect measures of learning (e.g., surveys) to direct measures (student demonstration of achievement) was significant. Moreover, most deans and faculty had no real idea what this evidentiary change even meant. (Martell, 2007: 189)

## Key AACSB AoL challenges

The widespread reaction to the AACSB AoL requirements ranged from apprehension, to reluctance, to strong resistance. There are a number of challenges that must be overcome in order to make real progress in assessment: (1) Comprehension of the real

purpose of assessment; 2 The change in focus from course grades to program assessment; and 3 The acknowledgement of the shift from indirect to direct measures.

A major challenge that must be overcome is helping faculty understand the true purpose of the assessment process. Some faculty are apprehensive that program assessment data will be used to evaluate their teaching or second-guess their grading (Pringle & Michel, 2007; Martell, 2007; Farmer, 1990), a response that has been characterized by some as 'paranoia' (Forgarty, 2003). Schools have systems in place as part of the evaluation, tenure, and promotion process – program assessment data should never be used for this purpose (Eder, 2005). Another issue related to perception of purpose is more subtle, but has the potential to reduce AoL to a bureaucratic exercise that adds little or no value to the curriculum. The purpose of AoL is not to prove to the AACSB that everything is going as it should, and that student learning is on track. Furthermore, it is not the intent to compare student learning in one school with that in another. The point of the AoL process is diagnostic; that is, to identify gaps in student learning and develop ways for which it can be improved in the degree program. This is the context and spirit in which AoL is intended to be approached, with an eye toward continual improvement.

A second challenge for many schools is the paradigm shift from strict course assessment to program assessment. Faculty routinely evaluate student learning of their subject material in the normal course of teaching. Usually a student's grade in a course is a compilation of various learning assessments including exams, assignments, presentations, group projects, and so forth. Anecdotally, many faculty members' response to the new AACSB assessment mandate was a variation of 'I already do assessment, I assign grades.' The focus of the AoL standards is learning *across* a curriculum, however; namely, a degree program:

> Learning goals can be established at different levels in the educational process. At the course or

single-topic level, faculty members normally have very detailed learning goals. These standards do not focus on such detailed learning goals ... AACSB accreditation is directed at program-level learning goals of a more general nature. These goals will state the broad educational expectations for each degree program. These goals specify the intellectual and behavioral competencies a program is intended to instill. In defining these goals, the faculty members clarify how they intend for graduates to be different as a result of their completion of the program. (AACSB, 2007: 62)

Course grades reflect students' learning within a class, not across a curriculum. It is an important distinction that if unrecognized can stymie progress in achieving the AoL standards.

The classical assessment of Ph.D. students provides a good illustration of program assessment. The key learning assessments for Ph.D. students are written and oral comprehensive exams, a dissertation proposal defense, and the dissertation. These assessment methods provide the basis for faculty to evaluate the students' expert knowledge in their field, their ability to evaluate others' research, and their ability to design and implement a sound research project. Thus, the key focus in assessing candidates for Ph.D.s is not what they are learning in individual courses, but on what they learned as a result of their Ph.D. program. It is the faculty (plural) who develop the standards of performance and who conduct the assessments. Some specialized Master's level programs (e.g., MS in Finance) also often utilize comprehensive exams or projects that evaluate students' learning across their curriculum. But when we look at the degree programs that form the bulk of most business schools' portfolios – the undergraduate and MBA degrees – assessments of student learning are often exclusively conducted in the classroom for the sole purpose of evaluating learning in a single course. Prior to passage of the new accreditation standards, an overall GPA that met or exceeded a minimal requirement was often the only evidence that students had appropriately learned. Schools can no longer maintain AACSB accreditation with this approach.

Unlike individual assessment, program assessment calls for a broader explication of the programmatic learning goals. Faculty are now charged with thinking more broadly about their programs and to establish overall learning goals that all students, regardless of their major or what courses they select, should fulfill. Answering this type of question requires that faculty think outside of what happens in their classroom and across the curriculum. And if it is difficult for many to think across an entire curriculum when determining learning goals, it is even harder for many to imagine having to modify one's courses to address some of the deficiencies that AACSB AoL processes may uncover. For example, the most popular learning goal for undergraduate degree programs is 'effective communication' (Martell & Calderon, 2005). If assessment of students' writing skills finds them to be deficient, it is up to the business school faculty to develop a solution. This is true even if the faculty holds the conviction that writing should be taught elsewhere, identifying a skill as a learning goal means the faculty will be held accountable for students' performance.

Finally, a challenge facing many schools is providing the right form of evidence. The current standards call for a dismissal of indirect measures of learning such as focus groups and exit interviews. Accordingly, the AACSB maintains that such methods do not provide sufficient evidence of student learning. Gathering evidence on student learning through direct measures, however, is considerably more complex and administratively taxing than through the indirect measures which were in vogue prior to 2003. For most schools, these previous indirect methods of assessment were convenient and cost efficient and could be handled by administrative staff, whereas faculty play a pivotal role in collecting data through direct methods. Surveys conducted in the years following the passage of the new AACSB standards (Martell, 2005; Pringle & Michel, 2007) indicate that not knowing how to conduct direct assessments of program learning is a key source of faculty resistance to implementing

AoL programs. It is this final challenge of building capacity for direct assessment practices that is the focus of the remainder of this chapter.

## Building capacity for direct assessment practices

As recent surveys indicate, the current state or quality of AACSB AoL practices in schools of business is rather meager. A careful examination of these data reveals information about ubiquitous faculty resistance and fear of the process, apathy toward learning evaluation, and an apparent lack of perceived capability (Pringle & Michel, 2007). As one administrator recently remarked, 'a faculty member paid to do undergrad assessment didn't have a clue and wasn't respected by peers' (as cited in Pringle & Michel, 2007: 207). That assessment represents such a burden for institutions and their personnel alike is rather surprising given the professional training of most of its personnel, administrators, and faculty. Specifically, although the term 'assurance of learning' may be recently and inextricably tied to AACSB standards and accreditation, the process of evaluating student learning is by no means a new or convoluted endeavor. As noted above, the AACSB standards state, 'In defining these goals, the faculty members clarify *how they intend for graduates to be different as a result of their completion of the program* [emphasis added].' That is, how effective was the intervention of the degree program in bringing about its stated objectives?

In other words, the AACSB standards are at first more concerned with a summative rather than formative assessment. *Formative* assessment refers to the process of collecting information that can be used to improve the process of the intervention itself (Brown & Gerhardt, 2002). In more familiar terms, formative assessment examines both the process and content of what is taught in the curriculum. It is focused on the delivery of content and seeks to identify ways in which to improve it. *Summative* assessment, as the name implies, is focused on understanding whether or not the learning objectives set forth have been accomplished (Noe, 2006). It is true that the ultimate purpose of educational assessment is to generate data that are useful in improving the overall quality of the program; however, from an AACSB standards perspective, the place to start is with summative assessment that should ultimately inform a more focused formative assessment. Thus, following the AASCB, building an institution's assessment practices begins with the outcomes or effectiveness of the business degree program.

When framed this way, faculty and administrators should take some comfort in what it is that they are charged to do, namely, conduct applied research. Aside from the administrative burdens that are synonymous with documenting evidence, business school faculty and administrators readily have the tools to competently engage in assessment practices. Such tools were likely learned in their doctoral seminars and research meetings and are the same tools used to conduct their own research projects and evaluate individual student learning. Our view is that when institutions conduct assessment projects that generally meet good scientific standards of rigor and quality, they will *de facto* fulfill AACSB requirements.

Fortunately, the science of training and evaluation has much to offer in the domain of evaluating learning. Indeed, researchers have been actively seeking ways to target and measure learning in all types of occupational and educational settings for decades (Salas & Cannon-Bowers, 2001). Although disparate in nomenclature and steps, the extant literature suggest that comprehensive assessment of learning generally involves four critical practices, including: (1) Explication of learning objectives; (2) Development of evaluation criteria; (3) Selection of appropriate (matched) assessment methods; and (4) Decisions and use of data. In the paragraphs below we draw on this literature to address the key steps toward developing a successful assessment program that in the process will also fulfill AACSB requirements.

## DEVELOPING STATE-OF-THE-ART ASSESSMENT PRACTICES

### Learning goals and objectives

For purposes of this chapter, we take for granted that an institution has taken sufficient time to comprehensively conduct a needs analysis by establishing their mission, understanding who they serve and the critical knowledge, skills, and behaviors they hope to inculcate in their students at the program level. The outgrowth of this work leads to the first most critical practice in assurance of learning, establishing learning objectives. Learning objectives serve a number of important purposes. First, they help the school clearly delineate and communicate the most essential knowledge, skills, and behaviors that they hope their students will currently or ultimately possess (Quiñones & Tonidandel, 2003). Second, they establish the criteria from which all future evaluation will focus. As such, establishing good learning objectives should not be an afterthought, but is the foundation of good assessment practice.

The AACSB standards call for learning goals to be mission driven. To date, however, many business schools utilize mission statements that speak only in generalities about student learning. A survey conducted by the second author in 2004 (Martell & Calderon, 2005) found that the most popular learning goals for undergraduate business programs are knowledge about business concepts, communication, ethical reasoning, critical or analytical thinking, and teamwork. Further, Martell and Calderon (2005) also report that while 88 percent of AACSB accredited schools participating in the survey had identified learning goals, less than two-thirds had translated them into objectives. This is the second, critical stage in defining learning goals. Faculty must articulate what, exactly, they mean by concepts such as 'critical thinking,' 'ethical reasoning,' or 'leadership.' This process, which AACSB refers to as translating learning goals into learning objectives, must focus on student outcomes that are observable. For example,

what could a student do, that faculty could observe, to indicate they possessed a global perspective? In debating this question, faculty may propose some of the following learning objectives: 1 Students will be able to identify the different aspects of national culture that affect work behaviors, and discuss how these cultural components impact motivation; 2 Students will be able to develop a marketing plan that is appropriate for a specified consumer good in an overseas market; 3 In a simulated setting, students will be able to exhibit culturally appropriate behaviors; and 4 Students will be able to correctly identify the impact of foreign exchange rate fluctuations on the income statement and balance sheet of a US company that manufactures and sells product in that country.

Transforming the above ideas into quality learning objectives usually requires attention to three key concepts (Noe, 2006). First, a quality learning objective is a statement of what the student is expected to know or do. Second, a specification of the level of quality to be demonstrated. Third, a clarification of the conditions under which a student is expected to demonstrate the knowledge, skill, or behavior, if necessary. This does not have to be a complicated or lofty statement. To the contrary, in order to apply across a degree program, most learning objectives are broad statements of student capabilities. Moreover, some have argued that there is often an overemphasis on writing highly detailed behaviorally-based learning objectives. As Kraiger (2002) remarked, one should, 'feel free to write instructional objectives to reflect desired changes rather than a restrictive behavioral framework' (p. 355). For example, the Kellstadt Graduate School of Business at DePaul University has established the following learning objective for communication in their undergraduate business degree program: *Students will be able to communicate effectively both orally and in writing. They can produce a coherent written statement and oral presentation of the analysis of a complex business issue.* Notice that both what the student is expected to know or do and the specification of quality (i.e., coherent), though general in nature, are included. In many cases, the third component to learning objectives (i.e., conditions) will be rather straightforward (e.g., business environment). As programs increase in their specificity (e.g., Masters in Human Resources) the conditions may also increase in specificity (e.g., 'in a unionized environment').

## Assessment criteria

Perhaps the most important and least understood aspect of assessment involves the specification of evaluation or assessment criteria. Important to remember, under the new AACSB standards, AoL is inherently learner-centered. In other words, although other target outcomes of assessment are important, such as institutional success (e.g., alumni giving, increased enrollment etc.) and educational delivery (e.g., number of courses, types of courses, etc.), the immediate goal of an assessment program is to focus on changes in the learners to demonstrate program efficacy. Although many models have been proffered to guide the explication of target outcomes (e.g., Kirkpatrick, 1976), one recent model developed by Kraiger, Ford and Salas (1993) has served to significantly augment understanding of learner-centered criteria. Importantly, this model draws its value from greater than 50 years of learning theory (e.g., Anderson & Krathwohl, 2001; Bloom, 1956; Krathwohl, Bloom & Masia, 1964; Gagne, 1984). Thus, the most significant contribution of the Kraiger et al. (1993) model is the extensive synthesis of prior research (e.g., Bloom's Taxonomy) resulting in a comprehensive yet parsimonious model of the most time-tested learning taxonomies and classification systems. Specifically, Kraiger et al. outline three overarching learning outcomes and their related learning concepts: 1 Cognitive outcomes; 2 Skill-based outcomes; and 3 Affective outcomes. Each of these outcome categories is discussed in more detail below.

*Cognitive learning outcomes.* Cognitive outcomes refer to the acquisition of knowledge, both in terms of the quantity and the type of knowledge learned. In addition, cognitive outcomes represent the degree to which learners demonstrate the relationships among particular knowledge components (Kraiger et al., 1993). As such, cognitive learning outcomes can be categorized into three major domains: 1 Verbal knowledge; 2 Knowledge organization; and 3 Cognitive strategies. Verbal knowledge, often referred to as *declarative knowledge*, is the traditional focus of university-based assessment and involves assessing the amount and/or accuracy of knowledge acquired. Most college instructors' exams are aimed at measuring students' declarative knowledge. Knowledge organization refers to the way in which students organize or categorize their knowledge. This differs from declarative knowledge in that it goes beyond simply possessing the knowledge to include an understanding of the interrelationships between knowledge structures. Finally, cognitive strategies involve learners' capabilities to select the most appropriate form of knowledge to apply to learning, remembering, and problem solving (Gagne, 1984). Often referred to as *metacognitive* skills (Brown, 1975), this form of cognitive outcome involves planning and revising one's actions based upon previous knowledge of the problem or situation. Although the reader may be less familiar with the specific aspects of cognitive outcomes, they are perhaps the most commonly and easily captured in an academic setting as we discuss in the section under assessment methods.

*Skill-based learning outcomes.* Sometimes called behavior outcomes, skill-based learning outcomes involve the demonstration of technical or motor skills that learners had not previously held or demonstrated as well as the capacities to perform these skills with fluidity under real conditions (Kraiger, 2002). Learning objectives focused on students actually 'doing' are generally attempting to capture some form of skill-based outcome. Two forms of skill-based outcomes are important to note. First, *skill-acquisition* involves both proceduralization (i.e., the ability to perform newly acquired behaviors) and compilation (i.e., the increasing capability to demonstrate behavior without error). For example, as learners acquire skills in programming a spreadsheet, they learn to apply various steps in the process (proceduralization). With practice, learners begin to move away from the separate steps involved and treat the entire process as a whole (compilation). Second, ultimately learners' skill leads to *automaticity* whereby the skill learned requires increasingly less effort thereby freeing capacity for other tasks. Although universities routinely purport to measure skills, few institutions focus their assessment efforts on these types of outcomes (Bommer, Rubin, Bartels, 2005).

*Affective learning outcomes.* Affective outcomes refer to learners' attitudes or motivation toward the particular learning objective. These outcomes include understanding the direction or strength of particular attitudes such as a learners' conviction. In addition, the motivation aspect of affective outcomes includes learners' confidence levels, also known as self-efficacy. Such outcomes, sometimes called 'reaction measures' (Kirkpatrick, 1976) are usually quickly dismissed by those who seek 'hard evidence.' However, significant research indicates that attitudes are related to subsequent performance and skill acquisition. For example, there is strong evidence linking individuals' levels of task-specific self-efficacy to subsequent attempts and performance of the task (Martocchio & Hertenstein, 2003; Stajkovic & Luthans, 1998). Further, affective outcomes have been narrowly defined in previous research (Kraiger et al., 1993) and thus are often seen as inconsequential earning terms such as 'smile sheets.' But as Gagne (1984) notes, 'schools do a great deal to establish attitudes. Schools are fairly successful in establishing socially beneficial attitudes' (p. 383). Indeed, with the heightened emphasis on ethics, corporate social responsibility, and citizenship, many institutions are in fact highly concerned with the attitudes and motivations of their students. Measuring affective outcomes in ways that are useful and valid can be difficult. For this reason, affective outcomes are often discouraged

by AACSB examiners in favor of skill and cognitive outcomes. This is unfortunate, as much can be learned from rigorously designed affective assessment outcomes.

*Problems in criteria development.* In selecting criteria that will sufficiently capture the complexity of the established learning objectives, it is important to be aware of some common problems associated with criteria development. One area of particular importance is that of criteria deficiency and contamination (Noe, 2006). *Criteria deficiency* is present when the specified criteria only measure part of what is hoped to be learned and expressed by the learning objective. For example, consider the following learning objective, '*students will be able to use analytical and decision-making skills in problem solving.*' Clearly this objective involves cognitive and skill-based criteria. To capture only cognitive criteria for instance would be a rather incomplete assessment of this learning objective. Conversely, *criteria contamination* involves measuring criteria that are not reflected in the desired learning outcomes or criteria that are impacted by outside factors. Using the above example, the learning objective does not seek to measure issues surrounding affective outcomes such as motivation or attitudes toward decision making or problem solving. Measuring learners' attitudes toward problems-solving, while valid in its own right, would introduce criteria not called for by the learning objective itself. Problems of contamination and deficiency can be avoided by ensuring that the criteria chosen are the most relevant to measuring the stated learning objectives.

## Assessment methods

As we noted above, in order to truly assess learning, one must specify the actual knowledge, skill, or behaviors associated with a given learning objective. This process entails identifying *what* will be measured (e.g., non-verbal communication) and also *how* it ultimately gets measured (e.g., a classroom presentation). How the learning goal gets measured is a process we refer to as selecting appropriate assessment methods and should not be confused with the establishing criteria (i.e., what gets measured). Assessment methods are neutral; that is, they are a mechanism by which a particular capability is elicited and captured. Further, many methods can and should be used effectively to capture more than one capability. For example, an institution hoping to measure decision making may use a written test to measure knowledge of the specific target (e.g., stakeholder analysis) and a case study to elicit proceduralization of the decision-making steps (e.g., determining the appropriate stakeholders for a technological change effort). In addition, since the learner is providing a sample of writing, written communication might be assessed as well.

Selecting appropriate assessment methods can be confusing. The most important factor to consider in choosing the right method is the specific learning objective that is being targeted. The goal is to match the objective capability with the assessment that will best elicit and measure that capability (Quiñones & Tonidandel, 2003). For example, institutions routinely target interpersonal *skills* such as leadership and teamwork in their learning objectives, yet when it comes time to assess these skills, they employ methods more suitable to cognitive outcomes such as written exams (Bartels, Bommer & Rubin, 2000). That is not to say that a body of knowledge in the realm of leadership or teamwork is irrelevant; there is of course an important and extensive knowledge base to master. Yet, if the goal is to develop individuals who can influence people effectively, a method such as role-play or work-sample (e.g., vision speech) provides a much more salient context for which to display these skills.

Another important aspect of choosing the right method is to focus on the most appropriate source of evidence to support that learning has taken place. If the learning objective is targeting awareness of ethical issues, for example, the most appropriate data source would be the learner (e.g., self-report survey). However, if the learning objective is more concerned with communicating an ethical message, the data source may be ratings from an instructor (e.g., rubric of communicating ethical ideas).

The process of selecting an appropriate method can be simplified by relying on classification schemes. The classification scheme by Kraiger et al. (1993) later elaborated by Kraiger (2002), can easily be modified to suit the university learning environment and can serve as a road map for selecting the most appropriate method. In Table 19.1 we provide a summary of assessment criteria and potential methods most appropriate for assessing the criteria. As mentioned above, some methods are more conducive than others for capturing certain types of criteria. The best approaches use multiple methods in an effort to 'triangulate' the learning objective. Further, Table 19.1 should be viewed as illustrative rather than exhaustive since skilled assessors and well-crafted assessments can often elicit and capture multiple forms of outcomes. Below, we briefly describe some advantages and disadvantages common to assessment methods.

*Measuring cognitive outcomes.* The quintessential cognitive assessment is the written examination or 'paper-and-pencil' test. Traditional methods familiar to the reader such as multiple-choice, true-false and so on are best suited for learning objectives which require a demonstration of accurate recall or recognition. Working knowledge of most disciplines is captured quite well by these tests. In attempting to measure learners' cognitive strategies, however, it is more difficult to create multiple-choice test to appropriately elicit such criteria. Appropriate methods might include problem sets whereby students can show their work or case scenarios where students can explicate their higher-order thinking to solve a case (for an example of more sophisticated methods see Davis, Curtis & Tschetter, 2003). It should be noted, however, that research suggests that knowledge examinations are best administered close in time to the point of learning (Kraiger et al., 1993).

**Table 19.1   Classification of assessment learning outcomes**

| Learning outcome category | Learning concept | Measurement focus | Potential assessment methods |
|---|---|---|---|
| Cognitive outcomes | Verbal (declarative) knowledge | Quantity of knowledge, recall accuracy, speed of recall | Exams testing recognition (e.g., multiple-choice) or recall (e.g., essay, fill-in-the-blank). |
| | Knowledge organization | Idea similarity, knowledge interrelatedness, hierarchical ordering | Concept mapping or card sorting |
| | Cognitive strategies | Forming concepts and procedures, problem solving | Case scenarios, problem sets |
| Skill outcomes | Skill acquisition | Proceduralization compilation | Assessment centers, work samples, role plays, behavioral checklists, presentations |
| | Automaticity | Automatic processing | Behavioral observation, performance ratings |
| Affective outcomes | Attitude | Targeted object (e.g., ethics), attitude strength, self-efficacy | Self-report, task specific self-efficacy |
| | Motivation | Effort, tenacity, goal difficulty, motivation to learn | Self-report, observation, time-on-task, goal-difficulty ratings |

*Source*: Adapted from Kraiger (2003) and Kraiger et al. (1993)

*Measuring skill-based outcomes.* Assessing skill-based outcomes usually involves a more active form of testing that includes observing student behavior and utilizing some form of standardized rating system from which to form judgments about skill capabilities. Skill-based measures might include work samples, role plays, behavioral checklists, presentations, or even observation. Whether judging student proceduralization or some deeper internalization, skill-based outcomes most surely involve collecting multiple observations. The reader is likely familiar with the use of role plays and oral presentations in assessing skills. Two methods less familiar, but highly effective are work samples and assessment centers. As the name implies, a work sample is a sample of an actual piece of a job (Guion, 1998). Used to select employees, work samples are designed to test discrete job behaviors through the demonstration of particular skills in a realistic environment. Work samples are among the best predictors of future work performance, as those who can demonstrate the skill today will likely be able to demonstrate it in the future (Roth, Bobko & McFarland, 2005; Schmidt & Hunter, 1998). As such, translating

this process to academics holds promise for effective assessment. For example, using work sample technology to assess students' specific vocational skills in technical areas such as marketing presentations, financial analyses, or performance appraisals would allow for broad assessment of a set of important skill-based outcomes.

Another emerging technology in the use of skill-based outcome measurement is that of the assessment center. Used for decades as an employee selection tool, the assessment center can also be used to collect systematic information about student skills (Waldman & Korbar, 2003), particularly interpersonal or 'soft' skills (Bommer et al., 2005). Assessment centers place students in a hypothetical scenario where they typically adopt the role of a manager or employee in a fictitious company. Through interactive exercises such as meetings and oral presentations designed to elicit specific skills, trained assessors evaluate student skill domains such as initiative, leadership, planning and organizing and decision making.[1] Since performance in student assessment centers is linked to important career outcomes (Waldman & Korbar, 2003), performance results can be fed back to learners in a meaningful way for skill development (Kottke & Schultz, 1997; Mullins, Shaffer & Grelle, 1991). Although assessment centers hold a great deal of promise for assessing certain skills, they do come with considerable administrative barriers, such as costs, faculty time, and expertise. Hence, to date their prevalence as an assessment technique remains rather low (Bommer et al., 2005).

Like cognitive outcomes, unless skills are truly practiced throughout a program's curricula, measuring skills close in time to when they were learned is vital to gain an accurate picture of the skill. In fact, meta-analytic research demonstrates that after one day of training little to no skill decay exist. Yet, one year post-training results show a 92 percent decrement in skill demonstration (Arthur, Bennett, Stanush & McNelly, 1998). This research highlights the potential problems inherent in the so-called 'end of program' exam and comprehensive field exams. Students who do not continue to utilize the knowledge and skills taught early in the program will not likely demonstrate those skills later in their program. This may in part explain the trend away from field tests toward course-embedded assessment (Pringle & Michel, 2007).

*Measuring affective outcomes.* Since affective criteria exist solely within the person, the demonstration of change in affective criteria is most typically measured by self-report instruments. As noted above, the most common form of affective outcome measures are reaction outcomes whereby learners indicate their satisfaction with the content and process of a particular exercise, course, and/or program. Such measures are routinely captured by universities post-term to gauge student experiences with the course. Although useful toward understanding what learners believed to be valuable in enhancing learning, such measures provide little evidence of actual learning. Indeed, reaction measures have received strong criticism in the assessment literature (Holton, 1996) for their lack of association with actual learning (Alliger & Janak, 1989).

Recent developments in affective criteria, however, have given way to more viable forms of affective outcome measurement. One particularly useful affective outcome is that of *self-efficacy*, generally defined as a learner's belief in his/her ability to accomplish a given task (Bandura, 1977). Self-efficacy has been conceptualized to be a vital motivational factor that directly influences how individuals approach challenges in different learning situations. Empirical research has supported this notion showing positive relationships between self-efficacy beliefs and learner task choice, effort, and persistence in overcoming challenges (Bandura, 1991; Gist & Mitchell, 1992), training performance (Tannenbaum, Mathieu, Salas & Cannon-Bowers, 1991), and reactions to training (Gist, Schwoerer & Rosen, 1989). Within the learning environment, it is often the case that objectives directly seek to increase learner confidence in a particular task (Kraiger et al., 1993) such as public speaking or business writing. Thus, given the extant research, assessment programs may benefit greatly from the inclusion of self-efficacy measures as a gauge of learning.

Another important affective outcome to consider is that of motivation to learn which has been defined as the desire to learn content within a given program or developmental environment (Noe, 1986). Motivation to learn is thought to influence learners' decision-making processes critical to the effectiveness of the developmental program and is positively related to learning (Colquitt, LePine & Noe, 2000), participation in developmental activities (Noe & Wilk, 1993), positive reactions (Cole, Field & Harris, 2004), and completion of programs (Baldwin, Magjuka & Loher, 1991). In addition, learning motivation has been shown to be associated with increased transfer (actual use of the acquired knowledge, skills, or behaviors) to work environments (Colquitt et al., 2000). In light of these findings, it is important to note that learning motivation is generally seen as a malleable attitude (Cole et al., 2004). Thus, efforts to assess change in learning motivation can provide meaningful information as part of a comprehensive assessment program.

Although we have discussed multiple methods for assessing learning outcomes, we by no means have provided an exhaustive review. As we noted, the 'best' method will always depend on the specific learning goal and the method(s) most suitable for measuring it. Further, we hasten the reader to note that assessment methods, regardless of how sophisticated or elaborate, contain imperfections. As with any evaluative domain, errors associated with the assessor and deficiencies in the instrument can skew results. Concerns about adequate reliability (i.e., consistency in measurement) and appropriate discriminability (i.e., that the measure reflects actual differences in the criteria) are always important considerations in selecting or developing an assessment method (Noe, 2006).

## Assessment designs

Aside from determining the appropriate criteria and the methods that best measure the criteria, the design of assessment efforts plays an important role. The design of an assessment effort refers to a plan for the circumstances under which assessment information will be elicited and collected. The reader is no doubt familiar with the various evaluative design paradigms available, such as post-tests, single group pre-test-post-tests, pre-test-post-tests with comparison groups and so forth. Each of these designs is associated with various costs and benefits as they relate to controlling threats to the internal and external validity of assessment results. A full discussion of these designs is beyond the scope of this chapter and is discussed extensively elsewhere (see for example Cook & Campbell, 1979; Cook, Campbell & Peracchio, 1990). Thus, rather than provide full treatment here, we instead discuss some recent alternatives to the classic quasi-experimental designs. First, however, we discuss designs put forth by the AACSB under the new standards.

It should be noted that the language we use in this chapter is not entirely consistent with the AACSB's documentation. This is intentional as we aimed to be more precise in our language. In particular, the AACSB refers to the designs below as 'assessment approaches.' Unfortunately, this language obscures the distinctions we have made between matching criteria to the appropriate method (methods such as written exams for cognitive-based outcomes) and design choice (structure of the research). Nevertheless, because of their criticality toward accreditation, we briefly discuss the AACSB AoL standards with respect to assessment design. Three assessment designs have been offered by the AACSB as ways to collect assessment data: 1 Selection; 2 Course embedded; and 3 Determination. These are briefly discussed below followed by a section devoted to increasing assessment design rigor.

*AACSB assessment designs.* Selection designs refer to an assessment that takes place at the point of entry. For example, to gain admission to the Neely School of Business at Texas Christian University (Wakefield, 2005), students must demonstrate their proficiency with business software packages. Another example is provided by the C.T. Bauer College of Business at the University of Houston (Anderson-Fletcher, 2005), which requires applicants to demonstrate a minimal level of writing competency in order to be admitted. The selection design is not frequently used for AACSB AoL purposes (Martell, 2007; Martell & Calderon, 2005), and is only a viable option for undergraduate business programs that admit students in their sophomore or junior years.

The second design approach listed in the AACSB documentation, course-embedded, is the most widely-used design in business schools. In recent surveys (Martell, 2007; Pringle & Michel, 2007) 70 percent of the respondents indicated they used the course-embedded design. In the course-embedded design, products generated by students to fulfill requirements for a course are also used for AACSB AoL purposes. The course-embedded design collects student performance data across multiple courses using an established performance standard.

For example, a course product (e.g., a case write-up) is assessed by one professor for his/her course using his/her own performance criteria for the purposes of assigning a grade, while a second copy of the paper is assessed by someone else using the criteria determined by the faculty at large. A comparison of the outside evaluation against the professor's grade is not part of the assessment process. In other words, the course serves as the mechanism by which student assessment data are elicited. Course embedded methods do have many practical advantages. First, they take advantage of student products already incorporated in the curriculum which simplifies the assessment process. Second, they tend to be closely tied to the school's curricula. Third, by utilizing student work that impacts their course grades, students' motivation tends to be high thereby capturing students' best efforts.

Demonstrations or tests are the final direct assessment design discussed in the AACSB AoL standards. These assessments take place outside of the classroom, in spirit if not in actuality. Often referred to as the single-group post-test design, demonstrations are rather straightforward – a single group (e.g., senior business students) completes a test or battery of tests designed to evaluate multiple learning objectives. As we noted above, Doctoral programs rely on demonstration designs when evaluating candidates via qualifying or comprehensive exams. In undergraduate assessment programs, the most commonly used method within a demonstration design is the Educational Testing Service (ETS) Major Field Achievement Test in Business (MFAT-B). More than 500 business schools use the MFAT-B to evaluate their students' cognitive-based outcomes.

Methods such as the assessment center used by the Kellstadt Graduate School of Business at DePaul University, the Stillman School of Business at Seton Hall's assessment panel (Boroff et al., 2005), and the mock interviews used at the School of Business at Montclair State are all methods that lend themselves nicely to the demonstration (i.e., single group post-test) design. Demonstration designs have some key advantages, namely, they are comparatively easy to set up and, depending on the method used within, can assess students on multiple learning goals simultaneously. For example, the assessment center used at DePaul University assesses oral communication, teamwork, and decision making in the same exercise, and the Stillman panel evaluates oral communication, knowledge, teamwork, and critical thinking. Potential drawbacks include costs (the MFAT-B is more than $25 a student, developing an assessment center is very time intensive, the Stillman School's use of alumni as outside assessors is a time-consuming administrative task), lack of alignment between the school's curricula and measures developed elsewhere, and student motivation. Once assessment activities are taken outside of the classroom, students' motivation to provide their best performance may be diminished. Even if the school makes participation mandatory, the issue of motivating students to give their best effort must be addressed by other means. A typical response is to incorporate students' performance on the demonstration into a course grade (see Rotondo, 2005 for a discussion of other motivating techniques).

### Increasing assessment design rigor

Although we encourage institutions to think in terms of increasing the rigor associated with their assessment designs, such rigor does not necessarily require multi-group pre-post quasi-experimental designs. Indeed, when one reflects on the considerable costs, feasibility, and availability of resources to conduct such assessment, the process can be rather daunting. Thus, institutions should determine whether or not they actually need to demonstrate change in the learner or whether achievement of a particular standard is sufficient. For many institutions, their concern is that students achieve a particular level of competence in relation to some standard, rather than improvement or that future student learning will be improved.

In such a situation, a single group post-test (course embedded or determination design) can suffice. However, it is important to keep in mind that such a design does not evaluate the efficacy of the program in inculcating the criteria it espouses, rather it evaluates the level of knowledge, skills, or behaviors in its students, regardless of how or where it was acquired.

Institutions interested in showing changes in the learner can employ some alternative approaches which can improve rigor but do not require a classic pre-post test control group design. Haccoun and Hamtiaux (1994) introduce an alternative design called the internal referencing strategy. This design allows for increased causal inferences as the authors describe:

> The [internal referencing strategy] may be described as a pre-post single group design in which the evaluator purposefully incorporates in the pre- and post measures items which are relevant to the training (i.e., which ought to change because the course content will cover them) and items which are not expected to change (because the course will not deal with them). Comparisons are then established between pre-post differences on the relevant items as well as on the irrelevant items. Effectiveness is inferred when changes on relevant items are greater than changes on irrelevant ones. (p. 595)

As might be apparent, this strategy applies most readily to assessment of cognitive-based outcomes, though as Haccoun and Hamtiaux (1994) note it may with some effort be applied to behaviorally-based outcomes.

Another alternative design to consider in lieu of an actual control group (i.e., who never receives the educational intervention) is to adapt the staggered training or rolling group design (Kraiger, McLinden & Casper, 2004; Quiñones & Tonindandel, 2003) to educational environments. In this design, training is given to all participants; however, training groups start at different points in time. Groups waiting to begin training can serve as the comparison group to groups who are already in progress. Educational environments provide natural rolling groups, particularly for course embedded or program

assessment. For example, a group that completes post-test measures at the end of a term as part of a business writing course could be compared against a group's pre-test measure at the beginning of the term.

## Use of assessment data for program improvement

The AACSB, in addition to other accrediting bodies and assessment scholars, are clear about the ultimate purpose of assessment: to *assure* student learning.

> Measures of learning have little value in and of themselves. They should make a difference in the operations of the school. Schools should show how AoL results impact the life of the school. Such demonstrations can include uses to inform and motivate individual students and uses to generate changes in curricula, pedagogy, and teaching and learning materials. (AACSB, 2007: 69)

From this perspective, analyses should focus on what has been learned about students' learning. In doing so, areas for curriculum improvement will most certainly be identified. This process, which is referred to by the AACSB as 'closing the loop,' is one of the greatest concerns that business school Deans have about assessment (Martell, 2007). Utilizing assessment results is critical because the AACSB requires 'the impact of assessment outcomes on continuing development of the degree programs … be evident' (AACSB, 2007: 69).

In other words, it is not enough to examine a single outcome and implement a change as a result of the examination; rather, continual systematic efforts must be made to develop the degree program until evidence can be shown that the intervention(s) has achieved its goal. More complex is that the summative evaluation often gives way to formative evaluation as schools seek answers to *why* there are particular deficiencies in knowledge, skills, or behaviors. In such a process, institutions will likely explore issues related to andragogical techniques, course integration, as well as admission procedures and the rigor of the program.

Matching the appropriate method to criteria as discussed previously allows for a more parsimonious search for future interventions. For example, if a particular cognitive-based outcome such as knowledge of employment law is relatively low among students, the interventions proposed will logically follow this finding (i.e., interventions design to improve learning and retention of employment law). The improvement process is a cyclical one much like those championed by the total quality management movement. Here the goal is to make data-driven decisions toward improvement, track the data and feed it back into the decision-making system. In this spirit, many institutions are adopting a two-year cycle in which progress on learning goals are routinely and systematically assessed and development interventions implemented.

## CONCLUDING THOUGHTS

Throughout this chapter, we have attempted to illuminate the trends associated with assessment and clarify the requirements for accomplishing assurance of learning toward accreditation. We have of course omitted a great deal of information related to assessment concerns, such as andragogical approaches and their impact on student learning, as well as practical and logistical recommendations for accomplishing assessment. For example, recent research has shown that capturing individual difference variables such as grade point average (Bacon & Bean, 2006) alongside other assessment information can allow for increased understanding of the outcomes of interest or effect of a particular intervention. In addition, we did not provide a comprehensive list of tools or techniques to accomplish assessment. Although important, we hoped that this chapter would provide a more basic foundation for the accomplishment of assurance of learning. Indeed, it has been our experience that institutions, in their haste to establish an assessment process, often benchmark other universities and blindly adopt the assessment tools they uncover. Rightfully so, off-the-shelf tests and

techniques tested elsewhere are seductive and seemingly come with turn-key solutions to assessment. Unfortunately, not unlike corporations who rely heavily on benchmarking, institutions who adopt methods without a thorough consideration of criteria are not likely to effect real change in their programs (Pfeffer & Sutton, 2006). We hope that the information presented here assists schools in employing a more thoughtful and systematic approach to their assessment programs.

## NOTE

1 For more extensive reviews of assessment centers in academia see Bommer et al. (2005) and Riggio, Mayes, and Schleicher (2003).

## REFERENCES

Anderson, L.W. & Krathwohl, D.R. (eds) (2001). *A Taxonomy for Learning, Teaching, and Assessing: A revision of Bloom's taxonomy of educational objectives.* New York: Longman.

Anderson-Fletcher, E. (2005). Going from zero to sixty in twelve months: Implementing assessment at the Bauer College of Business, in K. Martell & T. Calderon (eds), *Assessment of Student Learning in Business Schools: Best practices each step of the way,* (Vol. 1:2, pp. 64–83). Association for Institutional Research.

Association to Advance Collegiate Schools of Business (AACSB) International (2007). *Eligibility procedures and accreditation standards for business accreditation.* Revised January 31, 2007. [Electronic version].

Alliger, G.M. & Janak, E.A. (1989). Kirkpatrick's levels of training criteria: Thirty years later. *Personnel Psychology, 42,* 3331–42.

Arthur, W.Jr., Bennett, W.Jr., Stanush, P.L. & McNelly, T.L. (1998). Factors that influence skill decay and retention: A quantitative review and analysis. *Human Performance,* 11, 57–101.

Bacon, D.R. & Bean, B. (2006). GPA in research studies: An invaluable but neglected opportunity. *Journal of Marketing Education, 28,* 35–42.

Baldwin, T.T., Magjuka, R.J. & Loher, B.T. (1991). The perils of participation: Effects of choice of training on trainee motivation and learning. *Personnel Psychology,* 44, 260–7.

Bandura, A. (1977). *Social Learning Theory.* Englewood Cliffs, NJ: Prentice Hall.

Bandura, A. (1991). Social cognitive theory of self-regulation. *Organizational Behavior and Human Decision Processes, 50,* 248–87.

Bartels, L.K., Bommer, W.H. & Rubin, R.S. (2000). Student performance: Assessment centers versus traditional classroom evaluation techniques. *Journal of Education for Business, 75*(4), 198–201.

Bloom, B. (1956). *Taxonomy of Educational Objectives: The cognitive domain.* New York: Donald McKay.

Bommer, W.H., Rubin, R.S. & Bartels, L.K. (2005). Assessing the unassessable: Interpersonal and managerial skills, in K. Martel & T. Calderon (eds) *Assessment of Student Learning in Business Schools: Best practices each step of the way* (pp. 103–29). Tallahassee, FL: Association for Institutional Research.

Boroff, K.E., Strawser, J., Wisenblit, J. & Onimus, L. (2005). Undergraduate assessment at the Stillman School of Business, in K. Martell & T. Calderon (eds), *Assessment of student learning in business schools: Best practices each step of the way* (Vol. 1:2, pp. 99–118). Association for Institutional Research.

Brown, A.L. (1975). The development of memory: Knowing, knowing about knowing, and knowing how to know, in H.W. Reese (ed.), *Advances in Child Development and Behavior* (Vol. 10, pp. 103–52). San Diego, CA: Academic Press.

Brown, K.G. & Gerhardt, M.W. (2002). Formative evaluation: An integrative practice model and case study. *Personnel Psychology, 55,* 951–83.

Cabrera, A.G., Colbeck, C.L. & Terenzini, P.T. (2001). Developing performance indicators for assessing classroom teaching practices and student learning. The case of engineering. *Research in Higher Education, 42,* 327–52.

Cole, M.S., Field, H.S. & Harris, S.G. (2004). Student learning motivation and psychological hardiness: Interactive effects on students' reactions to a management class. *Academy of Management Learning & Education, 3,* 64–85.

Colquitt, J.A., LePine, J.A. & Noe, R.A. (2000). Toward an integrative theory of training motivation: A meta-analytic path analysis of 20 years of research. *Journal of Applied Psychology, 85,* 678–707.

Cook, T.D. & Campbell, D.T. (1979). *Quasi-experimentation: Design and analysis issues for field settings.* Boston: Houghton Mifflin.

Cook, T.D., Campbell, D.T. & Peracchio, L. (1990). Quasi-experimentation, in M.D. Dunnette & L.M. Hough, (eds). *Handbook of Industrial and Organizational Psychology,* (2nd ed.). Vol. 1, 491–576.

Davis, M.A., Curtis, M.B. & Tschetter, J.D. (2003). Evaluating cognitive training outcomes: Validity and

utility of structural knowledge assessment. *Journal of Business and Psychology, 18,* 191–206.

Eberhardt, B.J., McGee, P. & Moser, S. (1997). Business concerns regarding MBA education: Effects on recruiting. *Journal of Education for Business, 72*(5), 293–6.

Eder, D. (2005). A culture of assessment, in K. Martell & T. Calderon (eds), *Assessment of Student Learning in Business Schools: Best practices each step of the way* (Vol. 1:1). Association for Institutional Research.

Elsbach, K.D. & Kramer, R.M. (1996). Members' responses to organizational identity threats: Encountering and countering the Business Week rankings. *Administrative Science Quarterly, 41*(3), 442–76.

Farmer, D.W. (1990). Strategies for change, in D. Steeples (ed.) *Managing Change in Higher Education,* pp. 7–17. Jossey-Bass Publishers.

Fee, C.E., Hadlock, C.J. & Pierce, J.R. (2005). Business school rankings and business school deans: A study of nonprofit governance. *Financial Management, 34,* 143–66.

Fogarty, T.J. (2003). Why faculty resist assessment, in T. Claderon, B. Green & M. Harkness (eds), *Best Practices in Accounting Program Assessment* (pp. 56–63). American Accounting Association Publishers.

Gagne, R.M. (1984). Learning outcomes and their effects. Useful categories of human performance. *American Psychologist, 39,* 377–85.

Gioia, D.A. & Corley, K.G. (2002). Being good versus looking good. Business school rankings and the Circean transformation from substance to image. *Academy of Management Learning & Education,* 1, 107–20.

Gist, M. & Mitchell, T.R. (1992). Self-efficacy: A theoretical analysis of its determinants and malleability. *Academy of Management Review,* 17, 183–211.

Gist, M., Schwoerer, C. & Rosen, B. (1989). Effects of alternative training methods on self-efficacy and performance in computer software training. *Journal of Applied Psychology,* 74, 884–91.

Gross, M.A. & Hogler, R. (2005). What the shadow knows: Exploring the hidden dimensions of the consumer metaphor in management education. *Journal of Management Education,* 29, 3–16.

Guion R.M. (1998). *Assessment, Measurement, and Prediction for Personnel Decisions.* Mahwah, NJ: Erlbaum.

Haccoun, R.R. & Hamtiaux, T. (1994). Optimizing knowledge tests for inferring acquisition levels in single group training evaluation designs: The internal referencing strategy. *Personnel Psychology,* 47, 593–604.

Holton, E.F. III. (1996). The flawed four-level evaluation model. *Human Resource Development Quarterly*, 7, 5–21.

Kingsbury, A. (2007). The measure of learning. *U.S. News & World Report* (12 March), 53–7.

Kirkpatrick, D.L. (1976). Evaluation of training, in R.L. Craig (ed.), *Training and Development Handbook*. New York: McGraw-Hill.

Kottke, J.L. & Schultz, K.S. (1997). Using an assessment center as a developmental tool for graduate students: A demonstratio, in R.E. Riggio & B.T. Mayes (eds), Perspectives on assessment centers [Special Issue]. *Journal of Social Behavior and Personality*, 12, 289–302.

Kraiger, K. (2002). Decision-based evaluation, in K. Kraiger (ed.), *Creating, Implementing, and Managing Effective Training and Development: State-of-the-art lessons for practice* (pp. 331–76). San Francisco, CA: Jossey-Bass.

Kraiger, K., Ford, J.K. & Salas, E. (1993). Application of cognitive, skill-based, and affective theories of learning to new methods of training evaluation. *Journal of Applied Psychology*, 78, 311–28.

Kraiger, K., McLinden, D. & Casper, W.J. (2004). Collaborative planning for training impact. *Human Resource Management*, 43, 337–51.

Krathwohl, D.R., Bloom, B.S. & Masia, B.B. (1964). *Taxonomy of Educational Objectives: The classification of educational goals*. White Plains, NY: Longman.

Martell, K., and Calderon, T. (2005). Assessment in business schools: What it is, where we are, and where we need to go now, in K. Martell & T. Calderon (eds), *Assessment of Student Learning in Business Schools: Best practices each step of the way*, (Vol. 1:1). Association for Institutional Research.

Martell, K. (2005). Overcoming faculty resistance to assessment, in K. Martell & T. Calderon (eds), *Assessment of student learning in business schools: Best practices each step of the way* (Vol. 1:2, pp. 210–26). Association for Institutional Research.

Martell, K. (2007). Assessing student learning: Are business schools making the grade? *Journal of Education for Business*, 82(4), 189–95.

Martocchio, J.J. & Hertenstein, J.E. (2003). Learning orientation and goal orientation context: Relationships with cognitive and affective learning outcomes. *Human Resource Development Quarterly*, 14, 413–34.

Mathieu, J.E., Tannenbaum, S.I. & Salas, E. (1992). Influences of individual and situational characteristics on measures of training effectiveness. *Academy of Management Journal*, 35, 828–47.

*MBA Alumni Perspectives Survey. Comprehensive Data Report*(2006). Graduate Management Admission Council (GMAC). Accessed Oct 1, 2006.

Mullins, R.G., Shaffer, P.L. & Grelle, M.J. (1991). A study of the assessment center method of teaching basic management Skills, in J.D. Bigelow (ed.), *Managerial Skills: Explorations in practical knowledge* (pp. 116–53). Newbury Park, CA: Sage.

Noe, R.A. (2006). *Employee Training and Development* (4th ed.). New York: McGraw-Hill.

Noe, R.A. & Wilk, S.A. (1993). Investigation of the factors that influence employees' participation in development activities. *Journal of Applied Psychology*, 78, 291–302.

Pfeffer, J. & Fong, C.T. (2002). The end of business schools? Less success than meets the eye. *Academy of Management Learning & Education*, 1, 78–95.

Pfeffer, J. & Sutton, R.I. (2000). *The Knowing-doing Gap*. Boston: Harvard Business School Press.

Pfeffer, J. & Sutton, R.I. (2006). Evidence-based management. *Harvard Business Review* (January), 63–74.

Porter, L. & McKibbin, L. (1988). *Management Education and Development: Drift or thrust into the 21st century*. New York: McGraw-Hill.

Pringle, C. & Michel, M. (2007). Assessment practices in AACSB-accredited business schools. *Journal of Education for Business*, March/April, 202–11.

Quiñones, M.A. & Tonidandel, S. (2003). Conducting training evaluation, in J.E. Edwards, J.C. Scott & N.S. Raju (eds), *The Human Resources Program-Evaluation Handbook* (pp. 225–41). Thousand Oaks, CA: Sage Publications.

Riggio, R.E., Mayes, B.T. & Schleicher, D.J. (2003). Using assessment center methods for measuring undergraduate business student outcomes. *Journal of Management Inquiry*, 12, 68–78.

Roth, P.H., Bobko, P. & McFarland, L.A. (2005). A meta-analysis of work sample test validity: Updating and integrating some classic literature. *Personnel Psychology*, 38, 1009–37.

Rotondo, D.M. (2005). Assessing business knowledge, in K. Martell & T. Calderon (eds), *Assessment of Student Learning in Business Schools: Best practices each step of the way* (Vol. 1:1, pp. 82–102). Association for Institutional Research.

Rubin, R.S., Baldwin, T.T. & Bommer, W.H. (2002). Using extracurricular activities as an indicator of interpersonal skill: Prudent evaluation or recruiting malpractice? *Human Resource Management*, 41, 441–54.

Rubin, R.S. & Dierdorff, E.C. (in press). How relevant is the MBA? Assessing the alignment of required curricula and required managerial competencies. *Academy of Management Learning & Education.*

Rynes, S.L. & Trank, C.Q. (1999). Behavioral science in the business school curriculum: Teaching in a changing institutional environment. *Academy of Management Review*, 24(4), 808–24.

Safón, V. (2007). Factors that influence recruiters' choice of b-schools and their MBA graduates: Evidence and implications for b-schools. *Academy of Management Learning & Education*, 6(2), 217–33.

Salas, E. & Cannon-Bowers, J.A. (2001). The science of training: A decade of progress. *Annual Review of Psychology*, 52, 471–99.

Schmidt, F.L. & Hunter, J.E. (1998). The validity and utility of selection methods in personnel psychology: Practical and theoretical impolications of 85 years of research findings. *Psychlolgical Bulletin*, 124, 262–74.

Stajkovic, A.D. & Luthans, F. (1998). Self-efficacy and work-related performance: A meta analysis. *Psychological Bulletin*, 124, 240–61.

Tannenbaum, S.I. (1997). Enhancing continuous learning: Diagnostic findings from multiple companies. *Human Resource Management*, 36, 437–52.

Tannenbaum, S., Mathieu, J., Salas, E. & Cannon-Bowers, J. (1991). Meeting trainees' expectations: The influence of training fulfillment on the development of commitment, self-efficacy, and motivation. *Jouranl of Applied Psychology*, 76, 759–69.

Thompson, K. (2004). A conversation with Milton Blood: The new AACSB standards. *Academy of Management Learning & Education*, 3, 429–39.

Trank, C.Q. & Rynes, S.L. (2003). Who moved our cheese? Reclaiming professionalism in business education. *Academy of Management Learning & Education*, 2, 189–206.

Urgel, J. (2007). EQUIS Accreditation: Value and benefits for international business schools. *Global Focus*, 1, 32–7.

U.S. Department of Education (2006). *A Test of Leadership: Charting the future of U.S. Higher Education.* Washington, D.C.

Wakefield, G. (2005). (Almost) painless assessment: Using intake processes for assessment purposes, in K. Martell & T. Calderon (eds), *Assessment of Student Learning in Business Schools: Best practices each step of the way*, (Vol. 1:2, pp. 24–46). Association for Institutional Research.

Waldman, D.A. & Korbar, T. (2003). Student assessment center performance in the prediction of early career success. *Academy of Management Learning & Education*, 3, 151–68.

Zell D. (2001). The market-driven business school: Has the pendulum swung too far? *Journal of Management Inquiry*, 10, 324–48.

Zell, D. (2005). Pressure for relevancy at top-tier business schools. *Journal of Management Inquiry*, 14, 271–74.

# 20

# The Research-Teaching Nexus: Tensions and Opportunities[1]

Roy J. Lewicki and James R. Bailey

## Abstract

To deny that there is a tension between research and teaching activities and demands at most management education institutions would be disingenuous. But it would be equally disingenuous to deny the productive synergies and reciprocities between knowledge creation, dissemination and application. Scholarship and education are the twin pillars that serve as the foundation of most academic management education institutions. Yet there are two trends prevalent in the more prestigious research universities: that excellence in scholarship and education are both critical to faculty selection and promotability, and that one of these pillars (research) is more strongly encouraged and rewarded than the other, exacerbating the tension and impeding the realization of effective institutional balance. This chapter examines the apparent dichotomy between teaching and research and the relationship between them. In the chapter, we assess the dominant paradigm for faculty recognition in leading business schools, and question the assumptions on which it is grounded. Examining data from studies that have explored the relationship between faculty research productivity and teaching excellence, we discuss those findings and their implications for current and future faculty reward systems and institutional priorities.

One of the most strongly held ideologies – and values – in the academic community of the modern research university – embraced by faculty and administrators alike – is that there is a strong, positive, and mutually reinforcing relationship between a faculty member's teaching effectiveness and research accomplishments. The belief is embodied in the hiring practices of most academic units in these institutions, and most visibly endorsed in their annual review, promotion and tenure standards. While these academic units occasionally take the initiative to hire lecturers and clinical professors (whose only responsibility is teaching) or research professors (whose only responsibility is to secure grants and publish in leading journals), the premier and most prestigious academic appointment is in the primary tenure-track, where both research productivity and instructional effectiveness are regularly monitored and assessed. See Bailey and Lewichi (2007) for additional treatment of these issues.

The origins of this perspective are deeply rooted in the history of the university itself, although not necessarily traceable to its origins. Newman (1853), in his book, *The Idea of a University*, commented that:

> ... to discover and to teach are distinct functions; they are also distinct gifts, and are not commonly found united in the same person. He, too, who spends his day in dispensing his existing knowledge to all comers is unlikely to have either leisure or energy to acquire new (p. 10)

Leinster-Mackay (1978), examining the origins of the university, claims that it can be traced back to Arabic cultures and that the primary function was as a teaching institution; in fact, the baccalaureate degree takes its name from the Arabic *baccalaureus*, meaning 'with the right to teach on the authority of another' (as quoted in Hattie & Marsh, 1996). However, the increased emphasis on research began with the German universities at the turn of the 20th century. Since that time, a number of educators have commented on the importance of knowledge acquisition among faculty, and increasingly, an importance on knowledge *creation* as well as acquisition (e.g., Barnett, 1992; Gell, 1992).

In the modern elite, research university, while the sacred trilogy of 'research, teaching and service' are all given strong administrative endorsement, most faculty are aware that the prevailing ideology is that it is the quantity and quality of one's scholarly research which will be the ultimate determinant of contract renewal, promotion and tenure. Moreover, many institutions are moving to recalibrate their annual review and compensation systems to reflect this emphasis, offering smaller teaching loads and lowered teaching expectations for strongly productive research faculty. As a result, most faculty evaluation systems have developed complex and sophisticated mechanisms for discerning and measuring research quantity, quality and impact, while 'satisficing' on measures of teaching effectiveness by treating anything more than 'bad' teaching ratings as fully acceptable evidence of teaching quality and impact.

The prevalence of this 'great person' or superstar approach to faculty selection and development (i.e., that one person is capable of being both an excellent teacher and researcher) across higher education cannot be underestimated. Indeed, several critics have suggested that the belief in the existence of, and search for, 'great person' faculty is reflective of ongoing discussion about the core values of higher education itself. Rowland (2000) conducted interviews with heads of university departments about their star researchers and teachers. The department heads characterized successful researchers as 'driven', 'self-motivated', 'confident', and 'someone who has a passion for something and wants to pursue it at all costs'. In contrast, successful teachers were described as 'open', 'concerned for students', 'caring', and 'carrying out their obligations with a sense of duty'. Rowland goes on to note (as cited in Badley, 2002):

> Such qualities are more often associated with female stereotypes. It cannot be altogether coincidental that these representatives of a large male preserve of senior academics reflect a view of research (which has been the main criterion of their gaining seniority) in terms of mainly male qualities. There would seem to be no obvious epistemological basis for this view of knowledge and its production. Such a perspective is no doubt self-reinforcing of the male hierarchy that produces it. (Rowland, 2000, 16–17, quoted in Badley, 2002: 445)

While this view may be somewhat extreme – and Badley goes on to wax elegantly about the implications of the male/female characteristics and their literary and cultural significance – the questions remain. Is the search for 'great persons' – the 21st century's academic version of the 'war for talent' (Michaels, Handfield-Jones & Axelrod, 2001) – a meaningful search? Is there empirical support for the validity of the 'great person' model (cf. Fairweather, 2002, for one answer to this question)? Why have universities not pursued alternative staffing models for managing this talent problem?

When one questions the origins and validity of this 'great person' approach, one discovers that current day faculty and administration tend to embrace a set of underlying assumptions (not necessarily supported by more than anecdotal evidence) that can be grouped into three general categories: that research contributes to teaching, that teaching contributes to research and that the two major role activities embrace a common underlying set of cardinal values that bind the two (cf. Hattie & Marsh, 1996, 2004). They agree that research should contribute to teaching for a number of reasons. Past research serves as the content base for what is taught. Active researchers will know this content base more thoroughly and understand its nuances. Lectures are the primary basis for transmitting this knowledge, and active researchers are more likely to incorporate the most recent research findings and debates into their teaching presentations. Moreover, active researchers are more enthusiastic and energized about their areas of research, and will communicate this excitement in their classroom performance. This excitement will generate interest among students, who see the instructor as more knowledgeable, credible and interesting than an instructor who is merely conveying the work of others.

Similarly, the prevailing wisdom is that that teaching should contribute to research. Effective teachers must be able to explain the 'big picture' of various topics and sub-fields in their discipline. As a result, preparing these explanations will help teachers understand the background and context of their research specialty, and perhaps relate it to topics and approaches that were previously seen as unrelated. Moreover, the process of describing this work to students, and fielding their questions and critiques often will help to sharpen new areas of inquiry, raise untested questions or suggest new methodologies. Enthusiastic engagement of the research issues by students stimulates and motivates the researcher toward new pursuits. For those faculty who are teaching outside their research area, teaching may help to reframe existing areas of research or even help to formulate new research questions because of the challenges that may be presented from those outside the discipline.

Finally, the argument is that research and teaching activities are complementary because they embrace common academic values (cf. Braxton, 1996; Badley, 2002; Leslie, 2002). These values endorse the acquisition of knowledge for its own sake, seeking 'truth' through rationality and systematic investigation, and they argue that each reinforces the other by virtue of adherence to these values. Moreover, it is clear, they argue, that almost all strong teachers and strong researchers support the importance of both activities, and endorse the development of mechanisms to encourage and nurture strength in both areas.

However, critics (cf. Braxton, 1996) have noted that there is mounting evidence that the two activities can also be strongly incompatible. In fields where many of the interesting research problems have already been mined, researchers must focus on a very narrow set of problems, and discussing these with students may consume one class period at best. Meanwhile, as noted earlier, teaching demands may require the instructor to teach courses out of his immediate area of expertise, or broad survey courses that do not generate intellectual excitement for faculty or students. Time required for teaching activities (class preparation, grading, office hours) often directly competes with time necessary for research activities (writing, study preparation, data collection and analysis). This stress is often felt most strongly by younger faculty who have non-academic and family obligations that require strict time budgeting of their professional commitments. And when one examines the actual work required to design and conduct high-quality research, the portfolio of activities is quite different from the actual work required to be a strong teacher; preparation activities are different, 'performance' of those activities are different, different personalities may be required to excel at each activity, and totally different audiences must be satisfied to sustain and underwrite the critical work in each domain.

The fundamental belief – by academic administrators and many senior faculty leaders – that quality scholarship facilitates quality teaching – is being challenged from inside and outside the academic community. A chorus of prominent voices has charged that business education has minimal, if any, impact on students' success or performance once they reach the job market, and that the majority of academic research is so particularized and divorced from practical realities that it adds little practical value (Pfeffer & Fong, 2002). Bennis & O'Toole (2005) charge that too much emphasis on research has led to schools designing curricular delivery mechanisms around paradigms consistent with conducting scientific research but inconsistent with delivering professional education, and, correlatively, abandoning the teaching mission to a portfolio of untenured clinical instructors while rewarding full-time faculty for sustained research productivity. Ghoshal (2005) went so far as to claim that in pursuit of academic credibility via rigorous research, theories of effective management have adopted a set of assumptions about human nature that provide intellectual justification for a class of behaviors that sour the corporate ethical climate (e.g., that increased attention to transaction costs and agency theory may have created an increased pressure on results at the expense of ethics, Ghoshal, 2005). Furthermore, business schools face a rapidly shifting demographic in terms of enrollment, fragmentation among providers, segmentation of markets, globalization, advances in delivery technology, a declining supply of doctorally qualified faculty and increased importance of non-degree education (AACSB, 2002). Finally, at the broader institution level, Badley (2002) comments that research and teaching are headed toward 'divorce' in many institutions, leading to two different types (and classes) of institutions which emphasize one or the other,

but that inherently (with certain exceptions), teaching institutions are seen as inferior and underfunded. This trend, he claims, is leading to the conclusion that:

> In effect, only the rich [top research universities] can afford to maintain a strong marital relationship between high class research and good quality teaching. For the rest, a divorce, if not actual, appears to be pending. (Badley, 2002: 446)

These criticisms and challenges require formulating effective strategic and operational responses that necessitate bringing the precise nature of the research-teaching nexus into sharp relief.

In this chapter, we will present and discuss in detail the tensions and compatibilities between faculty research and teaching activities.[2] The next section selectively reviews empirical research that questions whether productive researchers are, in fact, better teachers. (While there is no shortage of eloquent invective on this question, the focus on empirical studies both narrows the range of studies to be reviewed and applies sophisticated research methodology to this important question.) This review will lead us to expand the definition of what constitutes 'research' and 'scholarship', and we will draw heavily from Boyer's (1990) classification scheme to point out that there are other forms of scholarship beyond what is traditionally defined as 'research' in modern business schools. We then propose three major courses of action for the business school community: (1) A rich empirical examination of the relationship between traditional and non-traditional definitions of 'research excellence' and 'teaching excellence' among business school faculty; (2) A broadening of the definition of scholarship in business schools that entails full institutional support; and (3) The development and support of formal and informal recognition and reward systems for *both* highly skilled teachers and researchers, rather than continue to pursue a uniform model of faculty selection and promotion.

## THE EMPIRICAL RELATIONSHIP BETWEEN RESEARCH AND TEACHING

The empirical relationship between research productivity and quality teaching is certainly a testable research proposition. Although no single effort has focused on this relationship in the management disciplines *per se* (see Arnold, 2008 in press for one exception in a college of economics), several excellent studies in the broader higher education literature have examined this relationship. It is beyond the purview of this chapter to thoroughly review the overlapping and often contradictory streams of this literature. Fortunately, Hattie & Marsh (1996, 2004; Marsh & Hattie, 2002) provided exhaustive and authoritative reviews and meta-analyses of this literature (see also Allen, 2006, for a more recent but less complete review).

Hattie & Marsh (1996) reviewed 58 empirical studies of the research-teaching relationship. In order to make sense of the possible explanations for various patterns of results, Hattie & Marsh posited three distinct classes of possible explanatory categories for the research-teaching relationship: those that argue for a negative relationship (i.e., that good researchers are not good teachers), those that argue for a positive relationship (i.e., that good researchers are also good teachers) and those that argue for no relationship (i.e., that strength in one domain is not directly related to strength in the other). These categories are reviewed below.

Three models fell within the category that argued for a possible negative relationship. The first is the *Scarcity Model*. The logic here is that research and teaching compete for three critical resources: time, energy and professional commitment. Not unlike many other managerial decision-making models, the Scarcity Model assumes that faculty have limited and fixed resources (time and energy), and thus assumes that time, energy or commitment invested into either teaching or research largely comes at the expense of the other. The possible second negative relationship approach is the *Differential Personality Model*, which suggests that researchers and teachers are fundamentally different kinds of personalities with different work preferences and styles (recall the Rowland quote, above); the personal qualities associated with excelling at research are different from those that require excellence at teaching. The third is the *Divergent Reward System Model*. This holds that different incentive contingencies exist for research and teaching. However, because research activity has gained higher status in many institutions, the reward systems are not necessarily 'separate but equal'. Instead, in many institutions, the research-oriented faculty are privileged by the formal reward system (e.g., annual compensation, tenure and promotion), including a reduction in their teaching responsibilities, whereas teaching faculty bear a greater teaching load (and perhaps reduced obligations to produce publishable research), but not necessarily equal compensation or stature.

Two primary models represent a possible positive relationship between research and teaching. The first is the *Conventional Wisdom Model*. The prevailing assumption among the professoriate is that there is an essential connection between excelling at research and teaching; that the content derived from the former is critical to sustaining excellence at the latter, and that the institution seeks to hire and reward those whose combined skill set represents the true 'scholar-educator'. *Prima facie* evidence to sustain the search for these 'chosen few' is provided by surveys that find that as many as 90 percent of faculty believe an active research program is necessary to be a good instructor (Halsey, 1992, cited in Hattie & Marsh, 1996). Predictably, though, the relationship is conceived to be unidirectional, not bidirectional. That is, the core belief is that strong research skills drive good teaching, but not necessarily the reverse. A good researcher will also make a good teacher, and therefore faculty selection should be driven by demonstrated research talents. The second model which might explain a positive relationship is the '*G*' model, which argues that the fundamental constellation of personal abilities, interests and values required for quality research is the same as that required for quality teaching. That constellation of approaches includes personal qualities and habits, such as perseverance, dedication, discipline, imagination, originality, inventiveness, investigative inquisitiveness and critical analysis.

The last category, also containing three possible models, would posit that there is no special relationship between research and teaching. First, the *Different Enterprises Model* would hold that knowledge creation and generation, and knowledge dissemination and application, are fundamentally different activities that neither promote nor distract from one another. In an organizational analogy, one need not be involved in the formulation of strategy in order to execute the operational details it entails. Second, the *Unrelated Personality Model* would suggest that excellent researchers and strong teachers have uniquely different personality profiles; while there is some overlap between the qualities within each profile, the similarities are not necessarily tied to effectiveness in either domain. Finally, the third model, the *Bureaucratic Funding Model*, begins with the premise that research and teaching are divorced activities, and thus that they should be institutionally separated so as to encourage more research depth and release educational curriculum design from the research interests of faculty.

In an effort to distinguish the relative validity of these eight different models, Hattie & Marsh (1996) conducted a meta-analysis of the extant studies that met the following criteria: data were collected in universities or similar institutions of higher education, complex ratings of research and teaching activities were available and the data were sufficient to derive correlations. Indices of research productivity mainly included the number of publications or overall productivity (a weighted composite measure), but citation counts, quality assessments of publication outlets and grants were also used in some instances. Indices of teaching were predominately student and peer evaluations, although a few studies also included self-ratings.

From the 58 published studies that met these criteria, Hattie & Marsh calculated 498 correlations between the research and teaching indicators. The resultant weighted average was a correlation of .06. The mean correlation between research and teaching was somewhat higher in liberal arts colleges as compared to that in major research universities, and somewhat higher in the social science disciplines as compared to that in natural sciences or the humanities. They also reported that time spent on research is related to research productivity, but is not related to teaching quality. In contrast, actual time spent on teaching is not related to teaching quality, and is negatively related to research productivity. Further, results indicated that compared to non-researchers, good researchers were also well-prepared teachers and had strong presentation competencies, and that good researchers and good teachers were enthusiastic, employed broad topic coverage, were committed to teaching, and appeared more knowledgeable. However, as they noted in a follow-up article (2002):

> The overall conclusion of a zero relationship was found across disciplines, various measures of research output (e.g., quality, productivity, citations), various measures of teaching quality (student evaluation, peer ratings), and different categories of university (liberal, research). Based on this review, we concluded that the common belief that research and teaching are inextricably entwined is an enduring myth. At best, research and teaching are very loosely coupled. (Marsh & Hattie, 2002: 606)

The studies that comprised Hattie & Marsh's meta-analysis (1996) and the follow-up review (2002) could be criticized on a host of methodological grounds. One predictable concern is the measurement of teaching quality. Although student evaluations are important, they are only a proxy for actual student learning, which is the outcome of ultimate interest. Further, measuring research mainly through indices of productivity, like a number of publications, is a fairly blunt representation of quality. In addition, many of the studies used to prepare the meta-analysis did not use measures of either teaching or research effectiveness that allowed them to be included because of unique qualities of data aggregation or analysis. But be that as it may, the fact remains that the picture is bleak for those who insist on an unambiguous positive or negative connection between research and teaching, or even more poignantly, a directional relationship. That the traditional justification for professorial duties might simply be erroneous deserves the most serious attention.

The results of the study created signifi-cant discomfort in the academic community, largely because the results challenged the deeply held beliefs of many academics, that a positive, mutually supportive relationship between the areas of professional practice exist (cf. Neumann, 1992; Jensen, 1988), and that the two sets of practices could not even be effectively separated (Braxton, 1996; Gray, Diamond & Adam, 1996). Many also ques-tioned whether the 1996 meta-analysis was adequate to convincingly embrace the conclu-sion of 'no relationship', because that analy-sis: (a) drew from data collected across many institutions; (b) drew data from studies that did not allow the researchers to test for more complex relationships between research and teaching activities (i.e., possible mediators and moderators of the relationship); and (c) that while the relationship may be close to zero as determined by a meta-analysis of a number of studies, a stronger result might be obtained if a more complex, single-sample data set were collected from a research institution.

In response to this critique, and also to provide help to academics and university administrators who want to emphasize or shape those elements that might make the relationship more positive, Marsh (1997) explored the impact of the earlier findings and proposed an agenda for future hypothesis testing. Marsh & Hattie (2002) set out to test elements of this more defendable and elaborate agenda of the relationship between the two activities. Their intent was twofold: to examine the effects of potential mediators and moderators of the relationship between teaching and research which might explain

why the relationship between the two was not more visible (analyses which were not possible in the 1996 study because of the zero-order correlation between the major variables) (Baron & Kenny, 1986), and to examine the cultures and contexts of different departments and universities to determine whether certain academic units can create a more positive relationship because of the structural or environmental characteristics of those units. They also indicated that they hoped to take advantage of advances in statistical research methodologies, such as structural equation modeling, that would allow more sophisticated analyses of data at the instructor, department, faculty and institution levels of analysis. With regard to mediators and moderators, Marsh & Hattie chose to focus on several possible hypothesized (predicted) mediated or moderated relationships that could be grouped into two categories: back-ground variables of the specific faculty who bring differential talents to teaching and/or research, and resources committed to each of these processes. The nine proposed mediators and moderators were:

1  Perceived self-efficacy at teaching or research. Faculty who believe they are skilled at either activity might be likely to be more motivated to complete the required tasks, to spend more time and resources on activities related to each activity and hence to be better at either activity.
2  Satisfaction with teaching or research activities. The more satisfaction faculty derive from com-pleting each activity, the more time, energy and motivation they might be likely to invest.
3  Personal goals. The higher the sense of priority for each activity, the more time they might invest in it.
4  Extrinsic rewards for teaching or research. The greater the extrinsic rewards for an activity (recognition, salary, promotion), the more the activity might be pursued.
5  Constraints to teaching and research. The greater the constraints to engaging in an activity (difficulty in obtaining adequate time, materials, funding, etc.), the lower the probability that they might be likely to engage in the activity.
6  Beliefs about the nexus between research and teaching. A faculty member's beliefs about the relationship between the two activities might, in effect, create self-fulfilling beliefs for proving

either a positive or a negative relationship. Those who believe that teaching and research are compatible would probably pursue these activities in ways that are mutually reinforcing and supportive, while those who believe they are incompatible may be very conscious about the lack of compatibility and clearly favor one over the other.

7  Departmental ethos for teaching and research. These departmental characteristics may include beliefs about the teaching-research nexus at the department level, or beliefs about the greater importance of teaching-research which lead to more informal rewards and recognition for excellent performance in either activity.

8  Time actually spent on teaching and research activities. In an earlier study that developed the analytical model, Marsh (1987) proposed that time actually spent on research would be negatively related to time spent on teaching. This finding was actually confirmed by Hattie & Marsh (1996), reporting that time spent on research was seen as more critical to career success, and there was a weaker positive correlation between time spent on teaching and improved teaching effectiveness, compared to the stronger positive correlation between time spent on research and improved research effectiveness. In short, incremental improvements in teaching seem to be achievable with less direct time investment per unit time, compared to incremental improvements in research per unit time. Time invested may also be a proxy for the different levels of interest and motivation noted above. The authors note a number of studies in which time spent on either activity is correlated with time spent on the other, and to overall measures of teaching and research productivity, etc. As they note:

> the overall message appears to be that time on research is related to research productivity but not to teaching effectiveness, whereas time on teaching is not related to teaching effectiveness but may be negatively related to research productivity. … In summary, those who spend more time on research do have higher research outcomes, but those who spend more time on teaching do not seem to be more effective teachers. There seems to be a non-reciprocal pattern of relations in that time on research has more critical outcomes than time on teaching. (Marsh & Hattie, 2002: 613)

9  Activity in teaching and research. Finally, while the actual time spent on either activity appears to

yield different results, there may be a relationship between specific activities spent in teaching (e.g., class preparation, preparation of course materials, grading, meeting with students, etc.) and teaching effectiveness, and between specific activities spent in conducting research (grant writing, student supervision, editorial duties, data collection and analysis, presentation to meetings, etc.) and research effectiveness.

To investigate these relationships, Marsh & Hattie collected new data from 182 faculties at a research university, spread across 20 academic departments. Faculties reported that on the average, they spent a total of 48.3 hours working each week, of which 46 percent was on teaching, 28 percent on research and 27 percent on 'administration' (service, record keeping, etc). Teaching effectiveness was assessed with student evaluations using a standard university form, plus assessment of other instructor practices. Research productivity was assessed by faculty publication activity, and by the university's assessment of departmental-level research strength and research funding. To access the proposed mediators and moderators, a separate measure completed by each faculty member assessed time spent on research and teaching activities, internal and external 'motivations' for working on each type of activity, satisfaction with research and teaching performance and personal assessment of one's own effectiveness as a teacher and researcher. They also aggregated the teaching and research data into two major indices: teaching effectiveness (overall teacher rating, overall course value, evaluation of teaching materials and teacher presentations), and research effectiveness (number of published journal articles, conference papers, book chapters, edited books and authored books).

The results of these analyses were dramatic. First, the correlation between overall teaching effectiveness and total number of publications was .03; there was no strong correlation between any of the component elements that comprised the teaching effectiveness rating or the research publication index. When the elements of the 'teaching effectiveness' and 'research productivity' measures were combined into an overall factor score for each, the correlation between the factor scores was .02.

Second, they explored whether the teaching-research relationship might differ as a function of the type of academic department. But when the two overall indicators of teaching and research were assessed at the department level, variance at this level was not statistically significant for teaching effectiveness, research publications, or for the teaching-research relationship. Moreover, differences in 'department ethos' (culture) that might be seen as supporting a stronger emphasis on research or teaching productivity had little or no relationship to the teaching-research correlation.

Third, there appeared to be strong support for the hypothesis that time spent on research and teaching was negatively related, but no indication that the time spent on either activity had any significant impact on teaching effectiveness or research productivity.

Fourth, self-perceived ability at teaching or at research did relate to actual effectiveness at either one, but the perceived ability ratings were not significantly correlated with each other. The self-perceived rating of teaching ability was the only rating significantly related to actual teaching effectiveness. Stronger emphasis on research goals and research outcomes were negatively related to teaching outcomes.

Fifth, research publications were more consistently related to self-ratings of research ability, personal research goals, time spent on research and belief in the 'research nexus' (the belief that research facilitates teaching). Perceived research ability appeared to drive many of these high ratings, and these ratings were negatively correlated with teaching variables.

Finally, the authors tested the possible moderator variables, particularly the individual-level 'nexus' variables. Marsh & Hattie (2002) predicted that the more a faculty member believes research contributes to teaching or that teaching contributes to research, the stronger the relationship should

be between these variables and actual teaching effectiveness and research productivity. The authors tested the teaching × research interaction against 20 potential moderating variables of teaching effectiveness and research productivity; none of the relationships was statistically significant. Moreover, the teaching × research interaction was not significant for either of the nexus variables, and in fact, the direction of the non-significant interaction was negative (betas = –0.17 and –0.10); to quote the authors, 'the teaching-research relation is actually more negative for those who have the more positive beliefs that good teaching contributes to good research' (Marsh & Hattie, 2002: 626). The interaction effect was positive for academics who spend a greater proportion of their time teaching, suggesting that those who teach more may be more able to devise strategies to allow teaching to contribute to their research productivity.

The collective impact of the two Hattie & Marsh studies indicates a robust set of findings that suggest no direct *or* mediated/moderated relationship between teaching effectiveness and research productivity. Moreover, despite several literature searches, we found no significant comprehensive research since the Hattie & Marsh studies to challenge their findings. More distressingly, we found only one study examining this relationship in a professional school environment, including business schools, to examine whether or not these findings apply to professional schools versus arts and sciences disciplines. Arnold (2008, in press), studying undergraduate and graduate-level courses in a school of economics, found that there was a negative relationship between research and teaching in the first two years of a bachelor's degree program, but the relationship was positive for the later two years and for graduate courses. Arnold suggests that the results may derive from the tendency to assign more senior faculty, who are by definition more productive researchers, to upper division and graduate courses, and that these faculty may be able to integrate their research into these classes, and gain research ideas from their teaching. This study, and others which might be developed in professional schools, might be in a better position to address the hypothesis that research and teaching activities in a professional school might be more synergistic than in arts and sciences. We suggest, however, that by broadening the conception of what constitutes 'legitimate academic scholarship', business schools can fashion a robust and meaningful relationship between research and teaching activities and the reward systems that motivate them.

## BROADENING THE CONCEPT OF SCHOLARSHIP

In his seminal work, Ernest Boyer (1990), President of the Carnegie Foundation for the Advancement of Teaching, lamented the shift in the professoriate from a balanced conception of research, teaching and service, to one that emphasizes research and publication at the expense of the other two. Tracing the evolution of the conception of scholarship to the current day, he observes that research is firmly entrenched at the top of the hierarchy of academic functions, and teaching is understood as the communication of that research to others. Boyer credits this shift to a narrowing definition of scholarship among the nation's elite academic institutions, and a remarkable tendency for all leading research universities to embrace this narrow view.

In an effort to move beyond this constricted conception, Boyer argues that universities must rethink what it means to be a scholar and embrace a more expansive definition of the construct. Rather than viewing scholarship as merely 'research', Boyer offers four forms of scholarship: discovery, integration, application and teaching. We shall review the basic definition of each, and then elaborate on how they are being integrated into academic institutions and their measurement, promotion and reward systems.

The *scholarship of discovery* is probably the most familiar, as it is generally synonymous with what current academics describe as 'research'. Pursuit of this form of scholarship

is generally considered to be the essence of the professional academy: the freedom to think about problems from unrestricted, new and different perspectives, the ability to pursue knowledge for its own sake and the capacity to investigate ideas without constraint on the type of questions one can ask. The support and growth of this form of scholarship has made premier research universities – particularly in the United States – world leaders in the generation of new knowledge and insight about the human condition. Numerous Nobel Prize winners, literary stars and patent holders populate the faculties of these first class universities. They contribute both to the intellectual vibrancy of the academic culture and to a stream of financial support that cyclically sustains high-caliber research and holds tuition at an affordable level. The work performed by these academics is generally what is most highly recognized and rewarded through the awarding of tenure, promotion and compensation.

The *scholarship of integration* emphasizes the need to '... make connections across the disciplines' (p. 18), to extend knowledge obtained through discovery to comparable knowledge derived from other disciplines and paradigms. Such work is often called 'interdisciplinary research' in that the scholarship of integration is about discovering the boundaries of a particular field or tradition and then either to relate them to comparable ideas and theories in other traditions or to put them in larger perspective to infuse broader meaning. Boyer reports the results of a survey across faculty at many different types of academic institutions: 85 percent of faculty at research institutions believed that multidisciplinary work had significant value and importance and give research streams within a discipline a larger meaning and context (yet considerably fewer actually attempted it), and it tends to be somewhat less rewarded in promotion and tenure considerations.

The *scholarship of application* is the third form of scholarship. Here the scholar inquires about the ways that research findings can be applied to important practical or social problems. Not only is this form of scholarship concerned with how to direct the consequences or outcomes of research to specific issues, but the reverse is equally valid – that is, how can practical or social problems be used to dictate and direct the basic research agenda. Boyer draws a sharp distinction between 'citizenship' activities – participation in the ongoing governance and management of the university through committee work and administration – and genuine pursuit of the scholarship of application. This third form of scholarship is most visible through efforts to apply the findings from discovery and integration to significant practical or social problems, and to create and sustain an agenda for future discovery and integration that is informed from this application.

The scholarship of application is very similar to the process of action learning (Revans, 1980; Raelin, 2000). In action learning, participants in a learning process study their own actions and experience and use it to improve their performance. This process is usually done in 'action learning sets', small groups which discuss and review what they have done and then use that learning to guide future action. Action learning is a process of combining traditional knowledge (derived through books, lectures and presentations) with the constant use of questions about application in order to create new insights, ideas, approaches, refinements, etc. The approach has proved to be very effective in learning complex tasks, and for working in environments where constant improvement, refinement and fine tuning are required to improve individual and team performance.

Finally, Boyer's fourth form of scholarship is the *scholarship of teaching*, which emphasizes the dissemination of knowledge derived through discovery, integration and application. As Boyer indicates, teaching both educates and entices future scholars. It must start with intellectually engaged, well-read faculty. They must understand their field and its nuances, and they must be capable of finding creative and engaging ways of communicating complex knowledge to others. Effective teaching is a communicative

and communal act. Good teachers must be intellectually engaged and active learners. But they also must be able to transform and extend their own learning so that they are able to stimulate others to think, understand and explore. These activities may be directed at a wide variety of audiences – to those who will become practitioners, purveyors of the four forms of scholarship, or who simply seek to become wiser and more broadly educated. Effectively engaging in this scholarship requires more than effective transmission of knowledge. As Boyer emphasizes, faculty must also actively participate in the examination and evaluation of those knowledge dissemination activities so as to improve the very practice of the scholarship of teaching.

Over the past quarter century, the scholarship of teaching and learning has received significant attention. Barnett (2000) & Badley (2002) have nicely elaborated the complexity of the role responsibilities for teaching and research, and created a justification for each as different forms of inquiry. In the business school environments, Bilimoria & Fukami (2002) have traced some of the origins of the scholarship of teaching and learning movement to the creation of the Organizational Behavior Teaching Society in the mid-1970s, and the subsequent creation of the *Journal of Management Education*. Since that time, the Academy of Management professional organization has devoted significantly more program time to teaching and learning activities. Numerous other new teaching and pedagogy journals have been created in related business fields (accounting, international business, MIS, marketing and public administration), and new scholarly books, monographs, personal portraits of teaching and other teaching-related scholarship have appeared. Finally, critics of the adequacy and effectiveness of management education – beginning with Porter and McKibbin (1988) and continuing to the current day (Ghoshal, 2005; Bennis and O'Toole, 2005; AACSB, 2002) have challenged whether business schools have 'lost their way' by over-emphasizing research and under-emphasizing teaching. These critiques have led to several important innovations. First, many business schools are now encouraging and rewarding teaching and 'knowledge dissemination' activities as a regular part of faculty performance evaluation and management. Second, management educators are treating the 'classroom as an organization', applying research-derived best practices to the faculty's management of the classroom environment. These practices include processes of participative management, reward and punishment practices, teamwork, addressing cultural diversity and individual differences in learning styles. Relatedly, experienced researchers are providing instruction to teaching faculty on ways to use the classroom environment as a site for data collection and hypothesis testing in areas, such as negotiation and conflict management, teamwork and learning styles (Loyd, Kern & Thompson, 2005). Finally, the number of articles on teaching practice, technology, methods and evaluation of impact has increased significantly, as has the theoretical and empirical rigor with which these topics are addressed. Bilimoria & Fukami (2002) point to important trends in the continued development of scholarship in the management domain, and address what must be done at the department and institution level to support these developments (cf. Fukami, 2004).

## RECOMMENDATIONS

Ideally, quality acquisition and generation of knowledge ('research') is a necessary partner to quality dissemination of knowledge ('teaching'). The entire educational endeavor is based on the premise that to develop and expand what is known about a domain should go hand in hand with how to disseminate that knowledge. Knowledge must be communicated to students in a fashion that improves their ability to understand and act within a domain; in turn, students, practitioners and their teachers must ask new questions about effective action, questions

which drive future research. Ideally, this intimate and intrinsic reciprocity is indisputable, and represents the full cycle of knowledge creation, dissemination and application. As we noted throughout this chapter, however, the university began with a dominantly teaching mission, expanded to incorporate research, but is currently shifting to a heavier focus on research. This has been accompanied by a second tendency, to select faculty whose expertise is in both sets of skills. However, there are many alternative ways for the two to feed each other synergistically without them having to co-occur *within* individual faculty. As we will note, the opportunities for variation and innovation are more dramatic when we look within and across academic departments, schools and universities.

In this chapter, we examined the empirical research on the relationship between research and teaching in the broad university context. We noted that the available analyses of this data suggest that the relationship is extremely weak. At the same time, critics of business school's commitment to its educational mission are calling for fundamental transformations in the emphasis given to teaching and research activities. The combined effect of these two factors suggest that it is hard to defend the notion that knowledge creation – in the exclusive form of the scholarship of discovery – should be the dominant model encouraged and rewarded by all business schools. We believe that it is highly problematic for business schools with varying institutional characteristics and market demands to *all* value research productivity above other forms of scholarship. In this final section, we describe several ways the business disciplines can move forward around this debate.

First, the existing research on the relationship between traditional calibrations of research and teaching indicates that the two dimensions are more independent rather than correlated, much less directionally or causally related. As Hattie & Marsh (2004) note, the correlation is fundamentally zero, indicating that for some faculty, research and teaching are positively correlated, for some the two are negatively correlated and for some there is no correlation. Moreover, not all faculty are productive in either activity. Fairweather (2002) examined faculty productivity of over 25,000 faculties across 817 institutions that differed across the different classifications of universities identified by the Carnegie Commission (1987): research, doctoral-granting, comprehensive colleges and universities, liberal arts colleges, etc. They note that about 46 percent of all faculties across these designations are productive researchers, and 54 percent are productive teachers, ranging from over 50 percent at research universities to 39 percent at liberal arts colleges.[3] In order to examine the prevalence of the 'great person' model, Fairweather examined the percentages of faculty who met the standards for both high productivity in research and teaching across institutional type. On average, about 22 percent of all faculty met the criteria for high productivity in both areas. He then added a second teaching criterion: that the faculty member used more collaborative instructional practices (i.e., group discussion, class presentations, apprenticeships, internships, fieldwork, role playing, simulations, group projects or cooperative learning experiences). For this second group, the number of those highly productive in both drops to about 6 percent who meet this criterion. Faculty members in liberal arts were more likely to make this designation. Slightly more men made the first criterion (high productivity in both); slightly more women made the second group (high in both and using collaborative instructional practices).

Given the overall statistics on the relationship between teaching and research activity, and the small number of faculty in the more prestigious universities who meet the 'great person' criterion, it is not clear why more institutions do not espouse a broader view of scholarship in faculty hiring, performance review, tenure and promotion. Boyer's framework offers those involved in management education – scholars, educators and administrators alike – an opportunity to expand, recognize, and legitimate different forms of scholarship. Moreover, as we note below, institutions are

exploring ways to create the infrastructure, reward and performance evaluation systems to support this differentiation. Nevertheless, as Boyer (and others cited here) lament, the scholarship of discovery has become the most privileged criterion for allocating formal and informal internal rewards (e.g., promotion, compensation, release time, chaired professorships and discretionary budgets) and external esteem (e.g., 'Fellow' designations in major associations, keynote address invitations, editorships of major journals; cf. Gómez-Mejia & Balkin, 1992).

We urge that the research evidence on the relationship between research and teaching drive a re-examination of this privilege system, and particularly in business schools. If good teaching is as instrumental to business school success as research, more should be known about how to select and nurture both sets of skills. Good researchers can be taught to be master teachers (cf. Jaffe, 2004), and to link research to teaching (cf. Healey, 2005). Further, business schools may have to broaden their understanding of what the scholarship of discovery means in the context of business research. Most professional schools – law, education, medicine – produce research that focuses on applied problems. However, the trend in many business schools – particularly high-status research universities – has moved away from applied problems of the profession and 'backed into' the creation of new knowledge in the core disciplines from which that knowledge was drawn. Traditionally, fields like management and marketing drew basic research from psychology, sociology and economics to understand business problems. But increasingly, these fields have set out to directly compete with the basic social sciences disciplines, studying core problems that may or may not directly relate to a recognized business issue. In fact such 'basic' research is now seen as more prestigious and critical to first-class scholarship than are studies oriented toward real-world problems. A report by the British Center for Excellence in Management and Leadership described this as the difference between

Mode 1 and Mode 2 research (CEMM, 2001). Mode 1 research emphasizes academic understanding for its own sake. Its key consumer is its own kind – often a very small academic community that shares the same interest in an increasingly narrow definition of research problems. Mode 2 research, in contrast, emphasizes knowledge produced for the purpose of application. Explicitly designed for the practitioner, it requires a constant dialogue between scientist and manager to ensure understanding of the problem and application of solutions (CEMM, 2001). Bennis & O'Toole (2005) bemoan the significant drift toward Mode 1 research, suggesting that it is a core reason to explain why tenured faculties are moving away from engaging the business world. The implications are clear both for a decreased emphasis on knowledge dissemination and for an increasingly widening gap between knowledge creation and its application at the individual faculty level.

One might argue that the more the focus of scholarly business research turns toward the core disciplines and away from a firm grounding in applied business problems, the less that research also directly informs the process of instructing students (the business practitioner-to-be). Given that we found no serious scholarship examining the research-teaching relationship in the domain of management education, we argue that these implications should drive a blue-ribbon empirical investigation into this relationship – within and across management disciplines and types of business schools. We also argue that many institutions might choose to broaden their institutional scholarship so as to challenge the pre-eminence of basic theory scholarship, and to more visibly value and reward applied scholarship.

Second, research productivity requires a critical mass of faculty who are well trained in scientific conceptualization and execution. Thus, the institution must commit to supplying doctoral students or research assistants, attracting grants and independent funding and affording release time for junior faculty and highly productive scholars. Top research

universities have these resources and use them to nurture a culture that emphasizes the scholarship of discovery as a dominant criterion for faculty reward and promotion. However, it is particularly remarkable that such pressures for faculty research productivity inhere in institutions that lack a strong research ethos or the resources to attract, support and nurture a research faculty. In response to such confusion, professional associations and accrediting bodies should re-affirm a broader standard for what is recognized and rewarded, consistent with the Boyer model. The scholarships of integration, application and pedagogy are equally valid forms of inquiry. Because of their varied orientations toward breadth, practice and delivery respectively, this variety may provide mechanisms for some institutions to define excellence in their mission in a manner that does not unduly or maladaptively privilege the scholarship of discovery. Several mechanisms can be pursued here:

*Research funding.* Institutions should not necessarily be required to support research endeavors out of their own funds. In Europe, and increasingly in the United States, research is funded by industry and non-government organizations rather than by government or university-based grants. Although business academics often see such funding as 'tainted', this perception is not shared by colleagues in other professions such as medicine or engineering. These funding sources might be more likely to be 'relevant' and applied forms of business research.

*Subject populations.* The increasingly diverse nature of the business student population (undergraduate, MBA, Executive Masters, continuing education, etc.) creates a readily available population for participants in behavioral science research and organizational entry for the functional area disciplines. One notable study provided excellent guidance for how teaching venues can be employed as valuable sites for hypothesis generation and testing (Loyd, Kern & Thompson, 2005). It suggests that classroom research has had a long and honorable tradition, and also presents unique methodological considerations for researchers – those that can be managed in a way to make the classroom a fruitful arena for research.

*Training and culture change.* Teachers can not only use classrooms as data collection environments, but to be more sophisticated in the way that they extend research into the classroom by helping students learn how to do some or all of the following: define an issue, conduct a literature review, find and draw insights from the literature, propose a hypothesis, collect data, analyze the data, draw conclusions and make a presentation to peers, either individually or in groups (cf. Zamorski, 2002).

Third, we explored the veracity of the prevailing assumption in many leading research universities – that the excellent researcher and the teacher must be one and the same person. And we noted that at least one study (Fairweather, 2002) suggested that only 22 percent of faculty met the standard when loosely defined, and that the number dropped to 6 percent when he applied a more rigorous definition of 'teaching productivity'. (Since his study did NOT incorporate student evaluations of teaching effectiveness as a measure of teaching productivity, one might expect that this percentage would drop even further if that criterion were incorporated in the index.) Yet, many of the institution's leading business schools are committed to this 'superstar' theory of promotion and tenure – ideally, research *and* teaching excellence must be embodied in the same individual, and that knowledge creation should necessarily be carried out by the same person who is responsible for knowledge dissemination. As previously asserted, quality education must be linked to quality research, but there is no reason to assume that active researchers have sole custody of either the knowledge or the delivery skills most appropriate and relevant for undergraduate, masters, doctoral or exec-utive student constituencies. As researchers naturally and progressively focus their studies to gain greater depth, they might sacrifice the breadth that would place that knowledge into a context more conducive to learning. Thus, a more valid proposition would be that active

discovery scholars may not be better teachers, but those who are actively engaged in one or more of Boyer's forms of scholarship, or employ the collaborative teaching practices described by Fairweather (2002), are more likely to bring a critical, rigorous research mind-frame to the classroom and are better teachers .

The prospect that research and teaching expertise must not necessarily reside in the same person proffers both opportunities and problems. A given school might appoint, recognize and reward faculty with differ-ential responsibilities for creating and dis-seminating knowledge. Excellence in either or both areas would be rewarded with equally esteemed and valued senior professor endowed chairs, tenured status and signif-icant discretionary funds and perquisites. This approach would allow those with increased research responsibilities to devote their time and talent to top-quality research, relatively unencumbered, whereas the out-of-class activities of those with increased teaching responsibilities would focus around staying abreast of relevant literature and developing innovative instructional courses and programs. This portfolio model would, if properly managed, create a balanced human resource infrastructure capable of addressing an array of institutional missions. However, the success of this portfolio approach requires a supportive institutional culture–at both formal and informal levels. Research and teaching faculty must enjoy mutual respect and admiration for differential contributions as critical to overall institutional advancement and success. If this condition were met, the knowledge transfer between those pursing the scholarships of discovery, application and pedagogy would be remarkably productive. In contrast, the most obvious potential pitfall of this arrangement would be the unintentional creation of a 'caste' system where one designation of faculty is perceived as superior to the other. This situation already exists in many institutions that devalue teaching contributions or have subcontracted the major instructional mission to instructors whose titles, compensation and diminished voice speak volumes to a 'separate and unequal' faculty culture.

Lastly, it goes without saying that pursuit of this approach is going to require institutions to become significantly more sophisticated at evaluating teaching capability and rewarding its excellence. Faculties are quite skilled at evaluating research quantity and quality, but complex approaches for evaluating and developing teaching have lagged. Most institutions use quantitative student evaluations. A fewer number have augmented ratings with qualitative comments from student written evaluations, student focus groups, and periodic faculty observation. Fewer still endorse the development of teaching portfolios or have broadened their definitions of teaching excellence to recognize more complete 'knowledge dissemination' activities (cf. Lucal, Albers, Ballantine, Burmeister-May, Chin, Dettmer & Larson, 2003 for a review in the field of sociology). For institutions to improve the respect high-quality teaching deserves, teaching practices must be subject to peer review, and with the same degree of rigor as we currently review research grants and publications (see Van Fleet & Peterson, 2005 for one paradigm). Thus, institutions would recognize the development of new instructional materials and approaches, textbooks, simulations and authorship of articles on teaching as valid and significant contributions. Another standard for teaching excellence that has clearly lagged is to develop mechanisms for evaluating whether a faculty member's teaching materials are current and contemporary. Many administrators fear that some effective teachers may not have updated their lecture notes or readings packets in 20 years. While an experienced executive MBA student might recognize this immediately, a naive undergraduate may not. Reading, summarizing or re-interpreting current research literature in any area enhances the likelihood that teaching materials are current. Although currency may not be a concern for the active researcher who is typically reading the journals and summarizing contemporary knowledge, further work is needed to ensure that these standards are met for strong

teachers. Third, faculty compensation systems may also have to be realigned such that excellent teachers are eligible for the same level of salary increase as excellent researchers. At least one recent study (Fairweather, 2005) shows that spending more hours teaching leads to lower base salaries for faculty in research, doctoral-granting and comprehensive universities. Only teaching of graduate students saw any improvement in their pay, and the use of the more collaborative teaching techniques had little impact on pay. Developing and refining these standards becomes even more critical as many institutions turn to an increasing number of part-time and clinical faculties to bear the major burden of an institution's instructional load, since comparable criteria should be applied to both full- and part-time faculties. Finally, at the department and institution levels, faculty leaders (department chairs and deans) must work to transform the cultures within these units to support excellence in both domains. One study has shown that when there is strong congruence between individual values and the organizational priorities to support research or teaching, faculties were significantly more satisfied and productive than when they experienced incongruence (Wright, 2005).

## SUMMARY

The dominant paradigm in the faculty recognition and reward systems of most business schools is rooted in three assumptions: (1) Institutional excellence is a result of research productivity; (2) Encouraging and rewarding faculty research will yield permanent faculty who are also quality educators committed to the institution; and (3) All business schools must follow this model if they wish to improve. This paper questions these assumptions in several ways. First, the available literature suggests that a meaningful correlation or directional relationship between research excellence and teaching excellence cannot be isolated. We call on the management education community to conduct serious empirical research to explore these relationships, given the multiple demands on faculty and their institutions for increased accountability to students, their professions, their institutions and the business community. Second, faculty scholarship can be conceptualized more broadly than traditional creation of new knowledge, and it is possible to select, evaluate and reward faculty based on broader definitions of productive and contributing scholarly performance. This broadening will require improved processes to calibrate different types of scholarship, as well as by enhancing the reward and recognition to those who may excel at teaching excellence comparable to those who excel at traditional research. Third, many institutions that define the scholarship of discovery as the primary criterion for faculty performance do not have the resources to attract, nurture or support this activity. We suggest several possible alternatives for these institutions. These institutions should consider a faculty incentive and reward system which recognizes multiple forms of scholarship. and seeks to create a culture that enables rich co-existence, exchange and debate among them, thus better serving a variety of important stakeholders.

## NOTES

1 The authors wish to thank the following for their comments on earlier drafts: Mitlon Blood, Dan LeClair and Jerry Trapnell of AACSB; Dean Fred Evans of the College of Business at California State University-Northridge; and Steven Watson, Special Advisor to the President, AACSB and former Dean, Henley Management College, U.K.; two anonymous reviewers, and the editors of this volume.

2 We will NOT examine teaching effectiveness, *per se*, or whether students can effectively apply the knowledge they obtain in business schools. However, this is an important focus for both academic institutions and their accrediting agencies, as accreditation practice moves toward requiring the assessment of outcomes of various educational programs and practices.

3 'Research productivity' was defined as the number of refereed publications during the previous two-years, and 'highly productive' was defined as someone who exceeded the median number of teaching hours for the relevant program area and institutional type over a two-year period. Highly productive teachers were designated as those who exceeded the relevant median in classroom contact hours, independent studies or dissertation committees.

## REFERENCES

AACSB (2002). *Management Education at Risk*. St. Louis, MO: AACSB-International.

Allen, M. (2006). Relationship of teaching evaluations to research productivity for college faculty. In B.M. Gayle, R.W. Preiss, N. Burrell and M. Allen (eds), *Classroom Communication and Instructional Processes: Advances through meta-analyses*. (pp. 345–358). Mahwah, NJ: LEA Associates.

Arnold, I.J.M. (2008, in press). Course level and the relationship between research productivity and teaching effectiveness. *The Journal of Economic Education*.

Badley, G. (2002). A really useful link between teaching and research. *Teaching in Higher Education*, 7(4), 443–55.

Bailey, J. & Lewicki, R. *The Scientist and the Sage. BizEd*, VI, 4, pp. 32–38.

Barnett, B. (1992, June 3). Teaching and research are inescapably incompatible. *Chronicle of Higher Education*, p. A40.

Barnett, R. (2000). *Realizing the University in an Age of Supercomplexity*. Buckingham: SRHE Open University Press.

Baron, R.M. & Kenny, D.A. (1986). The moderator-mediator variable distinction in social psychological research: Conceptual, strategic and statistical considerations. *Journal of Personality and Social Psychology*, 51, 1173–1182.

Bennis, W. & O'Toole, J. (2005). How business schools lost their way. *Harvard Business Review*, May, 96–104.

Bilimoria, D. & Fukami, C. (2002). The scholarship of teaching and learning in the management sciences: Disciplinary style and content. In M. Huber & S. Morreale (eds), *Disciplinary Styles in the Scholarship of Teaching and Learning: A conversation*. (pp. 125–142). Washington, DC: American Association of Higher Education.

Boyer, E. (1990). *Scholarship Reconsidered: Priorities for the professoriate*. Princeton, NJ: Carnegie Foundation for the Advancement of Teaching.

Braxton, J.M. (1996). Contrasting perspectives on the relationship between teaching and research. *New Directions for Institutional Research, 90*. (pp. 5–14). San Francisco: Jossey-Bass.

Carnegie Foundation for the Advancement of Teaching (1987). *A Classification of Institutions of Higher*

*Education*. Princeton: Carnegie Foundation for the Advancement of Teaching.

*Do we need a separate Research Council for management research?* (2001). Center for Excellence in Management and Leadership, United Kingdom.

Fairweather, J.S. (2002). The mythologies of faculty productivity: Implications for institutional policy and decision-making. *Journal of Higher Education, 73*(1), 26–48.

Fairweather, J.S. (2005). Beyond the rhetoric: Trends in the relative value of teaching and research in faculty salaries. *Journal of Higher Education, 76*(4), 401–422, July/August.

Fukami, C.V. (2004). The scholarship of teaching and learning: Putting your money where your mouth is on teaching effectiveness. *Decision Line*, March, 20–22.

Gell, C. (1992). Faculty research. In B.L. Clark & G.R. Neave (eds), *Encyclopedia of Higher Education*. (Vol. *3*, pp. 1634–41). Oxford, UK: Pergamon.

Ghoshal, S. (2005). Bad management theories are destroying good management practice. *Academy of Management Learning & Education, 4*, 75–91.

Gómez-Mejia, L.R. & Balkin, D.B. (1992). The determinants of faculty pay: An agency theory perspective. *Academy of Management Journal, 35*, 1–36.

Gray, P.J., Diamond, R.M. & Adam, B.E. (1996). *A national study on the relative importance and research and undergraduate teaching at colleges and universities*. Center for Instructional Development, Syracuse University.

Halsey, A.H. (1992). *Decline of Donnish Dominion: The British academic profession in the twentieth century*. Oxford, UK: Clarendon.

Hattie, J. & Marsh, H.W. (1996). The relationship between research and teaching: A meta-analysis. *Review of Educational Research, 66*, 507–542.

Hattie, J. & Marsh, H.W. (2004). One Journey to unravel the relationship between research and teaching. Paper presented at a colloquium, Research and Teaching: Closing the Divide? An International Colloquium, Marwell Conference Center, Coldon Common, Winchester, Hampshire, SO21 1 JH, 18–19 March 2004.

Healey, M. (2005). Linking research and teaching to benefit student learning. *Journal of Geography in Higher Education, 29*(2), 183–201.

Jaffe, E. (2004 September). Those who can, teach. *American Psychological Society, 17*(9), 21–27.

Jensen, J. (1988). Research and teaching in the universities of Denmark: Does such an interplay really exist? *Higher Education, 17*, 17–26.

Leinster-Mackay, D.P. (1978). The idea of a university: A historical perspectives on some precepts and practices. *Vestes, 20*(4), 28–33.

Leslie, D.W. (2002). Resolving the dispute: Teaching is academe's core value. *The Journal of Higher Education, 73*(1), 49–73.

Loyd, D.L, Kern, M.C. & Thompson, L. (2005). Classroom research: Bridging the ivory divide. *Academy of Management Learning & Education, 4*, 8–21.

Lucal, B., Albers, C., Ballantine, J., Burmeister-May, J., Chin, J., Dettmer, S. & Larson, S. (2003). Faculty assessment and the scholarship of teaching and learning: Knowledge available/knowledge needed. *Teaching Sociology, 31*(2), 146–161.

Marsh, H.W. (1987). Students' evaluations of university teaching: Research findings, methodological issues, and directions for further research. *International Journal of Educational Research, 11*, 253–288.

Marsh, H.W. & Hattie, J. (2002). The relation between research productivity and teaching effectiveness: Complementary, antagonistic or independent constructs? *Journal of Higher Education, 72*(5) September/October.

Michaels, E., Handfield-Jones, H. & Axelrod, B. (2001). *The War for Talent*. Boston: Harvard Business School Press.

Neumann, B. (1992). Perceptions of the teaching-research nexus: A framework for analysis. *Higher Education, 23*, 159–171.

Newman, J.H. (1853). *The Idea of a University*. Garden City, NY: Doubleday.

Pfeffer, J. & Fong, C.T. (2002). The end of business schools? Less success than meets the eye. *Academy of Management Learning & Education, 1*, 78–95.

Porte L.W. & McKibbin, L.E. (1998). Management Education and Development Drift or Thrust into the 21st century. Highstown, NJ: McGraw-Hill.

Raelin, J.A. (2000). *Work-based Learning: The new frontier of management development*. Reading, MA: Addison Wesley.

Revans, R. (1980). *Action Learning: New techniques for management*. London: Blond & Briggs, Ltd.

Rowland, S. (2000). *The Enquiring University Teacher*. Buckingham: SRHE Open University Press.

Van Fleet, D.D. & Peterson, T. (2005). Increasing the value of teaching in the academic marketplace: The creation of a peer review infrastructure for teaching. *Academy of Management Learning and Education, 4*(4), 506–514.

Wright, M. (2005). Always at odds?: Congruence in faculty beliefs about teaching at a research university. *The Journal of Higher Education, 76*(3), 331–353.

Zamorski, B. (2002). Research-led teaching and learning in higher education: A case. *Teaching in Higher Education, 7*(4), 411–427.

# PART III

# Management Development: Non-Credit-Based Learning

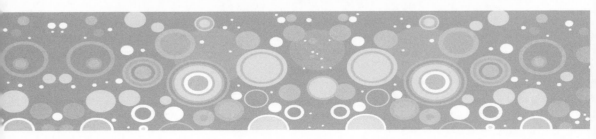

# 21

# Reflexivity, Learning and Reflexive Practice

Ann L. Cunliffe

## Abstract

In this chapter I explore three questions: What is reflexivity? Why is reflexivity important to managers and management learning? And how can we encourage and support reflexive practice in management learning? In relation to the first question, I offer a way of thinking about reflexivity from a constructionist and deconstructionist perspective. The former is situated in the sociological, existential, and phenomenological literature, the latter in poststructuralist and postmodern work. I move on to argue that reflexivity is fundamental to management and management learning because it is about who we are, how we relate to others, and what we do, and thus forms the basis for ethical and responsive management. Finally, I explore the implications of reflexivity for management learning, suggesting that one way of making reflexivity relevant to managers is to focus on reflexive practice. I suggest the basis for this is an understanding of how we make sense of our experience, and offer ways of incorporating reflexive practice in management learning.

To begin any paper with the question 'What is Reflexivity?' can lead the author and reader along a rocky road with many converging and diverging paths. It's a question I've been grappling with for a number of years, and one that involves delving into sociological, philosophical (existentialism, phenomenology, poststructuralism, etc.), anthropological, and other fields. It highlights not only a wide-ranging debate across the natural and social sciences on the meaning of reflexivity, but also differing interpretations and claims about its value and its problematic nature. Most of this debate has been an intellectual one, centered around various conceptualizations of reflexivity, its epistemological consequences, and its methodological possibilities (see Chia, 1996; Lawson, 1985; Linstead, 1994; Pollner, 1991). The critics of reflexivity claim it to be abstract, obscure, irrelevant, and encompassing overly self-indulgent introspection – a political and linguistic game played by academics with nothing better to do (Samuels, 1991; Searle, 1993). But I think these criticisms miss the point. Yes, reflexivity can be obscure if viewed in a particular way, but over the last ten years or so, I've found myself drawn more and more into believing there's a need for reflexivity in all aspects of our lives, and this plays through my research, teaching, and personal life. I've moved toward the belief that whatever else we may teach, reflexivity is fundamental to management learning because it is about who we are, how we relate to others, and what we do – and this is why reflexivity is a cornerstone for ethical and responsive management. I've also come to the realization that it's far easier to *talk about* reflexivity and to debate its merits, than it is *to be* reflexive. What I will argue in this chapter, is that *being reflexive* is at least as important, if not more so, as *doing reflexivity*, and that we need to address both in management education and learning. Of course, as a 'good' reflexive scholar I recognize mine is a situated position and therefore both fallible and contestable; nevertheless it is one that I offer as a possibility for incorporating a reflexive stance in management learning.

I will therefore explore three questions: What is reflexivity? Why is reflexivity important to managers and to management learning? And how can we encourage and support reflexive practice through management learning?

## WHAT IS REFLEXIVITY?

*'Just do it' (Just offer the lived world and write). (Latour, 1988: 170)*

The question 'What is reflexivity?' has been explored in some depth elsewhere by a number of authors, each offering a different range of reflexivities (e.g., Alvesson and Sköldberg, 2000; Cunliffe, 2003; Hardy and Clegg, 1997; Holland, 1999; Lynch, 2000; Woolgar, 1988). This is therefore not a straightforward question to answer. What I would like to do here, rather than review the various conceptualizations of reflexivity and its nuances (I've covered this ground elsewhere in Cunliffe, 2003), is to offer my own situated and ideologically bound perspective, and examine its implications for managing and management learning. This perspective is based on a number of years

working with the concept and trying to figure out how to incorporate reflexivity into my own research and teaching. During this period, my interest has moved from categorizing and critiquing reflexivities, to exploring the possibilities for *reflexive practice* – and by this I mean incorporating reflexivity not only into our research, but also into learning, teaching, as well as into managing organizations and living our lives in general. I will then offer and build on a way of thinking about reflexivity (Cunliffe, 2002, 2004) that seems to be useful in helping students understand what it means to be reflexive and why this is important. So this is not an academic monograph, rather it is more of an essay, offering ideas that might be useful in thinking about the possibilities of reflexivity for management learning.

Let me begin with a brief overview of reflexivity before moving on to discuss a way of thinking about how we make sense of our experience that moves us toward reflexive practice. Pollner's (1991) definition offers a useful start point for exploring reflexivity:

> An 'unsettling,' i.e., an insecurity regarding the basic assumptions, discourse and practices used in describing reality. (1991: 370)

This 'unsettling' can take a number of forms based on the body of literature underpinning the process. We can trace the conceptual roots of reflexivity back to two main fields: sociologically oriented work (mainly US based), and philosophically oriented work, in particular poststructuralism (mainly European based). Each orientation leads to a different approach to reflexivity: sociologically oriented work to constructionist approaches and philosophically-oriented work to deconstructionist approaches. Table 21.1 summarizes the orientations and forms a basis for the following explanation.

Cultural anthropologists and sociologists such as James Clifford (1986), George Marcus (1986), Harold Garfinkel (1967) and Clifford Geertz (1983) questioned our relationship with our social world and the ways in

**Table 21.1   A summary of the assumptions underlying constructionist and deconstructionist approaches to reflexivity**

| Constructionist | Deconstructionist |
|---|---|
| **Social and Organizational Realities:**<br>Emerge in everyday conversational and textual activities. Shaped through language use. Language communities and/or communities of social practices. | **Social and Organizational Realities:**<br>Discursively constructed sites of power, discipline, normalization, marginalization, and resistance. |
| **Self:**<br>Selves and identities shaped in everyday interaction. | **Self:**<br>A subject constructed and normalized through discursive practices. |
| **Language:**<br>What we say and how we say it shapes meaning and realities. | **Language:**<br>Separation of words and objects. Meaning is constantly deferred and constructed through binary oppositions. |
| **Knowledge:**<br>An implicit, contextual, and indexical knowing. | **Knowledge:**<br>A political process of production and consumption. |
| **Reflexive Concern:**<br>Exploring how we constitute social and organizational experience in everyday interaction.<br>Exploring multiple meanings and interpretations.<br>Exposing the situated, tentative, and provisional nature of research and knowledge. | **Reflexive Concern:**<br>Destabilizing and deconstructing Truths, ideologies, language, overarching narratives, single meanings, authority, and disciplinary practices. Revealing and interrogating assumptions that privilege particular groups. |

which we account for our experience. They were particularly concerned with unsettling our notion of 'reality': whether there are 'real' social realities and identities that exist separately from our experience of those realities; whether we experience realities in the same way; and whether we are able to explain social realities accurately and with neutrality. They argued that social realities are constructed as we interact with others and try to make sense of what is going on around us. This meant that, as Garfinkel suggested, we need to consider the 'ongoing accomplishments of organized artful practices of everyday life' (1967: 10) – practices that are indexical because they consist of shared taken-for-granted meanings that vary depending on the context in which they are used. The classic example is when we use the word 'I'. The meaning of 'I' varies depending on who is talking, in what context, and in relation to whom. As a result of this 'unsettling' of reality, cultures and social realities are loose and often contradictory 'assemblages of texts' (Clifford, 1983: 133) that shape and are shaped by people in their dialogue in particular contexts. Language therefore plays a formative role, and speech is intersubjective and performative – shaping

and being shaped by our social realities as we interact with others. This sociological orientation questions our ways of being and acting as participants in the lived world, and in addition, sees research itself as a social accomplishment with its own indexicality. Social constructionist orientations to reflexivity therefore unsettle:

- The certainty of an external and commonly shared social reality.
- The idea that language describes an already existing social world.
- The certainty of a direct relationship between knowledge and social experience, i.e., that we can write truthful and accurate accounts of our world.
- The certainty of our assumptions and knowledge claims, suggesting instead that knowledge is contextualized and tentative and so we should not claim to write authoritative accounts or generate definitive, generalizable theories.

Deconstructionist approaches to reflexivity, although holding similar assumptions about the nature of reality, unsettle in a different way. Many poststructuralists using a Foucauldian perspective argue that realities and subjectivities are constructed by discursive (linguistic systems and ways of talking, texts, ways of thinking, etc.) and non-discursive (institutional structures, social practices, techniques, etc.) practices that regulate what is 'normal' and what is not. Knowledge plays a disciplining role in this process because it consists of unconscious rules and practices that determine: what is 'good' knowledge, what are 'good' standards for judgment, who are experts, and therefore who can control meaning and speak for others. These practices are riddled with power, because they privilege particular ideologies, social structures, institutional practices, and groups over others (Foucault, 1970, 1972). Language is unstable because meaning is always deferred, moving away from any 'original object' because in defining that object we use words that are themselves defined through the use of other words with other meanings. Meanings arise from a play of différance between binary oppositions (Derrida, 1973, 1976), for example, organization is created through a tension between organization and disorganization; as we attempt to subdue the latter, we privilege the former, but both are always in contention with each other – as we attempt to organize our lives, disorganization always raises its head! Poststructuralist-based reflexivity therefore deconstructs language, texts, signifiers (iconic and linguistic symbols), and signified (the original object or concept) to reveal the fractures, contradictions, assumptions, and lack of original meaning (Lawson, 1985: 92–102). *Deconstructionists also challenge single and absolute ideologies* (e.g., capitalism) truth claims (e.g., that there are true 'facts' and 'right' ways of doing things), *and hegemonic practices* (e.g., hierarchical forms of power) *to highlight paradoxes* and *absurdities* of such claims.

To summarize, deconstructionist orientations to reflexivity aim to unsettle:

- Ideologies and 'T'ruths – that there is one best way.
- Single meanings of language and texts by revealing assumptions, contradictions, exclusions, and multiple readings.

- How knowledge, theories, and categories are constructed and marginalize groups.
- How apparently benign texts and practices privilege some groups over others.

A survey of the literature on reflexivity highlights the range of work across both perspectives, and in the final section, I will offer a number of excerpts from student papers as a means of illustrating each perspective and its relationship to reflexive practice.

## WHY IS REFLEXIVITY IMPORTANT TO MANAGERS AND MANAGEMENT LEARNING?

Let us define 'ethical intention' as *aiming at the 'good life' with and for others, in just institutions.* (Ricoeur, 1992: 172)

Management learning is not just about teaching management techniques and helping managers develop the appropriate managerial competencies; it also involves helping managers become critical thinkers and moral practitioners. The latter is important given the influence of organizations on the environment, society, and on the lives of individuals. Alasdair MacIntyre (1981) suggested that managers are one of the characters (a representative of cultural and moral ideals) of the modern age. They are perceived (and often see themselves) as morally neutral technicians engaged in the business of achieving organizational goals of efficiency and effectiveness, without necessarily engaging in moral debate on these goals or on the means by which they are achieved. This is perhaps one of the explanations for the numerous ethical scandals over the last few years. As Ghoshal states controversially, 'By propagating ideologically inspired amoral theories, business schools have actively freed their students from any sense of moral responsibility' (2005: 76). If we believe this is so, then reflexive practice is fundamental to managing and to management learning because it not only draws attention to the privileging of certain groups and the marginalization of others, but highlights the relational, and therefore moral, nature of our social and organizational experiences. This sentiment is echoed in the quote by Ricoeur (above), whose work on identity and selfhood (being who we are in the experiential moment) offers a way of thinking about reflexive practice and highlights the basis for moral leadership.

Ricoeur (an hermeneutic phenomenologist) argues that selfhood unfolds through *attestation,* an awareness that I am the author of my own discourse and actions. He also suggests that achieving selfhood is intersubjective – we come to know who we are through others – and involves an ethical intention that relates to living a good life with others. A good life is not solely about behaving according to universal norms or to creating equitable institutions, but is about being able to judge our actions in relation to others; to be responsible for our actions; and to treat others with solicitude and mutuality – to respect people for who they are rather than for their 'utility' (1992: 173–83). Attestation and ethical intention can be linked to reflexive practice because each centers around the notion that if we construct our social realities with others, then we have a moral responsibility to make available *communicative opportunities* and *socio-ontological resources* (Shotter 1993: 163) i.e., to create opportunities for others to speak and participate in shaping meaning, realities, and identities. In the context of management education and development, reflexive practice is therefore about encouraging students to:

- Challenge their conceptions of reality and organizations.
- Think about what 'just' organizations might look like.
- Explore what moral leadership might mean, and how our actions might lead to the 'avoidance of the suppression of alternative conceptions and possibilities' (Deetz, 1995: 223).
- Examine their own assumptions and taken-for-granted actions, who they are (as managers, friends, colleagues, etc.) and who they would like to be in relation to others.

And in doing so, emphasizing responsibility for helping shape new, more collaborative, and inclusive forms of reality.

## Reflexive practice in management learning

Having outlined the roots of reflexivity and its importance for managing organizations, I'd like to move on to explore the idea of reflexive practice, because it is this aspect of reflexivity I find to be of most relevance to management learning. When discussing reflexive practice with students, I spend some time defining reflexivity, particularly how it differs from reflection, and as a basis I find it helpful to compare ways in which we make sense of our experience. Figure 21.1 offers a way of doing so.

I recently attended a conference panel presentation on reflexivity, where the comment was made that some people have spent a lot of time differentiating between reflection and reflexivity – but that the issue is unimportant. This was followed by a discussion about how reflexivity involved researcher bracketing – a phenomenological concept involving a recognition of our own biases as researchers so we can be more objective in collecting data, be aware of the impact of those biases on data interpretation, and be able to offer a more authentic explanation. I mention this discussion because it highlights an issue I find problematic. I am one of the 'some' who believe there *is* a difference, and that this difference *is* an important and fundamental

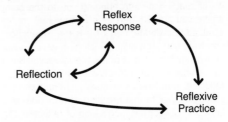

**Figure 21.1   Making sense of experience: Situating reflexive practice**

one, because reflection and reflexivity incorporate:

- very different understandings of the nature of our social realities;
- very different understandings of who we are in relation to our world and others;
- and these understandings carry different implications and responsibilities for our actions and interactions.

Whether we are engaging in reflection, reflexivity, or both, means we go about our research and teaching in different ways. And while much of management learning is based on a tradition of reflecting about our experiences (see Chapter 5), reflexive practice is less prevalent and more complex. Figure 21.1 can be a useful start point in refining understanding of reflexive practice.

As a means of illustrating these ways of making sense, I'd like to offer excerpts from research conversations that took place over a number of years as part of two different studies. I have selected these excerpts because they have particular relevance for the ways in which managers make sense of their organizational lives. The first was a conversation with Mike, Vice President of a health care organization. This conversation was about the uncertainties of managing organizations, but we moved on to talk about how he knew what to do as a manager.

**Ann:** '... so how do you know what you know?'
**Mike:** 'How you come to that knowing, is in my case 49 years, 3 months and 25 days. I think it's all that's gone into bringing you to the point where you are. So, part of it is how well you've acquired knowledge, part of it is the experiences you have had – experiential learning which is not knowledge bound, part of it is the values you bring to the situation, some of it is your own ability to be reflective in different situations ... I don't know a snappy answer to that question of how does one know. ... My conversation's kind of reflective, I'm trying to think "what do I believe about knowing, what do I know about knowing?" so I'm trying to access knowledge, do some synthesis and say this is what seems right to me'.

*And later:*

**Mike**: '... knowing is an ongoing process, it's more synthetic, contextual [than knowledge], what you're doing at the time, almost with that knowledge and the experience you're having at the time – almost the intersection of experience, environment and knowledge becomes knowing'.

What follows is a discussion of how these excerpts help explain the notions and differences between reflex response and reflection.

(a) **Reflex Response: 'Experiential learning which is not knowledge bound ... an ongoing process ... what you're doing at the time ...'**

I suggest that one of the ways in which we make sense is intuitive, and embedded in action and interaction. Reflex responses are those embodied reactions, a tacit knowing which is difficult to articulate because it's a form of knowing that often involves instantaneous and intuitive action – as Mike says, a knowing at the 'intersection of experience, environment and knowledge'. Reflex responses are part of the ongoing, practical, and indexical accomplishments discussed by Garfinkel, and are unselfconscious in the sense that we are often unaware of the performative impact of words, gestures, and responses on others and ourselves. What to say, how to act, how to respond, is spontaneous to the moment of interaction (Cunliffe, 2002). We are so at home in our surroundings, and our actions, ways of relating and speaking are so much a part of who we are, that we do not think about how to act in advance, nor do we notice what we are saying or doing in the moment. Merleau-Ponty suggests we attune ourselves to situations through skillful and embodied responses: responses not based on reflection – representation, thinking, and then reconstruction – but on an understanding in which we 'experience the harmony between what we aim at and what is given, between the intention and the performance' (1962: 167).

Much of our everyday interaction can be seen in this way. We interact and react in ways that, in the experiential moment, we may not be able to articulate. As Merleau-Ponty says, just as musicians 'feel', not measure, where the keys and pedals are and use them to achieve musical and emotional responses, so we 'feel' our way around our relationships and interactions with others. This is instinctive – a gut or reflex action – but an action or reaction not entirely random or ungrounded, because as we speak and act in-the-moment we may unconsciously draw on our tacit knowing of people, organizational practices, or the problem at hand. For example, in a recent discussion with a retired senior executive now working in a business school, I asked her for her thoughts about a meeting we had just attended this is part of a study of identity with a colleague; the name has been anonymized.

> **Helen:** 'I got quite frustrated because we had heard some various pieces of input from the students and I wanted that to be incorporated. And some of it was, no question, fairly basic information— effective meetings and time managements and things like that. And I can remember very strong push-back … saying, 'Well, that's dumbing it down', or something. I can remember finger in the socket and sort of reacting and saying, 'You know, at the end of the day, to be successful you have to be able to run an effective meeting. You have to manage your time. And if that's what they need, that's what they need'. You know? And then you step away and say, you know, in the meeting [I'm] disappointed in the approach I took'.

In this instance, her references to the 'finger in the socket' response and 'sort of reacting' are good examples of reflex responses. They also illustrate Merleau-Ponty's notion about the connection between intention and performance: her embodied response was based on her (skillful) management experience and her aim (articulated in a number of our discussions) to prepare students for the business world. She later reflects back on the situation (as she's doing in our discussion) 'And you step away and say … disappointed in the approach I took'. This highlights the interwoven nature of reflex responses and reflection.

(b) **Reflection: 'I'm trying to think "What do I believe …" so I'm trying to access knowledge …'**

*Active, persistent, and careful consideration of any belief or supposed form of knowledge in the light of the grounds that support it, and the further conclusions to which it tends,* constitutes reflective thought. (Dewey, 1997: 6, italics in original)

As seen in Chapter 6, contemporary work on reflection has built on early work by Dewey, and is more nuanced than I will outline here. Chapter 6 also speaks to the impact of reflection on management education – more recently the role of critical reflection. What I offer here is some aspects of reflection that help differentiate it from the other forms of sensemaking identified in Figure 21.1. I'd like to begin with Dewey's work (originally published in 1910) because he was concerned particularly with the role of reflection and education in broadening critical thinking skills.

In Dewey's exposition of how we think, he argues that the aim of education is a logically-trained mind. Central to this aim is reflective thought, which involves a balance between analysis and synthesis, concrete and abstract, experiential and experimental (empirical and scientific) thinking. A disciplined mind involves a way of thinking that involves an 'ability to "turn things over," to look at matters deliberately, to judge whether the amount and kind of evidence requisite for decision is at hand' (1997: 66–7). He states that the basis for this is reflection, and the basis of reflection is discovering facts to confirm or disconfirm beliefs. As Mike says in the excerpt above, he's thinking about what he knows, what he believes, and synthesizing information to see 'what seems right to me'.

In talking about the nature of reflective thought, Shotter (1993) aptly summarizes its key assumptions:

- That there is a single reality to be discovered. This idea of reflective correspondence incorporates the view that there is an object we can think about, measure, categorize, and develop theory to explain.

- That our minds work on discovering an objective viewpoint of that reality. Reflection has also been defined as *benign introspection* the goal of which is to improve 'the adequacy of the connection between analysts' statements and the object of those statements', which 'sustains and enhances the Scientific axiom of the research effort' (Woolgar, 1988: 22).

- That reflective thought can discover a deeper form of 'underlying order from which all human thought and activity *must* in fact spring' (Shotter, 1993: 24).

- And that there are 'already determined meanings' to describe what is. (p. 25)

Reflection is therefore associated with assumptions of a rational and reasoning being with an inner consciousness, making logical sense of an outside world. It assumes a knower, a known, and a set of accurate statements, and is viewed as a cognitive or intellectual activity in which critical reflection should be objective, logical, and rational.

The need for reflection and reflective practitioners underpins much of management education. Schön (1983) implies that reflection is a means of examining situational requirements; of connecting the ideas and experiences of a manager or a professional with the conditions of the environment, with customers or clients, and with organizational policies and practices. This process involves *reflecting-in-action*: constructing an understanding by drawing upon cumulative personal and organizational knowledge and engaging in a reflective conversation with the situation (see Chapter 5). Reflecting-in-action incorporates an experimental logic of exploration, move testing and hypothesis testing (p. 147) – part of the synthesis Mike mentions (above). For Schön and others (e.g., Kolb, 1984), reflection-in-action provides a stimulus for viewing professional and management practice from an active and contextualized perspective and forms a basis for more effective problem solving by developing a 'new theory of the unique case' (p. 68). We often ask our students to engage in reflection on case studies or in

self-reflection on their own actions and traits as a means of developing their skills and competencies.

We also engage in reflection on an everyday basis, as the excerpt from my discussion with Helen – where she was reflecting-on-action (see Chapter 6) illustrates:

> **Helen:** 'So there are times where, yeah, I'd be dishonest if I didn't, it's a struggle sometimes to say, "I used to be listened to by an awful lot of people. And my opinion isn't listened to here…" '
>
> 'The self-reflection that probably occurs for me is to step away from it and say, "But that's not what this is about." You know? So I will deliberately have to pull myself out … that's probably a good example where you say, "But that's not my domain. I can give suggestions or thoughts about it. But really, at the end of the day …" So there would be a good example where I would even sit back here in the office this afternoon and say, "I could have handled that [meeting] better. I could have maybe not worried quite as much." But I'm not entirely there yet in terms of my transformed self'.

As Helen implies, it can be 'a struggle' in the experiential moment to separate yourself from your feelings (her reflex response), and it's only later she's able to 'pull myself out', to 'step away' and reflect on how she handled the situation. This 'stepping away' requires some degree of separation from our feelings and ourselves, to think more objectively about how we act. Yet herein lies a paradox, 'The paradox of self-identity is that the state of seeing or thinking can never see or think itself, for when it tries to do so it must necessarily take itself as its own object and thus lose sight of its active subjectivity' (Cooper, 1987: 407). In other words, self-reflection becomes a disembodied process because it involves turning ourselves into objects of study – an individual at large – by identifying and comparing our traits and actions with generalized psychological and personality characteristics (e.g., introvert, high self-monitors, etc.). This reflective separation provides a basis for self-development, but I suggest that in practice we cannot be objective – our view is always situated, positioned, and part of who we are.

Reflection can therefore be enhanced by reflexive practice.

## (c) Reflexive Practice:

Social constructionists loop the circle of reflexivity around onto themselves. From our point of view, it thus becomes a problem as to why, at this moment in history, we account for our experience of ourselves in the way we do … . (Shotter, 1992: 177)

Both constructionist and deconstructionist approaches to reflexivity are based on the assumption that social and organizational realities are linguistically constructed. They are, however, based on very different assumptions about how this takes place, on the nature of language, and on the form of 'unsettling' reflexivity should take. As seen in Table 21.1, deconstructionist approaches view realities and selves as discursively constructed sites of power and aim to destabilize realities, language, agency, and ideologies. I suggest this can be equated with critical reflexivity, which often takes the form of an intellectual critique of ideologies and texts. Constructionist approaches view realities and selves as constructed by people in their interaction, and aim to explore the process of constituting social and organizational realities. Melvin Pollner (1991) argues that we need to engage in *radical reflexivity*, which 'enjoins the analyst to displace the discourse and practices that ground and constitute his/her endeavors in order to explore the very work of grounding and constituting' (p. 370). In other words, Pollner is asking us to recognize our own situated position and its impact on our research. Elsewhere, I have argued that radical reflexivity forms a basis for reflexive inquiry (Cunliffe, 2003); here I wish to take this further by exploring the implications of radical reflexivity for management learning. I suggest that this means helping managers become aware of how their assumptions and how these play into their conversations, interactions, and the responses of others, and how they shape meanings and organizational 'realities' in everyday conversations. As educators we

also need to think about how our positioned assumptions play into our teaching. This is *reflexive practice* – which I believe is about *being* reflexive in the way we manage organizations, interact with others, and live our lives in general. It involves both critical and self-reflexivity.

Critical reflexivity, based on deconstructionist approaches, offers a way of critiquing ideologies, normalized social and organizational practices, and their consequences. In this way, we can begin to think about how overarching narratives, for example of efficiency, profit, and managerial authority, legitimate our 'social and political institutions and practices, laws, ethics and ways of thinking' (Lyotard, 1992: 18). Critical reflexivity also means uncovering the ways in which organizations are sites of power, disciplining members to be good (normalized) performers, (e.g., Martin, 1990; Townley, 1994). We need only look at the systems and practices within organizations to see how this operates: we are hired based on normalized selection criteria; we work to job descriptions; are evaluated and rewarded through performance management systems; and are trained to be competent and behave in appropriate ways. These organizational practices, often seen to be objective processes, can privilege some and marginalize others. For example, Ashcraft and Mumby (2004) talk about the often taken-for-granted gendered nature of organizations:

First, gender is constitutive of organizing; it is an omnipresent, defining feature of collective human activity, regardless of whether such activity appears to be about gender. Second, the gendering of organization involves a struggle over meaning, identity, and difference; this ongoing discursive struggle occurs amid, and acts upon, gendered institutional structures. Third, such struggle (re)produces social realities that privilege certain interests. (p. xv)

Foucault suggests the real political task of critique (critical reflexivity), is to surface and examine the techniques and practices of power and discipline (e.g., Deetz, 1998; Mumby, 1988) or explore how organization culture manipulates and controls meaning and provides a forum for competing hegemonic stories (e.g., Boje, 1994). By engaging in critically reflexive practice managers can reveal opposing and multiple perspectives; offer alternative ways of thinking about these practices; and create possibilities for managing organizations in more equitable ways through collaborative and responsive discourse (Deetz, 1992). Critical reflexivity can therefore lead to new possibilities for changing organizational practices and transforming hierarchical values into new, more democratic, and socially relevant values (Jun, 1994: 20). One of my MBA students talked about the need to critique accepted practices and their consequences in his paper (I will explain the use of reflexive papers and journals in more detail later):

In law school, we were taught to address issues by applying a template, a framework known as IRAC. IRAC stands for Issue, Rule, Analysis, and Conclusion. You were tasked with pinpointing the issue, finding the rule, applying that rule to the issue, and formulating a conclusion. This 'master program' (Argyris, 1991) is a product of single-loop learning because it tends to create organizational defenses when things go wrong. ... In my example, I (and many other students) took for granted the IRAC rule as a way to solve problems. IRACking, as it is commonly known in law school circles, became a habitual practice for me. It was the only way I knew how to solve problems. Reflexivity would have required me to question this framework, explore limitations in [its use], and remain open for change. Perhaps reflexivity would have led me to ignore the IRAC framework and forced me to analyze my client's situation through a different perspective. Perhaps, a dialogue with my clients would have helped me better understand the issue(s) my clients were facing.

Self-reflexivity incorporates Pollner's (1991) notion of radical reflexivity in that it centers around recognizing the part we play with others in shaping (and being shaped by) our social realities, meanings, and our sense of who we are. In being self-reflexive, we are attesting (Ricoeur, 1992) to our ability to act and to understand that we are always selves-in-relation-to-others – 'others' being both particular people and generalized others such as groups, categories (white, female,

extrovert), language systems, culturally and historically-situated discursive and non-discursive practices (Cunliffe, forthcoming). *Being* self-reflexive also involves:

- Questioning our own ways of being, relating, and acting. How our assumptions, words, and responses in living conversation influence others (Bakhtin, 1981). It also means surfacing our defensive responses and their impact.
- Questioning how we make sense of our surroundings and the multiplicity of meanings and voices we may or may not hear. Becoming aware of the limits of our knowledge, of how our own behavior plays into organizational practices and why such practices might marginalize groups or exclude individuals.
- Examining how we may act responsibly and ethically.
- Understanding how we relate with others, and between us shape organizational 'realities' – shared practices and ways of talking.

Thus, we recognize, we are active in shaping our surroundings, and begin to critically take circumstances and relationships into consideration rather than merely reacting to them. Another excerpt from an MBA student's paper helps illustrate this notion of attestation and self-reflexivity:

My challenge in this situation is in identifying ways to change this habit, this rigid, ingrained pattern of thinking ... [That] my way is the only way because it works for me. Yet, not only was this mode of thinking harmful to my group members, it doesn't benefit me, particularly in my interactions with others. ... I honestly believe it is easy to look back at a situation and identify things I could have done better, such as showing more patience or trust in my group members, or holding my tongue, but this doesn't seem to address the heart of the issue, which is why do I act out of the belief that my ways are right, and that the only reasonable way to accomplish a goal is by following my pre-determined timetable and method? 'If we practice the discipline of remembering ourselves, we will become amused witnesses to the folly of many of our actions. (Chatterjee 1998: 6)

By engaging in self-reflexivity we help create new possibilities for action, new ways of being and relating, while recognizing the ethical responsibilities associated with these new ways.

Managers and students alike may engage with reflexivity as an intellectual, a social, and/or a personal practice. As an intellectual practice, they can draw on deconstructionist approaches to write critical essays, analyze case studies and current events from a critically reflexive perspective. This involves examining possible underlying assumptions, normalizing, and disciplining practices. They can also analyze their own organizational experiences from a critical perspective, identifying contradictions in organizational policies and practices, exploring différance and multiple readings of texts, organizational documents, and practices. Critical reflexivity means complexifying rather than simplifying, questioning rather than answering or accepting, looking for paradoxes and contradictions rather than order and patterns, thinking about what lies unsaid as well as what is said, and recognizing multiple perspectives rather than imposing a world view.

Thinking and acting self-reflexively means thinking from *within experiences* about who we are and how we relate with others. I have used reflexive journals and papers for a number of years with undergraduates, MBA and MPA, and Executive MBA students. Journals can be powerful in helping students think both more reflectively and reflexively about the way they interact with others. Not only do they personalize reflexive practice, but as Locke and Brazelton (1997) suggest, writing itself is a learning process because it offers a way of surfacing, articulating, and rethinking our conceptualizations of the world: a way of thinking about thinking. Journals relying on reflection usually ask students to apply concepts and theories to particular situations as a means of identifying patterns of behavior, systems, and structures; analyzing those situations and/or their own actions, competencies, and personality traits. Reflexive journals involve attestation (Ricoeur, 1992) – accepting and taking responsibility for the part we play in constructing social realities. They begin with the premise that 'The basic practical-moral

problem in life is not what to do but what kind of person to be' (Shotter and Cunliffe, 2002: 20). This means questioning our own assumptions; thinking reflexively about how these assumptions influence the ways in which we relate to others and influence each other's responses; how we construct meaning about what is happening; and thinking about our role in creating communicative opportunities and ethical discourse. It also involves writing from the first person rather than the objective (reflective) third person. I have written about the approaches, issues, and grading of reflexive journals in depth elsewhere (Cunliffe, 2004). As a means of illustrating the difference between reflective and reflexive journals and papers, I will outline the requirements and offer two examples.

I ask students to do the following in their reflexive journals:

1  Identify personal insights, issues, instances of critical questioning and revelation, connections with ideas or comments (by you, other course members, readings …) that struck you and offered the potential for reflective/reflexive insight or learning.
2  Discuss why these are important to you. What impact did they have and/or what dilemmas, questions or possibilities did they raise? Have these resulted in order or chaos for you?
3  So what are you going to do now? What issues, questions, and dilemmas are you going to explore further – why and how? How will this influence who you are and how you relate to others? What relational nets can you construct/connect with to continue this process of reflective and reflexive learning?

As a means of illustrating this form of writing, I offer two excerpts from student journals. The first is an example of self-reflexivity, of questioning his way of being. If written from a reflective perspective, the student would probably have talked about his results from self-assessment questionnaires (e.g., the Myers Briggs Type Indicator®, or the Big 5 Personality Model) to identify strengths, weaknesses, and areas of improvement. Here he writes from his own insight and discusses the paradoxical nature of his strengths and weaknesses:

> I will begin by listing the strengths with the weakness with which those strengths are entangled. I am:
>
> Confident yet insecure; respected for my abilities and knowledge yet quiet in eliciting them; well-liked with a good sense of humor yet shy; honest yet too forthright at times; hardworking and motivated yet disinterested; organized yet a procrastinator; resourceful but too independent; always willing to help yet sacrificing my own work; and finally, smart yet cocky.
>
> Looking at the list above, I realize the dichotomy that exists within me, and it evidences qualities I feel can be unleashed if I am attentive to the strengths and work to limit my weaknesses. Many of the weaknesses I have are masked by my strengths (confident yet insecure, hardworking yet disinterested) while some of the strengths, when misused, can become weaknesses (smart becomes arrogance, honesty becomes opinionated). I recognize that most of my strengths are apparent to others because those I have listed above have been used to describe me in performance reviews. But deep down, I know that sometimes I can procrastinate, be disinterested in the task at hand, and be too forthright. My weaknesses are often hidden and controlled, but the fact that they are there and sometimes hold me back, is a concern of mine. I do not perceive my weaknesses as terribly bad qualities but as I listed them above, I realized that I had more of a façade (Luft & Ingham, 1955) that I originally thought.

My second example blends critical and self-reflexivity and is taken from another student's paper. This excerpt addresses her initial assumptions and her experience of the lack of information sharing amongst course members, which she connects with Foucault's notions of knowledge/power. In doing so, she writes from within her experience: her questions, dilemmas, and insights.

> I assumed we were here first and foremost to learn; last and finally, to compete against each other. I did not anticipate that there would be a power structure, and that this power structure would be based in part on information sharing, and that it could potentially interfere with the desire to learn through exchange. I did not know that by openly sharing information, power could be lost. I had never really thought of information sharing

> as having any relationship with power … yet, from my observations during the first ten weeks of the program, (they) are clearly linked. Lastly, I trusted that my openness and desire to share (my theories in action) would earn respect and be reciprocated. I was wrong. …
>
> Have we been socialized to act and respond in a specific manner? Does our response correspond to some ultimate desired result – do we have an agenda? Is it dependent upon our culture? Are our actions and reactions predicated on our insecurities and/or vulnerabilities? … Foucault believes that power is inescapable and seeps through into the core of our being. We think in language so we think in terms of power. …
>
> As I worked through my struggles with regard to information sharing … I have made several realizations. *(She discusses these in some depth)* It is only through these realizations, and my learning through such, that I am better able to understand the dynamics of information sharing and am better prepared to move forward …. (Originally published in Cunliffe, 2002)

Once students grasp the notion and practice of critical and self-reflexivity through their journals, they also recognize their ability to change themselves and create new ways of relating.

In summary, I suggest reflexivity is fundamental to managers and management learning because not only does it require us to 'unsettle' and 'question' our ways of relating, acting, managing, and organizing, it also carries with it an ethical and moral responsibility for both our personal and organizational actions. This responsibility centers around attestation and self-reflexivity – it is based on recognizing the active role we play with others in shaping our social and organizational realities. Another MBA student aptly summarized this responsibility:

> Early in this paper, I was expressing concern over others' perspectives of me – *who they think I am.* That was a subtle expression of fearing the hidden. I reiterate that the best way for others to actually know *who I am,* is for me to first know *who I can be over time,* and then to *speak* and *act* consistently within that range. To overcome concerns and fears requires such action. In my experience, negative outcomes magnify when they are accompanied by fear. If the hidden is exposed – subjected to the light – then we can make a more measured decision

as to whether or not the object of our concern merits attention.

Self- and critical reflexivity can form an impetus for developing more responsive, creative, and ethical ways of managing organizations. In this sense, reflexive practice can and should be an integral part of management learning and management practice.

# REFERENCES

Alvesson, M. and Sköldberg, K. (2000) Reflexive Methodology: New Vistas for Qualitative Research. London: Sage.

Argyris, C. (1991) 'Teaching smart people how to learn', Harvard Business Review, 69: 99–110.

Ashcraft, K.L. and Mumby, D. (2004) Reworking Gender: A Feminist Communicology of Organization. Thousand Oaks, CA: Sage.

Bakhtin, M.M. (1981) The Dialogical Imagination: Four Essays by M.M. Bakhtin. Edited by M. Holquist. Trans. by C. Emerson and M. Holquist. Austin: University of Texas Press.

Boje, D.M (1994) 'Organizational storytelling. The struggles of pre-modern, modern and postmodern organizational learning discourses', Management Learning, 25 (3): 433–61.

Chatterjee, D. (1998) Leading Consciously: A Pilgrimage Toward Self-Mastery. Boston, MA: Butterworth-Heinemann.

Chia, R. (1996) 'The problem of reflexivity in organizational research: Towards a postmodern science of organization', Organization, 3: 31–59.

Clifford, J. (1983) 'On ethnographic authority', Representations, 1: 118–46.

Clifford, J. (1986) 'Introduction: Partial truths', in J. Clifford and G. Marcus (eds), Writing Culture: The Poetics and Politics of Ethnography. Berkeley, CA: University of California Press. pp. 1–26.

Cooper, R. (1987) 'Information, communication and organization: A poststructuralist revision', The Journal of Mind and Behavior, 8: 395–416.

Cunliffe, A.L. (2002) 'Reflexive dialogical practice in management learning', Management Learning, 33: 35–61.

Cunliffe, A.L. (2003) 'Reflexive inquiry in organization research: Questions and possibilities', Human Relations, 56: 981–1001.

Cunliffe A.L. (2004) 'On becoming a critically reflexive practitioner', Journal of Management Education, 28: 407–27.

Cunliffe, A.L. and Jun, J. (2005) 'The need for reflexivity in public administration', Administration and Society, 37: 225–42.

Cunliffe, A.L. (forthcoming 2008) 'Orientations to social constructionism: Relationally-responsive social constructionism and its implications for knowledge and learning', Management Learning,

Deetz, S. (1992) Democracy in an Age of Corporate Colonization: Developments in Communication and the Politics of Everyday Life. Albany: State University of New York Press.

Deetz, S. (1995) 'Character, corporate responsibility and the dialogic in the postmodern context: A commentary on Mangham', Organization, 2: 217–25.

Deetz, S. (1998) 'Discursive formations, strategized subordination, and self-surveillance: An empirical case', in A. McKinlay and K. Starkey (eds), Foucault, Management and Organizational Theory. London: Sage. pp. 151–72.

Derrida, J. (1973) Speech and Phenomena. Evanston: Northwestern University Press.

Derrida, J. (1976) Of Grammatology. Baltimore, MD: John Hopkins University Press.

Dewey, J. (1997) How We Think. Mineola, NY: Dover Publications, Inc. (originally published 1910).

Foucault, M. (1970) The Order of Things. An Archaeology of the Human Sciences. London: Routledge.

Foucault, M. (1972) The Archaeology of Knowledge, trans. by A.M. Sheridan Smith. New York: Pantheon Books.

Garfinkel, H. (1967) Studies in Ethnomethodology. Englewood Cliffs. NJ: Prentice-Hall.

Geertz, C. (1983) Local Knowledge. New York: Basic Books.

Ghoshal, S. (2005) 'Bad management theories are destroying good management practices', Academy of Management Learning and Education, 4 (1): 75–91.

Hardy, C. and Clegg, S. (1997) 'Relativity without relativism: Reflexivity in post-paradigm organization studies', British Journal of Management, 8 (Special Issue – June): S5–S17.

Holland, R. (1999) 'Reflexivity', Human Relations, 52: 463–84.

Jun, J.S. (1994) Philosophy of Administration. Seoul: Daeyoung Moonhwa International.

Kolb, D.A. (1984) Experiential Learning: Experience as the Source of Learning and Development. NJ: Prentice-Hall.

Latour, B (1988) 'The politics of explanation: An alternative', in S. Wooigar (ed.), Knowledge and Reflexivity: New Frontiers in the Sociology of Knowledge. London: Sage. pp. 155–76.

Lawson, H. (1985) Reflexivity: The Postmodern Predicament. La Salle, IL: Open Court.

Linstead, S. (1994) 'Objectivity, reflexivity, and fiction: Humanity, inhumanity, and the science of the social', *Human Relations*, 47: 1321–45.

Locke, K. and Brazelton, J.K. (1997) 'Why do we ask them to write, or whose writing is it anyway?', *Journal of Management Education*, 2: 44–57.

Lynch, M. (2000) 'Against reflexivity as an academic virtue and source of privileged knowledge', *Theory, Culture & Society*, 17: 26–54.

Lyotard, J.F. (1992) *The Postmodern Explained*. Ann Arbor, MI: University of Minnesota Press.

MacIntyre, A. (1981) *After Virtue: A Study in Moral Theory*. Notre Dame, IN: University of Notre Dame Press.

Marcus, G.E. (1986) *Anthropology as Cultural Critique: An Experimental Movement in the Human Sciences*. Chicago: University of Chicago Press.

Martin, J. (1990) 'Deconstructing organizational taboos: The suppression of gender conflict in organizations', *Organization Science*, 1: 339–59.

Merleau-Ponty, M. (1962) *Phenomenology of Perception*. Trans. by C. Smith. London and New York: Routledge. (Reprinted 2004).

Mumby, D.K. (1988) *Communication and Power in Organizations: Discourse, Ideology and Domination*. Norwood, NJ: Ablex.

Pollner, M. (1991) 'Left of ethnomethodology: The rise and decline of radical reflexivity', *American Sociological Review*, 56: 370–80.

Ricoeur, P. (1992) *Oneself as Another*. Trans. by K. Blamey. Chicago: University of Chicago Press.

Samuels, W. (1991) 'Truth and discourse in the social construction of economic reality: An essay on the relation of knowledge to socioeconomic policy', *Journal of Post Keynesian Economics*, 13: 511–24.

Schön, D.A. (1983) *The Reflective Practitioner: How Professionals Think in Action*. New York: Basic Books.

Searle, J.R. (1993) 'Rationality and realism: What is at stake?', *Daedalus*, 122: 55–84.

Shotter, J. (1992) 'Social constructionism and realism: Adequacy or accuracy?', *Theory and Psychology*, 2: 175–82.

Shotter, J. (1993) *Conversational Realities: Constructing Life through Language*. London: Sage.

Shotter, J. and Cunliffe, A.L. (2002) 'Managers as practical authors: Everyday conversations for action', in D. Holman and R. Thorpe (eds), *Management and Language: The Manager as Practical Author*. London, UK: Sage. pp. 15–37.

Townley, B. (1994) *Reframing Human Resource Management: Power, Ethics, and the Subject at Work*. London: Sage.

Woolgar, S. (ed.) (1988) *Knowledge and Reflexivity: New Frontiers in the Sociology of Knowledge*. London: Sage.

# 22

# Action Learning and Related Modalities

Joseph A. Raelin

## Abstract

In this chapter, I hope to first locate action learning within the range of prevailing 'action modalities' in management development that conceive of practice as having its own epistemology. They all more or less emphasize the value of concurrent reflection on experience to expand and create new knowledge while improving practice itself. I will then succinctly describe action learning both in theory and practice, highlighting and illustrating its prospective outcomes, its project orientation, and its reliance on learning teams. Next, I will survey other selected action modalities, namely: action research, action science, developmental action inquiry, and cooperative inquiry. In the last sections, I will take up three contemporary topics: the emergence of critical theory within the action dimension, which bounds action learning's humanistic aspirations; the global application and resulting cross-cultural implications of the use of action learning; and the challenge to the action modalities of their not yet having widespread adoption in the field.

Action learning fits within a management development cluster of strategies that I have chosen to refer to as the 'action modalities.' Although this chapter is primarily dedicated to action learning, it is important to locate it within an emerging tradition in management development that sees practice as having its own epistemology. Distinct from the more fixed world of classic academic scholarship, which has long been viewed as being accessed through reason and intellect rather than through experience (Damasio, 1994; Letiche & Van Hattem, 2000), the action modalities embody the 'practice turn' in social theory. Using language as an ends, not as a means of transference, they acknowledge that concurrent reflection on experience can expand and even create knowledge at the same time that it is engaged in improving practice (Gramsci, 1973; Bourdieu, 1990; Bergson, 2001).

Although not always credited, Kurt Lewin (1946) is this author's nomination as the founder of these so-called action modalities in his reference to action research as a means of conducting systematic inquiry into group and organizational phenomena. However, the original source of the epistemological tradition that undergirds these modalities is likely to be American pragmatist, John Dewey (1897), who as founder of the experiential education movement believed that learning should be active and that learners should be involved in real-life tasks and challenges (the 'social life'). Another common basis unifying these modalities is that knowledge is to be produced in service of, and often in the midst of, action (Peters & Robinson, 1984). Often, the knowledge generated is from real-time data that can support participants' reflection on feedback helping them make sense of what has happened and what can be done next. Through the interplay between action and feedback, participants acquire more valid social knowledge, more effective social action, and greater alignment among self-knowledge, action, and knowledge of other.

Action learning can produce new knowledge whether it arises from reflection on theory or reflection in practice, and whether its producers are academics or practitioners or both. The nexus between theory and practice results from a dialectical process of inquiry in which the context may predispose particular parties to contribute their points of view. Thus, at times, researchers will dialogue with other researchers, at other times faculty will interact with students, theorists with practitioners, generalists with locals, professionals with managers, observers with actors, and so forth.

The action modalities are thus inherently participatory. Theorists and practitioners mutually open themselves up to an inquiry process that seeks to 'unfreeze' the assumptions underlying their actions. Their methodologies are experimental and predominantly conducted in a group setting. Each encourages the presence and skillfulness of a facilitator or any facilitative participant who can help the group make use of actual situations as opposed to simulated experiences. There is also considerable focus on re-education and reflection. This means that the participants, who are normally adult practitioners, seek to improve themselves especially in regard to their human interactions and practices.

They accomplish this through impartial self-observation, critical reflection with others, and intentional, real-world action experiments which in raising consciousness tend to permit more control over one's actions.

The action modalities are concerned with interventions in action that are useful to the client, but action researchers also value theory. In particular, they are interested in conceptualizing their experiences in a way that is meaningful and valuable to the members of their learning community as well as to third persons who might be interested in the results of their interventions (Eden & Huxham, 1996).

The final similarity to be considered here among these approaches is the role of context and feelings in the inquiry process itself. Positivist science for validity purposes requires the 'subject' to be as detached from the inquiry as possible so as not to contaminate the data. In a similar vein, the context of the inquiry needs to be controlled so that findings can be generalized. The action modalities purposely engage learners and participants in both the inquiry and its context so as to incorporate subjective feelings and points of view. In Argyris and Schön's terms (1974), learners and facilitators working in the action modalities are thus more able to get at participants' 'theories-in-use' rather than their 'espoused theories.' The inquiry process is thus not hypothetical, arising from a hunch or premise about subsequent action, as it is 'parathetical,' arising from proposition and action presented alongside one another (Raelin, 1999a).

## ACTION LEARNING

Action learning is typically offered in corporate management development programs, but also can be offered as a methodology in whole or in part within formal programs in higher education (Conger & Benjamin, 1999; Johnson & Spicer, 2006). What distinguishes action learning from other experiential pedagogies is its application of real-world experience.

Since practitioners are stakeholders in the problems which they are attempting to solve, real problems, according to action learning proponents, should become the focus of study (Korey & Bogorya, 1985; Raelin, 1997).

There are many variants of action learning, but all seem to have four common principles (Pedler, Burgoyne & Brook, 2005; Raelin, 2008):

- That learning be acquired in the midst of action and dedicated to the task at hand.
- That participants work on problems aimed at organizational as well as personal development and the intersection between them.
- That learners work in peer learning teams to support and challenge each other.
- That its users demonstrate a learning-to-learn aptitude entailing a search for fresh questions over expert knowledge.

Action learning is thus contextualized learning that seeks to generate learning from human interaction arising from engagement in the solution of real-world work problems (Pedler, 1996; Marquardt, 1999; Yorks, O'Neil & Marsick, 1999; Boshyk, 2002; Raelin, 2008). Although its proponents can appreciate the value of 'active' learning strategies that bring a sense of live experience into the classroom through cases, simulations, and the like, they contend that the best way to test theories and make them actionable is through real experience. Although simulated experience can be useful to help students learn from their tacit handling of challenging situations, simulated events often risk defusing or abstracting live conflicts. Cooperation may be obtained where it otherwise may be impossible, and emotionally laden and vexing problems may end up neatly analyzed into solutions. Learners ultimately need to confront real risks and take real and often moral positions.

Practitioners and working students thus need the opportunity to merge theoretical principles with an understanding of the social construction of the organizations in which they work. Most principles about organizations, for example, cannot anticipate the particular circumstances unique to each organization. In action learning, principles become most useful when they help learners become more effective in action. Further, practitioners often learn best by sharing their principles and experiences with each other. Colleagues can be most helpful to one another when they become sensitive to each others' area of operation and provide new perspectives and stimulate inquiry regarding practice experiences (Nonaka, 1994).

In action learning's original conceptualization proposed by Revans (1982, 1998), learning results from the independent contributions of programmed instruction (designated P) and spontaneous questioning (designated Q). P constitutes information and skill derived from material already formulated, digested, and presented typically through coursework. Q is knowledge and skill gained by apposite questioning, investigation, and experimentation. Most action learning theorists consider Q to be the component that produces the most behavioral change since it results from interpretations of experience and knowledge accessible to the learner. These interpretations are bolstered by feedback from fellow learners who participate in a debriefing of the learner's workplace experiences. Thus, any actions taken are subject to inquiry about the effectiveness of these actions, including a review of how one's theories were applied into practice. Action learning relies upon feedback that by focusing on the participant's values and behavior ensures that any actions are seen not as neutral stances but as positions with points of view and anticipated consequences. So, in action learning, the 'action' is there as the pathway to learning. Solving the problem is fine, but it isn't as critical that there be problem resolution as much as there be learning from experience. Another way to state this is that it is preferable to fail at finding a solution to a problem yet obtain learning rather than to fail to learn while obtaining a solution to the problem.

In this way action learning addresses the pitfalls of conventional training and even of experiential learning, which often overlook the need to engage in mutual reflection as a means to surface the tacit knowledge embedded in live experience. By having peers serve as a sounding board to one another regarding the operating assumptions underlying their project interventions, participants become more equipped to produce the outcomes they desire (Argyris & Schön, 1996). They learn from each other how to overcome the blockages that they themselves and others erect to deter project accomplishment (Coghlan & Brannick, 2001). They challenge each other by subjecting the real issues brought up to scrutiny from alternative perspectives, giving members a chance to question their underlying perceptions and assumptions (Marsick, 1990). Their learning is tied to knowledge collectively and concurrently co-constructed in service of action (Tsoukas & Mylonopoulos, 2004).

Because of both the variety and inconsistency in action learning delivery (Revans himself eschewed any single definition), it is challenging to depict a typical action learning program (Weinstein, 1995; Revans, 1998; Marsick & O'Neil, 1999; Willis, 2004; Pedler, Burgoyne & Brook, 2005). Nevertheless, here is a characterization of a modal delivery platform. Initially, a series of presentations constituting what Revans referred to as programmed instruction might be given on a designated theory or theoretical topic. In conjunction with these presentations, managerial or professional participants might be asked to apply their prior and new knowledge to a real live project that is sanctioned by organizational sponsors and that has potential value not only to the participant but to the organizational unit to which the project is attached. Throughout the program, the participants continue to work on the projects with assistance from other participants (who are either working on the same project as part of a team or on an individual project in their own organization) as well as from qualified facilitators or advisors who help them make sense of their project experiences in light of relevant theory (Coghlan et al., 2002). This feedback feature principally occurs in learning teams or 'sets' typically composed of five to seven participants that hold intermittent meetings over a fixed program cycle (Smith & O'Neil, 2003). During the learning team sessions, the participants discuss not only the practical dilemmas arising from actions in their work settings, but the application or misapplication of concepts and theories to these actions.

## Outcomes

Various research accounts have placed the business-wide return on investment from action learning as anywhere from 5 to 25 times its cost (Alder, 1992; Fulmer & Vicere, 1996; Brenneman, Keys & Fulmer, 1998; Raelin, 2008). These ratios are largely calculated on the basis of costs removed or savings generated from project work. Anthony Fresina (2001), founder and president of the firm KnowledgeWorks, believes that the return on investment from action learning is dependent on: bold, stretch assignments given to a motivated team of participants who do not know the business under consideration but who are given free rein to tackle the problem as they see fit while focusing on their individual and team learning through the assistance of a trained facilitator.

From many accounts in the domain of executive development, it appears that action learning has been deployed effectively in organizations of varying sizes across a wide range of business applications, such as: early career programs, new manager assimilation, skill development, high-potential development, team effectiveness, continuous improvement, knowledge management, and organizational transitions (Dotlich & Noel, 1998; Vicere, 1998; Marquardt, 1999; Fulmer, Gibbs & Goldsmith, 2000; Boshyk, 2002; Davey, Powell, Powell, & Cooper, 2002; Hernez-Broome & Hughes, 2004).

Action learning's exponents claim that it can also produce institutional or cultural change since it represents a form of intra- and inter-organizational learning (Lawrence, Hardy & Phillips, 2002). Over the course of time, especially when action learning program managers attempt to collect, store, and disseminate the knowledge originating from projects, action learning can add to an organization's institutional memory. The sharing of knowledge and practices can transfer intelligence across generations of employees. Further, as activities seep into organizational practices, there is the genuine opportunity for shifts in culture to occur as well as performance improvements.

Besides these organizational and institutional effects, action learning as a management development approach produces change at individual, interpersonal, and managerial levels of experience. Johnson (1998), for example, found that action learning yielded such benefits as increased empathetic listening, enhanced ability to formulate more informed actions, and higher readiness to take responsibility and initiative. Lewis & March (1987); Weinstein (1995); Davey et al. (2002) from a managerial perspective reported on a number of participant outcomes, to wit:

- how to better organize teams
- how to relate better to staff, especially to listen and take criticism
- how to be more open with co-workers
- how to effectively present ideas to upper management
- how to take on more responsibility in one's role
- how to effect culture change more effectively within one's organization.

Since the project and learning team are so critical to action learning methodology, I will next turn my attention to these two features.

## The action learning project

In order to replicate real-time conditions, most projects are designed to have strategic value to the organization or unit within the organization that sponsors the project; in other words, they are expected to contribute to, perhaps even challenge, the goals and policies established by the sponsoring unit. The Executive Leadership Institute at service giant ARAMARK, according to its architect Al Vicere (Hayes, 2004), uses action learning projects to help the leadership team

assess how the competitive environment is changing, in particular to know 'when to shed skins' and shift to a new segment or grow a business.

Participants can work on projects individually or in groups. Either way, other organizational members and stakeholders not directly affiliated with the program may be drawn into the project. Projects span any number of critical problems arising in the organization, be it a strategic decision to enter a new market or a new application connected to one of the company's functional areas. Projects have recognized sponsors – the departments and respective executive managers from which they originate. The sponsors take a genuine interest in the assignments and are expected to apply normal business pressures to ensure a high-quality outcome within a particular period of time.

Projects almost always require some kind of output which can be evaluated. Often, a lengthy written statement detailing project aims, performance, and recommendations is prepared. This report, however, is not meant to merely describe the 'results,' as much as detail the learnings and competencies addressed in the experience as well as the real constraints that may have blocked proposed interventions.

The advantages of working on such 'real' problems, therefore, become obvious. Participants are forced to find real, workable answers, not easy, hypothetical ones; leadership and teamwork skills are developed along with the more technical skills; the company benefits immediately from the participants' contribution to the project; and the lessons learned from the experience tend to stay with the participants longer than if they had learned them from a book or lecture. Moreover, solving problems *per se* is not necessarily as much the focus in action learning as 'dissolving' them. Consistent with Ackoff's notion of 'messes' (1981), organizational problems are rarely stand-alone events but rather messy, dynamic, interdependent entanglements. Action learning participants might just as readily change the nature of the system or the environment in which the problem resides as directly 'solve' the problem.

The project thus does not always address the initial problem that was presented by the sponsor. The potential solution that the individual or team comes up with may not work or may not be endorsed. Perhaps the team has come up with a solution, but one that addresses another problem. Nevertheless, action learning works if it is composed of participants: (1) who care about the problem, (2) who are given the authority to work on it at their own discretion even to the point of being transformed by participation in the project, and (3) who are committed to inquiring about the most fundamental assumptions behind their practices (Pedler, 1996). What is critical is that the experience should confront learners with the constraints of organizational realities, leading oftentimes to the discovery of alternative and creative means to accomplish their objectives.

As noted at the outset of this section, projects may be initiated as individual ventures or may be staffed by a team of participants from the same company. Occasionally, the project might be initiated with the help of either internal or external consultants. One project variant is to have a team from the program actually engage in the project while also meeting as a learning team. The team may be constituted of employees from the same department or may be entirely cross-departmental or even cross-divisional. Cross-functional teams are encouraged where practical because they expose participants to different ways of thinking and enlighten them to knowledge processes outside their own boundaries.

It might be noted that if the format is team-based, each individual must take responsibility to ensure that he or she is working on a specific component of the overall group venture. Otherwise, individual initiative and learning may be lost within the team effort. It is for this reason that some project exponents believe that individual projects tend to produce greater individual learning as compared to group projects. I believe there is ultimately no best way to constitute a project team. There is perhaps a natural efficiency in having a team work on a project while also meeting as a learning team. Further, there is a benefit in having team members mutually observe and offer constructive feedback on each others' actual job performance. Reflections on plans, assumptions, and practices can be more spontaneous and immediately contextualized. However, it may not be practical for an organization to release an entire group to work on one project.

Hence, the scope of project activity must also be considered as a program feature. Not only must an organization decide whether to release a full team to work on a project, but it may need to decide how many projects to have going at any one given time. For example, it is possible to suffer 'action project overload' (Tucker & Taylor, 1997). This can occur if management becomes distracted by the frequent requests for information, interviews, customer visits, and the like which are associated with project requirements. For example, projects often send out members to obtain information from organizational or unit data banks or directly from top management. Although managerial staff are generally happy to accommodate such requests, there are limits to how much distraction from one's current job one can tolerate. Since projects have been characterized as typically strategic in character, there is also a need to retain sufficient staffing to do the tactical and operating work of the company, especially in instances when projects are being undertaken on a full-time basis.

A relatively new operating issue in action learning is the constitution of 'external' action projects, or projects made up of managers from different organizations or agencies. Such an approach seems to be very applicable at senior levels where top managers may not have anyone with whom to share personal and confidential problems. There is also a strategic side to external projects that give top managers an opportunity to discuss trade-related topics of mutual concern, be it trends analysis, marketing and distribution strategy, talent management and retention, or even mergers and acquisitions. The Home Office, Britain's principal criminal justice agency, and the Association of Chief Police Officers organized a year-long action learning program for senior police officers focusing on illegal drug activity in 37 districts (David, 2006). Participants were purposely divided into cross-regional sets to promote inter-agency information sharing. Results of the program from participants were universally enthusiastic because of the opportunity to exchange knowledge that was put to immediate use, such as: improving cross-force activity against drugs, identifying gaps in suspicious activity reporting systems, or funding the financial investigation of suspects.

Finally, the duration of projects is often debated in the literature, but there is no optimal time frame. Some programs support lengthy projects of six months to a year, as in the case of ARAMARK's Executive Leadership Institute or SUPERVALU's Work-Based Learning program; some are mid-range as in UBS's 12- to 15-week business challenge component of its ASCENT talent development program; others can be quite short, in the four- to six-week range (Meister, 2007; Raelin, 2008). The shorter time frames support full-time participation, whereas the longer ones tend to require participants to work on their projects in addition to their regular jobs. The longer programs are also deemed to provide more conceptual development and in-depth experience but suffer the risk of loss of participant intensity and/or supervisory support (Raelin, 1999b).

Projects can also take on a life of their own once the program is over. In fact, full implementation of a project, once it has been completed through the program, may represent the highest form of success. It indicates that the team's work has been so critical that it requires institutionalization within the unit or organization. Projects, then, should incorporate within their presentation a plan for implementation of their findings and recommendations. The property and casualty insurer, the Chubb Corporation, runs an action learning Global Executive Program focusing on strategic innovation and critical thinking. In a recent instance, following the approximately 18-week program, three SBU-related project teams remained intact for three to six months after the program formally ended to experiment further with their business models and to ensure a successful handoff to their respective SBU (Kuhn & Marsick, 2005).

## Learning teams

As noted earlier, the primary vehicle for providing collective reflection in action learning is the learning team or set, a group of five to seven participants who support each other in their workplace project activity. Learning team members, often assisted by a facilitator or coach, help each other make sense of their action learning project experiences in light of relevant theory. Set members become skilled at the art of questioning in order to challenge the assumptions underlying planned interventions in members' projects. Subsequent actions taken tend to be clearer, better informed, and more defensible as a result of the set dialogue (McGill & Beaty, 1992).

Participants in action learning, then, learn as they work by taking time to reflect with like-minded peers who offer insight into each others' workplace problems. Reflection can be enhanced by the recollection of past theories or by the creation of new theories to inform spontaneous inquiry and offer alternative frames of problems (Smith, 1988; Sutton, 1989). The typical conversational device in most learning teams is questioning rather than advice giving. Through apposite questioning, the problem solver is led to reflect on a problem from different perspectives. The type of question used in an action learning team matters in that questions are not designed to place the focal person on the defensive nor to illustrate the cleverness of the questioner. Rather, questions are designed to open up the focal person's own view of the situation. They should keep the focus on the focal person and not on the questioner. Questions tend to be open-ended, rather than closed (requiring a 'yes' or 'no' answer), tend to ask for specifics, and, when asked in a 'why' format, are typically applied to future behaviour rather than past actions. The idea is to create an environment for exploration rather than rationalization (Beaty, Bourner & Frost, 1993). As the process unfolds, the questioners might themselves come to appreciate, through the very process of inquiry, particular nuances that affect their own problems and environments.

Ultimately, a good question leads to possible changes in action as one is led to challenge the assumptions of practice. In a set for small business consultants, one of the members was asked in a non-judgmental way why she engaged in constant note-taking. Did it not prevent her from active engagement in the set? The set's facilitator summarized what happened next (Weinstein, 2005):

> A brief upset from the challenged person was followed by her abandoning pen and paper. However, what was so unexpected was how she then participated and offered some of the most helpful questions and insights. She had always taken notes. Following feedback from the set on how helpful she had been, she admitted that although she felt slightly bereft, she was bemused at how she had successfully changed her behavior. Her note taking, she admitted, had been a smokescreen to hide behind, in case her comments were silly or of no use.

In an in-service program for teachers using a community of practice approach, Lauriala (1998) reports how one teacher, in her own words, experienced her learning team's inquiry process:

> I felt my own teaching at that moment, when I started to compare it to this [inquiry-led] system, quite absurd. When I was looking at that system, I started to question myself how could teaching be carried out otherwise.

The support generated among members in a learning team establishes close bonds which subsequently may account for dramatic expressions of teamwork and encouragement from one member to another. In a learning set organized through the Britvic Soft Drinks' Developing to Lead action learning program, the following anonymous quote was recorded by the company's training manager (Meehan & Jarvis, 1996):

> I was seriously considering defaulting. I sent Jane an e-mail, just saying the word 'help.' She responded immediately: 'We cannot complete without you, we all do it together or not at all. Don't give up now, we are so close. Where can I help you most?'

Thus, in observing a typical action learning team, members will be seen listening, posing questions, and offering suggestions to another team member whose project is under scrutiny. Occasionally, the focal individual might listen as the other set members brainstorm ideas regarding his or her issue or project. Participants often decide to experiment with new approaches in light of the group discussion, leading to new theories or ideas to be tested in action during the intervening periods between set meetings. The results are then brought up at subsequent meetings.

Beyond the contribution of learning teams to project approaches, teams also provide feedback to members to help them assess their effectiveness in a group setting. Participants are encouraged to develop personal agendas or development plans for individual and managerial change and share these with the rest of the group. Team members then discuss each others' plans, identify potential pitfalls, and suggest improvements. Occasionally, participants may even be called back together six to eight months later to report on the successes and frustrations in implementing their personal development plans.

Learning teams thus provide many opportunities for members to develop their interpersonal and managerial skills. Learning tends to be enhanced because, compared to other teams, the learning team explicitly focuses on member development. Among the lessons available to members are such skilled practices as providing and accepting positive and negative feedback, negotiating with others, dealing with internal and external politics, testing publicly one's espoused values and beliefs, fielding a new strategy, and managing change. The experience is designed to encourage the participant to challenge his or her own actions and consider novel views and processes. At the same time, participants are encouraged to be critical of academic theories placed into their use. Finally, the experience makes ample room for making mistakes, provided that participants learn from them.

Learning teams also develop a team culture in their own right which presents participants with lessons regarding group dynamics. As such, they are not unlike other groups which must confront the inevitable processes of their own development (Schein, 1967). However, as learning teams, again there tends to be explicit focus, in this case on group learning. Hence, learning teams, as a special form of team, might reflect a different set of norms compared to performance or task teams.

Finally, as a method of reflective practice, learning teams allow participants to engage in critical reflection. Some organizations, though sponsors of action learning interventions, are not always hospitable to the probing that characterizes the dynamics of this form of learning. Hence, participants appreciate the opportunity to try out their ideas and examine their values and assumptions in the learning team. With the help and encouragement of their team members, especially their facilitator, they can also try out some new interpersonal skills or managerial competencies based on 'reframed' assumptions derived from public reflection within the team (Dixon, 1990). After rehearsal, they can bring their new ideas and competencies into the organization with renewed confidence. There is no better experience in learning about a new idea (or even a personal competency) and its practicality than by attempting to use it in a work environment where it may initially be considered unworkable.

Having completed my discussion of action learning, I turn next to some of the other principal action modalities, though there is not sufficient space to discuss all of them, existing or emerging. They share with action learning an emphasis on inquiry in the moment from real-world experience, accomplished in service of actionable knowledge creation.

## ACTION RESEARCH

Action research, as the grandfather of all action modalities, has been traditionally defined as an approach to knowledge generation that is based on a collaborative problem-solving relationship between researcher and client and that aims at both solving a problem and generating new knowledge. It developed largely from the work of Kurt Lewin and his associates and involves cyclical processes of diagnosing a change situation or a problem, planning, gathering data, taking action, and then fact-finding about the results of that action in order to plan and take further action (Greenwood & Levin, 1998; Lewin, 1946; Peters & Robinson, 1984). A critical feature is that it focuses on important social or organizational issues as they are being planned and implemented with those who experience these issues directly.

The intended change in an action research project typically involves re-education, a term that refers to the requirements of a critical knowledge that can change patterns of thinking and action that are presently well-established. Effective re-education depends on participation by clients in diagnosis, fact-finding, and free choice to engage in new action. Often, it ends up challenging the *status quo* from a participative perspective, which may lead to challenging the premises of current belief systems. It also contributes simultaneously to the creation of new knowledge in social science, to actionable research within the affected system, and to personal and interpersonal development in everyday life. Rigorous standards for developing theory and empirically testing propositions organized by theory are not to be sacrificed, nor is the relation to practice to be lost (Argyris, Putnam & Smith, 1985; Raelin & Coghlan, 2006).

## ACTION SCIENCE

Action science is a work-based intervention approach for helping learners increase their effectiveness in social situations through heightened awareness of their action and interaction assumptions. Although initially aimed at the individual level of experience, action science is ultimately concerned with improving the level of public discourse both in groups and in organizations. Individuals' mental models – the images, assumptions, and stories carried inside our minds about ourselves and about others – are often untested and unexamined and, consequently, often erroneous. In action science, these mental models are brought into consciousness in such a way that new models are formed which may serve us better (Senge, Kleiner, Robert, Ross & Smith, 1994).

Action science thus calls for the deliberate questioning of existing perspectives and interpretations, referred to by Argyris & Schön (1978) as 'double-loop' learning. When a mismatch occurs between individuals' values and their actions, most people attempt to narrow the gap by trial-and-error learning. They also prefer to maintain a sense of control over the situation, over themselves, and over others. In action science, the governing values underlying actual behavior are subjected to critical reflection resulting in free and informed choice, valid information, and high internal commitment to any new behavior attempted.

Donald Schön (1983) preferred the term 'reflection-in-action' to characterize the rethinking process of action science which attempts to discover how what one did contributed to an unexpected or expected outcome. In order to engage in reflection-in-action, practitioners might start by offering a frame of the situation at hand. Then, if in a group situation, group members might inquire as to how others see it. Members might thereupon collectively reflect upon these frames and subsequently begin to surface and test their own underlying assumptions and respective reasoning processes. The ultimate aim is to narrow inconsistencies between one's espoused theories and theories-in-use. Espoused theories are those characterizing what we say we will do. Theories-in-use describe how we actually behave although their revision of our espoused values is often tacit. The goal of action science is to uncover our theories-in-use, in particular to distinguish between those which inhibit and those which promote learning.

Action scientists also make direct comparisons between individual and organizational learning. Argyris and Schön (1974) find that people tend to learn and, in fact, are socially conditioned to use a cognitive model referred to as 'Model I.' Mostly concerned with detecting errors in our problem solving, Model I is unfortunately characterized by a need to control, maximize winning, suppress emotions, and be rational. Its consequences tend to be defensive behavior, miscommunication, and in actuality, the escalation rather than the reduction of error (Argyris, 1982), which can have deleterious implications for organizational change. Model II behavior, on the other hand, is based on directly observable data and requires that people support their advocacy of positions with illustration and with inquiry into others' views. Accordingly, Model II practitioners tend to more reliably produce intended consequences and thus increase their learning.

## DEVELOPMENTAL ACTION INQUIRY

Closely related to action science is the modality referred to as developmental action inquiry (DAI), or just action inquiry, attributed to the work of Bill Torbert (1999). DAI is the systematic attempt to enrich a person's, group's, organization's, or society's awareness of the interplay among transpersonal awareness, subjective interpretations and strategies, intersubjective practices and politics, and objective data and effects. More specifically, DAI seeks to blend and align first-person, subjective inquiry; second-person, intersubjective inquiry; and third-person, objective inquiry among four so-called 'territories of experience,' namely: intuitive vision, rational strategy, artistic performance, and concrete outcomes.

Engaging in DAI involves the steps of:

1   Affirming the vision of a lifetime of self-transforming action and inquiry in association

with friends of similar commitment and with the help of liberating spiritual/performance disciplines that exercise one's attention to encounter and span the four territories of experience from moment to moment.

2 Developing and testing in one's own practice an analogical theory of the timing of processes.

3 Developing a performance artistry in movement, tone, and speech that is simultaneously vigilant and spontaneous, and that blends one's own idiosyncratic passion with archetypal-observational dispassion and with timely compassion.

4 Developing dialogical and empirical measurement methods for assessing success in the object-ing world. (p. 203)

## COOPERATIVE INQUIRY

This action modality invites participants to engage in self-critical examination in the presence of a group which, itself, invites spontaneous inquiry into its own patterns (Reason, 1994; Heron, 1996). In cooperative inquiry all those involved in the research are both co-researchers, generating ideas and designing and managing their projects, and also co-subjects, participating in the activity that is being researched. Rather than accepting pre-ordained content and methods, cooperative inquirers search for their own patterns of knowing while continually examining their practices, asking such questions as: 'Who am I that is engaged in this knowing?' Thus, participants become decentered from a narcissism that characterizes human agency. They learn to view themselves as self-referents and as observers of each other in a community that persistently constructs and shares its own interpretations of the world.

As a methodology, cooperative inquiry groups engage in progressive cycles of action and reflection made up of a four phases (Reason, 1999). In phase 1, the 'co-researchers' decide on the issues they wish to explore. They talk about their interests and concerns, agree on the focus of their inquiry, and develop together a set of questions or propositions. They next agree to undertake

some action that will contribute to this exploration and agree to a set of procedures by which they will observe and record their own and each other's experience.

In phase 2, the group members apply their agreed upon actions in their everyday life and work: they initiate the actions and observe and record the outcomes of their own and each other's behavior. They may at first simply watch what it is that happens to them so they develop a better understanding of their experience; later, they may start trying out new forms of action.

In phase 3, the co-researchers become fully immersed in their experience. They may become more open to what is going on and they may begin to see their experience in new ways. They deepen into the experience so that superficial understandings are elaborated and developed. They may also be led away from the original ideas and proposals into new fields, unpredicted actions, and creative insights. In phase 4, the co-researchers re-assemble to consider their original questions in the light of their experience. As a result, they may change their questions in some way or reject them and pose new questions. They then agree on a second cycle of action and reflection. They may choose to focus on the same or on different aspects of the overall inquiry. The group may choose to amend or develop its inquiry procedures – forms of action, ways of gathering data – in light of its experience of the first cycle.

## CRITICAL ACTION LEARNING

In the last three sections, I take up first an evolving tradition in action learning – its potential critical nature, explore its global applications, and finish with a discussion of the challenge of enacting action learning in management development circles. Although not yet pervasively incorporated into practice, 'critical action learning' has been seriously broached by a number of academics. This tradition derives from a criticism of conventional action learning in its presumed acceptance of current managerial orthodoxies that conceive of organizational actions and changes as largely depoliticized and accepting of current power relationships. In this way, it may give learners a false sense of their participation in a social structure that feigns involvement while sustaining performance coercion (Garrick & Clegg, 2001). Critical theorists would have action learning focus more upon management as a lived experience that is capable of challenging conventional wisdom (Willmott, 1997).

Criticism in action learning can take two forms; it can focus on critical pedagogical content, which tends to politicize the curriculum, or it can focus on critical reflection, which embraces dialogic and emancipatory approaches to teaching and learning (Anderson & Thorpe, 2004). In the former instance, critical pedagogy has as its intent the freeing of people from unnecessarily restrictive traditions and power relations that inhibit opportunity for need fulfillment. As such, it often requires a resistance to established power structures, which may even unwittingly prevent the release of human aspiration (Alvesson & Willmott, 1992). Emancipatory discourse, meanwhile, has a compatible but more social psychological agenda of freeing people from internal forces that may limit their personal control and autonomy (Habermas, 1974; Fromm, 1976). It is a reflective process that rejects any form of fixed knowledge residing only in those who presume to construct it for others.

Critical action learning in either instance encompasses a reflective, denaturalizing experience that can encourage participants to find their distinctive voice in tones separate from those of their teachers (Tosey & Nugent, 1997; Willmott, 1997; Fournier & Grey, 2000; Meyerson & Kolb, 2000). They learn to reconstruct their taken-for-granted assumptions even in the moment so as to address the socio-cultural conditions that may constrain their self-insight (Habermas, 1971; Raelin, 2001; O'Neil & Marsick, 2007). Participants in such a venue can search for individual and collective meaning that may arise from a discourse among competing interests, one that

goes after the tough questions, not the easy answers (Heifetz, 1994).

Unfortunately, the evidence regarding how effective action learning participants have been in questioning the historical, cultural, and political conditions within their own organization has been mixed (Lakes, 1994; Nash, 2001). Gutierrez (2002), in an experimental graduate course in critical analysis of both the corporate organization and the classroom, found it difficult to alter the traditional professor–student dependent relationship. In particular, emancipatory change required students' capacity to engage in deep self-analysis at the individual level, to exhibit sensitivity and relinquishment of control at the interpersonal level, and to appreciate the constraints of deep enculturated social processes at the organizational level. Students who have achieved a level of critical awareness have at the same time reported both discomfort and dissonance when their newfound social awareness and political acuity were contraposed against the utter reality of their powerlessness to effect consistent and substantive change in their work environment (Brookfield, 1994; Buckingham, 1996; Reynolds, 1999).

Nevertheless, Caron & Fisher (2006) in their report of an internship program in business administration that emphasized critical reflection found that enhanced self-awareness and political consciousness were an important achievement that could lead to behavioral change. Rigg & Trehan (2004) in their ethnographic case study of several post-graduate programs in management development also found that critical action learning could lead to perspective and personal transformation since it gives participants a language to frame how their long-held assumptions can be challenged when mapped against their professed values. Thus, action learning projects can focus as much on the meaning of live accomplishments as the accomplishments themselves. The ensuing dialogue can minimally raise such critical questions as: how are we relating to one another as humans; who has been excluded from our deliberations that ought to be included; why have we and our managers organized in the way we have; are there alternative ways to manage our work processes; what cultural or historical processes have led to our current state of being (Reason, 1994; Nash, 2001; Fenwick, 2004).

## GLOBAL ACTION LEARNING

One of the benefits of action learning is that it can afford participants critical lessons in cross-cultural understanding as well as give them broad exposure to the organization's international operations. Using social learning theory, Black & Mendenhall (1990) argue that cultural sensitivity is best learned from experience because individuals use the consequences of live experiences to shape current and future behavior. Having exposure to projects in other cultures gives action learning participants a chance to make sense of their interactions – teaching them, for example, what is appropriate and inappropriate in these settings or which behaviors to execute or suppress. The resulting cross-cultural experience is not simulated as in a classroom exercise but is real, emanating from the rough-and-tumble of actual practice in the field. Participants gain experience in a number of ways, be it from on-site interviews inquiring about the viability of a project prospectus, or from having to sell the findings from a project to a local management.

Further, the experience of working with a global, cross-cultural team can present participants with critical lessons in intercultural competence. Intercultural competence entails the capacity to analyze communication behavior within a new culture, resulting in an ability to respond to messages as if from within that culture (Beamer, 1992). Working with learning teams, Smith & Berg (1997) found that there are three processes that can lead early on to growing intercultural competence. First, the team members learn how to learn together. As members think of situations in which they had the opportunity to learn something of value but did not, they gradually learn to be more patient with each other when group crises occur. For example,

they may begin to recognize features of some environments that are not hospitable to productive group life.

Second, members begin to explore their interdependence, which can be accomplished by exploring each other's unique cultural contributions. As they reflect upon the socio-political issues within their respective cultures, they may begin to recognize their connectedness. Finally, they also learn to work through their differences as they consider cultural norms that are sacred to each respective culture. In this way, they can deal with the inevitable polarities embedded within the group environment, such as confrontation versus conciliation or individuality versus collectivity. In the former case, some members may believe that it is preferable to confront conflicts or irritations directly, where others may strive to accommodate differences. In the latter instance, some members may be culturally disposed to preserve the centrality of the individual, whereas others may expect individuals to subordinate themselves to the well-being of the group.

In a learning team affiliated with a university-based action learning program that is highly multicultural, one of the members reflected on her experience in the learning team as follows:

> Learning teams constitute a fertile environment where people can develop the ability to diagnose important differences and appreciate cultural diversity. Being part of a team with members from all over the world has allowed me to reconsider certain personal aspects and forced me to become more adaptable according to the team's needs. From different eating habits and vegetarian preferences to working schedules and family issues, a team will always remind you that you cannot be self-centered and that there are different people with various needs in their lives which you have to respect.

Nevertheless, caution is in order whenever a Western-based practice, such as action learning, is deployed in other cultures, such as in the developing world. An implicit ethnocentrism may lead program managers to force-fit some familiar action learning principles. The main concern is that in many cultures and subcultures, learners are viewed as (and may even view themselves as) passive and dependent, whereas teachers are considered active and authoritative (Jones, 1990). In such environments, learners have difficulty with pedagogical approaches such as action learning, which ask them to take responsibility for their own learning and self-reflect. In a similar vein, teachers find it difficult to let go of their control of the learning process for fear that it would undermine their authority. Indeed, in some cultures there is wide deference to those with presumed expert authority. Moreover, there is also tremendous respect for book knowledge over knowledge emanating from work itself.

In terms of the specific practices of action learning, three of them – learning teams, projects, and public reflection – may be accompanied by some inherent Western-based assumptions that may need revision when applied in other parts of the world (Marquardt, 1998; Yiu & Saner, 1998; Yiu, 2006). Let's consider each of them in turn:

*Learning teams*: In constituting learning teams, we tend to mix people of differing ages, genders, levels, and roles. The inherent philosophy of such teams recognizes such Western values as egalitarianism and informality and such practices as offering different perspectives and promoting give-and-take among members. In most other cultures, however, mixing people of different status groups may disturb their sense of hierarchy, their respect of differences, and the role of power and authority in the workplace. Further, formality among the different statuses in groups may be the expected communication mode.

In an action learning intervention in China reported by Lichia Yiu of the Centre for Socio-Eco-Nomic Development (CSEND) in Geneva, Switzerland, she found that in order to improve the effectiveness of management training among China's economic and administrative cadres, learning team members were much more prone to sharing their questioning insights with their learning team facilitator than with one another. Meanwhile, facilitators were observed as having a more paternalistic,

nurturing, and less confrontational style, compared with their Western counterparts, and were more comfortable working on challenging personal issues with members individually than with the team as a whole.

*Projects*: Action learning projects tend to focus on real organizational problems within real time frames. The project team is advised to assume authority to act within its sphere of responsibility. Yet in some non-Western cultures, having a group take on a managerial task might reflect poorly on the manager, who might lose face if having to admit an inability to handle the problem himself or herself. In addition, the sharing of personal difficulties might be seen as culturally crass. Having someone outside one's immediate environment work on an internal problem might also be seen as an unnecessary incursion.

*Public reflection*: Public reflection, by promoting a thinking about one's thinking, calls for public examination of the most fundamental assumptions and premises behind our practices. Co-participants in work-based learning are viewed as learning resources who can help us bring things into perspective and draw out our questioning insight. In some cultures, however, a manager's authority or professional competence are seen as personal possessions. He or she may be reluctant to share information that might compromise one's status. Moreover, questioning one another, especially pointing out a weakness to those of superior status, would be seen as disrespectful or insulting. One also does not wish to be seen asking a foolish question. There is also value, among some Asian countries, for example, to withholding one's feelings and thoughts and to respect personal boundaries by not prying into the feelings and thoughts of others.

Transformation in non-Western cultures toward more reflective practices is nevertheless possible, especially as these practices are contextually adapted. In some instances, the practice may just require a reframing.

Thinking of a question as a challenge may be reframed as a sign of interest or curiosity, even a gift. Consider the example of the work of Arphorn Chuaprapaisilp (1989), who combined action research with the Buddhist teaching known as Satipatthana to transform nursing education at the Department of Medical Nursing, Prince of Songkla University in Thailand. According to Chuaprapaisilp, there are few action learning components in clinical teaching in Thailand and instead content learning and academic excellence are stressed. Chuaprapaisilp's intervention entailed moving the traditional approach to learning – based on observing, remembering, and copying – to a critical approach represented by reflection on experience.

According to the new approach, known as the Critical Experiential Learning Model, teachers initially created a democratic learning atmosphere wherein they clarified together with their students the objectives, structures, processes, roles, and assumptions in the conduct of the students' subsequent clinical work. The model included a process of gaining emancipation through experience such that teachers and students together challenged existing structures, identified contradictions, established clear communication, and engaged in the reflective process of Satipatthana, or mindfulness. Satipatthana promotes contemplation of the body, feelings, mental states, and mental events. The Critical Experiential Learning Model, according to Chuaprapaisilp, not only demonstrated that participants in this Eastern culture were able to improve their learning practices but it also demonstrated that such practices could enhance the quality of nursing care.

## THE CHALLENGE OF ACTION LEARNING

Although growing in popularity, action learning and its allied action modalities may not have as many on-site adherents as some of the other management development approaches discussed in this section of the *Handbook*.

There are many reasons to be offered for this condition. For example, locating learning in a specific place, namely within a classroom, seems to dominate most of our educational enterprises from the first days of formal schooling. It is both easier and cheaper to offer teaching from a single platform and from a text. We can measure the results from rote instruction far more easily than we can from experience (Mabey, 2002; Mintzberg, 2004). And, of course, learning from standard training is the way we have always done it!

A more profound reason for its modest adoption is that, if implemented reliably, action learning can become a political undertaking that can bear on questions of power and social relationships in its client organizations. There could be an inevitable threat to managers resulting from action learning project work, especially when managerial roles and responsibilities become challenged by the recommendations forthcoming from the project. Even though most projects are not typically designed to re-engineer anyone's current job in that they tend to be 'white space' endeavors, they may nevertheless invoke risks to present operating conditions. As noted in the prior section, at the individual level of analysis, the reflective dialogues in learning teams may come across as overly blunt or even forced to participants unaccustomed to this level of interpersonal directness. Participants who have experienced action learning tend to report having gone through a much deeper and holistic exercise than ever anticipated. In a way, as Weinstein (1995) once warned, action learning can even be considered subversive by conformist organizations because of what it values; namely:

- it examines everything
- it stresses listening
- it emphasizes questioning
- it fosters courage
- it incites action
- it abets reflection
- it endorses democratic participation.

On the other hand, it could be argued that action learning should be managed in a way that leverages whatever the prevailing culture allows; that part of the learning process should be to learn how to be effective in local environments and, in particular, how to sell proposals to senior management (Peters & Smith, 1998). Although action learning projects might start out as local ventures, their effects often flow into the surrounding environment. Participants begin to question things beyond their local contexts.

Thus, action learning, if it is to have strategic impact, does not operate in vacuum. Indeed, it is seldom designed as a one-time, individual learning opportunity. Most designers see it as having organizational learning implications. Participants tend to follow through on the problems that they are confronting. Project success, when defined as a learning opportunity for the sponsoring unit or organization, is dependent on releasing the talent and experience on the part of the individual or team involved. Projects gradually take on a life of their own and, at times, even diverge from the question originally posed to the team. What tends to be consequential to participants is a sense that whatever they discover in their study, they will have the opportunity to see the project through to its natural conclusion, even if it means challenging the *status quo*. Project recommendations need not be automatically accepted. Team members just need to know that their recommendations will get a fair hearing by their sponsors even when they conflict with existing norms and plans. Action learning, then, requires an organizational culture of risk-taking and openness that permits occasional surfacing of ineffectual rules and practices. There is no place for reflective practice in a closed culture; action learning works best when all organizational members, including those at the top, agree to submit even their governing values to scrutiny.

# BIBLIOGRAPHY

Ackoff, R.L. (1981). *Creating the corporate future.* New York: Wiley.

Alder, H. (1992). The bottom line. *Training Tomorrow,* November, 33–4.

Alvesson, M. & Willmott, H. (1992). On the idea of emancipation in management and organization studies. *Academy of Management Review, 17,* 432–64.

Anderson, L. & Thorpe, R. (2004). New perspectives on action learning: Developing criticality. *Journal of European Industrial Training, 28*(8/9), 657–68.

Argyris, C. (1982). *Reasoning, Learning and Action.* San Francisco: Jossey-Bass.

Argyris, C. & Schön, D.A. (1974). *Theory in Practice: Increasing professional effectiveness.* San Francisco: Jossey-Bass.

Argyris, C. & Schön, D.A. (1978). *Organizational Learning. A theory of action perspective.* Reading, MA: Addison-Wesley.

Argyris, C. & Schön, D.A. (1996). *Organizational Learning II.* Reading, MA: Addison-Wesley.

Argyris, C., Putnam, R. & Smith, D. (1985). *Action science.* San Francisco: Jossey-Bass.

Beamer, L. (1992). Learning intercultural communication competence. *Journal of Business Communication, 29*(3), 285–303.

Beaty, L., Bourner, T. & Frost, P. (1993). Action learning: Reflection on becoming a set member. *Management Education and Development, 24,* 350–67.

Bergson, H. (2001). *Time and Free Will: An essay on the immediate data of consciousness.* Meneola, NY: Dover.

Black, J.S. & Mendenhall, M. (1990). Cross-cultural training effectiveness: A review and a theoretical framework for future research. *Academy of Management Review, 15*(1), 113–36.

Boshyk, Y. (ed.) (2002). *Action Learning Worldwide: Experiences of leadership and organizational development.* New York: Palgrave.

Bourdieu, P. (1990). *In other words: Essays towards a reflexive sociology.* Stanford, CA: Stanford University Press.

Brenneman, W.B., Keys, J.B. & Fulmer, R.M. (1998). Learning across a living company: The Shell Companies' experiences. *Organizational Dynamics, 27*(2), 61–9.

Brookfield, S.D. (1991). *Understanding and Facilitating Adult Learning: A comprehensive analysis of principles and effective practices.* San Francisco: Jossey-Bass.

Brookfield, S.D. (1994). Tales from the dark side: A phenomenography of adult critical reflection. *International Journal of Lifelong Education, 13*(3), 203–16.

Brooks, A. & Watkins, K. (1994). *The Emerging Power of Action Inquiry Techniques.* San Francisco: Jossey Bass.

Bruner, J., Goodnow, J. & Austin, A. (1956). *A Study of Thinking*. New York: Wiley.

Buchanan, D. & Badham, R. (1999). *Power, Politics and Organizational Change*. London: Sage.

Buckingham, D. (1996). Critical pedagogy and media education: A theory in search of practice. *Journal of Curriculum Studies*, *28*(6), 627–50.

Burgoyne, J.G. (1994). Managing by learning. *Management Learning*, *25*(1), 35–55.

Burgoyne, J. & Reynolds, M. (eds) (1997). *Management Learning: Integrating perspectives in theory & practice*. London: Sage.

Caron, L. & Fisher, K. (2006). Raising the bar on criticality: Students' critical reflection in an internship program. *Journal of Management Education*, *30*(5), 700–23.

Chuaprapaisilp, A. (1989). Improving learning from experience through the conduct of pre- and post-clinical conferences: Action research in nursing education in Thailand. Unpublished Doctoral Thesis, University of New South Wales, Australia.

Coghlan, D. (2001). Insider action research: Implications for practicing managers. *Management Learning*, *32*, 49–60.

Coghlan, D. & Brannick, T. (2001). *Doing Action Research in Your Own Organization*. London: Sage.

Coughlan, P., Coghlan, D., Dromgoole, T., Duff, D., Caffrey, R., Lynch, K., Rose, P., Stack, P., McGill, A. & Sheridan, P. (2002). Effecting operational improvement through inter-organizational action learning. *Integrated Manufacturing Systems*, *12*(3), 131–40.

Coghlan, D., Dromgoole, T., Joynt, P. & Sorensen, P. (2004). *Managers Learning in Action: Management education, learning and research*. London: Routledge.

Conger, J.A. & Benjamin, B. (1999). *Building Leaders: How successful companies develop the next generation*. San Francisco: Jossey-Bass.

Cross, K.P. (1982). *Adults as Learners: Increasing participation and facilitating learning*. San Francisco: Jossey-Bass.

Damasio, A.R. (1994). *Descartes' Error: Emotion, reason, and the human brain*. New York: Putnam.

Darling, M.J. & Parry, C.S. (2001). *From Post-mortem to Living Practice: An in-depth study of the evolution of the after action review*. Boston: Signet Consulting.

Davey, C.L., Powell, J.A., Powell, J.E. & Cooper, I. (2002). Action learning in a medium-sized construction company. *Building Research & Information*, *30*(1), 5–15.

David, H.T. (2006). Action learning for police officers in high crack areas. *Action Learning: Research and Practice*, *3*(2), 189–96.

Delahoussaye, M. (2001). Leadership in the 21st Century. *Training*, *38*(9), 60–67.

Dewey, J. (1897). My pedagogic creed. *The School Journal*, *54*(3), 77–80.

Dixon, N.M. (1990). Action learning, action science and learning new skills. *Industrial and Commercial Training*, *2*(4), 10–16.

Dotlich, D.L. & Noel, J.L. (1998). *Action Learning: How the world's top companies are re-creating their leaders and themselves*. San Francisco: Jossey-Bass.

Eden, C., & Huxham, C. (1996). Action research for the study of organizations. In S.R. Clegg, C. Hardy & W.R. Nord (eds), *Handbook of Organization Studies* pp. 526–42. London: Sage.

Fenwick, T.J. (2004). Toward a critical HRD in theory and practice. *Adult Education Quarterly*, *54*(3), 193–209.

Fisher, D., Rooke, D. & Torbert, W.R. (2000). *Personal and Organizational Transformations Through Action Inquiry*. Boston: Edge\Work Press.

Flanagan, J. (1997). *Quest for Self-knowledge*. Toronto: University of Toronto Press.

Fournier, V. & Grey, C. (2000). At the critical moment: Conditions and prospects for critical management studies. *Human Relations*, *53*(1), 7–32.

Fresina, A.J. (2001). *A Letter to the CEO Regarding Action Learning*. Crystal Lake, IL: Executive KnowledgeWorks.

Fromm, E. (1976). *To Have or to Be?* New York: Harper & Brothers.

Fulmer, R.M. & Vicere, A.A. (1996). Executive development: An analysis of competitive forces. *Planning Review*, *24*(1), 31–6.

Fulmer, R.M., Gibbs, P.A. & Goldsmith, M. (2000). Developing leaders: How winning companies keep on winning. *Sloan Management Review*, *42*(1), 49–59.

Garrick, J. & Clegg, S. (2001). Stressed-out knowledge workers in performative times: A postmodern take on project-based learning. *Management Learning*, *32*(1), 119–34.

Gerber, R. (1998). How do workers learn in their work? *The Learning Organization*, *5*(4), 168–75.

Gramsci, A. (1973). *Letters from Prison*. Selected, translated from the Italian, and introduced by L. Lawner. New York: Harper & Row.

Greenwood, D. & Levin, M. (1998). *Introduction to Action Research*. Thousand Oaks, CA: Sage.

Grimmet, P.P., Erickson, G.L., Mackinnon, A.A. & Riecken, T.J. (1990). Reflective Practice in teacher Education. In R.T. Clift, W.R. Houston & M.C. Pugach (eds), *Encouraging Reflective Practice in Education: An analysis of issues and programs* pp. 20–38. New York: Teachers College Press.

Gutierrez, R. (2002). Change in classroom relations: An attempt that signals some difficulties. *Journal of Management Education*, *26*(5), 527–49.

Habermas, J. (1971). *Knowledge and Human Interests* (J. Shapiro, Trans.). Boston: Beacon Press.

Habermas, J. (1974). *Theory and Practice*. London: Heinemann.

Hayes, T. (2004). Conversation with a change agent: Al Vicere on ARAMARK. *Human Resource Planning*, *27*(2), 5–8.

Heifetz, R.A. (1994). *Leadership without Easy Answers*. Cambridge, MA: Belknap Press.

Hernez-Broome, G. & Hughes, R.L. (2004). Leadership development: Past, present, and future. *Human Resource Planning*, *27*(1), 24–32.

Heron, J. (1996). *Co-operative inquiry: Research into the human condition*. London: Sage.

Johnson, C. (1998). The essential principles of action learning. *The Journal of Workplace Learning*, *10*(6/7), 296–300.

Johnson, C. & Spicer, D.P. (2006). A case study of action learning in an MBA program. *Education + Training*, *48*(1), 39–54.

Jones, M.L. (1990). Action learning as a new idea. *Journal of Management Development*, *9*(5), 29–34.

Ketelhohn, W. (1996). Mastering management: Toolboxes are out, thinking is in. *Financial Times*, 20 (22 March), VII.

Knowles, M.S. (1998). *The Adult Learner: The definitive classic in adult education and human resource development* (5th edition). Houston: Gulf Publishing.

Kolb, D.A. (1984). *Experiential Learning*. Upper Saddle River, NJ: Prentice-Hall.

Kolb, D.A. & Fry, R. (1975). Toward an applied theory of experiential learning. In C. Cooper (ed.), *Theories of group process*. London: John Wiley.

Korey, G. & Bogorya, Y. (1985). The managerial action learning concept – theory and application. *Management Decision*, *23*(2), 3–11.

Kuhn, J.S. & Marsick, V.J. (2005). Action learning for strategic innovation in mature organizations: Key cognitive, design, and contextual considerations. *Action Learning: Research and Practice*, *2*(1), 27–48.

Lakes, R.D. (1994). *Critical Education for Work: Multidisciplinary approaches*. Norwood, NJ: Ablex.

Lakoff, G. & Johnson, M. (1980). *Metaphors We Live By*. Chicago: University of Chicago Press.

Lauriala, A. (1998). Reformative in-service education for teachers (Rinset) as a collaborative action and learning enterprise: Experiences from a Finnish context. *Teaching and Teacher Education*, *14*(1), 53–66.

Lave, J. & Wenger, E. (1991). *Situated Learning: Legitimate peripheral participation*. Cambridge, UK: Cambridge University Press.

Lawrence, T.B., Hardy, C. & Phillips, N. (2002). Institutional effects of interorganizational collaborations: The emergence of proto-institutions. *Academy of Management Journal*, *45*(1), 281–90.

Lee, A.S. (1991). Integrating positivist and interpretive approaches to organizational behavior. *Organization Science*, *2*, 342–65.

Letiche, H. & Van Hattem, R. (2000). Self and organization: Knowledge work and fragmentation. *Journal of Organization Change Management*, *13*(4), 93–107.

Lewin, K. (1946). Action research and minority problems. *Journal of Social Issues*, *2*, 34–46.

Lewis, A. & Marsh, W. (1987). Action learning: The development of field managers in the Prudential Assurance Company. *Journal of Management Development*, *6*(2), 45–56.

Lombardo, M.M. & Eichinger, R.W. (2000). High potentials as high learners. *Human Resource Management*, *39*(4), 321–30.

Loughran, J.J. (1996). *Developing Reflective Practice: Learning about teaching and learning through modelling*. London: Falmer Press.

Mabey, C. (2002). Mapping management development practice. *Journal of Management Studies*. *39*(8), 1139–60.

Marquardt, M.J. (1998). Using action learning with multicultural groups. *Performance Improvement Quarterly*, *11*(1), 113–28.

Marquardt, M.J. (1999). *Action Learning in Action*. Palo Alto, CA: Davies-Black.

Marquardt, M.J. (2004). Harnessing the power of action learning. *T + D*, *58*(6), 26–32.

Marsick, V. (1990). Action learning and reflection in the workplace. In J. Mezirow (ed.), *Fostering Critical Reflection in Adulthood: A guide to transformative and emancipatory learning*. San Francisco: Jossey Bass.

Marsick, V. & O'Neill, J. (1999). The many faces of action learning. *Management Learning*, *30*(2), 159–76.

Martineau, J.W. & Hannum, K.M. (2003). *Evaluating the impact of leadership development: A professional guide*. Greensboro, NC: Center for Creative Leadership.

McGill, I. & Beaty, L. (1992). *Action Learning – a practitioner's guide*. London: Kogan Page.

Meehan, M. & Jarvis, J. (1996). A refreshing angle on staff education: Action learning at Britvic Soft Drinks. *People Management*, *2*(14), 38.

Meister, J.C. (2007). Experiential learning integrates action coaching to maximize results. *Chief Learning Officer*, *6*(4), 58.

Meyerson, D. & Kolb, D.M. (2000). Moving out of the 'armchair': Developing a framework to bridge the gap between feminist theory and practice. *Organization, 7*(4), 553–71.

Mintzberg, H. (1973). *The Nature of Managerial Work.* New York: Harper & Row.

Mintzberg, H. (2004). *Managers Not MBAs: A hard look at the soft practice of managing and management development.* San Francisco: Berrett-Koehler.

Nash, A. (2001). Participatory workplace education. In P. Campbell & B. Burnaby (eds), *Participatory Practices in Adult Education* pp. 185–96. Mahwah, NJ: Lawrence Erlbaum.

Nonaka, I. (1994). A dynamic theory of organizational knowledge creation. *Organization Science, 5*(1), 14–37.

Nonaka, L. & Tageuchi, H. (1994). A dynamic theory of organizational knowledge creation. *Organization Science, 5*(1), 14–37.

O'Neil, J.A. & Marsick, V.J. (2007). *Understanding Action Learning.* New York: American Management Association.

Pedler, M. (1996). *Action Learning for Managers.* London: Lemos & Crane.

Pedler, M., Burgoyne, J. & Brook, C. (2005) What has action learning learned to become? *Action Learning: Research and Practice, 2*(1), 49–68.

Peters, J. & Smith, P.A.C. (1998). Action learning and the leadership development challenge. *Journal of Workplace Learning, 10*(6/7), 284–91.

Peters, M. & Robinson, V. (1984). The origins and status of action research. *Journal of Applied Behavioral Science, 29*(2), 113–24.

Pettigrew, A. M. (1990). Longitudinal field research on change theory and practice. *Organization Science, 1,* 267–92.

Piaget, J. (1969). *The Mechanisms of Perception.* London: Routledge & Kegan Paul.

Pleasants, N. (1966). Nothing is concealed: De-centering tacit knowledge and rules from social theory. *Journal for the Theory of Social Behaviour, 26*(3), 233–55.

Polanyi, M. (1966). *The Tacit Dimension.* Garden City, NY: Doubleday.

Popper, K. (1959). *The Logic of Scientific Discovery.* New York: Basic Books.

Raelin, J. A. (1997). Action learning and action science: Are they different? *Organizational Dynamics, 26*(1), 21–34.

Raelin, J.A. (1999a). The action dimension in management: Different approaches to research, teaching, and development, Preface (as Editor) to the Special Issue of the journal. *Management Learning, 30*(2), 115–25.

Raelin, J.A. (1999b). The design of the action project in work-based learning. *Human Resource Planning, 22*(3), 12–28.

Raelin, J.A. (2001). Public reflection as the basis for learning. *Management Learning, 32*(1), 11–30.

Raelin, J.A. (2008). *Work-based Learning: Bridging knowledge and action in the workplace.* San Francisco: Jossey-Bass.

Raelin, J.A. & Coghlan, D. (2006). Developing managers as learners and researchers: Using action learning and action research. *Journal of Management Education, 30*(5), 670–89.

Reason, P. (1994). *Participation in Human Inquiry.* London: Sage.

Reason, P. (1999). Integrating action and reflection through co-operative inquiry. *Management Learning, 30*(2), 207–26.

Reason, P. & Bradbury, H. (2001). *Handbook of Action research.* London: Sage.

Reber, A.S. (1993). *Implicit Learning and Tacit Knowledge: An essay on the cognitive unconscious.* New York: Oxford Unviersity Press.

Reingold, J. & Bongiorno, L. (1997). Where the best B-School is no B-School. *Business Week,* October 20, 68–9.

Revans, R.W. (1982). *The Origin and Growth of Action Learning.* Brickley, UK: Chartwell-Bratt.

Revans, R.W. (1998). *ABC of Action Learning.* London: Lemos and Crane.

Reynolds, M. (1999). Grasping the nettle: Possibilities and pitfalls of a critical management pedagogy. *British Journal of Management, 9,* 171–84.

Rifkin, G. (1996). Leadership: Can it be learned? *Fortune ASAP, 8* (April), 100–12.

Rigg, C. & Trehan, K. (2004). Reflections on working with critical action learning. *Action Learning: Research and Practice, 1*(2), 149–65.

Salaman, G. & Butler, J. (1990). Why managers won't learn. *Management Education and Development, 21,* 183–91.

Sanders, D.D. & McCutcheon, G. (1986). The development of practical theories of teaching. *Journal of Curriculum and Supervision, 2*(1), 50–67.

Schein, E.H. (1967). *Process Consultation,* Volume I. Reading, MA: Addison-Wesley.

Schein, E.H. (1995). Process consultation, action research and clinical inquiry: Are they the same? *Journal of Managerial Psychology, 10*(6), 14–19.

Schön, D. (1983). *The Reflective Practitioner: How professionals think in action.* New York: Basic Books.

Senge, P.M., Kleiner, A., Robert, C., Ross, R.B. & Smith, B.J. (1994). *The Fifth Discipline Fieldbook.* New York: Doubleday.

Smith, K. & Berg, D. (1997). Cross-cultural groups at work. *European Management Journal, 15*(1), 8–15.

Smith, P. (1988). Second thoughts on action learning. *Journal of European Industrial Training*, *12*(6), 28–31.

Smith, P.A.C. & O'Neil, J. (2003). A review of action learning literature 1994–2000. *Journal of Workplace Learning*, *15*(2), 63–70.

Sutton, D. (1989). Further thoughts on action learning. *Journal of European Industrial Training*, *13*(3), 32–35.

Sveiby, K.E. (1997). *The New Organizational Wealth*. San Francisco: Berrett-Koehler.

Tannenbaum, S. & Yukl, G. (1992). Training and development in work organizations. *Annual Review of Psychology*, *43*, 399–41.

Torbert, W.R. (1998). Developing wisdom and courage in organizing and sciencing. In S. Srivastva & D.L. Cooperrider (eds), *Organizational Wisdom and Executive Courage* pp. 222–53. San Francisco: New Lexington Press.

Torbert, W.R. (1999). The distinctive questions developmental action inquiry asks. *Management Learning*, *30*, 18–206.

Tosey, P. & Nugent, J. (1997). Beyond the threshold: Organizational learning at the edge. In J. Holford, C. Griffin & P. Jarvis (eds), *Proceedings of the Lifelong Learning: Rhetoric and public policy conference* pp. 271–76. Surrey, UK: University of Surrey.

Tsoukas, H. & Mylonopoulos, N. (2004). Introduction: Knowledge construction and creation in organizations. *British Journal of Management*, *15*(1), 1–9.

Tucker, V.M. & Taylor, M.W. (1997). *Action Project: Common pitfalls and ways around them*. ISOE Working Paper, WP-97/001, The Pennsylvania State University, University Park, PA.

Van Mentz, M. (1983). *The Effective Use of Roleplay: A handbook for teachers and trainers*. London: Kogan Page.

Vicere, A.A. (1998). Changes in practices, changes in perspectives: The 1997 International Study of Executive Development Trends. *Journal of Management Development*, *17*(7), 526–43.

Vicere, A.A., Taylor, M.W. & Freeman, V.T. (1994). Executive development in major corporations: A ten-year study. *Journal of Management Development*, *13*(1), 4–22.

Viljoen, J., Holt, D. & Petzall, S. (1990). The MBA experience: Participants' entry level conceptions of management. *Management Education and Development*, *21*(1), 1–12.

Vince, R. & Martin, L. (1993). Inside action learning: An exploration of the psychology and politics of the action learning model. *Management Education and Development*, *24*(3), 205–15.

Weinstein, K. (1995). *Action Learning: A journey in discovery and development*. London: HarperCollins.

Weinstein, K. (2005). The power, and dilemma, of honesty: Action learning for social entrepreneurs. *Action Learning: Research and Practice*, *2*(2): 213–19.

Whitley, R. (1988). The management sciences and managerial skills. *Organization Studies*, *9*(1), 47–69.

Willis, V. (2004). Inspecting cases: Prevailing degrees of action learning using Revans' theory and rules of engagement as standard. *Action Learning: Research & Practice*, *1*(1), 11–27.

Willmott, H. (1997). Critical management learning. In J. Burgoyne & M. Reynolds (eds), *Management Learning: Integrating perspectives in theory & practice* pp. 161–76. London: Sage.

Willmott, H. (1994). Management education: Provocations to a debate. *Management Learning*, *25*(1), 105–36.

Yiu, L. (2006). Cultural variance of reflection in action learning. Paper presented at the Annual Meeting of the Academy of Management, Atlanta, GA, 14 August.

Yiu, L. & Saner, R. (1998). Use of action learning as a vehicle for capacity building in China. *Performance Improvement Quarterly*, *11*(1), 129–48.

Yorks, L., O'Neil, J. & Marsick, V.J. (eds) (1999). *Advances in Developing Human Resources: Action learning: Successful strategies for individual, team and organizational development*. San Francisco: Berrett Koehler.

# 23

# Developing Emotional, Social, and Cognitive Intelligence Competencies in Managers and Leaders

Richard E. Boyatzis

## Abstract

Various combinations of emotional, social, and cognitive intelligence competencies have been shown to predict effectiveness in leadership and management throughout the world (Boyatzis, 2008). Although billions of dollars are spent each year in attempts to develop them, and in graduate management education to prepare people for these roles, little longitudinal research has been done to show what works and what does not.

Using 20 years of longitudinal studies of people 25–65 years old at the Weatherhead School of Management (Boyatzis, Stubbs & Taylor, 2002), supported by other Model Programs from the Consortium on Research on Emotional Intelligence in Organizations (Cherniss & Adlenr, 2000), and a review of other published, longitudinal, multi-trait studies, the chapter will show that: (1) most approaches at training or management education do not affect these vital competencies; (2) some studies show significant improvements in competencies that sustain at least seven years; and (3) the change process that seems to work most effectively requires both Intentional Change Theory and concepts from complexity theory to understand.

While billions are spent trying to develop competencies each year, the results have been less than satisfactory. This does not even measure the millions of person hours spent in pursuit of competency development through performance reviews, training programs, coaching sessions, or workshops and courses in graduate or executive education. Some conclude from all this that effective leaders, managers, and professionals cannot be developed. This conclusion leads to a belief that effective leaders, managers, and professionals are either born that way or people should just focus on their current, evident strengths and find jobs, careers, and organizational settings in which they will be effective (Buckingham & Cliftox, 2002).

This chapter will bring a message of hope, by building on earlier longitudinal studies (Boyatzis, Stubbs & Taylor, 2002; Boyatzis, Cowen & Kolb, 1995). The competencies related to effective leaders, managers, and professionals can be developed in adults, but it is not easy. As the many longitudinal studies reviewed and reported in this paper show, even dramatic success in developing these competencies can be eroded by destructive organizational practices.

## PREPARING PEOPLE TO BE EFFECTIVE

One of the primary objectives of training and graduate management education is to prepare people to be outstanding managers, leaders, and professionals. This means helping people develop the functional, declarative, procedural, and meta-cognitive knowledge needed. Examples of these types of knowledge are, respectively, market segmentation for a new product, the time it takes a polymer to set, calculating the present value of a capital acquisition, and ethical principles as applied in international business transactions. This knowledge is necessary but not sufficient for the leader, manager, or professional to add value to organizations. In this sense, knowledge bases are threshold talents.

To be an effective leader, manager, or professional, a person needs the ability to use knowledge and to make things happen. These can be called competencies, which Boyatzis (1982) defined as, 'the underlying characteristics of a person that lead to or cause effective and outstanding performance.' A set of competencies have been shown to cause or predict outstanding leader, manager, or professional performance in the literature (Bray, Campbell & Grant, 1974; Boyatzis, 1982; Kotter, 1982; Thorton & Byham, 1982; Luthans, Hodgetts & Rosenkrantz, 1988; Howard & Bray, 1988; Druskat, Mount & Sala, 2005; special issue of the *Journal of Management Development* in February, 2008 on 'Competencies in the 21st Century,' and the special issue of the *Journal of*

*Management Development* in April, 2009 on 'Competencies in the EU') Boyatzis, 2008) or meta-analytic syntheses (Campbell, Dunnette, Lawler & Weick, 1970; Spencer & Spencer, 1993; Goleman, 1998). Compiling these findings and summaries, it can be said that the important competencies fall into three clusters: (1) Cognitive intelligence competencies, such as systems thinking or pattern recognition; (2) Emotional intelligence competencies, or intrapersonal abilities, such as adaptability, emotional self-control, emotional self-awareness, positive outlook, and achievement orientation; and (3) Social intelligence competencies, or interpersonal abilities, such as empathy, organizational awareness, inspirational leadership. influence, coaching and mentoring, conflict management, and teamwork. In addition, there are several cognitive capabilities that appear to be threshold competencies from the research cited above. That is, they are needed to be adequate in performance, but using more of them does not necessarily lead to outstanding or effective performance. Given research to date, these would include: knowledge (technical and functional); deductive reasoning, and quantitative reasoning.

Beyond knowledge and competencies, the additional ingredient necessary to outstanding performance appears to be the desire to use one's talent (McClelland, 1985). This seems driven by a person's values, philosophy, sense of calling or mission, unconscious motives and traits (Boyatzis, Murphy & Wheeler, 2000; Boyatzis, 1982; McClelland, 1985). These three domains of capability (i.e., knowledge, competencies, and motivational drivers) help us to understand *what* a person can do (i.e., knowledge), *how* a person can do it (i.e., competencies), and *why* a person feels the need to do it (i.e., values, motives, and unconscious dispositions).

## CAN A PERSON GROW AND DEVELOP THEIR TALENT?

Decades of research on the effects of psychotherapy (Hubble, Duncan & Miller, 1999), self-help programs (Kanfer & Goldstein, 1991), cognitive behavior therapy (Barlow, 1988), training programs (Morrow, Jarrett & Rupinski, 1997), and education (Pascarella & Terenzini, 1991; Winter, McClelland & Stewart, 1981) have shown that people can change their behavior, moods, and self-image. But most of the studies focused on a single characteristic, like maintenance of sobriety, reduction in a specific anxiety, or a set of characteristics often determined by the assessment instrument, such as the scales of the MMPI. But there are few studies showing sustained improvements in the sets of desirable behavior that lead to outstanding performance.

In management training, there is no fundamental question about purpose. The aim of development efforts is to help people become more effective. It requires development of competencies, as well as arousal of the appropriate motivation and value drivers. The question is whether the methods are effective or not. Do they produce an improvement in the competencies in use at work?

In schools, many faculty members still see competency development as the responsibility of the career placement office or adjuncts hired to conduct non-credit workshops. So in universities, there is a double challenge. First, there is the question as to whether or not the methods yield graduates who can and will use the competencies to be effective. Second, are these competencies integrated into the curriculum? Is it a main element in the program or school's mission? If faculty adopt the challenge of developing 'the whole person,' competency development would be as fundamental to objectives and methods as accounting Boyatzis, Cowen & Kolb, 1995).

Outcome assessment in higher education asks, 'What are our students learning?' The early results from such studies were sobering with only one clear conclusion – students graduating from our colleges were older than they were when they entered. Evidence was reported of knowledge acquisition, improvement in competencies, including critical thinking, and shifts in motivation, but these were far less frequent than was predicted

or expected (Winter, McClelland & Stewart, 1981; Mentkowski et al., 2000; Pascarella & Terenzini, 1991; Banta, 1993).

To address program impact, as of the early 1990s, only a few management schools had conducted student-change outcome studies which compared their graduates to their students at the time of entry into the program (Albanese, et al., 1990). Today, many schools have conducted other types of outcome studies, namely studies of their alumni or studies with employers and prospective employers (Kridel, 1998). Some schools have examined the student-change from specific courses (Bigelow, 1991; Specht & Sandlin, 1991). Student-change outcome studies have been a focus in undergraduate programs (Astin, 1993; Banta, 1993; Pascarella & Terenzini, 1991; Mentkowski & Strait, 1983; Mentkowski et al., 1991; Winter et al., 1981), but still relatively little has been documented about the effects of graduate programs.

This leaves the major question: Can MBAs and participants in executive education develop competencies that are related to outstanding managerial, leadership, and professional performance? And the related question, can people engaged in management training develop the competencies related to outstanding leadership, management, and professional performance?

## IMPACT OF MANAGEMENT EDUCATION AND TRAINING

The 'honeymoon effect' of typical training programs might start with improvement immediately following the program, but within months it drops precipitously (Campbell et al., 1970). Only 15 programs were found in a global search of the literature by the Consortium on Research on Emotional Intelligence in Organizations to improve emotional intelligence (Cherniss & Adler, 2000). Surprisingly, only five of them are still being offered or delivered. Most of them showed impact on job outcomes, such as number of new businesses started, or life outcomes, such as finding a job or satisfaction

(Cherniss & Adler, 2000), which are the ultimate purpose of development efforts. But showing an impact on outcomes, while desired, may also blur *how* the change actually occurs. Furthermore, when a change has been noted, a question about the sustainability of the changes is raised because of the relatively short time periods studied.

The few published studies examining improvement of more than one of these competencies show an overall improvement of about 10 percent in emotional intelligence abilities three to eighteen months following training (Noe & Schmidt, 1986; Hand, Richards & Slocum, 1973; Wexley & Memeroff, 1975; Latham & Saari, 1979; Young & Dixon, 1996). More recent meta-analytic studies and utility analyses confirm that significant changes can and do occur, but not with the impact that the level of investment would lead us to expect nor with many types of training (Morrow et al., 1997; Baldwin & Ford 1988; Burke & Day, 1986). The author does not claim this is an exhaustive review, but suggestive of the percentage improvement as a rough approximation of the real impact.

The results appear no better from standard MBA programs, where there is no attempt to enhance emotional intelligence abilities. Even before the humbling Porter & McKibbin (1988) report showed that MBA graduates were not fulfilling the needs of employers or the promise of the schools, the American Assembly of Collegiate Schools of Business started a series of outcome assessment studies in 1978. They showed faculty to be effective in producing significant improvement of students with regard to some abilities (Boyatzis & Sokol, 1982; Development Dimensions International-DDI, 1985). Boyatzis & Sokol (1982) showed that students had significantly increased on 40 percent to 50 percent of the competencies assessed in two MBA programs, while DDI (1985) reported that students in the two MBA programs in their sample had significantly increased on 44 percent of the variables assessed.

But, they also decreased significantly on 10 percent of the variables in the Boyatzis

& Sokol study. When the overall degree of improvement in these abilities was calculated (Goleman, Boyatzis & McKee, 2002) , these studies showed about a 2 percent increase in emotional and social intelligence competencies in the one to two years students were in the MBA programs. In fact, they showed a gain of 4 percent in emotional intelligence (i.e., self-awareness and self-management abilities), but a *decrease* of 3 percent in social intelligence (i.e., social awareness and relationship management) (Boyatzis & Sokol, 1982; Boyatzis, Renio-McKee & Thompson, 1995). Studies from another two highly ranked business schools behavior showed similar results, only improvements of 2 percent in the skills of emotional intelligence (DDI, 1985).

There is some doubt as to knowledge retention of MBAs. In one study, professors administered the same final exam from the required course in accounting at a later point than when the MBAs took the exam (Specht & Sandlin, 1991). They reported that the half-life of knowledge was six weeks.

A series of longitudinal studies underway at the Weatherhead School of Management of Case Western Reserve University have shown that people can change on this complex set of competencies that distinguish outstanding leaders, managers, and professionals. And the improvement lasted for years. A visual comparison of the percentage improvement in behavioral measures of emotional intelligence from different samples is shown in Figure 23.1. The 1–2 year data was from the full-time MBA cohorts. The 3–5 year data was from the part-time MBA cohorts. The 5–7 year data was from 2/3 of the part-time MBA cohorts (the same as assessed for the year 3–5 sample). The latter was interviewed two years following their graduation. Again, critical incident interviews were conducted to solicit work samples. The audiotapes were coded by the same reliable coders as the other samples. The behavioral code used for all of these samples, from 1990 through 1996, and the two-year follow-up sample, were the same. When coders were coding the graduating samples (or the two-year follow-up sample) they had to recode the entering (or in the case

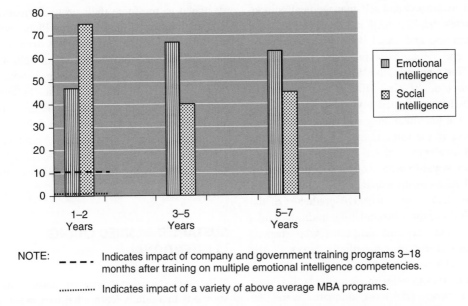

NOTE: - - - - Indicates impact of company and government training programs 3–18 months after training on multiple emotional intelligence competencies.

.............. Indicates impact of a variety of above average MBA programs.

**Figure 23.1 Percentage improvement of emotional and social intelligence competencies from behavioral measurement of different groups of MBA graduates taking the LEAD course[1].**

of the two-year follow-up, recoding was done on the entering and graduating interviews) to ensure minimal interference from coder interpretation drift. That is, a shift over time in interpretation of the codebook. Again, inter-rater reliability was calculated each year of these longitudinal studies.

MBA students, averaging 27 years old at entry into the program, showed dramatic changes on videotaped and audiotaped behavioral samples and questionnaire measures of these competencies as a result of the competency-based, outcome-oriented MBA program implemented in 1990 (Boyatzis, Baker, Leonard, Rhee & Thompson, 1995; Boyatzis, Leonard, Rhee & Wheeler, 1996; Boyatzis, et al., 2002). The coding of these audiotapes of work samples through critical incidents, videotapes of simulations were accomplished by advanced doctoral students with an average inter-rater reliability of 89 percent on a behavioral code for the competencies (Boyatzis, 1998). The code was

developed from earlier inductive studies of the behavioral indicators that distinguished outstanding from average performing managers (Boyatzis, 1982; Spencer & Spencer, 1993; Goleman, 1998).

Four cadres of full-time MBA students graduating in 1992, 1993, 1994, and 1995 showed 47 percent improvement on self-awareness competencies like self-confidence and on self-management competencies such as the drive to achieve and adaptability in the one to two years to graduation compared to when they first entered. When it came to social awareness and relationship management skills, improvements were even greater: 75 percent on competencies, such as empathy and team leadership.

Meanwhile with the part-time MBA students graduating in 1994, 1995, and 1996, the dramatic improvement was found again in these students who typically take three to five years to graduate. These groups showed 67 percent improvement in

---

[1]For 'n' and description of measures, see Boyatzis, Stubbs & Taylor (2002) *AMLE* article; comparison references are listed in Goleman, Boyatzis & McKee, 2002.

self-awareness and self-management competencies and 40 percent improvement in social awareness and social skills competencies by the end of their MBA program.

That's not all. Jane Wheeler tracked down groups of these part-timers two years *after* they had graduated (Wheeler, 1999). Even all that time later, they still showed improvements in the same range: 63 percent on the self-awareness and self-management competencies, and 45 percent on the social awareness and relationship management competencies. This is in contrast to MBA graduates of the WSOM of the 1988 and 1989 traditional full-time and part-time programs who showed improvement in substantially fewer of the competencies.

Changes in assessment methods did occur over time. The most dramatic were the shift from tests (1987 to 1989) to tests and interviews and simulations (1990 to 1998) to only the 360 informant assessments (1999 to present). The same 360 was used from 1990 through 2001, when an improved version was used, called the ECI-U (Boyatzis & Goleman, 2001; Boyatzis & Sala, 2004).

The positive effects of this program were not limited to MBAs. In a longitudinal study of four classes completing the Professional Fellows Program (i.e., an executive education program at the Weatherhead School of Management), Ballou, Bowers, Boyatzis & Kolb (1999) showed that these 45–55-year old professionals and executives improved on self-confidence, leadership, helping, goal setting, and action skills. These were 67 percent of the emotional intelligence competencies assessed in this study.

In the case of the MBAs, the entire program was organized around the competencies and values in 1990. Most courses required experiential activity in the form of team projects or field work. Career development activities, clubs, service work, and other program design changes contributed to the reinforcement of the message about competency development. For the Professional Fellows Program, the leadership course was one-fourth of the program activity. In addition, the remaining program components were all designed to reinforce their group formation and exploration of their Learning Plan. Once the year-long formal program was over, they were all inducted into the Society of Fellows. This was a self-directed learning society. Approximately two-thirds of the Fellows ending the program continued to be involved in development activities in the following years through the Fellows Society. About one-third of the Fellows were heavily involved in the years following their completion of the program.

## SUSTAINED DESIRED CHANGE IS INTENTIONAL

What the studies referred to above have shown is that adults learn what they want to learn. Although this sounds trite, the important distinction is that often people engage in learning or development activities for other reasons. That is, they attend a program to get a degree, not necessarily learn something. They attend a training program because they think their boss wants them to do it or it is expected by the corporate human resources department.

Other things, even if acquired temporarily (i.e., for a test), are soon forgotten (Specht & Sandlin, 1991). Students, children, patients, clients, and subordinates may act as if they care about learning something, go through the motions, but they proceed to disregard it or forget it – unless, it is something which they want to learn. This does not include changes induced, willingly or not, by chemical or hormonal changes in one's body. But even in such situations the interpretation of the changes and behavioral comportment following it will be affected by the person's will, values, and motivations.

In this way, it appears that most, if not all, sustainable behavioral change is intentional. *Sustained desired change is an intentional change in an aspect of who you are (i.e., the Real) or who you want to be (i.e., the Ideal), or both.*

Another feature of this theory is that most changes (i.e., the discoveries) are best understood through complexity theory

(Boyatzis, 2006). A preliminary concept is that most of the time the process of sustained, desired change unfolds in discontinuous and non-linear ways. This was called punctuated equilibrium by Gersick (1991). The nature of the non-linear change and the suddenness of the emergence of the various stages may be easier to notice when observing sustained, desired change through ICT on changes in teams, organizations, or communities (Amis, Slack & Hinings, 2004).

The process of intentional change is graphically shown in Figure 23.2 (Boyatzis, 1999, 2001, 2006; Goleman et al., 2005). The description and explanation of the process in this chapter is organized around five points of discovery. A person might begin intentional change at any point in the process, but it will often begin when the person experiences a discontinuity, the associated epiphany or a moment of awareness and a sense of urgency. This theory was first described in several articles in the late 1960s (Kolb & Boyatzis, 1970). It was built on ideas of William James (1890), and later enhanced

based on the research of Albert Bandura (1977).

This model describes the process as designed into a graded, required course and the elements of the MBA and executive programs implemented in 1990 at the Weatherhead School of Management. Experimentation and research into the various components have resulted in refinement of these components and the model as discussed in this paper. For a detailed description of the course, read Boyatzis (1995, 1994). Again, the course was the stimulus and source of the student's learning plan. But it took the remainder of the program to enable them to work on the learning plan and practice the desired changes. Without the surrounding system of the program (including both formal program requirements and informal in-school and out-of-school activities), the desired changes could not be practiced and internalized. This course was taught by 23 different faculties over the 18 years of the longitudinal studies. It is believed, therefore, that the results could

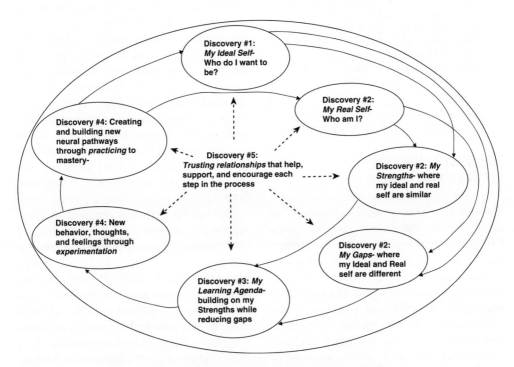

**Figure 23.2   Boyatzis' intentional change theory (Boyatzis, 2001, 2006)**

not be attributed to one faculty member, which is often a problem with developmental programs. In addition, the same course is now a required part of most of the degree programs at ESADE in Barcelona, Spain. Although they have not completed sufficient outcome studies to date to show the comparable impact, they are underway. At ESADE, with a dramatically different student base than WSOM, of mostly Spanish, Latin American, and European MBAs. Their EMBA consists of mostly Spanish and Latin American students with some Europeans currently working in Spanish companies. At least seven different faculties are teaching the course at ESADE. Faculties from other universities in the US, Europe, and Malaysia have used this course design.

---

### Research Questions

Because a major objective of this chapter (and the book) is to inspire future work, research questions that remain unanswered will be raised at the end of each section of this chapter.

1 Is intentional, desired change more sustained than unintentional desired change?
2 How much self-awareness or consciousness of the desired change is necessary and how much is sufficient for sustained change?
3 What are the ways in which a coach or teacher can help a person move through the process?

---

## THE FIRST DISCOVERY: MY PERSONAL VISION

Franklin is wrestling with redirecting his career for an old reason. He has been Executive Director of a foundation for ten years. Donors, program recipients, and policy makers consider him a distinctive success within the foundation world. His emotional intelligence is considered a model to be emulated by others, as is his incisive intellect. And yet he is restless. During a coaching session that was part of an assessment and development program, he identified two

possible career paths for the future: he could leverage his expertise and join a larger, global foundation as Executive Director; or he could become an executive for a company. The attraction of corporate life would be higher compensation.

When asked if he was feeling pressure from his family about money, Franklin said, 'Not at all.' Asked why he considered leaving the arena he felt passionate about with a deep sense of social mission and if there were any challenges a company can give him that he did not feel in a foundation, he looked toward the ceiling and shook his head. He realized that he was reacting to frustrations of his current situation. Once free of considering 'doing time' or 'paying his dues' in a company as a desirable option, he began to brainstorm ideas for adding to his personal income while leading foundations. He thought of expanding his writing to include books and giving speeches as ways to supplement his income.

Franklin was having trouble identifying his ideal work for the future. His deep, inner commitment to the not-for-profit world was ignored in considering the attractiveness of the private sector. But these attractions were things others found desirable, not Franklin. The first discovery of the change process is determining our Ideal Self, an image of the person we want to be. It emerges from our ego ideal, dreams, and aspirations (Boyatzis & Akrivou, 2006). Sometimes this appears as a wake-up call, alerting us to the observation that we have lost the enthusiasm or passion we once had for what we are doing and how we are living (Boyatzis, McKee & Goleman, 2002).

The last 20 years has revealed literature supporting the power of positive imaging or visioning in sports psychology (Loehr & Schwartz, 2001, 2003; Le Duff, 2002), meditation and biofeedback research, and other psycho-physiological research. It is believed that the potency of focusing one's thoughts on the desired end state of condition is driven by the emotional components of the brain (Goleman, 1995; Boyatzis & McKee, 2005). Visioning or positive imagery works through creating new neural circuits that the person can then use later when wanting to engage the related actions (Bennis & Nanus, 1985; Roffe, Schmidt & Ernst, 2005; Meister, et al., 2004; Carter, Macdonald, Ursu, Stenger, Ho Sohn & Anderson, 2000). They also work by arousing hope (Groopman, 2004; Curry, Snyder, Cook, Ruby & Rehm, 1997) which in turn stimulates the PSNS and its resulting increase in cognitive openness, cognitive power, and flexibility. In this aroused state, a person can grow new neural tissue, referred to earlier as neurogenesis (Erikson et al., 1998), and the healing powers of engaging a person's immune system (Manniz, Chadukar, Rybicki, Tusek & Solomon, 1999).

This research indicates that we can access and engage deep emotional commitment and psychic energy if we engage our passions and conceptually catch our dreams in our Ideal Self-image. It is an anomaly that we know the importance of consideration of the Ideal Self, and yet often, when engaged in a change or learning process we skip over the clear formulation or articulation of our Ideal Self image. If a parent, spouse, boss, or teacher, tells us something that should be different, they are telling us about the person *they* want us to be. As adults, we often allow ourselves to be anesthetized to our dreams and lose sight of our deeply felt Ideal Self.

---

### Research Questions

1 What are the necessary and sufficient components of a person's Ideal Self or Personal Vision that drive desired change?
2 Can wake-up calls be a sufficient motivator of change or must they be converted, first, into a positive image of a desired future to be effective?
3 How can a coach or teacher help a person realize or develop their Ideal Self?

---

## THE SECOND DISCOVERY

Joe started a doctoral program to propel him into his new life. His friends and family thought he was crazy. He owned and ran three health care companies, a nursing home, a temporary service agency specializing in health workers, and a small consulting practice. The nursing home had some problems including cash flow and a quarrelsome partner. It was not clear who was the antagonist between the two partners, but the relationship felt like a bad marriage staying together 'for the children.' He began teaching management part-time at a local university and loved it. The university made him a full-time faculty member. He was pursuing an Executive Doctorate in Management to refine his research and writing skills. This is a doctoral program designed for scholar-practitioners with typically 20 or more years of work experience of which at least ten are in management or leadership positions.

He loved the program but was running himself ragged with all of the responsibilities. When Richard Boyatzis asked him, 'Joe, what do you most want to be doing in five to ten years?' Joe did not hesitate, 'I love teaching. I would like to contribute through writing. I can translate complex concepts into language that people understand. I would love to do some research and test my ideas. But mostly, I love teaching.'

'Why are you keeping all these businesses?'

He turned with a questioning look, 'What do you mean?'

Pointing to the draft of his essay on his desired future, Professor Boyatzis clarified, 'You are a full-time faculty member. You want to be a full-time faculty member. You want to spend more time writing and doing some research. You are currently in a doctoral program. And yet, you are still involved in running three businesses. Don't you think this is too much? Haven't you made a choice already as to which you want? So why the ambivalence?'

He listed the contractual complications and financial implications leading to his conclusion that he must continue all three businesses. But then he added, 'I have considered handing the temporary services business to my son, letting the consulting business drop away to nothing by just not taking any new projects.' Once provoked in this way, he started to consider speeding the timeline. He brainstormed a few steps that would remove him from running the nursing home within a year, and from ownership of the nursing home within two years. Nodding his head with a growing smile, Joe said, 'This could work. This could really work! Boy oh boy, do I look forward to two years from now!'

Joe had changed but was confusing his old self with the person he had become. Joe knew that he was not as exciting a leader in his businesses as he had been in the past; while in the classroom, he engaged students using his humor and playfulness. Facing his Real Self, looking in the mirror was difficult.

The awareness of the current self, the person that others see and with whom they interact, is elusive. For normal reasons, the human psyche protects itself from the automatic 'intake' and conscious realization of all information about ourselves. These ego-defense mechanisms serve to protect us. They also conspire to delude us into an image of who we are that feeds on itself, becomes self-perpetuating, and eventually may become dysfunctional (Goleman, 1985).

For a person to truly consider changing a part of himself or herself, you must have a sense of what you value and want to keep. These areas in which your Real Self and Ideal Self are consistent or congruent can be considered Strengths. Likewise, to consider what you want to preserve about yourself involves admitting aspects of yourself that you wish to change or adapt in some manner. Areas where your Real Self and Ideal Self are not consistent can be considered Weaknesses.

The sources of increased awareness often come from developing the comparison of the Ideal and Real selves (Higgins, 1987, 1989, 1991). Acknowledging discrepancies can be a powerful motivator for change. But as this line of research by Higgins has shown, the distinction between the person's Ideal Self and their Ought Self become an

important additional discovery. The Ought Self is the accumulation of the Ideal Self for a person that others around him/her impose.

All too often, people explore growth or development by focusing on the 'gaps' or weaknesses. Organizational training programs and managers conducting annual reviews often make the same mistake. There is an assumption that we can 'leave well enough alone' and get to the areas that need work. It is no wonder that many of these programs or procedures intended to help a person develop result in the individual feeling battered, beleaguered and bruised, not helped, encouraged, motivated, or guided.

The second discovery can be achieved by finding and using multiple sources for feedback about your Ideal Self, Real Self, Strengths, and Weaknesses (Taylor, 2006). The sources of insight into your Real Self can include systematically collecting information from others, such as 360 degree feedback currently considered fashionable in organizations. Other sources of insight into your Real Self, Strengths, and Weaknesses may come from behavioral feedback through videotaped or audiotaped interactions, such as collected in assessment centers. Various psychological tests can help you determine or make explicit inner aspects of your Real Self, such as values, philosophy, traits, motives, and the like.

Sources for insight into your Ideal Self are more personal and more elusive than those for the Real Self. Various exercises and tests can help by making explicit various dreams or aspirations you have for the future (Boyatzis & McKee, 2005; McKee, Boyatzis & Johnston, 2008). Talking with close friends or mentors can help. Allowing yourself to think about your desired future, not merely your prediction of your most likely future, is the biggest obstacle. To be most helpful, these conversations and explorations must take place in surroundings that you feel are psychologically safe.

## THE THIRD DISCOVERY: MINDFULNESS THROUGH A LEARNING AGENDA

Karen was describing her career goals during an MBA class. At 27, she was energetic, poised, and ready to take on the world. She identified her long-term career goal to buy or open an art gallery in Chicago or a big mid-western city. When asked why an art gallery, she embarrassingly admitted she loved art but could not paint or sculpt.

Karen explained that she would approach her career goal by working for a large bank for a number of years to learn more about finance, not to mention make some money. Others in class thought it made sense until the Professor said, 'So in order to learn to be an entrepreneur in the arts, you want to work in a large, bureaucratic organization that values conformity, where most people wear gray or blue suits with red ties or scarves and managers demand adherence to policies, rules, and regulations? In this environment, you might extinguish the entrepreneurial spirit and confidence that you have and need to run an art gallery successfully.'

Karen's original draft of her learning plan would not have led to her desired future. She had absorbed an image from her reference group of fellow students and her general image of business – she thought she needed to master finance to be an entrepreneur. The MBA mythology has placed banks as one of the best places to work to master finance.

So Karen had written her original plan to work in an organization that was not of interest to her. Later conversations with her professor resulted in a learning plan more directly aimed at a future toward which she had passionate commitment.

The third discovery in intentional change is development of an agenda and focusing on the desired future (Boyatzis & McKee, 2005; McKee, Boyatzis & Johnston, 2008). While performance at work or happiness in life may be the eventual consequence of our efforts, a learning agenda focuses on development. A learning orientation arouses a positive belief in one's capability and the hope of improvement. This results in people setting personal standards of performance, rather than 'normative' standards that merely mimic what others have done (Beaubien & Payne, 1999). Meanwhile, a performance orientation evokes anxiety and doubts about whether or not we can change (Chen, Gully, Whiteman & Kilcullen, 2000).

As part of one of the longitudinal studies at the Weatherhead School of Management, Leonard (1996) showed that MBAs who set goals desiring to change on certain competencies, changed significantly on those competencies as compared to other MBAs. Previous goal-setting literature had shown how goals affected certain changes on specific competencies (Locke & Latham, 1990), but had not established evidence of behavioral change on a comprehensive set of competencies that constitute emotional intelligence.

A major threat to effective goal setting and planning is that people are already busy and cannot add anything else to their lives. In such cases, the only success with self-directed change and learning occurs if people can determine what to say 'no' to and stop some current activities in their lives to make room for new activities.

Another potential challenge or threat is the development of a plan that calls for a person to engage in activities different than their preferred learning style or learning flexibility (Kolb, 1984; Boyatzis, 1994). In such cases, a person commits to action steps in a plan that require a learning style which is not their preference or not within their flexibility. When this occurs, a person becomes demotivated and often stops the activities, or becomes impatient and decides that the goals are not worth the effort.

---

### Research Questions

1 How many 'learning goals' are optimum for increasing effectiveness?
2 Do differences in planning, cognitive, and/or learning styles mean that the form and format of goal setting should be varied for those with the different styles to result in sustained change?
3 How does a mentor guide a person in developing a meaningful learning plan?

---

## THE FOURTH DISCOVERY: METAMORPHOSIS

Bob wanted to build a portfolio of man-ufacturing companies in which he would have significant ownership and meaningful involvement in the management. A passive approach to providing venture capital was not enough. But Bob knew he was often impatient and not as sensitive to others as he would like. He wanted to develop a style that was collaborative with others, not managing them. Too many companies acquired by venture capitalists languish from inattention or falter from too much 'help.' Bob said, 'An owner will be reluctant to sell his or her business to someone with whom they have a poor rapport, and the envisioned "advisory group" will become dysfunctional.' So he wanted to build his empathy and patience with others as a step-ping stone to a more collaborative leadership style.

To experiment with this enhanced or new talent in understanding others, he decided to start with an opportunity closer to home – actually at home. Bob's relationship with two of his children, in particular his two daughters, should be more fun and supportive than it had been recently. He saw a way to work on his leadership style while rebuilding family relationships.

Bob declared a learning goal to 'identify an activity of mutual interest that I can do with my daughters on a routine basis (i.e., two or three times a month).' He knew they had expressed interest in two sports, golf and horseback riding. Bob talked to his daughters, more importantly he opened up the possibility and listened to their responses. They then set up a schedule to go riding and golfing on a monthly basis. He committed to watching movies with them that they wanted to see and even watch MTV with them.

The fourth discovery is to experiment and practice desired changes. Acting on the plan and toward the goals involves numerous activities. These are often made in the context of experimenting with new behavior. Typically following a period of experimentation, the person practices the new behaviors in actual settings within which they wish to use them, such as at work or at home. During this part of the process, self-directed change and learning begins to look like a 'continuous improvement' process.

To develop or learn new behavior, the person must find ways to learn more from current, or on-going experiences. That is, the experimentation and practice does not always require attending 'courses' or a new activity. It may involve trying something different in a current setting, reflecting on what occurs, and experimenting further in this setting. Sometimes, this part of the process requires finding and using opportunities to learn and change. People may not even think they have changed until they have tried new behavior in a work or 'real-world' setting.

Dreyfus (1990) studied managers of sci-entists and engineers who were considered superior performers. Once she documented that they used considerably more of cer-tain competencies than their less effective counterparts, she pursued how they devel-oped some of those competencies. One of the distinguishing competencies was Group Management, also called Team Building or Teamwork. She found that many of these middle-aged managers had first experimented with team building in high school and college, in sports, clubs, and living groups. Later, when they became 'bench scientists and engineers' working on problems in relative isolation, they still pursued use and practicing of this competency in activities outside of work. They practiced team building and group management in social and community organizations, such as 4-H Clubs, and professional associations in planning conferences and the like.

The experimentation and practice are most effective when they occur in conditions in which the person feels safe (Kolb & Boyatzis, 1970). This sense of psychological safety creates an atmosphere in which the person can try new behavior, perceptions, and thoughts with relatively less risk of shame, embarrassment, or serious consequences of failure.

---

### Research Questions

1 Are there personality dispositions, like Optimism, that would affect a person's ability to proceed through sustained, desired change?
2 How long should a person practice new behavior in a relatively safe environment before trying it at work?
3 What can mentors do to facilitate experimentation and learning at work and in other settings?

---

## THE FIFTH DISCOVERY: RESONANT RELATIONSHIPS

Our relationships are an essential part of our environment. The most crucial relationships are those in which we feel trust and safety in conversation. These are called 'resonant relationships' (Goleman et al., 2002; Boyatzis & McKee, 2005). They are often a part of groups that have particular importance to us. These relationships and groups give us a sense of identity, guide us as to what is appropriate and 'good' behavior, and provide feedback on our behavior. In sociology, they are called reference groups. These relationships create

a 'context' within which we interpret our progress on desired changes, the utility of new learning, and even contribute significant input to formulation of the Ideal (Kram, 1996).

In this sense, our relationships are mediators, moderators, interpreters, sources of feedback, sources of support, and permission of change and learning (Boyatzis, Smith & Blaize, 2006; Boyatzis & McKee, 2005). They may also be the most important source of protection from relapses or returning to our earlier forms of behavior. Wheeler (1999) analyzed the extent to which the MBA graduates worked on their goals in multiple 'life spheres' (i.e., work, family, recreational groups, etc.). In a two-year follow-up study of two of the graduating classes of part-time MBA students, she found those who worked on their goals and plans in multiple sets of relationships improved the most and more than those working on goals in only one setting, such as work or within one relationship.

In a study of the impact of the year-long executive development program for doctors, lawyers, professors, engineers, and other professionals mentioned earlier, Ballou, Bowers, Boyatzis & Kolb (1999) found that participants gained self-confidence during the program. Even at the beginning of the program, others would say these participants were very high in self-confidence. It was a curious finding. The best explanation came from follow-up questions to the graduates of the program. They explained the evident increase in self-confidence as an increase in the confidence to change. Their existing reference groups (i.e., family, groups at work, professional groups, community groups) all had an investment in them staying the same, meanwhile the person wanted to change. The Professional Fellows Program allowed them to develop a new reference group that encouraged change.

Based on social identity, reference group, and now relational theories, our relationships both meditate and moderate our sense of who we are and who we want to be. We develop or elaborate our Ideal Self from these contexts. We label and interpret our Real Self from these contexts. We interpret and value Strengths (i.e., aspects considered our core that we wish to preserve) from these contexts. We interpret and value Weaknesses (i.e., aspects we wish to change) from these contexts.

---

### Research Questions

1 What competencies of the coach or teacher have the most impact on effectiveness of the coaching?
2 How many coaches should a person have at any point in their lives? Does their life or career stage affect this number?

---

## WHAT IF LEARNING WERE THE PURPOSE OF EDUCATION OR TRAINING?

Borrowing from the title of Chapter 10 of Boyatzis, Cowen & Kolb's (1995) book for the subtitle of the implications section of this paper, we can offer a promising answer. An MBA education or management training *can* help people develop cognitive, emotional, and social intelligence competencies needed to be outstanding managers, leaders, and professionals. But we cannot use the typical lecture and discussion methods with their focus on knowledge acquisition only in education. Nor can we use the 'data dump and run' approach typical of assessment and feedback processes in training. A more holistic approach can help dramatically improve our impact and the relevance of an education or training to their future work organizations.

For practitioners or educators, the major implications lay in the design of the training or developmental assessment programs. Designing and conducting outcome research may be humbling, but it keeps you honest. When you offer a development program, you could have the outcome data to know what participants are learning and how much of it is sustained. If you do, it is likely that you will find the impact will be improved by following the discoveries and sequence described in Intentional Change Theory.

## REFERENCES

Albanese, R. (chair), Bernardin, H.J., Connor, P.E., Dobbins, G.H., Ford, R.C., Harris, M.M., Licata, B.J., Miceli, M.P., Porter, L.W. & Ulrich, D.O. (1990). *Outcome measurement and management education: An Academy of Management Task Force Report.* Presentation at the Annual Academy of Management Meeting, San Francisco.

Amis, J., Slack, T. & Hinings, C.R. (2004). The pace, sequence, and linearity of radical change. *Academy of Management Journal, 47*(1), 15–39.

Astin, A.W. (1993). *What Matters in College? Four critical years.* San Francisco: Jossey-Bass.

Baldwin, T. & Ford, J.K. (1988). Transfer of training: A review and directions for future research. *Personnel Psychology, 41,* 63–105.

Ballou, R., Bowers, D., Boyatzis, R.E. & Kolb, D.A. (1999). Fellowship in lifelong learning: An executive development program for advanced professionals. *Journal of Management Education. 23*(4), 338–54.

Bandura, A. (1977). *Social Learning Theory.* Englewood Cliffs, NJ: Prentice-Hall.

Banta, T.W. (ed.) (1993). *Making a Difference: Outcomes of a decade of assessment in higher education.* San Francisco: Jossey-Bass.

Barlow, D.H. (1988). *Anxiety and Disorders: The nature and treatment of anxiety and panic.* New York: The Guilford Press.

Beaubien, J.M. & Payne, S.C. (1999). Individual goal orientation as a predictor of job and academic performance: A meta-analytic review and integration. Paper presented at the meeting of the Society for Industrial and Organizational Psychology, Atlanta, GA. April, 1999.

Bennis, W. & Nanus, B. (1985). *Leaders: Strategies for taking charge.* New York: Harper & Row.

Bigelow, J.D. (ed.) (1991). *Managerial Skills: Explorations in practical knowledge.* Newbury Park, CA: Sage.

Boyatzis, R.E. (1982). *The Competent Manager: A model for effective performance.* New York: John Wiley & Sons.

Boyatzis, R.E. (1994). Stimulating self-directed change: A required MBA course called Managerial Assessment and Development, *Journal of Management Education, 18*(3), 304–23.

Boyatzis, R.E. (1995). Cornerstones of change: Building a path for self-directed learning, in R.E. Boyatzis, S.C. Cowen & D.A. Kolb (eds) *Innovation in Professional Education: Steps on a journey from teaching to learning* (pp. 50–94). San Francisco: Jossey-Bass.

Boyatzis, R.E. (1998). *Transforming Qualitative Information: Thematic analysis and code development.* Thousand Oaks, CA: Sage Publications.

Boyatzis, R.E. (1999). Self-directed change and learning as a necessary meta-competency for success and effectiveness in the 21st century, in R. Sims & J.G. Veres (eds), *Keys to Employee Success in the Coming Decades* (pp. 15–32). Westport, CN: Greenwood Publishing.

Boyatzis, R.E. (2001). How and why individuals are able to develop emotional intelligence, in C. Cherniss & D. Goleman (eds), *The Emotionally Intelligent Workplace: How to select for, measure, and improve emotional intelligence in individuals, groups, and organizations* (pp. 234–53). San Francisco: Jossey-Bass.

Boyatzis, R.E. (2006). Intentional change theory from a complexity perspective. *Journal of Management Development, 25*(7), 607–23.

Boyatzis, R.E. (2008). Competencies in the 21st century. *Journal of Management Development. 27*(1), 5–12.

Boyatzis, R.E. & Akrivou, K. (2006). The ideal self as a driver of change. *Journal of Management Development, 25*(7), 624–42.

Boyatzis, R.E., Baker, A., Leonard, D., Rhee, K. & Thompson, L. (1995). Will it make a difference?: Assessing a value-based, outcome oriented, competency-based professional program, in R.E. Boyatzis, S.S. Cowen & D.A. Kolb (eds), *Innovating in Professional Education: Steps on a journey from teaching to learning.* San Francisco: Jossey-Bass.

Boyatzis, R.E., Cowen, S.S. & Kolb, D.A. (1995). *Innovation in Professional Education: Steps on a journey from teaching to learning.* San Francisco: Jossey-Bass.

Boyatzis, R.E. & Goleman, D. (2001). *The Emotional Competency Inventory-university Version.* Boston: The Hay Group.

Boyatzis, R.E., Leonard, D., Rhee, K. & Wheeler, J.V. (1996). Competencies can be developed, but not the way we thought. *Capability, 2*(2), 25–41.

Boyatzis, R.E., Murphy, A. & Wheeler, J. (2000). Philosophy as the missing link between values and behavior. *Psychological Reports, 86,* 47–64.

Boyatzis, R., McKee, A. & Goleman, D. (2002). Reawakening your passion for work. *Harvard Business Review. 80*(4), 86–94.

Boyatzis, R. & McKee, A. (2005). *Resonant Leadership: Renewing yourself and connecting with others through mindfulness, hope, and compassion.* Boston: Harvard Business School Press.

Boyatzis, R.E., Renio-McKee, A. & Thompson, L. (1995). Past accomplishments: Establishing the impact and baseline of earlier programs, in R.E. Boyatzis, S.S. Cowen & D.A. Kolb, (eds), *Innovation in Professional Education: Steps on a journey from teaching to learning.* San Francisco: Jossey-Bass.

Boyatzis, R.E. & Sala, F. (2004). Assessing emotional intelligence competencies, in G. Geher (ed.), *The Measurement of Emotional Intelligence,* (pp. 147–80). Hauppauge, NY: Noves Sciences Publishers.

Boyatzis, R.E., Smith, M. & Blaize, N. (2006) Developing sustainable leaders through coaching and compassion. *Academy of Management Journal on Learning and Education, 5*(1), 8–24.

Boyatzis, R.E. & Sokol, M. (1982). *A pilot project to assess the feasibility of assessing skills and personal characteristics of students in collegiate business programs.* Report to the AACSB (St. Louis, MO).

Boyatzis, R.E., Stubbs, E.C. & Taylor, S.N. (2002). Learning cognitive and emotional intelligence competencies through graduate management education. *Academy of Management Journal on Learning and Education, 1*(2), 150–62.

Bray, D.W., Campbell, R.J. & Grant, D.L. (1974). *Formative Years in Business: A long term AT&T study of managerial lives.* New York: John Wiley & Sons.

Buckingham, M. & Clifton, D. (2001). *Now Find Your Strengths.* New York: Free Press.

Burke, M.J. & Day, R.R. (1986). A cumulative study of the effectiveness of managerial training. *Journal of Applied Psychology, 71*(2), 232–45.

Campbell, J.P., Dunnette, M.D., Lawler, E.E. III & Weick, K.E. (1970). *Managerial Behavior, Performance, and Effectiveness.* New York: McGraw Hill.

Carter, C., Macdonald, A., Ursu, S., Stenger, A., Ho Sohn, M. & Anderson, J. (2000). How the brain gets ready to perform, presentation at the Thirtieth Annual Meeting of the Society of Neuroscience (New Orleans, November).

Chen, G., Gully, S.M., Whiteman, J.A. & Kilcullen, R.N. (2000). Examination of relationships among trait-like individual differences, state-like individual differences, and learning performance. *Journal of Applied Psychology, 85*(6), 835–47.

Cherniss, C. & Adler, M. (2000). *Promoting Emotional Intelligence in Organizations: Make training in emotional intelligence effective.* Washington DC: American Society of Training and Development.

Curry, L., Snyder, C.R., Cook, D., Ruby, B. & Rehm, M. (1997). The role of hope in academic and sport achievement. *Journal of Personality and Social Psychology, 73,* 1257–67.

Development Dimensions International (DDI) (1985). *Final report: Phase III.* Report to the AACSB (St. Louis, MO).

Dreyfus, C. (1990). *The characteristics of high performing managers of scientists and engineers.* An unpublished doctoral dissertation, Case Western Reserve University.

Druskat, V., Mount, G. & Sala, F. (eds) (2005). *Emotional Intelligence and Work Performance.* Hillsdale, NJ: Erlbaum.

Erikson, P.S., Perfilieva, E., Bjork-Eriksson, T., Alborn, A-M., Nordburg, C., Peterson, D.A. & Gage, F.H. (1998). Neurogenesis in the adult human hippocampus. *Nature Medicine, 4,* 1313–17.

Gersick, C.J. (1991) Revolutionary change theories: A multilevel exploration of the punctuated equilibrium paradigm. *Academy of Management Review, 16,* 274–309.

Goleman, D. (1985). *Vital Lies, Simple Truths: The psychology of self-deception.* New York: Simon & Schuster.

Goleman, D. (1998). *Working With Emotional Intelligence.* New York: Bantam.

Goleman, D., Boyatzis, R.E. & McKee, A. (2002). *Primal Leadership: Realizing the power of emotional intelligence.* Boston: Harvard Business School Press.

Groopman, J. (2004). *The Anatomy of Hope: How people prevail in the face of illness.* New York: Random House.

Hand, H.H., Richards, M.D. & Slocum, J.W. Jr. (1973). Organizational climate and the effectiveness of a human relations training program. *Academy of Management Journal, 16*(2), 185–246.

Higgins, E.T. (1987). Self-discrepancy: A theory relating self and affect. *Psychological Review, 94,* 319–40.

Higgins, E.T. (1989). Continuities and discontinuities in self-regulatory and self-evaluative processes: A developmental theory relating self and affect. *Journal of Personality, 57,* 407–44.

Higgins, E.T. (1991). Development of self-regulatory and self-evaluative processes: Costs, benefits and tradeoffs, in M. Gunnar & L.A. Sroufe (eds), *Self-processes and Development: The Minnesota symposium on child psychology, 23* (pp. 125–65). Hillsdale, NJ: Erlbaum.

Howard, A. & Bray, D. (1988). *Managerial Lives in Transition: Advancing age and changing times.* New York: Guilford Press.

Hubble, M.A., Duncan, B.L. & Miller, S.D. (eds) (1999). *The Heart and Soul of Change: What works in therapy.* Washington DC: American Psychological Association.

James, W. (1890). *The Principles of Psychology.* New York: Henry Holt.

Kanfer, F.H. & Goldstein, A.P. (eds). (1991). *Helping People Change: A textbook of methods,* 4th Edition. Boston: Allyn & Bacon.

Kolb, D.A. (1984). *Experiential Learning: Experience as the source of learning and development.* Englewood Cliffs, NJ: Prentice-Hall.

Kolb, D.A. & Boyatzis, R.E. (1970). Goal-setting and self-directed behavior change. *Human Relations, 23*(5), 439–57.

Kotter, J.P. (1982). *The General Managers.* New York: Free Press.

Kram, K.E. (1996). A relational approach to careers, in D.T. Hall (ed.), *The Career is Dead: Long live the career* (pp. 132–57). San Francisco, CA: Jossey-Bass Publishers.

Kridel, J. (1998). Personal communication from the director of professional development, Programs for the AACSB.

Latham, G.P. & Saari, L.M. (1979). Application of social-learning theory to training supervisors through behavioral modeling. *Journal of Applied Psychology, 64*(3), 239–46.

Le Duff, C. (2002). A pile of medals for a positive thinker. *New York Times,* February 21, 2002, C-17.

Leonard, D. (1996). *The impact of learning goals on self-directed change in management development and education.* Doctoral dissertation, Case Western Reserve University.

Locke, E.A. & Latham, G.P. (1990). *A Theory of Goal Setting and Task Performance.* Englewood Cliffs, NJ: Prentice-Hall.

Loehr, J. & Schwartz, T. (2001). The making of the corporate athlete. *Harvard Business Review* (January/February): 120–28.

Loehr, J. & Schwartz, T. (2003). *The Power of Full Engagement: Managing energy, not time, is the key to high performance and personal renewal.* New York: Free Press.

Luthans, F., Hodgetts, R.M. & Rosenkrantz, S.A. (1988). *Real Managers.* Cambridge, MA: Ballinger Press.

Manniz, L., Chadukar, R., Rybicki, L., Tusek, D. & Solomon, O. (1999). The effect of guided imagery on quality of life for patients with chronic tension-type headaches. *Headache: Journal of Head and Face Pain, 39,* 326–324.

McClelland, D.C. (1985). *Human motivation.* New York: Cambridge University Press.

McKee, A., Boyatzis, R.E. & Johnston, F. (in press). *Becoming a Resonant Leader and Renewing Yourself and Others.* Boston: Harvard Business School Press.

Meister, I., Krings, T., Foltys, H., Boroojerdi, B., Muller, M., Topper, R. & Thron, A. (2004). Playing the piano in the mind – An fMRI study on music imagery and performance in pianists. *Cognitive Brain Research, 19*(3), 219–28.

Mentkowski, M. & Strait, M. (1983). *A longitudinal study of student change in cognitive development, learning styles, and generic abilities in an outcome-centered liberal arts curriculum.* Final Report to the National Institutes of Education from Alverno College.

Mentkowski, M., Rogers, G., Deemer, D., Ben-Ur, T., Reisetter, J., Rickards, W. & Talbott, M. (1991). Understanding abilities, learning and development through college outcome studies: What can we expect from higher education assessment? Paper presented at the Annual Meeting of the American Educational Research Association, Chicago.

Mentkowski, M. & Associates (2000). *Learning that Lasts: Integrating learning, development, and performance in college and beyond.* San Francisco: Jossey-Bass.

Morrow, C.C., Jarrett, M.Q. & Rupinski, M.T. (1997). An investigation of the effect and economic utility of corporate-wide training. *Personnel Psychology, 50,* 91–119.

Noe, R.A. & Schmitt, N. (1986). The influence of trainee attitudes on training effectiveness: Test of a model. *Personnel Psychology, 39,* 497–523.

Pascarella, E.T. & Terenzini, P.T. (1991). *How College Affects Students: Findings and insights from twenty years of research.* San Francisco: Jossey-Bass.

Porter, L. & McKibbin, L. (1988). *Management Education and Development: Drift or thrust into the 21st century?.* New York: McGraw-Hill.

Roffe, L., Schmidt, K. & Ernst, E. (2005). A systematic review of guided imagery as an adjuvant cancer therapy. *Psycho-oncology.* DOI: 10.1002, 889.

Specht, L. & Sandlin, P. (1991). The differential effects of experiential learning activities and traditional lecture classes in accounting. *Simulations and Gaming, 22*(2), 196–210.

Spencer, L.M. Jr. & Spencer, S.M. (1993). *Competence at Work: Models for superior performance.* New York: John Wiley & Sons.

Taylor, S. (2006). A conceptual framework and empirical test of leader attunement: Toward a theory of leader self-awareness. An unpublished doctoral dissertation. Case Western Reserve University.

Thornton, G.C. III & Byham, W.C. (1982). *Assessment Centers and Managerial Performance.* New York: Academic Press.

Wexley, K.N. & Memeroff, W.F. (1975). Effectiveness of positive reinforcement and goal setting as methods of management development. *Journal of Applied Psychology, 60*(4), 446–50.

Wheeler, J.V. (1999). *The impact of social environments on self-directed change and learning.* An unpublished doctoral dissertation. Case Western Reserve University.

Winter, D.G., McClelland, D.C. & Stewart, A.J. (1981). *A New Case for the Liberal Arts: Assessing institutional goals and student development.* San Francisco: Jossey-Bass.

Young, D.P. & Dixon, N.M. (1996). *Helping Leaders Take Effective Action: A program evaluation.* Greensboro, NC: Center for Creative Leadership.

# 24

# A Framework for Leadership Development

George A. Hrivnak Jr., Rebecca J. Reichard and
Ronald E. Riggio

## Summary

Despite the tremendous amount of time, money, and energy spent by practitioners and scholars alike to understand, promote, and facilitate effective leadership development, the field is still far from fully understanding what is often regarded as both art and science. That is not to suggest, however, that the field's efforts have failed to result in substantial progress. Indeed, after defining some salient concepts and the overall scope of this chapter, we review some of the major theoretical and empirical advances in leadership development. Furthermore, the trends and 'best practices' dominant in today's organizations in leadership development are then summarized and considered in light of the current academic trends to identify points of congruence and disconnect. With this foundation, we offer an approach to leadership development that builds on this current understanding. Our model does not offer a specific set of methodologies or instructional tools *per se*, but rather a framework to incorporate these modalities in a thoughtful, goal-driven, and comprehensive instructional approach designed to achieve specific, measurable, organizational objectives. Finally, we conclude this chapter with recommendations for future efforts to advance relevant research, to focus the teaching of leadership in the university classroom, and to improve the efficacy of current and future leadership development programs in practice.

## INTRODUCTION

Effective leadership is commonly believed to be an essential element of organizational success. The positive outcomes associated with effective leadership are numerous, including higher levels of individual commitment (e.g. Chen, 2004); satisfaction, (e.g. Fuller & Patterson, 1996); effort (e.g. Bass, 1999); effectiveness (e.g. Bass, 1985; Lowe, Croecke, & Sivasubramaniam, 1996); and team outcomes (e.g. Burke et al., 2006) to name but a few. Not surprisingly, leadership development is often the focus of a significant amount of organizational resources with respect to attracting, retaining, and developing leaders at all levels of the organization. In fact, U.S. organizations spend an estimated $30 billion (Training, 2005) to $50 billion (Lockwood, 2006) on leadership development annually. This premium on the value of leadership exists in organizational contexts ranging from business to government to the military and across many, if not all cultural boundaries. Given the importance of leadership and the amount of time, attention, and resources devoted to its development, it is easy to appreciate why the study of leadership has become one of the most heavily researched areas within the social sciences over the last few decades (Reichard & Avolio, 2005). Due to these efforts, our collective understanding of leaders, followers, and leadership has advanced significantly, if somewhat disjointedly (Burns, 1978).

In response to the query, 'are leaders born or made?', the appropriate response seems to be 'both'. While some dispute the 'trainability' of leadership (e.g. Barker, 1997), it appears that successful leaders across a variety of cultural contexts are likely to possess some common abilities and characteristics (e.g. House & Aditya, 1997; House, Hanges, Javidan, Dorfman & Gupta, 2004). But perhaps a more important ingredient is the amount and type of developmental experiences that one accumulates to enable personal growth as a leader (Caliguri, 2006; McCauley, Drath, Palus, O'Connor & Baker, 2006). Researchers have suggested that approximately 30–32 percent of leadership role occupancy is determined by genetics while the remaining majority is due to environmental factors (Arvey, Rotundo, Johnson, Zhang & McCue, 2006; Arvey, Zhang, Avolio & Krueger, 2007). Furthermore, the evidence from a number of studies has demonstrated that at least some elements of leadership can be trained (e.g. Dvir, Eden, Avolio & Shamir, 2002; Parry & Sinha, 2005; Thomas & Greenberger, 1998). More recently, a meta-analysis of leader development interventions found that leaders undergoing training have a 73 percent chance of positive outcomes compared to those in a control group (Reichard, Hughes, Avolio, Hannah, Chan & Walumbwa, unpublished manuscript).

Other recent leadership perspectives based on individual identity, social identification processes, and stages of adult development (Collinson, 2006; Lord & Hall, 2005; McCauley et al., 2006; van Knippenberg, van Knippenberg, de Cremer & Hogg, 2004) seem to emphasize the individual and collective change within and between leaders and followers through social psychological processes. While we respect these and other extant views and acknowledge that the field is far from having a unified position on the matter, we contend that sufficient evidence and theory exist to offer some informed guidance on the development of leadership that draws from multiple perspectives. We begin this chapter with the well-supported assumption that leaders and leadership *can* be developed.

## CONCEPTUAL DISTINCTIONS

Within the leadership domain, there are a number of conceptual ambiguities. Before continuing, it may be useful to address some important conceptual distinctions and assumptions underlying our ideas. The first, perhaps overemphasized distinction is in regard to the overlapping concepts of leaders and leadership as compared to managers and management. Managers and the processes of management have been characterized as mechanistic and primarily focused on efficient performance. In contrast, leaders and leadership are frequently defined as being principally concerned with vision, direction, and the organic growth of followers and the organization (Locke, 1999). These broad, overly simplified views are captured in the oft-repeated maxim that managers 'do things right', while leaders 'do the right thing' (Bennis & Nanus, 1985). While there seems to be some value in these definitions, these roles are often much more ambiguous and overlapping than implied. Rather than joining the debate, we recognize that the position of power and authority granted through a managerial role is not a necessary or sufficient condition for effective leadership. Similarly, one can be explicitly recognized or implicitly perceived as a leader without the trappings of a formal title or position. For the purposes of this review, we do not highlight distinctions between management and leadership development.

Another important distinction is the difference between training and development. The human resources literature commonly distinguishes these two areas along a few important dimensions (Fitzgerald, 1982). Training typically refers to targeted activities designed to remediate a skill or performance gap in an employee's current job. Alternatively, while development activities may help employees in their current role; the emphasis of these efforts is usually on preparing employees for future assignments or enabling long-term organizational goals (Bartz, Schwandt & Hillman, 1989). Thus, the choice of terms in the concept of leadership development seems appropriate. While leadership development activities may improve an individual's leadership effectiveness in his or her current role, the focus of such activities is in cultivating leadership capacity for future organizational assignments. The distinction is important because it impacts not only the design and implementation of leadership development programs, but also the time frame for which the impacts should be measured in assessing program effectiveness.

More recently, Day (2000) differentiated between the concepts of leader development and leadership development. By the former, he referred to an individual-based focus on developing such human capital as the knowledge, skills, and abilities required by formal leadership roles. For example, leader development refers to formal training, job rotation, and off-site workshops. In contrast, when defining *leadership* development, Day focused on the building of social capital, which refers to the networked relationships among employees. Leadership development emphasizes building and using interpersonal competence. It also entails enhancing the capabilities of all group members with respect

to leadership (McCauley & Van Velsor, 2004). In sum, leader development focuses on an individual level process of building human capital, and leadership development expands the collective capacity of employees and the building of social capital. While this conceptual distinction is valid and important, we will use the term leadership development inclusively of both leader and leadership development here.

The remainder of this chapter is structured as follows. First, we summarize some of the major theoretical developments regarding leadership and compare these with the dominant trends and 'best practices' of leadership development in an attempt to identify points of congruence and disconnect. We will then offer an approach to leadership development that builds on this foundation. Our model does not outline a specific set of methodologies or instructional tools *per se*, but rather provides a framework to incorporate these modalities in a thoughtful, goal-driven, and comprehensive approach designed to achieve specific, measurable, individual and organizational objectives. We conclude the chapter with recommendations for future research, pedagogy, and practice in regard to leadership development.

## THEORETICAL AND CONCEPTUAL DEVELOPMENTS

While some have argued that there are no comprehensive existing theories of leadership development (Day, 2000; Day & Halpin, 2004), practitioners have oftentimes relied on existing theories of leadership as a framework for content and evaluation of developmental interventions. For example, training based on the Situational Leadership Model prescribes to leaders the appropriate balance of task versus relationship-oriented behavior to engage in depending on the maturity level of followers (Hersey & Blanchard, 1982; Hersey, Angelini & Carakashansky, 1982). Other examples include Fiedler and colleagues' LEADER MATCH program based on the contingency theory of leadership (Fiedler & Mahar, 1979) and Avolio's (1999) full leadership development program was based on transformational leadership theory. More recently, Avolio and colleagues proposed an approach to leadership development based on the nascent concept of authentic leadership development (Avolio, Gardner, Walumbwa, Luthans & May, 2004; Gardner, Avolio, Luthans, May & Walumbwa, 2005; Luthans & Avolio, 2003). So while the focus of scholars has historically favored explicating the process of leadership itself, the field seems to be directing increasing attention to specifically bridging the gap between theory and practice in regard to the processes by which leadership is *developed*.

The focus of this chapter is not to debate the single best theory or definition of leadership. As others have already observed, there are myriad definitions, with few consistent themes (Yukl, 2006). Rather, we feel it is far better to follow the recommendation of Yukl & Van Fleet (1992) to use these various perspectives to our collective advantage so as to eventually develop sufficient understanding to begin to arrive at some type of consensus in our thinking. Furthermore, this diversity in perspectives may actually prove beneficial to both theory and practice. Simply making people aware of the theoretical variety and lack of consensus can help emphasize the point that there is no one best way to lead. As a result, recognizing and examining our current understanding of leadership and its shortcomings may actually help to break down our implicit theories of leadership and allow more nuanced ways to think about the topic.

## FUNDAMENTAL ISSUES IN LEADERSHIP DEVELOPMENT

While theories and definitions of leadership abound, the scholarly literature regarding leadership *development* is relatively scarce. As with the broader field of leadership, leadership development still lacks a generally accepted comprehensive model to guide research and practice (Lord & Hall, 2005). Much of the existing empirical research has largely focused on singular methods of leadership development rather than on more comprehensive approaches. The extant leadership development literature is heavily skewed toward research investigating specific development technologies, such as multi-rater feedback, coaching, job rotation, action learning, and classroom training (Day, 2000). Similarly, formal classroom training, executive development programs, and off-site meetings are the norm for many leadership programs. Thus, lacking a broadly accepted guiding logic, it seems that scholars and practitioners alike too often fail to address the basic questions of *who, what, where, when, how,* and *why* of leadership development. In the sections that follow, we do hope to advance this discussion by identifying and discussing the essential elements to be considered in such a model.

### Who?

Some authors have suggested that because leadership is a participative process, it can be enacted regardless of role (Day & Halpin, 2004). Pearce and Conger (2003) have argued that in today's organizations, leadership is more likely to be shared among organizational members rather than being concentrated among top leaders. Since the argument can be made that most, if not all leader competencies are just as important to followers (i.e. non-leaders), all organizational members should ideally be included in leadership development efforts. While this sounds like a fine and egalitarian idea, the cost of any significant leadership development effort would likely be prohibitive for most organizations. On the other hand, failing to have a strategic rationale for selection criterion will undoubtedly result in various forms of organizational conflict. Thus, the question of who should be included in an organization's leadership development program is yet another reason why such programs need to be defined in relation to the organization's goals and environment. A classic example is AT&T's

well-documented program initiated in the 1950s to identify and develop potential leaders early in their careers (Bray, Campbell & Grant, 1974).

Needless to say, the question of who should be included is not singularly focused at the individual level. That would simply be *leader* development. Our emphasis includes leader*ship* development, and is thus relational. In other words, it must consider the social context of the leader and must incorporate group-level, multi-level, and organization-level considerations as appropriate. Although much of this development comes from the establishment and growth of organizational relationships over time, awareness of these issues and approaches to fostering these relationships would seem to be topics amenable to developmental interventions.

Unfortunately, organizations cannot assume that all of its members are interested in or capable of continuous learning. This idea has been referred to by Avolio (1999) and others as developmental readiness. Hannah (2006) defined developmental readiness as both an ability and orientation to attend to and make meaning of feedback. Reichard (2006) stated that developmental readiness is based on the leader's level of learning goal orientation, developmental efficacy, and most importantly, motivation to develop. Consequently, participation selection focused on those individuals with relatively higher degree of readiness is likely to be more successful and reduce the chance of squandering organizational resources. Thus, these considerations serve as a starting point for determining the organization's leadership requirements.

## What?

There are two general considerations when determining the content of leadership development. First, asking what leadership competencies should be incorporated in a leadership development program assumes, of course, that such capabilities can be learned. This inevitability leads to the so-called state versus trait debate. While many traits, such as

intelligence and personality, have been shown to be positively associated with leadership, the relative stability of such constructs precludes development (Fleishman, Zaccaro & Mumford, 1991, 1992a, 1992b). Leadership development efforts should, therefore, be focused on building those facets of leadership which are viewed as more malleable, state-like, and open to development. So while intelligence may be regarded as fairly stable, related skills, such as critical thinking, decision making, and a systems perspective may be more responsive to development efforts. Further, Luthans and colleagues demonstrated the development of the positive psychological capital states of hope, optimism, efficacy, and resiliency through a micro-intervention (Luthans, Avey, Avolio, Norman & Combs, 2006). At a higher level of analysis, another state-like outcome of leadership development programs should be an increase in the density of the social network of organizational members . Much of the focus on these types of characteristics is on leader development.

The second consideration – which arguably faces less dispute – is the importance of social competencies. These interpersonal skills (e.g. communication, empathy, conflict management) enable individuals to establish the relational ties among group members through which communication, trust, and commitment can be developed (Brass & Krackhardt, 1999). Embedded within this emergent network of social relationships is the information, control, and other resources collectively referred to as social capital (Burt, 1992, 1997). Thus, the significance of Day's (2000) distinction is the recognition of the necessity of a dual focus on developing both human capital (leader development) and social capital (leadership development).

In any case, the lack of consensus regarding these issues has certainly not prevented academics, consultants, and organizations alike from defining and advocating their opinions. Acknowledging the inherent ambiguity of the situation, we contend that some set of salient competencies for a given organization can be determined through appropriate task and personnel analysis to understanding the gap between existing leadership capacity and estimated requirements. Ultimately, the content of a specific leadership development program should generally be driven by that organization's specific goals and context. However, we also believe that at least three areas deserve specific consideration in any leadership development effort.

*Emotions.* Research and debate in affect, mood, and emotions has risen exponentially in the management literature. Subsequently, researchers and practitioners alike have made extensive efforts focused on understanding and enhancing the emotional competencies of leaders and their followers (Boyatzis, 2007; Lord & Hall, 2004; Riggio & Lee, 2007). While an ability-based model of emotional intelligence appears to have some merit and emotions undoubtedly plays a role in the relational processes of leadership, the field is far from agreeing on the precise nature of its influence. Indeed, a recent review of the emotional intelligence literature cautioned against embracing unsubstantiated claims regarding the concept and encouraged a more evidence-based approach to its explanation (Jordan, Ashton-James & Ashkanasy, 2006). Chapter 9 in this volume by Ashkanasy and colleagues is a thorough review of this important topic and highlights some of the major issues and concerns.

*Culture.* With the rise of globalization and the increasing propensity for cross-cultural interactions, developing leaders for international assignments is another area of growing importance for leaders and followers alike (Javidan & House, 2001; Jung & Avolio, 1999; Offermann & Matos, 2007). Although relatively few studies have examined leadership in or across various cultures (Gerstner & Day, 1994), addressing this shortfall in the literature appears to be a focus for a growing number of researchers. Of this work, the GLOBE study of leadership and culture in 62 countries is the most recognized of these recent contributions. The findings of the GLOBE research program suggest that while leadership universals may exist in all forms of

leadership, the status and influence of leaders varies considerably across cultures (House et al., 2004). This study provides a wealth of findings with important implications for leadership cultural contexts and leadership development efforts. As Schein (1992) aptly noted, culture is the context of leadership and one cannot be thoroughly understood without consideration of the other.

*Diversity.* Of course, cultural values are not the only source of difference among individuals. Gender, age, race, religious belief, sexual orientation, and other factors all combine to various degrees to reflect a rich diversity in most, if not all leadership contexts. Given the mechanisms of globalization mentioned above and other ongoing socioeconomic trends, social diversity is a reality that must be incorporated into our understanding of leadership (Chin & Sanchez-Hucles, 2007) and must be systemically embraced by practitioners and researchers alike. Successful leadership development efforts not only must help leaders understand how to address diversity issues, but must also help to remove barriers to minority participation in leadership. These barriers include social stereotypes, a lack of mentors, inadequate networking opportunities, work–life balance challenges, and other barriers (Kilian, Hukai & McCarty, 2005). It is, therefore, incumbent upon all of us involved with the development of leadership to address these issues in our work so that the outcomes of such efforts reflect the diversity of today's organizations.

## Why?

From an organizational perspective, the answer to the question of why a leadership development program should be implemented often involves a desire to improve an organization's leadership capability in terms of quality, quantity, or both. However, having a clear understanding of the organization's goals and what role leadership plays in the achievement of those goals is the essence of a more meaningful answer to this question. Leadership development ultimately needs to be driven by the specific goals, strategies, and needs of the organization and the salient elements of the organizational environment. Interestingly, it is often the case that a shift in one or more of these driving factors results in a crisis that becomes the impetus for the creation of a leadership development process. This could be a shortage of experienced leaders to support the firm's international expansion strategy or a shift to a new organizational structure with an emphasis on self-managed teams. Whatever the case, the contextual dependence of leadership development also helps to answer the question of 'where' leadership development should occur. Although this issue will be addressed again later, it is important to ensure that much of leadership development takes place in the organizational environment in which the leadership behavior is expected to occur, increasing the likelihood of transfer of learning.

Another important consideration here is a major concern of all training and development interventions: implementing a leadership development program is not the solution, if the problems affecting leadership in the organization are a result of some other performance-related issue. These types of issues often involve poor or inadequate goals, roles, tasks, feedback systems, reward or recognition mechanisms, and other related issues. Another benefit of conducting a proper organizational assessment is the identification of these instances where the root issue cannot be addressed through the intervention of a leadership development program.

## How?

What methods should be employed in fostering leadership development? As with many other aspects of leadership development, it is useful to draw from the adult learning literature. Our assumption is that consideration of relevant adult learning factors can aid comprehension, internalization, retention, and the likelihood of appropriate application of the learning experiences that are incorporated into a well-designed leadership development program. For example, adults like individuals at other stages of development seem to have preferred learning styles (Kolb, 1984). While there are numerous typologies of these learning styles and significant debate exists among scholars regarding the construct and its assessment (Cassidy, 2004), the concept nevertheless seems worthy of consideration. Still, our contention is that when an individual's preferred learning style is engaged, overall learning effectiveness and efficiency is enhanced. Also, when an individual's preferred learning style is understood, the learning experience in a leadership development program can be tailored to this preference to improve effectiveness. However, when the learner's preferred style is unclear or there are multiple types of learners involved in a learning activity, a variety of methods and techniques should be employed to address the multitude of styles.

Another important consideration in adult development is that adults have accumulated knowledge and experience that can either contribute to or hinder a learning experience. Indeed, Dewey (1938) noted that all genuine learning is derived from experience (though not all experience provides learning). Prior experience can serve as a useful starting point or framework for future learning. However, experiences that contribute to inappropriate schemas or perceptions may need to be reevaluated and modified in order for new learning to take place (Dewey, 1938). The significant influence of personal experience also suggests that an emphasis on informal, experiential learning methods that build on the existing knowledge and experience of the learner are likely to be more effective than formal training methods (Kempster, 2006; Kolb, 1984). These types of learning environments can help to convey the application and value of what is being learned and makes the transfer of new skills or knowledge easier for the participants in the leadership development program. Interestingly, classroom and similarly artificial environments are often used for leadership training. While these settings may have their usefulness for conveying facts and information or for reflecting on recent learning activities, they cannot provide the developmental impact of experience.

## When?

When should these competencies be developed? Are some skills more important for certain roles within the organization? Is there a sequencing of competency development that enables development or maximizes the impact of the overall effort? Like the other questions of leadership development, there are numerous interacting considerations in the answer to this question. Despite the fact that considerable research is needed, some initial answers to this question can be inferred from the context, structure, and processes of the organization. Other insights can be inferred from existing evidence and best practices.

Defining the organization's sequence of leadership competency development is only part of the answer to these questions. Another important consideration here is the notion of changing social roles and individual values. The notion that adults have multiple and shifting social roles and progress through periods of transition and stability as they mature exists in psychology, education, management, and other fields (e.g. Erikson, 1982; Hoare, 2006; McCauley et al., 2006). These dynamics suggest that the personal value and meaning that an individual derives from his or her job, career, and organization of employment is likely to change over time. These shifting priorities influence the amount of effort and sacrifice that an individual is likely to commit toward leadership development. In the same way, since motivation can be enhanced by offering rewards that are valued by the individual, the nature of these rewards needs to be tailored to the needs and values of that individual. For these reasons alone, it is important to remember that the timing and pace of leadership development is unique to each individual and is significantly impacted by factors outside of the organizational context.

In summary, addressing these fundamental questions of leadership development is a useful starting point for identifying relevant issues and implicit assumptions. Even if the existing theoretical and empirical support is lacking in regard to many of these questions, the extant literature and lessons from current best practices do provide sufficient basis to begin to develop a guiding framework for more rigorous testing and continued development.

## A FRAMEWORK FOR LEADERSHIP DEVELOPMENT

Building on these core issues, we now present our conceptual framework for designing an effective leadership development program. Our objective here is not to outline a specific set of methodologies or instructional tools *per se*, but rather provide a way to incorporate these modalities in a thoughtful, goal-driven, and comprehensive instructional approach designed to achieve specific, measurable, organizational objectives. Although the field still lacks a universal theory of leadership development, we hope that the proposed framework helps to move us closer to this goal.

Before presenting this framework, it is important to explicate a few critical assumptions derived from the previous section. As already suggested, leadership development is contextually dependent. As such, it would be unrealistic to propose a 'one-size-fits-all' model of leadership development. Rather, our framework identifies key considerations for each individual organization to consider in the design, development, delivery, and evaluation of a comprehensive and systematic approach to leadership development. Second, successful leadership is far more dependent on the progressive development of relational and sociological competencies than on acquiring specific technical knowledge or skills. More specifically, the process of leadership is about influencing others, directly and indirectly, through a variety of contextually dependent mechanisms. Thus, our framework focuses on assessing and developing these competencies to the extent that they have been identified as important within a given context. Third, as with the concept of continuous or lifelong learning, there is no 'end state' in leadership development. Lastly, our contention is that leadership development efforts are future-oriented. The majority of the benefit from efforts made today is reaped during subsequent leadership situations and also by providing a basis for continued development and learning of these competencies.

## Beginning with a mutual commitment

Leadership development, like all learning, is ultimately the responsibility of the learner. It is not something that an organization 'does' to current or future leaders, but rather something that it helps to foster within each potential leader. Success is largely dependent on the willingness of the individual leader to invest the time and energy in the endeavor, with continual support and resources provided by the organization in the interest of achieving long-term organizational goals. This suggests the value of mutual commitment between the individual and the organization to pursue a long-term relationship. So if individuals have responsibility for their development, what are the obligations of the organization in this relationship?

First, organizations demonstrate a commitment to leadership development by openly acknowledging the importance of leadership and supporting the development of leaders from within the organization. A stated commitment is further substantiated by a significant commitment of resources to the leadership development program. This is accomplished by recognizing that leadership development is a long-term strategic investment not unlike a commitment to research and development. Beyond direct program expenses, this commitment entails creating sufficient organizational 'slack' to allow for learning and growth. This is largely

a staffing consideration that allows for sufficient organizational personnel to enable individuals to both participate in the program and serve various support functions, such as mentoring or providing assessments and feedback. It also involves the development of systems and processes to manage the 'pipeline' of developing leaders and the job and project opportunities that provide the essential context for experiential learning.

In addition to the commitment of resources, it is imperative that the program has the attention and focus of leaders and managers throughout the organization. This is achieved by integrating the leadership development process within the organization's other strategic operating processes. For example, staffing decisions should be considered as job rotation or development assignment opportunities for developing leaders. Another example of organizational focus is shown when leadership development is made part of each leader's job description. This includes identifying potential leaders, mentoring and coaching junior leaders, leading by example, and being cognizant of their respective roles in managing the organization's leadership pipeline. Thus, there are instances where the leadership development process must be separate from the performance evaluation process (e.g. with respect to leaders in the program) as well as instances when they are strategically linked (e.g. when identifying, mentoring, and otherwise developing future leaders is part of a manager's performance objectives). Finally, leadership development programs will be ineffective without an overarching culture of support for learning and continuous development. Such an organizational environment enables and recognizes the need for decisions to continue investment in leadership development even during difficult situations. It also helps to facilitate difficult staffing and other strategic decisions that are in the organization's (and the leader's) long-term interest.

An important consideration in this regard is whether the organization's leadership development model is one that is needs-based (i.e. deficit) or strengths-based. A needs-based model takes the view that leaders lack certain required competencies that must be developed in order to improve leadership quality. Historically, this has been the dominant perspective of many organizational training and development programs. A significant assumption here is that individuals are capable of developing all of the identified competencies. This view has been challenged by the strengths-based model of leadership development which recognizes that some people may not be able to develop the required competencies to the desired level. More importantly, this perspective focuses on an individual's inherent strengths and focuses on finding ways to leverage these strengths to compensate for deficiencies in other areas. In our view, both perspectives have their merits. Perhaps the best solution is to use a blended approach. Try to develop deficient competency areas, but recognize that development may have unique limits for each individual. When the development is insufficient, focus on leveraging the person's strengths and others forms of augmentation (e.g. additional organizational support, redefining job roles) to compensate for the deficiency.

With this multi-faceted obligation recognized and embraced, the organizational commitment to support the individual's leadership development efforts is defined. We will continue to refer to aspects of the roles of both the individual and the organization throughout the rest of the chapter. Nonetheless, the foundation for the design and implementation of the leadership development process has been set.

## Assessing organizational requirements

The effectiveness of any type of development program or learning activity begins with how well it is designed. Effective design requires a thorough understanding of the problem. In this case, defining the problem involves understanding the organization's leadership needs and priorities, as well as the context in which that leadership will be required. The context of leadership is largely defined by the organization's operating environment, mission, goals, strategy, and other related elements. The leadership needs of the organization are then defined as an input to the strategy that has been developed to achieve the organization's goals.

In order to fill these leadership needs, qualifying and quantifying the organization's leadership requirements is an essential task. This involves both determining the number of leaders desired at each level or section of the organization and defining the specific leadership competencies required at each. Similarly, it should also clarify the expected competencies – leadership, technical, and otherwise – to be developed at each level. Care should be taken in the sequencing of these activities to both ensure the ordered acquisition of prerequisite competencies and to be reflective of the tasks and objectives of the possible roles at each level. Figure 24.1 is a graphic example of how these competencies might be defined at each level of the organization.

In this hypothetical example, the organization has four basic organizational levels; organization member, manager, director, and executive (i.e. the CEO and other executive officers). The descriptions of these levels are irrelevant and merely selected for convenience of differentiation and explanation. At each of these levels (indicated by a disruption in the diagonal line), a different stage of leadership development is identified (e.g. project leadership, portfolio leadership, etc.) that is in addition to the typical job descriptions that are representative of that level within the organizational hierarchy. The competencies (shown to the right of the diagonal) below the disturbance in the diagonal line can be thought of as prerequisites of that organizational level. The competencies above the disturbance represent the development priorities within that level. The model is not intended to imply a fixed number of levels or competencies, nor does it suggest distinct association between organizational levels and competencies sets. It is representative, not definitive.

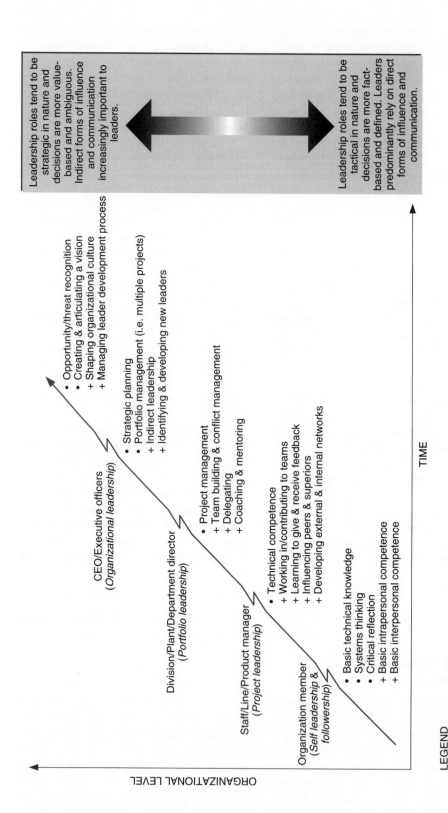

**Figure 24.1 A model of leardership development**

As an example, an individual participating in the leadership development program who is promoted to the position of manager would be expected to have already gained or developed relevant technical competence, experience working in teams, an understanding of how to give and receive feedback, as well as the rest of the competencies listed. In her new position as manager, she would be expected to have the development priorities of project management skills, team building, conflict management, delegation, and mentoring.

To the right of the graph is a continuum designed to offer a brief explanation of the rationale behind the sequencing of competencies. As the leader progresses through the organizational hierarchy, decisions become more value-based, strategic, and ambiguous. Also, indirect forms of influence and communication become more critical to effective leadership due to the increasing span of control. The objective here is not to suggest new forms of leadership, but to provide an example of a typology that an organization might use to define the progressive, sequential stages of development that it determines appropriate for its leaders.

The organizational needs assessment is a critical step in the design of the leadership development program and can yield numerous benefits if conducted thoroughly and effectively. For one thing, this step helps to clearly define needs and expectations and allows individuals progressing through the leadership development stages to anticipate leader competency expectations of future roles. It also provides a framework that allows for individuals to be recruited internally or externally, because the competencies at each organizational level are clearly defined. More importantly, this assessment can also serve as the mechanism for identifying and selecting potential leaders within the organization.

## Conducting the gap analysis

Once the organizational needs are defined with respect to leadership, the existing leadership capability within the organization can be assessed. This leadership needs or 'gap' analysis can be further delineated between short-term (immediate to less than one year) and long-term (more than one year) needs. While the term may imply a shortfall of leadership capability, a gap analysis may also reveal a surplus of leadership at a given organizational level. Given the competitive operating environment of most organizations, such a situation might occur as a result of a significant shift in organizational goals, strategy, structure, or similar change. Thus, it is important to recognize that the design and configuration of the leadership development program is an ongoing process that adapts to changes in the organization's environment and shifts in its strategic objectives.

Based on the results of the gap analysis and similar forecasts, a leadership development plan can be created to fulfill the identified requirements. Given the future orientation of an effective leadership development program, short-term needs are difficult to fill unless there is an available surplus of leaders in other areas of the organization that are capable of taking on the new role. Lacking an available pool of internal talent, it is often necessary to hire an individual from outside the organization to fulfill these relatively urgent needs. From this scenario, it may be inferred that it is easier for the organization to plan for and address long-term needs as opposed to short-term needs. While this may be the case in some respects, it can also be more difficult in others. One of the most significant challenges to long-term planning is the development of accurate forecasts of future leadership requirements. Nevertheless, this is a challenge that organizations face in many other strategic decisions and is but one more consideration that should be clearly explicated to ensure the long-term success of the organization.

## Methods of leadership development

Once existing and potential leaders are identified within the organization and selected for participation in the program, the real work of leadership development begins. As mentioned previously, organizational learning typically takes one of two basic types: training and development. While a review of these methods here would be a redundant contribution to the literature (see Day, 2000 & Yukl, 2006), a brief summary is useful. Training is often exemplified by workshops, seminars, classes, or degree programs offered by the organization, consultants, or educational institutions. These activities typically are designed to address well-defined learning objectives in a relatively short time frame. The instructional techniques used in these training sessions include lectures, cases, simulations, exercises, games, role playing, and various types of multi-media presentations.

Alternatively, development activities may help employees in their current role, but the emphasis of these efforts is usually on preparing employees for future assignments or enabling long-term organizational goals. In an organizational context, terms, such as development assignments, job rotation programs, and project assignments (i.e. action learning; Dotlich & Noel, 1998) are often cited as typical development methodologies (we will collectively refer to these methods as development assignments throughout the remainder of this chapter). Essentially, these methods involve using existing and specially created positions and projects within the organization as a context for development using an experiential learning process. This approach seems especially relevant to leadership development because organizational leadership is a set of applied knowledge, skills, and abilities that need to be practiced and developed *in situ*.

As a form of pedagogy, experiential learning usually suggests some type of process that begins with an initial experience, followed by reflecting on the experience from a variety of perspectives, abstracting relevant learning and principles from the experience, and then testing this new learning by applying it in a new situation (Kolb, 1984). Research suggests that the effectiveness of this type

of approach is a function of the amount of challenge involved in the assignment, the variety of tasks involved in the assignment, and the quality of feedback relative to the individual's performance of the assignment (Yukl, 2006).

The degree of challenge involved in a development assignment can result from such factors as ambiguously defined goals, tasks, or roles; the degree of risk involved (e.g. economic, career); the relative importance to the organization of a successful outcome; and the overall difficulty of the assignment. Since the amount of challenge is difficult to control in experiential approaches, additional organizational support and guidance may be necessary in some assignments. The organization can help mitigate some of the other factors, for example, providing greater clarity regarding goals or tasks. However, other factors – such as risk and importance – may simply be a function of increasing levels of responsibility. Consequently, supervisors, mentors, and coaches must be constantly vigilant in their awareness of when a developing leader needs more help.

A wide variety of learning experiences is beneficial in a number of ways. Increased variety provides a greater number and type of situations, problems, decisions, and outcomes from which leaders can learn. Through proper reflection on the experience, the learner can help distill universal principles and techniques and identify the limitations and dependencies of those that are more contingent in nature. This variety can also be increased by learning from both positive and negative exemplars. Just as one can learn from both good and poor role models, leaders can learn from experiences that result in either failure or success. However, it is unclear as to the best way to combine and sequence assignments in the interest of creating a more effective development program. Whether or not there is an optimal mix of tasks or assignments either in general or for a specific stage of development remains an open question for leadership scholars.

## Providing feedback

Feedback helps to facilitate the reflection process necessary to extract the lesson from experience. Feedback can be provided through a number of sources and methods. Individual feedback can be acquired from superiors, mentors, coaches, peers, and other relevant perspectives. Other sources and mechanisms include multi-rater (360°) feedback and assessment centers. For example, 360° feedback refers to the process by which followers, peers, supervisors, and even customers provide confidential feedback to the target leader, who in turn uses the feedback to make leadership improvements (see Atwater, Brett & Waldman, 2003, for benefits and risks of 360° feedback). Assessment centers involve leadership simulations with assessors providing evaluations and feedback (Thornton & Rupp, 2006). One drawback of several of these feedback mechanisms is that characteristics (e.g. personality or implicit leadership theories) of the individuals providing the feedback may bias or otherwise influence their comments. It may, therefore, be necessary to determine the extent of the bias of these factors and attempt to take this into account when considering such feedback in order to gain a more accurate picture of a leader's strengths and development needs.

One source of potential feedback and leadership development for leaders comes from mentoring (Cf. Ensher & Murphy, 2005); traditionally a process whereby a more experienced individual (i.e. the mentor) guides a less experienced individual (i.e. the mentee or protégé). In fact, previous research on organizational mentoring has demonstrated its positive impact on promotions, salaries, and job mobility (Allen, Eby, Poteet, Lentz & Lima, 2004) and has suggested its use in addition to other career self-management strategies (Murphy, Ensher & Reichard, unpublished manuscript). Mentors and coaches can provide additional value to leaders through their guidance, advice, and organizational support. Thus, in a way, mentors are somewhat of a personification of the organization's commitment to support of the individual's leadership development. In a leadership development context, mentors are typically senior managers that have some combination of extensive technical, leadership, or organizational knowledge. A mentor can be a source of guidance and encouragement for the mentee or can help facilitate the socialization and acceptance of her mentee within the organization. Depending on one's role and influence in the organization, the mentor might also be able to help the mentee obtain coveted or valuable assignments to help advance their leadership and career development. On the other hand, coaching, while similar to mentoring as a form of one-on-one learning, differs in that it is typically much more limited in duration and specific in its scope or purpose. Also, due to the obvious lack of available mentors for leaders high in the organizational hierarchy and the cost of many external coaches, executives tend to rely more on coaches than on mentors. Beyond traditional mentoring as described here, other types of mentoring used in leadership development include peer, step-ahead, reverse, group, and e-mentoring (Ensher & Murphy, 2005).

## An emphasis on experiential learning

While the benefits to the leader are obvious, the coaches and mentors also benefit in various ways as well. This satisfaction is not unlike a teacher who enjoys guiding the development of a promising student. Yet these methods are not without their issues. Personality and other relationship conflicts can often result in unsuccessful mentoring and coaching outcomes. While it would appear obvious that some combination of selection and training of mentors might be beneficial in obtaining more positive and consistent results, there is limited empirical understanding of precisely *how* a mentor or coach actually facilitates leader development.

While experiential methods can be a powerful form of learning, especially for adults, the relative lack of structure in experiential learning and lack of understanding in how to employ it as a learning method limits its use. This is one reason that organizations too often seem to overemphasize discrete training methods, while neglecting or underutilizing the potential of experiential learning. This is unfortunate because the role of experience in adult learning is axiomatic with but a cursory review of theory. Still, it is important to recognize that while leadership is primarily developed through experiential methods, formal (e.g. classroom) training methods can be used to help prepare for, augment, and interpret these learning experiences. Finding the right balance of methods is an ongoing process in search of a dynamic solution, and largely depends on the characteristics of the learner and their organizational context.

## Assessment of leadership development outcomes

Assessment is a critical element of successful leadership development programs that is often underdeveloped, if not altogether omitted. The purpose of assessment in the leadership development process is to determine whether or not the efforts have yielded the desired effect. However, the goals, objectives, and measures of leadership development activities are often poorly defined, if defined at all. One potential tool that is often suggested to help determine the impact of these efforts is Kirkpatrick's (1976) model of evaluation.

Essentially, Kirkpatrick's model provides a typology of approaches to measuring training and development outcomes. Designed to be considered in succession, beginning with the lowest level, the four-levels are intended to measure: (1) reaction of trainees, with respect to what they thought or felt about the training; (2) trainee learning as reflected by an increase in knowledge or capability; (3) behavioral change; and (4) the impact of the change in trainees' behavior relative to their organizational roles. Obviously, measurement of the true impact of the training and development effort is improved with each successive layer. Unfortunately, progressing through each layer involves increasing levels of time, expense, and

challenge. Furthermore, it does not eliminate the need to have clearly defined learning objectives and measures.

At a minimum, leadership development programs should be designed to measure changes in leader behavior (i.e. level 3). Depending on the competency being developed, efforts should be made to assess the organizational impact of that behavioral change. This decision should be made in recognition of the cost of assessment relative to importance of measuring the behavioral effects. The danger lies in the risk of overzealously pursuing performance measurement in lieu of leadership development. The reality is that in addition to the lack of clarity regarding which leadership competencies are most important, practitioners and scholars often lack the technology and understanding to measure some of these competencies. This presents a paradox: it is important to measure the change in leader behavior and the organizational impact of that behavior, yet we often lack the tools to do so. Nevertheless, the challenge must be addressed. Indeed, it is only through the continuing efforts of organizations, consultants, and scholars to address this challenge that this problem will be resolved.

## Effective program management

Managing the long-term development process can be a challenging task for individual leaders. Learning contracts (Knowles, 1991) or similar types of individual development plans can be used to define a strategy for personal development as a leader. Effective learning contracts are essentially well-designed blueprint for self-directed learning. The process of constructing a learning contract is very similar to the methodical approach used at the organizational level to design the leadership development program. Beginning with an assessment of development needs, a set of learning objectives is defined along with the learning resources and strategies that will be used to achieve these goals. Of course, it is important that the resources and strategies also consider the learning styles and preferences of the individual and are adapted to these factors in mind. The final portion of the contract is the specification of how evidence of learning and change will be collected including the methods, validation, and timeframe of this assessment.

Learning contracts can help to add structure to a program of leadership development for those who are seeking greater clarity of the process. Creating or updating these plans requires the individual to reflect on personal values and help him or her to define their development goals and priorities. It also serves as a way to assess alignment between an individual's personal development goals with the organization's development goals. This process can also help to establish or strengthen relationships with supervisors, mentors, or coaches who help guide the individual through the creation of the plan. It can also help to clarify the individual's priorities at a given stage of development which can suggest the type of development or training that is needed, allowing for improved planning by the organization to help ensure the appropriate development assignments will be available.

Obviously, managing the various types of experiential opportunities available to leaders is a difficult task. One potential solution to this problem is for the organization to implement a system to aggregate these development assignments into a central repository to help facilitate effective program management. This solution would provide a single source of current and upcoming experiential opportunities (both job and project assignments) for individuals in the pipeline. As another example of integration to other organizational processes, this system could be a special extension of the firm's job posting system. The program management system should also be able to monitor individual and collective (i.e. all leaders in the organizations) development progress. Comparing this development status to a current assessment of organizational leadership needs provides a measure of the surplus or deficit of leadership capacity in terms of both quantity and quality at each level

of the organization (e.g. succession planning). Thus, senior management is able to track the preparedness of the organization to sustain effective operations and pursue future growth opportunities.

## IMPLICATIONS FOR TEACHING AND PRACTICE

In providing an understanding of leadership development for management students, it is imperative that undergraduate and graduate students appreciate the reality of lifelong learning and what it entails. Teachers can help prepare students for this journey by ensuring that students have learned how to learn and think. This involves providing greater exposure to critical reflection, rhetoric, systems thinking, learning styles, experiential learning, and similar concepts, as these techniques play a critical role in leadership development efforts. It is also important to promote the development of intrapersonal and interpersonal skills that are essential to the social influence mechanisms of leadership (Day, 2000). Specifically regarding leadership, students would likely benefit more if faculty put less emphasis on the details of traditional leadership theories, and instead focused on the practical aspects of these theories and how they are applied. This could lead to further discussions of implicit leadership theories and promote awareness of personal leadership stereotypes and their potential impact on perceptions of actual leader behavior.

For too long, scholarly efforts regarding leadership development have significantly lagged behind the work of practitioners in the field. While some pressing research needs have already been mentioned, we will summarize some of them again here and suggest others that seem particularly salient. For one, researchers need to continue to explore the relative efficacy of leadership development methodologies (e.g. multi-rater feedback, coaching, mentoring). While this has arguably been the area of greatest activity, there are numerous unanswered questions. In particular, is there an optimal mix, sequence, or timing of developmental techniques? If so, does this optimal solution vary across different organizational contexts or national cultures? Another area that requires significant attention is leader competencies. What competencies are most salient to effective leadership and is this affected by various contextual factors? While several researchers have advocated a competencies approach, (Burgoyne & James, 2006), others question its utility. Is there a core subset of 'universal' leadership competencies that are important regardless of the situation? The work of House and colleagues (House et al., 2004) suggests that this is the case, but the leadership literature is far from agreement on the matter.

Methodologically, researchers need to move beyond cross-sectional studies and expand their research designs to include more appropriate methods for the subject under examination. Effective learning involves behavioral change and change occurs over time. In the case of leadership development, these changes occur over relatively long periods of time. Therefore, the lack of studies employing true longitudinal and latent growth modeling designs is more than a little disappointing. Fortunately, some scholars have begun to employ these and other novel approaches in their research designs, so perhaps the field is beginning to recognize the limitations of earlier approaches (e.g. Atwater, Dionne, Avolio, Camobreco & Lau, 1999; Harris & Cole, 2007; Keller, 2006; Liden, Wayne & Stilwell, 1993).

While scholars continue to struggle to answer these and numerous other questions, practitioners, executive coaches, and other consultants will undoubtedly press on with their own prescriptions for developing effective leaders. Although this may be disconcerting to some, these efforts do have their benefits, as recent meta-analyses of training interventions suggest (e.g. Reichard & Avolio, 2005). Assuming we can infer some degree of effectiveness based on the amount of resources that are increasingly committed to leadership

development, practitioners are often at the forefront of developing new techniques and methodologies to organizational challenges. Unfortunately, weighing the utility of this myriad of techniques is nearly impossible because of the lack of evidence to support many of the practitioner and organizational claims. One potential solution to this dilemma is greater cooperation and coordination between scholars and practitioners in collectively designing, implementing, and assessing leadership development programs for the benefit of client organizations. Perhaps such an approach will enable the field to produce the actionable knowledge necessary to make a qualitative difference for both theory and practice.

# REFERENCES

Allen, T.D., Eby, L.T., Poteet, M.L., Lentz, E. & Lima, L. (2004). Career benefits associated with mentoring for protégés: A meta-analysis. *Journal of Applied Psychology, 89*(1), 127–36.

Arvey, R.D., Rotundo, M., Johnson, W., Zhang, Z. & McGue, M. (2006). The determinants of leadership role occupancy: Genetic and personality factors. *The Leadership Quarterly, 17*(1), 1–20.

Arvey, R.D., Zhang, Z., Avolio, B.J. & Krueger, R.F. (2007). Developmental and genetic determinants of leadership role occupancy among women. *Journal of Applied Psychology, 92*(3), 693–706.

Atwater, L.E., Brett, J.F. & Waldman, D. (2003). Understanding the benefits and risks of multisource feedback within the leadership development process, in S.E. Murphy & R.E. Riggio (eds), *The Future of Leadership Development*. Mahwah, NJ: Lawrence Erlbaum.

Atwater, L.E., Dionne, S.D., Avolio, B.J., Camobreco, J.F. & Lau, A.W. (1999). A longitudinal study of the leadership development process: Individual differences predicting leader effectiveness. *Human Relations, 52*(12), 1543–62.

Avolio, B.J. (1999). *Full Leadership Development: Building the vital forces in organizations*. Thousand Oaks: Sage.

Avolio, B.J., Gardner, W.L., Walumbwa, F.O., Luthans, F. & May, D.R. (2004). Unlocking the mask: A look at the process by which authentic leaders impact follower attitudes and behaviors. *The Leadership Quarterly, 15*(6), 801–23.

Barker, R.A (1997). How can we train leaders if we do not know leadership is? *Human Relations, 50*(4), 343–62.

Bartz, D.E., Schwandt, D.R. & Hillman, L.W. (1989). Differences between 'T' and 'D.' *Personnel Administrator, 34,* 164–70.

Bass, B.M. (1985). *Leardership and performance beyond expectations.* New York: Free Press.

Bass, B.M. (1999). Two decades of research and development in transformational leadership. *European Journal of Work and Organizational Psychology, 8*(1), 9–32.

Bennis, W.G. & Nanus, B. (1985). *Leaders: The strategies for taking charge.* New York: Harper & Row.

Boyatzis, R.E. (2007). Developing emotional intelligence competencies, in J. Ciarrochi & J.D. Mayer (eds), *Applying emotional intelligence: A practitioner's guide* (pp. 28–52). New York: Psychology Press.

Brass, D.J. & Krackhardt, D. (1999). The social capital of twenty-first century leaders, in J.G. Hunt & R.L. Phillips (eds), *Out-of-the-box challenges for the 21st century army* (pp. 179–194). Stanford, CT: JAI Press.

Bray, D.W., Campbell, R.J. & Grant, D.L. (1974). *Formative years in business: A long-term study of managerial lives.* New York: Wiley.

Burgoyne, J. & James, K.T. (2006). Towards best or better practice in corporate leadership development: Operational issues in Mode 2 and design science research. *British Journal of Management, 17*(4), 303–16.

Burke, C.S., Stagl, K.C., Klein, C., Goodwin, G.F., Salas, E. & Halpin, S.M. (2006). What type of leadership behaviors are functional in teams? A meta-analysis. *The Leadership Quarterly, 17*(3), 288–307.

Burns, J.M. (1978). *Leadership.* New York: Harper & Row.

Burt, R.S. (1992). *Structural holes.* Cambridge, MA: Harvard University Press.

Burt, R.S. (1997). The contingent value of social capital. *Administrative Science Quarterly, 42*(2), 339–65.

Caligiuri, P. (2006). Developing global leaders. *Human Resource Management Review, 16*(2), 219–28.

Cassidy, S. (2004). Learning styles: An overview of theories, models, and measures. *Educational Psychology, 24*(4), 419–44.

Chen, L.Y. (2004). Examining the effect of organization culture and leadership behaviors on organizational commitment, job satisfaction, and job performance at small and middle-sized firms of Taiwan. *Journal of American Academy of Business,* Cambridge *5*(1), 432–8.

Chin, J.L. & Sanchez-Hucles, J. (2007). Diversity and leaership. *American Psychologist, 62,* 608–9.

Collinson, D. (2006). Rethinking followership: A post-structuralist analysis of follower identities. *Leardership Quarterly, 17*(2), 179–89.

Day, D.V. (2000). Leadership development: A review in context. *The Leadership Quarterly, 11*(4), 581–613.

Day, D.V. & Halpin, S.M. (2004). Growing leaders for tomorrow, in D.V., Day, S.J. Zaccaro & S.M. Halpin (eds), *Leadership development for transforming organizations: Growing leaders for tomorrow* (pp. 3–22). Mahwah, NJ: Lawrence Erlbaum Associates.

Dewey, J. (1938). *Experience and education.* New York: Collier Books.

Dvir, T., Eden, D., Avolio, B.J. & Shamir, B. (2002). Impact of transformational leadership on follower development and performance: A field experiment. *Academy of Management Journal, 45*(4), 735–44.

Dotlich, D. & Noel, J. (1998). *Action learning.* San Francisco: Jossey-Bass.

Ensher, E.A. & Murphy, S.E. (2005). *Power mentoring: How successful mentors and protégés get the most from their relationships.* San Francisco: Jossey Bass.

Erikson, E.H. (1982). *The lifecycle complete: A review.* New York: Norton.

Fiedler, F.E. & Mahar, L. (1979). A field experiment validating contingency model leadership training. *Journal of Applied Psychology, 64*(3), 247–54.

Fitzgerald, W. (1992). Training versus development. *Training & Development, 46,* 81–4.

Fleishman, E.A., Zaccaro, S.J. & Mumford, M. D. (1991). Individual differences and leadership. *The Leadership Quarterly, 2*(4), 237–45.

Fleishman, E.A., Zaccaro, S.J. & Mumford, M.D. (1992a). Individual differences and leadership II: An overview. *The Leadership Quarterly, 3,* 1–4.

Fleishman, E.A., Zaccaro, S.J. & Mumford, M.D. (1992b). Individual differences and leadership III: An overview. *The Leadership Quarterly, 3,* 77–80.

Fuller, J.B. & Patterson, C.E.P. (1996). A quantitative review of research on charismatic leadership. *Psychological Reports, 78*(1), 271.

Gardner, W.L., Avolio, B.J., Luthans, F., May, D.R. & Walumbwa, F.O. (2005). Can you see the real me? A self-based model of authentic leader and follower development. *The Leadership Quarterly, 16*(3), 343–72.

Gerstner, C.R. & Day, D.V. (1994). Cross-cultural comparison of leadership prototypes. *The Leadership Quarterly, 5*(2), 121–34.

Hannah, S.T. (2006). *Agentic leadership efficacy: Test of a new construct and model for development and performance.* Unpublished doctoral dissertation, University of Nebraska, Lincoln.

Harris, S.G. & Cole, M.S. (2007). A stage of change perspective on managers' motivation to learn in a leadership development context. *Journal of Organizational Change Management, 20*(6), 774–93.

Hersey, P. & Blanchard, K.H. (1982). Leadership style: Attitudes and behaviors. *Training and Development Journal, 36*(5), 50–2.

Hersey, P., Angelini, A.L. & Carakushansky, S. (1982). The impact of situational leadership and classroom structure on learning effectiveness. *Group and Organization Studies, 7*(2), 216–24.

Hoare, C.H. (ed.) (2006). *Handbook of Adult Development and Learning.* Oxford: Oxford University Press.

House, R.J. & Aditya, R.N. (1997). The social scientific study of leadership: Quo vadis? *Journal of Management, 23*(3), 409.

House, R.J., Hanges, P.J., Javidan, M., Dorfman, P.W. & Gupta, V. (2004). *Culture, Leadership, and Organizations: The GLOBE study of 62 societies.* Thousand Oaks, CA: Sage.

Javidan, M. & House, R.J. (2001). Cultural acumen for the global manager: Lessons from Project GLOBE. *Organizational Dynamics, 29,* 289–305.

Jordan, P.J., Ashton-James, C.E. & Ashkanasy, N.M. (2006). Evaluating the claims: Emotional intelligence in the workplace, in K.R. Murphy (ed.), *A Critique of Emotional Intelligence* (pp. 189–210). Mahwah, NJ: Lawrence Erlbaum.

Jung, D.I. & Avolio, B.J. (1999). Effects of leadership style and followers' cultural orientation on performance in group and individual task conditions. *Academy of Management Journal, 42*(2), 208–18.

Keller, R.T. (2006). Transformational leadership, initiating structure, and substitutes for leadership: A longitudinal study of research and development project team performance. *Journal of Applied Psychology, 91*(1), 202–10.

Kempster, S. (2006). Leadership learning through lived experience. *Journal of Management and Organization, 12*(1), 4–22.

Killan, C.M., Hukai, D. & McCarty, E.C (2005). Building diversity in the pipeline to corporate. *Leadership Quarterly, 17*(2), 179–89.

Kirkpatrick, D.L. (1976). Evaluation of training, in R.L. Craig (ed.), *Training and Development Handbook:* 18.1–18.27. New York: McGraw-Hill.

Knowles, M.S. (1991). *Using Learning Contracts: Practical approaches to individualizing and structuring learning.* San Francisco: Jossey-Bass.

Kolb, D.A. (1984). *Experiential Learning: Experience as the source of learning and development.* Englewood Cliffs, NJ: Prentice-Hall.

Liden, R.C., Wayne, S.J. & Stilwell, D. (1993). A longitudinal study on the early development of leader-member exchanges. *Journal of Applied Psychology, 78,* 662–74.

Locke, E.A. (1999). *The Essence of Leadership: The four keys to leading successfully.* Oxford: Lexington Books.

Lockwood, N.R. (2006). Leadership development: Optimizing human capital for business success. *2006 SHRM Research Quarterly.* Alexandria, VA: Society for Human Resource Management.

Lord, R.G. & Hall, R.J. (2004). Identity, leadership categorization, and leardership schema, in D. Van Kinjppenberg & M.A. Hogg (eds), *Leadership and Power: Identity processes in groups and organizations.* Thousand Oaks, CA: Sage.

Lord, R.G. & Hall, R.J. (2005). Identity, deep structure and the development of leadership skill. *The Leadership Quarterly, 16*(4), 591–615.

Lowe, K.B., Kroeck, K.G. & Sivasubramanian, N. (1996). Effectiveness correlates of transformationsl and transactional leadership: A meta-analytic review of the MLQ literature. *Leadership Quarterly, 7*(3), 385.

Luthans, F. & Avolio, B.J. (2003). Authentic leadership: A positive developmental approach, in K.S., Cameron, J.E. Dutton & R.E. Quinn (eds), *Positive Organizational Scholarship* (pp. 241–261). San Francisco: Barrett-Koehler.

Luthans, F., Avey, J.B., Avolio, B.J., Norman, S.M. & Combs, G.M. (2006). Psychological capital development: Toward a micro-intervention. *Journal of Organizational Behavior, 27*(3), 387–93.

McCauley, C.D. & Van Velsor, E. (eds), (2004). *The Center for Creative Leadership Handbook of Leadership Development* (2nd ed.). San Francisco, CA: Jossey-Bass.

McCauley, C.D., Drath, W.H., Palus, C.J., O'Connor, P.M.G. & Baker, B.A. (2006). The use of constructive-developmental theory to advance the understanding of leadership. *The Leadership Quarterly, 17*(6), 634–53.

Murphy, S.E., Ensher, E.A. & Reichard, R.J. *The combined impact of career-self management strategies and mentoring relationships on job satisfaction and perceived career success.* (Unpublished manuscript).

Offermann, L.R. & Matos, K. (2007). Best practices in leading diverse organizations, in J.A. Conger & R.E. Riggio (eds), *The Practice of Leadership: Developing the next generation of leaders* (pp. 277–299). San Francisco: Jossey-Bass.

Parry, K.W. & Sinha, P.N. (2005). Researching the trainability of transformational organizational leadership. *Human Resource Development International, 8*(2), 165–183.

Pearce, C.L. & Conger, J.A. (eds), (2003). *Shared Leadership: Reframing the hows and whys of leadership*. Thousand Oaks, CA: Sage.

Reichard, R.J. (2006). *Leader Self-development Intervention Study: Impact of discrepancy and feedback.* Unpublished doctoral dissertation, University of Nebraska, Lincoln.

Reichard, R.J. & Avolio, B.J. (2005). Where are we? The status of leadership intervention research: A meta-analytic summary, in W.L. Gardner, B.J. Avolio & F.O. Walumbwa (eds), *Authentic Leadership Theory and Practice: Origins, effects, and development.* Amsterdam: Elsevier.

Reichard, R.J., Hughes, L., Avolio, B.J., Hannah, S., Chan, A. & Walumbwa, F.O. *Impact of leadership research at multiple levels of analysis.* (Unpublished manuscript).

Riggio, R.E. & Lee, J. (2007). Emotional and interpersonal competencies and leader development. *Human Resource Management Review, 17*(4), 418–26.

Schein, E.H. (1992). *Organizational Culture and Leadership* (2nd ed.). San Francisco: Jossey-Bass.

Thomas, P. & Greenberger, D.B. (1998). A test of vision training and potential antecedents to leaders' visioning ability. *Human Resource Development Quarterly, 9*(1), 3–19.

Thornton, G.C. & Rupp, D.E. (2006). *Assessment Center in Human Resource Management: Strategies for prediction, diagnosis, and development.* Mahwah, NJ: Lawrence Erlbaum.

Training (2005). Industry Report 2005. *Training,* December, 14–28.

van Knippenberg, D., van Knippenberg, B., de Cremer, D. & Hogg, M.A. (2004). Leadership, self, and identity: A review and research agenda. *The Leadership Quarterly, 15*(6), 825–56.

Yukl, G. (2006). *Leadership in Organizations.* Upper Saddle River, NJ: Pearson.

Yukl, G. & Van Fleet, D.D. (1992). Theory and research on leadership in organizations, in M.D. Dunnette & L.M. Hough (eds), *Handbook of Industrial and Organizational Psychology,* Vol. 3 (2nd ed.) (pp. 147–197). Palo Alto, CA: Consulting Psychologists Press.

# 25

# Coaching and Mentoring in Support of Management Development[1]

David Clutterbuck

This chapter aims to provide an overview of two closely related and often confused forms of developmental intervention within organisations. Both coaching and mentoring appear in a number of forms, influenced by culture, context and purpose. We explore the origins of supported mentoring and coaching, the applications, the benefits, competencies and some aspects of efficacy.

Ask an assembled group of managers how many have a clear perception of the difference between coaching and mentoring and at the least a substantial minority will admit that they are very confused. The two terms are often used interchangeably. Members of a particular professional group may attempt to seize the practitioner high ground by depicting coaching as a highly skilled, non-directive endeavour and mentoring as a directive, instinctive form of advising; only to be refuted by another group, which entirely reverses the definitional characteristics. Even the European Mentoring and Coaching Council,

the most active body in bringing the worlds of coaching and mentoring together, cannot achieve a single definition acceptable to all.

The origins of this confusion lie in recent history and in the ways that different cultures and professions have established the one-to-one developmental alliance in the light of their own experiences. But the story of mentoring in particular goes back much further. Mentor was a character in the Odyssey, the old courtier, in whose care King Odysseus leaves his son Telemachus, while he fights the Trojan wars and finds his way home. Even the name Mentor has more than one interpretation. Homer no doubt meant it to signify a *minder* – someone who looked after the prince – but European tradition, through the adaptation of the Mentor story by a French cleric in the 17th century (Fenelon, 1699) interprets it more as someone, *who makes you think*. To make matters more complicated, the character Mentor was depicted in both accounts as a blithering old fool; it is the goddess Athena (who represents wisdom, amongst other virtues), who takes the lead role in developing Telemachus.

The term coaching is reported to have originated in the Universities of Warsaw, where the best teachers were compared to the most luxurious and well-constructed horse-drawn vehicles of the time. However, it has also attracted an association with the concept of coaxing – leading by encouragement.

Mentoring and coaching became established as learning tools long before they gained the names we give them today. The apprenticeship system of the Middle Ages in Europe, for example, was based on a relationship which, at its best conflated the two concepts. The master craftsman was both coach (passing on skills) and mentor (providing wider personal development).

Within a developmental alliance, the more experienced or more powerful partner can have strong influences on a learner's behaviour, simply by the force of their belief, in what the other person can do. Experiments in schools have found that, where a teacher demonstrates enhanced expectations of children, then their performance improves, sometimes by as much as twice that of a control group. Reversing the groups produces the same effect – performance of the individual is significantly dependent on the expectations of the teacher. In the workplace, subtle clues from the supervisor are absorbed consciously or unconsciously by employee. His or her expectations become translated into actual behaviours by the team, producing a self-fulfilling prophecy. This phenomenon is called the Pygmalion Effect (Livingstone, 2003)

The coach or mentor in the Pygmalion Effect can be a hard taskmaster. Their belief in what the learner could be is sometimes so strong that they may lose sight of whose benefit the learning process is for. For example, when sports coaches are heard saying 'I'm not going to allow you to let me down', it is arguable that they have become too emotionally involved with the learner's goal – that is, that it has instead become the coach's goal.

## COACHING AND MENTORING IN THE LATE 20TH-CENTURY

The term mentoring only began to be used and understood widely in the academic and business literature in the late 1970s, although there had been occasional previous scattered mentions. All of these early references were to informal relationships. Only in the late 1970s and early to mid-1980s did academics turn their attention to the topic (Levinson, 1978; Kram, 1985) and only in the early 1980s did a number of US organisations begin to formalise mentoring for their young male graduates.. Under these programmes, new recruits were assigned a more senior, influential person to act as a godfather or sponsor – 'to oversee their career' (Gray and Gray, 1990). A model of mentoring emerged which emphasised the use of the mentor's influence on behalf of the protégé, required a level of loyalty in return and involved significant levels of advice giving and professional role modelling. This model is sometimes called *sponsorship mentoring*. (This is not the same as sponsorship *per se*. a narrower role, which Kram's seminal (1985) study differentiates from the mentoring role.) A relatively directive approach, often conflated with the line manager role, sponsorship mentoring places substantial emphasis on the mentor's authority and influence. It remains popular in some US corporations and in cultures, which have a high power-distance.

Cultural factors made this model of mentoring unsuitable for northern European countries, where elitism was frowned upon and where employers were investing heavily in encouraging people to take responsibility for the own careers and for self-development. A different model evolved, which placed greater emphasis on two-way learning, the value of different experience rather than influence and the stimulation of reflection and action through learning dialogue – that is, a questioning, exploring style rather than an instructional or advising one Hands-on interventions by the mentor are unwelcome and seen as unhelpful. This model of mentoring is commonly called *developmental mentoring* and tends to avoid the term protégé, preferring instead mentee (one who is helped to think) (Hay, 1995; Clutterbuck, 1985; Garvey, 1998; Clutterbuck and Megginson, 1999).

In recent years there has been a marked shift in the US, particularly in terms of academic attention, towards the developmental mentoring model and other less directive, power-based relationships (Eby, 1997; Kram, 1996; Higgins and Kram, 2001). This shift in definitional focus can be characterised as a gradual broadening from:

- *directive to non-directive* (e.g., James, 2000; Skerrit and Draper, 2000). Both these case studies emphasise the importance of mentees taking control of their own learning and career management (also Stoddard and Tamsey, 2003; IDS 2004). Barham and Conway (1998) link the degree of directiveness to the mentor's normal working style. Where they normally view themselves as an expert the style of the mentoring relationship will be more didactic and less empowered from the mentee's perspective. Where the culture of the organisation expects managers to act more as facilitators, however, the balance of the relationship will be more equal and it will be about mutual learning and sharing and there will be an empowered 'feel' to the mentoring relationships.
- *career-focused to wider developmental focus* (Wellin, 2001; Gibb and Megginson, 1992). From the latter perspective, career progression occurs as a result of the expansion of the learner's capabilities and gaining relevant experience, rather than as a result of instrumental help by the mentor. Career success is a secondary outcome of the relationship, rather than its dominant rationale. Implicit in the wider perspective is the concept of a more extensive choice of career paths and trade-offs between work and non-work ambitions. Kram's original study (1985) identified both career and psychosocial elements to the sponsorship mentoring role. However, the psychosocial functions (a word she now perceives as too vague) she describes (offering friendship, providing challenging assignments, being a role model, giving advice) do not necessarily require a significant depth of learning dialogue. Developmental mentoring has much in common with counselling and mentor training often borrows heavily from the counselling theories of Egan (1994) and others.

- *hierarchical to humanistic.* That is, the hierarchical level of the players becomes less important than the learning potential between them. Studies of peer mentoring (e.g., Beattie and McDougall, 1995) and upward or reverse mentoring begin to appear in the literature (Proctor & Gamble, 2002). Mutuality and reciprocality of benefit, becomes a core theme – for example, Applebaum et al. (1994). McManus and Russell (2007) make an important distinction between relationships that begin as peer mentoring, and traditional mentoring arrangements, which evolve into peer relationships. In my work guiding organisations in the design of mentoring programmes, there is an increasing requirement to ensure that both forms are encouraged.
- *one-way learning to mutual learning.* Whereas early texts emphasise the transfer of learning from the mentor to the mentee/protégé, we now see a greater expectation that learning will be two-way. (Hawken, 2000; Apter and Carter, 2001; Garvey and Galloway, 2001). Fletcher and Ragins (2007) suggest that all high quality developmental interactions involve a fluidity in roles between expert and learner.
- *exclusive to inclusive.* From an emphasis on the highly talented young man (Levinson, 1978; Collins, 1979) mentoring is seen as a resource for a much wider range of individuals and circumstances. In particular, mentoring becomes an important tool in the management of equal opportunities and diversity. Indeed, the literature on mentoring and diversity now forms a substantial proportion of published academic papers. (e.g., Ragins and McFarlin, 1990; Clutterbuck and Ragins, 2002).
- *one very powerful relationship to a network of supportive/learning relationships.* A number of authors have taken the view that a single mentor is inadequate for the learning needs of people operating in complex work and career environments. Effective learners, they propose, have one or more mentors simultaneously within a learning net of relationships, some of which may be highly intense and others much less so. Some of these relationships, such as formal mentoring, may be recognised; others may be tacit (Caruso, 1990; Higgins and Kram, 2001; Higgins, 2004).

A similar process of evolution has occurred within coaching. Ellinger and Bostrum (1999: 754), reviewing the coaching literature, identify an early model, which emphasises managerial control and directiveness, giving way to one, which emphasises empowerment. Line manager: 'coaches help create enabling relationships that make it easier for people to learn'.

Coaching had gradually emerged during the early and mid-20th century as an instructional process, which used feedback from an experienced person to a less experienced. The coach assigned a task, observed performance and then gave feedback, which he or she discussed with the learner, with a view to determining how to do better next time. Effective coaches had the skills of breaking tasks into manageable chunks, pacing learning according to the coachee's ability and providing motivation. They also tried to move the coachee towards greater ownership of their learning, by encouraging and supporting them in defining their own learning tasks, observing their own performance and bringing their own feedback for discussion with the coach. This general model is often described as *traditional coaching*.

The link with superior expertise was broken initially in sports coaching, where both individuals and teams were assisted in achieving higher performance by people, who had moderate personal competence in the sport but high ability in assisting others to focus on areas of improvement potential. Some sports coaches, such as Timothy Galwey (1975), went further and developed styles of coaching that used questioning techniques to help players access their intuitive competence and to overcome the mental barriers that prevented excellence. These approaches were rapidly adapted to the business context, particularly for senior managers, and have in recent years been badged as developmental coaching.

It is (hopefully) obvious that sponsorship mentoring and traditional coaching have a lot in common. Both are relatively directive, in that control of the process rests more with the helper than the learner. The standards which the learner is expected to meet are not set by the learner, but by the organisation, the mentor or some external stakeholder, such as a sports governing body. Similarly, developmental mentoring and developmental coaching have much in common. Both rely heavily on asking insightful questions, holding back on advice giving and giving as much control of the process as possible to the learner. They use very similar techniques and make very similar assumptions about the nature of learning and the role of the helper.

So what, if any, are the differences between coaching and mentoring, particularly in the context of management development? One critical difference relates to purpose. Coaching almost always relates to some aspect of performance – it answers the questions: *What do you want to achieve?* or *What do you want to do better?* It therefore tends towards the specific. Mentoring has much more holistic intentions and tends to address the question: *Who or what do you want to become?* Mentoring is also much more closely associated with career outcomes than coaching. Ellinger and Bostrum (1999: 753) cite previous definitions of coaching as 'a process for improving problem work performance' (Fournies, 1987) and as a process of empowering employees to exceed prior levels of performance' – that is, performance management is seen as the critical link between traditional and developmental coaching. They distinguish mentoring from coaching as 'a longer-term process that is developmental, career-focused and covers all life structures'. Another critical difference relates to scope of the helping intervention. For example, mentors often help mentees network, either by making introductions, or assisting them in designing and pursuing networking strategies; coaches rarely stray into this territory. In general, mentoring relationships tend to be longer lived than coaching relationships (typically two years versus six months, in formal arrangements).

Do the differences matter? Anecdotal evidence from coaches and mentors from all four of these roles suggests that the boundaries between one style and the next are often breached. In particular, developmental coaches may temporarily shift role into developmental mentor and vice versa. Sometimes it is necessary for a developmental coach to take a more directive style – for example, if the learner has low competence and low motivation to learn. However, mismatched expectations of role and behaviour are also associated with relationship failure, so it would appear important to have some degree of clarity. One organisation, for example, makes a distinction between:

- Skills coach – someone expert in an area, who will spend time passing on know-how to others; typically a technical area or a very specific managerial skill, such as negotiating; usually a relatively short-term intervention.
- Line manager coach – responsible for performance management and creating the opportunities for putting new knowledge and skills into practice.
- Developmental or career mentor – someone who works with the learner on their wider and longer-term development.
- Sponsor – someone at senior level, who undertakes a general oversight of the person's career, ensuring, for example, that people in the talent pool are moved on within the organisation, when it is appropriate for their learning.

## FORMAL V. INFORMAL COACHING AND MENTORING

A great deal of research effort has been undertaken in the US, in particular, to assess the relative virtues of formal and informal mentoring. No significant studies have attempted to examine these issues in coaching and this may be in large part a result of different expectations from the coaching relationship, which is almost always referred to in a formal context. Informal coaching – *ad hoc*, unsupported by the organisation – does occur, of course, especially between peers in the same team, but it has not attracted the same level of academic interest.

A plethora of studies in the 1990s suggested that formal mentoring would always be inferior to informal, because it did not have the emotional substrate of a relationship that develops out of an evolving friendship. (e.g., Chao et al., 1992) These studies almost all asked large numbers of people about their mentoring relationships and compared them on the basis of either 'receipt of mentoring functions', as a surrogate for

relationship quality, or specific outcomes, such as career advancement. The researchers' conclusions were that formal relationships and programmes should aim at duplicating, as much as possible, the spontaneity and behaviours of the informal.

Yet case studies from Europe, which measured the outcomes from structured mentoring programmes (e.g., Browne, 2000) reported very high levels of benefit for both participants and for the organisations. These organisations did not measure informal mentoring to compare with formal, although in at least one case a major reason for launching the formal programme was the failure of employees to acquire and make effective use of informal mentors.

One reason for this divergence of conclusions was methodological – it is not uncommon for two different research methods to produce conflicting results. Another is a basic flaw in the method used in most of the US studies, which did not include failed attempts at initiating informal relationships in their calculations. We still don't know how many frogs a potential mentee or protégé has to kiss before they find a prince! Relationships perceived as informal mentoring by the mentee/protégé are almost by definition likely to be successful to a degree, in the sense that they deliver some value. Formal relationships, which do not work out, are a lot easier to identify and measure and there has been a considerable literature on failed mentoring relationships (e.g., Eby et al., 2004; Scandura, 1998; Ragins et al., 2000). A third reason may be the different cultural expectations and models of mentoring in the US and Europe – the constituents of a successful relationship are not the same.

In addition, defining formality and informality proved a problem. Rather than clearly differentiated variables, there are spectra. For example:

- How people come together (by chance, by mentee purposeful approach, by mentor purposeful approach, through an 'informal' introduction by human resources, or through a matching scheme based on preset criteria).

- Who sets the objectives (the mentee, the mentor, the organisation or all of these).
- Provision of training (from none, through voluntary participation to mandatory participation).
- Support (from none, through having a library or similar resource to search, through to having a steering group and/or programme coordinator).

However, Ragins et al. (2000) largely resolved this conflict in a study that demonstrated that the critical issue was not the level of relationship formality. What matters is the quality of the relationship, whether it be formal or informal. This general independence of context has been supported more recently by my own longitudinal studies of mentoring relationships, which find that expectations of organisational supportiveness show no significant correlations with relationship quality or participant outcomes (Clutterbuck, 2007).

The inferences of our current understanding of the formal–informal debate include:

- It is important to ensure that all people likely to participate in a mentoring relationship have the skills to manage their respective roles, regardless of whether they do so in a formal or informal capacity.
- Having a support mechanism – for example, a source of advice, technique training – promotes the quality of both formal and informal mentoring.

There has been some speculation, supported by anecdote, that a critical mass of formal mentoring can trigger a culture change, which supports widespread informal coaching and mentoring. It remains to be seen whether this is indeed the case, and whether what constitutes a critical mass is generic, wholly situational, or somewhere in-between.

Ragins advises that formal and informal mentoring should be seen as mutually supporting activities. Both have advantages and disadvantages. Informal mentoring tends to last longer, and hence has time to acquire depth. At extremes, this may also be a disadvantage, because it can in some circumstances encourage dependency. Formal mentoring can focus more narrowly on specific career goals – because of constrained expectations about duration; but informal relationships may lack sufficient sense of purpose and direction. Informal relationships tend to take place within the same business area, so there are more opportunities for role modelling and the mentor is likely to understand the issues (particularly the politics and personalities) the mentee is grappling with. However, formal mentoring, which typically and deliberately matches people outside their business area, provides the advantage of a different perspective. Oil company Petronas, which experimented with giving managers two mentors (one in the same business area, but not their boss) and one in a completely different area, found that the latter was felt by participants to be the most valuable.

Participants in structured programmes – both mentors and mentees – may be less committed to the relationship than informal partnerships, but the evidence for this being more prevalent than in informal mentoring is unconvincing. Many informal mentoring relationships are also casual. However, the danger that organisational objectives may subvert or smother individual objectives is real – I have seen a number of rigidly designed programmes that leave little scope for person-centred dialogue. On the other hand, if an organisation is investing in encouraging mentoring, it is not unreasonable to expect some organisational benefits to emerge.

Perhaps the strongest argument in favour of some level of formality is that informal matches tend to occur for reasons related to the emotional gratification of the mentor. For example, they may see in the protégé or mentee themselves 20 years before. This may lead them to play too strong a role in steering the protégé's career; it may also stimulate cloning. Most troubling of all, however, is that people choosing in their own image perpetuate race and gender imbalances in the organisation. Unless it occurs in a culture, where there is already formal mentoring with a strong diversity flavour, informal mentoring can simply reinforce the old boy network and undermine diversity management objectives.

In their extensive, but largely US-centric review of mentoring research, Wanberg et al. (2003) point out that 'there is a striking dearth of research on formal mentoring' (p. 85). They also describe the conflation of formal and informal mentoring as a significant limiting factor on the validity of much mentoring research in general.

The constituents of an effective formal mentoring programme, according to Kram and Bragar (1992) are:

- 'Specific objectives and a defined target population
- a process to select and match protégés with mentors
- an orientation that involves suggestions on maintaining the relationship as well as expectation setting
- communication with involved parties about the intent of the programme
- a monitoring and evaluation process
- a co-ordinator to provide support to participants'.

It is perhaps significant that these characteristics are all contained in the International Standards for Mentoring Programmes in Employment.

## BENEFITS OF COACHING AND MENTORING

One of the problems with defining the benefits of coaching and mentoring is that they are contingent on the relationship or programme purpose. However, some generic benefits can be identified. For convenience, it is normal to break these into four categories of beneficiary: organisation, learner, coach/mentor and line manager. Evidence of outcomes for each of these audiences tends to be scattered in reports and case studies to conferences, or in small numbers of empirical studies (Wanberg et al., 2003). However, taken together the volume of literature suggests that mentoring delivers a wide range of positive outcomes to participants and to the organisation. In general, strongly positive mentee outcomes are more clearly delineated

and more frequently recorded than for mentors (Clutterbuck, 2007).

## Benefits for the organisation

*Retention*: Mentoring is strongly associated with improved retention, with case studies of evaluated mentoring programmes showing increased retention of 30 percent and in one case 1,300 percent by comparison with control groups (e.g., Browne, 2000). Wider, general multi-company studies of employee motivation indicate that people who have a mentor are only half as likely to be considering leaving the organisation (Emerging workforce study, 1999).

*Job commitment*: Both coaching and mentoring have been shown to increase the learner's engagement with their work and with their employing organisation, and this in turn has an impact on employee retention (Aryee and Chay, 1994). Job commitment has been used in numerous research studies as one of the principal ways of measuring the impact of mentoring and/or coaching.

Among the ways coaching and mentoring influence job commitment are:

- By reinforcing the positive cycle of exploration, understanding, competence, self-confidence, self-esteem and personal performance (see below).
- By providing recognition for the learner's achievements.
- By helping the learner identify and value opportunities for learning even in difficult or routine situations.
- By clarifying and strengthening the links between today's work tasks and tomorrow's career aspirations.
- By providing positive role models.

By helping the learner to develop their skills in collaborating and getting on.

*Performance*: Coaching is generally associated in the handful of empirical studies conducted with increases in performance, either specific skills or behavioural elements of a competence framework (e.g., Elliott, 2006; Jarvis et al., 2006).

*Recruitment and induction*: Having a mentoring programme is a significant factor in selection of an employer. Mentors also provide a very cost-effective resource to re-capture talented employees who have moved to other organisations. When these employees are ready to move again, the first person they often talk to is their former mentor, if they have had a good mentoring relationship.

Induction into the organisation is typically improved by mentoring. People become acclimatised up to twice as fast as normal. At senior management levels, where the track record of success in external appointments is not high in general, mentoring is believed to make a substantial difference in acceptance of the new manager.

Other key areas of organisational benefit include:

- Succession planning – many companies find that mentoring provides a clearer picture of the talent pool available, and helps people position themselves more clearly against the likely needs of the business.
- Merger and acquisition – establishing mentoring relationships across the two organisations helps build trust and overcome cultural differences, making the integration process faster and more efficient. (It also helps keep key people, who might otherwise have left through uncertainty about their future.)
- Diversity management – mentoring has proved to be one of the most important elements of diversity programmes. A number of major employers, such as the UK's National Health Service, have targeted mentoring particularly at the transitions into senior management and top management.

## Benefits for the mentee/coachee

These are very wide, but the most commonly reported are:

- Greater clarity about personal development and career goals.
- Being able to discuss, in an open and unthreatening environment, issues about their career and development.
- Improved networking.

- Practical advice on organisational politics and behaviour.
- The opportunity to be challenged constructively.
- Increased self-confidence.
- Transfer of knowledge and, in particular, judgement.
- Having a role model.
- Greater clarity (within a coaching relationship) about how they are actually performing and what is preventing them from achieving more.

Various research data suggest that mentees achieve greater confidence in their own potential and ability; feel more secure in their role (especially at senior levels) and earn more than their non-mentored counterparts (e.g., Bartram and Garreffa, 2004).

Dougherty and Dreher (2007) provide a valuable overview of the literature relating to mentoring and career outcomes. Many of these studies suffer from methodological problems (e.g., an over-reliance on protégé self-report and inadequate definition of mentoring). However, there emerges a broad picture of multiple benefits. Chao et al. (1992), for example, report stronger career-related outcomes than psychosocial. The context of the majority of these studies, however, is sponsorship mentoring. In my own longitudinal study of developmental mentoring, the opposite results emerge – career outcomes are of less significance than personal development outcomes. This may be partly to do with the difference between the two constructs of sponsorship mentoring and developmental mentoring (and the data show that mentees and mentors both perceive them as separate constructs); or it may be related to the fact that supported mentoring programmes have a shorter duration (typically 12–18 months) than those in the predominantly US studies reviewed (and hence career outcomes have not had sufficient time to occur). In Europe and Australasia, there seems to be much less expectation that the mentor will be instrumental in what happens to the mentee's career, and a greater emphasis on achieving career goals independently.

## Benefits for the mentor/coach

The most frequently cited benefits for mentors and coaches are:

- Their own learning (often mentors and coaches report as much and more learning than mentees and coachees).
- The opportunity to practise good developmental behaviours outside their direct line responsibilities.
- Development of their own self-awareness.
- Greater understanding of other areas of the business and/or of other cultures.

## Benefits for the line manager

Line managers, whose direct reports take part in mentoring or off-line coaching schemes, typically comment upon:

- The value of a 'second opinion' – someone the mentee can take issues to, who does not have a direct involvement.
- Improvements in the mentee's relationships with peers and the line manager him/herself.
- A clearer sense of purpose and direction on the part of the mentee.

Line managers acting as coaches to their direct reports often find that they:

- Gain a greater understanding of the work tasks and what really happens in work processes.
- Can delegate more and worry less.
- Can identify and act to reduce team conflict at an earlier stage than normal.
- Can acquire more honest feedback about their own management style and behaviour.
- Build stronger relationships with their teams.

There are, however, significant difficulties in the role of line manager as coach. Because they have such a stake in the team's outputs, it is easy for the line manager coach to impose his or her agenda on the coaching conversations. In addition, some of the principle barriers to a direct report's performance may lie in the manager's own attitudes, assumptions and behaviours, which they may be reluctant to address or may even be unaware of (Farrar, 2006). This is

also a strong argument against attempting to conflate the roles of mentor and line manager, a practice strongly advised against in the practioner literature (Klasen and Clutterbuck, 2002; Cuerrier, 2003). In the mentoring context, the different perspective a mentor can bring from *not* being involved in the mentee's direct work environment or reporting line is valuable. The Malaysian national oil company Petronas has routinely provided senior level mentees with two mentors – one off-line, but within the same general functional area and one much more distant. The majority of mentees report that the more distant mentor is the most valuable, not least because of the greater psychological safety they experience.

## EVOLUTION OF COACHING AND MENTORING RELATIONSHIPS

While only the evolution of mentoring relationships has been studied empirically (Kram, 1985), and then in the context of informal, sponsorship mentoring only, the general principles seem to apply equally to supported, developmental mentoring. The five stages depicted in Clutterbuck (1985) are:

- Initiation – building the rapport and particularly the trust necessary to establish psychological safety; contracting, if appropriate; and getting to know each other. Critical in this process is an exchange of values (Hale, 2000). Recommended good practice is for the dyad in a formal programme to review the relationship at the end of the second meeting, with a view to either dialogue about how to build rapport, or a 'no-fault divorce'.
- Goal-setting – establishing a general or specific purpose for the relationship. Although many coaching textbooks (and the most famous model of the coaching conversation, GROW) maintain that SMART goals are essential for effective coaching, there is little evidence for this. My own longitudinal studies of mentoring relationships (Clutterbuck, 2007) find no correlation between goal clarity (specificity) or goal commitment on the part of the mentee and either relationship experience (quality) or mentee outcomes.

Megginson (2007) draws upon a range of studies to suggest that goals in effective mentoring and coaching relationships are emergent. Having overly defined goals, it seems, focuses attention such that other opportunities are missed.

- Progress-making – The dyads have established a clear sense of direction, which focuses their conversations. Issues that occur on a meeting-by-meeting basis are now placed in the context of the relationship purpose, and broader learning takes place. The interchange of learning becomes more balanced, rather than primarily from coach or mentor to coachee or mentee.
- Winding up – In a detailed study of relationship endings (Clutterbuck and Megginson, 2004), a clear differentiation emerged between relationships regarded positively by both parties and those regarded negatively. Positive relationships were associated with a planned and well-managed disengagement from the formal process. Typically, participants reviewed what had and had not been achieved and discussed where the learner would look next for their one-to-one development needs – that is, what will take the place of the coach or mentor? Negatively perceived relationships were associated with a gradual drifting away.
- Moving on – Kram (1985) describes this phase as redefinition. Having achieved (to a greater or lesser extent) its original purpose, the relationship evolves into a more *ad hoc*, informal form, akin to a strong friendship. Gratitude on the part of the mentee or coachee, and the generative effect on the coach or mentor (Levinson, 1978) combine to establish a loose relationship, in which either party may use the other as a sounding board from time to time.

However, the validity of the phase model approach has been questioned by Bullis and Bach (1989), who found that, while the phase model may be *generally* descriptive, the progress of individual relationships was much more random. Surprisingly, this early work has not stimulated other studies, although it has significance in the design and deliverer of training and support for mentors and mentees.

Professional coaching relationships in the workplace (and particularly in the context of executive coaching) tend to be of relatively short duration – typically between six months and a year and sometimes only two or three meetings. Hence it is not possible to extrapolate a similar pattern of evolution of coaching relationships. In the absence of relevant empirical research, we can postulate an alternative general dynamic:

- A brief *contractual* phase, in which the objectives of the relationship are defined and the dyad determine whether they can work together. (Essentially an amalgamation and truncation of the rapport-building and goal-setting phases above.)
- A *transactional* phase, in which the coach helps the client explore specific issues of behaviour, leadership or skill, maintaining the goal focus.
- A brief *review* phase, in which the outcomes of the relationship are assessed, from the perspective of coach and coachee and, where appropriate, other stakeholders, such as the coachee's direct reports and boss.

## RESEARCH INTO COACHING AND MENTORING

One of the major distinctions between coaching and mentoring is the volume and nature of the research, which has been carried out into each. The great majority of research into mentoring is quantitative and US-centric. (A recent *Handbook of Mentoring* (Allen and Eby, 2007) almost completely ignores the growing volume of mentoring research from Europe, Australasia, South Africa and elsewhere.) Some of the major criticisms with this body of research include:

- Failures of definition (e.g., not specifying what kind of mentoring or coaching is being studied).
- Confusion over what kind of relationship is being measured (e.g., relations between boss and subordinate are often conflated with off-line relationships – two very different dynamics).
- Lack of triangulation.
- Misuse of instruments (e.g., confusion of what mentors do, with what the relationship achieves).

There is a much smaller volume of research into coaching and most of this is qualitative (Megginson, 2006). The few quantitative studies are focused on attempts to demonstrate return on investment on executive coaching

(Wasylyshyn, 2003; Parker-Wilkins, 2006; Jarvis et al., 2006).

## SHARED PRINCIPLES OF DEVELOPMENTAL COACHING AND DEVELOPMENTAL MENTORING

Both coaching and mentoring in their non-directive forms adhere to the principle that they are focused on helping the learner with the quality of his or her thinking. Hence the emphasis in much of the literature on the importance of crafting and posing insightful questions. Observation of effective mentors and coaches indicates that they:

- Ask relatively few, but very concise questions.
- Avoid offering solutions until they and the learner have established a strong, mutual understanding of the issues under consideration; and even then prefer to assist the learner to identify to their own solutions.

It can be very difficult for a line manager to behave in this way, not least because he or she is conditioned to solve problems and is likely to see his or her role from that perspective. However, it is broadly accepted (although not empirically proven, to my knowledge) that solutions, which the individual has thought through in their own mind, with or without the assistance of a developmental partner, receive greater commitment and are more likely to be the basis of new behaviour patterns.

## CREATING TIME TO THINK

Management development is difficult to achieve in an environment of frenetic action. As Argyris and Schon (1996) have shown, change at anything but a superficial level requires a process of reflection. Yet most managers and professionals struggle to find any real thinking time during their working hours. Coaching and mentoring provide opportunities to find personal reflective space (PRS) and to operate on the quality of the learner's thinking.

## CORE COMPETENCIES OF COACHING AND MENTORING

The situational nature of coaching and mentoring mean that the competencies required vary according to the level at which the coach or mentor intends to work, the kind of intervention required (e.g., skills transfer, strategic thinking or therapeutic) and the purpose of the relationship. The wide spread of competencies has been captured by the European Mentoring and Coaching Council and is downloadable from its website www.emccouncil.org. However, in *The Situational Mentor* (Clutterbuck and Lane, 2004), we attempted to identify, from an extensive series of workshops, some generic skills, which appear to apply to all coaches and mentors.

### *Self-awareness (understanding self)*

Mentors need high self-awareness in order to recognise and manage their own behaviours within the helping relationship and to use empathy appropriately. The activist, task-focused manager often has relatively little insight into these areas – indeed, s/he may actively avoid reflection on such issues, depicting them as 'soft' and of low priority. Such attitudes and learned behaviours may be difficult to break.

### *Behavioural awareness (understanding others)*

Like self-awareness, understanding how others behave and why they do so is a classic component of emotional intelligence. To help others manage their relationships the mentor must have reasonably good insight into patterns of behaviour between individuals and groups of people. Predicting the consequences of specific behaviours or courses of action is one of the many practical applications of this insight.

### *Business or professional savvy*

The experience and judgement that come from having been around for some time – whether in an organisation, a profession, or simply in life – can be very valuable in helping a coachee or mentee learn the ropes, understand the politics and focus on what matters. Passing on 'coping strategies' – how to get by – can be equally valuable.

## Sense of proportion/good humour

It's important that participants should *enjoy* the sessions they have together, because learning is generally more effective in a relaxed atmosphere. Laughter, used appropriately, is invaluable in developing rapport, in helping people to see matters from a different perspective, in releasing emotional tension.

In practice, good humour is a vehicle for achieving a sense of proportion – a broader perspective that places the organisation's goals and culture in the wider social and business context. People acquire this kind of perspective by ensuring that they balance their day-to-day involvement with work tasks against a portfolio of other interests. Some of these may be related to work – for example, developing a broader strategic understanding of how the business sector is evolving; others are unrelated to work, and may encompass science, philosophy or any other intellectually stimulating endeavour. In general, the broader the scope of knowledge and experience the mentor can apply, the better sense of proportion s/he can bring.

## Communication competence

Communication isn't a single skill; it is a combination of a number of skills. Those most important for coaches and mentors include:

- Listening – opening the mind to what the other person is saying, demonstrating interest/attention, encouraging them to speak, holding back on filling the silences.
- Observing as receiver – being open to the visual and other non-verbal signals, recognising what is *not* said.
- Parallel processing – analysing what the other person is saying, reflecting on it, preparing responses. Effective communicators do all of

these in parallel, slowing down the dialogue as needed to ensure that they do not overemphasise preparing responses at the expense of analysis and reflection. Equally, they avoid becoming so mired in their internal thoughts that they respond inadequately or too slowly.
- Projecting – crafting words and their emotional 'wrapping' in a manner appropriate for the situation and the recipient(s).
- Observing as projector – being open to the visual and other non-verbal signals, as clues to what the recipient is hearing/understanding; adapting tone, volume, pace and language appropriately.
- Exiting – concluding a dialogue or segment of dialogue with clarity and alignment of understanding (ensuring message received in both directions).

## Conceptual modelling

Effective coaches and mentors have a portfolio of models they can draw upon to help the mentee understand the issues they face. These models can be self-generated (that is, the result of personal experience), drawn from elsewhere (e.g., models of company structure, interpersonal behaviours, strategic planning, career planning) or – at the highest level of competence – generated on the spot as an immediate response.

According to the situation and the learning styles of the mentee, it may be appropriate to present these models in verbal or visual form. Or the mentor may not present them at all – simply use them as the framework for asking penetrating questions.

## Commitment to their own continued learning

Effective coaches and mentors become role models for self-managed learning. They seize opportunities to experiment and take part in new experiences. They read widely and are reasonably efficient at setting and following personal development plans. They actively seek and use behavioural feedback from others. They see the coaching or mentoring relationship more as an opportunity for their own learning than for 'putting something back' (Engstrom, 1998).

## Strong interest in developing others

Effective coaches and mentors have an innate interest in achieving through others and in helping others recognise and achieve their potential. This instinctive response is important in establishing and maintaining rapport and in enthusing the mentee, building his or her confidence in what they could become.

While it is possible to 'switch on' someone to self-advantage of helping others, it is probably not feasible to stimulate an altruistic response.

## Building and maintaining rapport/relationship management

The skills of rapport building are difficult to define. When asked to describe rapport, in their experience, managers' observations can be distilled into five characteristics:

- Trust:       will they do what they say?
             will they keep confidences?
- Focus:      are they concentrating on me?
             are they listening without judging?
- Empathy:    do they have goodwill towards me?

do they try to understand my feelings, and viewpoints?
- Congruence:   do they acknowledge and accept my goals?
- Empowerment:  is their help aimed at helping me stand on my own feet as soon as practical?

## Goal clarity

The mentor must be able to help the learner sort out what s/he wants to achieve and why. This is quite hard to do if you do not have the skills to set and pursue clear goals of your own.

Goal clarity appears to derive from a mixture of skills including systematic analysis and decisiveness. Like so many of the other mentoring competencies, it may best be developed through opportunities to reflect and to practice.

The mentoring or coaching relationship is a partnership, however. The effectiveness of the relationship also depends on the competencies exhibited by the mentees or coachees, who need to have at least a basic level of communication skill, to articulate their issues. Coachees/mentees also need to be open, to be prepared to challenge constructively and to reflect on their issues both

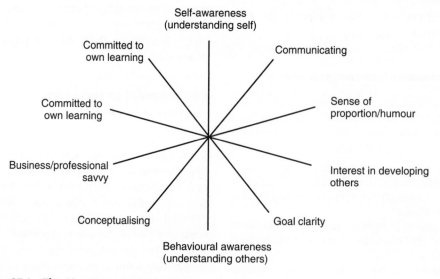

Self-awareness
(understanding self)

Committed to own learning

Communicating

Committed to own learning

Sense of proportion/humour

Business/professional savvy

Interest in developing others

Conceptualising

Goal clarity

Behavioural awareness
(understanding others)

**Figure 25.1   The 10 mentor competences**
*Source*: © Clutterbuck Associates 2007.

before and after coaching/mentoring sessions (Clutterbuck and Lane, 2004). Empirical study of mentee and coachee competencies is patchy and inconclusive. Some behaviours and attributes suggested by the literature include:

- Communication skills and self-esteem (Kalbfleisch and Davies, 1993).
- Willingness to engage in personal developmental activity (Maurer et al., 2003).
- In the context of sponsorship mentoring, particularly, ingratiation (in this context meaning using emotional intelligence to manage personal reputation with the relationship) (Aryee et al., 1996).
- Ambition (high need for power and achievement) (Fagenson, 1992).

Whereas the behaviours required to be an effective mentor are relatively constant throughout the relationship, the mentee may (need to) evolve behaviours and competencies as the relationship progresses (Clutterbuck and Lane, 2004). Personality factors may also influence mentee efficacy at different phases of the relationship (Turban and Lee, 2007). In community mentoring, an issue of considerable concern is that people who need mentoring most may not have the qualities either to attract and motivate a mentor or to contribute effectively to the mentoring process.

There is a small but significant body of literature on dysfunctional mentoring (Scandura, 1998; Eby et al., (2004)). The assumptions behind most of this literature relate more to sponsorship mentoring than to development mentoring. Anecdotal evidence from developmental mentoring suggests that problems arise most frequently from failure in the education of the mentor into the role. The mentor's motivation may be an important factor here. Engstrom (1998) indicates that motivation to learn is closely associated to relationship success and an emphasis on altruistic motives to relationship dysfunction. Mentors, who use phrases such as 'I want to prevent her making the same mistakes as I did', may stifle the spontaneity of the relationship and learning dialogue, for example.

Much also depends on the quality of the matching process. In structured programmes, mentors and mentees are supported in finding an appropriate match. While the ability to work closely together to achieve personal growth for the mentee may depend on a variety of factors, the most critical in establishing the relationship appears to be the sense that both parties share similar values (Hale, 2000).

## COACHING THE TEAM

Team coaching differs from individual coaching in a number of ways. Confidentiality is more difficult to manage, the scope of discussions is likely to be narrower and the speed at which individuals within a team consider and reach decisions may vary widely. Team coaching is often confused with team facilitation, which involves a much lower level of engagement with the team. There is very little empirical research on team coaching and what there is focuses on project teams (Hackman and Wageman, 2005) – there are at least five other types of team in the workplace.

## VIRTUAL COACHING AND MENTORING

The assumption that coaching and mentoring need to be carried out face to face, to be fully effective, is increasingly being challenged, with more and more organisations implementing some form of IT-based programmes or support, and a small but growing literature on the subject (e.g., Fagenson-Eland and Lu, 2004). The face-to-face meeting has the virtue of length – people usually set aside an hour or more, which is difficult to sustain using distance media – so it is possible to explore issues in depth. It is easier to build rapport and to get into flow – sparking ideas off each other. And the visual clues of body language can provide valuable insights into the other learning partner's emotions and reveal inconsistencies between what they say and what they think.

However, there are advantages to e-coaching and e-mentoring as well. There is built-in reflective time, so participants can think more deeply about their questions and their answers. As a result, coaches and mentors tend to ask better, more insight-provoking questions. There is a written record, which can be analysed subsequently to reveal hidden patterns (taking copious notes in a coaching/mentoring session undermines the attentiveness of both parties). There are no visual distractions. And the dialogue can take place on more of a just-in-time basis, rather than wait until the next scheduled meeting.

Telephone mentoring and coaching has the disadvantages of both face-to-face and virtual approaches. It tends to work really well only when both parties are experienced coaches or mentors. One of the big problems is that people struggle to cope with the silences.

Many large programmes now encourage participants to use a mixture of media, including face-to-face, e-mail, video-conferencing and even podcasts. This allows for considerable flexibility.

## EFFECTIVE COACHING AND MENTORING PROGRAMMES

Effective mentoring schemes:

- begin with **clarity of purpose**. What exactly does the business expect to achieve from investing in this activity? Objectives vary widely, from the relatively general, such as raising the competence of our people, to the very specific, such as achieving targets for increasing the number of women or racial minorities in senior positions. Having a clear set of programme goals is critically important in helping each relationship develop its own clear sense of purpose and direction. (Otherwise mentor and mentee struggle to find anything to talk about after the first few meetings);
- have **top management champions,** who are prepared not only to support mentoring with encouragement and resources, but who become role models for mentoring. At District Audit, which

has one of the most successful schemes in the UK, the chief executive attended a high proportion of training sessions and talked openly about his own current experience as a mentee;
- are clear about who their **audiences** are. Although there are examples of all-comers schemes that work well, it is not normally realistic to expect everyone to have a mentor at the same time;
- manage well the three key processes of **selecting, matching and training**. The selection criteria will normally depend on who the target audience is, but a pragmatic groundrule is that mentors should be substantially more experienced than the mentee, but not so far ahead that it is difficult for the two of them to empathise with each other's work issues. The practice, now largely abandoned in most countries, of placing young graduate recruits with very senior managers, led to very little real learning, because the experience gap was too great. They allow participants at least some choice of mentoring partner and to build in a **'no-fault divorce'** process. A broad rule of thumb is that without any focused training, less than one in three mentoring relationships delivers real value. With appropriate mentor training, the proportion rises to two out of three and with in addition training for the mentee and some form of education in mentoring for line managers, success rates of 90 percent are common;
- **measure and review using** both hard outcomes (e.g., retention rates) and key processes, such as whether people meet sufficiently frequently, help on three levels. First, review within each relationship helps in re-assigning those that don't work. Second, measurement and review at the six-month point helps the coordinator adjust the scheme. Finally, measurement at 12 months and beyond provides the data to demonstrate that mentoring is delivering results for the business.

The effectiveness of mentoring relationships can also be affected significantly by the attitudes of participants and influential third parties. Some of the most important issues include:

- Whether participants are volunteers or press-ganged. The quality of learning and of the relationship itself is likely to be much lower, when participants did not actively select into the programme.

- How supportive influential third parties are. For example, a resentful line manager can make it very difficult for the mentee and mentor to meet.
- Participant expectations – If mentors do not expect the relationship to be one of equality or of two-way learning, it will achieve much less. Equally, if the mentee is expecting some form of sponsorship, which the mentor is unwilling to offer, then it will be difficult to retain rapport and a sense of mutual purpose.
- The mentoring 'ambiance' – do people see having a mentor as a sign of positive support for individual development; or as a remedial (or worse, a means of helping people exit the organisation)?

Attitudes towards mentoring need to be identified before a mentoring programme is launched. Training of mentors and mentees should help shape participants' expectations; as should briefings for influential third parties.

## CREATING A COACHING AND MENTORING CULTURE

The stark reality, however, is that most managers put very little effort into coaching. Even though the company may have provided coaching training for them, unless there is a robust coaching climate, there will be very little overall impact on the performance of the business, on retention of talent or on the achievement of strategic goals.

So what exactly is a coaching culture? Some of the signs identified in our research (Clutterbuck and Megginson, 1999), include:

- Personal growth, team development and organisational learning are integrated and the links clearly understood.
- People are able to engage in constructive and positive confrontation.
- People welcome feedback (even at the top) and actively seek it.
- Coaching is seen as a *joint* responsibility of managers and their direct reports.
- There is good understanding at all levels about what effective developers and developees do.
- Coaching is seen primarily as an opportunity rather than as a remedial intervention.
- People are recognised and rewarded for their activity in sharing knowledge.

- Time for reflection is valued.
- There are effective mechanisms for identifying and addressing barriers to learning.
- People look first inside the organisation for their next job (a typical average would be that only one in five does so!).
- There are strong role models for good coaching practice.

Some of the most useful interventions include:

*Ensuring that all managers have at least the basic skills of coaching.* Just running a training course isn't enough. Managers need to put what they have learned into practice. Initial training needs to be reinforced with opportunities to review each coaching session and to reflect upon feedback from the coachee. Good practice typically involves either follow-up group sessions, or the use of a mastercoach to sit in on coaching sessions and provide immediate feedback.

*Equipping all employees with the skills to be coached/mentored effectively.* CA's research indicates that coaching works best when the coachee is both a willing and an informed participant. The more the coachee understands about the coaching process, the easier it is to help the coach help them. For example, effective coachees learn how to phrase questions in ways that will elicit the kind of help they want. Greater impact can also be gained by regarding coaching as a team activity (most coaching is actually done by peers, not by superiors, anyway) and engaging the whole team in learning how to make coaching a day-to-day activity.

*Providing an advanced coaching/mentoring skills programme for senior managers.* The more senior a manager is, the more important it is that they coach well – the cost of mistakes and lost talent rise exponentially the higher up the organisation one goes. An advanced coaching skills programme builds on the existing knowledge and competence of the manager, providing a range of techniques and approaches that broaden his or her portfolio of responses. In some cases, a whole day is devoted to practising these techniques, with expert feedback to each pair from a mastercoach, who observes them.

## Developing a cadre of mastercoaches/mastermentors

A number of organisations, such as Kellogg in Europe, have developed some line managers and HR professionals as mastercoaches, giving them a wide enough experience of coaching and related developmental approaches to tackle most problems they may encounter, both as coaches in their own right and in helping other managers grow in coaching skills. As a group, they also provide a valuable resource of experience to support each other and less experienced coaches.

The core process is action learning – participants share the learning burden and explore issues together in a series of one-day meetings. There are also opportunities for contributions of knowledge from outside experts. At the end of the programme, they have the confidence and competence to act as real champions for coaching.

*Providing opportunities to review good coaching/mentoring practice.* Bringing coaches – of all levels of experience – together from time to time helps to spread good practice and remind people of what is expected of them. This is particularly true around the time of annual appraisal. A coaching practice review can help managers prepare direct reports more effectively for their appraisal, and thus extract much greater value from it.

## Recognising and rewarding managers who demonstrate good coaching/mentoring practice

If managers who do not coach or invest significant effort in developing others still receive promotions and high rewards, it sends a very negative message. Some organisations are now making developmental performance an integral part of their succession planning and annual bonus systems.

## Measuring and providing feedback on the quality, relevance and accessibility of coaching/mentoring

It's important to have a clear picture of what coaching is happening, and how effective it is, especially from the perspective of the coachee. Identifying pockets of good and poor practice allows for remedial action.

## Ensuring that top management provide strong, positive role models

Top management can choose to be coached by a professional external resource, by a peer, or by someone more junior, who can educate them in other perspectives. (This is especially useful when the more junior person comes from a different gender or racial origin.)

A positive example from the top is critical. Unless people see that top managers are investing in their own development, and in coaching/mentoring others, their own motivation will inevitably be muted.

## Identifying cultural and systems barriers to developmental behaviours

The excuses managers give for not devoting sufficient time to coaching or to encouraging coaching between members of the team are many. Top of the list is usually inadequate time and much can be achieved by helping managers develop better skills of prioritising, general time management and establishing regular and sacrosanct periods of reflective space.

Other barriers to coaching behaviour are often more subtle – for example, a general reluctance to address difficult behavioural issues, or to admit to weaknesses. Initial research to establish these most common such barriers can prove invaluable. From this understanding, it is possible to conduct educational and motivational campaigns and to coach managers to overcome their own specific barriers.

Interestingly, although Kram's (1985) original study of mentoring suggested that organisational culture was an important contextual variable in effectiveness of mentoring relationships, my own qualitative studies show no correlation between a scale of organisational supportiveness (Clutterbuck, 2007) and find no significant correlation with mentor or mentee behaviours, with quality of relationship experience or with outcomes for either mentor or mentee. It seems that, where participants have been well-trained in their roles, the relationship is insulated from the organisational context. A moderate level of correlation can be observed, however, between strength of participants' perception that the organisation's purpose in supporting mentoring is aligned with their relationship purpose, and the relationship dynamics.

## MEASURING THE IMPACT OF COACHING AND MENTORING

Measurement in coaching and mentoring is important for three purposes: to troubleshoot relationships that aren't working well; to improve the overall programme; and to demonstrate return on investment. Hence it makes sense for organisations to use a balanced portfolio of measures, both hard and soft, process-related and outcome-related. My own organisation's clients have access to a database that allows them to compare metrics, using validated scales of participants' behaviour, relationship experience and outcome, both amongst participant groups and against other participating organisations. Another useful resource is the International Standards for Mentoring Programmes in Employment, which provides a benchmark for assessing programmes. Similarly, the European Mentoring and Coaching Council (EMCC) has a quality assurance programme to assess coach and mentor training against common standards.

Standard advice for measuring the impact of individual coaching interventions is that they should start with an initial assessment of the learner's competence in the area to be focused on; should involve regular progress reviews; and should conclude with a repeat of the original competence measures. It is important in this context to use a wide range of inputs and observations – a common error is to use only the perceptions of the coachee's boss(es). However, a recent case study (Ertam, 2007), in which members of a management talent pool were assessed using 360° feedback at the beginning and end of a 12-month coaching/mentoring relationship found that direct reports saw very substantial positive changes, while bosses saw almost none. We have called this phenomenon 'relationship drag'. It appears that bosses' initial perceptions take a lot more time and effort to shift.

Another problem with measuring coaching impact is that defining output measures at the beginning of the relationship tends to close down opportunities for wider learning. Professional executive coaches report frequent problems of conflict between the measures imposed by the organisation and the learning needs that emerge for the coachee.

## ROLE OF STANDARDS AND PROFESSIONAL BODIES

There is a growing army of executive or managerial coaches with a plethora of qualifications. A number of bodies have arisen to regulate and professionalise the sector, notably the International Coach Federation, originating from the US and the EMCC, which has a much wider remit. Other organisations, such as the Association for Coaching, exist to promote good practice in a particular area of coaching. Increasing collaboration between these bodies is beginning to establish some commonality of standards for individual practitioners, but *caveat emptor* still applies within the marketplace as a whole. In carrying out assessment centres to select pools of external coaches for large employer organisations, it is evident that the proportion of truly effective (and not dangerous!) executive coaches within the market is relatively small. The EMCC has carried out extensive research to map the range of competencies required at different levels and in different applications of coaching and mentoring. These standards have subsequently been used to establish a quality award to accredit coaching and mentoring educational programmes.

The International Standards for Mentoring Programmes in Employment (ISMPE) provide an assessment, accreditation process for in-company mentoring. Compiled by an array of practitioners, providers and academic observers, they allow programme coordinators to benchmark against other programmes. A similar awarding body has been discussed for in-company management of coaching and may be created in the future.

## CONCLUSION: THE CHALLENGES TO COME

Coaching and mentoring are increasingly popular instruments of management development, used in some fashion, according to surveys by the American Society for Training and Development and the Chartered Institute for Personnel and Development, in most large- and medium-sized organisations. Critical challenges for organisations include:

- Raising the competence of all employees, particularly those in management positions, to coach/mentor and be coached/mentored, so that these behaviours become endemic within the culture.
- Integrating coaching and mentoring more coherently with other business and people management systems, from strategic planning to succession planning and performance management.

For the coaching and mentoring profession, the critical challenges lie in:

- Achieving common standards of accreditation and qualification, to remove customer and client confusion about what to expect.
- Establishing the business case for coaching in ways that are credible to senior managers and leaders.

## NOTE

1 Sections of this chapter are reproduced with permission from CAMeO (Coaching and Mentoring Oracle).

## REFERENCES

Allen, T.D. and Eby, L.T. (2007) *The Blackwell Handbook of Mentoring*, Oxford: Blackwell.

Appelbaum, S.H., Ritchie, S. and Shapiro, B.T. (1994) 'Mentoring revisited: An organizational behaviour construct', *The International Journal of Career Management*, 6 (3): 3–10.

Apter, M.J. and Carter, S. (2001) 'Mentoring and motivational versatility: An exploration of reversal theory', *Proceedings of the 8th European Mentoring Centre Conference*. Cambridge, UK.

Aryee, S., Wyatt, T. and Stone, R. (1996) 'Early career outcomes of graduate employees: The effect of mentoring and ingratiation', *Journal of Management Studies*, 33 (1): 95–118.

Argyris, C. and Schon, D. (1996) *Organizational Learning II: Theory, Methods, and Partice*. Reading MA: Addition-Wesley Longman.

Aryee, S. and Chay, Y.W. (1994) 'An examination of the impact of career-oriented mentoring on work commitment, attitudes and career satisfaction among professionals and managerial employees', *British Journal of Management*, 5: 241–9.

Barham, K. and Conway, C. (1998) *Developing Business and People Internationally – A Mentoring Approach Research Report*. Ashridge Management College.

Bartram, A.T. and Garreffa, T. (2004) 'The effects of mentoring on perceived career success, commitment and turnover intentions', *Journal of the American Academy of Business*, Sept: 164–70.

Beattie, R.S. and McDougall, M. (1995) 'Peer mentoring: The issues and outcomes of non-hierarchical developmental relationships', *Paper to British Academy of Management Annual Conference*.

Browne, S. (2000) *Paper to 7th Annual European Mentoring Centre Conference*. Cambridge, UK, November.

Bullis, C. and Bach, B.W. (1989) 'Are mentoring relationships helping organizations? An exploration of developing mentee-mentor-organizational identification using turning point analysis', *Communication Quarterly*, 37: 199–213.

Caruso, R. (1990) 'An examination of organisational mentoring: The case of Motorola', PhD Thesis, University of London.

Chao, G.T., Walz, P.M. and Gardner, P.D. (1992) 'Formal and informal mentorships: A comparison on mentoring functions and contrast with non-mentored counterparts', *Personnel Psychology*, 45: 619–36.

Clutterbuck, D. (1985) *Everyone Needs a Mentor*. Wimbledon: CIPD. Revised 1991, 2001 and 2004.

Clutterbuck, D. (2007) 'A longitudinal study of the effectiveness of developmental mentoring', PhD thesis, University of London.

Clutterbuck, D. and Ragins, B.R. (2002) *Mentoring and Diversity: An International Perspective*. Oxford: Butterworth-Heinemann.

Clutterbuck, D. and Megginson, M. (1999) *Mentoring Executives and Director*. Oxford: Blackwell.

Clutterbuck, D. and Megginson, D. (2004) 'All good things must come to an end: Winding up and winding down a mentoring relationship', in D. Clutterbuck and G. Lane (eds), *The Situational Mentor*. Aldershot: Gower, 178–93.

Collins, E.G. (1978) 'Everyone who makes it has a mentor', *Harvard Business Review*, 56 (2), July–August: 89–101.

Collins, A. (1979) 'Notes on some typologies of managerial development and the role of menter in the process of adaptation of the individual to the organisation', *Personnel Reveiew*, 8 (4): 10–14.

Cuerrier, C. (2003) *Starting Point for Mentoring*. Quebec: Fondation de l'entrepreneurship.

Dougherty, T.W. and Dreher, G.F. (2007) 'Mentoring and career outcomes', in B.R. Ragins and K. Kram (eds), *The Handbook of Mentoring at Work*. Thousand Oaks, CA: Sage. pp. 51–93.

Eby, L.T. (1997) 'Alternative forms of mentoring in changing organizational environments: A conceptual extension of the mentoring literature', *Journal of Vocational Behavior*, 51: 125–44.

Eby, L.T., Butts, M., Lockwood, A. and Simon, S.A. (2004) 'Proteges' negative mentoring experiences: Construct development and nomological validation', *Personnel Psychology*, 57: 411–47.

Egan, G. (1994) *The Skilled Helper: A Problem Management Approach to Helping*. Pacific Grove, CA: Brookes & Cole.

Ellinger, A.D. and Bostrum, R.P. (1999) 'Managerial coaching behaviors in learning organizations', *Journal of Management Development*, 18 (9): 752–71.

Elliott, A. (2006) 'How coaching drives high performance at Portman', *Strategic HR Review*, 5 (4): May/June.

Emerging Workforce Study (1999) www.spherion.com

Engstrom, T. (1998) 'Personality factors' impact on success in the mentor-protégé relationship', MSc thesis, Norwegian School of Hotel Management.

Ertam, B. (2007) 'Mentoring in DHL', *Paper to Turkish Institute of Personnel and Development Annual Conference*. Istanbul, November.

Fagenson, E.A. (1992) 'Mentoring: Who needs it? A comparison of protégés' and non-protégés' needs for power, achievement, affiliation and autonomy', *Journal of Vocational Behavior*, 41: 48–60.

Fagenson-Eland, E. and Lu, R.Y. (2004) 'Virtual mentoring', in D. Clutterbuck and G. Lane (eds), *The Situational Mentor*. Aldershot: Gower. pp. 178–93.

Farrar, P. (2006) 'The paradox of manager as coach: Does being a manager inhibit effective coaching?', PhD thesis, Oxford Brookes University.

Fenelon, F. de. (1699) *Telemachus, Son of Ulysses*. Republished Cambridge University Press, 1994.

Fletcher, J.K. and Ragins, B.R. (2007) 'Stone center relational cultural theory: A window on relational mentoring', in B.R. Ragins and K. Kram (eds), *Handbook of Mentoring*. Thousand Oaks, CA: Sage. pp. 373–400.

Fournies, R.F. (1987) *Coaching for Improved Work Performance*. Liberty Hall Press.

Gallwey, T. (1975) *The Inner Game of Tennis*. New York: Random House.

Gallwey, T. (2000) *The Inner Game of Work*. New York: Random House.

Garvey, B. 'Mentoring in the marketplace: Studies of learning at work', Doctoral thesis, Durham University, July 1998.

Garvey, B. and Galloway, K. (2001) 'Mentoring at the Halifax plc (HBOS): A small beginning in a large organisation'. *Proceedings of the 8th European Mentoring Centre Conference*. Cambridge, UK.

Gibb, S. and Megginson, D. (1992) 'Inside corporate mentoring schemes: A new agenda of concerns', *Personnel Review*, 21 (7): 65–79.

Gray, M.M. and Gray, W. (1990) 'Planned mentoring: Aiding key transitions in career development', *Mentoring International*, 4 (3): Summer.

Hackman, J.R. and Wageman, R. (2005) 'A theory of team coaching', *Academy of Management Review*, 30 (2): 269–87.

Hale, R. (2000) 'To match or mismatch? The dynamics of mentoring as a route to personal and organisational learning', *Career Development International*, 5 (4/5): 223–34.

Hawken, D. (2000) 'The advanced collegial mentoring model: Reciprocal peer mentoring', *Proceedings of the 7th European Mentoring Centre Conference*. Cambridge, UK.

Hay, J. (1995) *Transformational Mentoring*. Maidenhead: McGraw-Hill.

Higgins, M. and Kram, K. (2001) 'Reconceptualizing mentoring at work: A developmental network perspective', *Academy of Management Review*, 26 (2): 264–88.

Higgins, M.C. (2004) 'The more, the merrier? Multiple developmental relationships and work satisfaction', *Journal of Management Development*, 19 (4): 277–29.

Incomes Data Services (2004) *Mentoring*. London: IDS HR Studies No. 778.

James, R. (2000) 'Mentoring – Getting it right. The Barclays' experience', *Proceedings of the 7th European Mentoring Centre Conference*. Cambridge, UK.

Jarvis, J., Lane, D. and Fillery-Travis, A. (2006) *The Case for Coaching: Making Evidence-Based Decisions*. Wimbledon: CIPD.

Kalbfleisch, P.J. and Davies, A.B. (1993) 'An interpersonal model for participation in mentoring relationships', *Western Journal of Communications*, 57: 399–415.

Klasen, N. and Clutterbuck, D. (2002) *Implementing Mentoring Schemes*. Oxford: Butterworth Heinemann.

Kram, K. (1985) *Mentoring at Work: Developmental Relationships in Organisational Life*. Glenview, IL: Foresman Scott.

Kram, K.E. and Bragar, M.C. (1992) 'Development through mentoring: A strategic approach', in D.J. Montross and C.J. Shinkman (eds), *Career Development: Theory and Practice*. Charles C. Thomas. IL: Springfield, pp. 221–54.

Kram, K.E. (1996) 'A relational approach to career development', in D. Hall and Associates (eds), *The Career Is Dead – Long Live the Career*. San Francisco, CA: Jossey-Bass. pp. 132–57.

Kram, K. and Isabella, L.A. (1985) 'Mentoring alternatives: The role of peer relationships in career development', *Academy of Management Journal*, 28: 110–32.

Levinson, D.J. (1978) *The Seasons of a Man's Life*. New York: Ballantine.

Livingstone, J.S. (2003) 'Pygmalion in management', *Harvard Business Review*, 81 (1) (January): 97–106.

Maurer, T.J., Weiss, E.M. and Barbeite, F.G. (2003) 'A model of involvement in work-related learning and development activity: The effects of individual, situational, motivational and age variables', *Journal of Applied Psychology*, 88: 707–24.

McManus, S. and Russell, J.E.A. (2007) 'Peer mentoring relationships', in B.R. Ragins and K. Kram (eds), *The Handbook of Mentoring at Work*. Thousand Oaks, CA: Sage.

Megginson, D. (2007) 'Researching coaching and mentoring', *Paper to 12th European Mentoring and Coaching Council Conference*. Cologne, October.

Parker-Wilkins, V. (2006) 'Business impact of executive coaching: Demonstrating Monetary Value', *Industrial and Commercial Training*, 38 (3): 122–27.

Proctor and Gamble (2002) 'Mentoring up at Proctor and Gamble', in D. Clutterbuck and B.R. Ragins (eds), *Mentoring and Diversity: An International Perspective*. Oxford: Butterworth Heinemann. pp. 195–202.

Ragins, B.R. and McFarlin, D.B. (1990) 'Perceptions of mentor roles in cross-gender relationships', *Journal of Vocational Behavior*, 37: 3231–339.

Ragins, B.R., Cotton, J.L. and Miller, J.S. (2000) 'Marginal mentoring: The effects of type of mentor, quality of relationship and program design on work and career attitudes', *Academy of Management Journal*, 43 (6): 1117–94.

Scandura, T.A. (1889) 'Dysfunctional mentoring relationships and outcomes', *Journal of Management*, 24: 449–67.

Scandura, T. (1996) 'Perspectives on mentoring', *Leadership and Organization Journal*, 17 (3).

Scandura, T.A. (1998) 'Dysfunctional mentorind relationships and outcomes', *Journal of Management*, 24: 449–67.

Skerrit, I. and Draper J. (2000) 'Mentoring within a professional development scheme', *Proceedings of the 7th European Mentoring Centre Conference*. Cambridge, UK.

Stoddard, D. and Tamsey, R. (2003) *The Heart of Mentoring: 10 Pronen Principles for Developing People to Their Fullest Potential*. Colorado: Navpress.

Turban, D.B. and Lee, F.K. (2007) 'The role of personality in mentoring relationships: Formation, dynamics and outcomes', in B.R. Ragins and K. Kram (eds), *The Handbook of Mentoring at Work*. Thousand Oaks, CA: Sage. pp. 21–50.

Wanberg, C.R., Welsh, E.T. and Hezlett, S.A. (2003) 'Mentoring research: A review and dynamic process model', *Research in Personnel and Human Resources Management*, 22: 39–124.

Wellin, M. (2001) 'Mentoring and coaching at a conscious level to enhance relationship skills', *Proceedings of the 8th European Mentoring Centre Conference*. Cambridge, UK.

Wasylyshyn, K.M. (2003) 'Executive coaching: An outcome study', *Consulting Psychology Journal: Practice and Research*, 55 (2): 94–196.

# 26

# Rethinking the Role of Management Development in Preparing Global Business Leaders

Kathryn Aten, Luciara Nardon and
Richard M. Steers

## Abstract

As today's business environment becomes increasingly global, experts have advocated that managers cultivate a global mindset. A global mindset is the ability to analyze problems and reach conclusions that are independent from the assumptions of a single country, culture, or context and to implement solutions appropriately in different countries, cultures, and contexts. Whereas in the past, managers needed to grasp the particularities of a country or culture before doing business, today's rapidly changing, multicultural business environment often requires managers to interact with multiple cultures with little time to immerse themselves in the foreign context. For this reason, we argue that traditional immersion methods of developing cross-cultural knowledge are insufficient. We contend that managers operating in a multicultural environment require a more efficient path that allows them to learn cultures 'on the fly' in the course of, rather than prior to, multicultural assignments and interactions. We present an intercultural interaction learning model as a potential solution to this dilemma. We then discuss the implications of the model for management development and identify the skills required for learning cultures on the fly. We conclude with examples of experiential exercises to develop these skills.

The plight of today's global managers is evident from the legions of stories about failures in cross-border enterprise. Global managers are responsible for utilizing human, financial, and physical resources in ways that facilitate their organization's overall objectives in turbulent and sometimes hostile environments about which they often understand very little. Nonetheless, ignorance or unfamiliarity with local business customs is seldom an acceptable excuse for failure, and with the current global infatuation with a fairly narrow definition of leadership – 'Lead, follow, or get out of the way' and 'Just do it!' – there is seldom any room for anything but success. Indeed, particularly in many Western cultures, lack of success is more often attributed to personal failure than external considerations beyond management's control.

As globalization pressures increase and managers spend more time as frequent flyers and flexpatriates, the training and development community has increasingly advocated more intensive analyses of the criteria for managerial success in the global economy. As more attention is focused on this challenge, an increasing cadre of management experts are honing in on the need for managers to develop perspectives which stretch beyond domestic borders (Black and Gregersen, 2000). This concept is called a global mindset (Srinivas, 1995; Levy et al., 2007; Javidan et al., 2007).[1]

In this chapter we discuss the relevance of a global mindset and the challenges of developing it. We argue that immersion methods of developing cross-cultural knowledge are well suited to traditional expatriate assignments or situations requiring that managers interact with a defined set of cultures, but insufficient in today's business environment in which many managers must interact with multiple cultures and with short notice.

## CULTIVATING A GLOBAL MINDSET

Business leaders and researchers have increasingly recognized the need for managers who are sensitive to and knowledgeable about the global context in which their companies operate. Global mindset training has emerged to address this need (Mendenhall and Stahl, 2000). A *global mindset* has been defined as an ability to develop and interpret criteria for personal and business performance that are independent from the assumptions of a single country, culture, or context; and to implement those criteria

appropriately in different countries, cultures, and contexts (Maznevski and Lane, 2003). An alternative yet similar definition is a way of viewing the world with a particular emphasis on broadening one's cultural perspective as it relates to intercultural behavior (Levy et al., 2007). In other words, a global mindset allows managers to think in global terms, beyond the boundaries of a local context.

### Global mindset training

The increasing prominence of the global mindset concept raises the question, how can we develop managers to function effectively in a multicultural world? Various scholars' interpretations of the concept suggest different paths to achieving this objective. Some propose that a global mindset represents a cognitive or knowledge structure that contains information about several cultures and realities (Rinesmith, 1992), which allows managers to interpret situations using multiple cultural frameworks and then select the most appropriate action for a particular situation. This view suggests that managers must acquire in-depth knowledge of multiple contexts in order to develop a global mindset. Others focus on personal characteristics such as a high level of curiosity, awareness and acceptance of diversity, acceptance of complexity, and systems thinking (Early, et al., 2007; Srinivas, 1995). This view supports the notion that developing a global mindset requires managers to radically change their existing mental maps. From this perspective, the objective of global mindset training 'is stretching someone's mind past narrow domestic borders and creating a mental map of the entire world' (Black and Gregersen, 2000: 175). Training programs have emerged to address both perspectives.

Traditionally, practitioners and scholars have suggested that managers should deal with cultural conflicts by adapting to the other's culture. Academic and management training programs have long recognized a fairly typical pattern of behavior and accommodation referred to as *culture shock*. That is, new expatriates initially experience stress and anxiety as a result of being immersed in an unfamiliar environment. Over time, they learn new ways of coping and eventually feel more comfortable living in the culture of the host country. Expatriate managers are able to be effective in dealing with people from another country by learning the foreign culture in depth and behaving in ways that are appropriate in that culture. For example, a manager assigned to work in France for several years would be advised to study the French language and culture and then begin to make French friends upon his or her arrival in the new location. The first perspective described above suggests that to develop a global mindset, managers should follow this traditional prescription with the added requirement of developing knowledge about multiple cultures.

Recently, practitioners and scholars have begun to explore methods for developing global mental maps. Black and Gregersen (2000), describe three principles involved in the remaking of mental maps: contrast and remapping, confrontation and remapping, and conceptual framework and remapping. The authors argue that in order to remake mental maps people must encounter a map that differs substantially from their existing map, they must confront the contrast in a compelling manner, and they must be given a conceptual framework with which to reformulate their original mental map. Organizations have utilized a variety of training designs to assist managers in reformatting mental maps including; action learning involving foreign travel, computer-simulated business games, and class room training involving multiple nationalities (see Black and Gregersen, 2000 for examples), in-country, real-time personal coaching, utilizing repatriates and reverse expatriates – foreign subsidiary managers – in-training programs, and cultural skills assessment centers (see Mendenhall and Stahl, 2000 for examples).

While we concur that both deep cultural knowledge and global mental maps are desirable characteristics in global managers, developing these is a complicated and lengthy process requiring considerable time and effort (Black and Gregersen, 2000; Mendenhall and Stahl, 2000). Many managers today must operate in an extremely dynamic global environment, working with multicultural and temporary project teams as well as peers in countries around the globe. This type of work requires that managers be able very rapidly to create successful working relationships with individuals from many cultures with which the manager may be unfamiliar. We argue that programs designed to cultivate a global mindset by developing new knowledge structures and mental maps are insufficient. Today's managers require skills that will allow them to succeed and learn from multicultural interactions while in the processes of cultivating a global mindset.

## Challenges of a cultivating a global mindset

Although having a global mindset, understanding a great deal about the world and its cultures, and using this knowledge in appropriate ways may be ideal, efficiently achieving this is difficult. The traditional approach to cross-cultural training is useful for extended expatriate assignments or situations in which a manager must deal with a limited number of cultures. Sequential assignments and lengthy training programs devoted to changing mental models will likely facilitate the development of a global mindset over time. However, the increasing intensity and diversity that characterizes today's global business environment requires an approach suited to managers that must succeed immediately and simultaneously in multiple cultures.

Gone are the days when a manager prepared for a long-term assignment in France or Germany – or even Europe. Today, this same manager might need to deal simultaneously with partners from multiple cultures around the globe. Thus, learning one language and culture may no longer be enough. In addition, the timeline for developing business relationships has declined from years to months – and sometimes to weeks, and few managers can afford the considerable time and commitment required to develop new mental maps prior to taking on work assignments. This reality signals to us the need for a new approach to developing global managers, one that acknowledges the admirable goal of global mindset training and also provides skills to support more immediate business success in today's multicultural environment.

The evolution from a principally bicultural business environment to a more global one presents today's global managers with at least three new challenges:

1   *Many intercultural encounters happen on short notice, leaving little time to learn about the other culture.* Imagine that you just returned from a week's stay in China where you were negotiating an outsourcing agreement. As you arrive at your home office you learn that an incredible acquisition opportunity just turned up in Argentina and that you are supposed to leave in a week to explore the matter further. You have never been to Argentina, nor do you know anybody from there. What do you do?

2   *Sometimes it is unclear to which culture one should adapt.* Suppose that your company has asked you to join a global project team to work in a six-month R&D project. The team includes one Chilean, one Polish, one Korean, and one Swiss national. Every member of the team has a permanent appointment in their home country but is temporarily assigned to work at company headquarters in Belgium for this project. Which culture should team members adapt to? In this case, there is no dominant cultural group to dictate the rules. Considering the multiple cultures involved, and the minimal exposure each manager has likely had to the other cultures, the traditional approach of adaptation is unlikely to be successful. Nevertheless, the group must be able to work together quickly and effectively to produce results (and protect their careers) despite their differences. What would you do?

3   *Intercultural meetings increasingly occur virtually (by way of computers or video conferencing)*

*instead of through more traditional face-to-face interactions.* Suppose you have been asked to build a partnership with a Thai partner that you have never met and that you know little about Thai culture. Suppose further that this task is to be completed on-line, without any face-to-face communication or interactions. Your boss is in a hurry for results. What would you do?

Taken together, these three challenges demonstrate just how difficult it can be to work across cultures in today's rapidly changing business environment. The old ways of communicating and doing business are less effective now than in the past. The question before us, then, is how to facilitate management success in such situations.

## LEARNING CULTURES ON THE FLY

Traditional methods of developing cultural expertise and knowledge structures, which enable global thinking, are rarely sufficient in today's business environment. While one might eventually develop the characteristics embodied in a global mindset by sequentially acquiring deep knowledge of multiple cultures, we contend that today's managers require a path that is more efficient, although recent developments in global mindset training seem likely to generate new conceptual frameworks. However, we contend that today's managers require a path that is more efficient and supports success while learning.

Successful managers will be those who can learn to accomplish goals working with others from different cultures in the course of minimal interactions, as opposed to through the traditional approach of lengthy immersion. In other words, we argue that successful managers must learn to learn cultures 'on the fly.' Nardon and Steers (2007) recently developed a model of interdependent learning which suggests an alternative avenue for developing cross-cultural management skills and global mindsets. Key to this model is the contention that managers can compensate for a lack of knowledge about a specific culture by developing and drawing on their learning skills. The model focuses on learning to interact with people from different cultures. We contend that when managers are able to successfully interact with people from foreign cultures, the acquisition of business and local knowledge is facilitated. While local contexts' particularities need to be understood and taken into account for business success, business and institutional knowledge is transmitted through interpersonal interactions. Mastering learning skills is thus possibly the best strategy available to managers who want to succeed in the multicultural reality of today's business environment.

In the remainder of this chapter, we first present the intercultural interaction learning model, beginning with a brief review of experiential learning theory, which provides a theoretical grounding for the model. We then discuss the implications of the model for management development. We identify the skills required for learning cultures on the fly and conclude with examples of experiential exercises to develop these skills.

## EXPERIENTIAL LEARNING THEORY

Knowledge is typically defined as familiarity that is gained by actual experience. In accordance with this definition, experiential learning theory holds that knowledge is created when individuals learn from experience. Learning occurs when individuals grasp and transform their experiences into new knowledge. Experiential learning theory elaborates this process.

When it was originally proposed, experiential learning theory focused on individual learning. However, as we discuss below, recent adaptations take into account social, interdependent aspects of learning. While we draw primarily on more recent conceptions, these are strongly grounded in the original theory. We thus briefly review the individual experiential learning model before proceeding to our discussion of interdependent learning.

## Individual learning: experiential learning model

According to experiential learning theory, knowledge is grasped through concrete experience and abstract conceptualization and is then transformed through reflective observation and active experimentation (Kolb and Kolb, 2005). The process of knowledge creation consists of four stages: experience, observation, reflection, and abstract conceptualization. While learning can begin in any of the four stages, learning is above all else a *process*: an individual has an experience, observes and reflects on the experience, develops theories and conceptualizations to explain the experience, and finally tests theories through active experimentation. The example below illustrates the experiential learning process in a cross-cultural setting.

Consider the following scenario: You come from a culture that values direct, straightforward communication. When you converse with others, you ask direct questions as you have learned from experience that this behavior usually results in straightforward answers. Now, imagine that you engage in a conversation with an individual from a culture that values indirect communication and 'saving face.' This person has learned through experience that indirect and subtle suggestions yield comfortable interactions allowing all parties to save face. Neither of you are sufficiently knowledgeable to adapt your communication styles to fit the other's culture.

In this scenario, you are likely to ask a direct question and get what you perceive to be an unsatisfactorily vague response. You are then likely to experience an emotional reaction – discomfort, perplexity, offense, or surprise – to the results of your actions. This *concrete experience* will likely prompt you to try to understand what is happening through *observation* and *reflection*. You recognize that there is a mismatch between what is happening and what you thought would happen, and then observe the other person to try to ascertain why she is responding as she is: maybe she did not hear you, maybe she did not understand the question, maybe she does not speak English very well, maybe she is shy, maybe she is not comfortable with the question. You then search for other clues in her behavior and in the context of the situation that can help explain her behavior. Your observation and reflection provides a foundation for *abstract conceptualization* and *generalization*. You develop a theory to explain what is happening: you identify a plausible explanation for her behavior and search for alternative solutions to your communication problem. Let's suppose that you conclude that your partner is uncomfortable with your question. Her body language suggests that she feels embarrassed, so you theorize that you should pose the question in a different way. Your theory will guide you future actions when dealing with this individual and others from similar cultures.

Learning through experience is a process of trial and error in which individuals' experience do not meet expectations leading to reflection, identification of solutions, and experimentation with new behaviors. Individuals identify successful behaviors and incorporate them into theories of how to behave. When the individual next engages in a similar situation, he draws on his latest theories for guidance. One tests the implication of new concepts by practicing new actions. For instance, in the example above, you might decide to formulate your question in a different way, and observe the results, beginning a new learning cycle which continues until you are satisfied that you have identified successful behaviors.

## Interdependent learning: intercultural interaction learning model

While experiential learning theory has remained one of the most influential theories of management learning (Kayes, 2002: 137), it has been criticized for its failure to account for the social aspects of learning (Holman et al.,

1997). Kayes (2002) addresses these concerns by incorporating the social context into the original model. Kayes argues that concrete experience is manifested in an emotional state of need, the need to be understood for example, which becomes an internalized representation through observation and reflection. He relates abstract conceptualization to identity, which serves to organize experience. For example, if I identify myself as a good communicator, I am likely to organize the experience of not being understood in a way that will lead me to experiment with alternative behaviors. Finally, Kayes equates active experimentation to social interaction through which experiences arise. Thus, in our example, active experimentation is no longer the act of the individual; rather it is a social interaction involving the interactions and feedback between at least two people.

These ideas form the theoretical foundation of the intercultural interaction learning model. The model focuses on the interaction of two or more individuals who are simultaneously experiencing problems, reflecting on them, theorizing about them, and engaging in corrective actions. The learning process is interdependent and interactive, rather than independent or linear (Thomas, 2006; Kayes, 2002; Schwandt, 2005). The learning of one party leads to an action that will influence the learning of the other party in a cycle of interdependent learning. This interdependence is illustrated in Figure 26.1.

An intercultural interaction is an opportunity for interdependent learning in which individuals both learn about the other's culture and negotiate effective ways of relating to one another. Ideally, as individuals from different cultures interact they develop better ways of communicating with each other. However, if learning is short-circuited, the interaction fails and the relationship suffers. For example, if after asking a question and receiving an unsatisfactory answer, the individual does not observe and reflect on the other party's behavior, she may engage in actions that are detrimental to the relationship.

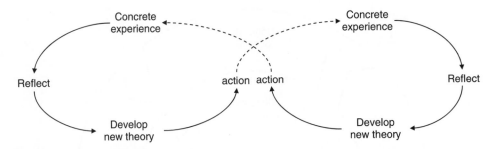

**Figure 26.1 Interdependent learning**
*Source*: Adapted from Kayes, 2002. Copyright 2002 Academy of Management. Used with permission.

An effective intercultural interaction is the result of successful interdependent learning, through which two or more parties negotiate ways of working together. Managers can learn culture on the fly – creating successful intercultural interactions without the benefit of lengthy cultural immersion – by negotiating identities, meaning, rules, and behaviors. The learning skills, which support these negotiations, can substitute for the knowledge gleaned from lengthy immersion training.

Additionally, these learning skills offer the flexibility to account for the interactions of multiple layers of cultures and individual personalities. One of the dilemmas managers face when working abroad is that while they may have mastered the generalities of one particular culture there is no guarantee that the organizations and people they encounter will comply with the generalizations of the local culture. Cultures are not homogeneous and people and organizations within particular countries vary considerably. Learning in the course of interactions eliminates this problem. These learning skills are shown as part of the Intercultural Interaction Learning Model illustrated in Figure 26.2.

*Negotiating identity.* An individual's identity is the set of attributes that is central, enduring, and distinctive (Ashforth and Mael, 1989). Identity is the answer to the question, 'Who am I?' Identity is constructed through social interactions, through which individuals create categories and define themselves in relation to others. This categorization process influences one's perception of his or her position in relation to others as well as how he acts and feels about interactions. Identity is closely linked to one's interpretations of reality (Schwandt, 2005). Individuals make sense of the world based on how they see themselves and one's actions are usually congruent with one's identity. Individuals tend to engage in activities that are harmonious with their self-concept and to support institutions that embody their identities (Ashforth and Mael, 1989).

Because of this, intercultural interactions are often challenging. When a person engages with another from a different cultural background, her assumptions, values, and beliefs may be questioned. Her perceptions about who she is, her competence, status, and self-worth may be challenged. An intercultural interaction is likely to produce strong feelings about one's identity and expectations. For these feelings to be positive, individuals must negotiate identity (Ting-Toomey, 1988).

For example, to a Spanish manager, arriving 30 minutes late for a meeting is normal and acceptable. A Spanish manager who arrives 30 minutes late can be a competent, professional person. However, a manager of a Japanese partner would find this to be extremely inappropriate and disrespectful, signifying either that the Spanish manager is unprofessional or that the Japanese partner is of low status and importance. Either interpretation threatens the identity of one of the parties and may jeopardize communication, impede learning,

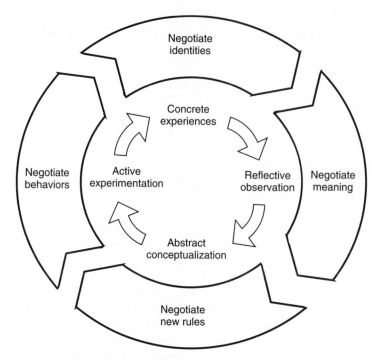

**Figure 26.2    Intercultural interaction learning model**

and compromise the success of the interaction. In order for the interaction to succeed, the parties must negotiate acceptable identities for themselves in the context of their interaction. This involves the identities of both parties. For an intercultural interaction to be successful, each must preserve a satisfactory identity while respecting and preserving the identity of the others.

*Negotiating meaning.* Meaning refers to the interpretation individuals assign to their experience and observations. For example, in some cultures the signing of a contract signifies the end of a negotiation, in others it signifies the beginning of a relationship. Assignments of meaning are based on current and past experience. Jointly understood meaning is constructed through interaction, as individuals exchange information (Berger and Lukeman, 1966). When two individuals from different cultures interact, they are likely to have different interpretations of the meaning of the concrete things, such as a contract, that they discuss. To be effective, they will need to negotiate and find common meaning.[2]

Meaning cannot be transmitted from one person to another: only messages are transmitted (Gudykunst, 1998). When we send a message to another person we attach meaning to it based on our interpretations, and when another receives the message, he attaches meaning to it based on his interpretations. For example, a Western party to a negotiation says, 'I am glad we were able to sign a contract,' she may mean 'I am glad the negotiations are over and I can get back to other business.' However, an Asian counterpart may hear 'I am glad we agreed to initiate a relationship and negotiations that will continue for a long time to come.' A common meaning must be negotiated in order for cross-cultural interactions to be effective.

*Negotiating new rules.* Once individuals agree on acceptable identities and meanings, they need to negotiate new rules that will inform their relationship. These rules are akin to theories of action (Argyris, 1995) and over time create a common context. For example, the Spanish and Japanese managers in the previous scenario need to establish rules about acceptable behaviors regarding time. They might agree, for instance, that arriving 15 minutes after the appointed time is acceptable, but that further delays should be avoided – or at a minimum deserve an apology. Alternatively, they may agree on a more clear specification of time when making appointments: 8:00 am Spanish time, means that delays are expected, while 8:00 am Japanese time means that they should arrive 10 to 5 minutes prior to the meeting time. Over time, rules regarding the most important cultural obstacles to the success of a relationship can constitute a new shared culture (Casmir, 1992; Klimoski and Mohammed, 1994; Adler, 2002; Earley and Mosakowski, 2000) for the individuals involved. However, at minimum even in the time-sensitive situations in which today's global managers operate, recognition of the need to negotiate rules and imperfect attempts to do so supports successful interaction.

*Negotiating new behaviors*. Finally, once individuals develop new theories of action and agree on a common set of cultural rules to guide interaction, they must negotiate new behaviors. For example, if the negotiated rule is that delays of more than 15 minutes should be avoided, managers must learn to engage in behaviors that will allow arriving on time, such as using a scheduling system or bringing work to occupy delays, depending upon their initial custom. It is easier for most individuals to engage in some behaviors than others (Kolb, 1976; Kolb and Kolb, 2005). To be successful in intercultural interactions, managers must recognize their weaknesses and compensate with other behaviors. For instance, individuals who find it difficult to communicate indirectly may compensate by searching for opportunities to discuss issues one on one and prefacing their direct statements with an apology.

## THE ROLE OF MANAGEMENT DEVELOPMENT

In today's global environment managers frequently do business in multiple countries and interact with people from multiple cultures simultaneously. The examples in this chapter may appear to suggest simple solutions. For instance, expect that Spaniards may be late for appointments. However, actual intercultural encounters are extremely complex. Culture is very complex and may seem paradoxical to an outsider (Bird and Osland, 2003). Additionally, individuals are influenced by regional, organizational, functional, and professional as well as national culture. And, people in all countries vary in their beliefs, values, and behaviors. People are different, regardless of their origins. Finally, business professionals around the world are learning how to interact with foreigners and may behave in ways that are not typical of their own culture.

Therefore, while simplistic categorizations of cultures may provide an introductory understanding of behavior and initial explanation (Adler, 2002) they are not good predictors. Thus, a learning module on cross-culture interaction with the objective of making managers aware of different cultures and exposing them to theoretical categorizations of cultural types will not meet the needs of today's global managers. While the content present in these types of courses are important and necessary, it is not sufficient (Maznevski and Lane, 2003; Cant, 2004). And, as we have discussed, today's global managers do not have sufficient time to develop deep, context-specific knowledge of several cultures *a priori* or even the ability to predict on which cultures to focus their attention. Rather, in order to succeed in today's complex, global environment, managers need to develop context general skills and abilities, which can be applied to facilitate successful multiparty interactions with people from any culture. By learning to negotiate identities, meanings, behaviors and rules, managers will be able to uncover cultural assumptions allowing them to learn *while* interacting with people from diverse cultures.

Managers today require a global mindset, and traditional means of developing mangers for foreign assignments do not meet the requirements of today's global business environment. Rather than relying on deep *a priori*

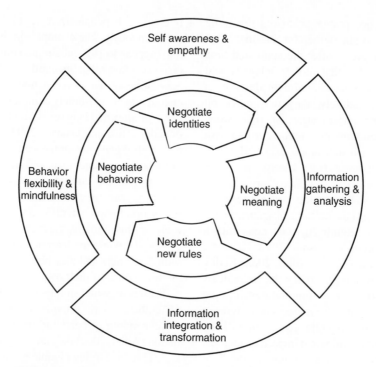

**Figure 26.3   Skills and abilities for negotiating interactions**

knowledge, managers must learn to learn in context. Much of the work done inside and, we argue, between organizations, requires learning in context (Brown and Duguid, 1991). To learn in context, managers must learn how to learn from and make sense of varied and changing environments (Schwandt, 2005), learn how to learn with others, (Brown and Duguid, 1991), and learn how to develop unique mental models (Brown and Duguid, 1991). Management development then must impart to managers learning skills that will help them to comprehend management issues from a global perspective and implement globally sound decisions even when they have not had time to develop deep knowledge of alternate ways of doing and being.

### Required skills and abilities

To successfully negotiate identities, meaning, rules, and behavior, and learn cultures on the fly, managers must develop four essential abilities. These are the ability to recognize and empathize with diverse cultural perspectives;

to gather and analyze information from multiple sources and with global reach; to recognize and choose actions that are culturally acceptable and globally responsible, and to implement these actions in multiple contexts. In the next section, we elaborate the skills and abilities for negotiating intercultural interactions (summarized in Figure 26.3) and provide examples of exercises to support the development of these skills.

*Skills for negotiating identities*. Successfully negotiating identities in cross-cultural interactions requires self-awareness and the ability to empathize. Deep self-awareness allows one to preserve one's own identity when faced with experiences that contradict existing beliefs and values. Empathy toward others allows one to assist the other party in preserving his or her identity.

To preserve ones own identity in the course of an uncomfortable intercultural interaction, one requires a deep self-awareness (Cant, 2004; Adler, 2002). Self-awareness refers to an understanding of one's identity, values, and beliefs about our social position and social interactions. Global managers must understand that they are complex cultural beings and that their values, beliefs, and assumptions are a product of their cultural heritage. A manager who understands that his identity and beliefs are strongly influenced by his cultural experiences is better equipped to separate his sense of worth from an uncomfortable situation. For example, a Japanese manager faced with a tardy Spanish partner may think 'As a Japanese manager, I do not like to wait,' rather than 'only people that are not important are kept waiting.' The first statement preserves his identity, while the second challenges it.

To preserve the other's identity, managers must develop empathy. Empathy refers to the ability to identify and understand others' feelings and motives. Skilled managers empathize with others not based on shared values and assumptions, but based on the common fact that we are all complex cultural beings who behave in accordance with a complex web of cultural values and beliefs.

To be empathetic, managers must understand that others are also complex cultural beings whose actions are a product of deep-seated cultural values and beliefs. When misunderstandings occur, competent global managers will search for cultural explanations of confusing or offensive behavior, before judging it. For example, if an Egyptian counterpart failed to deliver a promised report on time, rather than concluding that he is not dependable, trustworthy, or competent, an empathetic American counterpart would assume that he is acting consistently within own cultural rules and seek a culturally driven explanation. For example, perhaps the Egyptian manager decided indirectly that he could not finish the report. Maybe the American request was not appropriate or the time expectations were not clear. Managers that are open-minded and willing to suspend judgment are more likely to be successful in today's global environment.

To negotiate identities effectively managers must understand that all people are cultural beings. Managers must be aware of their cultural values and empathize with the other,

understanding that he or she is also influenced by culture. Culturally self-aware, empathetic managers can negotiate acceptable identities in which their own and the other's sense of self are preserved. When each party's both parties sense of self is preserved, the interaction is more likely to generate positive feelings and it becomes easier to continue learning.

***Skills for negotiating meaning.*** To successfully negotiate meaning, managers must uncover hidden cultural assumptions to become aware of how culture is shaping the perceptions, expectations, and behaviors of all involved parties. This requires the ability to inquire and advocate (Friedman and Antal, 2005). Managers must inquire, by exploring and questioning, to fully understand their own reasoning and the reasoning of others. Managers must advocate, expressing and supporting, their own thoughts and desires. New meaning is created when managers explore: How do I/you perceive the situation? What do I/you wish to achieve in this situation? Which actions am I/are you taking to achieve this goal? This requires the suspension of judgment, release of previous understanding, and tolerance of the uncertainty that will exist until a new understanding is created.

Engaging in inquiry and advocacy is challenging because it requires that managers explore and uncover their perceptions and the assumptions on which they are based.

Successful managers must be receptive to others' perceptions and willing to depart from the safety of their own previous interpretations in order to construct jointly acceptable meaning. Culturally based preferences influence how individuals accomplish this. For example, in some cultures, individuals prefer to express themselves using open and direct communication, whereas in other cultures individuals are likely to share their assumptions indirectly. While direct communication may be uncomfortable or offensive to indirect communicators, indirect communication may be difficult for direct communicators to fully understand (Hall, 1959, 1981; Hall and Hall, 1990). Additionally, cultural-based preferences may influence the circumstances in which inquiry and advocacy are more likely to be successful. In some cultures formal meetings may be the most preferable setting, while in other cultures it may be late at night over drinks, and in yet in others it may be through informal one-on-one conversations.

When managers successfully combine inquiry with advocacy they share information about their cultural assumptions, the meanings they associate with the issue, and the reasoning for their thinking. Competent managers gather information by observing context, body language, facial expressions and behavioral cues, and actively listening, summarizing and asking questions when and in a manner that is appropriate. Negotiating meaning requires the ability to explore what lies under the surface of the cultural iceberg by asking questions when appropriate, observing others, testing assumptions, and stretching frames of reference. It requires the ability to gather and analyze information from various sources. When managers reflect on an intercultural experience by gathering and analyzing information, it becomes possible to change the mental models that guide their future actions (Schwandt, 2005).

*Skills for negotiating new rules.* To develop new rules, managers must become competent at integrating and transforming information in order to assimilate the information gathered in the negotiating meaning stage into a coherent theory of action. For example, during an intercultural interaction, when a manager answered her phone during a meeting she noticed that her counterpart looked annoyed and signaled to her assistant that she should not be interrupted. This information can be integrated into a theory: the counterpart does not appreciate interruptions. The integrated theory about the other must then be transformed into a theory of action: the managers should avoid interruptions that are not important and always apologize for any interruption that might occur. As this theory is tested and the behaviors are practiced new rules are created and fine-tuned.

*Skills for negotiating new behaviors.* Engaging in new behaviors requires a high level of behavioral flexibility; that is, the ability to engage in different behaviors, to switch

styles, and to accomplish tasks in more than one way (Thomas, 2006). For most individuals it is easier to engage in some behaviors than others (Kolb, 1976; Kolb and Kolb, 2005). Successful managers must recognize those behaviors they find challenging, and compensate with other behaviors. For example, some individuals find it very difficult to communicate indirectly. A successful manager who recognized this limitation might compensate for it by searching for opportunities to discuss issues one on one – where embarrassment is avoided – and by prefacing direct statements with an apology. To be successful, global managers must be mindful of themselves, the other, and the interaction (Thomas, 2006; Thomas and Inkson, 2004). They must pay close attention to their feelings and actions and the actions and reactions of others.

The effectiveness of cross-cultural training has proven difficult to assess. Few organizations assess the effectiveness of their training programs and such assessments are rarely available to researchers (Morris and Robie, 2001). The effectiveness of programs to cultivate a global mindset either through new knowledge structures and mental maps or learning culture on the fly is untested.

The criteria for evaluating cross-cultural training performance suggested by Black and Mendenhall (1990) could prove useful. They find that successful cross-cultural skill training supports cross-cultural skill development, including maintenance of self, fostering relationships with host nationals, and cognitive skills to promote correct perceptions of the host country environment and social systems; cross-cultural adjustment, the development of comfort and proficiency regarding expected behavior, values and assumptions; and work performance. Morris and Robie (2001) add measures of stress and perception of cultural competence, awareness of cultural differences, and technical knowledge of other cultures. It is our contention that the learning cultures on the fly model will enable managers to more rapidly achieve cross-cultural skills and expertise and acceptable work performance in a multicultural business environment than would traditional immersion training or programs designed to create new mental maps alone. An assessment and comparison of the approaches should therefore include longitudinal measures of cross-cultural skill development, cross-cultural adjustment, and improvement in work performance in multiple cultural contexts in order to assess the transfer of learning to multiple contexts and the rapidity of improvements.

## Sample learning exercises

While management development programs cannot support the development sufficient context-specific knowledge to meet the needs of today's managers, they can prepare managers so that they can learn through their intercultural and international experiences. Managers require concrete experience from which to hone their skills in understanding their own culturally based assumptions and negotiating alternative identities, meanings, rules, and behaviors. However, this experience does not have to be *a priori* in another country.

Management development programs can assist managers in developing the above mentioned learning skills in other, simpler ways. For instance, they can provide managers with exposure to a variety of perspectives and contexts and opportunities to try out perspectives and practice applying skills. In most organizations today, multiple values, beliefs, and cultures are represented in the workforce. Managers can also be encouraged to stretch their cultural boundaries by venturing outside of their comfort zone in their own neighborhoods. For example, managers may be asked to spend time in a nearby location, which is 'foreign' to them (Ratiu, 1996). This foreign culture does not have to be from a different nationality, but can be a place frequented by a group of people that share different assumptions about life or live a very different lifestyle. To gain intercultural experience close to home one could attend an unfamiliar religious function, heterosexual individuals could visit a gathering place popular with homosexuals,

and people could visit ethnic neighborhoods, shops or gathering places. These experiences should be designed to allow managers to experience the discomfort of culture shock (Ratiu, 1996) and to encourage them to examine their own cultural assumptions.

Below we describe some simple exercises designed to increase managers' awareness of their learning processes. New conceptual frameworks must be developed over time and a global perspective requires cross-cultural experiences. The exercises described below are aimed at helping managers prepare for learning from such experiences. The complete procedures can be found in the referenced texts.

*Enhancing skills for negotiating identities*. As discussed above, the ability to negotiate identity is predicated on a high degree of self-awareness. In order to successfully negotiate an acceptable identity in a cross-culture interaction, a manager must be aware of his own assumptions, expectations, and values. A manager lacking a high degree of self-awareness will likely become defensive when strongly held beliefs are questioned, feeling a threat to his identity. Only with a high self-awareness can a manager recognize beliefs and habits for what they are and separate them from self-worth. The two examples summarized below are illustrative of management development exercises that can provide cultural self-awareness in the home country, which could then be applied in many cultural contexts. After completing these exercises, participants should be able to identify previously unnoticed cultural values and assumptions:

Exercise 1: Discovering Cultural Values Through Media. Culture is learned, and values and assumptions are disseminated through the media. Select a short segment of a movie or TV show that is 'typical' of your particular culture. Analyze the show looking for values, assumptions, and other cultural characteristics (based on Kohls and Knight, 1994: 55).

Exercise 2: Discovering Communication Styles Through Media. Select ten minutes of a movie or TV show that is typical of your culture and analyze the communication style used in the interactions. How representative do you think this scene is of your culture? Are the communication styles found in the film clip characteristic of you, your friends, and family? (Based on Saphiere et al., 2005: 171).

***Enhancing skills for negotiating meaning.***
Negotiating meaning requires an understanding of how culture is shaping the behaviors and assumptions of parties to an intercultural interaction. Successful managers must learn to gather cultural information through observation and sensitive questioning and then analyze information to determine how the interaction is shaped by culture. The exercise below is designed to enable participants to gather and analyze information and infer culture from observation.

Exercise 3: *Grocery Store Ethnography.* Provide participants with a list of local ethnic grocery stores. Explain that the local grocery store chain is considering oversees expansion. In groups of three, send the participants to the 'foreign country' to learn about grocery shopping habits, observing as much as possible. After the visit, they should write a report and prepare an informal presentation detailing their observations and explaining differences between the foreign and home country. They should consider the following:

1   How is the store organized? How is it different from mainstream American stores?
2   How are food items categorized? Is it easy to find what you want?
3   How are the food items packaged? What differences do you notice in how products are presented? Do they seem attractive to you?
4   Did you find items you did not expect? Did you expect to find items that were not available? How do you think store managers decide what should be offered?
5   Based on your observation, describe the typical shopper? Young, old, male, female? How does this compare with American shoppers?
6   How do people behave? What behaviors seem appropriate and polite? How does this differ from what you would observe in a mainstream American store?
7   Note any other areas in which this store seems to be different from mainstream American stores (adapted from Kluver, 1998).

***Enhancing skills for negotiating rules.***
To be successful in intercultural interactions,

managers must learn to integrate the information they have gathered and analyzed to form new theories of actions. The first exercise below illustrates that group culture is a learned result of group experience, and is a dynamic phenomenon, enacted through interactions with others. Participants will become aware that individuals in a group negotiate rules of behavior even if they are not aware they are doing it. The second exercise provides an opportunity to practice negotiating new rules.

Exercise 4: Emergent Rules. Divide participants into groups of 10–15. The groups must be large enough to require rules of behavior. Give participants 15 to 20 minutes to perform a very ambiguous task. For example, instruct them to 'experience the emergence of group culture' and be prepared to discuss the experience. It may be helpful to assign an observer to each group. The observer should note key decisions, participants, conflict and emergence, and changes in leadership. Debrief the activity as follows, drawing on the observer to highlight examples of the rulemaking process:

1   How did this activity feel? Participants usually find ambiguous group tasks to be very uncomfortable. Explain that the purpose of the exercise was to illustrate our dependence on rules we unconsciously rely on to complete group tasks. The absence of a clear task and leader created a culture-free environment with no rules or norms of behaviors. In such an environment people usually feel very uncomfortable because we do not know what is expected, how we should behave, and if we 'belong' in this group.
2   What happened? (Call on participants first, then observer for elaboration and examples). Address the following:

    •   How did you decide on what to do?
    •   Was there conflict?
    •   What process emerged?
    •   Did anyone emerge as a leader?
    •   What norms or rules emerged?
    •   How did you feel at the end of the exercise?

3   Conclusion. Explain that while each individual comes to a group with a cultural heritage, a new group's culture must be defined. Goals, means, procedures, and rules of interaction must be forged out of common experience, and only once you start understanding each other can you integrate this into a shared culture. The

group reacts to the initial actions or inaction of group members. For example, when someone makes a suggestion, the group reacts to it. This shared emotional experience is the first common experience of the group and defines this group as different in some way from other groups. Inter-actions begin as individuals make suggestions, disagree, or attempt to make decisions or gain agreement. These activities manifest this group's culture. Ways of interacting and understanding are proposed through explanation and example and, if they are accepted and practiced, become taken for granted. (Adapted from Schein, 2004: 64–70). Exercise 5: Negotiating Group Rules. Divide participants into groups of at least six people of as diverse backgrounds as possible (nation-ality, ethnicity, profession, age, gender). Instruct participants to state and analyze their cultural preferences, communication styles, and individual preferences, and come up with rules for interacting and accomplishing team tasks. After some time to work in groups with the agreed-upon rules (approximately half of the available course time works well) revisit this activity. Ask participants to identify their initial assumptions regarding the meaning of the rules, discuss misperceptions, and renegotiate.

***Enhancing skills for negotiating behaviors***. Successfully accomplishing tasks in a variety of cultural contexts requires behavioral flexibility. managers must learn to try to practice new and sometimes uncomfortable behaviors. The following exercise affords the opportunity to practice a new behavior.

Exercise 6: Translating Direct and Indirect State-ments. First, instruct participants to individually read the groups of statements below. Participants should rephrase the first group of direct statements to communicate the same message in a more indirect manner. Participants should decode the second group of sentences, attempting to determine what the speaker means. Next, divide participants into pairs of direct and indirect communicators. Participants may self-select or may assign a com-munication inventory. Have partners evaluate and give feedback to each other's statements. (Adapted from Peace Corps Training Manual).

*Direct statements:*

- I don't think that is such a good idea.
- That's not the point.

- I think we should.
- What do you think, Mr. Cato?
- Those figures are not accurate.
- You are doing that wrong.
- I don't agree.

*Indirect statements:*

- That is a very interesting viewpoint.
- This proposal deserves further consideration.
- I know very little about this, but …
- We understand your proposal very well.
- We will try our best.
- I heard another story about that project.
- Can we move on to the next topic?

## CONCLUSION

In summary, we have argued that success in today's global business arena is predicated in large measure on the ability of managers to understand and then work effectively in multicultural environments. We agree with the growing number of scholars – and managers – who advocate the development of a global mindset. Having said this, however, we argue that prevailing methods of management development are insufficient. Today's managers do not have time to become inculcated with an in-depth knowledge of the cultures to which they will be assigned prior to their assignments. And, although developing new mind maps based on new conceptual frameworks is an ideal goal, achieving this ideal requires considerable time and commitment. The applicability of both of these methods of developing a global mindset to the increasing numbers of frequent flyers or flexpatriates is uncertain.

Toward this end, we suggest that managers and their organizations should increasingly focus on developing broader, flexible learning skills that will enable a capacity to learn cultures 'on the fly.' This developmental strategy provides today's mobile managers with learning and adaptation skills, rather than focused knowledge of particular cultures or regions. While, ideally, these strategies would be combined, today's whitewater business environment frequently simply does not allow managers sufficient time to develop focused, in-depth knowledge, or a global mindset prior to performance. In such cases, having a capacity to learn cultures on the fly – to learn as we go – offers managers the ability to meet the competitive challenges facing them in today's global business environment.

## NOTES

1 Scholars disagree as to whether this general phenomenon should be referred to as a global mindset or cultural intelligence (see, for example, Early, et al., 2007). While advocates of both approaches offer useful arguments in support of their positions, the basic concepts remain the same and we will use the term global mindset in this chapter.

2 This idea has been referred to previously as negotiating reality by Friedman and Berthoin Antal, 2005.

## REFERENCES

Adler, N.J. (2002) *International Dimensions of Organizational Behavior* (4th ed.). Cincinnati, OH: Southwestern.

Adler, N.J. (2008) *International Dimensions of Organizational Behavior* (5th ed.). Cincinnati, OH: Thompson-Southwestern.

Argyris, C. (1995) 'Action science and organizational learning', *Journal of Managerial Psychology*, 10: 20–6.

Ashforth, B.E. and Mael, F. (1989) 'Social identity theory and the organization', *Academy of Management Revieiw*, 14: 20–40.

Berger, P. and Lukeman, T. (1966) *The Social Construction of Reality.* New York: Doubleday.

Bird, A. and Osland, J.S. (2003) 'Teaching cultural sense-making', in N.A. Boyacigiller, R.A. Goodman and M.E. Phillips (eds), *Crossing Cultures: Insights from Master Teachers.* New York, London: Routledge. pp. 89–100

Black, J.S. and Mendenhall, M. (1990) 'Cross-cultural training effectiveness: A review and a theoretical framework for future research', *Academy of Management Review*, 15 (1): 113–36.

Black, H. and Gregersen, B. (2000) 'High impact training: Forging leaders for the global frontier', *Human Resource Management*, 39: 173–84.

Brown, J.S. and Duguld, P. (1991) 'Toward a unified view of working, learning, and innovation', *Oraganization Science*, 2: 40–57.

Cant, A.G. (2004) 'Internationalizing the business curriculum: Developing intercultural competence', *The Journal of American Academy of Business*, September: 177–82.

Casmir, R. 1992 'Third-culture building: A paradigm shift for international and intercultural communication', *Communication Yearbook*, 16: 407–28.

Earley, P.C., and Mosakowski, E. (2000) *Academy of Management Journal*, 43 (1): 26–49.

Early, P., Murnieks, C. and Mosakowski, E. (2007) 'Cultural intelligence and the global mindset', in M. Javidan, R.M. Steers and M.A. Hitt (eds), *The Global Mindset.* Amsterdam: Elsevier. pp. 75–103.

Friedman, V.J. and Berthoin Antal, A. (2005) 'Negotiating reality: A theory of action approach to intercultural competence', *Management Learning*, 36: 69–86.

Gudykunst, W.B. (1998) *Bridging Differences: Effective Intergroup Communication.* Thousand Oaks, CA: Sage.

Hall, E.T. (1959, 1981) *The Silent Language.* New York: Doubleday.

Hall, E.T. and Hall, M.R. (1990) *Understanding Cultural Differences.* Yarmouth, Maine: Intercultural Press.

Holman, D., Pavlica, K. and Thorpe, R. (1997) 'Rethinking Kolb's theory of experiential learning: The contribution of social constructivism and activity theory', *Management Learning*, 28: 135–48.

Javidan, M., Steers, R.M. and Hitt, M.A. (2007) (eds), *The Global Mindset.* Amsterdam: Elsevier.

Kayes, D.C. (2002) 'Experiential learning and its critics: Preserving the role of experience in management learning and education', *Academy of Management Learning and Education*, 1: 137–9.

Klimoski, R. and Mohammed, S. (1994) 'Team mental model: Construct or metaphor?', *Journal of Management*, 20: 403–27.

Kohls, L.R. and Knight, J.M. (1994) *Developing Intercultural Awareness: A Cross-Cultural Training Handbook.* Yarmouth, Maine: Intercultural Press.

Kolb, D.A. (1976) 'Management and the learning process', *California Management Review*, 18: 21–31.

Kolb, A.Y. and Kolb, D.A. (2005) 'Learning styles and learning spaces: Enhancing experiential learning in higher education', *Academy of Management Learning and Education*, 4: 193–212.

Kluver, R. (1998) 'Grocery store ethnography', in T.M. Singelis (ed.), *Teaching about Culture, Ethnicity & Diversity: Exercises and Planned Activities.* Thousand Oaks, CA: Sage. pp. 23–8.

Levy, O., Beechler, S., Taylor, S. and Boyacigiller, N.A. (2007) 'What we talk about when we talk global mindset: Managerial cognition in multinational corporations', *Journal of International Business Studies*, 38: 231–58.

Maznevski, M.L. and Lane, H.W. (2003) 'Shaping the global mindset: designing educational experiences for effective global thinking in action', in N. Boyacigiller, R. Goodman and M. Phillips (eds), *Crossing Cultures: Insights from Master Teachers*. London, UK: Routledge. pp. 171–84.

Mendenhall, M.E. and Stahl, G.K. (2000) 'Expatriate training and development: Where do we go from here?', *Human Resource Management*, 39: 251–65.

Morris, M.A. and Robie, C. (2001) 'A meta-analysis of the effects of cross-cultural training on expatriate performance and adjustment', *International Journal of Training and Development*, 52: 112–25.

Nardon, L. and Steers, R.M. (2007) 'Learning cultures on the fly', in M. Javidan, R.M. Steers and M.A. Hitt (eds), *The Global Mindset*. Amsterdam: Elsevier.

Levy, O., Taylor, S., Boyacigiller, N. and Beechler, S. (2007) 'Global mindset: A review and proposed extensions', in M. Javidan, R.M. Steers and M.A. Hitt (eds), *The Global Mindset*. Amsterdam: Elsevier. pp. 11–41.

Peace Corps Training Manual. http://www.peacecorps.gov/wws/educators/enrichment/culturematters/Ch3/tocCh3.html. Accessed 12-12-17.

Ratiu, I. (1996) 'Simulating culture shock', in Seelye (ed.), *Experiential Activities for Intercultural Learning*. Yarmouth, ME: Intercultural Press. pp. 101–3.

Rinesmith, S.H. (1992) 'Global mindset for global managers', *Training and Development*, 46 (10): 63–9.

Saphiere, D.H., Mikk, B.K. and DeVries, B.I. (2005) *Communication Highwire: Leveraging the Power of Diverse Communication Styles*. Yarmouth, ME: Intercultural Press.

Schwandt, D.R. (2005) 'When managers become philosophers: Integrating learning with sensemaking', *Academy of Management Learning and Education*, 4: 176–92.

Schein, E. (2004) *Organizational Culture and Leadership*. San Francisco, CA: Jossey-Bass.

Srinivas, K.M. (1995) 'Globalization of business and the third world', *Journal of Management Development*, 14 (3): 26–49.

Thomas, D.C. and Inkson, K. (2004) *Cultural Intelligence: People Skills for Global Business*. San Francisco: Berret-Koehler.

Thomas, D.C. (2006) 'Domain and development of cultural intelligence: The importance of mindfulness', *Group and Organization Management*, 31 (1): 78–99.

Ting-Toomey, S. (1988) 'A face negotiation theory', in Y. Kim and W.B. Gudykunst (eds), *Theory in Intercultural Communication*. Newbury Park, CA: Sage. pp. 261–76.

# 27

# Community of Practice or Practices of a Community?

Silvia Gherardi

## Abstract

Ideas travel globally and they take root locally. Following the journey of the ideas engendered by the concept of CoP illustrates how it has taken root differently in different communities of researchers. The original idea of CoP, born within a predominantly anthropological literature, underlined the social and situated dimension of learning. Its translation into management studies shifted its emphasis to the problem of identifying and managing/cultivating the dimension of community. Finally, its translation in the context of on-line communities stressed the social competences necessary to make up for a missing interactive dimension with technology. The debate that developed on the absent, undervalued, or taken-for-granted dimensions of CoPs, had the effect of demonstrating that the types of CoPs vary greatly, and that it is also necessary to distinguish between the theoretical concept and its use to denominate an empirical phenomenon. The chapter discusses a literature, smaller in numerical terms, which proposes a reversal of the concept: from community of practice to practices of a community. The shift from community of practice to practices of a community is more than a play on words. It verbally expresses a change of perspective and epistemology leading towards an extension of the initial formulation toward a wider understanding of it within practice-based studies. This change has been illustrated in relation to the theme of management seen as practice, practices, and practising.

## INTRODUCTION

Ideas travel globally and they take root locally. Their meanings must consequently be sought in the local context and within the community of speakers that gives shape to those ideas. Therefore, to retrace the trajectory that the concept of 'community of practice' (CoP) has followed since 1991, when it first appeared, until the debate in progress today, we may reconstruct how its meaning has changed with its gradual incorporation into local discourses.

The concept of CoP has been crucial in giving impetus to the diversified field of research and theory which goes by the name of 'practice-based studies'. The term initially served to communicate in concise form a complex theorization which sought to shift the debate from cognitive theories of learning and knowledge to social theories. The great success enjoyed by the term upon its appearance was due to the metaphor on which it rested, namely that the community should replace the individual as the learning subject and the repository of knowledge as a collective heritage. The collective subject thus became the source of agency, and knowledge was not necessarily confined to the head and mental mechanisms of an individual. In this image, the social coincided with the collective, even if strictly speaking a social theory of learning (Bandura, 1986) is related as much to the individual as to the collective. In organization studies, however, the term CoP took hold because it immediately communicated the ideas that communities learn and that an organization can be considered a community of communities.

The harshness, at times excessive, with which the term was subsequently criticized paradoxically contributed to its diffusion and operationalization as a key to interpretation of organizational development. Now, some time after that wave of criticism, the term CoP must be credited for opening the way for a strand of research which – through the controversies provoked among scholars of learning and knowledge in organizations – has led to what is today termed the 'practice turn', and which gathers scholars from diverse disciplinary backgrounds around rediscovery of the concept of practice as a form of learning and practical knowledge as a situated activity.

Some scholars wonder whether, in this process of diffusion and appropriation that has shifted attention from the first term – community – to the second – practice – the concept has not lost its original sense and its heuristic capacity as well. Whilst the worry that the original notion has been traduced or abandoned is legitimate, it is difficult to give a non-ideological answer to this question. Perhaps a new controversy is imminent, but if we consider a disciplinary field as a conversation in progress, in which a plurality of voices and points of view participate, we can see that this conversation unfolds unpredictably. We can thus seek to answer the question by tracking the voices taking part in this debate

and thereby reconstruct the scenario in which this conversation takes place.

Therefore, unlike an exegetic method whose purpose is to reconstruct the 'original' meaning of a text, I shall use a method inspired by the metaphor of translation (Ricoeur, 2004) and based on the image of the journey of ideas (Czarniawska and Joerges, 1995; Czarniawska and Sevón, 1996) and material-semiotic change in their meanings as an effect of local translation, as in the tradition of actor-network theory (Latour, 1987).

I shall first reconstruct the cultural context which gave shape to the concept of CoP within the community of anthropologists/educationalists addressed by the work of Lave and Wenger. I shall then move to analysis of how the concept has travelled and how it has been appropriated by the community of management scholars; and then, as the final stage of the trajectory, how it is used by those who study virtual communities as empirical objects of research. This analytical approach will contextualize the three debates in relation to the knowledge interests of scholars: the empirical terrain of research, who/what constitutes 'the Other' from which the concept differs, and in comparison to which it acquires identity. The aim is to show the fertility of the concept, also in light of the criticisms brought against it, but above all to propose a reversal of the concept whereby the emphasis shifts from communities to situated practices.

I therefore intend to argue that the change from CoP to PoC (practices of a community) continues the debate in progress by shifting attention away from the acting subject to the practices that perform a situated subjectivity. The heuristic fertility of this reversal will be illustrated in relation to management as practice, practices, and practising.

## CoP IN THE LEARNING LITERATURE

Few scholars remember that, within the debate between science and technology, the term CoP has an antecedent in the expression 'community of practitioners' (Constant II, 1984), which denotes the locus of technological knowledge nurtured and reproduced by the developers of a particular technology.

It is instead customary to date the origin of the term CoP to the book by Lave and Wenger (1991) titled *Situated Learning* and subtitled *Legitimate Peripheral Participation*. The idea is certainly contained in the book, but it is not given the salience that it subsequently acquired. Already in their acknowledgements, Lave and Wenger write:

> the idea of exploring and developing the notion of legitimate peripheral participation would not have happened in any other context but that in which we were both working in 1988: the Institute for Research on Learning in Palo Alto, California. (Lave and Wenger, 1991: 25)

These first lines therefore express the knowledge interest which motivates the authors – the process of learning as a trajectory of participation – and its local embeddedness in a context of scholars concerned, according to the acknowledgements, with cultural psychology (Cole, 1996), activity theory (Engeström, 1987), and history of technology and distributed cognition (Mukerji, 1983).

Moreover, the book was published as part of a series significantly titled *Learning in Doing: Social, Cognitive, and Computational Perspectives* edited by Roy Pea and John Seely Brown. Previously published in the series had been the book by Newman et al. (1989) on cognitive change in school, the book by Suchman (1987) on plans and situated action, and the collection by Chaiklin and Lave (1993) on the theme of understanding practice.

The two editors write in their foreword (page 11) that: 'the *situated* (emphasis in the original) nature of learning, remembering, and understanding is a central fact. It may appear obvious that human minds develop in social situations, and that they use the tools and representational media that culture provides to support, extend, and reorganise mental functioning'. They continue by declaring that cognitive theories of knowledge representation and educational practices (both at school and in the workplace) are inadequate to interpret our relations with the objects

and technologies that mediate knowledge. These few words enable us to contextualize the concept of CoP within a vision of situated learning, and also to identify how the same concept of situatedness then acquired a twofold meaning of situated-in-social-situations and situated-in-materiality, that is, in the instruments that mediate with the external world. Explanation of how the new ICT technologies change the ways in which we know and understand is stated as being one of the aims of the series.

When we then read the excellent foreword by William Hanks (an anthropologist) we find who/what constitutes 'the Other' of the concept of CoP more clearly expressed: namely the context from which the book intends to distance itself, and from which it assumes meaning by difference. This is the cognitive theory of learning. Hanks (1991: 13) writes that Lave and Wenger's work is interesting 'because it located learning squarely in the process of co-participation, not in the heads of individuals'.

If we therefore circumscribe the birth of the idea of CoP to its historical-cultural context, we note how it differs on the one hand from cognitive theories of learning and on the other from the conception of learning as individual learning. Hence, by means of this concept a shift is accomplished both with respect to where learning takes place (in the community, not in the head) and in respect to who learns (the community as a collective subject, not the individual).

The notion of community of practice emphasizes that the process of learning is at once social and cognitive:

> a community of practice is an intrinsic condition for the existence of knowledge, not least because it provides the interpretive support necessary for making sense of its heritage. (Lave and Wenger 1991: 98)

Lave and Wenger postulate a close relationship between knowledge, the technology of practice and the culture of that practice:

> Knowing is inherent in the growth and transformation of identities and it is located in relations among

practitioners, their practice, the artifacts of that practice, and the social organization and political economy of the communities of practice. (1 p. 22)

If the historical-cultural context in which an idea develops is important for tracing its pedigree, equally important is the research context that has constituted the terrain from which the idea has grown. Lave and Wenger develop their argument by analyzing five cases of apprenticeship: Yucatec midwives, Vai and Goia tailors, naval quartermasters, meat cutters, and non-drinking alcoholics. This gives rise to the notion that learning through apprenticeship is a matter of legitimate peripheral participation, and this term is used as a synonym for situated learning, where 'learning is an integral and inseparable aspect of social practice' (Lave and Wenger, 1991: 31). The authors are concerned with the process whereby novices become full practitioners through participation – as a way of belonging – to a community of practices. Their social theory of learning was concerned with extending the notion of learning outside schooling and outside traditional places, and also Brown and Duguid's (1991) understanding of CoP stresses the 'non-canonical' nature of learning.

We may therefore conclude that the idea of CoP in the literature on situated learning 'concerns the process by which newcomers become part of a community of practice' (Lave and Wenger, 1991: 29). And as Fox (2006: 428) noted, learning is a reciprocal relation between persons and practices because as learners move towards full participation, the practice itself is in motion.

## CoP IN THE KNOWLEDGE MANAGEMENT LITERATURE

How did the term CoP travel to management literature, and how in so travelling did its meaning change? In order to clarify this process, I shall refer to an article by Wenger (2000) and one by Wenger and Snyder (2000), which show how the author,

having left the Palo Alto institute to become a consultant, collaborated with authors of diverse disciplinary backgrounds to produce a book titled *Cultivating Communities of Practice: A Guide to Managing Knowledge* (Wenger et al., 2002).

Wenger's 1998 book began with description of an insurance claims processing office as a CoP and highlighted its various distinctive features: sustained mutual relationships, shared ways to engage in doing things together, rapid propagation of innovation, mutual defining identities, local lore, a shared discourse reflecting a certain perspective on the world, and others besides. Wenger argues that organizations always participate in, and are constituted by, such social learning systems. From this springs the fixation of many empirical researchers who, on the basis of the features described by Wenger, have debated the issue of whether or not a certain set of workers can be defined a community of practice, assuming that the term CoP designates an entity endowed with 'real' existence. Of course, Wenger is much more cautious than his followers, but he nevertheless leaves a margin of ambiguity in his work.

In fact, Wenger writes that a CoP is not a stable or static entity, that it evolves over time, that its existence may not be evident to its members, and that it should not be reified. He also maintains that management cannot establish a CoP but only facilitate its spontaneous emergence. Nevertheless the analytical framework that he later developed (Wenger, 2000: 227–8) for managerial purposes is built on a conception of CoP as a mechanism through which knowledge is held, transferred, and created.

He introduces three distinct 'modes of belonging' through which this learning process takes place, and each of which contributes a distinct aspect to the evolution and social coherence of a CoP:

- engagement: doing things together, talking, producing artifacts;
- imagination: constructing an image of ourselves, of our communities, and of the world, in order to

orient ourselves to reflect on our situation, and to explore possibilities;

- alignment: making sure that local activities are sufficiently aligned with other processes so that they can be effective.

Each mode establishes a distinct foundation for the community, creates a distinct kind of bridge across boundaries between practices, develops a distinct aspect of identity, and requires a different kind of work. Wenger then uses this foundation to examine three structuring elements of social learning systems: communities of practice, boundary processes among these communities, and identities as shaped by participation in these systems. About each of these elements he asks three questions (and produces three 3 × 3 tables): Why focus on it? Which way is up: that is, how to construe progress in this area? And finally, what is do-able, that is, what are the elements of design that one can hope to influence?

On being translated to the managerial literature, CoP becomes a concept used to enable managers to understand and intervene in knowledge management processes. Communities of practice add value to organizations in the following ways (Wenger and Snyder, 2000: 140–1):

- they help drive strategy,
- they start new lines of business,
- they solve problems quickly,
- they transfer best practices,
- they develop professional skills,
- they help companies recruit and retain talent.

In the title of their article the authors define CoPs as 'the new frontier'. And from what CoPs 'do' one can reconstruct what they 'are', namely organizational forms. And as such they are compared to formal work groups, project teams, and informal networks, with which they share forms of complementarities:

Communities of practice are emerging in companies that thrive on knowledge. The first step for managers now is to understand what these communities are and how they work. The second step is to realize that they are the hidden fountainhead of knowledge development and therefore the key to

the challenge of the knowledge economy. The third step is to appreciate the paradox that these informal structures require specific managerial efforts to develop them and to integrate them into the organization so that their full power can be leveraged. (Wenger and Snyder, 2000: 145)

With these words the authors conclude their article, and from these words we may infer who/what is 'the Other' of CoP (once the concept has been translated into the managerial literature) that define its identity by difference. This 'Other' is disorder, that cannot be managed. But 'management' of CoP is a contradiction in terms.

Although defined in the terms of a paradox, it is only an apparent paradox because a management cannot form a CoP, it can only cultivate one. The numerous successes achieved in the nurturing of managers testify that CoPs are manageable and that their 'Others' are unmanageable formations.

## CoP IN THE ON-LINE COMMUNITIES LITERATURE

Even if it is difficult to define what is and what is not an on-line community, since they are so disparate, I shall try to make a reference to the vast literature around them without entering into details.

The literature on on-line communities has enthusiastically appropriated the idea of the CoP in that many themes of interest – such as the learning and sharing of knowledge – are shared, to the point, indeed, that it is difficult to distinguish which community has influenced the other. It becomes easier to see the intersections when we bring to light who/what constitutes 'the Other' of the concept of CoP in this literature. When communities of practice are virtual communities, their 'Other' is face-to-face interaction and the relative sociality (trust, social capital, 'warm' communication, and so on). It is evident therefore that the empirical research object is constituted by those communities which meet only on-line or have mixed modes of on-line and off-line collaboration. The research questions are whether or not these can be called communities of practice, and what facilitates or obstructs their becoming 'communities' in the absence of face-to-face interaction. The objective is often the implementation of some knowledge management device which, to work efficiently, requires a community that has new technology among its consolidated practices.

To summarize the debate within this community of scholars, one must start from the role of technologies in relation to the potential social connections:

- work groups increasingly use ICT technologies to collaborate 'normally', so that the sharing of information and knowledge takes place on an everyday basis;
- ICT technologies make it possible to work at a distance in a relatively stable and continuous way, or in more sporadic and limited form, and the groups thus brought into in contact may constitute a CoP;
- ICT technologies are also used outside work, and around them communities which share interests and engage in intense social exchanges are spontaneously developed;
- technology itself, with its variability that facilitates synchronous interaction (telephony, whiteboard, slides, and video links), asynchronous interaction (e-mails, discussion boards, e-mail lists, wikis and blogs), and access to stored information (file sharing, document archives, newsletters), and different forms of interaction (talking, writing, listening), can differently mediate the formation or otherwise of a CoP.

These four themes are treated in the literature in regard to a single question: is the quality of knowledge generation in proximate communities superior to that associated with distanced interactions? Clearly, the management of distributed communities involves much more than choosing the right technological tools. For example, in a detailed survey of the literature on Virtual Communities of Practice (VCoP) Dubé et al. (2005) describe 21 structuring characteristics (i.e. stable elements that can be used to describe a VCoP) and find that each community has different strengths

and challenges during its life development and therefore needs a specific level of organizational and managerial support. The aim of their work is to counter the 'one size fits all' model of advice on how to develop intentionally formed VCoP and to show how each has a unique 'personality', and therefore how to identify strategies, challenges, and practices contingent upon their specific characteristics. We may conclude from this study that the initial question – which assumes interaction in the CoP to be the standard model with which VCoPs should be compared – is badly formulated. Consequently, the comparison between exclusively on-line and off-line communities can be better understood if we position both on a continuum, and if we do the same with the idea of sociality. In this regard, the literature review conducted by Amin and Roberts (2006) is careful to distinguish between communities whose purpose is the development of learning and the exchange of knowledge, on the one hand, and those in which learning simply 'happens' on the other.

When learning becomes the purpose of the community, VCoPs are similar to epistemic communities, and they share problems of leadership and management with them. Classic examples are the communities that have formed around open source (Hakken, 2003) or the communities of software developers (Faraj and Sproull, 2000), or the self-help communities which use the Web to communicate on a theme of common interest (Josefsson, 2005).

As in all knowledge teams whose work is technologically mediated, the most crucial resource is expertise, but its mere presence is not enough to guarantee success. Skills and knowledge interdependencies must be effectively managed through expertise coordination. In fast-response organizations, Faraj and Xiao (2005) distinguish between expertise coordination in the form of reliance on protocols, community of practice structuring, plug and play teaming and knowledge sharing, and what they call dialogic coordination practices, i.e. epistemic contestation, joint sense making, cross-boundary interventions, and protocol breaking. Research in this area is most innovative when it discards the concept of CoP as an entity in itself, and with it the problem of how to turn a group into a community, and returns to the initial view of learning as a situated activity. In this regard, the study of the spontaneous and often self-managed communities that Preece (1999) calls 'empathic communities' – like the medical support group that she studied – focuses on the practices mediated by the ICT technologies which perform empathy by providing emotional as well as informational support. It therefore contributes to the literature on the CoP by showing that instrumentality is not enough to hold a CoP together. This kind of analysis also furnishes better understanding of the many failures of technological systems for knowledge management (McDermott, 1999), which on their own are unable to produce the socio-technical system that makes them work.

We may therefore conclude that the original idea of CoP in a predominantly anthropological literature underlined the social and situated dimension of learning. Its translation into management studies has shifted its emphasis to the problem of identifying and managing/cultivating the dimension of community. Finally, its translation in the context of on-line communities has stressed the social competences necessary to make up for a missing interactive dimension with technology, but without forgoing the managerial dream of being able to create and manage a CoP by simple diktat or via technology.

## CRITICISMS TO COMMUNITIES OF PRACTICE AND BEYOND

The concept of CoP has been much debated and harshly criticized, also because, as just said, its translation from one disciplinary context to another has created an ambiguity which has left ample room for the iconoclasm long characteristic of organization studies. The main reason adduced for abandoning

the concept of CoP is that it has become the symbol of a 'new type' of governance of corporate knowledge – management-by-communities (Amin and Cohendet, 2004), and especially management-of-communities. And the blanket use of the term has weakened the original conceptualization of CoPs in relation to learning and knowing situated in all kinds of social practices.

Paradoxically, the criticisms have contributed to the vitality of the concept and they can be regarded as suggestions to continue the translation of the concept of CoP, if we no longer require it to have a single and original meaning.

These criticisms have been well documented (Handley et al., 2006; Roberts, 2006) and I will now summarize the main points brought against the term 'CoP', and then make the radical proposal of overturning the concept so that its use can continue in a next translation.

The themes that have been contested can be summed up as follows:

*Community.* the concept itself of community has been harshly criticized because it has been assumed in the non-problematic sense of synonymous with a harmonious, welcoming place where conflict neither exists nor is allowed. Bauman's (2001) critique of the contemporary society that expresses a need for community is often invoked to criticize the concept itself of community as a place of natural solidarity. In sociology 'the Other' of the concept of community, understood as a common, subjectively felt sense of belonging, is society – meaning a convergence of interests, conventions, contracts, and institutions. Opposed to mechanical solidarity, therefore, is the organic solidarity based on institutions, while conflict (or its absence) is a dimension independent from the community/society pairing. If we return to Weber or Marx, struggle is conceived as typical of human society in its forms of *Gemeinschaft* or *Gesellschaft*. The term 'community' within the concept of CoP has been widely discussed in its various meanings by Lindkvist (2005), who proposes that the term CoP should be reserved for the occupational communities studied by Lave, in which apprenticeship and the master/pupil relationship establish a stable sociality. In this context of 'tightly knit' and 'value-laden' sociality, knowledge is mainly embodied and homogeneous knowledge. Instead, Lindkvist proposes the concept of 'collectivity of knowledge' to denote project groups and similar collectives which meet for limited periods of time, and among which knowledge is diversified and distributed. These project groups are increasingly common in contemporary organizations. They raise problems for the management of specific knowledge specifications and are fundamentally different from occupational communities.

Other authors who have criticized the concept of community (Contu and Willmott, 2003; Cohendet et al., 2004; Handley et al., 2006) have done so mainly to move from the absence of conflict to the absence of the power dimension in the concept of CoP.

*Power.* The significance of power in shaping the legitimate peripheral participation of a newcomer was present in the early work by Lave and Wenger, as Contu and Willmott (2003) document in detail, but it subsequently faded. For instance, taking the classic study of Orr (1996) on photocopier repair technicians, Contu and Willmott reinterpret its description by highlighting power dynamics. Marshall and Rollinson (2004) likewise stress the idea of the negotiation of meanings present in the concept of CoP, but they are excessively consensual and do not consider power relations within organizations or between these and external sources of knowledge/power. The distinction that Yanow (2004) draws between local knowledge and expert knowledge is indicative of a line of inquiry, which investigates power in relation to knowledge, learning, and the development of competence. Yet another example is the endeavour to manage professional health-care communities (Swan et al., 2002) through the rhetorical use of the concept of CoP as a source of identity proposed from outside. This set of criticisms on the one hand stresses the close link between knowledge and power (reprising Foucault's conception of

knowledge/power), and on the other prompts reconsideration of the link between trust and knowledge sharing.

*Trust.* The main criticism in this case concerns the fact that the relation between trust and knowledge sharing is taken for granted, without considering that trust is not an attribute of a group, nor an automatic social effect, but the contingent product of a social construction of trust. As such, it relates to power dynamics within the group between newcomers and old-timers (Carlile, 2004), and between workers and management (Coopey, 1995).

*Participation.* How does participation differ from socialization? Centring on this theme in particular are the criticism and proposal of Handley et al. (2006, 2007), who contest the use of the concept of CoP as an apprenticeship model that leads linearly from being a novice to being an expert. Their intention is to show that the concepts of participation and practice are connected, and that both are linked to the idea of identity development as both an individual and social process with uncertain outcomes. Also based on this idea is the proposal that the CoP should be viewed in light of the concepts of habitus and predisposition (Mutch, 2003). Hence, if participation is to be viewed as a discretionary, negotiative, and path-dependent process, the theme of the extent to which the CoP reproduces the same knowledge and the extent to which it innovates through constant adaptation becomes a dynamic way to look at the concept of CoP.

*Size, spatial reach, duration.* There are limits to the size of the communities, as well as to their spatial reach. Amin (2002) suggests that location, proximity, and distance should be considered relationally, rather than as geographically determined. Similarly there are 'fast' communities – at times of accelerating business – and 'slow' ones when identity, trust, and community take time to develop. These criticisms suggest that CoPs as empirical phenomena are highly differentiated along all the dimensions considered. They should therefore be analyzed in their specificities and variability (Roberts, 2006). Or the concept of CoP should be abandoned for different definitions (collectivities, networks, configurations) that focus on the nature of knowledge and the processes of its creation and treatment.

The debate that developed on the absent, undervalued, or taken-for-granted dimensions of CoPs, and sought them empirically in specific communities of practice, had the effect of demonstrating that the types of CoPs vary greatly, and that it is necessary to distinguish between the theoretical concept and its use to denominate an empirical phenomenon.

## FROM THE CoP TO PoC

Now that the fashion has passed, and with it the persuasive power of the rhetoric associated with the label CoP, I shall discuss a literature, smaller in numerical terms, which proposes a reversal of the concept.

The proposal to reverse the emphasis on the two terms has been present for some time in the literature (Brown and Duguid, 2001; Gherardi et al., 1998; Roberts, 2006; Swan et al., 2002). It has recently given rise to a broader debate which has rediscovered within organizational studies the heuristic value of practices and envisages a 'practice turn' in the social sciences (Schatzki et al., 2001).

The idea of reversing the concept has been motivated as follows:

> Our emphasis is hence on the term 'practice' [...] than on that of 'community': knowledge, activity, and social relations are closely intertwined, and in a sense the common activity provides the medium and the resource for both the reflective linguistic act of generating a 'sense of community', and the inevitable conflicts and power struggles between those who know and those who don't. (Gherardi et al., 1998: 278)

Other authors have argued for a shift of emphasis to practices (Brown and Duguid, 2001) or shown that such a shift also allows development of a different way of considering the concept: for instance

as a linguistic artifact that sustains both a rhetoric and a disciplining effect (Swan et al., 2002).

The concept of practice and practices is just as problematic as that of community, since it has a distant origin and therefore has been subjected to many interpretations and contrasting definitions. If it becomes fashionable in organization studies, it may suffer the same fate as the concept of community. Consequently, in order to argue that it can contribute to the theme of knowledge as situated activity, one must explain how the concept of practice has taken shape within a theoretical sensibility informed by actor-network theory, and how this in turn continues on Foucauldian themes.

In my discussion thus far, I have deliberately neglected the crucial contribution of actor-network theory (ANT), a conceptual vocabulary that constitutes a form of 'relational materialism' committed to the project of understanding how humans and non-humans are connected in contingent, material, and processual ways in networks. The author who has most effectively developed ANT in connection with practice is Fox (1997, 2000), who, while acknowledging the importance of learning *in situ* in the context of work practices rather than in the classroom, argues that the emphasis that situated learning theory places on the social context of learning is problematic and ambiguous.

In fact, Lave and Wenger view learning as situated, but they assume a realist ontology of learning: although learning is situated in social relations and not in the heads of individuals, they have no doubt that it 'happens' even when asserting that 'agent, activity, and the world mutually constitute each other' (ibid.: 33). Their concern is to distance themselves from a model of scholastic and cognitive learning in which persons receive a body of factual knowledge about the world and introduce a more active and more global conception of learning. But the fact remains that – as Fox (1997) stresses – their study is situated within a modernist project. Consistent with a modernist project is the view of context as pre-given, although the effects of objective social structures are not determined but take shape within socio-economic relations. On the other hand, the concept of context as 'emergent' is more in keeping with a post-modernist project. 'In the postmodern view, "context" is no longer "out there" in the messy, complex surface of an objective world; rather, that very surface complexity and confusion are a projection of language itself, the inconsistencies of its classifications, taxonomies, dichotomies, and more' (Fox, 1997: 741). Both Fox (1997), Fox and Grey (1999) and other authors such as Contu and Willmott (2000) and Gherardi (2000) have pointed out an ambiguity in Lave and Wenger's work: the ambiguity between realist and constructionist assumptions, with respect to consideration of the context as sometimes pre-given and sometimes emergent, or as a two-faced Janus (Contu, 2000). The difference can also be expressed as a question of emphasis, depending on whether use of the term 'community of practice' gives priority to the 'community' or to the activity comprised in the 'practice'. Stressed in the former case is that community constitutes the context and the community pre-exists its activities. In the latter, it is the activities themselves that generate a community in that they form the 'glue' which holds together a configuration of people, artefacts, and social relations. Moreover, this shift also changes the emphasis placed on knowledge: in the former case, learning is viewed as access to and the mastering of expert knowledge possessed and nurtured by the community; in the latter, the attention is directed at the practical knowledge contextually employed during performance of a practice. Knowledge, therefore, is not an 'asset' of the community, but rather an activity (a 'knowing'), and an activity that itself constitutes the practice ('knowing-in-practice').

There are therefore three types of relations established between practices and knowledge (Gherardi, 2006: 38):

- A relation of *containment*, in the sense that knowledge is a process that takes place within situated practices. On this view, practices are constituted as objective entities (in that they have been objectified) about which practitioners already have knowledge (i.e. they recognize them as practices) and which comprise bits and pieces of knowledge anchored in the material world and in the normative and aesthetic system that has elaborated them culturally.
- A relation of *mutual constitution*, in the sense that the activities of knowing and practising are not two distinct and separate phenomena; instead, they interact and produce each other.
- A relation of *equivalence*, in the sense that practising is knowing in practice, whether the subject is aware of it or not. Acting as a competent practitioner is synonymous with knowing how to connect successfully with the field of practices thus activated. The equivalence between knowing and practising arises when priority is denied to the knowledge that exists before the moment of its application, so that when applying it something already existent is not performed, but the action instead creates the knowledge formed in the action itself and by means of it.

A shift has therefore come about from considering a CoP as the context where learning takes place to considering how the situated and repeated actions create a context in which social relations among people, and between people and the material and cultural world, stabilize and become normatively sustained.

The contribution that actor-network theory can make to the concept of CoP, through criticism of the conception of 'context', consists in showing how practices are tightly interwoven to constitute a field of practices or a network of more or less closely connected practices enduring in time and variously sustained by power and material anchoring effects. The community is one of those effects, as well as being a device for the reproduction of the field of practices. It is therefore through the conceptions of power in actor-network theory, which derives from Foucault, and of materiality, that the concept of CoP has been progressively redefined until it has been reversed.

Both for Foucault and for ANT, power is not a possession, but an effect. It is manifest only when it is used. The same conception is applied to materiality, and it is in this regard that ANT can contribute most to the theory of situated learning, when it allows communities of both humans and non-humans to be treated equally as an ecology of practices (Gherardi and Nicolini, 2005). Knowledge, therefore, is not only in the heads of people but also in the material world that anchors knowledge to the technologies, artifacts, techniques, socio-technical devices that weave a material-semiotic network together. For ANT, 'theorising should not presume the existence of either an objective socio-historical context nor the existence of macro-actors on that stage, rather their existence is what analysis should seek to explain by reference to nests of practice' (Fox, 2000: 858).

To illustrate how practices are tightly interconnected and form a texture (Gherardi, 2006) – that is, a fabric of connections in action – I shall borrow an example from Swidler (2001):

- Take a hypothetical architect's plan for a house. Long before the architect can draw up plans for the house, constraints on the possible design for the house are built into taken-for-granted practices which involve standard kinds of materials (bricks, door frames, steel girders, etc.). Like composers who cannot write music for which there are no instruments (Becker, 1982), architects assume the standard kind of materials that are available, and ignore the potentially infinite set of materials that are unavailable.
- The plans that architects draw up are inevitably incomplete. Even when the competence of a contractor or a builder is brought in, the plan for a house leaves most of what will be required to build it unspecified: the skill of the craft-workers, the ways in which different workers with different specialities coordinate their activities, what they consider to be the appropriate uses of standard objects and materials.
- Behind the plan lie other, almost invisible, practices. The architect's knowledge of what a house is, how people use one, whether sleep should take place in a room different from those reserved for eating or washing. Numerous cultural differences are inscribed in such a common, universal activity as living in a house.

- Also lying behind the plan is the set of professional practices against which the architect's aesthetic judgement is compared and which furnishes the vocabulary of meanings with which s/he works in order to produce the aesthetic effect valued by his/her professional community.
- Another set of practices links the architect to the client: who decides what, how payments should be made, who and how to own a house. A large set of practices then link both the architect and the client to the capitalist market economy, mobilizing the work of other persons and institutions.

The example is a telling one for at least two reasons. First, it prompts reflection on the role of ideas versus material factors in causal explanations, and on the interpenetration of the material and ideational worlds (against idealism). Second, it raises the question as to whether in a field of practices the researcher should abandon him/herself to an endless deferral of nested practices, or if in concrete instances of practices there are some which anchor, control, or organize others. In the case of the house, practices associated with capitalism, such as paying for a house or owning it, are more enduring and powerful than others.

We may therefore conclude from the above example that a field of practices arises in the interwoven texture that connects practices to each other, and that this texture is held together by a certain number of practices which provide anchorage for others.

Management as a set of managerial practices, as a profession, as professional knowledge, and as a situated activity can be studied as practice, practices, and practising. The professions are in fact formed to establish boundaries around a body of knowledge. They use the term 'practice' as in the current usage of medical or legal practice to denote how the practices of which it is made up correspond to a shared and normatively sustained mode of practising it, and how, with the support of the state, the professional practice regulates access and the correct ways to participate in and exercise specialist expertise (Abbott, 1988).

## MANAGEMENT AS PRACTICE, PRACTICES, AND PRACTISING

The final translation of the concept of CoP has taken place in the literature given the label of 'practice-based studies', where different strands of analysis share a predominant interest in situated activity and the role of technologies and artefacts in mediating the relationship with knowledge and the world (Gherardi, 2000). Once the reversal of the concept of CoP has been accomplished, what changes come about in research interests, and what problems are raised by the reversal? I shall provide an example of how the interpretative frame can change by examining some research studies, without implying that the respective authors work within the frame that I propose, or that their interests are in some way connected with the concept of CoP. My intention is to show how the overturning of the concept causes an inversion in research approach, and how from the interest that it was presumed that managers should have in managing CoPs as 'objects' comprising knowledge useful to them, one moves to enquiring what type of CoPs managers are if we analyze the situated practices that construct 'management'.

If we take the term 'practice' in the singular, it denotes a body of theoretical knowledge, often institutionalized, which is translated into a set of 'knowledges' normatively sustained by customs (a praxis). In regard to management as practice, we can enquire how social support is given to this body of knowledge, which only recently, and not in all the Western countries, has been recognized as a scientific discipline and therefore worthy to be taught at universities and formally transmitted to aspiring managers. There are many ways to answer this question, but one of them consists of looking at situated practices of knowledge transmission.

Let us therefore consider the analysis conducted by Sturdy et al. (2006) on management education, in the UK, on the perceived relationship between managers' formal studying and their day-to-day organizational practices – what they call learning into practice. Sturdy et al.'s analysis is based on managers studying part-time on a two-year Executive MBA programme and on their perception of knowledge transfer. Their thesis is that what is considered to be 'explicit management knowledge is more the development of a form of self-confidence, but a form which both disguises and reproduces the fragility of knowledge and identity' (Sturdy et al., 2006: 844). Gaining an MBA involves performance of 'the trick of self-confidence', a term that the authors employ to refer to the identity work that provides the student with 'an existential tool of management control, often fuelled by career progression and the material privilege it brings' (idem.: 854).

We already know from the literature on anticipatory socialization (Becker et al., 1961) that what students learn at university before entering a profession is primarily a way to believe, to use language, and to think of the terms of the future professional self that they will develop. What is specific to this work is not so much this process as showing that managerial knowledge and the policies that sustain MBA courses are strategically positioned as a primary conduit for new management ideas and techniques to nourish management practice. In spite of this strategic discourse to funnel explicit learning of managerial ideas into national competitiveness, MBA is a form of therapeutic language training within life projects, sustained by others through specific practices within power relations.

We can see in this example how the shift from CoP to PoC entails a change of perspective that, in the case of institutionalization of the professional knowledge that sustains the identity, asks: what are the situated practices, the organizational forms enacted, and the discursive practices through which managerial knowledge is developed and transmitted?

I now consider management as a set of practices, as specific techniques which have been standardized, disembedded from their country- and time-specific context and rendered generalizable (Brunsson and Jacobsson, 2000; Wilmott, 1997). Through the creation of standards, management knowledge has been reified in forms of quasi-objects: TQM, BPR, JIT, and many others (Grint, 1997) are more than just acronyms, since this black-boxed knowledge materializes in practices. For example, Hodgson and Cicmil (2007) analyze the politics of standards by taking project management as their point of reference. There has in fact been a great expansion of project management as a managerial and organizational technique alternative to the hierarchy outside the domain of the constructions in which they have originated (Lindkvist, 2005), and many authors speak of the 'projectification of society' and also of life (Beck and Beck-Gernsheim, 2002; Lundin and Söderholm, 1998; Midler, 1995). The project, this new 'iron cage' for rationality, which exists ready-made instead of being conceived as being 'constituted by the action of interdependent actors' (Kreiner, 1995: 344), establishes standards and an infrastructure for a technology of control in the workplace. As Bowker and Star (1999) forcefully put it, this infrastructure is a significant site of political and ethical work.

As Hodgson and Cicmil (2007: 445) illustrate, the 'establishment of universal knowledge of this kind implies a loss of a reflexive and embodied rationality in favour of abstract principles and blind faith in universal techniques'. And this has direct consequences both on managerial practice, which restricts the resources of legitimation for the practitioner who wants to be approved, and on the conception of responsibility that they deploy. Standardization, in fact – as Hodgson and Cicmil (ibid.: 446) conclude – also entails self-disciplinary control, so that the responsibility of project managers may become centred on following the best practices as enshrined in the authorized body of knowledge, and they may lose reflexivity and critical control over their own practices. What has been analyzed in relation to a specific managerial technique extends to all the managerial knowledge reified in black boxes and 'universal' practices.

In this case the reversal of the concepts of CoP in PoC directs attention to the set of practices that constitute management as a set of ready-made utensils, tools, techniques, and discourses waiting to be applied uncritically. Practices in this sense are decontextualized techniques. When we instead view them as situated practices, the attention moves to 'doing-in-situation' to the way in which contextual rationality adapts the activity to the circumstances. In this way we move to 'practising'.

To understand in what situated ways management as a practice and as an institution is reproduced, I shall refer to a classic in the literature: *Moral Mazes* by Jackall (1988). In the large American corporations – those studied by the author, but the analysis applies to many others – one of the main concerns of the manager is to be in the 'right' group, and for this team work is necessary.

In Jackall's (1988: 76–83) anthropological analysis, playing the 'team game' is an activity inspired by the following behavioural principles:

(a)  interchangeability with managers of equivalent level. Corporations discourage specialization as one ascends the hierarchy, and interchangeability is not so much a general ability as a flexibility of perspective that allows rapid adaptation to external and internal demands;

(b)  a large amount of time spent at the office. This kind of ritual forges the social bonds and professional intimacy which make group work possible and gives reliability to everyday interaction;

(c)  playing the team game means being considered an effective member of the group, as someone who knows his/her place and does not act the *prima donna*;

(d)  playing the team game means adapting to the ideology of the moment, bowing to the ruling divinity. Bureaucracies enable those who belong to them to act differently, provided they accept the rules and the official versions of reality;

(e)  the genuine team player exhibits a cheerful, optimistic, and zealous attitude. Adopting the correct style is a way to reflect the kind of image that makes others feel at ease and to show that one is in harmony with them. It is to display a certain *savoir faire*.

This reference to a classic of the management literature on the great American corporations shows us how the practising of management is realized through what one does, what one is, and what one becomes by doing. The social dimension of networking, the political dimension of alliances, and belonging to managerial teams highlight both the internal fragmentation of the professional community and the ethical choices that sustain the situated practices which make up managerial practice. This example induces us to conclude that managerial identity is formed as an effect of a network of action-interactions grounded in practices and in their practising. In this case, too, the concept is overturned, in that managerial identity is not the source of action but rather the result of it.

The focus on the ethical dimension that sustains practices warrants particular attention, because it enables us to specify a theoretical conception of practices. The debate on business ethics and on the performances of top managers that has filled the pages of newspapers in recent years enables us to see how practices are socially (i.e. culturally, ethically, and aesthetically) sustained.

The easy answers put forward on what has caused the recent rash of corporate wrongdoing perpetuate the mythology of business ethics management. This is what Treviño and Brown (2004) describe in the form of five myths:

1 It's easy to be ethical! Therefore if it is easy, it does not need to be managed.
2 Unethical behaviour in business is simply the result of 'bad apples'! The implication is that if we rid the organization of one or more bad apples, the problem will be solved.
3 Ethics can be managed through formal ethic codes and programs! Creating a formal program, by itself, does not guarantee effective ethics management.
4 Ethical leadership is mostly about leader integrity! The implication being that ethical behaviour is a matter of individual characteristics.
5 People are less ethical than they used to be! The implication is that unethical conduct is nothing new and maybe that the stress on ethics is just another managerial fad.

In light of these myths on ethics and ethical management we can discuss the difference between conceiving practices as a set of activities that form a pattern, and look at practices as ways to do the things that respond to criteria of good or bad practice. In the latter case, a practice is such when it is reproduced on a customary base within a network of human and non-human actors which sustains, disputes, rewards, and punishes a certain way of doing things. This stress on the normative accountability of practices directs research to questions about how the social criteria evaluating practices and the instruments of practices are formed, and about how the accountability of practices is constantly disputed within the community of practitioners as consonance and dissonance among ways to appraise and to sustain practices (Gherardi and Nicolini, 2002). It produces situated identities and engenders change in the practices themselves as they are being repeated.

## CONCLUSION

Following the journey of the ideas engendered by the concept of CoP has illustrated how it has taken root differently in different communities of researchers. The researchers inspired by this concept have focused on sometimes very distant thematic areas (learning as situated activity, management of communities as management of the knowledge possessed by the community, interactions and cooperation at a distance in virtual communities), but they are linked by the common theme of what constitutes practical knowledge.

It often happens in scientific debate that a term which becomes dominant in a certain period and opens up a strand of research, then dwindles away. The criticisms made of the concept of CoP have weakened it by showing its limitations; but at the same time they have contributed to its translation into something else. As the concept has circulated, it has been put to different uses and has exhibited good interpretative flexibility. This process has given rise to a line of inquiry which, in reversing the concept, has led to the contemporary debate on the 'practice turn', or to the field called 'practice-based studies'.

The shift from community of practice to practices of a community is more than a play on words. It verbally expresses a change of perspective and epistemology. In fact, placing the stress on the community implies the ontological priority of the subject as the source of action and knowledge, while placing the stress on practices implies that the becoming of the subject results from the connections-in-action among the material world, knowledge, and the actors present, according to a principle of symmetry (Latour, 1987). The subject is thus decentred, ecologically embedded in a network of interactions among humans and non-humans (Strati, 2007).

The criticisms brought from an actor-network theory perspective against the concept of CoP have made it possible to connect it with the emerging debate on practices (Nicolini et al., 2003). The point of convergence is of interest in knowing-in-practice. In fact, since the initial debate on how to dispense with cognitive models of learning, the idea of learning as situated and collective activity has continued in a broader form, where not only learning but knowledge itself is the effect of doing-in-situation. In turn, every doing-in-situation is an expression of a practical expertise that creates connections-in-action. The attention thus shifts to how practical knowledge is enacted in situated contexts of action, and how it changes in relation to the context of action that the action itself creates. Alternatively, if one prefers, one may say that the attention has not moved very much since its first formulation, because the theme of the knowledge produced, nourished, and reproduced in action and through action is still the same. What has perhaps been produced by the debate is a different way of looking at the same problem, and therefore a change in the relation with it. This process of reciprocal redefinition between perspective and object has been illustrated in relation to the theme of management seen as practice, practices, and practising.

For instance, if it is practice, as a body of knowledge institutionalized in a discipline and taught through an educational system, which produces management as its effect, research on knowing-in-practice concentrates on analysis of the ecology of actors, tools, and practices that transmit managerial knowledge and, through it, distribute career opportunities and social positions. If the focus is instead on practices as standardized bodies of knowledge which produce managerial techniques, analysis is conducted on what type of manager is produced (and presupposed) by the use or otherwise of a particular managerial technique. To paraphrase Foucault, we may ask: what is a project manager? Finally, if we consider the activity of practising to be a process inseparable from knowing and doing, we view management as a subjectivity which is a situated effect of the knowledge/power relations that materialize within a system of normative accountability of managerial practices.

## REFERENCES

Abbott, A.W. (1988) *The System of Professions*. The University of Chicago Press.
Amin, A. (2002) 'Spatialities of globalisation', *Environment and Planning A*, 34: 385–99.
Amin, A. and Cohendet, P. (2004) *Architectures of Knowledge: Firms, Capabilities and Communities*. Oxford: Oxford University Press.
Amin, A. and Roberts, J. (2006) 'Communities of practice? Varieties of situated learning', Paper presented at Dime seminar, Durham, October.
Bandura, A. (1986) *Social Foundations of Thoughts and Action*. Englewood Cliffs, NJ: Prentice-Hall.
Bauman, Z. (2001) *Community. Seeking Safety in an Insecure World*. Cambridge: Polity.
Beck, U. and Beck-Gernsheim, E. (2002) *Individualization. Institutionalized Individualism and its Social and Political Consequences*. London: Sage.
Becker, H., Geer, B., Hughes, E.C. and Strauss, A. (1961) *Boys in White. Student Culture in Medical School*. Chicago, IL: University of Chicago Press.
Becker, H. (1982) *Art Worlds*. Berkeley: University of California Press.
Bowker, G. and Star, L.S. (1999) *Sorting Things Out: Classification and its Consequences*. Cambridge, MA: The MIT Press.

Brown, J. and Duguid, P. (1991) 'Orgnizational learning and communities of practice: Toward a unified view of working, learning and bureaucratization', *Organization Science*, 2: 40–57.

Brown, J.S. and Duguid, P. (2001) 'Knowledge and organization: A social-practice perspective', *Organization Science*, 12 (2): 198–213.

Brunsson, N. and Jacobsson, B. (2000) *A World of Standards.* Oxford: Oxford University Press.

Carlile, P.R. (2004) 'Transferring, translating, and transforming: An integrative framework for managing knowledge across boundaries', *Organization Science*, 15 (5): 555–68.

Chaiklin, S. and Lave, J. (1993) *Understanding Practice: Perspectives on Activity and Context.* Cambridge: Cambridge University Press.

Cohendet P., Creplet, P., Diani, M., Dupouet, O. and Schenk, E. (2004) 'Matching communities and hierarchies within the firm', *Journal of Management and Governanc*, 8: 27–48.

Cole, M. (1996) *Cultural Psychology.* Cambridge, MA: Harvard University Press.

Contu, A. (2000) 'L'apprendimento situato e la semiotica della pratica: "nuovi vocabolari" per l'apprendimento organizzativo', *Studi Organizzativi*, 2: 83–106.

Contu, A., Grey, C. and Ortenblad, A. (2003) 'Against learning', *Human Relations*, 56 (8): 931–52.

Contu, A. and Willmott, H. (2000) 'Comment on Wenger and Yanow. Knowing in practice: A "Delicate Flower" in the Organizational Learning Field', *Organization*, 7 (2): 269–76.

Contu, A. and Willmott, H. (2003) 'Re-embedding situatedness: The importance of power relations in learning theory', *Organization Science*, 14 (3): 283–96.

Constant II, E.W. (1984) 'Communities and hierarchies: Structure in the practice of science and technology', in R. Laudan (ed.), *The Nature of Technological Knowledge. Are Models of Scientific Change Relevant?* Dordrecht: Reidel.

Coopey, J. (1995) 'The learning organization, power, politics and ideology', *Management Learning*, 26 (2): 193–214.

Czarniawska, B. and Joerges, B. (1995) 'Winds of change', in S. Bacharach and P. Gagliardi (eds), *Research in the Sociology of Organizations.* Greenwich CT: JAI Press.

Czarniawska, B. and Sevón, G. (eds) (1996) *Translating Organisational Change.* Berlin: de Gruyter.

Dubé, L., Bourhis, A. and Jacob, R. (2005) 'The impact of structuring characteristics on the launching of virtual communities of practice', *Journal of Organizational Change Management*, 18 (2): 145–66.

Duguid, P. (2005) 'The art of knowing: Social and tacit dimensions of knowledge and the limits of the community of practice', *The Information Society*, 21: 109–18.

Engestrom, Y. (1987) *Learning by Expanding: An Activity Theoretical Approach to Developmental Research.* Helsinki: Orienta-Consultit Oy.

Faraj, S. and Sproull, L. (2000) 'Coordinating expertise in software development teams', *Management Science*, 46 (12): 1554–68.

Faraj, S. and Xiao, Y. (2006) 'Coordination in fast-response organizations', *Management Science*, 52 (8): 1155–69.

Fox, S. (2000) 'Communities of practice, Foucault and actor-network theory', *Journal of Management Studies*, 37 (6): 853–67.

Fox, S. (1997) 'Situated learning theory versus traditional cognitive theory: Why management education should not ignore management learning', *Systems Practice*, 10 (6): 749–71.

Fox, S. (2006) 'Inquiries of every imaginable kind: Ethnomethodology, practical action and the new socially situated learning theory', *The Sociological Review*, 54 (3): 426–45.

Fox, S. and Grey, C. (1999) 'Emergent fields in management: Connecting learning and critique', *Management Learning*, 31: 1.

Gherardi, S. (2000) 'Practice-based theorizing on learning and knowing in organizations: An introduction', *Organization*, 7 (2): 211–23.

Gherardi, S. (2006) *Organizational Knowledge: The Texture of Workplace Learning.* Oxford: Blackwell.

Gherardi, S. and Nicolini D. (2002) 'Learning in a costellation of interconnected practices: Canon Or dissonance?', *Journal of Management Studies*, 39 (4): 419–36.

Gherardi, S. and Nicolini, D. (2005) 'Actor-networks: Ecology and enterpreneurs', in S., Gherardi, D. Nicolini, and F. Odella (1998) 'Toward a social understanding of how people learn in organizations', *Management Learning*, 29 (3): 273–98.

Grint, K. (1997) 'TQM, BPR, JIT, BSCs and TLAs: Managerial waves or drownings', *Management Decision*, 35 (10): 731–38.

Hakken, D. (2003) *The Knowledge Landscapes of Cyberspace.* New York: Routledge.

Handley, K., Sturdy, A., Fincham, R., and Clark, T. (2006) 'Within and beyond communities of practice: Making sense of learning through participation, identity and practice', *Journal of Management Studies*, 43 (3): 641–53.

Handley, K., Sturdy, A., Fincham, R. and Clark, T. (2007) 'Researching situated learning: Participation, identity and practices in client-consultant relationship', *Management Learning*, 38 (2): 173–91.

Hanks, W. (1991) 'Foreword', in J. Lave and E. Wenger (eds), *Situated Learning: Legitimate Peripheral Participation*. Cambridge: Cambridge University Press.

Hodgson, D.E. and Cicmil, S. (2006) *Making Projects Critical*. Basingstoke: Palgrave.

Hodgson, D.E. and Cicmil, S. (2007) 'The politics of standards in modern management: Making "The Project" a reality', *Journal of Management Studies*, 44 (3): 431–50.

Jackall R. (1988) *Moral Mazes*. Oxford: Oxford University Press.

Josefsson, U. (2005) 'Coping with illness online: The case of patients' online communities', *The Information Society*, 21: 143–53.

Kreiner, C. (1995) 'In search of relevance: Project management in drifting environments', *Scandinavian Journal of Management*, 11 (4): 1–31.

Latour, B. (1987) *Science in Action: How to Follow Scientists and Engineers through Society*. Milton Keynes: Open University Press.

Lave, J. and Wenger, E. (1991) *Situated Learning: Legitimate Peripheral Participation*. Cambridge: Cambridge University Press.

Lindkvist, L. (2005) 'Knowledge communities and knowledge collectivities: A typology of knowledge work in groups', *Journal of Management Studies*, 42 (6): 1189–210.

Lundin, R.A., and Söderholm, A. (1998) 'Conceptualising a projectified society: Discussion of an eco-institutional approach to a theory of temporary organizations', in R.A. Lundin and C. Midler (eds), *Projects as Arenas for Renewal and Learning Processes*. Boston: Kluwer.

Marshall, N. and Rollinson, J. (2004) 'Maybe Bacon had a point: The politics of interpretation in collective sensemaking', *British Journal of Management*, 15: 71–86.

McDermott, R. (1999) 'Why information technology inspired but cannot deliver knowledge management', *California Management Review*, 41 (4): 103–17.

Midler, C. (1995) ' "Projectification" of the firm: The Renault case', *Scandinavian Journal of Management*, 11 (4): 363–73.

Mukerji C. (1983) *From Graven Images: Pattern of Modern Materialism*. New York: Columbia University Press.

Mutch, A. (2003) 'Communities of practice and habitus: A critique', *Organization Studies*, 24 (3): 383–401.

Newman, D., Griffin, P. and Cole, M. (1989) *Working for Cognitive Change at School*. Cambridge: Cambridge University Press.

Nicolini, D., Gherardi, S. and Yanow, D. (eds) (2003) *Knowing in Organizations: A Practice-Based Approach*. Armonk, NY: ME Sharpe.

Orr, J.E. (1996) *Talking about Machines: An Ethnography of a Modern Job*. Ithaca, NY: Cornell University Press.

Preece, J. (1999) 'Emphatic communities: Balancing emotional and factual communication', *Interacting with Computers*, 12: 63–77.

Ricoeur, P. (2004) *Sur la traduction*, Paris: Bayard.

Roberts, J. (2006) 'Limits to communities of practice', *Journal of Management Studies*, 43: 623–39.

Schatzki, T., Knorr Cetina, K. and von Savigny, E. (eds) (2001) *The Practice Turn in Contemporary Theory*. London and New York: Routledge.

Strati, A. (2007) 'Sensible knowledge and practice-based learning', *Management Learning*, 38 (1): 61–77.

Sturdy, A., Brocklehurst, M., Winstanley, D. and Littlejohns, M. (2006) 'Management as a (self) confidence trick: Management ideas, education and identity work', *Organization*, 13 (6): 841–60.

Suchman, L. (1987) *Plans and Situated Action*. Cambridge, UK: Cambridge University Press.

Swan, J., Scarbrough, H. and Robertson, M. (2002) 'The construction of "Communities of Practice" in the management of innovation', *Management Learning*, 33 (4): 477–96.

Swidler, A. (2001) 'What anchors cultural practices', in T.R. Schatzki, K. Knorr Cetina and E. von Savigny (eds), *The Practice Turn in Contemporary Theory*. London and New York: Routledge. pp. 74–92.

Treviño, L. and Brown, M. (2004) 'Managing to be ethical: Debunking five business ethics myths', *Academy of Management Executive*, 18 (2): 69–81.

Wenger, E. (1998) *Communities of Practice. Learning, Meaning and Identity*. New York: Cambridge University Press.

Wenger, E. (2000) 'Communities of practice and social learning systems', *Organization*, 7 (2): 225–46.

Wenger, E. and Snyder, W.M. (2000) 'Communities of practice: The organizational frontier', *Harvard Business Review*, January/February.

Wenger, E., Mc.Dermott, R. and Snyder, W.M. (2002) *Cultivating Communities of practice*. Boston: Harvard Business School Press.

Wilmott, H. (1997) 'Rethinking management and managerial work: Capitalism, control and subjectivity', *Human Relations*, 50 (11): 1329–59.

Yanow, D. (2004) 'Translating local knowledge at organizational peripheries', *British Journal of Management*, 15: 9–25.

# 28

# Assessment and Accreditation of Non-Formal Management Education and Development Programmes

Lichia Yiu and Raymond Saner

## Summary

This chapter provides an overview of the non-formal management education and in-service training and identifies various assessment tools used in western Europe and northern America. The chapter ends with an examination of options of safeguarding the value of non-formal management education and management development programmes in the spirit and context of lifelong learning.

## INTRODUCTION

Impacted by rapidly evolving technology, global competition and instant communications, workers and managers alike are finding it more difficult to keep up with their job requirements. Learning has become a synonym for survival. Acquisition of knowledge and skills through formal management education (initial formal education at MBA schools) is no longer sufficient for future managers to ensure successful careers and adequate performance at the job site for the remaining years of their work life. Continuous education and training is a must. However, satisfactory learning outcome judging from the transferability of learning to the workplace is not necessarily assured. Literature on non-formal management education and training and its overall performance are scarce, especially outside of the North American context.

While the demand for continued management learning has been growing, the supply has also been increased. Many adult education institutions and private service providers sprang forward to fill the need that was too vast to be satisfied by the formal education institutions. In a little more than a decade ago, continuing education for adult learners has taken a giant step forward to fill the vacuum and has since blossomed into a full industry in its own. One of the most dynamic and thriving sector of adult education no doubt is management studies and management training. Revenue for the adult learning sector is substantial. In the United Kingdom alone, it was estimated that 43 billion Euros are spent on training of adults each year. The market size for leadership development alone for the FT top 500 European companies is estimated to be around 105 million Euros (ECUANET, 2006). Spending for adult training in the United States is also high. According to the ASTD estimate, the market turnover reached $280 billion in 2006. Management development and training on-the-job constitute a substantial share of this total amount spent on adult learning.

A variety of the adult learning organisations are dedicated to management education and development programmes. Among them are corporate universities, a hybrid between a 'real' university and an 'upgraded' training unit. It was estimated by experts that in the United States alone there are more than 2,000 corporate universities (Knight, 2007) while Europe has about 36 corporate universities, with France having the highest number (ECUANET, 2006).

The spread of management education and training was made easy by the integration of the internet and related communication technologies at the workplace and the rapidly lowering cost of providing an ICT platform for delivering training and education across geographic divide. Today, access to on-line management education and training is unhindered in most countries, and commercialisation of higher education is gaining momentum driven both by the institutions' need for mobilising social resources and by the consumers' demand for more education and qualification.

In the midst of this development, concerns over credibility of business schools have been voiced leading to broader reflection about the essence of managerial learning and the core mission of the business schools. Key proponent of calling for change is Mintzberg (2004) who criticised business schools for failing to educate and develop true managers.

While Mintzberg's concern centres on the MBA programmes of formal education institutions like universities and colleges, his criticism does not extend to the growing field of non-formal management education which so far has eluded the critical eye of management scholars and researchers even though the field of informal management training has grown in size without adequate quality assessments and practically without any form of accreditation systems. What follows is an attempt to take a closer look at this under-researched and under-published field of management education and training.

## NON-FORMAL EDUCATION AND INFORMAL LEARNING

There is a confusion of terminology between informal learning and non-formal learning. It is important to clearly define the meaning of each term used before proceeding with the discussion of assessment and accreditation.

In 2001, the European Commission defined the terminology used in the discussion about training within the EU countries (Bjørnåvold, 2001: 21) as follows:

**Formal learning** is typically provided by education or training institutions, structured (in terms of learning objectives, learning time or learning support) and leading to certification or an academic degree. This is intentional from the learner's perspective.

**Informal learning** results from daily life activities related to work, family or leisure. It is not structured (in terms of learning objectives, learning time or learning support). Typically, it does not lead to certification. Informal learning may be intentional. But in most cases it is incidental or at random. It comprises 'all forms of more or less conscious self-learning outside of the formal educational settings, in direct relation to life

**Facets of informal learning**

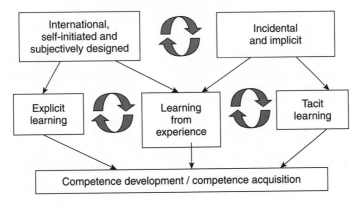

**Figure 28.1    Facets of informal learning**
*Source*: (Frank in Wittwer (2003): 177).

and experience – from unconscious, tacit learning on the one hand to conscious, self-organised learning on the other hand' (adopted from Fietz et al., 2006).

Informal learning was conceptualised into three elements (Frank, 2003. see Figure 28.1): explicit learning, learning from experience (reflection) and tacit learning.

**Non-formal learning** on the other hand, is not provided by an education or training institutions and typically is not leading to certification. However, it is structured, in terms of learning objectives, learning time or learning support, and intentional from the learner's perspective. It refers to any activity involving the acquisition of understanding, knowledge or skill which occurs outside the curricula of formal educational institutions and without necessarily the presence of an institutionally authorised instructor.

An important distinction was also made between informal and non-formal or education, which is the theme of this chapter. According to UNESCO, non-formal education implies:

> Any organized and sustained educational activities that do not correspond exactly to the definition of formal education. Non-formal education may therefore take place both within and outside educational institutions [and cater to persons of all ages]. Depending on country contexts, it may cover educational programmes to impart

adult literacy, basic education for out-of-school children, life-skills, work-skills, and general culture. Non-formal education programmes do not necessarily follow the 'ladder' system, and may have differing duration. (Coombs, Prosser and Ahmed, 1973: 185)

Simkins (1977) compared non-formal education with formal education in terms of purpose, timing, content delivery systems and control, and developed *ideal type models* of formal and non-formal education (see Table 28.1). In short, non-formal education and training are therefore courses or programmes that are not part of a universally recognised programme and involve little or no reliance on pre-determined guidelines for its organisation, delivery or assessment and do not lead to any formal qualification or certification.

Both informal (intentional aspect) and non-formal learnings have been greatly supported by the availability of information on the internet (informal learning) and have been facilitated by access to educational materials and courseware through the internet (non-formal learning or education). Formal educational institutions, such as MIT, have made available their whole teaching and course material on-line free of charge to aid individuals due to life circumstances who could not afford or attend the formal education programmes. Actions taken by institutions

**Table 28.1   Simkins (1977) ideal type models of formal and non-formal education**

|  | Formal | Non-formal |
|---|---|---|
| Purposes | Long-term and general<br>Credential-based | Short-term and specific<br>Non-credential-based |
| Timing | Long cycle/preparatory/full-time | Short cycle/recurrent/part-time |
| Content | Standardised/input-centred<br>Academic<br>Entry requirements determine clientele | Individualised/output-centred<br>Practical<br>Clientele determine entry requirements |
| Delivery System | Institution-based, isolated from environment<br>Rigidly structured, teacher-centred and<br>   resource-intensive | Environment-based, community-related<br>Flexible, learner-centred and resource-saving |
| Control | External/hierarchical | Self-governing/democratic |

Adapted by Fordham (1993) from Simkins (1977: 12–15). Reprinted with permission.

such as MIT in the public interest have contributed in providing the field of informal learning possibility also for a more structured and coherent learning in terms of subject matter mastery.

Taking into account the difficulty in discerning the complexity (due to its heterogeneity) and the diversity of non-formal education and training, the question arises as how to strengthen the accountability of this form of learning delivery which has become more relevant and urgent. In the past few years, most developed countries have increasingly emphasised the crucial role of learning that takes place outside formal education: in light of the increasing demands for updating knowledge and upgrading skills of their working population in general and the more mature workers in specific. How to recognise informal and non-formal learning so that adults can continue their more advanced learning in a formal education setting that has become a hot topic.

This emphasis of enriching the human capital and re-enrolling large number of working population into systematic learning processes has led to an increasing number of political and practical initiatives in the field of informal and non-formal learning and education; thus gradually shifting the practice of lifelong learning (in other words, providing lifelong learning opportunities) from the stage of experimentation to implementation. For the purpose of improving and ensuring quality of adult training and education, different

measures have also been put into action, such as more effective accreditation systems, better monitoring and evaluation, improved statistical systems, better performance evaluation at the institution level and better monitoring of student outcomes and destinations (OECD, 2003).

## ACCREDITATION AND QUALITY ASSURANCE OF NON-FORMAL TRAINING AND EDUCATION

Although accreditation services for formal management studies and programmes have matured, the same cannot be said of non-formal education. The United States is one of the few countries providing accreditation specifically for this purpose in a formalised manner and with dedicated accreditation bodies. For example, the Accrediting Council for Continuing Education & Training (ACCET, www.accet.org) is one of such organisations specialised in continuing education. ACCET was founded in 1974 and provides institutional accreditation for organisations whose primary function is for educational purposes and also for organisations offering continuing education as a clearly identified institutional objective within the operational entity, such as in-service corporate training.

ACCET accreditation can include educational institutions that offer programmes at locations other than the main headquarters under specified conditions and controls.

ACCET also accredits non-collegiate continuing education and training organisations throughout the United States and accredits programmes abroad. Institutions that may be eligible for accreditation include: (a) Trade and professional associations; (b) Private career schools; (c) Corporate training departments; (d) Intensive English programmes; (e) Labour union training programmes; (f) Religious organisations and ethical societies; (g) Public affairs and cultural societies; and (h) Social service, volunteer and personal development organisations.

Accreditation of non-formal training and education is an effort to safeguard the public interests and to provide a minimum guarantee of educational and training quality through third-party actors. Often these third-party actors also seek certification of their own management systems in order to demonstrate their commitment to certain quality standards and in turn strengthen their reputation and credibility. These third-party accreditation bodies could be public or private entities. What follows is a short survey of the accreditation of non-formal education by different European countries.

## Switzerland

Switzerland has established a special monitoring and certification instrument for adult learning in the 1990s. The Swiss Certification for Institutions of Continuing Education was the entity to offer quality certificate service named EduQua (http://www.eduqua.ch) to the adult continuing education institutions in Switzerland. Its members are 800 schools, institutions and academies throughout Switzerland. In Geneva, the Foundation for Adult Training (IFAGE) is one of the many EduQua certified non-formal institutions that provides courses either for professionals or beginners in business and finance.

EduQua assesses training and education providers by using the following six criteria, which it considers to be keys to the quality of an institution: (1) the course offer, (2) communication with clients, (3) performance-based value, (4) staff – meaning the educators,

(5) learning success, and (6) quality assurance and development. Increasingly, EduQua certification has been put forth as a prerequisite for public funding in different Swiss cantons[1] (EduQua, 2007). There is also talk among educational officials about applying the same quality criteria to the providers in the education sector in all of Switzerland and make national subsidies dependent on a proof of quality.

A different approach was taken by experts focusing on quality of training from an ISO perspective. A team of international experts developed the ISO 10015 Standard which is an international standard approved by ISO member states. ISO certification is an internationally recognised quality label which demonstrates an organisation's commitment to quality and a well-functioning quality assurance system.

The ISO 10015 Quality Standard for Training was published in December 1999. The Centre for Socio-Eco-Nomic Development (CSEND) is the first organisation to become a certification body for ISO 10015-related quality assurance work. CSEND received its accreditation from the Swiss Accreditation Agency (SAS) in February 2003 and has since certified training systems in China, India, Bahrain and conducts seminars on the application of ISO 10015 to management training. In contrast to the EduQua, ISO 10015 focuses not only on the four-stage training process, i.e., defining training needs, designing and planning training, providing for training and evaluating training outcomes; it puts equal emphasis on the alignment of training to the needs of the organisation. By so doing, training is focused not only on the individual acquisition of knowledge and skills, but equally on the application of these acquired knowledge and skills in solving individual performance issues and in enhancing organisational performance (Saner, 2002; Yiu and Saner, 2005) (see Figure 28.2).

## Europe

In the rest of Europe, certification of educational institutions is a relatively new concepts.

It is not common in Europe to see accreditation organisations cater specifically for the adult learning and non-formal sector. In Nordic countries and Austria, accreditation bodies usually have the dual role of accrediting both formal and non-formal training. For example, in Austria, accreditation of non-formal training programmes is given by the Bundesministerium für Wirtschaft und Arbeit (Federal Ministry of Economics and Labour) according to the Austrian Akkreditierungsgesetz (Accreditation Act).

In other countries, institutions delivering accreditations in the non-formal system concentrate their task primarily on management of the learning environment, such as classrooms and educational facilities, but taking little into account the quality of actual training and learning. For example, in the United Kingdom and also recently in Germany, regular inspections by the public authority constitute part of the approval procedure for non-formal training bodies to apply for public financial support. These inspections are targeted mostly at the institutional management systems and do not focus specially on the training programmes themselves. Nevertheless, in the United Kingdom, there is an established practice of adhering to an output-oriented and performance-based model to education and training. This is not the case in Germany, however, where validating informal learning still appears to be rather low (Fietz et al., 2006). On the whole these particular cases reveal the excessive diversity in the monitoring of non-formal training all over Europe. A focus on specific European countries and regions that have different background in non-formal training will show evidence for improving the coherence of training and education monitoring both at a national and at an international level.

## United Kingdom

In the United Kingdom, there is general acceptance of learning outside formal education and training institutions as a valid and important pathway to competences. Non-formal and informal learnings are considered as basic features to increase individual skills and work competences. Recently, the Learning and Skills Council (LSC, www.lsc.gov.uk) has taken a strategic interest in the recognition of non-formal learning for adults. The LSC has therefore become an accreditation agency focusing on non-formal training and education. The Adult learning Inspectorate (ALI), now merged with the Office for Standards in Education (Ofsted, www.ofsted.gov.uk), is another quality control body for both formal and non-formal education funded by the public funded provisions in the United Kingdom.

British Accreditation Council (BAC, www.the-bac.org) is a registered charity (non-profit-making organisation) in the United Kingdom which was established in 1984 to act as the national accreditation body for independent further and higher education. Until 2000, BAC accreditation was only available to colleges in the United Kingdom, but there are now accredited colleges in different countries including Switzerland. At present, BAC accredits over 200 colleges in the United Kingdom, and nearly 30 overseas. These accredited independent colleges include business and professional education and training.

## Scandinavian countries

Adult education and training in the Scandinavian countries is mostly regulated with the same tools and the same institutions involved in the formal educational system. Nevertheless, it is not possible to speak of a 'Nordic model'. Finland, Norway, Denmark and Sweden have chosen different approaches and are working according to different schedules. These differences do not change the fact that 'all four countries have taken practical steps through legislation and institutional initiatives towards strengthening the link between formal education and training and learning taking place outside of schools'(Colardyn and Bjørnåvold, 2004). In fact, these countries have created institutes in charge of evaluating the quality of education and training both in the formal and informal sector. Documenting and recognising high qualifications acquired through non-formal and informal learning has been emphasised for decades in the Scandinavian countries (Fietz et al., 2006).

In Denmark, for example, the Danish Evaluation Institute (EVA, www.eva.dk) is an independent agency formed under the auspices of the Danish Ministry of Education in 1999 under national legislation (Act on the Danish Institute of Evaluation, Consolidated Act of September 2000). It is responsible for external quality assurance at all levels of education in Denmark, including higher education (public and private subsidised higher education institutions). It initiates and conducts systematic evaluations of higher education programmes. Their activities may include institutional, auditing and other forms of evaluation.

Accreditation of all programmes leading to a professional Bachelor's degree began in 2004. EVA conducts the accreditation/ evaluation, and the Ministry of Education makes the accreditation decision. EVA also conducts accreditation of private courses as part of the Ministry of Education procedure determining whether students at private teaching establishments should be eligible for Danish state study grants. Business schools, for example, the Copenhagen Business School (CBS), may go for double accreditations. In the case of CBS, it has the national accreditation from EVA, but also obtained EQUIS accreditation for international recognition.

The Norwegian Agency for Quality Assurance in Education (NOKUT, www.nokut.no) was created in 2003 to be responsible for the evaluation and accreditation of all higher education institutions. As from 1 January 2002, an accreditation has become mandatory and universal for all formally recognised higher education in Norway which covers both institutional and programme-based accreditations. Non-formal learning is recognised on the individual basis; there is no formal accreditation procedure for non-formal education providers. The Finnish case shows a recent reform process that increasingly takes into account the non-formally

and informally acquired competences. The vocational qualification system is widely appreciated and the tendency is that all kinds of skills and competences should get formally validated credits.

## France

In several respects, France can be characterised as one of the most advanced European countries in the area of identification, assessment and recognition of non-formal learning (OECD, 2003). Concerning the 'opening up' of the national vocational education and training system including management-related training for competences acquired outside formal institutions, nowadays there are several different forms of recognition for competences acquired outside formal courses of study. The bilan de compétences and the Validation des Acquis Professionnels (VAP) legally regulate the recognition of vocationally acquired competences in order to undertake certain courses of study in the formal educational system. Since 1992, vocational certificates like the Certificat d'aptitude professionelle can be obtained (to various degrees) on the basis of assessments of non-formal and prior learning. Another important initiative was taken by the French Chambers of Commerce and Industry where the aim was to set up procedures and standards to assess independently the informal education and training system (OECD, 2003). Concerning the competences strictly in management and business, there has been an initiative in 1999 of the French employers' association MEDEF (Mouvement des Entreprises de France) under the title of 'Objectif Compétence' that aims to anchor this competence aspect more strongly especially in small- and medium-sized enterprises.

## Mediterranean countries

In the Mediterranean countries, despite the fact that informal training and education are very spread, there is still a lack of monitoring and evaluating. Nevertheless, some countries in the South of Europe have taken important initiatives. In Spain, institutional level work led to the creation of a system for assessment, recognition and accreditation of vocational skills acquired through non-formal and informal channels ('The Law on Qualifications and Vocational training of June 2002'). An important further step could be marked with the set up of the ERA programme – 'Evaluación, Reconocimiento y Acreditatión de las competencias profesionales'(Fietz et al., 2006). Recently, Portugal has undertaken a programme for Certification of Training Institutions named QUALFOR that can be compared to the EduQua certification in Switzerland.

Many firms and financial institutions deliver learning programmes for their employees. Some of them aim to set up corporate universities to deliver specific training in management and leadership. This informal scope of management development is generally not aligned to standardisation or accreditation because their education and training are strictly focused on their employees. As a result, the quality of the teachings and the training mostly depends on the quality and the success of the firm in its fields. Nevertheless, some major firms or banks have voluntarily asked for accreditation of their training units and programmes. EFMD through its CLIP (Corporate Learning Improvement Process) programme provides accreditation of corporate learning function. So far 12 leading corporate learning organisations from across Europe have been awarded the Corporate Learning Improvement Process.

A summary list of the accrediting institutions and quality assurance systems of non-formal management training is presented in Table 28.2.

According to Business Podium Boards (BPB, www.business-podium.com), there are more than 100 *unrecognised* accreditation associations of higher learning in the United States, United Kingdom and Europe (see Table 28.3). Some of the accreditation associations listed by BPB are discipline or professional specific. A large number of them are dealing with the general

topic of higher learning. It is obvious that knowledge production and related services, including accreditation and recognition of non-traditional learning, have become one of the major drivers of the Western economy. This sector, i.e., accreditation, could warrant greater regulatory control.

## SHOULD NON-FORMAL MANAGEMENT TRAINING INSTITUTIONS BE ACCREDITED OR SUBJECT TO QUALITY CERTIFICATION SCHEMES?

The proliferation of the 'private' accreditation bodies reflects the reality of the increasingly deregulated education market worldwide, making it easier to provide non-formal management training and course work. This proliferation has also created challenges and difficulties in recognition of learning attainments, making it more of an increasing concern regarding the compatibility of diplomas, certifications and qualifications by the employers.

Seeing it from the providers' point of view, organisations which manage training programmes would like to differentiate their products by acquiring quality certification through an accreditation procedure offered by an independent entity. Accreditation could help screen out sub-standard or unqualified management education and development programme suppliers. Yet, it does not necessarily address the question of learning outcome or that of an active instrument in protecting the public and private interests of achieving quality non-formal management education or learning. It is also questionable whether the self-regulated accreditation bodies abide by stringent standards of good governance imposed by international organisations, such as the International Organisation for Standardisation and affiliated international metal organisations or government bodies. Unless verification mechanisms exist to monitor and regulate these non-state 'soft' regulators, accreditation of the non-formal training and

**Table 28.2  Examples of accrediting institutions and quality assurance systems of non-formal management training in western Europe and North America**

| Organisation | Scope of work | Methods of regulation | Accreditation procedure | Validity | Level of recognition | Accreditation of informal education/training | Territory and size of the users | External quality assurances measures | Oversight | Type of programme | Status of recognition | Organisational status |
|---|---|---|---|---|---|---|---|---|---|---|---|---|
| **Accrediting council for continuing education & training (ACCET)** | ACCET accredits non-collegiate continuing education and training organisations throughout the United States and accredits programmes abroad | Independent peer review and evaluation | 1. Inquiry 2. Application 3. Accreditation and evaluation workshop 4. Analytic self-evaluation report (ASER) 5. Examination team 6. On-site examination 7. Team report 8. Accrediting commission action 9. Time schedule | 3 to 5 years | Recognised by the US department of education Certified as an ISO 9001-quality management system | Specifically informal schools and programmes | USA 248 | No | – | All sorts of private career schools corporate training departments For our interest: trade and professional - associations labour union training-public affairs and cultural societies | Private initiative | Private accrediting agency |
| **EduQua** | EduQua is the first Swiss accreditation/ label for adult education | Voluntary | 1. Subscription within a certification organisation 2. Adult education type of programme 3. Work on the type of programme 4. Sending off the final work | 3 years | Secrétariat d'Etat à l'Economie (SECO) | Schools and programmes of all sorts | Switzerland 49 business and management schools for 800 institutions of all sorts | No | Proformation SQS SGS ProCert IQB-FHS SCEF | All sorts of | Label | – |
| **Qualifications and curriculum authority (QCA)** | QCA develops criteria which awarding bodies and their qualifications must meet, and processes they must go through. Examinations and qualifications | Voluntary | A two-stage process must be completed: the recognition process; the application for accredited qualifications | Variable | Sponsored by the department for education and skills (DfES) | Specifically informal: schools programmes Personals: accrediting for example ILM dedicated to advancing the capability of managers and leaders | UK | No | – | All sorts of programmes in business and administration | QCA is a non-departmental public body | It is governed by a board whose members are appointed by the Secretary of State for Education and Skills, and managed on a day-to-day basis by an executive team |

*(continued)*

**Table 28.2  Continued**

| Organisation | Scope of work | Methods of regulation | Accreditation procedure | Validity | Level of recognition | Accreditation of informal education/training | Territory and size of the users | External quality assurances measures | Oversight | Type of programme | Status of recognition | Organisational status |
|---|---|---|---|---|---|---|---|---|---|---|---|---|
| **EFMD-CLIP- Corporate learning improvement process** | A quality improvement tool for the corporate learning function | Independent peer review and evaluation | 1. Application 2. On-site briefing and initiation of the process 3. Eligibility 4. Guided self-assessment 5. On-site peer review 6. Awarding of the quality label 7. Follow-up: quality improvement and institutional development | Accredited: 3 years reaccredited 5 years | Supported by a broad international body of academics and professionals. ENQA | EQUIS is not primarily focused on the MBA or any other specific programme. Its scope covers all programmes offered by an institution | Worldwide 11 | Granting of the EQUIS award is made by an independent EQUIS accreditation awarding board | EFMD | Banks and firms | An international not-for-profit association | A voluntary affiliation of organisations |
| **International organisation for standardisation, (ISO 10015)** | ISO 10015 is a quality assurance tool for the in-service training system and custom-tailored training programmes | Voluntary | Third-party audit on annual basis for certification purpose | Certified and registered for 3 years cycle | Recognised by national standard setting authorities and international mutual recognition system | Applicable for all training functions | Worldwide | Yes. National authority accredits ISO certification bodies. National authority is also subject to international peer review in order to sustain good governance | IAF (International accreditation forum) and respective national authority responsible for standard-isation | All | International recognition | International NGO, governed by a board and Swiss laws |

**Table 28.3   Unrecognised accreditation associations of higher learning according to BPB Survey as of 30 September 2007**

- Accrediting Commission International (ACI) (in Beebe, Arkansas) (aka International Accrediting Commission)
- Accrediting Council for Colleges and Schools (ACCS)
- Accreditation Governing Commission of the United States of America
- Alternative Institution Accrediting Association (AIAA)
- American Accrediting Association of Theological Institutions (AATI) (in Rocky Mount, North Carolina)
- American Association of Bible Colleges
- American Association of Drugless Practitioners Commission on Accreditation (AADPCA)
- American Association of Independent Collegiate Schools of Business
- American Association of International Medical Graduates (AAIMG)
- American Association of Non-Traditional Colleges and Universities (AANCU)
- American Association of Schools (AAS)
- American Council of Private Colleges and Universities (ACPCU) (connected to the operator of Hamilton University, now called Richardson University)
- American Federation of Colleges and Schools (AFCS)
- American Federation of Colleges and Seminaries (AmFed)(AFCS) (in Lakeland, Florida)
- American Naturopathic Certification Board (ANCB)
- American Naturopathic Medical Certification and Accreditation Board (ANMCAB or ANMAB)
- American Naturopathic Medicine Association (ANMA)
- American Universities Admission Program (AUAP)
- Arizona Commission of Non-Traditional Private Postsecondary Education
- Asia Theological Association (ATA)
- Association for Distance Learning (ADLP) (aka National Academy of Higher Education and Association of Distance Learning Programmes)
- Association for Online Academic Excellence (AOAE) (in Wales)
- Association of Christian Colleges and Theological Schools (in Louisiana)
- Association of Christian Schools International (ACSI) (in Colorado Springs, Colorado)
- Association of Distance Learning Programs (ADLP) (aka Association for Distance Learning and National Academy of Higher Education)
- Association of International Education Assessors
- Association of Reformed Theological Seminaries
- Board of Online Universities Accreditation (BOUA)
- Board of Theological Education of the Senate of Serampore College (BTESS)
- British Learning Association (BLA)
- Central States Consortium of Colleges & Schools (CSCCS) (connected to the operator of Breyer State University)
- Centre of Academic Excellence UK (CAEUK)
- Central States Council on Distance Education (CSCDE)
- Christian Accrediting Association (CAA)
- Commission on Medical Denturitry Accreditation (COMDA)
- Council for Distance Education Accreditation (CDEA; connected to Association of International Education Assessors)
- Council for International Education Accreditation (CIEA)
- Council of Online Higher Education (COHE)
- Council on Medical Denturitry Education (COMDE)
- Distance Education Council (DEC) (connected to the operator of Saint Regis University) (not to be confused with the legitimate Distance Education Council recognised by the Indian Department of Education)
- Distance Graduation Accrediting Association
- Distance Learning Council of Europe (DLCE) (connected to University Degree Programme)
- European Committee for Home and Online Education (ECHOE) (connected to University Degree Programme)
- European Council for Distance and Open Learning (ECDOE) (connected to University Degree Programme)
- Examining Board of Natural Medicine Practitioners (EBNMP)
- Global Accreditation Commission (GAC)
- Higher Education Accreditation Commission (HEAC)
- Higher Education Services Association (HESA) (connected to University Degree Programme)
- Integra Accreditation Association (IAA)
- Inter-Collegiate Joint Committee on Academic Standards (ICJCAS)

(continued)

**Table 28.3    Continued**

- Interfaith Education Ministries (IEM)
- International Academic Accrediting Commission (IAAC)
- International Accreditation Agency for Online Universities (IAAOU) (connected to operators of Ashwood University, Belford University, and Rochville University)
- International Accreditation Association (IAA)
- International Accreditation for Universities, Colleges and Institutes (IAUCI)
- International Accreditation and Recognition Council (IARC)
- International Accrediting Association for Colleges and Universities (IAACU)
- International Accrediting Commission (IAC) (aka Accrediting Commission International)
- International Accrediting Commission for Postsecondary Institutions (IACPI)
- International Association of Educators for World Peace (There are different groups by the same name though none are authorised accreditors)
- International Association of Universities and Schools (IAUS)
- International Commission for Higher Education (ICHE)
- International Commission of Open Post Secondary Education (ICOPSE)
- International Council for Accrediting Alternate and Theological Studies (Kerala, India)
- International Council for Open and Distance Education (ICODE)
- International Distance Learning Accrediting Association (IDLAA)
- International Interfaith Accreditation Association (IIAA) (closed down operations at the end of May 2007)
- International University Accrediting Association (IUAA) (in California)
- Kingdom Fellowship of Christian Schools and Colleges
- Middle States Accrediting Board (MSAB)
- Midwestern States Accreditation Agency (MSAA)
- National Academy of Higher Education (NAHE) (aka Association for Distance Learning)
- National Accreditation Association (NAA)
- National Association for Private Post-Secondary Education (NAPSE)
- National Association of Alternative Schools and Colleges (NAASC)
- National Association of Open Campus Colleges (NAOCC)
- National Association of Private Nontraditional Schools and Colleges (NAPNSC; Grand Junction, Colorado)
- National College Accreditation Council (NCAC)
- National Council of Schools and Colleges (NCSC)
- National Commission on Higher Education (NCHE)
- National Distance Learning Accreditation Council (NDLAC) (Glenndale University and Suffield University claim NDLAC accreditation)
- National Learning Online Council (NLOC)
- Naturopathic National Council (NNC)
- Non-Traditional Course Accreditation Body (NTCAB)
- Online Christ Centered Ministries
- Pacific Association of Schools and Colleges (PASC)
- Regional Education Accreditation Commission
- Southern Accrediting Association of Bible Institutes and Colleges (SAABIC) [6]
- The Association for Online Distance Learning (TAODL)
- Transworld Accrediting Commission International (TWACI)
- United Congress of Colleges (UCC) (Ireland, UK)
- US-DETC – Nevada (not to be confused with the legitimate DETC, based in Washington DC)
- Universal Council for Online Education Accreditation (UCOEA)
- Virtual University Accrediting Association (VUAA)
- West European Accrediting Society (WEAS)
- Western Association of Private Alternative Schools (WAPAS)
- Western Council on Non-Traditional Private Post Secondary Education (WCNPPSE)
- Virtual University Accrediting Association (in California) (VUAA)
- World Association of Universities and Colleges (WAUC) (in Nevada; operated by Maxine Asher)
- World Online Education Accrediting Commission (WOEAC)
- World-wide Accreditation Commission of Christian Educational Institutions (WACCEI)

education might not fulfil its mandate in assuring quality of learning experience and outcomes.

For instance, accreditation of a corporate university is no guarantee either in ensuring that an enterprise's training inputs will actually result in the attainment of strategic objectives of the corporation or productivity improvement of the manager. It is the view of the authors that accreditation has not yet fulfilled the expectation of ensuring a return on training investment. There is a need to strengthen both the outcome assessment and the quality assurance of the learning process. While the outcome assessment is complex and not fully reliable, in-process quality control and assurance become all the more important and urgent.

The analysis of the individual countries relating to the goal of ensuring quality of non-formal learning/education in continuing education and higher education shows that further development is required, even in those countries that have already implemented national systems for validating informal and non-formal learning. In contrast to the fragmented approach that can be observed in many countries, a holistic approach–encompassing both non-formal and informal learning, as well as general education, vocational education and enterprise training – requires co-ordination at a national level.

Approaches used in Scandinavian countries could serve as model for this combination of accreditation and recognition of formal and informal leaning and the corresponding service providers. Moreover, developing a co-ordinated approach at an international level between the different actors involved in non-formal learning process could be a preliminary step towards standardisation of professional qualification in different fields of management studies. Based on a transnational model, public and private agencies that provide certification and accreditation in tertiary education and management studies need to agree upon a professional qualification standard for various branches of management studies in order to benchmark different offers and to provide guidance for curricula development.

Initiatives to create an international common professional competence standard, such as certification of project management managers (PMM), has gained credence. Similar trends could be predicated for other management applications.

No amount of accreditation, however, would be able to guarantee minimum standards of non-formal management training or outstanding learning outcome of in-service management education. The former is influenced less by the subject matter expertise yet more by the ability of the faculty to communicate his material in a motivating manner and connected to the actual practices and issues of the business.

Many young management teachers started their career without proper training in pedagogy or with little experience in actual practice as managers. Their teaching remains theoretical and to some extent, hearsay. Situation in the non-formal management training programmes are similar, even though these programmes tend to have a greater mix of academicians and practitioners. Experienced managers or practitioners are often asked to conduct these courses because of their personal reputation or because of the firms that they represent. Often their teaching is rich in anecdotes but poor in reflection and short in generalisable conceptualisation. This shortcoming does not seem to matter, since non-formal management education and development programmes are designed with a commercial purpose where entertainment value is supreme.

Accreditation of non-formal management education and development programmes is only half of a measure, necessary but not sufficient. It is time also to look at the other end of the pipe: What competencies are actually acquired by graduates of the non-formal management education and development programmes? What difference would this type of learning make to the persons, to their work organisations and to the economic development of their society? The institutional arrangements and basic infrastructure for quality assurance for this sector are yet to be completed. The emergence

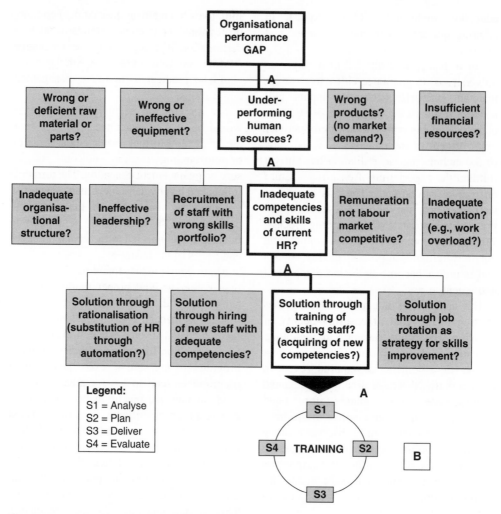

**Figure 28.2 ISO 10015-Based training management process**
Source: ©Centre for Socio-Economic development, 2003.

of ISO 10015 quality standard could fill part of the gap (see Figure 28.2).

## CONCLUSION

Non-formal education and training became part of the international discourse on education policy in the late 1960s and 1970s in the context of recurrent and lifelong learning. The twenty-first century, with its changing international economic conditions, has not only revived this policy discussion but also heightened the demand for continued education, especially in the management field. Countries with knowledge-based economies have come to rely on education production as one of the major engines of their economic performance and well-being. Individuals from the emerging markets wanting to benefit from the economic opportunities are also eager customers for these management training programmes and education. In this context, short-term, focused non-formal education is also thriving.

Proliferation of service providers formed a diverse landscape in terms of management training and education, with formal business schools offering short courses or executive programmes at one end of the spectrum to private operators at the other end. In between, corporate universities occupy the space in providing their own brand of management education and training. Proliferation caused difficulty in consumer choice and recognition of qualification, certificates and diploma. As a result, both business schools and non-business school-based management education and development programmes have been seeking accreditation in order to boost its credibility and competitiveness in the marketplace.

Does accreditation post an entry barrier for the unqualified service providers? Does accreditation guarantee effective use of education and training resources? Does accreditation assure quality of management education and relevance of learning outcome? Does accreditation strengthen the quality of non-formal management education and protect the public and consumer interests? These are questions that beg further inquiry and answers. A review of accreditation and quality assurance measures in the formal education sector could generate new insights which could also benefit the non-formal training and education sector.

## NOTE

1 In the Swiss political system, cantons enjoy the autonomy in managing most of its public affairs. A canton is similar to a province in France or state in the United States. Education is considered to be a cantonal competence and its policy and management are decided by the canton authority.

## REFERENCES

ACCET (Accrediting Council for Continuing Education & Training): http://www.accet.org/index2.cfm, accessed 30/08/07.

Accredited qualification databases, UK. *Awarding Body Directory*. Retrieved June 12, 2007, from accredited qualifications web site: http://www.accredited qualifications.org.uk/AwardingBodyDirectory.aspx#

Association of Collegiate Business Schools and Programs (ACBSP). Accreditation. Retrieved June 6, 2007, from

ACBSP web site: http://www.acbsp.org/index.php?module=sthtml&op=load&sid=s1_020acc

Bjørnåvold, J. (2001) Cited in Fietz and Junge (2006) 'The changing institutional and political role of non-formal learning: European trends', in P. Descy, and M. Tessaring (eds), *Training in Europe*. Second report on vocational training in Europe 2000. Background report (CEDEFOP Reference series): Luxembourg: Office of Official Publications of European Communities.

Coombs, P.H., Prosser, C. and Ahmed, M. (1973) *New Paths to Learning for Rural Children and Youth*. West Haven, CT: International Council for Educational Development Publications.

Colardyn, D. and Bjornavöld, J. (2004) 'Validation of formal, non-formal and informal learning: Policy and practices in EU member states', *European Journal of Education*, 39 (1): 69–89.

Danish Evaluation Institute (EVA) 'Adult education and continuing training'. Retrieved June 6, 2007, from EVA web site: www.eva.dk/Methods/Adult_Education_and_Continuing_Training.aspx

Department for Education, Lifelong Learning, and Skills (DELLS) 'Learning and qualifications'. Retrieved June 17, 2007, from DELLS web site: http://new.wales.gov.uk/topics/educationandskills/learning_and_qualifications/?lang=en

ECUANET (2006) 'An overview of corporate university'. Accessible at p://www.google.ch/search?q=How+many+corporate+universities+in+the+world&hl=de&start=20&sa=N.5.

EduQua (2007) Good grades for good school, EDUQUA at http://www.eduqua.ch/002alc_0101_en.htm, accessed on 30/09/07.

European Quality Link (EQUAL), European MBA guidelines. http://www.fibaa.de/ger/downlo/european mbaguidelines.pdf

Fietz, G., Junge, A., Nicholls, B. and Reglin, Th. (2006) 'Promoting visibility of competences – the Exemplo toolkit for SMEs'. EU Leonardo da Vinci Programme, pilot project. *Impuls*, 25. Retrieved July 4, 2007, from Exemplo web site: http://www.exemplo.de/exemplo/Website_Produkte/impuls25_screenpdf.pdf

Fordham, P.E. (1993) 'Informal, non-formal and formal education programmes', in YMCA George Williams College, *ICE301 Lifelong Learning Unit 2*. London: YMCA George Williams College.

Frank, I. (2003) 'Erfassung und Anerkennung informell erworbener Kompetenzen – Entwicklung und Perspektiven in ausgewählten europäischen Ländern', in W. Wittwer and S. Kirchhof (eds), *Informelles Lernen und Weiterbildung. Neue Wege zur Kompetenzentwicklung*: München/Unterschleißheim. pp. 168–209.

Knight, R. (2007) 'Corporate universities: Move to a collaborative effort', *Financial Times.* 19 March.

Mintzberg, H. (2004) *Managers Not MBAs: A Hard Look at the Soft Practice of Managing and Management Development.* San Francisco: Berrett-Koehler Publishers Inc.

OECD (2003) 'Thematic review on adult learning: Germany'. Country Note. Retrieved June 12, 2007, from OECD web site: http://www.oecd.org/dataoecd/44/5/36341143.pdf

OECD (2003) 'Thematic review on adult learning: UK'. Background report. Retrieved June 12, 2007, from OECD web site: www.oecd.org/dataoecd/49/49/2471965.pdf

OECD (2003) 'Thematic review on adult learning: USA'. Country Note. Retrieved June 12, 2007, from OECD web site: www.oecd.org/dataoecd/60/23/35406014.pdf

OCDE (2003) 'The role of national qualifications systems in promoting lifelong learning: Australia'. Retrieved June 12, 2007, from OECD web site: www.oecd.org/dataoecd/13/45/34327618.pdf

OCDE (2003) 'Les rôles des systèmes nationaux de certification pour promouvoir l'apprentissage tout au long de la vie: Rapport de base de la France'. Téléchargé le 13 Juin 2007 sur le site de l'OCDE: http://www.oecd.org/dataoecd/13/44/34327758.pdf

OCDE (2003) 'Les rôles des systèmes nationaux de certification pour promouvoir l'apprentissage tout au long de la vie: Rapport de base de la Suisse'. Téléchargé le 13 Juin 2007 sur le site de l'OCDE: www.oecd.org/dataoecd/53/10/33874774.pdf

Saner, R. (2002) 'Quality management in training: Generic or sector-specific?', *ISO Management Systems*, July–August. pp. 53–7.

Saner, R. and Fasel, S. (2003) 'Negotiating trade in educational services within the WTO/GATS context', *Aussenwirtschaft*, pp. 275–308.

Simkins, T. (1977) *Non-Formal Education and Development. Some Critical Issues.* Manchester: University of Manchester.

The Austrian Accreditation Council: http://www.akkreditierungsrat.at/

The Council for the Curriculum, Examinations and Assessment (CCEA): http://www.ccea.org.uk/

Yiu, L. and Saner, R. (2005) 'Does it pay to train?' ISO 10015 assures the quality and return on investment of training, *ISO Focus: Education – Foundation for the Future*, April. 7–10.

# 29

# The Pluralistic Future of Management Education

James O'Toole

Let a hundred flowers bloom, and a hundred schools of thought contend.

(Slogan from Chinese classical history appropriated by Mao Tse-Tung in 1956)

Only one thing is known for certain about the future: *It cannot be predicted.* All the forecaster can do is to extrapolate current trends, and then assign odds to the probability of the occurrence of various events in coming years that would alter the course of those trend lines. Not a very scientific exercise, is it? Nonetheless, the temptation to do so is irresistible. So, looking through the distorted lens of the present, I train my telescope on the most probable future scenario for business schools. What do I see? Sorry to report, the future looks rather grim.

But before we gaze more deeply through my flawed telescope, some distinctions must be made. Note that my forecast above concerns *business schools* and not *management education* (which is the stated subject of this volume). That is because there is no such thing as 'management education,' a term which is an artificial construct, a Platonic idea that exists only in the mind. In reality and in practice, what exists are such things as training programs, undergraduate business programs, MBA programs, corporate universities, on-line courses, tele-courses, workshops, seminars, and dozens if not hundreds, of other formal and informal ways to learn about management. Each is different from the others, each can be researched, and each has its own unique future. Hence, it is no more logical to forecast the future of management education, as if that were real and singular, than it is to forecast the future of 'the arts,' ignoring the fact that dance, drama, opera, poetry, music, and the several graphic arts all have quite different futures in store for them.

Similarly, to generalize about management education around the globe is to ignore the inconvenient fact that the challenges and opportunities in Asia are quite different from those in Europe, let alone making distinctions between the real differences in the futures of Japan and India, or the differences found within India between programs housed in institutions of higher education, and those located inside corporations. Given these complexities which, in fact, I actually have *simplified* here, the fearless forecaster has three options: (1) Throw in the towel, (2) Offer hundreds of narrow, specific predictions; or (3) Focus on the dominant form, offering prominent caveats concerning the limits as to its universality. Not surprisingly, I have chosen here to do the latter, focusing in on the traditional American MBA, the program with the longest history and the most available information. For good or ill, it is also the model for most formal programs around the world.

## THE FORECAST

Let's start with the situation today. Business schools housed in traditional American institutions of higher education are besieged on all fronts. On one side, for-profit, non-accredited training institutes are proliferating and grabbing larges chunks of total market share. Promising quick and easy programs, marketable skills, and good jobs, these proprietary schools – many offering on-line programs – are growing faster than one can say Topsy. In addition, there has been tremendous growth in overseas business schools, particularly in China, Asia, and Eastern Europe, all threatening one of this nation's largest exports: education. In sum, more and more potential business students at home and abroad are doing a quick cost/benefit calculation ... and deciding not to invest in traditional American b-schools. So, the immediate future looks good for proprietary schools and for b-schools on four continents, and not so rosy for those of us ensconced in Ivory Towers situated on the fifth.

On the other side, more and more corporations are establishing their own internal 'universities,' teaching business skills to liberal arts graduates who they hire on the

cheap and then train to the specifications they believe are required for success in their particular businesses. These programs are particularly threatening to the future of MBA programs, which are the flagships of American business higher education. Why is this happening? Mainly because an increasing number of employers feel they don't get sufficient bang for the big bucks they pay for MBAs. In fact, recent studies at *Business Week* (2006) show a negative correlation between long-term corporate performance and the presence of MBAs in a company's C-suite.

If all that weren't bad enough, the performance of b-schools – in particular, those with MBA programs – is being increasingly criticized from inside those institution themselves by a growing chorus of deans (even from such prestigious institutions as Northwestern's Kellogg School) and management professors, among the latter Henry Mintzberg (2004), Pfeffer and Fong (2002), Rakesh Khurana (2007), and the late Sumantra Ghoshal (2005). My colleague Warren Bennis and I also have chimed in (2005). Significantly, while these deans and scholars all offer notably different critiques of the b-school, their criticisms are mutually consistent, an indicator that the chances of them all being right are rather high. In any event, they are in agreement about the lack of relevance of the MBA curriculum. At the core of all their arguments is a call for the re-conceptualization and re-definition of the purpose of management education. That runs against the current tide. While little creative effort is being devoted to reforming what and how MBAs are taught, the nation's top b-schools are caught up in a high-stakes competition to better their relative rankings in the business press – spending a fortune to hire big-name researchers, on the one hand, and to recruiting students and then place them in the best paid jobs, on the other. In short, the focus of the top b-schools is on prestige, and not on substance. Given all of the above, it is hard to paint a rosy future for the American business school. And, in the long run, the future is probably not so good for the many b-schools around the world that have copied the U.S. model.

## WHAT IS TO BE DONE?

In their introduction to this volume, our editors review the criticisms leveled at management education and, in that context, usefully remind us that '*how* we teach, and the tools we use, must closely mirror important aspects of *what* we teach.' As promised, the chapters in this book offer classroom-based 'solutions' to what ails management education, which is a promising shift in focus away from the current efforts to build prestige by hiring better researchers and recruiting more promising students. My assignment was to comb through these articles in search of clues that might point to 'the future of management education.' My conclusion will seem obvious to anyone who has read even a few of these pieces: *there is no single future of management education but, instead, a plurality of futures*. The numerous articles found in this colloquy are variously practical, theoretical, research-based, anecdotal, philosophical, prescriptive, descriptive, abstract, concrete, derivative, original, discipline-based, broad-based, and narrowly focused. This eclectic grab bag examines undergraduate, graduate, and continuing management learning, jumping from education to training, to personal and professional development. There is surely something here to fit every interest and bias: every thoughtful reader can find something that is personally useful, as well as something that is idiosyncratically upsetting. In short, the diversity of viewpoints and perspectives represented in these pages is a perfect reflection of the fragmentation that exists in the field of management education.

Before I go further, I must come clean: I wish more of the authors had followed the lead of the editors and focused on the marriage of 'the what' and 'the how' of management education. For my money, the emphasis here is so heavily on the how that we lose complete sight of the what and, thus, the essential relationship of the twain. In the end, what one learns here is how to more effectively deliver a flawed product. In general, we are given numerous intriguing 'solutions' but, in the process, we lose sight of *the problem* with management education. If it is not too late to do so, let me take on that task here at the end. Again, for the sake of precision, I restrict my comments to traditional MBA programs.

## THE PROBLEM

To my mind, the central problem of management education is the corrosive impact, in turn, that 1950s managerialism, 1970s management science, and 1990s investor capitalism have had on the MBA curriculum, cumulatively driving out the initial high purpose of business schools which was to create a true profession of management. The effects of this legacy became apparent during the Enron, Arthur Andersen, WorldCom, Tyco, and other turn-of-the-millennium corporate scandals. At the time, almost everyone – corporate investors, regulators, employees, citizens, media-talking heads – were outraged by the behavior of American executives. Of course, business leaders were not the first to be caught engaging in unethical behavior – politicians, doctors, journalists, lawyers, and others have taken embarrassing turns in the public spotlight in recent years. But when those high-profile miscreants betrayed the ethics of their respective professions, it has been their peers in the government, medical, media, and legal communities who typically have been the first to condemn their behavior. In sharp contrast, the collective silence of American business leaders was deafening during the early 2000s corporate scandals. Nary, a CEO, spoke out publicly against the illegal and unethical practices of the likes of Messrs. Lay, Kozlowski, et al. Instead, as Federal Express's CEO Fred Smith recently admitted, he and his fellow executives decided 'to lay low' until the storm blew over. Why did business executives fail to speak out in defense of the integrity of the management profession? Was it, as some observers suspected, because their own ethics were so badly compromised that none could afford to cast the first stone?

Rakesh Khurana's institutional history of the American business school, *From Higher Aims to Hired Hands* (2007), suggests a different reason: *management isn't a profession.* Unlike the 'learned professions,' management lacks a systematic and established body of knowledge, a community of practitioners with standards of expertise and conduct, qualifying examinations, and 'attitudes of communalism, disinterestedness, and a societal orientation.' In essence, the malefactors at Enron couldn't be read out of their profession because they were not, in fact, members of a profession to begin with – even though the convicted Jeffrey Skilling and Andrew Fastow held MBAs from prestigious 'professional' schools of business. Thus, instead of thinking of corporate executives as professionals who lead institutions with high social purpose, it is probably more accurate today to characterize them as self-interested technicians and hired guns. Sadly, as Khurana documents, that's what they are assumed to be by many leading scholars in top-tier b-schools, and, by extension, that is how they are taught and, in too many cases, how they end up acting.

Things didn't start out that way. The stated purpose for founding the first b-schools in the late nineteenth and early twentieth centuries was not to help fledgling managers to get rich quick but, rather, to educate a class of business leaders intellectually and morally equipped to address the nation's fundamental social and economic problems. The founders of the University of Pennsylvania's Wharton School (1881), Dartmouth's Tuck School (1900), and the Harvard Business School (1908) were public-spirited men with the intent of turning management into a respected 'calling' with the higher purpose of public service similar to the law, medicine, and even theology. Indeed, Kuhrana relates the near-religious beliefs some of those founders held about the potential for business leaders to make great contributions to society, *if* they were broadly and liberally educated *and* socialized to see themselves as members of a professional community.

That belief – or, more accurately, *hope* – remained alive until the end of World War II. Then the world changed, and with it the *raison d'être* of the b-school. Khurana documents how this 'very-ill-defined institution' has reflected both the changing social order of its times and the changing role of business in society. For example, as America sought to meet the scientific challenge presented by the Soviet Union in the 1960s, the country's business schools were called upon to play a major role. The agent of change, in this instance, was the Ford Foundation which used its significant financial leverage to encourage radical curricular reforms at the nation's leading b-schools. Drawing on the defense work of Robert McNamara's Whiz Kids, the Ford Foundation provided incentives too rich to refuse to schools willing to put management science at the heart of their programs. In the blink of an eye, almost all the top-tier schools were teaching quantitative analysis, decision theory, model building, operations management, and the like. The old professoriate – who had been schooled mainly in the operating trenches of big business – were extruded and replaced by a young generation of 'quantoids,' primarily those with degrees in engineering and economics. This was a positive reform in that it introduced intellectual rigor to the educational enterprise, but it was negative in that the non-quantifiable stuff of leadership – judgment, ethics, the 'people factor' – was lost. And out with the old went the original high purpose of the institution: to create a true profession.

From there it was a simple hop, skip, and jump to where we are today: top-flight b-schools recruit faculty whose prime, if not sole, interest is publishing articles in scientific journals. Reflecting the interests of faculty, the schools now turn out graduates who have little understanding of general management and, thus, have become recruiting grounds for the investment banks and private equity firms whose myopic focus on short-term profit and the interests of shareholders has led, more than anything else, to the behavior we now simply lump under the category 'Enron.'

## THE DECLINING IMPORTANCE OF TEACHING

The most controversial and difficult to address consequence of the changes that have occurred in business schools is a shift in the balance of the relative importance of teaching versus research. Medical schools effectively deal with this tension by acknowledging the necessity and virtue of professorial pluralism. The faculties of the best medical schools are home to both pure researchers – the genetic biologist who only does cutting edge work published in leading scientific journals – and clinical professors – the surgeon who develops practical operating room techniques and publishes in practitioner journals. The former teaches pre-med science classes and Ph.D. seminars, the latter carries the teaching load with MD candidates and interns. In contrast, and largely a legacy of the Ford Foundation reforms, the best b-schools only have room for those professors whose main interest is publishing discipline-based, quantitative research in journals read by fellow academics. There is no room in the enterprise for the professor whose primary audience is students and business executives, and who publishes in practitioner journals, even ones as respected as the *Harvard Business Review*.

The assumption that there is a singular standard of professorial excellence – namely, publishing in 'A' journals – has had a devastating impact on the quality of teaching in the nation's leading business schools. Given the centrality of this problem, it is curious that only one of the numerous articles contained in this volume addresses it. But Lewicki and Bailey hit the nail on the head in their review of 'the research-teaching nexus' in which they 'explore the inherent tensions and compatibilities between research and teaching.' They discover – and who should be surprised? – that there is no evidence that productive researchers are better teachers than members of the faculty who publish less. This counters the myth promulgated by many deans in top-flight research universities that the best researchers are, *ipso facto*, also the

best teachers. But the problem goes deeper than that: for example, at the University of Southern California's business school (where I was on the faculty for nearly 30 years) there is a growing consensus that *only* those who publish in 'A' journals are competent to teach MBAs. That the empirical evidence shows otherwise is no deterrent to those who hold this view (they simply ignore the data Lewicki and Bailey review, and the anecdotal evidence of famous Nobelists who mumble, and discipline-based specialists so caught up in the esoterica of their own theories they leave their classes befuddled and uneducated). The declining quality of teaching found at such institutions as USC is the result of expecting good researchers also to be good teachers.

It should be noted that this aspect of the American business school model is the most imitated around the world. Professors in Asia, Europe, South America, Australia and southern Africa now compete to get their articles published in the *ASQ* and other scientific A-journals. And top-flight b-schools around the world are increasingly adopting American-style standards for hiring and promotion. (For the life of me, I have never understood why it is that perfectly sensible people overseas who are rightly critical of American cultural and economic hegemony then will insist on importing the very worst aspects of this nation's culture and its economic institutions!)

So here's my conclusion: If the deans of business schools around the world really want to improve the quality of their offerings it will be necessary for them to challenge the assumption that Good Researchers=Good Teachers and, in its place, adopt a pluralistic model of professorial excellence. Fortunately, as Lewicki and Bailey point out, such a model exists. The late, respected educator Ernest Boyer identified four forms of scholarship, all worthy of inclusion in the academic enterprise. In addition to *the scholarship of discovery* (the traditional, discipline-based view of research as the generation of new knowledge, the prime audience for which is other scholars), Boyer calls attention to *the scholarship of integration* (interdisciplinary studies that put research results in broader perspectives), *the scholarship of application* (what business professors call applied research), and *the scholarship of teaching* (the creative activity involved in communicating effectively to non-technical audiences). In a true *professional* school, all four of these forms of scholarship would be recognized as legitimate. But that is not the case at the leading business schools today. (Let me stress that my generalizations are true only at top-tier schools and the wanna-bes. While the research standards and the MBA curriculum is much the same at all the 30 or so top-flight schools, there is, in fact, a tremendous amount of variation in the programs offered by the second tier. Indeed, in those schools there are heartening examples of professors doing applied research useful to practitioners, and offering curricula infused with ethical values and the importance of service to society.) Which brings us to the corrosive role of accreditation in nurturing this system.

## ASSESSMENT AND ACCREDITATION

Rubin and Martell's thought-provoking Chapter 19 in this volume on assessment and accreditation causes the reader to reflect on the fact that the supposed gatekeeper of the b-school enterprise is adrift in a Sargasso sea of confused and counter-productive assumptions about management teaching and learning. Unfortunately, there is no equivalent of the ABA or AMA to oversee, and set professional standards in, the field of management. The institution that does exist, the AACSB, is a misguided and poor substitute for a professional body. Having abandoned its founding purpose of creating and maintaining high professional standards, the AACSB's current *raison d'être* is accreditation. Having found the challenge of defining the higher purpose of business education to be a values-laden 'hot potato,' the AACSB has become involved in institutional assessment by

'hard evidence' – basically because that is a relatively safe, non-controversial exercise.

Sadly, the AACSB's current demand for 'assurances of learning' in its accreditation of b-schools threatens to lead to standardization around an 'assessable' norm which, by definition, must be a mediocre benchmark. At worst, the assessment process is a pro-forma, bureaucratic exercise unrelated to the quality of teaching, or to any higher purpose of the enterprise. More than that, the AACSB's willing embrace of the hard, cold facts of quantification of student learning plays to the strengths, and worst instincts, of many members of the professoriate. The AACSB's prescribed pre-tests, post-tests, and pre-test post-tests reflect the increasing scientism of b-school profs. Overemphasis on rigor of assessment is much like overemphasis on scientific rigor in social research, in general: there is the danger of losing sight of relevance. What fun it is to measure the measurable, seeking great precision in quantification of the trivial, and ignoring the hard-to-measure important! The way things are headed, the AACSB could end up accrediting schools that use the best assessment methods, while decertifying those that concentrate their resources on doing the right things for all their stakeholders. Already, it is acting a lot like many of the nation's largest grant-giving foundations, which spend massive percentages of their time and resources on program assessment, and too little of those on creatively using their considerable leverage for the greater good.

Of course, one can imagine some true metrics of learning. In an ideal world, one would like to measure what graduates have retained from their classroom experience, and what they actually use in their careers. And wouldn't it be useful to know how b-school education affects the later behavior of executives? (When I was the director of executive seminars at the Aspen Institute, we did an assessment of the long-term effect of our programs on the behavior of past attendees. We found the most common measurable was that our programs created dissatisfaction among our 'grads' with the status quo at their companies, and they tended to quit their jobs within a year of attending an Aspen seminar. Since companies spent a fortune sending their high potential executives, and their spouses, to Aspen for our two-week programs, we did not think it prudent to advertise this fact!) In a similar vein, one can imagine checking up on the later behavior of MBAs from leading b-schools, say, by documenting the numbers of their criminal indictments, citations for regulatory infringements, companies and careers destroyed by misguided M&A activity, and ratio of their salaries to those of typical workers in their companies. Or, one could measure the percentage of MBAs that each b-school produced who took jobs with ethically rotten companies just because they paid well, versus those who took jobs with good companies, but at lower salaries. Publish those numbers, and Harvard and Stanford might not look quite so good. Then, again, this is a tricky business: if students attend top b-schools primarily to get credentialed, they won't learn much in class even given the best teachers and most engaging methods. Besides, changing behavior is difficult: is it fair to blame the H.B.S. for the quality of G.W.B.s leadership? Hey, this assessment stuff is tricky!

## WHAT IS THE PURPOSE OF THE B-SCHOOL?

Of course, at base, the problem is not one of metrics at all; rather it is one of purpose, or the lack thereof. Because b-schools don't have a clear mission, there can be no consensus around desired learning outcomes. And because they lack a compass, b-school leaders are overly responsive to the curricular desires of university administrators, students, corporate recruiters, and their narrowest, academic discipline-oriented faculty. It wouldn't be that way if curriculum design started with the question of what the b-schools' key constituencies truly *need* in the long term, and not what they *want* this week, or the next. In this regard, many of the authors of the

papers in this volume reflect the curriculum development process at the business schools in which they labor. They leap to offering solutions in terms of the delivery of course content before asking such essential prior questions as:

- What does it mean to be an educated manager?
- What is the purpose of the MBA degree?
- What is the essential, core content of an MBA curriculum?

Only when such questions about content have been answered can one then usefully ask, *how is the best way to deliver it?* These papers put the cart before the horse. Still, this book is about management learning, after all, and not about curricular reform, so it is natural that the authors tend to focus on alternative modes of learning. And while that focus is obviously useful, in the long run (and in practice) making appropriate choices among the many alternatives presented here will depend on b-school decision makers having clearly identified the purposes of their enterprises. If they know the why of the MBA, they then will have the essential guidance needed to choose the how. Method follows vision, not vice versa.

Besides a willingness to ask tough questions, what also is needed are b-school faculty and deans with the vision, integrity, and courage to resist pressures to provide miseducative programs. For example, top corporate executives say they want MBA grads who are ethical leaders, effective communicators, good team members, and willing innovators – yet, the recruiters who represent their companies routinely hire only MBAs who have specialized in finance, marketing, accounting, and IT, and who have none of the broader abilities CEO's say they want, and manifest little interest in developing those capabilities. Because ranking-conscious deans want their graduates to get high-paying starting jobs, too many b-schools design curriculum to make recruiters happy, rather than giving their graduates the broad-gauged skills and knowledge they will need to be effective and ethical leaders in the long run.

## A TEACHER-LESS AND CONTENT-FREE CLASSROOM?

There is much welcome discussion in this volume about putting the learner back at the center of management education. Who could disagree? Yet, in fact, it is the traditional researcher, and not the student or teacher, who is front and center in so many of these chapters. Indeed, the true subject of many of these papers is not really learning, teaching, or management education, at all; instead, the subject is *the researching* of those issues. In reading some of these papers, I couldn't help but imagine this dystopic future scenario for management research: studies of researchers studying researchers studying researchers studying …

The emphasis in these papers is on learning, and not on teaching. In many ways, that is a logical and important change of perspective. Clearly, there is a lot of bad teaching in b-schools, much of it easily correctable. If learning is the goal, then traditional lecturing is the worst form of teaching, and the quality of the classroom experience can be greatly increased by minimizing the use of that method. In this regard, the problem- and project-based learning methods described here by DeFillippi and Miller are great ideas that enhance learning and should be used more often and more widely. The use of technology in the classroom is more problematic. Technology is here to stay, and its use will only increase. Hence, the issue becomes one of using technology *appropriately*. Alas, the most common educational use of technology today – PowerPoint presentations – is almost always inappropriate. If lecturing is the worst form of teaching, adding PowerPoint to a lecture is merely to automate the process by which learners and teachers disengage. We are now seeing that 'Power corrupts, and PowerPoint corrupts absolutely.'

Doubtless, educators are just scratching the surface of the potential uses of technology, but they must also understand that the growing use of such approaches as distance learning and on-line management education present not only opportunities, but also threats, to the quality of learning and the quality of student life. While it is incumbent on educators to embrace technology where it is appropriate, it would seem prudent not to lose sight of the fact that there is real value in face-to-face learning, in the direct interactions of students and teachers, and in the interactions of students outside the classroom. A future in which all learning occurred in rooms – each one containing only one person and a computer – would be sterile and inhuman. Just because proprietary schools are succeeding, using on-line programs doesn't mean that traditional schools should, or have to, copy them. In this case, imitation is a form of flattery that universities can't afford to engage in.

And while focusing on the learner, we must not lose sight of the fact that teachers and teaching count; indeed, for many of us, the most influential people in our lives have been our teachers. They are the rare authority figures in our lives who are not authoritarians. We get excited to learn about a subject when our teachers are clearly enthusiastic about it. They show us the value and joy of learning and, by the example of their own lives, encourage us to learn difficult things. And they give us the confidence that we are able to do so. Teaching machines can't do that. Curiously, the most time-tested form of teaching, the Socratic method, gets only one mention in these chapters (and the related case method also receives short shrift). That might be because the Socratic method is the hardest form of teaching – teachers need to be fully prepared and to have mastered their material. But, if what we read here is true, the role of the teacher in the future will be more hands-off.

In some of these chapters, the role of the teacher appears limited to setting up the classroom, asking students to organize themselves into teams, letting them define what they want to learn and how they want to learn it, and making sure the class has the Internet access … *et voila*, the teacher's job is done! It used to be that teachers had to have learned something before they came to class. Now, teachers and student are assumed to be equally qualified (or equally ignorant). The newly prescribed mutual learning, peer mentoring, non-directive, non-hierarchical teaching fits perfectly with post-modernist thinking with regard to the value of intellectual authority and received wisdom. Indeed, for me, the most frightening future trend identified in these pages is the introduction of 'critical theory' into the management curriculum. I have a difficult time seeing how post-modernism is a relevant, or useful, response to the current shortcomings of management education. Please don't ask me to choose between Jacques Derrida and Michael Jensen! As CBS newscaster Charles Osgood's young son once asked him, 'Hey Dad, what's worse: alligators or tigers?'

There is so much in these pages about critical studies, cross-cultural education, emotional intelligence, cognitive neuro-science, positive psychology, web-based collaborative, action, and experiential, learning, but so little on showing the relationship of those topics to learning the basics of business: the making and selling of goods and services. There is also surprisingly little recognition of the fact that a great deal of the MBA curriculum must continue to be devoted to learning economics, finance, accounting, marketing, and IT, and it is not always clear how all the new exciting stuff described here relates to teaching this rather traditional material. Indeed, the focus in these pages is mainly on self-knowledge. Indeed, many of these papers use the disciplinary language of psychology, rather than the practical language of business. If all of this is a reflection of reality, one thing seems likely about the future of management education: business professors won't be spending much time teaching the quotidian activities involved in buying and selling.

Many of these articles seem to complicate things unnecessarily. Sadler-Smith discusses customizing management education based on the observed differences in cognitive learning styles found among managers. Recognizing that people learn in different ways, and echoing our editors, he concludes that 'the processes of *how* managers learn are as important as the content of *what* they learn.' This is a clear reaction to the left-brained approach to learning management science which aims at logic and ends up in management-by-the-numbers. It is obvious that rote drilling in accounting principles won't make people effective managers, let alone ethical leaders, and that's why there is also need for the soft, emotional, right-brained learning that is more likely to lead to good judgment and intuition. However, I don't think that is what is being proposed here. Instead, the authors of some of these papers are interested simply in the techniques of learning, irrespective of the content. For example, they are silent about what the intrinsic value of learning the ins and outs of the derivatives game might, or might not, be – what they care about is how effectively and efficiently the game is taught. Given the preference for delivery method over content, it isn't surprising to find so little interest in these pages in such topics as ethics, social responsibility, values, corporate culture, and the quality of work life.

Of course, a central tendency of pragmatic American culture is to ask 'how to?' instead of 'why?' or 'to what end?' Perhaps that is why so many of these papers seem to be circling-in perilously close to the idea of content-free teaching. But don't ideas and content – *substance* – ultimately count more than form, method, and technique? Both are necessary, of course, but shouldn't form follow content? But here we have Hrivnak, Riggio, and Reichard faithfully capturing the state-of-the art in leadership development – which amounts to training that is both content and ethics-free. Of course, the methods they outline can be shown to *work* in terms of assessable learning. In fact, they work equally well in terms of training *both* dictators and virtuous leaders! But there seems to be no need to bother with values in these approaches to leaning: leaders don't need to learn about pursuing moral ends that are good for their followers, since the moral basis of the relationship of leaders to followers is a non-assessable, non-researchable topic.

Clearly, the learning-centered course design is better than a design that ignores student needs; but wouldn't a well-designed course that also teaches something useful be even better? And, if that something useful was also virtuous, wouldn't that be best? But few of the authors of these pieces appear willing to go there. As in the Tom Lehrer song about the lack of concern on the part of space scientists about the effects on those where 'the rockets go down' … 'that's not my department, said Werner von Braun.'

Almost all of these papers are so forward looking that one cannot help but be struck by the odd mention of out-moded practices that seem still to hang on. For example, there is more than one reference to 'standard textbooks' in these pages. Doubtless, textbooks are needed, and may be appropriate, in fields like accounting with established bodies of knowledge and facts that need to be memorized. But what could be more anachronistic today than using a textbook in such fields as leadership, management, history, sociology, ethics, and psychology? Indeed, probably the most progressive single change in management education would be to throw out all textbooks and replace them with real books. In this regard, I found Gallos's article on 'artful teaching' one of the most useful pieces in the volume. She demonstrates numerous ways in which imaginative teachers can use drama, fiction, philosophy, films, and graphic arts in the classroom to gain fresh perspectives on business and organizational problems. She could have added history books and biographies, as well.

## BEYOND THE MBA

One of the most marked – and unsettling – trends in formal management education is the steadily declining average age of those who are receiving it. Until recently, top American business schools insisted that applicants to their programs had had several years of work experience under their belts. This requirement was based on the documented fact that students need to have a first-hand understanding of organizations before they can fully appreciate how to manage them. The schools also insisted that their applicants had had solid liberal arts educations, recognizing that business leaders need to be fully rounded individuals. Today, however, in an attempt to meet growing competition from non-traditional programs, most of those schools now admit MBA students directly after receiving their bachelor degrees and, increasingly, admit students into MBA programs during their junior and senior undergraduate years. Far worse is the growing trend among undergraduate students to choose business as their major field of study. They are doing so, for the most part, because their parents insist that they earn a 'marketable degree' to justify the high and rising cost of university tuition. All this is as understandable as it is short-sighted on the part of students and parents, and miseducative on the part of universities and colleges. It means not only that those institutions are trying to teach management to young people too inexperienced to benefit from what they are learning, but that the students are missing out on their one chance in life to become truly and broadly educated human beings. Dealing effectively with those trends is one of the most difficult tasks university administrators will face in the coming decade. And, yes, this issue is different (or non-existent) in other lands and other cultures, which conveniently brings me to the next topic.

There are many references in these pages to the growing practice of multi-cultural business education. How could it be otherwise? Globalization is the dominant trend of the age. Doubtless, all business students today need to be sensitive to differences in foreign customs and, in particular, the need to obey foreign laws. Beyond that, real learning about other cultures becomes difficult: for example, to fully understand Chinese culture if one is a Westerner, or to understand Western culture if one is Chinese, requires serious and formal study, as Harvard professor Tu Wei-ming has demonstrated (O'Toole, 1999). Yet, sadly, most of what is taught to globe-trotting executives is anthropologically naive and substantively shallow, and doesn't even address the major 'cultural' problems global managers face – which most often are a function of their inability to speak the language of the people with whom they are doing business. The simple truth is that if you don't speak their language, the behavior of 'others' is always difficult to understand. That has created a great market for trainers who develop courses to explain the curious customs of others to tongue-tied managers (a set composed mainly, but not exclusively, of mono-lingual American and Japanese business people). The good news is that business people around the world now all share a common business culture based on Western premises. Thus, if the global manager simply avoids boorish behavior, respects local laws and the few customs that every literate person should be aware of, the rest of what passes as multi-cultural business education is either unnecessary, or an exercise in politically correct cultural relativism. In short, all the fuss about preparing business students for the global economy of the future is yesterday's news: that economy is here and they already 'get it.' The wave of the future in global business education is the hard slog of learning foreign languages.

I have stressed the necessity to make clear distinctions between related concepts, the most significant of which are the terms *education* and *training*, which are often conflated to the disadvantage of institutions of formal education. The definition of training is 'forming habits of thought and behavior by discipline and instruction.' Education, in distinction, means to 'develop the faculties and powers of a person.' The difference between the two concepts is one of kind, and not simply of degree.

Training is an applied, practical process with immediate results. It has to do with right and wrong answers and behavior. It has to do with facts, a set body of information, and how-tos and how-to-dos. It is appropriate for routine and repetitive tasks and is appropriate when the right outcome is known in advance by a trainer who can tell if the trainee has answered a question correctly,

or behaves properly. Because clear outcomes are identifiable, precise lessons plans can be drawn up by trainers and learning outcomes measured. *McDonald's Hamburger U. trains workers to make Big Macs correctly.* There is nothing developmental in the training process: it doesn't prepare burger flippers for subsequent, more advanced jobs if they know how to cook raw meat for x minutes at x degrees.

Education comes from the Latin *educe*, to 'draw out.' It is a maieutic process that is not immediately practical. It is designed to develop the capacity to learn. What one learns in formal education is how to learn by asking fundamental questions and by challenging assumptions. The process equips the learner to explore issues from multiple perspectives. It is not about learning the right answers; it is about learning to ask the right questions in order for the student to become more innovative, creative, and responsive to change. The process broadens and, thus, is developmental. The MBA curriculum educates (or it should educate) tomorrow's managers so they can continue to learn throughout their careers.

There is danger in equating the two types of learning. Training has to do with indoctrination, while education encourages the challenging of established ideas. What happens within corporate walls is almost always training. Corporate trainers assume a single, right outcome and favor pedagogical methods (lectures, simulations, games, outdoor 'rocks and ropes') the results of which are predictable and controllable, and doubtlessly appropriate when trying to achieve certain types of behavioral change (for example, to discourage sexual harassment). In sharp contrast, education has to do with sharpening the mind in a way that creates the flexibility needed to cope with change and with ambiguous situations in which the right outcome is not known in advance. Educators use such methods as assigning reading materials that reflect diverse opinions and values, analyzing history, and case and seminar discussions.

Education is the business of formal higher education institutions. It cannot be done effectively by proprietary schools, corporate universities, or on-line b-schools. It is the purpose, function, and *raison d'être* of universities and colleges. In the future, the only way those institutions can thrive is to stick to their last, and leave training to others. Trying to incorporate training methods and techniques into the classroom is to abandon the comparative competitive advantage that degree granting institutions of higher learning historically have enjoyed. Significantly, it is to the long-term advantage of businesses for those institutions to truly *educate* their future managers.

## SUMMARY

What I find missing in these pages is a sense of the future *of business*. Since history shows that business schools mirror changes in the corporate world, it would seem to make sense to think first about the future of those institutions whose influence on the programs of b-schools is the greatest. But few of our authors began with the question: 'What will managers need to know, and what skills will they need to possess, to be successful in the future?' Failing to start there, the alternative is for b-schools to take control of their own destiny by creating bold and innovative programs the value of which will be obvious to companies and students. Doubtless, most deans would prefer the latter course; realistically, however, there is little evidence that they are willing to break with established norms and do little but to tinker at the margins with what everyone else is doing. Most pertinently, professors whose identity is based on their status as researchers in their respective disciplines have little incentive or interest in the hard work of curricular reform.

Doubtless, the future of business education promises to be one of greater competition between traditional college- and university-based programs, on the one hand, and unaccredited for-profit providers, particularly on-line programs, on the other. I believe there is no way the traditional university

programs can win this competition by aping their low-cost competitors' offerings. Instead of playing me-too and offering more speed or convenience, they must offer greater value, which is, after all, their comparative competitive advantage. For the many reasons I've given, I don't believe there are technical, or technological, fixes for the problems with business education. It avails no one to improve the delivery of a poor product.

All my quibbling aside, it is truly impressive to see how much thought and research is being directed to the techniques and practices of management education. Unfortunately, I suspect that all this concern about how to teach may reflect the fact that there is so little agreement about what to teach. Clearly, there is general agreement that the current, dominant mode of management education isn't working, but no agreement on what should replace it. The problem is, without agreement on the what, there can never be closure on the how. Hence my fearless forecast: *Faute de mieux*, pluralism will be the wave of the future.

## REFERENCES

Bennis, W.G. and O'Toole, J. (2005) 'How business schools lost their way', *Harvard Business Review*, May : 96–104.
*BusinessWeek* (2006) 'Is the MBA overrated?', March 20: 78–9.
Ghoshal, S. (2005) 'Bad management theories are destroying good management practices', *Academy of Management Learning & Education*, 4: 76–91.
Khurana, R. (2007) *From Higher Aims to Hired Hands: The Social Transformation of American Business Schools and the Unfulfilled Promise of Management as a Profession*. Princeton University Press.
Mintzberg, H. (2004) *Managers, Not MBA's*. San Francisco, CA: Berett-Koehler.
O'Toole, J. (1999) *Leadership A to Z*. San Francisco, CA: Jossey-Bass. 276–79.
Pfeffer, J. and Fong, C.T. (2002) 'The end of business schools? Less success than meets the eye', *Academy of Management Learning & Education*, 1: 93.

# Index

# Supporting researchers
# for more than forty years

Research methods have always been at the core of SAGE's publishing. Sara Miller McCune founded SAGE in 1965 and soon after, she published SAGE's first methods book, Public Policy Evaluation. A few years later, she launched the Quantitative Applications in the Social Sciences series – affectionately known as the "little green books".

Always at the forefront of developing and supporting new approaches in methods, SAGE published early groundbreaking texts and journals in the fields of qualitative methods and evaluation.

Today, more than forty years and two million little green books later, SAGE continues to push the boundaries with a growing list of more than 1,200 research methods books, journals, and reference works across the social, behavioral, and health sciences.

From qualitative, quantitative, mixed methods to evaluation, SAGE is the essential resource for academics and practitioners looking for the latest methods by leading scholars.

**www.sagepublications.com**

# Research Methods Books from SAGE

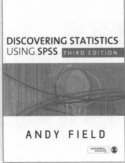
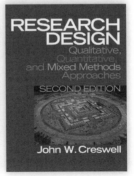

# The Qualitative Research Kit

Edited by Uwe Flick

www.sagepub.co.uk